FORGING AHEAD IN READING

J. ALLEN FIGUREL, *Editor*

Indiana University, Northwest Campus

Volume 12, Part 1

Proceedings of the Twelfth Annual Convention

International Reading Association

Newark, Delaware 19711

INTERNATIONAL READING ASSOCIATION
OFFICERS
1967-1968

President: H. ALAN ROBINSON, Hofstra University, Old Westbury, New York
President-elect: LEO FAY, Indiana University, Bloomington, Indiana
Past President: MILDRED A. DAWSON, Sacramento State College, California

* * *

Executive Secretary-Treasurer: RALPH C. STAIGER, University of Delaware, Newark, Delaware
Assistant Executive Secretary: RONALD W. MITCHELL, International Reading Association, Newark, Delaware

DIRECTORS

Term expiring June 1968

Althea Beery, Cincinnati Public Schools, Cincinnati, Ohio
Brother Leonard Courtney, FSC, The Christian Brothers, St. Paul, Minnesota
Grace McClellan, Child Guidance Clinic of Greater Winnipeg, Manitoba

Term expiring June 1969

Margaret J. Early, Syracuse University, Syracuse, New York
Theodore Harris, Washington State University, Pullman, Washington
Eve Malmquist, National School for Educational Research, Linköping, Sweden

Term expiring June 1970

Millard H. Black, Los Angeles City School Districts, California
Amelia Melnik, University of Arizona, Tucson, Arizona
Virginia D. Yates, Prairie District Schools, Prairie Village, Kansas

* * *

Publications Coordinator: Faye R. Branca, International Reading Association, Newark, Delaware

* * *

Foreword

THE SHRINKING WORLD is making effective communication a vital necessity. And among the communication components reading stands out as the most necessary. With the explosion of knowledge has come, as a corollary, the explosion in publications of all kinds, each demanding the attention of the reader. The complexity of the total reading act and the greater holding power of the school has increased the difficulty of teaching reading effectively to everyone. Now there is greater interest in methodology, reading materials including special media, teacher training, in-service programs, research and its applications, contributions of other disciplines to reading, and many more. In fact, almost everyone is getting into the reading act, professional and lay people alike. This volume and its three companion publications is a reflection of such wide-scale activities throughout the world. The volumes are by far the most up-to-date collection of ideas on reading.

Forging Ahead in Reading, the largest of the volumes, contains the Featured Addresses of the Seattle Convention, sections on Instruction in Reading, Curriculum and Organization, Teacher Education, Special Interest Areas, and Research on the psychology and sociology of reading, the pedagogy of reading, linguistics in its application to reading, and the application of research to classroom situations. The papers here presented represent broad viewpoints on the teaching of reading at all levels, from the kindergarten through college and graduate school. Much material is contained in this volume. The manuscripts have been edited but not abbreviated. In reading the volume, the teacher can be as selective as she chooses to be. The reading of any one paper is not a prerequisite for reading another, although reading related papers will serve as background for evaluation. The three companion volumes, which may be purchased separately, are Part 2, *Ivory, Apes, and Peacocks: The Literature Point of View;* Part 3, *A Decade of Innovations: Approaches to Beginning Reading;* and Part 4, *Perception and Reading.*

Conventioneers found Seattle a truly remarkable city, abounding in many interests and having pleasant May weather. The officers of the Association, the program committee, and the many local committees had done their homework well, resulting in one of the most profitable conventions of IRA. The program provided an array of choices. Special effort had been made to provide opportunity for divergent ideas to be presented and critically evaluated. The fine program combined with the luncheons, convention dinner, school visitations, and general hospitality made going to Seattle a profitable trip both professionally and socially. The city was truly a benign host, as were the universities, colleges, and schools of the area. Sincere and warm thanks go to them.

Neither this foreword nor the papers herein presented can transmit the enthusiasm and spirit of the convention. The report will however give you a totality of the papers presented and discussed. The editor hopes you will find encouragement in reading them.

J. ALLEN FIGUREL
Editor

CONTENTS

Foreword iii

v

CURRICULUM AND ORGANIZATION

RESEARCH

THE INTERNATIONAL READING ASSOCIATION came into being January 1, 1956, through the merger of the International Council for the Improvement of Reading Instruction and the National Association for Remedial Teaching. It is a professional organization for individuals and groups who are genuinely concerned with the improvement of reading programs—both developmental and remedial, for children and adults—and with providing adequate guidance in all situations in which reading serves as a vital aid to learning.

The Association publishes three professional membership journals. *The Reading Teacher* and the *Journal of Reading* are published eight times a year—October through May. *The Reading Teacher* is a publication devoted to all aspects of reading at the elementary school level; the *Journal of Reading* is concerned with the improvement of reading programs in high schools and at the college and adult levels. *Reading Research Quarterly* is issued each year in fall, winter, spring, and summer and is a scholarly journal concerned with experimental research and theoretical speculation in reading and related areas.

Membership is open to all persons engaged in the teaching or supervision of reading at any school level, to parents, and to other persons interested in the purposes of the Association. Members and council affiliates represent all fifty of the United States and many nations, such as Australia, Canada, England, Germany, New Zealand, Nigeria, Japan, Denmark, and others. For complete information about membership in the Association and subscriptions to IRA journals write to Dr. Ralph C. Staiger, Executive Secretary-Treasurer, International Reading Association, Six Tyre Avenue, Newark, Delaware 19711.

All parts of Volume 12, as well as a limited number of the back issues of the Proceedings, are available from the publisher, International Reading Association, Inc., Six Tyre Avenue, Newark, Delaware 19711. The early volumes, 1 through 8, of the Proceedings were published in cooperation with Scholastic Book Services.

MILDRED A. DAWSON, *President*
International Reading Association
1966-1967

FEATURED ADDRESSES

Forging Ahead in Reading

MILDRED A. DAWSON
Sacramento State College

WE ARE LIVING in a fast-moving world. Before we know it, men will take up residence on the barren moon, their lives sustained by huge rock crushers which will reduce the moon's crust to fine powder, then to basic elements, in the process of producing air, water, soil, and fuel from the rocks. Tomorrow, perhaps, a flying saucer will deliver a flock of beings superior in ability and achievement to us human folk, and from them we will learn to soar over the universe with the greatest of ease. Ere long we will not take the trouble to sit down to a superb banquet like this one, but will pause only to swallow a capsule which will sustain us for long hours. Soon man will work no more, except possibly a two-hour week in rotation in order to repair the mechanisms charged with producing the wherewithal for our continued existence. Social security as we know it will disappear because all will have wealth; poverty and ignorance will disappear; no more dull or defective children will be born since we will have mastered the principles of selectivity in delivering the offspring of man and beast into the world.

All of this sounds fantastic; yet wonders do exist, even in our field of reading. We have this remarkable development at Indiana University where research reports are being assembled in the ERIC Clearinghouse on Retrieval of Information and Evaluation on Reading. Soon all we will have to do in getting background for a proposed study is to write to the center and IBM types of machines will feed out all the summary cards pertinent to the problem in hand. We are already programing materials and reading instruction; automation is springing up everywhere. Innovations greet us on every hand and there might sometime be a single innovation that will prove to be the panacea for all our reading ills; but I doubt it.

All of these developments are challenges to us in IRA. They provide us with opportunities for progress in many instances, but possibly more important they put on us the responsibility for evaluating them and determining to what extent they work and under what conditions.

In an entirely different vein, there are other challenges which we must accept and meet if we are to forge ahead in reading. On the one hand, there are schools where administrators and teachers seem ready to jump on every new bandwagon that comes along, where the school personnel are constantly looking for a single panacea which will cure all troubles in teaching reading. On the other hand, there are still classrooms where reading is taught in routine, old-fashioned ways and where change and progress seem impossible. The new and the old—both challenge us in this organization to investigate, try out, accept change where it is merited, reject change to the extent that innovations are futile or harmful. We must accept the fact that certain procedures and materials are valuable under particular circumstances, valueless in others. I have always enjoyed the capsules of wisdom in Pope's *Rape of the Lock*. This one seems pertinent here.

Be not the first by whom the new is tried
Nor last to throw the old aside.

In past months as I pondered this matter of forging ahead, I often recalled a talk I heard at an initiation in a girls' honorary society. The speaker was a gentle-mannered, retiring little woman who was known over our state as a leader in PTA's program for library development in schools. She started out by telling an anecdote about her early days in local PTA work. She was a mother of primary children and the president of a local PTA. She knew of a bill being debated in the legislature, one that might do

1

2 FORGING AHEAD IN READING

great harm to library programs in schools. So she went to listen to the debate. One speech so alarmed her and so aroused her indignation that, before she knew it, she was striding down the aisle calling out, "No! No! You mustn't do that!" And then she launched into a speech that expressed what she had in her heart. She got results, made a deep impression on the legislators, but went home trembling and upset because of her experience. This quiet little woman then went ahead talking to the senior girls in the honor society about what they must do if they were to succeed as members of their prospective school communities. "Get involved," she advised them and told them how. And that is my message to you, each of you. *Get involved.* Involve yourself in the IRA purposes of improving reading in every classroom in every nation.

What should your commitment be? Possibly you have a bent for research and have facilities for it. Then commit yourself to doing research that will promote progress in the field of reading. There are multitudinous opportunities. Innovations already at hand need thorough testing and evaluation; others will be constantly emerging; possibly you can experimentally devise additional innovations. We have little truly definitive research on the innovations that are seeking a place on the market and in the schools. Or you may prefer to follow the suggestions made by the late William S. Gray and David Russell who stated that all research on reading should be repeated and brought up to date. Conditions have changed; materials and procedures have been revised; we know much more now about setting up controls, devising effective techniques, applying appropriate statistical formulas, and the like. Besides, many of the studies we constantly cite were much too narrow to permit sweeping generalizations. Are you interested in readiness throughout the spectrum of reading, in phonic applications, in the effectiveness of various linguistic approaches, in

critical reading, in the development of interests and taste in reading, in diagnosis and remediation, or in developmental reading at secondary and college levels? There is room for research in all of these and other aspects of reading. We are far from having the last word.

Let us hope you do not confine yourselves to solo performances in the research to which you commit yourself. We need cooperative research which is well coordinated, fully controlled, longitudinal, far-reaching. This may be in the way of having several competent persons working on different aspects of the same problem in one institution of higher learning or within a single foundation. Better still, a large group of public schools or several universities will plan together and carry to completion a comprehensive and conclusive study. I should like to see a chair set up at IRA Headquarters to be occupied year by year by different leaders in the field of reading. Each leader would plan and implement a program of cooperative research in the aspect where he is especially competent. He would turn to public schools, universities, foundations, governmental agencies, or any other organization to act as cooperative participants in a widespread investigation. Why shouldn't IRA take leadership in research—not to do it as an organization, but to bring to focus a program of coordinated and definitive research by having a key person at Headquarters with time to plan and to implement the research we so badly need?

This would take money and IRA does not and never will have sufficient funds. Maybe this is where you can commit yourself. If you have a flair for raising funds, if you have winning ways with directors of foundations or heads of governmental agencies or with persons rich from writing basal reading series, IRA can use you. Seriously, there is a certain know-how in writing up proposals, in approaching various sources for funding research; and we would welcome suggestions and help in locating funds and in soliciting them in effective ways. I have asked the Long-Range Planning Committee to consider seriously this problem of financing IRA's projects in the years ahead.

Possibly your interests lie in another direction. Are you interested, as am I, in the international opportunities and responsibilities of IRA in future years? Our Board is international with Canada, Sweden and the United States represented. The Organization Committee consists of persons in all the nations where we have affiliates and councils already formed or imminent. As a result, we are at this moment having translations of IRA materials published in various languages abroad; we have the biennial World Congress on the way; the United Kingdom is holding annual conferences with representation from other countries.

I envision a great extension of such activities, and they should not be on a one-way street. It is fine to translate IRA publications into other languages; but there are developments of great moment in other countries, and we can profit greatly from sharing their wisdom. I recall how impressed I was by the address given by Dr. Sakamoto in Paris and how I wished that every council in IRA could take on the enterprise shown in Japan. I recall two projects: the promotion of reading interest on the part of the adult, out-of-school population; the selection and carrying out of a major research project by each separate council. Here is an idea for our Regional Planning Committee.

In a troubled world, such cooperative endeavors on the part of reading personnel the world over should do much to cultivate understanding and promote friendship among the peoples of the entire globe. Possibly IRA can do much to bring the millennium that we hope for.

Those of you able and ready to commit yourself to the international aspects of IRA work may be more interested in attacking the problems of illiteracy. Think of the almost hopeless efforts to set up democratic governments in recently de-colonized countries where most of the people can neither read nor write. There is a crying need for expert help by reading personnel willing to spend from two to four years abroad helping new governments to organize for curriculum development so that appropriate materials in the native tongue (possibly) and appropriate teacher education may be set up. We are setting up institutes to study the best ways to proceed in fighting illiteracy over the world; but really this is so small a beginning. Is it you who should commit yourself to thought on the problem of fighting illiteracy at the source, of raising funds to underwrite the expenses of some other persons who are free to go abroad, or developing helpful bulletins and curricular materials? Surely there are several among you who will commit yourselves to such projects.

Perhaps you, like me, have spent years in teacher education, and here is where your commitment should lie. We know all too well that our prospective teachers learn too little about how to teach reading before they start teaching. We realize that too few are trained and that schools who seek reading teachers for the secondary school and college find them in short supply. We are disturbed that standards for training reading specialists are so low in many states. Now let us commit ourselves to doing something definite to remedy these situations. It does little good to wring our hands and lament over the situations. Now commit yourself to go home and do something about it. Possibly you can help to work up a program where methods courses and practice teaching are concomitant and the prospective teacher utilizes each procedure as she learns it in theory. Maybe you can work with school boards, legislators, school administrators, teacher training institutions to convince them that there should be an internship or some definite follow-up procedure for each newly installed teacher. It is likely that you can upgrade your own work by going out into schools and taking over classes from time to time so that you sense and understand the management problems of the teacher, absorb the actual impact of individual differences among children, and get a truly definite idea of the nature of the reading materials with which teachers work. It is so easy to abide in an ivory tower when we are working with our teachers-to-be, when we need to keep our feet on the ground. As teacher education personnel, too, you and I have the responsibility of keeping up with the innovations like the various phonic adaptations and programing so that we help our students evaluate them and know how to use the better ones appropriately; we should keep abreast of the various controversies, know the facts on either side, take a stand if and when duly convinced—without legal complications, please! Commit yourself to being alert, dynamic, practical, forward-looking, well informed, and above all active in promoting betterment wherever you see deficiencies.

Here is an area where each of you can and should make a definite commitment—legislation. In general, school people are somewhat fatalistic and resignedly accept legislation which they do not approve. Why should you bemoan the insufficient preparation to teach reading, the low standards for certification in some quarters, the lack of provision for diagnostic and remedial attention? Get busy and do something about it. Talk reasonably but persuasively wherever talking will do some good—to an influential person in PTA, a school board member, a perceptive member of a service club, a local legislator, your principal or superintendent or dean. Once I had a hard-headed, conservative dean. When he was not receptive to an idea I was sure to be worthwhile, I did not argue; but I managed to send in a genial person who had evidence or left persuasive publications on the dean's desk. I don't recall a single instance when I didn't get my way, usually by

having him call me to his office and say, "I wonder why you haven't been trying this." And then he would cite the evidence that I had subtly brought to his attention. He never did catch on to my tactics. Or take the time when a certain principal campaigned against a policy that the superintendent and school board had decided to be a wise policy. I asked the superintendent and president of the school board if I might take a hand in getting community support. I started simply and concluded massively. The county chairman in the dominant political party was also the husband of the president of AAUW; so I went to the AAUW president and explained the constructive action which the school board wished to take. Her husband approached Tom Dewey's right-hand man at Albany, the lieutenant-governor, and the school board action got the approval necessary.

So, do something about matters that need attention, not in a combative way but a way likely to get smoothly functioning action. For instance, write letters to the governor, members of the assembly or Congress, the state superintendent of instruction, or whatever person can promote desirable change. One matter many of you can work on is the study, revision, and final adoption of the professional standards that IRA is setting up.

Each of you here is undoubtedly a member of a local IRA council. So here is a commitment for everyone. Work to improve reading instruction in your own area because, unless IRA touches classroom procedures, all our more grandiose schemes avail us little. How many classroom teachers in your area are not members of IRA? We find that teachers a few miles from a national or state convention do not know the organization exists. That should not be. If you are to get these nonmembers to join, you must help to see that the programs of meetings are valuable, intriguing, too good to miss. You may want an outside speaker once a year, but see that it is someone with a real message—inspirational or informative or both. Have most of the meetings handled by local personnel in panels, demonstrations, or just plain talks with meat in them. The Council Program Aids Committee has three kits that should be invaluable helps in setting up fine programs. The numerous publications of IRA are a limitless source for subject matter for meetings.

Help IRA to reach out into every school in an enlightening, stimulating, constructive way. Help it to span the earth in a fight on illiteracy and in programs that feature cooperation and mutual understanding and assistance. Help to get the legislation and financial support that will make IRA a vital force. Lend a helping hand if only by writing letters to persons in authority. I am committed. Your Board is committed. Won't you join us in commitment to the betterment of reading on every hand? Only thus can we "forge ahead in reading."

The New Frontiers of Print

ARNOLD EDINBOROUGH
Saturday Night Publications, Limited

WHEN I ATTENDED the university, a friend of mine became embarrassed at his inability to swim. An asthmatic child, he had been forbidden to stay in the water at his summer cottage for longer than a few minutes. But by the time he got to college he was a husky six-footer whose asthma had blessedly disappeared. He felt out of it when he sat around the swimming pool near the gym.

The spring of his sophomore year he went, unknown to us, to a private gymnasium and took an intensive course. He was determined to surprise us all—and he did. One early summer afternoon, he roared out of the locker room, raced down the springboard, and dived into the pool. Unfortunately it had been drained for cleaning—he was in a cast for the rest of the summer.

I thought of that incident as I looked over the impressive program for the International Reading As-sociation's Twelfth Annual Convention. A great number of people are really getting themselves and masses of other people into shape to read and to read well. But, when today's kindergarten and primary children have grown to university age, will reading be necessary?

Is there a future for print?

Consider first the technology which militates against it

The technology of sound

Much of what used to be written can now be recorded and replayed as often as print can be reread. In schools, all language skills can be better taught with tape in a language lab than with a book in a classroom. In universities and public libraries, an archive of actual speeches and special audio-material will soon replace transcripts or accounts of such events. In business, the voice-writer into which a voice can speak, a tape can be punched, and with which either a visual transcript or an aural file can be produced is not far away from commercial production and application.

The technology of sight

Television already moulds a great many children's attitudes more than the classroom does. Indeed, the gap between what is absorbed from TV and what is taught in the classroom is widening. Only very few teachers are aware of the amount of information and the range of opinions and attitudes built up by television in children, both preschoolers and those in school. Even the global environment of television—so often talked about by Marshall Macluhan—is more consistently apprehended by the 3- to 15-age group than by any other. For them, reading in many subject areas only says again, after infinite pains, what they already know from their osmotic, hypnotic watching of the box. There is also the controlled television teaching now going on in many universities. Scarborough College in Toronto does 50 percent of its total instruction by television, and even in such differing areas as the teaching of poetry and biology, instructors have evolved audio-visual techniques which have enormous impact. The use of tapes, audio-visual material, and effective programing, for instance, can make poetry the musical act it once was and should be, eliminating the rigidities of print which have long interposed themselves between poet and reader.

There are also closed-circuit television applications in industry where, linked with the tape-memory of a computer, the study of records and the assessing of performance can be greatly simplified. As Shakespeare would say on behalf of the anti-print people, "fie upon but yet, it does allay the good precedence"—and so it does.

The status of print

Secondly, in the face of all this audio-visual technology, let us look at some interesting facts.

Newspapers. First, on the North American continent, despite the novelty and the amazing speed with which television has become almost universally available in the past fifteen years, the circulation of newspapers has increased—and increased in percentage of coverage, not just in actual numbers. In other words, more people read more newspapers than they did before television.

Magazines. Second, though there have been some losses—mainly due to managerial ineptness rather than audience rejection—magazines have consolidated their position. Compare *Time's* circulation now or *The New Yorker's* with their figures for the thirties. Canada's *Saturday Night* fifteen years ago had a circulation of 45,000 when the population of Canada was some 13 million; today it has 95,000 while the population has increased to only 20 million—a 120 percent increase for the magazine, just over 50 percent for the nation.

Supplements. Again, weekend supplements came into operation in Canada at the very same time as television, and now two are published every week—both with circulations over two million.

In Great Britain, Lord Thomson took the colored supplement idea and, against all the critics, not only introduced it but made a success of it and forced other Sunday newspapers to include a supplement. Elsewhere, the same innovations and extensions of the daily and periodical press have caught on. *Link* in India, *Der Spiegel* in Germany, and—in a different area—*Encounter* in London and *Commentary* in the United States.

Books. But it is in book production that the full impact of print is seen.

In Canada there were only 684 titles published in 1952, before television was nationally available. In 1962, the publication of 3,600 titles evidenced an increase of 426.2 percent. The United States increased production from 11,840 to 21,904, or 85 percent; and Britain, France, and Germany all increased book production by varying amounts from five percent to 35 percent.

These spectacular increases were nothing, however, compared to the increase in some other countries. In Africa, fourteen newly independent nations which had no publishing program in 1952 published a total of 1503 titles ten years later. These varied from programs of a handful in Libya and the Cameroons to several hundred in Ghana, Ethiopia, and Nigeria. In China, the number of titles increased tenfold (from 2,500 to 26,000) on the mainland and fivefold in Formosa (427 to 2625).

These statistics, mainly supplied by UNESCO, are buttressed by the statistics on paper consumption in the world supplied by the International Institute for Economic Studies. Though North America has only increased in paper consumption by 44 percent, Europe has increased by almost 100 percent; Africa by 242 percent; and Asia by 512 percent. Obviously, then, print is not on its way out and reading is not going to be a superfluous skill.

New frontiers of print

The reasons the increases have taken place vary from area to area and an analysis will perhaps show the way ahead—the way to the new frontiers of print.

The undeveloped world

In the world of emerging nations, the phenomenal increase is due to the growth of literacy. The peasants of Russia, the masses of China, the Negroes of Africa are all emerging slowly into the industrial era: for China it is a reawakening of an old and skilled civilization; for Russia it is a change in the methods of production; for Africa it is the assumption of independent political and economic action. Millions are learning to read in order to acquire the training for which reading is itself the basic skill. Many are reading in a foreign language as well as their own.

For these people, reading is essential; and they must be provided with literally thousands of millions of instructional pamphlets, workbooks, and textbooks. Since they will be learning about already established technical processes and will have to relate those processes to thinking patterns established in a preliterate culture, I hope there will be a crosscurrent of ideas which will make for a new flexibility of approach. Maybe our technical writing can be improved by the rejection of stereotypes we have created. I say "we" because English is still a powerful language in the world. One in five of all literate persons anywhere on the globe reads English.

But economic advance does not come from machines alone. In fact machinery or, more precisely, technology, can often defeat its apparent aims in underdeveloped countries. (What is needed in India, for example, is a very selective group of technological processes which demand the minimum of capital and minimum of labor.) The newly independent masses of Africa and Asia, not to mention those of Latin America, need a vison too.

There is another new frontier of print: the export of books and magazines in sufficient quantities to convey the vision of freedom, both political and economic, which has brought this continent and Europe to their present highly developed states. Merely sending what we publish for ourselves won't do. In the struggle for men's minds expert plans for attack must be carefully laid. Friends who have been to Africa report new books from Red China and Russia are numerous; books from the West are not nearly so obvious. Yet our whole Judeo-Christian heritage, that heritage of individual dignity and freedom, is based on the Book; Christians and Jews alike are people of the Book, and it is the Bible which has made us free.

The developed nations

The increases in the printed word are not so spectacular in the developed nations; but they are solid and, in the face of the growth of other media of mass communication, perhaps even more surprising. There are, to my mind, two main reasons for the increase, technical and psychological.

Technical advances in the developed world. The art of printing is changing as rapidly in this last half of the 20th century as it did in the first quarter of the 19th. Then, the mechanical steam press so increased efficiency that Robert Escarpit says in his excellent monograph *The Book Revolution,* ". . . before the end of Napoleon's reign, more sheets could be printed in an hour than had been possible in a day fifteen years earlier."

In the past ten years we have broken the hold of metal. Instead of setting type in lead, then transferring it to paper-mache and later by metal again to press, we can now set and print type from film. What is more, we can use an ordinary typewriter keyboard to punch a tape which can then be typeset, the words properly hyphenated in the setting by feeding the tape first through a computer where all possible syllabications (or breaks) are held in the computer's memory.

By the refining of inks and paper and with the use of film instead of metal, it is now possible to print four-color reproductions at the rate of 50 per second.

It will not be long before it will be possible to print newspapers from the same copy simultaneously in New York and Seattle, Los Angeles and Boston.

But the greatest advances have been more in the production of paperback books; and though paperbacks are taken for granted, they rely on several new techniques in order to be as saleable as they are. It was necessary to have a cheap coated paper before they could be illustrated—a paper which has only recently been practicable at its present prices. New lithograph techniques to make use of this paper were also required. The revolution in chemistry was necessary to produce the glue which holds the books together and the plastic coating which makes their covers so attractive. Also needed were new materials-handling techniques to ship the books and computers to process the inventory.

With all those things, what happened? A paperback revolution! In the United States it is reckoned that almost half of all books published this year will be in paperbacks. Look at the sales figures for the past ten years: from 250 million to 600 million, from less than 50 million dollars to over 100 million dollars. Anyone who has been to an European book fair knows that what is now true in Canada and the United States has been true in Europe for some time. It was after all, Sir Allen Lane who launched Penguin Books, the "quality" paperback, in 1935.

Psychological factors in the developed world

But the spread of the newspaper, the success of new magazines (Look at *Playboy*), and the paperback revolution did not all come about because of new techniques. Producing print is one thing; getting people to read it is another.

Responsibility. Much speculation exists on why people read. Large leadership surveys have been conducted on the subject, especially by newspapers. The one overriding quality expected of the print media is that it be right. Television and radio can show you something happening, but for most people the event needs putting into context. The fragmented world of television actuality is not coherent enough for linear man, to use Macluhan's phrase. As far as TV news is concerned, the medium is not the message: it is still the envelope in which the message comes. People who saw the shooting of Oswald couldn't wait until the papers next day told them how and why it had happened.

A heavy responsibility rests on the journalist who must act ethically in researching, backgrounding, and commenting on an event. It also puts a heavy onus on the teacher of reading to see that all students be taught to detect and evaluate the slanting which goes into every newspaper report or magazine article. If publishers and teachers and researchers can produce a responsible press, *that* will be a new frontier of print.

It is not just that people want to see happenings in black and white; it is that they can select their own pace or differing paces, considering what it is that is being read. They can choose their own level of reading. While there is now a very heavy insistence on speed-reading (inspired, I think, by John F. Kennedy), I would like to ask for a reassertion of the values of contemplation. As Bacon said: "Some few are to be chewed and digested."

Overall on the North American continent there is the need to be solitary, the need to individualize oneself again. Television does not allow this: you are either a willing or unwilling participant. You are involved, but involved often in such a way as to reject the involvement and be alienated.

Too-real actualities, like Napalm-burned children in the news, you may reject. Vulgarity, like that of Jimmy Durante, you may reject. And the commercials have been almost totally rejected in many categories, especially by young people.

A paperback book—print in any form—involves us. It is an effort to read it or an effort not to, an existential choice. We can argue with it; we can be informed by it; and we gradually build the content into our own consciousness. This solitary activity enhances our individuality since the book is making us even more different from our fellows who haven't read it. Because it is an object, it also helps us to build a hearth for ourselves. The collection of books is an indication to character because it builds character.

Above all, the book, the word, appeals to our imagination in a way which nothing else can. Language puts us above the apes; the recording, transmittal, and later enjoyment of that language make us human. It is this area of imagination which is the last frontier of the printed word.

Walt Rostow has posited several states of economics from primitive, through take-off, to sophisticated development. I would like to do the same for man's mind, his spiritual and psychological economy.

First, comes mere literacy, where reading is a tool: *that* represents an immense frontier for the emerging nations. Until they can cross it, their new-found independence won't do them much good. Neo-colonialism or economic colonialism is much like old-style imperial colonialism. Technology and ideology can bring them, with our help, into the family of aspiring if not affluent man.

Second, comes inquiring literacy, where reading is not just a bread-and-butter matter but a skill whereby one can become totally involved with his environment. That is the frontier facing Europe, North America, and some scattered countries of Africa and Asia, chiefly those where Western settlement is still a dominant influence as in South Africa, Australia and Singapore. It is an important one for it builds national feeling and a generally accepted ethical and moral framework in which the nation has its being and from which it can conduct its international affairs. The paperback revolution and the increase in the periodical press show this to be so.

Third, comes committed literacy, where there is a power in words which transcends all other influences and sends us back to ourselves to find out what we know. Montaigne was such a committed man. *"Que-sais-je?"* he asks; so was Milton, who tried to justify God's ways to man; so were the 19th century liberals under the influence of John Stuart Mill; so was T. S. Eliot; in different areas but in no different sense, so were C. S. Lewis, Teilhard de Chardin, Albert Camus, Aldous Huxley, and Robert Frost, all of whom are now in print in millions of copies of paperbacks.

This I take to be the last frontier of print: where reading instructors, writers, publishers, and the readers themselves can be led to think of the human condition and to make everyone so conscious of his own human dignity that he will not try to limit someone else's. It is not an impossible task. The techniques and resources are open to us all, and there may be in your classes at this moment a dozen or so writers who have the genius to write what we would all wish to read and see read. Professor Escarpit, in the book to which I have already referred, sums it up this way:

> Books are like bread. Throughout the world, the production of grain and the basic foodstuff derived from it was primitive man's great victory over hunger. The result was that bread became something almost holy, the symbol of liberating labour, survival and communion. The instinctive reactions of many peoples still embody this sort of innate respect for bread, which is obscurely enshrined in their collective memory as a saviour. Books are the object of the same sort of unacknowledged veneration since they were the bread of the mind, the great victory achieved by somewhat less primitive men over ignorance and the slavery it means. A book which does

not last, an ephemeral book, a book which is an act and not necessarily a lasting reality, a treasure to be preserved a possession for all time—*ktema es aei*—is something which profoundly shocks our instinctive feelings and may even disgust us.

At the same time, we are very well aware that the poor man's bread in the present-day world has ceased to be a symbol and has become a mere metaphor, and a bad one at that. We know that the world's hunger will not be overcome this time by the individual magic of the ear or the loaf, but by a vast collective effort bringing into play all the scientific, technical, and mechanical resources of the advanced civilizations, by a profound and systematic reform of social structures, by a concerted world policy which will affect many other sectors besides those of agriculture and food.

Nor can the great hunger of the mind be overcome in any other way. The individual demands of writers, the refined tastes of cultivated book-lovers, should be given neither more nor less weight in our plans for the future than the majestic gesture of the sower or the gastronomy of Brillat-Savarin in the discussions of the Food and Agriculture Organization. We must deny nothing, but nor must we interpose anything between books and life, and especially not myths. We are living in an age when great things are being done by teams assisted by machines. We readily accept this for the arts which have developed along with mass civilization, such as radio, television and films, not to mention the theatre, where there is direct contact with the audience and where the principle has always been more or less accepted. We must now go on to accept it in respect of books. It goes without saying that the very nature of reading will always necessitate a greater measure of solitude than other forms of communication or artistic expression, but the solitude of the writer, like the solitude of the reader, is not anti-social. It is only the means whereby each may find the other. A man reading alone in his room often has more companions than if he were watching a film with a thousand other spectators in a cinema.

It is this inherent virtue of books which must be maintained and developed. Dissemination, limitless and ceaselessly renewed communication among all men—that is the true function of the book. Once it ceases to fulfil it, however fine its appearance and however noble its content, it is merely so much waste-paper, a soul-less treasure. One might as well put a stone in its place.

It is that communication, that individual, refreshing, searching communication you and I are both concerned with. Out of it comes any hopes we may have for a sane, free, peaceful world. I hope we make it.

Effective Study—
Its Nature and Nurture

A. Sterl Artley
University of Missouri

In the days of computerized education, programed learning, and audiovisual aids of various sorts and types one begins to wonder if in the year 1967 a paper on study has any place on the program of IRA. Yet, on second thought, the process of assembling ideas and using them in forming generalizations and resolving issues is one that will be forever with us regardless of how the ideas are clothed and regardless of whether we are referring to a third grader or a graduate student. The Education Research Information Center (ERIC) may reduce some of the tasks involved in study, particularly in locating and summarizing information; but the major task of synthesizing and using it cannot be reduced to a mechanical process.

Much has been written already about the process of study; but in spite of the attention it has received as a specialized reading activity, major changes in school programs designed to improve study procedures have not taken place in widespread fashion. A few sporadic and transient programs are the best we can find. Karlin (8) in a paper presented at the Miami meeting of IRA quoted Ruth Strang as saying, "The most discouraging circumstance is that so little has been done to implement sound ideas that were advocated and tried years ago." In the same paper Karlin also refers to a survey made by McGinnis in 1961 in which she reported 61 percent of a total of 1,029 college freshman said that their high school teachers had not showed them how to improve reading skills. In addition, less than 10 percent of the high school teachers surveyed claimed to have had any training in teaching reading and study procedures.

It is not to be presumed that another paper on study will effect major changes in practice. However, there are several aspects of study that have not been sufficiently emphasized. These I would like to explore with you.

The nature of study

First, I should like to discuss the use of the term study. Literature uses several terms somewhat synonymous in reference to this subject—*study, study skills, reading-study abilities,* and *reading abilities in the content areas.* All these terms relate to what one uses in terms of skills, abilities, and understandings in the process of study. But study itself, what is it? What does one do or should one do when he studies, whether at the fifth grade level or the eleventh? Strangely enough it is at this precise point that some of our study-skills problems lie, for we are not in agreement as to what the process is, in the first place. Even dictionaries are of limited help, for they define the process in different ways. One states that it is " . . . a process of acquiring . . . knowledge of a subject." Another defines it as " . . . the application of the mind to the acquisition of knowledge, as by reading, investigation, or reflection." The *Dictionary of Education* defines it as "the application of the mind to a problem or subject." Note that the first two definitions stress the idea of study as the process of "getting" knowledge, while the last one connotes the idea of problem solving.

In reading a number of articles and reports dealing with the subject, I have been particularly sensitive to the definition of study that the writer either states or implies. In the majority of cases it seems to be assumed that study is the act in which one engages to accumulate facts, information, or ideas. The end result is a score on a test of factual information or the number of questions that can be answered

correctly after one has read a geography or science text. A study-skills course may be devoted to teaching the pupil or student how to locate information or to use a table of contents or to secure data from charts, graphs, diagrams, and the like, after which a study-skills test is administered and progress is noted in the learner's ability to engage in each of these tasks more efficiently, the implication being that he now has at hand a set of skills that will enable him to acquire facts more expeditiously.

On the other hand, we find statements to the effect that study should be considered as something more than information gathering, or as the dictionary says, "knowledge acquisition." Fay (*4*) wrote, "Students must be shown that there is more to study than merely reading the pages of an assignment." He contends that study in social studies is an active thinking process of following an author's line of reasoning in relation to a well-defined and clearly understood purpose. In other words, the process of study is engaged in when there exists some purpose or need to be satisfied.

In like manner, Robinson (*11*) in an article in *The Reading Teacher* said, " . . . a meaningful reading program in social studies or the other content areas will focus on problem-solution as the end, and skill development as the means, not vice versa." He, too, sees study in broader terms than the acquisition of information.

In a paper that I fear has been lost in the welter of literature on reading and study is the one presented by Preston (*10*) as the keynote speech at the Miami meeting of IRA. In "Reading for What?" Dr. Preston discussed what he called the "low ebb of reading as an intellectual activity." As an intellectual activity, he said, reading was at a low ebb for several reasons, one being that reading people are preoccupied with technical problems, the mechanics of the act, information getting, rather than the end result. He wrote, "We should not take our chief satisfaction in bringing about mere literacy, desirable though literacy is. It is only half the job. We need to conceive of our role in broader terms and not rest content until the learner is eagerly *applying reading to some worthwhile goal.* [italics mine] The real miracle of reading lies less in the process than in what can be accomplished through it." Translating this concept of reading into the language of study, we have the generalization that study is being carried on at its highest level when the reader is doing something with the writer's ideas.

In fact it is almost in these terms that Nila Banton Smith (*15*) defined study. In differentiating between reading and study she described a housewife perusing a household periodical for entertainment. Later the housewife returned to the magazine and studied an article having a recipe which she wanted to use in preparing the evening meal. In the latter situation she has put information to work and has utilized skills where the intent was "to do something" with the content read.

What we have then are two points of view with regard to the means and the end of the study act. One, that information, knowledge, facts, and ideas are the end; the other, that these are the means to the end of use, application, problem solving, question answering, or issue resolving. One has engaged in the act of study when he has derived information or ideas and has put them to use for some purpose that has relevance and significance to the learner.

Perhaps if we were to look at the study act apart from reading, it might be helpful; for we engage in study many times where no reading as such is involved. Many of us engaged in study when we faced the question as to whether we would attend the Seattle meeting of IRA. For some there were deterrents: it is a long way to Seattle from New York, Florida, and even Missouri, and cost was a major factor. Some were engaged in major projects where time away from the job had to be considered. But at the same time

there were reasons why we should come: there were excellent meetings to attend; there was a paper to present; there were friends that we see only once a year; and the State of Washington is pleasant in May. And so we assembled facts from various sources: we used our past experiences; we talked with friends; we checked to see if there was money in the travel fund; we looked over the program; we may even have read the promotional literature about Seattle, and eventually we came to a decision. Can anyone say that this activity was not the process of study in every sense of the word?

On analysis, what was involved in this act? What were the steps? First, there was a problem, a question, or an issue. Second, there was the securing and marshalling of facts and information needed to solve the problem. Third, there was the evaluating and weighing of the bits of information, since each bit was not necessarily of equal value or merit. Finally, there was a resolution of the problem. All of this together composes the act of study.

Take note, if you will, of the second step in the study act. We called it the securing and marshalling of facts and information. There is no doubt that this was a very important part of the study process; but there would have been very little, if any, reason for it *had there not been a problem to resolve.* Study took place when there was a purpose or motive, and the collection of information was a means to the end of problems solving. Isn't meaning hereby given to Robinson's generalization that study should focus on problem solving as the end and skill development as the means? And in the same way isn't a partial answer provided, at least, to Preston's question, "reading for what?"

I don't wish to labor the place of idea intake in study or in the receptive area, as Herber (*7*) calls it, yet I do feel that it is in this step that the study act on all levels of instruction—from the elementary grades through college—so frequently begins and ends.

It is reflected in the sixth grade teacher's assignment, "For tomorrow study to the middle of page 126," meaning that tomorrow be prepared to hand the material back in a discussion. It is reflected in the high school teacher's admonition, "Be sure to 'cover' the material carefully, for tomorrow we are going to have a test," which frequently ends up being a series of true-false items measuring little other than factual recall. It is reflected in research in which the researcher matches a control and experimental group to which he gives a series of lessons on the use of the card catalog, use of the dictionary, and map reading. After post-testing the two groups, he enters the data on Hollerith cards, puts them through a computer, and comes out with the fact that the 3.78 points of difference between the two groups is statistically significant at the one per cent level. Truly, studying for what?

Facts, knowledge, ideas, all are useful, in fact essential, in the study act because they constitute the raw material in the process of problem solving. But accumulated for their own sake to be regurgitated later, they are no better than the miser's coins which he counts each Saturday night and returns to his sack since they serve neither himself nor society to any useful purpose.

In fact, they represent a kind of pseudo erudition dramatized in radio days by the Quiz Kids and today in television on the College Bowl program, where for preparation the group dredges up every particle of isolated and undigested information that the questioner might possibly ask. Understanding the process of study would in a dramatic way modify the assignments that we make, the study act in which the students engage, and our teaching methods in general.

The reading-study purpose

The term *purpose* in relation to reading and study also is used in different ways by different writers. Some speak of study as being a purposeful activity when the reader approaches his material with a definite question in mind; such as, "To what extent did Germany's decision to attack the Soviet Union and Japan's decision to attack the United States make possible the defeat of the Axis in World War II?" Others use the term in reference to the reading set or study objective that the reader keeps in mind as he studies, as, for example, to note details, to verify a statement, and to answer a specific question. Still others refer to purpose as adjustments that the reader makes in reading, such as to skim or to recognize devices and words that indicate certain types of idea relationships. Certainly before one can help students establish a purpose for study one needs to know what a purpose is to begin with.

Perhaps the following may help in clarification. The student begins with a study *objective* or study task, which may be a question for which he wants an answer or a problem situation in need of resolution. It is the reader's basic motivation for reading. Examples of these kinds of reading tasks might be: Why does a satellite orbit the earth? What steps are involved in baking a cake? or, What factors made possible the defeat of the Axis in World War II? The reading or study objective, on the one hand, may be met with a minimum amount of reading; or it may require the use of several sources and a prolonged period of study. It may be one that is established by the teacher as part of an assignment. It may be one set by the student himself as something he needs to find out or understand. At any rate it is an essential prerequisite for study. Being without it is like beginning a vacation trip with no idea of where one is going or what one wishes to see.

The study task or objective determines, in turn, the study *purpose*. The purpose may be to determine the main idea, to note details or facts, to trace out the writer's organization, to distinguish between fact and opinion, or to sense idea relationships. The purpose supplies the mental set for the act of study. If the study objective or task calls for tracing out the writer's organization, the student puts his mind to the job of searching for the main ideas being developed and the various levels of subordination used by the writer in developing his ideas. But, of course, a reading purpose cannot be determined until the student clearly has in mind his study objective.

Knowing the study objective and the study purpose, the student now needs to make certain adjustments as he proceeds. An obvious adjustment would be in the area of rate, for some purposes may call for rapid reading while others may call for a slow, study-type reading. The student may need to reread to determine the level of subordination of a given point, or he may need to skim to determine whether a particular bit of information is supplied by the article. The adjustments, then, are those required in order to satisfy the study purpose which in turn is conditioned by the study objective.

The most recent and possibly the most complete piece of research dealing with reading purposes is that of Helen K. Smith (14). She was concerned with student ability to identify appropriate reading purposes from the nature of the content, to comprehend material, and to make necessary reading adjustments in the light of the reading purpose. Using ninth graders from a suburban Chicago high school, Smith divided them into experimental and control groups, fourteen classes composed of 204 students being experimental and fifteen classes of 307 students being control. From these two sets of classes she matched two groups—an experimental group of 62 students and a control group of like number. All comparisons were between both experimental and control classes and groups. All students were pre- and post-tested with the Cooperative English Test: Reading Comprehension, and a "Test of Purpose" developed by the researcher. This test was made up of two parts: Part I, to assess the ability of students to identify appropriate reading purposes for which a given selection should be read; and Part II, to determine the ability to comprehend passages when given a pre-stated purpose, as well as to determine the procedures and adjustments used in reading those passages. Over a period of a year the experimental students were given instruction in purposeful reading through work in their regular English classes.

Comparisons made at the end of the experimental period indicated that those between the experimental and control classes were much more significant than those between the smaller groups of experimental and control subjects. As a result of the instruction given in the experimental classes, the students were better able to identify appropriate purposes for reading, to read significantly better for the purposes studied, and to comprehend on a higher level than could the students in the control classes.

As an overall conclusion from this comprehensive study, Smith concluded that well-planned assignments should be made in which students are given reading purposes or are given direct instruction and guidance in setting their own purposes. Moreover, she recommended that instruction in purposeful reading should be given below and above the ninth grade, the grade in which this study was carried out.

Other studies than Smith's confirm the value of study objectives and purposes. Schlesser and Young (13) working with college students found that higher levels of achievement accrued from helping students develop motives for study than from instruction in specific study techniques. They said, " . . . steady, vigorous, highly motivated effort is the outstanding trait of the student whose achievement is high relative to his abilities."

Spache (18) made several pertinent observations concerning study objectives. He pointed out that accurate comprehension assumes clear-cut purposes (reading objectives), established either by the teacher or by the student himself. "Without directions," he wrote, "he is likely to retain neither main ideas, nor details, nor relationships since he knows not what he is seeking." And then he continued discussing the importance of clarifying study objectives for each assignment. He suggested that the instructor ask himself, "What are the reasons for having the pupils read this assignment?" And then he added a statement with which I thoroughly concur, "If the instructor has not a particular purpose in mind, it is doubtful whether the assignment is justifiable."

To my way of thinking, the point Spache made regarding the importance of reading objectives underlies one of the most troublesome problems facing a student in the act of study. When questioned about their study problems, students frequently list as one of the first their inability to concentrate. What they don't know and what we many times don't realize is that unless they are asleep, they are always concentrating on something; but what they are concentrating on may have little relation to the learning task. Rather than thinking about the precipitating causes of the Civil War, the major problem is "How will I ask Susie to go to the spring formal, and what will I do if she says, 'No'?"

It is a well known principle that one focuses his attention (concentrates) on those things that are of most significance to him. Consequently, if one is to concentrate one must make the learning task preeminent. Granted this is difficult to do when the learning task is in competition with the spring prom, but the principle still remains. If learning tasks are to be competitive with other questions and problems confronting the learner to which his attention might be drawn, two things must be kept in mind. First, the learning task or study objective should be one that focuses on problem solving, issue resolving, or generalization forming rather than memorization of details. Tyler (19) showed, for example, that facts and rote learnings were eroded away by the passage of time while generalizations and principles were retained to a much greater degree. Second, and most important, the learning task must have relevance to the learner. It must be one to which he sees some point, some purpose in doing. Otherwise it becomes another assignment to do, to get out of the way, and to forget. As Spache says, if there is no good purpose for doing it, it is doubtful whether the assignment is justifiable.

When discussing reading-study objectives, the question frequently arises as to whether, to be most effective, the study objectives should have their origin with the teacher or the student. A study reported by Henderson (5) throws some light on this question. Taking 24 good readers and 24 poor readers on the fifth grade level he subjected them to four different types of purpose-setting behavior. In one of these situations the subjects read the first half of a story and then conjectured and declared a reading purpose. In another the reading objectives were supplied by the teacher. A check of comprehension indicated that the differences between the two treatments were insignificant whether the pupils set their own purposes or were given purposes by the teacher.

Similar findings to those above were reported by Smith (14) in the study to which we have already referred. From her findings, you will recall, she concluded that well-planned assignments should be made in which students either were given reading purposes or were given direct instruction and guidance in setting their own purposes.

It would appear logical to assume that the younger children would profit from study objectives supplied largely by the teacher. Eventually the objectives will be cooperatively derived by teacher and pupils; and still later, as pupils become more mature, they will assume increasing responsibility for formulating their own study objectives.

Skills involved in study

In the area of study skills, there is likewise confusion growing out of the inconsistent use of terminology and the overlapping of skills from one learning area to another. Nila Banton Smith (16) helps to clarify the issues here by categorizing skills needed to study effectively as common reading skills, common study skills, and specialized skills and competencies needed for study in the various curricular areas. The common reading competencies utilized in study are those used in any type of reading in any type of content, nontextual as well as textual, and for any type of objective. Important here would be the various word perception abilities, vocabulary, basic comprehension skills, and critical evaluation. To a large degree the comprehension skills are those growing out of the reading purpose we have already discussed— reading for the main idea, following direction, following a sequence of ideas, forming generalizations, and the like.

One can find almost as many lists of comprehension skills assumed to be important in reading and study as there are writers on the subject. Niles (9) contends, however, that at the heart of the ability to comprehend content of any kind there are three major skill areas. The first is the ability to find and understand thought relationships (comparison-contrast, chronological, cause-effect, etc.) The second is the ability to set specific study objectives and purposes. These we have already discussed at length. The third is the ability to make use of the backlog of real and vicarious experiences that relate to and serve to amplify the new materials. Without a doubt these are essential competencies that would serve well the purpose of reading or study in any area.

The common study skills are those to which frequent reference is made in the literature. They are skills and abilities used in study rather than casual reading and used similarly regardless of the area or subject. Usually these are referred to as location of information with reference to a particular reading task or objective; selecting and evaluating information in the light of the objective; and organizing information (facts, principles, generalizations) in a form or manner demanded by the situation. This task may be in the form of an outline for an oral report, notes for a discussion, an investigative paper, a dramatization, or a cartoon or drawing to illustrate a synthesis of ideas.

Frequently, recall or retention is listed as one of the common study skills. I am omitting it here for it has always seemed to me that recall is inherent to the act of organization. Recall is a by-product of the organization process rather than a separate competency to be developed. In the second place it carries the connotation of memorization for later rote recall or recitation of such things as lists, isolated facts, and statements. These we would hardly accept as the end toward which the study process should be directed.

I am omitting from our discussion anything having to do with the actual teaching procedures for the development of the common study skills, chiefly because the monograph on study skills in the Perspectives in Reading series, prepared under the sponsorship of IRA and compiled and edited by Harold Herber (6), covers this area so completely. This is a monograph that should be in the hands of every classroom teacher, particularly those on the secondary level. Well-written and extremely helpful chapters cover the development of word study skills, the use of book parts, sources of information, and visual aids. I recommend it highly as a source of practical help. Suffice it to say here that there is ample evidence that study abilities can be taught (2) and that the teaching of them contributes to improved learning.

Within the past twenty-five years or so we have become increasingly aware of the fact that efficient reading in the content areas calls for more than the general or common study skills referred to above. A considerable body of research evidence is available that competent reading in one area, literature for example, does not necessarily insure competent reading in science or mathematics. Though there may be skills that overlap one area with another, there are others quite unique to a given area. This is so because each content has its own specialized vocabulary, its method of treating ideas, its pattern of writing, and its own particular objectives which structure the kind of approach required (1).

Further evidence of this is in a study by Smith (17) who made an analysis of 52 tests in science, 60 in social studies, 49 in mathematics, and 45 in literature and arrived at a set of writing patterns used by authors in the development of content in each of these areas. From these writing patterns she derived the various response types demanded of the reader in dealing with the content. For example, social studies requires the reading of pictures, maps, and atlases; the analyzing of content for cause-effect relations, comparisons, sequence of events; and the critical analysis of content where different viewpoints are expressed, where facts are mixed with opinions, and where propaganda is used. This analysis is extremely helpful to teachers in aiding their students to read the subject matter in each of their teaching areas.

Other lists of skills and abilities assumed to be necessary for interpreting content in the various subject areas are found in any text in reading methods. I would want to call particular attention to another monograph in the Perspectives in Reading series titled *Reading Instruction in Secondary Schools* and edited by Margaret J. Early (3). Chapters by Bamman on reading in the science and mathematics areas, Herber in history, and Burton in literature are very comprehensive.

But in the final analysis, as helpful as these sources may be, it is quite difficult to tell Mr. Harris, teaching history in P.S. 46, precisely what study competencies *he* will need to develop. In the first place, the curricular design he follows will determine to a great extent the skills he will need to teach. If he follows a single text, the skills will be quite different from those he would

need to develop were he using a problem centered approach. They will depend on the level of students in his class and to a large extent on their prior instruction. Consequently, Mr. Harris' best guide will come from the answer to a question he asks of himself: "What competencies do my students need in order to study my subject as I teach it?" Following this is the second question: "In which skills and abilities are my students sufficiently competent to deal with in my area?" These remaining skills then become the teaching responsibility of that teacher as they are required, keeping in mind of course that there may be students who will require individual help apart from that given to the group.

Study skills programs

The literature contains a number of action studies and a few pieces of well-controlled research attesting to the value of school programs devoted to the development of study skills and abilities. Many of these are described by Catterson (2). She points out that some programs are carried out under the aegis of English classes and others in special reading classes. She notes, however, a trend toward programs handled by classroom teachers in the regular content areas. If content area teachers are involved with content that students use for study purposes and if study competencies are to a substantial degree specific to each content area, then it must follow, as night the day, that the major responsibility for developing study competencies will be within the context of subject content on all grade levels.

But content area teachers have not been overwhelmingly responsive to this idea. One reason is, they say, that they lack the knowledge to conduct instruction. This, I think, is a rationalization; for if the doing of it is important, as evidence and sheer logic shows, then there are ample resource materials available for help. The two IRA Perspectives monographs to which we have frequently referred, to say nothing about the treatment of study in any reading test, would provide ample help. Moreover, reports of most of the successful reading and study programs on the secondary level have indicated that in-service training of teachers was an essential part of the program. Frequently such instruction was provided by the reading supervisor or coordinator.

Another reason, implied if not actually stated, for letting the task go by default is that the subject matter teacher feels that he hasn't time to develop study procedures along with the teaching of his subject content. The task is assumed to be something extra added to an already overextended course outline. Like selling football tickets on Saturday afternoon, it goes over and beyond the call of duty. But Catterson makes a statement that I think takes away the potency of this as an argument. She says, "The authors of these papers have made it obvious that they think of study skills not as *something* to teach, but as a *way* to teach—a way of teaching which advances not only the student's knowledge of subject matter but his ability to learn other subject matter independently and at will." In other words she was not talking about a unit on study to be added to an already overloaded course outline but something that should be a part of just good teaching.

But if we need to clinch the argument that the teaching of subject content cannot be divorced from the development of study competencies, the following question is offered as the *coup de grace*. What is the teaching of a particular subject such as social studies, science, literature, or home economics other than that of teaching the pupil or student to recognize and face issues, questions, or problems inherent to that body of content; to locate appropriate informative content; and to derive from that content ideas, generalizations, and principles that will help him answer his questions, resolve the issues, or form valid bases for opinions or judgments? It would seem, then, we are saying only in another way that *the teaching of a particular subject is the teaching of the study of that subject;* and that makes inescapable the fact that every teacher is a teacher of reading and study.

REFERENCES

1. Artley, A. Sterl. "Influence of the Field Studied on the Reading Attitudes and Skills Needed." in W. S. Gray (Ed.), *Improving Reading in Content Fields.* Proceedings of the Annual Conference on Reading. Chicago: University of Chicago Press, 1947.
2. Catterson, Jane. "Successful Study Skills Programs," in H. L. Herber (Ed.), *Developing Study Skills in Secondary Schools,* Perspectives in Reading No. 4. Newark, Delaware: International Reading Association, 1965.
3. Early, Margaret J. (Ed.) *Reading Instruction in Secondary Schools,* Perspectives in Reading No. 2. Newark, Delaware: The International Reading Association, 1964.
4. Fay, Leo. "How Can We Develop Reading-Study Skills for the Different Curriculum Areas?" *The Reading Teacher,* 6 (March 1953), 12-18.
5. Henderson, E. H. "A Study of Individually Formulated Purposes for Reading" *Journal of Educational Research,* 58 (July-August 1965), 438-441.
6. Herber, Harold (Ed.), *Developing Study Skills in Secondary Schools,* Perspectives in Reading No. 4. Newark, Delaware: International Reading Association, 1965.
7. Herber, Harold. "Developing Study Skills in Secondary Schools: An Overview." In H. L. Herber (Ed.), *Developing Study Skills in Secondary Schools,* Perspectives in Reading No. 4. Newark, Delaware: International Reading Association, 1965.
8. Karlin, Robert. "Nature and Scope of Developmental Reading in Secondary Schools." In J. A. Figurel (Ed.), *Reading As An Intellectual Activity,* Proceedings of the International Reading Association, 8 (1963), 52-56.
9. Niles, Olive. "Comprehension Skills," *The Reading Teacher,* 17 (September 1963), 2-7.
10. Preston, Ralph. "Reading for What?" in J. A. Figurel (Ed.), *Reading as an Intellectual Activity,* Proceedings of the International Reading Association, 8 (1963), 13-20.
11. Robinson, H. Alan. "Reading Skills Employed in Solving Social Studies Problems," *The Reading Teacher.* 18 (Jan. 1965), 263-69.
12. Romano, M. J. "Reading and Science: A Symbiotic Relationship," *Education,* 81 (Jan. 1961), 273-76.
13. Schlesser, G. E., and C. W. Young.

"Study and Work Habits," *The School Review,* 53 (Feb. 1945), 85-89.

14. Smith, Helen K. *Instruction of High School Students in Reading for Different Purposes* (Cooperative Research Project No. 1714), Office of Education, United States Department of Health, Education, and Welfare, 1966.

15. Smith, Nila Banton. *Reading Instruction for Today's Children.* Englewood Clifs: Prentice-Hall, 1963, 307.

16. Ibid. p. 312.

17. Smith, Nila Banton. "Patterns of Writing in Different Subject Areas," *Journal of Reading,* 8 (Oct. 1964) 31-37; 8 (Nov. 1964), 97-108.

18. Spache, George. *Toward Better Reading, Champaign:* Garrard, 1963, 77.

19. Tyler, Ralph W. "Permanence of Learning," *Journal of Higher Education,* 4 (April 1933), 203-204.

Phonics Problems in Beginning Reading

DONALD D. DURRELL
Boston University

THE CENTRAL PROBLEM in learning to read is the mastery of phonics. Any child who can speak English can learn to read it, if an adequate program in phonics is provided for him. The fact that he can speak demonstrates his intellectual capacity to use symbols for objects, actions, ideas. Since his speech is made up of phonetic elements combined to produce words and sentences, he has a working basis of phonemics, even though he may be unconscious of the separate elements. The task of phonics is one of attaching these sounds in speech to printed symbols.

The elimination of poor readers, reading failures, or nonreaders usually requires only the improvement in the effectiveness of phonics instruction. In the early days of the study of reading failures, we pursued the question, "What is wrong with the child?" This approach brought elaborate psychological inquiry: tests of eye-hand dominance, motor tests, visual and auditory perception tests, neurological theories, psychiatric concern, sociological studies. We find this approach repeated in the current reincarnation of "dyslexia." There is usually nothing wrong with the child; what he needs is precisely adjusted and highly motivated lessons which establish relationships between sounds in speech and words in print. Our present crude knowledge of phonics is adequate to overcome difficulties in individual tutoring where constant adjustments may be made to the child's learning needs, but the elimination of failures in classroom teaching requires better services than our current phonics programs offer. We still have too many unanswered questions about phonics.

If there are any lingering doubts about the value of phonics in beginning reading, the Bond-Dykstra report *(3)* should dispel them. In this analysis of the national study of first grade reading, it is noted that the reading approaches which stressed phonics had the highest yields. The differences among the programs were not great, but the general order seems to be the following: basal readers plus supplementary phonics, linguistic approaches, the initial teaching alphabet, language experience approaches, and basal readers without extra phonics service. The only individualized reading program was that of Spencer *(15)* who provided a foundation of intensive phonics. All programs provided phonics instruction; even the language experience programs included systematic phonics instruction.

Apparently we need a definition of phonics. We find some authors of reading approaches which stress phonics denying that they use a phonics approach. College students of the current generation often believe that they had no phonics in their reading programs. The basic definition of phonics might well be "attaching speech sounds to printed words." If one is learning to read by any method, he is learning phonics; if he has learned to read, he *has* learned phonics. It is the only way a phonetically-based reading system can be learned. Even the "look-say" approaches match speech elements to printed words, although both pupils and teachers may be unaware of the fact. All approaches to reading are phonic approaches, just as all are "linguistic" approaches; phonics and language are basic elements in beginning reading. The learning of phonics begins with speech and continues as long as a person reads; advanced language scholars constantly add to their phonics learnings.

The child's phonics program begins with learning to speak. When he learns to say "mamma," "daddy," and "bye-bye," he has started his phonics program. He has mastered the trick of producing the phonemes /m/, /d/, and /b/ plus the vowels. As other phonemes are added and words come clearly, the phonetic background for reading is being established, but often unconsciously. A child may develop a wide speaking vocabulary with clear enunciation and still be unaware of the phonemes in his speech, just as most adults are unconscious of the lip-tongue-teeth-breath gymnastics in their speech. Until the phonemes in speech are brought to the child's attention, he will not learn to read; he has no phonemes to attach to graphemes. About one third of children entering first grade need special training to bring the sounds in spoken words to their attention (12). This lack of ability to identify phonemes in spoken words is the major cause of reading failures. There is nothing wrong with the child; all he needs is help in becoming aware of the sound elements in his spoken words. The need is easy to discover; simply ask the child to give the first sound in *money* or *magic* and the last sound in *steam* or *drum* and then test for other consonant phonemes in a similar manner. Oddly enough, some of our linguists seem unaware of this difficulty; some even deny the need for "ear training."

The child's preschool phonics also consists of familiarity with letter names. The average American child comes to first grade knowing the names of twenty-one capital and fifteen lower-case letters (12), but some children know no letter names. Despite the continuing evidence of the relationship of letter name knowledge to learning to read, some people see no tie between letter names and phonics. In a recent textbook, one of our top scholars acknowledges the relationship of letter names to success in reading but adds this footnote, "Yet undoubtedly letter names is a symptom rather than a cause of reading success." Apparently we need a rationale and evidence for letter names as a part of phonics. The rationale is easy, and we have some beginning evidence of the relationship. All consonant letter names, except *h, q, w,* and *y,* contain their phonemes plus an extraneous vowel and, of course, the names of vowels are their "long sound." In the names of the "long-*e*" letters—*b, c, d, g, p, t, v, z*—the phoneme precedes the vowel in the name; to say these letters, the child uses exactly the same speech mechanisms as in giving the "sounds." The names of the "short-*e*" letters—*f, l, m, n, s, x*—have a similar value, with the phoneme following the vowel in the name. The names of *r, k,* and *j* also contain their phonemes. The close association between name and sound in twenty-two of the twenty-six letters surely should help phonics; it does. Wylie (16) shows that when the letter name is known, the sound is easier to learn. He finds that the names of *h, q, w,* and *y* also helped in learning sounds, although to a lesser extent; the name may indicate high familiarity with letter form, making the sound easier to attach. Someone who notes the advantage of letter names in phonics will surely ask Congress to rename *h, q, w,* and *y*: perhaps *hay, kwee, way,* and *yuh* might do; and at the same time they might change the names of *c* and *g* to *kee* and *gay,* to take advantage of their more frequent hard sounds!

The ability to identify phonemes in words and to recognize letter names represents a prereading phonics achievement which can be inventoried at school entrance. The value of this early phonics learning in predicting reading success is shown in the Bond-Dykstra (3) report: "The best single predictor of first grade reading success among the premeasures used in this study was the Murphy-Durrell Letter Names Test. Likewise, in four of the six treatment groups, the Murphy-Durrell Phonemes Test ranked as the second best predictor of reading achievement." (It is evident here that modesty has been set aside for the satisfaction of the supporting evidence!) What is measured by these tests is early phonics achievement, the completeness of the phonics foundations for beginning reading and for more advanced phonics. Successful "look-say" pupils always have this phonics background; all of the children who learn to read before coming to school are quite proficient in phoneme perception and letter name knowledge; they can even "spell by ear." It is this phonics background that makes it possible for the child to master the "fifty to seventy-five sight words before phonics instruction" which some people insist upon. The phonics actually comes before the sight words; without this prereading phonics, sight words are very difficult to acquire. Of course there is no need to quarrel about "words first" or "phonics first"; phonics *comes* first, but both prereading phonics and more advanced phonics may be taught through techniques using whole words so that sight vocabulary and phonics may be learned at the same time.

Problems and controversies abound in the teaching of phonics. Vowels seem to invite the hottest conflicts; the amount of the heat indicates the depth of our ignorance about how vowels should be taught. The undependability of spelling vowel phonemes is, of course, the cause of the trouble. Horn's (9) finding that "the short *i* sound is spelled at least fifteen ways," is confirmed by Hanna (8) who reported twenty-two different spellings of short *i*. The hope that vowel rules will solve the problem seems to fade with each new study: Clymer (5) and now Bailey (2) find the two-vowel rule, "the first says its name, the second is usually silent," to be more often wrong than right. They find that oth-ers among our traditional rules lack desirable dependability. Hanna's team (8) derived 111 vowel rules and 92 consonant rules to assist their computer to spell; even with these 203 rules the computer spelled only one half of the 17,000 words correctly! Shumway's finding (14) that fifth grade children could spell correctly in September more than half of the spelling words for the year is rather comforting; one wonders what rules were built into their computers. And it is reassuring to contemplate McKee's demonstration (10) that one can get on quite well in reading when dashes are substituted for vowels.

In addition to rules, many other solutions have been proposed and developed to meet the varied spellings of vowels. Diacritical marks to distinguish different vowel sounds in beginning reading was found by Fry (7) to be one of his less effective approaches. Different colors of print to indicate different vowel sounds is another approach. Some linguists establish the more dependable short vowels in three-letter words before moving to other vowel sounds. George Bernard Shaw suggested simplified spelling, a proposal which is constantly revived. Dewey (6) presents scholarly support for simplified spelling, discussing, and illustrating both ends of the problem: difficulties in putting sounds into print and in obtaining sounds from print. The initial teaching alphabet is a modification of simplified spelling, suggested as an approach to stabilize the phoneme-grapheme relationship for early stages of reading. All of these approaches are successful in teaching reading, but none more than another nor more than phonics in standard spellings and print. There is the persistent question of why so many children acquire superior abilities in reading and spelling despite the vowel variations. What perceptual abilities, what insights, do such children acquire which eliminate most of the trouble? Can we identify these and teach them to others?

Our studies indicate that the phonogram is the unit most children depend upon in recognizing words in beginning reading. The phonogram stabilizes the vowel quite dependably; in one-syllable words, the consonants which *follow* the vowel set the vowel value. In the ancient *ca-t* versus *c-at* controversy, our evidence favors *c-at*. In studying the abilities of first grade children to read unfamiliar words, Canham (*4*) found that even those children who were taught a *ca-t* approach could get from *cap* to *map* easier than from *man* to *map*. Of course this is a featherweight problem; there are fewer than 150 three-letter words with medial short vowels in the child's speaking vocabulary. Yet the fact remains that *at* says *at,* but *ca-* says different things in *came, call, car, care, catch*. In most of the 225 phonograms from which stem three or more primary grade words, the vowel is stable; relatively few change vowel sounds with initial consonants, such as the *-ant* phonogram shifting the vowel in *want*. Of course, the same sound cluster may be spelled different ways; for example, the *air* sound is spelled many ways, the most frequent being *-ear, -are,* and *-air*. However, Santeusanio (*13*) found that children have little difficulty with this problem in *reading;* spelling presents more difficulties. The utility of the phonogram as a recognition unit is further supported by Wylie's finding (*16*) that children can identify whole phonograms easier than they can identify the vowels within the phonogram. If the phonogram which includes the vowel is known, why bother with the separate sound of the vowel?

Wylie also provided some light on the question of teaching long vowels first or short vowels first. In his test of recognition of 140 phonograms by first grade children in May, the long vowel phonograms and the short vowel phonograms were almost equally easily mastered. The same finding was shown for long vowel phonograms formed by silent *e* and those formed by vowel digraphs. The only significant differences in ease of learning was in frequency of appearance of phonograms in words. Phonograms which were common to many words were more readily learned than those from which few words stemmed. If stability in vowel sounds is desired in beginning reading, the selection of which to present first seems to be one of frequency of appearance in words; whether they are long or short makes little difference.

We have thus far ignored the consonant problems; perhaps we should continue to do so. That they present difficulties of phonemes being represented by different letters, silent letters, doubled letters, or letters representing different sounds is amply shown by Hanna's need (*8*) for ninety-two consonant rules for his computer.

There are other more intriguing concerns in phonics, some of which may be trivial but others significant. The order of teaching letters, "stick letters before circle letters or stick-and-circle letters," is trivial; children's knowledge of letter names bears no relationship to form (*16*). Which consonant phonemes to teach first is also a trivial question; the child must know them all within a short period, and the difficulty of learning one seems little different from learning another. Vowels first or consonants first also is of little concern; both must be learned and in a phonogram or whole-word phonics approach, they are presented together. Regardless of the programed order, each child has his own unique order of learning, so the program seldom fits any individual. Where does writing come into the phonics program? Is it an earlier or later learning? Child development studies find that the desire to write comes by the fourth year, long before the desire to read; phonics programs possibly should include writing very early.

Of greater import are the questions concerning methods of teaching phonics. First, as for the matter of keeping meaning foremost in words used in phonics instruction, shall we stress meaning or eliminate it? Shall we provide "automatic response to phoneme-grapheme ties" ignoring word meanings, even teaching nonsense syllables? Or shall all phonics instruction be done within meaningful words, with meaning being maintained by various types of context clues? My preference is for the latter, although we have no clear evidence to support the choice. Shall phonic elements be taught separately or always within words which are seen by the child? Again, my preference is for whole-word phonics, but we lack conclusive evidence. Word element practice should be more than the study of the anatomy of meaningless symbols. It loses the advantages of the differential learning potential provided by the whole-word approach which allows the child to pick up the phonogram and the sight word as well as the consonant being taught. That this differential learning potential is important is shown by Arkin (1) and Murphy (11) who found that children acquired phonograms incidentally and a large sight vocabulary as well when whole-word approaches were used in a phonics program.

Shall we require children to "sound out" words? Or shall we encourage a word recognition technique, based upon response to larger word elements? This question reveals a rather profound problem about the value of phonics: is its chief value in "unlocking" new words or is it found in more accurate perception of sight words? We are all aware that phonics is a crude tool for "unlocking" words; it will unlock words in one's speaking vocabulary if a context clue is provided, but in new words one can never be sure of vowel values, variable consonants, or accent. This brings up the doubtful merit of phonics practice which asks the child to mark the vowels and accents in words. If he can't read the words, he can't be sure of vowels and accents; if he can read the word, he doesn't need to "unlock" it! Possibly the unlocking aspect is overrated and we might do just as well without sounding-out words. If sounding is done, the unit of the syllable

or the phonogram or even root word seems more promising.

There are dozens of other unanswered questions about phonics, but one is paramount—the ability of the teacher presenting the phonics program. In the national study of first grade reading, the project directors who reported differences among classrooms found that the differences were greater among teachers using the same approaches than the differences between approaches. For example, Fry (7) found that the achievements in the lowest classroom often was less than half of that in the highest classroom, even when pupils were equal on premeasures. Murphy (11) found that the lowest teacher in one approach delivered an achievement below primer level at the end of the year, while the top teacher produced an achievement above grade three; yet the two classrooms were made up from randomized groups in the same building, with exactly the same scores and distributions on premeasures. Before we attribute the results to teacher personality traits, it is well to observe the differences in learning activities in the classroom. The chief difference seems to be in economy of classroom learning time. The teacher who produces low pupil accomplishments seems to have a genius for wasting learning time: her pupils are always "waiting turns," waiting until others are ready, waiting while the problem of one pupil is being settled, waiting for materials, waiting while milk-money is being collected, waiting even in a line of pupils in front of the toilet. The teacher who produces high pupil achievement yields avoids all this waiting: she uses every-pupil-response techniques in much phonics instruction; she keeps all pupils busy with self-directing, self-correcting lessons; she uses pupil teams for many types of activities, involves mutual aid in learning constantly; her pupils keep at work while milk-money is collected, keep at work while other pupils go to the toilet! In addition, the high-yield teacher adjusts the instruction to differing levels and learning rates; pupils who come with inadequate prereading phonics get early help in letter names and phoneme identification, while such instruction is omitted for those who don't need it. There are many other differences in the economy of the use of classroom learning time, but these will illustrate some differences in practice. A careful study would probably show that there is more learning opportunity provided in a single hour in some classrooms than there is in a week in other classrooms. Of course there are desirable personality qualities as well as undesirable ones among teachers; we all prefer attractive pleasant teachers to frowsy ones with nasty dispositions; but pupil achievements are more likely to vary with what the teacher *does* in using learning time than with her personality.

The teacher variable will continue to be the most significant factor in phonics learning until our instructional materials are improved. Some phonics programs depend almost entirely upon teacher-built materials, offering only sample lessons and general advice. Some offer hit-or-miss lessons, unrelated to differences in phonics backgrounds brought to first grade or to the amounts of practice required for mastery. Many programs have low economy techniques built in when every-pupil-response techniques and self-directing, self-correcting lessons might well have been included. Few programs take advantage of the mutual aid in learning provided by pupil teams. Even the most carefully structured programs offer the same service for all children, ignoring individual differences. Each must make choices among the unanswered questions about phonics, providing a plausible rationale rather than evidence for the choice.

We need many innovations in phonics programs, but with the innovations we have the responsibility to evaluate. No current phonics program warrants uncritical school-wide adoption. All offer plausible advantages, evidences of higher achievements as compared to undefined alternative programs, and

testimonials from satisfied and delighted users. We need well-designed studies to evaluate phonics programs—studies which use many approaches in direct comparisons, which utilize more precise measures of phonics growth and transfer, and which control many essential variables. Many of the unanswered questions will require the precision of inventories of small elements of growth. Clearly there are rich opportunities for research studies, both large and small, in the area of phonics.

While searching for more perfect phonics programs, we should not fail to recognize that we have done well with current ones. All newly-standardized primary reading tests show that children at the end of first grade now achieve nearly as well as did children at the end of second grade fifteen years ago. If we can make this progress with our imperfect phonics programs, we can make still higher gains as our knowledge and services improve.

REFERENCES

1. Arkin, Susan, *et al.* "Growth Patterns in First Grade Reading," unpublished Ed.M. thesis, Boston University, 1964.
2. Bailey, Mildred Hart. "The Utility of Phonic Generalizations in Grades One Through Six," *The Reading Teacher,* 20 (February 1967), 413-418.
3. Bond, Guy L., and Robert Dykstra. *Report of the Coordinating Center for First Grade Reading Instruction Programs.* Minneapolis: University of Minnesota. February 1967.
4. Canham, Alice E., *et al.* "Phonogram Clusters in Beginning Reading," unpublished Ed.M. thesis, Boston University, 1966.
5. Clymer, Theodore. "The Utility of Phonic Generalizations in the Primary Grades," *The Reading Teacher,* 16 (January 1963), 252-258.
6. Dewey, Godfrey. *English Heterografy or How We Spell.* Lake Placid, N.Y.: Lake Placid Club Educational Foundation, 1964.
7. Fry, Edward B. *Reading Instruction Using Diacritical Marking System, Initial Teaching Alphabet and Basal Reading System,* Project 2745, U.S. Office of Education, 1966.
8. Hanna, Paul R., *et al. Phoneme-Grapheme Correspondences as Cues to Spelling Improvement,* OE Bulletin No.

32008. Washington: U.S. Office of Education, 1967.

9. Horn, Ernest. "Phonetics and Spelling," *Elementary School Journal,* 57 (May 1957), 424-432.

10. McKee, Paul. *Reading: A Program of Instruction for the Elementary School.* Boston: Houghton Mifflin Co., 1966.

11. Murphy, Helen A. *Reading Achievement in Relation to Growth in Perception of Word Elements in Three Types of Beginning Reading Instruction,* Project No. 2675, U.S. Office of Education, 1966.

12. Murphy, Helen A., and Donald D. Durrell. *Manual of Directions, Reading Readiness Analysis.* New York: Harcourt, Brace and World, Inc. 1965.

13. Santeusanio, Nancy E. "Evaluation of a Program for Teaching Homophones in Beginning Reading," unpublished Ed.D. thesis, Boston University, 1962.

14. Shumway, Frances B. "Sixth Graders' Ability to Spell Unstudied Words," unpublished Ed.M. thesis, Boston University, 1949.

15. Spencer, Doris U. and L. Doris Moquin. *Individualized Reading versus a Basal Reader Program at the First Grade Level in Rural Communities,* project No. 2673, U.S. Office of Education, 1966.

16. Wylie, Richard. "Word Element Perception in Beginning Reading," unpublished Ed.D. thesis, Boston University, 1967.

Five Decades of Remedial Reading

ALBERT J. HARRIS
The City University of New York

THE YEAR 1965 marked the close of the first fifty years of American interest in remedial reading. When I was invited to choose a topic, it occurred to me that an historical overview of the 50-year period might be appropriate. As I read again some of the contributions that were written over 30 years ago, I rediscovered many an idea that had been new and exciting when I had first encountered it. I developed a new respect for the pioneers and a conviction that much of our present thinking has roots that go far back. It began to appear that each of the five decades had its own distinctive characteristics.

Since this paper is an attempt to provide an historical overview and perspective, the five decades will be discussed in sequence. For each ten-year period, major trends will be noted and the particular developments that seem to me most noteworthy will be briefly described. Obviously, the selection of what to include from a vast and nearly overwhelming literature is a matter of personal opinion; and while I have tried to be objective, my own beliefs and interests necessarily have influenced my choices and what I shall say about them.

The first decade: 1916 to 1925

The idea that some children have special difficulty in learning to read and can be diagnosed and given special teaching seems to have sprung into prominence in American education almost full grown. The first journal article on the subject appeared in 1916; by 1922 there already were two books and a body of periodical literature on the subject.

Concern with reading disability did not originate on this continent. A case study written in 1896 by a British physician, W. Pringle Morgan, is generally thought to be the first writing on the subject (41). Morgan used the term "congenital word-blindness" to describe a fourteen-year-old boy who had not learned to read although he seemed intelligent in other respects. But for the next twenty years interest was confined almost entirely to a few European medical practitioners and did not cross the Atlantic.

The first American paper on remedial reading was probably one written by Willis Uhl and published in the *Elementary School Journal* in 1916 (59). Uhl gave silent and oral reading tests to all pupils in grades three to eight of an elementary school, listed ten kinds of faults, and suggested remedial procedures. Within the next four years diagnostic procedures, case studies, and school survey results were published by such people as Augusta Bronner (5), Charles Judd (31), W. S. Gray (25), Clarence T. Gray (34), and Laura Zirbes (62). By 1921 William S. Gray authored a book of case studies (26), and in 1922 Clarence T. Gray attempted to cover the field in a book entitled *Deficiencies in Reading Ability: Their Diagnosis and Remedies* (24).

The first American paper in the European mode was by Clara Schmitt and appeared in 1918 (50). She used the terms "developmental alexia" and "congenital word-blindness" and advocated a systematic phonic method of remedial instruction. She introduced one new sound at a time in a continued story in which bells rang (*l*), dogs barked (*r*), cows mooed (*m*), etc.

At the same time Grace Fernald, who had worked under Dr. Shepherd Ivory Franz in the retraining of soldiers with head wounds, was developing the kinesthetic method for teaching nonreaders. Her first paper, published in 1921, was widely read and influential (18).

The first decade drew to a close with the publication of the Report of the National Committee on Reading in 1925—the famous 24th Yearbook of the National Society for the Study of Education (46). In this highly influential volume there was a chapter entitled "Diagnosis and Remedial Work." That chapter consisted mainly of a table with three parallel columns: *evidences of deficiency, diagnosis* and *remedial suggestions*. The table occupied ten pages and contained suggestions that are still worth reading.

There is an interesting contrast in the basic approach of the early medical and educational writers on reading problems; one which I believe continues to this day. The physicians were concerned primarily with differential diagnosis and only secondarily with remedial help. The educators were concerned mainly with developing tests to measure reading skills and with practical teaching techniques. They were interested in diagnosis—especially the kind of diagnosis that tries to establish causation—to a far lesser degree. This difference is still quite evident in the 1960's.

The second decade: 1926-1935

The later 1920's saw the development of many new ideas. Most important, probably, was the development of batteries of tests for use in diagnosing reading difficulties. First to appear were the *Gates Reading Diagnosis Tests* in 1927 (21). Monroe's *Diagnostic Reading Examination* was published in 1928 (39), and the *Durrell Analysis of Reading Difficulty* was first copyrighted in 1933. These three batteries are still used widely in reading clinics, two of them in revised editions.

Among the research studies of the decade, perhaps the most valuable was Monroe's *Children Who Cannot Read* (38). This book summarized previous research, reported on a detailed study of hundreds of severe reading disability cases, and described in detail a teaching method emphasizing phonics with a good deal of kinesthetic reinforcement. It ranks, in my opinion, among the best researches on reading disability. Other important research contributions were made by Gates and his doctoral students, one of whom was Guy L. Bond. These studies systematically studied visual, auditory, readiness, and lateral dominance factors in relation to reading problems.

Samuel T. Orton, a neurologist, published his first paper on reading problems in 1925 (43). The development of his ideas has recently been summarized usefully by Mrs. Orton (42), who was instrumental in founding the Orton Society in his memory. Orton's theoretical formulation is based on rivalry between two cerebral hemispheres, neither of which has established a clear dominance over the other; as dominance shifts, the child shows a fluctuating reversal tendency. Orton's followers have generally favored a synthetic phonic or sounding-blending method of teaching.

At about the same time, Walter F. Dearborn of Harvard was reporting a high incidence of mixed dominance and left-handedness in cases of reading disability (11). He explained their reversals in terms of conflicting motor tendencies, a theory that was for many years the main alternative to Orton's ideas. Dearborn also studied aniseikonia, a condition in which the two eyes form images of unequal size, and found that children with this condition were handicapped in reading (12). My own first introduction to reading problems came about through Dearborn's assistant who in 1929 let me take all of the tests they were using and explained their research methodology to me.

By the early 1930's there was enough published on reading problems to make summaries very useful. Integrative summaries of research on remedial reading were published by Miles A. Tinker in the 1930's (56, 57).

Still another feature of the second decade was the founding of the first reading clinics. Among the earliest were those founded at Boston University by Durrell and at Shaker Heights, Ohio, by Betts.

Aside from Monroe's monograph, referred to earlier, the most influential book on remedial reading of the second decade was Gates' *The Improvement of Reading,* first published in 1927 and revised in 1935 (22). Although Gates concentrated mainly on his own tests and teaching materials, his was the best textbook on remedial reading for many years.

The third decade: 1936-1945

The period from 1935 to the beginning of World War II was marked by a continued output of new books. First to appear were Betts' *Prevention and Correction of Reading Difficulties* (2) and the first book on remedial reading in secondary schools, by McCallister (35), both of which were published in 1936. The next year came *Remedial Reading* by Monroe and Backus (40), and *Prediction and Prevention of Reading Difficulties* by Stanger and Donohue, two followers of Orton (54). In 1938 Luella Cole's *The Improvement of Reading* called for multilevel boxed materials for individualized practice and predicted the coming of reading laboratories which arrived commercially about 20 years later (9). Russell, Karp, and Kelly issued a compendium of useful reading exercises and games in the same year (49). In 1940 two textbooks appeared, *How to Increase Reading Ability* by Harris (28) and Durrell's *Improvement of Basic Reading Abilities* (16). During the early 1940's, the years of World War II, the only other important new book was Fernald's definitive description of her kinesthetic method (17).

The mid- and late-1930's also saw the development of the first large-scale remedial program in a public school system. The presence of many hundreds of unemployed college graduates led to some bold ventures in finding useful things for them to do while receiving federal aid. Under the supervision of some of Gates' assistants, the Federal Writer's Project prepared a series of 80 practice booklets for use in remedial reading. Several hundred people with no previous teaching experience were put through a short training program and then were assigned to teach small groups of retarded readers in the public schools of New York City. Most of my earliest students in remedial reading courses were involved as teachers or supervisors in that remedial program, which lasted for several years until our entry into World War II caused the program to be discontinued.

The accelerating pace of research and writing on all aspects of reading instruction during the 1930's produced an appreciative welcome for Traxler's *Ten Years of Research in Reading,* which appeared in 1941 (58). This summary and annotated bibliography listed and briefly summarized more than 100 articles on remedial reading and 18 articles on diagnosis and included in addition references on many other topics. Traxler was encouraged to prepare three later volumes of the same kind, each covering a period of several years (58). These have been extremely valuable to scholars and research workers in reading.

During this decade the mental hygiene movement discovered reading disability; and case studies, theoretical discussions, and research reports began to appear in such journals as *Mental Hygiene, American Journal of Orthopsychiatry,* and the *International Journal of Psychoanalysis.* Blanchard's case studies of children with reading problems of apparently emotional origin attracted wide attention (3). In 1941, Gates estimated that among children with marked reading disabilities about 75 percent show personality maladjustment and that in only about 25 percent is the emotional difficulty a contributing cause of the reading failure. He was widely quoted in educational circles (23). Child guidance specialists, however, regarded his figures as marked underestimates. While in educational situations remedial teaching was the preferred treatment, child guidance clinics often gave priority to psychotherapy for child and parent.

This decade also saw the development of what may be called the machine approach to remedial reading. For diagnosis, the major development was the production of a commercially manufactured eye-movement camera called the *Ophthalm-O-Graph,* designed by Earl A. Taylor; previously such cameras had to be individually designed and custom built. Taylor's 1937 book provided new information on the use of eye-movement photography in diagnosis (55).

On the remedial side, there were three main machine developments. One was the first reading pacer, designed by Guy T. Buswell (6). It contained a motor-driven shutter that would come down over a page of print at a rate that could be controlled. A second was the first set of motion picture films for reading practice at controlled speeds, developed at Harvard for use with college students. A third was Earl Taylor's *Metron-O-Scope* (55). This was a large and cumbersome device which had three shutters and could expose a line of print one third at a time at a controlled rate.

All of these appeared between 1935 and 1940. Improved devices to accomplish the same purposes are currently in wide use, particularly in college and adult reading programs.

In 1940 I summarized the results of the research then available on the effectiveness of improving reading by attempting to train eye movements or by controlling the exposure of reading material, as follows: "Experimental evidence indicates that motivated practice produces as much improvement in rate of reading as programs of eye-movement training do, while it has a somewhat more favorable effect on comprehension. Another point of practical importance is the fact that motivated practice requires no special material while eye-movement drills require the use of specially prepared material or expensive apparatus. There is no reason for the teacher who relies on motivated practice to feel that his method is inferior to the formal methods of training eye movements or the use of complex machines to pace the reader" (28). Now, 27 years later, I have found no reason to change that opinion.

America's entry into World War II caused a depletion of the graduate schools; and during the war and for a couple of years after it, little that was new about remedial reading appeared in print.

The fourth decade: 1946-1955

Of the research studies that appeared during the ten years that followed World War II, the one that had the greatest influence in America was Helen Robinson's *Why Pupils Fail in Reading,* published in 1947 (47). The first part of the book contained a scholarly review of the literature on the causation of reading disability. The rest of it was a detailed report of the intensive study of 22 cases, by a staff representing ten different professional specialties. Robinson stressed the absence of any one causal factor present in all cases. In these children many anomalies were present that were not considered to have causal importance for the reading problem, as well as many that were. For example, while 73 percent of the cases had visual problems, the visual problem was considered *causally* significant in only 50 percent. Social, visual, and emotional problems appeared most frequently. Inappropriate teaching methods, neurological difficulties, and speech or functional auditory difficulties seemed less frequently to be causal. Endocrine disturbances, general physical difficulties, and insufficient auditory acuity appeared to be least important. Robinson's book provided strong support for a pluralistic view of the causation of reading disabilities.

The major European research study of the decade was Hallgren's monograph on the inheritance of specific dyslexia, which was published in 1950 (*27*). Hallgren's study of 79 clinic cases and 43 other "word blind" cases included family histories. He reported some evidence of reading disability among the parents or siblings in all but 13 cases and concluded that a primary reading disability is inherited as a unitary Mendelian dominant characteristic. He also accepted the idea that there are other reading disabilities caused by such factors as emotional disorders or environmental conditions.

Hallgren's monograph is widely cited by recent writers on dyslexia, such as Hermann in Denmark (*30*), and Critchley in England (*10*), as providing evidence of a special kind of "pure" reading disability. I am inclined to agree with M. D. Vernon, who commented, "What seems much more plausible is that there is a congenital disposition in certain cases towards the occurrence of certain related defects: reading disability, speech defects or infantile speech; motor incoordination; left-handedness or ambidextrality" (*61*).

In the textbook field, 1947 saw the publication of Kottmeyer's *Handbook of Remedial Reading* (*33*), as well as revised editions by Gates and Harris.

This decade saw the birth of the two organizations which later merged to become the International Reading Association. The National Association for Remedial Teaching, known as NART was started in New England by a group among whom Elva E. Knight was prominent and shortly attracted to its board of directors many of the leading authorities on reading problems. The International Council for the Improvement of Reading Instruction (I.C.I.R.I.) was started around 1947 by graduate students at Temple University. Following the naming of its publication as *The Reading Teacher* in 1951 and its issuance as a printed magazine in 1952, I.C.I.R.I. grew steadily. By 1954 the majority of the people on the board of one of these organizations were also on the board of the other, and the desirability of a merger was evident. The last day of their independent existence was December 31, 1955, a fitting close to the decade.

The Orton Society was also founded during this decade and issued its first bulletin in 1950.

The preference of many psychiatrists and clinical psychologists for emphasis on emotional causation and treatment of reading problems by psychotherapy continued strongly through these ten years. One of the most influential papers was by Gerald Pearson, a highly regarded psychoanalyst, and described several kinds of personality deviations that could produce reading disability as a symptom (*44*). I can recall being a member of a symposium on ego problems in reading difficulties at the annual convention of the American Orthopsychiatric Association in 1953; I described remedial reading as a form of non-interpretive, ego-strengthening psychotherapy. Numerous theses were done about that time in which personality tests were given to a reading disability group and a group of normal readers. Nearly all of those studies found a wide range of scores in both groups and no significant differences in group averages. By the end of the decade the suspicion was growing that the psychology of personality was not providing the key to the understanding of reading disability.

This decade from 1946 to 1955 was also marked by a general expansion of interest in remedial reading, an expansion which was shown in many ways. Scores of colleges and universities organized reading clinics, and many started graduate training programs for reading specialists. The number of remedial teachers in public school systems continued to grow. Remedial reading programs began to spread upward from elementary schools to the secondary schools. Commercial organizations offering everything from tutoring the nonreader to speed reading for executives sprang up in the larger cities.

With a growing market, materials written specifically for use in remedial reading began to appear, and several writers compiled lists of books that combined a mature interest level with low difficulty.

As this decade ended, in 1955, a new theory burst upon the public: children were failing to learn to read just because they weren't being taught phonics. Rudolf Flesch's *Why Johnny Can't Read* (19) became a best seller, and public and parental criticism of the schools quickly intensified. Looking back, it is easy to see both that the argument was a gross oversimplification, put across with blatant use of propaganda techniques, and that it had a partial basis in fact. The merger resulting in the birth of IRA came just when public interest in reading was reaching a peak of intensity. So closed a most interesting decade.

The fifth decade: 1956-1965

The year 1956 opened the fifth decade on a level of high emotional tension. Reading specialists were busy showing that disabilities existed in countries where the grapheme-phoneme relationship was regular and phonic instruction was the rule and informing the public about all the factors that may help to produce a reading difficulty other than method of teaching. Flesch had, however, done remedial

reading a great service: he had convinced hundreds of thousands of parents that when Johnny had trouble with reading, he was not necessarily stupid; and this viewpoint led to public pressure both for improved developmental reading programs and for more diagnostic and remedial facilities.

On January 1, 1956, IRA officially came into existence; and its phenomenal growth since then has been a source of continuing amazement to me, as well as of satisfaction. Before and shortly after the merger some remedial specialists expressed fears that their interests would be neglected in the new organization. By now, I hope, such fears are things of the past.

New books continued to appear. New textbooks included one by Bond and Tinker in 1957 (4) and one by Roswell and Natchez in 1964 (48). Revised editions were brought out by Harris in 1956 and 1961 and Kottmeyer in 1959. The 1962 University of Chicago Reading Conference was devoted to underachievement in reading (60). Scholarly contributions included Vernon's review of the literature on backwardness in reading (61), Malmquist's study of reading disability in the first grade (36), the books by Hermann and Critchley mentioned previously, and a useful collection of papers edited by Money (37). Although papers on diagnostic and remedial reading continued to appear in scores of educational, psychological, and medical journals, the various IRA publications became increasingly helpful. Annual reviews of reading research by Helen M. Robinson for IRA* and Theodore Harris for the *Journal of Education Research* continued the pioneer efforts of Gray and helped to keep reading specialists in touch with new developments.

The major shift in theory was away from psychodynamics and toward renewed emphasis on physiological, neurological, and constitutional factors. In 1956 Rabinovitch first published his

---

*In *The Reading Teacher* through 1964 and in the *Reading Research Quarterly* from 1965 on.

distinction between primary reading disabilities, which he considered to be the result of constitutional deviations in neurological functioning, and secondary reading disabilities which may be induced by a variety of environmental factors (45). The next year Lauretta Bender attributed severe reading disability to a maturational lag, a delayed development of certain brain centers (1). Rabinovitch and Bender were both psychiatrists with excellent reputations and their papers were influential. Both avoided the trap of attributing deficiencies in perceptual or motor skills necessarily to brain damage, a diagnosis made all too often on flimsy evidence.

In 1959 a brave effort was made to explain all reading disabilities with a single theory. Smith and Carrigan, after an intensive study of about 40 cases, concluded that all of the varied symptoms could be explained by a lack of balance between two chemicals controlling the transmission of nerve impulses in the brain (52). The theory was impressive; the evidence, unfortunately, was less than convincing.

Another unconventional approach was that of Delacato, whose background was in work with brain-damaged children. Delacato attributed reading disability to an arrest of neurological development (14). Some children were thought to be arrested at a level of one of the lower brain centers; their treatment might start with practice in creeping, crawling, and sleeping in a preferred position. For other children the problem was thought to be failure to establish unilateral dominance, and unconventional measures to enforce unilateral dominance were used, including such practices as forbidding the child to listen to music. Delacato's theories have been widely discussed, but most specialists on reading disability remain skeptical.

At IRA pre-conference institutes efforts were made by Harris in 1961 (29) and deHirsch in 1962 (13) to clarify the nature of the perceptual difficulties in reading cases. Both stressed the Gestalt aspects of perception, particularly with regard to part-whole relationships and failures in integration of one experience with another.

Experimentation with drugs as an adjunct to remedial treatment was started but did not get very far. Smith and Carrigan were encouraged by their results with a few cases; Staiger, on the other hand, obtained negative results (53). Considering the variety of drugs now used in psychiatric settings, this area of reading research has barely been started.

New trends in diagnostic testing included growing skepticism about intelligence tests, a new and warmly greeted test based on psycholinguistic principles, and considerable attention to testing of perceptual abilities. While reading clinics continued to rely on the Stanford-Binet and Wechsler intelligence scales which are individually administered, there was growing recognition that group tests of mental ability are not very satisfactory with retarded readers. The Illinois Test of Psycholinguistic Abilities measured nine aspects of visual, auditory, and motor functioning relevant to language development and was welcomed in many reading clinics (32). The Frostig Developmental Test of Visual Perception attempted to provide measures of five aspects of visual perception: eye-hand coordination, figure-ground, form constancy, position in space, and spatial relations (20). Auditory perception tests were found useful, and favorable validity data were reported for the Wepman Auditory Discrimination Test (8), and an auditory blending test devised by Roswell and Chall (7).

The outpouring of new ideas about how the teaching of beginning reading can be improved that has taken place since 1960 has had its counterpart in remedial teaching. Advocates of perceptual training—i.t.a., words in color, materials based on linguistic principles, programed materials, programed tutoring, talking typewriters, and specific phonic systems—have all been clamoring for attention. Most of these approaches are still too new to be properly evaluated, and we will have to wait a few years for the dust to settle.

The 1960's have also seen an outburst of interest in the massive reading retardation among disadvantaged children, particularly those belonging to minority groups. So far, most of this attention has been focused on improving the developmental reading program, providing preschool enrichment, and working with the school dropout and adult illiterate. We need to take a careful look at the child who is both disadvantaged and a case of special disability.

Remedial reading began during this decade to be accepted as a field of special education, requiring specially trained teachers and deserving financial support. The first state certification of remedial teachers was begun, although most states still do not certify remedial teachers as such.

The climax of the decade, however, came with the passing of the new education acts of 1965. The Elementary and Secondary Education Act provided hundreds of millions of dollars for new programs to meet the needs of the disadvantaged. Much of this money under Title I and Title III has gone into an almost infinite variety of remedial reading projects and programs. One of the immediate results was that the previously inadequate supply of trained reading specialists was totally insufficient to meet the demand, and hundreds of untrained or insufficiently trained people have had to fill a great many of the new positions. How seriously this condition may have affected the quality of the new programs is still a matter of guesswork.

In 1965, also, federal recognition of the critical need for reading personnel was shown by the addition of reading to the fields of study in which special training institutes could be supported under the National Defense Education Act. The December 1965 issue of *The Reading Teacher* listed 67 NDEA

institutes in reading to be held in 1966. This institute program, which is continuing, holds promise of lessening somewhat the critical shortage of trained reading specialists.

Thus, the fifth decade closed with recognition by the public and by the government that remedial reading is a necessary special service and that it should be staffed with properly trained teachers.

We have taken a birds-eye-view of five decades. The year 1916 marked the first publication on reading difficulties in America; 1965 ended with federal support for a vast program of new diagnostic and remedial services and with support also for the training of needed personnel in this field. We have come far in these 50 years.

As the 50 years came to a close, however, much remained open and unsolved, and still is. We still do not have definitions of reading disability and remedial reading which everyone is willing to accept. Controversy continues over the causation of reading failure. Many varieties of remedial treatment are in use, some long established, others very new. While reading clinics and remedial programs have proliferated, there is no set of standards as to how they should be organized, how they should operate, or how they should be staffed. Research is lagging far behind innovation, making it possible for the program with the best press agent to get the most attention. The many professions interested in reading problems are just beginning to pay attention to one another's findings and opinions.

There is, then, a great deal still to be accomplished. The work of predicting, preventing, diagnosing, and correcting reading failure has been well started. But final answers are a hope for the future rather than a present reality. Much remains to be done.

REFERENCES

1. Bender, Lauretta. "Specific Reading Disability as a Maturational Lag," *Bulletin of the Orton Society*, 7 (1957), 9-18.
2. Betts, Emmett A. *Prevention and Correction of Reading Difficulties.* Evans-

ton: Row, Peterson & Co., 1936.

3. Blanchard, Phyllis. "Psychogenic Factors in Some Cases of Reading Disability," *American Journal of Orthopsychiatry,* 5 (1935), 361-374.

4. Bond, Guy L., and Miles A. Tinker. *Reading Difficulties: Their Diagnosis and Correction.* New York: Appleton-Century-Crofts, Inc., 1957.

5. Bronner, Augusta F. *The Psychology of Special Abilities and Disabilities.* Boston: Little, Brown & Co., 1917.

6. Buswell, Guy T. *Remedial Reading at the College and Adult Levels: an Experimental Study.* Supplementary Educational Monographs, No. 50. Chicago: Department of Education, University of Chicago, 1939.

7. Chall, Jeanne; Florence G. Roswell; and Susan H. Blumenthal. "Auditory Blending Ability: A Factor in Success in Beginning Reading," *The Reading Teacher,* 17 (1963), 113-118.

8. Christine, Charles and Dorothy Christine. "The Relation of Auditory Discrimination to Articulatory Defects and Reading Retardation," *Elementary School Journal,* 65 (1964), 97-100.

9. Cole, Luella. *The Improvement of Reading.* New York: Farrar and Rinehart, 1938.

10. Critchley, Macdonald. *Developmental Dyslexia.* London: William Heinemann Medical Books Ltd., 1964.

11. Dearborn, Walter F. "Structural Factors Which Condition Special Disability in Reading." *Proceedings of the American Association for Mental Deficiency,* 1933, *38,* 266-283.

12. Dearborn, Walter F., and Irving H. Anderson. "Aniseikonia as Related to Disability in Reading." *Journal of Experimental Psychology,* 1938, *23,* 559-577.

13. de Hirsch, Katrina. "Psychological Correlates in the Reading Process." *In Challenge and Experiment in Reading,* J. Allen Figurel, (Ed.). *International Reading Association Conference Proceedings,* 7 (1962), 218-226.

14. Delacato, Carl H. *The Treatment and Prevention of Reading Problems.* Springfield, Illinois: Charles C. Thomas, 1959. *The Diagnosis and Treatment of Speech and Reading Problems.* Charles C. Thomas, 1963.

15. Durrell, Donald D. *Durrell Analysis of Reading Difficulty.* Tarrytown, New York: World Book Co. (Harcourt, Brace & World), 1937.

16. Durrell, Donald D. *Improvement of Basic Reading Abilities.* Yonkers-on-Hudson: World Book Co., 1940.

17. Fernald, Grace M. *Remedial Techniques in Basic School Subjects.* New York: McGraw-Hill Book Co., 1943.

18. Fernald, Grace M., and Helen B. Keller. "Effects of Kinesthetic Factor in Development of Word Recognition," *Journal of Educational Research,* 4 (1921), 355-377.

19. Flesch, Rudolph. *Why Johnny Can't Read.* New York: Harper & Bros., 1955.

20. Frostig, Marianne; Welty Lefever; and J. R. B. Whittlesey. *Administration and Scoring Manual for the Marianne Frostig Developmental Test of Visual Perception.*

21. Gates, Arthur I. *Gates Reading Diagnosis Tests.* New York: Bureau of Publications, Columbia University, 1927.

22. Gates Arthur I. *The Improvement of Reading.* New York: The Macmillan Co., 1927; 2nd Ed., 1935.

23. Gates, Arthur I. "The Role of Personality Maladjustment in Reading Disability," *Journal of Genetic Psychology,* 59 (1941), 77-83.

24. Gray, Clarence T. *Deficiencies in Reading Ability: Their Diagnosis and Remedies.* Boston: D. C. Heath and Co., 1922.

25. Gray, William S. "Diagnostic and Remedial Steps in Reading," *Journal of Educational Research,* 4 (1921), 1-15.

26. Gray, William S. *Remedial Cases in Reading: Their Diagnosis and Treatment.* Supplementary Educational Monograph, No. 22. Chicago: Univ. of Chicago Press, 1922.

27. Hallgren, Bertil. "Specific Dyslexia," *Acta Psychiatrica et Neurologica,* Supplement 65 (1950).

28. Harris, Albert J. *How to Increase Reading Ability.* New York: Longmans, Green and Co., 1940.

29. Harris, Albert J. "Perceptual Difficulties in Reading Disability." In *Changing Concepts of Reading Instruction,* J. Allen Figurel, (Ed.). *International Reading Association Conference Proceedings,* 6 (1961), 282-290.

30. Hermann, Knud. *Reading Disability: A Medical Study of Word-Blindness and Related Handicaps.* Springfield, Illinois: Charles C. Thomas, 1959.

31. Judd, Charles H. *Reading: Its Nature and Development.* Supplementary Educational Monographs, No. 2. Chicago: Univ. of Chicago Press, 1918.

32. Kirk, Samuel A., and J. J. McCarthy. "The Illinois Test of Psycholinguistic Abilities—An Approach to Differential Diagnosis," *American Journal of Mental Deficiency,* 66 (1961), 399-412.

33. Kottmeyer, William. *Handbook for Remedial Reading.* St. Louis: Webster Publg. Co., 1947.

34. Lloyd, S. M., and C. T. Gray. *Reading in a Texas City: Diagnosis and Remedy.* University of Texas Bulletin No. 1853. Austin: Univ. of Texas, 1920.

35. McCallister, James M. *Remedial and Corrective Instruction in Reading.* New York: D. Appleton-Century Co., 1936.

36. Malmquist, Eve. *Factors Related to Reading Disabilities in the First Grade*

of the Elementary School. Stockholm: Almqvist & Wiksell, 1958.

37. Money, John (Ed.). *Reading Disability: Progress and Research Needs in Dyslexia.* Baltimore: Johns Hopkins Press, 1962.

38. Monroe, Marion. *Children Who Cannot Read.* Chicago: Univ. of Chicago Press, 1932.

39. Monroe, Marion. *Monroe Diagnostic Reading Examination.* Chicago: C. S. Stoelting, 1928.

40. Monroe, Marion, and Bertie Backus. *Remedial Reading.* Boston: Houghton, Mifflin Co., 1937.

41. Morgan, W. Pringle. "A Case of Congenital Word-Blindness," *British Medical Journal, 2* (1896), 1378.

42. Orton, June L. "The Orton-Gillingham Approach." Chapter 8 in *The Disabled Reader,* John Money, (Ed.) Baltimore: The Johns Hopkins Press, 1966.

43. Orton, Samuel T. "'Word-blindness' in Children," *Archives of Neurology and Psychiatry,* 14 (1925), 581-615.

44. Pearson, Gerald H. J. "A Survey of Learning Difficulties in Children," *Psychoanalytic Study of the Child, 7* (1952), 372-386.

45. Rabinovitch, Ralph, *et al.* "A Research Approach to Reading Retardation," *Neurology and Psychiatry in Childhood.* Proceedings of the Association for Research in Nervous and Mental Disease, 34, 363-396. Baltimore: Williams and Wilkins, 1956.

46. *Report of the National Committee on Reading.* Twenty-fourth Yearbook, Part I, of the National Society for the Study of Education, Guy M. Whipple, (Ed.). Bloomington, Illinois: Pub. Sch. Publg. Co., 1925.

47. Robinson, Helen M. *Why Pupils Fail in Reading.* Chicago: Univ. of Chicago Press, 1947.

48. Roswell, Florence, and Gladys Natchez. *Reading Disability: Diagnosis and Treatment.* New York: Basic Books, Inc., 1964.

49. Russell, David H.; Etta E. Karp; and Edward I. Kelly. *Reading Aids through the Grades.* New York: Bureau of Publications, Teachers College Columbia University, 1938.

50. Schmitt, Clara. "Developmental Alexia: Congenital Word-Blindness or Inability to Learn to Read," *Elementary School Journal,* 18 (1918), 680-700, 757-769.

51. Sievers, Dorothy J., *et al. Selected Studies on the Illinois Test of Psycholinguistic Abilities.* Madison: Photo Press, Inc., 1963.

52. Smith, Donald E. P., and Patricia M. Carrigan. *The Nature of Reading Disability.* New York: Harcourt, Brace & Co., 1959.

53. Staiger, Ralph C. "Medicine for Reading Improvement," *Journal of Developmental Reading,* 5 (1961), 48-51.

54. Stanger, Margaret, and Ellen K. Donohue. *Prediction and Prevention of Reading Difficulties.* New York: Oxford Univ. Press, 1937.

55. Taylor, Earl A. *Controlled Reading.* Chicago: Univ. of Chicago Press, 1937.

56. Tinker, Miles A. "Diagnostic and Remedial Reading, I and II," *Elementary School Journal,* 33 (1932-33), 293-306, 346-357.

57. Tinker, Miles A. "Trends in Diagnostic and Remedial Reading as Shown by Recent Publications in This Field," *Journal of Educational Research, 32* (1938), 293-303.

58. Traxler, Arthur E. *Ten Years of Research in Reading: Summary and Bibliography.* Educational Records Bulletin, No. 32. New York: Educ. Rec. Bur., 1941. *Another Five Years of Research in Reading,* Educational Records Bureau Bulletin, No. 46 (1945). *Eight More Years of Research in Reading,* Educational Records Bureau Bulletin, No. 64 (1955). *Research in Reading During Another Four Years,* Educational Records Bulletin, No. 75 (1960).

59. Uhl, Willis W. "The Use of the Results of Reading Tests as a Basis for Planning Remedial Work," *Elementary School Journal,* 17 (1916), 266-75.

60. *The Underachiever in Reading.* Compiled by H. Alan Robinson, (Ed.). Supplementary Educational Monographs, No. 92. Chicago: Univ. of Chicago Press, 1962.

61. Vernon, M. D. *Backwardness in Reading: A Study of Its Nature and Origin.* Cambridge. Cambridge Univ. Press, 1957.

62. Zirbes, Laura. "Diagnostic Measurement as a Basis for Procedure," *Elementary School Journal,* 18 (1918), 505-552.

Tomorrow's Reading Instruction: Paradox and Promise

NILA BANTON SMITH
Glassboro State College

THIS IS AN AGE of explosions. There is a knowledge explosion, a transportation explosion, a communication explosion, a chemical explosion, a psychological explosion, a medical explosion, and an educational explosion, of which reading instruction is one part. While trying to adjust ourselves to these explosions, other explosions will burst forth—all new and exciting.

Paradoxes usually accompany explosions.

In discussing "Tomorrow's Reading Instruction: Paradox and Promise," I plan to point out some of the paradoxes of the future and to attempt to evaluate their promises and dangers in reading.

In order to consider paradoxes of tomorrow, we must first visualize the world of tomorrow. The "tomorrow" that I have in mind is the year 1985. Children born in the present year of 1967 will be eighteen years old in 1985 and receiving their high school diplomas in June of that year. These are the children that we shall be teaching in the years ahead. In what kind of a world will they be living? What kind of reading instruction must we provide if these young people are to cope with changes that are racing by in supersonic speed? Surely it will be paradoxical to what we are doing now.

First, let us discuss the kind of world in which these children will be educated and then the kind of reading that we shall need to provide.

The world of tomorrow

Transportation and communication. Travel of all kinds will have undergone striking change by 1985. Man will not only have landed on the moon but he will have established bases there. Because of man's ardent craving to explore new worlds, perhaps astronauts will have landed on Mars. Surely this visitation will happen before the end of this century, and perhaps other planets will have been reached, also.

Atomic powered planes will flash through the air with supersonic speeds, taking us any place in the world in fantastically short times. Huge carriers many times bigger than the biggest plane at present will carry large groups of people to conventions or on excursions to different parts of the world. Helicopters will be commonly owned and used in carrying people to and from work. In cities the copters may land on rooftops.

Luxury trains will travel from coast to coast in a few hours. Some trains now under experimentation travel 150 miles per hour. Undoubtedly these speeds will be greatly increased by 1985.

Automobiles will be streamlined, self-driving, and so heavily equipped with safety devices controlled by the government that it will be practically impossible for a person to get himself killed in an accident on the highway. Because of air pollution the electric car may come back. A Ford Motor official says that there will be automated tracks between major cities. A computer will guide the car to the right track and take over its speed at 75 miles per hour while the driver plays cards, dictates letters, or eats a lunch taken from the car's refrigerator.

Telephones will be equipped with photographic devices, and we will be able to reach a person by dialing any place in the world. Business conferences by video phone will take place commonly. Men in the conference will see and hear one another while sitting in their respective offices all over the country.

Talking typewriters will take dictation, changing spoken words to printed symbols; and computers will take care of bookkeeping and recording in business offices. Storage of information will undergo phenomenal change. Even now the National Cash Register Company has perfected the art of microphotography to a point it is able to store on a single 4 x 6 inch film the entire contents of the *Encyclopaedia Britannica*.

Satellites will flash educational programs, entertainment, and propaganda into far distant homes which now have little contact with the rest of the world. Satellites equipped with strong physical sensors will be able also to survey farms to detect diseases in crops. They may also be used to locate sources of minerals, drought areas, and forest fires.

Chemical and psychological developments. The chemical revolution may result in spectacular changes in learning with use of the new drugs. One of the most publicized drugs with which chemists are experimenting at present is their memory-enhancing pill. This drug has the trade-name Cylert. Researchers discovered it at Abbott Laboratories in North Chicago. Cylert appears to produce a chemical found in the brain called ribonucleic acid, and so it is given the abbreviation RNA.

When N. Plotinkoff, a scientist in the Abbott laboratory (10), tested the drug on rats, he discovered that it improved their learning capacity up to five times the learning capacity of untreated rats. And this learning was permanent.

Now the memory pill is being tried in human beings. Results will not be available for some time, but hopes are high that the drug will do for humans what it did for rats.

Retarded children are likely to be given the memory pill under experimental conditions. If most retarded children are slow because of underdeveloped brain cells, the drug may offer some benefit to them.

Perhaps in this period of stepped-up effort by biochemists and biophysicists, control or modification of specific personality characteristics may become a possibility. And perhaps scientists may one day even reach into the genes and change the very matter we're made of.

Environment, social contacts, and dendrites seem to have something to do with learning, also. The neurons appear to be the most likely candidates for the thinking process, but it is not known whether they reproduce. Dendrites which extend into the arms and legs do grow back after being severed or mangled. Therefore, scientists think that possibly neurons may send out new shoots also, thus increasing learning ability.

Anyhow, there is some evidence linking dendritic growth with intelligence. Rats raised in enriched environments and in company with other rats were found more adept at learning tricks than were their brothers and sisters raised in complete isolation. Dr. Krech and his co-workers at U.C.L.A. examined and compared the brains of these rats. They found a striking difference in the dendritic growth in the two groups of rats. The enriched environment social group had much greater dendritic growth than the deprived rats had and, as already stated, they were more adept at learning.

And so dendrites, RNA, and other memory drugs all fit into the picture. Nature seems to make use of all these elements in her own way. By 1985, scientists may have probed into nature and forced her to reveal her secrets in ways which will raise intelligence and increase learning ability.

The possibility of using chemistry and psychology to improve learning is, indeed, a paradox of great significance.

Medical developments. Equally exciting will be the developments in medicine. No doubt the class of 1985 will have much longer lives than any preceding class will have had. Chemical control of aging will take place. Resistance will be made possible in many kinds of disease and unhealthy hearts, kidneys, livers, and spleens will be replaced with healthy ones from other people, or it may be that synthetic organs or electronic devices may be used instead of natural organs.

All of this means, of course, that our population of older people will be greatly increased. Environment will change rapidly over their span of years, and it will be necessary for them to go back to school periodically to keep up with the changes, particularly in the areas of social studies and the sciences.

The possibilities of computers in everyday living. This may be an appropriate point at which to discuss the computer and some of its characteristics and to indicate some of its possibilities in future years. The first commercial computer in the United States was installed just thirteen years ago. Now almost 20,000 are in use—in factories, banks, business offices, government—and 7,000 more are on order. Scientists are working on models that will, it is predicted, develop their own intuition, design their own descendants, and make their own decisions.

Some experts predict that eventually we will have high IQ computers. These computers will be able to comprehend IQ tests and make unbelievably high scores on them.

It is said that individuals will not be handling money or even checks in the years ahead. Each person will have a computer number. He will give this number when he makes a deposit, and he will use the number and perhaps a thumb print in lieu of cash whenever he makes a purchase. The computer will keep a record of deposits and expenditures. It also will warn the person, himself, and the people with whom he is dealing when his deposits are reaching a dangerously low level in relation to his expenditures.

Schools and reading in 1985

School architecture. In order that the flexible kind of education which we visualize for 1985 may proceed, we shall need new architectural arrangements in school buildings. One of the boldest new plans being proposed is the educational park, which would assemble on a single large site children from a broad attendance area. In this park-like setting there would be clusters of schools—a high school which would accommodate several thousand students, intermediate schools for several thousands of middle-grade pupils, and perhaps only one primary school which would still serve as a neighborhood school. Students would be taken to and from school by buses or, perhaps, by helicopters.

One indication of the transition from old buildings to new ones in order better to meet the coming instructional programs is that they are "open-ended"—leaving opportunities for easy adaptations in the curriculum and instructional methods. Space will be fluid with flexible, sound-proof partitions moved to make large or small rooms as desired. Traditional classrooms will be replaced by instructional spaces designated as learning centers, seminar rooms, research areas, and learning laboratories. Air conditioning will be the rule. Large spaces will be broken into a series of operational units. Interiors will be broken by courts, lounges, snack bars, and general service areas. Drapes, interior glass panels, brick walls, murals, and varying color schemes will add softness to the interiors. Office space, lounges, and classrooms will be carpeted.

The study hall will disappear. It will be replaced with student carrels (small, enclosed structures for individual study), cubicles for computer work, seminar rooms, reading lounges, and more extensive library and research facilities.

Thus, the architecture of the new schools in communities that can afford them will be conducive to reading improvement. The provision for flexibility in room size will make it possible to organize small groups who have special needs in reading. Small rooms and carrels will permit some students to work individually and progress at their own rates. Better libraries, learning laboratories, and ready lounges will permit independent study, research, opportunities to pursue solutions to problems, and the enjoyment of reading for just pleasure and relaxation.

Organizing for instruction. Some of the new grouping procedures at present are paradoxes. So many of these are appearing at this time that it almost seems as if we are groping for grouping. This is quite paradoxical to our philosophy of the past.

Our first concern about grouping arose in the 1800's. The Westward movement, industrialism, more rapid transportation, the birth of new towns, and mounting hordes of youth—all of these factors together brought about public, tax-supported schools and mass instruction began. Organizing classes into grade levels was ushered in as the solution to our problems, and McGuffey wrote the first series of graded readers to fit in with the new school organization. Elementary teachers, striving to meet individual differences, divided their classes into three groups each. The three-group plan has stood as an invincible bulwark ever since, but it will be gone by 1985.

Many new scheduling and grouping plans, already underway, stand as paradoxes to former arrangements. I will mention two of these. One is the flexible scheduling plan which may serve as a harbinger of the future. This plan schedules the day into short modules of time. In Norridge, Illinois, schools have 20-minute modules or 21 periods per day, instead of 7 as formerly. In the Indiana plan, 15-minute modules occur (9). One short module may be used for something that doesn't require much time. Other modules may be connected to make longer periods as desired. Grouping varies, also.

Such flexibility in scheduling offers excellent possibilities for teaching reading. Perhaps a few students who want power reading might meet for fifteen minutes twice a week. Perhaps those needing corrective reading could meet fifteen minutes daily. Possibly remedial cases could meet with an instructor individually or in very small groups for thirty minutes daily. I suspect that when all schools have more flexible schedules, the problem of trying to find time in which to teach reading in the secondary school will no longer exist, and that such flexibility will also be a valuable aid in meeting individual differences in the elementary grades.

Along with flexible time scheduling, we find many other new grouping plans emerging. One of these innovations at present is team teaching, in which (1) there are new groupings of both teachers and students. I suspect that many are already experimenting with team teaching. I think this method has great promise for tomorrow's teachers of reading.

A team of teachers may request a single student or as many as 350 students for lengths of time which vary from twenty minutes to a whole day. The team teachers decide what activities will best meet the needs of their students for any particular day. They then plan on groupings and procedures in terms of these needs. Thus, the amount of time for reading and the elements of reading to be given practice are varied in terms of pupil requirements.

These examples of flexible scheduling and team teaching, I believe, are harbingers of future arrangements which hold much promise for successful teaching of reading to children of varied abilities.

New methods and materials. The reading explosion of the sixties has been responsible for an outcropping of many new approaches to beginning reading. Authors and publishers hope that their respective products will enable children to learn to read better and in a shorter time.

We have the Initial Teaching Alphabet, linguistic reading materials, programed instruction, Words in Color, and several other new approaches. All of these are paradoxical to the use of a graded basal reading series which has been with us ever since the publication of McGuffey's set of readers. What about the future of these paradoxical methods and materials that are already with us? Some of them may be with us in 1985, but perhaps integrated within frameworks broader than word recognition which most of them are primarily designed to teach. Others of them may remain much as they are now and be provided to teachers along with several other sets of material. Under these conditions, the teacher may choose from several methods those materials best suited to teach word recognition to children having different styles of learning. Some of our present paradoxical methods may disappear entirely and then come back in fifty or a hundred years wearing a different cloak of philosophy. I have found in my research that there are such things as historical cycles in reading. In addition, some new approaches that we don't even dream of at the present time will have appeared by 1985 and will begin their cycles of modification, integration, or obsolescence, as the case may be. Our knowledge of teaching reading will be richer, however, because of all of them.

As for promise, the fact that so many people are trying to find better ways of teaching reading is in itself promising. I hope that we may continue to search.

Teaching reading at different age extremes. For the past four decades, children have entered first grade and started their reading instruction at six years of age. During the early twenties, instruction in reading was supposed to have been concluded at the end of third grade. Later the endpoint came to be sixth grade, and eventually high school, and then on to college freshmen who needed to upgrade their reading skills. A few adults began coming to reading centers to improve their speed and comprehension. Now we have strong directives to teach all adult illiterates to read, and this work is presently being done with vigor and the involvement of thousands of individuals. As a paradox of 1985, we may see the complete obliteration of illiteracy in our country, including all adults as well as children.

As for young children at the other age extreme, the government, in its Head Start project, has already set the pattern for sending three- and four-year-olds to school. By 1985 all public schools will probably have nursery schools.

In some quarters pressure is now being made by parents to teach their three- and four-year-olds to read, and some schools are teaching reading in kindergarten. Specialists in early childhood deplore this situation. On the other hand, children are more sophisticated today than they were when the six-year-old readiness age was established in the 1920's. Studies and articles report that many children are reading early. We find accounts in popular literature as well.

You will probably recall that the author of the Pulitzer Prize winning novel *To Kill a Mockingbird* amusingly portrays the experiences of a preschool reader. You will remember that Jem said of his four-and-a-half year old sister, ". . . Scout there's been reading' since she was born, and she ain't even been to school yet." Then, upon entrance in first grade Scout, whose real name was Jean Louise, was asked to read something that Miss Caroline wrote on the chalkboard; and she read it so well that Miss Caroline was visibly vexed. Miss Caroline then had her read most of the first reader and the stock market quotations in the *Mobile Register.* All of this time Miss Caroline's irritation was building up, and she finally exploded, "Tell your father to stop teaching you. It will interfere with your learning to read in school." Jean Louise said that her father didn't teach her and then she began soliloquizing to herself as to how she did learn to read and finally decided that it just came like learning to fasten the flap on the back of her union suit without looking around.

There are other children like Jean Louise, and they should not be denied reading if they want it. On the other hand, we must bear in mind that there are great masses of children in the United States who are not ready for reading, even at six years of age and perhaps not until seven or later. In these cases the school must catch up the lag.

Without a doubt, our concept of reading readiness needs revision. In the meantime, let us hold fast to the assumption that there is no one chronological or mental age at which reading instruction should begin. Readiness for reading is a matter of individual qualifications.

By 1985, when all schools provide nursery schools, perhaps some children will be ready for reading earlier than otherwise would be the case. Simultaneously, by 1985 we shall have new tests for assessing reading readiness, new materials to use in strengthening certain readiness factors, and new administrative arrangements to take care of children who are immature in the readiness constituents.

Nationalized, factualized, computerized instruction

Without a doubt, our schools are becoming more nationalized, more factualized, and more computerized. As one example of these trends, "National Testing" will be discussed.

National testing. As you undoubtedly know, a Carnegie-supported exploratory committee on preparing tests for national assessment was appointed. This committee requested specific organizations to produce specifications for instruments for each assessment. The Educational Testing Service and three other agencies were given contracts and have set up panels of specialists in each subject field. Although primary attention is focused on the Carnegie-supported "Assessment of Educational Progress," efforts to set up national testing has the support and encouragement of the U. S. Office of Education.

Several educational organizations and individual leaders in education violently disapprove of such a measure. Some of their reasons are as follows:

1. Any national testing program will inevitably lead to a standardization of the curriculum.
2. Such a program will be used to compare one school with another.
3. The art of group testing is too poor to justify a national program.
4. It places great emphasis on only a part of the true objectives—the acquisition of knowledge and measurable skill, neglecting the important factors of total physical, social, and emotional development, as well as personality growth and self-actualization.

Those who support the movement give reasons such as these:

1. At present we are without data to tell us where we as a nation stand in education or how we compare with other nations.
2. In view of planning for education at local, state, and national levels, we must have accurate information.
3. The government needs some uniform test data from the schools of the nation so that it may judge properly the effectiveness of subsidies.

So you see there are two sides to the matter.

The baselines for the first major assessment are well underway and the assessment will be made this fall (5).

1. *Samplings will be taken* from age levels of 9, 13, 17, and adult (about 30 years old). It is hoped that the school-age samples will be conducted through the schools; the adults will be reached by population sampling techniques.
2. *Sampling will be at three levels*—what 90 percent of the population should know, what the majority of the population should be expected to know, and what a small percentage (10 percent) should know.
3. *The sampling also will be taken by four regions* (Northeast, Southeast, Midwest, and Far West); by four levels of urbanization (city, rural, etc.), which also will take into account the socioeconomic level; and by both sexes.
4. *The first measurements will be in nine areas*—reading, writing, literature, vocational education, fine arts, social studies, math, citizenship and science.
5. *No participant will be expected to take more than a small part of the battery,* a maximum of 40 minutes. The full assessment would require about 10 hours.

The first assessment will be voluntary, given to schools whose administrators approve it.

This planned assessment will require from $2 to $3 million. Floyd N. Marrisett, Vice-President of Carnegie, admits that some comparisons will be made, " . . . and that there is some possibility of conformity to a national standard." Henry Dyer of ETS says that "teaching should be pointed very specifically at the tests the students will take as measures of output . . .," and he believes that this is the only way to determine outcomes, which must be known before objectives can be set. So it is that the leaders involved in this project are still talking about comparison, conformity to a national standard, and to test results pointing toward our teaching goals. If the national tests are pointing toward teacher goals, then our education is bound to become increasingly factual.

So, from what I can gather, I suspect that the reading teacher of tomorrow will have the results of his efforts tested by national tests. The most promising feature of this movement is that the poorer schools will probably get more financial aid from the government in order that they may produce better test results. I trust that each of us will hold fast to and strengthen our own personal ideals in regard to the development of physical, mental, linguistic, social, and emotional growths.

Technology and reading instruction. Now I shall discuss the paradox that overshadows all others mentioned so far —the technological revolution. Many people are predicting that all learning in the future will be administered by satellites and computers and that books as we know them will become obsolete. We'll simply have microdots on computers.

Companies hoping to make a fortune in school hardware are buying up the publishers of school textbooks. RCA bought Random House; Litton Industries, Inc., bought American Book Company; Time, Inc., bought Silver Burdett and placed it in a joint venture with G. E.; Zerox bought American Education Publishers, together with their smaller subsidiaries; Raytheon bought D. C. Heath. Between 1964 and the end of 1966, 120 arrangements of this type were made, and they are still going on. Recently CBS bought Manhattan's venerable publishing house of Holt, Rinehart, and Winston; and Bell & Howell bought Charles Merrill.

Big business is pushing the concept of technological revolution in schools with great vigor. Last August, I listened to representatives of Ford Foundation, Carnegie, Western Union, and others as each presented to a committee of Congress his company's plan for an educational satellite program. Such a program would reach many people who are in need of education. It would, of course, also make a fortune for the company or organization that is permitted to develop it. Millions of receivers must be bought to make use of satellite programs; many new television sets must be purchased.

According to these plans, the costs of educational satellite programs are to be paid in one form or another by people exclusive of big business. One plan is to place a tax on television sets to support the program; another plan is to run a satellite commercial program concurrently with the educational program and use funds from the commercial program to finance the educational program. Another plan is to have the government finance the educational program out of taxes. Regardless of the plan, big business will make the profit and others will finance the program.

As for computers: the computer enthusiasts say that practically all education in the future will be achieved through the use of programed material served by computers as the student sits by himself in a carrel or cubicle. Much experimentation in teaching *reading* with the use of computers is now underway in all elementary grades and high school.

The very latest experiment that I have heard about is the one underway in Brentwood School, East Palo Alto, California. IBM is the company that is financing this experiment. Here is a quotation about the experiment from *Look magazine:* "The IBM Corporation is especially happy since it has invested some $30 million in the research and development of computer-based instruction. 'There may be a lot of profit in this one day,' says Leonard Muller, Director of Instructional

Systems Development for IBM. Executives of other heavyweight electronics corporations agree. They have begun to hear the rustle of the new money that is falling like autumn leaves onto educational ground."

Now to describe briefly how the children in this experiment are learning to read. The master computer that does the teaching has 18 terminals. As the children come to the classroom, each one sits down before a screen at the end of his terminal. Various pictures begin to dance on this screen in front of him. Soon he is asked by the computer to make a response. This he does with a light-projecting pen. If the response is correct, the computer says "Good!" If it is wrong, the computer says "Nooooo." If there is a hesitation of more than 5 to 10 seconds, the computer says decisively, "Do it now!" If the child still sits and does nothing at all, the computer taps out a distress signal calling the teacher. I suspect that in computer teaching the teacher would be receiving such calls very often, because as I previously mentioned children have different styles of learning.

It seems that the government is aiding and encouraging the hastening of automated instruction. In the *Saturday Review* for January 14, 1966, there is a report of a sub-committee of economic development. This committee had as its charge to make recommendations in regard to "Efficiency and Innovations in Education." The committee was made up of 200, mostly business men.

To give you an idea of the tone of their recommendations, I will read you the opening paragraph of the report by the chairman of this committee (*11*).

Five centuries ago, when the first book was printed with movable type, the groundwork was laid for the greatest forward surge in education that the world has known up to now. Today we are seeing the beginning of another forward surge that may prove even greater. The electronic age is changing our traditional notions of education. The role of the teacher, the role of the classroom, the nature of the learning process, itself, must be re-examined in the light of the new technology.

The implication is that books are dead and will be replaced by technology. Several articles by other members of the committee follow, pointing out new directions in education in terms of electronic devices. I don't know why the committee on economic development should be telling the profession of education what the new directions in education should be, but they are. There are several other indications that big business is overstepping its bounds somewhat in trying to control education. I don't believe, however, that we need to fear the future possibilities of this situation. I am confident that our leaders in education, buttressed by the support of classroom teachers and college professors, will hold the front lines to a healthy balance.

I am pleased, already, at some of the responses that are coming forth from our professional leadership. The American Association of School Administrators, one of our most prestigious groups, held its annual convention in Atlantic City in February, 1967. Many of the speeches given by the members emphasized software as well as hardware. The January 1967 issue of the Phi Delta Kappan devoted its entire contents to "Big Business, Technology and Education."

Fritz Ianni, Research Chief in the Office of Education, expressed himself quite bluntly after attending a management convention. Among other things that were said at this convention in regard to the future of education was the remark of one business executive who blurted out, "There's a billion dollar market at our feet." Another explained, "*We've* been in education for years. *We* train thousands of people every year, teach them to operate computers, build jet engines; we've got one machine with a tape recorder and color slides that show how to do industrial soldering in 35 steps." Ianni, being justifiably alarmed, exploded in effective, if not elegant, language. He said, "Those guys who think you can teach kids in school just like you'd set up an industry program for 50 men in industrial soldering, they're nuts."

These are just a few examples of the expressed attitudes of some of our leadership people in regard to the aggressiveness of big business in our professional field. I think all of us should be aware of this situation.

There is no doubt at all that we shall find many of the new electronic devices helpful. But I hope that we, as teachers, may always be able to choose which ones we want to use, what we want to use in them, how we want to use them, and with whom. These decisions I think must be left with us, irrevocably.

The role of the reading teacher. Some people are asking "Will teachers of reading be needed in the future? Will teachers of reading have any role to play at all? Will books become obsolete? Will technology do the entire job of teaching reading? Will the teacher become just a buttonpushing robot?"

In my opinion, teachers of reading will be needed in the future, but they will have different roles to play. It is obvious, for one thing, that teachers should learn to be mechanics. They must understand computers and other technological devices thoroughly so that they may use them to advantage, maintain them, and possibly repair them when minor breakdowns occur. Teacher preparation will require courses in computerization. In connection with such a course, or in a separate course, teachers should be taught how to prepare programed material for use in the computer.

It is imperative, in my opinion, that teachers put their creative talent to work in preparing materials for electronic devices. Computers at present are too expensive for schools to buy. So, those firms dealing in computers rent them to schools under the condition that the schools buy from them their programed materials to use in the computer. And by whom are these materials prepared? By programers, generally, not by educators!

There is a heavy demand at the moment for programers. Big business needs 50,000 programers at once. It is advertising for programers and often saying that no special education or math is required. I know a young man who had great difficulty in getting through high school. He went to work for a computer company, where he was to learn how to be a computer mechanic. Soon afterwards he told me that instead of working with the mechanical aspects of computering, he was now programing material. I asked him what he was programing, and his reply was "Anything they give me. All I have to do is to break it down into tiny bits and ask a lot of questions over and over again."

At the present time in our schools, we are using reading materials which have been prepared by authorities in the field of reading educators who know children, and who are well acquainted in the broad, but specialized, field of reading. The computer people are making a big mistake in assuming that all that is needed in preparing reading material for the schools is someone who knows how to program. I am not alone in passing this judgment. Many others are saying the same thing.

In a talk given by Harold Howe (6), U. S. Commissioner of Education, I heard him say, not in so many words, but to this effect:

> I spoke to a bunch of business men the other day about setting up an organization for evaluating the educational tools that big business will be coming up with in the future. The Food and Drug Administration keeps an eye on what we put in our bodies. This organization I am talking about would take care of what we put in our minds. The speech made everybody pretty nervous. That's what I wanted to do—make them nervous.

Here is another quotation; this one is from H. Thomas James (12), Dean, School of Education, Stanford University:

$50 billion to spend

The word seems to be going out to the schools that they are expected to buy $50 billion worth of hardware in the next decade, and that they should get busy and figure out how they are going to use it. I have no doubt that $50 billion worth of equipment would help improve education in this country; my plea is that we put the geniuses to work studying the education process, as some few of them are doing, and asking, not, "What can this piece of equipment I happen to have too much of do for education?" but, "Given present needs and opportunities in education, what kind of equipment might I invent that would be useful?"

Wanted: Bigger Storerooms

Unless the latter question gets attended to, we will have to build even larger storage rooms for unused hardware than we already have (and one has to see what we even have now to believe it!) or else invent some new kind of disposal unit to grind it.

I don't know whether big business will ever take educators into partnership with them in preparing electronic devices and material to be used in them. I do know that teachers have much unused creative ability and ingenuity. If they will put their latent talent to work preparing materials, themselves, in terms of needs of their special groups or individual pupils and then process these through the computer or other electronic device, I can see much more promise in the whole situation.

Don't you believe the shibboleth that computers are going to free you from drudgery and leave you free to do other things. This is a paradox in itself, for many of the people who are saying this are saying at the same time that computers have the possibilities of doing everything.

Let's consider for a moment what the computer can do in reading and what you as teachers will need to do. The computer can drill children in recognizing whole words, in learning phonetic elements, and perhaps in working with word structure. It can give a lot of practice in following directions. It can check literal comprehension with set answers.

But how about interpretation, critical reading, and creative reading? In order to answer this question, I would like to take a moment to define these different kinds of comprehension as I

see them. *Literal comprehension* is the skill of getting the primary, direct, "literal" meaning of a word, idea, or sentence in context. *Interpretation* is used to include those skills necessary in getting deeper meanings than in literal comprehension, such as supplying or anticipating meanings not stated directly in text, drawing inferences, making generalizations, reasoning cause and effect, speculating on what will happen next, detecting the significance of a statement or passage or selection, and so on. *Critical reading* is the third level in the hierarchy of reading-for-meaning skills. According to my thinking, critical reading includes literal comprehension and interpretation; but it goes further than either of these in that the reader evaluates—passes personal judgment on the quality, the value, the accuracy, and the truthfulness of what is read. *Creative reading* is different again. In the first three types of reading that I have mentioned, the student is working with the author's text and his thinking. In creative reading, the student leaves the author's text and branches out on his own in thinking through to different solutions to a problem or to sensing new relationship.

One of our most important objectives in reading at present is to teach students to think; hence, the emphasis on all of our teaching should be on the last three types of thinking, and I can't see how a computer can develop these types of reading for which there may be many answers. The computer may offer a child three answers from which he is to choose one. In this case, the child is confined to the three answers resulting from someone else's thinking, rather than doing his own thinking and coming up with his own unique answer.

Thinking, discriminating, decision-making individuals are what we need in future America. Our students can only develop in these ways through participation in group thinking where each one expresses his own thinking orally, checks others' thinking and is checked by others, adds to others' thinking and lets others add to his—all of this guided by an astute teacher who will throw in a remark or question at the proper moment to stimulate deeper reflection. Mental interaction is necessary in working with deeper meanings in reading, but arriving at one set answer usually is not necessary. A variety of answers may come forth; but if straight thinking and sound judgment is shown, the variety that comes from uniqueness should be praised and not condemned. Under conditions described above students will have had practice in thinking rather than merely trying to find the one right answer set by someone else. Computers or no computers, the teacher will have the major responsibility for teaching interpretation of reading content and the thinking processes attendant upon critical and creative reading.

Then what about the children for whom the computer taps out a distress call to the teacher? Certainly not *all* children are going to learn by computerized instruction or by TV programs administered by satellites. There never will be any one panacea for teaching *all* children to read.

Perhaps while the majority are busy with the computer or other electronic device, the teacher may make case studies of those who are having difficulty in reading. She should be equipped during her college days to do a comprehensive case study of each child's qualifications for learning to read, including the social and emotional factors which affect reading success. Perhaps numberless prospective remedial reading cases might have been prevented from developing if their teachers had made case studies of them at the outset of their troubles. We hope that teachers of the future may have time to make such studies and that their colleges will have prepared them to do so and to correct the difficulties that are revealed, as well.

Psychotherapy has proved to be valuable also in working with remedial reading cases. Just being with someone who is sympathetic and encouraging aids the child in improving. Teachers should have more instruction in and more practice in using therapy during their college years. Warm, friendly, personal companionship is something that a computer or a satellite T.V. program cannot give. Teachers should be equipped to do more in the way of therapy. This is an area of teacher specialization which cannot ever be touched by automation.

There are other human influences of good teachers, that cannot be duplicated by electronic devices. As Harry Brandy says (2)

> . . . it is hard to imagine a conversation between a machine and a pupil; it is difficult to imagine the machine and the learner growing together, interacting with each other so that the experience of each changes irreversibly with each moment of instruction. It is even more difficult to conceive of a machine toward which the pupil feels respect and from which he expects understanding and respect. It is difficult to imagine how a machine could, without a word, pass a judgment on a pupil that the pupil will feel more keenly than the most detailed of reports from the battery of tests that the electronic counselors can emit on a second's notice.

We shall always need perceptive teachers of reading to guide and encourage students to invent questions as well as to answer them; to reflect, infer, and predict; to string together beads of information in arriving at generalizations; to aid independence in study; to foster creativity; to nourish values; and to refine sensitivities. In my opinion, no automated device can ever take the place of a tolerant, understanding, dedicated, inspired teacher of reading.

One more point, "Are books dead?" This is a question which we as teachers of reading must face.

"The printed word is passing", say the technologists. Is this true? If not, what is the function of books in this automated world? Frank Jennings says (7)

> . . . the value of a book in the changing world is in its ability to hold things still long enough for them to be understood, until fear and confusion can be replaced by something less paralyzing.

The book can make yesterday's seven thousand years a golden tapestry for the hero's hall. With it we can measure today's dilemma against yesterday's defeats. It may not diminish the press of our anguish, nor tarnish the glow of our achievements, but it can show us connections, it can point out perspectives.

The function of books, both for adults and children, has been stated well in this quotation.

Insofar as children alone are concerned, never before have so many books been written for children, never have so many books been read by children.

As Jeane Dunn has so aptly said (3):

> From the very tiny who point with petal fingers to intriguing details of illustration and inquire: 'What's dat?' to the young girl or lad with the just-perceptible mantle of adulthood resting on them, engrossed in the fifth dimension of *A Wrinkle in Time,* from these I have derived an uncrushable belief that Man's great gift to himself—the printed word—will never die.

I agree heartily with this sentiment. Books are not dead! Teachers are not dead! God is not dead! God-given teachers of reading and interest-laden books will walk down the aisles of time together in happy communion so long as civilization may endure.

REFERENCES

1. Beggs, David W., III. *Team Teaching.* Bloomington, Indiana: Indiana University Press, 1965.
2. Braudy, Harry. *Threat of Promise.* Englewood Cliffs: Prentice-Hall, 1961, 151.
3. Dunn, Jeane B. "Why the Printed Word Will Never Become Obsolete," *Woodbury Daily Times,* December 16, 1966, 1.
4. Dyer, Henry. Annual Conference of the U. S. Testing Service reported in *Education, U.S.A.* Washington, D. C., 1966, November 3, 1.
5. *Education, U. S. A.* National Assessment of Education. Next Fall, 1967. October 27, 1.
6. Howe, Harold, II. *Life* (February 10, 1967), 42.
7. Jennings, Frank. *This Is Reading.* New York: Teachers College, Columbia University, 1965, 74.
8. *Look Magazine,* February 1, 1966, 5-7.
9. Manlove, Donald C. and David W. Beggs. III. *Flexible Scheduling.* Bloom-

ington, Indiana: Indiana University Press, 1965.
10. McBroam, Patricia. "Understanding Memory," *Science News,* 12 (March 19, 1966), 186-87.
11. *Saturday Review,* January 14, 1966.
12. Thomas, James H. "Federal Policy and the Public Schools," *The School Administrator,* 24 (January, 1967), 66.

Skillful Teaching: Theory and Practice

RUTH STRANG
The University of Arizona

RECOGNIZING the relationship between reading disability and emotional disturbance, clinical psychologists and psychiatrists are emphasizing the importance of skillful instruction. A child's feeling of inadequacy in school can become pervasive and lead to a consistent pattern of failure to work up to his level of ability. As a basic process of the reeducation of emotionally disturbed children, Hobbs (5) mentioned competence in teaching that results in competence in learning. Psychiatrists, too, have recognized that disability in reading, which often underlies failure in other school subjects, is the root of many problems referred to mental hygiene and guidance clinics. From his experience in the Langley Clinic, Berlin reached the conclusion that "The educative efforts of our skilled teachers play an important part in the recovery of even psychotic children. Beginning to learn academic material is one way of beginning to deal with the real world. . . . I would, therefore, again emphasize that the teacher expects of herself that she learn to teach as effectively and skillfully as possible and that, in teaching, she is performing an important mental health task" (1).

Conditions for effective learning

A major emphasis in the teaching of reading today is on how pupils learn. Understanding the learning process is basic to effective teaching. We should, therefore, first ask what conditions are prerequisite to effective learning?

1. *Attention* is basic to learning. If we can get and hold the pupil's attention, then the way is open to learning. Movement attracts attention. Contrast captures a child's attention—contrast between capitals and lower case letters, between words that are alike except for a single letter (*fat* and *fate, hat* and *hate,* and between different kinds of sentences and paragraphs (*10,* pp. 125-128). Instead of drilling on one form, the pupil learns by having to distinguish one form from another. This skill requires active attention.

A mild discrepancy, novelty, or surprise also attracts attention. That is one reason why any new method so often get results. A new approach is especially important for pupils who have failed to learn by methods previously used. However, if the stimulus situation is so completely unfamiliar that the pupil has no response to make to it, it causes anxiety. The best way to find out whether a task is stimulating or frustrating to a pupil is to observe his response. If he becomes bored, the reading material may be dull or too easy or too difficult. Bright children sometimes avoid getting bored by discovering or creating some variation in a monotonous routine task. Less able learners may not get bored because they have not yet learned the response needed; the task still has some novelty to them.

2. *A background of correct oral English* is another prerequisite to success in learning to read. The spoken language is primary. By listening to selected TV programs, recordings, and stories read aloud to them, children gain a feeling for the sound and structure of English sentences. They also learn to associate the sound of words and phrases with printed forms as they follow the lines of print while listening to the passage read with natural intonation and stress. Pupils from non-English speaking homes especially need much experience in listening and speaking.

3. *The spirit of discovery* lightens learning. It is intellectually stimulating; it associates the experience with satisfaction; it aids memory; and it makes learning more personally meaningful. Even the study of phonics may have an element of discovery as when a child learns for himself that the same letter may have different sounds in different words as *e* in *ever, eve, fear, end,* and *player.* He has this feeling of discovery when he finds that he can read many new words as soon as he knows the consonant letter-sound associations and a single vowel sound. It is also exciting to realize that he can completely change the meaning of a word by adding a different initial consonant to a familiar cluster: *ame* as in *name, same, game,* and *tame.* Merely using word recognition skills to identify an unfamiliar word is an act of discovery, as is also locating and interpreting clues of character, mood, and plot in a story. Thus many aspects of reading can be presented as a process of discovery.

4. *Reinforcement of progress* in reading is another basic condition for effective learning which requires skill in making the consequences of the reading act satisfying or rewarding. Much has been written on the psychology of "operant conditioning," and a few experiments along this line in the field of reading have been reported. Severely retarded readers in several classes were given check marks on a chart for coming to class on time, for handing in their homework, and for even looking quite steadily at a book during a library period. They received extra credit for reading and reporting on a book. These check marks added up to some special privilege such as going to a school movie or football game. The result was that these students became more receptive to learning, more accessible to reading instruction. The teacher's hope is that the students will have acquired a new mode of response and will eventually become interested enough in reading to continue on their own initiative.

Reinforcement is most effective when it follows almost immediately after the desired behavior and is specific and relevant to the individual.

5. *Social reinforcement* based on identification with an admired person also provides a favorable condition for learning. Having established a number of points of identity with the pupil, the teacher may then describe *his* method of reading: "When I come to an unfamiliar word, I stop and think 'what word might make sense in the sentence; does that word begin and end with the sounds these letters stand for; does the word have some common parts I already know?' I don't attempt to say the word until I've applied my word recognition skills." This procedure was employed effectively with an impulsive boy who made many errors in reading because he did not stop to think and analyze the unfamiliar words.

6. *A positive expectancy of progress* promotes learning. A pupil who expects success is willing to attack new tasks. Even when he meets difficulty, he will put forth effort because he has built up ego strength in earlier years. But what of the pupil who has previously met more failure than success? He needs immediate experience of success through carefully chosen reading material and skillful instruction. In one experiment a teacher's expectation that certain pupils would make unusual growth in reading during the year actually did result in higher achievement than would normally have been expected of them.

7. *Reading must be functional and have personal significance and value* in the life of the child or adolescent. The undisciplined Maori children described by Sylvia Ashton Warner learned readily words like *mommy, fight,* and *ghost;* they failed to learn the words in a primer foreign to them. Adolescents whose ways of perceiving, thinking, and remembering have been shaped by a lifetime of TV and other mass media require the stimulus of reading material relevant to their world. They learn because reading has personal value for them. Unless the teacher looks at the world through their eyes, he fails to make connection with them.

8. *Understanding the individual in his environment.* This involves diagnostic teaching. Learning tasks must be commensurate with the individual's capacity, challenging but not overwhelming. But an exclusive analysis of his internal dynamics as in psychotherapy is increasingly being replaced by an analysis of the individual with reference to environmental conditions that may be facilitating or inhibiting progress in reading.

There are individual differences in the learning process used by children of different ages, abilities, and backgrounds. Some individuals tend to perceive the situation as a whole; others notice only details, often trivial, insignificant details (9). Some individuals tend to learn more easily through a visual approach; others, through auditory channels (2). If the teacher is aware of children who strongly favor either the auditory or visual modality, he may provide experiences in learning through their preferred channel. In addition, he may give special practice to strengthen the aspect in which they are weak; for example, exercises and games in auditory perception for boys who are weak in this basic ability. In general, the teacher "accentuates the positive" and eliminates the negative behavior by not giving attention to it.

Because of the effect of age differences on the learning-teaching process, this article will attempt to describe some examples of skillful teaching at different stages of child and adolescent development.

Infancy and preschool prereading experiences

Preparation for successful reading begins at birth. Apparently an individual's cognitive style—his ways of perceiving, reasoning, and remembering—has its genesis very early in life. Unless his environment provides appropriate stimulation, these abilities, which underlie reading achievement, do not begin to develop. With opportunities to manipulate things, to look, and to listen, the child's visual, auditory, and related perceptions develop.

Concomitant with the cognitive development is the affective aspect involving human relationship. The tender loving care of the mothering one is the basis of a sense of trust. A sense of trust encourages freedom to explore and an openness to new experiences.

During preschool years qualities of an inquiring mind, an outgoing attitude, a feeling of self-confidence and competence are further developed. The work of Hess and his associates (4) at the University of Chicago illustrates concretely the teaching process involved. Mothers were asked to teach their preschool children a simple task such as putting together a simple puzzle. Their methods varied greatly. Some mothers practically completed the task for the child or told him exactly what to do while others guided his learning by questions and comments which eventuated in the child's successful performance. Some mothers made disparaging remarks such as, "Why are you so slow!" "You're not half finished yet." Others encouraged the child by comments such as "You found just the right piece." "You're half finished already." Wilma Miller (6) continued experimentation along the same line by studying the relationship of parental language patterns and control to reading readiness and reading achievement at the end of the first grade. She found that the mother's teaching style and the prereading activities in the home were related to the child's initial reading readiness and to reading achievement near the end of the first grade.

Other preschool environmental conditions conducive to success in learning to read are opportunities for children to become familiar with the sound of language by hearing stories and poems read aloud to develop their speaking vocabulary and facility in the spoken language. The child's desire to learn to read grows as he sees others enjoying reading, discovers the delight that lies between the covers of books,

and begins to have a practical need to know words in print.

If a child has not had the opportunity to develop these abilities and interests—and this lack is true of most disadvantaged and bilingual children—he needs earlier rather than delayed school entrance, provided that his experiences in the preschool group develop the prereading competencies needed for successfully learning to read.

"Skillful instruction" during infancy and preschool years consists in providing a "responsive environment" for the child—a stimulating environment in which the child takes the initiative and the adult responds appropriately.

The primary grades: mastery of basic reading skills

Skillful instruction in beginning reading follows the preschool pattern of providing a responsive environment. In school there are new words, phrases, and sentences that the first grader wants and needs to read: his name on his locker, *girls, boys, up, down,* details of the daily schedule, and the like. He can learn these by sight. To aid him the teacher may illustrate and discuss the meaning of the word and call his attention to its configuration, the sequence of letters, and any distinguishing characteristics; she writes the word on the board, pronouncing it as she writes. She may ask the children to trace the word with their fingers. The aim is to make the first impression as vivid as possible. The value of starting reading instruction in this way is to introduce reading as a personally significant, thought-getting process.

Realizing that no learning takes place without attention, she selects the words most interesting to the children. She uses movement, contrast, and novelty to attract and hold their attention.

Because of wide differences in children's abilities and preschool background, skillful teaching in the primary grades must be diagnostic teaching, that is, teaching based on an understanding not only of the child's present competencies and learning capacity but also of the ways in which his environment is influencing him. The teacher can gain such understanding by combining readiness training with diagnosis. As she uses various readiness exercises, she will note which children respond quickly and which need further practice in a small group or as individuals. A standardized readiness test serves as a check on the teacher's informal appraisal.

The following procedures used by a first grade teacher, Mrs. Dorothy Maxson of the Tucson public schools, provided practice in preliminary reading skills and also in some of the underlying mental abilities needed in learning to read.

An action song, "Where Is Thumbkin?" involved attention, memory, repetition of familiar words and phrases with emphasis on natural intonation and coordination of voice, eyes, and bodily movements.

Listening to and following directions required close attention, comprehension of the directions, memory, and motor ability to carry them out.

An exercise in distinguishing beginning sounds of pairs of words such as

fox—box, which is an animal?

hair—chair, which can you sit on?
required a background of experience, word knowledge, and ability to recognize the category in which a given word belonged.

A simple kind of closure exercise consisted of supplying the rhyming word omitted in nursery rhymes. This exercise also gave practice in the recognition of ending sounds of words.

Recalling, in proper sequence, the events of stories heard previously helped in developing a sense of sequence in reading. The children's attention was called to sequence by leading questions: "What animal did Sambo meet in the jungle? What happened then? What did the tiger say?, etc."

Discrimination of differences in the position of objects and letters was taught with pictures of one animal facing right and the other three facing left and with a series of letters: *b b b a* (one letter shorter than the others); *m m n m* (one letter with one hump missing); *d d b d* (the same letter form but in a different position). This last exercise is especially important to teach the principle that changing the position of certain letter forms changes their meaning. For example, the letter form *d* when facing in the opposite direction becomes *b* and when turned upside down, becomes *p*. The children were asked not only to identify the form that was different but to tell why they thought it was different. They were encouraged to verbalize the methods of learning that brought success.

The same letter was presented in different forms: capital *B,* small *b;* and *b* in print, script, and manuscript. This, too, was an important principle for children to learn, namely, that the same letter meaning may be presented in different forms (*3,* pp. 404-409).

Asking children to tell what they saw in a picture quickly detected the "whole perceivers," those who looked at the picture as a Gestalt or whole, and the "part perceivers," those who picked out separate and often trivial details.

In addition to the appropriateness and sequence of instructional methods and materials, this teacher's enthusiasm, encouragement, and sensitivity to individual children provided an ideal environment for learning.

Skillful teaching recognizes individual differences in children's need for practice. There is danger in overdrilling. If a child overlearns a habit where flexibility is necessary, it becomes rigid and detrimental to other learning. For example, practice in sounding out words may be continued when they should be recognized by the child's noting fewer and fewer clues. Once a child builds a rut in the road, it is hard for him to get out of it.

Skillful teaching is sequential. It progresses from auditory and visual perception, discrimination, and memory to the integration of auditory with visual symbols, to simple categorization and concept formation.

Skillful instruction in the primary grades exposes children to complexity as well as to the specific sequential learning of vocabulary and word recognition skills. Sound-letter associations are taught in words. Words are taught in sentences; sentences are used to build paragraphs, and the sequence of ideas in a passage as a whole is recognized.

Intermediate grades

Skillful instruction in the intermediate grades introduces advanced reading skills incidentally, gives specific instruction in location of information and study skills, and reinforces and applies skills taught in the earlier grades.

Perhaps the most serious criticism of teaching in the intermediate grades is that little or no real instruction in reading is given. Instead of having the dual objectives of knowledge of the subjects and development of effective methods of reading each of these subjects, the focus is on content.

Children in the intermediate grades need specific instruction. Skillful teaching of the new technical vocabulary in science and social studies— through objects, pictures, dramatizations—makes words come alive in the context in which they are used. These children need instruction in *how* to read a sentence, and *how* to get the author's thought from a paragraph, and *how* to recognize the structure of a selection as a whole. Skillful teaching of sentences involves linguistic study of the structure of the English language as an aid to comprehension. Skillful teaching of paragraph reading leads the students to explore and discover the various purposes for which paragraphs are written and the various forms they may take (*10*), pp. 125-128).

The intermediate grades are not too early to teach an approach to a reading selection—the preliminary exploration, thinking, and speculation as to the content and contribution of the selection; the raising of questions which the selection might answer; the reading followed by review and finally by putting the knowledge gained in the form in which it might be used. This is the familiar Survey Q3R method, though it may not be introduced to the children by that name. But the teachers would go through the process with the class many times and remind them of the method when giving assignments.

Skillful instruction develops and encourages reading interests in children of this age who usually reach a peak of voluntary reading about twelve years of age.

Junior high school

Reading problems pile up in junior high school. Whether they have learned to read, students are required to attend school until they have reached the legal school-leaving age. Effective reading instruction during these years is crucial; it may be the school's last chance to salvage potential ability. Research has shown that a large percentage of dropouts have potential reading ability (*7*).

Skillful instruction in junior high school must recognize a) the students' values and ways of thinking and feeling, shaped by the mass media of communication; b) their sense of inadequacy engendered by years of failure to succeed in school; c) their embarrassment at having to read material below their interest and difficulty level; d) their impatience with methods of teaching reading that have failed to help them make progress; and e) their fear of or lack of hope for their future.

English S, a course of study developed for potential dropouts in the Detroit schools, explores these students' current interest in TV programs, part-time employment, recreation, family relations, boy-girl relations, and similar areas of young adult interests. This approach to reading has been reported as very successful with the group for whom it was designed. Practically none of the potential dropouts who were enrolled in this course left school prematurely.

Skillful teaching of retarded young adolescents aims to assure immediate success; another experience of failure confirms their feeling of inadequacy. For this reason the learning tasks must be selected carefully; they must be challenging yet possible of achievement with reasonable effort. If a book is too easy, the student obtains no real sense of accomplishment; if it is too difficult, he will feel only frustration.

When the student's progress in reading is blocked by lack of basic reading skills in simple sight vocabulary and word recognition, the teacher must find a different way to teach these skills. Junior high school students will reject primary methods and materials. One teacher introduced the Phono-Visual Charts as a scientific method developed by experts in speech. Another teacher preceded drill with the Fernald Method by a psychological explanation of how a person learns better by using several sensory avenues.

Novelty of method not only attracts attention it also revives hope. (On the other hand, a method that has previously resulted in no improvement in reading tends to be rejected.) This is one reason why any new gadget or machine or method of instruction often results in some initial progress with retarded readers.

Thoughts of the future depress some adolescents' effort but stimulate others to put forth more effort to learn to read. Their reaction depends upon how they view their future and what the future actually offers them. For months one ninth grade Spanish-American boy had made no effort to improve his reading. One day in a conversation with him, his teacher, Mrs. Betty Frey, learned that he had given up hope of making anything of himself. He could see no use for reading or any need for school learning. A few days later his teacher read an article in the local paper about a Mexican-American who had been elected to a position of some prominence. She

cut out the clipping and put it on the boy's desk without comment. From that time on the boy's interest and effort to improve in all the language arts increased.

Skillful teaching of able learners is aimed at developing greater proficiency in reading and study skills and in preventing waste of precious years in which childish habits are discarded or revised and more mature habits and skills are developed.

Senior high school

Although some senior high school students are merely "serving their term," many are anxious about entering and succeeding in college or a vocation. They realize the value of efficient reading and study habits; they are impatient with the reiteration of general rules about study methods, paragraph reading, and the like. They want specific help over and above what they have been able to work out for themselves.

Skillful teaching requires much more understanding of the reading process than we possess at present. Students can help teachers to acquire this understanding through contributing introspective reports regarding their own most efficient reading methods.

One high school student, obviously a bright boy, was making a very poor academic record. Some conflict regarding his ambitious mother and his vocational choice was evident. He described his previous instruction in reading as "too vague and general." His present teacher, taking the clue from the boy's own comments, went through the process of reading a rather difficult paragraph from his history book. She guided each step in the intensive study of this paragraph. He skimmed, noting key words, to get an overview; approached the reading with a question in mind; varied his rate, pausing to fix in mind the information he was looking for; related the illustrations to his own experience; and reacted to the specific ideas, interpreting words and phrases as he read. The teacher emphasized recalling what he had read rather than spending the same time in the common practice of merely re-reading. The boy's response to this specific instruction was markedly different from his previous lackadaisical attitude toward reading.

Although instruction in simple aspects of interpretation of literature and critical and creative reading begins as soon as children have acquired a minimum of proficiency in "reading the lines," there is room during high school years for more intensive instruction in the higher level reading skills. Many high school students do not know what clues of character and motive to look for or how to locate and interpret them. Instruction of this kind can be given on a story read by the entire class. The teacher repeatedly demonstrates the process of interpretation with the whole class until the students have mastered the skills sufficiently to use them in their outside reading.

Creative reading is encouraged by calling attention to imagery of various kinds which students can reproduce in their own minds and describe in words, drawings, or paintings. Since the interpretation of poetry is many-sided, the teacher encourages students to make their own unique responses to a given poem or piece of literature. However, there may even be a place for programed instruction in the initial study of poetry (8).

Skillful instruction in higher levels of critical reading is also needed by most high school and college students.

Summary

Skillful teaching of reading begins with an understanding of the individual student's reading abilities, difficulties, and potential; with his values and concept of himself; and with school, home, and neighborhood conditions that are facilitating or hindering his progress in reading.

Having this understanding, the teacher sets the stage for success by providing appropriate reading tasks and by giving skillful instruction. Whenever possible, he ignores the behavior that is interfering with the student's learning. Instead of calling attention to errors, he "accentuates the positive." He tries to attach satisfaction to the consequences of behavior that lead to improvement by reinforcing any move in the right direction. To accomplish this reinforcement he enlists the aid of appropriate motivation ranging anywhere from tokens, material rewards, recognition, and approval to the satisfaction that comes from success and self-realization.

In response to such teaching, the highest praise a student could give would be to say, "I made this progress in reading myself."

REFERENCES

1. Berlin, I. N. "Unrealities in Teacher Education," *Saturday Review,* (Dec. 1964), 57-58.
2. Budoff, Milton, and Donald Quinlan. "Reading Progress as Related to Efficiency of Visual and Aural Learning in the Primary Grades," *Journal of Educational Psychology,* (Oct. 1964), 247-252.
3. Duane, Alexander, and John Money. "Reading Disability and the Problem of Direction Sense," *The Reading Teacher,* 20 (1967), 404-409.
4. Hess, Robert D., and Virginia Shipman. "Early Experience and the Socialization of Cognitive Modes in Children," *Child Development,* 36 (1965), 869-886.
5. Hobbs, Nicholas. "Helping Disturbed Children: Psychological and Ecological Strategies," *American Psychologist,* 21 (1966), 1105-1115.
6. Miller, H. Wilma. "Relationship between Mother's Style of Communication and Her Control System to the Child's Readiness and Subsequent Reading Achievement in the First Grade," unpublished doctoral dissertation, University of Arizona, Tucson, 1967.
7. Penty, Ruth. *Reading Ability and High School Dropouts.* New York: Teachers College Press, 1956.
8. Reid, James M., John Ciardi, and Laurence Perrine. *Poetry: A Closer Look.* New York: Harcourt, Brace and World, 1963.
9. Robinson, Helen M. "Perceptual and Conceptual Style as Related to Reading," in J. Allen Figurel (Ed.), *Improvement of Reading through Classroom Practice,* International Reading Association Conference Proceedings, 9 (1964), 26-28.
10. Strang, Ruth, and Dorothy Bracken. *Making Better Readers.* Boston: D. C. Heath, 1957.

INSTRUCTION IN READING

WORD RECOGNITION

A Critical Look at Instruction in Word Recognition at the Elementary Level

JUANITA LEWIS
Colorado State College

WORD RECOGNITION, the same as any other term in the field of reading, can become ambiguous when one examines it in the many different pieces of literature of a reading program. For the purpose of this paper *word recognition* refers to the child's ability to recognize a word and its meaning in context. Before a child can recognize a word, he must first have the opportunity and skills necessary to identify that word, or someone must tell it to him. Actually, one could hardly talk about word recognition without getting into word identification skills. Therein lies the ambiguity of *word recognition;* it is a result of word identification.

Instruction in word recognition

Consider the ways a child learns to recognize or identify a word. There are four major areas to be considered as far as instruction in word recognition is concerned. They are 1) Context, 2) Phonetic Analysis, 3) Structural Analysis, and 4) Comprehension.

Context

Anyone who has examined one or more of the available reading programs being used by children today is aware of the fact that attention is given to helping children through three different kinds of context.

Oral Context. The purpose of oral context is to give the child practice in using verbal clues to identify words. Frequently, it is supplemented with picture and/or printed context, structural and/or phonetic analysis, or in some cases any miracle that comes to the teacher's mind.

Picture Context. The purpose of this activity is the give the child practice in using picture clues to identify words. Most readiness programs and preprimers offer opportunities for the child to develop this skill. It, too, is frequently supplemented with oral and printed context.

Printed Context. The purpose of printed context is two-fold:
1. To give the child practice in using printed context to identify new words, and
2. To give the child practice in comprehension.

Oral and picture context used along with printed context seems to be a means to an end—what end? Reading!

Phonetic Analysis

Varying degrees of phonetic analysis appear in reading programs. A consensus seems to be that children need help with at least three skills:

Identifying likenesses and differences in beginning sounds. Attention is devoted here to giving children skill in sounding out the beginning of a word to enable them to identify words.

Identifying likenesses and differences in sounds in the medial position. Attention is devoted here to giving children skill in sounding out the "middle" of a word of syllable to help them identify words.

Identifying likenesses and differences in ending sounds. Attention is devoted here to giving children skill in sounding out the ending of a word to help them identify words.

Structural analysis

Again, almost any method of teaching reading that could be mentioned gives attention to structural analysis. This skill enables the child to take a word apart and sound out the parts to help him identify it. Children are helped with five different kinds of structural analysis:

Root words. It is believed that to

find a root word in a strange word will help a child identify the strange word.

Prefixes. After the child has learned to identify the root word, he, identifies the prefix to further aid him in identifying the strange word.

Suffixes. Again the child is encouraged to find the root word plus the suffix to help him identify the strange word.

Compound words. Children are also given practice in discovering that the strange word may consist of two words that they already know.

Syllabication. Attention is devoted to helping children develop skill in dividing words into syllables as a means of identifying strange words.

Comprehension

The advocates of any method of teaching reading would strongly agree that their approach to reading leads to comprehension; otherwise, what is the purpose of context, phonetic analysis, or structural analysis? Some are happy if the child understands a word. Others are not happy unless the child understands the whole sentence. Many are not satisfied until the child comprehends a whole paragraph, a whole story, or the main idea of a selection. Literature shows that authorities expect the child to understand what he reads. Most authorities agree that it is from the printed context that comprehension comes.

Picture Context. Programs devote a sizable amount of time to helping children develop comprehension with picture symbols.

Oral Context. Programs devote time to helping children develop comprehension through listening to oral context.

Printed Context. No method ignores printed context and the role it plays in comprehension. The most common use made of printed context is.

1. Silent Reading. The child is given a purpose; he examines the printed context silently and through comprehension fulfills his purpose.

2. Oral Reading. Again the child is given a purpose for reading; he reads orally and fulfills his purpose.

3. Skimming. Sometimes the child is given a purpose and is called upon to skim the material with comprehension to fulfill his purpose.

4. Drill. The many different types of drill employed in helping children with comprehension would be too numerous to list at this time. Suffice it to say, the end result should be comprehension of the material which the children have handled.

A critical look at instruction in word recognition

Now for a critical look at instruction in word recognition. As was pointed out earlier in this paper, word recognition is the ability to recognize a word and its meaning in a particular context. It was also pointed out that there are four major areas in instruction in word recognition: 1) Context, 2) Phonetic Analysis, 3) Structural Analysis, and 4) Comprehension. Take a critical look at these four areas which have become sacred to people in the field of reading.

Context.

Picture Context. Let's look first at picture context. Couldn't we devote more time to printed context rather than picture context? When I examine a basal series, I never fail to ask myself this question. I will agree that in the beginning children do enjoy SOME picture reading, but through observing children during my classroom teaching experiences I found time after time that children became bored and restless when asked to read a picture to death. Agreed, some method needs to be used to "put words into the mouths of poor readers," but even they rebel after a while. I have nothing but sympathy for the six-year-old child who has to go through a reading readiness program where he is asked to read pictures and more pictures and more pictures.

Those who are first grade teachers have probably had the same experience I had in first grade reading: The child who can go through the whole story reading every detail in the picture plus adding numerous ones of his own, when asked to read the selection, looks at you with a question in his mind and asks, "What selection?"

Solution? Publishing companies and teachers must concentrate less on picture context.

Oral Context. How about oral context? Does it help the child or not? Have you ever sat in the back of the room and listened to a first grade teacher teach reading? If you have, I believe you will agree with me that much of the oral context given by the teacher is not what we are after at all. For example: when a child is reading a sentence and stops in the middle of the sentence because he can't identify a word, it would seem to me that he needs to know that word immediately for comprehension, otherwise, he loses his train of thought and begins to word call. In my opinion, teachers don't help by such oral context as "It begins with the same sound as ball, bird" or "We had that word yesterday, remember?" or "That's one of our new words." I'm concerned, too, when the teacher gives the child oral context that he will not have access to later when he is reading independently. In summary, I suppose my major criticism is the fact that teachers using detailed oral context during a silent or oral reading lesson can be interfering with comprehension rather than helping the child.

Solution? Tell the child the word now; help him later with his problem!

Printed Context. Couldn't we have more words in beginning reading, and couldn't we include more than just one-syllable words?

Sometimes I wonder what children think of our schools when we take them to a reading circle, build up their interest in reading, and then hand them a story with such limited vocabulary that it couldn't possibly compete with library books they are reading or are having read to them or with their conversations during recess. Please don't misunderstand me. I am not advocating a recording of the conversation at recess time followed by a printed chart from which the child reads and rereads and rereads what a group had to say during a particular recess in a particular situation. I am not advocating this approach at all. I have tried that approach and it didn't work for me.

Solution? I would like to see more reading readiness programs devote attention to the skills basic to beginning reading and less attention to picture reading of everyday situations or nursery rhymes.

As for two-or more-syllable words, I recall from my own classroom experience that *Washington* was a word that all of my first grade children could recognize when they saw it in printed form—yes, even the children in the low group.

Solution? Put more words in primary reading material, and let's not be afraid to try the big ones.

Phonetic Analysis

I have several questions concerning phonetic analysis:

Beginning Sounds. The r e a d i n g readiness program?

Why spend time in our reading readiness books with activities completely unrelated to beginning reading?

It seems to me that by the time a child completes his reading readiness program he should be on the road to reading. If this is true, it would seem to me that our reading readiness should get him ready!

How about teaching beginning sounds?

This makes sense to me, and since I have worked with kindergarten and first grade children, I know that many of them can successfully work with beginning sounds. Not only from observation do I know this, but I also know it from examining and conducting research. I have already heard the argument that all children cannot do this work at kindergarten level. Is this any reason for not letting those who can move forward? If we hold back for this reason, we can't have reading at first grade level or geometry at high school, can we?

Solution? Give the child more work with letter forms and sounds.

Medial Sounds. Why can't children be exposed to them earlier?

At first grade level it bothers me that we can't start working earlier with certain phonetic analysis skills—to be specific, with vowels. I don't recall too many words the child meets in his recreational reading where he wouldn't be confronted with vowels. I believe that if we would work with the vowels soon enough at early first grade level, we could help children become more independent in their reading habits. After all, aren't we supposed to give the child what he can put to use immediately? And surely one can't deny that even in the first word in the preprimer the child meets a vowel. I remember hearing a saying one time "get what you need but need what you get." "Needing what you get" brings me to my next comment. I am a little disturbed when I go into classrooms and see teachers using phonetic programs that are not in any way tied to the immediate needs of the child. I'm sure that teachers are using these highly advertised, colorful, phonetic programs with good intentions. I would just like to mention that according to the laws of learning, children tend to forget what they don't use and, secondly, that what they learn should be used immediately in a meaningful situation.

I would be happy to see a structural program in phonics *if* it is a program that goes along with the reading program the teacher is using at that time and *if* it concentrates on the high frequency needs of the children. Why should a child have to drill on a specific sound if he is not having trouble with it?

Solution? Give children practice in hearing likenesses and differences in words they are using now. Don't wait until that magic period, the second grade.

Structural analysis

I have three criticisms concerning structural analysis:

Why have children find little words in big words? I am concerned about programs that encourage children to find little words in big words. This procedure forms a BAD habit that children must break sooner than one expects. I can see no advantage in this activity whatsoever because the English language is not that consistent. The minute the child starts having two-syllable words he is going to run into trouble.

What about configuration? I am equally concerned about the series that wastes the child's time by having him look at a printed word and visualize a picture of that word that, probably, is completely unrelated to that word. When you have a child look at the word *been*, think of it with an outline around it, add wheels to it, and make smoke come out of the top, you're taking his mind off the word. Again, very rarely have I seen childrens books where, first of all the word was framed; and I never recall seeing one where the word's had wheels on them.

Why do we ask children to divide words in syllables? It is well and good to have children divide words into syllables, but many programs never go beyond this step. Children should then be taught to look at each syllable as an independent word that would be identified the same as any small word.

Solution? Have the child take the word apart in a logical manner and use these parts to identify the word.

Comprehension

Some of our programs make little, if any, provision for comprehension. Some of our teacher's manuals ask such regurgitative-type questions that the only thing a child has to do is to repeat a sentence whether it makes sense. Some of the drills provided by publishing companies and by teachers ask for such specific details that children lose the meaning of the whole story. Some teachers fail to help children see that the material they are reading silently or orally must make sense. Some of our teachers have resigned themselves to the fact that children simply can't use expression—therefore, "I'm not going to push the issue." Some teachers have become obsessed with *rate* at the expense of *comprehension*. And some teachers have not themselves fully understood what reading actually is.

Solution? Provide practice for children that will help them critically think and critically read so they will learn to demand meaning from printed material.

Summary

As I stated at the beginning of this paper, *word recognition* refers to the child's ability to recognize a word and its meaning in a particular context. We must realize that recognizing a word is only part of the job. Unless a child understands what he reads, we are not preparing him to cope with the printed material he will be meeting as he continues his education. Let's not be so involved in instruction in word recognition that we ourselves forget to take a critical look at it and the role it plays in helping children learn to read!

Word Recognition Skills for the Junior High School

KATHLEEN K. CLAYTON
Manilus (New York) Public Schools

WHEN considering the topic of word recognition skills for the junior high school, one has to think about what word recognition techniques these students have been taught in the elementary grades. Next, some type of evaluation or diagnosis, should be planned to determine if these junior high students have these skills. After administering a group or an individual instrument, the teacher has to plan the program around the needs of the students. Some groups of students may have little need for extensive work in word recognition techniques at the junior high level because their skills are already well developed. Some groups will need the kind of program that involves a heavy concentration on word recognition techniques.

What is word recognition? It has been defined as the "identification of a word by means of a context clue or skill in analysis of the word form" (2). Word recognition involves a number of techniques: the use of sight words, the use of phonetic analysis, the use of structural analysis, the use of context, and the use of the dictionary. Word recognition skills are those methods or techniques used by readers to identify, to pronounce, or to recall words. Before the reader can attach meaning to a word, he must be able to identify it. Learning to read and being able to read requires word recognition skills. Johnson has said:

> The ultimate aim of the reading program in relation to word recognition ability, should be the spontaneous recognition of virtually every word. Accompanying this ability to react effortlessly to the majority of words should be a reservoir of word analysis skills to unlock the few unfamiliar words which are met from time to time (5).

Let us consider the various word recognition techniques already mentioned that have been taught in the elementary school and that may need reviewing or reteaching in the junior high school.

Sight Words. Most professional books on reading and basal reader manuals have descriptive material on sight words in the discussion of teaching word recognition. Sight words are those words that are recognized as a whole. The sight word is the word that is told to the child and is the basis for teaching phonetic and structural analysis. The child becomes familiar with words already in his listening and speaking vocabularies by having the printed forms of the words presented to him as wholes in meaningful context. The sight word is used in a meaningful situation and discussed. Then there is the need for this word to be used frequently in different settings so that the word is recognized instantly and spontaneously.

Phonetic analysis. Phonetic analysis is a term that is a source of confusion in discussions on the teaching of reading. We talk about phonetics, phonics, and phonetic analysis. Phonetics is the science of speech sounds. Phonics is the science of speech sounds as applied to reading. Phonetic analysis is the analysis of a word into its phonetic elements for pronunciation purposes (2). Bamman says, "The recognition of symbols and the sounds which they represent is known as phonetic analysis (1)."

What we are to present or teach at a grade level will be dependent upon what the student already knows about phonics. Phonics is part of every sound reading program. The junior high school program needs to be concerned with phonics and phonetic analysis to the extent that the student should be able to use phonics as a word recognition technique.

The teaching of phonetic analysis proceeds from the known to the unknown or from the simple to the complex. Teach those phonetic principles that are more generally and universally applied before moving to less frequently used analytic skills. The development of skills in phonetic analysis is based on phonetic understandings. The student must have a knowledge of the sounds that are used in our English language and of the symbols that stand for those sounds. It is generally accepted that we have about forty-three separate sound units or phonemes in our language. Each of these phonemes is either a vowel or a consonant sound. We have only twenty-six written symbols in traditional orthography to represent these sounds. We have more sounds than symbols, and some symbols must be used to represent more than one sound. This situation naturally makes it difficult to teach phonetic analysis.

The student should have learned to associate sounds with various types of consonant and vowel symbols. He should know the single consonant letters that are used to represent a single consonant sound. He should know or

be taught consonant blends. Where two or three consonant letters are blended so closely that they are produced almost as one sound; e.g., *br, st, scr.* The special two-letter consonant symbols that are used to represent a single consonant sound should be known. The letters *sh* as in *shirt* or *shape,* for example, represent one sound that is different from that of either of the single letters in the symbol *sh.*

There are three general types of vowel symbols with which the student should be acquainted. These are single-vowel letters as *a* as in *cat* or *o* as in *go.* The student needs to understand that these single-vowel symbols can be used to represent variant single vowel sounds. He needs to know that two-vowel letters may be used to represent variant single vowel sounds; e.g., *oo* as in *book* or *food; ea* as in *tea, tear,* or *read.* The third general type is the knowledge of the dipthongs or two-vowel letters that are used to represent two-vowel sounds blended to form one speech sound; e.g., *ou* in *mouse.*

The understandings of silentness and variability of consonants and vowels are basic (4). Double consonants at the end of a word represent one sound; e.g., *sell, tall.* Words with double consonants followed by a vowel are likely to have two syllables, e.g., *middle, happen.* Silent consonant symbols in a word may have a meaning function. The student should know or be taught the hard and soft sounds of *c* and *g* and how he can determine these for pronunciation and meaning purposes.

He should know that vowel letters are sometimes silent and that they have a function. One should also know that each vowel letter represents several vowel sounds. Final *e* on a word is usually silent and usually prolongs the sound of the preceding vowel. If there are two vowels together in a word or a syllable, the first vowel is usually long and the second vowel is usually silent. If there is only one vowel in the syllable or word, the vowel is usually short unless it is at the end of the word. If the only vowel letter in a word or syllable is followed by *r*, the sound of the vowel is usually affected by the *r*. The teacher must be careful in teaching these principles as rules that are always true. They must be taught as principles that generally apply to word analysis, but there are exceptions to the rules or principles. The student needs practice and opportunities for applying these principles in his daily reading.

Many good sources list the phonetic principles that students should know and be able to use. Materials by Gray, Betts, Bamman, Karlin, Spache, and others are most helpful in the teaching of phonetic analysis.

Structural analysis. Structural analysis involves knowledge of compound words; inflected forms; derived forms including prefixes, suffixes, and roots; syllabication; and contractions. A compound word is a combination of two distinct known words that are joined to form one word. Students who do not recognize compounds are weak in word attack skills and have not learned to look at words for familiar parts. Students who are troubled by compound words need specific instruction if they are to learn to work with compounds which are a part of our everyday reading materials in the classroom.

Inflected forms of words have to do with person, case, gender, number, tense, and comparison. Common inflectional endings are *-s, -es, -er, -est, -ed,* and *-ing.* Usually, the basic meaning of an inflected form is contained within the root word. Derived forms are those words which have prefixes or suffixes. These are both referred to as affixes. This form differs from the inflected form in that the affixes have meanings of their own. Then these affixes are added to a root form the meaning of the total word or form may be entirely different. The meaning of the root form does not change. The addition of the affix is what changes the meaning of the total

word or form. Developing skill in the recognition of derived forms serves two purposes: expanding meaning vocabulary and gaining an understanding of the origin, or history, of words *(1)*.

Syllabication. Syllabication is dividing words into syllables for the purpose of identifying unknown words. It functions as an aid in word recognition by helping the student break words into smaller units, pronounce these, blend, and thus recognize words in his speaking and listening vocabularies. Syllabication helps students in their spelling and writing. As most students mature in reading in the upper elementary grades, they become increasingly dependent upon their knowledge of syllables and less upon letter phonics. The student needs to understand that every syllable must contain a vowel sound. With this knowledge, he has a method of breaking words into divisions for pronunciation purposes.

Principles of syllabication can be found in the professional books of Spache, Bamman, Karlin, Gray, and Betts. Be careful of having students memorize syllabication principles. Generalizations which are formulated by the students will be more meaningful than memorized principles. These generalizations should be kept as few and as simple as possible. Emphasize those generalizations which clearly help in pronouncing a word.

Context clues. Contextual analysis or the use of context clues is identifying a new word by anticipation of the meaning or through the words and ideas adjacent to the new word *(2)*. Readers frequently rely upon the context to help them with unknown or new reading words. Students should be encouraged to use context clues as an identification technique. We do need to teach students how to use contextual clues. Contextual clues should not be used alone to identify unknown words. Phonics and structural clues need to be combined with the contextual clues where possible. Spache states that most context clues demand some degree of inferential thinking.

Such inferential thinking is an essential part of the reading process at all maturity levels and should be strongly encouraged (7).

Jan-Tausch has indicated that words are learned best when introduced in conjunction with meaningful context. This remark applies to the teaching of all word recognition skills.

The dictionary. The dictionary is used as an aid in identifying unknown words met in reading and as a check on a pronunciation or a meaning tentatively arrived at by the reader through the use of context clues, word-form clues, and systematic analysis (4). The dictionary is a storehouse of the meanings of words but is a word recognition helper.

Skills needed in using the dictionary as a word recognition technique are 1) being able to locate the word by opening the dictionary to the section in which the word is contained and being able to apply alphabetical knowledge to find the word; 2) being able to use guide words as aids in the location of words; 3) being able to identify the root form from alternate forms of the word; and 4) being able to pronounce the word (6).

Evaluation of needs. As stated earlier, in order to plan a program the teacher must know what are the student's needs. Different types of testing or evaluative instruments can be used to determine these needs. Standardized tests can be administered and compared with national norms. Individual informal reading inventories can be administered where word recognition skills of the student are carefully studied. Johnson has suggested pertinent questions on word recognition skills as listed below:

> Does he see base words in affixed forms?
> Does he apply the final- e principle?
> Does he use the dictionary spontaneously to get the pronunciation of a word he cannot analyze on his own?
> Does he use his oral language background as checkpoint for his analysis of a printed form?

> Does he skip over unfamiliar words or use a slurred pronunciation rather than attempt to analyze them?

> Does he drop word endings (5)?

Reading is a series of many skills intermeshed with one another. It is a thinking process and not subject matter to be taught. Word recognition techniques must be taught, evaluated, and retaught where needed for effective use and reading skill development.

REFERENCES

1. Bamman, Henry A., Ursala Hogan, and C. E. Greene. *Reading Instruction in the Secondary School.* New York: Longmans, Green, 1961.
2. Betts, Emmett A. *Foundations of Reading Instruction.* New York: American Book Co., 1957.
3. Caroline, Sister M., IHM. "Word Recognition and Vocabulary Development," in J. Allen Figurel (Ed.), *Reading and Inquiry,* Proceedings of the International Reading Association, 10 (1965), 227-229.
4. Gray, William S. *On Their Own in Reading.* Chicago: Scott, Foresman & Co., 1960.
5. Johnson, Marjorie S. "Evaluating the Secondary School Reading Program," *Reading Instruction in Secondary Schools,* Perspectives in Reading No. 2. Newark, Delaware: International Reading Association, 1964, 117-128.
6. Karlin, Robert. *Teaching Reading in High School.* Boston: Allyn & Bacon, Inc., 1964.
7. Spache, George D. *Reading in the Elementary School.* Boston: Allyn & Bacon, Inc., 1964.

Matching Word Analysis Skills to Student Needs at the Secondary Level

Clifford J. Lorenz
Clarke College

"THEY ONLY TEACH us to talk about what we do not know." The words were Jean Jacques Rousseau's in his famous book *Emile.* The subject was the use of books, and perhaps he had a point when we consider the time and effort which is being expended by senior high school reading teachers. It is becoming painfully obvious to many of these teachers that this great expending of time and effort is not worth it. Perhaps it would be best, as Rousseau advocated, to take the pupil to a hill on a clear night and allow him to observe the wonders of heaven rather than have him read about astronomy from a book.

How often is heard the complaint from teachers of secondary reading that students in their classes find the phonetic and structural analysis of words tedious, unsophisticated, and unrelated to their present and future needs. Parents and school officials may believe in the importance of "remedial" reading, but the adolescent is not willing to accept this same belief. The curriculum, therefore, must be something the pupil does, not something that is done for him. It must be living as well as preparation for life. It was Rousseau who said that what we do in school should be designed to meet the natural needs of the pupil.

If a program of teaching reading skills is to become worthwhile, teachers should concern themselves first and foremost with an evaluation of the specific needs of the youth who are enrolled in their reading classes and secondly with the actual improvement of skills. Such an approach does not regard the acquisition of skills as a separate problem, but it does recognize the uniqueness of each child and his needs. It is not a problem of lack of material but of adapting available material to the student.

For purposes of this paper, I am assuming that the teacher to whom I speak is well qualified to teach word analysis and has a thorough knowledge of the sequential development of word analysis skills. I also assume that the reading teacher is familiar with the use of diagnostic procedures and has analyzed the problem correctly.

The concept of needs is not new, nor is the proposal that teachers meet the needs of youth a unique one. All secondary schools are organized on the vague premise that needs are present and must be met. We hear of track programs, computer programed schedules, college preparatory courses,

vocational education, and so forth. The National Society for the Study of Education pointed out approximately fifteen years ago the necessity of the concept of needs as a foundation of curriculum development and that a wider recognition of the implications of this concept for the education of youth must be achieved. And yet in 1967, one only has to look at the large number of students who do not finish high school to decide just how gradual needs are being met. The Office of Education estimates that only sixty per cent of those who enter high school actually continue until graduation. The question "Are we just paying lip service to this problem?" must, therefore, be asked. Many educators say this situation is as it should be. They claim the presence of children with learning problems results inevitably in a lowering of standards. If, however, we believe in the democratic ideals of education, we cannot accept this premise.

It is my contention that high schools are bound in a straight jacket of academic conventions and traditions and surrounded by rules, regulations, and requirements and are so compartmentalized, formalized, and non-functional as far as curriculum is concerned that the child with a reading problem has very little chance to make progress. The undeniable fact is present that most high schools have been very reluctant to accept the child who has a reading problem and make a serious effort to adapt instruction to this problem. Granted, reading classes have been established in many schools because of the large amount of money available through ESEA titles, but money alone is not the complete solution to the problem. As long as departmentalized instruction exists with the implication that each teacher teaches primarily only one specialty and that any particular child, unfortunately, has many different teachers during the course of a day, the child who has a reading problem is going to encounter an impersonal and routine environment. In other words, it really isn't doing much good to place a child in a reading class and then turn him loose the rest of the day to face teachers who are not aware of his problem and expect him to read from books far above his level. As Samuel Kirk said many times, rapid and frequent shifting of gears from one teacher to another and from one group to another places a severe strain on the mental and emotional adaptability of the child. This is not to say that the child who is in a corrective reading class should be put in the charge of one teacher exclusively. Nevertheless, a substantial reduction in the variety, complexity, and usual inconsistency of the personal relations of a typical senior high school is desirable.

It seems to me, therefore, before we can intelligently discuss the problem of providing corrective and remedial services on the senior high school level, our curriculum makers and administrators must sit down with the reading consultant and work in close accord for the child who has a reading problem. Enrolled with the reading teacher, the student now becomes the special concern for all his classroom teachers through the school day. Test results are shared. The classroom teacher is kept informed of the level at which the student is capable of reading. Suitable reading materials may be supplied by the consultant. Assignments are adjusted. Personal recognition is given when there are small successes. All have a part now in the complete program.

It was Kottmeyer who said, "At the secondary level, the rescue operation for the retarded reader is difficult and uncertain." The participation of each classroom teacher helps to bring the rescue infinitely closer. Every member of the staff should know what is being done for each student enrolled in a corrective or remedial reading classroom. Transfer will take place only as the school staff makes a direct effort to have the work of the reading teacher applied to the various lessons of the day.

If these ideas are brought into being,

then we can get down to the basic problem of matching word analysis skills to student needs and translate these needs into teaching goals.

Many teachers are ignoring the needs of the children in their classrooms. I think this condition is quite apparent among the large group of ESEA teachers who have been pressed into service during the past two years. Many simply have little or no awareness of the basic needs of adolescents. And yet, if we are going to reach the children in our classrooms, a defensible educational program must recognize both the personal needs of youth and the broader needs of society. We live in the tense balance of what the student is and what he may become because of our influence.

Let us take a look at what is meant by *needs*. Many authors have listed the needs of youth in countless studies. During recent years, for example, deficiencies in the amount and kind of vocational and educational guidance have been pointed out. Other studies, in light of campus riots and student rebellion, have expressed concern over the need for developing a more responsible behavior of juveniles and have led many to the conclusion that a reawakening of spiritual and moral values among youth is needed. When one looks at the amount of research conducted by psychologists, sociologists, guidance personnel, and philosophers, one is struck, however, by a conspicuous similarity to Robert J. Havighurst's developmental tasks of adolescence. The tasks of which Havighurst writes are those the individual must learn—the developmental tasks of life, those things that constitute healthy and satisfactory growth in our society. They are the things a person must learn if he is to be judged and to judge himself to be a reasonably happy and successful person. Havighurst points out that the period from twelve to eighteen is primarily one of physical and emotional maturing. The boy becomes ready for manhood and the girl, for womanhood. Emotional independence from parents is necessary.

Vocational choice becomes a worry. School loses its appeal to the wide open mind of the child and must cater to the selective interests of the teenager. (I think this last point is worthy of serious reflection.)

Specifically the nine developmental tasks are

achieving new and more mature relations with peers of both sexes,

achieving a masculine or feminine social role,

accepting one's physique and using the body efficiently,

achieving emotional independence of parents,

achieving assurance of economic independence,

selecting and preparing for an occupation,

preparing for marriage and family life,

developing intellectual skills and concepts necessary for civic competence,

desiring and achieving socially responsible behavior, and

acquiring a set of values and an ethical system as a guide to behavior.

These developmental tasks, then, become the needs of the students in your classroom. These needs become the motivating force in your remedial setting. With the above tasks as a guide, a technique which has been used successfully by psychologists and psychiatrists for years is employed. Listen. Oftentimes we spend too much time talking and not enough time listening. Teachers sometimes feel they are not accomplishing something unless they are talking. If we would take more time to listen, we would find out a great deal. Honesty is the best policy. The child has to discuss his needs. In word analysis, therefore, the teacher is guided by the individual and his needs, and a curriculum is devised to meet the twin motivational forces of needs and interests. Giving an adolescent a workbook, similar in content and style to one a younger brother or sister is using in elementary school, is not going to motivate him. Telling him to

look at a picture sequence of a "turkey," "tent," and "bottle" and requiring him to say each picture in the group and decide whether he hears a consonant sound at the beginning, middle, or end may be sound instruction for developing auditory discrimination of consonant sounds; but I do not believe the student is going to be particularly motivated or interested. The teacher must begin with listening to the student and discussing his needs and then relate these needs to the problem at hand. Then, using the basic principles of developing word attack skills, the teacher creates her program designed for the uniqueness of the persons with whom she is working. Obviously this is going to take time and a great deal of work. But as someone once said, "Education won't be much fun when we get where we want to go."

Getting to know the student is the first step in teaching word analysis skills. If you haven't discovered by now, most of the children enrolled in remedial or corrective reading classes have personality problems. The child who is in high school and has a reading problem of such magnitude that he still needs to be taken back to second, third, or fourth grade material is frustrated; and this frustration shows up in everything from a large yawn in the back of the room, to complete indifference, or to outright rebellion. He has been down the remedial road for seven or eight years and has just about "had it." The teacher of reading will not get very far if she assumes a smiling facade and mere tolerance and then plunges into a structured program of word attack skills. If she is going to succeed where others have failed, the teacher must get to know the students in her class. She must learn to minimize personality short comings and ease the tensions that result from having the students' inadequacies exposed for all to see. A knowledge of child growth and development is a must for all remedial teachers. As has been pointed out in the literature on this subject, once the student has found his niche in the class program and received the approbation of the teacher and the group, the child with a reading problem gradually learns that he can afford to forget himself and begin working. Each succeeding accomplishment, however trivial, is another segment added to the building of self-confidence.

The fundamental problem in the teaching of reading skills to high school students is one of listening and determining needs and using these needs as the motivating force. I am not advocating that every teacher should ascertain every specific need of every student. It would obviously be impossible to list all the needs of youth. The developmental tasks outlined earlier, however, illustrate general classification of needs. It is clear that general needs such as selecting and preparing for a vocation would expand in many directions upon careful analysis. Moreover, attempts to enable a youth to acquire essential competencies in this respect would take into consideration wide differences in the abilities and interests of students in your classroom. However, as Featherstone in his book *Functional Curriculum for Youth* states, "Insight, understanding, and generalized knowledge in terms of principles and laws are what give youth—or adults—effective control in dealing with today's and tomorrow's problems of living."

Let us ask, "Have we so stereotyped ourselves to such an extent that we cannot do what is being asked?" Has the role which we play every day taken over the person—his message, his meaning? Has the role of the teacher assumed boundaries so limited, so impregnable that the person playing the role acts and reacts in only one way?" In stereotyping ourselves and our students we do violence to the holiness of human nature. The role, although a haven for security, keeps up from commitments, adventures, and excursions which are valid and fitting and many times obligatory. We play the role and bury the person because we are either afraid or too lazy to try a new approach.

God has offered us a spirit of creativeness, a spirit of innovation. Use it! We must become personal toward one another. We must talk about ourselves, about our lives, about our emotions. Again, we must become personal toward one another. In the encounter of persons love becomes contagious and communication exists.

I would like to share with you a statement of Max Ehrmann. I think it says what I have been trying to say. "Go placidly amid the noise and the haste, and remember what peace there may be in silence. As far as possible without surrender, be on good terms with all persons. Speak your truth quietly and clearly, and listen to others; they too have their story."

The teaching of reading, therefore, must not just be an experience but an opportunity for dialogue between student and teacher.

REFERENCES

Alberty and Alberty. *Reorganizing the High School Curriculum.* New York: MacMillan Company, 1965.
Brink, W. G. "The Broadening Concept of Needs," *Adapting the Secondary School Program to the Needs of Youth.* Fifty-second Yearbook, Part I. National Society for the Study of Education. Chicago: University of Chicago Press, 1953.
Brink, W. G. "Developments in the Secondary School," *The Bulletin of the National Association of Secondary School Principals,* Vol. 39, No. 211, May, 1955.
Featherstone, W. B. *A Functional Curriculum for Youth.* New York: American Book, 1950, 77.
Featherstone, W. B. *Teaching the Slow Learner.* Columbia University: Bureau of Publications, 1951.
Turnbull, William. *New Approaches to Individualizing Instruction.* A Report on a Conference of May 11, 1965. Princeton, New Jersey: Educational Testing Service, 1955.

Word Attack Skills for the Retarded Reader in College

MILDRED B. FORD
Voorhees College

GOOD READERS not only must be able to recognize quickly and accurately the words they have met before but they must also have at hand tools with which they can determine the meanings of new words. One of the most important of these tools is the ability to pronounce the words because sometimes one knows a word when he hears it spoken and yet does not recognize it when he sees it in print.

Principles of word recognition

The terms *word recognition* and *word attack* are used somewhat interchangeably as applied to reading skills *(5)*. Word recognition is an important basic reading skill. It is in word recognition skills that retarded readers most commonly are deficient. Even though comprehension is the primary goal of reading instruction, word recognition is prerequisite.

We are primarily concerned with finding the method of teaching that best advances the retarded pupil in auditory and visual discrimination.

Bond and Tinker *(1)* identify word recognition with the following basic skills:

1. Associating the approrpriate meanings with the printed symbol;

2. Using the context clues and other meaning aids to anticipate the words to be recognized and then checking the accuracy of the recognition;

3. Becoming flexible and efficient in visually analyzing the word into usable recognition elements;

4. Developing knowledges of visual, structural and phonetic elements, knowledge of consonant and vowel sounds, blends and diagraphs, prefixes and suffixes, etc.;

5. Learning skills in auditory blending and visually synthesizing word parts to rapidly pronounce or recognize the word as a whole; and

6. Forming the habit of using the more analytical and the pronunciation techniques when and only when needed.

Word recognition problems are often found to be at the root of the difficulty of disabled readers who fall into the descriptive categories of limiting disability and complex disability. College readers (retarded) fall into these areas; some can be helped with individualized instruction and some have problems that are too difficult to cope with in a classroom situation.

Effective teaching techniques of word attack skills

To determine the degree of difficulty the college reader has in being able to attack words, systematic evaluation should be administered. The evaluation techniques must be informal or standardized. *Reader's Digest* self-testing section is suggested as an eclectic procedure. Teacher observations should be used to determine what methods are used by the reader to attack new words. Does the student use context clues? Or phonetics? Or structural analysis? Does he know and use the rules syllabication?

Knowledge of word attack skills is important, but skill in using them while reading makes the knowledge of value *(6)*.

Scholastic Scope (Scholastic Magazine), a weekly periodical for high school students, is one reading media which has been used successfully in teaching the use of word meaning and context clues to retarded college readers.

Training in the utilization of context clues should be stressed in teaching word attack skills. The student at this level should be encouraged to employ shrewd guesses in an attempt to determine the meaning of a word from the way it is used in the text *(3)*. A student proficient in utilizing context clues can usually derive enough sense from a word to satisfy his need at the moment. One method of increasing his ability is to present the student with a list of sentences in which the critical word is omitted and have the students fill in the blanks or have them read short interesting articles with words they should know, may not, but can determine the meaning of because of the context.

The problem a college student faces when he meets a new word is likely to be different from that of a child seeing a word for the first time. When a child first starts to read, the words that he encounters are, for the most part, strange to him in form only. That is, most of the words that a child finds in his beginning reading assignments are already in his speaking vocabulary. The words that are new to a college student, however, are usually strange in both meaning and form (6). When the college freshman enters his history class, the vocabulary is as foreign as German. He has had no previous experience which would give him familiarity to the concept or the abstraction for which the word stands. His success in the course is partially dependent upon his ability to understand the technical terminology.

In attempting to develop word recognition for college students, the requisite is to stimulate interest in learning new words and to make the student aware of the words he does not know.

The inherent factors which the student possesses when he enters college have not prepared him for college reading. More than one half of the students entering the small colleges are taking remedial courses. High school preparation has not been efficient; therefore, the student is in "trouble" with reading.

In structural analysis, words should be taught in terms of their components, prefixes, suffixes, and roots so that students can see the effects of prefixes and suffixes upon the meaning of the root, learn the meaning of common Latin and Greek roots and affixes, and get the meaning and pronunication of a word when the surrounding context is not enough (2). The students can build their own derivations, place them in original context, and exchange them with one another to try out their skills.

In order to use roots, prefixes, and suffixes most effectively the student must be proficient in syllabication. If he possesses scanty knowledge in this area, syllabication as means of word attack should be demonstrated and the rules for dividing words into syllables should be presented.

Roberts (4) has outlined the principles of syllabication with examples and exercises on the college level. Sometimes the student is so deficient that an individual approach should be adopted. He also suggests exercises using Greek and Latin roots so that students who have problems unlocking new words may review the rules.

If the college student cannot recognize words quickly and accurately and cannot begin the attack of new words by dividing them into syllables and pronouncing them, it is very probable he has never become a mature reader, with reading skills developed beyond those of the elementary school child. The student will not gain much from training in vocabulary, rate, and comphrehension unless he can recognize a key word by its context, by structural or phonetic analysis, or by syllabication, the next thing to do is look it up in the dictionary and learn how to pronounce the unfamiliar word. Independent use of the dictionary requires skills in the use of guide words, use of the pronunciation key, and the use of several definitions given for aid in word recognition. These four techniques should be stressed with the retarded reader if the techniques have been forgotten.

In the reading laboratory several levels of dictionaries should be available so that students may refer to them as they are needed.

The retarded reader should have at his disposal many kinds of reading materials of low levels but of high interest. The Globe Book Company (New York) has all of the classics on these levels. Careful selection of reading material is important so that the student will not feel that he is reading "child stuff."

One step of correcting a disability in word recognition is to make the student sound conscious (3). He must learn to hear sounds and to think of letters in terms of sounds, and his lessons may vary with a series of exercises that teach him the various sounds

attached to the vowel and the consonants. After he has learned to hear
the sounds and to associate them with
the proper letters, he must be taught to
blend them in combination. All this
activity can be achieved through the
use of simple words whose pronunciation he already knows; he simply
learns to break their sounds down into
their component parts until he can
hear the value of each letter and combination of letters.

Next, the student should be given
the basic rules for building these into
words, that is, the rules of syllabication, accent, and pronunciation. These
rules should be simple and general as
possible, taking account of only the
most common exceptions. "The student is not to be made a specialist in
phonetics," states Triggs (6).

Once the basic facts have been mastered, the lessons become a matter of
practicing their application in forms as
varied as the instructor's ingenuity can
supply and for as long as the student's
disability requires. This application
should include drill in discriminating
among words of similar configuration
and in retaining the visual image of the
word once it is learned. This work
must be done first with words in isolation, but it should be applied immediately in sentences so as to approximate
the reading situation. Workbooks are
recommended for this practice, along
with teacher made exercises.

Materials for the retarded reader

Word Attack (Harcourt, Brace and
World, 1956) is acceptable to college
students because of its hard cover and
format. It contains lists of words and
permits the student to develop
clues—an aid to word identification.
The idea of becoming a word detective
appeals to students and helps them develop the important concept that figuring out words is a responsibility each
person must accept if he is to read independently.

Mentioned earlier, *Scholastic Scope*
(Scholastic Magazine, Inc., 1966-67)
is desirable because context clues and
word meaning skills are presented in
such a way that students are enthusiastic about performing those tasks.

*Basic Reading Skills for Junior
High School Use* (Scott, Foresman,
1957) contains exercises which may be
used in reviewing and developing word
attack skills with older pupils.

Oral reading is necessary to assure
the application of word attacks skills.
Preparing a newspaper report, short
book review, excerpts from magazine
articles to read before a group helps to
give the student the confidence he
needs to read aloud in his regular
classroom situation.

Reading Laboratory IIIb (Science
Research Associates) has been accepted by retarded college readers as
an aid to word attack skills because of
its multilevel activities. The exercises
are designed for culturally deficient
readers. After completion of Laboratory IIIb the student is moved to Laboratory IVa, a more difficult reading
aid, to promote learning of higher levels of prefixes, suffixes, context clues,
and word meaning skills.

The use of *Flash X's and a Tachistoscope* (Educational Developmental
Laboratories) with some of the college
students for improving concentration
and quickness in perceiving words and
associating them with meaning has
been used. Students like the feel of a
machine; they think that this device is
something new and scientific that will
help them to learn to read better.
Students at this age need motivation if
results are to be expected.

Phonics We Use—Book F (Lyons
and Carnaham—1964) is an excellent
refresher course for students who are
in need of independent attack on words.
Analytical inspection of words plus
context clues are used in attacking new
words in a modern program of phonics.

The college retarded reader is often
culturally inefficient because he has
been carelessly taught by teachers who
are not proficient in the teaching of
reading.

Evaluation of progress

The appraisal procedures are as broad as the concept of reading and the program planned to achieve the broad objectives. Standardized text should not be used alone. Observation is of greatest importance; informal tests, practice exercizes, and interest inventories would give evidence of progress in word attack skills.

Concluding statement

Developing word attack skills for the retarded college reader is a slow and difficult process. Rapport should be established among the teachers and student to acquire the best results. The physical condition of the classroom should be conducive to learning. A soundproof room is rec-ommended. Instruction should in-clude the utilization of context clues, structural and phonetic analysis and the teachings of suffixes, roots, pre-fixes, and dictionary skills; and the de-vising of supplementary exercises by the instructor. Reliable measurement of growth should be provided for at in-tervals of nine-week periods.

REFERENCES

1. Bond, Guy L., and Miles A. Tinker, *Reading Difficulties: Their Diagnosis and Correction.* New York: Appleton-Century, Croft, Inc., 1957.
2. Fitzgerald, Frances. "In Corrective and Remedial Classes," *Reading Instruction in Various Patterns of Grouping,* Supple-mentary Educational Monographs, Vol. XXI, No. 89, The University of Chicago Press, 1959, 134-137.
3. Reed, James C. "In College," *Corrective Reading in Classroom and Clinic,* Supple-mentary Educational Monographs, Vol. IV, No. 79, The University of Chicago Press, 1953, 140-144.
4. Roberts, Clyde. *Word Attack: A Way To Better Reading.* New York: Har-court, Brace and World, Inc., 1956.
5. Smith, Henry P., and Emerald V. De-chant. *Psychology in Teaching Reading.* Englewood Cliffs, New Jersey: Pren-tice-Hall, Inc., 1961.
6. Triggs, Frances Oralind. *Remedial Reading: The Diagnosis and Correction of Reading Difficulties at the College Level.* The University of Minnesota Press, Minneapolis, 1943.

Word Attack Skills for the Junior College

MARGARET F. PORTER
Junior College of Broward County,
Florida

WORDS LIE! (*1*) We are all aware of this condition but have we honestly faced up to the problem which con-fronts the young inexperienced reader? For instance, in Florida the ocean is handy and fishing is not a rare sport. With the EDL films (*2*) our reading students are faced with the word "gaff." Few, if any, of the students have a problem in defining this word as "a barbed hook for securing a heavy fish to lift the fish into the boat." On the other hand, if I use "gaff" by say-ing, "Have my pay ready by four o'clock! I can't stand the gaff any longer," students are bewildered and go fishing for a meaning.

Power and speed in reading by Doris Gilbert (*4*) in the first vocabu-lary test presents the word "depauper-ate" and gives the student a choice of meanings. Now, let's face it! If you are a pauper, you are certainly depen-dent on the charity of the community; in fact, you can't own the shirt on your back. How much poorer can you pos-sibly get? Yet, the prefix "de" has many meanings: "send away" as in the word deport, "out of" as in the word detrain, "down" as in the word depose, or in "depauperate" apparently it means "deeper into poverty" or "im-poverished (*7*)." What can this pos-sibly mean when a man is already a pauper? How much deeper into pov-erty can he go?

Perhaps you have now begun to re-call how many different meanings even prefixes have, let alone words.

Arthur S. McDonald in his article "Vocabulary Development: Facts, Fal-lacies and Programs" (*6*) states " . . . a word is not an entity with a mean-ing. Few, if any, words have absolute unchangeable meanings. Rather, words serve as stimuli to call up a cat-egory of meanings, the appropriate one of which must be selected by the individual in accord with the context." The same article defines six different approaches to teaching vocabulary now in use; viz.:

1. Historical
2. Wide reading
3. Memorization of word lists
4. Dictionary
5. Word analysis
6. Context approaches

George D. Spache in several of his articles on promoting vocabulary growth (*11*), but particularly in "Frontiers of Research" (*10*), recommends very much the same approach as McDonald but specifies Latin roots, prefixes, suffixes, and inflectional endings. He also goes on to suggest that present approaches to promoting vocabulary development at the college-adult level are not working and that the results achieved are not very encouraging. Spache further hints that perhaps the fault lies in the tests we are using to measure such growth. This hint opens up for us a new line of reasoning since we are well aware that vocabulary portions in tests reflect the background, training, and prejudices of the test-maker. We discover considerable variance if the test supplies the word only and permits choice of meaning or if the student is given additional assistance by having the word to be defined used in a phrase or sentence. You will note the differences in the students' scores.

With these few facts facing us, then what are the problems we are faced with in individual sections of the country, and what experiences have each of us had wherein we have arrived at some possible partial solutions.

Junior College Problems

We in Broward County have an up-and-coming wide-awake community, fighting for better educational facilities. The majority of high schools have had reading programs for many years. The students have taken from these programs the urge for speed above all other things. They come to the junior college with fairly adequate rates of reading, but they have achieved the speed at the expense of other reading skills. The majority of students make the same mistakes that young inexperienced younsters make in the elementary grades. They fail to note median vowels, a practice which results in confusion of such words as adapt, adept, and adopt. They fail to note endings or skip them entirely. They believe "pogrom" (*2*) is a misspelling or a misprint of the word "program."

The first great error, failure to really see the word, is lack of perception. To elminate this error we train for acuity of vision through perception exercises. Using the perceptoscope and its accompanying filmstrips, the training begins with numbers at varying flashed speeds, advances to geometric designs which the student is asked to reproduce, then moves to words and phrases. This machine, however, has its limitations.

The exercises are short, rather sketchy, and certainly lack depth. Thus when using perceptoscope materials, we feel that we should expose our students to other reading experiences. WE extend the perception training through the use of workbooks, three or four in many cases (*4, 5, 8, 12*), and through teacher-made exercises. The commercial workbooks train in timed perception exercises with a given word to the left, and the students match this word with one of a group. After approximately two weeks of this type of training, we move into word meaning exercises—the word to the left matched with a definition or synonym from a group. Again, after approximately two weeks of this type of training, we move into word association exercises. This word association is so planned that a general term is supplied, such as bakery or mine, and groups of specific words are supplied which fit into the general category.

These types of exercises sound long and complicated. Actually, in working with a group they consume only five to ten minutes of the class period. They serve to alert the student, offer valuable training in building up experience, while at the same time also serve as a "warm up" for the vocabulary and reading sessions which immediately follow.

Readiness or reading readiness is something we rarely hear mentioned at college-adult level although it is used frequently in the elementary grades. Rather, we prefer the term "set." Our experiences tend to show that no matter what the age, experience, or level of the student, he does better work and gains confidence through the short exercises which give him time to become oriented and which provide "set." Perhaps the real secret of the success of these exercises is largely psychological. On the other hand, as the exercises increase in difficulty, we use them to teach the word attack skills. As we carefully check errors, the student is questioned about errors, and the mistake is used to explain some rule of syllabication, prefix, root, or suffix. Notice that the rule is offered at the time the mistake is made. These same words are made the responsibility of the student, and he is warned that later they will appear on a spelling test.

Spelling tests, or the threat of them, usually lead to long discussions of how to go about really learning to spell. With the students who will take the trouble to practice and who recognize themselves as "hopelessly" bad spellers, the old and yet ever new Grace Fernald technique (3) of kinesthetic learning is still a fine way to improve. Approached through the angle of good psychology and possible development of sensory involvement, college-adult groups become interested and experiment. If they can be encouraged to continue the practice with some modifications, their spelling really does improve.

We have been gratified to note that our experiences at JCBC closely parallel the findings of the Vineyard and Massey study in which they discovered that through teaching vocabulary and improving spelling the grade point average of students improves from one-half to one point as a general rule (13).

A check of the literature for the past six or seven years makes little or no mention of the levels of language usage or recognition of the levels of experience at which our college-adult students operate. Perhaps we have become so involved with methodology in the teaching of vocabulary that we have forgotten the old adage that we take from the printed page in proportion to what we bring to it. Thus we maintain in the reading laboratory a large collection of paperback books, leaning toward the classics and do-it-yourself instructional books, all of which may be used for practices with individual accelerators or stopwatches.

We are primarily interested in the development of scholarship—the grade point average of the student who must attain 2.0 if he is to remain in school. In many cases we try to help him by telescoping background materials which he has refused or rejected in the past. To keep this student in the program, he must be shown immediately that he can improve. This improvement must be self-evident in what he scores in his regular credit courses. Thus our choice of materials is always guided into articles, exercises, vocabulary, and discussions to build quickly facts and figures which have some carry-over into his regular academic disciplines. On the obverse side is the fact that the student has already achieved a fairly high level of sophistication in spoken language which he fails to recognize when he sees it in print. We try to make use of this speaking and listening skill by encouraging the student to use it in this theme writing, in answering the questions in the comprehension checks, and in his written summaries. Usually the student is so surprised to discover how much he already knows that he rarely forgets once he sees himself in print. In fact, at this very moment most of our JCBC students are suffering from "ennui" after the exciting moments of the "pogrom."

In summing up what I have tried to say, students at college-adult levels are aware of their shortcomings. They arrive at the reading laboratory highly motivated to set the world on fire. If they fail to achieve, it is in most cases the fault of the teacher. The teacher must make the work meaningful; students at this level will not stand for nor endure dull, uninteresting classes. They know that they do not know; they are ready, willing, and very able—it is for us to supply them with interesting and fruitful experiences.

REFERENCES

1. Babcock, Havilah. *I Want A Word.* Columbia, South Carolina: R. L. Bryan Company, 1958.
2. Educational Developmental Laboratories, Long Island, New York.
3. Fernald, Grace M. *Remedial Techniques in Basic School Subjects.* New York: McGraw-Hill Book Company, Inc., 1943.
4. Gilbert, Doris Wilcox. *Breaking the Reading Barrier.* Englewood Cliffs: Prentice-Hall, Inc., 1964.
5. _____. *Power and Speed in Reading.* Englewood Cliffs: Prentice-Hall, Inc., 1963.
6. McDonald, Arthur S. "Vocabulary Development: Facts, Fallacies and Programs." Thirteenth Annual Yearbook of the National Reading Conference, 1963.
7. Merriam-Webster New Collegiate Dictionary. Springfield, Mass.: G. & C. Merriam Company, 1961.
8. Miller, Lyle L. *Increasing Reading Efficiency.* New York: Holt, Rhinehart, Winston & Company, 1954 (Revised Edition).
9. Radke, Frieda. *Word Resources.* New York: The Odyssey Press, Inc., 1961.
10. Spache, George D. "Frontiers of Research." Fifteenth Yearbook of the National Reading Conference, 1965.
11. _____. "Clinical Work with College Students." Newark, Delaware: *Prospectives in Reading, No. 1,* International Reading Association, 1964.
12. Stroud, James B., Robert B. Ammons, and Henry A. Bamman. *Improving Reading Ability.* New York: Appleton-Century-Crofts, Inc. 1956.
13. Vineyard, Edwin E., and Harold W. Massey. "The Interrelationship of Certain Linguistic Skills and Their Relationship with Scholastic Achievement When Intelligence is Ruled Constant," *Journal of Educational Psychology,* XLVIII (May, 1957).

Vocabulary Development in the Primary Grades

MARGUERITE B. BOUGERE
University of Chicago

THERE IS A wryly humorous and revealing story of the first grader who burst into tears on the first day of school when her teacher told the children to "get into line behind each other." Upon being asked why she was crying, the little girl sobbed out: "I don't know where *each other* is!" The story provides a point of departure for a discussion of vocabulary development in the primary grades—a discussion which will focus upon relationships between the spoken and the written language.

In considering means to promote vocabulary development, it should be stressed that such development cannot proceed merely by accretion of isolated words. In speaking and listening, as in reading and writing, individual words have meaning only as they are related to one another and to the ideas expressed. The meaning of the phrase each other, for example, is not taught by giving definitions of *each* and *other* separately; it is learned as a whole in the context of meaningful experience. The job of the primary teacher is to help children develop competence in receiving ideas through listening and reading and in expressing ideas through speaking and writing. Vocabularies grow as children share experiences which broaden their interest in and understanding of their world. In the school setting, the teacher structures experiences in such a way that children are stimulated to use language and to express and receive communication with ever-increasing skill and satisfaction.

In this frame of reference the reading teacher is seen first and always as a language teacher, and vocabulary development is seen as an integral part of total language development in listening, speaking, reading, and writing.

Reading is viewed as an extension of the child's previously achieved and still-developing skills in oral language. This view is reflected in some of the well-known series of reading texts which incorporate specific instructional procedures in speaking, listening, and writing as part of a total plan for reading development.

The use of such a frame of reference does not imply that vocabulary develops "just naturally" as maturation and experience bring increasing competence in language abilities. As long ago as 1938, William S. Gray and Eleanor Holmes conducted a series of studies of the development of meaning vocabularies that function in reading. Their findings, which have been corroborated by subsequent investigations, indicate that a close relationship exists between knowledge of word meanings and reading achievement and that direct methods of teaching vocabulary, where the teacher plans for and reinforces the learning of words in context, give pupils greater command of vocabulary than do methods which depend upon incidental learnings only.

Evaluating language development

The teacher who wishes to develop forces the learning of words in constant evaluation is needed to identify strengths and weaknesses, to chart progress, and to provide guidelines for helpful learning experiences. A pupil language development chart or a notebook with a page for each child can provide a graphic record of each child's language status and development. Marion Monroe and Bernice Rogers, in *Foundations for Reading*, suggest a simple and workable plan for recording and evaluating a pupil's use of language, including his ability to verbalize ideas, his knowledge of word meanings, and his mastery of sentence structure. Time here does not permit a full discussion of this plan, but careful study of this or of the similar suggestions contained in teachers' manuals of language arts series is suggested. Such study will prove rewarding to the teacher interested in fostering language growth.

The special case of the disadvantaged child

For those teachers who are working with children from lower socioeconomic backgrounds, it is important to emphasize that evaluation of language use should be made in terms of the child's power to communicate and comprehend rather than merely in terms of middle-class standards of "correct usage." The cataloging of what the teacher considers "errors" does not provide an adequate base for planning situations which will develop greater language competence. Although we do not as yet know enough about the complex process of language learning to pinpoint exact procedures for measuring and increasing language competency, linguistic and educational research strongly suggest that a positive, accepting approach to the child's language is more beneficial than a critical or wholly correction-oriented approach.

English sociolinguist Basil Bernstein has provided some insights into the school language problems of the disadvantaged child:

> The child has to translate and thus mediate middle-class language structure through the logically simpler language structure of his own class to make it personally meaningful. . . . The expressive behavior and immediacy of response that accompany the use of (the child's) language may . . . be wrongfully interpreted by the teacher. This may lead to a situation where pupil and teacher each disvalue each other's world, and communication becomes a way of asserting differences.*

I recently observed a first grade reading lesson, an overview in which children were discussing the pictures. During the lesson the teacher rejected every single verbal offering made by the children. The children's comments were couched in non-standard

* Basil Bernstein. "Some Sociological Determinants of Perception: an Enquiry into Subcultural Differences," *British Journal of Sociology* (1958), 249.

but often delightfully colorful language. Sample responses were, "He popin' the battercakes!" "That's a mighty big icebox!" "She got on her high heels!" The teacher, wearily and grimly correcting every expression, uttered, "He is *tossing* the *pancakes.*" "The *refrigerator* is *very* big." "She *is wearing* her *good shoes.*" At the end of the session the teacher was exhausted and discouraged; the children were apathetic and confused. The teacher said to the observer, "It's so hard to teach these children anything—you have to pull everything out of them." Her communication with the children, was indeed a way of asserting differences; she was, furthermore, implicitly saying to them, "Of course, you'll never learn to read. You can't even talk.

The teacher might have made an attempt to mediate between the children's choice of words and that preferred by the school. She might have recognized that they were responding and communicating at the only level they knew. She might have welcomed the opportunity to extend and enrich their vocabularies by discussing alternative expressions pleasantly and positively. For example, she might have said, "Yes, he's having a good time with the battercakes. You know, lots of people call these 'battercakes,' but they have another name, too. Lots of people call them 'pancakes.' Isn't it fun to know two names for something that's so good to eat?"

Personalizing vocabulary development

Pupil-made reading materials can help bridge the gap between the child's oral language and the written language. This condition is equally true for the "disadvantaged" child who needs constant reinforcement of the basic notion that reading is "talk written down" and for the verbally able youngster who needs scope for self-expression so that school remains an exciting challenge to his abilities. A good beginning at any primary grade level is a booklet; perhaps entitled "All about Me;" illustrated with snapshots or drawings of the child, his family and friends, including a map of his neighborhood; and containing references to games he plays, books he likes, and activities he enjoys. Such booklets and others based on group experiences, learning from class work, or the child's own creative imagination become part of the class library. They are displayed, read aloud, and discussed in specially planned language periods. The alert teacher uses them for evaluation of individual language growth and selects from them "Mary's new word" and "Joe's interesting sentence" to use in enriching vocabulary development for the entire group.

How do teachers find time to help chilren prepare such booklets? Some teachers plan a few minuttes each day in which children can dictate material for their own books. Other teachers, in schools where the concept of the teacher aide is being put into practice, have older children, parent volunteers, or paid aides who can transcribe the children's own language into their booklets.

Using story time to develop vocabulary

The practice of telling and reading stories to children can be an important aid to vocabulary development if the teacher plans for effective listening by actively involving children in such activities as retelling, dramatizing, assisting in, and illustrating the stories heard. Allowing the children to manipulate puppets or place figures on the flannel board to go along with the sequence of the story promotes full involvement. The teacher sets the stage for comprehension and vocabulary development as she clarifies and illustrates the meaning of unfamiliar words before relating the story in which they appear. Asking questions afterwards, such as, "How did the princess show that she was *disappointed*?" or "Why do you think the money is called "Curious George?"

gives opportunities for reusing and further strengthening meaning associations with new words.

Encouraging young children to join in a refrain, such as, "Run, run, run/ As fast as you can/ You can't catch me/ I'm the Gingerbread Man," promotes unselfconscious oral expression for children who may seldom "speak out" alone. Choral reading by more mature groups serves a similar purpose. Selected words and phrases from favorite storybook passages or refrains can be related to the vocabulary used in school texts. Presenting such words and phrases on the blackboard, charts, flash cards, and sentence strips transfers what has been heard and spoken to the visual realm. The enjoyment of listening and speaking thus motivates meaningful reading experiences.

Capitalizing on enjoyment of songs and rhymes.

The teacher can capitalize on children's love of rhyme and rhythm to develop vocabularly through listening to records and other musical activities. New words learned in songs can become words a child uses frequently and can become part of the reading vocabularly when their printed forms are subsequently introduced on board or chart. The use of familiar folk songs and of the chants and rhymes the children use in games is often helpful in making the culturally different child feel more at home in the classroom. The introduction of these songs and the reuse of their words in other language activities can help build common vocabulary for the entire class.

Developing vocabulary through shared experiences.

Planning and carrying out a class trip or a special event such as a program or holiday celebration can build a background of shared experience which promotes vocabularly development. The planning phase provides a meaningful setting for discussion and interchange of ideas which the teacher may organize by writing out "What We Will See at the Zoo," for example. The trip itself will provide many opportunities for verbal descriptions and discussion of what is seen and done. A recapitulation of the experience through class discussion, dramatization, illustration, and preparation of a story chart or of individual booklets can give further opportunities for use of the newly learned words and concepts which can thus become part of each child's vocabulary.

Developing vocabulary in the content areas.

At one time it was often supposed that "reading in the content areas" was begun at the intermediate level. Today, it is understood that the basis for successful achievement in the content fields must be firmly established in the primary grades. The meaning vocabulary that is needed for reading social studies, science, and other content materials can and should be introduced through oral language activities very early in the child's school life. Beautiful new picture books and easy-to-read science texts and trade books for young children, children's weekly newspapers, discussion and chart presentation of new words and concepts currently in the political or science news, and well-planned class units of study in science and social studies, all provide a basis for learning specialized vocabulary. This vocabulary, comprehended and used in the daily speech of the primary youngster, is the firm foundation for successful reading in the content areas.

Creative book-reporting activities can develop vocabulary.

As children mature in their reading skills, the sharing of stories through a variety of book-reporting activities gives opportunities for vocabulary development. The creative teacher does not limit book reporting to a sterotyped retelling of the story but lets children share their enthusiasm for books through group activities. The youngest children enjoy drawing their favorite characters and mounting them on sticks. They can then, individually or in groups, use the puppets as foils to recount a humorous or exciting scene or bit of dialogue. By third grade some children are socially and linguistically mature enough to take part in panel discussions of books. Book reporting can be particularly useful in helping both reporters and listeners clarify the meanings of abstract words such as *pride, curiosity, danger,* or *courage.* It can further give opportunities for better understanding of figurative language and implied meanings. The alert teacher will capitalize on the children's interest in storybook characters and situations to broaden and deepen their understanding of abstract concepts. Those children who cannot yet read "on their own" need not to be left out of participation in book-reporting activities. They may show pictures from a picture book or occasionally report on a story that has been read aloud to them, and always they are included as active listeners and discussants at book-reporting time, an activitiy bolstering both their interest in reading and their vocabulary growth.

Conclusion

The foregoing suggestions are but a sampling of the means thoughtful teachers use to foster vocabulary development within the framework of all the language arts. Oral vocabulary development has been viewed as the foundation for and the accompaniment to the development of reading skills. As primary teachers recognize the importance of oral language to growth in reading, they seek throughout the school day to accept, encourage, evaluate, and build upon the children's ability to understand and produce spoken language and thereby promote their ability to perceive, comprehend, and respond to the written language as well.

Vocabulary Growth through the Use of Context in Elementary Grades

PAUL C. BURNS
The University of Tennessee

ACCORDING TO HARRIS (19), "If the total vocabulary of representative children grows 15,000 words or more during the first six grades . . . this means an average of at least 2,500 words a year, 66 words a week, or 13 words a day—excluding vacations, weekends, and holidays." This statement suggests that although the vocabulary of basal readers may be controlled, the total reading done by children involves a great number of words. The important fact is that if teachers had to teach all the words that children learn, the time required would be exorbitant.

Children who read widely can learn a great many words through use of context. Wide reading provides the opportunity for context, or all of the elements which give support to meaning, to illuminate word meaning when it is essential to the flow of thought. Through wide reading, the reader can begin to recognize the subtleties and varied meanings of words. This idea has its basis in semantics: "We learn the meanings of practically all our words not from dictionaries, not from definitions, but from hearing these noises as they accompany actual situations in life and learning to associate certain noises with certain situations (23)."

Types and uses of contextual aids

Artley (1) suggests four types of contextual aids: pictorial context, verbal context, experimental context, and organizational or structural context.

Logical reasoning and research evidence support the validity of pictures as a way of supporting word meaning. Some recent writers obviously question this premise in favor of children's reading materials which omit pictures presumably to focus attention strictly upon "decoding symbols." It is a well established fact that many primary school pupils lack ability to use pictures in constructing the meaning of strange words (4, 33, 34). In its broader sense, pictorial context includes maps, charts, graphs, and statistical tables; and inadequate "reading" and interpreting of these may be hindered by the omission of or de-emphasis of foundational "picture reading" experiences. "Visual context" examples are emphasized in such programs as Gibson-Richards' *First Steps in Reading English* (14).

Of verbal context, a distinction may be made between the two types of acts in which context can be used to figure out the meaning of a word: first, using context in figuring out the meaning of a word is (The lecturer leaned upon the ———[podium, lectern, etc.] as he spoke.); and second, in using context in unlocking a word which is strange only in print (Jim opened his ———[Book, magazine, etc.] and began to read.) In the first case, context is used as an explainer of a meaning unfamiliar to the reader or as a determiner of which of several familiar meanings is needed for a given word; in the second situation, the reader uses context as a clue which along with his use of sounds represented by letters stimulates the reader to call to mind simultaneously the familiar spoken form and the familiar meaning of a given word (30).

By experience cues, Artley refers to the idea that the reader may rely on his past concrete experience, perhaps to a crow's harsh voice, to help clarify the meaning of the last word in the sentence "The crow cawed *raucously.*" Organizational or structural context refers to such clues in the presentation of the material as sectional or marginal headings, paragraphing, typographical aids, and those aids that are in the familiar patterns of language as appositive, nonrestrictive, or interpolated phrases or clauses and other language expressions.

A little explored type of context may be referred to as "spoken context," a foundational experience particularly needed at the beginning instructional levels but appropriate at all grade levels. Examples of use of this orally presented type of context (Bill can play———[ball, tag, etc.] with me.) can be found in McKee and Harrison's *Preparing Your Child For Reading (29)*.

Another context type may be labeled as "set context"; that is, the particular circumstances under which the reader does the reading. This type of context provides much of the content of the study of semantics which deals with physical and psychological contexts as well as verbal context.

From consideration of such types of context, it can be reasoned that the uses of context include 1) perceiving new words on the basis of reasoning and logical inference; 2) checking meanings derived through other word analysis skills; 3) checking on word perception, particularly in case of homographs (*tear, hail, lead,* etc.) where one must choose the pronunciation and meaning which makes sense in the sentence; and 4) trying to find a clue to the meaning of a word which leads to sensible use of the dictionary. It would seem that these uses of context are legitimate ones to promote in the elementary school if reading is considered a reasoning act, if multiple tools of vocabulary development are desirable, if the vagaries of our language are to be understood, and if one's reading should make sense.

Importance and need for developing the use of context

Reading authorities have emphasized for many years the importance of developing effective use of context. For example, McKee (*31*) writes ". . . use of context is the chief means for increasing vocabulary through reading. . . ." McCrimmon (*26*) states, " . . . in practice we learn the meanings of words by their context. . . . This is exactly how the writers of dictionaries got their defini-

tions." Spache (*39*) points out: "Eventually contextual analysis becomes one of the most frequently used methods of derivation of word meanings, as phonics and structural analysis decrease in use." Leary (*24*) advocates, "Train a child to anticipate probable meaning, to infer an unknown word from its total context, to skip a word and read on to derive its probable mean, to check the context clue with the form of the word, to search the context for a description or explanation that will identify the word, and he will have acquired the most important single aid to word recognition. For regardless of what word he perceives, if it doesn't make sense in its setting, his perception has been in error." Fay (*11*) and Gates (*12*) have made similar statements supporting the use of context. In speaking of the poor reader, Harris (*21*) cautions, " . . . there may be a temptation to assume that pupils who need training in word recognition should be discouraged from attempting to utilize the context at all. Nothing is farther from the truth. . . . All good readers make use of context clues, so there is no reason to discourage poor readers from doing the same. . . ."

Other advantages that accrue to the reader who learns to use context wisely include 1) understanding that a word has no permanent meaning which reflects a *living language;* making use of available material instead of having to go to another source, such as the dictionary; and 3) improving learning to read while reading to learn and thereby facilitating integration of skill learning with content learning.

Classroom experience and research investigations suggest that lack of skill in using context is quite prevalent among elementary school pupils. In an early study, Gray and Holmes (*16*) found that when a context clue was available (in this case, an appositional statement), it was not necessarily used to infer a correct meaning. Bradbury (*6*) found that in attempting to read his textbooks, the average child in the fourth grade can use the context successfully to construct the meaning of a strange word in about one out of three opportunities. According to Spache and Berg (40) the average high school graduate uses the context to derive meanings in only about 50 to 60 percent of the words that are unknown to him. Gibbons (13) found about the same results for the average college freshman. Several studies give us reason to believe that more guidance in the use of contextual analysis provides for growth in this technique. Porter (35) found that primary children can learn to use contextual analysis of simple types quite effectively. When words were completely omitted from the context, these pupils correctly deduced the exact word omitted 23 percent of the time. They were able to deduce probable meanings of the omitted words 83 percent of the time. In other words they were successful in contextual analysis for meanings in 8 out of 10 attempts. Harrison (22) also found that context can illuminate word meaning if the necessary guidance is provided for children. Hafner (18) concluded that short-term instruction in the use of context aids seemed to hold promise of improving pupil reading comprehension.

Analysis of nature of text material

What are the kinds of situations, oral and verbal, that need to be presented and practiced if contextual analysis is to become an important tool and means of vocabulary growth? Types of context clues have been analyzed by Artley, McCullough, and Deighton on the basis of their use in books.

Artley (2, 3) has proposed seven types of contextual aids to word meanings from an earlier listing: 1) typographical aids, as parentheses or footnotes; 2) grammatical aids, as appositive phrases or clauses; 3) substitute words, as synonyms or antonyms; 4) word elements, as roots, prefixes, and suffixes; 5) figures of speech; 6) pictures, diagrams, and charts; and 7) inference, as in "Due

to the mountain ranges and the cold climate, the amount of *arable* land is limited." McCullough (27, 28) has categorized types of contextual clues as experience clues, comparison or contrast words or phrases, synonyms, summary clues, reflection of mood of a situation, definition, and familiar expression as "He kept his *cool.*" Deighton (9), analyzing the types of context clues found in textbooks on an eighth grade to adult reading level, stated context illuminated word meaning through definition; example, modification, restatement, and inference.

It can be noted that there are similarities and overlappings among these listings. Depending upon one's definition of *context*, some clues may appear more appropriate than others. Other similar classifications of the instructional specifics in this area of context clues are suggested by McKee (32) and Betts (5). Which listing or which particular clues are most usable for the elementary school teacher has not been determined. It would seem that inference as a context clue is one of the least used but more promising and that study of word elements (roots, prefixes, and suffixes) has not produced good results. It would be helpful to teachers if they knew the context types which appear most commonly in pupil materials and what degree of difficulty each type of contextual clue presents for the pupil. One study (44), for example, suggests that the most difficult context situation for sixth grade children involves use of contrast, such as, "Is John *clumsy* or is he *agile*?" The connecting word "or" deserves careful treatment as it can join words of similar meaning or words of different meanings as "I had never seen him so *depressed* or *melancholy.*" and "Is Jim *talkative* or *taciturn*?" There is no clue for the reader to use in determining which of the two possible functions *or* is performing. Another problem that has received little study is how to help the young child conceive of an unknown word as referring to a circumscribed meaning rather than to regard the word as carrying with it the whole of a major part of the context in which it appears (*42*).

Ways of developing effective use of context

It appears to me that there are some basic ideas to be considered in developing the skillful use of context. These would include:

1. Continue to emphasize reading for meaning. While in the strict sense it may be true that context doesn't give meaning to a word any more than the dictionary does, it is safer to suggest that "symbols signify something" rather than "symbols signify nothing."

2. Provide large quantities of readable material appropriate to interests in "reading class" and in teaching the content subjects (*17*). The pupil simply *cannot* use context every fourth or fifth word. Content books frequently present such a high vocabulary load that they seriously hinder the use of context clues by the reader.

3. Outline a carefully designed delineation of the set of aids as a context syllabus in the reading area; pre-test to find strengths or weaknesses of the pupils; and then afford practice with the needed abilities through the reading textbooks, workbooks, and other supplementary materials as needed.

4. Provide greater emphasis to context clues development with oral and listening situations, prior to and along with application of verbal reading m a t e r i a l s. Further exploration is needed into the area or "spoken context," for the pupil who cannot use the clues of context in listening will likely have little if any more control of them in the reading act. On the contrary, it has been suggested (*37*) that better training in "spoken-listening context" can be used to improve the

pupil's ability to understand adequately what he attempts to read.

5. Teach the child to go beyond the single word in search for the meaning by context. One study (*41*) suggests that the words that follow a strange word are more likely to aid in contextual analysis than those that precede it. This study confirms the desirability of teaching pupils to read the entire sentence (or rest of paragraph) before attempting to derive the meaning of an unknown word. The practice of immediately stating, "Look it up in the dictionary" is a poor one. It would be better to say, "Try to find a clue to the meaning of the word through the context." The pupils need to know that the context needed for constructing the meaning of a given strange word may appear before, after, or both before and after the strange word (*15*). It should be recognized that there is some evidence that the influence of context upon word meanings seems to decrease rapidly with the distance of the context, and context more than about five words distant has relatively little effect upon clarifying an unknown word.

6. Provide time for discussion of how meaning can be derived through context. Discuss with pupils what is meant by using context to figure out the meaning of a word, what the helpful parts of the context may be, and where they appear. Also pupils need to recognize the situation where no clue is provided, as in "Bill was *reluctant* to do it."

7. Capitalize upon context in all types of content reading situations. Teach pupils the common ways textbooks make new meanings easy to acquire. Study the content books used to see how the new terms are made understandable, and let the pupils in on this study.

8. Delay discussion of the meaning of a strange word in the reading material or content subjects if the context is provided by familiar words for building that meaning. Pupils must have an opportunity for application for taught skills in the normal reading situation. Occasionally the teacher might select a half dozen difficult words from future reading assignments and ask pupils to write their definitions. After the reading, pupils may correct of revise their earlier definitions. This is a particularly applicable assignment at the intermediate school level.

9. Develop a general appreciation for words and language structure. Through experience and instruction the pupil needs to appreciate denotations and connotations of specific words and multiple meanings for the same word. He needs to be guided to anticipate the fact that pronunciation and meaning of homographs, such as, *bow, refuse,* and *wind* cannot be verified until seen in "use situations." He needs to recognize that homonyms may be spelled alike (cold *hail* or *hail* a cab) or may be spelled differently *(stake, steak)*. He certainly should expect irregularities in the alphabetic representations of English sounds *(head, break, early,* etc.) Further, the pupil needs to sense the importance of the order of words to the structure of language and/or meaning. By the position or function of a word in a sentence, and to this extent, its meaning is suggested *(27)*. "The igg ogged the ugg" type of presentation may help pupils recognize the "nounness" or "verbness" of the words. This feeling helps the pupil sense that nouns and verbs are most essential for meaning. The structure of the phrase, sentence, or paragraph often serves as a clue to the

meaning of what is written. Rhetorical terms of coherence are also guides to reading comprehension of a paragraph, pure conjunctions and certain adverbs being very common links *(36)*. The fact that many of the contextual clues to word meaning have their origin in such concepts provides a strong argument for the development of general knowledge of language structure, and suggests again the interrelationships of the language arts *(45)*.

Cautions in the use of context clues

It is not possible to develop effective use of context clues in situations where the child is bogged down with the mechanics of reading. Wide independent reading—where little difficulty with word recognition or meaning is presented—gives the pupil an opportunity to use contextual aids. But *opportunity* alone is not enough. As in other skills of r e a d i n g , children in the intermediate grades vary greatly in their ability to identify words and to derive meaning from context as reaffirmed by studies from Boston University *(7, 8, 10, 25, 43)*. Children with poor reading ability usually cannot identify words they do not know. Unless children are taught to notice unfamiliar words and to be alert to the connection between the context and the unknown word it bears upon, they are unlikely to develop large vocabularies from extensive reading.

It must be clear that the child will not always gain the correct meaning of a word from the context. Context always determines the meaning of a word but doesn't always reveal that meaning. Context generally reveals only one of the meanings of an unfamiliar word. It is worth saying to children over and over again that no word has one fixed or unalterable meaning, that no one context revelation will suffice for all the later uses of the word which may be met. Also, context seldom clarifies the whole of any single word meaning. Context will often provide a synonym, but synonyms are never exact equivalents.

Finally, vocabulary growth through context revelation is a gradual one. It is a matter of finding one clue here and another there, of fitting them together, and of making tentative judgments and revising them as later experience requires. It is building meaning into a word over a period of years through the combined experiences of the writer and the reader.

REFERENCES

1. Artley, A. Sterl. "Developing the Use of Context" in *Developing Vocabulary and Word-Attack Skills, A Report of the Eighteenth Annual Conference and Course on Reading.* Pittsburgh: University of Pittsburgh, 1962, 91-98.
2. *Ibid.,* 95.
3. Artley, A. Sterl. "Teaching Word Meaning Through Context," *Elementary English Review,* 10 (February 1943). 68-74.
4. Beck, G. "The Ability of First Grade Pupils to Use Pictures in Constructing the Meanings of Strange Words," master's thesis, State College of Education, Greeley, Colorado, 1940.
5. Betts, Emmett A. *Foundations of Reading Instruction.* New York: American Book Co., 1957, 581-582, 601-611.
6. Bradbury, Helen. "The Ability of Fourth Grade Pupils to Construct the Meaning of a Strange Word from Context," master's thesis, State College of Education, Greeley, Colorado, 1943.
7. Burgand, Joan F. "An Investigation of Abilities of Fifth and Sixth Graders to Derive Meaning from Context in Silent Reading," master's thesis, Boston University, Boston, Massachusetts, 1950.
8. Butler, Huldah A. "Finding Word Meanings from Context in Grades Five and Six," master's thesis, Boston University, Boston, Massachusetts, 1943.
9. Deighton, Lee C. *Vocabulary Development in the Classroom.* Bureau of Publications, Teachers College, Columbia University, 1959.
10. Elivian, Jeannette. "Word Perception and Word Meaning in Silent Reading in the Intermediate Grades," master's thesis, Boston University, Boston, Massachusetts, 1958.
11. Fay, Leo C. *Reading in the High School,* Department of Classroom Teachers, AERA, Washington, 1956, 18.
12. Gates, Arthur I. *The Improvement of Reading.* New York: The Macmillan Co., Revised, 1947, 241.
13. Gibbons, Helen. "The Ability of College Freshmen to Use Context to Construct the Meaning of Unknown Words," doctor's field study, No. 2, State College of Education, Greeley, Colorado, 1940.
14. Gibson, C. M., and I. A. Richards. *First Steps in Reading English.* New York: Pocket Books, Inc., 1957.
15. Godfrey, Grace. "A Study of Context as a Means of Explaining the Meanings of Strange Words in Certain Children's Books," master's thesis, State College of Education, Greeley, Colorado, 1941.
16. Gray, William S., and Eleanor Holmes. *The Development of Meaning Vocabularies in Reading.* Chicago: University of Chicago Press, 1938, 1.
17. Gray, William S. *On Their Own in Reading.* Chicago: Scott, Foresman and Co., 1960.
18. Hafner, Lawrence E. "A One-Month Experiment in Teaching Context Aids in the Fifth Grade," *The Journal of Educational Research,* 63 (July-August, 1965), 472-474.
19. Harris, Albert J. *Effective Teaching of Reading.* New York: David McKay, Co., 1962, 220-221.
20. *Ibid.,* 194.
21. Harris, Albert J. *How to Increase Reading Ability.* New York: Longmans, Green and Co., Fourth Edition, 1961, 374.
22. Harrison, Janice Mantle. "Acquiring Word Meaning Through Context Clues," master's thesis, Ohio State University, Columbus, Ohio, 1960.
23. Hayakawa, S. I. *Language in Thought and Action.* New York: Harcourt, Brace and Co., 1949, 57.
24. Leary, Bernice. "Developing Word Perception Skills in Middle and Upper Grades," *Current Problems in Reading Instruction.* Pittsburgh: University of Pittsburgh Press, 1951, 25.
25. McAuliffe, Mary E. "Getting Meaning from Context in Grade Four," master's thesis, Boston University, Boston, Massachusetts, 1950.
26. McCrimmon, James M. *Writing with Purpose: A First Course in Composition.* Boston: Houghton-Mifflin, 1957, 157.
27. McCullough, Constance M. "Context Aids in Reading," *The Reading Teacher,* 11 (April, 1958), 225-229.
28. McCullough, Constance M. "Recognition of Context Clues in Reading," *Elementary English Review,* 22 (January, 1956), 1-5.
29. McKee, Paul, and Lucille Harrison. *Program in Skills Basic to Beginning Reading.* Boston: Houghton-Mifflin Co., 1960.
30. McKee, Paul. *Reading: A Program of Instruction for the Elementary School.* Boston: Houghton-Mifflin Co., 1966, 264, 258-268.
31. *Ibid.,* 262.
32. McKee, Paul. *The Teaching of Reading.* Boston: Houghton-Mifflin Co., 1948.
33. Miller, W. "Reading With and Without

Pictures in the Primary Grades," doctor's field study, No. 2, State College of Education, Greeley, Colorado, 1938.

34. Miller, W. "What One Hundred Third Grade Children Saw in Six Pictures," doctor's field study, No. 2, State College of Education, Greeley, Colorado, 1938.

35. Porter, Douglas. "The Instrumental Value of Sound Cues in Reading," paper read at the AERA Convention, Atlantic City, February 17, 1960.

36. Shaw, Phillip. "Rhetorical Guides to Reading Comprehension," *The Reading Teacher,* 11 (April, 1958), 239-243.

37. Sister Mariam, O.P. "Context Clues in Primary Reading," *The Reading Teacher,* 11 (April, 1958), 230-234.

38. Smith, Henry P., and Emerald V. Dechant. *Psychology in Teaching of Reading.* Englewood Cliffs: Prentice Hall Inc., 1961, 219.

39. Spache, George D. *Reading in the Elementary School.* Boston: Allyn and Bacon, Inc., 1964, 216.

40. Spache, George D., and Paul C. Berg. *The Art of Efficient Reading.* New York: The Macmillan Co., 1955, 109.

41. Weaver, Wendell. "The Predictability of Word Meaning," *New Developments in Programs, Training Aids and Procedures,* National Reading Conference Proceedings, 12 (1963), 152-157.

42. Werner, Heinz, and Edith Kaplan. "Development of Word Meaning Through Verbal Context: An Experimental Study," *Journal of Psychology,* 29 (April, 1950), 251-257.

43. White, Loretta M. "The Ability of Fifth Grade Pupils to Get Word Meaning from Context," master's thesis, Boston University, Boston, Massachusetts, 1950.

44. Wilson, Frank E. "The Ability of Sixth Grade Children to Acquire the Meaning of a Strange Word from Context," master's thesis, State College of Education, Greeley, Colorado, 1947.

45. Zames, Wilbur S. "A Study of the Process by Which Readers Determine Word Meaning Through the Use of Context," unpublished doctoral dissertation, University of Missouri, Columbia, Missouri, 1965.

Vocabulary Development through the Use of Multi-Level Materials (Secondary)

WILLIAM T. HOLDER
St. Louis Junior College

IN THE BOOK entitled *The Stages of Economic Growth* W. W. Rostow lists five steps involved in the growth of a traditional culture into a high order technological culture: 1) the traditional society, 2) the preconditions of take off, 3) the take off, 4) the drive to maturity, and 5) the age of mass consumption. J. D. Finn states in the collected works *Revolution in Teaching* (De Grazia and Sohon, p. 27) that "it is my thesis that American Education, considered as a culture in tradition, is now beginning the take-off stage into a high order, high energy culture, and that it is the first educational system in the world to reach this stage." It is true that a technological revolution is engulfing every aspect of education—low power translators, videotape, stratovision, language laboratories, language laboratories plus visuals, mobile laboratories, individual listening and view devices, teaching machines, thermoplastic recordings, and data and data transmission systems. Exciting instructional systems include the EBF series in physics, AIBS series in biology, UICSM for mathematics, PSSC system in physics, Heath de Rochemont in Parlons Francois. There are the Stoddard organizational proposal, the Trump organizational proposal, and team teaching. Too, there are the operating organizations—the Ford Foundation, the NSF, the LRI, the EMC, and the EFL. Instructional systems are concentrating on mass data presentations, individual and small group automated teaching, human interaction, and individual study and creative periods.

Grounded?

Yet amidst the great curriculum reform movements, Robert Karlin in *Teaching Reading in High School* (p. 21) states that "it is estimated that between ten and twenty percent of every school population may be considered disabled in reading." He also writes (p. 2) that "probably from twenty percent for forty percent of our high school population is reading below grade norm." Even with SRA, the controlled reader, the Perceptoscope, the Tach X, the shadow scope, and the SQ3R procedure, reading teachers cannot endorse the following resolution—"Existing technical equipment has been shown to be an effective decay preventive that can be of significant value when used in a conscientiously applied program of reading skills and regular supervisory care." Educational institutions, nevertheless, are probing more deeply into the reading process than every before and more broadly into the factors that affect it. There can be no misinterpretation of the evidence that words are symbols, that the meaning of symbols results only from experience with that symbol, that the way to increase vocabulary is to read and to use, and that the individualized methodology correlated with multi-level materials can provide unlimited achievement in vocabulary growth.

Needs

A typical high school class consists of from twenty to thirty students. Obviously it cannot be taught as though all members of the class had the same interests, desires, intellectual capabilities, or physical characteristics; nor can it be taught as though each youngster had reached the same level of attainment in reading or possesses identical instructional needs. Each girl and boy must be given material that is as nearly suitable to his level of reading growth as is possible and must be taught by methods compatible with his characteristics and capabilities.

As previously stated, the way to improve vocabulary is to hear and see words and to use them until they become familiar. Almost anyone can learn hundreds of new words, but the purpose of vocabulary development is not to memorize two or three hundred words. The ultimate goal is to develop the techniques to deal with unfamiliar words and to deal with new meanings for familiar words as they appear in different context.

Comprehension in any field requires adequate vocabulary, and the accumulation of a recognition vocabulary in a textbook is built on the concept of a controlled vocabulary. The student must learn the vocabulary to understand the important ideas in his reading. The teacher usually starts a reading activity by putting new words on the blackboard and devoting part of the lesson to the study of new words. Novice teachers tend to teach the new words of a story before the student has had an opportunity to meet the unfamiliar word in the context of the story. The bright and energetic student acquires the vocabulary at a rapid rate, and the less capable student becomes so overwhelmed that he becomes stagnated. Ultimately, the limited individual in terms of the intelligence constellation tends to have a low vocabulary, and the bright learners tend to have a rich vocabulary.

Even though word recognition is difficult and complex learning, multilevel materials provide pacing so that each youngster can profitably learn with comfort and self-respect. Each teacher must determine the placement of students in the various achievement groups. He must discover the level of materials high school students can read and the stage of development of reading skills which they manifest. Each student is put to work in a congenial learning situation.

An approach

The class consisted of twenty-five students. Seven of the students were reading one year or more above grade norm; twelve were reading at grade level; three were from 1.1 to 2.0 years below grade level; and three, from 2.1 to 3.7 years below grade level. The assignment was to read an article entitled "The Wings of Madness," by Hallowell Bowser that appeared in the October 24, 1964 issue of *Saturday Review of Literature*. The article described the reaction of individuals toward the U. S. Army's Operation Water Moccasin. The vocabulary included the following words to be understood: maneuver, presumably, fantastic, venerable, insurgency, sinister, deluged, conspirators, progenitors, promulgated, lemmings, infrared, impassioned, pagan, and parched. The students reading at or above grade level were asked to form groups of five, to read the article silently, and to apply their skills in using context clues and other meaning aids to anticipate the words to be recognized. The groups were to determine the correct pronunciation and the correct definition for the particular context in which the word was used. The entire group then used the pre-prepared master track recording cards and the Language Master to check the pronunciation and the definition of each word. The teacher could have written the words on the board, pronounced, and defined them, however. This procedure, if consistently used, however, would interfere with the development of independence in word attack. Following the vocabulary exercise, the students worked on exercises to draw conclusions from what they had studied, make comparisons and inferences, evaluate the facts, and participate in follow-up activities that provided for the development of critical reading skills.

With the exception of one student, the remainder of the class—slow readers tending to have shorter attention spans, lacking strong motivation, and needing more direction-were asked, because of their interest in law enforcement, to read silently an editorial that appeared in the November 29, 1966 issue of the *St. Louis Globe-Democrat*.

> Do we really live in a *civilized society* when a night clerk in a *fashionable* motel on North Kingshighway is robbed not once or twice but three times in a three-month period—shot and killed in the last holdup early Sunday?
> The victim, Elmer Glen Rosenblum, *sought* only to make a *decent* living. Now he is dead from bullet wounds in the back and chest.
> We are living in a *society* where criminals *apparently* have so little fear of the law that they return to rob the same businesses over and over—and shoot their *hapless* victims for little or no cause.
> Who will stage a march to *protest* the *violation* of the *civil rights* of Elmer Glen Rosenblum?
> And what about the rights of John N. Dougherty, who was trying to make a living driving a taxicab, when one of two robbers stabbed him to death in order to take about $30 from his pockets.

> As things stand today, the *perpetrators* of this *savage* crime can expect the arresting officers to find them an attorney *promptly* and to advise them *immediately* of their right not to give *evidence* against themselves.
> This bending over backward, to spare the criminal the *inconvenience* of making a confession, thus has had the effect of greatly *increasing* the danger to a person being robbed. The robbers, as in these two *instances*, may decide to take the life of the only witness, the victim.

Again the students were asked to decipher word meaning through context clues. As weakness in the word recognition techniques appeared—phonics, word structure, sight words, or context—teaching or reteaching took place. While the class was working on the assignment, the teacher did not become detached from the group. After the words were discussed, supplementary exercises assured the students and the teacher that the newly acquired vocabulary could be used—understood in context, explained in isolation, and practiced and understood in a functional situation.

The student's success is dependent upon the selection of instructional materials to facilitate sequential learning of new skills. The reading material must be current and over a wide range of interests as predetermined through interest inventories and concerned with anxieties and experiences.

Reading and the deprived

But in this class, one child, Johnny, remained. Johnny is a severe reading disability case who, according to his school report, has made no appreciable progress in reading. He is the fourth of eight children; he lives in a deteriorated tenement; he gives the appearance of being under nourished, and during the past year he was severly injured when he fell down a flight of stairs. Any ability? On the Wechsler Intelligence Scale Johnny obtained an IQ of 105, but he is reading about 3.7 grades below his capabilities. Since Johnny's retardation is so great, it would probably be better to have him taught in a clinic. There is no clinic, but Johnny does receive individual help each day. As the groups were forming, a member of the senior class and president of the 'F.T.A. came into the room, motioned for Johnny, pulled two chairs out into the hall, and went to work on special materials pitched at a level of difficulty Johnny could handle. He was working on generalizations of phonics, principles of syllabication, principles of phonics, principles of accents, and comprehension. But the teacher had distinguished between a workbook-controlled approach and an experimental-functional approach. Monotonous and unnecessary practices which prevented progress had been eliminated. This disabled reader was interested in the assignment because he was being exposed to the experience of discovery. Often he was cognizant of his knowledge, and on many occasions he could not verbalize his findings; but he did experience it and, therefore, remembered it and made use of it. Johnny likes high school, his teacher and his tutor. He can't read adequately, but he will.

Mechanical or Creative?

The development of vocabulary is of obvious importance. Traditional reading programs incorporate four basic approaches to vocabulary development —rate learning, etymological approach, linguistic approach, and the incidental technique. In practically all of these the content has become supplementary to the drill—the exercise, the workbook. The following poem written by an anonymous writer may convey to you what I mean:

Adventure

Here's an adventure! What awaits
Beyond these closed, mysterious gates?
Whom shall I meet, Where shall I go?
Beyond the lovely land I know?
Above the sky, across the sea,
What shall I learn and feel and be?
Open, strange doors, to good or ill!
I hold my breath a moment still
Before the magic of your look
What shall you do to me, O Book?

Do not focus on the science of words as expressed in formulas. Enrich the students' experiences, and you enrich their vocabularies. Do not become so busy with the knowledge of mastering facts, skills, words, and formulas in a skewed curriculum that you forget to realize yourself and your students as persons. You, the teacher, must react to the message of the reading matter intellectually, aesthetically, and emotionally; and you must permit each individual in your classroom, regardless of ability, to react to the message of the reading matter intellectually, aesthetically, and emotionally. The intimate relationship of the reader to the reading matter must not be neglected, for it is through this relationship that meaningful and productive reading occurs.

A Three-Pronged Attack on Vocabulary Development (Secondary)

ROBERT KARLIN
Queens College of The
City University of New York

"IN ALL PROBABILITY, an inadequate vocabulary is the greatest single cause for failure to read with comprehension in either general or technical fields" (1). This belief is commonly held by classroom teachers and reading authorities on the basis of their experiences with students and the results and implications of vocabulary research.

Each of us—whether we are teachers of English, science, social studies, or reading—is concerned with our students' command over their language. And one aspect of this language is meaning vocabulary that is, words which have meaning for those who hear, use, or read them. We know that speaking and writing vocabularies, as measured by actual use, are exceeded in size by listening and reading vocabularies; but the size of our high school students' reading vocabulary is a matter of dispute, depending upon the way in which it has been measured. Estimates vary. Dale questions Seashore's figure of 80,000 words known by twelfth graders and suggests a number somewhat larger than Thorndike and Lorge's estimate of about 15,000. Regardless of the actual figure, an average is no indicator of what students can manage. Besides, we are not as much interested in how many words students know as we are in their ability to cope with the reading demands school and society make. These demands at the secondary level become increasingly greater as students sample larger varieties of narrative and expository materials containing words used in specialized ways. Serra (6) came to the conclusion that the "concept burden of instructional materials is too heavy" while other students of vocabulary reported a decrease in the rate of specialized vocabulary growth during the later high school years.

Word meaning involves percepts and concepts. While a delineation between the two is not sharp, students of language development define the former as "what is known of an object, a quality, or a relationship as a result of sensory experience" (5). Concepts grow out of percepts which lead to generalizations about objects, qualities, or relationships. Before children arrive at school, they learn percepts and develop concepts naturally by listening, speaking, and exploring. First-hand experiences account for almost all they acquire. Their horizons broaden upon entrance into school: first-hand experiences continue, but vicarious ones begin to shape their ideas more and more until a stage is reached wherein the latter dominates. That *meaning vocabulary* grows during these periods is established; that *precision of meaning* keeps pace with this growth is not as readily defined.

The work of Piaget and others suggests the close relationship between vocabulary and concept. Word meaning can be provided by definition and explanation—the use of words to explain words—but definition and explanation do not make up completely for deficiencies in concept weakness which could be the result of experiential deprivation. It becomes clear that our task as teachers of language includes attention to concept development, for without a referent to which vocabulary can be tied, meaning is unlikely. Of course we deal with several levels of meaning, and to expect all our students to reach these same levels in the face of variations in experiences and intelligence is hardly realistic. Some vague understandings of words might be realized without the acquisition of firm concepts. But the results are necessarily superficial and account for some of our frustration as we seek to help students better understand what they read.

It would appear, then, that one main attack to improve word understanding should be directed at developing some concept understanding. And this work teachers of different subjects can do. For years now they have been urged to provide experiences—both direct and vicarious—that would better prepare their students to deal with the content they were expected to master. This building of background prior to reading can make a significant difference between merely reading words and truly establishing meanings.

Methods of vocabulary development

Research studies on vocabulary development have sought to test ways by which improvement might be realized. The results of these studies show that it is possible to increase meaning vocabulary through several avenues. It seems clear, however, that dependence upon a single formula, regardless of its apparent values, is not so likely to bring results as multi-pronged attacks of a sustained nature. With regard to this last point, hit-and-run tactics such as devotion to vocabulary building for six-weeks or a similar period cannot be expected to produce lasting outcomes.

Wide reading in combination with direct and indirect programs constitute a three-pronged attack on vocabulary development. For reasons detailed earlier, we would not expect deep inroads into vocabulary weakness without accompanying efforts to expand concept formations. To rely upon a so-called "best" means reduces chances even more. Let us now examine each of these prongs as bases for a comprehensive vocabulary development program.

Wide reading

The facts that children acquire meaning vocabularies in an easy and natural way prior to and during the early years of school by listening to and experimenting with words, that words require a context and repeated settings, and that some intensive vocabulary programs have failed to produce expected results might have led to the suggestion by a number of reading and language students that wide reading is one of the best ways to develop vocabulary. Perhaps this conviction receives even greater support from the observation that avid readers appear to be masters of considerably more words than their less reader-oriented brothers are. Status studies of the relation between vocabulary size and extent of reading would be likely to support this belief even though causality could not be inferred from such investigations. Studies, however, of direct effects to increase vocabulary through wide reading alone have not proved fruitful.

We can raise objections, furthermore, against the singular dependence upon reading to build vocabulary. We assume that if the reader meets a word for the first time or an old word in a new setting, he will determine its meaning from either the context or the dictionary. Context is only useful it if is familiar; in addition, context can provide imprecise meanings which, when repeated, further reinforce them. To what extent students will halt their reading to look up unknown words in a dictionary is problematic. Some persons have suggested that to check dictionary meanings during reading interferes with one's thinking. The amount of reading each student does will vary, so will its quality. Uneven and unreliable results are predictable.

What then do we recommend? Wide reading by all means within a comprehensive vocabulary program and for other reasons, too. Wide reading complements vocabulary activities of a direct or incidental kind. It increases our chances for providing meaningful learning through need and application.

Direct and indirect approaches

Students of vocabulary development have been divided on the question of the merits of direct teaching of vocabulary and incidental treatment of words. By direct teaching some mean the deliberate presentation of words taken from lists or other sources for study. Incidental treatment, they say, involves the study of words which appear in the textbooks and other sources students read. It seems to me that this differentiation is an artificial barrier. Who would question the desirability of helping students acquire initial and deeper meanings for words which appear in daily reading? Who would suggest that no gains are to be derived from efforts to broaden vocabulary if words are taken from other sources? The souces of words do not seem so crucial to vocabulary building as do methods teachers pursue to help students increase their understanding. Personally I prefer meeting vocabulary needs as they occur. What better time and reason are there for dealing with them? But this preference does not preclude any attention one might give to so-called direct approaches to vocabulary building.

A number of investigations provides support for direct vocabulary instruction. But the research which provided little support for indirect instruction was not comparing the sources from which words were drawn; it compared direct instruction with casual or *laissez-faire* instruction. In the latter instance students were left to their own devices for dealing with unknown words. Who c o u l d not have predicted the results under these conditions? For purposes of this discussion, we view planned efforts, regardless of word source, as direct; and it is with these that we are concerned.

Demonstrations and investigations on vocabulary development do not point up overwhelming superiority of one method over another. They do appear to suggest these underlying guidelines - that we might follow regardless of method:

1. All students are not required to deal with indentical words since weaknesses should determine degree of involvement in vocabulary study.
2. Words are studied in context rather than in isolation.
3. Emphasis is placed upon working rather than esoteric vocabulary.
4. Application of word learning is stressed.

Let's turn now to procedures (whose limitations one must remain cognizant of) for helping students broaden and extend their reading vocabularies.

We acquire vocabulary through verbal contexts; it seems reasonable to teach students to use these contexts as they read in order to seek meanings for unknown words. The key to word meanings in context are clues that might be joined to focus in on the unknown. If students require help in locating these clues and generalizing from them, one might provide a text for them in which several clues appear, discuss how these clues are related, and then decide through choices what possible meaning for the unknown word the clues offer. The following example contains a number of clues in brackets which students can use to determine the meaning of *subsidence*. Note how the larger context provides multiple clues not ordinarily found in single sentences.

Coral reefs appear in mid-ocean

Rocks and land formed by coral are some of the most interesting deposits in the sea (Figure 12-11). Study of cores taken by drilling holes through coral reefs down to 1400 meters tell us of the structure of these deposits. These cores were taken from Eniwetok Atoll. [Reef-building corals live only in tropical waters and at shallow depths (to 80 meters). Corals were found throughout the length of the core from Eniwetok.]

The length of the core and the presence of coral indicated to earth scientists that conditions in the surface waters of the tropical seas had not changed for 60 million years.

How do we know this? How is it possible to find, at depths of 1400 meters, coral rock that was formed within 80 meters of the surface? To Charles Darwin, who visited coral atolls in the 1830's as a young man of 22, it seemed that the sea floor and the islands had slowly *subsided*. [The corals grew upward, keeping pace] with the *subsidence* (Figure 12-12). He recognized three types of coral reefs: reefs growing along the shores of volcanic islands; reefs that were some distance from a volcanic island with a lagoon behind the reef; and circular reefs, or *atolls,* which surrounded lagoons with no central island. Darwin believed that atolls had originally been shoreline reefs that were now at the last stages of *subsidence*.

A hundred years of argument followed the publication in 1842 of Darwin's ideas on atolls. [The borings on Eniwetok in the 1950's reached volcanic rock after passing through 1400 meters of coral.] Thus Darwin was proved correct and his idea was shown to be a great example of scientific reasoning. [More important, in proving him right, we have learned that the sea floor does not sink uniformly. Instead it sinks an amount that depends on the mass of lava making up the individual island.]*

subsidence means stopping, settling, raising.

After students have learned to interpret clues which we have called to their attention, we might provide other contexts in which similar clues appear but which students now seek to identify themselves. Some teachers have offered variations of these lessons with success: one is the presentation of possible meanings for the unknown word followed by a search for clues to support one of them; another is the removal from the text of the new word and from the clues a meaningful word found for it from a suggested group of words. We might expect variation in approaches to contribute to motivation and learning. A point to remember is that discussing and exploring are likely to lead to better results than do mere telling or performing.

* *Investigating The Earth,* Earth Science Curriculum Project, American Geological Institute, 1965, 12-12—12-13.

Recently, the desirability of raising to conscious levels that which students seem to know has been suggested. Assuming such is the case, we might offer for study and discussion examples of structural and language clues which aid meanings through context: synonym and antonym, subordinate clauses, phrases in apposition, definition, illustration, position, typography.

We do not know to what extent the context offers meaning clues. Background of experiences can be a delimiting influence. And some texts might not contain clues or, if present, are so elusive that most students will not recognize them. And incomplete meanings might be products of contextual study. But few will deny some values in spending time with students who have not learned to take advantage of context mechanics and their interpretation.

Perhaps more attention has been given to the study of *word origins* as a vocabulary building technique by teachers and producers of materials then to any other method. It is reasoned that a large number of English words have their origins in Latin and Greek roots and affixes and that study of these sources will provides avenues through which meanings are secured.

All too frequently students are required to memorize the meanings of these prefixes, roots, and suffixes, and compile words containing them. This practice is dull and boring to most students and has not been shown to be a productive means of enabling them to determine the meanings of new words not previously encountered. Instead, some gains might be realized through a study of words as they appear in context in order to build relationships between the literal meaning as determined through analysis and actual meaning. Exercises in which the roots and affixes of these words are sought might be prepared (*mission, converts, intangible*). In this connection, students should realize that a source might change in form and/or meaning. By providing a limited number of roots with their meanings, as well as sentences and paragraphs, we can build new words and substitute them for known words. In addition, by adding prefixes and suffixes to know words we can extend their meaning (form + al, hero + ic, ante + date). Meaningful application of word sources can develop insights which help some students unlock some words.

A related vocabulary development program involves the study of the *history* of words. Perhaps you recall the punishment Tantalus, son of Zeus, suffered in the lower world. Out of this Greek myth comes our word *tantalize*. It is possible that some students will be spurred on by such exposures. But to assume all students will, especially those who need help the most, is not realistic. Interesting and little-known facts about words can enliven the study of words, but they are not likely to be enduring motivators. Personal need has greater possibilities.

Breadth and depth of vocabulary become a major concern in the middle grades and continue thereafter. One aspect is tied to *multiple meanings* of words. As materials become more complex, words take on meanings not commonly associated with them. There has been some research to suggest that general vocabulary knowledge and knowledge of multiple meanings are not intimately related. Assistance in extending meanings can be provided in conjunction with *dictionary* use. Obviously, a curriculum in which provisions for varied activities exist will include reading of all types, and words that are familiar in one sense will appear in contexts that require others. The examination and study of different meanings for such words—the word *take*, for example, is said to have 106 meanings—in order to determine an appropriate one could be a meaningful experience. Context clues, if present in conjunction with dictionary choices, will yield good results.

We need not only wait for words to appear in new contexts. We can provide contexts in which familiar words appearing in students' reading are used in different ways. Thus a word such as *charge* whose meaning is known in such contexts as *charge five dollars* or *charged up the hill*, is presented in less familiar contexts: *charged with murder, charge the jury, set off a charge.* Total contexts plus meanings provided by the dictionary will suggest the sense in which the word is used. Additional experiences—oral, written, and read—will tend to reinforce the new meanings students acquired for old friends.

The study of *lists of words* for which students are required to provide dictionary meanings and on which they are tested periodically has not proved to be a productive process when these words are studied in isolation and without purpose. Lists of words common to a particular area can be compiled by subject-matter teachers and studied by students in relation to their reading and writing. Graphic aids, models, descriptions, and in some instances dramatizations can help to reduce verbalizations. Some educators have suggested exercises that require students to seek analogies among words and to compare and categorize them in order to provide multiple exposures. How effective these approaches are will depend upon the extent to which they are meaningful—that is, tied to what students are doing. There is little justification for expending time and energy on learning specialized uses of words if the words are not those which are relevant to topics being studied and on knowledge of which completion of tasks depend.

A more recent development in vocabulary development is the introduction of *programed materials.* These materials consist of items, called frames, which are placed in sequential order and are intended to elicit responses that are verified immediately. Usually on the basis of a given statement responses intended to develop understanding are made in order of difficulty:

These words contain prefixes: *postpaid, postdate.*

1. Which of the following words contains a prefix? *swim, postwar*

    1._____

2. The prefix in the word *postmortem* is   2._____

Additional frames built on preceding ones will develop the concept of the prefix as well as its specific meaning.

It is possible to create programed materials which stress relationships among words and their meanings. How effective their use is will depend on a number of factors such as student motivation and relevancy of content. It has been shown that some students seem to learn more through programed than other modes. Perhaps we need to experiment more with the process in order to ascertain the conditions needed to promote effective learning.

Summary

Vocabulary building is an integral part of the reading-learning process. Its importance to continous growth in reading has led to a recognition of the contributions nature and nurture make to fulfillment. We teachers know that the sole responsibility for vocabulary development is not ours; however, we share this responsibiltiy. Our task is to offer as meaningful and comprehensive a vocabulary development program as possible. We ought not to settle for less.

REFERENCES

1. Cole, Luella. *The Elementary School Subjects.* New York: Rinehart, 1946, 40.
2. Gage, N. L. (Ed.). *Handbook of Research on Teaching.* Chicago: Rand McNally and Co., 1963, 883-898.
3. Karlin, Robert. *Teaching Reading in High School.* Indianapolis: The Bobbs-Merrill Co., Inc., 1964, 115-124.
4. McDonald, Arthur S. "Vocabulary Development: Facts, Fallacies and Programs," *New Concepts in College-Adult Reading,* Thirteenth Yearbook of the National Reading Conference, 1964, 77-85.
5. Russell, David. *Children's Thinking.* New York: Ginn and Co., 1956, 66.
6. Serra, Mary. "The Concept Burden of Instructional Materials," *Elementary School Journal,* 53 (May 1953), 508-512.
7. Simmons, John S. "Word Study Skills," *Developing Study Skills in Secondary Schools,* Perspectives in Reading No. 4, International Reading Association, 1965, 13-31.

Dialogue in Words
(College)

JOHN H. MATTHEWS
Ohio University

Cast: a professor of English and an ex-student, a young lady, who is also teaching.
Scene: in the professor's office.
Time: afternoon.

LADY

Actually, I suppose my real reason for coming to see you is the problem I'm having with my freshman students. I think the problem centers on one thing—vocabulary. At least this is the thing I've been brooding over lately. I can't seem to teach it the way I would like.

PROF

Have you used any texts?

LADY

Oh, I've tried them. And they all seem to do *some* good. One that *I* like best is a text on historical linguistics. I've been concentrating on roots and affixes—all very fascinating but I'm not sure how effective for my students.

PROF

I'm certain that's a good method.

LADY

I am, too. But—I don't know—it doesn't seem good enough. For one thing, the students who seem to profit most from the work we've been doing are the ones who are doing the best work to begin with.

PROF

Isn't that a paradox you find in all teaching?

LADY

I suppose. But it still bothers me. I think that, above all, we have to get our students *interested* in language—in words. I suppose this is obvious, but I don't think there is any subject in which interest is more obviously a condition for learning than in this business of vocabulary development.

PROF

I'm sure that's true. But that doesn't seem to say very much, does it, when you consider that in this case *interest* might be just the obverse of *understanding*.

LADY

I know; I know. Which gets us back to where we started. I want to reach the middle fifty percent in my classes, not just the top twenty-five. Of course, really, I want to reach *all* of them, but . . .

PROF

No, stick with what you just said. The middle fifty, as well as the top twenty-five. Then allow for the possibility of having a class with no bottom twenty-five.

LADY (laughs)

What if it doesn't have a *top* twenty-five?

PROF (laughs)

Ignore the evidence. But seriously, you want to reach the majority of your students, and you're not doing it. Is that right?

LADY

I'm afraid it is.

PROF

Of course, the first thing we have to find out is what vocabulary is if we're going to teach it.

LADY

Oh, that's obvious! Believe me, I've gone through that maze. Don't forget, I had you as a professor.

PROF

And you were one of my best students, too. But I don't think you can go back to the elementals of a subject too often. Sometimes I actually look forward to an opportunity to explain parts of my work to an ignorant, but intelligent, person. It keeps me alert, as well as honest.

LADY

All right. What is your question, then?

PROF

What is vocabulary? That's the first question, surely.

LADY

Well, I'd say vocabulary is the . . . reservoir of words one can make use of. Something like that, anyway.

PROF

Okay. And developing a larger or more resourceful or more efficient vocabulary means adding to the number of words in this reservoir. Would you say that?

LADY

You almost lost me with that string of adjectives, but I see what you're getting at. It isn't just increasing the number of words in your collection but also knowing their meanings.

PROF

Good. I'm glad to see that teaching hasn't destroyed either your ability or your inclination to be wary. Words are symbols, of course, and one hardly gains anything by just increasing his store of symbols if he doesn't know what they mean.

LADY

Forgive me, but isn't that all very obvious?

PROF

You're forgiven; and the answer is "Yes, it is very obvious." But it has to be stated now and then. It's one of the elementals, I just mentioned, that you have to come back to periodically. You know, touch base. I don't think anyone is so sophisticated or wise that he doesn't forget the obvious now and then. But also, the fact is a lot of vocabulary building techniques actually do, by implication, focus upon the simple accumulation of new words, as if this is vocabulary enrichment. They might give token attention to the fact that it is subtly distinguished meanings that matter in vocabulary, but their emphasis is too often on a simple multiplication of symbols.

If a student learns a word that he believes is totally and exclusively syn-onymous with another and proceeds to use it in this way, has he increased his vocabulary? Not at all. Suppose he learns the word "ingenuous" and thinks that it is totally and exclusively synonymous with the word "naive." He has learned a new symbol but not a new meaning. So in the important sense of the word, his vocabulary is not richer. If, however, he learns that "naive" is more likely to have a pejorative connotation of gullibility than the word "ingenuous," he has increased his vocabulary.

LADY

But these two words *are* synonymous, aren't they? I mean, in most contexts they seem to be.

PROF

Yes, in most contexts they are; and that statement brings to mind another truism: context carries a tyrannous authority of meaning, particularly in the realm of connotation. I used to refer to the authority of context as "ultimate" but that overstates it. If this were true, we wouldn't be able to communicate or articulate (a different matter) at all. I mean, no matter how often I say that I am raising coffee breaks in my garden, and you know that I mean "marigolds" when I say "coffee breaks," my disruptive context has not exercised any lasting authority on either term. You merely translate "marigold" for "coffee break" and let it go at that. But it is context that will tell you whether "ingenuous" has a bad connotation. The word "naive," however, will carry more of a bad connotation with it (if we agree that gullibility is bad) and will carry some potential of this pejorative connotation right into any context, rendering the context less authoritative by this fact. Clearer examples would be the words "skinny" and "slender." Context is almost helpless in giving "skinny" an honorific connotation or "slender" a pejorative one.

LADY

Forgive me once again, please. I don't want to sound impatient, and all of this is very interesting, but I really am concerned about these students of mine and their vocabulary problems. I don't think anything you've said so far has helped much. And I feel like a fraud and a failure standing up in front of the class knowing what it is they need and not being able to give it to them.

PROF

Once more, you're forgiven. But I think you overstate the case. I think we've agreed on at least one important matter, even if it does seem to be a truism. Vocabulary is essentially the availability of meanings, along with the agreed-upon symbols for these meanings, to a person's mind. I think we have to insist that these meanings are available to the mind (even if mind is a kind of hypostatizing, rather than an entity, as psychologists seem to agree) . . . available to mind, rather than just to speech. As it is a matter of meanings, vocabulary development ideally must refer to a particular kind of intellectual development . . . the kind that expresses itself in the logics of grammar, diction, and syntax.

LADY

Please. You've unloaded too much on me all at once. I agree that we must be concerned with meanings rather than empty symbols, and . . .

PROF

All right. Let me put it this way. A single word not only can, but inevitably *will*, have many different meanings. Is that right?

LADY

Yes. Although I would say a word like . . . well, "father," for example, has a stable meaning.

PROF

Insofar as it designates a specific relationship it does. But we use the word to refer to the person who holds this relationship, and the actual meaning of the word is, therefore, as manifold as the personalities and characters of the men that can be called "fathers."

LADY

Yes, I see that. But I seem to be drifting farther and farther from my poor inarticulate students.

PROF

Patience, please. We have agreed, and we agree that we agree, that in vocabulary development we are concerned with minds acquiring meanings. That is a far remove from mere word collecting and from the person who feels his vocabulary is richer because he can now call everything that he used to call strange "eldritch" and every knowledgeable man a "cognoscente."

LADY

All right. That is a start, I agree.

PROF

Let's look at a particular word— "command," for example. I open my Webster's Third Unabridged and find four more-or-less distinct meanings listed for the intransitive form of the verb: one, "to have or to exercise direct authority: *Govern;* two, to give an order or orders, three, to be commander (the general will command in person at the western front) ; and four, to dominate as if from an elevated position (far and wide his eye commanded—John Milton)."

LADY

Yes, I understand. To know how and when to use this verb with all four intransitive meanings is to have four meanings available, even if there is only one word for them . . . one symbol.

PROF

Yes. One should command all four meanings, you might say.

LADY (laughing)

Please. I'm really anxious to learn something about vocabulary, and I have the feeling you know something that could prove useful to me, and yet . . .

PROF

Through sheer perversity refuse to divulge the secret. Is that it?

LADY

No, I wasn't going to say perversity. But I don't see how your insistence on these ideas is going to help me with my students.

PROF

Well, let me go on. You say that, according to our dictionary, the word "command" has four more-or-less distinct meanings as an intransitive verb. Is that right?

LADY

Yes.

PROF

Do you collect sentences?

LADY

No, but I remember your talking about collecting sentences in class. I know what you mean, though. I *do* respond to good prose. Partly thanks to you, I'll admit.

PROF

Good. But I'm disappointed that I wasn't able to infect you with my mania for collecting examples of good prose. Good sentences, for example. Sentences that are sharp and hard with muscular syntax and a rich and precise diction.

LADY

Or vocabulary.

PROF

Yes. I don't think a person can ever use language well—read it or write it or think it well—without learning to be *interested* in it. Maybe even loving it, if that doesn't sound too enthusiastic, in a professorial way. At least being able to respond to the unique powers of language.

LADY

I suppose. But basically I'm concerned right now with having language work for me and for my students. I don't want them to become critics or scholars or poets. I'm not any of those things myself. I'm simply a teacher who's trying to be a better one, and I . . .

PROF

I know, and you want to help your students develop a more powerful vocabulary in ten days or less.

LADY

Well, I'm not *that* impatient. Although I'll confess that I want to hear something about how I might teach them to improve . . . in less than ten days.

PROF

Touché.

LADY

Not only that, I'm wondering what happened to your discussion of the word "command." You seemed to get side-tracked on your hobby of collecting sentences. Or did I miss something?

PROF

You haven't missed a thing. I'm coming back to one of my favorite sentences, which was written by Isaac Walton in his essay on John Donne. Have you read it?

LADY

No, I haven't. What is the sentence?

PROF

Let's see. It goes something like, "His fancy was unimitably high, equalled only by his great wit; both being made useful by a commanding judgment."

LADY

Yes, I see we've come back.

PROF

Indeed we have. And the rhetorical question I have to ask is this: which of the four meanings of the word "command" are we to attach to the word in Walton's sentence?

LADY

Do you want me to answer? I thought rhetorical questions implied their answers because of the way they're formulated.

PROF

You're quite right. Maybe this question isn't really rhetorical after all, so answer if you like. I'll repeat the sentence: "His fancy was inimitably high, equalled only by his great wit; both being made useful by a commanding judgment."

LADY

Well, I'm not sure I can. I don't think I know exactly what's happening in the sentence.

PROF

I'm glad you perceive the difficulty. The fact is, "commanding" in this sentence has no specific, literal meaning. It's a metaphor, of course, and because it is figurative, or metaphorical it actually partakes of all four meanings listed in our dictionary.

LADY

Of course. So that this makes a fifth meaning, you might say. That is, the word "command" can mean any one of the four meanings listed, or it can mean all four together when used metaphorically, or . . .

PROF

Keep going.

LADY

Or it can mean any combination of the four, can't it?

PROF

You're absolutely right.

LADY

Does having this word as a vital part of your vocabulary include knowing all its metaphorical possibilities?

PROF

I would think so in the best of all possible worlds. However, who can map all the metaphors available to a word? Some of the metaphors haven't been invented yet, but their meanings will be immediately apparent—if they are good metaphors—the first time they are used.

LADY

This is all so complicated.

PROF

You can't have a simple theory for something as intimately involved with human thinking as language is.

LADY

I'll never get back to my students. By the time you get through explaining things to me, I'll be so confused I won't be able to open my mouth.

PROF

Hang on. There's something even more bewildering. Webster's Third has oversimplified.

LADY

I don't think I want to hear about it.

PROF

Be patient. There's light ahead. The dictionary oversimplified by saying there are only four meanings for the intransitive verb "command." Earlier we agreed that in one very important sense there are as many meanings for the word "father" as there are men who can be designated as fathers. So "command" like almost any other word has an indeterminate number of meanings.

LADY

I think I'm about to cry.

PROF

I'm glad you've kept your sense of humor.

LADY

But language isn't that bewildering, really. Most of the times I've heard the word "father," or read it I haven't known anything about the particular person being talked about, and I haven't *needed* to know.

PROF

Of course you haven't. Because in most situations you don't have to know very much about the man. If your sorority sister said, "My father is sending me a check next week," you didn't need to know much of the meaning behind her use of the word. And that is an important point. But the meanings available to you from that word generally are now vastly richer and more subtle than they were at the age of three or four, when you first learned basically what the word "father" designated. It is reasonable to say that your vocabulary for the word "father" has grown enormously throughout the years.

LADY

I'm sorry. I think I agree with almost everything you've said, but when you start speaking about the "vocabulary of a word," it just sounds too strange.

PROF

And yet, we agreed that vocabulary is a matter of meanings, basically; and if this is true, one can speak quite clearly about the vocabulary of a word. We have been discussing the vocabulary of the word "command," as a matter of fact. Haven't we?

LADY

I would probably have agreed with you that Isaac Walton's sentence was beautiful prose, but now I'm beginning to wish he had left writing alone and stuck to his fishing.

PROF

This complexity is related to the unique conceptualizing power of language. The only way to account for it is with what some linguists call "an expanding grammar," which I believe we have built into our thinking, anyway, even though we can't formulate it. Because the next time we encounter a new metaphorical use of the word "command," we will immediately recognize the felicity of this new usage—if the metaphor is a good one, I repeat (and we will call it good by the inevitability with which we recognize the meaning . . . this is something of a circularity, I'm afraid).

PROF

Will you please, please, *please* tell me how this is going to help me teach my freshman students meanings for both old and new words?

PROF

That's good. "Vocabulary development is the learning of meanings for both old and new words." I like it.

LADY

I feel as if an egg beater has been run through my thoughts, and here you compliment me for being able to communicate my despair.

PROF

All right. I think you understand a lot more than you think you understand. But you want some more tangible advice, and I'll try to help.

LADY

Thank you.

PROF

Most of the methods for vocabulary development have some merit. That's the plain truth. Some students will respond particularly well to the study of word roots and affixes; others will learn best when the material appears in a contextual situation. A good programed text has excellent possibilities here . . . depending, of course, on the intangibles of student response. I would think a programed text, working with words in a context which is in itself concerned with information about word development, roots, affixes, etc., would be good. I don't know of such a text, but there are so many books coming out I really can't claim to command a sufficient knowledge of the current literature.

LADY (laughs)

Please. Spare me that word!

PROF

Your wish is my . . . well, never mind. But to continue, one of the most effective methods for developing a good vocabulary is also one of the oldest and most obvious: reading. You yourself mentioned that there is no subject which needs interest more than this one of vocabulary development. And I quite agree.

LADY

Oh, there must be more than this!

PROF

Well, perhaps there is. And I'll get to it in just a minute. But to touch base once again, we'll have to acknowledge the importance of reading. For one thing, it gives us words in their natural habitat—flowing, living speech.

LADY

So it's the teachers of literature, as much as anyone else, who bear the responsibility?

PROF

Of course. And don't omit the first teachers of literature, the parents, who have so many opportunities to . . .

LADY

Excuse me, but now I really *do* feel like crying. After leading me through that thorny jungle of philosophy or semantics or whatever it was, you surely won't deposit me right back where I started from?

PROF

No, there's more to be said. Do you know anything about the education of French boys before World War II?

LADY

Well! That's as surprising a change of subject as your question about collecting sentences. No, I can't say I do.

PROF

Well, you know about *explication de texte*, do you not?

LADY

Yes. In fact, we ourselves had some schooling in *explication de texte* in a poetry seminar last summer when I was picking up some graduate credits.

PROF

What is it, then? How would you define it?

LADY

That's hard. I suppose it consists of analyzing a poem or literary work and trying to find out . . . trying to find out . . .

PROF

How the language works?

LADY

Well, that, of course, but . . . it's trying to discover the meanings of the words isn't it? You're saying it's vocabulary!

PROF

You are precisely right.

LADY

Because in *explication de texte* we are discovering all the meanings that the words can have in the particular contexts of that poem or that story.

PROF

Not only the meanings they *can* have but *insist on having* in their particular contexts. Because they *can* have irrelevant or adventitious meanings for our more subjective and paranoid temptations.

LADY

And in a literary work, you presumably have language used with a greater responsibility for clarity and richness than in more utilitarian situations, where the language is used as a kind of transfer between some need and a specific action, and . . .

PROF

Hold on, there! *Now* who's beginning to gallop?

LADY

Well, I mean, that's good. But when I stop to think, I've been doing this kind of thing in one way or another all along. I don't call it *explication de texte* or anything like that, but when I get my freshmen to discussing a poem and looking hard at the language, I am really getting them to explicate . . . in a modest way, of course.

PROF

I'm not so sure it's very modest.

LADY

Now don't be polite, because I certainly haven't been. And I have more to ask. Are you saying that I have been teaching vocabulary development all along as I have been using explication?

PROF

Unquestionably.

LADY

But this is so frustrating. I came to you hoping you could recommend something new and something better for helping my students develop vocabulary, and now I find that you recommend my doing exactly what I *have* been doing.

PROF

Maybe not exactly.

LADY

What do you mean?

PROF

Well, the mere fact that you weren't aware that, in the last analysis, you were teaching vocabulary kept you from doing a lot of valuable things that you might otherwise have done. I mean to say, this fact gave to every one of your approaches a certain cast, which was maybe a fraction off target . . .

LADY

What you want to say, but are being too polite to say, is that I was on the right track; but since I really didn't know what I was doing, I wasn't teaching as effectively as I might have.

PROF

You do call a tub a tub, don't you?

LADY

Well, I think you're right. If I understand that every time I analyze a literary work, I am really involved in vocabulary study then I can work more effectively.

PROF

This is perhaps an obvious idea to some people, but it is a terribly important one. I think you'll agree.

LADY

It's like touching base again, isn't it?

PROF

Right. Now let's turn once more to the idea of explication and to something else the French schools can teach—a kind of discipline that leads naturally and by degrees into *explication de text.*

LADY

What is that?

PROF

Rollo Walter Brown wrote a book in 1927 titled *How the French Boy Learns to Write.* I recommend that you read it since you're interested in vocabulary. Well, in this book, Mr. Brown describes a particular approach to what is in reality vocabulary building. The French give it the marvelous name, *Lecons de Choses*—"lessons in things." These "lessons in things" consist of the teacher discussing a particular body of information with his young elementary-age pupils. One day, they might talk about policemen and the vocabulary associated with their work. Another day, they will discuss the preparation of vegetables; another day, meats and all the particular vocabularies associated with these common activities. The subjects naturally become more challenging and complicated as the students advance. Notice once more what these lessons are called: not "lessons in words," but "lessons in things." They are what the semanticists would call "extensionally oriented."

LADY

Yes, I see. They are studying meanings not just words in themselves. Something you have been emphasizing all along.

PROF

And because of this constant drill (that's still a scare word in education today, but I believe it's the appropriate term for the French teacher's assiduous approach to the task) . . . and because of this constant drill in words as symbols of *things,* Mr. Brown states, these young French boys are given splendid vocabulary training in noticing details, in perceiving distinctions between things, and generally preparing themselves for general intellectual effort in either the sciences or the humanities.

LADY

That's very interesting, and I think I might look at that book. But I am still disturbed to think that in teaching explication I have really been working with what is potentially a very effective vocabulary developing instrument, and I didn't know it. I could have done so much more!

PROF

You can start tomorrow. Meanwhile, listen to me just a little longer, and I will promise to shut up. When I was reading Mr. Brown's book, I was struck by something. This idea isn't really new with the French, even though they give it their own stamp. It's a very old idea.

LADY

I'm sorry. I've lost you. What idea, lessons in things?

PROF

No, I was being vague. These ideas—lessons in things and *explication de texte*—are not new. They are, in some important ways, at least, as old as Plato.

LADY

You mean dialectic?

PROF

Precisely. Dialectic.

LADY

Are you saying, then, that dialectic itself is a vocabulary developer?

PROF

I really can't imagine a better one.

LADY

Well, you certainly see vocabulary in a lot of places!

PROF

I can consider it an axiom that the *academic* knowledge of any subject—no matter how non-verbal it might appear—is essentially a matter of possessing the vocabulary of that subject.

LADY

Because, as you've been drumming in my head, vocabulary is the understanding of meanings, which in itself means relationships, because it always appears contextually, and . . .

PROF

And how would you define the word dialectic?

LADY

Oh, I was afraid of that. Let me see. I would say dialectic is discussing a particular subject until two or more people can come to some important agreements about it.

PROF

Not bad. And usually this is a semantic exercise, is it not? You know, Socrates insisted upon Glaucon's arriving at a viable definition of the word "justice" or "truth." Incidentally, you're a lot smarter than Glaucon.

LADY

I'll ignore that. Yes, I see what you mean. And dialectic is of course an inquiry into vocabulary. Into the implicit resources of language.

PROF

You said that beautifully. I wasn't joking; you *are* smarter than Glaucon. It just might happen, you know, that you will some day become a sentence collector.

LADY (laughs)

I must agree that the rigorous way you have to look at words when you are studying a poem or trying to arrive at some kind of agreement concerning the definition of an important or troublesome word, as in dialectic . . . I must agree that this is a problem of vocabulary. As you have defined the work, at least. And I think your definition makes sense, I must say.

PROF

Now *you* are turning polite.

LADY

That's exactly what we've been doing, isn't it?

PROF

Turning polite?

LADY

No, you know what I mean. Dialectic. You've been goading me and leading me on to admit one thing after another, and all the while we have been inquiring into the viable meanings of certain words . . . like the word "vocabulary" itself and . . .

PROF

And "command."

LADY

And "command," and . . .

PROF

And I would like to know what you mean by the word "viable," which you have tossed around a few times this afternoon.   Or was that me who tossed it around?

LADY

Professor! "Or was that I?" And I think it *was* you.

PROF

Precisely the obverse of what I asked.

LADY

I am going to escape while I can. And thank you very much.

PROF

It was a pleasure. I only hope I can remember what we said.

LADY

So do I. Believe me.

Special Materials to Aid in Vocabulary Development at the College Level

JORDAN UTSEY
University of Oregon

THE IMPORTANCE of an adequate listening, speaking, writing, and reading vocabulary to learners at all levels is well known by reading specialists. We know that the correlation between ability to succeed in virtually any subject and vocabulary is very high. In a very real sense, if one has command of the technical vocabulary of a field, he is in control of the area.   Unfortunately, many college students exhibit various types of deficiencies in their reading vocabularies. The inadequacies in their vocabularies may be lim-

ited to certain special areas or subjects such as geology, philosophy, or biology; or the deficiency may he more general—a limited speaking, writing, and reading vocabulary in all areas. In either case the problems of improving the students' vocabularies are ones of degree, not of kind.

Problems of instruction

There are at least two problems related to instructional materials in vocabulary development at the college level to which I would like to address myself before looking at specific materials.   The first of these is the influence of program organization upon materials in vocabulary development. The second is the influence of learning theory upon materials.

The first problem, the organization of college reading-improvement programs, is of crucial importance because organization either facilitates or hinders the use of certain vocabulary development materials.   College reading improvement programs are typically organized in one of two ways, either as a separate, special course or as an integral part of several different subjects. The organization of a reading course as a special service appears to be the most common approach.   In such a course, vocabulary development is an essential part of the work, and attention is devoted to direct instruction. Work in vocabulary development is typically focused upon the study of word lists, antonyms and synonyms, root words, the etymology of words, and the use of dictionaries and glossaries; studying the denotation and connotations of words, workbooks and vocabulary builders, and the most used English prefixes and suffixes; and learning to listen for new words and to derive the meaning of words from context; and other such activities (1).

There are some problems associated with this approach, however.   First, Kingston (4) has pointed out that "Direct vocabulary instruction probably will be more effective in assisting the student who has rich and varied concepts but a more limited number of verbal symbols associated with them. It is doubtful how much it helps the student who lacks the necessary store of concepts." Our work with Upward Bound students has amply demonstrated the truth of Kingston's observations.

Second, following a review of a number of vocabulary improvement workbooks and chapters, Johnson (3) concluded that the reading materials used for vocabulary development should be in the specific area in which improvement is wanted—science, psychology, education, etc.—and that general vocabulary development may be less effective.

And finally, Cuomo (2) has pointed out that any system is no better than the list used. If time is spent learning words that do not reflect individual needs, the efforts will be largely wasted. Moreover, learning the definition of a word only from a list or a dictionary often gives a distorted idea of its correct use.

The major advantage of the separate courses in reading improvement is that the responsibility for teaching reading rests with an instructor who devotes some time and attention to the task. His prime responsibility is usually the teaching of reading, and he works at it. Another advantage is that the instructors of separate reading courses are usually up-to-date on the latest instructional materials and techniques. They typically make available to students all kinds of workbooks, study guides, programed materials, man-machine systems, etc. This form of organization lends itself to and encourages the use of all kinds and types of materials and seems to be limited only by the imagination, creativity, or budget of the instructor.

The second rather common form of organization for teaching reading at the college level is a program wherein vocabulary is taught as an integral part of each course by subject matter teachers in their own classrooms. It has long been recognized, if I may use a cliché, that all secondary teachers and college instructors should be teachers of reading in their particular disciplines. This notion has been substantiated by Spache (7), for, as he indicates, reading specialists have not been overly active in discovering methods or materials for teaching students to read or study effectively in such areas as math, history, etc.

It would appear that there are certain advantages for students when each instructor assumes responsibility for teaching the vocabulary relevant to his discipline. Direct vocabulary study is closely related to the subject being taught and, therefore, highly relevant; the words are learned as they are needed for understanding the discipline; and the terms are in a meaningful context (5).

There are, however, several disadvantages which seem to be difficult to overcome. College instructors are not always aware of their students' vocabulary needs. They may be occupied with outside-the-classroom activities, or they may have such large classes that their best efforts fall short of what is needed if students are to be helped. Moreover, instructors may not have the time or the inclination to consider which instructional techniques and materials would best meet the students' needs. In contrast to the separate courses in reading in which an instructor may very easily oversupply the students with materials and systems for learning, the instructor in the subject matter courses may not even be aware of the alternatives available.

Clearly then, the instructors in the separate reading courses are likely to utilize many effective materials and techniques but are also likely to find it difficult to relate their instruction to other courses, subjects, and experiences in the students' college curriculum. Subject matter teachers, on the other hand, are more likely to make vocabulary study relevant to at least one discipline but are less likely to take advantage of the materials which would make their teaching really effective.

The second problem I mentioned which is related to vocabulary development is that of the influence of learning theory upon materials. Most, if not all, of the current commercial vocabulary development materials available appear to be based upon the notion that vocabulary expansion or development is a getting process—a kind of accumulation—that one gathers vocabulary or words as he may collect coins or acquire more acres of land. According to this view, vocabulary development results from being told word meanings and remembering what one has been told; or it consists of looking up word meanings in the dictionary and remembering what one has found there. It presupposes that people and books have all the word meanings, and we learn meanings from them.

What often happens, however, is that vocabulary building based upon this type of material actually amounts to expanding vocabulary without increasing meanings or understandings. For example, one may tell a student that a short statement is succinct. He now has a new word, but his stock of meanings is not increased. Similarly, if the student looks up succinct in the dictionary, he may find the synonym concise; he has again expanded his vocabulary but not his meanings. Of course, the student has benefited for he can now understand these new words when he reads them—that is, he gets some meaning rather than none, but it is an old meaning already attached to a known word or words.

A second approach to teaching vocabulary is based upon the notion that meaning is the crucial aspect and that meanings are acquired through experience. Thus, since words are symbols for meaning, words are symbols for experiences. To expand vocabulary it is, therefore, necessary to expand experience.

Singleton (6) has hypothesized, and I tend to accept his premises, that there are basically only three ways to increase one's vocabulary:

1. Learn new terms to describe known or new experiences.
2. Learn new uses or meanings for word symbols already known.
3. Move word symbols from the understanding vocabulary to the speaking, reading, and writing vocabularies.

College students, I am convinced, tend to acquire new vocabulary rather spasmodically over a long period of time. This new vocabulary is most frequently acquired as there is a real change in their lives. The normal conduct of their lives often embodies a routine for which they know the vocabulary. To expand vocabulary we structure the students' course work so that they are continually involved in new materials and learning experiences.

If one accepts the foregoing view of vocabulary development, we again are forced back to the conclusion that effective instruction in vocabulary is most likely when subject matter instructors are involved in teaching the terms and concepts related to their individual disciplines.

There still remains, however, the major problem pointed out previously, that is, the lack of knowledge on the part of the regular college instructor about students' needs, materials, and instructional strategies.

Some special materials

I surveyed some fifty-two different commercial workbooks, texts, man-machine systems, programed materials, and college courses in an effort to find some really special materials I could report to you. Nearly all were rather traditional in their approaches and directed students to

1. Study antonyms and synonyms.
2. Study denotation and connotations.
3. Study the etymology of words.
4. Work cross word puzzles.
5. Learn new words by studying dictionaries and glossaries.
6. Study word roots.
7. Learn various types of study techniques, SQ3R, etc.

The foregoing is not intended as a criticism of current materials. I would simply point out that the content options or alternatives open to commercial publishers aiming at a mass market are somewhat limited.

There was, however, one set of materials not commercially prepared which did appear to me to be special in several ways.

The materials are not the product of a single reading specialist or content teacher working in isolation but rather are the result of a team approach to help freshman college students learn the vocabulary needed to succeed in their various courses. The personnel of the Reading Center of the San Bernardino Valley College in California, in cooperation with various subject matter instructors, have created several sets of guidelines, study helps, and vocabulary lists focused upon the instructional problems of specific courses.

For example, instructors of freshman literature courses have provided the reading specialists in the center lists of words and concepts crucial for an adequate understanding of required readings. The reading specialists, using several different kinds of media for presentation and testing, have organized the terms and concepts into various study units for effective learning. The terms and concepts the students are asked to learn are thus both relevant to their course work and effectively taught. The materials are divided into levels of difficulty, and students are pretested and placed in the program in terms of their achievement.

The work at San Bernardino is being expanded and other materials written to expand the offerings in other disciplines besides English. The cooperation between the reading specialists and subject matter teachers has led to increased awareness on the part of academicians that each instructor is responsible for helping his students increase their ability to read in his particular field, develop the special vocabulary needed, and cultivate interests in voluntary reading.

The foregoing, then, appear to be the most recent and significant materials specifically created to aid in vocabulary development at the college level. The materials were developed through a combining of the strengths of several disciplines focused upon a single problem—helping college freshmen achieve an acceptable degree of performance in their first literature courses.

The materials as well as the approach would appear to hold considerable promise for improving reading at the college level.

REFERENCES

1. Colvin, Charles R. "The 'Ideal' College Reading Program," *Journal of Developmental Reading,* 5 (Winter 1962), 81.
2. Cuomo, George. *Becoming a Better Reader.* New York: Holt, Rinehart and Winston, Inc., 1965.
3. Johnson, Harry W. "The Hidden Consensus on Vocabulary Development," *Problems, Programs and Projects in College-Adult Reading,* Eleventh Yearbook of the National Reading Conference. Milwaukee: The National Reading Conference, Inc., 1962, 106-07.
4. Kingston, Albert J. "Vocabulary Development," *Journal of Reading,* 8 (March 1965), 265-266.
5. Shaw, Phillip. "Reading in College," *Development In and Through Reading,* The Sixtieth Yearbook of the National Society for the Study of Education, Part I. Chicago: The University of Chicago Press, 1961, 336-354.
6. Singleton, Carlton M. "Vocabulary Development for the Mature Student," *Research and Evaluation in College Reading,* Ninth Yearbook of the National Reading Conference for Colleges and Adults. Fort Worth: Texas Christian University Press, 1960, 75.
7. Spache, George. "Improving Reading Skills in the Subject Matter Areas," *Significant Elements in College and Adult Reading Improvement,* Seventh Yearbook of the National Reading Conference for Colleges and Adults. Fort Worth: Texas Christian University Press, 1958, 32-33.

Mobilizing All the Language Arts

Shelton L. Root, Jr.
Wayne State University

I MUST CONFESS that I was bemused by the topic assigned—mobilizing all the language arts. Somehow, it conjured up visions of commanding speaking, listening, reading, and writing to fall in, come to attention, march forward, and pass in review before our eyes.

But in the context of other topics in this section on word recognition and vocabulary development and the present topic, comprehension skills, it seemed that I should explore some "how to's:" how to mobilize these four language arts and use them to sharpen such comprehension skills as observing single details and relating them using context clues, how to identify main ideas; how to understand organizational elements; how to draw inferences; and how to distinguish between primary and supporting ideas.

Such would be a most worthy undertaking. It is an assignment that I should like to see someone tackle. I had, indeed, intended to address myself to some of the "how to's," until I came upon a study conducted by Gerald W. Brekke at the University of North Dakota. This study, as it is reported in *The Reading Teacher* of January, 1963, changed my thinking. It challenges us to consider whether the time now spent in the reading programs is time well spent.

The purpose of Brekke's study was, ". . . to identify and compare current practices in time allotments for basal and other reading with the optimum amounts of time recommended by reading authorities."

More than sixty reading authorities were asked to make recommendations concerning the number of minutes per week that should be devoted to reading in grades one through eight. These recommendations were made for two areas: first, time devoted to basal reading instruction; second, time devoted to other reading. "Other reading" was defined as "reading done outside of specifically designated reading classes—either in free reading periods or in other subject areas. . . ." Average time allotments for each grade level were found and were used to determine what relationships existed between what the authorities recommended and what the situation was in actual practice.

To determine what was going on in the schools, Brekke obtained data from more than seven thousand classrooms in more than a thousand schools across the United States. His findings raise some fundamental questions concerning the relationships among basal instruction, "other reading" which includes "free reading," and the purpose of this paper—namely, mobilizing the language arts as they relate to various comprehension skills.

Let me report some of the findings. First, and only as a matter of interest, 99.5 percent of these schools employed to some extent the basal reading approach. Second, far more time was devoted to basal instruction in the primary grades than was recommended by the authorities. Third, there was *no* correlation between time allotments beyond the recommended norm for basal reading instruction and improved reading achievement as measured by standardized tests. Remember, please, that the measure of reading achievement depends largely upon comprehension. It seems fairly safe, therefore, to extrapolate that there was no correlation between raising comprehension and increasing basal instruction beyond recommended norms. Fourth, at every single grade level the amount of time devoted to "other reading" was far below that suggested by the authorities.

Theodore Clymer commented on this study: "Perhaps we are overteaching and underusing reading skills." What one is taught seldom, if ever, makes any difference to him unless he is able to use the newly learned skill in situations that make a difference, situations that are important. I contend that we can teach isolated comprehension skills until doomsday but that teaching will make a difference in the child's ability to comprehend what he reads only when what he reads makes a difference to him! And, what he reads will make a difference to him only when the content of what he reads has some direct relevance to his immediate life—be it to find pleasure, to acquire information, or both. Children simply do not long attend to the business of acquiring reading skills for the purpose of stock-piling them for use at some future time. Children need time— now—to use those skills in other reading situations.

The average child in the typical classroom, as reported by this study, would have fared this way as he passed through the grades. In the first grade, he would have had forty-two hours less time for "other reading" than was suggested by the authorities; in the second grade, he would have had twenty-five hours and twenty minutes less time for "other reading" during the year than was recommended; in grade three he would have lost thirty-six hours; in grade four, thirty-seven hours and ten minutes; in the fifth grade he would have given up forty-nine hours and forty minutes, and sixth grade would have seen him lose fifty-one hours and twenty minutes.

These figures seem startling enough, but see what would have happened to him in grades seven and eight. Grade seven would have taken seventy-six hours of other reading away from him, and grade eight would account for the staggering sum of eighty-four hours lost from other reading.

Taken singly, by grade level, it is obvious that our typical reader is getting a good bit less time than the authorities think he should for "other reading"—time when he should be using his comprehension skills. When the sum of lost hours is totalled, the result is appalling.

During the first eight years of school the average reader would have four-hundred and one hours and thirty minutes less to devote to other reading than he should have had. Let's look at it another way. If, at the ninth grade we were to repay those hours, we would have to let him read all day, every day, for nearly fourteen school weeks. This amounts to one third of the school year!

There is cause for concern here. None of us would take it lightly if during eight school years a child lost a third of a year of basal reading instruction, or a third of a year of social studies, or a third of a year of instruction in mathematics. Most of us might, in fact, question whether the average child could cope well enough with such a loss to be qualified for promotion. But, it would be relatively easy to know if such a loss were taking place, to guard against it, and to make up for it.

The loss of time for other reading is more insidious. It takes place gradually. Its effects, while certainly cumulative, are not easily measured. And, one wonders, whether there is any way to make up for the loss. I suspect there is not.

We can only speculate upon what is lost, but I think that speculation is in order. First, during the primary grades where reading habits are formed, the child is being "basalized" better than half an hour a week more than the authorities recommend while he is losing nearly an hour a week of other reading. These are years when he may be learning that *the game is not worth the candle*—that being taught to read leads only to more teaching, the mastery of which leads only to more of the same.

Second, the child may *not* be learning that there are books worthy of comprehension—*comprehension* meaning *to grasp mentally and emotionally*, to be attuned to the nuances of language.

Third, the teacher may well be

learning that reading instruction is little more than a monotonously repetitive affair that calls for great endurance and little originality. Basal instruction may, indeed, become monotonous.

Fourth, teachers may not be finding the time to enjoy the satisfaction that comes from bringing the right child together with the right book and watching him exercising his skills of comprehension.

Fifth, because of overcommitment to basal reading instruction we may not be finding the time to mobilize *all* the language arts to improve reading comprehension.

To bring all this matter into sharper focus if we are to effect any new and dramatic changes in the acquisition of reading skills, such as, word recognition, vocabulary development, and comprehension, we must shift our concern from direct instruction in the skills of reading to what most of us have treated as peripheral—the language arts.

By this, I am not suggesting that we discontinue direct instruction in reading skills. Rather, I am suggesting that our classroom teaching should more nearly reflect reality: the reality that the acquisition of reading skills is, like the acquisition of writing skills, a highly sophisticated business. It can be learned and practiced successfully only after the skills of speaking and listening have been satisfactorily developed. Then these more natural language arts must continue to hold an important position in our classrooms while the language arts of reading and writing are developing. It is a mistake to think that the basal reading program alone will develop comprehension skills. To develop such skills we must turn to the interrelationships that exist among the language arts and the area we call other reading.

It is in this area of other reading that children can be led to discover that what they have read can be worth talking about and that what others have to say about what they have read can be worth listening to. It is in this area of other reading that children can be led to discover that what they have read can be worth writing about.

And, no less important, it is from this area that contact is established with all of the esthetic media that are so important in the building of comprehension. Music, dramatics, sculpture, painting, and dance help build the broad and deep experiential background so necessary to the development of true comprehension.

Because the skills of reading comprehension are dependent upon all the language arts, we must back off from overemphasis on direct reading instruction. We must provide time for children to read for profit and for pleasure. We must provide time for listening, time for speaking, time for writing. Only then can we be sure that children will become effective readers.

Clustering Comprehension Skills to Solve Problems

ALTHEA BEERY
Cincinnati Public Schools

IMPLICIT IN THE WORDING of this topic are several assumptions: 1) that elementary children can solve problems and that it is desirable for them to have training in doing so; 2) that reading will help in children's inquiry; 3) that comprehension skills in reading are necessary in this quest; and 4) that these skills are not separate and disparate but tend to cluster around related skills. Let's examine these assumptions for a moment.

First Assumption: Elementary children can solve and should have training in solving problems. Those of us who have worked with children need no further evidence that children *can* attack problems and that, within the limits of their experience and a challenging situation, they enjoy the opportunity with considerable success. Research backs this up (*17, 22*). In fact, the characteristics and attitudes favorable toward inquiry can be developed in quite young children. Banta

(2) has built and is norming a test (CATB) for children from three-to-six years of age that measures the following characteristics which he considers significant for problem solving and believes to be amenable to training: curiosity, exploratory behavior, persistence, resistance to distraction, control of impulse, reflectivity, analytic perceptual processes, and innovative behavior.

Second Assumption: Reading helps in children's inquiry. Provided that children have the requisite literacy skills, reading is an important tool which children use in problem solving, whenever their search extends beyond their previous experiences or one immediately at hand, including observation or inquiry of adults or other children (21, 26). How limited, indeed, their search for answers to their problems would be without access to the printed page.

Third Assumption: Comprehension skills are necessary for solving problems. Children use a great variety of comprehension skills when they read to find answers to questions, including reading for general ideas, for significant details, for the author's plan of development, to summarize, to judge or evaluate, to identify possible solutions and test them out, to use reference skills, to get the literal meaning of a sentence or paragraph, etc.

Fifty years ago Thorndike (28), from a study of errors which elementary school children made in reading single paragraphs, concluded that reading a single paragraph with understanding involves many elements of thought, including the weighing of words in terms of the context, the organization of each element in its proper relation to others, the selection of certain connotations of words, and the rejection of others. He said that in effective reading the mind selects, softens, emphasizes, correlates, and organizes—all under the influence of the right mental set or perspective. He compared the processes required in comprehending a paragraph to those of solving a problem in mathematics.

Fourth Assumption: Comprehension skills are not used separately but tend to cluster. Fortunately for children and teachers alike, these skills can be grouped around basic steps involved in problem solving. They do not need to be taught in isolation. In fact, for the most part, they should be developed together. A flexible reader shifts from one skill to another as he gains insight into the nature of the problem, the difficulty of the reading matter, and its development by the author and as he develops or rejects "hunches" he has concerning the best solution. Not only does the understanding of what is read involve many of the higher mental processes it also involves them in close conjunction with one another. As the situation demands, we analyze, organize, criticize, reject, reason, and judge with one process merging imperceptibly into another and employing the appropriate reading or study skills.

What problem solving involves

Where does problem solving fit into all this? Reading to solve problems is never a simple form of comprehension. It involves many of the skills needed for critical reading. Indeed, problem solving *is* a form of critical reading although it may impose more restrictions than some other types of careful reading. Dale (5) gave *problem centered* as a characteristic of critical reading.

The essential steps in problem solving have been listed in different ways by authorities in reading and psychology. In this article, they have been classified under those centering around the problem itself, locational skills, comprehension of the printed page, organizational skills, evaluation of materials in relation to the problem, and finally, application of findings so that attitudes, values, and behavior are changed.

The problem situation

Reading for problem solving emphasizes the *purpose,* in this case the problem to be answered. Whether the problem originates with the introductory material in the text, with the teacher as an assignment, by the class setting the problem, or even with an individual pupil himself is not crucial, so long as the child accepts the problem as his own. The clarification of the problem may include exploratory reading and class discussion or some other method of sharpening so that the direction of the search is clearly defined.

If the solution of a problem is to call forth effective reading, the problem or purpose must have relevance to the pupil and his interests. Roma Gans (9) in a landmark study discovered that high achievement on a standard test is no guarantee that the pupil has the ability to reject material which does not contribute information on a selected topic. It should be equally clear that the problem should not be so simple as to require no thought or investigation nor yet so complex that it cannot be truly understood; nor should the reading materials and thought processes involved be too complex for him to handle. If reading is to be a part of problem solving, there must be appropriate material available.

Location of suitable reading materials

In the early elementary grades, guidance may well be given in a group situation with children reading a given selection in search of pertinent facts. Or, following the reading of the selection, the group may discuss whether the facts in the article supported or contradicted information gleaned from a previous selection.

For a successful quest, a child must have at his command a variety of reference skills such as using a card index in the library, a dictionary, an encyclopedia, chapter headings, side headings, and the index of a book. None of these abilities is spontaneously acquired. On the other hand, neither does each of them have to be taught meticulously and sequentially to every child in every class. Needed, of course, is a teacher who is adept at diagnosing the level which different pupils have attained in these skills and at knowing when to give guidance in a

particular skill to an individual, a small group, or even the entire class.

Comprehension of material read

In the first place, comprehension in any real sense involves the ability to recognize words and attach meanings to them in relation to other words and their function in an English sentence. The richer the word meanings, the more likely that full comprehension will be achieved.

Except for a small minority who would *limit* the term "reading" to simple decoding of letters to sounds, there is general agreement that reading involves getting information from the printed page. Many persons call this "literal comprehension." Edgar Dale (4) calls it "reading the lines." A few writers would also include under literal comprehension some elements of the higher thought processes, such as seeing the relationship between ideas and sensing the purpose which the writer had in mind. Constance McCullough (15), in an article in a recent issue of *Elementary English,* points out how necessary to even literal comprehension is the knowledge of our language and how it works, i.e., *linguistics.* She illustrates with the following sentence: "In . . . its . . . hose-like . . . gray . . . trunk . . . the . . . little . . . figure . . . on . . . the . . . matchbox . . . carried . . . a . . . Republican . . . banner." In her own inimitable way she gives the steps which the listener or reader might take in understanding this sentence—cumulative, tentative, revised steps with later words in the sentence modifying or expanding earlier meanings. The example illustrates that the reader leans heavily, although often unconsciously, on his knowledge of our language and how it patterns itself.

Organization of materials

Too many children read along absorbing the ideas as they appear without building mentally an outline of the selection. Studies show that children tend to read all material at the same rate, regardless of their purpose of the nature of the material itself (6, 12).

Certainly, as elementary teachers, we are responsible for helping children decide whether a particular selection should be scanned rapidly merely to locate material which is important in the solution of a given problem or should be read more carefully for pertinent matter. At the same time children must carry in their minds some feeling of where this point fits into the general problem. At first this activity can probably best be done as we guide a group of children in reading a common selection. Later they should be responsible for the same activity when reading or studying independently. Certainly by the end of the elementary school at least the better pupils should be able to organize the information which they have obtained from several sources without duplicating ideas.

Evaluation of materials read

In a third-grade-class discussion about wild animals, one child said in response to another's statements, "But that isn't a *fact*. I read something different in another book." This remark led naturally to a discussion of which author was better qualified to make such a statement and to a comparison of the copyright dates of the two books. Further investigation involved the use of additional books and encyclopedia and included an interview with the director of the local zoo. Of course, pupils do not always need to go this far in deciding between fact and opinion.

In evaluating, the reader must constantly check the statements of the author against what he has learned from experience or other reading. As he reads critically, he weighs what the author said and challenges his ideas. He notes whether the author is making sweeping generalities which he does not back up with sufficient facts or whether he uses propaganda devices. The reader follows the author's line of reasoning and accepts or rejects his conclusions. He asks whether the material is written from a biased point of view. Studies have shown that young people color what they read by

their own attitudes and biases (*3, 11, 16, 18*). Even so do we as adults. The least we can do is to be on guard against letting prejudice color our own reading and to be committed to giving pupils opportunities to weigh what they read or hear reported on the scales of objectivity in an honest search for truth.

Application

When children are reading to solve a problem, they test what they have read by checking whether they have solved the problem they set for themselves. Young children are tempted to accept the first solution that they find. Older boys and girls are increasingly able to hold hypotheses tentatively and to test them more logically. Even when they have reached an apparently satisfactory solution, they learn to limit it by a statement such as, "This seems to be the answer. . . ," *or* "As far as we can find out, the solution seems to be. . . ." Gray (*10*), Gans (*8*), and others stress the fact that reading should make a difference in attitudes, values, and behavior. When children read wisely and thoughtfully and reach a conclusion, they must learn to incorporate it into their attitudes and values, contingent upon subsequent experience and evidence from further reading. Too few of us act on the basis of what we have learned from our reading. We should teach children to stand up and be counted when a controversial problem they have studied is under discussion. Further, reading should influence what children *do*. For example, it is of little use for a child to learn how bacteria is spread if he continues to be negligent in personal cleanliness, the handling of food, and the like.

Problem solving related to subject fields

Whatever the content field in which reading is done to solve problems, it will require certain comprehension skills. Examples are recognizing and understanding the general and technical vocabulary; getting the sense of the material; evaluating it in the light of the purpose or problem, such as judging the relevance and worth of the ideas; and seeing the relationships among ideas.

Granted that there are comprehension skills common to all content areas, there is still variation from field to field in the skills to be emphasized. The nature of the reading material and its function tend to differ from subject to subject, as Nila B. Smith and others have pointed out (23, 24).

Science and arithmetic

Science and arithmetic texts are typically compact in form with a rather heavy burden of technical terms and with precise, sequential steps to be followed. Usually a varying but slow rate is required (7).

Social studies

Social studies materials can often be read at a faster pace, but not always. Frequently, the pupil must interrupt his reading to study a picture, a graph, a chart, or a map. Cause and effect, especially in historical writing, must be traced. Here, too, authenticity is important (14, 20).

Children's literature

We are accustomed to think of critical, evaluative reading in relation to arithmetic, science, and social studies—the so-called content fields. Recently, increased emphasis has been placed on analysis and a more probing interpretation of literature by children. Some of us have feared that this emphasis might result in lessening children's love for good stories and books, if such analysis is within their powers. Evidence is accumulating, however, that with careful selection of materials and wise guidance elementary children can learn to use the problem solving approach in evaluating materials: comparing characters in two books with similar themes, tracing the development of plot and character, and reacting to the quality of a selection. Children seem to enjoy savoring the appropriate word and the vivid description and examining the point of view of the author. All this without lessening their competence in reading and at the same time increasing the range and amount of voluntary reading! An interesting study has been in progress at Ohio State University under a grant from the U.S. Office of Education (13, 29, 31). In fact, this study group has developed and normed a test on the critical reading of literature. The study was a comprehensive one which included control groups and guided classroom observation. To members, evaluation of literature to be valid must be done in accordance with criteria, hopefully criteria which the children have helped to set up.

Children compared Madeline, quite a character but always the same, with *Crow Boy* who changes believably into a more mature yet still shy boy. They learned how to identify realistic *vs.* imaginative roles. They found that trying their hands at writing their own modern folk tales or fables enhanced their ability to discriminate. Such problems as why the author chose to write a story from a given point of view proved interesting and profitable.

Van Gilder (30) found that the differences in the skills required in various fields lie not so much in the materials themselves as in the type of thinking required. He rejects the notion that the reading act can be packaged, parceled, or isolated into separate compartments. The teacher not specifically charged with the development of reading power may take comfort from Artley's (1) statement that the teacher need only ask himself, "What competencies must my students have to carry out the learning tasks in this course as I teach it?"—and then, presumably, help students build the competencies when lacking. We would hope that the tasks set would frequently be problem solving in nature.

Inquiry as an individual matter

Suchman (27) defines inquiry as learning that is initiated and controlled by the learner himself as a means of expanding his own understanding.

He believes that the more active, autonomous, and responsible the learner becomes for decisions regarding the collection and interpretation of information, the more meaningful the learning and the better motivated the pupil. Stauffer (25) also distinguishes between group and individual inquiry.

Conclusion

In summary, can children in the elementary grades be taught to use reading and other modes of inquiry to solve problems? The answer to this question is affirmative (19)—granted that young children, as indeed any of us, cannot think beyond the acquired experiential background and that they do not always have the verbal skills with which to express their ideas; their thinking nevertheless, does not vary in kind from that of adults.

Problem solving skills are not limited to reading. If we wish children to use these skills when they do read, we must capitalize on every opportunity for them to develop a spirit of inquiry t h r o u g h manipulation, observation, conversation, and discussion. Situations throughout the school day and in out-of-school life give countless opportunities for children to practice the skills involved in critical thinking. As adults, we must permit differing opinions and cherish a questioning attitude.

A recent convention of this Association was centered around the theme "Reading and Inquiry." *The Annual Proceedings,* issues of *The Reading Teacher,* and other IRA publications, contain numerous articles related to critical, discriminative reading, many with practical suggestions for classroom procedures. Let us apply what we have read and what our experience has taught us as we guide children's reading in the classroom. If we do, in addition to *who, what,* and *when* questions, we will add ones which ask *why* or *how.* We will release imaginations as we give such leads as *I wonder why. . . ? What if . . . had not finished his job?* Above all, we will strive to create an atmosphere in which "read-

ing between the lines" and "reading beyond the lines" (4) are taken for granted, a climate in which children's ideas are encouraged and examined. In these ways we make reading and all learning an adventure which leads to lifetime commitment to inquiry.

REFERENCES

1. Artley, A. Sterl. "Influence of Specific Factors on Growth of Interpretation," *Reading: Seventy-five Years of Progress.* Proceedings of the Annual Conference on Reading. H. Alan Robinson, (Ed.) Supplementary Educational Monographs. Chicago: University of Chicago Press, 1966.
2. Banta, Thomas J. "Tests for the Evaluation of Early Childhood Education: The Cincinnati Autonomy Test Battery (CATB)," *Educational Therapy,* Vol. 2, Special Child, Chapter 2 (in press).
3. Crossen, Helen J. "Effects of the Attitudes of the Reader upon Critical Reading Ability," *Journal of Educational Research,* 42 (December 1948), 289-298.
4. Dale, Edgar. "The Art of Reading," *News Letter,* 32 (December 1966). Columbus: O h i o S t a t e University, School of Education.
5. ————. "The Critical Reader," *News Letter,* 30 (January 1965). Columbus: Ohio State University, Bureau of Educational Research and Service.
6. Ellinger, Bernice, and Charlotte Huck. "Does Johnny Evaluate?," *Grade Teacher,* 82 (March 1965), 101-105.
7. Fay, Leo. "Reading S t u d y Skills: Math or Science," *Reading and Inquiry,* International Reading Association Conference Proceedings, 10 (1965), 92-94.
8. Gans, Roma. *Common Sense in Teaching Reading,* Indianapolis: Bobbs, Merrill, 1963.
9. ————. *A Study of Critical Reading Comprehension,* Contributions to Education, 811. New York: Bureau of Publications, Teachers College, Columbia University, 1940.
10. Gray, William S. "Theme of the Conference," *Promoting Growth Toward Maturity in Interpreting What Is Read,* Supplementary Education Monograph 74. Chicago: University of Chicago Press, 1951, 2-5.
11. Groff, Patrick J. "Children's Attitudes Toward Reading and Their Critical Reading Abilities in Four Content-Type Materials," *Journal of Educational Research,* 55 (April 1962), 313-318.
12. Herculane, Sr. M. "A Survey of the Flexibility of Reading Rates and Techniques According to Purpose," *Journal of Developmental Reading,* 4 (Spring 1961), 207-210.
13. Huck, Charlotte S., and Martha L. King. "Observation of the Critical

Reading of Children," *AERA Paper Abstracts,* American Educational Research Association, 1967, 45.

14. Huus, Helen. *Skill Development in Social Studies,* 33rd Yearbook of the National Council of Social Studies, National Education Association, 1963, 94-113.

15. McCullough, Constance. "Linguistics, Psychology, and the Teaching of Reading," *Elementary English,* 44 (April 1967), 353-362.

16. McKillop, Anne S. *The Relationship Between the Reading Attitude and Certain Types of Reading Response,* Contributions to Education. New York: Bureau of Publications, Teachers College, Columbia University, 1952.

17. Payne, Rebecca. "Primary Children Can Solve Problems," *Childhood Education,* 41 (May 1965), 479.

18. Piekarz, Josephine. "Getting Meaning from Reading," *Elementary School Journal,* 56 (March 1956), 303-309.

19. Raths, Louis E., *et al. Teaching for Thinking: Theory and Application.* Columbus, Ohio: Charles E. Merrill, 1967.

20. Robinson, H. Alan. "Reading Skills Employed in Solving Social Studies Problems," *The Reading Teacher,* 18 (January 1965), 263-269.

21. Russell, David H. "Research on the Processes of Thinking with Some Applications to Reading," *Elementary English,* 42 (April 1965), 370-378, 432.

22. _____. *Children's Thinking.* Boston: Ginn and Company, 1956.

23. Smith, Nila B. "Patterns of Writing in Subject Fields I," *Journal of Reading,* 8 (October 1964), 31-37.

24. _____. "Patterns of Writing in Different Subject Fields II," *Journal of Reading,* 8 (November 1964), 97-102.

25. Stauffer, Russell G. "Reading as a Cognitive Process," *Elementary English,* 44 (April 1967), 342-348.

26. _____. "Reading as Experience in Inquiry," *Educational Leadership,* 24 (February 1967), 407-412.

27. Suchman, J. Richard. "Learning through Inquiry," *Childhood Education,* 41 (February 1965), 289-291.

28. Thorndike, Ed. L. "Reading as Reasoning: A Study of the Mistakes in Paragraph Reading," *Journal of Educational Psychology,* 8 (June 1917), 323-332.

29. Usery, Mary Lou. "Critical Thinking through Children's Literature," *Elementary English,* 43 (February 1966), 115-118, 120.

30. Van Gilder, Lester L. "Meeting Reading Demands of the Content Subjects," in *Vistas in Reading,* J. Allen Figurel, (Ed.) International Reading Association Conference Proceedings, 11 (1966), 39-42.

31. Wolfe, Willavene. "Teaching Critical Reading to Elementary School Children," *Paper Abstracts.* Washington, D.C.: American Educational Research Association, 1967, 11.

Three Important Levels of Comprehension

LEONARD W. JOLL
University of Rhode Island

THE ROLE OF THE TEACHER in the secondary school is closely related to the entire reading program of the student. In considering this aspect there are three levels of comprehension which should be given careful attention. First, there is the level of literal reading where the student gets full and accurate meaning from the lines. Second, there is that of critical reading which involves the ability to read carefully and to reaact intelligently to the presentation of the author. Third, there is that of reading interpretatively which not only involves the previous two levels but requires a sensitiveness and involvement on the part of the reader. It cannot be assumed, under any circumstances, that a student who reads without error is fully competent in all or any one of these areas.

What are the involvements of literal reading? Each teacher who expects students to get information from the printed page will involve these students in literal reading. Gray called particular attention to this function in the Forty-Seventh Yearbook (3). It was further emphasized by Karlin (5) and Stauffer (7).

In teaching literal reading the following areas must be carefully considered.

Vocabulary: There are many words which have many meanings. Some of these meanings may be exact or denotations while others may be implied or connotations. Each area of concentration has its own vocabulary. In order to get full meaning from the printed page in any area, a thorough understanding of the vocabulary must be had by each student. The development of this understanding becomes the resonsibility of the teacher working in the area of content. If this teacher is the expert in the area, then he should be the expert in developing the right concept for each word of the vocabulary in this area.

Use of context clues: The use of context clues is of vital importance to a student in developing competency in literal reading. Not only must the student be able to use context clues but at the same time he must be able to judge if the meaning he is deriving is reasonable. It must be remembered that in many cases the use of contextual clues is actually little better than an outright guess. Because of this factor, when a student arrives at some conclusion as to the possible meaning of the word from the contextual setting, he should check the dictionary if the meaning does not seem reasonable.

Dictionary skills: Dictionary skills are not only needed in literal reading, they are needed in every phase of word attack as a final resource. It is regretable that not all students are facile in the use of the dictionary. The first instruction in its use may have been somewhere between the third and fourth grade. This work does not in any way guarantee that the skill was well developed or that the student has continually tried to improve himself in this skill.

Materials: In selecting materials to develop literal reading care should be taken to avoid those which go into a considerable amount of elaborate description or which tend to be debatable. A frequent error of secondary pupils is to read into materials ideas and thoughts which do not exist. Material which is highly factual and well organized lends itself very well for the development of literal reading. It is a common failing of students in reading science to react to what they think is in the chapter. The same holds in reading mathematical problems. In developing materials in these fields the authors have neither time nor space to go into nonessentials. The facts are all there; it is up to the student to identify them. In developing competency in literal reading we must aim for a high degree of comprehension and accuracy. There is no place for assumptions in literal reading.

Probably one of the areas which has drawn the most comments in the teaching of reading in the secondary school is that of critical reading. It would appear that we have three areas in critical reading: the first is to be able to read and question; the second is the ability to pick and choose those materials which best serve our purpose; while the third is to be counted and to pass judgment upon. Even though they are frequently classified under the heading of critical reading, they are in fact quite different. Teaching a student to read and question certainly should come before teaching him to read so that he can pass judgment. When a student is able to read and question, then, and only then, has he fully involved himself in thinking about the topic which is being presented. As has been so well expressed by Roma Gans, he sees relevance in what he reads. He is able to determine if what he reads is satisfying his need for reading. Gans has given us four excellent points to consider in teaching the second aspect of critical reading (2). The first is the awareness of the need to evaluate the source of material read. The second is the ability to assess the ways in which words influence ideas. The third is the ability to select wisely what is to be read. The fourth, which is without a doubt the highest level in this aspect of critical reading is the ability to make selections which are based upon the reader's own intellectual processes and not upon authority.

The third area of critical reading is the willingness to be counted and to pass judgment on what has been read. In our fast-moving world we too frequently find multitudes of readers who do not appear to know the difference between fact and opinion. It is one thing to be able to sift through thousands of words and to derive some general ideas, but it is far more important to be able to cut through this verbiage and arrive at a conclusion which is well founded and backed up by carefully organized and clearly presented facts.

One might ask how is it possible to arrive at a stage where this ability to cut through is well established. Certainly it does not come overnight. The reader not only must be proficient in literal reading but also he must have added a great amount of breadth and depth to his reading. One would not expect a lawyer to present a case in which he had not previously done research. The critical reader must be able to bring to bear the fruits of considerable reading in many areas. The critical reader must realize that if he is to make his point, then the tools he uses must be very sharp and well honed. Denberg and Jones (1) have summarized this skill very well with the following points: 1) precision with word meanings, 2) an awareness of possible semantic confusion, 3) careful structure of thought, and 4) recognition of implicit assumptions.

We frequently hear critical reading referred to as the ability to read between the lines. In order to do this the reader must closely observe the several points which have been developed. Yes, it is the ability to read *between* the lines but never to read *into* the lines. Materials to teach critical reading should involve newspaper editorials, commercial advertisements, investigation reports, inferences, and establishment of proof.

Without doubt, interpretive reading is probably one of the highest levels of competency in the reading skills scale. There are many who attempt to teach this skill, but few have many of the necessary qualifications.

William S. Gray (4) pointed out that since 1917 many studies have been reported on teaching and developing competency in interpretive reading but that there did not appear to be too much agreement on how it should be done. Time and again we have heard the old story of the many rich experiences one may have from reading: that from the printed page the reader may vicariously partake in any of the experiences known to man. One could be led to believe that all that is necessary is to make a student an accurate and fairly flexible reader and the task will be accomplished. The development of effective interpretive readers is not this easily done. The development of the interpretive reader must have an early beginning. Rich, indeed, is the child whose parents surround him with a great variety of books and then take the time to enjoy these books with the child. To enjoy books is to live with them and to know their characters. Children both want and need to be read to. This is a practice that should not terminate in the lower grades. I have never known a group who did not enjoy being read to or being told a story provided that the stories were carefully selected and well told or read.

One of the greatest assets of a child is his imagination. If we are going to develop good interpretive readers, then we must never let anything interfere with this great gift. Fortunately, it exists in all children. If it does not, then some adult has killed it at a very early age. What a joy to the reader when his thoughts come from the page in color, when he gets the real feelings of the characters. We must constantly try to get readers to form their own reactions and not be forever telling them this is the way they should feel when they read. The true love of the beautiful has been stiffled more than once because of this approach. The truly effective interpretive reader must be accurate; he must have developed not only a critical reaction but a sensitive one. It has been said that the day is lost when we do not, for a few fleeting moments, indulge in a daydream or two. For these we can be thankful; at least they are our own. They have not been influenced by someone trying to tell us the exact purpose and mood of every detail. Why should we not observe some of these when we are attempting to develop effective interpretive readers?

The National Council of Teachers of English have given *us* several excellent suggestions in developing taste in literature (6). Reading in many ways can be compared to eating. Fortunately, we do not all like the same foods. A good connoisseur can, however, do much to make many foods more palatable but he cannot give us new taste buds. Why should we not take a few hints from this situation and apply the same philosophy in developing interpretive readers. We can guide, suggest, encourage, or maybe inspire. We can provide numerous experiences, both actual and vicarious; we can surround students with materials in both width and depth; in fact, we might even force them to read, but the full enjoyment and fulfillment will only come through complete involvement on the part of the reader. When this situation occurs, then, and only then, do we have interpretive readers.

We can teach literal reading; we can make an honest attempt to do the same with critical reading. We can plant the seeds of interpretive reading. We can furnish a healthy atmosphere, but then let us leave it alone and not in the hands of self-styled experts.

REFERENCES

1. Benberg, Robert, and Charles Jones. "Critical Reading in a Developmental Reading Course," *Journal of Reading,* 10, No. 6, 399.
2. Gans, Roma. "Developing Critical Thinking," *Reading in the Secondary School,* M. Jerry Weiss (Ed.). New York: The Odyssey Press, 1961.
3. Gray, William S. "Increasing the Basic Reading Competencies of Students," *The National Society for the Study of Education,* 47th Yearbook. Chicago: University of Chicago Press, 91-114.
4. _____. "New Approaches to the Study of Interpretation in Reading," *Improving Reading in Secondary Schools: Selected Readings,* Lawrence E. Hafner (Ed.). New York: The MacMillan Co., 1967.
5. Karlin, Robert. *Teaching Reading in High School.* New York: The Bobbs-Merrill Co., Inc., 1964.
6. Smith, Nila Banton, Helen Huss, Leonard Joll, and Angela Broening. "The Development of Taste in Literature." Champaign, Ill.: *National Council Teachers of English,* 1963.
7. Stauffer, Russell G. "Concept Development and Reading," *The Reading Teacher,* 19 (No. 2, Nov. 1964), 100-105.

Developing Critical Reading Power through Newspaper Reading

CARL SAILER
Jersey City State College

MY FAVORITE WAY to start developing critical reading power through newspapers is with a careful consideration of the claims made in advertising. Let us look at a few examples to see several things which can be done to stimulate thinking about what has been read in an ad.

INTRODUCING OUR JENNY LIND COLLECTION EARLY AMERICAN ELEGANCE IN LAMPS
$24.88 to $35.88
Regularly $32.50 to $44.95

"How do you read this ad?" can be the opening question. Differing interpretations will get the discussion going. Does this advertisement mean that the lamps were formerly priced at the higher figures and are now reduced? That may be the impression some uncritical readers get, and that may be the one the writer wishes to create. But the ad does not say that the lamps have been marked down, and we readers would be well advised to consider the "regularly" as mere "sales talk"—if not purposefully misleading.

In the same category is "usually." Other phrases to be wary of include: "manufacturer's list price," for it is a misleading price to be marked down from; "special bargain," for it has little value; "special purchase" *may* indicate a real sale with savings but, "specially priced" has little validity. From this study of the meaning of words in varying situations it is an easy step to the fascinating fabrication of the realm of semantics, a step which can be an enjoyable and revealing excursion.

Now what about this ad?

STIR, PUREE, GRATE, CHOP, MIX, BLEND, LIQUEFY
This 5-cup Oster blender has 8 recipe-tested speeds
You get 4 bowls at no extra charge
SALE $39.88 reduced from $49.88

Questions: Believable? Reasonable reduction? Verifiable?

Thinking: The original or standard price can be easily checked at another store. The reduction is probably less than the usual markup, the difference between the store's purchase price and selling price. It is, therefore, believable.

There are complications, however, when we read about a toaster reduced from $13.99 to $10.99 when no brand name is given and when we cannot check the stated original price. Moving from the relatively simple to the more complex, read this ad on a much higher priced article.

MINK JACKETS
SALE-PRICED TOMORROW
$400 $500 $600

With every fur you receive a guarantee regardless of price. We'll replace and repair skins that wear out through natural causes for two whole years from date of purchase. We'll refund your money in full for any reason at all up to six weeks from date of purchase.

Intelligent buying requires the aid of critical reading and critical thinking. After cost and need have been considered, comparative shopping must be done. The critical reading problem involves untangling terminology such as natural cerulean, bleached white mink, natural blue mink, silverblue, natural pastel, autumn haze, ranch, dyed, let-out, etc.

The critical reading problem continues with this question: What does the guarantee mean in terms of protection? What does it mean to the purchaser and does it mean the same thing to the advertiser? Interpret "natural causes." Does this phrase mean ordinary, daily, double or normal wear? What does "wear out" mean? Does it mean completely worn out or worn through or easily visible or somewhat ragged or shabby or what? Can it be both replace *and* repair or must it be replace *or* repair? Who decides? Here there is room for close reading and closer reasoning.

By design I would not talk about the refund aspect of the guarantee, I would wait for a student to mention that this ought to be discussed. But if I did not get the question from the group, I would raise it myself.

The 3-C and the 3-D ways

A critical reading of the ads is not quite so simple as it seems at first sight. To protect our own best interests, we must be able to distinguish the good ad from the poor, the better ad from the bad, and the best from the misleading. This skill demands both penetration and reservation, much intellectual penetration and more mental reservation. My further recommendation is that every reader use the 3-C and the 3-D ways of critical reading or critical decoding. The 3 C's are careful, circumspect and critical. Careful means cautious, thorough; circumspect means considering all sides; critical means involving skillful judgment as to truth and merit. All these are dictionary definitions. The 3 D's are decode, dissect, and discount; decode the advertising jargon; dissect minutely the terminology; and discount the claims.

Armed with a sword having the blade of keen penetration and the handle of substantial reservation, protected by the breastplate of 3-C and the buckler of 3-D, with all these on your side, you are ready to engage in an interesting and challenging "battle of wits" with the ad writers. Be advised that they are sharp and that you, too, will need to be. Be sharp—stainless steel sharp—and cut your cost of living. With a little practice in this critical reading skill you can "eat higher on the hog" and "live beyond your means" without landing in jail.

If better living were indeed to be the outcome, then I agree with *The Wall Street Journal,* "The best thing that ever happened to an advertising program: a creative (critical) reader."

Cartoons: the more manageable material

Assuming you have reluctant readers and you are looking for easier and more manageable material, try starting with cartoons. Regular cartoons, better known as "the funnies," could be a point of departure from which to go to editorial cartoons. Ask the students to point out the absurdities and the incongruities which they see in such three-to-four panel cartoons as *Nancy, Ferdinand, Donald Duck, The Girls, Big George,* and *Grin and Bear It.*

Several examples will suffice, Nancy and two of her friends are at ski school, and the instructor appears on the scene with his arm in a sling, bandages around his head and left leg, and using a crutch as a ski pole. He says, "Now for the first lesson." If the students make application—even current and localized—of the main thrust of the cartoon, be prepared to concede the truth in whatever degree it exists. Some of us do teach writing but do not write well. Some of us do teach reading without doing too much of it. And let's not talk about speaking or listening. Are we teachers good listeners in our classes?

Ferdinand is paddling up the river in a birch-bark canoe, and he is passed by an Indian going down stream in a rowboat propelled by an outboard motor. (Title the cartoon "Curriculum"?) Donald Duck, stranded on a tropical island, sees a huge wooden packing crate float up to his little island refuge. His unpacking reveals the compact auto from which he uses the tires for his raft. The last panel shows Donald paddling away—to home presumably. (Whither, Education?) Two women, passing a taxi stand, say, "Since our husbands want us to economize this year, why don't we just walk the five blocks to the hat shop?" (Fill in your own title.) In a school room a mother, accompanied by her son, is saying, "I don't see why Junior is a problem, Miss Finch! Good grades are due to heredity and bad ones to poor teaching."

Editorial cartoons as transitionals

These cartoons would of course be fun, but they would also be mild, intellectual gymnastics for flexing somewhat flabby mental muscles. They could be introductory to editorial cartoons, which demand a more mature type of interpretation. Let me try to describe one of these in a few sentences. One is a picture of a hallway showing several doors with names on them and 1968. One door has Nixon's name on it and outside is a pair of spiked running shoes. The next door down the hall has what appears to be Romney's name and a pair of shoes—not spiked. Further down the hall is an indistinct name and a pair of loafers. Here there are a few subtleties to challenge the mind.

A second editorial cartoon is a drawing of an auto speeding down the highway with two passengers, Mr. Taxpayer and Mr. Economy. They have just passed over a road-wide wire which leads up to a timing device and a motorcycle policeman named Income Tax Hike who is standing behind a billboard labeled Prices. "I think you slowed down just in time," says Mr. Taxpayer. Some knowledge of rising prices and inflationary pressures is needed here to stimulate thinking.

"Then high school, college, marriage, Vietnam . . ." says the father to the mother about the baby in the crib. With this situation most high school students can identify and react.

Editorial cartoons, not side-by-side with an editorial, are intermediate ("funnies" first) to editorials and commentaries by columnists. Start with an editorial which has a cartoon to accompany it, probably on the same page. Discuss the cartoon first and then the editorial.

Seated at a desk is a man labeled Congress holding a report entitled "President's Plan to Finance Educational and Non-Commercial TV." Another man standing beside the desk is urging, "Why not? After all, we're dealing with a disaster area!" The editorial is called "For Better TV" and offers comments on a number of points: shortcomings of commercial TV, excise tax on new TV sets, diverting income from satellite relay of commercial TV, how to spend the limited funds of $9 million, and freedom from government interference. Even if there is agreement that there should be more educational and non-commercial TV, there is obviously plenty about which the students can read critically and react. Read and react. Read and think. These are the key processes.

The critical reading concept

And isn't this what we want when we try to develop critical reading power? Don't we want the students to weigh and consider, to reflect upon, to line up the pros and cons, to assess the value of the arguments and reasons, to assay the fine metal in the ore, to determine the strong and weak points of the exposition, and to run up a box score of the runs, hits, and errors? This, then, brings me to my major premise: Reading is thinking, and critical reading is critical thinking. A companion basic idea, if not a corollary, is that teaching must result in student thinking; i.e., teaching is student thinking.

Now it will be easy to "get students going" on another companion cartoon and editorial, for it is about Adam Clayton Powell. Here the teacher's problem will be to keep the discussion on the track and to slow it down so that it can be looked at thoughtfully and thoroughly, completely and deeply. Here the teacher's problem will be to keep down the heat and friction and to turn on the light, enlightment, and tolerance. A difficult and monumental task! One possible way is to use a wide range of different newspapers so that several editorials, a number of columnists, and many points of view are represented and available. This task will constitute a real test of critical reading, critical thinking by the students, and a stern test of masterful teaching. It is here that the teacher must be a superb example of a rational appraisal of all the facts and all the arguments given on both sides of the question.

But do not try one as difficult as the Powell discussion is bound to be until

you have done a number of others on less emotionally charged areas, ideas, or persons. Both the teacher and the students need practice before they plunge. Here you will have to feel your way and be sensitive to the stage of development of the ability of your group to discuss subjects more rationally than passionately. Perhaps California's Clark Kerr represents a good intermediate step between educational TV and Powell.

The Powell controversy had its center in the East, whereas the Dr. Clark Kerr case had its origin in the University of California. Both cases, however, became national and international, Both are fine but difficult material for students practicing the art of critical reading and thinking. The student has to function in reading on at least three different (but not necessarily distinct) levels: He must first comprehend, then interpret, and finally evaluate. Any reader must first understand what has been said; secondly, he must be able to interpret its significance; and then he must evaluate its importance. Without this depth of three-fold reading, a student cannot be said to be reading critically. And he must have the patience to learn how. This will entail a great deal of practice from day-to-day, over an extended period of time, and on many kinds of materials.

Other eligible material

What are some of these materials over and beyond the ads, the cartoons, the editorials, columns, controversial issues, and persons? Several present themselves immediately: political news; the sports pages, particularly sports editorials and columns; certain kinds of news articles and stories where there is an admixture of straight, strict reporting coupled with unwarranted editorializing; feature and human interest stories; and certain special, syndicated features and columns.

Most certainly the student must be exposed to the two (or more) sides of the political news, to a Republican and a Democratic newspaper, to a conservative and a liberal point of view, to the sports pages, editorials, and columns of more than one newspaper. The student must be taught how to detect the intrusion of opinion into news items where it does not belong. He must have repeated practice in discovering it for and by himself. To better understand illicit editorializing the student might try his hand at writing an opinion-filled news story. Human interest and feature news stories can be evaluated against a background of "hard news." The syndicated columns and special features offer golden opportunities for critical reading.

Use plenty of examples and discussion

While learning the art of reading critically and creatively is going on—with its daily ups and downs, its monthly progress and regressions—the teacher must practice patience. He must have understanding and insight, give opportunities for reactions and encouragement to thinking, and be exemplary. In fact, and in the final analysis, the teacher may have only two major functions to perform in terms of developing critical reading power: exemplification and discussion. Set the example many, many times and give all the students time to talk and plenty of time to discuss. With these two "fists" a strong teacher can knock out "Knuckle-Head," the non-critical reader.

A Study Technique to Enhance Comprehension at the College Level

MARVIN EPSTEIN
Hahnemann Medical College &
Hospital

THE APRIL MAIL brings joy and relief to Charlie Collegebound and all his family. The tensions of the past two years evaporate in the warm sunshine of his acceptance by the college of his choice.

Does this acceptance mean that Charlie is ready for college? No, it simply means that some harassed admissions officer somewhere is betting (on the strength of Charlie's college boards, high school transcript, and letters of recommendation) that the odds are better than even that he won't flunk out.

Unless Charlie is an exception, he still has to learn that reading is a two-way channel of communication, a conversation or even an argument with the author, and that studying is a much more sophisticated discipline than cramming at the zero hour for tomorrow's exam.

The problem

It has been the writer's experience in working with college students in a reading improvement and study skills laboratory that they have never developed literal and critical comprehension skills or an efficient method of using them. The fact that recall and application of the information acquired are essential ingredients of reading comprehension seems to be learned more by osmosis than formal instruction.

The average college student who comes to the reading laboratory uses inefficient methods to obtain the author's ideas. He is frequently a word-by-word reader; he has no clear understanding of why he is reading. In essence, he lacks a purpose for reading. He has difficulty in determining what is important and relevant and in distinguishing essential facts from the nonessential. After wandering through a maze of facts he has difficulty integrating the information into a cohesive whole, a task which should have been his purpose for reading the selection in the first place. In struggling to acquire the facts and to integrate them, the student is deflected from retaining the information; so he resorts to rereading the text again and again. When satisfied that he finally has the information he wants, he then becomes perplexed as to how this body of knowledge, polished and refined by his thinking and reasoning, may be incorporated into his memory and eventually applied to the solving of his problems.

The reading laboratory college student also has little understanding of sentence comprehension, paragraph structure, the use of typographical clues, the determining of meaning of words from context, the use of full and half signals, and key words and phrases. We have all seen textbook pages festooned with underlined words and sentences, even covered with transparent yellow brush strokes to aid in the comprehension, recall, and review of the material.

Students who employ these devices are merely looking at the words, not reading. They are not comprehending what the author has to say; they are not using their higher mental abilities to reflect upon and embellish the author's thoughts with their own inferences, conclusions, and implications. Many students lack the skills to classify and index ideas, to make inferences, to draw conclusions, to determine the author's tone and intent, to analyze cause and effect, and to apply syllogistic reasoning.

Another essential skill too often undernourished in the reading laboratory student is an efficient method for reorganizing the ideas obtained from the author. In other words, he has difficulty outlining, summarizing, making notes, and utilizing graphic means to aid comprehension, recall, and review.

Skills, techniques and methods

There is a hierarchy in the development of skills and the utilization of efficient methods and techniques in reading. Depending upon the stage of development of the reader's skills and his use of technique, instructional help should start wherever the student's needs are in the hierarchy.

First, the student should be helped to understand that reading is a process and *purpose* is a vital aspect of this process. It is imperative for the reader to determine what he wants from the selection he is going to read and to gear his reading rate to the degree of difficulty of the material. The selection should be read aggressively and alertly. Where possible, the reader should attempt to visualize what the author is communicating directly or by implication. In other words, he needs to interact with the author's ideas and thus become involved both mentally and emotionally.

Second, the reader must understand that the questions *who, what, when, where, why,* and *how* are basic to comprehension. The first four of these provide the facts, while the *why* and *how* require the integration of facts and the use of thinking and reasoning skills.

Third, the use of the five W's and the *how* should be related to sentence comprehension by the initiation of phrase reading. Students must learn to read by phrases to obtain meaning immediately. Meaning is more difficult to extract from isolated words. Phrase reading reduces the number of visual fixations needed for a sentence and thus increases both reading rate and comprehension. The powers of attention and concentration are best utilized in this manner because the opportunity for the mind to wander or be distracted is reduced and interferences to the thought processes are minimized.

Fourth, the structure of a paragraph neds to be fully understood by the student. The "ingredients" of a paragraph consist of a main idea, supporting details, and elaborations in the form of examples, illustrations, and further explanations. The good reader must develop the ability to obtain the main idea quickly and efficiently and to recognize the details and elaborations which support the main idea. To accomplish this end, the skills for detecting key words and phrases, full and half signals, and typographical clues should be fostered. In accordance with the reader's purposes, relevancy (distinguishing between the essential and nonessential ideas) should be paramount. Only when relevancy is determined, can the higher mental abilities of obtaining the sequence or chronological development of the ideas, determining the cause-effect relations, making valid inferences, drawing conclusions, etc., be applied. When students have difficulty classifying and indexing ideas and/or using syllogistic reasoning or other thinking processes, special skill development in these areas should be introduced.

Vocabulary development must be part of the program of comprehension skill development. The student should be helped to determine the meaning of a word from context. It may be necessary to have him develop an analytic method of determining word meaning through the use of affixes and roots. Some dictionary skills may have to be taught as well.

Fifth, larger reader selections should now be introduced. These may include selections of two or more paragraphs, chapters in a textbook, magazine articles, or selections from professional journals. Again, the student has to learn to establish a purpose for reading, determine the degree of difficulty of the material, note the organizational plan of the author, be versatile in his reading rate, and reorganize the ideas obtained from the selection in accordance with his purposes.

Sixth, for study purposes, the student must know how to make notes by means of outlining, summarizing, and drawing graphic representations such as tables, diagrams, and graphs.

To aid the student in developing comprehension skills, it is this writer's experience that a hierarchy of instructional techniques is most rewarding. A comprehension check on the selection should progress from the aided recall—multiple choice answers to specific—questions—to the unaided recall where the reader is required to reorganize the i d e a s in accordance with the purposes initially established. This task may be accomplished best by using the discussion method in a group situation where the members of the group interact with one another by asking for clarification. This process requires the students to furnish supporting data from the selection read; to determine the accuracy of the con-

clusions, inferences, implications, main ideas, etc., they have drawn; to extract the precise meaning of words used in the selection; and to develop many other r e a d i n g comprehension and thinking skills. In addition, graphic representations may be used to help clarify, integrate, and reinforce the ideas obtained. In an unstructured situation, such as this, the variety and extent of the discussion are determined by the members of the group. So long as it is related to the selection that has been read, is this not the most natural way to apply and use the information acquired from reading?

A reading-study method

Once the college student has developed the skills of phrase reading, understands the structure of a paragraph, knows how to use full and half signals, and can identify key words and phrases a reading-study method may be introduced which is a combination and adaptation of Robinson's SQ3R technique and George Cuomo's basic reading plan. Included in the method is the employment of outlining and summarizing skills, as well as the use of diagrams and tables and other graphic representations. The use of vocabulary skills is also included. This method is efficient in developing adequate comprehension and study purposes, provided the student is guided step-by-step through the method beginning with easy materials or with subject-matter with which he has little or no conceptual or vocabulary difficulty. It is recommended that initially the student use the reading-study method with one content field so that he may master the procedure and coordinate the many skills required. When this goal has been accomplished, the student should apply the method to a second content field slightly more difficult than the first, and so on gradually to the most difficult.

It has been found by this writer that unsuccessful reading-study techniques and habits used by college students are deeply ingrained. Since students are resistant to change, progress can be effected only when they are carefully guided and given many experiences in the use of the method.

This is the recommended reading-study method: first, the student should survey the material to be read; e.g., the chapter of a textbook including its title, sub-titles, bold-faced headings, italicized words, graphic representations and the captions which accompany them, introduction and summary, and the questions, if any, at the end of the chapter. This summary enables the student to determine what the chapter is about, how much he may already know about the topic, and what else he may want to learn. It also defines the boundaries of the topic about which the author is communicating and serves to motivate the student by creating interest and by stimulating questions.

Second, the student looks at the first boldface heading he encounters. The heading should be turned around in the form of a question using one of the five *W's* and the *how*. It is better to ask the *why, how,* or *what* in that order as they apply to the heading. The broader the question, the better as more of the pertinent details and evaluations may be used in answering. Raising a question in this way provides a goal-directed purpose for reading the selection.

Third, the student then reads efficiently to answer the question(s) he has raised. There has to be a flexibility of approach in all reading which takes into consideration the experiential background of the reader, the concept and vocabulary of the material, and the degree of difficulty imposed by the writer's style and organizational patterns. These organizational patterns may include a direct statement, question and answer, chronological or sequential development, comparison or contrast of ideas, use of example or illustration, or the use of analogy.

The reader first obtains the main idea of each paragraph under the boldface heading from the topic sentence and the key words and phrases within that sentence. He then integrates the main ideas by relating one to another and, at this point, tentatively attempts to answer the question by talking it out with himself, a process similar to explaining it to someone else. In this way the reader recognizes how much of the information he has obtained and whether he wants to obtain more details and elaborations or proceed to the next boldface heading.

Let us assume the reader wants to obtain the supporting details and elaborations contained in the paragraphs under the boldface heading. Keeping in mind the initial question, the main ideas, and the author's organizational pattern, he seeks the details from the full and half signals, key words and phrases, and typographical clues. He skips or skims passages he already knows, skips or skims difficult passages, and concentrates on those passages that help to answer the question originally asked. Should the reader encounter an unfamiliar word, he attempts to obtain its meaning from context. If unsuccessful, he ignores it for the moment. Again, he talks out the ideas he has obtained from reading the selection, fits them into the broad patterns of the main ideas, and relates them to the question obtained from the boldface heading. At the same time the reader is actively using his higher mental abilities. He is communicating with the author by using the author's organizational pattern to draw conclusions and implications and make inferences which may support or disagree with those of the author.

If the reader has difficulty with a passage, he should ignore what is familiar and funnel in on the sentences that present some difficulty to him as he rereads the paragraphs under the bold face heading. He studies the passage thoroughly, determines its meaning by clarifying concepts, and applies his thinking and reasoning skills. He should again attempt to unlock the meaning of unfamiliar words from context by applying analytic methods;

only when all else fails, should he resort to the dictionary. When all the difficulties are cleared away, the student should recapitulate what he has gathered from the selection by talking it out aloud with himself or a willing listener.

Now, satisfied that he comprehends what he has read and can answer the questions in the boldface headings, the reader is ready to make notes for future study and review. The paper used should be the standard 8½" x 11" size, arranged as shown in the illustration.

KEY WORDS	OUTLINE	SUMMARY
Name(s)	I Main Idea	
Date	A. Detail	
Place	1.	
Fact(s)	2. (Elaborations)	
Vocabulary	3.	
Formula	B. Detail	
	1.	
	2. (Elaborations)	
	C. Detail	
	1.	
	2. (Elaborations)	
	II Main Idea	

A line is drawn down each side about an inch and a half in from the edge of the pages. The left is called the "key words" column; and the right, the "summary" column. The space between the two lines is used for the outline.

After integrating all of the ideas and applying his own thinking to the material he has read, the student makes an outline using his own words and *not* those of the author (except where a direct quotation is needed). Using short phrases and sentences, he should write the main ideas first, not necessarily in the author's sequence, but in the sequence which makes the most sense for his purposes. The details are added in the same manner, with each detail supporting the main idea. Elaborations in the form of examples, illustrations, and further explanations are filled in if needed. If the data are

suitable for graphic representation, a diagram or table may be sketched under or alongside the details. When the note making has been completed, the reader no longer needs the textbook, magazine article, journal, or reference book; all of the pertinent memory triggers are contained in the outline. It is important not to *copy* directly from the text.

To prepare for review and further study the student then lists in the left column key words (one-word clues) taken from the outline. These may be the names of persons, places, dates, facts, vocabulary words, or formulas. In the right-hand column he writes a two- or three-sentence summary parallel to the vertical line. These two columns are later used for periodic reviews. The student looks first at the key words in the left column. These clues set his memory to work, and he talks out with himself what he learned originally. If his memory needs refreshing, he may then scan the outline and summary. There should be no need to go back to the original text. When a graphic representation is used, he should look away and try to reconstruct it in his mind's eye, noting the labels used, comparing and contrasting the ideas presented, talking out aloud the applicable processes involved, and then referring back to the notebook page only for supplemental details until it is firm and clear in memory.

The reader then proceeds similarly to each succeeding boldface heading until he has finished the material under a subtitle. He will probably then want to reorganize his data because, in thinking about what he has learned, he may wish to rearrange the sequence again to suit his own (not the author's) purposes. This process will entail making new notes in outline form and perhaps using new key words and summaries. The reader, perhaps raising broad new questions and answering them with further refinements and reorganization of the ideas and his own thinking on a chapter-wide basis, continues with this procedure until all the subtitles in the chapter have been covered.

The method described appears to be a formidable and time-consuming task, according to students' frequent claims; skillful guidance by the instructor however, will help the student overcome his impatience, will result inevitably in more efficient comprehension of the material read, and will virtually eliminate the time that otherwise would go into inefficient reviewing. The thinking and note-making process of this method puts the significant new information the student has read into his memory, where it belongs and where it can be retrieved instantly by a glance at the key words. Gone forever are the all-night vigils with underlined paragraphs spread over hundreds of textbook pages.

Summary

Higher education is a job. For a job, you need tools. When Charlie Collegebound arrives on the campus of Old Podunk U., no matter how good a craftsman his IQ has made him, the work he turns out will be inferior, if he doesn't have the tools of comprehension and efficient reading-study techniques.

There is a hierarcy of skill development. Charlie is somewhere up the ladder, not because anyone taught him in the lower grades, but because he had to learn by trial and error how to study somehow.

Each college student should be informally evaluated or observed to determine where he stands in the hierarchy. It is then the task for the reading laboratory instructor to take up where Charlie's self-taught skills are weak. The fashioning of the tools of learning is worth every minute it takes, for learning never stops.

REFERENCES

1. Cuomo, George. *Becoming A Better Reader.* New York: Holt, Rinehart and Winston, 1960.
2. Robinson, Francis P. *Effective Study.* New York: Harper and Row, 1949.

Developing Structured Guiding Questions As An Aid in Reading and Discussion at the College Level

E. F. HJERMSTAD
Illinois Teachers College, Chicago-South

ONE CENTRAL IDEA in teaching comprehension skills established thus far has been that the emphasis is on making what the students read a valid personal experience, rather than on what they read or what they have to read. The key to these experiences lies in structuring the student's experiences so he can go much deeper into literature and college reading assignments with a constructive purpose in mind other than just reading some work for a grade or the completion of an assignment.

The idea which should come across strongest to the student is that he should never take a book or writing at its face value. The student should be encouraged to find the errors in what he has read. He should study the technique the author has employed, question his motives and take into consideration bias, emotion, and other personal reasons which might interfere with the author's objectivity.

After the student has enumerated the good and bad qualities in a reading, he is in a better position to decide just what value the reading has as it is used in a class or individually, Whether this can be called a clinical or a cynical way to approach a written work is debatable, but it is necessary to start the student thinking about what he is reading in a new perspective during his college career.

The lectures or discussions in college reading courses should be not so much about what the student is reading as the *application* of what he is reading. College reading teachers should expose the student to the ideas which have evolved from the type of critical reading his courses are trying to get him to do. It is possible in this regard to think of the class discussion as serving more as a prolog for the dialog in reading which follows. The student should get the impression he is learning through discussion in much the same way as students of the philosophers did: by listening to his teacher and himself argue so he can test his knowledge and interpret the subject matter with greater clarity. Instead of lecturing and telling the student exactly what he should be looking for, the teacher should encourage the student to arrive at answers by discussing with him what he got out of a reading and coming to some conclusion. Teachers should pose probing questions to spark a discussion or to keep the student moving in the right direction. Teachers should also offer the student opinions on which he could elaborate or reject and build his own theory.

Obviously, not all students are as vocal as some in each reading section. Nor are teachers always able to cover every possible problem an assignment may present. The structure of the discussion, however, should give the student a chance to organize and express what he has found important in the readings.

Preparing for discussion

In preparing a reading for the student it is necessary to go over what was assigned to the student; so preparing for the reading also becomes an excellent way of preparing for class discussion. In making preparations, the teacher should constantly be alert in selecting the wording he wishes to use to create worthy discussion questions. Many teachers are prone to pull grand-sounding phrases out of space and fit them in wherever they look good. College reading sections should argue a great deal about terminology and the meaning of phrases. Initially, when the student begins to realize that it might be his reading that could undergo the scrutiny of the group at any session, he should find himself spending more time in organizing his thoughts and trying to be more precise in his terms. It is one of the basic responsibilities of the teacher to be as concise as possible in his own verbalization and serve as a proper model for his students to emulate.

To create a preciseness and an organizing principle for discussion it is necessary to organize and explain to the students how critical reading demands that one know a *method* for analyzing an author's stated or implied arguments. Technically, the student needs some logical network to follow that will allow him to unlock the deeper meanings to be found in reading and discussion. These formulations can be brought about quite readily if the teacher knows how to create guiding questions which can be used especially well in c l a s s discussions. These guiding questions should also identify worthy starting points for the student with ineffective comprehension skills who has not, in the past, *purposefully* engaged in logical exercises or attempted many critical reading assignments.

Structured guiding questions are useful in unlocking in the reading act that mystical internal conversation between reader and author which is carried on through modes of informal language analysis. Formal language analysis, on the other hand, refers to those precise exercises one performs in practicing syllogistic reasoning, as in a course in logic. Through class discussions and assignments it is necessary to get the student to practice using his language as it really exists—as an informal mode of analysis. Exercises devoted to formal logical analysis, such as those found in such tests as Applied Logic by Little, Wilson, and Moore, are valuable; but these exercises are basically useful as prereading influences to *key* the student to apply himself to the critical reading situation. How simple life would be if we could turn every piece of writing or every language situation into a neat syllogistic framework.

The teacher should structure questions so the student will be *forced* to react critically to the works of various authors. The questions used should draw forth other questions from the student; and if the student can begin to use some of the questions consistently, he will soon discover he is being critical within a basic logical continuum. The teacher, in turn, can usually judge the effectiveness of the student's work by discovering whether oral work improves and judging whether the student follows the teacher's questions rationally and can formulate his own ideas within the guidelines of the discussion.

Basic types of structured questions

The primary framework for developing guiding questions for class discussions is found in what might be termed the analytic structure of argumentation. Analytic arguments are usually organized in print in the inductive or deductive mode. In analytic arguments the author sets up the criteria for analysis based on his sustaining powers of reason and expertise so the reader can cope with his material within a rational setting. In preparing questions for discussion in this area, the teacher should organize questions that will identify the terms the author uses and the *way* he uses them. Secondly, the teacher should prepare questions that will aid the student in discovering the author's method of inquiry; and, lastly, the teacher should develop questions that will help the student understand the author's purpose.

To insure that workable questions are formulated in the analytic area, the teacher must consciously establish in the student's reading selections and in the discussions a balance in argumentative structures between generalizations, judgments, and opinions on one side and facts, details, illustrations, and evidence on the other. Primarily, it is important that the student be able to draw conclusions from what he knows or can discover about a subject; secondly, he must also support or clarify each conclusion with samples of the thinking behind it, especially as he is trying to unite his purposes for reading the selection with the author's purpose for writing it.

The teacher's questions in the analytic area should aid the student in learning to distinguish between fact and judgment in a workable manner. When one notes daily how easily facts are aborted or changed through careless reading and listening, it seems only logical that the student learn to approach factual material with a sustaining method of analysis. In building questions relating to facts and judgments, the teacher can constantly relate factual material to at least these four areas:

1. That facts are reports on what has happened or exists.

2. That facts result from observation or measurement.

3. That facts can be tested or verified.

4. That facts are usually quite specific.

It is the teacher's responsibility to ask questions, either guiding questions before the reading or direct questions during class period, to insure himself that attention is being paid to factual material. The questions concerning factual material are also important when the teacher and class are discussing the basic literal meaning of some selection.

The teacher's questions concerning judgments in and of the printed word (remember, of course, that judgments use language predominately in an informal mode of analysis) should constantly relate to these five areas of judgment development:

1. The teacher should note that judgments are, in the main, opinions, decisions, and pronouncements.

2. Judgments characterize or even classify the author's purpose, bias, method of analysis, etc.

3. Judgments usually express approval or disapproval.

4. Judgments usually make a very *general* statement about something.

5. The truth or falsity of a judgment cannot always be demonstrated.

With just a few disciplined questions in the two areas of fact and judgment, the teacher can aid the student in disciplining himself as he reads, notes his literal interpretations of generalizations and details, and begins to base his conclusions on analytic rather than generalized reading skills.

By disciplining himself both in reading and discussion to think through the generalizations and details in a selection, the student can usually see how unwarranted assertions or rash judgments impair reading unless they introduce factual material. The student should also be able to see the limited usefulness of judgments and begin to *prefer* statements which can develop with facts.

The student can also become acquainted with methods of inquiry by recalling how specific details are harder to collect than judgments because they require very careful reading or other investigation. Finally, and most important, the search for developing details helps the reader and author clarify and discipline generalizations. Really a dual purpose is served by working in this area: the student learns to generalize from details, and he also learns to *use* details to explain or support generalizations.

The other major area for structuring questions may be called the synthetic argumentative mode. Synthetic arguments are those arguments that usually arise in reading when one has passed from literal interpretation to implied meaning. Most of the dialog in this area takes place after the student realistically identifies the *particular* criteria the author uses for establishing meaning which is consistent with the text or meaning coherent in itself.

Questions concerning arguments of the synthetic type should relate to the following major questions; namely, what are the *effects* of this reading on the reader? Questions in this area should relate experiences in reading to situations or experiences in the student's life, if possible. The questioning should start with *just* criticisms that can be made about statements the student has brought forth through discussion and reading. The teacher must then decide if these statements coordinate with details and other supporting evidence from the reading to indicate the formulation of a correct or valid *personal* evaluation on the part of the student. For example, in discussing the psychological and sociological ramifications of LSD on our populace, it would be important to organize questions which would force the student to look at the primary and secondary references in the readings which were assigned in this subject field. This active *search* for supported references in several areas can be controlled by using some of the prior questions on facts and judgments. By knowing these chronological procedures, the teacher can then ascertain the worth of the value judgments or subjective points the student may proffer during discussion. In other words, the teacher can show the student that the judgments he makes *away* from the reading must also contain a logical framework for his observations.

Important areas for recall

A format for the type of questioning just noted should consider these questions:

1. Why are the arguments valid or invalid? (The students should conceptualize and reconceptualize their ideas from the *criteria* they deem important in the selection.)

2. What is the author saying to you? (To answer this question the student *must* constantly review the factual material in the reading.)

3. What is the author doing to you? (The answer to this question is discovered through some understanding of the author's thought patterns.)

The student's success in developing strong comprehension skills depends on the types of questions he begins to ask himself as he is trying to read critically. The student who has not developed constructive habits of asking questions while reading by the time he gets to college might be handicapped simply because he has never been led into the deeper resources of the printed word in any *structured* manner. The conscientious college reading teacher will note this difficulty and probe any opening that will bring about good practices in the sequential development of reading skills.

Point of view

A student cannot master anything without much practice. He certainly cannot master language without it. Children, once they begin to speak, keep up a constant chattering and so get the necessary practice in language. Now what practice do college students get?—A little in their daily recitations in class, a little in writing compositions, a little while typing, a lot by reading a vast amount of material for different purposes; all good practices as far as they go but certainly not enough to give most students a mastery of comprehension skills in reading.

To the college student trying to fathom a difficult reading assignment, it does not make too much difference whether he can identify the significant reading skills he uses to master the reading selection. In the main, he wants to solve a trying and personal reading problem on which he is expending a considerable amount of physical and intellectual energy. The sympathetic teacher knows this and therefore must be able to *evaluate* and *structure* these personal explorations the student undertakes in establishing those relationships which are necessary to institute a starting point for inquiry into personal thought processes. Anything less than this attainment cheats the student.

Criteria for Selecting Materials to Teach Reading (Elementary)

HANS C. OLSEN
Wayne State University

EVERYONE AGREES that materials of one sort or another are needed in the reading program of the school. This need is evident to professionals and laymen alike. Obviously children can neither learn to read nor refine their reading skills without something to read.

Despite the wide recognition that materials are indispensable in teaching reading, a fundamental problem remains: which of the available materials are most appropriate and effective. This problem has long plagued classroom teachers, school administrators, and reading specialists and is growing more acute.

Several types of materials have been on the market for some time, and new forms appear with increasing frequency. Among the former are basal series, supplementary readers, trade books, workbooks, review materials, tests, charts, filmstrips, and teachers' guides. Two of the newer forms are reading laboratories and programed materials. Each type of reading material is designed to help teachers achieve certain instructional goals. Some purport to provide a total reading program; others are less inclusive.

The pressure of the present

A tremendous number of reading materials are now on the market. New ones come to our attention almost daily. Older ones are revised and refined; seldom are they discontinued. Increased attention to education, including the availability of Federal funds, has helped to promote this deluge of materials. There appears to be no slackening in this trend; if anything, it promises to continue at an accelerating rate.

Several other factors compound the problem of teachers, administrators, and reading specialists. One of these is the rather marked similarities of materials within types listed earlier. Even when new and different approaches appear within one or another type, a movement of accommodation begins. The older, established materials are revised to include the new approaches, and/or advertising materials and teachers' guides are developed to show how the publicized innovation always has been or is now an integral part of the older materials. Successive revisions of the new materials tend to modify them in the direction of the older materials, and a new synthesis is reached.

Publishers' representatives, promotional literature, and samples of materials compound the problem. We are battered by a barrage of words, pictures, and examples designed to demonstrate and support claims of superiority for each of the materials. This continuous flood of advertising extolling the special characteristics and strengths of materials to teach reading is replete with statements such as "the most complete program," "the most widely used," "modern materials," and "the most recent thing."

Each of the materials on the market reflects more or less accurately a particular concept of what the instructional program in reading ought to be. New knowledge about reading, learning, society, language, literature, and instructional technology results in changing emphases in the reading programs advocated by various authorities and publishers. The new knowledge thus leads directly to the rash of new materials as well as to the revision of older ones.

Criteria and analysis of materials

These factors taken together make the selection of appropriate materials a difficult and time consuming task. Many lists of criteria have been developed to assist selectors in their work.

Some lists are quite extensive; others, more limited. Each list, however, mirrors the biases and preferences of the person or group who developed it. This fact accounts for the differences among the lists. Those who elect to use an available list "buy" the point of view of the compiler. Not all selectors, however, find an orientation or philosophy that is acceptable to them in criteria developed by someone else. Many believe they must devise their own set of criteria. In either case, one criterion or more is basic to the selection process.

These criteria may not be fully spelled out or consciously applied but they are used, nevertheless. Numerous criteria may be employed, or only a few, or perhaps one. Each criterion is a principle accepted by the selector. It serves as a standard to measure materials and provides a basis for analyzing them. The first task of a selector, then, is to bring together a comprehensive set of criteria. The second is to use these criteria consciously to objectively analyze available materials. It is only after the principles have been assembled in a list of criteria and the materials analyzed that selection should take place. Major emphasis must be placed on the first two steps. The third follows naturally.

This means that those responsible for choosing new materials must be analysts first and selectors second. The list of principles they have assembled determines what they look for in their examination and to some extent how they conduct their examination. Analysts must identify the strengths and weaknesses of the materials and their suitability for specific situations. All of this points out the fact that selection itself is much less involved and difficult than are the tasks of developing a comprehensive, consistent set of criteria and then using them to analyze the available materials.

Analysts of reading materials have at their disposal far more principles than they can use. They will be swamped by sheer numbers if they attempt to use all possible principles. In addition, some principles conflict with others. Thus, choices have to be made among principles. The goal is a complete, coherent framework for analyzing materials.

Developing criteria for specific situations

Knowledge of three elements in the situation in which the materials will be used help the analyst determine what is essential, what is inconsequential, and what is unacceptable in available materials. These elements are the children, the teachers, and the reading program. Certainly the materials should be appropriate to the needs, interests, and backgrounds of the children for whom they are selected. Materials should also be compatible with the preparation, experience, and preferences of the teachers who will be directing children in their use. The objectives and pattern of the reading program in the school building or system should be reflected in the materials. If the analyst has accurate knowledge of these three elements in his own school situation, his analysis is likely to identify the most suitable materials.

Analysts will almost always use several criteria to guide their examination of materials. The materials are measured against these standards. The validity of the materials is established by this measurement. It is logical to select the materials closest to the norm created by these standards or criteria.

Rarely will materials exactly fit the norm. It is improbable that any materials give these principles exactly the same emphasis as did the analyst who compiled them. For example, one set of basal readers may include many colorful pictures, fitting one criterion. Phonics, however, is not stressed in the readers. Since a strong emphasis on phonics is another criterion, this set of readers does not fit the norm perfectly. Obviously, certain principles that support some materials may not be included among the criteria accepted by an analyst; conversely, an analyst may have included a specific criterion not basic to some materials.

The fact that several criteria must be considered means that those who prepare and those who use materials for reading instruction are forced to establish priorities among the criteria they select. They must decide what they want most, what is less important to them, and what they do not want. Seldom will analysts or authors agree completely on a list of criteria or the priority assigned them. This means that except in rare instances most analysts will not be completely satisfied with any materials. They must decide which of the available materials most nearly meets the norm they have established.

Criteria for special consideration

Four of us at Wayne State University recently identified and made available in a book more than two hundred principles that analysts might use as criteria.* We learned several interesting things in the course of our work. First, there are far more principles that might be selected than can be used easily or advantageously. We also learned that a great many of the more-than-two-hundred principles are seldom used as criteria either because they are not widely known or because they are not compatible with dominant current thinking about reading. Another thing that came to our attention is how often contradictory principles are found in working lists of criteria. Perhaps the most surprising thing is the frequencey with which unstated, even unrecognized principles slip into the framework of criteria. In this latter category the criterion of lowest cost often may be found.

Giving attention to two groups of principles may be especially profitable for all who are responsible for selecting reading materials. The first of these groups consists of those principles that are obscure and, therefore, seldom used. Many of these would

*Kenneth S. Goodman, et al. *Choosing Materials To Teach Reading.* Detroit: Wayne State University Press, 1966.

probably be used more often as criteria if analysts knew about them. The second group of principles is made up of those that are contradictory. These must be recognized by analysts, and a choice is required between them. They cannot be used together.

Little-known criteria

Lack of familiarity with seldom-used principles dooms them to obscurity. A primary task of all analysts is to acquaint themselves with all possible principles. The work of the four of us from Wayne State was an attempt to provide some assistance. Here are some questions that embody representative examples of little-known principles that we have identified.

What provision is made for controlling grapheme-phoneme (symbol-sound) correspondence? Some materials rigorously control this relationship. Others give no attention to it. This material should not be confused with a formal, systematic phonics program. Perhaps the most widely known attempt to maintain a consistent grapheme-phoneme relationship is the i.t.a.

Is there a recognition of and provision for dialect differences in the materials? Students of language point out that marked differences exist in the way in which language is used by various groups of people in the United States. Many dialects exist. Provision for dialect differences is now evident in some materials. Most of the available materials, however, give little consideration to this principle.

Do the materials contain deliberate attempts to stimulate children to read widely outside of school? Relatively few materials designed for the reading program in early grades present such guides for children. Yet, wide individual reading is a stated goal for most reading programs.

Contradictory criteria

Analysts must steer clear of the tangle caused by choosing conflicting, contradictory principles when they compile criteria to guide their examination of reading materials. The task of analyzing materials takes enough time, effort, and patience without compounding the difficulty by including opposing criteria. The contradictions must be identified and resolved before the norm is established. Here are two examples of conflicting principles that illustrate the choices analysts must often make.

Children should always gain meaning from materials used for reading instruction. This principle underlies most basal series today. Other reading materials, such as some with a linguistic base, emphasize a conflicting principle; the early stage of the reading program should concentrate on helping children learn the grapheme-phoneme relationship. Meaning is unimportant, even detrimental to acquiring this basic knowledge. These principles are difficult to reconcile.

Reading materials should have a carefully controlled vocabulary. Materials based on this principle present a limited number of words. They are repeated many times to assist children in building a large stock of sight words. A contradictory principle is that the content of reading materials should be of high literary quality. They should consist of selections that have stood the test of time, excite the imagination, and touch the emotions. These two principles are clearly incompatible.

Conclusion

Selecting suitable reading materials can be a bewildering task. Great numbers of available materials and conflicting advertising claims make it difficult to choose among them. Selectors need some basis for analyzing and comparing materials. Deliberately chosen, consciously applied criteria serve that purpose.

Selectors of reading materials have, therefore, a threefold responsibility. First, they must carefully devise a comprehensive, consistent set of appropriate criteria. Then they must objectively analyze available materials and measure them against this norm.

After that, they simply select the materials that fit the norm most closely. This process sounds easy. It is not. Selectors, however, who carefully and wisely spell out the criteria they will use to guide their analysis of materials can proceed with confidence and dispatch.

Aspects of Books That Affect Readability and Use

Ned D. Marksheffel
Oregon State University

THIS PAPER is confined to a brief look at six pertinent aspects of books that affect readability and use.

1. What is a book?
2. Readability formulas
3. Format
4. Availability of books
5. The author's role
6. The reader's role

What is a book?

Many people have little difficulty in defining a book. They tend to think of it as something containing a certain number of written pages that are prevented from blowing away or becoming lost by two stiff covers of paper, cloth, leather, plastic, or any other available material.

Those who love reading rarely think of a book in terms of paper, print, ink, and binding unless there is something strikingly different about these items. To these people, a book is so complex that it almost defies definition because its meanings vary with one's interests, moods, purposes, background, etc.

How do you look upon a book?

From the writer's viewpoint, a book is an enigma. Surely the first one must have been concocted from a witch's brew, stirred by a wizard, and edited by a sorcerer.

If we examine the contents of the progeny of the first book, we find that books are really made of flesh, blood, tears, sorrow, and tribulation. At the same time they contain joy, happiness, dreams, hopes, aspirations, and triumphs.

Sometimes books are both destroyers and builders of nations. Sometimes they reveal secrets for alleviating pain and wiping out crippling diseases. At other times they are misused and become horrendous instruments of torture that rack inefficient readers' minds and bodies.

At the very least, books are bits and collections of magic that reveal knowledge, inspire man to greater heights of love and compassion for his fellow man, and give him a better understanding of himself and his role in the universe. And all the while they accurately and inaccurately record man's reaction and interaction with life.

The definition of *book,* therefore, depends upon the user and his purposes for using.

Readability formulas

Teachers and students are probably the greatest users of books. And because teachers are practical people, they are interested in the reading level of books that they use with students. Publishers and authors, therefore, had to devise an instrument that would give teachers some kind of an answer about the reading difficulty of a particular book. Such an instrument was developed and is called a readability formula. The formula is supposed to indicate that a certain book is not too difficult for the average student in a specific grade.

Teachers, however, know that when they have three different textbooks of the same level of readability according to readability formulas, one of the texts will be easier to read than either of the other two. Likewise, one of the books will prove to be the most difficult to read.

A readability formula *is* of value, but because it is a mechanical measure of difficulty based upon such factors as numbers of prepositions, numbers of personal nouns, numbers of syllables in words, and numbers of words in a sentence, it is subject to errors. It cannot, for example, make allowances for an author's organization of material, introduction and use of new words, style, or use of synonyms. Two different authors using almost identical lists of words and writing about the same topic and for the same grade level will produce two books with widely different degrees of difficulty. Readability, therefore, cannot be judged solely by a readability formula.

Format

Several other aspects of books that are more or less mechanical and that affect readability and use also need to be mentioned. A reader's choice or rejection of a book may be due, at least originally, to the format of the book. The kind and size of print; the amount and balance of darkness and lightness on a page; the arrangement and use of pictures, graphs, charts or other illustrations; the amount and kinds of color in the illustrations; and even the choice of paper tend to influence the use and readability of books. The degree to which these aspects operate varies with each reader. Some readers, for example, crave illustrations in their reading material; some are rather indifferent in this respect while others almost automatically reject any book that is "cluttered with illustrations." Thus, we might note that the so-called mechanical aspects of books affect their use.

Availability of books

Many times the priceless ingredients in books remain unused and inert because they are not available to an acceptable reader. Unless a book can team up with a reader, it is not serving its purpose and is quite useless except as a dust catcher, something to throw at a cat, or an object to hold an uncooperating door ajar.

Too often, the kinds of books that are needed for certain students are not available. This lack is a rather common complaint of teachers at all levels of education and in all fields. Such is the case, I've been told, even with graduate students and reading experts.

Many times publishers have been blamed for not producing the kinds of books teachers need and want, and this situation has been more true in the past than at present. Publishers will publish that which is saleable. After all, the consumer of books, can and should determine to a great extent the kinds of books that leave the presses. But as I see some of the junk (and I use the word *junk* deliberately) that is being thrust upon unwary or uncritical readers, I question my preceding statements. Surely people do not desire some of the books that are published, or do they?

Succinctly stated, more of the proper kinds of books should be available to teachers and students. Availability, as I use it, means not only that someone has published certain books but that the books have been purhcased and are in the hands of readers who can and will read them. If books are to be used in any manner, they must be available to readers.

The author's role

The author's role in the use of books is an important and a demanding one. He must not only know thoroughly the subject about which he is writing but he must be absolutely honest. Being absolutely honest does not rule out fiction or fairy tales. Being honest, as it is used here, means that the author writes clearly, creatively, and interestingly. He writes to inform and interest his readers, not to impress them with his superior vocabulary and unique style.

It is a simple matter for an author to assume unwittingly that his readers are more knowledgeable and more efficient readers than they really are. On the other hand, he must be careful not to insult the reader or emasculate content by oversimplification. Experience, however, shows that even highly efficient, sophisticated readers can be interested in and learn from books of comparatively low readability levels. Highly intelligent and efficient readers often become engrossed with books of no greater than fifth- or sixth-grade difficulty because of the content and the author's mastery of expression.

I am not implying that all books should be aimed at low-level readability, but I am saying that oftentimes high-level concepts and knowledge may be of more value to greater numbers because the authors wrote clearly, honestly, and interestingly. Some of our greatest and most cherished books are so written. An author may *encourage* reading, *foster growth* in reading, and *improve his readers'* knowledge by the manner in which he introduces new vocabulary and develops concepts. Many times authors attempt to simplify content by reducing the amount of space devoted to a particular topic. The results can be devastating. Those who are in doubt about this view-point need only to read critically almost any sixth grade social studies textbook. Highly abstract concepts that take years to develop are showered like thunderbolts upon the immature reader.

One sixth grade social studies textbook, used by the writer, had at least 39 difficult concepts on one page. Staggering, isn't it? A history textbook that is now being used with tenth graders covers World War I and the League of Nations in 13 pages!

At this point it appears pertinent to state that we have unwittingly been too harsh on many authors, because there are numerous excellent writers of all kinds of books. To these people we, the teachers and readers, owe our gratitude.

Authors should also recognize that today's readers demand material that begins quickly, uses colorful vocabulary, and includes sufficient detail to make the message realistic. Students crave interestingly written action stories that are spiced with humor and conversation. They like biographies, historical events, scientific events, space exploration, western adventures, mysteries, and stories about boys and girls of their own age.

The reader's role

The reader not only has an opportunity but also a responsibility to learn to read to his maximum. One good reason is that all higher levels of learning are dependent upon his ability to read, and he should learn this fact early. He should also learn that not only his future but his life may be in jeopardy if he fails to learn to read efficiently. Most of you, for example, have noted that the containers and conveyors of inflammable materials are now being labeled flammable because too many people mistakenly thought inflammable meant *not* flammable. In such instances, the lack of reading ability actually cost people their lives.

The reader needs to be taught how, why, and when to use the clues that authors provide for getting the most out of the reading material. And when we talk about the reader, we must include his teachers.

The knowing teacher attempts to provide each pupil with reading materials at a level at which he can pronounce a minimum of 95% of the words and can comprehend at least 70-75 percent of the material without excessive help.

The teacher knows, as should the pupil, when to select more difficult material for the student in order that he be sufficiently challenged to learn but not be defeated by materials that are too difficult for him.

If only teachers could realize that many, many times the difference between total reading failure and success hinges upon the slim margin of but a single grade level of difficulty! Those who have worked extensively with reading problems know that a student may become so perplexed and upset by the difficulty of a particular book or selection that he temporarily loses all control of the few reading skills he possesses. If he is forced to continue to try to read these kinds of materials for any length of time, he usually becomes a desperate, frustrated reader. He may learn to abhor the sight of any book. He may become so emotionally disturbed that he is unable to do any directed school learning successfully.

On the other hand, the same student may choose a book loaded with difficult and strange vocabulary and sup-posedly beyond his reading skills and yet read the material with relish and growing understanding. His inability to initially pronounce many of the words becomes a challenge rather than an obstacle. Why? Because *he* chose the book and because he is keenly *interested* in the subject. He is thus able to draw upon what he already knows and associate that understanding with the new information and concepts found in the book. He may, for example, be completely frustrated by certain fifth grade general reading books and yet read successfully eighth or ninth grade materials in another area.

The student's own background, his interests, goals, and attitudes toward reading definitely affect the readability and use of books.

Conclusion

In conclusion, it is apparent that many factors need to be considered about aspects of books that affect readability and use. Only a few of these factors have been developed but it is hoped that those aspects chosen are pertinent to you.

The Printed Page and the Poor Student (Secondary)

JOHN E. COOPER
Des Plaines, Illinois Public Schools

PROGRESS IN TEACHING language skills to *poor* secondary students will be made only when teachers stop speaking in terms of generalities and begin communicating through an exchange of specific classroom materials and techniques based upon needs. This theme will be developed in three steps by (1) showing the dangers of the generalities, 2) suggesting specific student needs, and 3) describing a sample lesson to show how these specific needs can be met.

The questions asked in the three subheads of this paper are those which I have asked myself in the process of identifying the basic-skills student and developing language arts materials for him. I have chosen to use the term *poor* when referring to this basic-skills student for reasons which will be revealed.

Who is the *poor* student?

The *poor* student has been called a lot of things. Over the years all of these tags have been used by different teachers in varying circumstances to identify this one student:

slow	underachieving
limited	needy
remedial	deprived
basic	underprivileged
fundamental	culturally deprived
vocational	culturally
nonacademic	unmotivated culturally
nonverbal	disadvantaged
manual	disadvantaged
noncollege-oriented	noncompetitive
academically	linguistically
unsuccessful	untalented
reluctant	

Because I have been interested in accurately identifying the student, I have become cautious about the use of educational tags like these. Rather than pinpoint the needs of this student, such tags have, in practice, often hidden his needs. Take the first tag, "slow," for example. "Slow" was invented at a time when teachers accepted the notion that each student had a built-in ceiling or rate of learning: he could go only so high, so fast. To be very objective, we teachers assigned a number to this student, and we called the number IQ. Even though we observed this student at certain times going far higher and far faster than his number allowed, we were reluctant to give up the tag. In spite of the newer research into learning patterns, we still feel comfortable with the catchall "slow." I think this is one reason why materials for this student remain so bland and limiting.

Or, pick another tag from the list. Pick "vocational." A number of years ago students forced us to admit that the straight college prep high school was missing the mark. A certain student was not succeeding; that is, he was getting F's in academic courses.

So we began building shops for this student, and we tagged him and his English texts "vocational." We didn't modify the academic courses for him; we just added the shop courses. Now we were giving him a mixture of John Milton and Henry Ford. He still got F's in Milton. And the sad thing was he was only getting D's in Ford because he couldn't read the automotive manuals. We academic teachers shrugged. "At least he's good with his hands," we said.

Take "underachieving" as another example. This tag became popular when educators tried to isolate a thing called "motivation." To tag a student with "underachieving" we needed two numbers; this *was* scientific! One number was a score from some standardized test. The other number was based upon a thing we called performance. In between lay "motivation." To make the two numbers match, all the English teacher needed to do was motivate. But how? Many were disappointed when pretty pictures did not supply the easy answer.

We began a search for the educational adrenalin which we could shoot into the veins of the underachiever. We didn't find many ways of increasing the scholastic metabolism of this *poor* English student; but as we searched, we learned that it was a risky business trying to separate the "can'ts" from the "won'ts" with a tag like "underachieving."

More recently, we teachers have been trying for identification of a deeper kind. We have been studying the cultural elements which have shaped Jim Jones's learning patterns. These studies excite us because they hold the promise of identity for Jim.

But the old danger is still with us. In practice, we have tagged Jim "disadvantaged" and lumped him with millions of other students. Just picture them: a homogeneous group of several million high school students! Unless we do something, Jim will remain anonymous long after the tag, "disadvantaged," has been replaced by other tags.

This, then, is the danger of educational tags as they are applied to the *poor* student. It's not that the tags weren't honestly conceived. It's not that tags aren't necessary at times. They are necessary—for the covers of books and for labels on educational courses and for titles of speeches. The danger of tags is that we have fooled ourselves into believing that we can use them to communicate about the one significant problem: what does Jim Jones need in the English class?

Tags for the *poor* student have been largely a product of desperation. Prove this to yourself this way: for every eight tags which you can think of that have been used in an attempt to identify the *poor* student, think of only one tag which has been applied to the top student. See if you don't run out of top tags first. Tags have been easier to invent than materials.

What will the next tag for the *poor* student be? It doesn't really matter unless we are willing to go beyond the tag to take a hard, honest look at the student.

What are the *poor* student's needs?

In my work, I have found that one of the best ways to identify the *poor* student is to let him speak for himself. The following are actual excerpts from papers my basic-skills students have written this year. They are without benefit of red pencil.

Student 1: Now since I am getting kicked out of school my grades are starting to lower. I am doing bad in english, in math, in art etc. Getting kicked out is what is ruining my grades. I hope that I can catch up in all of my work. Sooner or later.

Student 2: . . . my mother and fother work in the factory in Chicago. . . . I was born in Poland in the Circus. . . . My English is not this good because I'm only here no more then two years. . . . The school for me is lot of fun. . . . I'm doing fine in school everithing is going o.k. But I dont like one thing that I dont get any frends in school. . . .

Student 3: My older brother was presidunt of sudent counsel last year my pareents say I should be like him. He got a sholarship this year. . . .

Student 4: I don't have a mother or father my mother died when I was 4. I never sceen my father. I admit I get long some some times because I look at other kids familys they have a mother and father to give them love and help when they need it I don't. . . .

Student 5: It is just great going to school here at Maine West. . . . Everythings about the same at home too. Our dog had his first birthday in February. My mother is a den mother for one more month.

Student 6: Mr. Cooper I am not good at anything except to burn garbage at my house. I am poor at everything. I will be lucky if I make it through Maine West that is how poor I am in doing everything.

Student 7: Well, so you want to know what's new right? Right! I can tell you that everythings going ok, my grades well, there fair. Im getting C's in everything but English. And Im getting Ds in there because of my big mouth I guess, right?

Student 8: As you know I don't speak to much english, but I am trying to make my best in school. I going to start saing that I don't like this english class not because of the teacher. I don't like this class because it is difficult. It is difficult because the only thing we do is reading, making a lot of project. . . . I am in a spanish excelerate class and all the student there are the briliants in school and I fill embarase when they see something of the things we do in english low and in Fundamentals of Algebra.

Student 9: . . . Thats when my dad was murdered while we were with my mom. She remarried again for the third time, a little after two years ago. Ever since then, we've had a lot of better things since she remarried. but none of us like the man she married.

Student 10: In Wood Shop there is some trouble with lamps like the one I'm making. The bottom is high in the middle and lopsided on the edges it's a little hard trying to get it level with only a file. I've been working on it for about 3 months. . . .

Student 11: An other one of my sisters got in trouble and leave school. . . . There is just one thing I hate and thats being pittied because I am from a boarding school.

Student 12: At home too, I got in trouble with the police and got put on probation, and grounded by my perents. . . .

Student 13: Before seven or eitht months a big change was in my life. It was when I came for the first time in U. S. A. It was very difficult for me because I di'n't understand English at all. The English I had in Greece were too little to make me understand the American people. . . . And that's why I am alway silent. I do not say that I am unhappy with my new life but I am not as happy as I was before. . . . The Greecs have a different life they live very free even if they don't spend so much mony in one night as they do here.

Student 14: And know my dad just gave my brother me car a 63 chevy super sport 709 4 speed and so I have two cars and I don't know what to do with my ford I have 1200 dollars in it. . . . I make and ware from 36 to 45 dollars a week and that all go's to my car. but this summer I am going to work with my dad on the rail road and than I will be making good money for the cars.

Student 15: I'm poor at winning.

These youngsters are typical of the ones in my basic skills classes. They are probably also typical of at least one third of the high school students in this country. I think these excerpts show why I have not found tags like "slow," "vocational," "underachieving," and "disadvantaged" to be helpful in identifying my students. Photographs of them would point up the danger of those further generalities based upon skin color and physical features. I have tried, therefore, to set aside the tags and instead have sought to identify these students on the basis of their common needs. Over a period of several years my students have revealed a pattern. The pattern always contains these three areas of need:

1. *This* poor *student needs to improve verbal skills greatly.* My student hasn't had the kind and variety of language experiences that other students have. He is weak in reading, writing, speaking, and listening. He needs materials which pick him up at his point of development and give him basic work with words.

2. *The* poor *student needs success.* He has been bucking up against an educational system that is not designed for his needs or background. In our zeal to reach for the moon, literally, we are reaching right past him. We have been playing a vicious alphabet game.

It goes like this. We give the academically oriented student the dice. He rolls and gets an "A." The student I am describing usually has to play the same game, only he is using different dice. He rolls and gets "F." It doesn't surprise him; he always rolls an "F." He learned long ago that these dice are loaded. After awhile he stops playing the game.

Now, about success. My experiences with this student have convinced me that he appreciates a teacher's efforts to provide him with basic skills. Whenever I have been able to break through his defenses and have given him work which challenges him *at his level,* he has always responded by working hard to produce a product of which he and I can be proud. He enjoys being told "Well done!" as much as you and I do.

3. *The* poor *student needs to feel a personal value in subject matter.* By this I mean that the teacher has to select materials which interest the student, not the teacher. You have to take him at his own level of experiences—with his own set of values—and relate things from there.

These three elements are what the *poor* student needs: lots of basic language experiences, success, and subject matter with personal appeal. I try to build these three elements into all of the materials that I develop.

What materials work with the *poor* student?

This is the point at which most discussions of the *poor* student fail. The classroom teacher is able to see the danger of generalizations about this student. Often, the classroom teacher is also able to see that the existing curriculum is not designed for this student. But this place is where desperation sets in. The typical English teacher keenly feels the need to communicate about specific materials for this student. "Can you show me some materials that work?," many teachers have asked me.

Let me describe for this typical teacher a lesson that works with the *poor* student. I will try to show just exactly how the three areas of need—skills, success, and subject matter—can be incorporated in one type of lesson which I call the *extended activity*. The *extended activity* has this general structure: 1) it is a *unit* built around one theme; 2) it requires extended use of language for about five class periods; 3) it calls upon the student to use reading, writing, speaking and listening skills to produce a product; and 4) the central product in each *extended activity* is made of cardboard.

The theme of this particular *extended activity* is "The Internal Combustion Engine." This activity has five teaching goals: word study, writing skills, reading comprehension (nonfiction), speaking-listening skills, and following written directions.

I start the extended activity by passing out five parts to each student: word hunt sheets, cardboard model sheets, the central story, a final quiz, and a listening drill.

This is exactly how I teach with the gas engine extended activity.

Step one. The student does the word hunt.

This is a word study sheet based upon ten words selected from the story. For each word the student is given a picture clue, a meaning clue (short definition), and a spelling clue (the partially spelled word). There is also a number referring to the central story page upon which the word can be found in context. The student uses the clues to identify the word. He spells it correctly by supplying the missing letters. He writes it clearly in a blank and uses it in a sentence. The ten words are selected for general usefulness to the student and because they represent the specific vocabulary of the story. This is vocabulary work in its most basic sense: What are the combinations of letter symbols which represent the sound of the word? What is the meaning behind the sound symbols? How does the student accurately represent these sounds on paper so that meaning is communicated?

The word hunt also serves as an orientation to the activity.

Step two. The student reads the central story.

This is a simple story in which two boys acquire an old one-cylinder engine and discuss its function. In three pages, the student is presented with the function of a gas engine three different times.

Step three. The student does the listening drill.

This listening drill occurs midway in the story. It takes the form of a rough drawing of a gas engine which one of the boys in the story has drawn on the garage floor to help the other boy understand its function. The script which I, the teacher, read is supposedly part of the conversation. While I describe the function of each part of the engine, students listen and choose terms from a list with which to label each part on the drawing. Students then are scored on the basis of the number of parts which they were able to identify in this listening drill. Correct spelling of terms also affects the score.

Step four. The student builds the cardboard model.

After he finishes the story, the student takes the three sheets of cardboard. Sheet #1 contains a picture of the outline of a one-cylinder engine. Sheet # 2 is the parts sheet. It contains the moving parts and detailed written directions for building the model. Sheet # 3 is a backing sheet.

The student begins at the top of Sheet # 2 and follows the written directions independently. At first I must resist giving help. This is the student's project. He is going to demonstrate to himself and me that he can use printed words to produce a product. As he progresses through the steps, the student will probably come to me with his partly completed model. "What's wrong here?" he may ask, to which I reply, "Look at this part right here. Go back and check the words near the end of Step Three."

Or, often the student will come to me for encouragement: "Teacher, it says to join these three parts. Is this what it means?" In a case like this a quick nod from me will send him back to his seat trusting the written words more.

Often, the best possible teaching situation develops when one student will lean toward another and say, "Boy, did you mess that up! Can't you see what it says to do right here in Step # 4? It says put this part *down* through here not *up*."

Finally, the student brings his model to me for evaluation and I either praise an accurate job or send him back to read part of the instructions again. When he is done, he can say, "I used words to produce this product!"

Step five. The student takes the final quiz.

The quiz for this activity is a short "open book" essay quiz in which the student describes the four steps, or strokes, in the cycle of an internal combustion engine. To do this quiz he refers to the story and to his finished model. He does this carefully because he knows that he may need these sentences later to communicate to his classmates.

Step six. The student gives an oral demonstration.

Finally, several students are asked to give oral demonstrations using their cardboard models and the information they wrote on their final quizzes to describe for the rest of the class how a gas engine works. Other class members and I listen and criticize these short talks: Can the demonstrator communicate main ideas? Can he put things in the right sequence? Can he use specific words like "valve" and "cycle" instead of catch-all words like "things"?

When the student has finished this activity, he has had the kind of language experiences which meet his needs. He knows that both spoken and written words are useful tools. He trusts words better now. He will probably retain the meanings of special words like "cycle." He may, to some small degree, associate pleasure with reading now. He has *succeeded*, not failed, when he produced a product through the use of words. He has been willing to accept the teacher's help with all of this because he has felt, personally and immediately, the value of this lesson. When he hands in this activity for my final evaluation, it always gives him and me pleasure when I say, "Well done!"

Conclusion

To summarize this paper, I would like to go back to the title, "The Printed Page and the *Poor* Student." As you probably sense by now, this title is a fraud. With my theme being what it was, I didn't dare use one of the conventional tags; so I selected *poor*. However, I also selected this title so that I could accent what I have been saying about the abuse of educational tags as they are applied to basic-skills students. Here's what I mean. The tag *poor* can have at least three different connotations. It's all in how you say it. If, when you first saw this title you said "the *poor* student," you were thinking of social or cultural matters. If you said "the poor *student*," you were thinking about ability or achievement. If you said "the poor student!," you might have been reflecting upon the dearth of materials available which meet his needs. You see, the tag hinders communication just as the other tags for the basic skills student do.

You are welcome to my tag. It will be of no further value to me as I search for materials that contain the three elements: basic verbal skills, success through words, and subject matter with personal value.

What Materials Should Be Used In College Reading Courses?

LAWRENCE E. HAFNER
University of Georgia

TOO OFTEN a college freshman of some undiscovered potential turns up at college an intellectual ninety-seven pound weakling who wants to become a one-hundred-eighty-pound strongman. His mentors in some schools may be likened to an assortment of "doctors," "nurses," "dietitians," and "physical culture specialists" who are going to whip him into intellectual shape.

The "nurse" [testing specialist] examines him at the college induction station and finds that he is in fact a ninety-seven pound weakling in the information department; or as the German expression goes, *Er hat alles in Armen und nichts im Kopf,* and she duly notes this in his "medical" record. What about the doctors? He doesn't get to the doctor until he is decimated by the "ace-type critters" we are now going to vilify.

What does our "dietitian" [the student's advisor] do? She assigns him a carefully worked-out, tailored-to-his-needs (Eeny, meeny, miney, mo) diet comprised of 1/10 English Composition, 1/5 Socratic Dialogs, 1/5 Western Civilization, 1/5 College Algebra, and 1/10 Chemistry. What about the other fifth? Guess.

Enter the *ersatz* "physical culture specialists" [some of his professors] who forthwith drop three-hundred-pound barbells [texts] into his arms (crushing him, of course,) with instruction [assignments] to "lift these twenty times tonight as warm-up because tomorrow brings five-hundred-pound barbells, thirty times!" Then comes the *coup de grace,* the test of how he is developing, a nearly totally unrelated task of juggling five 50-pound cannon balls (taking an objective test when his study questions were essay, or vice versa) while doing a *piroutte.*

"Help! Help!" [Enter the doctor—a wise counselor or reading specialist.]

These good guys know that many of the ninety-seven-pound weaklings can develop into one-hundred-eighty-pound strongmen. They also know it cannot be done by the procedures just mentioned.

Students' problems and needs

The learner in college must receive ideas and transmit ideas. We say he must become adept in the language arts of reading, listening, writing, and speaking if he is to succeed in college. What, then, characterizes the ineffective student?

Lack of language arts skills

He lacks *reading-study* skills. Lacking these skills, we find him deficient in these ways: he doesn't like to read; he doesn't vary his approach according to difficulty of material and varying purposes; he doesn't know how to set these purposes; he is deficient in vocabulary and in general information; he doesn't support the main idea with relevant details; he reads only for facts or details; he can't get the gist of the material he is reading; he can't paraphrase ideas; he can't boil down material; he does not utilize available chapter aids.

He lacks *listening* skills. Many of the deficiencies in listening are related to the deficiencies in reading. Ralph G. Nichols has listed ten bad listening habits in an article titled, "What Can Be Done About Listening?" Some of these habits are those which characterize the inefficient listener in college: calling the subject dull (used as an excuse to let the mind wander); criticizing the speaker (should listen to *what* is said); listening only for facts (listen for main ideas); and tolerating distraction (the good listener "zeroes in"), etc.

He lacks *writing* skills. We find him unable to write a clear, coherent sentence; he is unable to classify ideas; consequently he cannot outline material; he cannot write a summary paragraph; he does not employ transitional devices; he cannot make reading notes; he cannot write a library paper; he cannot write essay examinations.

He lacks *speaking* skills. Some of the reading and writing skills enter into the picture here. In addition to lack of ability to organize and to deliver clear, forceful sentences, we find the student unable to make suitable introductions, to choose words effectively, to use rhetorical devices, to use appropriate illustrations, to use humor, to illustrate his points, to make concrete applications, to "wrap up" his speech, etc.

Skills related to understanding ideas, organizing them, and expressing them run as golden threads through these language arts strands. Although the college teacher of reading does not have primary responsibility for developing skills other than the reading-study skills, he finds it increasingly difficult to separate these interrelated language arts. He finds, too, that he can make substantive contributions in these development areas.

Lack of concepts that underlie specialized vocabulary terms

Levine (*7*) has pointed out that words for which we know the meanings separately can become meaningless in combination in a particular contextual setting if we do not understand the underlying concept. He points out that a person might know the meaning of "intermediate" (coming between) and of "frequency" (repeated occurrence of a thing at short intervals or periods) and still not know the the meaning of *intermediate frequency* as it is used in technical radio work. He favors, and I concur, subject matter teachers becoming responsible for teaching subject matter reading.

Personal problems and personality deficiencies

Although a college student probably will not manifest all of the language arts deficiencies previously noted or the various kinds of problems discussed in the following sections, he will manifest a certain number of them

and probably in clusters. Some of the *personal* problems which plague the college student are

1. *Anxiety associated with poor achievement in college.* Such anxiety can have a debilitating effect on the student's ability to think flexibly and to concentrate on his work. Anxiety, as measured by the Cattell 16 PF, appears to be associated with poor achievement in college (*2*).

2. *Lack of motivation.* An ill-defined purpose for being in college (*6*), lack of curiosity—those not profiting from a reading-study skills course did not like to read (*3*)—, and failure to accept long range goals (also characteristic of psychopathic personalities), are some behaviors associated with lack of motivation to pursue academic studies. On the other hand, Heil's (*4*) study of achieving scholars showed that "students admitted to the Scholar's Program, in contrast to those admitted to the regular program, appear to have . . . greater power needs and drive, and greater orientation toward inquiry."

3. *Lack of ego strength.* Hafner (*3*) made comparison on several personality variables of students who showed effective gains in grade point during the quarter they were enrolled in a reading-study skills course with those who showed ineffective gains. He concluded that his findings tend to corroborate those of Woolf (*12*) which showed a correlation between low ego strength and lack of success in intellectual endeavors. Heil's scholars, on the other hand, appear to have greater self-sufficiency and inner strength than students in a regular program. However, Hafner (*3*) found another type of self-sufficiency in non-achieving students which was characterized by rejection of ideas which, if accepted and applied, could have helped these students. Experience shows us, too, that many students do not realize that academic work in a first-rate college requires much diligent application of sophisticated reading-study skills.

Jackson (*5*) studied the gains or

lack of gains made by students with varying degrees of maladjustment symptoms (according to the MMPI) and found that reading gains were a function of personality. He concluded that forty percent of the participants needed to be diagnosed and treated for their personality deviations if the reading programs were to be effective with them. Hafner (3) came to similar conclusions as the result of his study. These findings make sense. Personality deviations can interfere with the ability to concentrate, and the ability to concentrate may well be the *sine qua non* of reading and study endeavors.

The preceding ideas were presented prior to the discussion of materials so that materials could be viewed in their proper perspective. No attempt will be made to relate personality problems to types of materials. People with personality problems, however, or even those without them, probably should not be subjected to either a speed reading program or a program emphasizing advanced organization skills if the students have comprehension deficiencies; *i.e.,* if they are not pretty good readers.

One or two pointers might be given. In addition to having the personality problems treated, the advisor and/or reading specialist should probably insist that the student who takes a reading-study course should be required to reduce his course load for that term. Too heavy a load greatly reduces the chances that he will carefully, thoughtfully, and diligently apply the skills he is being taught to the reading and study of his text materials. In addition, the one type of "self-sufficient" student probably should not be in the course unless he experiences a felt need and volunteers for help. Of course, there may be some exceptions to this idea. The anxious student may need a more structured course, and, above all, he will need to feel safe and unthreatened by the experience. The instructor would do well not to "come on too strong" with this type of student. Finally, what you do and the materials you use most not only have

real validity they must have *face* validity for the student.

Materials to use in a college reading program

After brief mention of some of the kinds of material available and a divagation into computer-assisted instruction, I would like to go into some detail in describing two kinds of materials, reading manuals and boxed materials (reading laboratories).

1. *Reading manuals.* Reading manuals are usually designed to help the student improve such skills as vocabulary, comprehension, interpretation, and critical reading.

2. *Study manuals.* Study manuals try to help a student schedule his time effectively, read efficiently, listen well, make effective notes, apply a study skill such as SQ3R, write objective and essay examinations insightfully, and write a term paper in an organized manner.

3. *Reading-study manuals.* Authors who try to combine reading and study helps into one volume usually have to sacrifice scope and depth to some extent.

4. *College texts.* The students' own textbooks and/or a variety of basic texts used in college work can be the main focus of a course or can be used in conjunction with other materials.

5. *Boxed materials.* Some reading and study materials have been graded, placed on neat and durable cards, and packaged. These kits, also called laboratories, can be used independently as practice materials or as the basis for direct teaching to an individual or small group.

6. *Reading machines, teaching machines, and computer-assisted instruction.* Technology has come a long way since the tachistoscope and the accelerator. Examples of present day accelerators are the SRA Rateometer and the Burson Electronics Reading Timer. Increasingly sophisticated *hardware* [machines] and *software* [programs and materials used in conjunction with the hardware] are being designed and manufactured.

Electronic Futures, Inc. (EFI), of North Haven, Connecticut, has developed the Audio Notebook System, a portable tape-recorder reproducer system powered by flashlight batteries or 110-220V AC. It is designed to help the student improve his language arts skills. EFI has developed remedial and developmental reading materials for children and adults. It also has a Wireless Multi-Channel Reading System which allows the teacher to simultaneously direct *separate* lessons from any source (Audio Notebook, phonograph, TV, tape recorder) to *various* groups regardless of their seating arrangements. In this system, each student learns independently at his own maximum learning rate as he receives simultaneously the audio and visual presentations of the material in question. Although I know of no research reports on the effectiveness of this material, I must say it does have face validity. Researchers should test out the other validities. College reading people should experiment with these systems and develop additional materials to use with them.

Educational Development Laboratories of Huntington, N. Y., has had a number of reading-study systems on the market for several years, and they are probably better known than those we have been discussing.

Another system that college reading people should know about, although they may not utilize it (depending on how ambitious they are), is the computer-assisted instructional (CAI) system. An example of this is the IBM 1500 Instructional System. In this system, a subject matter instructor utilizes a special author language called Coursewriter Language to program courses by entering data on instructional station keyboards. R. J. Siegel of IBM states that the IBM 1500 CAI system presents "lesson material at 'student stations.' A station may consist of a television-like viewing screen, an image projector, and an audio system. A student can respond to questions by typing an answer on a keyboard or by using a light pen to identify information on the viewing screen." He further states that lesson materials may be prepared and organized by educators into a series of statements and questions to be presented by the computer. In writing the lesson, the author anticipates a variety of student responses. If a student answers a question correctly, he proceeds with the lesson. If the answer is incorrect, an alternate sequence of instruction is provided automatically by the system to guide him to the correct answer and ultimately to a full understanding of the subject matter. Research data regarding the value of this system are available from IBM.

As with any type of material, these kinds of material can be used to advantage or to no advantage. Excellent machines plus excellent programs plus excellent methodology plus excellent, insightful teachers plus motivated students with promising capacity equal excellent results. The results will be less than excellent to the extent that any one of the variables in the equation is less than excellent. The same is true with other kinds of materials.

7. *Newspapers.* Excellent for developing vocabulary, critical reading skills, and informational backgrounds are the various metropolitan newspapers. Some of the top English language newspapers are the *New York Times, Christian Science Monitor, Milwaukee Journal, St. Louis Post-Dispatch, Washington Post, Atlanta Journal, Minneapolis Star, Seattle Times, Seattle Post-Intelligencer, San Francisco Examiner, Los Angeles Times, Manchester Guardian,* and *London Times.*

8. *Files of teacher-made exercises.* Can be prosaic or imaginative.

9. *Current events magazines. Newsweek* is veridical and varied in content. *Time* is exciting and controversial. *U. S. News and World Report* bulges with authoritative articles on business, economics, and government.

10. *Paperbacks.* "A hole is to dig," and a paperback is to carry around

with you and read. Keep a good supply of quality books around (which you read, too) and you and your course may be labeled AUTHENTIC.

Descriptions of selected reading manuals, study manuals, and boxed materials

BERINGAUSE, ARTHUR F. and DANIEL K. LOWENTHAL. *The Range of College Reading—Exercises in Improvement.* Boston: Houghton Mifflin, 1967.

This book contains reading selections from college texts in the humanities, business, social sciences, science, mathematics, and technologies. Each of these areas is further subdivided into subjects. For example, humanities contains reading selections from speech, English, music, and art. Range One, or part one, contains selections easier than those in Range Two or Range Three. After each selection one finds the following activities or exercises which are titled: 1. Short Answer Questions, 2. Vocabulary Study, 3. Mechanics, 4. Style, 5. Questions for Class Discussion, 6. Composition. An appendix contains references to selected supplementary readings. The selections contain a goodly number of pictorial illustrations, the ones accompanying the original texts.

CHRIST, FRANK L. *Study-Reading College Textbooks.* Chicago Science Research Associates, 1967.

This volume contains "exercises in chapter study and textbook reading." Christ points out that many a student reads a college text but neglects the "two thirds of the process that would make his efforts fruitful: *preparation* before reading and *summarizing* after reading."

First, the author explains the Study-Reading Method, including brief discussions on previewing and the SQ3R method. The body of the book is devoted to exercises in which the student applies the SQ3R method to excerpts from typical college textbooks.

Appendix A contains a comprehension exercise for each excerpt in the body of the work and also model survey question and review exercises.

FARQUHAR, WILLIAM W.; JOHN D. KRUMBOLTZ; and C. GILBERT WRENN. *Learning to Study.* New York: Ronald, 1960.

The authors state that their ideas concerning efficient study habits are ground upon important research findings. Could be useful to students in schools which espouse "non-teach," since it clearly places upon the student the responsibility for improving his study habits. This volume does not contain exercises for improving comprehension, but it does contain many practical suggestions for 1) developing self-understanding, 2) improving skill in remembering, 3) preparing for and writing examinations, 4) notemaking, and 5) writing effective reports.

HILL, WALTER, and WILLIAM ELLER. *Power in Reading Skills.* Belmont, California: Wadsworth, 1964.

The avowed purpose of this volume is to provide a comprehensive set of learning-practice materials in the advanced reading skills underlying powerful reading. The first power area explains a reading-study system called the Point procedure. Subsequent sections are devoted to the teaching of comprehension and organization skills using exercises constructed to move 1) "from smaller to larger reading units, 2) from specific comprehension to the organization of larger ideas, 3) from literal interpretation to inference and critical analysis, and 4) from slower rate of performance to faster rate of performance." The instructor who uses material such as this will need to experiment carefully to make sure he uses it to best advantage with·the particular types of students he has in his classes.

JONES, EVERETT L. *A New Approach to College Reading.* New York: Holt, Rinehart, and Winston, 1964.

Jones' approach to college reading does seem to be new. It strikes at the heart of a basic problem in reading improvement—the need to develop concepts and to improve language facility. This volume contains interesting essays on a variety of topics. Each essay is accompanied by ten-to-twenty topical suggestions for discussion and writing plus ten theme titles. A twenty-five item multiple choice test of vocabulary terms accompanies each essay.

For the unsophisticated student and teacher this approach may lack face validity. Many college students, however, could profit from the language development which could be induced through the discussions and other types of activities.

McDONALD, ARTHUR S., and GEORGE ZIMNY. *The Art of Good Reading.* Indianapolis: Bobbs-Merrill, 1963.

The authors have made "understanding and flexibility, the two main ingredients of effective reading, . . . the subject of this book." Chapter one contains selections which are pretests. Chapters two through nine contain four types of reading selections which form the basis of exercises designed to help a person develop into an effective reader. (Additional exercises are found in the last part of the book.) The types of selections are fiction, biographical sketches, social science, and commercial.

The various exercises are designed to help transform a person into a reader who overviews, reads flexibly, is well motivated, determines his purposes for reading, understands and critically evaluates what he reads, discovers the organization in what he reads, gives full attention to his reading, and remembers what is important to him in his reading—in short, is an effective reader.

ROBINSON, FRANCIS P. *Effective Study.* Revised Edition. New York: Harper & Brothers, 1961.

Robinson's approach to *quality* study is based upon research conducted by himself and others. In part one of the book he discusses higher-level work skills, including his oft-quoted, much copied, SQ3R method of studying. In the section on effective skill in examinations, Robinson discusses 1) the effect of type of examination upon review method, 2) techniques for taking essay examinations and objective examinations, and 3) making use of returned examinations. Part one also treats such topics as motivation to study and preparing reports. Part two is devoted to such topics as reading ability and writing skills. " . . . much of the student's practice and application must be done outside this book . . ., preferably (in) the student's actual textbook." The seven-page bibliography contains 177 entries, largely research studies.

In Appendix One can be found quizzes on chapters two through seven. Appendix Two contains a comprehension test, special reading skills tests, an English Survey Test, and a spelling test.

PARKER, DON H. *Reading Laboratory IV A, Grades 9-12.* Chicago: Science Research Associates.

In this kit one finds material designed to develop power of reading, rate of reading, and ability to listen and take notes. Each card in this series of graded exercises contains a reading selection, comprehension checks, exercises designed to increase vocabulary, and activities for improving word recognition skills. The reading selections use a variety of subjects and are usually read with considerable interest. Also included in the laboratory kit are placement tests, student record books, and a teacher's handbook.

PAUK, WALTER. *How to Study in College.* Boston: Houghton Mifflin, 1962.

This book tells the reader how to study effectively and efficiently. Pauk has developed well-written sections on such topics as taking lecture notes, taking reading notes, remembering what you learn, studying for and writing examinations, writing papers,

reading a textbook, and studying foreign languages, mathematics, and the natural sciences. The book does *not* contain exercises for developing comprehension and vocabulary skills although it does give some hints on developing these skills. The sections on taking notes and how to read a textbook appear to be particularly effective ones.

THURSTONE, T. G. *Reading for Understanding,* Grades 5 through College. Chicago: Science Research Associates.

This is a series of 400 graded lesson cards which fit neatly into a small box. Each card contains ten challenging paragraphs in a number of areas such as philosophy, science, sports, politics, and education. The student reads the paragraphs. The last word of the paragraph has been deleted. If the student fully understands the paragraph, he will be able to select the correct response from the four multiple choice responses provided. This material is interesting, in compact form, and does stimulate the reader to read in a careful inquiring manner. Placement tests, record booklets, and answer keys are provided.

SPACHE, GEORGE D., and PAUL C. BERG. *The Art of Efficient Reading.* Second Edition. New York: Macmillan, 1966.

Spache and Berg have treated many topics in this large (323-page) book—and have done so in a distinctive manner. The book is written on the premise that students need to "understand more clearly various ways of approaching their reading tasks" and that they need "sufficient practice in these techniques to enable them to achieve flexibility." The first section of the book is devoted to developing a number of reading approaches that can be applied to the acts of studying and reading. Section two emphasizes a system for analyzing difficult words, suggestions for gaining meaning clues from affixes and roots, and exercises on how to use the dictionary effectively. Section three contains hints on and exercises in reading materials in a variety of college subjects. The appendix discusses phonics clues in reading.

TAYLOR, STANFORD E., et al. *EDL Listen and Read Program.* Huntington, New York: Educational Developmental Laboratories, 1962.

The Listen and Read program is a developmental program in both reading and listening. It consists of thirty tape recordings and a student workbook which is used in conjunction with the tapes.

The program is designed to acquaint the student with the need for good listening and to "develop the ability to listen with greater attention, discrimination, organization, and retention." At the same time, a variety of reading skills, appreciations and understandings should be developed, according to the authors.

The topics covered in the tapes are important. For example, one finds topics such as Unlocking Sentence Meaning, Spotting Topics in Paragraphs, The Art of Notemaking, and Reading Between the Lines.

This material is intended for the secondary level but can be used on the college level.

Other useful books

BROWN, JAMES I. *Efficient Reading.* Revised Edition. Boston: D. C. Heath, 1962.

JUDSON, HORACE. *The Techniques of Reading.* Second Edition. New York: Harcourt, Brace & World, 1963.

LEEDY, PAUL D. *Read with Speed and Precision.* New York: McGraw-Hill, 1963.

MONROE, MARION; GWEN HORSMAN; and WILLIAM S. GRAY. *Basic Reading Skills for High School Use.* Revised Edition. Chicago: Scott, Foresman, 1958.

SCHICK, GEORGE B., and BERNARD SCHMIDT. *A Guidebook for the Teaching of Reading.* Chicago: Psychotechnics Press, no date.

SMITH, NILA BANTON. *Be A Better Reader.* Book VI Englewood Cliffs, New Jersey: Prentice-Hall.

SMITH, NILA BANTON. *Faster Reading Made Easy.* Englewood Cliffs, New Jersey: Prentice-Hall, 1963.

VAN GILDER, LESTER L., and SISTER M. LUCY ANN WASINGER. *Achieving Maturity Through High School Reading.* Dubuque: William C. Brown, 1967.

WEDEEN, SHIRLEY ULLMAN. *Advanced College Readers.* New York: G. P. Putnam's Sons, 1963.

Some notes on a sequence of courses

Hafner (3) found that his reading study skills course was successful in raising the grade point average of the participants enough to keep them in college. It did not, however, succeed in raising their reading comprehension significantly. Since a great emphasis was placed upon organizational and other kinds of study and examination skills and since the reading tests tend to have a speed element in them that seems to play havoc with individuals who have developed a study set, the foregoing results are not entirely unexpected.

Pauk (10) reported related findings. He compared the effectiveness of two courses designed to improve G.P.A.

Post-Course G.P.A.'s were compared in each instance with the G.P.A.'s of control groups. He found that the study-skill-only course yielded a mean increase in G.P.A. that was significantly better at the .01 level than the control group's efforts. The reading-and-study skills course yielded increases significantly better at the .05 level than the control group's results.

Wedeen (11) found that a six-week reading improvement course utilizing accelerators, films, lectures (to increase eye span), reading manual exercises for speed and comprehension, and the students' own texts resulted in short term gains in rate (.01 level) and very insignificant gains (.90 level) on vocabulary and comprehension. In both the short term and long term studies the experimental group was statistically superior to the control group in rate and vocabulary but inferior in comprehension.

Maxwell (8) has indicated that from twenty to thirty percent of the students who enter the University of Maryland Reading and Study Skills Laboratory "need intensive help in spelling and word attack skills prior to starting reading improvement work." She has developed an individualized course for helping students overcome these deficiencies. This course is considered to be a prerequisite to further work in reading study skills.

Earlier in this paper it was suggested that college reading people may not know whether they should try to incorporate computer-assisted instructional systems into their regimes. We could infer that Maxwell would say yes, for in another paper (9) she states that a reading-study skills lab can expand its services, although this might require more physical facilities eventually by making available to students for use in the laboratory tape recordings of the lectures of the various professors. Students enrolled in these courses can listen to these tapes as many times as they like. As the result of such activity at the University of Maryland, nine class members earned A's, compared with the prediction of three. Incipient, but not insipid! Furthermore, Maxwell has introduced a library of learning programs (tutor texts) in different subject areas. "Students find these valuable for reviewing course work and mastering fundamental principles. For example, a student may review college algebra or calculus, chemistry or physiology, or work on his vocabulary in German."

The studies by Hafner, Pauk, Wedeen, and others not cited here indicate to me that probably 1) study sets and reading test sets are antithetical, 2) rates gains are sometimes gotten at the expense of comprehension, 3) too many instructors try to accomplish too much in one course, and 4) study skills instruction yielded better G.P.A.'s than reading-study skills instruction. If I couple these conclusions with the studies done by Maxwell in spelling and word attack, Woolf in low ego strength, and Levine in technical vocabulary study, I conclude that there are many facets to reading-study-G.P.A. improvement and that certain of these facets are propaedeutic for others; this implies that for best results these reading-study improvement courses should be taken in sequence. Such a sequence might well be 1) Concept Learning and Vocabulary Study, 2) Spelling and Word Attack Skills, 3) Comprehension and Interpretation I, 4) Comprehension and Interpretation II, 5) Study Skills I, and 6) Study Skills II.

You may want to mix this up, bake it, and slice in a slightly different way. I would want you to. But I think one cannot deny that 1) as much or more instruction is needed in the receptive language arts as in the *transmissive* languages arts (speech, composition); 2) not all facets of the language arts can be taken up at once; 3) some logical and/or psychological sequence needs to be worked out; and 4) credit should be offered for these courses as they are for composition and speech. (Happily, there is a growing tendency

for colleges to offer credit for such reading-study courses.)

Summary

Many students who now do poorly in college because of skills deficiencies, personality deficiencies, personal problems, lack of concept background, and lack of sympathetic intelligent help from administration and faculty can do better. Psychologists, advisors, and reading specialists can team up to uncover and remedy personal, program, and skills deficiencies.

There is a wealth of materials and techniques which can be used to help the student improve step-by-step until he utilizes his talents efficiently and effectively. As reading specialists experiment with curricular offerings in their areas and with the prospects of putting their "receptive" courses into the regular curriculum, a new day will dawn for college students, a day of sunshine and hope, a day when their talents burst forth and they make the contributions they have wanted to make but didn't always know they were capable of making.

REFERENCES

1. Brown, Frederick G. "Study Habits and Attitudes, College Experience, and College Success," *Personnel and Guidance Journal, 43* (November 1964), 287-292.
2. Hafner, Lawrence E. "Relationships of Various Measures to the 'cloze,'" in Eric L. Thurston and Lawrence E. Hafner, (Eds.), *New Concepts in College-Adult Reading,* Thirteenth Yearbook of the National Reading Conference. Milwaukee: The National Reading Conference, Inc., 1964, 135-145.
3. Hafner, Lawrence E. "Improving Grade Point Average Through Reading-Study Skills Instruction," in George B. Schick, and Merrill M. May, (Eds.). *New Frontiers in College-Adult Reading,* Fifteenth Yearbook of the National Reading Conference, Inc., 1966, 46-57.
4. Heil, Louis M. "Scholastic and Personality Variables Associated with Acceptance to and Success in the Brooklyn College Scholar's Program," *The Superior Student, 7 (March-April 1965),* 34-40.
5. Jackson, Boyd B. "Reading Diagnosis, a Dilemma?" in J. Allen Figurel (Ed.), *Improvement of Reading Through Classroom Practice,* International Read-

ing Association Conference Proceedings, 1964, 156-158.

6. Kim, Ki Suk. "The Use of Certain Measurements of Academic Aptitude, Study Habits, Motivation, and Personality in the Prediction of Academic Achievement," *Dissertation Abstracts,* 18:150, January 1958.

7. Levine, Isidore. "The Limits of Individual Reading," *Journal of Reading, 10* (December 1966), 156-160.

8. Maxwell, Martha J. "A Self-Help Approach to Better Spelling as a Preliminary Step Toward Reading Improvement for College Students," *Journal of Reading, 6* (Winter 1963), 134-136.

9. Maxwell, Martha J. "The College Reading Laboratory," *Journal of Reading, 9* (May 1966), 402-405.

10. Pauk, Walter. "Study Skills and Scholastic Achievement," *The Reading Teacher, 19* (December 1965), 180-182, 186.

11. Wedeen, Shirley U. "A Two-Year Basic Skills Study," *Journal of Reading, 4* (January 1967), 231-237.

12. Woolf, Maurice. "Ego Strength and Reading Disability," In Eric L. Thurston, and Lawrence E. Hafner, (Eds.), *The Philosophical and Sociological Bases of Reading,* Fourteenth Yearbook of the National Reading Conference, Milwaukee: The National Reading Conference, Inc., 1965, 73-80.

Fair Use of Copyright Law and Instructional Materials

ROBERT E. SHAFER
Arizona State University

I WOULD LIKE to discuss the problems of selecting and evaluating materials for instruction in college reading courses with particular reference to certain provisions of the forthcoming new copyright law. These provisions at this writing have been passed by the house and are awaiting passage by the senate. Bill 597 has new and startling implications for teachers and college professors in all fields as they select and evaluate copyrighted materials for instruction. Particularly in those fields where the reading of printed material forms the primary basis for instruction, the college teacher needs to look carefully at the provisions of the newly prepared law. As we shall see, however, its provisions not only cover printed material but also extend to the uses of phono-records and films and any pictorial, graphic, or sculptural works, or any combination of these in any multimedia system.

Background for change

The current bills embodying the proposed new law represent more than six years of study conducted under the auspices of the Register of Copyrights in the Library of Congress with the participation of such interested parties as the Authors' League of America, the American Book Publishers' Council, the National Textbook Publishers' Institute, and the Ad Hoc Committee on Copyright Revision formed under the aegis of the National Education Association in 1963, and 35 to 40 educational organizations of which IRA is one.

All interested parties were in agreement that changing conditions, especially the new copying technologies, were creating situations which had been impossible to imagine in 1909 when the existing law was passed. As Dean Fred S. Siebert of the School of Communication Arts at Michigan State University noted:

> The present law was enacted when motion pictures were in their infancy and before the advent of radio and television. In addition, the 1909 act has not kept pace with the provisions of similar acts in most western countries or with the protection afforded artistic and creative works in the international conventions on this subject (*1*).

After many years of deliberation and study, we are on the threshold of a new copyright law. What are some of its implications for teaching professors, researchers, and others who select copyrighted materials for teaching?

In order to discuss the full significance of many of the proposed changes in the law, some further background is necessary. The first copyright law of the United States was enacted by the first Congress in 1790, in an exercise of the constitutional power "To promote the progress of science and useful arts, by securing for limited times to authors and inventors the exclusive right to their respective writings and discoveries" (*2*). Perhaps the key words in these lines are "limited times" and "exclusive right," for it is over the meanings of these terms that many teachers face problems in selecting and evaluating copyrighted instructional materials.

The concept of fair use

It seems clear that those most closely associated with the administration and application of the copyright law consider it basically a protective law "to insure that authors receive the encouragement they need and the remuneration they fairly deserve for their creations" (3). Section 106 of the proposed law sets out the following exclusive rights of the copyright holder: 1) the right to reproduce the work in copies or phono-records, 2) the right to prepare derivative works based on the copyrighted work, 3) the right to distribute copies or phono-records of the work to the public, 4) the right to perform the work publicly, and 5) the right to display the work publicly. These exclusive rights of the copyright holder are spelled out in Section 106 of the proposed law. Sections 107 through 116 deal with limitations on the exclusive rights of the copyright holder and may be considered to bestow certain rights and privileges on those members of the general public who must use copyrighted material. In certain cases these rights and privileges have been developed through judicial law in a body of cases over a long period of time. Such is the case with the concept of "fair use" which for the first time has been incorporated into the proposed new law. It is necessary for every teacher who uses or intends to use copyrighted materials without first obtaining the permission of the copyright holder to be acquainted with the doctrine of fair use.

Section 107 of the proposed new copyright law is currently phrased as follows:

Limitations on exclusive rights: fair use

Notwithstanding the provisions of Section 106, the fair use of a copyrighted work, including such use by reproduction in copies or phono-record or by any other means specified by that section for purposes such as criticism, comment, news reporting, teaching, scholarship, or research, is not an infringement of copyright. In determining whether the use made of a work in any particular case is a fair use, the factors to be considered shall include:

1. The purpose and character of the use;
2. The nature of the copyrighted work;
3. The amount and substantiality of the portion used in relation to the copyrighted work as a whole; and
4. The effect of the use upon the potential market for or value of the copyrighted work (4).

Whether a teacher or college professor can use a portion of a copyrighted work for the purpose of "criticism, comment, news reporting, teaching, scholarship, or research," without first obtaining written permission of the copyright holder and be secure in the knowledge that he is not an infringer, depends upon his estimate of the way a judge would apply the above four criteria in an infringement suit by the copyright holder. It will, therefore, be essentially impossible for any user of copyrighted materials to know *for certain* whether his copies of a portion of a newspaper editorial on the ditto machine or on a transparency really are fair use unless he can convince the copyright holder to take him to court. As a recent report of the committee on the judiciary states the issue:

> The expanded statement of the fair use doctrine in amended section 107 offers some guidance to users in determining when the principles of the doctrine apply. However, the endless variety of situations and combinations of circumstances that can arise in particular cases precludes the formulation of exact rules in the statute. . . . Beyond a very broad statutory explanation of what fair use is and some of the criteria applicable to it, the courts must be free to adapt the doctrine to particular situations on a case-by-case basis (5).

Since it is not possible for a teacher or professor to know precisely whether any given instance of his use of copyrighted material is a fair use, he must rely on his own judgment and knowledge of the new law (as well as the old) and of the intentions of those who drafted the new law when he makes his own estimate of fair use. It behooves all, therefore, who regularly select and evaluate and use copyrighted material for instructional or other purposes as stated above to become familiar with the provisions of the new law regarding fair use as well as the stated intentions of those who were most closely concerned with drafting the new law. (The specific intentions of the committee on the judiciary of the House of Representatives as regards the fair use section of the proposed new law are stated on pages 61-66 of the report of the committee. I have drawn upon them for the preparation of this paper.)

The application of fair use criteria

As stated previously, one of the criteria which would need to be considered by any teacher or college professor in selecting or evaluating instructional materials is *the purpose and nature of the use*. According to the report (p. 62), the proposed law would recognize "that the making of copies by a teacher for classroom purposes can, under appropriate circumstances, constitute a fair use. . . ." Other important points which would need to be considered by a judge deciding a fair use case or a teacher attempting to decide whether any projected use would indeed be fair would be the nonprofit character of the school and whether any charge was made for copies distributed.

An additional point raised is the element of spontaneity. Did the teacher make copies for himself and/or his students "acting individually and at his own volition," or did he do so because his department chairman suggested it? Other considerations would be whether the teacher made a single copy for himself (to read to the class or project on an overhead projector) or made multiple copies which were limited to the size of the class and were recalled or destroyed after a single use.

For example the complete reproduction of a fairly long poem in examination questions distributed to all members of a class might be fair use, while the distribution of separate copies of the poem without restrictions might not be (6).

The report goes on to point out that spontaneous copying which might be fair use in an isolated circumstance would become an infringement if the copies were accumulated over a period of time and incorporated so as to constitute an anthology.

The nature of the copyrighted work

Another fair use criterion which is essential in selecting and evaluating copyrighted instructional materials under the proposed new law is that of the "character" and "availability" of the copyrighted work. Questions which would undoubtedly be asked might be the following: 1) Is the copyrighted work intended to be consumable in the course of classroom activities, e.g., a workbook, standardized test answer sheet, etc.? If so, the principles of fair use "would have little if any application." 2) Would material in current newspapers and periodicals be more allowable under fair use than the type of text material mentioned above (7)?

Yes, as the register's report states:

With respect to material in newspapers and periodicals the doctrine of fair use should be liberally applied to allow copying of items of current interest to supplement and update the students' textbooks, but this would not extend to copying from periodicals published primarily for student use (8).

If the copyrighted work is "out-of-print" and unavailable for purchase through normal channels, the teacher or professor selecting it for classroom use may have more justification for copying it than in the ordinary case. The committee's report (9) points out that "the existence of organizations licensed to provide photo-copies of out-of-print works at reasonable costs is a factor to be considered." This would mean that the professor or teacher selecting an out-of-print copyright work would need to find out whether any organization was providing the out-of-print work for sale at a reasonable cost. If so, the doctrine of fair use would be less applicable to his own copying activity than if the work were not being offered for sale by such an organization. The committee's report also notes that "the applicability of the fair use doctrine to unpublished works is narrowly limited since, although the work is unavailable, this is the result of a deliberate choice on the part of the copyright owner" (10). In most cases, apparently, the copyright owner's "right for first publication" would outweigh any needs of copying material for classroom purposes.

The amount and substantiality of the material used

Can a teacher or professor, in the course of selecting and evaluating copyrighted instructional material, make a single copy of an entire copyrighted work for reproduction for an overhead projector or for other visual display purposes? In three and one half years of discussion and deliberation among the members of the educational community, the publishing community, and the committee on the judiciary, there is as yet no agreement on the exact meaning of the term "entire work or complete work" or the term "excerpt." The report of the committee on the judiciary states the following interpretation:

> The committee understands that this was not generally intended to extend beyond a "separately cognizable" or "self-contained" portion (for example, a single poem, story, or article) in a collective work, and that no privilege is sought to reproduce an entire collective work (for example, an encyclopedia, volume, a periodical issue, or a sizable integrated work published as an entity) a novel, treatise, monograph, etc. With this limitation, and subject to the other relevant criteria, the requested privilege of making a single copy appears appropriately to be within the scope of fair use. (11).

It should be kept in mind that this portion applies only to the making of a single copy and that the making of multiple copies under fair use applies only to excerpts. Considerable debate was also present during the three and one half years of deliberation between the various groups about the exact meaning of the term "excerpt." Once again, the report of the committee is enlightening in demonstrating consensus on what the problem is, if not on a satisfactory resolution of the problem.

> In general, and assuming the other necessary factors are present, the committee agrees that the copying, for classroom purposes, of extracts of portions, which are not self-contained and which are relatively "non-substantial in length," when compared to the larger, self-contained work from which they are taken, should be considered fair use. Depending on the circumstances, the same may also be true of very short, self-contained works such as a four-line poem, a map in a newspaper, a one-half page "vocabulary builder" from a monthly magazine, etc. (12).

This excerpt would seem to place the committee on the judiciary in the extremely hazardous position of judging that a four-line poem is less a "self-contained work" than a five-line poem and, therefore, more applicable to the doctrine of fair use. Would the committee, one wonders, restrict teachers to copying only four-line poems (as self-contained works) or should the committee not attempt to make a determination of this sort and, rather rely on the competencies of those teaching poetry to make a differentiation between a short poem and a long poem for the purposes of copying?

Effect of use on potential market or value of a work

This factor has long been considered to be the most important criterion of fair use and certainly, as the report of the committee on the judiciary points out, "With certain special exceptions (use in parodies or as evidence in court proceedings might be examples), a use which supplants any part of the normal market for a copyrighted work would ordinarily be considered an infringement" (13).

In the long course of debate over this particular provision between the representatives of the publishing industry, education, and various copyright attorneys, the representatives of the educational community serving on the Ad Hoc Committee were often convinced that neither the representatives of the publishing industry nor the copyright attorneys really understood that teachers were attempting to copy copyrighted material for nonprofit teaching purposes and not, by design, to deprive copyright owners of their legitimate profits. In fact, the point was made by both school and college teachers over and over again that only by using copyrighted material from literature, news media, etc., could literate audiences ultimately be produced. The fact that this point has not yet sufficiently penetrated the judicial mind is seen clearly in the report of the committee on the judiciary in the following statements, which reveal much about the legal attitudes toward this issue:

> Fair use is essentially supplementary by nature, and classroom copying that exceeds legitimate teaching aims, such as filling in missing information or bringing a subject up to date, would go beyond the proper bounds of fair use. Where the unauthorized copying displaces what realistically might have been a sale, no matter how minor the amount of money involved, the interests of the copyright owner need protection. Isolated instances of minor infringements, when multiplied, in many times become in aggregate a major inroad on copyright that must be prevented (14).

In this statement, we note that the committee on the judiciary apparently believes that "filling in missing information" or "bringing a subject up to date" "exceeds legitimate teaching aims." Most teachers and professors would thoroughly disagree with the fact that legitimate teaching aims do not include supplying needed information or being historically accurate in one's subject. How the latter aims could be considered "unauthorized copying" and not under fair use is difficult to reason. Perhaps the most controversial statement in the committee's statement as to judging the effect of use on the potential market or value of a work, however, is in asking the teacher or user of copyrighted material

to make a judgment about "what realistically might have been a sale, no matter how minor the amount of money involved." It would seem almost impossible for a teacher or professor to make such a judgment accurately, particularly when the term "no matter how minor the amount of money involved" has to be estimated. It is conceivable that many instances of fair use might involve the loss of a minor amount of money. This might not be the case, however, as in the example of a school system which simply could not afford to purchase newspapers for each student in a class. Under the proposed law the teacher will be forced to estimate whether the newspaper publisher would lose sales if he duplicates an excerpt from the paper. The teacher would also need to estimate the significance of the school system's wealth and intentions with respect to buying newspapers. So variable is piled upon variable, and the teacher's task in making a decision becomes enormously complicated, probably to the point of hopeless confusion on the part of many teachers.

Many of the most astute copyright attorneys, publishing house presidents, and others involved in copyright law revision continue to use language which clearly indicates that they have not yet seen some of the larger issues behind the pleas of the teachers, professors, librarians, and others who are primarily concerned with using copyrighted materials. Such terms (noted in the previous quotation) as "unauthorized copying" and "minor infringements" fly in the face of the accepted doctrine that there is a legal test for fair use. If the teacher or professor knows that some uses of copyrighted material are fair in teaching, research, commenting, criticizing, and news reporting, he also knows that he would not be doing "unauthorized copying" in certain situations. He is also aware that deciding whether his copying might be displacing "what might realistically have been a sale, no matter how minor the amount of money involved" places him in an almost untenable situation as regards making a decision in advance of doing the actual copying. The statement "Fair use is essentially supplementary by nature" is certainly not clear. As Harold Wigren (15), Chairman of the Ad Hoc Committee on Copyright Revision representing educational organizations, stated in his recent testimony before the subcommittee on Patents, Trade Marks, and Copyrights of the Senate Judiciary Committee:

> While the new section 107 and the house report are helpful in making determinations as to what might be used and what should not be allowed, there is nevertheless widespread disagreement still between publishers and educators despite several summit conferences to resolve our differences, as to what constitutes "fair use" of a work. Teachers still will have no positive assurance that a given use of a work is fair or permissible use. It is argued in some quarters that it is impossible to guarantee such certainty. Yet, if the experts cannot agree as to what constitutes the "fair use" of a work, how can a teacher in Pocatello, Idaho, know the answer?

It seems clear that almost any use of a given copyrighted work should in effect be ruled out by the statement *"where the unauthorized copying displaces what realistically might have been a sale, no matter how minor the amount of money involved* the interests of the copyright owner need protection" (16). That is, almost any use of a copyrighted work might involve a minor amount of money *if the work was to be used.*

Why use a small portion of one of the criteria to wipe out the doctrine of fair use when one has spent so much writing it carefully into the law and developing a variety of criteria which could be applied to a great variety of cases using copyrighted material for classroom purposes? At best this section of the committee's report seems inconsistent with what has gone before.

Selecting and evaluating new materials outside the classroom

The doctrine of fair use of copyrighted materials is also applicable to other kinds of uses, as for example, all stages in the operation of information storage and retrieval systems. The Committee's report states that "Reproduction of small excerpts or key words for purposes of input and output of bibliographic lists or short summaries might be examples of fair use in this area" (17). Also, the fair use doctrine applies to excerpts of copyrighted works used in educational broadcasting activities and photocopying in libraries. With regard to library copying, the following excerpt from the committee's report is helpful in understanding the problem:

> . . . an earlier effort to specify limited conditions under which libraries could supply photocopies of material was strongly criticized by both librarians and copyright owners, through for opposing reasons. The effort was dropped, and at the hearings, representatives of librarians urged that it not be revived; their position was that statutory provisions codifying or limiting present library practices in this area would crystallize a subject better left to flexible adjustment. On the other hand, both the American Council of Learned Societies and the Department of Health, Education, and Welfare argued that the problem is too important to be left uncertain and proposed adoption of a statutory provision allowing libraries to supply single photocopies of material under limited conditions. . . . Unauthorized library copying, like everything else, must be judged a fair use or an infringement on the basis of all of the applicable criteria and the facts of the particular case. Despite past efforts, reasonable arrangements involving a mutual understanding of what generally constitutes acceptable library practices in providing workable clearance and licensing conditions have not been achieved and are overdue. The committee urges all concerned to resume their efforts to reach an accommodation under which the needs of scholarship and the rights of authors would both be respected. (18).

Note that in this quotation the committee accepts the needs of "scholarship" as a legitimate use of copyrighted material but still uses the term "unauthorized" to describe the copying which would take place for scholarly purposes while recommending that each case is decided on its own merits after the application of the previously mentioned critera. In selecting and evaluating one does not know whether the copying is "unauthorized" until after the decision has been made by the court. As in the case of classroom copying, matters of the fair use criteria are applied only after the copyright holder has sued the copier as an infringer and as a result of the case the court renders a decision.

The Ad Hoc Committee on Copyright Law Revision, of which the International Reading Association is a member, is making further recommendations to the senate regarding the selection and evaluation of copyrighted materials in libraries and on educational broadcasting stations by means of the computer. It is clear, however, that the doctrines of fair use described above are considered applicable to all of these uses, but there are many questions remaining as to the ways in which they are applicable. New educational technologies are exploding, and one of the fears of members of the Ad Hoc Committee is that these educational technologies will not be provided for in the new bill. As Wigren points out in his testimony:

The bill makes no provision for new technology in teaching and learning; in fact, under the present paragraph D of section 110, entitled "Time and Content," the uses of copyrighted material without clearance or payment of royalties—on dial access retrievable systems or in computer assisted instruction, closed circuit television, 2500 megahertz, or on most audio-visual devices designed for individualized and independent learning are virtually eliminated.

If guidelines are needed to protect the copying of copyrighted materials for classroom uses, one would hope that they could be worked out by means of continued meetings with representatives of the various affected groups. Help will be needed in resolving some of the serious questions which lie ahead as educational technology develops. For example, as Wigren also points out, "the bill makes no mention of computers; nor does it provide language applicable to computers and computer uses, yet computers are one of the fastest growing technological advances in American education" (20).

Protection of innocent infringers

If a teacher or professor selects and evaluates instructional materials thinking that his use of these materials may be under fair use as stated earlier, he would be able only to project that the use actually would be as a result of a court decision. The copyright owner must bring an infringement suit against the user; and after the various fair use criteria above are applied in the individual case, the court will decide whether the use was indeed fair. Under section 504 of the proposed law, the copyright owner would be entitled to recover actual damages as well as "any profits of the infringer that are attributable to the infringment and are not taken into account in computing the actual damages." The report continues, the copyright owner may elect

at any time before the final judgment is rendered, to recover, instead of actual damages and profits, an award of statutory damages for all infringements involved in the action with respect to any one work for which any one infringer is liable individually, or for which any two or more infringers are liable jointly and severally, in a sum of not less than $250.00 or more than $10,000.00, as the court considers just (21).

If the court finds that the infringement was committed wilfully, the court may increase the award of statutory damages to a sum of not more than $20,000.00. The court also has the right in cases of alleged infringement involving teachers and professors to waive all statutory damages "in whole or in part." This applies

where an instructor in a non-profit educational institution, who infringed by reproducing a copyrighted work in copies or phonorecords for use in the course of face-to-face teaching activities in the classroom or similar place normally devoted to instruction, sustains the burden of proving that he believed and had reasonable grounds for believing that the reproduction was a fair use under Section 107 (22).

Although this provision would exempt classroom teachers and professors from the payment of statutory damages for infringements, it would not apply to librarians or to teachers on television and radio or to others operating under the doctrine of fair use who are not using copyrighted materials for teaching face-to-face teaching purposes in the classroom.

Summary

Although there are other educational uses of copyrighted materials in a variety of situations such as educational broadcasting, the primary emphasis in this paper has been to show how the doctrine of fair use is being written into the new and forthcoming copyright law currently passed by the House and under consideration in Senate Bill 597. This new law would apply to the copying of copyrighted materials by classroom teachers and professors in the course of selecting and evaluating various printed and audio-visual copyrighted materials for instruction with their students. Although many aspects of the application of these criteria to various types of classroom uses of copyrighted material were dealt with in the testimony before the house and senate committees and are therefore dealt with in some measure in the report of the house committee before the judiciary, it seems clear that most teachers and professors copying copyrighted material without permission in the expectation that their use is fair would not be sufficiently informed by the guidelines which currently exist in the committee reports so that they would know whether their potential uses of copyrighted material would be fair. If they guessed wrong, they could be liable for statutory damages between $250 and $10,000 per instance of copying. A distinct need remains to clarify both the intent of Congress as regards fair use and the development of specific guidelines for fair use.

Perhaps one of the most insightful statements on fair use by a copyright expert was published this year by Benjamin Kaplin, Royall professor of law in Harvard University in the James S. Carpentier lectures at Columbia University, in addressing the question of the varied rights of producers and consumers of copyrighted materials he said:

Educators pay a very large toll annually to copyright proprietors; but in certain respects, as non-profit users, they have long been favored by copyright doctrine and legislation, and they have long acted as though they were entitled to other favors that are perhaps not too clear under the law. Having already mentioned photocopying, I shall not touch the question of multiplication of tangible copies of works for teaching purposes except to say that the fact of an educational non-profit motive is generally considered to work towards excuse from liability in the sense of fair use. Here the revision bill would leave particular interpretations to the courts, as we have seen. . . . Under these arrangements, a great many educational uses are free of copyright accountability. Now, impressed by the sheer spread of educational uses, the Register thinks education should devote more of its money—always and inevitably in short supply—to compensating copyright owners; he is no longer satisfied with the simple statutory lines. The result in the revision bill is specific exemptions in lieu of the general. There would be an exemption for the performance or exhibition of any works in face-to-face non-profit teaching activities, but beware too strong a recreational element or having a lot of parents in the room at the time. Performance of non-dramatic literary musical works or exhibition of works by transmission as a part of the systematic non-profit instruction of students would be allowable within certain limits; but much of the programming of educational broadcasting stations would lose its existing exempt status. Now it is no wonder that the teachers and others who would be deprived by the new detailed code of some existing benefit are making loud moan; at the same time publishers claim to see their own eventual extinction in the encouragement given to the use of devices which can make one tangible copy serve in the place of many. It is hard to know where the ideal line of exemption should run; the Register's line, being nervous and finical, would probably begin to irk very soon. However, the notion held by some publishers, that the preferment of some educational users springs entirely from sentiment, not reason, seems to me wrong. It is wrong if we posit that copyright seeks an optimum combination of producers incentive with users benefits; that will justify preferment under conditions which can be generally described. At a certain point, no doubt, exact reason fails; and there I would join in the Register's call to all those here in battle to recognize that authorship, publishing, education, and research are inter-dependent and mutually supportive endeavors (23).

In our selection and evaluation of copyrighted materials, we need to remember that we work in an "interdependent" situation where the rights of both the creator and the user of copyrighted materials must serve the needs and interests of the public.

REFERENCES

1. Siebert, Fred S. "The Copyright Law," *The Educational Forum*, XXX, Number 1, 17-21.
2. *United States Constitution*, Article I, Section 8.
3. *Copyright Law Revision*, Committee on the Judiciary, House of Representatives, 89th Congress of the United States, 2nd Session, p. 32.
4. *A Bill for the General Revision of the Copyright Law, Title 17 of the United States Code*, Senate of the United States, 90th Congress, 1st Session, p. 8.
5. *Copyright Law Revision*, Committee on the Judiciary, House of Representatives, 89th Congress of the United States, 2nd Session, May 1966, p. 61.
6. *Ibid.*, p. 62.
7. *Ibid.*, p. 63.
8. *Copyright Law Revision*, Committee on the Judiciary, House of Representatives, 90th Congress of the United States, 1st session, March 1967, p. 31.
9. *Ibid.*, p. 34.
10. *Ibid.*, p. 34.
11. *Ibid.*, p. 35.
12. *Ibid.*, p. 35.
13. *Ibid.*, p. 35.
14. *Ibid.*, p. 35.
15. Wigren, Harold E. *Testimony before the Subcommittee on Patents, Trade Marks, and Copyrights*, Senate Judiciary Committee on S. 597, March 16, 1967, p. 5.
16. *Op. Cit.*, p. 5.
17. *Ibid.*, p. 35.
18. *Copyright Law Revision*, Committee on the Judiciary, House of Representatives, 90th Congress of the United States, 1st session, March 1967, p. 36.
19. *Op. Cit.*, p. 6.
20. *Ibid.*, p. 7.
21. *A Bill for the General Revision of the Copyright Law, Title 17 of the United States Code*, Senate of the United States, 90th Congress, 1st session, p. 8.
22. *Ibid.*, p. 44
23. Kaplin, Benjamin. *An Unhurried View of Copyright*. New York: Columbia University Press, 1967. 106-108.

Values and Limitations of Standardized Reading Tests

ADDIE S. MITCHELL
Morehouse College

IN THE HALF CENTURY since the pioneering efforts of men like Edward L. Thorndike and Arthur S. Otis in group testing of achievement and intelligence, the prevailing attitude toward standardized tests in general and the standardized reading test, in particular, has passed through several well-defined stages. After an early period of indifference and even suspicion, teachers and school officials often tried out tests merely because they were new. Later there developed in many quarters a childlike faith in the efficacy of objective tests and an uncritical acceptance of the results of standardized testing. This excess of faith gradually became less common, and a more critical and cautious attitude developed and still prevails. In most areas, there can be noted a healthy skepticism and a growing concern relative to the values and limitations of standardized reading tests, accompanied by greater care in interpreting test scores and choosing tests to be used. While there cannot be discerned any decrease in the use of reading tests, more emphasis than ever before is being placed on the need to improve the effectiveness of the construction, the administration, the interpretation, and the application of standardized test results.

What is a standardized reading test?

There are several main ways in which commercially distributed standardized reading tests differ from the tests made by the individual teacher for use with his class. Inherent in these features are some of the strengths as well as limitations of these evaluative instruments.

1. Typically, the standardized test is one which is produced by a test-publishing agency. While tests are sometimes developed and standardized in a mimeographed form for use by some restricted population, the standardized reading test, as we know it in the field of reading, is a published instrument.

2. It provides norms for various groups that are broadly representative of general reading performance throughout the country, as determined by the extent of the population on which the test was tried. Prior to publication, it has been given according to prescribed directions to a representative group of students; scores obtained from this "standardization" program comprise the norms that permit test users to compare the performances of their students with those of the larger, representative group.

3. In developing a standardized test, a careful study is made of all test items, and student performance on a preliminary form of the test is analyzed and evaluated so that the final instrument contains items designed to make the test both reliable and discriminating.

4. The standardized test is developed through the cooperative efforts of a number of persons, including test experts and editors of test items and aims to cover instructional objectives of a greater range than those typically covered by any teacher-made test. It is based on general reading skills, using fairly general content and objectives common to many schools over the country.

5. The standardized reading test makes possible the observation of a single sample of behavior on a predetermined set of reading activities, under a single set of circumstances, by one or more observers or examiners.

These distinctive features of the standardized test represent important advantages for some purposes and disadvantages for others. For example, the content of a published test is fixed or set, a condition making it an inflexible tool. Unless there are frequent revisions, content becomes out of date, and it is likely that certain older concepts will be unfamiliar to the examinees. Results from one standardized test may not be comparable to those secured from another; such tests, furthermore, cannot be adapted to special current needs, to local emphases, or to particular limited units of study without lessening their validity. Certain evaluative needs must be met through the teacher-made informal test.

There are at least four attributes of the standardized test which should be considered here: *validity* (the ability of the test to do the job we want it to do), *reliability* (the ability of the test to yield dependable and consistent scores), *objectivity* (the ability of the test to eliminate the influence of an examiner's opinion or prejudice, and thus allow equally competent users to obtain the same results when scoring), and *usability* or *practicality* (the ability of the test to provide for ease of administration, scoring, interpretation, and application). Included also under the quality of usability are the practical considerations of test costs and a satisfactory mechanical format.

Significant values of standardized reading tests

The values of standardized reading tests lie particularly in situations in which comparisons must be made—comparisons of reading achievement in one school with that of other schools, comparison of achievement in different areas of study, and comparison of reading achievement with apparent potential to determine approximate degree of reading retardation. By ascertaining the discrepancy which seems to exist between reading achievement and level of reading expectancy, an estimate may be made of whether a given student might be considered a disabled reader who could profit from special reading help in small-group or individual situations, whether he is a slow learner in need of a complete educational program adjusted to his slower

rate of progress, or whether retardation appears to be so slight as to render the case simply as corrective and capable of being handled in the regular classroom setting.

Standardized reading tests are also especially valuable when the following types of comparisons are to be made for individuals and groups and when decisions affecting the school curriculum must be made: 1) study of reading growth over a period of time after instruction to determine whether progress is more or less rapid than might be expected from pretest to post-test, 2) further identification of reading needs pursuant to complete diagnosis of reading disabilities, and 3) evaluation of the reading status of students from schools or classes on a common basis, as when a student transfers to a new school.

Since standardized reading tests fall into at least three broad categories— the reading survey, the survey test with diagnostic features, and the diagnostic test,— the reading teacher is provided with a wide spectrum of testing techniques and materials for reading evaluation. For example, there are study skills tests, vocabulary tests, oral reading tests, tests designed to measure competence in handling certain comprehension skills in work-type and narrative materials, and rate of comprehension tests. At lower levels, there are reading readiness tests, tests of perception and reading aptitude, word recognition tests (both visual and auditory discrimination being emphasized in particular ones), and tests designed to measure the extent of mastery of the basic sight vocabulary.

Limitations of standardized reading tests

While some of the limitations of standardized reading tests have been referred to elsewhere in this discussion, there are others of which we as reading teachers and potential users of these instruments should be cognizant. Though the better reading tests currently on the market cover a wide range of skills from perceiving symbols, getting meaning from them, and evaluating or interpreting this meaning and reacting to it, *no* standardized reading test can cover all of the specific objectives of reading instruction. Thus, a reading test may fall short of determining a student's responsiveness to reading; it does not, in fact, reveal the extent to which given students integrate reading into their total life experiences. Standardized reading tests, while making an effort to measure study skills, are quite useless in appraising *how* the student actually uses these skills to solve an intellectual problem. Such tests do not measure the affective domain—those aspects of feeling, appreciation, and reaction to printed matter which are so vital to the total act of reading. Even less adequate is the standardized test at the point of ascertaining the degree to which the individual *will* read and the type of reading material he will choose, after having measured the extent to which he *can* read. From still other points of view, standardized reading tests are limited; sampling of reading performance is often too short and time limits too demanding to reveal actual reading behavior comparable to that found in a typical school setting or a variety of situations. The teaching of reading is a complex undertaking, aiming to develop multiple outcomes. A specific existing test will provide one type of appraisal for only certain ones of these desired outcomes, while other goals are likely to be measured only through informal testing, teacher observation, and judgment. The choice of any particular standardized test must be made with these limitations in mind while raising questions concerning the objectives of instructions which the test can and cannot measure and analyzing the test itself to see the types of responses elicited, the relevance of questions to types of reading skills taught, and the extent to which content conforms to those outcomes which the reading program seeks to achieve.

Specific considerations

Measuring Vocabulary or Word Meaning. The commercial survey reading tests undertake to appraise only limited aspects of the whole range of reading skills. The subtests most frequently included in survey reading tests are word knowledge, paragraph reading or level of comprehension, and rate of comprehension. The test of word knowledge is usually of the multiple-choice variety; and because of the nature of the test (the time limits of the total test being of salient importance and usually constituting a period of sixty minutes or less), only a limited number of words can be provided. How adequate is a vocabulary measure which establishes one's knowledge of words on the basis of such a limited sample as thirty words? Should not this kind of standardized test be followed by additional measures of vocabulary? To what extent is the vocabulary score earned contaminated by word recognition difficulties? Is the student actually unfamiliar with items missed on the test or is he unable to pronouce the words? Only the teacher's ingenuity can determine the answer to the latter question; no provision is made on the standardized test of vocabulary or word meaning to ferret out word attack difficulties. It is at this point, then, that the vocabulary sections of standardized reading tests and pure vocabulary tests are limited, even though they may contain a fairly adequate sampling of words from various fields. To really answer the question of whether word recognition or word attack difficulties are hampering reading growth, the teacher must read aloud to the student at least a fair share of the items missed. If he responds correctly by providing an acceptable meaning of many of the words originally missed, it may well be concluded that he knows the meanings of these words, is not so impaired in vocabulary as his earned score indicates, but is in need of help with word attack. While this procedure introduces an informal element into the standardized test and cannot serve to alter the earned score, it provides the insight which the teacher needs to get at the root of the particular problem.

Second, a student may know quite a different meaning for a word from that provided among the multiple-choice items listed on the test. For example, let us suppose that the term "apprehension" is provided in a list of vocabulary items and that the correctly-keyed response is "misgiving." It is very likely that some students would be less familiar with this particular meaning than with that which relates to the "arrest or capture" of a criminal who has previously eluded the policeman. Or still others may be more accustomed to hearing the term "apprehension" used synonymously with "comprehension." In other words, word-meaning sections of standardized reading tests, as well as pure vocabulary tests, 1) are often limited by inadequate sampling of word knowledge through a highly circumscribed list of words, 2) do not provide opportunities within their structure for differentiating between word attack problems and word meaning difficulties, and 3) fail to make provisions for multiple meanings of given words.

Paragraph comprehension

The test of paragraph reading designed to yield a level-of-comprehension score usually involves silent reading of paragraphs of increasing length and difficulty, purporting to measure various comprehension skills through responses to questions which follow the reading. Only a critical examination of the single test items comprising a particular test will enable the potential user to tell how many items call merely for rote memory, the answering of factual questions covered in the passage, or the drawing of inferences and conclusions based on information given in the passage. To what extent is the student required to think, understand, apply, and trasfer rather than merely recall? The examination of the items of a test will reveal whether test items require the reader to ascertain the author's mood, tone, purpose, or intent; to understand main ideas and support-

ing details; or to understand literary devices, such as figurative language, the rhetorical sentence, and idiomatic expressions peculiar to our language. Reading with understanding is all of this and more. The components of the reading process are represented in different proportions in various standardized tests in varying degrees of effectiveness. The reading teacher must examine the actual test items to get a clear understanding of what skills and abilities the test is measuring; it is only as he so examines that he can judge whether the given standardized test is valid for *his* purposes.

Rate of comprehension

There is not always a positive relationship between rate of reading and comprehension. In fact, in certain disciplines there is an inverse or negative relationship between the two. When materials are difficult for the reader and the concepts, new and the vocabulary is technical, there is little relationship between rate and comprehension—the faster the student reads in such cases, the less he tends to comprehend. The positive relationship between rate and comprehension appears to be present only in very easy reading materials. How does the nature of the standardized test currently on the market influence the interaction of rate and comprehension? Few tests of rate of comprehension make any provisions for or give any insight into flexibility of rate, which is the ultimate goal in improving rate of comprehension. Often the time required in answering questions enters into the score earned for rate of reading; thus, a pure rate of reading score is not attained. On the other hand, when questions are asked at the end of a selection and these questions are untimed, there is little direct relationship between rate and comprehension since power, not speed of comprehension, is measured. The rate of reading score which one earns on a standardized test is dependent upon the requirements of the test, the length of the time sample, the type of reading material used, the difficulty of the material selected, and the types of questions asked. It appears that at present no single standardized test of rate of comprehension is available to take into account and measure adequately the flexibility of rate necessary for the wide variety of types of reading with which the mature reader is called upon to cope.

Summary

Standardized reading tests cannot be considered recent innovations in the process of evaluating reading achievement. It appears that at present standardized reading tests are more widely used than those in any other area, although achievement tests have been developed for practically every subject in the school curriculum. A great variety of both survey and diagnostic tests has been developed in the field of reading, ranging from tests of visual and auditory discrimination to tests of rate of comprehension. In view of the stated values and limitations of standardized reading tests, the reading teacher is making increased use of informal or teacher-made test exercises to supplement formal or standardized instruments in order to achieve effective evaluation. Some surveys show that the average classroom teacher uses five or six teacher-made tests for every standardized test employed. In a comprehensive program of reading evaluation which would facilitate forging ahead in the field of reading in the modern classroom, teachers must continue to utilize other techniques for assessing reading growth in conjunction with standardized reading tests. These include records and observational methods, oral and essay examinations, discussions, questionnaires, inventories, interviews, checklists and rating scales, personal reports, and projective-type techniques. For each of these and other evaluation techniques, many uses may be discerned in current practice for administrative needs, instructional purposes, guidance, and research. The adequacy of each method, each test, each procedure used in evaluation must be judged in relation to established objectives and the extent to which the test adequately measures these objectives.

REFERENCES

1. Crook, Frances E. "The Classroom Teacher and Standardized Tests," in Test Service Notebook, Number XXI. New York: World Book Company, 1956.
2. Figurel, J. Allen, (Ed.). Improvement of Reading Through Classroom Practice. International Reading Association Conference Proceedings, IX. Newark, Delaware: International Reading Association, 1964.
3. Horrocks, John E. Assessment of Behavior. Columbus, Ohio: Charles E. Merrill, 1966.
4. Lindvall, C. M. Testing and Evaluation: An Introduction. New York: Harcourt, Brace and World, Inc., 1961.
5. Lyman, Howard B. Test Scores and What They Mean. New Jersey: Prentice-Hall, Inc., 1963.
6. Mitchell, Addie S. "The Effects of Rate Training on the Academic Performance of Good Readers at the College Level." unpublished doctoral dissertation, The University of Chicago, 1965.
7. Robinson, Helen M., (Ed.). Evaluation of Reading, proceedings of the Annual Conference on Reading, XX, The University of Chicago Press, 1958.
8. Ross, C. C., and Julian C. Stanley. Measurement in Today's Schools. Prentice-Hall, Inc., 1961.
9. Spache, George D. Toward Better Reading. Illinois: Garrard Publishing Company, 1963.
10. Stauffer, Russell G., (Ed.). "Diagnosis of Reading Problems with Classroom Materials," The Reading Teacher, XIV. Newark, Delaware: International Reading Association, 1960.
11. Strang, Ruth. Diagnostic Teaching of Reading. New York: McGraw-Hill Book Company, 1964.
12. Thorndike, Robert L., and Elizabeth Hagen. Measurement and Evaluation in Psychology and Education. (Second edition) New York: John Wiley and Sons, Inc., 1962.

Interpreting the Results of Standardized Tests

STANLEY I. MOUR
University of Louisville

"... Relieve my languish and restore the light"
Sonnets to Delia, Samuel Daniel

THE PRECEDING QUOTATION reflects, I believe, the feelings of most teachers on each occasion requiring the interpretation of a standardized test. There is no task, save the preparation of grades, which is more painful. There is much languish but little light.

The purpose of this discussion is to express some ideas and opinions concerning important, but unheralded, factors which influence performance on standardized tests and, therefore, must be considered in the interpretation of such test results. Unfortunately, circumstances of time and space and the limitations of my competencies preclude the restoration of light as a result of this discussion; perhaps, however, a small spark may be kindled.

Purposes of standardized tests

Standardized tests are most often used by the teacher in order to 1) obtain information concerning the current status of general development in a particular skill or area, 2) obtain information concerning specific strengths and weaknesses in a particular skill or area, and 3) estimate expected levels of performance or predict particular behaviors.

While the specific purpose of a test may be stated in the title or in the manual, the premise upon which this paper is based is that the sole justification for administering *any* test is to obtain a deeper and more complete understanding of the child.

General considerations

Most teachers, through college course work, journal articles, and presentations at conferences and meetings, are aware of general considerations in the selection and use of standardized tests. Such considerations have most often been presented as a set of rhetorical questions concerning reliability, validity, administration, and scoring. In addition, the teacher is provided with a test manual; this manual, however, gives little information beyond the statistical data of the test—the portion least understood and consequently least read. While the manual does indicate at which grade level, percentile rank, or stanine a particular child has performed, it offers little else of value for a fair and adequate interpretation of the results.

Such considerations are, of course, important. They have, however, been reiterated so often that they approach being trite; and, perhaps more important, such criteria are too often emphasized to the exclusion of other equally pertinent criteria.

There is, for example, little in any test manual which aids the teacher in understanding the influence and importance of his role in the testing situation as a factor in the interpretation of the test scores. There is less which provides an understanding of the test and testing environment as a factor in test performance and, therefore, as a factor in interpretation of results. There is practically nothing which provides a basis for the teacher to understand the child and his background and environment as factors in the interpretation of standardized tests.

Factors related to the child

It is difficult for many teachers to imagine children coming from environments in which the values, behaviors, and attitudes are not similar to those held by the teacher. The blunt truth, however, is that not every child is from the middle class and all do not enter school ready and eager to learn. Nor does every child perceive school as the means by which the "good life" can be attained. On the contrary, there are children from families which are openly hostile to school and the concept of education. There are children from families where there is little intellectual stimulation, little language background, and few experiences which help provide the basis for readiness to learn. There are environments in which children merely exist.

When such learned behaviors as these are transferred to the school environment, a child's negative attitudes may very likely be manifested in disinterest, lack of motivation to perform, and even readiness to fail. It should be expected, then, that in a test situation this child generally reacts in a manner which inhibits rather than promotes his test performance; and, consequently, such a negative approach invariably results in a poor score, low performance, or failure. Unfortunately for this type of child the most frequent interpretation of his performance is "he just doesn't have it," *even though his inadequate performance may have absolutely no relation to his ability nor to the amount of knowledge he has assimilated.*

Conversely, assume for a moment that this same child with the same score came from an environment which, while favorable to the school, was not one in which more than a hint of intellectual stimulation could be provided. Does his score *mean the same* as it did previously?

I fear that too many teachers, largely because they have not been provided with the necessary background, make a surface interpretation of a test score and fail to consider whether the child has had ample opportunity to be exposed to the skills or behaviors required of him in the school environment. Many children, for a variety of reasons, have not been exposed to simple tasks and behaviors which we as teachers expect of children. When such a child is required to perform on a test which is designed to evaluate such skills and behaviors, he will perform poorly or not at all. But without sufficient knowledge and information about a child's development and background one cannot know whether the child performed at a low level because he lacked opportunity to learn and, therefore, had not developed the necessary skills, whether the child had such opportunity and failed because he lacked the ability to perform, or whether the child had the opportunity and the ability but would not perform. There is a vast difference between the child *who does not perform because he can't and the child who can perform but won't.*

I wonder, too, how many of us consider the child's perception of the test situation as a factor in his performance and, therefore, a necessary factor in the interpretation of the results? We assume that "children take tests in their stride and are not concerned." But is this true? For many children the test is always perceived as an experience filled with frustration and anxiety. On the other hand, there are individuals who possess a considerable amount of "test sophistication" and who perform well under such pressure and anxiety. Yet such factors are rarely, if ever, considered in the interpretation of a test score.

Children must also possess certain skills if they are to be successful on the standardized tests of today. To be sure, the child must possess knowledge; but he must be able to express this knowledge, and to do so he must possess certain skills of a physiological nature.

In order to perform adequately on a test, a child must first be able to interpret the directions adequately. He may possess all the knowledge necessary for a high level score on the test, but he must first understand what he is to do. This step may involve auditory or visual skills, or it may involve a combination of both. In any case, the child needs sufficient auditory and visual development to proceed beyond the set of directions.

Second, following the comprehension of the directions, the child must respond to a set of questions or tasks in order to express his ability to function on the test. On most of our present standardized tests such response is written, and the child must be able to grasp and guide a pencil in the production of the proper response. In the case of a required verbal response, he must have sufficient language development and background to produce and communicate a response.

Imagine for a moment a child whose eyes do not focus properly or a child whose auditory skills are inadequately developed, and imagine how he might approach a test which requires a high level of visual or auditory skills in order to perform adequately. Or worse, imagine a child experiencing a disorder or dysfunction of motor movements about to take a test as he is cautioned there is a time limit of twenty minutes on the test. How might his performance be affected, and how, in turn, might his performance affect the outcome of the test? Just what does his test score reflect?

Factors related to the test

In addition to the usual rhetorical questions one must ask about the statistics of a test, it is important in the interpretation of the results that the teacher understand what a test is and it is not, what a test can do and what it cannot do.

At best a test is an evaluation of a *sample* of skills or behaviors. No test can adequately or accurately measure all skills and behaviors in even one area. One, then, should expect a test to be fallible in that it samples a given behavior at a particular time and at a particular stage of a child's development. It is possible and probable, therefore, that a child might have strengths which could compensate for the weaknesses indicated by the test but that the test would not so indicate.

Another consideration concerning the nature of the test, and a consideration often overlooked, is whether the test is culturally fair. We have by now, I hope, become reconciled to the fact that no test can be "culture free" since everyone must develop within the framework of some culture; but rather, we should consider the cultural basis for the test and determine whether it can adequately and fairly evaluate individuals from different cultures. Assessing the cultural fairness or lack of cultural bias of a test is becoming increasingly important since many children who enter school are to some degree alienated from the cultural mainstream of the nation. Many, though native born, do not even speak standard American English.

A final factor relating to the test that we should consider in this brief discussion concerns the testing environment created by the test.

Mentally examine for a moment a reading test you currently use and consider the following questions: 1) How closely does the test approximate the day-to-day reading situations required of the children? (If the test environment is not reasonably close to the regular routine and environment of the classroom, then this fact must be considered in the interpretation of the test results.) 2) How realistic are the time limits of the test, if any; and how might the children react individually to the time limits? and 3) Are the test materials reasonably similar to the kinds of materials read by the children in class? (Not every story requires the child to respond to a multiple-choice item. Not every child responds as well to the essay-type of question; however, the types of materials and the types of responses required should be considered in the interpretation of the test results.)

I cannot answer these questions for you; but they are questions which you must answer if you are to make a fair and impartial evaluation of each child—and no child should receive less.

This brings me to the final area I wish to consider in the interpretation of standardized tests—you.

The teacher and the interpretation of test scores

While the purpose of testing, according to this paper, is to gain a deeper and better understanding of the child and while the child is the singularly most important individual in the school milieu, it is the teacher who has the power to regulate the testing situation and to make it a meaningful experience or merely another educational trauma. It seems, then, that the teacher has several important responsibilities.

First, the teacher must control the current impulse to overburden children with tests. He must make decisions concerning the value of the test in providing information necessary to understanding the child. The teacher must decide whether such information as the test can provide is significant and essential or whether the same information could be obtained through other equally valid means.

Second, it is imperative that the teacher know everything possible about each child in the testing situation in order to consider the emotional and intellectual impact of the test upon the child. The teacher must learn more about the child's perception of the test situation.

Third, it is imperative that the teacher be thoroughly familiar with every aspect of the test ranging from the statistics as explained in the manual to an understanding of the test passages and questions. Only then can the teacher understand what the test is and what it is not.

Finally, it is incumbent upon each teacher to interpret to each child the purpose of the test, the reason it is being given, what the test scores mean, and how such scores are to be used.

Summary

In the limited space permitted, I have attempted to outline and discuss briefly some of the factors I believe a teacher must consider in the interpretation of standardized tests. I have mentioned, but not discussed, some of the very familiar criteria which have been used over the years to the exclusion of other important criteria. This paper, however, has focused upon factors which I believe need to be considered. These factors relate to the nature of the teacher in the test environment.

It is my hope that this paper will serve as a catalyst in bringing about a better understanding of test results and will, perhaps, cast light on other factors which need to be considered in the interpretation of standardized tests.

Ascertaining Instructional Levels

MORTON BOTEL
University of Pennsylvania

ARE THESE TRUTHS self-evident?

1. Each pupil is unique, and his reading program must be tailored to this uniqueness.
2. The reading program includes library books, readers, subject matter textbooks, and newspapers.
3. If so, it follows that each pupil must be reading materials in which he is fluent in oral reading and in which his comprehension of vocabulary, details, and main ideas is very high.

Interestingly enough, we find many teachers, supervisors, and school systems who affirm these ideas in written and oral statements of beliefs but whose programs do not reflect such verbal affirmations. For example, in these same schools we find pupils whose oral reading can be characterized as dysfluent and whose comprehension is fuzzy or worse in one or more of the reading-media forms mentioned above. In too many instances such crippling performance is evident in all reading media. It is also true at the other extreme that pupils may be using materials which offer no challenge. Either extreme illustrates how a school, in practice, tries to fit the pupil to a nonfitting book rather than to fit the book to the pupil.

Our rationale for fitting books to the pupil is based on both psychological and linguistic evidence. From a psychological point of view we have evidence that the most efficient learning takes place where pupils are highly motivated, where their self-esteem is enhanced, and where they have rather full comprehension of what they are doing. For those who are overplaced in reading, such lack of success leads to discouragement, loss of dignity or ego support, withdrawal, and often to hostility. At the opposite extreme, to the underplaced the lack of challenge offers inadequate opportunity for involvement, and the effect is to dampen the enthusiasm of these able pupils.

From a linguistic point of view we know that pupils who are dysfluent will find it difficult to make the proper connection between the melodies of oral language and the incomplete representation of these language structures in writing. Some of the fundamental meaning in language, as we know from our studies in linguistics, as expressed through the intonational structures of stress, pitch, and juncture. If we encumber the poor reader with written material which he cannot decode easily from the point of view of word recognition and attack, how can we expect him to provide for himself these missing intonational features?

Given this psychological and linguistic rationale as the basis for matching pupils with readable books, we need to adopt or invent procedures for accomplishing this purpose for each pupil at every grade level in every subject. It has been my experience that this goal will not be achieved generally in a school unless it is spelled out as a matter of policy and implemented in well-defined ways.

In general these procedures are all variations of the informal reading inventory which usually defines the limits of three reading levels for each pupil as summarized in the following chart:

Levels	Performance in Context	
	Oral	Silent
	Fluency	Comprehension
Independent	99-100%	95 to 100%
Instructional	95- 98%	75 to 94%
Frustration or Overplacement	less than 95%	less than 75%

Some significant schoolwide procedures which are concerned with ascertaining and placing pupils at their instructional levels are: 1) informal teacher appraisal, 2) check-out procedures, and 3) the Informal Reading Inventory and placement tests.

Informal teacher appraisal

There is no doubt in my mind that informal teacher appraisal in every subject and in every grade is the ideal approach to the continuous problem of ascertaining instructional levels. Every time a pupil reads aloud and answers a questions or completes an activity sheet independently the teacher can determine whether the criteria indicated in the preceding chart are being met. If not, the sensitive teacher can immediately provide such needed help in overcoming the problems leading to lack of fluency or inadequate comprehension as the following:

a). The use of an easier book in a series,

b). More preparation before the pupil is asked to work independently,

c). The substitutions of easy, wide reading experiences for a time, and

d). The substitution of other more appropriate media for the frustrating book.

Check-out procedures

Many of the school systems I have served have instituted check-out procedures by which reading specialists, master teachers, or principals share with the teacher the responsibility of advancing pupils when they have "mastered" a book in a structured series according to the IRI criteria chartered earlier.

Sometimes this check-out is done in the classroom; sometimes it is done in the principal's office. Sometimes the teacher and class listen in as each pupil reads; sometimes the pupil reads only to the collaborating specialist. To check his oral reading fluency a pupil may be asked to reread familiar stories in the back of his "completed" reader; sometimes he may be asked to read orally at sight in the next reader.

As a check on extent of comprehension, nothing seems to us a more valid criterion or more reliable a measure than the average performance of a pupil on the pages of the workbook he has completed *independently*. Additional comprehension checks may be obtained by asking the pupil questions about stories he has just read or by asking him to summarize briefly the most important ideas or events in a paragraph, a page, or a story.

I have used a variation of this check-out procedure as a basic element in evaluations and surveys I have conducted for schools. These schools are asked to keep a record of the percentage of accuracy of each pupil on five pages of the reading workbook he is using and to record the percentage of accuracy of the oral sight reading of each pupil on 100 running words in the next story in his reader.

comprehensiveness, and practicality for the classroom teacher. All, however. provide an estimate of the instructional levels of pupils. Our own Botel Reading Inventory (3)—a measure easy to administer and interpret and consider-

READING FLUENCY AND COMPREHENSION SURVEY

Directions: 1. *Under Oral Reading Fluency* record the percent of words in 100 running words in a new story which the pupils read correctly. Errors are words which pupils mispronounce, refuse to pronounce within five seconds, omit, or insert.

2. *Under Comprehension* record the percent of accuracy on each of five successive pages in the pupil's workbook which he has completed independently.

Pupil	Percent of Oral Reading Fluency	Percent of Comprehension					
		1	2	3	4	5	Average

Pupils failing to achieve a score of at least 75% in average comprehension *and* at least 95% in oral reading are regarded as probably overplaced. In some schools, particularly in so-called culturally disadvantaged areas, I have found instances in some classes in which almost every pupil is overplaced in basal readers and in textbooks in the subject areas.

A simple and useful variation of the check-out which I recommend to parents and librarians is this: after a pupil has chosen a book from the library or for purchase, he should be given the "five-finger" check. You do this by marking off or noting a 100-word sequence of words that looks typical of the book and have the pupil read it aloud at sight. If you count more than five errors, the book is probably too difficult and the child should be guided to a more appropriate book.

Reading inventories

Anyone may develop reading inventories by using pages from structured or scaled reading materials as described in many sources (1, 2, 4, 5). Others may be obtained from reading clinics and some publishers (37). Reading inventories vary in length,

ate of the time pressures of the teacher of 25 or more pupils—was developed with the classroom teacher in mind.

In any event, and this is most important, we must regard the results on these reading inventories as starting points. Nothing can take the place of the continuous informal teacher appraisal after the first estimate has been made by the use of the reading inventory. Only if we follow this procedure are we assured high validity and reliability of our appraisals. Continuous appraisal provides the most meaningful validity in that it is based directly upon the materials and methods we are using and provides high reliability in that our pace and even our level can be modified if a pattern of unsatisfactory fluency or comprehension develops.

The significance which we have come to attach to ascertaining instructional levels and to effective placement of pupils using such methods as described in this paper is probably best expressed by the fact that we believe the eleventh commandment is: Thou shalt not overplace pupils.

REFERENCES

1. Betts, Emmett A. *Foundations of Reading Instruction.* New York: American Book Company, 1957, 438-485.

2. Botel, Morton. *How to Teach Reading.* Chicago: Follett Publishing Company, 1959, 15-24.
3. Botel, Morton. *The Botel Reading Inventory.* Chicago: Follett Publishing Company, 1961.
4. Harris, Albert J. *How To Increase Reading Ability.* New York: Longmans, Green & Co., (Fourth edition) 1961, 152, 161.
5. Johnson, Marjorie, and Roy Kress. *Informal Reading Inventories.* Newark, Delaware: International Reading Association, 1965.
6. Karlin, Robert. *Teaching Reading in High School.* Indianapolis: Bobbs-Merrill Company, Inc., 1964, 73-78.
7. McCracken, Robert. *The Standard Inventory.* Bellingham, Washington: Western Washington State College, 1966.

Pinpointing Specific Skill Needs

NITA M. WYATT
University of Kansas

LATER IN THIS SERIES "The Diagnostic Teaching of Reading" is discussed. It seems quite appropriate that the topic "Pinpointing Specific Skill Needs" should precede such a presentation, for in the classroom the pinpointing of specific needs certainly must precede diagnostic teaching. It makes little sense to teach a child what he already knows, but avoiding such repetition requires a "diagnostic" frame of mind on the part of the teacher. She must be able to determine what the child already knows and can do, and plan the instructional program for the child around that knowledge.

It also seems significant to me that this discussion follows one entitled "Determining Instructional Level." The determining of instructional level is a starting point for diagnostic teaching, but much more information is needed about a child after the instructional level is determined. A study done in 1953 by Mary Watkins at Minnesota pointed up this need very emphatically (2). Her study compared the reading behavior of third grade children making normal progress in reading with that of children in grades four, five, and six reading at the third grade level. She selected 64 pairs of students, each of which was composed of a retarded reader and a normal-progress reader. The children were matched on mean reading grade, IQ, and sex. The Gates Diagnostic Reading Tests, Monroe's Diagnostic Reading Examination, and the Bond Silent Reading Diagnostic Tests were administered. She found that the same total reading score is no indication that the readers possess similar reading patterns. It is conceivable that when instructional level is determined through an informal inventory technique, two readers operating at third grade level may have quite different skill needs.

Pinpointing the skill needs of a child reading at the third grade level would involve a study of the total reading process. Space does not permit the discussion of all the skills which need to be assessed. I would, therefore, like to assume the reader is familiar with some diagnostic procedures and turn his attention to an area which has been of particular interest ot me recently. This is the area of phonics teaching and, specifically, the equating by some teachers of teaching phonics with teaching reading.

Watkins found in her study that there is a distinct difference between normal progress readers and retarded readers. When she pinpointed the skills which differentiated one group from the other, she found that retarded readers were slower readers than normal-progress readers. She also found that "retarded readers seem to possess more phonetic knowledge than the normal-progress group but the retarded readers *do not apply this knowledge.*" This finding would lead one to hypothesize that teaching "phonics" may not be all there is to the teaching of reading skills.

There is some evidence that we can accelerate word study skills or "phonics" knowledge as measured by the reading of word lists. We can do this by developing an instructional program which devotes time and attention to sound-symbol correspondence and the teaching of various rules or generalizations. The following graph depicts the results of an intensive use of

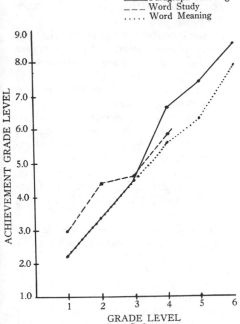

_____ Paragraph Meaning
_ _ _ Word Study
. . . . Word Meaning

GRADE LEVEL

an extraneous phonics program along with a basal reader in a suburban school district. It is interesting to note that there was not automatic accompaniment of increased skill in reading meaningful connected material with the increase in word study and word reading skills. At second grade level the ability of the children to sound out words seemed far in advance of their abilities to apply this knowledge in connected reading.

The same tendency was noted in the results of one of the First Grade Reading Studies. One experimental approach, called the "linguistic phonic" approach, emphasized sounding from the beginning. The children were expected to use their knowledge of sound-letter relationships immediately in connected reading—the sounding program was not an extraneous one. The table below indicates the results at the first and second grade levels:

At each of the grade levels it can be noted that the linguistic phonic approach produced significantly greater mean scores in word reading and word study than the other two approaches, which used commonly known basal readers. It was possible to produce significantly better performance in "word reading" through emphasizing phonics, but there was no significant gain in reading-connected material through producing greater skill in sounding. Perhaps, as Eisenberg says in commenting about several instances in which brain-damaged children were observed to be fluent in oral reading but quite deficient in comprehension, ". . .they indicate the complex nature of the reading process, in which word recognition and sentence comprehension are separable skills" (1).

Observation of the reading skills of children involved in the first grade study just discussed led to the hypothesis that the bright children in the linguistic-phonic approach behaved differently from the slow children. One would expect the bright children to read better, of course, but there seemed to be a qualitative difference in

Scores on the Stanford Achievement Test for Three Groups of First Graders
Taught With Three Approaches to Reading Instruction

Group	Word Reading	Word Meaning	Paragraph Meaning	Word Study
FIRST GRADE				
Sex grouping*	24.4		25.5	40.8
Linguistic-phonic	27.4**		25.8	42.7**
Control*	23.0		23.9	40.4
SECOND GRADE				
Sex grouping*		19.3	33.7	38.5
Linguistic-phonic		22.1*	35.3	42.1**
Control*		18.4	31.0	37.2

* Groups using basal readers.
** Score significantly greater than scores of other groups (.05 level).

their behavior. This observation prompted a study of the scores on a standardized test of two groups called "good readers" and "poor readers." Good readers were arbitrarily defined as those who scored at or above grade level 3.1 on the Paragraph Meaning subtest of the Stanford Achievement Test. Poor readers were defined as those who scored at or below grade level 1.7 on the same test. The mean scores of both groups on the Word Reading and Paragraph Meaning subtests were then determined and are reported in the following table:

Group	Number of Students	Word Reading	Paragraph Meaning
Good Readers	25	3.1	3.4
Poor Readers	35	2.7	2.5

It is interesting to note the reversal of position of the two groups on the Word Reading and Paragraph Meaning subtests. The poor readers seemed better able to read word lists than to read connected material, but this ability did not seem to be true of the good readers. Further evidence of this trend was provided through the observation that 19 of the 25 good readers had higher scores on paragraph meaning than on word meaning. Among the poor readers, 28 of the 35 had higher scores on word reading than on paragraph meaning.

These observations and those cited earlier lead to the hypothesis that we need to give more attention to what a child *does* as he is reading connected material rather than to what he *knows* about reading. These "application skills" need to be pinpointed if we are to help children become better readers. The assessment of such skills must be done largely through individual contacts with children as they read or talk about how they read. The emphasis of the remainder of this will, therefore, not be upon what tests can be administered but upon what kinds of behavior a teacher may look for in observing the child in the reading process.

Although the "application" or "integration" skills are not well defined,

there are some behaviors that I believe I have observed more often among good readers than among poor readers. It seems to me that the good reader more often

1. uses context to predict what an unknown word may be *before* the analysis process begins or *as* the process beings,
2. visually disects a word into pronounceable units,
3. measures the sounds he is producing through phonetic analysis of a word against his store of familiar pronunciations, and
4. varies the sound value given to a particular letter or cluster of letters until a recognizable word is produced.

Although most children possess some knowledge associated with these skills soon after they enter school, what they know, in some cases, really cannot be used in the process of reading because of the way it was presented originally. Let us consider each of the skills listed above and note some possible ways of assessing the child's performance of each. We must also be concerned throughout the discussion with the child's ability to combine the skills into a usable technique.

The good reader uses context to predict what an unknown word may be before the analysis process begins or as the process begins.

The use of context may well be the major skill which distinguishes connected meaningful reading from reading of word lists. It implies that a reader mentally interprets groups of words rather than one word at a time, In silent reading, the reader stores up his visual impressions until he has a meaningful group of words to interpret. In oral reading the eyes are traveling far enough ahead of the voice to give the mind time to group the words and to decide upon the appropriate pitch, stress, and pause patterns to give to the words when they are said. This grouping procedure provides a valuable clue in word analysis, for it tells the reader what type of word to expect in a particular place in a sentence. Word order and structural clues can tell a child whether an unknown word is a noun, a verb, an adjective, or an adverb; and this identification gives him some idea of what the word is. Whether a child groups words in reading can be detected in oral reading through the intonation he produces. Word-by-word reading is often indicated by the use of the same pitch and stress for every word.

Assuming that a child does group words into a meaningful context, we may still find that he does not use this tool as fully as he might in word analysis. Quite often the teacher advises the child to adopt a procedure which puts checking the context after the analysis of the word in question or minimizes the use of context. "Sound it out" is often the first response of a teacher to a child's failure to recognize a word. "What would make sense?" would be a better response. The child's analysis of a word may be a more cursory one, a more speedy one, if he has the word in mind before he begins to try to pronounce it from an analysis of the letters representing it. With this skill the assessment may need to involve the teacher's behavior as well as the characteristic behavior of the child or the habit of blindly groping at sounds will be constantly reinforced by the teacher. Some indication of the presence of the skill of using context as a springboard into word analysis may be inferred from observing a child pronounce just one syllable of a word and then produce the whole word without further study of the spelling of the word. Adults may approximate for themselves the difficulties of word analysis without the use of context by revealing the letters of an isolated word one-by-one and trying to pronounce them. This task may be contrasted with the revealing of the letters of a word after the surrounding context has been studied.

The good reader visually disects a word into pronounceable units.

A child may know what a syllable is and may know the rules of syllabica-

tion; he may be able to say a word and tell how many syllables it has without being able to use syllabication in reading. In the reading process a child must look at a string of letters printed on the page and produce some sounds from the looking. If the string of letters is a long one, he may need to look at only a few of them, pronounce the sounds, then look at more letters, pronounce more sounds, and so on. The real problem for the child then is "How many of these letters should I consider in the first attempt at pronouncing?" How far should he "look into" this word? Exercises in which the child looks at a word in a list, pronounces it from past contact with it, listens to the sounds, and then marks off the syllables in the printed word have little relevance to the task of "looking into" a word which is unknown. Again the instructional program as well as the child's characteristic behavior needs to be assessed. The lack of the skill of dissecting a word visually *while* reading may be inferred from the child's performance. Such behaviors as refusing to attempt a pronunciation of a new word, consistently producing a sound for the first consonant only, or erratic visual searching for any known element in the word reveal a lack of skill. Skill with visual analysis may be inferred from attempts to pronounce hunks of words as they occur from left to right. Skill in *word analysis* may be inferred from the combination of this visual analysis with checking of context.

The good reader measures the sounds he is producing through phonetic analysis of a word against his store of familiar pronunciations.

Since there are so many ways of representing a particular sound in English spelling, a child's first attempt at pronouncing may produce only a distant approximation of the word which is recorded. The good reader seems to have the habit of listening to such an approximation and trying to match it with some word stored in his vocabulary bank. For example, a first grade child attempting the word *secret* said *sĕc'ret* and then changed immediately to the appropriate pronunciation. She produced *kīnd jer gar* for *kindergarten* and, again, after pronouncing only a part of the word, moved to an accurate pronunciation. Another child, who had difficulty using her word analysis skills in connected reading, said *fac tó ry* for *factory.* She proceeded with the rest of the sentence without adjusting the word. When she was asked whether she knew a word that made sense which sounded like the one she had produced, she immediately said, "Oh, that's *factory,* isn't it?"

Although this first grade child was able to produce *kindergarten* and *secret* from approximations of the words, she was not able to produce accurate pronunciations of *career* and *financial.* These words were far above her experience level and were not yet words that belonged to her oral vocabulary. Her extensive vocabulary helped her with the analysis of many words but not every word which she encountered. The child who has a very meager oral vocabulary finds word analysis a difficult task. He often has no word against which to match his attempts at sounding. The instructional program for such a child might well concentrate upon vocabulary building through an enriched oral language program.

The good reader varies the sound value given to a particular letter or cluster of letters until a recognizable word is produced.

If you came to the unknown word *gead* in something you were reading, how would you pronounce it? Context would not help much because this word is meaningless. Your first attempt at pronunciation would probably lead to rhyming it with *bead,* but it might also rhyme with *bread* or have the vowel sound heard in *break.* The good reader tries several pronunciations, trying to make the word fit into a pattern he knows. The poor reader often stops with one pronunciation, if he gets that far. Maturity in this skill is indicated when a child attempts several pronunciations of a

word and then goes to a dictionary or glossary if none of his attempts produces a word he recognizes. Of course, he must also be able to *use* diacritical markings to produce an accurate pronunciation when he does go to a dictionary.

Summary

In discussing the topic "Pinpointing Specific Skill Needs" I have deliberately ignored many of the specific skills which the teacher needs to consider in teaching reading. I have hypothesized some skills which are not readily measurable but which seems to me to be important as I observe reading disability cases. An accompanying hypothesis that they are also teachable is implied. Major points suggested for further study, both in the classroom and in controlled research, follow:

1. Connected reading requires an integration of several skills which may not be required in reading word lists.

2. The good reader more often relies on use of context and a broad oral vocabulary than does the poor reader.

3. A poor reader may be a poor reader because he has a meager oral vocabulary.

4. The good reader produces several approximations of a word and constantly matches his approximations with words he knows which would make sense in the context he is dealing with.

5. It seems possible to teach phonics knowledge without teaching the application of such knowledge in connected reading.

REFERENCES

1. Eisenberg, Leon. "The Epidemiology of Reading Retardation and a Program for Preventive Intervention," *The Disabled Reader,* John Money (Ed.). Baltimore: Johns Hopkins Press, 1966, 14.
2. Watkins, Mary. "A Comparison of the Reading Proficiencies of Normal Progress and Reading Disability Cases of the Same IQ and Reading Level," unpublished doctoral dissertation, University of Minnesota, 1953.

New Developments in the Evaluation of Critical Reading

MARTHA L. KING
Ohio State University

DEVELOPING A NATION of critical readers appears to be an educational aim more lauded than comprehended, more sought-after than accomplished. For despite the improvement in general literacy statistics of the nations, teachers and other thoughtful citizens are showing increasing alarm over the inability of Americans to read critically. Much has been written about the probable causes of this special reading deficiency. Vague and ambiguous concepts of the nature of critical reading, inadequate definition of the specific skills involved, insufficient instructional materials and techniques, and the limited abilities of teachers to instruct pupils in these higher level reading skills are commonly identified as inhibiting factors. A fifth deterrant has undoubtedly been the lack of procedures and instruments to use in evaluating the achievement of pupils in this area.

Teachers tend to teach best those subjects and skills that are regularly and directly evaluated in the schools' organized testing programs. In reading this means, then, that word recognition skills, literal comprehension skills, knowledge of vocabulary, and some interpretation and study skills are the facets of reading best taught because these are the skills that are covered in the standardized tests most frequently used in elementary schools. Only rarely do such tests include items that require pupils to identify the author's opinion, detect hidden meanings, interpret figurative language or tone, or make generalizations from the facts given. Items which require the examinee to identify omission of important facts, irrelevant data, discrepancies in information, inappropriate analogies, and persuasive use of words are completely missing from elementary school reading tests. Yet, through newspapers, magazines, and television, youngsters daily confront reading materials in which such reading skills are needed.

It is the purpose of this paper to describe two types of evaluation instruments that were developed at Ohio State University as a necessary part of a research study of the feasibility of teaching critical reading at the elementary school level. When the researchers began designing procedures for teaching critical reading skills to pupils in grades one through six, it soon became apparent that new instruments for measuring effectiveness of instruction were needed. Recognizing that critical reading is a complex dynamic process involving various types of thinking, two very different kinds of evaluation instruments were devised. One was a battery of three tests, which were constructed for grades one through six, to measure the growth in achievement of the identified critical reading skills. The second technique was developed to measure the quality and kind of thinking that occurred when children were engaged in critical reading and discussion activities in the classroom. This second instrument also enabled the teacher to assess to a limited degree the effectiveness of her verbal behavior in stimulating the critical reading-thinking habits of her pupils.

Developing a test of critical reading

Developing a test of critical reading skills for elementary school pupils was an arduous task because the skills of critical reading had not been identified and precisely clarified. Moreover, finding reading matter or writing new materials that would test critical reading ability and still be within the readability competence of the examinees was extremely difficult. The first step in test construction was that of clarifying that aspect of reading ability commonly referred to as critical reading. What knowledge and skills were essential for the critical reader? From a search of the literature a long list of reading skills, thought to be basic to critical reading, was compiled. This list was sent for validation to a panel of reading experts across the nation. They were asked to critically analyze the list, to rate the importance of each skill, to suggest other skills that should be added, and to indicate those that should be omitted. The revised group of critical reading skills was further validated by classroom observations of critical reading lessons, in which the completeness of the list of skills was checked. Despite the care that was used in developing the list of skills, duplication and overlapping were evident in the resulting list. Some skills, moreover, were very similar; others were quite distinct. To assure both balance and preciseness in the definition, the skills were categorized into three major groups. All of the items that concerned the validity (reasonableness) and reliability (trustworthiness) of reading materials were classified as *logic* skills. Included were drawing conclusions from stated premises, identifying unstated premises, identifying fallacies in reasoning, and recognizing persuasive devices in writing. The language skills were classified either under logic or the second major classification, *literary analysis* skills. Skills that involved recognizing and judging persuasive use of words, vague and imprecise words, and the multiple meanings conveyed by a single word were included with the logic skills. The literary analysis category contained such language-related skills as interpreting and evaluating metaphor, symbolism, personification, alliteration, and authentic speech. Other skills included under literary analysis were related to identification, analysis, and evaluation of 1) forms of writing; 2) the components of literature such as characterization, plot structure, setting, and theme; and 3) the literary devices that make up the author's style.

Those skills that involved going beyond a single piece of writing and comparing or evaluating it according to external factors were designated *general skills*. This group consisted of such abilities as identifying, comparing, and evaluating sources; judging the author's viewpoint and competence; determining the publisher's (or sponsor's) commitments; and comparing multiple sources in order to verify information.

Constructing test items

Critical reading *ability* results from the readers not only knowing about and identifying such features of writing as logical fallacies, literary form, or the point-of-view of the author but also from their skill in analyzing, comparing, and judging various aspects of the written material. Constructing a useful evaluation instrument, then, called for devising test items that required the reader not only *to recognize* faulty reasoning, discrepant information, and elements of the author's style but also *to judge* the trustworthiness, truthfulness, and quality of materials. An example of a question which requires the reader *to recognize* and judge a statement—in this case a false analogy—is the following:

> A boy is like a tree. He must stand straight and tall.
> What is wrong with these sentences?
> 1. Trees are always straight, but boys are not.
> 2. Trees are always straighter than boys.
> 3. Boys are not as tall as trees.
> 4. Boys are not like trees in most ways.

The next question expects the reader to *analyze* statements and *apply* knowledge to reach a valid conclusion from a series of statements:

> Anyone who is on a TV show is rich. Captain Kangaroo is on a TV show.
> If the above statements are true, what else must be true?
> 1. Captain Kangaroo is rich.
> 2. People who are not on a TV show are poor.
> 3. Captain Kangaroo may be rich.
> 4. Anyone on a TV show may be rich.

In the example that follows the children are expected to make a *judgment* about the kind of question Bill's mother asked:

John told his mother about his new friend, Bill. His mother said, "Is your friend a good boy or a bad boy?"

What is wrong with this question?

1. Bill may be good one time and not so good at another time.
2. Bill might be better than John.
3. John's mother knew Bill was a good boy.
4. Bill was John's friend, so he was good.

Other questions in the test asked the examinee to compare two sources for likenesses and differences in content, form, author's purpose, and facts provided. The following illustrations from the primary form of the test show that students also were expected to go beyond the text provided in making judgments about the material.

LET'S READ ABOUT SEA SHELLS

What are sea shells? Sea shells are the hard coverings of many kinds of sea animals that belong to the mollusk family. Mollusks are animals with soft bodies. They are animals without backbones. The shell is the house that the mollusk lives in. There are many things that you can learn by looking at sea shells. One sea animal, the nautilus, grows a new room each time he gets bigger. When he adds a new room, he closes up the old one. Some shells have 30 rooms in them.

HOUSES FROM THE SEA

My sister and I walked along the beach with our empty pails. The ocean waves rolled in and out. The waves surprised us by leaving many shells lying on the wet sand. Many of the shells reminded us of butterflies, angel wings, Chinese hats, staircases, fans, tops, castles, and boats. We filled our pails with all kinds of shells. We found one large beautiful shell. When we held it up to our ears, we could hear the sound of the ocean. We want our friends to see our shells. We will tell you the funny names we made up.

Pretend you want to share a shell collection with your class. Which story would you read to find out more about sea shells?

1. The first story because it tells more about the sea shells.
2. The second story because there are funny names we can use.
3. The first story because mollusks are funny animals.
4. The second story because it talks about the ocean waves.

In what way do you think the two stories are different?

1. One is about a girl and a boy, and one is about backbones.
2. One is about a family, and one is about a house.
3. One has information about sea shells, and one is a story about collecting shells.
4. One has facts about angel wings, butterflies, Chinese hats, fans, and castles; and the other story has facts about houses.

What should the person who wrote the *first story* have done?

1. Gone deep sea fishing.
2. Studied about sea animals.
3. Studied about the nautilus.
4. Made a collection of sea shells.

Due to the practical necessity of constructing a testing instrument that could be administered to elementary school pupils within reasonable time limits, only a sampling of the extensive list of critical reading abilities could be included. Selection of items for the initial forms of the tests was based upon criteria of appropriateness for the grade levels tested and the uniqueness of the skill. For example, if two abilities were judged to be very similar, such as recognizing the propaganda devices of namecalling and plain folk technique, only one item was included. Parallel items were written for each of the skills selected for both primary and intermediate grades. These were then organized into four trial forms of the test—two for pupils in grades one through three, and two for pupils in grades four through six. The tests were then administered to a population of 3,017 pupils in ten elementary schools in a four-state area. Results of this administration furnished data for both item analysis and coefficients of reliability of the two forms at each grade level. Following the item analysis, final forms of the primary test and intermediate test were constructed on the basis of two additional criteria: the discriminating power and the difficulty of the test items. The reliability of coefficients for the two trial forms ranged from .72 to .86 for the different grade levels. Although these were not exceptionally high, they were considered adequate for the purpose of this test, which was to assess growth of pupils in specific skills.

Norming the final forms

Three forms of the Critical Reading Test were finally constructed. There were two primary forms, which differed primarily in the readability of the items, and one intermediate form. Both of the primary forms contained 10 questions pertaining to "general" skills category; 17 questions in the *logic* classification, which included propaganda devices and semantics questions; and 15 in the *literary analysis* category, which included literary form, plot structure, theme, characterization, and literary devices. The intermediate test was longer than the primary and was divided as follows: 15 items tested the general skills of comparing sources, determining author's competence and purpose, and selecting relevant sources; 21 questions were focused on logic skills; and 18 items pertained to literary analysis. The revised tests were administered to a second national sample for purposes of norming. Forty-six school systems in eight states in four geographical regions provided norming data from 3,527 pupils. Detailed data pertaining to grade level norms, coefficients of reliability of the final forms, and factor analysis are not given here but are available in a paper written by Bernice Ellinger (2).

How adequate is the test?

Comparison of the mean scores across grade levels shows that the level 2 primary test was very difficult for grade two in both spring and fall administrations and that the intermediate test was difficult for fourth graders in the fall testing, especially. Further investigation will show whether the forms of the test should be further revised for readability or moved up one grade level each.

The main criterion for judging the adequacy of a test is the degree to which it measures what it professes to measure. The skills that are included in the Ohio State Critical Reading Test were submitted to a group of recognized reading authorities for validation before items were written. In other words, the skills included in the test were judged by these authorities to be essential to critical reading. How successful the item writers were in devising questions that actually test the skills identified is yet to be determined. Factor analysis of the test, which is still in progress, will provide better data regarding the internal validity of the instruments.

Ralph Tyler has said that evaluation of learning should be considered a dynamic process that continues to change according to changing educational concepts, conditions, and purposes of evaluation. The developers of this test of critical reading view it as an embryonic effort that will change and improve as it continues to be used, researched, and revised.

Classroom observations as an evaluative technique

Paper and pencil tests provide one kind of evaluation data about pupils—that is, an indication of their level of accomplishment in selected skills or learning tasks at a given time. Such instruments do not provide appraisal data about the learning conditions that foster a specific type of behavior, nor do they furnish information about the thinking processes that pupils use as they are engaged in such cognitive tasks as critical reading. Inasmuch as critical reading is a thinking act in response to written communication, it is highly important that teachers have tools for analyzing and evaluating children's thinking processes as revealed, not only by written responses, but by verbal responses, also. Research in the areas of teacher behavior and children's thinking has emphasized the importance of the teacher's language in fostering intellectual growth in children. From her studies of teaching strategies and the development of cognitive processes, Taba concluded that a teacher's questions play a crucial role in the development of pupil's thinking skills because her questions circumscribe the mental operations which pupils can perform and determine which modes of thought they learn (3).

It follows reasonably, then, that evaluation procedures, designed to give the teacher feedback about the kind and quality of thinking that was observable in the verbal interaction between herself and the students, should provide clues to ways of improving the instructional process. Such evaluation techniques should not only reveal the pupil's growth but should furnish data about the effectiveness of the teacher's language.

The second type of evaluation instrument that was developed and used in the Ohio State University Research Study of Children's Critical Reading was an observation scale. This tool enabled the researchers to analyze the relationship between the teacher's verbalizations and the pupils' responses and to assess the changes (or improvements) in both teacher and pupil utterances that occured during the eight months of study. To fulfill the purposes of the research study an observation instrument, which would permit the classification of both qualitative and quantitative verbal behaviors, was devised. The scale consisted of two related category systems: one for recording the teachers' utterances and the other for noting the pupils' responses. The eight categories for classifying the teachers' talk show some influence of Bloom's *Taxonomy (1)*; the definiitons of the terms, however, have been altered and limited as is shown in the following definitions:

Specific facts: All talk that is intended to bring specific information to the learners.

Clarifying: Statements or questions used to refine previously discussed ideas or those misinterpreted by individuals; included are definitions, illustrations, rephrasing, or emphasis on a prior point.

Interpreting or Inferring: Providing meanings that go beyond the literal ones given in the written material. Included are the personal meanings which the reader associates with the text and his interpretation of the author's hidden meanings.

Analyzing: The statements or questions that require an identification and examination of component parts of a piece of writing, a situation, or a phrase; the nature of the relationship of the parts; and the internal consistency of the whole piece.

Applying: The statements or questions that require a direct application of information or criteria to another situation or piece of information.

Summarizing: A synthesis of preceding information and ideas, often showing relationships between parts, is the object of such questions and statements.

Evaluation: Statements or questions in which a judgment based upon criteria is made or expected. Both personal values and public criteria are bases for making judgments.

The main criterion for determining the five pupil categories was the differentiation of levels of thinking that were observable in their responses. Here the mental operations as identified by Guilford in the structure of the intellect proved useful in defining the separate types of thinking. The five different types of thinking—cognition, memory, convergent and divergent production, and evaluation—were arranged in a continuum horizontally across the top of the observation scale. *Cognition and memory,* which were grouped together and defined as literally understanding and relating what had been read or previously stated, were classified as level 2; *convergent responses,* those that indicated interpretation, illustrations, or reorganization of the content, were designated as level 3; *divergent responses,* those that revealed theorizing, hypothesizing, or making new and unique applications information and ideas, were classified at level 4. Level 5 was reserved for responses that showed that pupils had made an *evaluative judgment* based upon personal or public criteria. Responses were classified at level 1 when there was evidence of guessing or random thoughts. Both level 3 and 4 responses were considered essential prerequisites to critical reading, but level 5 responses were judged to be the most desirable because of the evaluative nature of critical reading.

During the experimental year of the critical reading research study, 24 classroom teachers, four at each of the first six grade levels, were regularly observed while teaching reading. One half of the teachers (the experimental group) were given special materials and instruction in critical reading while the remaining twelve (the control group) had no special instruction in critical reading but were provided an equal amount of instruction and materials in selected areas of children's literature.

The purpose of the observations was to collect data pertaining to the similarities and differences in the verbal behavior of both teachers and pupils in the two groups and to ascertain what kinds of changes, if any, occurred during the time of the study. Each teacher was observed six times, providing a total of 144 observations for analysis. Two trained observers at each session made on-the-spot categorization of the teachers' statements or questions and the pupils' responses. Teachers' statements and questions were classified according to the seven types designated above. Pupils' responses were recorded in the same horizontal rows as the preceding statement or question made by the teacher; the responses, however, were classified within the rows according to the level of thinking exhibited. The observation instrument provided a graphic representation of the type of utterances the teacher made, the quality of responses given by the pupils, and the reciprocal relationship between the two.

The analysis of the 144 observations produced some interesting and encouraging data, which have implications for the evaluation of critical reading. First of all, the study revealed that both groups of teachers improved their questioning behavior. They decreased their use of specific fact questions and increased their use of more thought-stimulating questions. Experimental teachers changed in the direction of asking more interpreting, analyzing, and evaluating questions; control teachers moved toward asking more applying questions. Apparently, knowing how to ask different kinds of questions for various purposes leads to greater improvement than do intuition or desire. The control teachers wanted to teach increasingly better lessons and did improve; the experimental teachers who had some training in the art of asking questions asked significantly more questions, however, that demanded analytical and evaluative responses.

The findings further revealed a significant relationship between the teachers' questions and the intellectual effort exhibited in the pupils' responses. Those teachers who asked more interpreting, analyzing, and evaluating questions elicited from their pupils higher levels of thinking which could be classified as inferring, illustrating, hypothesizing, theorizing, and evaluating. Improvement in pupils' ability to engage in higher levels of thinking was noted during the time of the study, also. The experimental pupils, especially, were observed to give significantly more responses at the highest evaluative level. It appears that pupils may become increasingly aware of the goals of reading instruction through the questions the teacher asks; and that when they clearly understand the expectation to think more deeply or in a variety of ways, they are motivated to meet the expectation.

The observation procedures just described involved several outside observers because they were used to collect research data; the techniques, however, are adaptable to regular classroom situations. By recording reading instructional sessions on audio or video tape, the individual teacher can replay, listen to the recordings, and analyze the verbal exchange between herself and the children. If she samples instructional sessions regularly over a period of time, the teacher will be able to evaluate changes in her language and that of the children. One first grade teacher who regularly sampled the discussion in one reading group for a period of two months observed that when she asked better questions, the children responded with more independent and thoughtful contributions. She noted further that the parroting of answers, which was common among the first graders, decreased; children who seldom spoke at the beginning of the observations made worthwhile contributions after six weeks; children increased the length and number of sentences used; and pupils moved in the direction of responding to one another rather than to the teacher. Also, growth of individual pupils in analyzing, comparing, and evaluating reading materials was revealed through the comparison of recordings. After listening to more than a dozen tapes, this teacher concluded that the pupils became more highly motivated and interested in reading when they were challenged to interpret, apply, and evaluate and that success in these thinking processes brought the children more satisfaction and confidence in their reading.

Experimentations with two procedures in the evaluation of critical reading have been described. Although different, both of the two devices will provide the teacher with feedback essential to the improvement of the teaching learning environment. Together, the two instruments measure both knowledge and process objectives of critical reading.

REFERENCES

1. Bloom, Benjamin, *et al.* *Taxonomy of Educational Objectives: Cognitive Domain.* New York: David McKay (Longmans, Green), 1954.
2. Ellinger, Bernice. "Development and Refinement of a Test of Critical Reading Ability of Elementary School Children," Occasional Paper 67-102. Columbus Ohio: Ohio State University, School of Education, 1967.
3. Taba, Hilda; Samuel Levine; and Freeman F. Elzey. *Thinking in Elementary School Children,* Cooperative Research Project No. 1574 (Mimeographed). San Francisco, California; San Francisco State College, 1964.

CURRICULUM AND ORGANIZATION

CURRICULUM

Ends and Means: Developing Specific Objectives for Reading Instruction

VICTOR M. RENTEL
University of South Carolina

T. H. HUXLEY once remarked that the great end of life was not knowledge but action. This statement is only partly true, for action, to be purposeful, must be directed by knowledge. The two, knowledge and action, cannot be separated so easily, even if the match at times becomes awkward. This balance between knowledge and action is a major concern for educators who must constantly keep the balance mechanism adjusted to the social and philosophical changes that influence education in every period. If, in the coming years, educational technology holds our fancy, as it seems likely to—given our lust for specialization and our preoccupation with measurement—specific behavioral objectives in education will increasingly shape society's larger goals as they are interpreted by the schools.

Because the objectives of reading instruction will play so large a part in determining both the academic and human possibilities of the children we teach, formulating these objectives demands careful and sensitive thinking. Objectives commonly serve four functions: a) they define and give direction to learning; b) they provide a mechanism for selecting content and experiences for the curriculum; c) they focus on the kinds of learnings which will receive emphasis; and d) they detail specifications for evaluation (10).

There is almost universal agreement that society's needs and demands are the primary sources of educational goals; but at this point universal agreement ends. The development of objectives, based on deep convictions arising out of previous experience and an interpretation of society's ideals, methods of thinking, attitudes, and current needs, is a matter of choice on the part of a teaching staff (1). Final selection of objectives ultimately depends upon a faculty's convictions and its philosophy of education.

Learning and learners

What is known about learning and learners, as well as the nature of content and its contribution to the education of an individual, will determine in part the selection of objectives, but, even more, will order, relate, and give them dimension (1). Most educators consider what we know about learning to be crucial in the selection of objectives to such an extent that current methods of teaching reading retain vestiges of nearly every learning theory which historically has achieved some prominence. The psychology of learning, in one guise or another, forms the basis for most instruction in reading—regardless of the timeliness or established proof of the theory. Taba makes this observation:

> The study of the psychological principles underlying curriculum and teaching is somewhat akin to an archeological expedition: one can find the fossilized remains of almost any learning theory that ever existed, no matter now outdated or how discredited it may be (14).

The warning here is clear. Before objectives are selected for reading instruction, their theoretical antecedents should be examined carefully, for quite possibly, the theories underlying these objectives may be little more than historical curiosities.

Briefly, is there a precise, consistent, unified theory of learning upon which the formulation of objectives in reading can be based? While many advances leading to a greater understanding of the learning processes have been made over the past few years, the answer to this question still remains a rather unsatisfactory *no*. If this is the case, of what practical value are theories of learning to instruction in general and reading in particular? Cantor, writing on the contemporary status of research in learning, skeptically concludes:

> In this writer's opinion, an honest appraisal of basic psychological research on learning indicates that, at the present time, such research activity produces little of significance for educational practice. (2).

Mowrer, in this connection, advised students of learning theory that they would do better in practical fields to make use of "enlightened and informed common sense." On the other hand, Hilgard does not regard differences among theorists as particularly vexing. Instead, he suggests that on many important points crucial to educators, most theorists are in substantial agreement. Theorists may differ with regard to interpretation, but they agree in principle on most matters. Havighurst, too, believes that sufficient "ground work" has emerged from research of the past few decades to enable educators to relate "intellectual development" to practical instruction (5).

Because of the intramural conflict between learning theorists, a tendency arises among those who are responsible for developing programs of reading instruction to ignore research findings in the psychology of learning. This is an extreme view. No unified theory of learning is likely to emerge from basic research for years to come, but where current theory is incorporated into curriculum planning, where the best evidence available is considered, where objectives consonant with theory are subjected to a rigorous tryout before their acceptance, the selection of objectives using learning theory as one of the bases seems to me to be sound.

Attempts to develop suitable objectives for instruction must be based on selection criteria which include, in addition to what we know about learning, what we know about the learner. In particular, objectives must be based on what is both logical and appropriate to the growth potential of a given level of maturity: specific objectives are developmental statements of general objectives. Mirroring the physical, social, and emotional concomitants of these needs, they reflect basic needs at various developmental levels. Then, to be attainable, objectives must also be statements of *behavior* which students at a given level of development can achieve.

Objectives—general or specific?

Both curriculum experts and specialists in educational measurement generally recommend that specific instructional goals be defined in behavioral terms. But this advice conceals a major problem. It is all but impossible, nor is it advisable, to specify fully and exactly all of the behaviors that might apply to a skill or concept Ebel makes this observation:

> Behavioral definitions tend to be books, not paragraphs, sections, or even chapters. . . . The virtue of concreteness involves the burden of complexity. Abstractions for all their faults do have the virtue of simplicity. The virtue of definiteness involves a danger of overemphasis on conformity (3).

The level of generality appropriate for an objective is one of the most troublesome questions facing educators today. Fifteen years ago it was popular—and still is if my topic today is any reflection of current thinking—to draw a contrast between highly specific objectives and those whose reference is a more generalized mode of behavior. Tyler suggests that it may be more useful to think of defined levels of generalization, verified experimentally, and aimed "at as high a level of generalization as experiments show to be successful." The purpose would be to help students use generalized modes of behavior as those modes are reflected in the ability to cope with specifics. An objective might then be "stated in the curriculum plan with specifics used as *illustrations* [italics mine], rather than treating the specifics as ends in themselves" (15).

This matter suggests that the goals of reading should be concerned with processes as well as products, with perspective as well as pertinence, and with simplicity as well as specificity. Most important, in relation to Tyler's suggestions, reading instruction needs to focus on adaptability, not merely on an adaptation.

Where specific behaviors are used to illustrate objectives, their function is largely one of clarifying the verbal meaning of a larger outcome. There have been at least three productive attempts to define educational goals in behavioral terms, one at the elementary level (7), one at the secondary level (4), and one (most appropriate) at the college level (1). These classification systems may be of great value to those responsible for the development of reading instruction in helping them to define substantive content, to specify objectives, and to plan learning activities for specific units of work. Referring to Bloom's *Taxonomy,* to which he was a contributor, Krathwohl (8) sees the *Taxonomy* as a concise model for the selection, analysis, and refinement of objectives. Further, it provides a system by which objectives can be compared both with learning content and the means used to measure the mastery of that content.

Though a possible "hierarchy of learning experiences" from the lower to the upper levels of the *Taxonomy* is suggested, only general support has been demonstrated in research for this hypothesis, but in no instance has the hierarchical structure of the *Taxonomy* been supported by various factor matrices (12, 13). If this system or similar classification ones suggest a readiness relationship between lower and higher objectives in the hierarchy, then these systems can hardly be ignored in framing objectives for reading instruction.

Behavioral illustrations in reading

There are listings in the literature of reading which catalog and classify the outcomes of reading instruction. In most of these lists, little or no attempt has been made to distinguish between general and specific goals, between content and behavior, or between lower and higher order objectives.

French provides many excellent examples of these distinctions and illustrates general objectives with specific behaviors. One such example states the general objective and illustrates behavior as follows:

> Commands and uses the basic skills of reading for information, ideas, opinions, stimulation, and leisure.
> Illustrative Behaviors
> a. Adjusts his reading rate and his method of reading (skimming, taking notes for detail or for enjoyment only) to the material at hand.
> b. Seeks consciously to attain his best reading rate and comprehension.
> c. Reads with increasing speed, comprehension, and appreciation.
> d. (Other illustrative behaviors are included) (4).

At the primary level, as one of the goals of modern reading instruction, David Russell states that teachers should provide "for the gradual increase in skills and acquisition of valuable habits in silent and oral reading" (11).

This objective may be illustrated behaviorally as follows:

1. Reading
   a. He does assigned reading by himself.
   b. Anticipates the story from its title, picks out chief sentences, and is able to tell what each says.
   c. Reads to find answers—what, when, where, and why.
   d. Distinguishes the chief elements in a story and can repeat them.
2. Word Recognition
   a. Recognizes and produces the individual letter signs for consonants and consonant blends.
   b. Can fuse two- or three-letter sounds into a single word and can recognize letters by their sound.
   c. Uses context to pronounce and locate meanings for words.

After developing specific illustrations for set objectives, the next logical step would involve placing these objectives in some hierarchy consonant with what is known of development and maturation. If the objectives selected are consistent and noncontradictory, they can then be compared with and classified according to one of the previously mentioned systems.

A concept of the learner

Systems, however, can only aid in the *formulation* of objectives. They cannot insure what will happen when objectives come face-to-face with a learner. Tyler, speculating on the changes that have occurred in his thinking over the past two decades, notes that beyond the planning of objectives students must have the chance to do what is implied in the objective, that what they do must be satisfying to them, and that what they have done must become an impelling force, stimulating them to try new ways to reach the same objectives (*15*). He urges that the learnings be sequential and that each learner set standards that compel him to go beyond his past performance. Finally, if learning is to continue beyond the teacher's "poor power to add or detract," the individual must have some means of judging his own output.

No recognition, no concept, no insight is more meaningful than the realization that in education we must deal with a live, squirming, purposeful human being in whom go our hopes for critical judgment, our needs for creative innovation, and our freedom to change as the world changes. And humans exert a powerful influence on one another, regardless of their ages. When we plan and develop programs of reading instruction, children and young people must be the constant focus of our attention.

If our attention is fixed on curriculum, on technology, and on reaching specific goals at every turn, students who vary from our conception of them but who, nevertheless, are expected to conform to a pattern of objectives will find themselves lodged on one of Procrustes' infamous beds. And if you recall, Procrustes had a marvelous way of fitting a traveler to his bed. If the traveler was unfortunate enough to have his legs extend beyond the footboard, Procrustes and his men would cut them off to make the sleeper fit the bed. If, on the other hand, he was too short, ropes were tied to his head and feet and Procrustes would conveniently stretch him until he reached the proper length. When we adjust students to programs rather than programs to students, when the curriculum in reading becomes a rigid lockstep sequence of goals, what happens to the child is analogous to what happened to Procrustes' travelers. We all need to remember that what happens to the child in schools is the final criteria for judging what we have practiced there. Children do not learn an objective but what they do in response to one.

REFERENCES

1. Bloom, B. (Ed.) *Taxonomy of Educational Objectives: The Classification of Educational Goals Handbook I: Cognitive Domain.* New York: David McKay Company, Inc., 1956, 26-28.
2. Cantor, G. M. "Basic Learning Research and Mental Retardation," in E. Trapp and P. Himelstein (Eds.), *Readings on the Exceptional Child.* New York: Appleton-Century-Crofts, Inc., 1962, 172.
3. Ebel, R. L. "The Relation of Testing Programs to Educational Goals," *The Impact and Improvement of School Testing Programs.* National Society for the Study of Education. Sixty-second Yearbook, Part II, University of Chicago Press, 1963, 34.
4. French *et al, Behavioral Goals of General Education in High School.* New York: Russell Sage Foundation, 1957, 96.
5. Havighurst, R. J., *et al.* "The Nature and Needs of the Disadvantaged," *The Educationally Retarded and Disadvantaged.* National Society for the Study of Education. Sixty-sixth Yearbook, Part I, University of Chicago Press, 1967, 33-35.
6. Hilgard, E. *Theories of Learning.* New York: Appleton-Century-Crofts, Inc., 1956, 486-487.
7. Kearney, N. C. *Elementary School Objectives.* New York: Russell Sage Foundation, 1957.
8. Krathwohl, D. H. "Stating Objectives Appropriately for Program, for Curriculum and for Instructional Materials Development," *Journal of Teacher Education,* 16 (No. 1) (1965), 83-92.
9. Mowrer, O. H. *Two-Factor Learning Theory: Reviewed, Revised, and Extended.* Urbana, Illinois, 1955 (Mimeographed).
10. Ragan, W. B. *Modern Elementary Curriculum.* New York: Holt, Rinehart, and Winston, 1963, 86-89.
11. Russell, D. *Children Learn to Read.*

New York: Ginn and Company, 1961,
144.

12. Smith, R. B. "An Analysis of Scability of the 'Knowledge' and 'Comprehension' Levels of the *Taxonomy of Educational Objectives: Cognitive Domain*," paper read at the National Council of Measurement in Education, 1965.
13. Stoker, W. H., and R. P. Kropp. "Measurement of Cognitive Processes," *Journal of Educational Measurement,* (No. 1) (1964), 39-42.
14. Taba, H. *Curriculum Development: Theory and Practice.* New York: Harcourt, Brace, and World, Inc., 1962, 77.
15. Tyler, R. W. "New Dimensions in Curriculum Development," *Phi Delta Kappan,* 61 (September 1966), 26-27.

Differentiating Objectives and Behaviors in a City-Wide Curriculum Guide in Reading

GLORIA E. FRIED
Trenton, New Jersey, Public Schools

THE DESIGNING of a reading curriculum and its presentation as a written guide constitute a vital aspect of curriculum development. The change in personnel involved is more important, however, than the concrete evidence provided by the written guide of the philosophy underlying the teaching of reading in a large city school system and tested approaches toward stated goals. Although measurement of change in the philosophy and attitude of teachers of reading is not readily assessed, its importance ranks with any other outcome in the writing of a curriculum guide. Although partly prescriptive, a reading guide should primarily be an intelligent, working consensus of teachers of reading.

The differentiation of objectives and behaviors—i.e., the desired outcomes and the effective approaches to their realization—is in essence the crux of any published guide for the instruction of reading. "Only with knowledge of goals," states Smith, "can the instructor know what he is to teach, the student what he is to learn, and the evaluator what he is to use as a criterion of training success" (5). The exploration of the topic is a natural dichotomy: goals and patterns.

The goals are the achievement of greater efficacy in the use of fundamental reading skills. These fundamental skills include the development of word perception and comprehension and their use in the content areas and in the quest for personal values.

Because reading involves sequential skills and is taught in stages, the Reading Guide of the Trenton, New Jersey, school system is patterned as a chart for each of the five stages described, preceded by a description of the developmental characteristics of children at the level concerned with implications for the most effective instruction of reading.

Each chart is divided into two areas and four columns.

Developing Fundamental Skills
Word Perception   Comprehension
Skills   Skills
Using Fundamental Skills
Reading in Content   Reading for Personal
Areas   Values

The guide lists the expected actions or desired behaviors at each stage. It is the responsibility of each teacher to supply the experiences and use the activities suggested which will allow children to reach the desired behaviors most effectively.

Developmental reading

All students in the Trenton school system receive instruction in developmental reading from grades one through twelve. In the elementary schools, the classroom teacher and a reading coordinator are responsible for this program. Because the role of the reading coordinator is a relatively new one, the role should be delineated.

Role of reading coordinator

The reading coordinator's responsibilities include 1) demonstrating reading skills in classroom situations; 2) planning reading programs with classroom teachers; 3) conducting inservice seminars with classroom teachers; 4) diagnosing reading skills of children; 5) assisting in identification of reading problems through standardized and specialized testing programs;

and 6) providing evaluation and feedback to teachers through conferences, workshops, consultant services, and research.

The philosophy of the coordinator program is that better reading performance throughout the school will be achieved more rapidly and more effectively by strengthening the knowledge and resources of the classroom teachers rather than by relying on a corps of special teachers to take over the classroom teacher's problems. The emphasis is on an improved developmental reading program helping teachers to understand and to know what to do about developmental needs of students at various stages in reading.

In the junior high schools special classes have been established for the teaching of developmental reading skills. On this level, too, a coordinator is available for in-service help and suggestions.

Content reading

Mastery of content skills must be nurtured throughout the grades. With their knowledge of improved techniques of reading instruction, corrdinators are assigned to the junior high schools to aid teachers of subject-matter courses.

For years it has been recognized that reading in content fields imposes demands not met by training in developmental reading programs. Research has shown, too, that general reading ability is not a predictor of success in all academic areas and that even students of good reading ability show variations in comprehension, vocabulary, and rate depending on the content. Yet, little has been done in actual content classes to help secondary students and teachers satisfy these needs.

A coordinator in each junior high school conducts seminars with teachers of various subject areas to help them identify reading skills needed in various subjects. Coordinators are available to all classes for demonstrations of "how" to help students handle necessary materials. They make available a variety of instructional materials for

students who need specialized instruction.

In the senior high school the team-teaching approach encourages the teachers and provides reading instruction in content classes with help for all ability groups. Students are purposefully guided through assigned material and are stimulated to read at varying rates for a variety of purposes.

"Team teaching," says Margaret J. Early, "is a concept of vital importance to the secondary reading program. Because reading cuts through all curriculum areas, the improvement of reading has been a task for team teaching. Or it should have been. For even though reading may be taught as an 'extra subject', instruction is ineffectual unless it is integrated with the teaching of content. Accomplishing this integration requires teamwork" (3).

Corrective reading

Realizing that the program would be remiss without a total approach, a corrective and an enrichment program have been included.

Each junior and senior high school has a staff member skilled in handling youngsters with mild to more severe corrective needs. Tutors are recruited from several nearby colleges for elementary age children. With some "on the job" training these students often provide the extra "pull up by the bootstraps" and the attention that help solve younger children's needs.

Enrichment reading

In an attempt to add variety to the program, a corps of volunteers, all college graduates, has been recruited to work with small groups and individuals. Use of community resources in this way adds new dimensions to the experience approach and gives additional service to potentially "able" students.

Federal funds have been utilized for additional summer programs to focus on the special reading needs of the language-and experience-impoverished child to help him build a frame of reference for learning "how" to read, especially in the readiness and beginning reading stages. "The first three years of the elementary school are critical. If learning is not successful and satisfying in these years, the entire educational career of the child is seriously jeopardized. The child's interest in school learning, the problems of the school dropout, and the educational and vocational career of the individual are largely determined by what takes place in the first few years of public school.

"A longer school day, summer programs, small group instruction, teacher assistants and tutoring programs, the aid of specialists, the use of diagnostic instruments, and the development of more effective instructional materials for this age group should all contribute to the educational development of these children" (1).

The differentiation of learning behaviors

In a survey of this limited scope, the described goals must be viewed as minimal, and the learning behaviors implementing and fulfilling these goals must be evaluated. A guide on the instruction of reading may well consider the following actions or behaviors: In the area of word perception skills, behavioral outcomes may include the pupil's ability to recognize, perceive, associate, identify, and discriminate. In the area of comprehension skills, he should be able to recall, use, understand, interpret, apply, and analyze. In his reading in content areas, the pupil should grow in his powers of selecting, determining, using, adjusting, locating, and organizing. In his reading for personal values, he should grow in his ability to listen, join, appreciate, enjoy, gather, and evaluate.

Any guide listing behaviors and objectives is merely suggestive. It is the responsibility of each teacher to modify, delete, and add to the list.

Examples of desirable behavioral activity on the various levels of reading are stated as follows in the Reading Guide of the Trenton Schools:

> Associates printed forms with sounds and meanings of spoken words. The teacher's objective is implementation to attain this goal. Suggested to her in the "Guide" as activities to achieve this are: bulletins and signs; pictures accompanied by captions; printed signs needed in play, "Stop," "Jump"; child's dictated story, experience, or poem accompanying his picture; labeled containers from which materials are obtained; titles on books, names of songs in music, records, books.

> Observes likenesses and differences in sounds of words. The teacher's objective is implementation to attain this goal. It is suggested in the "Guide" that she might accomplish her goal through tone games, rhyming words, and records to distinguish familiar sounds.

Further aids are included in a special section of the guide. They include the following topics: Developing Auditory Perception and Discrimination; Developing Visual Perception and Discrimination; Teaching Vocabulary; Teaching the Use of Context Clues; Teaching Main Ideas; Teaching Organizational Skills; Teaching Locational Skills; and the Development of Abilities in Critical Reading.

Teaching techniques are included for writing experience charts; the directed reading activity; SQ3R and other study techniques; and building study guides. Some typical classroom activities (on various levels), basal readers, audio visual aids, instructional materials, diagnostic measures, library books, and references for teachers complete this section.

Preparation of the written guide

The preparation of the written guide had a twofold purpose: first, the in-service training of teachers about new practices and new findings about the learning processes for the betterment of each individual through a realistic instructional program for all youth in the advancing technological culture; and secondly, the creation of a repository of philosophy, goals, and practices for the ready reference of all teachers.

Experience has revealed that guides, written by a select group, appointed by a central authority, and handed down for classroom use are unsatisfactory. Consequently, the preparation of the Reading Guide for the Trenton Schools involved the people most intimately concerned and held the belief that the interaction of personalities and the exchange of ideas in the preparation of the guide was as important as the final product, the guide itself. With these thoughts in mind, the teachers of reading in Trenton commenced the creation of the guide with three ideas: first, it would be a total all-city approach to reading; secondly, it would include a curriculum committee of as many as possible of those who were directly involved with reading practices in the schools; and thirdly, there would be a "built-in" in-service program.

Motivating concepts

Motivating concepts which guided the work in preparing the guide included these beliefs:

1. Continuous instruction in reading for all pupils from kindergarten to grade twelve is necessary.
2. Learning to read is a highly complex process, completely interrelated with the other language arts and closely integrated with all aspects of growth.
3. The reading process is developmental and continuous, building upon past increments of skills, habits, attitudes, and experiences.
4. Children learn to read at different rates; the rate of the individual child varies.
5. Learning to read through first-hand experiences and through direct contact with the environment facilitates the process.
6. Reading skills are learned through consistent and systematic practice and help.
7. Reading skills should be taught in connection with content subjects throughout the grades.
8. Reading skills and concepts peculiar to special areas, such as, shop, home economics, music, health, physical education, fine arts, etc., should be taught in the classrooms through the activities and by the teachers where these subjects are taught.
9. Reading develops critical thinking, expands interests, stimulates tastes, extends sources of pleasure and satisfaction, and broadens learning.

Use of periodic brochures

In an urban system there is generally the infusion of many ethnic groups which pose varying learning problems. There are varying ability groups who must also be considered. While guides must be written developmentally to include all learners, provisions for special needs must be made. It was decided that brochures accompanying guides or written periodically would serve this purpose.

The slow learner, the gifted, the underachiever, all warranted special treatment with individually written guides to accompany the major resource book. The disadvantaged child became the subject of many additional brochures. As Deutch points out, "The culture of his environment is a different one from the culture that has molded the school and its education technique and theory" (2). These children have relatively little intellectual stimulation of the kind valued by the school. They show language deficiencies and poor reading and achievement levels since "the lower class is not a verbally oriented environment" (2).

"Methods and materials which serve the average child will not seem to help the culturally deprived child acquire the critical communication and computational skills which are so necessary to achievement of educational goals. . . . The gaps between the learning tasks and the 'readiness' of the children are a source of frustration to the teachers as well as the children. All too quickly, the teacher and the child are ready to give up the struggle both with a terrible sense of being defeated" (6).

Continual evaluation

The curriculum designed, the guide written, the experiences must still be arranged daily to allow all children to respond to their environment and to interact favorably with the school. The focus is on the teacher who initiates the change. Robert Karlin of

Queen's College stated recently: "Programs are not as important as the teachers who administer them" (4).

It is the teachers themselves who must plan together, assess programs, and effect improvements. They must continue to study new approaches and improve instruction. They must review professional materials and attend workshops and conferences. A curriculum program is primarily an in-service program. As a prime objective it has the goal of continuous improvement of its offering to the pupils. As a result, it anticipates the supplying of all teachers with excellent reference material. Continuing teacher education, planning, and in-service programs are important conditions influencing reading development in a school system.

Summary

The writing of the guide was primarily a systematic structuring of objectives or goals to be attained. The reading curriculum, not the written guide alone, must be the paramount factor which fuses all skills, study habits, appreciations, and thought processes which the student needs to read efficiently.

The committee which wrote the guide was composed of those persons responsible for the reading program in the Trenton Schools. Coordinated by the director of reading, the group included reading coordinators, representative principals, teachers representing self-contained classrooms, and some personnel from departmental set-ups in the secondary schools.

Emerging as a resource book, the guide became a publication which included descriptive statements of learner characteristics, charts to be read horizontally for skills at each developmental level and vertically for skills progressing from kindergarten through grade twelve, varieties of teaching techniques, and instructional books and materials. To meet the needs of pupils from varying socio-economic levels and those with wide-ranging learning abilities, periodic brochures brought additional information and materials to those concerned.

Differentiated objectives and their related behaviors were explored on a city-wide basis. The objectives, it was agreed, may arise from inferences about the needs of the groups, but the specific behaviors must be unique. Behaviors which might be reasonably expected were listed sequentially on charts. The teacher was free, however, to implement the objectives through any creative classroom teaching techniques.

REFERENCES

1. Bloom, Benjamin S.; Allison Davis, and Robert Hess. *Compensatory Education for Cultural Deprivation.* New York: Holt, Rinehart, and Winston, 1965, 22, 28.
2. Deutch, Martin P. "The Disadvantaged Child and the Learning Process," *Education in Depressed Areas.* New York: Teachers College, Columbia University, 1963, 163-180.
3. Early, Margaret J. "Through Methods and Materials," in *New Frontiers in Reading.* J. Allen Figurel (Ed.). Conference Proceedings, International Reading Association. New York: Scholastic Magazines, 1960, 40-44.
4. Karlin, Robert. *"A New Look at Reading Research,"* Bridgeport, Connecticut: The Council of Experimental Research in Reading, 1966.
5. Smith, Henry Clay. *Sensitivity to People.* New York: McGraw-Hill Book Company, 1966.
6. Similansky, Sarah. "Evaluation of Early Education." New York: *Unesco Educational Studies and Documents,* 42 (1961), 8-17.

Writing and Revising a Curriculum Guide in Reading

BERNICE T. CLARK
New York State
Education Department

THE NEW YORK STATE Education Department is continually reviewing the various areas of the curriculum and has become increasingly aware of the fundamental role of language in all learning. As an important phase of the effort to provide quality education for the students of the state, a major project, the reevaluation of the English language arts program in kindergarten through grade twelve, was undertaken.

Planning for the writing of this guide began in 1962. Consultants selected for the Ad Hoc Committee on the English language arts were individuals vitally involved in the utilization of language: those who spend their professional lives writing or projecting the written word. It was considered important to hear from a group of distinguished, nationally-known authors, editors, directors, and experts in the mass media and in the field of communication.

The committee meeting was characterized by the deepest interest and enthusiasm. As one reflects on the insights of the committee with respect to the goals of language and its use in education, the more convinced one is that by no other means could the more significant implications for the revision of the English program be obtained.

Under the leadership of Associate Commissioner Walter Crewson, participants from the fields of literature, theatre, and mass media; educators who specialize in the language arts in schools and colleges; Assistant Commissioner Warren W. Knox; and members of the education department staff met in Albany. Commissioner James E. Allen, Jr., met with the group for a portion of the session.

The advisory committee members were Edward L. Bernays, public relations expert and author; Theodore Dahl, manager, Management Communications, International Business Machines Corporation; John Charles Daly, Columbia Broadcasting Company; William Gibson, author of "The Miracle Worker;" Rosamond Gilder, past editor of "Theatre Arts" magazine; George H. Henry, professor of education, University of Delaware; Robert F. Hogan, executive secretary, The National Council of Teachers of English; Joseph Mersand, chairman, English Department, Jamaica High School, New York City Public Schools; Mabel S. Noall, director, Secondary Reading Clinic, Boston University; Joseph Papp, director, New York Shakespeare Festival;

Walter Pauk, School of Education, Cornell University; Louise M. Rosenblatt, professor of English education, New York University School of Education; and Alan Schneider, director of Broadway plays. There were also guests from colleges and members of the State Education Department.

Visiting artists and educators at the conference, in their own way and through their own creative work, symbolized the various approaches to revitalizing the language arts program, kindergarten through grade 12. Each member of the advisory committee represented unique and productive experience in using the medium of language with live audiences, with readers, with great segments of the public, or with students in institutions of learning.

Differing views

Committee members challenged one another with some interesting differences of opinion. For example, there was a call for concentration on the precise study of word meaning, followed by the quick warning that excessive focus on word study *per se* might restrict the student's view too narrowly. There was an expert description of the careful, systematic use of selective language, geared to various publics for purposes of interpretation and persuasion and the counter plea that language should often be used solely for sheer pleasure and enjoyment. There was a spirited dialog on the selecting and utilizing of words to convey specific ideas with clarity and the description of an ephemeral and creative process of first placing words on paper and through them seeking to discover inner thoughts and then using the words to organize the thoughts which are discovered. There was the assertion that the program somehow misses the essence of language-feeling—or the emotional experience which can create joy in students. But there was the counter-assertion that joy can only come after basic skills are mastered and that the real problem is to teach pupils the practical communication skills needed in daily life: writing a clear, descriptive paragraph and making an acceptable oral presentation. A compromise view held that the joy and the skills can be built simultaneously.

Areas of general agreement

These were some of the rare individualisms that made the conference exciting. But the feeling of the entire group upheld such general insights and agreements as these: 1) Children come to school with motivations that are destroyed somewhere; let us seek their stimulation. 2) English is not merely a subject to be taught; it is the activation of ideas. It is not mechanical; it is creative. 3) Teaching English means affecting individual behavior, for the use of language is a form of human behavior tied in with experience, including the experience of the classroom. 4) The basic language arts program must be planned to give the increasing masses of children attending school a reasonable adequacy in the ability to communicate. 5) The syllabus will be a broad framework upon which additional plans and ideas may be built by teachers. 6) The areas in the syllabus should be carefully planned to motivate deepening interest in the language arts and to meet the realistic needs, wishes, interests, and desires of youth.

Specific recommendations

Most of the specific recommendations reflected a deep desire for creativity in the construction of the program and in the teacher's presentation, as well as a respect for the inner emotional life of the child. After a review of the existing program by Warren Knox, Walter Crewson emphasized that the department wanted to "mine" the recommendations of the visiting artists and experts in order to "find new directions."

The program

The group felt that the language arts program should be carefully articulated and developed in direct relation to current research which describes the nature and character of today's children. They said that interesting methods of presenting the program and a clearly organized outline of content should be prepared for teachers in a number of creative units related to the syllabus outline.

The committee felt that in building the program the following concepts and ideas should be given the most careful consideration: 1) English is not merely a subject to be taught. It is the creation and the stimulation of ideas. It is not a mechanical tinkering with structures or the analyzing of sentences out of context. It is the larger dimension of meaning and interpretation. 2) The language arts should be taught and treated as a concept designed to broaden and deepen the individuality of each learner. Language is not external; it is inextricably bound with the vitality of living. 3) The written language should be approached as something personal, tied to the way we speak. It should not become dull, impersonal, and passive, resulting in two languages—the language of daily usage and the passive, written language which uses such phrasing as "It has been announced that. . . ." 4) Language should be used as a searchlight pointing to the inward discovery of thought and then conveyed to others after nebulous ideas are clarified. It is a tool used in inward searching, not a conveyor belt. 5) Drill without feeling is a sterile process; language can be exciting to both students and teachers. 6) The mass media can be used effectively to develop feeling and excitement related to language. 7) The theatre uses words before they become literature; it is a dramatic, graphic expression of a people, their language, and their culture. The lack of theatre in many school programs often results in a long-delayed introduction to this art form. Then it may come too late to attract an abiding interest. Living language is conveyed through drama, either by children's acting in plays or watching the gestures and live performances of actors. Until children observe or participate in drama, their ability to communicate will be limited.

The student

It is felt that the inner life of the child enables him to undertake tasks which are frequently thought of as far beyond him and that the realistic inclusion of vital areas of life, too often side-stepped in the teaching process, results in the development of student confidence in teachers and deep interest in the program. The challenge was made to start with the valid inner life of the child and then to lead the way to grammar and precision.

It was believed that students need to 1) create an inner joy through language, which can become a kind of food that nourishes and possesses an internal dimension; 2) learn to keep listening in its pristine state and nourish the valuable faculty of listening attentively and thoughtfully as in the early stages of childhood when listening preceded the imitative process that led to speech; 3) learn to organize and convey thoughts logically because language is a social phenomenon—an effective tool in organizing experiences, thoughts, and emotions—with a structure of its own; 4) develop the same degree of confidence in the ability to write as in the ability to speak in order to overcome the average American's reluctance to put something down on paper; and 5) learn to read critically and analytically.

The teacher

It was agreed by all that teaching the language arts is a highly creative job and that the crux of the situation is that instruction and its results depend ultimately upon the enthusiasm and skill of the individual teacher.

The following recommendations were made regarding the teacher of language arts: 1) The teacher's approach should be an inspired one. A statewide in-service program involving the state's 13,000 English teachers should be organized. 2) A sense of greatness should be infused into teacher preparation. 3) A lay visiting faculty of distinguished artists and practitioners in the language arts should be organized to ignite, inspire, and deepen the language arts program in the high schools and in teacher training institutions. 4) Regional conferences and summer courses should be held for teachers of the language arts; and education department conferences should be organized for teachers of method. 5) Resource units should be prepared for teachers.

It was further suggested that a follow-up session be held with newsmen and leaders in radio and television in search of additional ideas and reactions to the recommendations of the advisory committee.

A report of the Ad Hoc Committee was reviewed by a group of representatives of the press, radio, and television at a meeting of the state education department in March of 1965. The meeting was chaired by Associate Commissioner Walter Crewson. Other department personnel present were Warren W. Knox and William E. Young.

The group stressed the importance of developing in students 1) a mastery of and respect for language as a tool of communication with the purpose of insuring an improved and more creative use of language; 2) the ability to write simple declarative sentences and to interrelate them in paragraphs which express clearly a thought of reasonable complexity; 3) the ability to find joy in some type of reading (students should be able to *race, gallop,* and *run* when they read), 4) the ability to express themselves clearly to peers and, conversely, the willingness to listen to a speech and the desire to see a play; and 5) increased interest in language and in reading through the discriminative use of television in the classroom as a motivating force.

The study of formal grammar does not necessarily result in effective writing; however, writing tends to improve in relationship to clear oral expression and the reading of good literature.

General guidelines were set up that

were translated into a working plan by a professional advisory committee the following spring. These guidelines were designed for working committees who were called into the department the following summer to write a preliminary manuscript. The professional committee was comprised of personnel from college and school systems— persons known to have an interest in this particular curriculum area. This professional committee worked on the following five major areas of the syllabus revision, all K-12 in scope: 1) reading 2) literature, 3) language, 4) composition, and 5) speaking and listening.

The working committees—one elementary, one junior high and, one senior high school—prepared initial manuscripts based on the guidelines and utilized the results of sound research to help structure the syllabus.

The first portion of the developmental reading section was edited and prepared for general distribution in an experimental edition. It contained vocabulary, word attack, comprehension, critical, and interpretative reading skills.

The third portion of the reading material completed the experimental edition of the syllabus and was distributed later in the school year. It contained locational skills, work study skills, oral reading, and rate of reading.

The reading syllabus was distributed to the schools of the state along with an invitation to chief school officers, inviting their districts to come into the official tryout. Many other districts and individuals indicated a desire to evaluate the materials. They were encouraged to do so. The experimental schools were in large and small cities, suburban and rural districts and were located from the tip of Long Island to the Pennsylvania and Canadian borders.

Implementation

The need to implement the program was then felt in the department. A team composed of Walter Eddington, Robert Johnstone, Vivienne Anderson, and Edna Morgan was charged with this responsibility. An orientation conference for school systems involved in the tryout was held in Albany on October 5, 1964; 150 were expected, but 300 came!

Ten regional conferences were then planned and held across the state in cooperation with local professional organizations and school districts. It is interesting to note that over 5,000 teachers, supervisors, and college professors attended these conferences.

All material (K-12) in each broad skill area is within the covers of one publication so that all teachers can familiarize themselves closely with the complete skill development process and be able to place youngsters on the continuum.

The whole is organized for ease of teacher use; 1) table of contents, 2) ample blank space for comments, and 3) evaluation sheets at the conclusion of each level in each portion of the material.

The philosophy as it appears in the introduction to the materials is explained this way: "It is believed that the best way to teach reading to all children, under the circumstances that exist at the present time, is that of systematic, sequential skills development, beginning in kindergarten and continuing through grade 12."

The purpose of this philosophy is not directed toward establishing separate reading classes (particularly at the secondary schools), but rather it is intended to aid in the organization of instruction to the end that a sequential and systematic program of skills development will result within the existing classroom situations.

The definite trend in reading instruction in this country bears out this theory. Recent research studies indicate that the integration of skills in current school programs is more effective than the practice establishing separate developmental reading classes at the secondary level. Attention to reading skills in the content areas is also gaining necessary momentum. It is also believed that the total program should make use of all reading experiences, oral and silent, that lend themselves to continued growth in major areas where reading is vital.

At various levels of development, instruction must certainly be adapted to the maturity of the student. This adaptation does not mean that skills are different but rather that the handling of the various skills takes into account the varying maturity levels of the student.

In some cases it is recognized that corrective and remedial programs, as well as provision for the gifted child, will be needed in addition to this program.

Total school program

There is a problem involved here. The elementary school cannot be expected to teach the more mature reading abilities needed in secondary school; nor can the secondary school teacher of English or the "reading period teacher" in elementary school be-expected to develop in students those reading abilities needed in the study of other disciplines. The teacher in the content area must assume the responsibility for teaching the skills that are necessary for full comprehension of the subject matter of that particular discipline. No one else knows that subject matter as well.

In the summer of 1964, three 3-week workshops were conducted on the campus of Vassar College. Literature, composition, and reading sections were held with the aid of a staff of 18 consultants, a librarian, an administrator, and two college professors. One thousand New York teachers (K-12) took part in these workshops.

The topics covered in the one-week reading section were chosen on the basis of the problems that arose in the regional conference: 1) innovations in the field of reading; 2) overview of the syllabus; 3) diagnosis for placement on the skills ladder; 4) skills areas, including context clues, vocabulary building, critical reading, and study

skills; and 5) materials such as tests, machines, visual aids, films, etc. Each area was given K-12 attention with regard to the syllabus.

The initial rewriting of the syllabus began on the basis of the evaluation sheets and tryout school reports. Although there were no changes in basic philosophy, there were some changes in sequence. All skills were carefully traced through each level, and it is hoped that the revised manuscript will be far superior to the experimental edition.

The New York State Education Department dreams of the day when every child in the state will be able to read as efficiently as his abilities will permit. The department is working for the day when it no longer will hear of reading retardation. It believes with Keppel that "Education must make good on the concept that no child is *unteachable* or *unreachable.*" New York State Education Department is providing the leadership to insure that Johnny *is* going to be able to read.

The Reading Program Spans the Total Curriculum

J. LOUIS COOPER
University of Connecticut

THERE IS GENERAL AGREEMENT among authorities in the field of reading instruction that in any well-balanced reading program there are three essential types of training: 1) the program in the fundamentals of reading; 2) guidance of reading in the content subjects, sometimes referred to as the program in the work-study skills; and 3) wide provision for both directed and independent recreatory reading, frequently referred to as the program in children's literature.

In most present-day reading programs a great deal of emphasis is placed on the first of these types of training throughout the elementary school. On the other hand, the other types of training often receive only token attention.

The program in the fundamentals of reading has a major function—the teaching of the mechanics of reading, that is, the process of decoding the printed symbols and reading them smoothly and fluently in both oral and silent reading situations. Throughout this program the uppermost problem is the establishment of basic skills and attitudes, and, particularly at the primary levels, the instructional load is heavily flavored with experiences already familiar to the child. Hence, the burden of new information is not a major factor.

At the intermediate levels the second type of training, reading in relation to the content subjects, becomes increasingly important. Here the child encounters texts in history or geography, an informative text in science, a basic text in arithmetic, and many others. Here he learns to use such sources as encyclopedias, dictionaries, reference books, and library card catalog and such tools as tables of contents, indexes, study guides, charts, maps, graphs, tables, and diagrams. This use is continued throughout the upper elementary grades and the secondary school, and the more highly specialized the subject matter becomes and the more highly departmentalized the program becomes, the more independence the learner is expected to assume for the use of these skills.

Reading in the content areas demands the basic skills that are common to all reading, those which are stressed in the program in the fundamentals of reading, but it also demands certain so-called study skills that are not necessarily essential for effective reading of story-type material. To some degree, materials in each of the areas such as the social studies, the natural sciences, mathematics, and literature make unique demands upon the reader. Is it not too much to expect children to read successfully the directions for doing a science experiment, to interpret maps, to read graphs, to read and interpret arithmetic problems, to establish purposes for reading a study assignment, to make use of headings and other typographical aids, and to adjust their rate of reading to the nature of the material if they have been brought up on nothing more than a steady diet of story-type materials?

Study-type reading and special skills required

Since development of the skills for effective reading and study in the content subjects requires something more than the typical program of basic reading instruction as it is commonly known, one basic question comes to mind: just what kinds of reading tasks are required for effective reading in the various subject matter areas?

It is difficult to classify into a few major categories all of the reading one must do in connection with the content subjects because each presents its own unique reading problems. Nevertheless, most such tasks will generally fall into one or more of the following categories:

1. Interpreting a single study-type selection, such as a chapter in a textbook.
2. Securing from a wide variety of printed sources information about a particular problem or topic.
3. Reading short, specific selections, such as mathematics problems, directions for a science experiment and the like, which require careful and detailed reading.

Each of these types of reading requires special skills. The best procedure for studying a chapter in a history or science book is quite different from the best process for reading several chapters in each of several books for comparative purposes or for extracting pertinent portions from several sources as they relate to a particular problem. It also differs from the process one would use if he were reading directions for doing an experiment, following directions in baking a cake, or solving a problem in arithmetic. If each of these types of reading requires special skills, just what are they? In this regard, it should be noted that although each subject area presents certain unique reading problems, there is considerable overlapping among reading abilities in different subjects.

Special skills needed for reading a single study-type selection

Although the use of a wide variety of reading materials and other learning aids is common practice in teaching the content subjects, most schools continue to use a basic textbook as the framework for such courses. Reading assignments are made from time to time in these basic texts, and children are expected to be able to read them with reasonable understanding.

In order to be able to cope with this type of reading, the pupil must acquire some systematic approach to reading, interpreting, and recalling the content of a single study-type selection, such as the SQ3R procedure or one of its many variations. Though these procedures differ slightly from one to another, all of them have the following basic ingredients:

1. A systematic preview of the selection for the purpose of establishing specific purposes for reading.
2. A systematic procedure for reading the selection, in which the reader reads one section at a time to find the answer to a major question or questions.
3. A series of steps for practicing immediate and delayed recall for the purpose of fixing in the mind of the reader pertinent portions of the material read.

Ordinarily, the special skills required for effective reading of a single study-type selection are not acquired by the pupil on his own. Careful guidance must be provided until the procedure has been well established.

Special skills needed for securing information from a variety of sources

In addition to having children read basic textbook materials, schools today place a good deal of emphasis on independent study and research. This kind of reading requires that the pupil secure information about a particular problem or topic from a wide variety of printed and other sources. In such reading, all previously mentioned basic reading abilities and study skills are needed, but these are not enough. Additional skills of three main kinds are required: 1) the skills of locating information, 2) comparing and evaluating the pertinent information from the several sources, and 3) organizing this information for some particular purpose.

To find the material he needs, the pupil must be able to locate items in an index, table of contents, encyclopedia, card catalog, various guides, atlases, almanacs, and etc. Once he has found the appropriate references, he has to pick out from the whole that which is pertinent to his particular problem and evaluate this material in terms of how up to date and authentic it is. He must then compare the pertinent information from the various sources to determine the extent of agreement or lack of it. Following the reading and evaluation of the material, the reader must organize these bits of information for a particular purpose.

Special skills required for reading short, specific selections

In all subject areas there are many situations in which one must read directions and follow them to the letter. Examples are recipes in cookbooks, directions for doing science experiments, directions for assembling a piece of equipment, and directions for operating a machine.

Unlike the reading one must do in textbook selections, one interesting thing about reading directions is that, although they need to be read carefully and for detail, frequently they do not need to be remembered. Another interesting fact is that few individuals can plead "not guilty" to the charge that we are a nation of instruction ignorers, despite the fact that we live in a world guided by directions and instructions. Since following directions is an important *skill* that many people have not mastered, the school reading program has a definite and clear-cut responsibility for teaching it.

Who should be responsible for teaching the work-study skills?

Granting that there are special reading and study skills required for effective use of materials in the content subjects, who should be responsible for teaching these skills?

For many years some have said that it is the job of the special subject teacher to develop these skills as needed in the study of the subject. It has been assumed that the mathematics teacher, science teacher, and social studies teacher will teach those reading skills essential for proper interpretation of the materials used in their courses. This theory, good though it may sound, simply has not been fruitful.

Since there is a great deal of overlap in the skills needed from one subject area to another and if every subject matter teacher is expected to teach the skills needed for his particular area, there are likely to be needless repetition of some skills and perhaps a neglect of other important ones. This is particularly true in the case of programs where departmentalization is practiced. More often than not, however, the assumption that every subject matter teacher is a teacher of reading has resulted in the good old American custom of "passing the buck." Everybody's business becomes nobody's business.

Then, too, if the teacher is subject-matter oriented, he may not recognize the specific skills to teach or just how to teach them so that the child will make the transfer to a functional application. Leaving the identification of the skills to be taught to the individual content subject teacher is likely to result in lack of sequential development of the necessary skills. Also, if study skills are to be taught as part of the content subjects, specific lessons for their introduction and development must be prepared by the teachers. Frequently, subject matter teachers lack the skill, time, energy, and proper facilities for the preparation of such instructional materials.

In the self-contained elementary school classroom where all the child's instruction is under the direction of one teacher, there is, of course, the possibility that these skills might be taught in their natural setting. Even here, however, there is the question of whether the skills should be taught in connection with the time allocated for each of the subject areas or during the time normally assigned for systematic reading instruction.

If we depend on the teaching of the essential interpretative skills in the subject matter classes, there is grave danger that the job won't get done. The teacher who is involved in putting across the concepts of science or mathematics is likely to find his allegiance divided between the ends and the means to the end if the content must be interrupted to teach the special reading skills that may be needed at a particular moment. If the emphasis in the arithmetic class is put on how to read the problem, the problem itself may never get solved. If the emphasis in the social studies class is put on finding the author's pattern and use of headings or some related reading skill, the major concepts and problems involved may become secondary.

The position held here, therefore, is that the essential reading and study skills for effective study of content materials should, wherever possible, be developed at a time apart from that normally used for the content subjects and should then be applied during the content area period without need for further attention except for refinement and the development of the habit of utilizing the skills. This appears to be a necessary answer whether the teacher who teaches the reading is the same person or a different person from the one who teaches the social studies, or the arithmetic, or the science.

Materials for teaching the study skills

Although the point of view of the writer is that the special skills needed for content area reading can best be taught during the regular reading instruction period, it must be recognized that the content of typical basal reading books is not particularly suitable for teaching many of the study skills.

Reading matter used for the lessons and for practice exercises should be quite similar to the materials the child is expected to use in his study of science, social studies, and mathematics. One cannot easily teach children the use of headings, the relationship of paragraph headings to center headings, and center headings to titles if the book being used as a teaching tool makes little or no use of headings. Such is the case of the typical story-type basal reader. A text in reading may teach the child to read a story, to recognize words, and to analyze vocabulary for pronunciation and meaning, but it does not teach him the special skills needed to read other kinds of materials.

This being the case, one might assume that the reading teacher would turn to the social studies, science, and mathematics books to find specific selections through which the special skills might be taught. This procedure would be quite appropriate except that it would leave the reading teacher with the responsibility for identifying the skills to be taught, finding the appropriate materials to use in doing the teaching, and providing the variety of books needed. While this task is possible in the self-contained classroom of the elementary school, it is time consuming and certainly not very convenient.

It appears that an appropriate solution would be for the reading teacher to have specially prepared materials in the form of a reading textbook, a kit of carefully developed materials, or perhaps a series of programed lessons, which would 1) carefully delineate the specific skills to be taught, 2) provide well-organized lessons for teaching the skills, 3) include reading selections consisting of appropriate content, and 4) suggest specific subject areas and situations for the application and integration of the skills.

Application of skills required for reading content area materials

It is imperative that the special study skills be taught, regardless of where or by whom. But the mere teaching of these skills is not enough. Provision must be made for the application of the skills in a truly functional setting. While it may be the major responsibility of the reading teacher to develop the initial understanding of the skills, it is surely the responsibility of the subject matter teacher to teach his subject in such a way that there is ample opportunity for children to use the various skills that have been taught to them.

One should not make the mistake of assuming that skills will be used just because they have been taught. For example, it is erroneous to assume that a child will brush his teeth simply because he has been given a toothbrush and a series of lessons on how to use it. We must, by some means or other, see to it that he develops the habit of brushing his teeth. So it is with the study skills. The subject matter teacher must set up situations which require the use of the special reading skills and provide guidance in using them until they are used with precision and until the habit of using them has been well established.

As reading assignments in textbooks are given, the teacher must make a special effort to help children apply those specific skills needed in reading a single study-type assignment. He must guide the children in setting up purposes for reading; aid them in finding the author's outline; remind them to be on the alert for signal words, statements of fact, and statements of opinion, insist that they make use of maps, graphs, charts; urge them to practice immediate and delayed recall; and show them how they might vary the reading rate in a particular selection. And, the teacher must keep a constant vigil to see that the skills are put to use.

In addition to helping the children develop skill in the effective use of basic textbooks, subject matter teachers must also organize their course content into problems, units, or topics which require and stimulate the use of a variety of learning aids and which encourage wide reading from a number of different sources. In this connection, let us assume that in science a pupil has a particular problem to be solved or a question to be answered. He should be encouraged not to accept the views of a single author. He must be led to see that different sources do not always agree and that, by going to different sources, one not only gets different points of view but also more information than can be had from a single source.

To get the answer to a particular question or problem, the individual must first locate information about that problem, a task which usually requires a number of locational tools. Once the information has been located, the pupil must evaluate it in terms of how much of each source is pertinent to the particular problem. He has to evaluate the material from the standpoint of validity; that is, who wrote it, when it was written, the status of the author as a recognized authority, evidence of author bias, etc. He has to compare the pertinent information from the several sources to determine the degree of agreement or lack of it; and he must draw conclusions based on these sources. In short, he must learn to read not to believe and take for granted, nor to accept or reject, but to weigh and consider. Finally, he must organize the information he has gathered from some particular purpose: to write a theme, to make a report, to prepare for an examination.

Under what better conditions could children develop a functional application of those skills needed for effective reading of content area materials than in courses organized and taught in a manner which requires their use? The answer is obvious. It seems clear that if children are to become effective readers, the reading program must span the total curriculum and must involve both special teachers of reading and subject matter teachers alike, whether they be the same or different people.

Building Reading into the High School Curriculum

LEITHA PAULSEN,
ZENA DORINSON, and
MARGARET FIEDLER

Bloom Township High School,
Chicago Heights

BLOOM HAS A VARIETY of reading services made possible by government funds: a reading laboratory for developmental students, a reading clinic for severely retarded readers, two reading consultants to work with classroom teachers, a learning aids center, and a program for students for whom English is a second language. All these services make valuable contributions to students and teachers. However, unless the effort of these fine, separate reading structures within a school are consolidated, results are scattered and the impact of individual effort is lost. Unless all reading services reinforce one another to help the student and provide in-service training to the teacher, a student's dramatic improvement in reading laboratory or clinic does not carry over to his course work and teachers are not brought to the point where they teach reading through their curricular content.

The developmental reading laboratory

One of Bloom's reading services is the Developmental Reading Laboratory. Instruction in this lab has become an accepted part of the freshman English program. But those of us concerned with coordinating reading and curriculum feel that it has not been as effective as it could be. How can we use the lab along with our other reading services so that it will better meet the individual needs of students and at the same time involve the reading specialist and the English teacher in a team effort that will build reading into the curriculum?

The plan calls for a preschool workshop week to orient teachers to the need for a diagnostic approach to read-

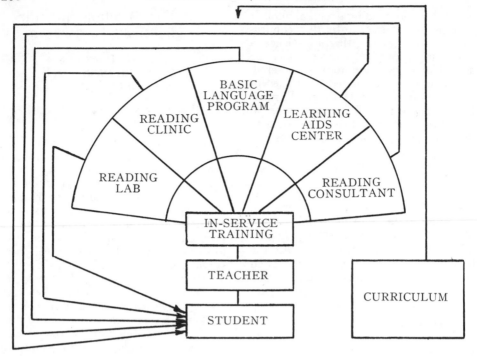

BUILDING READING INTO THE CURRICULUM

ing problems through the use of an informal reading inventory. Teachers are to inventory their own groups during the first three weeks of school and prepare a reading profile for each student. Then, in an individual conference, student and teacher are to use the profile to plan a program for improving skills of vocabulary, comprehension, and flexibility of rate. All procedures for inventorying are to be taught in a series of three in-service training sessions keyed to a step-by-step administration of the test.

Classes will then be scheduled into the reading laboratory for five periodic one-week sessions. Preceding each of these sessions there will again be in-service training to ready the classroom teacher for his role as a reading teacher in partnership with the reading specialist. The lab program is based on the sequence chart included in this article. Each group's reading instruction will start at the stage of development that shows most need for improvement and will move through the

sequence as the competency of the group permits.

The week's work will begin with a lesson based on the reading area in which the incoming group needs to extend skills. Then the student will work at learning stations stocked with materials that will individualize his instruction. Since these are *learning* stations rather than places for skill practice, the reading teacher and the classroom teacher must come to grips with the students' problems and carefully match instruction and materials to developing needs. The learning station lessons culminate with a short diagnostic test designed to give the student feedback on his progress in relation to his profile.

The reading specialist will complete the week's instruction with a reading lesson applying core skills to content which would ordinarily be taught in the classroom. This lesson should enable the teacher to see how to teach specific skills within the context of his ongoing units of work. In fact, the entire lab experience is only a launch-

DEVELOPMENTAL READING LABORATORY SEQUENCE CHART

1. VOCABULARY	2. COMPREHENSION	3. FLEXIBILITY OF RATE
Word Attack Skills Context Sounding Structure Dictionary *Vocabulary Extension* Denotation Connotation Symbolism	*Textbook Skills* Skimming Main idea and details Key words Topic Sentences Expressed Not expressed Author's purpose Sequence Comparison and contrast Cause and effect Conclusion Critical reading Fact and opinion Inference Judgment PQRST (Preview technique) Organizational skills Outlining Notetaking Summarizing Appreciation skills Visualizing Author's purpose Intent Mood Figures of speech Approaches in Poetry Drama Novel Essay	Materials Easy Difficult Purposes Study Recreation

ing pad to an improved classroom experience. We expect teacher and student to gain new insights, enabling the student to be more receptive to lessons designed to help him improve reading and enabling the teacher both to pick up cues which show when a student follows the steps in the development of a skill, when he is ahead, and when he is falling behind and to adapt instructional practices to these conditions.

When instruction does not reach every student, the teacher has alternative resources: he can use the consultative services of the reading specialist or the facilities of the Learning Aids Center. With the help of the reading specialist, he can plan programs for students who need further reinforcement or extension of reading skills: 1) to develop the same concepts, a student may be assigned a story or a chapter at a level easier for him to read; 2)

workbooks or programed materials may be brought in for single students or small groups; 3) the Language Master (Bell and Howell), Listen and Learn Tapes (Educational Developmental Laboratories), the Controlled Reader (Educational Developmental Laboratories), the Craig Reader (Craig Reader Corporation), filmstrips, or transparencies may be borrowed from the Learning Aids Center for use with selected students; 4) two or three students may be assigned to meet together to review material; or 5) the seriously retarded reader may be referred to the Reading Clinic for tutorial instruction.

We look upon this new plan as a vital part of an in-service training program which will enable teachers to become active partners in building curriculum. First, good instructional adaptations will be recorded and shared with other teachers who are teaching the same unit. Then these adaptations will be tried out by members of this group. Finally, those reading practices that have real worth will be taken by curriculum committees working during the summer and fused into content units.

The reading clinic

The Reading Clinic, designed to serve Bloom's most seriously retarded readers, functions also as an in-service training center for teachers. Funded by Title I, it is one of our newest services. The federal funds provided a relocatable classroom—a comfortable, carpeted room with a folding wall that converts it into two smaller areas—and equipped it with carrels, an orthorater, audiometer, controlled reader, tachistoscope, language master, shadowscope, high interest-low reading level library books, popular magazines, and a host of textbooks, professional books, workbooks, tests, and other instructional devices. These facilities were first used during the summer of 1966 for an in-service training workshop for both elementary and secondary teachers from our district. The teachers received one hundred dollars a week during the four weeks of the workshop and attended daily Monday through Friday from 8:00 A.M. until 1:00 P.M. During the first four days of the week they spent one hour preparing tests and lessons, two hours working with students, and two hours in seminar. On Fridays the students were not in attendance, and the teachers divided their time between work on case studies and lectures by visiting reading consultants.

The purpose of the workshop was to teach diagnostic and remedial procedures in an effort to broaden the teachers' concepts of reading so that they could bring better instructional practices into their classrooms. Each teacher was assigned three or four incoming freshmen whose pre-high school placement tests identified them as retarded readers. The teachers used the entire range of clinical diagnostic procedures to compile a reading

case history for each of their students, to diagnose individual reading problems, and to plan remedial instruction. They gave IQ and silent reading tests and learned how to find students' grade expectancies. They used the orthorater and the audiometer to check vision and hearing and conducted personal interviews with each child's parents to determine the physical and emotional factors affecting reading performance. A variety of tests was used to evaluate the students' word attack skills, visual and auditory discrimination, and silent and oral reading. The remaining workshop time was spent in appropriate remedial instruction. Thus, in a tutorial situation, each teacher could immediately apply principles learned. To support these experiences the five lectures, given by outstanding reading specialists from nearby universities, were carefully matched to each stage of instruction. There was general agreement that the workshop had deepened teachers' understandings of the skills involved in each area of reading and, in turn, would help them to improve their reading instruction even though they might not diagnose and remediate each of their pupils individually when they returned to their classrooms in the fall.

In addition to bringing improved reading to their own classrooms, some teachers were able to make even wider contributions. Several ordered new reading materials for their districts and informally guided teachers in their use; four teachers organized formal in-service reading instruction for all of their middle-grade colleagues. All of the teachers expressed a desire for another summer workshop, and we are now preparing our Second Bloom Workshop in Reading.

In the fall, the Reading Clinic began full-scale operation to help students. Students who seem to have severe reading problems are referred to the Reading Clinic by their teachers. The clinician writes full diagnostic reports for each student. These are sent to classroom teachers, as well as parents.

Teachers say that some of their most valuable insights on learning problems come from reading these reports; and as they visit the clinic to discuss individual students, their interest in reading grows. Many return for consultation on other students, for teaching materials, and for resource books from the professional shelf.

The reading consultant in the classroom

Title I not only funded services but, in a very real sense, became a major guideline for change because of its intent "to provide compensatory education for each educationally deprived student."

In the past, students assigned to freshman remedial English classes at Bloom had always been treated as slow learners who needed a remedial reading program. In the past few years, however, teachers reported students who were falling asleep in class, becoming behavior problems, and dropping out in increasing numbers. Traditional methods and materials were no longer reaching them. Our range of 5.5 to 6.7 grade levels no longer produced a homogeneous track of "slow learners," for the label "slow learner" hid groups of culturally disadvantaged and bilingual children—students from pockets of poverty, from the Brazos in Texas, and the Deep South—all exceptional children whose potential is unknown and whose progress requires something more than remedial reading instruction. Such students needed a "fresh start." This fresh start had to be given in a classroom where culturally deprived, bilingual, and slow learner were tracked together. Therefore, the remedial curriculum had to be designed to meet the needs of many different kinds of students.

Basic language development program

One of the most urgent needs was that of students for whom English is a second language. Polish, Italian, and Spanish speaking students were be-coming a large factor in our school. We discovered at least twenty-five students who could make no progress in any classroom until they learned to speak and read the English language. So a comprehensive sequential program with emphasis on independent learning of basic language skills was designed to supplement the remedial program.

The Basic Language Development Program was set up in the Learning Aids Center to help the student proceed through visual-oral learning experiences, to reading readiness experiences, and then to reading experiences. Students were scheduled at the Learning Aids Center during a studyhall period. The length of the course was flexible, adapted to the needs of the student; however, it was recommended that the student spend at least six weeks using the basic materials. The reading consultant made up individual programs, taught the student the procedures, and helped him to fill out his own program forms. The psychologist held several group guidance sessions. The teacher referred the student and was responsible to motivate, keep a close check on attendance in the Learning Aids Center, evaluate progress forms, and recommend adjustments in individual programs. As the student became familiar with the program, he was responsible for working more and more on his own. Student assistants were available to answer questions and help with problems.

The programed nature of the materials made the self-help assignments possible. For most students these materials were used in the following sequence: Language Master Word Picture Cards I, II, III; English Development Program, Set I, II, IV; Vocabulary Development, Set I; SRA Word Games 1-44; Conversa-phone records and guides; Co-Star records and guides; Conversation records and guides; and Sullivan Associates Programed Reading 2-14. Equipment used included the Language Master, earphones, record player, tape recorder, jack box, and extension cords.

The Basic Language Development Program is hard to evaluate objectively. However, a comparison of two pre- and post-tests, Burnett's Basic Reading Inventory and Peabody Picture Vocabulary Test, showed the trend of test results to be sharply upward. Success in the acquisition of abilities basic to language development and sentence reading may also be measured by the way in which assignments kept changing as learning occurred. Furthermore, teachers and counselors have commented about students' increased facility in the use of English.

Since this was a stopgap program undertaken to meet immediate and pressing needs and designed to make the most of limited equipment and facilities, our conclusion is that our stopgap objectives, met without hiring additional personnel or spending as much as $1,000, gave maximum results for minimum outlay. In a modest program under Title I—perhaps in the Basic Language Development Program—we have the blueprint for an experimental program which will qualify under Title III and thus leave Title I money for other reading improvement purposes.

Classroom adaptations for the culturally deprived

Next, we turned our attention to the culturally deprived within the remedial track. How could we unmask, identify, and make instructional plans for this type of deprived student? Teachers had to be shown that there were several levels and types of reading disabilities in their classrooms so that they would be willing to provide for individualized reading and small-group work. For this purpose we set up an informal reading inventory with a stress on tapping listening and speaking skills. Working as a team with the reading consultant, teachers learned a diagnostic approach that might identify the educationally deprived. One of the most dramatic revelations to teachers came through the use of the Wepman Auditory Discrimination Test, which we adapted for group use. When teachers found ninth graders confusing the vowel sound of e and i and the consonant sound of f and v, they began to recognize that weaknesses in auditory discrimination could possibly reveal a culturally deprived student. When other sections of the inventory uncovered deficiencies equally basic, teachers were convinced that they had to back up to the place where environment had taken its toll and, in many cases, start remediation at the very beginning of language development.

In this frame of mind, teachers were ready to plan lessons that would help correct many kinds of basic deficiencies. They began to adapt old materials, introduce new materials, and try new approaches. As they did so, a wealth of new ideas developed.

To individualize skill practice, teachers planned remedial lessons around "core" areas. Single copies of a variety of texts, workbooks, and audiovisual aids ordered as resource material before school started made this kind of lesson planning possible. In teaching syllabication, for example, we used a set of transparencies (visual aids) as introduction, Reading Spectrum as teacher's instruction, Be a Better Reader and Basic Reading Skills for High School Use as sources of individualized practice for students; board work from Phonics We Use and Conquests in Reading as reinforcements, and What's the Word filmstrips as review. Application lessons were taught with a vocabulary list taken from Goals in Spelling, Dolch's 2,000 Commonest Words for Spelling, and paperback books which the students were reading at the time. No longer did students use only two workbooks in which the whole class worked through the same pages at the same time.

To solve problems of both motivation and practice we bought six hundred paperback books, fiction and nonfiction, covering a wide range of titles but emphasizing adventure and sports for boys and romance for girls. These circulated as classroom libraries.

Teachers had to grow accustomed to the idea. Book reports were not assigned. Class time was given for reading. At the beginning all did not run smoothly; student librarians made mistakes; and books were lost. But students liked the books and said so in a student survey. They also reported that they did not want more time in class to discuss books; this fact we interpreted to mean that they needed instruction to develop skills of discussion.

To help students develop better concepts of themselves, one teacher took to heart the message summed up in "nobody knows my name." Beginning with discussions of pictures of people, she taught a combined vocabulary and spelling lesson. The student divided his paper into three columns. In the first he wrote (at the teacher's dictation) words about qualities which had been discussed that week, such as *kind, successful,* and *responsible.* Then students volunteered synonyms, and these were written in the second column. In the third column the student was asked to recall the name of the person contributing the synonym and to write it correctly. Through this activity, the students learned one another's names; they also began to look for and listen to one another's opinions and to see the value of having opinions of their own.

Although our search for a design to reorganize the remedial curriculum is not completed, we have taken a giant step forward. Our teachers are looking at their remedial students in a new light. Teachers have learned that they must start with the concept of "postponed achievement." This concept differs from that of "readiness;" it may be defined as *holding achievement as the goal while the student completes essential educational tasks in an ascending order of complexity to reach achievement.* With the disadvantaged reader there is no way of rushing head on to this goal. Time must be spent during the freshman year to develop prerequisites for success in reading, to compensate for lack of verbal facility,

to remediate, and to motivate. Only then can we emphasize developmental aspects of reading.

Pilot program: fresh start for freshmen

We recognize that there are many important questions that have not yet been answered. We need to know more about the learning process of our culturally deprived students and its implications for instructional change. We believe the Fresh Start for Freshman Program must provide learning experiences in which content, level, and rate are adjusted to individual needs. As in Head Start programs, our program must give students a broader conceptual base before, during, and after developing skills, abilities, and attitudes.

From this belief and our tentative explorations came plans for an experimental Fresh Start for Freshmen Program to answer questions in depth. The new pilot program will be developed in one freshman English remedial class of twenty students taught by a team of two teachers. Federal funds have provided personnel, materials, equipment, and supplies. One full-time teacher will take over the assignments created by freeing the project teachers for experimental work. All supplies, books, textbooks, workbooks, boxed programs, tapes, filmstrips, furniture, glass-enclosed conference areas, and student carrels are part of federal funding of the project, as well as a tape deck, Craig Readers, Language Masters, and a video-tape recorder.

We expect to improve self-concept and see changes in student behavior; but the big question is will academic improvement also occur and will it be measurable? With this in mind, we are planning to emphasize listening, speaking, and writing aspects of language instruction; to utilize principles of group dynamics during guided reading lessons for the whole class; and to provide individual remedial reading instruction as close to clinic practice as possible, diagnosing each student's difficulties, adjusting assignments, and placing him for small group or individual practice at learning stations stocked and equipped like those in the reading laboratory.

Another challenge of the Fresh Start for Freshmen Program is to find instruments that will identify levels of language development, interest, abilities, motivation, and potential of each student in order to establish the base from which we will measure individual growth.

To make it possible to work with whole group, small group, and individuals over a longer span, the class will be scheduled for a two-hour block of time. This scheduling will also facilitate the operation of an expanded team since, in addition to the two classroom teachers, the program will include the services of a counselor, the school psychologist, and the reading consultant. The counselor will work within the classroom setting at least once a week.

Since the aim of the program is to make an impact on the entire remedial curriculum, the project teachers' responsibility will not end with instruction for students. They must also use the special room and special conditions to originate curriculum materials, develop new evaluative techniques, and engage other teachers in their use.

This year we will attempt to disseminate information to other remedial teachers within the structure of departmental meetings. We hope, however, that another year the benefits of the program can be passed on by releasing our team teachers to go into other classrooms to demonstrate techniques, discuss problems, and incorporate other teachers' ideas into this developing curriculum.

Conclusion

The goal of all reading services is to help individual students with their specific reading problems, but we have added a new dimension by making all these services function as channels for in-service training to bring improved reading instruction into the routine of the classroom.

In this plan the teacher goes through a learning cycle which starts in the orientation reading workshop and culminates in his contributions to the curriculum. By changing locations for the in-service training lessons from workshop, to clinic, to laboratory, to the classroom, all reading specialists and resources are brought to bear on in-service problems. The learning cycle may be summarized as follows:

1. The teacher learns and teaches one skill with one child in the reading clinic.

2. The teacher then places that skill in a developmental reading perspective by teaching a small group in the reading laboratory.

3. The teacher learns and teaches the adaptation of that one skill to one classroom group.

4. The teacher applies his new knowledge to further instructional adaptations in the classroom.

5. The teacher reinforces skills by continued observation and practice in the reading clinic and by video-taped micro-teaching.

6. The teacher and his colleagues evaluate the results for incorporation into the curriculum.

Reading in the Total School Curriculum

SIDNEY J. RAUCH
Hofstra University

FOR MANY YEARS, it has been commonplace for reading specialists to list as one of the basic principles of reading instruction the following credo: *There is no one best program or method for teaching reading. Each program must, of necessity, be different, depending upon such significant factors as the individual pupil's abilities and needs, the strengths and weaknesses of the teachers, the purposes and objectives of the administrative and supervisory personnel, the materials available, and the interests and pressures of the community.* In his evaluation of the twenty-seven first grade reading studies sponsored by the U.S. Office of Education in 1964-65,

Russell Stauffer summarized his reactions as follows:

> I have become acutely aware of one tidy generalization—there is no one method of teaching reading. Regardless of the criterion used, there is no one method and this is so in spite of the tragic consequences of internal dynamism that some so-called methods have sought to advance—tragically, eccentrically, and captivatingly, . . . no approach has overcome individual differences or eliminated reading disability (1).

The more one reads about various types of reading programs and observes and evaluates programs in action, the more one becomes convinced that the ultimate success of any program is dominated by three factors: 1) the amount of time specifically devoted to the teaching of reading, with special emphasis upon the direct and systematic teaching of skills; 2) the moral and material support given to reading instruction by the administrators and supervisors responsible for the program; and 3) the awareness of content area teachers that they have a responsibility to extend and refine the reading skills of their students. However, this third factor does not imply or suggest that content area teachers are reading teachers, per se, or remedial reading specialists.

To involve the total faculty in the improvement of reading, the following three conditions must exist: 1) genuine interest and support of a school-wide reading program by the administrative and supervisory staff; 2) concentration on the classroom teacher's immediate and specific problems; and 3) realistic and effective in-service education.

Support of the administrative and supervisory staff

What does the administrator need to consider in initiating or extending a total reading program? Nila Banton Smith has offered the following suggestions: (Though these suggestions are in reply to administrators who wish to start reading programs in the secondary school, they appear to apply equally well to the elementary level.)

1. The administrator should have some background in reading gained through attending meetings and conferences dealing with secondary reading, and as a result of his own reading of recent books and articles on this subject.
2. The administrator should be enthusiastic about starting a reading program and confident of its success. He should take leadership in providing interest-stimulating activities such as those suggested in the appendix to *Corrective Reading in the High School Classroom* (Perspectives in Reading, No. 6, International Reading Association).
3. The administrator should make budgetary provisions for purchasing extra reading materials.
4. The administrator should schedule time for teaching reading except in schools where team-teaching is being used. In such schools, teams of teachers schedule the time with the approval of the administrator.
5. Support of the entire staff should be enlisted.
6. Support of the students and their parents should be obtained.
7. The undertaking should be a cooperative one in which all members of the faculty participate in planning the program from the beginning.
8. While the plan is cooperative, the responsibility for developing the program should be given to one person: the reading specialist, principal, curriculum director, classroom teacher, or someone else who is interested and competent.
9. The person to whom the above responsibility is given *must* be trained in reading.
10. When ready to start the program, care should be taken to make sure that each person involved knows what his responsibility is.
11. The administrator must be ready to accept small beginnings. A well-rounded reading program takes time to develop. The administrator needs to keep enthusiasm at a high ebb, but he often will find it necessary to temper enthusiasm with patience" (2).

It must be emphasized that the chief school administrator (i.e., the principal) sets the tone for the reading program. His interest and concern in better reading permeate the entire program. His sensitivity to the needs of his staff and realistic appraisal of the total school-community environment lead to the enthusiastic cooperation of all concerned. Above all, he provides the leadership necessary for the total involvement of the faculty. According to Ruth Strang, "The aim of the administrator is to provide the experiences every pupil needs to improve in reading." A list of "do's" and "don'ts" for the administrator is supplied by Dr. Strang on pages 77-78 of *The Improvement of Reading* (3).

Attacking immediate, specific classroom problems

The following question was asked of elementary teachers taking graduate courses in the teaching of reading at Hofstra University during the spring term, 1967: "What aspects of the teaching of reading concern you most?" The five major areas in order of importance were grouping, seat work activities, classroom diagnosis, teaching of phonics, and helping the slow learner.

The same question was asked of secondary teachers. Their responses in order of importance were critical interpretation, working with problem readers in the classroom, vocabulary improvement, improving reading in the content areas, and grouping.

Implicit in the above informal survey is the fact that the administration must be aware of these immediate needs and be ready with solutions for these problems. Classroom teachers will not respond to vague generalities. The want answers to problems they meet in the classroom every day.

It has been the writer's experience that content area teachers can contribute most to the improvement of reading by emphasizing the study skills. Basically, the study skills are those reading skills in which the primary aim is to obtain information. In a very helpful New York City Curriculum Bulletin, these skills are referred to as "reading for information, study, and research." (4). Of all the reading areas, improvement in the study skills seems to relate most directly to improvement of class work, resulting

in higher grades. Thus, both the student and teacher can see benefits almost immediately. These skills may be categorized as follows:

Skills of locating information
Using parts of the book (author's organization of materials, preface, introduction, table of contents, index, glossary, etc.)
Use of dictionary skills
Use of encyclopedias, almanacs, atlases and other references
Reading maps, charts, graphs, diagrams, etc.
Use of library techniques

Skills of evaluating information
Reading with a critical attitude
Using several sources to evaluate materials
Judging author's competency
Distinguishing between fact and opinion
Learning propaganda techniques
Evaluating relevancy of information to topic being studied

Skills of organizing information
Note-taking
Classifying facts and ideas
Arranging ideas in sequence
Knowing outline format
Knowing how to outline
Techniques of summarizing

Skills of retaining information
Use of Survey Q3R -See Spache, *Toward Better Reading*, pp. 345-346, for a good summary and evaluation of this study technique (5).
Systematic study vs. cramming
The need for rereading
Note-making vs. note-taking as a memory aid

Adjusting rate to purpose and to the difficulty of the reading selection
There is no such thing as rate in isolation. It must always be considered as *rate of comprehension*.
A good reader must have at least four basic rates of reading:

1) Skimming (skipping with judgment)
2) Rapid reading (timed-reading exercises —no skipping of material)
3) Intensive reading (the art and necessity of rereading)
4) Recreational reading rate.

In teaching the study skills, five basic principles should be kept in mind.

1. Instruction in the study skills should begin at that grade level in which the student begins to read extensively in the content areas. In most instances, this will be Grade 4.

2. Instruction in the study skills should be spread through several grades (i.e., Grades 4-12) rather than concentrated at one grade level. The teacher should think of the study skills as a "spiral curriculum" in which each major skill is reemphasized at each grade level, using more difficult material and proceeding at a faster rate.

3. It should be noted that each major study skill has levels of difficulty. The teacher should begin with the most obvious level of the skill and work toward the most difficult. For example, there is a world of difference between skimming a selection to find a name or date and skimming a chapter to get some idea of the author's pattern of organization.

4. Factual material, rather than narrative or story-type, is more conducive to effective instruction in the study skills. Such factual materials should have a minimum of word recognition problems for the student. The teacher's purpose is to teach a study skill, not to be bogged down in word recognition problems. Avoid materials that are at a student's "frustration level."

5. Though special materials and exercises may be used to teach the study skills, application should be made to the content areas. For example, teaching Survey Q3R is practically valueless unless application is made to a content area textbook.

Another effective way of involving the total faculty in a reading program is to make them aware of the major skills of reading instruction and to show that these skills are involved in practically all the subject areas. A very helpful guide to reading skills in the subject areas, including specific developmental lesson plans pertaining to many of these skills, can be found in the New York City Board of Education publication, *Reading in the Sub-ject Areas, Grades 7-8-9* (6). This curriculum bulletin lists the skills as indicated on the chart on page 216.

Realistic and effective in-service education

A group of reading specialists enrolled in the writer's course in the "Supervision of Reading Instruction" offered at Hofstra University during the fall semester, 1966, prepared a statement of basic principles for in-service education in reading. All involved were actively engaged in organizing and participating directly in their school's in-service programs. The IRA publication, *Conducting In-Service Programs in Reading* (7), was a helpful reference in the preparation of these principles:

1. In-service education must be responsive to the needs of the school or district. These needs could be established through
   a. surveys, including studies of the community;
   b. questionnaires to ascertain teacher needs;
   c. classroom observations by principals and reading specialists; and
   d. requests by teachers.
2. In-service education must have the whole-hearted support of the administration. The administration must indicate in every way possible that reading instruction has been given top priority
   a. in terms of participation of administrators in workshops, special courses, conferences;
   b. in terms of personnel made available to contribute to the reading program; and
   c. in terms of financial support.
3. In-service training should stress the *practical* aspects of the teaching of reading. For example:
   a. preparation of informal tests and other materials for particular grade levels,
   b. specific grouping procedures, and
   c. special activities and materials for the slow learner.
4. In-service training should stress complete involvement of those participating:
   a. participants should help in establishing the goals of courses or workshops;
   b. participants should help in planning the content as well; and
   c. groups should be small.
5. In-service training should include demonstrations, observations, pre-conferences,

GUIDE TO READING SKILLS IN THE SUBJECT AREAS (6)

Reading Skills	Language Arts	Social Studies	Science	Math.	Industrial Arts
WORD RECOGNITION					
1. recognize basic sight words	x				
2. use phonetic analysis	x				
3. use structural analysis	x				
4. use contextual clues for word meaning	x	x	x	x	x
5. use dictionary to check meaning	x	x	x	x	x
COMPREHENSION					
1. understand word and sentence meaning	x	x	x	x	x
2. find main idea and related details	x	x	x	x	x
3. organize and classify facts	x	x	x	x	x
4. perceive sequence of ideas	x	x	x	x	x
5. draw inferences and conclusions	x	x	x	x	
6. understand problems	x	x	x	x	x
7. form judgments	x	x	x	x	
8. predict outcomes	x		x	x	
9. read critically—distinguishing fact from opinion	x	x	x		
10. read for appreciation	x				
11. understand relationships	x	x	x	x	x
12. follow directions	x	x	x	x	x
WORK STUDY					
1. understand parts of a book	x	x	x	x	
2. understand the index of a text	x	x	x	x	
3. use of the dictionary	x	x	x	x	
4. use of the encyclopedia	x	x	x		
5. understand library techniques	x	x	x		
6. interpret maps	x	x	x	x	
7. understand charts	x	x	x	x	x
8. interpret graphs	x	x	x	x	
9. understand diagrams	x	x	x	x	x
10. adjust reading rate-skimming	x	x	x	x	x
11. select and evaluate information	x	x	x	x	x
12. use techniques of retention and recall	x	x	x	x	x

(The "x" under each subject area indicates that the reading skill is relevant to that particular subject.)

and post-conferences as integral parts of all in-service courses:

a. reading specialists must have the skills and experience for successful demonstration lessons; and

b. observations of master teachers should not be limited to one session. (Some activities need to be observed for several consecutive sessions.)

6. Evaluation should be an on-going concern in all in-service training through

a. evaluation of courses, workshops and conferences, etc. by supervisors and teachers; and

b. yearly testing of pupils.

7. In-service training should, for obvious reasons, be conducted during released time, rather than after school hours. Time must be provided not only for courses but also for visitations and conferences.

8. New teachers will be hired with the understanding that their inservice training will be an important part of their responsibilities. This training will be provided according to school and personal needs.

9. In-service training, especially for new teachers, should be defined not only in terms of workshops, courses, and institutes but also in terms of contacts with principals and reading specialists. More and better supervision by those who are well versed in the problems of teaching reading is the *sine qua non* for any program aimed at the improvement of reading instruction.

10. In-service training should have as its final goal the improvement of instruction in *all areas* of reading.

11. There must be a greater awareness of the fact that individual differences exist among teachers as well as they do among children.

To supplement the preceding matter Robinson and Rauch have offered the following suggestions:

1. An in-service program that threatens the security of staff members cannot succeed. The consultant must be sensitive and realistic in his demands upon the teaching staff. Programs that require too much of the teacher's "free" time are likely to breed resentment and failure. At the same time, participants in the in-service program should have the opportunity to share in both the planning and the evaluating of the program.

2. Programs that try to accomplish too much in too short a time will not have lasting results. It is better to concentrate on one grade level or one subject area at a time rather than attempt to reorganize the entire system-wide program in one year. A successful program in a limited area will mean much more in the long run than questionable progress on a broad scale.

3. The active support of teachers who are reputed to be extremely capable instructors and who are respected by other teachers greatly helps the reading consultant in organizing and conducting the in-service program.

4. In-service reading programs that involve persons who teach in a subject area must reflect the goals and objectives of that area. To help ensure fuller cooperation from content area teachers, the consultant should use the materials of their subject to demonstrate the application of specific reading skills (8).

To summarize; the chances for involvement of the total school faculty in a reading program will be determined to the extent that the following conditions are met: 1) teachers must recognize the need for such an effort; 2) realistic goals must be set; 3) the necessary teaching materials must be available; 4) in-service instruction must be down-to-earth and directed towards immediate classroom problems; and 5) school leaders must be sincerely and actively devoted to the cause of reading improvement on a school-wide basis.

REFERENCES

1. Stauffer, Russell. "Some Tidy Generalizations," *The Reading Teacher*, 20 (October, 1966), 4.
2. Smith, Nila Banton. "Questions Administrators Ask About Reading in Secondary Schools," *Corrective Reading in the High School Classroom*, Perspectives in Reading No. 6, H. Alan Robinson and Sidney J. Rauch, (Eds.). Newark, Delaware: International Reading Association, 1966, 124.
3. Strang, Ruth. *The Improvement of Reading*. New York: McGraw-Hill Book Company Inc., 1961, 77-78.
4. *Reading, Grades 7-8-9: A Teacher's Guide to Curriculum Planning*. Curriculum Bulletin No. 11, 1957-58 Series. Board of Education of the City of New York, 1959.
5. Spache, George D. *Toward Better Reading*. Champaign, Illinois: Garrard Press, 1963, 345-346.
6. *Reading in the Subject Areas, Grades 7-8-9*. Curriculum Bulletin No. 6, 1963-64 Series. Board of Education of the City of New York, 1964, 2.
7. Aaron, Ira E., Byron Callaway, and Arthur V. Olson. *Conducting In-Service Programs in Reading*. Newark, Delaware: International Reading Association, 1965.
8. Robinson, H. Alan, and Sidney J. Rauch. *Guiding the Reading Program: A Reading Consultant's Handbook*. Chicago: Science Research Associates, 1965, 47-48.

Innovative Programs in Oregon

ELEANOR JENKS
Oregon State Department of Education

NEVER IN THE HISTORY of the English-speaking world has so much emphasis been given to the importance of innovation in reading. Press, radio, television, pulpit, and political platforms, all give emphatic recommendations for the improvement of reading instruction. NDEA Titles III and XI; ESEA Titles I, II, III, IV, and V; and the Higher Education Act have provided a godsend of funds and encouragement to those of us long frustrated by financial want and ultraconservative curricular rigidity.

In Oregon, however, the wheels of innovation were already rolling. The State Board of Education in January of 1962 confirmed policy decisions which changed the course of Oregon education and altered the role of the State Department of Education. These policy decisions became the bases for development and implementation of The Oregon Program.

As The Oregon Program began to crystallize, it received the official endorsement of Senator Mark O. Hatfield, (then governor) and the legislature of the state which appropriated monies to facilitate planning and development. Twenty-six school systems and nine colleges and universities worked with the state department for over two years to develop budgets and plans that would reach into the classrooms of the state and effect constructive changes. The State Department of Education, under the guidance of Superintendent Leon P. Minear, provided direction and coordination for the wholehearted drive to upgrade Oregon schools and to accelerate change. A Ford Foundation grant of $3.5 million for a four-year program gave impetus to the concerted endeavor.

The State Department of Education has been immeasurable help in determining the needs of children in reading education in Oregon. Its work, conducted cooperatively with the schools and with college English and reading education personnel—the triad of cooperating institutions as envisioned and activated in The Oregon Program— has identified, largely by utilizing the *Evaluative Criteria,* 1960 Edition (1), both strengths and weaknesses. In the past year, eight district-wide workshops, three multiple-district workshops (Eastern, Central, and Western Oregon), and two statewide workshops have been held. These involved administrative, teacher, and to some extent, student participation.

Involving approximately 400 participants, one of these statewide workshops was held over a period of two weeks (July 25 to August 5, 1966) at Willamette University in Salem under the sponsorship of the State Department of Education and funded partially by the phasing-out of the five-year Oregon Program by the Ford Foundation and mainly by Title V monies from ESEA. This workshop focused on the fundamental communication skills of reading and writing and brought together *teams of participants*—teams composed of superintendents, principals, curriculum coordinators, supervisors, and teachers —to witness and evaluate presentations from on-the-spot Oregon and national authorities: Chief Consultant, Dwight Burton, Florida State University; Muriel Crosby, past president of the National Council of Teachers of English; Alvina Burrows, New York University; Robert Bennett, San Diego City Schools; Martha Maxwell, University of Maryland; Guil Hollingsworth, director of Boeing Scientific Research Laboratories in Seattle; Robert Myers, University of Oregon; Harold Covell, University of British Columbia; Marion Faustman, San Juan, California, Unified Schools; Richard Scott, superintendent at Fern Ridge, Oregon; Margaret Lane, University of Oregon; Dorris Lee, Portland State College; Leonard Rice, president of Oregon College of Education; and others, including (by tele-lecture) Julia M. Haven of the United States Office of Education. With the guidance of these consultants, teams evaluated their own needs and objectives and then prepared syllabi for curriculum improvement and in-service programs for their districts.

The other statewide workshop, held at Gearhart on Oregon's beautiful Pacific Coast, enrolled 56 teachers and administrators from 44 of the 64 small schools (those with enrollment under 200 students) who were involved in the ESEA Title III Small Schools Project. These people worked with seven consultants and Project Director Charles Haggerty of the State Department of Education.

Both of these statewide programs were evaluated by the participants. Resultant data compilation and summary comments equated with significantly enthusiastic reactions and follow-up curriculum and instructional innovations in reading and English. A substantial number of school districts, including a surprising number of rather small school systems, following in-service workshops and with consultant help, developed either initial or revised and definitely innovative curricula. Others are presently active or are contemplating such activity.

Let me describe two.

The Reynolds mobile reading classroom

Reynolds School District No. 7, Troutdale, Oregon, is located about fifteen minutes by freeway from downtown Portland. It is in East Multnomah County in a suburban area best described as the Greater Portland Metropolitan Area. In the eastern section of the district the area becomes more rural and the population less dense.

In this district there are approximately 3,000 youngsters from grades K through 12. These students are housed in five elementary schools, one new 7-8 grade intermediate school, and one high school. Previous to the 1965-66 school year the district provided what was probably an average kind of a reading program. A specialist was assigned to work with the elementary schools; each teacher in the primary grades had an adequate background and experience in teaching reading. At the high school special so-called "lab English classes" were organized and taught as reading classes. A summer remedial program, taught by three teachers, was available for a student fee of $15. Emphasis was remedial, rather than developmental or enriching. It was a fair program by most standards, but it lacked total teacher involvement, and it did not constitute a real attack on the problem.

With the advent of Title I of ESEA there came in the Reynolds District a bold undertaking, which changed each teacher's emphasis. The whole story cannot be told because it is still being written. It is a story of a rather small, suburban school district and its belief that every youngster is entitled to learn to read: not minimally, but *productively* for enrichment and *functionally* for survival as a happy, well-adjusted individual in a world in which every aspect has been and can be reduced to the printed page.

After discussing possible projects with teachers, the school board, state department officials, and reading specialists, it was decided to devote approximately $50,000 of the district's entitlement under Title I to an all-out attack on the reading problem, for initial testing revealed that over 600 youngsters needed better reading instruction.

As a focal point to launch their war on reading retardation the Reynolds District had constructed a mobile home type trailer 40 feet long and 12 feet wide, built to their specifications with book shelving, a projection booth, a teacher's desk, and thickly carpeted acoustical floors installed at the nearby factory. After completion, at a cost of approximately $6,000, they equipped this unit with over $10,000 worth of the most modern equipment, including five EDL listening booths with controlled readers, eight listening stations with headsets and built-in record players and tape recorders, several tachistoscopes, an audiometer, and shelves literally bulging with high-interest, low-reading-level books. This trailer with a reading specialist, a certificated primary teacher, and her assistant move from school to school in the district.

The laboratory remains at each school from six to eight weeks, and after it has left, its effect lingers; for not only does it leave equipment, books, and materials at each school but the unit is also utilized as a teacher-training device. As the reading specialist works with some of the children, their teacher observes and learns diagnostic and remedial techniques, while the assistant teaches the remaining children.

In the relatively short time that this mobile lab has been in operation, the results have been little short of miraculous. Youngsters are so enthusiastic that they request and are allowed to use the materials and read the books at recesses, lunchtimes, and after school.

One small fourth grade youngster from illiterate parents has actually learned to read—almost taught himself, his desire was so all-consuming. Prior to the lab's arrival he disliked school, was a discipline problem, and could barely read or write his own name.

As fabulous as the Reynolds people believe the idea has been, it does not represent their total commitment. Three full-time elementary librarians have been added; these librarians are teachers with reading experience, classroom experience, and librarian experience. Two full-time assistants were added to the high school and junior high school libraries. Lists of youngsters needing special help were circulated to all teachers. Hauton B. Lee, superintendent, declares that from these efforts has come a real renaissance in the faculties in all schools at all levels.

Last summer three reading teachers were employed for six weeks to instruct the children from these schools and a parochial school at no cost to the youngster. This summer there will be five.

Although the main emphasis in the program has been that of combating reading retardation, the district is moving definitely now toward a complete developmental program, and plans are being made for adult classes for both teachers and other members of the community.

The Lake Oswego RAM Center, 8mm. film loops, and developmental reading

The Lake Oswego Public Schools lie also in the emerald shadow of Portland's metropolitan fringe. Russell M. Esvelt, superintendent, and Scholastica Murty, high school English teacher and past president of the Oregon Council of Teachers of English—both educators renowned for their interest and participation in programs of innovation for educational change—speak pridefully of their "RAM Center." RAM, of course, decodes to *Research and Materials*.

Archie Matthew, director of the center, working with primary teachers in the district, hypothesized that the greatest factors in the success of teaching reading in the first and second grade are *motivation* and *identification*. The child has to be motivated to read, and identification with the material is paramount. Motivation, these people decided, has long been overlooked, and few steps other than outwardly making the material more attractive have been attempted in recent years. Identification in the form of experience charts and stories is at best a superficial attempt at individual involvement.

The Lake Oswego people observed that reading programs continue to be developed apart from the interests of individual students. Special equipment and commercially related materials designed as a "total reading program" and providing individual continuing-progress work are expensive. They studied the problem. What better motivation to read is there than reading one's own story? But what, other than self-identification, might stir the child toward writing his own story? Answers were found.

Take a look at an 8mm. film loop of a class trip to the farm. Listen to the children: "There's Jane and Tom . . . that can't be me actually milking a cow. . . . Boy! Wasn't that fun? . . . Jane looks like she didn't like the smell. . . . Not over already? . . . What? . . . We can watch it all over again, and the teacher says we can look at it by ourselves in our spare time, too!"

Now the stories are written. Thirty individual stories from thirty different experiences and the reliving of these experiences over and over. With guidance and sound judgment as to vocabulary, the thirty stories are cooperatively summarized by the children into one story that each child has had an intimate part in writing.

This story is then set in type, photographed with the 8mm camera, and spliced into the appropriate places in the original film. The trip to the dairy farm has become a reading story that is viewed and read over and over by the children—actors and authors. Printing the story in a booklet form with ample room for the child to illustrate each sequence is a follow-up activity.

Another approach by the Lake Oswego people in using the 8mm. film loop is to take *one child* from the classroom and place him in a situation where it is not feasible to take the *entire class*. By "starring" just one of their peers, the other children easily identify with the film—again achieving the objectives of identification and motivation.

Not counting a charge for time, the cost of the four-minute loop film may be as low as $6. The cost of the 8mm. loop projector with the stop frame feature is about $70.

Not nearly so expensive as many other reading devices, the 8mm. film loop is also used in Lake Oswego as a paced reader. Using child- or locally-oriented, teacher-developed stories, the material is presented in several ways. Two will be discussed here.

The first method involves the left-to-right oriented, sight word, reading story. Setting the story in type by line and covering all but the first word, the camera is turned on for 1½ to 2 seconds. The first word is covered, and the second, uncovered, with the same interval on film. Thus, the words of the story appear one at a time in a left-to-right direction, providing for the child this orientation. Again, these stories are only four minutes in duration and are used both individually and in groups. Student-produced art work is sometimes filmed and spliced in the story for added interest.

The second step in filming this type of reading story is to uncover one *phrase* at a time, still using the cover-uncover method with left-to-right movement as the film format. The time for each phrase is necessarily longer than for just one word at a time.

The second method of setting up the story for filming is to set the type one line at a time, uncovering each line slowly, and leaving it entirely visible before going on to the next line. Mr. Matthew develops subsequent films with shorter-line-visibility periods to increase the speed of reading.

The additional motivational factor of operating the projector by himself is undoubtedly an aid to increasing the reading interests and vocabulary of the child. In all cases, the teachers emphasize that the story filmed must have meaning to the child in order to be fully effective.

The success of this Lake Oswego innovation demonstrates that with a minimum of financial outlay and with the creative-imaginative minds of youngsters and good teachers a wealth of individualized reading experiences can be made available for the pupils.

Space limitation prevents detailed reporting of further Oregonian innovative programs. A few are listed: the Title I six-year longitudinal study to develop a cross-media individualized approach to reading instruction in Glide, where, working with teams of doctoral candidates at the University of Oregon, visual, auditor, and motoric experiences will be synthesized with the printed symbol in flexibly organized sequences of learning experiences; the Aud-X program, essentially a word recognition technique technologically adapted for continuing-progress individual learning, at the Bryant Elementary School in Lake Oswego, one of twenty-three such pilot programs in the nation; the NDEA Title III aided Study Skills Center with electronic tapes developed to the specifications of the professors and the needs of the students by Director Howard F. Bird at Lane Community College in Eugene; the teacher-trainee tutorial experience in a remedial reading summer workshop directed by Evelyn Egan at Clatsop College in Astoria; the simulation in reading instruction teacher-trainee program developed by Jordan Utsey of the University of Oregon, Carl Wollen of Oregon State University and H. O.

Beldin of Oregon College of Education; the ESEA Title III "Project Prometheus," which mobilizes the educational and cultural resources of the seven southwestern Oregon counties to provide an exemplary, six-week, residential summer school with unique cultural and intellectual experiences for able secondary students and coordinates in its structure fifty high schools, seven intermediate education districts, two regional curriculum councils, and seven cultural organizations in the development of interdisciplinary classes of timely significance; the many programs using i.t.a., "Words in Color," the development of gross motor skills, "Unifon," the locally developed and the commercially produced programed instruction, cross-grading, interest grouping, electronically equipped reading laboratories; and, of course, we should take note of the effects of the Knapp Library Project at Roosevelt High School in Portland and the ESEA Title III "Project Springboard," a mass media facilitation for member schools on student reading interests, quality, and quantity. And in Burns, Oregon, A. E. Starns, superintendent of the Harney County Intermediate Education District, steps to the music of yet "another drummer." He has envisioned and is presently blueprinting an *airborne reading and communications skills laboratory* which will serve the isolated rural schools of Eastern Oregon. Starns

will seek private and governmental financial aid to get his dream "off the ground."

You see, Oregon people have long recognized the right to step to the music we hear—a right we have so long as we do not align ourselves with those labelled by C. S. Lewis as "trousered apes." We make mistakes. We try to learn from our mistakes.

Carl Rogers, in his essay, "Toward a Theory of Creativity" (2), writes:

> With scientific discovery and invention proceeding, we are told, at the rate of geometric progression, a generally passive and culture-bound people cannot cope with the multiplying issues and problems. Unless individuals, groups, and nations can imagine, construct, and creatively revise new ways of relating to these complex changes, the lights will go out."

Today our nation has risen to the challenge with "new ways" in education, particularly in reading which is so necessary to beginning and continuing education.

As Plato said, "We can easily forgive the child who is afraid of the dark; the real tragedy of life is when men are afraid of the light."

REFERENCES

1. *Evaluative Criteria*. National Study of Secondary School Evaluation. Washington 6, D. C.: 1960 Edition.
2. Rogers, Carl. "Toward a Theory of Creativity," *A Source Book for Creative Thinking*. New York: Charles Scribner's Sons, 1962.

Teaching the Essential Reading Skills in Social Studies

ALVIN KRAVITZ
Amityville, New York
Public Schools

WITHIN THE PAST FEW YEARS teachers have become aware of the need for teaching reading skills in the content areas. One of the major content areas, social studies, requires an approach somewhat different from other subject areas. Let us view the topic from four interrelated, yet different, angles.

Directed reading activity

Elementary and secondary teachers who are involved in teaching social studies have found increasing success in presenting their subject matter through the use of a directed reading activity.

Whipple (18) states the format of present day social studies texts is similar to a reading book used for basal instruction. However, the reader's job is quite different. Children need guidance in selecting what to remember and then techniques in how to remember (17).

The New York State Curriculum Guides (8, 17) point out the advisability of a directed reading activity for basic instructional purposes. Spache (15) indicates the superiority of guided reading in the teaching of social studies.

All too often students are forced to plunge into complex materials with little idea of what to look for or even why they are reading a particular text. The involved structure of social studies texts requires preparation and assistance for the student. Strang (16) suggests that the teacher can guide the student through the use of prepared questions. Let us go a step further and prepare not only the questions for consideration during the lesson but the necessary matter prior to beginning any part of the lesson.

A plan for a directed reading activity in social studies is contained in Five Steps To Reading Success (2):

Step One: Readiness
Arousing pupil interest
Setting a purpose for the reading
Developing a background and a sense of continuity
Creating an awareness of the reading required

Step Two: Concept Development
Discussing the vocabulary and concepts which need clarification
Explaining how context may give a term meaning
Studying pronunciation and spelling when appropriate

Step Three: Silent Reading
Locating specific details
Finding the main idea and supporting details
Seeing a vivid picture through word concepts
Locating information by skimming
Determining accuracy of statements

Step Four: Discussion (Oral or Written)
Checking comprehension
Sharing different points of view

Step Five: Rereading (Silent or Oral)
Checking accuracy
Examining critically

Karlin (5) discusses a directed reading activity with a slight modification. His five-step process includes:

1. Readiness—vocabulary and purpose
2. Silent Reading—refer to question
3. Discussion—relating to silent reading
4. Rereading—for different purposes
5. Application—to the lesson

Gates (3) suggested that we cultivate student interest in each content subject. He believed that social studies texts needed to be reformed because of the too difficult readability, the poor literary quality, and the lack of organization of school materials. Since it is extremely difficult for the classroom teacher to rewrite texts while teaching the students in the classroom, perhaps the next best thing would be to circumvent the problem through the use of a directed reading activity.

Vocabulary

Each subject area has its own vocabulary which is unique. Social studies certainly is no exception to the rule. It is vital for the teacher to develop the vocabulary of the specific lesson within its own context, or comprehension of the total subject will be much less than expected (16). Smith (14) indicates the child's ability to deal with the content area improves as training is given in the vocabulary of that subject. *Reading in Secondary Schools* (8) shows the desirability of vocabulary development through the use of context meaning, word study, and the attainment of word attack skills as a means of improving overall comprehension.

Bamman (1) points out that reading social studies is more difficult than reading narrative material to which the elementary student is accustomed. The vocabulary is not controlled; the student must organize a mass of unrelated facts; the ideas are very complex; and much previous knowledge must be brought forward to assist the student in developing concepts.

Vocabulary is general term which covers various subdivisions. Bamman (1) has made six headings to include the types of difficult word areas the student may meet in his social studies work.

a. technical terms—
would include words such as feudalism, vassal, primogeniture, guild, and crusade.
b. multisyllabic words—
formidable words are totalitarian, accountability, telecommunication, endowments, and philanthropic.
c. abstract words—
maturation would help the student to understand such words as liberty, justice, equality, democracy, and despotism.
d. general terms—
multiple meanings arise in the use of elevator since the student may not realize we speak of a grain elevator.
e. mathematical terms—
usually included in the use of time designations, area, population statistics, graphs, and charts.
f. concepts—
these words produce mental images which are really abstractions such as "tolerance." A student's view will broaden as he begins the study of human relations. What is tolerance to one child may be intolerance to another.

Jenkinson (4) has an interesting approach to vocabulary development as she uses the term Functional Word Knowledge. She has divided the topic into three areas:

a. function words—
this area includes small words that are often ignored. Some examples of structure words are as follows:
(1) cause and effect—
because, since, so that
(2) suggest condition—
unless, if, although
(3) indicate contrast—
whereas, while
(4) time relationships—
as, before, when, after
(5) parallel ideas—
however, therefore, hence
b. shifts in word meaning—
the use of familiar words in unfamiliar context, i.e.
(1) cabinet — minister / clergy / furniture
(2) iron curtain? cold war? tariff wall?
c. classifying—
since learning often takes place through recognizing similarities and differences, it is essential to use this procedure.
(1) compare similarities and difference—
declaration and proclamation
(2) contrast differences—
a kingdom and a democracy
(3) paired qualities—
kind and gentle
humid and dank

No matter what procedure a teacher may wish to use for the introduction of vocabulary to any lesson it is vital that we understand the value of instruction in this area. If we wish to improve comprehension, we need to broaden our approach to include vocabulary development as a basic tool.

The SQ3R study formula

Students need to be taught how to study social studies as well as other subject areas. We often find elementary and secondary pupils who are so disorganized in their approach to the basic procedures that they do not know where or how to begin a study program. Robinson (9) proved the effectiveness of his study formula in his examination of college students' study habits. As a result, we have the SQ3R study formula in use throughout the entire educational strata.

Preston (6) suggests a modified approach for the elementary student beginning at the intermediate level. Strang (16) indicates a more difficult process whereby students at the high school level ask themselves a general question which cuts across the author's organization. We would not expect the same thoroughness or ability from an elementary youngster as we anticipate from a high school student. Since the application of the study method is one of degree dependent upon the grade level of the student, it is worthwhile to consider the following approach as a means of reaching most children.

Here is a sample lesson for the development of the SQ3R Study Formula that may be used from the intermediate level right on to the high school student. The language has been simplified in order that almost any child who reads at the fourth level or above might be able to understand the directions. Naturally, the teacher would direct the beginning lessons in the use of the procedure, but the student could retain the directional sheet for further study and reference.

S—Survey
Q—Question
R—Read
R—Recite
R—Review

Step I—Survey

Look through the whole assignment before you actually read to answer your questions. You should look for all of the following items before you begin to read.

A. *Boldface type*
This is the heavy, dark, large print at the beginning of each chapter, section, and paragraph. Look at the name of the chapter and the section heading.

B. *Pictures with Captions*
The picture and its caption, which is the explanation of the picture, will help to tell about the material you will soon read.

C. *Charts*
A chart will give you much information at a glance. When you read the chart before you read the story, you will have much information to help you understand the paragraphs.

D. *Drawings with Captions*
A drawing is considered the same as a picture when you survey the material before you read. Look at the drawing and its caption to help you understand the chapter or section.

E. *Maps and Diagrams*
A map or diagram will explain many paragraphs of written material if you look at it before you begin to read. A map or diagram may reduce half a page of writing into one small drawing.

F. *Summary*
At the end of most chapters there is a summary. The summary tells very briefly about the information that is in the chapter. After you have read the summary, you will usually have a very good idea of the main topics in the chapter.

G. *Questions*
The author has added questions to his chapter to direct your attention to some of the important ideas. Be sure to look at the questions before you read the selection. This step will help you to be ready for the new thoughts you are about to read.

Step 2—Question

Use the boldface type to make your question. If the heading of the section is "Great Plains Soil," use these words to make the following questions:

What is Great Plains soil like?
Of what is Great Plains Soil made?
What must farmers consider when using Great Plains soil?

If there is no boldface type to help you make a question, use this question: What does the author expect me to learn about *this* topic from studying this selection?

A. *Study Guide*
1. Fold or rule a sheet of large-sized

notebook paper lengthwise, down the middle.

2. Write your question on the left side of the page.
3. Answer your questions on the right side of the page.
4. When you write your answers use only key words to describe the ideas or facts you have decided are most important. *Do not write long answers.*
5. Be sure you have read the paragraph or section after your question and thought about it before you write the answer.

Step 3—Read

Read the paragraph or section to find the answer to your question. Do not stop to read every word carefully; concentrate on finding the main point. You cannot remember all the facts you find, so you must look for the important ones. There are usually *one or two main points* for each section.

Step 4—Recite

After you have finished the assignment, go back over the lesson immediately. Cover the right side of the paper where the answers are written, and ask yourself the questions on the left side of the page.

Answer the question orally. That means you must say the answers *out loud* so that you will know if you have made a mistake.

If you find you cannot answer the questions, look back at the key words which are your answers. Sometimes you will have to go back to the book to restudy the particular part which you did not understand or have forgotten.

Step 4 is very important. When you give yourself an immediate quiz on what you have studied, it is the best possible way to prevent forgetting.

Practice until you can recite the whole study guide without looking back to the key words. Then practice some more. This extra practice is what pays off.

Step 5—Review

About four weeks later, and also before every examination, go back to your questions and answers again and quiz yourself. Reread only those parts which you have forgotten.

If you have taken steps 1 (Survey), 2 (Question), 3 (Read), and 4 (Recite) faithfully, you will find that you do not have too much to restudy.

Study skills

Here is an area that encompasses all others previously discussed. In order for a student to apply himself to the full understanding of the material he has read in social studies, he must have basic knowledge of the study skills pertaining to his subject area.

Spache (*15*) states most students only receive training in reading of a basal reading type which often concludes by the fourth or sixth grade. This has been the situation until quite recently. The influx of federal aid money has encouraged many school districts to begin advanced training and even developmental programs at the secondary level. The writer would certainly agree with Spache (*15*) and Strang (*16*) that advanced reading training should be provided by all teachers for effective reading in the content fields.

Smith (*14*) has pointed out that study skills improve in a specific content area if they are pulled out and given special attention. She has indicated how teachers may help children if they are taught to recognize the major patterns found in elementary textbooks which deal with content areas. The necessary skills defined for social studies are indicated by Smith (*14*): reading pictures; reading maps, globes, atlases; reading for cause and effect content; reading for comparison; reading for sequence; reading to locate dates with events; and reading critically to determine different viewpoints, facts mixed with opinion, and when propaganda is used.

Smith's (*13, 14*) basic grouping of skills common to all areas appears wide enough to include many authors in the field of reading study skills. Five major areas are listed for classification purposes: selection and evaluation, organization, location of information, following directions, and specialized skills. Other authors have listed those skills necessary for learning social studies. Spache (15) has three categories which include a) locating information, b) organizing information, and c) retaining and using information. Russell's (12) emphasis for the social studies area is applied to the ability to locate information in reference books. Bamman's (1) suggested skills fall into the general pattern of information skills. Robinson (10) applied the major areas as established by Smith with a slight variation in the EDL Study Skills Library. Here the same concepts are involved, but they are classified under the headings of interpretation, evaluation, organization, and reference (locating information) with the theme of following directions throughout all the lessons. *A Teacher's Guide To Curriculum Planning* (7) has extensive listings of skills which should be covered by the teacher as instruction is given to students in the social studies curriculum.

Robinson's (11) pilot study attempted to determine the reading skills fourth grade pupils actually used as they tried to solve problems in social studies. Although many study skills were put into practice properly, it is interesting to note those skills in which deficiencies existed or application was not made by the student. This small group of intermediate students did not make maximum use of retaining details, comparing information, grasping unstated main ideas, remembering relevant details, making inferences, or using the table of contents, headings or guides, pictorial aids, and the index. The author of the pilot study suggests the teacher should be aware of the student's reading skills, analyze the skills necessary to carry out an assignment, and teach those skills required to carry out the assignment.

Karlin (5) has prepared a checklist of study skills based upon the classifications suggested by Smith (13, 14). It would be most helpful for the teacher to use this format in planning a program of instruction in study skills for the student.

CHECKLIST OF STUDY SKILLS (5)

I. Selection and Evaluation

Can the student do the following?
  a. recognize the significance of the content
  b. recognize important details
  c. identify unrelated details
  d. find the main idea of a paragraph
  e. find the main idea of larger selections
  f. locate topic sentences
  g. locate answers to specific questions
  h. develop independent purposes for reading
  i. realize the author's purpose
  j. determine the accuracy and relevancy of information

II. Organization

Can the student do the following?
  a. take notes
  b. determine relationship between paragraphs
  c. follow time sequences
  d. outline single paragraphs
  e. outline sections of a chapter
  f. outline an entire chapter
  g. summarize single paragraphs
  h. summarize larger units of material

III. Location of Information

Can the student do the following?
  a. find information through a table of contents
  b. locate information through the index
  c. use a library card catalog to locate materials
  d. use the *Reader's Guide to Periodical Literature* to locate sources of information
  e. use an almanac to obtain data
  f. understand and use various appendices
  g. use glossaries
  h. use encyclopedias to locate information

IV. Following Directions

Can the student do the following?
  a. see the relation between the purposes and the directions
  b. follow one-step directions
  c. follow-steps in sequence

V. Specialized Skills

Can the student do the following?
  a. understand the significance of pictorial aids
  b. read and interpret graphs
  c. read and interpret tables
  d. read and interpret charts
  e. read and interpret maps
  f. read and interpret cartoons
  g. read and interpret diagrams
  h. read and interpret pictures

Conclusion

Many factors are involved in teaching the essential reading skills in social studies. Teachers of this content area need to apply diverse methods and techniques in order that students may become more skilled as they read subject matter material. It would be useful to consider the overall approach which includes the directed reading activity, vocabulary development, a workable study formula, and applicable study skills for a worthwhile and effective program at the elementary and secondary level.

REFERENCES

1. Bamman, Henry A., Ursula Hogan, and Charles E. Green. *Reading Instruction in the Secondary Schools.* New York: David McKay Company, Inc. 1961, 135-154.
2. *Five Steps to Reading Success in Science, Social Studies and Mathematics.* New York: Metropolitan School Study Council, Teachers College, Columbia University, 1960, 8-9.
3. Gates, Arthur I. "The Nature and Function of Reading in the Content Areas," *New Frontiers In Reading,* in J. Allen Figurel (Ed.), International Reading Association Conference Proceedings (Scholastic Magazines, New York) 5, 1960, 152.
4. Jenkinson, Marion D. "Increasing Reading Power in Social Studies," in *Corrective Reading in the High School Classroom,* in H. Alan Robinson and Sidney J. Rauch (Eds.), Perspectives in Reading No. 6, International Reading Association, Newark, Delaware, 1966, 75-87.
5. Karlin, Robert. *Teaching Reading in High School.* New York: The Bobbs-Merrill Company, Inc., 1964, 236, 140-141.
6. Preston, Ralph C. "Sequence In Reading in the Content Areas in Social Studies," in *Sequential Development of Reading Abilities,* in Helen M. Robinson (Ed.), (Supplementary Educational Monographs, No. 90) December 1960, University of Chicago Press, 128.
7. *Reading—Grades 7-8-9. A Teacher's Guide to Curriculum Planning.* Board of Education of the City of New York Curriculum Bulletin, 1957-58, Series No. 11.
8. *Reading In Secondary Schools.* The University of the State of New York. Albany, New York: The State Education Department, Bureau of Secondary Curriculum Development, 1965, 44-47.
9. Robinson, Francis P. *Effective Study.* New York: Harper, 1961.
10. Robinson, H. Alan, Stanford E. Taylor, and Helen Frackenpohl. *Teacher's Guide EDL Study Skills Library.* Huntington, New York: Educational Developmental Laboratories, 1962, 4-5.
11. Robinson, H. Alan. "Reading Skills Employed in Solving Social Studies Problems," *The Reading Teacher,* January 1965. International Reading Association, 263-269.
12. Russell, David H. *Children Learn to Read.* New York: Ginn and Company, 1961, 339.
13. Smith, Nila Banton. "The Development of Basic Reading Techniques," *A Report of the Fifth Annual Conference on Reading.* University of Pittsburgh, 1949, 46-60.
14. Smith, Nila Banton. *Reading Instruction for Today's Children.* Englewood Cliffs, New Jersey: Prentice-Hall, Inc., 1963, 312, 348-349.
15. Spache, George D. *Toward Better Reading.* Champaign, Illinois: Garrard Publishing Company, 1963, 273-275; Chap. 18, 334-347.
16. Strang, Ruth, Constance M. McCullough, and Arthur E. Traxler. *The Improvement of Reading.* New York: McGraw-Hill Book Company, Inc., 1961, Chap. 6, 142-156.
17. *The Teaching of Reading.* The University of the State of New York, The State Education Department, Bureau of Elementary Curriculum Development, Albany, New York, 1963, 58-59.
18. Whipple, Gertrude. "Sequence in Reading in the Content Areas," in *Sequential Development of Reading Abilities,* in Helen M. Robinson (Ed.), Supplementary Educational Monographs, No. 90, December 1960. Chicago, Illinois: University of Chicago Press, 128.

Helping the Retarded Reader Read Social Studies Material

DAVID L. SHEPHERD
Hofstra University

THE RETARDED READER is one of the basic concerns of all content teachers. The pupil who cannot read the textbook puts his teachers in a quandary. "How can he," they say, "learn the information if he cannot read it?" Sometimes teachers seem to reach the point of desperation; they give up in the face of seemingly impossible odds. If the student cannot and does not read, they ask, "What can one do?"

The purpose of this paper is to investigate something that can be done in the classroom. We need to know who the "retarded reader" is, the degree of his difficulty, and the nature of his task. From such information we can determine some helpful approaches.

The term "retarded reader" includes a range of reading levels. It carries meanings that vary, depending on the point of view of the user. Obviously the retarded reader is the student whose reading level is likely to be below that of his enrolled grade. We also know that there is a continuum or range of levels which includes the pupil who must work harder than the average to accomplish his assignments to the pupil who is so deficient that he cannot accomplish his assignment in the textbook material no matter how hard he tries.

The severe case of disability needs other help in reading besides that of his regular class. He needs to be assigned remedial work in reading. But this addition does not solve the problem, at least not immediately. He still attends the social studies class; he still has social studies material to read. Specific reading help is needed. We find that the degree of severity seems to determine how soon special help will result in improvement in reading the social studies material. Those having more severe problems will need a longer time to reach a level when this special learning will manifest itself with more competence and independence in the social studies class. The social studies teacher must be prepared to meet the situation.

Complicating the picture further are the demands of the social studies; these demands often challenge the competent reader. With the retarded reader, the situation may be the *coup de grace*. Huus (5) lists a number of problems in reading the social studies; she speaks of the number of new concepts a pupil needs to learn and expand. This brings our attention to another problem, the background needed by the student for adequate comprehension. Peterson, (7) in her study of readability in social study materials, points out that pupils indicated difficulties in noting the main idea, in developing the data into a logical structure or pattern, and in seeing the relationship of one idea to another. Technical words were a problem. Relating details to main ideas caused difficulty, as did making inferences and using contextual clues. Peterson does indicate, however, that pupils were aided by illustrations and summaries as well as by paragraph headings and topic sentences. Yet, they did not use key words and leading questions from the textbook. Huus (5) also notes the problem of forming relationships with the various factual data the student reads. These relationships involve sequence with its use of signal words, chronology, cause and effect, space and distance, relative importance of ideas, and the application of the data to personal experience. Possibly, much of the difficulty with the skills of seeing the relationships in the social studies may be due to the paucity of the pupil's background. Another source of difficulty probably lies in the complicated style of social studies writing. The sentences tend to be long and involved. Abbreviations such as NATO may abound. And last, the vocabulary is a tremendous source of difficulty. The vocabulary consists of technical words peculiar to the social studies as well as general words which have a social studies application. Difficulty with the vocabulary is basic because the ideas and concepts of the social studies are labelled by the vocabulary. The concept is unexpressible without the knowledge of the proper words.

We have then a twofold problem in the social studies area. One part of the problem is the retarded reader. The other part of the problem is the nature of social studies material which is a challenge for even the competent reader, let alone the retarded one.

Considering this double-faceted problem, what can be done to help the retarded reader? What can we as teachers do when confronted with this situation? The remainder of this paper will be directed to these questions. First, basic criteria for effective remedial teaching will be reviewed. Second, a basic classroom procedure will be described.

Basic criteria

Imagine a situation in which you are the teacher of a social studies class. You meet the pupils for the first time, knowing little about them. You may suspect or know that a few of the pupils are not reading as well as they need to accomplish the usual expected reading assignments for the grade.

The first step is to diagnose. The teacher needs to find out as much as he can about the pupil's level of competency in reading; his attitude toward reading, schoolwork, the school, and himself; and his specific skills, strengths, and weaknesses. The teacher will consult the pupil's school record for test scores, teachers' comments, and general achievement in past subjects. The teacher will also wish to diagnose to find current and specific information regarding the students reading strengths and weaknesses. A teacher-made diagnostic inventory can be used in the social studies in which the pupil's competence in using the social studies reading material is checked. Examples of such diagnostic surveys can be found in Strang's (11) *Diagnostic Teaching of Reading* and Shepherd's (9) *Effective Reading in Social Studies.*

The next concern is to plan basic procedures which will help the pupil. The indication of the pupil's strengths and weaknesses, as shown by the inventory, helps the teacher to center his procedure around the pupil's instructional needs. In turn, with such attention on his problems, there is a greater likelihood that the pupil will experience success, will become motivated to a greater degree, and will begin to progress in reading skill as well as in social studies content. There is a chain-like development that occurs.

The social studies lesson becomes a reading skill lesson. The point of emphasis is that the procedure will no longer cover merely social studies content. Rather, a change of focus is made from teaching data to instructing the student in getting data from printed material. In the process of teaching the pupil such techniques, the content is learned because it is the instrument used to teach the skills. This new focus has sometimes been called a fusion—a fusion of reading skill instruction with content teaching. Abramowitz (1) says that we should teach subject matter as a skill lesson. Such a lesson follows the steps of a directed reading activity in which there are opportunities for reading, writing, and discussion.

An inference has been made that the procedure should provide for *individualization of instruction.* Such must be the case. Individualism and/or small group procedures in skill instruction can be based on the results of the diagnostic survey which shows each pupil's strengths and weaknesses. Hock (4) points out that the individualization process is accomplished through diagnosis, by the selection of content and material, and by the methodology used. He suggests the implementation of interest groups in which students do research in materials of wide variety in level and topic. Engaging in research through interest groups provides the framework for the direct teaching and application of the reading skills. Hock also points out that the pupils should be directed in the techniques of group dynamics. This idea indicates a departure from the recitation-type lesson. We know, also, that pupil-interest can lag under a procedure which becomes monotonous. Certainly the employment of pupil-interest is important and tends to increase as the pupil participates in group activities.

Procedure with the retarded reader should then have *variety* and *foster his interest*—hardly accomplished by lessons of rote drill. Interest, self-motivation, and self-application of skills are better accomplished in procedures which encourage the spirit of inquiry.

How basic is the concept of inquiry? We attempt to develop inquiry in an elemental way when we help pupils to read for a purpose. When we tell them to read to find out something about the topic, we are inferring the need to inquire. Our goal is ultimately to have pupils who want to know. Cultivating interest, using a variety of materials and methods, appraising the pupil objectively of his reading strengths and weaknesses help to develop in the pupil the attitude of wanting to know.

It is very important to develop this attitude in the remedial pupil. His retardation may have served and maybe is serving as a damper on his effort to achieve. His attitude may be "Let me out of here, but fast!" Consequently, we must organize our procedures and progress through the content in the manner which will insure success. We want him to see his progress, and he must see and know success.

Since success, interest, and the desire to know are so inextricably tied together, we look for procedures which will foster each of these three important ingredients. Watman (12) has suggested planning and executing civic projects. He maintains that such projects provide levers which propel the pupil into the content as well as insure his application of the skills. He suggests mock situations such as a session of congress with pupils taking various parts. Role playing is suggested as a valuable introductory device to stimulate discussion. (Caution is urged in the use of role playing because of the inherent emotion which may develop.) Watman suggests a well-structured procedure for the role playing. However, for our purposes, note the *variety of procedures*. These procedures would be used in the later steps of a directed reading activity.

The concern of many social studies teachers is covering information. The abstract areas of interest and motivation and the desire to know are important, they say, but there is a body of information to cover. Teachers meet great frustration with the retarded reader. "How can they," they ask, "do more than try to 'cover the course'?" Since the retarded reader cannot read well, he goes so slowly through the material that all of the interest-producing but time-consuming activities are impossible. One cannot do them. Lichtine (6) gives a partial answer to this concern. He maintains that the major emphasis in the social studies should be placed on a limited group of topics rather than the whole sweep of history. This, of course, requires possible replanning of the social studies curricula to include those periods of history, events, and persons which are significant to the pupil's understanding of the social institutions in his society.

It would be redundant to point out the influence and relationship of a selected topic curricula on the textbook material. Obviously, a single text cannot and should not be the course of study. Nor does this curricula infer a "watered down" version of a course. A watered down curriculum, to this writer, is a course which covers only the highlights and the broad generalizations of the entire historical account. The retarded reader has difficulty with the abstraction of the broad generalization. The vocabulary load of such an approach is staggering even to a competent reader. The retarded reader needs to have the vital and real human detail of history presented.

Actually, what I am saying is that history for the retarded reader should not be a panorama of facts which he must know. Rather, it must be presented as a series of happenings which involve people who have had similar feelings, desires, and problems that the pupils are experiencing. The pupils should be guided to see history as the interplay of peoples and that, as such, it is an account of both man's highest achievements and darkest moments.

Such a plan of selected topics and point of view requires a variety of materials. The materials should span a wide range of topics related to the history under study. Sloan (10) maintains that reading resource materials in the classroom should have a readability range from approximately grade 2.5 to grade 12. Each classroom should have from 50 to 100 different titles. Materials are available from many educational publishers. A teacher has only to consult the catalog of many publishers to note the growing wealth of supplementary material on different levels. Such materials are often listed as trade books, not as textbooks. However, some easy reading textbooks for high school pupils have appeared. One is the Abramowitz (2) material, published by Follett, and another is the Schwartz and O'Connor (8) history texts, published by Globe Publishing Co. Once we have the printed materials, our next step is to show the pupils how to use them.

Basic classroom procedures

One of the greatest helps to the retarded reader is the *textbook aids*. The author and the publisher of a well-written and designed textbook include a number of study helps. One study help is the graphic representations which include pictures, maps, diagrams, charts, and overlays. A great amount of information can be gained from these aids. For the retarded reader, there is a minimum of reading but a widening of his knowledge. To use these the pupil must be guided to have a purpose. For instance, a student can look at a map or picture and not see anything of significance unless he is looking for some specific item or condition. He needs to receive instruction in the use of picture legends, map keys, chart representations, etc. Often, many generalizations of content can be made from such materials in the text.

Another textbook aid is the typographical heading. Headings in boldface type give the author's outline which the pupil can use to determine how the material is organized. He is able to note the scope and areas of emphasis. These can be used in many ways. In one instance, pupils were first apprised of the topic, then asked to close their books and think of the items they would include if they had been the author. It is interesting to note that they chose, in different words

to be sure, the same topics the author included. There was only one step further to lead the students into the area of the nature of main ideas.

Question and vocabulary lists at the end of each chapter are study aids. The questions can be used by the student to note what the author thinks is important, as purpose questions to guide his own reading or as a self-evaluation of reading. The vocabulary list can be used in like manner.

Italicized words should be signals to the student. He should realize that these words are new and that they are defined in the same sentence in which he finds them. Other miscellaneous aids are the index, glossary, and special boxed items under such headings as "Important Points to Remember" or "Can You Answer These Questions?"

Coupled with the textbook aids, the student should receive instruction through effective procedures to get him ready to read the selection. One of the most effective, it seems, is a basic learning procedure which is more than merely a reading skill teaching procedure. The pupil should be prepared, motivated, and made ready to read and study a topic. Some teachers may think of this procedure as a method of assignment making. And, indeed, it is. The importance of preparation for reading a selection is basic. With the retarded reader it can be a matter of academic life or death.

The teacher's role is to help the pupil become ready to read. The pupil's background must be investigated because the teacher needs to know what information the pupil does not know. His background must be expanded to the point where he begins to have enough familiar knowledge at his command to use as hitching posts, as it were, for the new ideas. It is a basic learning theory that learners learn best when they can tie the new information to known and previously acquired information.

Because many times a retarded reader is characterized as knowing little or nothing of the school subject, we reason that we must present to an apathetic, incompetent, and indifferent pupil the basic facts of our heritage. This writer disagrees completely with the view that these pupils know nothing and care less. In this modern age of rapid communication, all pupils have picked up a great amount of information. We can *find out what they know* if we take the time to probe and dig it out. One of the essentials of making a pupil ready to read a selection is to help him bring to mind all that he knows about a subject. We must take the time.

Vocabulary development is a part of the preparation for reading. Two important points must be observed: the first is that in the preparation for reading only two or three words are introduced and syllabicated and meanings or concepts established; second, the words must be related to the student's own experiences.

We all know that a *preview of the material* to be read is part of getting the pupil to read. We direct his attention to the graphic aids. Next, the value of introductory paragraphs and summaries is brought out. Introductions that give an overview, the body of the material, and the summary which restates the essential ideas and conclusions compose the usual format of informational writing. Retarded readers can understand this concept. They can see the value of first notifying the reader of what is to be discussed, then discussing the information, and finally informing the reader of the important ideas. Such a format can be applied easily to their own writing as well as studying. In applying this format each of the four facets of the language arts can be used to reinforce one another.

Finally, the *pupil needs direction to his reading*. He should read with specific questions in mind. He should search for specific information. The teacher may need to do much direction here, though the pupil should be helped to become independent in guiding his reading as soon as he is able. Purpose questions serve the pupil in a number of ways. They help him to know what to get from his reading. They help him to hold his attention to the material. And they may begin to stimulate his thinking about the material. Our hope, of course, is for the student to think about what the author has written.

Summary

Helping the retarded reader in social studies requires the consideration and use of specific attitudes as well as procedure. John Dix (*3*) has summarized the twofold approach of attitude and procedures in a list of suggestions:

a. Provide frequent motivation in order to stimulate the pupil's interest and to insure as much as is possible the pupil's success. The experience of success is vital to the pupil's sustained interest and perseverance.

b. Establish simple cause and effect patterns. Thereby, help the pupil to see the interrelationships of the information. A technique which can help to set the stage for these simple patterns is to have the pupil anticipate from boldface headings the information he will get from his reading.

c. Assume nothing in the child's experience. In other words, be sure that an adequate background is always established for reading the material effectively. Proceed from the known to the unknown. At the same time, probe to uncover the information the pupil does have which he can then bring to bear upon the topic.

d. Avoid possible distraction. The teacher needs to plan the classwork so that the pupil will experience the minimum of distraction in the guise of frustration. Techniques to accomplish the lessening of distractions are included in the items of this list.

e. Give directions simply. Be sure that the pupils know what to do and how to go about it. Instruction must precede independent work.

f. Insure the pupil's competency in a reading skill by having him use it independently. The independent application of the skill follows intensive instruction in it. Further, provision for adequate help, if necessary, must be planned for in order to insure success.

g. Provide language development activities through project work which would require the pupil to read for information, write a report, speak in giving the report, and listen to other pupils as they give their reports. Have each aspect of the language arts reinforce the other.

h. Set short-term goals so that the pupils can experience quick success. The retarded reader, due to his past frustration in reading, is not usually in the mood to sustain interest and effort on long intangible assignments.

i. Emphasize essential concepts. Introduce only a few of these and their vocabulary labels at a time in order to insure the pupil's use of these terms and ideas in his own language patterns.

j. Show the pupils what they have learned and have them tell about it. In other words help them to know what they are doing and the reasons for it. Through informal diagnosis, help them to see objectively their strengths and weaknesses.

k. Prepare the pupils for their reading assignment. Most of the techniques we have discussed contribute to their important procedure.

What are we trying to do in our review of these ideas for helping the retarded reader in the social studies? Every teacher will know the answer—to help the retarded reader adequately gain information from printed materials. But, there is another goal that goes beyond teaching skills. The ultimate goal is to instill in the pupil the spirit of inquiry—the desire to know. Our techniques and procedures work toward that end.

REFERENCES

1. Abramowitz, A. "How Much Subject Matter Content for the Slow Learner," *Social Education, 27* (January 1963), 11-12.

2. Abramowitz, Jack. *The Follett Basic Learnings Program: American and World History.* Chicago: Follett Publishing Company, 1962.

3. Dix, John. "Helping the Can'ts and Won'ts," *School and Community, 53* (September 1966), 20.

4. Hock, L. E. "Using Classroom Committees to Individualize Social Studies Teaching," *High School Journal, 49* (October 1965), 22-29.

5. Huus, Helen, "Reading," *National Council of Social Studies Yearbook, 33* (1963), 94-114.

6. Lichtine, S. "What's Wrong With Our Social Studies Program?," *High Points, 48* (June 1966), 59-60.

7. Peterson, Eleanor M. *Aspects of Readability in the Social Studies.* New York: Bureau of Publications, Teachers College, Columbia University, 1954.

8. Schwartz, Melvin, and John O'Connor. *Exploring American History.* New York: Globe Book Company, 1963.

9. Shepherd, David L. *Effective Reading in Social Studies.* New York: Harper and Row, Publishers, 1960.

10. Sloan, F. A., Jr. "Nongraded Social Studies Program for Grades 4, 5, and 6," *National Elementary Principal, 45* (January 1966), 25-29.

11. Strang, Ruth. *Diagnostic Teaching of Reading.* New York: McGraw-Hill Book Company, 1964.

12. Watman, Thomas J. "Successful Techniques in Social Studies," *Catholic School Journal, 66* (January 1966), 48-49.

Teaching the Essential Reading Skills in Science

GEORGE G. MALLINSON
Western Michigan University

THE TOPIC OF THIS PAPER, "Teaching the Essential Reading Skills in Science," is currently subject to much debate. This debate arises from progress that has taken place since World War II. Twenty-five years ago no one would have disputed the merits of teaching the essential reading skills in science, nor would there have been much agrument concerning the premises on which the teaching might have been based. In general, it was agreed that reading represented the communication of ideas from the printed page via the processing of information through the visual mechanism and the transformation of that information into meaningful understandings. This general principle was translated into a number of sub-principles and skills, all of which served as general objectives of the teaching of reading. Specialists in the content fields applied these general objectives to their fields, and the literature contained many reports describing effective ways for teaching reading in the content areas. These ways were founded on the assumption that there were two major considerations in the teaching of reading:

1. *The recognition of the meanings of individual words:*

Support for this assumption is evident in the numerous general vocabulary studies published by Thorndike, Horn, Buckingham-Dolch, and the colleagues. The literature in science teaching contained numerous reports of research concerning science vocabulary and other problems related to reading science materials. Practically all of the earlier major studies were summarized in the milestone report of Curtis[1] in 1938 in which the findings of more than 100 studies of science vocabulary were synthesized. Although this study proved to be the high-water mark of vocabulary studies in science, nevertheless, it proved to be the basis for many other minor studies, most of which have since been forgotten.

2. *The organization of the word "stimuli" received from the printed page into meaningful patterns:*

It has been generally accepted that reading is a perceptual task. Hence, many of the traditional views concerning the teaching of the essential reading skills have been closely allied with gestalt findings. The influence of gestalt theorists is evidenced by the studies involving reading difficulty of Flesch, Dale-Chall, and Lorge. Their studies emphasized the structure of the materials to be read rather than the characteristics of the individual words.

In the past decade, however, a number of findings have cast doubt on traditional reading instruction and have suggested that reading instruction may change greatly from that of the present time. Some of these findings seem related only indirectly to reading instruction but their influence is evident if they are studied carefully.

[1] Curtis, Francis D. *Investigation of Vocabulary in Textbooks of Science for Secondary Schools*. Boston: Ginn and Company, 1938, viii, 127.

Perception and reading

Recently, there has been a great resurgence in the investigation of the theory and principles of learning. Many of the earlier ideas about learning behavior that emerged from the behaviorists and the gestaltists have been questioned. Much of the questioning has come from reading specialists. One reason for the concern is that it has not been possible to apply the findings of perceptual research to the teaching of reading, either in terms of general reading ability or reading in the content fields. This outcome seems strange, indeed, if reading is a perceptual task. However, an examination of many of these studies concerning reading and perception indicate that the designs may have been faulty. In general, they have dealt with one factor of perception and its relationship to the teaching of reading and have indicated that there is little relationship between this factor and reading success. Nevertheless, positive relationships might exist because perception is an extremely complicated process involving many different factors, and the distillation of one factor from the total realm of perception could destroy the significance of that factor. Thus, the limited range of perceptual phenomena tested may have been responsible for the apparent lack of relationhsip. It is well known also that findings of many perceptual studies suggest that learning involves wholes rather than parts of situations. However, these studies have generally involved adults. Yet, some of the more recent studies with children indicate that frequently they learn by parts rather than by wholes. Thus, the general applicability of findings from adult-centered studies may be somewhat doubtful.

Many of the studies involving perception have dealt with the organization of *objects* into patterns. Yet the teaching of reading, in which the findings of these studies have been applied, has been based on the word, phrase, sentence, or story methods, seldom on the use of objects. There is little evidence to indicate that an individual can mentally reconstruct words, phrases, sentences, and stories into analogous objects which, in turn, can be reconstructed into patterns. The symbol for an object, as found in reading material, may not be reconstructable into the wholes into which the objects themselves can be reconstructed.

McLuhan's work, which has affected television advertising greatly, has indicated that many of the ideas concerning perception are not tenable, at least over television. It has been assumed traditionally that a carefully organized didactic presentation of material would develop appropriate patterns of ideas in the individual and, thus, exert the desired influences on him. It has been found, however, that the individual does not necessarily develop the expected patterns. The factor of identification in many cases has more influence than the logical presentation of parts of idea development.

It may be, therefore, that the studies of perception themselves have been so atomistic as to destroy the possibilities of understanding the true role of perception.

The information explosion and educational communication

A major problem that besets educational communication, particularly in the sciences, is the knowledge explosion. Prior to 1940 it was believed that knowledge was doubling in volume every 50 years. If true, the volume of knowledge accumulated between the dawn of history and 1940 would be replicated in volume by 1990. However, the assumption proved to be incorrect. The development of computers in the middle of the 20th Century freed the scientist and researcher from lengthy periods of analyzing data. Prior to that development, the collection of data might have occupied 10 percent of the researcher's time, and the analysis of the data, 90 percent or more. However, with the development of the solid state computer, the analysis of data frequently takes less time than collection. Now, findings on

which future knowledge can be sought and revealed are immediately available to the scientist and researcher. Thus, by 1950 it was estimated that knowledge was doubling in volume every 10 years. In the early 1960's, with the new generation of computers, the rate of accumulation of knowledge was doubling every seven years. With the third generation of computers now appearing, scientific knowledge may be doubling every five years by 1970. As a result, the mass of information made available serves to complicate further the reading process.

The population explosion and educational communication

If you read at a rate of about 150 words per minute, by the time you finish this sentence the earth's population will have increased by about 23. One hour from now it will have increased enough to populate a city of about 8,000. One year from now the increase will be able to populate a nation the size of the United Kingdom and Sweden combined—countries with a total population of about 62,500,000 people. Recent, extensive investigations by UNESCO of the habits of *homo sapiens* suggest that the population increment is likely to increase in the years ahead. Many educational problems, particularly those involved with the teaching of reading, arise from the characteristics of the population, as well as from its size.

Nearly 50 percent of the world's population is below the age of 25. Altogether, more than 80 million persons in the United States are in some type of organized educational program supported by local, state, or federal funds or by private sources. Thus, education, at least in terms of student involvement, is an enormous business. It is expected that more than one trillion dollars from all sources will be spent on education in the United States before the end of the next decade. This figures is based on the assumption that 15 to 20 percent of the national income will be funneled into educational programs of various types.

Currently in the United States, nearly 40 percent of public monies, other than those for defense, is spent on some form of education. This fact has led to the development of new combines among publishers, computer manufacturers, and the electronics industry to exploit the potential market. Some of these combines are International Business Machines Corporation and Science Research Associates; Raytheon and D. C. Heath Company; and the Silver Burdett Company, Time, Inc., and the General Electric Company. Because of the information and population explosions and the continued growth of education, there is every reason to expect that the methods of education, particularly those in the sciences, will change and will be supplemented with media other than the textbook and traditional materials. This condition spawns a number of important problems. An investigation of the literature of science education indicates decreasing interest in the research in reading related to science education and more and more research on the use of outside objects, kits, and other multimedia for education. No doubt, this trend will continue, particularly with the sophisticated advertising and sales agencies in the newly formed combines. There needs to be a complete review of what constitutes the essential basic skills of reading in science in the years ahead and of what the most effective ways of teaching them are. This, perhaps, can be done only by surveying the role of technology and education in the years ahead.

Television and vocabulary load

The studies undertaken many years ago concerning the optimal number of scientific terms that a student could learn at any grade level are so outdated as to be useless. The impact of modern communication media, particularly television, now provides an entirely new environment in which youngsters are stimulated by vocabulary and, in turn, against which they learn this new vocabulary. Television viewing, which has become common, provides great reinforcement for the presentation of words. Thus, students currently in the early elementary school might learn scientific vocabulary far more readily than students at the seventh grade level formerly did. One only has to talk with elementary school children and examine the kinds of books they read to ascertain quickly that their comprehension of vocabulary is far beyond that of their parents at a similar stage. However, many of the vocabulary terms with which they now become familiar are not those found in the learning materials ordinarily used in the school. There is, of course, some overlap, but many of the terms found in the traditional teaching materials are not presented in the same stimulating environment as scientific terms are presented through modern communication media. The teacher may frequently be found in the embarrassing position of teaching terms, many of which are easier than those that appear on television, in an environment considerably less conducive to learning.

Technology and education in the next 100 years

No one in his right mind would attempt to predict specifically what is likely to happen in the technology of education during the next 100 years. However, by reviewing the past 100 and extrapolating, with due consideration for an acceleration of developments, some ideas may be postulated. The postulates are based on these assumptions:

1. There will continue to be shortage of qualified teachers to man the massive educational effort that lies ahead. Even if the anticipated supply were to expand greatly, one may expect that teachers will spend more time in updating their backgrounds and somewhat less in teaching. Also, the information explosion will require more teachers for science at the post-high school and post-baccalaureate levels.

2. In order to disseminate the ever-accumulating mass of knowledge, new methods will be needed to complement the teacher effort in accelerating its dissemination.

3. The role of education will increasingly change from teaching persons to store information in and retrieve it from their heads to that of acquiring new information. This change means new directions for teaching methods of inquiry.

The role of the book

As has often been stated, one would not think of advising friends to use new drugs as uncritically as one often recommends new learning devices. But, there is little doubt that the recommendations will continue, perhaps at an accelerated rate. Some devices will be useful and some will not. But, in all of these developments the book will continue to be an important teaching aid. However, the role and format of the basic textbook will change radically in the years to come. Some of the changes are likely to be these:

1. Textbooks in the natural sciences will increasingly de-emphasize the didactic presentation of information and will present more information in terms of problem and inquiry approaches. They will become more like textbooks of mathematics. Although many publishers have paid lip service to these approaches, there is little evidence yet of accomplishment. In general, the activities related to inquiry are found in the ancillary materials. One may expect that the textbooks of the future will contain mainly foundational problems and that the ancillary materials will contain problem-solving situations related closely to the student's everyday experiences. The latter will provide for cultural, geographical, and other differences among the students.

2. Modern printing developments will make it possible to increase greatly the numbers and types of illustrations in textbooks. This advancement will mean more four-color illustrations and the possible use of three-dimensional photography. Many of the problems in the textbooks will be focused on the analysis of these photographs.

3. There will be greater integration between the ancillary materials and the textbooks. Students will be expected to move from the textbook to filmloops and to other types of hardware, including science kits, and then back to the textbooks. A single problem involving the use of ancillary materials will occupy far more than the usual class period or even a day.

The role of electronics technology

The greatest change in sources of information input in the sciences will be in periodicals and serial literature to which the student is directed. These are the "monsters" that are placing overwhelming burdens on shelving and cataloging capabilities in libraries. They will be replaced by vast electronic banks of information in which this literature will be stored and to which students will direct questions. Such library systems will encompass these elements:

1. The purchase of subscriptions for periodical and serial literature in the form of a computer input device.

2. The storage of the "subscriptions" *in toto* in a ferromagnetic, or other domain, in a computer in a form suitable for extremely rapid examination, manipulation, and printout.

3. The availability of some type of index or bibliography which a student can scan to determine

which elements of the periodical or serial literature may be useful.

4. The issuance to a student, on receipt of a proper code number on one hand or a request based on diverse, custom, or subject specification on the other, a reproduced copy or copies of the periodical literature that he may keep.

The environments in which students gain information will be decentralized. Libraries may no longer be used for study, since the output mechanisms for the electronic banks can be placed in residence halls and homes. Much of the output may be on a television monitor rather than in the form of a printout.

Some suggestions

In the previous discussions the writer has attempted to list some of the major cultural pressures that affect vocabulary and hence the teaching of reading and also to make some predictions as to what may happen in the future with respect to learning materials. However, he has studiously avoided making any specific recommendations as to how to teach basic reading skills in science. To him the reason is obvious. Except for reviewing recommendations made in earlier reports, all of which would be redundant to those reading this report, he could do little. He firmly believes that extensive research must be undertaken to ascertain what needs to be done in a modern environment to teach basic reading skills of science before suggestions for implementation can be made. This opinion may be construed as an evasion but it seems to be the only outlet. Thus, the following suggestions for research and study are made:

1. The extensive vocabulary studies in science undertaken by Curtis and Mallinson and colleagues are hopelessly outdated. Although they may have been salutary and useful during the period when printed materials represented the primary learning sources, they are no longer significant contributions in view of the modern devices which are available for teaching science. Thus, it is suggested that a series of research studies be undertaken to ascertain the type of vocabulary youngsters use as a result of the total environmental impact upon them.

2. Studies need to be undertaken to determine how well youngsters can read terms and concepts with which they have been stimulated over different types of multimedia, including television and filmloops and other devices. It is obvious that these new multimedia offer entirely new patterns of perceptual stimuli which have not yet been investigated in this context.

3. Studies need to be undertaken to determine how familiarity with using these scientific terms in conversation and in being stimulated by them through the new multimedia is accompanied with understanding. The findings of the older studies in which word recognition was considered tantamount to understanding are no longer tenable.

4. Studies need to be undertaken to determine the ways in which modern graphic arts techniques can be incorporated into books and other printed materials so as to present science readings in a quasi-visual environment rather than remonstrances in print. Little has been done to determine how techniques such as three-dimensional printing may be used more effectively so as to complement verbal concepts. Textbooks, unfortunately, still rely on outdated formats rather than on making use of those that appear in modern media such as *Life, Time,* and *Fortune.* The picture essay technique has hardly been explored for providing a better visual environment

in which to develop science concepts.

5. Studies should be undertaken to review critically the literature involved with the teaching of the blind and making use of stimuli other than visual to develop science understandings. Generally, as indicated in the earlier part of this paper, reading was essentially visual communication through the medium of print. However, many techniques involving tactual and auditory stimulations may be combined with those from other sources to teach reading. Little has been done to explore this broader concept of perception.

Summary

In brief, this paper has said little about "how to do it." Should any of the readers be interested in ways for teaching the essential reading skills of two decades ago effectively through science materials, they may be found by reading several sources already mentioned. However, it seems that entirely new directions of research are needed if recommendations for techniques are not to be dinosaurian.

Promoting Reading Growth in Science Through Use of Multimedia

William A. Sapp
Project Uplift, Mt. Vernon, Illinois

IT HAS BEEN STATED by many reading professionals that if a teacher assigns reading, the teacher must teach reading. This statement is very true especially in the area of science. With today's growth and emphasis in the science area, students find themselves in a world filled with a special vocabulary and a method of solving problems which they have not acquired from their basal readers. It is the teacher's responsibility to aid the student in meeting the challenge which the science area holds.

How can the teacher meet this responsibility? How can he develop the special vocabularies and concepts? The teacher can best meet this responsibility with the combined techniques of reading and science with the aid of multimedia.

The teacher has one important factor on his side in this great task. "An examination of recent and earlier investigations of children's interest reveals science as the most persistent interest of girls and boys" (1). Here is an area that we as teachers can capitalize upon in more fully developing reading skills and needed habits. But, at the same time, we cannot let this interest in science overwhelm us. We still must aid the student in developing the special skills and background needed to read effectively in the science area.

Reading skills needed in science

We must aid the student in developing new vocabulary. One way is by the use of media to widen the student's understanding of science concepts, such as electricity and the water cycle.

We must build the student's locational skills and encourage their utilization. Students do not learn to use the table of contents, indexes, library card file, maps, and charts by osmosis. These are skills that must be taught. Teachers many times take locational skills for granted. One possible reason a major test company made the work study skills an optional part of their achievement test program was that teachers and administrators complained of the low scores in work study skills that appeared on the school's report form.

We must aid the student in developing skills of skimming. Students need to know how to overlook unrelated material to locate a specific piece of information.

Students need to develop the skill of critical reading. This skill is of primary importance when using current information from two sources with conflicting statements or in discussing group topics. When a decision concerning choices of material, statements, or points of view is to be made, the skills of critical reading and evaluation are needed.

With the interest students have for the science area, teachers should help to broaden this interest through reading. Students should be encouraged to become acquainted with the variety of new and interesting materials available today.

Design for a reading lesson in science

Teachers should use a predesigned plan of attack in promoting reading growth through science. This plan can accomplish two important objectives of textbook reading: "namely, the development of more skills in reading and the acquisition of important learnings in the field of secience" (2). This plan can be in as few as five steps or as many as twenty-five depending upon the individual teacher's necessity for detailed organization. I prefer a plan listed by Robert Karlin (3):

1. Readiness for Reading
   a. developing or relating experiences of students to content
   b. introducing vocabulary and clarifying concepts
   c. setting the purpose for reading
2. Silent Reading
3. Discussion
4. Rereading (new purpose)
5. Application

This plan fits my needs, but it may not fit yours. Every teacher should develop his own plan and change it as needs warrant.

Readiness for reading

It is difficult to realize but many students arrive at the classroom door with a speaking vocabulary larger, in many areas such as science, than their teacher's. While this is just a speaking vocabulary, more often than not developed by television and overlapped with fantasy, it is not necessarily an understanding vocabulary. As teacher of reading, we must aid the student in developing his understanding vocabulary. Such terms as elipse, eclipse,

weightlessness, and solar prominences require media to help the student develop total understanding and clarification.

Clarifying concepts is a prime responsibility of the reading-science teacher. This instruction must be initiated before the student begins to read the assignment. Most textbooks today do an excellent job in explaining concepts and word meaning with charts, pictures, and examples. But we as teachers cannot assume that this matter is understood by our students. Students will still need help in interpreting the meanings held within charts, pictures, and examples.

More explanation, developing concept experience, may be required even after the readiness and reading phase of the lesson, depending upon the concepts presented and the student it is presented to. It may require grouping of students according to their needs. Certain students may require easier reading material for a particular concept while others could use more difficult material to develop the concept further. Library resource books utilized correctly could serve a great advantage in both instances.

We must also realize that vicarious experiences, though excellent, cannot supplant real experiences. Even though real experiences, such as field trips, can become costly, we still should develop within the student an understanding of the relationship between the vicarious experience and the real experience. We should intermix vicarious experiences—developed by the text, films, study prints, and charts—with well-planned real experiences developed by experiments and field trips. If we plan a field trip we must still prepare the class by using the same variety of media to help combine vicarious learning with actual proof. Through these experiences the student may gain an understanding which will help him later when only vicarious experiences are available.

As an example, our local school district cannot afford to send all fifth grade students 200 miles round trip to the zoo to study animals of the earth. But this doesn't mean that none of the classes should make the trip. Some students may not need to visit the zoo because they have already had such an experience. The students who go to the zoo will see that these animals really do exist and this realization will fortify other experiences developed vicariously.

Galler (4) states, "The aim of science teaching is to enable a child to acquire these concepts which will explain his world of reality and enable him to deal effectively with his environment. It should challenge him to pose questions, to extend his curiosity so that further answers may be sought, and continued growth in problem solving may take place." We must use all resources to help the students in their quest for knowledge.

Use of multimedia in a science lesson

The use of multimedia is the teacher's greatest asset in developing reading skills in the area of science. It definitely enhances the development of science concepts since science concepts are built on relationships. Definitions, dictionary or written, will not suffice. Science concepts must be developed inductively from the specific to the general or from the concrete to the abstract. By using models, charts, films, (16mm, 8mm, single, concept, super, and strips) prepared transparencies, and study prints, the teacher is more able to present science concepts in a specific or a concrete way.

For example: How would you develop the total concept of *frost* to youngsters of our "concrete and asphalt cities," without the use of media? Whether you use films, charts, or a classroom plant placed outside the classroom window, the concepts of *killing frost* and *ground frost* must be developed as well as *window frost*. Coronet Film Company (5) has an excellent film titled "What the Frost Does." It guides elementary children's observations of the events leading up to frost and the effects of frost.

Summary

Teachers today are more fortunate than teachers of ten or twenty years ago, as I'm sure teachers of tomorrow will be more fortunate than we are today, in the aids that are available in building and relating experiences needed by the students in our classrooms. Multimedia are here to stay. Utilization of media will require many of us to change our philosophy and teaching techniques. But I assure you that you will notice the change in your students as you add *media-spice* to curriculum.

Research and experience prove the value of audiovisuals. The Nebraska Study and studies by Roulon and Wittich (6) have proven the values of media in retention of information and effectiveness of learning.

I challenge you as teachers of reading and as teachers of science to use media to their fullest advantages in your classroom. Instructional materials resources centers are "springing up" throughout school districts. Such centers provide invaluable aid to us in meeting the needs of our students.

To promote reading growth through science we must know the skills, realize the needs, and reach our students at their understanding levels.

REFERENCES

1. Lembesis, Anne C. "Reaching the Remedial Reader Through Science," *Education, 85,* No. 5 (January 1965), 288-293.
2. Dallmann, Martha, and John S. DeBoer. *Teaching of Reading,* Holt, Rinehart and Winston, Inc., 1965, 368.
3. Karlin, Robert. *Teaching Reading in High School,* Bobbs-Merrill, 1964, 237-238.
4. Galler, Albert A. "Reading a Science," in Albert Mazurkiewicz, *New Perspectives in Reading Instruction.* New York: Pitman Publishing Company, 1964, 44.
5. "What the Frost Does" in *Background For Reading and Expression.* Coronet Films, Coronet Building, Chicago, (11 min. color).
6. Schuller, Charles F. *The School Administrator and His Audio-Visual Program,* Department of Audio-Visual Instruction, National Education Association, 1954.

The Rationale for a System-Wide Reading Committee

J. Roy Newton
State University of New York
at Albany

BEFORE WE CAN determine what may be accomplished through the use of this committee, we must first determine what constitutes a reading committee. Many variations are possible depending upon the size of the school system and the existence of other committees.

The membership of the reading committee probably should include, at the elementary level, a representative from each grade with additional members if more than one school is involved. The middle school, where it exists, might have similar representation. At the secondary level the committee should involve someone from each subject area including the so-called "nonacademic" subjects. This may well be the chairman of the department although in some cases, at least, a stronger committee may result if representation of a department is delegated to a teacher who is "sold" on the importance of reading. In addition, teachers of language arts at all grade levels might be invited to belong. Intermediate grades and middle schools having departmentalization will tend to reflect the organization pattern suggested for the secondary school. To the above representation of classroom teachers should be added principals and supervisory personnel. Inclusion of the administration is vital to the success of the reading program. Reading related services such as the school psychologist, guidance counselor, school nurse-teacher, librarians, and audiovisual director should be added. At times, the reading committee may wish to include, for a specific meeting or series of meetings, lay people from the local community. Boys and girls, parents, and members of the medical profession have contributions to make.

Obviously the strength of such a committee lies in the breadth of its representation. Equally obvious should be that its size is at the same time a possible cause of weakness. However, only rarely will the entire reading committee need to meet, as when contemplating the evaluation of a whole-school reading program, or planning workshops, conferences, or in-service training programs. At other times a more effective organization is by a given grade; by primary, intermediate, junior, or senior high divisions; by supervisory and/or administrative personnel; or by departments.

The structure of the reading committee may be completed by the establishment of an advisory council which, itself, may serve as a planning committee. Important points to consider are those involving flexibility. Careful planning will avoid such pitfalls as unnecessary attendance at large meetings involving minutia of little concern to the majority of those in attendance. By careful planning, also, the reading committee will be able to focus attention relatively quickly upon those areas of the reading program which may be in need of immediate attention.

So much for the "what" of the reading committee. The next question to be answered is the one, "Why is a reading committee necessary?" Despite concern voiced in many quarters that change in reading procedures is accomplished relatively slowly, we have made considerable progress in the last ten or fifteen years. A few years ago a school administrator often felt he had "solved" the reading problems in his school by the hiring of a remedial teacher. This teacher was expected to work almost entirely with all the problem readers leaving the other teachers to go about the business of teaching. This philosophy had the effect of placing reading instruction on a treadmill. The reading teacher had to work faster, with larger groups, as more and more boys and girls were found to be in need of help. Emphasis was on correction rather than prevention.

Now schools are seeing that the professionally competent reading specialist is fully as important as are directors of curriculum and of instruction. The emphasis is shifting slowly but steadily from working with children to working with teachers— classroom teachers. Clinical work must be continued by highly trained technicians. However, the long term view, most productive in improving learning situations and hence involving preventive work, is in this area of improving instruction in the classroom.

Many school systems are taking advantage of the availability of ESEA funds to augment existing in-service programs. Special attention should be devoted to first year and nontenure teachers. As efforts are made to improve the quality and the amount of reading instruction in our teacher-training colleges, we must coordinate preservice and in-service experience. No matter how good we can make our preservice courses, an effective program demands the continuation of the professional training of teachers on an in-service basis. The reading committee appears to be a logical way of accomplishing this coordination in the area of reading instruction.

The concept of a committee devoted to the improvement and coordination of reading instruction is not new. In 1954, Simpson (3) suggested the formation of such a committee in connection with the improvement of reading skills among high school students. When Newton (1) enlarged the suggestion to include the whole school in 1960, the idea was criticized as being both impractical and Utopian. In 1965, Robinson and Rauch (2) indicated that schools are finding the reading committee to be a businesslike way of going about a job that is long overdue.

One more point must be accepted. It is about time classroom teachers, reading related services, administra-tors, and the lay public acknowledge the fact that reading is so important to learning that the organization of the whole-school reading program should be recognized as the responsibility of a competent reading specialist. The forward-looking administrator will delegate this responsibility while giving it his wholehearted support.

In this atmosphere, the reading committee is expected to function in the following ways as it:

1. Emphasizes the whole-school nature of the reading program.
2. Increases the effectiveness of reading personnel.
3. Unites, or helps unite, a school faculty.
4. Presents a structured organization that is flexible, efficient, and workable.
5. Provides channels for the dissemination of ideas, practices, and techniques.
6. Educates through involvement.
7. Aids in-service work in all areas.
8. Systematizes efficient operation.
9. Facilitates working closely with college personnel.
10. Expedites doing what has to be done.

REFERENCES

1. Newton, J. Roy. *Reading in Your School.* New York: McGraw Hill Book Company, 1960.
2. Robinson, H. Alan, and Sidney J. Rauch. *Guiding the Reading Program.* Chicago: Science Research Associates, Inc., 1965.
3. Simpson, Elizabeth A. *Helping High-School Students Read Better.* Chicago: Science Research Associates, Inc., 1954.

The Functioning of a Reading Committee

DOROTHY M. DIETRICH
Uniondale, New York,
School District

ONCE THE MAJOR TASK of organizing a reading committee has been completed, it becomes the responsibility of the school and the reading committee to find the means whereby the committee functions in the most feasible manner. Robinson and Rauch, in their book *Guiding The Reading Program (1)*, state that the function of the reading committee ". . . is to promote an ever progressing reading program." They then go on to say that, "The major task of the committee should be to evaluate the reading program continually and to take necessary steps towards improving the program—with the consultant taking a leadership role in making and implementing decisions."

In some school districts reading committees have been organized for the sake of having a reading committee listed on a committee roster. When this is the case, much friction can develop between the committee and consultant. Since neither one has been apprised of his responsibility, each is likely to resent what it considers the other's interference.

The reading committee should be a policy-making body who develops a broad framework within which the consultant is able to function. Rather than being concerned as to whether Miss Jones teaches phonics or Miss Brown individualizes instruction, their tasks should include such things as an evaluation of district-wide reading scores, adequacy of materials, innovations needed, experiments to be conducted, and areas to be strengthened. The consultant's role is to see that within this large framework each individual teacher is following through on the best teaching practices of which he or she is capable. Under no circumstances should the reading committee become involved in evaluation of individual performances of teachers. Should major areas of differences arise between the reading committee and the consultant, steps should be taken to involve a higher administrative officer or officers who can carefully evaluate the questions and suggest possible solutions. It is unfortunate that sometimes a consultant feels threatened by a reading committee. Such a committee is not there to evaluate the consultant's role, but rather to provide information

and insight which enable him to function more effectively.

One of the first responsibilities of the reading committee is to obtain information concerning the reading status within the school or school district. For this purpose many resources should be explored. Some of these include:

1. *Test results*. Results of standardized tests by grade and school as well as district-wide results often give indication of general areas of weaknesses. Comparison of test scores with national norms will help the committee determine whether theirs is a basic problem of overall improvement or one of refinement to improve only specific aspects of the program.

   Teachers might also be asked to evaluate the tests of pupils in their classes to determine discrepancies among scores obtained by individuals. They should be asked to report students whose scores are one or more years below the district norm or whose scores deviate from class performance.

2. *Reading consultant's records and observations*. If a reading consultant has been employed in the school for any length of time, no doubt he has been able to accumulate facts and information which should be passed along to the committee. These might include the number of students who are in need of remedial help; current teaching practices, either favorable or unfavorable; attitude of the teachers towards the improvement of reading; and areas of weakness he has noted.

3. *Teacher background*. Teacher background as it pertains to courses taken in the teaching of reading or experience in the teaching of reading would be helpful to the committee in order to determine in-service needs. Personal interviews, observations by impartial teams, or

questionnaires can be used to note ways reading is taught in the content fields, appreciation of literature is developed, materials are utilized, and/or instruction is individualized.

4. *Records.* A survey of available records indicating students' individual reading progress through the grades should be ascertained. Teachers should be asked what information concerning the child's reading progress they would find particularly helpful.

5. *Book inventory.* A complete inventory should be made of all basal and supplementary materials available as well as ditto materials, workbooks, trade books, films, filmstrips, records, and other machines which are used regularly by the teachers in the teaching of reading.

6. *Parent reactions.* By means of informal discussion groups, PTA programs, and individual contact with other parents, the community's attitude towards the reading program within the school should be explored.

7. *Administration reaction.* Administrators should contribute their ideas in relation to the total reading program and some of the areas they feel are in need of improvement. Determining the administration's attitude towards increased emphasis upon the teaching of reading is also important.

8. *Current reading practices.* An examination of the current practices carried out by teachers in their classrooms should be made to determine what methods and approaches are being utilized, what experimental projects are underway, or what approaches warrant experimentation.

From this mass of information, it is then possible for the reading committee to evaluate the present status of the reading program and note its strengths and weaknesses. A combination of factors will determine the directions in which the committee will probably decide to move. If the problem is one of a lack of materials which hinder teachers' performances, then this might become the first order of business; if teachers lack the background and experience in reading to use a sufficient supply of materials, the committee may want to consider in-service education; if the school is doing a good job teaching reading but parents react adversely to the reading program, then the committee might wish to explore means of informing the community about the school's total reading program. Thus it can be seen that the first direction of the committee will depend upon the reactions as obtained from the information gathered.

Often a reading committee which is just beginning to function will feel that the myriad problems presented to them are overwhelming. Committees have been known to try to focus upon all weak areas at once. It is often better to place major emphasis on one or two phases of the program, lightly shoring up the other aspects. The development of a sound reading program is something that takes place over a number of years and cannot be accomplished in one year.

During the phase when information is being gathered, the committee may wish to divide into small groups making it easier for a few people knowledgeable in specific areas to focus upon these needs. The full committee, working closely with the reading consultant, should then evaluate this material from a total school approach. Once the committee has focused its sights on the area or areas of concern, then new subgroups may be utilized to plan corrective devices. As an example, the committee decides its first order of business is the development of in-service courses; then teachers and administrators with special area consultants might divide the responsibility. One group may explore in-service courses for the elementary teachers and another, a program for secondary teachers. In this way it is possible for people who are most knowledgeable at each level to develop a program which fits the needs of their level. In smaller schools or school districts, it may be possible for the entire committee to work as a unit.

Whenever a committee has developed its plans in conjunction with the consultant, it then becomes the consultant's responsibility to see that such plans are carried out. In some instances this may mean the consultant will work with the principal of a building to see that sufficient materials are ordered or grade level meetings held. Sometimes it is helpful for the consultant and the principal to observe a reading lesson together. If in-service work is planned, the consultant might wish to investigate and recommend to the committee people eligible to teach the course or to appear as guest speakers. It may be that the reading committee will wish to use teachers from its own staff who practice good procedures. In this case the consultant, teaching particular areas himself, might be the person who would plan the course with the teachers.

The consultant constantly needs to feed information pertaining to the results of the implemented program to the committee and seek suggestions which will further the program. Programs initiated by the reading committee should be carefully evaluated from time to time to ascertain their effectiveness. If a course of action results in no appreciable improvement in the reading program, then it should be modified or discontinued.

As the reading committee delves into various aspects of the reading program, it will find itself often becoming involved in matters allied to reading but also encompassing other areas of the curriculum. The reading committee may wish to make suggestions concerning the teaching of reading to members of the content area departments or request that they be present at some meetings for consultation with the committee. Guidance people and psychologists will become involved in matters of record keeping and testing. As a result of parent involvement in the committee, it may be that adult education, PTA representatives, and other community groups will become involved.

Thus we can see that a reading committee organized to evaluate and guide a reading program within a district may have tremendous impact on the total school program. Its eventual outcome may be to change many areas of the curriculum. The committee can be of immeasurable help to the consultant, freeing him for more direct contact with teachers.

A reading committee's success depends upon the sincerity of higher administrative officials who support it, of members of the committee who believe in its importance, of the reading consultants who work toward the accomplishment of the committee's decisions, as well as the teachers who cooperate by complying with the decisions of the committee.

REFERENCE

1. Robinson, H. Alan, and Sidney J. Rauch. *Guiding the Reading Program.* Chicago: Science Research Associates, Inc., 1965.

The Role of the Educator in Diagnostic Appraisal and Remediation of Children with Reading Problems

ALICE J. WHITSELL
University of California
Medical Center

THE EDUCATIONAL CONSULTANT has a key position on a multidisciplinary team which evaluates and plans for children with reading problems. This consultant should be a teacher with a broad background of classroom teaching experience, a reading specialist who has had training and practical experience with a large variety of remedial techniques, and a diagnostician, The consultant should be familiar with the terminology of the medical and paramedical specialties represented on the team and must often act as the liaison member in translating unfamiliar terms into practical information for classroom teachers and parents. The presence of a teacher on the team has demonstrated in a remarkable fashion—especially to physicians and medical students—how helpful his diagnostic observations may be and how often and easily they may be overlooked.

The consultant confronts the child with an atmosphere as nearly as possible like the one he faces every day in the classroom. This provides a chance to observe him carefully in a school-like situation. Anxieties and frustrations as well as academic weaknesses are usually rapidly exposed. During the evaluation procedure the consultant also has a chance to envision the frustrations and anxieties of the child's regular teacher. This most important point is often overlooked by other members of the team who may not appreciate this type of problem so well.

During the course of the evaluation the consultant should

1. Take a careful school history from the school, the child, and the parents. This information may be quite different from that given to other team members.
2. Review carefully any previous records furnished by the referring source. This should include a report from the child's classroom teacher.
3. Find achievement levels in reading, spelling, and arithmetic or check readiness skills if the child is not reading. Test oral and silent reading, comprehension, word recognition, word analysis, listening skills, and motor proficiency—especially in regard to handwriting and ability to copy.
4. Note during testing: speech and language functioning, the child's reaction to stress and failure, how he compensates for his difficulties (how he holds his pencil or perhaps spells orally while writing), his attitude toward school (successes as well as failures), and his span of attention under varying circumstances.
5. Look for signs of possible difficulty in hearing or vision that may have been previously overlooked.
6. Try out and test various methods of teaching which place different demands on the child's input and output systems. The consultant's observations here may be more meaningful and valuable than standard psychological test scores.
7. Decide what kind of remediation would be most helpful and try it in a short teaching session.

The primary purpose of the evaluation is not only to get test scores but to obtain as clear an idea as possible of the child's problem—the nature as well as the degree. Then, the consultant can decide at what level to begin remediation and what teaching modality to stress.

In the summary and planning conferences, which are held jointly with the other members of the diagnostic team, the educational consultant is expected to exchange findings with the other team members, listen to and weigh their summaries and proposals, and join with them in an individualized, mutually agreeable, constructive plan for remediation. In this planning stage the educational consultant acts as a representative of the child's teacher in pointing out the feasibility of the plan. It is important, therefore, for her to know from the teacher as much as possible about the special services available in that school district as well as the structure of her class and how this particular child fits in. The classroom teacher can help by reporting on class size, grouping arrangements, and approximate achievement levels of the children. Other valuable information would be daily observations noted by the teacher, such as, he is clumsy on the playground; he frequently asks for directions to be repeated; his work is never neat; he loses his place frequently when reading; oral expression is better than written; and arithmetic concepts are good but computation is poor. Often these are the things that worry or even annoy a teacher. By themselves they may be meaningless but when put together with other findings they help in solving the puzzle.

The information gathered during the summary conference must be synthesized and translated into practical terms and transmitted to the parents, the referring source, and the child's school. The school contact is usually made by the educational consultant. This should not be done in the form of a formal pronouncement. It should include suggestions as to class placement and techniques.

The final report should include a summary of the medical, psychological, educational, and other special examinations. It should define the degree of the difficulty and the emotional climate of the family. It should include clear statements regarding the child's achievements and abilities, state clearly on what level to begin instruction, and what teaching modalities are most likely to bring success. Suggestions as to optimal class size or type are often given.

Even though these suggestions are specific they should not be considered arbitrary. The final implementation should be left up to the school administrators who are more familiar with what actually is available. Sometimes a modification of grouping within a classroom, a dropping back to easier material, use of a special teacher for short periods, use of an existing community service, or a tutor in the local community will rapidly ameliorate the situation if not provide the ideal solution.

The consultant usually assumes the responsibility of working out these details, often by personal contact with the person doing the teaching. After remediation has begun, it is necessary to check progress and be available for consultation with teachers, parents, and school administrators. In other words, it is necessary to keep all the lines of communication open and include the other team members if necessary. This continues through retesting and planning for the next block of work.

Teachers usually appreciate practical suggestions. Some examples of these may take the form of "Do's" and "Don'ts."

Don't	Do
Expect this child to sit and listen very long.	Try to improve his auditory memory span.
Expect twenty new spelling words a week.	Cut spelling list to four. *Increase gradually.*
Use whole-word method for teaching.	Try to improve visual and auditory skills and build up phonetic skills.
Teach phonics.	Teach sound blending first.
Expect a rapid *oral* response.	Accept short answers.
Expect this child to learn to read yet.	Go back to the readiness stage in visual perception.
Expect neat papers, yet.	Try to change slant, practice basic strokes in letter formation.
Have this child copy work from the board.	Work to improve eye-hand coordination—use markers if copying is necessary.

There is still no answer to the question of what is the best pedagogical procedure to use in helping any given child to remedy a learning disability. There is just no one universally successful method to help poor readers. However, there are many techniques which have been tried, tested, and proved to be of great value when fitted to a child's particular need. Short term goals are best, followed by frequent checkups and replanning. As careful as the planning has been, it doesn't always produce success. This doesn't mean it is time to give up; it means that plans should be changed and another approach tried. Although a multidisciplinary diagnosis is necessary to understand each problem fully, and each specialist helps in planning the program, it is the child's teacher who must bring about the remediation. The teacher must deal with the problem on a day-to-day basis. His position is greatly strengthened by a close relationship with a team of specialists who are available and ready to offer suggestions and advice as long as necessary.

Coordinating Reading Instruction and Content Teaching

Lester L. Van Gilder
Marquette University
and
Beatrice J. Wurtz
Menomonee, Wisconsin,
Public Schools

Today the united states has more students in colleges than any other nation. Educators are being made more cognizant of the need for helping college students improve their reading skills in all of the content fields. As the need arose during the past years, many colleges have been offering reading classes. According to A. J. Lowe (13), in 1945 a national survey reported only three college reading centers. But by 1954 there were 418 reading improvement programs in the colleges. In many instances the reading process has been worked to an appreciable extent. However, a number of students, according to Emery Bliesmer (3), are weak and can stand a degree of polishing or refining. Bliesmer further states that the degree or extent of their weaknesses will vary according to the type of college attended, admission standards, fields of study pursued, and many other related factors.

There are many pre-college experiences in reading necessary for academic success. If these have not been adequately mastered, two choices are offered: one is to consider students college failures and not offer any help in filling in the gap of unlearned or unpolished reading skills; the alternative is to consider each student worth saving and offer help in reading instruction.

When a student's marks are falling at the higher levels of education, it is generally because he is not keeping up with his class. Many colleges experience the "golden boy" student who attends college because mom and dad can afford to send him. The prestige of having a son in college prompts the parent into driving the son beyond his capabilities. Sometimes the son is unskilled, mentally inadequate, and on the road to becoming a frustrated adult. The "golden boy" is in the minority, but enough of them are slipping through admissions to cause concern to many of us. The great majority of students have trouble that usually stems from one of these basic causes as stated by Holmes (11):

a. a temporary disruption of learning habits because the student has been emotionally upset.
b. the application of the study habits which serve the students well in certain areas but which are not appropriate in others.
c. the fact that a student never has developed subskills, supportive abilities, value attitudes, and self-confidence necessary to good learning habits in general

We are aware of the reading difficulties of students at the college level. Therefore, the purpose of this paper is to investigate ways and means of coordinating the reading instruction within the content teaching at the college level.

Reading instruction in the social sciences

First, at this higher level, we must be aware that reading is based on power reasoning of the knowledge known and unknown within different disciplines. One must have a working knowledge of a subject. Also, one must be able to use this knowledge in the form of usable concepts as they interact within their subject area.

An example will be in the area of social studies. As early as primary grades the SQ3R method is presented in most social studies classes, but it would be possible for a student to have primary, intermediate, and high school teachers that never taught the SQ3R method.

McDonald (15) stresses, "If meaningful learning is to occur, emphasis must shift from accumulation of more and more data to better techniques of developing and using new knowledge."

The history teacher at the college level has a unique role to play. Lecturing to the class populace and requiring memorization of a mass of dates and events are becoming outmoded. Previous courses taken by our present day college students in the social studies areas have been an accumulation of facts and figures. Many college students have not been challenged to think conceptually. It is the college teacher's task today to engender the conceptual process by guidance through persistent searching questions that lead to critical reading.

In order to have students more adequately prepared for college-level reasoning, the Wisconsin State Department of Public Instruction has been strongly encouraging a conceptual approach to reading in grades 1 through 12. Many schools have already accepted the challenge while others are still in the process of in-service training. Ultimately the conceptual approach will enable the students to think on their own and not merely be satisfied to regurgitate long lists of factual data.

There is no concern at the college level that students do not read social science material using the necessary reading skills. This concern persists even though reading skills in the content fields can be identified and successfully taught.

Which has the highest priority, skills or content? Should reading skills and content be taught separately or together? Nila Banton Smith (17) found that "pulling out" of study skills yields improvement. Some studies show that too little time is allotted for the teaching of isolated skills in content material. It would seem imperative to teach content material and reading skills simultaneously in a functional way. There is a scarcity of research concerning teaching both skills and content together at the college level. It would seem feasible to assume that greater improvement in both skill of reading and knowledge of content would result if immediate practice of skills with course content were provided, whereby both skills and content would reinforce each other. From a realistic viewpoint, the functional approach would seem to be the propitious way.

Harold L. Herber (9) says, "When guiding skills development, the teacher cannot assume students' prior competence with the skills." He previews the text to identify the skill needed to comprehend a given selection. The application of the skill is reviewed with students before the reading assignment is given. Then, by means of a study guide, students are led through the process of applying the specific skill to the assigned selection. The guide provides for students' varied ability and achievement levels. Skill development at the collegel level can be adequately guided in a smiliar manner.

Van Gilder and Wasinger (19) state:

Distinctive skills necessary in reading the social sciences include skills in wide, rapid reading; skills in overviewing and previewing to sense the main ideas as well as the structure of extensive material, and the viewpoint and tone of the author. Finally, the highest echelon of these distinctive skills needed in reading the social sciences are those of critical evaluation and of relating what is read to an increasingly broad background of cultural and vicarious reading—that achieved through the experiences of another. Because social studies reading ought to be extensive, it is important to demand meaning of the whole selection, chapter, or book by utilizing the organizational structure of the book, the typographical and graphic aids to emphasis, as described in the study-reading approach to the SQ3R method of study.

The college teacher is in a position to teach the skills with the content of his subject to a mature mind. Using the content of the subject matter will not only save time for the college teacher but will help the college student with the interpretation, conclusions, issues, and values of the material at hand. At this higher level of reading there is a need to broaden the students' background with referents for interpretation. This task can only be done if the student has the knowledge of locational skills. Instead of the college teacher's handing out sheets for outside reading, all the while realizing that almost two thirds of his class will never set foot in the library, he should spend time during class periods at the beginning of the semester familiarizing the students with the library in general, the card catalogue, guides, (such as *The Readers Guide* or *Guide to Periodic Literature*), and other sources of material within the college library. A genuine interest in each class and in its ability to use effectively all of the available material and resources may induce another third of the class to do more than the required reading. Considering skills-teaching as a function of the English department alone is not realistic. Realistically, the reviewing of these skills in a functional way will bring unlimited results. Spache (*18*) relates, "Direct instruction and practice in the effective use of these reference materials which are fundamental to successful study are the responsibility of each teacher in the content fields." This task will require the college teacher to spend time reviewing skills that he undoubtedly feels the students should have acquired by this time.

It is the general consensus of all educators that one must start from where the student is—then one will continue to see growth in the vast amount of knowledge that overwhelms us today. Time spent reviewing, teaching with a sincere interest in the development of the needed skills in the specific content areas, will pay dividends in class performance and total results. For the mature reader to be able to read critically, he must do the required outside reading and more. The college teacher will then be able to effectively guide the mature student to study critically what the author is trying to say and to evaluate this "new" knowledge in the light of what the student has known or believed.

A college teacher is in a unique position to teach the mature student with readily accessible material. Most college libraries have an inexhaustible supply of reference materials including document bibliographies and biographical sketches. Helping each class build its skills by using the specific content used in class will help make reading skills and content truly functional.

Science: skill needs

Science, the field of many unknown challenges, has an immense fund of knowledge yet to be unfolded.

According to Hafner (*7*), "Science has many difficult concepts. Concept development should be rooted in experience, experiment, and discussion."

Poor readers at the college level generally have an inadequate science vocabulary. Building an adequate vocabulary is necessary for the classification of phenomena, for the testing of hypotheses, and for the understanding of large overall concepts developed through experimentation.

In Hafner's (*7*) reading improvement courses he finds able readers of science material have a good science vocabulary that enables them to "follow the thread of an argument, visualize a description, identify the antecedent of a pronoun, relate the text to illustrations, use transition words accurately, read involved sentences correctly, understand the mathematical aspects, and be persistent."

General reading skills, such as reading graphs or charts, are the same in science and the social studies. The rate of reading in science is considerably slower compared to that of reading in many other areas. Knowledge of word parts and derivation of words is very useful in scientific reading; many of our scientific terms are drawn from the Latin and Greek.

Mathematical needs

In the area of mathematics there is a change in the reading processes as great as in the social studies area. The use of modern math in a large percentage of our elementary and high schools will help train our students to react more intelligently and to employ quantitative reasoning for the use of the mathematical processes. According to Fay (5), the general study procedure in math develops the number system, basic arithmetic facts, vocabulary foundation, clue terms, symbols, and abbreviations before further building upon the mathematical and language foundations. The problem solving involved demands greater stress upon application of a range of comprehension and critical reading skills.

At the college level one must first be aware of the student's mathematical knowledge and his power to reason in using this knowledge in higher mathematics. Making our students more aware of why we use certain processes or formulas demands reading with a more definite purpose in order to improve reasoning and abstract thinking.

In earlier studies by Georges (6), Austin (1), and Leary (12), it was found that the training in reading in mathematics instruction should include the following: organizing details into working ideas, recognizing relationships, organizing processes to find solutions, adjusting rate to slow speed to secure a high degree of comprehension, understanding technical vocabulary and symbols, understanding common words with mathematical connotations or more precise mathematical usage, locating and selecting related readings, and evolving procedures for problem solving.

In lengthy problems it seems justified that the students should be trained in listing the steps of the solution and the formulas needed. The training in selection of the correct steps and correct formula should not be overlooked. Just as in any other area the students' confidence in their ability to make the correct choice is one of the first prerequisites to success in mathematics.

Reading improvement programs

Reading programs *per se* vary greatly within the colleges. They seem to be one of three types: a) textbook oriented or machine oriented with an untrained staff; b) well-trained teacher with the class load too large to individualize instruction or

diagnose weaknesses; c) program where guidance is individualized, weaknesses are diagnosed by trained personnel, and individualized instruction offered is expensive. The latter seems to be the trend because of the apparent need within our colleges.

Marquette University offers a reading improvement course for its college students. Comparable to many of our colleges' reading skills program, the Marquette offering is versatile in developing the skills needed in all the content fields. We have found that if content area teachers help with the building of the reading skills within their given field, in conjunction with the reading center work, the result is more success in helping our college students become mature, educated adults.

A study by McConihe (14) relates that "College students who come for reading instruction may expect to find the method in use dependent upon the aims and goals of the instructor." Whether in the reading centers or in the regular classrooms, this feature is a common denominator. Some reading centers stress vocabulary development, their belief being that higher education has a primary need for a more technical vocabulary. This belief is true, as is the assumption in other college reading centers that stress the flexibility of rate throughout the various content areas. There is also a trend toward emphasizing critical reading to make the student a more efficient reader.

Hill (10) states: "The difficulty experienced by many students in transferring flexibility skills learned in college reading laboratory to the broad college learning situation may indicate that problems of flexibility, in part, lie outside the realms of ordinary training and volition." Therefore, one wonders if the function in the reading center at the college level should include or be oriented toward flexibility in reading skills.

According to Ray and Martin (16), "Many reading improvement programs offered by American colleges and universities often described as remedial are composed of lower achievement and lower ability students, among whom the college dropout rate is in excess 50 percent." Is it really beneficial to the college or to the nation at large to offer this service to such a high percentage of potential dropouts? Beasley (2) and Heftel (8) have done research using low, middle, and high achievers as well as a wide difference in ability among the students. Their investigations showed gains by both groups. The results did stress the need for adjustment to the individual student through grouping and using a better developmental reading program.

Numerous factors found in juxtaposition to content reading skills have been investigated from elementary level through college level. Carter (4) finds cooperation between the reading clinics and the teachers of the content fields. The approach to the reading of content material is more developmental than remedial. We will be finding the trend away from college teachers being considered at the nadir in teaching reading skills. The college teachers are concerned and are starting to do something about better development of skills within their own specific area.

REFERENCES

1. Austin, Mary C. "Improving Comprehension of Mathematics," *High School Journal,* 29 (November 1955), 71-75.
2. Beasley, Charles E., Jr. "A Freshman Reading Program," *Journal of Developmental Reading,* 2 (Winter, 1959), 23-29.
3. Bliesmer, Emery P. "Experiences Needed for Comprehending Reading at Various Levels," *Reading and Inquiry,* J. Allen Figurel (Ed.), Proceedings of the International Reading Association, 1965, 64-65.
4. Carter, Homer L. J. "Cooperative Study, the Clinic and the Classroom Teacher," *Reading and Inquiry,* J. Allen Figurel (Ed.), Proceedings of the International Reading Association, 1965, 212-214.
5. Fay, Leo. "Reading Study Skills: Math and Science," *Reading and Inquiry,* J. Allen Figurel (Ed.), Proceedings of the International Reading Association, 1965, 92-94.
6. Georges, J. S. "The Nature of Difficulties Encountered in Reading Mathe-

matics," *School Review,* 37 (March , 217-26.
7. Hafner, Lawrence E. "The Ingredients of High Level Comprehension," *Reading and Inquiry,* Proceedings of the International Reading Association, 1965, 106-107.
8. Heftel, D. L. "Gains in Reading Compared with Academic Aptitude and Initial Rate," *Journal of Developmental Reading,* 5 (Spring 1961), 210-21.
9. Herber, Harold L. "Reading Study Skills: Social Studies," *Reading and Inquiry,* J. Allen Figurel (Ed.), Proceedings of the International Reading Association, 1965, 94-95.
10. Hill, W. R. "Influence of Direction Upon the Reading Flexibility of Advanced College Readers," New Concepts in College-Adult Reading, Thirteenth Yearbook, 1963, The National Reading Conference, Milwaukee, Wisconsin, 119-124.
11. Holmes, Jack L. "A Differential Diagnostic Program For Improving Speed and Power of Reading at the High School and College Level," *Reading and Inquiry,* J. Allen Figurel (Ed.), Proceedings of the International Reading Association, 1965, 495-498.
12. Leary, Bernice E. "Meeting Specific Reading Problems in the Content Fields," in Reading in the High School and College, Forty-seventh Yearbook, National Society for the Study of Education, Part II, Chicago: University of Chicago Press, 1948, 136-179.
13. Lowe, A. J. "State Survey of College Reading Improvement Programs," *New Developments in Programs and Procedures for College-Adult Reading,* 12th Yearbook, National Reading Conference, Milwaukee, Wisconsin, 85-86.
14. McConihe, Esther J. "Methods of Teaching College Reading Skills," *Reading and Inquiry,* Proceedings of the International Reading Association, 1965, 42-44.
15. McDonald, Arthur S. "Reading in History: Concept Development or Myth Making," *Reading and Inquiry,* J. Allen Figurel (Ed.), Proceedings of the International Reading Association, 1965, 102-103.
16. Ray, Darrel D., and Mavis D. Martin. "Gains in Reading Achievement," *Journal of Reading,* (January 1967), 238-242.
17. Smith, Nila Banton, *Reading Instruction for Today's Children.* Englewood Cliffs, New Jersey: Prentice-Hall, Inc., 1963, 311.
18. Spache, George D. *Toward Better Reading.* Champaign, Illinois: Garrad Publishing Co., 1965, 279.
19. Van Gilder, Lester L., and Sister M.

Lucy Ann Wasinger, C.S.A. *Achieving Maturity Through High School Reading.* Dubuqe, Iowa: William C. Brown Book Co., 1967, 133-137.

An Effective Whole-School Approach to Study Skill Development

NINA T. FLIERL
Delmar, New York Schools

EFFICIENT STUDY SKILLS hold the key to learning and to unlocking knowledge; one of the most effective ways of teaching study skills is with team teaching in a whole-school approach. Each study skill is taught in large group instruction classes with reinforcement and practice in the small classes of the school. In the latter, the students apply the appropriate study skill in subject area classes, such as, social studies, mathematics, science, or English. Whether at the elementary or secondary levels, the teaching of study skills in large group classes insures the teaching of each skill. Even more important to its application is every teacher's using the same approach for each skill. With this kind of sequential reinforcement of study skills in subject areas, students learn effective, independent study skills and apply them in all academic areas.

All too often with the continuous pressure of added curriculum topics, study skills is a "catch-as-catch-can area." Sometimes it appears that lip service only is paid to the importance of study skill instruction. The practice of "doing research" before a student has mastered the notetaking study skill is widespread. The sophomore boy dashes into a biology final examination without ever having heard about the study skill of taking examinations. The fourth grader laboriously copies from the encyclopedia in the name of "doing research." Honest educators will agree that these are not isolated examples.

It has been said that the country is losing some of its best minds with the post-sputnik educational push of "too much, too fast, too soon." If this is true or has a shade of truth, how many more minds are never developed because of a failure to master study skills.

The whole-school approach with team teaching of study skills is an economical and effective solution to study skill integration into the developmental reading program K-12.

From its earliest beginnings in 1955 teachers and educators have reported that large group instruction growing out of team planning produces superior learning. Large group instruction tied particularly to study skills can substantially strengthen a school's developmental reading program, for study skills are needed by every group and each grade or K-12 class.

Practice has indicated that study skills can be effectively taught in large group instruction with reinforcement in the students' regular classes which are small groups. A student learns how to write an essay question in the large group instruction. He then writes essay questions under teacher guidance, using the recommended study skill in a history class test, or in an English examination, or in any class requiring essay question writing. The student's knowing how followed by his doing each study skill incorporates it into his total academic approach.

Study skills which can be effectively taught in a whole-school approach with team teaching might include completing written and reading assignments, the SQ3R study method for content subject assignments, steps for reading and solving mathematics problems, guidelines for reading literature, writing the essay question, taking tests, and the research paper.

Two examples of study skill development resulting from team planning and adaptable to large group instruction follow.

Taking tests

Successful grades require knowing facts and writing facts. When you take a test, you are writing the facts which you know about a particular subject. The following steps in taking a test will help you to do your best in writing the knowledge which you have learned.

1. *Look* over the entire test.
   A scanning reading rate can be used. Plan your time schedule for doing the test. Notice all the directions for each part of the test, especially as to number of questions to answer.
2. Make *notes* for essay questions. Write down key words, listings, or phrases while they are fresh in your mind.
3. Start to *work*.
   Do objective part of the test first.
   Then write the answers to the essay questions from your notes.
4. *Reread* test.
   Look for misspelled words, omitted words, omitted question parts, and errors in figures

Look - notes - work - reread is useful study technique for taking a test.
If you misjudge your schedule plan for completing a test and do not have time to finish, write TIME on your paper and write a brief outline for the essay question from the notes you made at the beginning of the test.

Steps for reading and solving mathematics problems

To read a mathematics problem requires a particular kind of detailed reading. The following steps will help you to solve such problems:

1. *Scan* the problem to decide what you are to find.
2. *Read* the entire problem. Take your time and read carefully.
3. Decide what facts are *given*.
4. Decide on *operation* or *operations* you will use to solve the problem.
5. *Solve*.
6. *Check* reasonableness of answer and check your computation.

Scan - read - given - operation - solve -
check are the six steps to solve mathematics problems.

The whole-school approach of team teaching of study skills effectively insures that this all important area will be an integral part of the developmental reading program K-12.

Can Administrators and Teachers Plan the Reading Program Together?

Coleman Morrison
Rhode Island College

IN CONSIDERING THE QUESTION of whether administrators and teachers *can* plan a reading program together, it is presumed that such an arrangement is desirable—in other words, that teachers and administrators *should* plan the reading program cooperatively. In order to support this hypothesis one must examine the alternatives to such a proposal: that administrators should plan the reading program without teacher involvement or that teachers should plan the program without administrative assistance.

Although textbook authors hold little hope for the success of programs which are formed on the basis of either administrative or teacher selection, the fact remains that decisions pertaining to the formulation of the reading program are frequently determined in this manner in a large percentage of schools. The reason for the widespread adoption of either approach can be easily explained.

On the one hand, the administrator has traditionally been considered as the status leader and, consequently, the person who must get things done. A corollary to this concept of leadership can be found in the roles of dominance and subservience which have been assigned to, or assumed by, the administrator and teacher, respectively, from the time the American educational system was conceived. These roles tend to persist today despite all attempts to democratize school administration.

As an outgrowth of this concept of authoritarian leadership, the content and conduct of reading programs are frequently determined by school administrators. Objectives of the reading program are established by principals or, more frequently, by members of the central office staff; reading materials are selected by them; and teacher effectiveness is equated with the degree of compliance to the administrative program. Because no provisions are made to involve teachers in the planning of new reading programs, if indeed new programs are ever planned, there is every indication that teachers serve as obedient children in a role that affords them an element of security provided they do what is expected of them. However, our observations and follow-up interviews with teachers working under these conditions indicate that they go through the motions of instruction without having any firm commitment to the approach they may be using or, what is worse, any understanding of it. This is hardly a climate that is conducive to learning on the part of either the teacher or the children she is expected to teach.

In contradistinction to the authoritarian structure is the nondirective one where teachers are permitted or expected to formulate their own policies. In such systems these teachers often operate as small autocracies in deciding what components of reading to teach and how to teach them. Such policies are permitted to exist in so-called "democratic" school systems, although careful scrutiny of the personnel involved usually reveals an uninformed administrator with little, if any, knowledge of reading, who is ready and willing to leave the decisions relating to the reading program in the hands of the teachers. When such is the case, we have observed that frequently some teachers are too quick to adopt an unproved reading program, while others are unwilling to initiate change when better methods are available. In general, we have found little continuity in such teacher-directed programs. Unfortunately, most tend to flounder in directionless confusion

to the detriment of the children's reading progress.

Thus, we have found that reading programs which become a reality as a result of administrative fiat, or those which evolve when the administrator delegates authority to individual teachers and provides no subsequent guidance for them, have not produced the desired results—children who can read with acceptable skill and efficiency.

Since neither administrators nor teachers appear to be successful in planning the reading program without reliance on one another, it seems sensible to accept our original premise that they should plan the reading program cooperatively. From such cooperation should come the desired change and improvement—provided, of course, administrators and teachers *can* work together. "Ay, but here's the rub! Can this be done?" As a pragmatist, I have many reservations. These stem from a review of the professional literature relating to the necessary conditions surrounding successful planning sessions and some knowledge of the persons who must be involved in the cooperative process.

My answer to the question "Can administrators and teachers plan a reading program together?" is a very guarded and conditional "yes." Some of these conditional responses will be discussed in this paper.

Administrators and teachers can plan the reading program IF they can identify mutually acceptable goals of reading instruction. Such agreement is easy to make when the decisions involved are relatively simple and the people making them do not have strong diverse opinions. But, as so many of you know, this is not the case where reading is involved. The issue of beginning reading, for example, is an extremely complicated one. Here group thinking related to the question of whether to introduce reading to the five-year-old is frequently polarized at either end of the yes-no continuum; there is disagreement over whether the initial function of learning to read should be considered primarily a decoding process or whether it involves a commitment to help the child comprehend and interpret what he is reading in addition to recognizing the printed word; and the question of when and how to present phonic analysis remains a controversial issue.

Yet, these and other basic components of the reading program must be discussed and agreed upon in order that all concerned understand just what type of program is desirable and, consequently, what type of pupil behavior they should expect. Discussion alone is likely to produce nothing more than an impasse, however, unless members of the group have the opportunity to observe for themselves some of the changes that are taking place in the curriculum and then discuss them. Kindergarten teachers cannot be expected to accept the theory that some five-year-olds can profit from formal reading instruction unless they visit other classrooms where this work is being done. Nor are first grade teachers likely to modify their approach to beginning reading unless they can evaluate and accept for themselves any new program of instruction. What all of this means is that groups of people cannot arrive at mutually acceptable goals unless ways are found which will stimulate the modification of their existing perceptions—that is, their perception of the situation, of themselves, and of the probable effects of change. Such modifications in perception are believed to provide the stimulus necessary to overcome blind acceptance of, and the adherence to, the status quo.

Secondly, administrators and teachers can plan the reading program together IF they are both acquainted with a knowledge of modern theory and practice concerning the teaching of reading. This is a goal devoutly to be sought, but one that may only be realistic as it applies to those persons who are prepared as reading specialists. In this respect, I doubt if we can expect the self-contained classroom teacher to become sufficiently knowledgeable about all aspects of the curriculum, including the "new" math, the "new" so-

cial studies, the "new" science, the "new" reading, and I suppose if I were to investigate further, the "new" art, the "new" music, and the "new" physical education. To expect the classroom teacher to be well grounded in all of these disciplines would be akin to the expectation that the medical school graduate would be equally adept in dealing with problems related to the heart patient, the cancer patient, the ulcer patient, or the diabetic patient.

Hopefully, our colleges and universities which prepare elementary school teachers will soon come to regard the concept of the self-contained classroom as an anachronism, will assist prospective school teachers in indentifying one or two related areas of interest, and will help them develop some depth in their chosen field of specialization through course work and student teaching.

Success in this endeavor is the promise that lies behind the philosophy of team teaching and the efforts being made to capitalize on the strengths and avoid the weaknesses of teachers participating in the venture.

Just as it seems unreasonable to expect self-contained classroom teachers to be well grounded in every aspect of the reading program, neither is it sound to anticipate that the elementary school principal will be able to assist the staff in the development of a program of improved reading instruction. I single out the school principals because they are often in the most strategic position to provide the appropriate guidance to teachers and have, in fact, been assigned this responsibility which historically has passed from the superintendent to the elementary supervisor to the principal. Yet too many principals do not have the know-what to provide the know-how. We can also look for team leadership among school principals rather than expect each principal to guide the activities of all teachers in all areas of the curriculum. (Ironically enough, in those systems where reading consultants are employed, their major assignment is often to direct remedial programs rather than to guide developmental ones so that very few of these trained reading persons are utilized to guide either administrative officers or teachers.)

Keeping these points in mind, it might be reasonable to expect cooperative planning to be effective when administrators and teachers are certified as specialists in reading and teachers of reading, respectively. Together they can be assigned the responsibility for formulating reading policies and coordinating the reading program.

Third, adminstrators and teachers can plan the reading program together IF they can translate their agreed-upon objectives into pupil behavior which is consistent with appropriate and effective teaching-learning designs.

This condition presupposes that the cooperating group understand the structure and uses of knowledge, have a grasp of basic concepts of human development and learning, and possess a familiarity with teaching strategies appropriate to the formulation of skills, concepts, and attitudes.

To expect anyone to develop an appropriate reading program without a sound basis in the psychological disciplines would be as foolhardy as to expect a layman without adequate knowledge of anatomy or biology to set a broken bone. In both cases it is the recipient who suffers.

Unfortunately, however, we continue to prescribe courses of study in reading without taking into account the most efficacious models of teaching or the ways in which certain children react to methods of teaching or to the materials presented them. For example, there is currently a predilection on the part of many school systems to provide children with programed textbooks and teaching machines. These automated devices and their accompanying printed materials are designed to provide children with the opportunity to develop a selected number of reading skills with only minimal reliance on the teacher. Unfortunately, before such programs are adopted, no provisions are made to determine which children can profit from such independent instruction. Some children may find the novelty or continued use of self-manipulative activities academically rewarding; others may react favorably to a manner of teaching that can only be provided by an animate object, namely, the teacher. The question relating to which learners will profit more from one program of instruction and which will profit more from another must be established before we can adopt one or the other for *all* children. This statement is true not only in the reference to programed instruction but with respect to the adoption of any instructional materials. This caution appears justified especially in school systems which are eligible for federally supported programs and where the only criterion for the selection of materials appears to be the price tag.

Other conditions relating to cooperative planning can be stated more succinctly, although their importance should not be diminished accordingly. Here again we feel that teachers and administrators can plan the reading program together

IF they can recognize strengths and weaknesses of an existing reading program;

IF they are provided with reference materials to fortify them with background information;

IF released time is provided for planning periods; and,

IF affirmative action will result from suggestions or proposals made.

In an effort to correct those weaknesses which inhibit satisfactory group participation one can hope for improved preservice and in-service education programs. But, while we wait for these expediencies to develop, both administrators and teachers are eligible to participate in government sponsored NDEA institutes in reading. Here, the major objective is to improve the competencies of school personnel directly concerned with the teaching and administration of reading. Fortunately, provisions have been made to accommodate both experienced and inexperienced persons as well as specialized personnel responsible for the education of disadvantaged, handicapped, and exceptional children.

These programs, which consist essentially of workshops, practicums, seminars, symposia, colloquia, and the like, have been conducted on a nationwide basis since 1965 and will continue to be offered through June 1969, if not later. I might mention here that the International Reading Association has prepared a guide to assist interested persons in the preparation of institute proposals. This guide supplements the manual published by the office of education. Perhaps, Dr. Gunderson, the author, will write a similar guide instructing applicants how they can best be accepted in these institutes since it is my understanding that there are ten applicants for every available institute opening, a factor that should not, however, deter anyone with a gambling instinct.

The institutes held at Rhode Island College during the summers of 1965 and 1966 were conducted for elementary school principals on the basis that 1) the need for improvement was greatest at this administrative level and 2) that as a result of the institute the principal would be in a position to work more effectively with his staff and ultimately to favorably influence the progress of reading among more children than if the institute were restricted to teachers.

In evaluating the strengths of our institute and its effect on the participants, we feel that the most positive aspects of the six-week program would include the opportunities for principals to 1) come into contact with nationally known reading authorities; 2) receive a cross-country concept of reading instruction and administrative procedures through formal and informal discussion; 3) use and evaluate the most current instructional materials; and 4) expand their knowledge of reading instruction and broaden their knowledge of diagnostic and remedial services.

The kind of program we provided did not, however, insure that all of the participants would profit positively. It was our feeling that while most of the group would become innovators, there were several who would remain unmoved by the new ideas. Those in the latter category feel bound by real or imagined difficulties which, they probably rationalize, will prevent them from entering upon new avenues of reading instruction. It has been clear to those of us who participated in the program, however, that many will emerge to lead their faculties in the direction and guidance of appropriate modes of instruction.

I recently contacted our institute alumni and asked them the same question that I had hoped to answer in this paper: Can administrators and teachers plan the reading program together? All but one indicated some success in working cooperatively with their faculties. A reaction of one respondent representing the majority will suffice. "I think," this principal wrote, "that teachers and administrators can work together successfully if the teachers are convinced that the administrator has a genuine interest in the reading program, keeps abreast of things going on in the field, and acts more as a catalyst and a resource person than a directing genius."

A contrasting comment from another of the respondents was "I have not experienced any of the textbook-described patterns of working together to develop this or that facet of the reading program. No doubt it can be done, but I do not think that I have the leadership qualities to do it successfully. As a result, I operate in a different manner—either on a one-to-one basis or on an informal 'toss-it-out-for-consideration' basis with a small group. Unfortunately, my attempts to stimulate the faculty as a group have not been successful, so I have not pressed on along those lines."

Perhaps these two statements say more directly in two paragraphs what I have been trying to say in several pages; namely, some administrators and some teachers can plan the reading program together. For them, team planning has resulted in better instruction and, subsequently, in better education for children. To other administrators and teachers who have tried and failed, and to still others who have never tried, I can only refer them to the wisdom of Chester I. Barnard, who wrote in the dedication of his book *The Functions of an Executive:* "To try and fail is at least to learn; to fail to try is to suffer the inestimable loss of what might have been."

Improving Instruction through Cooperative Action

RICHARD L. WATSON
Kansas State College

NEVER HAVE WE SEEN a time in the history of man when so many materials and so many pieces of specialized apparatus have been amassed to teach a basic language skill. I would guess that better than seventy-five percent of all the instructional reading materials has come on the market in the past ten years. Much of this production, and we are certainly seeing only the beginning, has come as a direct result of Public Law 89-10. Some other things which are changing reading instruction have happened since this Elementary Secondary Education Act (in all of its titles). As with any change, we get a new set of strengths and weaknesses and a need for continuous evaluation. More than 10,000 new remedial reading programs have come into existence; more than 20,000 new remedial teachers have been hired.

Because tremendous amounts of money were rapidly fed into education (some 2.5 billion dollars to date) and because approximately 80 percent of this ended up in reading, many unique and perplexing problems have arisen. We have teachers without training, machines gathering dust, clothes closets housing reading programs, and directors of federal funds growing bald from pulling out their hair.

For the past two years I have been working closely with federally funded programs: first, as an interested college reading person in Title I; second, as a director of a Title IV reading program; and finally, as a consultant on seven Title III projects. I also was privileged to represent Kansas at the First National Conference on Education of the Disadvantaged held in Washington in July 1966. At times I wanted to laugh about the tremendous ineptness of which I was a part; other times, I felt we were making real improvements in reading instructions. All the time, however, I felt the pressure of deadlines and the need to succeed in obtaining funds to get a necessary job done.

Reading instruction has thrown school staffs into a crisis in the past two years, out of which shall come either gains of tremendous significance or merely a surge of change for change's sake, resulting in little more than a disappointing search for panaceas which do not exist. This crisis is a challenge which should be of great significance to all educators.

Most school systems are trying to meet the needs of the disadvantaged through remedial reading programs. Some of these programs have now been "umbrella'd" to include school nurses, school psychologists, speech correctionists, guidance counselors, and para-professional personnel. Some have been carefully constructed and thought through; some are part of a total, carefully planned school program in reading using well-qualified reading specialists in conjunction with skilled classroom teachers.

Judging from the programs I have seen and the people with whom I have talked, I feel that these are the exceptional programs. By and large (and I do not wish to be particularly critical of school administrators who have done the best jobs they could under the circumstances) programs have been hastily thrown together by people who lacked the expertise and the time to do otherwise. Two things cause me concern in regard to these reading programs: 1) they depend to too great a degree on a small number of remedial teachers (as opposed to the involvement of many or all teachers on a school system's staff) in preventive, as well as corrective, aspects of the program; 2) some of the programs have broken so many of the basic ground rules—from the principles of a remedial reading program through the purchase of materials—that for this reason alone they need to be revamped or abandoned. My fear is, primarily, that school systems will place the blame for failure on the remedial program because it did not function as they felt it should or would rather than to realize that it did not function because they were expecting too much or because they went about remedial structuring in the wrong way.

Let me give a few examples. One school I visited drew students out of many self-contained, middle-grade classrooms for reading. After being in the program six weeks, the administration discovered the remedial class had three more students than the largest class from which the students had been drawn. Another school system had so many remedial students it could only get each student, as one of a group of fifteen, into one thirty-minute session per week. Then there was the school system that, having no special education classes, assigned forty mentally retarded students to the remedial reading teacher along with an equal number of disabled readers.

We could go on and on and on to include all the schools that purchased materials before they appraised their needs or hired the teachers or even, perhaps, to the systems who turned the entire requisitioning job over to a "good" salesman.

We have many basic needs in the public schools right now. First, we need local assessments of what our *total* reading program looks like—its strengths and weaknesses in teachers as well as in individual students. It should include a survey of material and equipment *used* as well as what is *held* in buildings. It should include the relationships between staff, facilities, and functions totally as well as just the remedial phases of the pro-

gram in a few target area schools. We can make ourselves blind to need by losing track of the needs of either the school system's total reading program or of its total student population.

Secondly, local school systems need diagnostic guidance. We are spending far too little time on the diagnosis of reading skills, the identification of methods for instructing individual students, and the analysis of inhibiting factors which cause reading disability. This condition is due in part to a lack of knowledge among reading staff members, a lack of concern with detail, and an anxiety to get a complex job completed too quickly.

As a part of this diagnosis, home contacts need to be made with parents and some rapport setting and goal building need to be done with students. The staff of one school system, where careful diagnosis was made over a six-week length of time, achieved not only good results but a satisfied public. The staff morale was likewise helped. When questioned later, every member of the staff listed diagnosis as the single greatest strength of the program— they knew what to teach, whom to teach it to, and how to teach it. They wanted to repeat that six weeks' endeavor the next year.

The third need is for increased in-service training for teachers, not the one-day or one-week workshop type of training but the kind that takes place "on location" for an extended length of time.

All administrators should require reading teachers to pursue course work leading to the IRA reading specialist minimum standards. These teachers could be paid, as many have been, from ESEA monies. In addition all teachers should receive on-the-job help in coping with corrective problems within their classes. This training might need to start with some theoretical base, but it must basically end up solving or attempting to structure the solution of immediate and real classroom reading problems.

Such a program was begun in Lawton, Oklahoma, this winter. One thousand teachers in that general geographic area were involved in five distinct types of integrally related workshop experiences. The first workshop session consisted of laying a theoretical base through a large group lecture approach and contained the subsequent identification of local problems in small groups; the second session consisted of a team approach discussing the possible alternatives for solving each of the locally raised problems of the first session; during the third session each teacher got to look at and discuss materials and techniques which were directly applicable to her unique classroom problems; the fourth session consisted of giving a helper to each classroom teacher as she applied the corrective alternative she selected; finally, each teacher got help in appraising the results of her experimentation a year later. This program is typical of the in-service training which needs to be done more extensively.

We need to build more action research projects, especially in the majority of schools where little innovating is going on. Perhaps I should define my use of the term "innovative." By this, I am not thinking only—or even mostly—about those things which have never been tried or proven; I am most concerned about schools trying something which is new or innovative to them but which has been used successfully many times before. There are techniques which have been around in research and/or actual practice for thirty years or more but which would be innovative, practical, and helpful for many school systems.

In general, public school systems are not well adapted to the rigorous controls necessary for pure research and are not particularly interested in disrupting the ongoing program to establish them, but they do need to be concerned about improving their programs through experimentation. The guidelines for action research seem to lend themselves well to evaluating changes made through this type of locally originated experimentation.

Underlying these four proposals

(assessment, diagnosis, in-service training, and action research) is the need for expertise and leadership. There is concurrently another need, since the expertise and leadership never seem to be correctly located or available in sufficient quantity, and that is the need for cooperative action.

Some Title IV Regional Laboratories began working on these service-oriented aspects of the reading program but have been sharply criticized—even threatened with loss of funds by the USOE. Service-oriented successes apparently are considerably less tangible and objectively measurable than other kinds of programs and, as a result, are undesirable packages to sell to legislators. The fact remains that service programs which furnish help with assessment, diagnosis, in-service training, and action research are sorely needed in the public schools. The fact further remains that public schools are willing and able to pay for such services.

I would propose that all schools training teachers and/or certifying reading specialists, as well as all public and private school clinics with highly trained staffs, have an ethical and professional responsibility to aid school systems in the four areas of need just mentioned.

I would see them offering internships—"on location" training programs —helping with administrative decision making, and perhaps even explaining a complete reading program to someone else's board of education. Above all, I feel a tremendous need exists and that the entire survival of sound reading instruction may well depend on the willingness of "them who has" to share with "them who has not"—in the area of teachers and total school systems as well as the area of deprived children and target area schools. Kansas State College of Pittsburg will undertake a cooperative program of this kind this summer which is an extension of an earlier program forcefully abandoned by the Mid-Continent Regional Educational Laboratory of Kansas City.

The unique part of this story is that the program was shelved as "inappropriate" by the US Office of Education, only to be demanded by nearly every school system within a one hundred-mile radius of the campus.

The proposed program will call for at least one additional Ed.D. reading staff member and one graduate assistant on the Ed.S. level. These additions bring the total professional reading staff to six, including graduate assistants. The total staff will share responsibilities for elementary, secondary, and college clinic operations; the undergraduate and graduate reading programs; and the newly organized Reading Services Center.

The reading services function will hopefully contain a reading materials center recently amassed by the Regional Lab and will be located in a new school vacated through unification by the Pittsburg Public Schools and on lease from them to the college. This facility has been renovated for this use and contains offices, a duplicating room, and a combination classroom and material library. Already, the cooperative idea and attitude are an integral part of the operation, which is needed to underwrite the success of this type project.

In a recent survey in our area, school systems seemed to want all of the four projects presented earlier. Some of these projects were of greater concern to one school system than to another. Each apparently has some degree of uniqueness in its needs. This uniqueness should be highly respected by the staff of the Reading Services Center: local control must be a basic premise in the formation of this "grass roots" operation.

This program is expected to be self-supporting. There will be no basic membership charge or school system donation. The Reading Services Center will assess equitable charges for services rendered. These funds will in turn pay for staff, graduate assistants, facilities, and materials.

Colleges are not the only groups with the ability to form service-oriented centers. Recently while in Nebraska, I took note of two rather good public school clinic situations—one formed with Title I funds and the other funded from Title III. Both of these centers and their staffs could help outlying communities in need of services; a pay-as-you-learn program could be sponsored by each of these clinics. Monies would come from boards of education in the other communities in exchange for staff training, evaluative help, and perhaps even material appraisal. The same kinds of benefits as in the college program could be derived in this clinic plan, especially since each of these two facilities is adjacent to good graduate college reading programs.

Another new project in Kansas will band together the Topeka Public Schools, Washburn University, and the Menninger Foundation. This arrangement could very well be expanded to offer supplementary services of the sort mentioned to surrounding communities.

If we are to meet the crises that face us—to critically analyze, expand, and improve existing reading programs— then we must find more realistic ways of stretching existing reading "expertise." We must also be willing to share in the recent developments of significance, more extensively than the "model" school visitation concept; and we must be willing to tackle locally delineated problems, rather than only altering all problems to fit some grand design. Existing facilities must be used to lead others to equally valuable benefits. As we endeavor to build these cooperative arrangements, we will see more general reading progress as well as our federal and local dollars going further and doing more for the improvement of reading.

The PESO Story

EMMITT D. SMITH
West Texas State University

PESO STANDS FOR Panhandle Educational Services Organization. PESO, an agency of West Texas State University, is designed to provide services to public and private school systems in the area served by the university. West Texas State University is situated in Canyon, Texas, in the heart of PESO Country which includes some 40 counties in the Panhandle and South Plains of Texas. This region extends from Texline on the Texas-New Mexico line on the north to the cotton fields of Lynn and Dawson counties to the south—a distance of some 300 miles—and from the Oklahoma line on the east to New Mexico on the west—a distance of some 150 miles. It is said that this territory is larger than nine states in the union.

PESO is an experiment in organizational structure for educational services. PESO country is peculiarly well suited for an experimental program, for it includes a big city like Amarillo, many small towns like White Deer, and schools of all varieties between the old type, small rural two-teacher school to the new air-conditioned plant in town and city. It also has a growing complex of junior colleges, the latest one being located at Levelland, South Plains College. There are approximately 100 school districts in this vast area which, by affording educational opportunity to some 100,000 children involve the services of approximately 7,000 teachers and other school personnel and the valuable contribution of some 750 members of local boards of education.

Again, PESO is an agency of West Texas State University serving these 100 school districts in special ways. It came into being on January 1, 1966, when 94 of these 100 districts banded together to implement Title I, ESEA, in this region. This program was titled *Project Educational Improvement.* On September 6, 1966, a new program funded under Title III, ESEA, called the *Texas Cooperative Dissemination Project,* was initiated; and also in September, 1966, PESO became the applicant agency under the Department of Labor for 52 Neighborhood Youth Corps In-School programs

and four out-of-school programs in this area of Texas. Later still the OEO regional office in Austin asked PESO to become the applicant agency for all Head Start Programs in the region which do not fall directly under the Community Action Agency.

Project educational improvement

Because poor reading seemed to be at the root of all the problems of the educationally disadvantaged children in the area, the PESO group of schools decided to begin the attack on educational deprivation by attempting to improve the *reading levels* of the 10,500 children and youth in the region who were identified as being one or more years below the level of expectancy in reading skills. This decision formed the basis for the development of PESO's first component, Project Educational Improvement.

Procedurally, PESO assisted the 94 school districts to set up about 250 reading stations on campuses where there was a demonstrated concentration of children with reading disabilities. These central services were provided with 1) program development and supervision, 2) staff development, 3) fiscal services, 4) diagnostic services, and 5) evaluative services.

A well-equipped room

A reading station is a room in a school building. This room must be equipped properly and hold proper materials for the individual instruction of children in corrective reading. When needed, this room must afford privacy or opportunities for small groups of two or three or for the total group of eight to ten. It must have the elements of flexibility and mobility, for the creative and skilled teacher cannot function in a setting which is bound to one pattern.

A well-trained teacher

A reading station has a trained teacher in it. On January 1, 1966, when PESO began, it was realized that there were only a half-dozen well-trained corrective reading teachers in the entire Panhandle and South Plains. It was also realized that this was a typical situation all over the nation, so PESO did the natural thing—it decided to train its own corps of reading specialists. The 94 participating superintendents of schools selected from among their best elementary teachers to staff their reading stations, and PESO took it from there with a staff development program involving a number of study sessions during the spring of 1966 culminating with a well-planned six-weeks full-time work conference in June and July. One hundred and eighty teachers attended the summer conference at West Texas State University and some 50 at South Plains College in Levelland.

Out of this 1966 summer work conference came the proposal that West Texas State University design a preparation program for reading specialists. In Texas there is no special certificate for a reading specialist, but it was determined that such a program could be fitted into the state design for the professional certificate for teachers. In March 1967, the Teacher Education Unit at West Texas State University approved this program leading to a master's degree, the Professional Teacher's Certificate, and an institutional endorsement as a reading specialist. You will note that the components of this program follow rather closely those recommended by the IRA:

Developmental Reading in Elementary and Secondary Schools.

Diagnosis and Correction of Reading Disabilities.

Administration of the Reading Program.

Supervision and Curriculum Development in Reading.

Special Areas in Human Development.

Learning Disabilities.

Tests and Measurements.

Theories of Learning.

Advanced Educational Psychology.

Practicum—Clinical Seminar and Practicum in Diagnosis and Remedial Reading Procedures.

Again this summer, the 250 reading specialists-to-be who man the reading stations in PESO country will return to the campus to continue their preparation program. In a few years, the region will have a well-trained corps of corrective reading teachers.

Some of the best informed people in the nation were brought to the Panhandle and South Plains to start the long job of converting these 250 PESO teachers into good reading specialists. Don Hodes and Thurman Johnson from the Communicative Skills Project in Los Angeles County; Jeanne McCarthy, a specialist in learning disabilities from the Chicago area; George Spache, one of the nation's leading authorities in reading; and William Powell from the University of Illinois, were among the sixteen to twenty national-level people brought to PESO country to help develop a corps of well-educated reading specialists. Several members of the West Texas State University faculty in psychology, sociology, and speech therapy were used as well as all of the PESO staff people.

In addition to working with outstanding consultants from the state and nation, the 250 teachers were given the opportunity last summer to observe model reading stations at work in both locations—West Texas State University and South Plains College. These stations were supplied with equipment and materials by several commercial companies who have been most helpful in the PESO project. This summer program served simultaneously as a laboratory for teachers and an aid to children with reading disabilities.

The program for the summer of 1967 included 30 reading stations in Amarillo and Canyon which served some 900 children with reading disabilities and at the same time provided a planned practicum in corrective reading which is required in the preparation program for the institutional endorsement as a reading specialist.

Each station was staffed by a team consisting of a lead teacher chosen from the 250 in the region and at least two helping teachers. Each member of the team participated in these three planned experiences in the practicum: 1) working with the individual, 2) working with the small group, and 3) participating in a problem seminar involving visiting consultants.

Last summer each of the 250 teachers had to demonstrate proficiency in the use of equipment needed in diagnosis and treatment for reading disabilities. The eight unit coordinators served as tutors for all 250 teachers until each demonstrated ability in the use of some 10 to 15 different pieces of equipment.

Last summer the 250 teachers were producers of materials. A regular workshop period was scheduled for daily work. Many practical materials were developed including bulletin board displays and two teacher guides ready for use on September 1, 1966.

Some sixteen or twenty companies set up supervised displays of materials and equipment during the six weeks period in the summer workshop of 1966 and helped the teachers, working with their unit coordinator, to assemble requisitions for materials and equipment needed the following fall term.

Weekly opportunities to learn more about teaching reading were offered the school administrators in PESO schools each summer, for research indicates that change comes to the school where the school principal and superintendent are enthusiastic and knowledgeable about the change.

The program for children

The next important ingredient in the reading station is the program of instruction. The simple premise for the PESO, Project Educational Improvement, is that 1) if a child cannot read up to his expectancy level, there is a detectable reason; 2) if a disability can be detected, it can be diagnosed and described; and 3) if it can be diagnosed, it can be helped in most cases.

Diagnostic instruments such as the audiometer and the eye-movement camera are put to use along with a battery of standardized tests. Kenneth Waugh, WTSU, directs the guidance program for all 250 stations helping teachers to learn how to administer diagnostic procedures as well as interpret them.

After the reason for a child's disability is established, many approved techniques can be used, for children learn in many ways. A child may learn from listening. He may function best in a group or alone. He may need individualized attention. He may need to learn from discussion as he uses materials adjusted to his level. The need for improved word recognition, for comprehension, for speed, all must be considered by the trained reading specialist who works either with groups or with individuals in a well-equipped room designed for learning, such as the reading station.

This program goes on every day, five days per week in all kinds and sizes of school in PESO country—in a small rural school in Dawson County, in a predominantly Negro area, in any school where there is a child who cannot read as well as he should.

Evaluation

Project Educational Improvement has been developed on the basis of what people think they know about how children learn—particularly those children who have developed disabilities in reading. The evaluation of the impact of this project was a major concern of the PESO staff. Dr. Waugh developed the evaluation system used throughout the 250 reading stations in PESO. The design includes evaluation in the cognitive domain utilizing a battery of pre- and post-tests to evaluate the reading growth of the 10,500 PESO pupils. Two of these tests are intelligence tests to provide a basis for anticipated growth in reading and capability to learn. The other two measure achievement. In each group of two tests, one is group administered and one is individually administered.

Evaluation in the affective domain includes subjective judgments by teachers and administrators regarding changes in attitudes, motivation, interests, anxieties, and adjustments of PESO students.

The evaluation system also seeks to describe the growth of PESO pupils in areas other than reading. The staff is now in the process of developing a research design to try to shed some light on the optimum time to remove a child with reading disabilities from the corrective reading program.

Texas cooperative dissemination project

The next component of the PESO program is called the Texas Cooperative Dissemination Project and is financed by Title III, ESEA. Its purpose is to *multiply* and *accelerate* the impact of new information and new ideas on the school curriculum grades 1-12.

The procedures to be developed and demonstrated in this pilot project include the location, collection, screening, recasting (if necessary), storing, retrieving, organizing, and channeling new information, new ideas, and new materials to the public and private schools—grades 1-12.

The staff has elected to emphasize the so-called solids of the curriculum—the sciences, mathematics, social sciences, the English-Language Arts (including reading)—in the beginning efforts. It is planned to broaden the scope as experience is gained.

The fiscal agent for TCD, representing the 104 participating school districts in PESO country, is the superintendent of schools of the Canyon Independent School District in Canyon, Texas. The entire effort of TCD will be closely supervised by local school personnel working through their superintendents.

The inspiration for the design for the TCD Project came from the Agricultural Extension Service—a system which picks up the findings of research, organizes them around pertinent problems, recasts them in the language of the user, and channels them into the hands of the user in such a fashion that he will probably change his behavior. This is done successfully in agriculture, but no such system has been attempted in education.

In the location process, the TCD staff made early contacts with such national level endeavors as Project English, Project Social Studies, the Science Information Exchange, ERIC, the American Association for the Advancement of Science, and many other sources of new information, new materials, and new ideas. Complete new programs were studied, such as the program known as "AAAS Elementary Science: The Process Approach." After clearing this idea with the Texas State Department of Education, sets of materials and equipment were purchased and collected by the TCD arm of PESO. This same procedure was used in other areas such as English and Social Studies. Of course, the first step in *reading* had already been accomplished in the Title I program.

The attempt to channel new information and materials into the hands of teachers revealed some new problems. By survey, it was learned that many teachers were not aware of current happenings in their teaching fields. As a result, they felt no need for new information, new materials, or new ideas. To meet this problem, TCD organized the "Awareness Conference." New information, materials, programs, ideas, concerning some 10 or 12 specific areas (including reading) were assembled, researched, and organized into conference presentations. In this way, the staff was able to offer to our region a tailor-made, 12-section, study conference, deliberately planned to raise the awareness level of all teachers in the areas presented. Awareness conferences have been presented in 12 locations to some 5,000 teachers and administrators.

Out of the conferences came requests from schools to present pilot programs exemplifying the new ideas presented. To date, seven pilot programs exemplifying the Continuous Progress Elementary School, eight programs exemplifying "AAAS Science: The Process Approach," one program demonstrating planned use of NASA materials, and one program demonstrating use of cuisinaire rods in primary mathematics have been initiated. Three NDEA English Institutes with study centering on the linguistics approach are in progress sponsored by TCD. Other exemplary programs are in the planning stage.

After the exemplary program gains some maturity, present plans call for the organization of study clinics around the exemplary program allowing for maximum interaction between pilot program personnel and other interested school personnel. In this way, the TCD Project hopes to be instrumental in converting plans and ideas into action.

A number of professors from appropriate academic departments as well as the School of Teacher Education serve the TCD Project as their services are needed.

The Data Processing and Computer Center at West Texas State University is tied in to the PESO operation. Record keeping, fiscal services, development of computer assisted instruction projects, and other aids of this nature are provided.

Neighborhood Youth Corps

The Neighborhood Youth Corps Program is another component program under the direct administration of PESO. This program serves some 500 young men and women between the ages of 16-21 who otherwise might add to the startling number of dropouts. Some 52 school districts are involved in this program.

Head Start

Just recently, the Regional Office of the Office of Economic Opportunity asked PESO to coordinate the activities of all summer Head Start programs which do not fall directly under a community action agency. This category involved 13 counties and 610 preschool children. In addition, PESO serves as the delegate agency responsible for the operation of the long-term Head Start program in Amarillo.

The future

This year Texas will set up and finance with state funds 20 regional media centers. One of these centers will be located in Amarillo in the heart of PESO country. The long range plan is to build an intermediate unit educational service center around these media centers financed in the main by Title III (ESEA) funds along with the state funds provided for media.

PESO will merge this month with the regional media center; and, since the program has already started and has gained some maturity as an educational service center, PESO will provide a prototype for the other 19 regions to study. The functional design of this new PESO is presented here.

This service center will have these characteristics:

1. It will be an autonomous state agency with a lay governing board.
2. It will have the power to contract for services from the university.
3. It will be the fiscal agent for state, federal, and local tax funds, as well as funds from foundations or private gifts.
4. It will provide central services to participating schools which can be provided best regionally rather than by the separate schools.
5. It will be a service center, not an intermediate administrative unit.
6. Its mission will include the infusion of new educational ideas, current promising practices, and introduction of new materials, and information.

EXHIBIT D

TEXAS EDUCATION AGENCY

THE ASSEMBLY (The Joint Committee)——————————COMMUNITY RESOURCE COUNCIL

PESO
EDUCATIONAL SERVICES
CENTER

Governing Board
Regional Media Board
Director
Assistant Director
Seven Unit Coordinators

EDUC. PLANNING	CLIENT SERVICES	MEDIA AND MATERIALS	CURRICULUM DEVELOPMENT INSTRUCTIONAL SERVICES	FISCAL SERVICES DATA PROCESSING & COMPUTER SERVICES
AREA SURVEYS & STUDIES (demographic, economic, cultural)	DIAGNOSTIC SERVICES	DEMONSTRATION	CONTINUING EDUCATION	ACCOUNTING
FEDERAL & STATE RELATIONS	EVALUATIVE SERVICES	A-V MATERIALS PRODUCTION	LOCATING, COLLECTING, SCREENING, RECASTING NEW INFORMATION	RECORDS
SCHOOL-UNIVERSITY RESOURCES & RELATIONS	PSYCHOLOGICAL SERVICES	STORAGE & RETRIEVAL OF MATERIALS	ORGANIZING, PRESENTING NEW INFORMATION: SOCIAL SCIENCE, SCIENCE, MATH, LANGUAGE ARTS	CONTRACTUAL SERVICES
COMMUNITY RESOURCES & RELATIONS	MEDICAL SERVICES	PRINTING DUPLICATION	EXEMPLARY PROGRAMS	INTERNAL MANAGEMENT
PROGRAM PLANNING & ANALYSIS	DENTAL SERVICES	ERIC	STUDY CLINICS	
	GUIDANCE & COUNSELING	A-V CIRCULATION SERVICES	CONSULTANT SERVICES	
	LEARNING DISABILITIES CLINIC	LIBRARY SERVICES	CAI	
		EDUCATIONAL TELEVISION	CORRECTIVE READING STATIONS	
		AREA NEWSLETTER	OTHER PROGRAMS FOR DISADVANTAGED (NYC, HEADSTART INCLUDED)	

Developmental Reading: Definition for Sequence

CHARLES C. ROGERS
Euclid Central Junior High School
Cleveland, Ohio

THIS IS THE SECOND YEAR of operation for the Euclid English Demonstration Center without Federal funds. That there is a demonstration center pays testimony to the responsible acceptance by the board of education and by the Euclid School administration for continuing the work begun under George Hillocks. It is a tribute to Michael Flanigan, without whose efforts the work of this center would not have been continued. I single out these people (and I could mention others) because there are those who wonder what will happen when Federal dollars cease for worthwhile programs.

The Euclid experience has been that once progress is underway, there is little to fear—indeed, without a progressive board and administration, without the climate and without individuals with a commitment to better education for youngsters, the center could not have come into existence in the first place, with or without Federal money. Now that Federal funds are spent, nothing has changed in the effort being made except that we must sell our units at a modest price. This need only strengthens our desire to further improve our product for the consumer, ultimately the pupil.

What, then, is our direction, and what do we wish to accomplish? It becomes obvious from various journals that the function, or even the desirability, of a distinct junior high level is still questioned. And in our field, there are arguments as to whether junior high should include language arts or English.

It is time that we decide what must be done at each school level and still, at any given level, leave much for others to do. This is not a romantic plea for a return to an age of simplicity. Our English courses desperately need focus, for most pupils have not arrived at a gestalt.

Whatever we mean by English as a subject is of such a gestalt nature that it is nearly impossible for us to say what it is we should be doing at any given time. (We sometimes envy the college specialists.) Yet, we so often present materials in such a piecemeal fashion that the pupil cannot possibly put Humpty Dumpty together. Our map of the territory is incomplete; necessarily, his map is less complete than ours.

Separate we must; there is no magic way to teach a gestalt unless it be incidentally through that magic book which, once experienced, forever *hooks* the student on our way of knowing. But we seldom can plan for the occurrence of this event; we know too little of individuals or of how they are affected.

The Euclid Cooperative Research Project promised a total junior high curriculum in English. In retrospect, this ambitious aim is both weakness and strength. We are coming to believe the primary need in the teaching of English at all levels is to delimit, and while we pay lip service to totality, we have in reality limited goals. We deal with the tripod—language, literature and composition—but our primary goals all center around developmental reading.

At best, English is a study which helps the student organize and understand his experience, his world. It in turn provides experience which enlarges his world and makes growth possible. We teach the basic language structures and larger forms which are ways of knowing. In the Euclid Central Junior High program we deal with structures covering a range from morphemic to generic concepts.

Reading and writing are complexes of organizational skills. In dealing with them we come as close as one can to the general goal of teaching pupils to think. English is now complete as a subject because in language study we have the discipline, the way of knowing, of science. We now see the two great discipline areas of our culture, the humanities and science, married in our courses. I should think the humanities is still the most important for our pupils because of personal and cultural needs—science doesn't help one make value judgments.

At the elementary level much enrichment is possible, indeed necessary, but elementary remains the place for basic mechanical skills. Senior high and junior college seem the place for the heavy work of a liberal arts education. It seems to be, also, the time for specialization in the less demanding trades and occupations. The upper college years through the MA, or beyond, are essential for the professions. The PhD, or comparable degree, remains for the scholar. And so what of the junior high—is it distinct and worthwhile or is it a mere administrative convenience as so often seems the case? We believe it is a most necessary level, distinct from others.

At an NDEA Institute at a Midwestern university, a knowledgeable professor paid honest homage to the sixty junior high teachers in attendance and was, figuratively speaking, hooted off the stage. I tell this to make the point that there is an important transition period in formal education too little appreciated even by those who are involved in it. It seems that we either want to be teachers of children or subject matter specialists. We love kids or we love our subject. I don't know of any place where love will go better than in junior high. To badly use Frost—These *are* swingers of birches. But we don't teach kids, nor do we teach English: we teach English to kids.

Let us use the old-fashioned definition. Kids come to us able to read; if they can't, they are not, by definition, junior high level, and they go into remedial reading courses. If they can read, they read words. But words are not our way to understanding. Show me a bunch of words and their meanings, and I will show you the lexicon of the language which certainly is not the language. This is one of our wonderful ironies: we teach youngsters to read words. From present knowledge, what else can we do? But then we must correct this mistaken perception of language. They must learn to read words inter-inanimated in and from a context. Apperception, or more broadly perception or more commonly reading readiness, is still the most important concept in reading.

Reading, you will recall, is not so much what is on the page as what it is one takes to the page. We hear much about reading readiness in first grade where it is a relatively simple matter; oddly we hear little about it in the twelfth grade where a vastly greater amount of energy should be spent to guarantee it. We must make connections for the pupil and help him learn to make connections for himself. Words mean little except as used in particular structures and except as they are informed by experience prior to reading.

There is a gap, then, at the junior high level, a gap which produces the higher illiterate, which needs bridging above all others if we are not willing to trust to luck and nature. Both structure and methodology of the Euclid units are conceived as a means of bridging this gap in and through reading. The units provide the essential pre-writing experiences necessary for oral and written composition. They provide a progression from teacher direction to self-direction by the pupil with evaluation being inherently provided rather than being external and superficial to behavioral objectives.

Unit structure

Our units are of several types and might be generalized in the following way. Besides language study units, we have thematic, generic, and specific developmental reading units. An example of the latter would be a unit on symbolism in which the pupil is taught to read symbolic literature or understand literary symbols in various forms. Generic units present ways of understanding the world from the tragic, satiric, mythic, and heroic modes. Thematic units capitalize on threshold interests, such as animals; deal with value systems considered basic to our culture, such as power, justice, or courage; or deal with human developmental or social problem themes, such as coming of age or protest. Let me emphasize that regardless of the thematic content, whether it be social problems or pupil-centered or literary, units are structured so as to give primary emphasis to developmental reading.

In the unit *Protest,* for example, after reading short essays which protest various social ills, pupil attention is turned to how protest is made in literature; that is, the purpose of the unit is not sociological: our aim is not to put our pupils out into the streets with placards but to explore how men have structured the vehicle of literature to express ideas vital to their well being.

Work in all units is carried out inductively. The pupil understandings are of course directed but are drawn from or discovered by him from the careful choice of material and by directed study which allows him to come to personal choices within a framework of meaning, rather than his being taught "correct" understandings from some adult point of view.

The pupil is first taught the teacher directed understandings in the following way. From pretesting, from introductory nonreading lessons, and from discussion, present pupil knowledge is established. With introductory selections, this serves the purpose of letting the pupil in on the secret. He must understand direction as clearly as the teacher. Present definitions of concepts are usually established, to be revised later. These definitions provide direction in the reading.

Next, with teacher direction, concepts are explored and expanded. In *Courage,* for example, simply defined examples of physical courage are seen in stories before exploring those exemplifying more complex views of the concept. At the same time traditional understandings are established, such as Aristotle's "golden mean."

Thus, in the first, teacher directed phase of the units, background and concepts are discovered and explored which provide the direction for the balance of the unit work. Thus, too, our selections of themes must not be slight or frivolous because they provide the basis for exploring the levels of meaning contained in literary form. Further, they must contain concepts involved in later, more difficult reading. Courage leads into the generic study of heroic literature, for example. Herein, in part, lies the sequence which a developmental reading philosophy permits.

We want independently capable readers. The next phase attempts to free the pupil to direct his own efforts through group work. In this group work and throughout the units, we emphasize aid to the pupil before he reads, rather than examination after he has approached a work which for him is on a frustration level. Thus it is, too, that any given lesson provides background for a later one. Study guides which allow pupils to verbalize their problems together, and inventories to help them structure their understandings are widely used.

Works of considerable depth, surprising to some on the junior high level, are possible because of the established direction and group help provided. Levels of meaning are approached in an orderly progression with constantly directed attention to textual meaning rather than to flights of fancy which might break down the student's perception of structure. Pupil creativity is not absent, but it is freedom with discipline. Though what I am describing sounds rigid, pupil opinions are respected, solicited, and basic to further work in the units.

The third phase consists of redefinition, reevaluation (both from previously established concepts), and application. Having gained the direction of concepts and the discipline of structural knowledge as taught in the unit, the pupil now can operate on his own at a creative level and approach a work which will test his ability to use the knowledge gained. To some extent he will be setting purposes on his own; he will be discovering on his own.

Composition

When one conceives of reading and writing as organizational skills, he sees them as the two sides of the coin. Our unit structure provides important sequence in composition from pre-writing to writing to post writing. And incidentally, we find that with adequate pre-writing experiences, far less revising and correcting are necessary. Besides the careful development of concepts, opportunities for the pupil to express his ideas and cooperative group work to thoughtfully (that is, consciously) work out intellectual problems throughout the units are emphasized. These oral and written assignments range from easier to more difficult and from shorter to longer and are carefully placed through the units to lead to a culminating composition which the pupil can master because he has been practicing and revising without the drudgery of making this application to one assignment. With a modular scheduling system, all writing is done under teacher supervision, as is most reading.

The final composition is an effective evaluation of our efforts. While the pupil has supposedly been taught everything he needs to do it, the final reading and composition are on his own and call for application of what he has learned. Sometimes, even these final compositions are group efforts, thus guaranteeing that the problems of the composition will be objectified and discussed rather than merely being subconsciously mastered. Throughout, we want our pupils to know what they are doing and why.

Euclid Project English began as a cooperative research project of the Euclid Central Junior High School and of Western Reserve University. It was entitled "A Comprehensive Program in English for the 7th, 8th and 9th Grade: Literature, Language, and Composition; For Honors Students and Average Students." Its activities are a matter of published record.

To summarize, I should like to quote from our first bulletin, *An Introduction to a Curriculum,* which for me reads like a manifesto:

> The English curriculum at Euclid Central Junior High School deals with all the aspects of learning that are generally lumped under the broad title of language arts, but its major emphasis is the development of the student's ability to read and analyze independently.

Criteria for Effective Grouping

RICHARD C. WILSON
Florida State University

FEW ISSUES IN READING have gained more attention or have been embroiled in more controversy than grouping practices—perhaps because there are infinite reasons and ways to group children.

Grouping is more an organizational pattern than a method of teaching. Once a group is formed, regardless of the basis or criteria, what takes place is of more significance than the number, the interest, the age, the sex, the abilities, or grade placement of group members. Grouping is not a substitute for effective teaching. When groups are formed for a definite purpose to facilitate instruction, they are justifiable; otherwise, there are no defensible reasons for forming a special group.

Interclass and intraclass groups

Reading ability as measured by standardized tests or teacher judgment is the common basis for interclass and intraclass grouping. Interclass grouping may be vertical. The vertical, or across-grade plan, allows pupils from two or more grade levels to meet as a unit for reading. This arrangement is typical of the Joplin plan. Sometimes ability groups are formed within a specific grade level. This is a horizontal plan. For example, a school with five sections of fourth grade may decide to arrange all pupils in terms of total scores on a reading achievement test. The pupils are then sectioned; one teacher is assigned the top fifth; another, the next; and so on. Except for a formal reading period, the children function in a regular heterogeneous or mixed classroom.

The grouping arrangement should not be confused with methodology. Method is independent of grouping. Once a group meets, the teacher may use any number of procedures for direct or indirect instruction.

Interclass grouping is most common in departmentalized elementary and secondary schools. This arrangement lends itself well to a highly structured and scheduled program.

Grouping fallacies

In many typical interclass or departmentalized reading groups the instruction provides little or no variation in materials or procedures. The assumed homogeneity often precludes any emphasis upon individual requirements and needs.

Intraclass grouping is a common elementary school practice, especially where teachers employ a basal reader type program. The usual arrangement is three groups. The groups, labeled in a variety of ways, are established to narrow the range of reading abilities in order to facilitate teaching. Again, homogeneity is frequently based upon a single criterion—total reading achievement measured by formal testing or teacher judgment. Variations in interest, rate, comprehension, vocabulary recognition, and word concepts are rarely, if ever, a serious consideration.

The three-reading-group arrangement utilizes basal texts in about three ways: 1) The same text may be used for all groups, but the pacing varies, some groups may be reading at different rates and thereby the story topics taught vary among the groups at a given time. 2) The same text may be used for each group with pacing controlled for all, no group in this instance changes stories until all change. 3) Each group may have a different basal text and sometimes the texts are of different levels of readability. The pacing under these circumstances may vary.

Once intraclass groups are formed, the composition seldom changes. For many children, "Once a blue bird, always a blue bird!" Intraclass grouping in a traditional setting, like interclass grouping, does little to meet individual needs based on variables other than general ability.

Because standardized reading tests measure more than a single reading skill, it is unreasonable to expect a high degree of homogeneity where children are grouped according to a composite score. Yet, it is the rule rather than the exception to group on this criterion.

The values of grouping should not be lost because of limitations. Flexible grouping to meet a common, immediate need is widely recognized as a sound educational practice. Diagnostic teaching is the prerequisite. Obviously, grouping especially for a specific need cannot be done until common needs are determined. Why group for any reason if the grouping is planned to teach what the membership already knows? To do so is a needless waste. If a word skill, such as inflected endings, is to be taught, it makes sense to learn who needs the instruction rather than to teach everyone something needed only by a few.

Washburne (5) recognized the basic trouble inherent in any inflexible grouping plan when he wrote, "The difficulty with any attempt at grouping is that each child has his own characteristic profile of abilities and maturities." What is germane to grouping for one moment may be passe at another. An often overlooked danger in grouping is the tendency to see a child in a group as a member rather than as an individual. Wilhelm may have had this tendency in mind when he wrote, "Maybe the greatest hazard in this whole grouping business is that it causes some teachers to search constantly for similarity" (6).

Values

The limitations and pitfalls of grouping should not overshadow the worth and need for the grouping that facilitates and fosters learning and teaching. There are definite values in grouping that should not be forgotten. Here are some examples:

1. Many children participate more actively within small groups than within larger ones. The "auditorium" effect is lessened.
2. Often children need to be with others who have an interest in the same books or other reading materials.
3. The small group frequently facilitates interaction between teacher and pupils.
4. The exchange and sharing of materials is accomplished with greater ease within a small group.
5. Small group instruction minimizes the waste inherent in teaching a larger group for no greater reason than to regimentize teaching and keep all students reading the same materials at the same time (7).

Because of simple physics, sex, and the diversity of abilities, interests, instructional levels, personalities, social factors, and ages, groups should not be based on a single monolithic design. Grouping practices should serve all the variables to meet individual reading needs. The ability group should not be "the" group. No special group should be "the" group. As a matter of fact, it is worthy to consider McKim and Caskey's reminder, "All reading experiences do not call for groups" (4).

Guidelines

Here are some guidelines for grouping that may prove valuable at some appropriate time:

1. Every group should be flexible and subject to change. A stagnant group is as bad as no group.
2. Grouping should meet an immediate recognizable need.
3. Groups should be dissolved when their purposes have been met.
4. There should be no more groups operating simultaneously than can be judiciously handled.
5. Girls and boys sometimes like to be together for reading. On occasion they enjoy being separate. This is a good reason to group by sex sometimes.
6. Because the topic may be more important than "togetherness" on a reading test, grouping because of similar interests has merit.
7. For purposes of discussion, review, and some oral rereading, it makes

sense to group when each member has different material about different topics. Bookclubs encourage the practice; children like it, too.

8. No member of a group should feel overwhelmed by the tasks ˌ set for the group.
9. Groups should operate with some degree of leadership. They should not shift aimlessly without some direction.
10. Grouping for reading should not isolate reading skills from content. Children should think of reading as a tool for learning rather than as a subject. Reading is a part of every subject.
11. Labeling groups should be for simple short-term identification. The use of such terms as fast, average, and slow should be avoided. Such labels unnecessarily stigmatize and erode a child's self-respect.
12. When possible, provide an opportunity for children to participate in developing group plans and activities; personal involvement fosters interest and good working relationships.
13. Anticipate obstacles and prepare the membership for certain difficult tasks. Discuss possible solutions.
14. Keep in contact with groups working independently. Help when needed; transfer members to other groups when goals are met.

Keep in mind that good grouping practices, like good teaching, do not foster conformity and uniformity, but differences. "In fact," Gray wrote, "good teaching at any level increases the range in reading ability from the poorest to the best" (2).

REFERENCES

1. Burton, William H., Clara Belle Baker, and Grace F. Kemp. *Reading in Child Development.* Indianapolis: The Bobbs-Merrill Company, Inc., 1959.
2. Gray, William S. University of Pennsylvania Bulletin—Forty-second Annual Schoolmen's Week Proceeding, September 1955.
3. Hildreth, Gertrude. *Teaching Reading.* New York: Holt, Rinehart and Winston, 1958.
4. McKim, Margaret G. and Helen Caskey. *Guiding Growth in Reading.* New York, New York: The Macmillan Company, 1963, 152.
5. Washburne, Carleton W. "Adjusting the Program to the Child," Educational Leadership, December 1953, 138-147.
6. Wilhelm, Fred T. "Grouping Within the Elementary Classroom," *NEA Journal,* 58, September 1959, 19-21.
7. Wilson, Richard C. *Individualized Reading: A Practical Approach.* Dubuque, Iowa: William C. Brown Book Co., Inc., 1965, 29.

In-Class Grouping to Care for Individual Needs

JACK W. HUMPHREY
Evansville, Indiana, Public Schools

ABOUT TEN PERCENT of the pupils who enter high school in the Evansville Public Schools are unable to read well enough to be placed in regular English and literature classes. These pupils are assigned to a class called Reading I in their freshman year and may stay in Reading II, III, and IV for a total of four semesters or until they are able to read at a seventh grade level. No English credit is given for Reading II, III, or IV. Reading I is also offered during the summer so that an eighth grade pupil can be admitted to regular classes in the fall if he can work up to a seventh grade level.

Most of the teachers of Reading I-IV have reading specialist licenses which are issued by Indiana in accordance with standards presented by IRA. Each high school has one reading specialist who teaches all developmental reading classes and most of the Reading I-IV classes in a specially equipped reading room. Federal and local funds have been used to provide proper shelving, materials, and equipment. Figure 1 shows a diagram of a high school reading room which has ample space, shelving, and equipment.

The pupils who are enrolled in Reading I have had a combination of problems which have contributed to their lack of success in reading. One of the Reading I classes is located in a high school in the center of the city where a large number of pupils with reading problems enter high school; the members of this class of 15 pupils have backgrounds which have resulted in low academic achievement.

A number of different circumstances awaits pupils such as these in their high school language arts program. If they are not grouped according to abil-

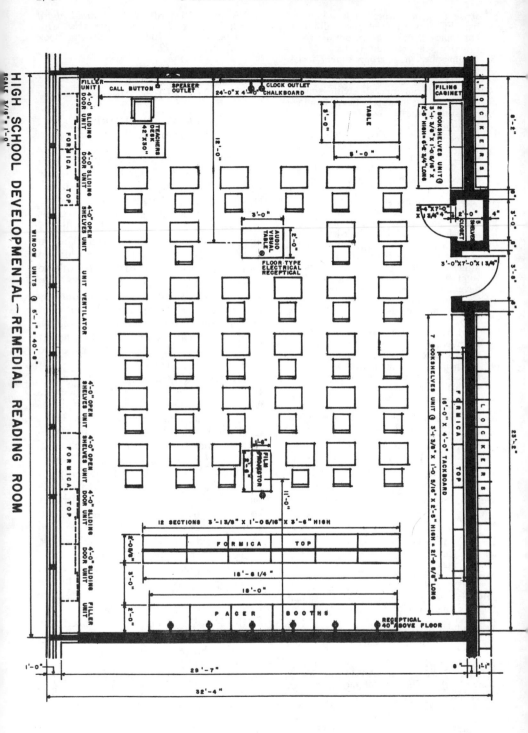

Figure I

ity, they must compete in regular classes and may become failures. Another doubtful way is to place them in ability groups and assign them to a new teacher on the staff who has neither the desire nor the training to work with "slow learners." Such methods as these will surely result in low achievement and poor attitudes. Even ability grouping and a variety of good materials cannot insure success unless they are utilized by a good reading teacher. A third way is to assign the pupils to a reading specialist who has materials and facilities to provide a good program. The remainder of this paper is a description of good reading programs for these 15 children using good classroom organization.

The pupils were tested at the beginning of the year with the Gates Reading Survey and the Lorge-Thorndike Non-Verbal Intelligence Test. Some had been given the Stanford-Binet Intelligence Test in past years, and the Botel Reading Inventory and Peabody Picture Vocabulary Test were given as needed. The mean for the Gates Reading Survey was 4.7 with a range from 2.0 to 5.7. The mean of the Lorge-Thorndike Test was 87.6 with a range of 71 to 106.

As a result of the testing, the pupils were divided into three groups. Group 1 had an instructional level of grade 5; Group 2, a level of grade 4; and Group 3, a level of grades 2 or 3. Six of the 15 pupils were placed in Group 1; six, in Group 2; and three, in Group 3.

The teacher found from the cumulative records and from talks with the school counselor that the pupils had many problems in school and at home. There was an average of 5.6 children in each family with a range of 2 to 11. Eight of the 15 children had no father in the home. Fourteen out of 15 had medical or dental work that had been done. Eight were discipline problems in other high school classes. The pupils had attended an average of four elementary schools with a range of one to 12. Most of the average reading grades on their cumulative records were low.

These statistics are interesting, but they have more significance when applied to individuals. Jim had five brothers and sisters and did not live with his father. His reading readiness score in first grade was average, but he had low grades in reading throughout his elementary career. He needed glasses which were provided with funds from Title I. Jim was assigned to Group 1.

Edith, a member of Group 2, came from a family with 11 children and now has two of her own. She attended five public and two parochial elementary schools. She had talked frequently with her counselor but seemed to continually get into trouble.

Shirley was a member of Group 3. She attended five different first grades and a total of 12 elementary schools in Indiana as well as some others in Kentucky. There were ten children in her family, and her parents were divorced. The school nurse and counselor helped her get a hearing aid this year, and she can now hear much better. Nurses in the past had attempted to get her hearing checked, but the family would move about the time that everything was arranged for her to see a doctor or get a hearing aid from a special Kiwanis fund.

As a result of information obtained from the tests, cumulative records, and other sources, the pupils seemed to need instruction in five areas. These were vocabulary, word attack skills, comprehension, oral and silent reading, and recreational reading. Emphasis was given to the improvement of attitudes and study skills in all phases of the program.

Vocabulary. The Reading I pupils needed a review of the basic sight words and basic sight phrases. Additional work was done in basic materials in conjunction with other areas such as comprehension and oral and silent reading. Vocabulary was reviewed before each story was read in skill books such as the *New Practice Readers* or in literature books.

Word attack skills. The Botel Phonic Mastery Test results showed very clearly those areas where specific help was needed. Many of the pupils needed work in phonics, and all seemed to need help in structural analysis.

Comprehension. Many skillbooks were available that were interesting and useful in the Reading I classes. It was important that the selections be high in interest and not too long. Comprehension needed to be stressed in all areas of the program, but some time was spent on specific exercises to improve in this area. The pupils

WEEKLY LESSON PLAN
GRADE 9—Reading I

Day	Group 1	Group 2	Group 3
MONDAY	Help Yourself to Read, Write, and Spell Shadow Scope, Use Better Reading Book 1 or Reader's Digest	⟶ Controlled Reader or Scope Magazine	⟶ Webster Word Wheels or Basic Sight Words or Flash X
TUESDAY	Dimensions in Reading Listen and Read Tapes	⟶ Flash X or Group Tachistoscope Reader's Digest 4 or Junior Reading for Understanding	⟶ Using Context B or Following Directions B or Working with Sounds B or Locating the Answer B
WEDNESDAY	McCall-Crabbs C or D Controlled Reader or Scope Magazine	⟶ B or C Practice Reader or Reading for Meaning	⟶ A Teen Age Tales A, B, C or Reader's Digest 2 or 3
THURSDAY	Help Yourself to Read, Write, and Spell Practice Reader C or D or Using Context D or E or Reading for Meaning 5 or 6	⟶ Ladder Books or Teen Age Tales 1-8 or New Worlds of Literature	⟶ Conquests in Reading
FRIDAY	Dimensions in Reading Ladder Books or Teen Age Tales or New Worlds of Literature	⟶ Using Context C or Following Directions C or Working with Sounds C or Locating the Answer C	⟶ Controlled Reader 2 or 3 or Scope Magazine

Figure 2. Weekly lesson plans for grade 9, Reading I

needed a variety of materials at various instructional levels.

Oral and silent reading. Most of the Reading I pupils did not read well orally. Poor readers usually have less opportunity (and desire) to read in content area subjects. High-interest material at an easy level was needed for these pupils to use in small groups.

Recreational reading. The pupils in the class did not read many books for pleasure. Most of the books in the high school library were too difficult for them, so it was important that high-interest books be made available in the reading room. *Scope Magazine* was used as a recreational material as well as for group instruction, and a variety of high-interest books were available for the use of the pupils to check out or to use when assignments were completed.

The bibliography contains a list of the materials and their publishers as shown in the weekly program in Figure 2. Provision was made in the weekly program to start all groups on the same materials each day. It was important for these pupils to feel that they were doing basic work along with the rest of the class. The *Help Yourself to Read, Write, and Spell* book contained work needed by all of the pupils. Group 3 usually needed additional help after directions had been given to the entire class. Directions for the work on any page of the various materials always included the working of several of the items with the entire group. The pupils were never assigned a page without being given this help.

After initial directions had been given, one of the three groups was called together for special help. For example, on Monday Group 1 began

Materials and publishers

Publisher	Material
Audio-Visual Research	Flash-Tachment
Barnell Loft, Ltd	Following Directions Locating the Answer Using the Context Working with Sounds

Bureau of Publications,
  Columbia University
	McCall-Crabbs Standard
	  Test Lessons in Reading

Educational Development Laboratories, Inc.	Controlled Reader and films Flash X Listen and Read
Garrard Press	Basic Sight Words
Ginn and Company	Help Yourself to Read, Write, and Spell
Harcourt, Brace, and World	New Worlds of Literature
D. C. Heath	Teen Age Tales
J. B. Lippincott	Reading for Meaning
Popular Library, Inc.	Limited Vocabulary Editions
Psychotechnics	Shadowscope Reading Pacer
Reader's Digest Services, Inc.	Reading Skill Builders
Scholastic Press	Scope Magazine
Science Research Associates, Inc.	Better Reading Book 1 Dimensions in Reading Junior Reading for Understanding
Webster Publishing Company	Conquests in Reading New Practice Readers Webster Word Sheels

work at the pacers while the other pupils were working on the basic assignment. When Group I pupils finished their work at the pacer, they returned to their desks to complete the assignment.

The second group worked with a student assistant, an upper-class volunteer working in the reading program instead of reporting to a study hall. She grouped them together and showed a controlled reader film. Group 3 got special help at a table with the teacher in order to finish the basic assignment and then reviewed the basic sight words using cards or the Flash X hand tachistoscope.

The rest of the week's program is outlined in Figure 2. A variety of materials and techniques was used to maintain the interest of the pupils. They were always broken into groups once the basic word had been accomplished so that instruction could best fit the needs of the pupils in each group.

The Reading I program is only as good as the teacher who is directing it. He must care for children and understand their problems. He must plan work at the level of each pupil so that progress can be made. As a result of having a good teacher who uses materials and techniques at the level of each pupil, many of these children, who had entered high school with poor reading skills, will be able to improve to the extent that they will complete high school. Jim, Edith, and Shirley may not all achieve this goal, but at least somebody cares enough to try to plan the best program possible.

Work with adolescents is difficult but rewarding. A poem by Richard Armour entitled *Time and Time Again* helps give us a perspective to this perplexing problem:

Adolescents, though kicking and screaming,
And often with ghastly results,
In time lose the battle, becoming
The thing they've most hated: adults.

Grouping for Remedial Reading on the Basis of Learner Needs

MIRIAM H. JELLINS
Atlanta University

CLASSROOM ORGANIZATION for purposes of instruction will be influenced somewhat by the general objectives and organization of the total reading program. These program organizational patterns modify, to a degree, the conditions and differences with which teachers must deal as intraclassroom organization is brought into focus. Further, the determinants of the nature and probable effectiveness of subgrouping plans are a combination of 1) factors which are inherent in specific instructional objectives of a given class or instructional unit and 2) those factors which derive from the specific reading and personal needs of the learner. In this discussion it may be a useful operation to consider how some of these factors in combination can contribute to the development of grouping strategies which could facilitate remedial reading instruction at the college level.

Providing for remedial and corrective instruction in reading on the college level has served as one of the primary reasons for establishing the college reading program. Poor performances on reading tests, low academic standings, difficulties in efficiently performing college reading tasks, and student attrition have served as justification for the reading improvement program for freshman students in many situations. Justification for continuation and expansion of college reading programs is founded in 1) concepts relating to the developmental nature of the reading process and 2) recognition that the college curriculum demands the efficient use of carefully selected clusters of reading skills.

It seems important to realize that correcting or remedying deficiencies in reading skills and abilities is a basic service of the college program. This service is provided for within the framework of various schemes of organization and at different stages in the classification and scheduling of students. Finally, provisions for more definitive differentiation of instruction are made within a smaller instructional unit or class.

Identification and classification

Grouping in smaller instructional units will depend upon the characteristics of students enrolled in or assigned to a particular unit. Enrollments or assignments are dependent upon institutional arrangements for the identification and subsequent classification of students. Three general conditions are typical. Condition one prevails where enrollment in a reading class occurs prior to any identification of level of reading proficiency. In situations where reading instruction is offered solely on a voluntary basis, through advisory and counseling procedures or through teacher referral, individuals may enroll in reading classes without direct prior knowledge on the instructor's part of competencies and deficiencies which exist in major reading skills. A student may enroll in any one of several sections, and the total enrollment of a given class may result in an extremely variable group of students insofar as the ranges of achievement levels and types of reading deficiencies are concerned. In this case, further classroom organization to provide for the differentiation of instruction would be imperative. Condition two is operative where there have been some evidences of reading deficiency as a result of screening measures. Assignments are made or voluntary enrollees are directed to sections in terms of a specific reading achievement level. Where students are directed to specific classes on the basis of their levels of performance in reading and/or the manifest nature of this reading problem, the resulting classes may not show as broad a range in achievement levels, but the variation in types of reading problems may be as great as in condition one. Condition three occurs more typically in clinical situations where a complete diagnosis

is made and assignment or recommendations are given on the basis of specific knowledge of reading strengths, weaknesses, and probable inhibiting factors. This condition is characterized by a situation wherein the student is assigned to particular instructional units after seeking help in reading following more intensive diagnostic procedures. Assignments may be to small groups or recommendations made for tutorial services.

Decisions made in regard to subgrouping in a class consisting of between ten and twenty students will have given consideration to equally as many sets of reading problems as revealed by individual reading profiles. Grouping does not eliminate the need for individualizing instruction; it is simply another stratagem which may serve the same purpose. There are likely to exist some common elements of possessed learnings as well as common deficiencies which may serve as bases for grouping and regrouping. Where classes have been established prior to the identification of reading needs, there may be more variation in levels of achievement than where the classes have been formed on the basis of results of survey and analytical reading measures. In effect, the least amount of subgrouping may be required where more characteristics of the reader have been considered in the initial identification of weaknesses prior to assignment of students to reading classes.

Categorizing needs for grouping among college students

Determining the types of subgroups to be formed within a class presupposes clearly defined program objectives as well as identifiable levels and variations of existing reading problems. Cues for grouping derive from program emphases, all of which may not be of a cognitive nature. There are important affective objectives which may influence the structuring of specific groups. More often the reading program seeks to effect positive changes in work-study skills, vocabulary development techniques, perceptual behaviors, and skills which promote accurate and rapid comprehension, selection, and synthesis of other skills appropriate for particular purposes. The reading program will further seek to effect positive changes in attitudes toward reading which are important as a major aspect of lifelong learning and enjoyment.

Although programs may be guided generally by similar lists of objectives, emphases upon certain aspects of development will vary from program to program. Subgroupings should reflect these variations in orientation. For example, there are programs which focus primarily upon the development of techniques in specific skill areas and offer intensive instruction in vocabulary development, rapid reading, and reading for various types of comprehension; or a multi-skills approach in which a unit of instruction is designed to foster each skill taught. In such an instance the student may be enrolled in either of the separate courses or in a multi-skills course where each skills unit must be completed according to prescription. In either case, the learner may engage in essentially the same activities although the pacing may vary from individual to individual.

A second kind of orientation is evidenced by the reading program which is structured around reading and study skills vital to achieving success in areas of content. Instructional units are then organized around skills-clusters thought to be valuable for purposeful reading in specific areas. Such an approach has been called a work-study approach (1).

Still another type of organization is the laboratory designed, more diagnostic approach. The procedures are clinically oriented and seek to focus instruction on the specific immediate reading needs of the learner after thorough and intensive diagnosis. An important variation of this more individualized approach is seen in the guidance-oriented program (2). In the diagnosis for this type of program, care is taken to ferret out what might be called inhibiting personality and emotional factors, in an effort to provide a learning climate through which the student can build positive attitudes toward reading and make favorable adjustments toward learning and success in the college community. Reading instruction within this program may be organized around interests or suspected reading needs as readily as around diagnosed reading deficiencies.

A particular college reading class, then, may be designed and described in terms of 1) the levels of achievement of students enrolled, 2) the types of reading and/or learning problems encountered among the enrollees, and 3) the scope of broader objectives which guide the total program. How do these factors combine to suggest possible subgroupings? It is conceivable that a broad range of instructional objectives would accommodate the formation of a larger number of subgroups for different instructional purposes. Such a possibility is quite important if adequate provision for learner needs is to be made in a more heterogeneous class. On the other hand, more restrictive objectives could accommodate only a limited number of groups with limited variation in purpose. Conceivably, these groups could offer possibilities for more intensive instruction and opportunities for substantial practice and stabilization of acquired skills. For more heterogeneous classes, these restrictions could be problematic in terms of provisions for differences in learner needs. For classes which have been formed with regard for particular learner deficiencies on the basis of a reading diagnosis, such restrictions may facilitate the attainment of instructional goals. It follows then, that some system must be devised for attending to the needs of remedial students when the class composition is highly heterogeneous and program objectives are restrictive in nature. Conversely, where program objectives are broad in scope and the units of instruction are of such design that each student must engage in brief, less intensive practice in many areas, a problem arises with relation to students whose needs have been identified and who would require intensive instruction and practice in a specific skills area.

Concepts of grouping

Some would contend that there should be as many subgroups within a classroom as there are individuals. Such a plan implies completely individualized instruction, which would be an ideal condition; however, there are values which may be credited to subgrouping. Among the more commonly recognized values are the following:

1. Efficiency. Students may exhibit common reading problems and evidence similar levels of competence. On certain occasions, where time and available space preclude individual instruction, intensive instruction may be given to subgroupings of students with common skills problems.
2. Student interaction. An actual need exists for subgrouping when interaction among students could enhance the development of certain vital interpretative, analytical, or evaluative skills.
3. Orientation and the development of desirable attitude patterns. At the beginning of a reading course it is perhaps essential that students become familiar with the reading process so they may recognize the kinds of problems likely to be encountered by their fellow students as well as themselves. This realization can serve to create an awareness of the universality of certain reading deficiencies, thereby setting conditions conducive to more positive attitudes toward reading improvement.

Grouping is justified only insofar as the grouping strategy will order conditions wherein the learner is directed toward the attainment of specific goals. The subgroup for instruction is more often a temporary, more restricted selection of students whose needs have constituted the primary data source for its formation. In addition to a recognition of common reading deficiencies, a full awareness of what the learner has already accomplished—his strengths—is vital to the successful

formation of an instructional group. Further, the effectiveness of a subgroup may well depend upon related factors such as 1) the amounts and kinds of tasks required of the student, 2) the kind and intensity of participation required of the student, and 3) the amount of teacher direction necessary for optimal productivity and progress of the group.

Grouping strategies

Means of implementing established program objectives, while considering learner needs, vary in terms of program orientation. Different approaches may be identified and possible types of groupings suggested on the basis of certain emphases of the program approach.

The skills centered approach

Throughout this kind of program, emphasis is upon the intensive study of specific sets of skills such as 1) vocabulary development, 2) basic comprehension, 3) interpretative, analytical, and evaluative techniques in comprehension, 4) selection and synthesis of appropriate reading skills for specific purposes, and 5) flexibility in the selection of rates of comprehension. Within this kind of program a variety of practice materials may be employed for intensive practice of skills related to the major area of emphasis. Instructional devices and programed materials are specifically selected to provide a variety of activities while focusing on one major problem area.

Since each major skills area is comprised of a cluster of subskills, the initial practice exercises for members of a class may be designed or selected to diagnose learner competence in each of the subareas. For example, component skills which promote vocabulary growth might be a) using a variety of clues to suggest special meanings of terms in a given context, and b) employing the technique of using structural elements of a word to aid in the determination of meaning and to be followed by the use of context and then dictionary verification of meaning. In many instances, subsets of skills can be arranged in such a sequence that the learner masters the least analytical skills first and then proceeds to the study of more complex operations. Utilizing the component skills of the problem area as the organizing elements for subgrouping facilitates the formation of short-term groups, where there is evidence of this need. This strategy for grouping is patterned after instructional procedures characteristic of individualized, clinical, diagnostic teaching.

Mechanically oriented programs.

There is evidence that mechanically oriented approaches make extensive use of visual and auditory instructional devices such as 1) rapid exposure devices for perceptual practice, 2) sequential visual presentations for purposes of establishing efficient eye-movement patterns, and 3) pacing devices for rate training in conjunction with specially selected exercises for practice under more natural reading conditions.

Using the same materials and instructional devices for all students with a common reading deficiency will not necessarily achieve desirable ends. Judicious and selective use of devices such as those described above might proceed on the basis of a) the students' need for external motivation, b) some knowledge of the learning style of the individual, c) comparability of the level of achievement and sophistication of the individuals considered for the group, and d) the probable functioning of each individual when working independently and under varying degrees of stress. Where such an approach is used, it is important to establish, at the outset, some awareness of the purposes for which the particular exercises are being undertaken and of their relationship to the total reading act.

Guidance oriented approaches

Objectives formulated for this approach appear to be more broadly conceived; that is, goals are not restricted to the attainment of a specific set of skills and techniques useful for efficient reading. The development of positive attitudes and behaviors with relationship to reading, personal adjustment to the demands of the college community, and competence in the performance of academic tasks are central foci in this more personality oriented approach. In effect, the development of reading skills appear to be consciously and deliberately related to, but subordinate to, the larger educational purpose. Spache maintains that the diagnosis for the guidance approach should attempt to determine whether reading problems are a reflection of other adjustment problems (2). It is determined whether the individual can learn to read better, whether it is advisable to initiate reading instruction, and whether reading instruction, if undertaken, will help with the individual's personal organization and college adjustment.

Where the total college reading program is directed by a guidance-centered approach, opportunities for subgrouping are numerous but the groups are not necessarily organized around major areas of reading skills. Rather, factors such as vocational or academic goals, interest, specific study habits, or complementary attitudes and skills may direct the formation of subgroups. Specific personal features are the basis for the organization of specific subgroups. For example, specific bases, which have been suggested in the literature, for grouping considerations in this kind of program show certain learning conditions which may be preferred or needed by different kinds of learners. Some individuals require directive textbook-oriented instruction while others may be more productive engaging in laboratory practice with a minimum of direction. Still another student may profit from "supportive machine training" as much as would some individuals who need closely supervised individual work (2).

The work-study approach

A work-study approach to reading improvement has been described by

Carter (1). This approach utilizes textbooks as the main materials and deals primarily in skills-clusters useful for proficient reading in specific subject areas. Carter identifies instructional emphases which reflect increasing levels of complexity: 1) identifying ideas, 2) interpreting ideas, and 3) evaluating ideas. Competencies in performing these tasks within each subject area become learning objectives for the student. The subject areas selected are dependent upon courses in which the student is enrolled so that he may apply learned techniques in the daily preparation of course assignments.

Through carefully designed diagnostic exercises based on selections from a variety of subject matter areas, estimates can be made relative to the extent to which a learner evidences proficiency at each of the levels identified above. Student profiles then become the data source upon which sub-groups will be formed. Variables influencing grouping decisions might be a) subject areas in which the student is enrolled, b) subject areas in which the lowest levels of proficiency are evidenced, c) learner's preference as to the subject area in which he feels most limited, d) common levels of achievement, and e) similar skills deficiencies in a particular subject area. Within this framework, grouping should provide conditions which are quite favorable for maximal learning.

Summary

Definitive grouping schemes for remedial instruction should be structured with respect for differences in 1) policies governing the selection and classification of enrollees for the college reading program, 2) the nature of instructional units or classes within the total program, 3) objectives guiding the selection of activities and materials for the program, and 4) the organizational elements of the program. Primary determinants of appropriate sub-groups for remedial instruction are 1) the specific personal and reading deficiencies of the learner and 2) the orientation and emphases within a particular college program. The formation of groups within the class must be directed toward specific purposes, the groups themselves being flexible and of a temporary nature. Probably no one grouping pattern will fit more than one particular set of circumstances; therefore, the reading teacher's strategy for making decisions relative to grouping must become an integral part of ongoing instructional procedures.

REFERENCES

1. Carter, Homer L. J. "Effective Use of Textbooks in the Reading Program," *Starting and Improving College Reading Programs,* The Eighth Yearbook of The National Reading Conference. Fort Worth, Texas: Texas Christian University Press, 1959, 155-163.
2. Spache, George D. "Reading Improvement as a Counseling Procedure," *Starting and Improving College Reading Programs.* The Eighth Yearbook of the National Reading Conference. Fort Worth, Texas: Texas Christian University Press, 1959, 125-130.

Capitalizing on Multi-Level Materials in Grouping for Instruction

EDWARD G. SUMMERS
Indiana University

THE TITLE of this presentation refers to two very important issues in developing and improving reading instruction at the secondary level. The first issue is the matter of effectively organizing reading instruction and the second is the issue of selection of adequate materials to meet the reading needs of students at this level. Both issues stem from the simple fact that students differ in their abilities to learn and profit from instruction and these differences increase even more markedly as students approach the junior and senior high school levels. The two issues have been attacked before in the literature on secondary reading and repeatedly in IRA conventions in recent years.[1] In the last seven

[1] Summers, Edward G. "International Reading Association Conference Proceedings Reports on Secondary Reading," *ERIC/CRIER Reading Review Series,* September 1967, Bloomington, Indiana. 28 pp.

years, beginning with the 1960 New Frontiers in Reading Conference, the IRA conventions have included more than 175 papers on reading at the secondary level. Since the Philadelphia convention in 1964 there has been a virtual explosion in papers dealing with secondary reading. One might attribute this to the fact that conventions are getting bigger and bigger. However, there is more to it than that. The actual percentage of papers on secondary reading in proportion to the number on other topics took a big leap at the Philadelphia convention and has been steadily rising since. Previous papers have dealt with topics such as: organizing reading programs, providing needed personnel in reading, methods and grouping for instruction, developing various skills in reading, materials for reading instruction, reading development in content areas, developing interests and tastes in reading, the library and reading program, diagnosis and treatment of reading problems, linguistics and reading, reading and the bilingual student, and reading and the disadvantaged. A glance through the Seattle program indicates that the interest generated in secondary reading continues. A look at the papers presented in the two areas of methods and grouping and materials substantiates the interest in these two topics.

The two issues of methods of grouping and materials stem from the recognition that individual differences exist in secondary school populations. One thing is certain—wherever in the secondary school we wish to look for individual differences we most certainly will find them. This is particularly true of differences in reading ability and achievement. The teacher might be facing students with a range in reading ability of from 3 to 8 years. What we do about the differences we find depends on several factors. One of the most crucial factors is the ability of the secondary teacher to recognize the importance of the reading differences and their effect on overall student achievement. The amount of

previous training in meeting individual differences, either during the undergraduate or graduate years or through in-service work, is another important factor. There are encouraging signs that increased training through all avenues is being more widely provided.

At the secondary level we do not find one group of adolescents but many different groups and subgroups. These vary within a school and between schools in different parts of a city and schools in different cities. The variability is particularly evident in the tool skill of reading. There is wide variation in the ability of students to utilize reading effectively in coping with the study materials of content areas. There is wide variation in the ability of some students to apply basic reading skills involved in even recognizing and working with common words found in printed materials. Some students with reading skills which may not be developed beyond the fifth grade level have to attempt to cope with tenth, eleventh, and twelfth grade textbooks—if they have not yet dropped out from the sheer frustration, anxiety, and boredom of making the effort of coping with an impossible task without the necessary tools. Although we have made remarkable strides since the early nineteen hundreds the fact remains that our holding power in the secondary schools is still not astounding beyond the age of sixteen. I'm not maintaining that if you have a dropout you automatically also have a reading problem. However, investigations have revealed in numerous instances that reading ability, or lack of it, is an important variable related to the constellation of factors involved in school leaving.

There is also wide variability in the ability of students to apply the reading skills needed in developing readiness for college. The next step in the academic ladder for better than fifty percent of our secondary students is the start of a four year college program. I believe we are gradually beginning to adopt the point of view that the secondary school has some responsibility in supplying instruction which will enable students to cope with the reading demands of college level learning. Although numerous problems still exist in developing effective programs of instruction.

The point I am stressing is that we do not have a single, large, rather generalized group of adolescents in secondary schools in terms of reading ability and needs but several groups and subgroups within groups. In looking at programs which are developing at the secondary level we see an increasing number of schools developing innovative, differentiated programs for subgroups of adolescents with different needs in reading. Two major adjustments are possible on the part of the teacher: 1) an attempt can be made to match the *instructional method* to individual differences; 2) an attempt can be made to match the *instructional material* to individual differences. The suggestion of this paper is that there is a logical interaction between the two and that we match both instructional materials and instructional methods to cope with individual differences.

In matching instructional method to needs and differences we attempt to group in some way for instruction. In essence, we are recognizing the existence of subgroups within the larger group of adolescents and attempting to at least individualize instruction as much as we are realistically able to. The ideal way to meet such differences is to provide instruction on a completely one-to-one Socratic basis. However, this is seldom possible economically in our educational system so we at least try to work with some gross grouping related to common needs.

Programs can be built around three familiar patterns: developmental, remedial, or corrective reading instruction. The patterns which have evolved in secondary schools to provide reading instruction are extremely varied.[2]

[2] Green, Ronald. "Reading Programs in Secondary Schools," *Occasional Papers in Reading*, Indiana University School of Education, July 1967. 25 pp.

We are all familiar with the reading laboratory pattern type of limited instruction where students are brought in for instruction either as a supplement to regular classes or in conjunction with instruction in a content area—usually English. In some schools reading instruction is offered as part of instruction in the regular English class using special materials with either an itinerant reading instructor or English teacher.

Reading instruction can be found at varying points throughout the secondary program. In some schools classes are offered at the transitional points in the curriculum—reading for seventh graders or reading for tenth graders. Classes are often found for college bound students at the upper secondary level.

You do not have to work in the area of secondary reading very long before you realize the "stop gap" or compromise nature of most of the programs offered and the need for better organization of instruction and adequately trained teachers. We are some way off from the ideal goal of providing reading instruction at the secondary level in the right amounts, at the right time for all students.

We need to better identify and at an earlier stage, those students in need of developmental, corrective, remedial, and even clinical instruction in reading. The real challenge is in developing adequate resources to attack the problem of needed reading skills at the base of the problem—in the content fields. We need more and better programs to prepare prospective teachers and to provide needed upgrading for teachers already teaching.

In addition to using grouping to develop manageable instructional units we can capitalize on multi-level materials to aid in adjusting to individual differences. I am not going to quote lists of materials that are available for use in working with different groups of students. Such lists are readily available in other sources. However, I would like to stress the use of multi-level materials that provide pretesting and random entry for students at varying ability levels. Once adequate instructional objectives are established, and needed reading skills identified, any number of multi-level materials can be constructive for use. Some good commercial kits are available but the teacher needs to be able to develop his own sets of material to use with differently diagnosed patterns of need. The reading teacher—and more increasingly in recent years, the content teacher at the secondary level—has the wherewithal to develop packages of varied materials broad skill areas to use in meeting the needs of secondary students *if* he has the training to assess reading needs of students, *recognizes* the importance of reading as a tool in subject achievement and personal growth and development, and if he is *concerned* about aiding students to solve their problems and improve reading ability. We do need to develop better sources of information on materials that are available and also develop better criteria in judging materials appropriate for use in reading programs.

The two topics, organizing reading instruction and selection of adequate instructional materials, have been and will continue to be important points for discussion and debate in implementing secondary reading programs.

A Grouping Plan Capitalizing on the Individualized Reading Approach

Lyman C. Hunt, Jr.
University of Vermont

THE FOLLOWING STATEMENT by one seventh grade teacher on the issue of grouping in the classroom is remarkably insightful:

I, personally, like an individual group, and whole-class organization depending on the learning situation. Time is precious—never more so than those fleeting minutes allotted to each class. The important thing is to have something "happen." It is dangerous to set patterns for an approach to teaching. Whereas the youngster feels security in an established schedule, the greatest danger is a development of detached boredom. The "best way" is the way that leads to an individual involvement (1).

Truly, little more needs to be said. However, an effort will be made to show specifically how the ideas so succinctly expressed relate to the individualized reading program.

In the individualized reading program, a variety of arrangements and organizations are used within the classroom. The watchword is flexibility. Grouping patterns must not become rigid. There are several important interactions between teacher and pupil or pupils. Other secondary interactions occur between and among pupils themselves when they work as partners or in friendship groups. In individualized reading, as the name implies, the primary interaction is a one-to-one relationship between teacher and pupil. Typically this relationship occurs during the individual conference and is the heart of the program but certainly does not preclude other arrangements.

The misconception persists that the teacher-pupil conference is the only kind of interaction between teacher and pupils in individualized reading. To the contrary, frequently the teacher will work with class subgroups. In addition, there are numerous occasions during the individualized reading program when the teacher works with the whole class. Our intent is to examine arrangements in some detail. But first something must be said about the importance of independence and self-reliance as displayed by pupils.

The importance of independence

The success of any reading program and the type of classroom organization which underlies it are a function of the degree of independence exhibited by the children. Certainly self-direction is particularly important to individualized reading. To succeed with individualized reading the teachers must help each child attain the highest degree of self-reliance possible. The goal must be for each child to work quietly, carefully, conscientiously, and consistently, with a sense of his own purpose and direction. Upon completing one task he must know how to move on to the next. He must learn to choose wisely from among several alternate tasks.

The following chart exemplifies activities suitable for quiet work time in the first grade.

QUIET WORK TIME
Use a soft voice.
Do your work without disturbing others.
Finish one job and go on to another job.
You can
   do a number paper
   draw a picture
   write a story
   paint at the easel
   look at a book
   read a book
   play with blocks
   work a puzzle (game)
   play a story
   play in the playhouse

The teacher soon realizes that she must take as much time at the beginning of the school year to teach independence and self-reliance as she does to teaching reading or arithmetic or anything else. By so doing she will have taken a long step forward toward guaranteeing positive results in the days ahead. Taking the extra few minutes to teach quiet independent work habits is crucial. The individualized reading program cannot be truly successful without this ingredient. Many teachers fail on this factor.

Classroom organization: teacher to total class

During the individualized reading program the teacher works with the total class as a unit on numerous occasions and for a variety of reasons. The opening moments of the quiet or silent reading time are most important. Here atmosphere is established; settling down is accomplished; directions are given. Each reader is reminded of the tasks he must accomplish.

A chart may be used for this purpose:

QUIET READING TIME
Have Conference
Read Silently
Select Book(s)
   Write Summary
Study Vocabulary
   Read to Partner

All must understand that these are the legitimate activities one engages in during the quiet reading time. Some will need a good deal more "instructional guidance" than will others prior to fitting neatly into this pattern. The gossips, wanderers, and time wasters will have to learn that there are better uses for their time. Daily reminders are necessary for a while.

This way of working is markedly different in structure; consequently, many pupils are unaccustomed to it. Much more self-direction and self-motivation are needed here than in the more typical three-group patterns.

There are always a few who will need frequent direction prior to learning these new patterns of behavior in reading time. Those lacking self-direction and independence will need more "instructional guidance," more firm direction. The teacher needs patience and persistence. It is a wise move for the teacher to spend a few moments with the class as a whole prior to becoming involved with individual or small group instruction. The dividends are worth it.

The total class conference following silent reading time

Through the personal conference the teacher really learns about the children as readers and about the books they choose to read. The richness of the personal contact makes the conference uniquely vital. There is so much to talk about and so many books to discuss that there is always the desire to prolong the conference. But always there are so many children that there is never enough time to talk sufficiently with each child. Many truly interesting conferences have to be cut short.

To augment suggestions given to individual children during individual conferences, a brief evaluation period can be held with the total class at the conclusion of the daily silent reading time. Here, as with the individual conference, the artistry of teaching is exhibited through the questions asked. Several suggested questions are listed which can be used effectively to prime the discussion. The teacher must realize that on any given day a different particular combination of questions could be used:

1. Did you have a good reading period today? Did you read well? Did you get a lot done?
2. Did you read better today than yesterday?
3. Were you able to concentrate today on your silent reading?
4. Did the ideas in the book hold your attention? Did you have the feeling of moving right along with them?
5. Did you have the feeling of wanting to go ahead faster to find out what happened? Were you constantly moving ahead to get to the next good part?
6. Was it hard for you to keep your mind on what you were reading today?
7. Were you bothered by others or by outside noises?
8. Could you keep the ideas in your book straight in your mind?
9. Did you get mixed up in any place? Did you have to go back and straighten yourself out?
10. Were there words you did not know? How did you figure them out?
11. What did you do when you got to the good parts? Did you read faster or slower?
12. Were you always counting to see how many pages you had to go? Were you wondering how long it would take you to finish?
13. Were you kind of hoping that the book would go on and on—that it would not really end?

By generating a discussion about the nature, quality, and quantity of reading accomplished by the class during silent reading time, the teacher helps to build a concept within each child about the kind of reader he is becoming and of what he needs to do to improve his own reading. Thus the development of the self-image, the concept of what the good reader does, emerges. This concept of the good reader, along with knowing what one must do to become one, is the foundation of improved reading performance by each child. Consequently, this evaluation session, while brief, can be invaluable. It should occur almost daily.

Book sharing by one pupil with total class

Book sharing time is second in importance only to quiet reading time. What are often rather routine and desultory descriptions by children of books read can eventually produce some near riots by several eager readers who want to be next in line to get their hands on a particularly popular book. True, some children never learn how to sell a book or make it seem exciting. But many do. Sharing a good book can be their big moment, and many children will be quite impatient while awaiting their turns to tell about an unusually good book.

Using a printed guide sheet can make the book-sharing period much more vital and dynamic. It may be posted on the chalk board or on a bulletin board. One teacher's chart reads as follows:

Hi! I'm Mr. Book. To share me, tell:
1. My name.
2. Who wrote me.
3. If I'm a good book.
4. About a very good part.
5. About a very good picture.
6. Then read a little bit so people can hear some of me.

It may take some persistent effort on the part of some children to learn to follow this form and yet make their books sound exciting to others. But it can be done. Emphasis is placed on practicing a part which, when read aloud to the group, stimulates others to read the book. Frequently during the individual conference the discussion centers on book sharing. The steps are reviewed with the child. Some have to be reminded to practice the part which will be read orally to the group. Some have to be urged to practice, and for a few practice is required. But stress is placed on the value of fluent oral reading of the part of a book to be shared with the whole class. The pupils must be keenly aware that the quality of oral reading may determine how well they sell their books to other readers.

Subgrouping within total class situations

The notion continues that class subgroups are not permissible within IRP structure nor that it is customary for the teacher to work with subgroups. The fact that stable, permanent ability groups are not used may be the source of confusion. There are, however, a variety of other class subgroupings which are frequently employed by teachers who use IRP.

Class subgroups can be organized along many different dimensions other than reading levels. Teachers may call groups together according to the particular reading skills or activities to be taught. At other times discussion groups may be formed according to types or classifications of books read. Such discussions can be based on large general classifications or can be more specific in nature. For example, one time discussion can center on factual or informational books and on fanciful stories the next day. Specifically, invitations can be issued to all children with animal, people (biography), funny (humor), adventure, mystery, family situation, science, or whatever type of book the teacher designates. Once again the reading circle is formed. But in this instance each child has a different book—a book he has chosen to read. The common element is the type of book being read and not the relative performance level of the reader.

The pattern of questioning is not highly structured but emanates from the kind of material being read and from the interest of the children in their books. The following imaginary discussion is based on a small group discussion where each child has read a fanciful or imaginary book.

Teacher: Each of you has a book which is imaginative, don't you? Some of the books are really fantastic, like Jean's Dr. Seuss book.

David, is your book more like reporting—telling what happened and how it happened—or is it quite imaginative? David: Boy, it's way out!

(Several other children are queried along the dimension of relatively factual to highly imaginative. The books vary with regard to this quality; the teacher emphasizes the reality-fantasy continuum.)

Teacher: How do we get books which are fanciful? Where do these ideas come from?

Debbie: From the author.

Teacher: Yes, but where does the writer get these ideas?

Ken: In his head.

Teacher: Yes, in his mind; he makes them up. Can we say that these books are really true; do the things in them really take place?

Children: No!

Ann: Most of the things in my book couldn't happen.

Teacher: Can we say these ideas are real ideas?

Albert: Ya! Some guy thought 'em up. He had 'em in his head. He got them from somewhere.

Teacher: But there is a difference between telling what actually happened and telling about something we just imagine happens.

Children in chorus: Yes.

Robin: But they sure make some wonderful reading.

Teacher: Now I want each of you to find in his book one or two places where the ideas are most fantastic or where the writer has told something that just couldn't happen. We'll see who has a part in his book with the most imagination.

(Children search for places in their books exemplifying the greatest degrees of fantasy. Turns are given to various children to read the fanciful parts; following several renditions according to limits of time, a decision is made regarding the greatest display of imaginative power by the various authors. Two or three children hold out for their particular book being most fanciful.)

This abbreviated, and to some extent simulated, discussion is intended to show how fundamental qualities basic to reading comprehension can be developed through group discussion.

The teacher, by observing reactions of various children, can add to her catalog of items about each child's reading. Does the child respond to the finer discriminations within the dimension of reality—fantasy? A teacher must observe these responses to know the child truly as a reader. All the cherished values of group interaction can be realized within this situation.

Similar dialog could have been presented for a variety of qualities found between the covers but below the surface print of hundreds of children's books. Several more important qualities are 1) Humor—extend understanding of what constitutes funniness and humor; 2) Biography—fidelity with which the qualities and characteristics of central person are developed. Is there an honest portrayal of positive and negative elements? 3) Mystery—manner by which the writer developed the aura of mystery and extent to which situations are contrived or natural, and 4) Family Situation—exploration of validity by the author in recording behavior and reactions of persons within the story to critical points. (How would the children who are reading react in similar conflicting situations?)

It is vital that teachers develop a facility for asking questions and generating discussion. The trick is to use questions which orient the reader to the nature and type of literature—i.e., what makes it funny or what makes it mysterious, or so on. The climax is to lead the discussion to a comparison of the extent or degree to which the underlying quality is present. By having each child find the most imaginative part in his book, comparisons can be made. After several children have shared their own fanciful parts, a decision can be made regarding whose is least realistic. Insight is gained relative to types and degrees of imagination. Such insights are basic to improved reading performance.

The summation of responses given by children over a series of group conferences becomes highly revealing. The generalized impressions the teacher gains about a particular child can be refined and verified within the scope of the individual teacher-pupil conference. Thus the group conference is a valuable part of the total classroom arrangement.

Skills Subgroups

Instructional groups are frequently formed to meet the particular needs of particular pupils. Teachers notice, as a result of accumulated observation and records, that some children need additional help with one or more particular word or contextual skill. To give them this particular instruction a temporary subgroup will be formed.

Skill groups may be formed when two or more children in a classroom need the same kind of extra assistance in order to progress in reading with greater ease and fewer tensions. To organize skills groups of this sort, the teacher must be alert to each child's responses and reactions in the various other reading situations. She must constantly be on the alert for barriers which prevent the child from reading fluently and efficiently.

Once grouped for instruction on a particular skill, the teacher continues with the group until the particular instructional goals have been accomplished. Then it is dismissed, restructured, or reorganized with another set of children and a new teaching objective.

Teachers frequently refer to this classroom arrangement as subgrouping by invitation. Once the lesson has been announced, all those who feel so inclined join the instructional setting. The teacher, of course, offers a special invitation to a selected few. And she makes sure that they accept. But others are welcome. By careful and constant referral to her checklist of skills, the teacher can visualize rather readily which basic reading skills she needs to teach and which children to invite.

Classroom arrangement:
the individual conference

The teacher-pupil conference is a highly personal matter; it is an expression of the two persons involved—the teacher and the pupil. The personality of each colors the situation and in essence determines the nature of each conference. No one can prescribe exactly what the teacher should say or do. No one should try. The teacher's personality must, of course, dominate and determine the pattern and tone for every conference. She is the constant factor: she is always there. On the other hand, the child's personality is the independent variable—the unpredictable ingredient which makes each conference a unique and highly individual teaching-learning experience. The child's reactions and responses to the books and materials being read become the focal point of the teacher-pupil conference—the object of the teacher's observations.

The intent here, then, is to present generalized patterns which typically occur during conference time. Hopefully, models or types can be established to aid teachers in developing skill and deftness in handling the conference situations, while at the same time cautioning each teacher once more that she must be the prime mover of the conference. She must be instrumental in developing it into a successful activity. Her art and power of asking questions and responding instantly and intelligently to the child's reactions with more questions are the key to success. It is her responsibility to initiate the action; most children will take off from the stimulus which she provides.

The conference time should not be a time for merely assuring oneself that the child has read and remembered every part of every page of his book. Undoubtedly the worst command that a teacher can give in conference time is "Tell me about your book," or phrased differently, "Tell me everything you can remember about your book." Nor is the conference the time to elicit answers to a long list of factual questions about every part of each book. The conference time is not the place where the teacher needs to sit with an individual child and listen to him read long passages orally or to record the

many mistakes he makes he seeing how many words he does not know. By contrast, the conference time must give the child an opportunity to reveal his strength as a reader through his personal responses to the book which he, himself, has chosen to read. The teacher's task is to assess the reader rather than the content of the book which has been read.

Much has been reported in the literature on the individual conference. For additional specific helps the reader is referred to material wherein the art of skillfull questioning has been described (2, 3, 4, 5).

Summary

The point, too frequently forgotten, to be remembered pertains to instructional procedures on the one hand and classroom organization on the other. First of all, the teacher teaches: she arranges the classroom to facilitate the teaching. To do otherwise is to reverse the order. Class organization is a consequence of instructional patterns. The rigid arrangement so frequently associated with the three-ability group arrangement must be avoided.

Successful teaching means fitting the classroom organization to instructional goals. Flexibility shown through utilizing many different organizational arrangements is the answer.

REFERENCES

1. Dutton, Merle (seventh grade teacher, Hunt Junior High, Burlington, Vermont). Unpublished paper.
2. Hunt, Lyman C., Jr. "The Key to the Conference Lies in the Questioning," *Educational Comment on Individual Reading—1966,* Herbert Sandberg (Ed.D.), University of Toledo.
3. Lazar, M., M. Draper, and L. Schwietert. *A Practical Guide to Individualized Reading.* New York: New York Board of Education, Bureau of Educational Research.
4. Veatch, Jeannette. "The Conference in IRP: The Teacher-Pupil Dialogue," *The Individualized Reading Program: A Guide For Classroom Teaching,* Lyman C. Hunt (Ed.), Newark, Delaware: International Reading Association Conference Proceedings, 11, Part 3, 1966.
5. Veatch, Jeannette. *Reading in the Elementary School.* New York: Ronald Press, 1966.

Reducing the Phoniness in Teacher Education

ALLAN MUSKOPF
Wisconsin State University

ONE OF THE MAIN PROBLEMS any teacher faces is how to make school, which by its very nature is *phony*, into something that is *real*. Gathering students together in a classroom to consider preselected content has all the inherent qualities of a phony situation.

In working with undergraduates in a teacher-education program, I have found this problem of phoniness to be greater than at any other level of teaching. Developing a course that has personal meaning for undergraduates is tremendously challenging and often frustrating.

Ironically, both professors and students are painfully aware of the phoniness of what they are involved in. Are we not aware that students still label their education courses "Mickey Mouse," or that they still complain, and rightfully so, that their professors in methods courses expound on the importance of motivation and individual differences, etc., and then proceed to ignore these factors in their own teaching?

The major roadblock in improving teacher education programs is the continued focus on *content* rather than on the *teacher* as the effective instrument in learning. Undergraduates find very little personal meaning in most of their professional education courses. Students in reading methods courses typically are confronted with such meaningless learnings as "The subskills of comprehension include. . ." or "The steps in teaching a phonic element are. . ." How can we expect them to become involved in such content?

There are several reasons for this continued focus on content. Probably, the major reason is the three-credit course structure in which we continue to operate. Student teachers tend to "turn on" reading for fifty minutes and then "turn it off" at the end of the hour; they seldom become immersed totally in the task of becoming an effective teacher. As Combs has pointed out, "Professional education is seriously hampered by the necessity of pouring it into the rigid forms of the traditional liberal arts organization, which does not fit the peculiar needs of a professional program. A program for the preparation of teachers must be much more dynamically oriented around the *person* of the student. It is time we recognized this need and found the courage to break with tradition sufficiently to put the principle into effect" (*1*).

Several attempts have been made recently to break through the discrete course structure and provide instead an integrated program (*3, 5, 6*). At the University of Rochester, for example, the program allows a group of seniors to work together for the entire year under a *team* of teacher-education professors. An attempt is made to combine the theoretical consideration of teaching with the real world of the classroom. This integrated structure allows a maximum of flexibility and individualization in the program.

The move away from the discrete course structure, however, requires a major renovation on the part of schools of education. There is little indication this will occur in the near future. In the meantime, what can the individual professor, working within the discrete course structure, do to reduce the inherent phoniness of undergraduate teacher education? I would like to describe some attempts I have made in that direction in my undergraduate course, "Teaching Reading in the Elementary School," at Wisconsin State University at Eau Claire.

1. Student teachers are involved in tutoring one student two afternoons a week. This tutoring experience is necessary in a preservice course for many reasons. Tutoring provides

reality. Students and professors no longer have to talk in a vacuum. "Word attack" takes on personal meaning for the student who must teach it that afternoon. Without the tutoring experience, undergraduate juniors and seniors can see no personal meaning in a discussion of phonics, diagnosing, etc.

Another reason for the tutoring experience stems from my concern to develop "teachers" rather than reading teachers *per se*. Students are confronted with the whole gamut of teaching-learning problems in the tutoring situation—motivation, materials, discipline, problems with parents, etc. This scope enables them to get a feel of what it's like to be a teacher. I am thoroughly convinced that teaching *one child* is the best way to learn how a child learns to read and to realize the frustrations he faces. The tutoring experience presents student teachers with real problems that force them into meaningful questioning and reading. For example, my students recently asked me to present a lecture on the teaching of phonics. As a result it was much more meaningful than it would have been if presented at a time when the students could see no real need for it.

I have found by trial and error that the earlier in a semester that I involve students in a tutoring situation, the better. My first anxious reaction was, "I have to get them ready. I have to tell them everything I know." I once took half a semester to get them ready for this experience and found it necessary to reteach most of what I had already presented as soon as they got involved with a real child.

2. Students must be provided with a climate of security. I think that the primary aim of teacher education should be to develop a secure sense of self in student teachers. Typically, undergraduates have very little confidence in their ability as a teacher, and they tend to discredit the value of the experience they have gained from almost twenty years of living. To a great extent, this climate of security is dependent on the instructor. Students will not feel secure if they know they are being evaluated at each step along the way. Therefore, I find that I must de-emphasize grades and tests and discontinue looking over the shoulder of a student when she is tutoring. Change of behavior is my goal rather than retention of information. If tests interfere with this change of behavior, then they must go.

3. One of the most important elements in my program is a makeshift student lounge equipped with a thirty-cup coffee pot and comfortable chairs. This lounge provides the milieu for informal, spontaneous discussion. I am convinced this informal discussion is more important than anything that goes on in the formal classroom. This lounge is available any time during the day when students are free.

4. I find that I have to be available many hours during the day when students drop in with problems concerning their tutoring, etc. This time factor is the main drawback of this type of program. Teaching this course requires many more hours than a typical lecture-type course. Some day, perhaps, administrators will recognize that a laboratory experience course is not equivalent to a three-credit lecture course and take this into consideration in determining course load.

5. Rather than have student teachers make out lesson plans (which they strongly rebel against and which I am convinced do a great deal to stifle spontaneous teaching), I have them "introspect" in writing following each tutoring session. This is the best method I have discovered to force students to analyze what they are doing and probe for answers. After some early criticism of their attempts at introspection, which in the beginning are usually no more than a description of what happened, and after providing them with models of good introspection, they opened up and really began exposing. This format has been so successful that I would like to share it with anyone who cares to write me.

6. I try to make sources of information readily available and then place the responsibility on the students to utilize these sources. Students must be trusted. Rather than put books on reserve in the library, I find it much better to cart them to the reading center and provide a small library in the center itself. I make wide use of handouts of excerpts, vital articles, etc. and also utilize tapes as another source of information.

7. I find that I resort to lectures less and less in my program. It seems that lectures impede student involvement.

8. I hesitate to mention the next experience because it is so new and radical. But it excites me. A few weeks ago a small group of students from this course approached me and said they wanted to get a group therapy session started. Since I had no experience as a leader of group therapy, I asked one of my friends in educational psychology to act as the group leader. For the past four weeks we have been meeting twice a week, and I am convinced that this experience provides an excellent means for understanding human behavior—both in others and in one's self. Perhaps those concerned with teacher education should explore the possibilities group therapy offers for changing behavior.

The program is far from perfect, but it is getting results. Students do get involved. They read, ask questions, worry about their student's progress, discuss teaching among themselves, and change—some of them quite dramatically.

Probably the best advice I can give anyone who plans to venture into this type of student-centered course in the teaching of reading is to read the books and articles listed in my bibliography. Of special importance are two books: *The Professional Education of Teachers* by Arthur Combs and the ASCT Yearbook, *Perceiving, Behaving, and Becoming.*

REFERENCES

1. Combs, Arthur. *The Professional Education of Teachers.* Boston: Allyn and Bacon, 1965.

2. Combs, Arthur (Ed.). *Perceiving, Behaving, Becoming.* Washington, D. C.: Association for Supervision and Curriculum Development, 1962.

3. Howard E. "To Feel Like a Teacher," *Journal of Teacher Education* (December 1965), 453-455.

4. Kelley, Earl. *Education for What is Real.* New York: Harper, 1947.

5. Lindsey, Margaret. *New Horizons For the Teaching Profession.* Washington, D. C.: National Commission on Teacher Education and Professional Standards, NEA, 1961.

6. National Commission on Teacher Education and Professional Standards. *Changes in Teacher Education.* Washington, D. C.: NEA, 1963.

7. Rogers, Carl. *On Becoming A Person.* Boston: Houghton-Mifflin, 1961.

8. Sarason, S. B., K. Davidson, and B. Blott. *The Preparation of Teachers.* New York: Wiley, 1962.

Preservice Instruction in Reading

M. JERRY WEISS
Jersey City State College

TEACHERS IN TRAINING let it be known quite clearly that they want a realistic presentation of situations and problems which will confront them and practical suggestions for coping with such matters.

Teachers in the field often let it be known that they feel things could be going better. They respond most enthusiastically to dynamic speakers who offer inspiring "how-to" suggestions.

We teachers are conditioned, so it seems, to view reading through an avalanche of maybe magical methods and materials, featuring potent packages and programed goodies, tons of tapes and tests, rarified research reports, sound structured stringent systems, guides to greater grouping, and wonderful workbooks. We have often shown students the twelve, or more or less, steps to would-be success as the text authorities and manuals tell us. And this is all we can do?

We have spent millions of dollars in research to prove what? And to whom? It should be apparent now to all that there is no one way to teach reading. We need to have creative, imaginative, flexible teachers who can think on their feet and try a variety of approaches to reach children and to develop lifetime readers.

To do this our own students need to experience teachers who are dynamic, creative, flexible, and imaginative and who can provide for individual differences. If we are speaking of philosophies, students want to see philosophies in action. They want to see ideas tested—live, not just in a series of pages in a text or through a lecture.

I believe it is important to be realistic and practical, and I believe students have to dig out a few answers to their own problems. They have to have the opportunity and the freedom to try their own approaches. If something doesn't work, they need to have time to analyze the situations and to draw certain conclusions for themselves.

Preservice instruction in reading requires a laboratory-like situation where 1) ideas and issues, philosophies, and problems are presented and 2) students pursue approaches to these problems and attempt to design meaningful programs which they hope to develop.

Programs are built upon sound objectives which fit particular situations, students, or community settings. The more that is known about students, their abilities, their interests, their attitudes, their experiences, and their needs, the more practical are the assignments. We do not merely discuss what one needs to know about one's students, but we also stress how to obtain such information and how to use such information in planning a total school curriculum. (Several of us at Jersey City State College do not believe that reading is a separate subject but that it is the entire curriculum. We realize that we use printed materials in all content areas and that experience charts reflect a variety of curriculum areas.) As a result, not only do all elementary teachers-to-be take a course in reading but also all secondary majors. Tremendous stress is placed on helping secondary teachers see the role of reading within their respective fields and as a total part of the entire school curriculum.

Diagnosis is important, but diagnosis is more than test scores. We are concerned with developing skills, but teachers need to know when best to teach which skills to which students. Skills need to be applied. When? Where? When do we best use drill material? How about games?

We are interested in developing critical readers. I believe our college students need to find the pleasures of reading and thinking for themselves. They need to have time to discuss their ideas and to examine a variety of sources of information. They need time to analyze, time to organize, time to synthesize. We do not merely talk about these activities; we let our students go through these processes. Then we discuss ways of applying these principles and activities to different situations.

For example, if we are going to talk about unit work, we need to let college students execute a unit for themselves to see what is involved. Many can make excellent outlines; few know what to expect when a unit is actually in operation.

Our reading center has many paperbacks. Students are free to read, to examine, to discuss, to challenge, and to become actively involved. When they see that there are many sources of materials and they handle a variety of books, unit teaching is possible.

Our reading center has many skill-building materials. Our college students work with many materials in live-tutoring situations. They see that some things work with certain children; others fail. They are taught not to discard any approach forever. In one situation there may be certain factors which cause failure; in another, that same approach may be most successful.

Students become familiar with teacher-made materials as well as commercially prepared materials. They learn to evaluate such materials in conjunction with their specific purposes and student needs. But it is interesting to note that our students view reading in terms of children's behavior—and they are concerned with skill development in conjunction with sound purposes and assignments based on meaningful diagnosis.

Books and the mass media are a part of the modern communications world. We talk of maturation that lasts. We talk of values, attitudes, and issues confronting modern man, not Dick and Jane. We look for a variety of resources—printed and otherwise—to help us to help each child to develop to his maximum potential. All language arts are related. Man reading is man thinking. It is important for us to understand why man thinks the way he does and what influences such thought. To understand, we must begin to measure the impact of learning (reading) upon the learner (reader). This approach leads to a study of evaluation.

Consider the following:

1. Preservice instruction should be realistic and practical.

2. Philosophies and problems are presented by college students as a basis for program planning.

3. Objectives that will develop skills, critical and creative thinking, self-selection, and appreciation are thought thorough.

4. We speak of diagnosis and apply our techniques in a laboratory or classroom setting where we work with *live* children; and we analyze the data as a means of planning realistic curricula for *all content* areas.

5. We become familiar with a variety of materials, *but mainly books,* which we can use to carry out interesting assignments and to provide for individual differences. We also try out a variety of methods.

6. We study motivational techniques and the psychology of learning in an effort to reach more students and to develop lifetime readers.

7. We recognize the mass media—tapes, records, television, and movies—as contributing forces in modern man's world of communication. We study the role of reading as one significant part of this world.

8. We evaluate our efforts and our proposed programs. We study child behavior, attitudes, and interests, as well as skill development. We look at the quantity and quality of materials read. We try to measure the impact of reading upon the reader.

Teaching begins with a concept of reality. Reality is the concept of being now. It is man existing, man thinking, man learning, and man performing. Reality is living and searching for an understanding of life's ways. Reality is not a panacea, pat answers, perfect research reports, guaranteed seals of approval, and degrees from the learned leaders in the field. Reality is not machines and packages, tests and grouping, grades and workbooks. Reality is the internal world enabling the external being to be honest with himself and then with others.

Reality is a philosophy that recognizes children as wonderful creations who bring certain feelings, certain abilities, certain interests, and certain experiences to the classroom. Life out of the classroom may be far more significant than life in the classroom, and the teacher should bring the two together. Only the teacher who takes the time to understand the child, his world, his skills, his values, and his hopes can ever make school, learning, and reading a magical, marvelous, meaningful experience for each child.

Preparing for Student Teaching: A Part of a Continuum

DOROTHY M. McGEOCH
Teachers College, Columbia University

STUDENT TEACHING is almost universally accepted as an essential, perhaps the *only* essential, component of a teacher education program. There is much less agreement, however, as to type, extent, or objective of the experience so described. For the purposes of this discussion, I would like to consider student teaching as one of a series of direct experiences, coming typically during the fourth year of a teacher preparation program and including "a period of guided teaching when a college student assumes increasing responsibility for directing the work of a group of learners over a period of consecutive weeks" (7). Hopefully, student teaching will be followed by a supervised internship and gradual induction into the profession. The part of the continuum which concerns us here, however, is the series of experiences which precede student teaching and provide the background needed for making the best use of the opportunities student teaching affords.

Three aspects of learning to become a teacher require special attention during the pre-student-teaching period: understanding the development of children and youth in their environment, developing a personal identification with the role of the teacher, and learning teaching strategies and skills. Let us look at some of the experiences related to each of these goals.

The child and the culture

Courses in human growth and development are typically included near the beginning of programs of teacher preparation. Educational sociology and cultural anthropology are beginning to be required, particularly in programs which prepare teachers for work in depressed urban areas. All of these have a contribution to make.

An understanding of minority group cultures is necessary in order to plan effective learning experiences for children of those groups. It is also important for the teacher of children whose culture is much more like his own to learn to use the conceptual tools of the sociologist and the anthropologist in assessing the environmental influences in any situation and in respecting the implications of cultural pluralism. Both knowledge and direct experiences are required.

The critical element at this stage is the focus on the growing individual in his environment. In some teacher education programs the student has a series of observation and participation experiences more or less related to his course work. It has been assumed that observation experiences in a

school supplemented by some community orientation will provide the needed understanding.

The evidence does not support this assumption. When placed in a classroom situation, the beginning student must be concerned with his own ability to perform the tasks which he perceives as being required of the teacher. His capacity to focus on the pupils as individuals is limited.

As an alternative to an early experience in the schools, a specified number of hours of service in a community center or in a tutoring program is sometimes required. These programs often have the limitation of putting students into a teaching situation with insufficient skill, or supervision, or both. The student may find his teaching role difficult because he does not know what to do and how to do it. He may, on the other hand, find it hard to understand and accept the children involved because of the limitations placed on him by his lack of competence as a teacher.

A third condition also results, particularly in the one-to-one contact of the reading-tutoring situation. The prospective teacher develops a close and sympathetic relationship with his pupil which, during the period of contact, is very satisfying to both parties. All too frequently, however, such an experience leaves the student teacher with few, if any, generalizable understandings to apply to the school situation and leaves the child with very few reading skills to help him in his school experiences.

Present programs may be attempting to combine two kinds of experience which might better be developed sequentially and later integrated in student teaching and the internship. A carefully planned community experience closely related to the development of concepts in the fields of child development, sociology, and anthropology might well precede experiences in the schools. For example, a summer experience similar to that of some VISTA workers could be accompanied by a continuing interdisciplinary seminar. In this way, the development and application of organizing concepts would proceed together, and the prospective teachers would acquire tools for analyzing the developmental and environmental factors which influence any pupil or group of pupils.

The role of a teacher

The student in the teacher education program must not only learn to understand the children he will teach, he must learn to be at home in the role of the teacher. For many young people the second is the much more complex and difficult task.

> What does it mean to feel like a teacher? It probably means different things to different people. The common factor, however, is an emotional identification with the perceived role of teacher. . . . To feel like a teacher means that the student must be aware of himself as a person who has the responsibility for decision-making, for guiding the behavior of learners, and for structuring the social milieu of the classroom; as a person who can formulate satisfying interrelationships with other adults and with children in the social institution that we call a school; and as a person who understands that his knowledge of subject matter is not a guarantee that the learners will be interested in it and will want to learn it (4).

Feelings about being a teacher develop through first-hand experience—experience as a person who confronts the ambiguities, satisfactions, and frustrations which are the teacher's lot. Provisions for gaining the experience which will enable the student to identify with the role of the teacher should follow the community assignment and be related to it.

As a teacher, the student will need to differentiate between the human needs which the school is equipped to deal with and those which are the major responsibility of other community agencies. The whole child, indeed, comes to school, but the teacher cannot single-handedly deal with all of the child's problems. The teacher may find at times that he must choose between what is best for a particular child and what is necessary in providing learning opportunities for a group

of thirty. The community experience is valuable in developing insight and understanding of the wide range of human needs, but subsequent experience with various aspects of the role of the teacher makes clear the extent to which such needs may be met by a single social institution—the school.

Service as teacher aides or assistant teachers provides opportunities both for involvement in classroom activities and for observation of a role model in the classroom teacher. Such experience may begin with many routine tasks but should include a chance to work with a group of learners for a reasonable period of time. Obviously the student will have very limited teaching skills at this time and will need carefully selected teaching tasks and continued guidance in his beginning activities.

Let me illustrate one way in which such initial experiences may be developed. Last fall, each student in my class in the teaching of reading was assigned to work two hours a week with a group of second graders who had not made normal progress in reading. The second graders were chosen for two reasons: help received at this stage is most effective in preventing cumulative retardation in reading, and second graders are easier for the inexperienced teacher to work with because they have not yet developed the negative attitudes of the older retarded reader.

Three children were assigned to each student with the intent of providing a simplified group teaching situation rather than the typical individual instruction of the reading tutor. Experience in dealing with three children was seen as a step toward teaching a regular class group.

Plans for the teaching were made in terms of hypotheses to be tested.

> If the children take home the stories they dictate to me, they will read them to their families and gain more practice in reading.
> If, at every session, I introduce three or four words which a child selects as his very own, the child will be able to read these words in succeeding sessions.

If the children learn the usual sounds of initial consonants, they will be able to identify words beginning with those consonants.

The students had a maximum of about sixteen sessions with their reading groups; many of their more comprehensive goals could not be realized. They found satisfaction in reconsidered objectives, however. One student summed up her reaction as follows:

While my original objectives for the group were quite specific—e.g., hoping to improve oral reading, accuracy of perception, vocabulary, etc.,—my later ones developed in a more general desire to motivate the children to want to read so that when I would no longer be there each Wednesday and Thursday they would still be enthusiastic about their reading experiences. . . . To restate some of the evidence I noted in my reports: (1) they began bringing in books to read, (2) they initiated the idea of making up their own play, wrote it, and are planning to present it to their homeroom class, (3) they started bringing in original stories and poems, (4) they began to discipline each other when one of the three was disturbing another, and (5) discussions about certain problems were carried on among themselves with far less direction needed from me.

This young teacher and others were beginning to feel like teachers as they planned, taught, and evaluated. Their summary statements at the end of the semester illustrate the meaning the experience had for them:

Thus, over all, I enjoyed the children, listening and hearing what they thought. The teaching gave me an opportunity to be with three second graders and, I think, perceive many characteristics about children in general. Though I will probably be teaching children in the upper grades next year, this three-month experience exposed me to problems similar to what I may encounter there. *Also, helping individuals who require assistance is satisfying, and teaching enabled me to experience this important, personal feeling.*

It is very difficult to judge the emotional effect one has had on children but I venture to guess that they gained from our experience just a taste of the ease of an emotionally secure relationship. As a result of our relationship I hope that perhaps they may be a little bit better equipped to recognize a sincere relationship when it is offered to them and not quite so quick to be aggressive.

My evidences of improvement were that they responded enthusiastically when I typed *their* play and put it into folders with their names typed on them; that one of the children asked to read a story she had written to the group—something she had never done before; and that the three children were able to discuss among themselves (without my help) some of the important things to note when reading a play dialog. Finally, their sincere disappointment at the end of the last session certainly revealed (in a most warm and wonderful way) that my objective had at least partially been attained.

Once when I was inadvertently ten minutes late, they said they were afraid I wasn't coming. I told them I'd always try to come, but I had the feeling that they were used to people disappointing them, and they may not have totally believed me at this time. However, by the end of the semester I had acquired their trust, as I tried to fulfill any ideas or plans I discussed with them.

The experience of working with these children gave me a strange sort of humility toward teaching—a humility in terms of the almost miraculous process by which a child learns to read; a humility toward the task which every teacher must face when she tries to reach a child, to make him expand outward from himself a little bit, to make him self-sufficient, and to initiate him further into the personalness of the spoken, read, and written word. I realize now that my approach to working with these children was almost like the attitude of the "method" actor: once one has competence in the "method" or "methods" one is equipped to cope with any situation.

There are other aspects of the teacher's role which may be experienced previous to student teaching or employment. Teachers' meetings, supervisory conferences, and meetings of professional organizations provide opportunities for the prospective teacher to identify his role as a member of a staff and a professional group. Student membership and active participation in a professional organization increase the probability of developing a positive identification.

Contact with parents is also important. Attendance at parents' meetings and parent-teacher conferences is helpful in giving the prospective teacher a sense of the way parents perceive the teacher and what they expect of him.

Recently I took a group of twelve students to meet with representatives of the parents of the school where the student teaching would be conducted. The parents, many of them Negro and Puerto Rican, instructed the young teachers in the attitudes they wanted teachers to show toward their children. They were very articulate and completely sincere. They also showed bitterness and a lack of satisfaction with the education their children were receiving. Many of the students began for the first time to feel like teachers as they listened and responded to the parents. It was an experience they will not soon forget.

Teaching strategies and skills

While he is coming to feel like a teacher, the student must also become increasingly competent in behaving as a teacher behaves—he must learn teaching strategies and skills. Until recently, teaching skills were developed by literally practicing in a classroom under the supervision of an experienced teacher. While the bulk of the practice took place during student teaching, a limited number of teaching experiences were often planned previous to the student teaching assignment. Recent technological advances have made available a number of alternative procedures.

Simulation techniques in many forms are being used increasingly in teacher education programs. Through films, recordings, video tapes, and case materials, programed sequences of problem situations to which the student must respond have been developed. In the more elaborate programs, the use of branching techniques has enabled the student to experience some of the logical results of the decisions he makes. In others, the gradual introduction of many types of information concerning a hypothetical group of pupils makes possible the presentation of increasingly complex problem situations (2).

Micro-teaching is another means of developing teaching skills in a controlled situation. The student prepares and teaches a single concept to a group of three to five students, and a video recording of the teaching is made. The student, profiting from previous experience, is able to obtain immediate feedback and to reteach the material. Dwight W. Allen of Stanford summarizes the advantages of this approach:

> Logistics are much simplified. Less complicated stimuli are presented for the novice teacher to cope with, and the supervisor can focus his supervision more precisely . . . micro-teaching can be controlled to provide as wide a variety of situations as desired. . . . Greater individualization is possible. Micro-lessons can be scheduled as needed, varying time and students for specific instructional purposes. . . . Experiments with micro-teaching have demonstrated that a high correlation exists between micro-teaching performance and performance in a full-sized classroom (1).

In a variation of the micro-teaching technique, students may be encouraged to try out various teaching styles with small groups of children. In what Bruce Joyce and Richard Hodges call "instructional flexibility training" students are encouraged to develop wider ranges of teaching behavior through analysis of their own teaching, development of goals for alternate behaviors, and provision for feedback about progress toward those goals.

> In order for better schools to be developed, teachers have to learn wider ranges of teaching behavior than we presently find. Some need to learn to radiate more kinds of social climate; some need to extend the ways they handle content; and some need to learn more teaching strategies (6).

Even where electronic equipment is limited, role playing and situational analysis are effective means of developing sensitivity to various teaching strategies and of formulating alternative responses in a defined situation. The procedures outlined by Hunter and Amidon are particularly useful during the pre-student-teaching period when a simplified hypothetical situation may provide a basis for more skillful behavior in the actual classroom (5).

It is apparent that all of the procedures for developing teaching strategies and skills depend upon the use of some means for analyzing teaching behavior. The recent advances in this field and the increasing number of systems of analysis which are available make it possible to teach students to view teaching through a number of frames of reference and to analyze their own teaching and that of others by means of the analytical schemes provided (3).

Considerable evidence shows that prospective teachers can learn to perform almost any specific teaching strategy effectively in controlled situations. It is less clear, however, how such strategies can be effectively integrated into continuing teaching behavior in regular classrooms. While the integration process is clearly a major function of the student teaching and internship periods, there can be no doubt that the development of a repertoire of skills and strategies in the early stages of professional preparation can make a valuable contribution to the gradually developing professional competence through a continuing series of teaching experiences.

Conclusion

The focus of this discussion has been on experiences which precede student teaching and provide the background needed to make the best use of the opportunities student teaching affords. Such experiences were defined as part of a continuum which extends into the first years of employment as a teacher. Some pre-student-teaching experiences designed to promote understanding of the child in his environment, development of a personal identification with the role of the teacher, and the acquisition of teaching strategies and skills were discussed. There was also a passing mention of the course work, seminars, conferences, and other expanding and integrating experiences which should give meaning and perspective to the direct experiences.

The two aspects of teacher preparation must reinforce each other. No experiences in school and community, however carefully planned and conscientiously executed, can make their desired contribution to the education of the prospective teacher unless concurrent opportunities for analysis and evaluation are given. A student in a class in the teaching of reading writes perceptively of this relationship in her evaluation of the course experiences:

> The best part of the reading course was its integration with the teaching, making each step a hypothesis to be kept or discarded. This integration and the constant evaluation and reevaluation forced me to *think* about each step of the teaching and face any discouragement or times when I felt that little progress was being made. Without the course backing up the weekly activity it would have been too easy to disregard false starts and flimsy hypotheses as the result of a first teaching experience. By consistently translating the things I did into analyzed experience, I was able to feel the cumulative effect of what I was doing on my pupils and myself. I was able to face the experience objectively and with other points of view in mind. The things we discussed in class related directly to what I was doing with my three pupils. They supplemented, disagreed, and reinformed; they forced me to consider what will happen when I have thirty children, not just three. . . . And the experience really made the future teaching a much more foreseeable event.

REFERENCES

1. Allen, Dwight W. "A New Design for Teacher Education," *Journal of Teacher Education,* 17 (Fall 1966), 297-298.
2. Bushnell, Donald D. "Computer-based Simulation: A New Technology for Education," *AV Communication Review,* 11 (March-April 1963), 45-55.
3. Gage, N. L. *Handbook of Research on Teaching.* Chicago: Rand McNally and Company, 1963.
4. Howard, Elizabeth Z. "To Feel Like a Teacher," *Journal of Teacher Education,* 16 (December 1965), 453.
5. Hunter, Elizabeth, and Edmund Amidon. *Improving Teaching.* New York: Holt, Rinehart and Winston, 1966.
6. Joyce, Bruce R., and Richard E. Hodges. "Instructional Flexibility Training," *Journal of Teacher Education,* 17 (Winter 1966), 415.
7. Sub-Committee of the Standards and Surveys Committee, John G. Flowers (Chairman). *School and Community Laboratory Experiences in Teacher Education.* Oneonta, New York: American Association of Teachers Colleges, 1948.

In-Service Education that Makes a Difference

DOLORES DURKIN
University of Illinois

AN INVITATION TO DISCUSS teacher education immediately engenders the feeling that the presentation ought to be very up-to-date and that, for instance, its content must give attention to matters like the influence of technology or, perhaps, of federal funds. However, I am going to bypass what might be a temptation for me and an expectation of yours and, instead, deal with much more ordinary matters related to the education of teachers.

The decision to concentrate on these more ordinary matters results from some contacts I have had with schools over the past few years as a researcher, as a consultant, and more recently as an instructor of college seniors who were preparing for student teaching. I want to describe just a few of these contacts and, in the descriptions, I will be selective. For instance, I am omitting references to some superb reading instruction that I have observed. Instead, I am going to describe a few samples of actual school practices which illustrate what I believe is *the* basic problem in the teaching of reading: the lack of match between instruction and children.

Examples of lack of match between instruction and children

For me, the most dramatic example of this lack of match occurred in the fall of 1957. At that time I was doing observational research in a first grade classroom. Although this research included boys only, it brought me into contact with a first grade girl who, while participating in the sixth week of a reading readiness program, was found to be able to read at a fourth grade level. In this instance the lack of match between what a child could do and what the school program offered her was embarrassing. However, for me it was also a reason

to begin some very interesting studies of children who learn to read at home before they start school.

I mention this research now because it has allowed for the identification of other illustrations of what I am calling a lack of match between instruction and children. More specifically, the focus of the studies has resulted in many invitations to consult with schools that are interested in reexamining their kindergarten programs to see whether reading ought to be introduced for some of the children. Generally these contacts have been very encouraging and full of hope—although every once in awhile I have been surprised, to say the least, at what I find. For instance, not so long ago I was asked by a school district to participate in some decision-making regarding the appropriateness of reading for its kindergartens. The consulting began with visits to kindergarten classrooms, a fact which made it apparent that decisions had already been made. In the first three classrooms, for example, I found very structured programs in which the whole class was drilling on things like the identification of letters and sounds. This circumstance was especially surprising because all three of the schools were in low socioeconomic communities suggesting that their kindergarten children probably needed many opportunities to extend speaking vocabularies, to express themselves freely, and so on. What I found, though, was this concentration on whole-class participation in rote learnings.

My surprise and, later, my concern prompted me to ask each of the three teachers why she was trying to teach reading to these kindergarten children. The first explained that the teacher next door to her started doing it, and so she decided to have some reading, too. When I asked the second teacher why she had selected materials requiring a great amount of phonics drill, she said a salesman had offered them to the school at no cost if they would be used in the kindergarten. When I asked the third teacher why she was using i.t.a. materials, she said her principal had been curious about them and decided to see what would happen if they were used in the kindergarten.

Frankly, I found it difficult to believe what I heard. However, the explanations were so spontaneous I had to conclude they must also be honest. I mention them now, by the way, not to support the idea that truth *is* stranger than fiction but, rather, to support my belief that decisions about school programs are often made with insufficient attention to the particular children who will be affected by them. The result can only be a serious lack of match between instruction and children.

Other examples

Because I want nobody to conclude that matching instruction to children is a problem only at the kindergarten level, let me move now to some of my other contacts with schools—in this instance to contacts achieved through student teachers recently. In particular, I would like to describe a reading methods course I taught to a group of college seniors who, in about the middle of the semester, left campus to do their student teaching in a wide variety of elementary schools.

In teaching the first part of this methods course I constantly emphasized that old and very familiar idea that children are very different in what they have achieved, even when they share the same classroom and grade placement. Consequently, when I discussed basal readers, I demonstrated how these texts might be used and I also reminded the students that a fourth grade basal reader, for example, is not written for all fourth graders but only for those who happen to be reading at a fourth grade level. With this in mind I showed these college students a variety of high-interest, low-vocabulary books that would be suitable for children not reading "at grade level." And I also showed them more advanced books which would challenge children lucky enough to be reading above the grade level to which they

were assigned. What I am trying to indicate, then, with just a few illustrations, is that the whole emphasis of the course was on matching instruction with children.

Then these college seniors left campus to do their student teaching. What did they find? With only one exception they found themselves in classrooms in which the same basal reader was used with all of the children, regardless of their particular abilities and achievements. Actually, some schools were so tightly structured that teachers used only one basal reader series. In other schools there were choices from among several series, but the same curtailments existed: If a child sat in a fourth grade classroom, for instance, he was not to read from a textbook above that level, even though his achievements obviously were above it.

Still other examples

To discourage the idea that I am picking on fourth grade teachers, let me move to another illustration of conflict between what I try to teach college seniors and what they subsequently find in the schools.

In 1967, a topic still requiring very detailed attention in reading methods courses is the content of phonics. Because college students now taking these courses attended elementary school when phonics was either deemphasized or, perhaps, simply bypassed, it is not uncommon to find that they barely know there are consonants and vowels in the alphabet. If a discussion moves to more technical matters like hard and soft sounds or to discussions of digraphs and diphthongs, they are completely lost. As one of the college students put it, "This is like taking a foreign language."

What the lack of background means, of course, is that attention must be given not only to the question of how to teach phonics but also to its content. In requiring students to learn the content, I constantly remind them that until they themselves feel very sure about their own knowledge of the whole of this content, they will not be able to select that part which ought to be taught to any given child. This is the sermon I preach.

Then out go the student teachers into schools. I'll cite just one illustration: out goes a student teacher into a first grade in which most children understand and can use consonant sounds, but nothing can be taught about vowel sounds because they are scheduled for second grade. Or I preach about the possible help that can come from workbooks, if and when assignments are made on the basis of what particular children need to practice, and then the student teachers find themselves in schools in which every page in every workbook must be completed by every child if he needs it or not.

It would be possible, even easy, to describe other conflicts between what I feel must be emphasized in methods courses and what student teachers then find in the schools. However, I think enough illustrations have been cited to make the point I want to highlight; namely, that a basic problem in the teaching of reading is the lack of match between instruction and children.

Coping with the problem

Assuming this indictment has validity, let me now move to a consideration of what might be done to cope with what I think is both a serious and a widespread problem.

I would like to suggest that the first step is to recognize how very difficult it is for a teacher to instruct at a level and at a pace that are suitable for the many different children assigned to one classroom. In fact, every time I visit a school I become reconvinced of the complexity of matching instruction with children. Such difficulty, however, does not mean that we abandon hope for achieving it but, rather, that we become more realistic in the in-service help we offer teachers.

Before discussing what I believe is one example of realistic help, let me stress an additional point; namely, the conviction that a teacher's efforts to match instruction with children will meet with success only to the degree that the whole school participates in these efforts. I mention this conviction because it affects my ideas about the kinds of help that must become available, if teachers are to achieve a maximum of instruction that really is appropriate for the children assigned to their classrooms.

Function of preservice course

Although the focus here is in-service education, I will comment on the *preservice* methods course in reading because I believe our notions about this preservice course affect our concepts of in-service needs.

In my opinion, the very best of preservice courses, even when they concentrate exclusively on reading, can make only a small contribution to the development of expertness in teaching—and, for now, I'm equating expertise with the ability to match instruction with children. It would be my guess that those who disagree with this judgment probably are individuals who have not had the experience of preparing undergraduates to teach reading in a classroom. With that experience it becomes very clear that the knowledge required to teach reading, coupled with the logistics of putting this knowledge to use with a large group of children, is simply too much for one course.

Presently, at least, I expect one preservice methods course to enable an undergraduate to participate with both knowledge and security in the student teaching situation—which is very different from having the full responsibility of a classroom. I would expect, too, that the content of the preservice course would make the student teacher very conscious of the positive features of the classroom program in which she is a temporary participant and, too, very sensitive to those aspects of the instruction which merit nothing but omission.

In-service education

If there is agreement about the inherent limitations of a preservice course, then there is no need to debate the question: Should there be an in-service methods course? Therefore, instead of making a plea for one methods course for teachers, I'd like to explain why I think there is need for two. Basic to this point of view are certain assumptions. I'd like to enumerate three of them now, even though two were noted earlier. The first is the common sense claim that one cannot teach what one does not know. The second assumption on which my proposals are based is the contention that effective teaching is directly related to the degree of match between instruction and children. The third is the conviction that this matching is possible only when the total faculty and administration of a school are working toward it.

Since "matching" seems to be the name of the game, let me now proceed to match these assumptions with the two in-service methods courses that I suggested earlier.

First course

The content of the first course would reflect the assumption that one cannot teach what one does not know. Consequently—and now I'll cite just a few illustrations—its students would learn about a topic like structural analysis with a scope and depth that would take them far beyond the usual unsophisticated treatment of prefixes and suffixes. Or, this course would give its students a knowledge of the full content of phonics. Or, this first course would deal with critical reading, not in some vague and general way but, rather, with a scholarly attention that would include such specific considerations as the techniques employed by propagandistic writers. In other words, one main goal of this first inservice methodology course would be to help teachers become specifically knowledgeable about possible content for their reading instruction.

Because I do not concur with the idea that "to know is to be able to teach," I want to suggest—with haste—that the other goal of this course would be to acquaint teachers with the various ways in which this content might be presented to children. Here the description "various" is underscored because I do not believe there is one best way to teach anything. Consequently, I would be of the opinion that the purpose of this first course is not to indoctrinate about methodology but, rather, to help teachers become aware of some of the instructional approaches that are possible.

Even with the broader focus, however, there still would be the need for specificity in the treatment of methodology. For instance, detailed help with a matter like question-asking ought to be included in the course. With this, attention could be given to the function of specific kinds of questions in relation to teaching the different comprehension skills. Or, since materials are a part of most teaching procedures, students ought to leave this first course knowing about available materials and how they can be used in a reading program.

To sum up, then, this first course would be a specific study of the possible content of reading instruction and, secondly, of some of the ways this content might be taught. Its special focus would be on *awareness:* helping teachers become aware of what might be taught and of how it can be communicated to children.

The second course

My conception of a second methods course needed by teachers is related to two of the three assumptions which I noted earlier. First, effective teaching is directly related to the degree of match between instruction and children. And, secondly, appropriate matching is possible only when the total faculty and administration of a school are working toward it.

As I reviewed these two assumptions, you probably saw implications not only for the content of a second course but also for the particular students who would be taking it. For instance, if there is agreement that a matching of instruction with children can only be attained when a total faculty is working to achieve it, then I assume there also would be agreement about the need for instructors of in-service methods courses to work with school faculties rather than, let us say, thirty teachers from thirty different schools.

As one suggestion, then, let me propose that the first in-service methods course would be open to all but that among its students would be at least one total faculty. At this time, in the first course, the members of this faculty would be growing in their awareness of the possible content of reading instruction and of how it might be taught.

In the second course, open only to faculties that participated in the first one, the emphasis would be on making choices about what to teach and how to teach it. Guiding the content would be the assumption that effective teaching is directly related to the degree of match between instruction and children.

What matching requires

Specifically, what might be included in the content of this second course? Actually, a more productive way to phrase the question is to ask what is required for this matching procedure? Obviously, if a classroom teacher is to make appropriate choices for the focus of her instruction, she must first know about the choices that are possible. And, in fact, this is why the content of the first course would concentrate on increasing teachers' awareness of what can be taught to improve a child's reading.

In making these appropriate choices, however, a teacher must also be knowledgeable about the existing achievements of the children in her classroom. This means that one major emphasis in the second course would be on diagnosis: what are the ways in which a classroom teacher can continuously learn about the specific achievements as well as the specific problems of the children she is teaching? In this instance, if the whole faculty of a school were involved in the course, its content could also examine how diagnostic information can be passed on from one teacher to another.

Additional topics in this second course would deal with other aspects of matching instruction with children. For example, once a teacher is aware of what can be taught and, in addition, has identified with needs to be selected for particular children, how can she then parcel out her time so that it becomes humanly possible to use what she knows? This question, of course, concerns the whole matter of classroom organization. And it suggests further content for this second course. More specifically, it suggests that time would be given to the various ways in which children can be grouped for instruction. The question suggests, too, that attention would be given to the kinds of materials that would be useful. And it suggests that very specific attention would be given to the kinds of assignments which would be suitable for children not working with the teacher and which would be productive in terms of what they needed to learn, relearn, practice, or whatever. Again, because a total faculty is involved, there could be a rich exchange of ideas and a profitable sharing of experiences related to this very important and also very difficult matter of classroom organization. Here, the intent would not be to promote one type of organization but, rather, to identify the various possibilities so that individual teachers could make choices which are not only suitable for the children they teach but, equally important, suitable for themselves as particular kinds of human beings.

Some final comments

Perhaps some of you might have reservations about the possibility of having two consecutive semesters of reading courses attended by total faculties. If so, then I would want to be very quick to emphasize that the particular form in-service help takes is not of paramount importance. That it is given in courses, or in workshops, or as part of a consulting service is not the important thing. What *is* of major importance, however, is that university and college personnel recognize the very real difficulty of achieving effective classroom instruction in reading and, in turn, that they provide a kind and amount of in-service help that will really make a difference. Naturally, for these hopes to be realized, there must also be elementary school faculties and administrators who recognize both the basic importance of reading and their need to learn more about the ways to teach it in the classroom setting.

Of course, I am aware that you might have other kinds of objections—for instance, to my view of what is the basic problem today in teaching reading. Here, I feel, I must be firm because I am convinced that at all grade levels there is a serious lack of match between what is being taught and what is really needed. I am firmly convinced, too, that the frequency of this problem is not accidental but, rather, that it is the result of our failure to recognize how very difficult it is to achieve appropriate instruction in the setting of a classroom. One result of our insensitivity to the complexities of classroom teaching is a lack of help which, in quality and quantity, would give all conscientious teachers the chance to create a reading program that has something for everybody, including tremendous satisfaction for the teacher herself.

An Experience in Teaching for Teachers and Students

JAMES R. LAYTON
Charlotte-Mecklenburg,
North Carolina, School System

HOW MANY BENEFITS can be received from a summer reading program without sacrificing quality for quantity? How many agencies and individuals can benefit from an effective program in reading? In the summer of 1966, Charlotte, North Carolina, was the scene of a unique summer reading program which was in its twelfth year of development.

The program was developed through the efforts of David Shepherd, now at Hofstra University, and Uberto Price of Appalachian State Teachers College, Boone, North Carolina. Shepherd and Price desired to train teachers in the teaching of reading and devised a program which would require the joint efforts of the Charlotte School System, of which Shepherd was reading director, and the college, A.S.T.C., where Price was and still is director of reading services. The summer reading program has undergone many changes through careful study and evaluation but remains basically the same as its originators designed it. This report is not of a crash program hurridly developed but one that has proved effective over the years.

Planning the program

Although the past summer program was jointly sponsored by Federal funds, Appalachian State Teachers College, and the Charlotte-Mecklenburg School System, the majority of the planning was the responsibility of the school system. Prior to beginning the program, the college and the Federal agency had to approve the plans. Each institution involved in the program had basic responsibilities to the overall design. Without prompt attention to their specific tasks, any one agency could have harmed the program severely.

Contributions to the program

The major contribution of the Federal agency was that of funds which, after approval of the plans, were delegated to the school system to furnish 1) tuition and transportation for 300 underprivileged students, 2) materials to be used by the scholarship students, 3) tuition for specified interning teachers, 4) an assistant administrator to act as transportation director and guidance counselor, 5) bus drivers who also aided the assistant administrator in minor duties, 6) a reading clinician, 7) library aids who served as bus chaperones, and 8) a secretary's aid.

The Elementary Language Arts Department of the school system, through the funds received from tuitional students not sponsored by Federal funds, was to supply the 1) administrative director, 2) secretary, 3) materials for non-scholarship students, 4) adequate building facilities, 5) buses normally used for schools during the regular term, 6) special teacher for phonics classes to teach interning teachers during the enrichment period, 7) book displays from major publishing companies, and 8) professional reading materials for extended study from the curriculum library.

Appalachian State Teachers College, under the supervision of its reading department, supplied 1) the professional director, 2) six nationally-known consultants, 3) nine quarter-hours or six semester hours of graduate credit for interning teachers upon successful completion of the program, and 4) professional reading materials from the college library.

The professional staff of the summer program was provided by the Elementary Language Arts Department of the school system with the approval of the college reading department. The professional director of the program was chosen by the college with the approval of the school system.

Specific qualifications for each staff member were agreed upon by the two organizations directly involved with the program. Job descriptions were outlined in order to eliminate the possibility of overlapping or conflicting duties which would impede the progress of the program. The responsibilities and qualifications required of the staff personnel were as follows:

I. *Program Administrator*
   A. Responsibilities
      1. Assigning pupils to classes based on test results.
      2. Assigning interning teachers to staff teachers.
      3. Selecting and procuring materials for instruction of the students.
      4. Working with the staff members and interning teachers to promote more effective methods of instruction.
      5. Assuming the responsibility for financial matters and bookkeeping.
      6. Arranging the schedule and housing facilities for the visiting consultants.
   B. Qualifications Required
      1. At least an A.B. degree from a recognized college.
      2. At least three years' successful experience as a classroom teacher.
      3. Successful completion of graduate courses in reading.
      4. Previous experience in a similar summer reading program.
      5. Strong background in reading instruction.
      6. Participation in Education 571, "Field Experiences in the Teaching of Reading," required by Appalachian State Teachers College.

II. *Professional Director*
   A. Responsibilities
      1. Continuous supervision of interning teachers and their staff supervisors.
      2. Instruction of all interns in the daily seminars.
      3. Assisting in daily planning of staff teachers and interning teachers.
      4. Scheduling regular conferences with program administrator, clinician, administrative assistant, librarian, staff teachers, and parents.
   B. The qualifications of the professional director are the same as those of the program administrator.

III. *Visiting Reading Consultants*
   A. Responsibilities
      1. Visiting classrooms and observing techniques and materials in use.
      2. Conducting the seminars for interning teachers and staff members.
      3. Suggesting ways of improving the caliber of instruction observed.
      4. Reviewing and recommending professional materials which may be helpful to participants in the program.
   B. Professional consultants are invited to the program in accordance with their individual talents in the field of reading. Consultants were scheduled in order to correlate their specialty with the overall design of the program. To date, all the consultants have been affiliated with a reading clinic in an outstanding college or university. Although there is added

expense in procuring nationally known authorities, their attendance keeps the program abreast of new ideas and problems in education across the nation.

IV. *Clinician*
  A. Responsibilities
    1. Administering and interpreting the various individual tests which are given in addition to the standardized placement tests. (Placement tests are administered in schools prior to closing for summer.)
    2. Consulting with interns and staff teachers concerning the various test results and securing the aid of school psychologists when the need arises.
    3. Recommending instructional techniques suitable for use with tested students who have special difficulties which may prevent them from progressing in the regular small group situations.
    4. Consulting when necessary with interning teachers, staff teachers, psychologists, social workers, and parents in order to diagnose, investigate, and develop an appropriate program for a child in need.
    5. Administering visual and audiometric tests with appropriate devices and interpreting the results of the tests.
    6. Teaching staff teachers as well as interning teachers to administer specific tests and interpret the results. These tests do not include psychological tests which should be administered by trained personnel; it is the intent of this program to teach the use of any test which could be used by the classroom teacher in order to become a more effective teacher.
  B. Qualifications of the reading clinician are the same as those of the professional director. In addition, the reading clinician must have had previous training and experience in a reading clinic as a clinician and diagnostician.

V. *Staff Teachers*
  A. Responsibilities
    1. Supervising the instruction of the children by the interning teachers.
    2. Planning with interning teachers to improve instruction in the use of varied and applicable materials.
    3. Conferring with the reading clinician as the need arises.
    4. Demonstrating specific techniques in teaching small groups of children and developing ways to transfer the learned techniques to a self-contained classroom.
    5. Attending daily seminar in order

to promote personal professional growth and acting as a liaison person between the interning teachers and the professional director in order to clarify and extend the text of seminar lectures.
    6. Insuring that the interning teachers meet the standards set by the cooperating college.
    7. Referring interns to professional materials applicable to problem readers and matters of interest.
    8. Familiarity with all instructional materials, equipment, games, and techniques proved effective for reading improvement.
  B. Qualifications
    1. At least an A.B. degree from a recognized college.
    2. At least three years of successful experience as a classroom teacher at the elementary level.
    3. Participation in Education 571, "Field Experiences in the Teaching of Reading," required by Appalachian State Teachers College.

Each year, new ways of working with children are used; new materials are brought into the program; new ideas in the teaching of reading are tried; and, for these reasons, personnel who have been associated with the program in the past are needed to evaluate and correlate the old with the new. Although new members have been added to staff at time of need, the experienced teachers in the program have proved to be more effective. The staff teachers are chosen from the corrective reading teachers who work in the elementary schools during the regular year and who are familiar with the curriculum of the school system. These teachers form the backbone of the summer program; without their energy and enthusiasm the program would not be possible.

VI. *Librarian*
  A. Responsibilities
    1. Developing skills of oral expression and listening during the story hour for the children.
    2. Conducting story time for the pupils.
    3. Supervising the selection of books by the pupils.
    4. Instructing children in library skills.
    5. Assisting staff and interning teachers in choosing suitable books for classroom and home reading.

6. Aiding interning teachers and staff teachers in choosing professional materials for extended study.
7. Helping to decide which professional books will benefit the program from past experiences in professional book circulation.

This program has benefited greatly from the services of the summer program librarian. She has been on the staff for four years and is an excellent resource person for consulting and assisting with the worthiness of professional reading materials in specific areas. A rotation program of persons to participate as the librarian is not feasible. An efficient, experienced librarian is of more benefit than a person who has the same qualifications but has never been involved with the professional aspects of reading instruction.

B. Qualifications
1. Certification as an elementary librarian.
2. Experience in library work in local school system.
3. Previous experience in a summer program.
4. Displays a high interest in children's literature.
5. Excels in storytelling and expressive reading skills.
6. Experienced and competent in fitting a book's reading difficulty, format, and interest to the needs of a child.
7. Is familiar with bibliotherapy and can consult with interning teachers and parents in this all-important but much-neglected area of reading.

VII. *Administrative Assistant*

A. Responsibilities
1. Working with the local director of school transportation in arranging for adequate buses for pupils entitled to transportation to and from the reading center. (This group of students was composed of those attending under Federal funds.)
2. Securing qualified bus drivers and orienting them to their duties and responsibilities.
3. Establishing bus routes and identifying convenient pick-up stations.
4. Supervising the bus drivers during the entire six weeks of the summer program.
5. Securing qualified parent chaperones for the students.
6. Serving as the liaison person between the reading program and the home in order to promote more interest in the program.
7. Arranging for bus drivers to vary their routes daily in order that scholarship pupils from deprived areas will have the opportunity to see their community and their county, probably for the first time.
8. Serving as the liaison person between the clinic and school-related personnel and organizations:
   a. Mecklenburg County Health Department
   b. The local school department of psychological services
   c. The local school department of social workers
   d. The local welfare department
   e. Family and children organizations
   f. The local organizations which provide free services for children with visual difficulties.
9. Assisting the administrative director, as time permits.

This position was designed solely to aid the deprived children who were attending the program through Federal grants. The children who paid tuition were not permitted transportation and oher free services under this aspect of the program. Federal financing made possible the employment of the administrative assistant and reading clinician, both of whose duties would have had to be absorbed by other personnel if the program had been entirely self-supporting.

B. Qualifications
1. Several years' experience in teaching, preferably with a background in the teaching of reading on the elementary level.
2. Knowledge of and previous relationships with school-related personnel and organizations.
3. Experience in counseling young people.
4. Previous experience in dealing with students and parents in geographic areas of deprivation.

VIII. *Interning Teachers*

The interning teachers, who were certified teachers seeking nine quarter-hours of graduate credit for certificate renewal or credit toward the master's degree, were responsible for promoting the reading abilities of children in their care and in fostering their own professional growth. Each interning teacher was expected to cooperate with the staff teacher in making plans for each day's lesson, including selection and presentation of all materials based on the needs of the individual children within the group assigned to her. Each interning teacher was expected to diagnose the needs of each child under the direction of the staff teacher and feel free to call on the staff member for help if a need arose. Each interning teacher was responsible for referring children to the counselor or clinician. It was strongly emphasized throughout the summer session that all teachers were expected to develop a classroom atmosphere conducive to good learning and to insuring a child's success by allowing him to see the progress of his efforts. Furthermore, each interning teacher was directed to use the professional growth period and the enrichment period wisely. Each intern was required to become proficient in the use of individual testing devices, especially the Keystone Telebinocular Visual Screening machine. Not only were the interning teachers to follow the directions set forth by the staff members and professional consultants but they were encouraged to explore ways for effective new methods of teaching. It was mandatory that each interning teacher attend the seminars and stimulate personal growth through study and extensive professional reading in order to become better teachers in their given areas the following year. Plans were also made to encourage and allow each teacher to explore ways for effective reporting to parents in conferences and written reports.

Operation of the program

For the duration of the six weeks, each staff teacher was assigned approximately six interning teachers. At each of the two daily periods, which were one hour and forty-five minutes in length, a teaching team worked with the children. Only one half of the interns taught at one time. During the first period while one half

of the interns was teaching, the other half was planning for the next day's lesson or participating in the professional growth or enrichment period. If a child was in need of individual attention, a teacher was taken from the studying group to work in the capacity desired by the staff teacher or clinician. In this manner, individual differences were provided for without harming the routine of the other children who had been assigned to the group according to the original tests. Approximately twenty students were assigned to the staff teachers during each time period. The total program saw fifty teachers involved in a period instruction with their respective staff teachers and pupils, while the other fifty were involved in self-improvement, guided study, research, and planning. All work by the interns was supervised by the staff members whose roles were explained earlier.

The techniques and materials used in the summer program were not duplications of materials in the regular classrooms. The intent was to introduce the interning teachers to new ideas and to allow them to share ideas which had proved effective. The transfer of these ideas, it was hoped, would enable the teachers to individualize their classrooms the following year and share their experiences with fellow teachers. Pre- and post-testing and continuous diagnosis of pupils were a must for this program and were constantly emphasized.

Daily schedule

A daily schedule was designed to aid in the fulfillment of responsibilities of each participant.

7:30	Staff reports
7:45	Interning teachers report
8:00- 9:45	First period of instruction
	A. One-half interns teaching
	B. One-half interns planning
9:45-10:15	Break
10:15-12:00	Second period of instruction
	A. One-half interns teaching
	B. One-half interns planning
12:00-12:30	Lunch and planning
12:30- 1:30	Supervised planning period with staff

1:30- 2:30   Seminar by director or con-
                sultants
2:30   Interns dismissed
3:00   Staff dismissed

Purposes of the program

The two major purposes of this program were 1) to help children with problems in reading or who desired to increase their reading ability and 2) to develop an in-service program for teachers who wished to improve and sophisticate their techniques of reading instruction and/or who wished to earn nine quarter-hours (six semester hours) of graduate credit. With the advent of Federal funds, the program no longer was forced to cater only to those students whose families could afford the tuition. Three hundred of the six hundred enrolled students were in attendance due to Federal funds. Tuition for a portion of the interning teachers was financed by the Federal agency. These teachers were volunteers from schools in deprived areas and were to return to the schools in the capacity of consultants to share the knowledge and ideas which were gained in the summer school.

The summer program was designed to benefit the 600 elementary students by developing 1) better attitudes toward reading, 2) efficient reading skills, 3) increased self-motivation through successful experiences, 4) an awareness of the value of reading as a tool, and 5) insight into personal reading problems and exploration of methods to overcome specific content area difficulties.

Although the benefits for the students were a main concern, it is felt that when one hundred teachers are trained in a practical approach to reading in a classroom atmosphere, the learned skills, if practiced, have an immeasurable impact on future instruction. It was the responsibility of each staff member of the program to aid the interning teachers in developing 1) a deeper understanding of individual needs and differences, 2) a better knowledge of reading skills and effective methods for teaching the skills, 3) a knowledge of diversified materials which could aid an individual or group in reading, 4) a knowledge of diagnostic tools applicable to classroom use, 5) an understanding of flexible grouping techniques to gear instruction in specific skills where it is needed most in a group of children, 6) a complete knowledge of word attack skills and proper methods of teaching them according to the school system's curriculum, 7) a complete knowledge of phonetic elements and the relationship of phonics to other word attack skills, and 8) a more effective method of counseling with and reporting to parents.

A public school system needs teachers who understand the reading curriculum used in that system. The system's program must be uniform and operate under specific guidelines if there is to be success. This qualification does not mean that newer methods of reading instruction cannot be under experimentation but the total program must be under the control of the administration and understood by the teachers within the system. The larger a school system becomes, the greater the responsibility of the classroom teacher to adhere to the curriculum designed by the administration. In-service training to insure that teachers understand the policies set forth is an excellent method of communicating these ideas. By developing summer programs specifically to meet the needs of the school system, the system is rewarded by having more resource personnel in the school system who understand the program. These same teachers are much better prepared to understand reading at many levels rather than at one or two levels with which they formerly were familiar. Training fifty teachers each year in a summer program slowly develops a strong core of personnel who can more effectively fulfill the needs of the school system.

Summary

A summer reading program as outlined in this report is no better than the personnel who plan it. It is no more dynamic than the enthusiasm of those who are in charge of its success. If a program is small, a more personal relationship of staff members to interning teachers is possible. A program with over fifty interning teachers has a tendency to lose its personality and offers less in the way of individual help to the interning teachers.

Too many administrative personnel with varying philosophies as to the correct approach to teaching reading can harm a program. Overemphasis on testing and not enough on teaching can cause serious problems in the teaching of the needed skills to the students. Too many academic and menial tasks required of the interning teachers may cause discontent. Care must be taken to waste no time which could cause the program to fall short of its goals. Steps must be taken to outline the goals of such a program, and methods should be developed to achieve success. Roles must be established and adhered to in order that each person feels comfortable in the position to which he is assigned. Each school system developing a program must pursue the design in such a way as to integrate its curriculum with the program in order for the gained knowledge to be useful. Interning teachers have no time for idealistic theory which can not be put into practice. An experience in reading for teachers and students should benefit teachers and students. Put their needs first and the experience will be rewarding.

(Additional information concerning the Charlotte-Mecklenburg Summer Reading Program may be obtained by writing James Suber, Director of Elementary Language Arts, Charlotte-Mecklenburg Schools, Charlotte, North Carolina.)

A Workshop Approach to Reading Problems

Sister Mary Edward, P.B.V.M.
Clarke College

THE FIRST STEP in beginning most worthwhile educational endeavors is the discovery of a need. Such a discovery was the beginning of the Clarke College NDEA Institute in Reading.

The summer of 1965 found the faculty at Clarke College greatly concerned about the educational development of elementary school children. A study of test data revealed that many children were not achieving according to their potential. This fact was especially true in reading, yet reading is the backbone of the whole elementary structure. Why did this situation exist? What did the education of reading teachers, or the lack of it, contribute to this problem?

Study

To discover answers to this question, Clarke College conducted a study in July 1965. Data were collected from a sample of 215 qualified elementary school teachers from 19 states and 77 cities. From this study the following facts emerged.

One hundred and four of the 215 teachers in the survey had never had a formal reading course. One hundred had had one, and only eleven had two or more. Of the 111 teachers in the study who had one or more courses in reading, 69 of them had no refresher courses in the past 10 to 25 years. Yet, 202 of the 215 teachers questioned taught reading in the elementary school.

Out of ten approaches to reading being used in various places, at the present time, 60 of the 215 teachers in the survey felt able to evaluate two; approximately 55 could evaluate three, and less than 18 were familiar enough with four or more of the methods to attempt any kind of evaluation.

Out of the ten rather widely advertised mechanical aids to reading, such as the pacer and the tachistoscope, very few felt sufficiently informed to comment regarding their functional value. The most popular device in the survey, the controlled reader, was familiar to 75 teachers. The film projector as an adjunct to reading instruction was familiar to only 63, and the number familiar with the Craig

Reader and the Language Master was 7 and 4, respectively.

From this study only one general conclusion could be drawn by a liberal arts institution devoted to teacher education: In-service education of elementary teachers of reading was imperative. The Clarke College NDEA Institute in reading was planned to fulfill the needs identified in this study.

Program

The findings of our study posed a great challenge. Participants in our institute would be classroom teachers of reading who had antiquated or inadequate formal training. How could they learn new theory, techniques, and materials and actually be convinced that these could be instruments for more effective learning in their classrooms?

Our plan of attack was threefold. We would attempt 1) to create a desire for change in the participants, 2) to give them facility in using the tools capable of bringing about change, and 3) provide them with the opportunity to experience change in themselves and in the children in their classrooms.

The key would be involvement—involvement in theory, practice, and materials. From the first day of the institute we would try to stimulate the participants to raise questions, search for answers, exchange ideas, observe suitable models, demonstrate proper techniques, create new materials, and apply skills in classroom situations.

Theory

How we used this functional approach can be illustrated best by pursuing one of the early problems the participants identified, "What is word recognition?" To answer this question we turned the participants loose in the curriculum library in teams of two or three. They were to make a comparative study of the word recognition programs in two recently published basal reading series of their choice. They were to discover the kinds of word recognition skills to be taught to children, the point at which the teaching of each skill was introduced and terminated, the teaching techniques used for introducing them, and the degree of continuity or lack of it in the development of each skill. Then the participants were to compare likenesses and differences between their two series.

Promptly, the participants began to dig; and, just as promptly, they began to see themselves in their antiquated and uninformed ways. Discussions were lively, humorous, open, and soul-searching. They quickly learned the meaning and role of sight words, context clues, phonetics, and structural analysis as means to word recognition. They experienced the sequential development of skills—or lack of it—in each basal series. They learned inductive and deductive methods of teaching word recognition. They also began to ask questions about why reading texts were designed as they were.

At this point, we guided participants into the professional reading books authored by the same men as the two series they had studied. Here they searched out the theoretical model the major author had used in writing the children's texts and identified the author's philosophy of word recognition.

Now the participants began to wonder how word recognition should be taught. They sought books and articles by the major authorities and tried to discover what part of each theory was based on opinion and what part was based on scientific research; their findings were interesting and disconcerting.

As an attempt to order the information gleaned from this experience, each participant worked out a blueprint for his own philosophy of word recognition. What was his definition of word recognition? What skills were involved? When should they be taught? In what sequence? What role did they play in the total reading act?

The culminating activity to our study of word recognition was a study of formal and informal instruments available to help discover gaps in children's backgrounds and to identify specific needs. Also studied in an informal period each afternoon were most of the mechanical aids, skill-building "boxes," workbooks, and games available for building these skills.

By the time the study of word recognition had been completed, so many questions had arisen concerning comprehension that the participants immediately began to pursue its study in the same manner. However, as an introduction to comprehension, questioning was studied in relation to its control of the expressive thought patterns and skills development of children. Emphasis was given to questions eliciting literal, interpretive, critical, or creative answers. The questions offered in the teachers' manuals were identified and evaluated from these four viewpoints.

Topics studied throughout the summer in addition to those mentioned previously were What are study skills? What is critical reading? What is creative reading? What is rate of comprehension? What are the language arts? and What is reading readiness? Each was probed in varying degrees of depth, but all were approached on theoretical and practical levels. We began each new venture with a question, searched out the answers as they were given in reading materials produced for children, studied the theoretical models used by reading authorities, evaluated their validity or lack of it according to scientific research, became acquainted with instruments available for assessing children's needs, and then produced statements delineating each participant's philosophy. Throughout all of the discussions there was constant interaction of staff with participants and participants with participants.

Lecturers

At appropriate times during the summer, four guest lecturers highlighted particular areas which the participants were studying. Dolores Durkin, drawing from the riches of her own research on children who read before they come to school, addressed herself to readiness for reading. H. Alan Robinson discussed reading study skills and impressed the participants with the fact that reading is not a separate subject to be taught at a particular time and a particular place but is a process which must permeate each subject in the total curriculum. A. Sterl Artley stressed the importance of developing critical reading at all grade levels and illustrated this by working through a directed reading lesson on critical reading. Bill Martin demonstrated a literature approach to reading, showing the relationship that exists between language patterns and reading. He delighted everyone with his own ability to tell stories and involve his listeners in the telling. Each speaker's ability to communicate with the participants and his willingness to discuss p r o b l e m s met by classroom teachers in the teaching of reading added depth and purpose to the accomplishments of the institute.

While our in-depth study of the fundamentals of reading was in progress, we also examined current theories and approaches to reading and evaluated them in the light of available research. Each committee of four or five participants chose the approach it preferred and presented it to the group in some creative way. Each presentation portrayed what the approached was—the theoretical model on which it was based, the materials used in it, its advantages and disadvantages as an approach to the teaching of reading, and an evaluation according to available research. Approaches studied included basal reading, individualized reading, language experience, i.t.a. programed reading, phonic, responsive environment, linguistic, neurological, and film.

It was during the discussions of our current approaches to reading that the real growth of the participants became evident. Initially they were concerned with trivia and superficialities. As the summer progressed, unimportant issues were glossed over and basic essentials became the heart of their concern.

Practicum

If changes in the participants' teaching behavior were to become a reality, they needed to experience change in themselves while teaching reading to children in their classrooms. The practicum was planned to provide such an opportunity.

The practicum involved seven classrooms, grades one through seven, with fifteen to twenty children in each classroom. The pupils of grades one, three, five, and seven were children of average reading ability. Those in grades two, four, and six were superior children. The master teachers, as well as the students, were from the Dubuque public and nonpublic schools. The principal of the school acted as coordinator.

Six participants worked daily in each classroom. Three of the six did team teaching and were responsible for activities in developmental reading. The other team of three guided reading activities in content areas. Midway through the institute the two teams exchanged tasks so those who had been engaged in developmental reading activities in the content areas and vice versa. Experiences in both developmental reading and reading in the content areas were provided for each participant.

During the first week of the institute, each participant chose his own grade level for the practicum. Practicum work did not begin for the participants until Friday of the first week, so they could get some depth in theory and become acquainted with new materials before moving into the practical aspects of the institute. This schedule also enabled the master teachers to become better acquainted with the children. Variations in the program occurred each Friday when the participants observed classes on some grade level other than the one in which they were teaching.

The practicum was organized to achieve three main goals. The first was to develop skill in the diagnostic teaching of reading to children in group situations. We worked with the participants to help them discover the reading needs of their children, select reading activities and materials appropriate for the fulfillment of these needs, and then evaluate their success or lack of it with objective evidence from the children's behavior.

A second major objective of the practicum was to provide the participants with experience in the sequential development of comprehension abilities and reading study skills within their own class and within the school. This was our motive for arranging observation each Friday in classrooms on a grade level different from that in which participants were teaching.

The use of a variety of techniques and materials with different kinds of learners was the third objective. To this end we had chosen superior students for some classes and average students for others.

During the institute the participants questioned, at times, the value of being so involved in classroom teaching. They felt that they would rather have more demonstrations by the master teachers and less teaching by themselves. In view of this, it was interesting to read their "in retrospect" evaluations made last December. The practicum took first place as a causative factor in change of their teaching behavior. One of the participants wrote: "I feel I must name the practicum as the most beneficial aspect of the institute. This is odd because, at the time of the institute, I felt this part to be the least valuable. However, in retrospect, the opportunity to view and use the various methods and materials in a classroom situation and to see student reaction to them has proven invaluable in evaluating their worth to my own situation."

Materials

In addition to classes, discussions, and teaching in the elementary school, the participants spent one period each afternoon examining the newer reading materials, checking out mechanical devices and evaluating their worth, making tapes and transparencies for use in their classrooms, launching creative projects, and conferring with the staff. Frequently the one period designated on the schedule was voluntarily extended to include others. This accommodation was especially true as the institute passed the midmark and participants became concerned that they might miss available opportunities.

Evaluation

Our institute had witnessed a great expenditure of human energy. The big question that remained to be answered was "Did the Institute accomplish what we hoped it would?"

The participants were asked to evaluate their experiences at the termination of the institute and again this past December. One of the most revealing questions asked was, "In retrospect, what was the most significant thing that happened to you during the Clarke Institute?" The following responses are typical of those received:

My idea of what reading is happens to have gotten completely changed.

What made the institute significant for me and far superior to all undergraduate and graduate work previously was the advantage of a lab school for practical purposes. This was extremely helpful.

Perhaps it was the opportunity for me to acquire knowledge about the basics of reading and learning in order to apply them effectively and give me some assurance and confidence to help others.

I have been of the opinion that most of our problems in education today (discipline, dropouts) are a result of children's not being able to read. It was most rewarding and inspiring to meet educators from all over the United States who were in earnest to do something about it.

It was good to be part of a professional group so keenly interested in going forward! The sum total of our courses left an influence that enriches a teacher in such a way that all aspects of her work should show improvement.

I gained confidence in my own ability to teach. The warmth, enthusiasm, and dedication of my fellow participants and the faculty helped me to "become" as no other single experience in my life. Because of this newly gained self-security, I now find myself able to give much more than ever before to my stu-

dents and my fellow teachers, not only in reading but in love and understanding.

This terminates my report on our attempt to upgrade our elementary teachers of reading through an NDEA Institute. William Gray once said that a teacher of reading should know the field of reading as thoroughly as any highly competent content teacher knows the field that he teaches. We did not achieve this ideal, but we did start our journey toward it.

The Illinois State-Wide Curriculum Study Center in the Preparation of Secondary School English Teachers

PAUL H. JACOBS
University of Illinois

THE ILLINOIS STATEWIDE Curriculum Study Center in the Preparation of Secondary School English Teachers is the only Project English Curriculum Study Center devoting itself to the preparation of curricula for *teachers* of English. It is a five-year cooperative research project involving twenty colleges and universities, all of which are in Illinois. "ISCPET," as it is called by those who are personally engaged in its activities, is jointly supported by a contract with the United States Office of Education and by local institutional funds. It officially got under way August 1, 1964.

Nature of the institutions

The twenty ISCPET colleges and universities vary a great deal in terms of their size, the source of their support, their location, and the scope of their academic programs. They include over half of the Illinois institutions that prepare teachers of English, and together they graduate about six percent of the nation's English teachers each year. Last year while one institution graduated approximately one hundred and sixty English teachers, another graduated only eight. Some are liberal arts colleges, either church-related or independent; some are universities, either privately supported or state supported. About half are in or near Chicago; about half are located in towns or small cities scattered about the rest of the state. While some offer only four-year undergraduate programs, others also offer master's degree work, and still others also offer doctoral programs in English or education or both.

Organizational structure

In every sense of the word, the Illinois center is a "cooperative" research endeavor. With its headquarters located at the University of Illinois in Urbana, ISCPET began under the general direction of J. N. Hook, director, and William H. Evans, associate director, with the author serving as the full-time research associate. Last summer, when Evans accepted a position at another university, the author became the associate director, and Raymond D. Crisp was employed as the research associate.

Contrary to what an outsider might think, the headquarters staff does not direct the work of ISCPET. Each of the twenty cooperating institutions has designated two professors, one each from the English and educational departments, as its official ISCPET representatives. It is these forty people, meeting together in extended sessions at least twice each year, who direct the countless activities of ISCPET. And surprising as this may be to some educators, they have proved that they can work in almost perfect harmony.

To provide for more frequent assistance and guidance than the forty representatives meeting only two or three times per year can possibly give, ISCPET has an executive committee composed of two permanent members (Hook and the author) and three members who are elected by the forty representatives for staggered terms ranging from one to three years. Before ISCPET can subcontract with a cooperating institution wishing to conduct a special research study, this committee must approve the proposal for the study. In addition to this type

of responsibility, the committee decides on major policies and handles any problems that might arise.

Assisting the two official representatives on each ISCPET campus is an *ad hoc* committee composed of from five to twelve members who, in most instances, come from the English and education departments but who, on some campuses, come from other departments as well. Although they vary to some degree from campus to campus, the principal duties of the committee are as follows: to recommend curricular changes in the institution's program for preparing secondary English teachers and to help in implementing the changes and in evaluating the results; to assist the two official representatives in the planning and the conducting of special research studies; to consider the institution's policies for admitting students or prospective teachers of English and for retaining them in the program; and, if desirable, to recommend changes in screening and in policies for retention.

Lest ISCPET personnel become inclined to think of English teacher preparation only in relation to the situation in Illinois and as a constant source for expert advice and assistance, ISCPET has an advisory committee made up of twelve nationally recognized educators, including at least one expert in every area of the preparation of English teachers from across the nation. The areas of specialization represented on the committee are linguistics, speech, literature, reading, junior high school English, senior high school English, national developments in the teaching of high school English, programs pertaining to all prospective teachers, programs pertaining to prospective teachers of English only, structure and articulation of courses, English teacher certification, and research design and evaluation.

ISCPET's raison d'être

Although at least eight national events, which occurred in the six-year period just prior to 1964, were influential in stimulating the creation of

ISCPET, here I will mention only two: the publishing in 1961 of *The National Interest and the Teaching of English (1)* and the publishing in 1964 of *The National Interest and the Continuing Education of Teachers of English (2)*. These unpretentious little volumes, which were prepared by a special committee of the National Council of Teachers of English, unveiled to the public for the first time a true picture of the sad state of affairs in English teaching and English teacher preparation across the nation. First, consider these findings reported in the first volume:

> Only a fourth of the nation's colleges require a course in the English language. Only 17.4 percent of the colleges require a course in Modern English Grammar. Fewer than 200 institutions are graduating teachers of English informed about modern language study. Only 41 percent of the colleges require prospective teachers of English to complete a course in advanced composition. Only 51.5 percent of the colleges require prospective teachers to complete a course in methods of teaching English. (p. 60)
>
> Only one-third [of the colleges] require work in world literature. Only one-fifth of the programs specify the need for a course in contemporary literature or in literary criticism or critical analysis. Few institutions provide for the study of the literature written for adolescents. (p. 75)

Now consider these findings from the second volume:

> Today, only half (51.9 percent) of the secondary teachers consider themselves well prepared to teach literature; slightly more than one-third (36.6 percent), to teach composition; slightly more than half (53.5 percent), to teach the English language. Fewer than one-third (32.7) feel well prepared to teach oral skills, and only one-tenth, to teach reading at the secondary level. Nevertheless, among the more experienced teachers, as many as 32.3 percent reported not taking a college English course since certification or not taking one for ten years. In his more than nine years of experience, the average secondary teacher of English has completed only 0.4 semester hours in composition and 0.7 semester hours in language. (pp. 5 & 6)

Finally, let us turn to another excerpt from the first *National Interest* volume.

> If the teaching of English is to be improved throughout the country, bold and immediate action must be undertaken on a national scale. This report on the status of English teaching indicates that assistance is urgently needed to achieve seven important goals:
>
> 1. To focus instruction in English upon the study of language, literature, and composition.
> 2. To educate teachers of English to the developmental and sequential nature of the study and to institute a national program for encouraging articulation of English studies throughout the school years.
> 3. To improve present preparatory programs for teachers of English.
> 4. To improve the preparation of practicing teachers of English.
> 5. To improve the services and supplies available to teachers of English.
> 6. To encourage significant research about the teaching of English.
> 7. To recruit and prepare *more* teachers of English. (p. 3)

Although ISCPET, as you will later see, is concerned to some extent with all of these seven goals, it is directing the greater part of its energies toward the first, second, third, fourth, and especially the third.

So much for the developments and events that provoked the birth of ISCPET! So much for ISCPET's *raison d'être!*

Objectives

Of natural and close relationship to its *raison d'être* are ISCPET's objectives. In brief, the problem faced by ISCPET is this: How can a college or university, regardless of its inherent or acquired characteristics, modify its program for preparing secondary school English teachers to bring that program closer to an "ideal," phrased in terms of common elements in the curriculum and in terms of desirable competencies in prospective teachers? Our center is going beyond the recommendations of *The National Interest and the Teaching of English* and other publications that present theory, in that we are searching constantly for application of *valid* theories.

We are making use of a study group of scholars and outstanding teachers to develop an "ideal" plan for teacher preparation and are considering carefully recommendations such as the ones in the NCTE's *The Education of Teachers of English for Schools and Colleges* (3). But we are taking two important *next* steps: 1) the implementation of a number of those recommendations through experimenting to discover how they may be put into effect in diverse institutions and 2) the measurement of the changes that result from following such recommendations.

Because the present English programs of our cooperating institutions vary so greatly, it is impossible for us to state in detail the curricular revisions that are being effected in each institution. We do not anticipate that a single, uniform program will be the outcome. Rather, we expect to develop several improved programs, with an agreed-upon commonality of content and emphasis but also with divergencies made necessary by institutional restrictions or made desirable by peculiar institutional strengths.

Basically, we are searching for answers to such questions as these:

a. What competencies are necessary and what additional ones are desirable in a teacher of English? What varieties of preparation are effective in producing these competencies? What preparation common to these varieties constitutes the ideal core of English teacher preparation?

b. What is the nearest approach to the ideal that can be made in a four-year undergraduate program? What permissible changes in present requirements would be necessary in each participating institution in order to approach the ideal as nearly as possible? How and when can these changes be effected? What changes in certification requirements would be necessary and desirable for approaching the ideal? How can we lead the

way toward improved certification requirements rather than remain subservient to existing ones?

c. What constitutes the strongest possible preparation for an English *minor* who may be required to teach English?

d. What constitutes the best program for a fifth year for 1) a person with an undergraduate major in English who has not taken courses requisite for a teaching certificate, 2) a person with an undergraduate major in English who already is certified to teach the subject, 3) a certified teacher who has only a minor in the subject, 4) a certified teacher with an English major but too poor an academic record for admission to graduate courses in English?

e. In what ways might a coordinated five-year program, or a two-plus-three arrangement, be preferable to a four-plus-one program? What differences might and should be involved? If Illinois (and other states now requiring only four years of preparation) moves eventually toward a five-year requirement for secondary teachers, what pattern of preparation will serve best?

f. What principles can be established for the most helpful supplementary preparation (refresher courses not leading to an advanced degree) for 1) the experienced secondary teacher who has been long absent from the college classroom and 2) the once-prepared teacher who has had no recent teaching experience?

g. What constitutes the best preparation for a doctorate in the teaching of English, intended to prepare persons for 1) working on the college level with students planning to teach secondary English or 2) serving as heads of secondary English departments or as supervisors of secondary English?

h. What are the best answers now determinable to a number of specific questions concerning the program for educating a teacher of English? Representative questions are the following:

—What preparation in literature is of particular value to prospective English teachers?

—What study of the English language best equips a teacher for a secondary English classroom?

—What training in rhetoric and c o m p o s i t i o n is especially needed?

—What audio-visual aids are particularly helpful in preparing an English teacher?

—What are the most relevant findings of educational psychology, especially about the learning process and about language learning?

—What sequence of courses in education best equips a prospective teacher to cope with the problems he will face in the classroom from day to day?

But, after setting tasks and objectives so ambitious as the foregoing, what has ISCPET actually accomplished in the first thirty-three months of its existence? I have already given you a partial answer to this question. Now let me try to complete it.

Accomplishments thus far

Throughout my remarks I have referred to the vast scope of ISCPET, not only in terms of its tasks and objectives but also in terms of its personnel. You will recall that it involves from eight to twelve persons on each of twenty different campuses with a total, roughly speaking, of 160-240 personnel. Yet, all of these people are working together with success and harmony. If we considered nothing but the differences in academic backgrounds of this number of people, I believe that all of us would agree that

ISCPET's accomplishment in this area alone is worthy of study and consideration. ISCPET's organizational structure, its first major accomplishment, could well serve as a model for other groups of institutions and agencies desiring to join hands to research mutual interests and problems.

During the fall of 1964, ISCPET representatives met in Chicago for several days and, with the guidance and assistance of the advisory committee, of English teachers, department heads, consultants, administrators, and of Illinois authorities on certification, agreed upon a list of competencies that any English teacher should possess. Although at times we seriously wondered whether we would ever get a consensus on certain of the competencies, we eventually did, and we called the list "Qualifications of Secondary School Teachers of English: A Preliminary Statement" (4). This four-page publication, our second major accomplishment, should not be considered "final" in any sense of the word. Revisions, perhaps even major ones, will be made to it in early 1969. In the meantime, thousands of free copies of the statement are being mailed to educators around the country, with the request that they send us their reactions to it.

Curricular revisions constitute the third major ISCPET accomplishment. Without exception, every institution has made some changes (most have made many) in both the academic and professional components of its program for training prospective English teachers. Let me cite a few examples. For its students who wish to major in literature, one institution has designed a special minor in rhetoric. This same institution is also revamping its program for candidates for the degree of Master of Arts in the teaching of English. Another institution has recently added a special course in the methods of teaching composition only. For the majority of its students, still another institution is abandoning freshman composition as a course; moreover, this same institution is completely overhauling the remainder of its program for training English teachers. A fourth institution recently reported seventeen major program changes, most of which deal with its offerings in literature, which will go into effect next fall. Almost all of our institutions now require courses in advanced composition, modern English grammar, and history of the English language. Although these are no more than representative examples, they do show the type and extent of curricular revisions now being made or implemented at ISCPET institutions.

ISCPET's fourth major accomplishment is in the area of evaluation and measurement. From the very beginning of our planning, we were aware that we would have to have a test for use in all of our participating institutions, beginning before any substantial changes in our then existing programs could be effected and repeated annually thereafter throughout the life of ISCPET. Consequently, at an early meeting of the institutional representatives, we considered the need and selected the new edition of the English Language and Literature Test of the NTE Battery, which is administered to all prospective English teachers during their senior year. The purpose in using this test the first year was to establish a norm or base line for each institution with which the scores of graduates in subsequent years of ISCPET can be compared in order to see what changes occur. Presumably, these changes will be largely attributable to curricular revision, and perhaps to policy changes, since the type and caliber of students within an institution are not changing markedly during the ISCPET years. Annual repetition of the test should reveal any statistically observable differences between pre-ISCPET and intra-ISCPET graduating seniors. No comparison of institutions is being made; each institution is competing only against itself. However, a cumulation of test scores is being maintained at ISCPET headquarters, and state-wide norms are being established. Thus, each institu-

tion is able to determine the position of its graduates on the scale.

Another type of measurement and evaluation device now being used by all our institutions is a set of six rating scales consisting of criteria based directly on the competencies listed in the ISCPET qualifications statement and, for the most part, on the ones in the "good" column. They are designed for use as follows: Form A, by the student teacher, to evaluate himself at the end of student teaching; Form B, by the "cooperating" teacher, to evaluate the student teacher at the end of student teaching; Form C, by the college or university supervisor, to evaluate the student teacher at the end of student teaching; Form D, by the graduate, to evaluate himself at the end of his first year of teaching; Form E, by a school administrator, to evaluate the graduate at the end of the first year of teaching; and Form F, by the chairman of the English department, to evaluate the graduate at the end of the first year of teaching. Thus, by the time he reaches the close of his first year as a full-time teacher of secondary English, each ISCPET graduate will have been evaluated six times—twice by himself, thrice by supervisory personnel, and once by an administrator—on essentially the same criteria. Data coming from this series of evaluations on each of our graduates should yield some extremely telling and valuable conclusions pertaining to curricular changes at our institutions.

Earlier, I referred to the special research studies for which the ISCPET headquarters office subcontracts with its cooperating institutions. Together these studies are considered ISCPET's fifth major accomplishment. From them will come our chief contributions to research. So far, there are twenty-eight studies under way at one stage or another. While some are short-term studies and are at or near the point of completion, others are long term and will not be completed until very near the termination date of our contract. Even at this date, proposals for additional studies are being drafted, a fact that leads us to predict a grand total of approximately thirty-five special research studies for our project.

Variety seems to be the predominant characteristic of ISCPET's special studies. Some of the studies are relatively simple, involving no more than a questionnaire or a status survey, together with tabulation and analysis of the data and interpretation of the findings. At the same time, however, others of the studies are quite sophisticated and require comparative or other measurements to assure validity.

There is a great deal of variety to be found even in the studies utilizing surveys. Some of these studies are collecting data from selected ISCPET institutions; others are collecting from all of our institutions; still others are soliciting data from hundreds of colleges and universities in every region of the country. While the survey is the major step of some special studies, it is only the initial step of several studies, with the subsequent steps being determined by the findings drawn from the data collected in the first step.

In case I have overemphasized the survey method of research, let me assure you that by no means do all ISCPET studies involve this approach. At the same time, however, I should empasize that all of our researchers must of necessity begin with close study and examination of all published research findings pertinent to the problems they have identified to research.

All of the special studies are designed and coordinated so that most components of the "ideal" program for preparing prospective secondary English teachers, as set forth in our qualifications statement, are being or will be explored. Of the already-approved studies, one involves reading; four involve literature; four, composition; five, language; two, oral communication; five, various aspects of methodology for prospective teachers; three, various aspects of methodology for in-service teachers; two, testing; one involves MATE programs; one, supervi-

sion of student teaching in English; and two involve fact-finding surveys of the present status of English programs in grades 7 through 12 of Illinois schools. (Persons interested in obtaining details of the studies should write to the ISCPET office at the University of Illinois.)

In addition to their standard final reports, many of the directors of our studies are preparing instructional materials that may be used by any interested college or university. The form of these materials, also, is characterized by variety. For example, some materials will be filmed and some, taped; most, however, will be prepared as syllabi for courses.

ISCPET's twenty institutions provide an ideal testing ground for programs in teacher education, for they represent a true cross-section of the nation's colleges and universities, and their graduates are employed in all of the fifty states. Whatever can be made to work in these institutions will almost assuredly work elsewhere. Therefore, for this reason and with the approval of the U. S. Office of Education, ISCPET is submitting to the office the final reports on its individual special studies at the very time they are completed rather than holding them until the overall ISCPET final report has been prepared. By doing this, we hope to make available all useful data at the earliest feasible time to all interested colleges, universities, organizations, and individuals throughout the nation, so that they may employ, as they see fit, those findings and recommendations pertinent to their needs. Thus the results of ISCEPT's endeavors will be given immediate national applicability.

REFERENCES

1. Committee on National Interest. *The National Interest and the Teaching of English.* Champaign, Illinois: National Council of Teachers of English, 1961.
2. Committee on National Interest. *The National Interest and the Continuing Education of Teachers of English.* Champaign, Illinois: National Council of Teachers of English, 1964.

3. Commission on the English Curriculum of the NCTE. *The Education of Teachers of English for Schools and Colleges.* New York: Appleton-Century-Crofts, 1963.
4. ISCPET. "Qualifications of Secondary School Teachers of English: A Preliminary Statement," *College English,* 27, November 1965.

Preparing for College Teaching

SAMUEL WEINTRAUB
University of Chicago

TEACHERS OF TEACHERS ought to be skillful at one thing more than any other: they should be excellent teachers. Unfortunately, this is not always the case. Methods courses often suffer from poor instruction as well as from lack of content.

Perhaps because of poor instruction, or possibly that factor along with others, u n d e r g r a d u a t e and graduate courses in reading methods do not appear to be so important in influencing beliefs regarding the teaching of reading as are the reading series used or the student teaching experience (*3*). Surveys of reading instruction in the United States point up the fact that the job of teaching today's children is not being particularly well done (*2*). Recent findings from the U.S. Office of Education Cooperative First-Grade Studies showed more clearly than ever the crucial role of the classroom teacher in influencing achievement in reading (*4*). Other studies clearly demonstrate that many classroom teachers are not well prepared to teach some of the most basic reading understandings and skills to children (*1, 5, 6*). When these three facts are considered together—the mediocre instruction in classrooms, the crucial role of the classroom teacher in improving reading skills, and the lack of knowledge of basic reading skills on the part of the classroom teacher—the urgent need for better preparation of teachers becomes apparent.

In addition to teacher preparation, other problems confront us as we try to upgrade reading instruction. There are problems in selecting students for entrance into the field of education. Other problems are due to the lack of constructive supervision of the profession once an individual has completed basic educational requirements and has been hired by a school system. Still other problems are created by the rapid turnover of teachers, the mobility of the teaching profession in general, and the inability to attract more men into teaching—particularly into teaching in the elementary schools. While these concerns call for constructive action, they are not the subject of this paper, which has as its focus the preparation of college instructors of reading methods courses.

The poverty of ideas and lack of originality as well as the questionable usefulness of some methods courses stem perhaps from several sources. Most often when an individual receives his doctorate with specialization in reading, he has had few, if any, guided experiences in thinking through the goals and content of a methods course. In many instances where the new college teacher is called upon to teach methods courses in reading, he leans heavily upon one or more professional texts for an outline of the course or he may go back to notes from a course in reading taken during his graduate or undergraduate schooling. The notes he draws from may or may not be particularly good. They are simply all he has. If the original course happened to be well done, the new instructor is, at best, a carbon copy of his mentor. If the course did not happen to be well thought through and well taught, the new offering is often no better and may well be much worse.

In order to break this unhappy cycle, the reading faculty at the University of Chicago decided to take some steps toward preparing future college teachers with the hope of upgrading instruction in professional courses. The focus of the rest of this paper is upon the planning and execution of this new program and on other suggestions for preparing college instructors.

In its first year, the program consisted of two related segments: a seminar and a practicum. In the seminar, the major emphasis was on college age students in general and then noted characteristics of the specific students with whom they would be dealing. It was known, for example, that most of the enrollees would be art and music majors who needed education courses to fulfill their certification requirements. A general look at developmental characteristics of college age students gave insights into the student population which members might be teaching in undergraduate courses. The importance of looking at a specific population of students, their interests, and backgrounds was pointed up in discussions about probable enrollees. The method of building the curriculum for the reading course was based on the Tyler rationale with some modifications.*

Having identified characteristics of the general college age population and then of the specific students to be served, the next step was to consider behaviors and academic knowledge desired as outcomes of the course. The group first determined general outcomes and then specific goals for the population enrolled. Far from being merely a routine listing of desirable behaviors and knowledge, the working through and discussion of these goals, upon which all of us agreed, took considerable effort and thought. The selection of behavioral objectives was basic to all that followed in setting up the content of the course.

Once the characteristics of the population to be served had been considered and the goals decided upon, the seminar members turned their attention to the content of the course. They reviewed secondary reading textbooks, elementary texts, and the syllabi developed by other teachers of professional courses in reading and then made a comprehensive listing of all the topics that might possibly be included. At this point the relevancy of

---

* Tyler, Ralph W. *Basic Principles of Curriculum and Instruction.* Chicago: University of Chicago Press, 1950.

a topic for a professional course in reading, rather than its importance, was the deciding factor.

Next seminar members turned their attention to the time allotted to the course, considered the background and needs of their students, and made decisions as to which topics were irrelevant and which were the least and the most essential.

When the most essential topics were decided upon, the general content of each topic was discussed, and the emphasis to be placed upon the content given, the u n i q u e population was evolved. Because this was to be a team teaching situation, each seminar member then selected the areas of greatest interest to him. Each person prepared in detail the specific objectives of a section of the course and ascertained the best means for realizing the general and specific behavioral outcomes. It was his responsibility, too, to elaborate the content of the particular segment or segments for which he had assumed primary responsibility. When this task had been done, each member prepared a detailed outline for discussion and evaluation by other members of the seminar. Included in the outline were assignments, specific points to be covered, and method of presentation. What finally evolved, then, was a particularized outline of behavioral objectives and specific skills, content to be covered, instructional methods, and concomitant assignments.

Evaluation of the course was to be in several forms, including informal and formal student feedback and self-evaluation by seminar members. The content of the final examination was considered in terms of how it could best measure the attainment of the specific objectives of the course. It should be mentioned, too, that while this syllabus was planned with a specific course and a particular population in mind, alternative ways of achieving and measuring the same objectives were discussed in seminar. Thus, given a different student population and setting, several substitute plans were available for consideration.

As we progressed in determining goals, sessions with college teachers who were conducting reading methods courses were scheduled. These visits served at least two functions. First, students in the seminar tapped the thinking of others concerning aims, content, and method. Thus one instructor's thinking did not dominate the group. Second, there was rather dramatic realization of the varied paths taken by different individuals in developing and teaching such a course. Instructors were asked the questions: What parts of your course made you happiest? What would you like to change if you had the opportunity?

Along with the planning experiences just outlined and the practicum which followed, members were involved in ancillary learning experiences. For example, they assumed responsibility for parts of a graduate elementary reading methods course being conducted by the instructor of the seminar. These experiences were highly practical. First, they read, wrote comments, and evaluated written assignments handed in by course members. Criteria for evaluating papers had to be established. Using these criteria, seminar members each read several papers, made a tentative evaluation, and then brought the papers and their problems back to the seminar for additional deliberation. This procedure was followed as each assignment was turned in.

Second, each seminar participant was responsible for conducting one instructional session with a small group of those enrolled in the graduate course. In the class were several who were simultaneously having their first teaching experience and taking their first education course. The content of the graduate reading methods course did not meet the needs of these relatively unsophisticated individuals. They were, therefore, scheduled for small-group instruction for part of each class period and given more individualized attention. Each seminar member was responsible for planning and conducting one such session.

Plans for the session were discussed and criticized beforehand by seminar members. An evaluation session followed. Unsolicited comments from the students who attended indicated how valuable they felt the small group sessions had been.

Third, students in the seminar assumed responsibility as a group for one three-hour meeting of the graduate methods course. The topic under consideration was the valuation of innovations in primary reading programs. Following the presentation, the session was evaluated in a free discussion by all seminar participants.

Another activity of the seminar was the development of a general syllabus for an undergraduate elementary reading methods course. A procedure similar to that in developing the secondary course was followed. Differences in aims, emphasis, and content between secondary and elementary courses were considered. Differences between graduate and undergraduate courses were also noted.

Summary

This paper, then, summarizes one attempt to prepare college instructors of reading methods courses. The seminar itself was evaluated in a discussion in which all aspects were scrutinized. One of the points emphasized by seminar members was the importance of the practicum aspects of the experience. In their opinion, the immediacy of purpose made the seminar far more valuable in content. As a result of the evaluation session, there will be several different emphases when the seminar is offered again.

This paper has not stressed the fact that seminar members looked carefully at many different ways of organizing professional courses as well as at many and varied types of experiences to be given undergraduate and graduate students. These experiences were evaluated in the light of the most effective ways to attain a specific goal and the general objectives of a course. At all times the attempt was made to note and evaluate the many paths to the same ends.

The basic principles used in building the undergraduate secondary reading methods course described in this paper appear to be generally applicable. They are 1) identify the characteristics of the population to be served; 2) determine learning objectives and behavioral goals desired as outcomes of curriculum experiences; 3) build learning situations which attempt to attain the desired objectives for a specific population; and 4) evaluate to determine whether goals have been attained.

In this writer's estimation, it is of critical importance to prepare and prepare carefully tomorrow's teachers of teachers. If tomorrow's teachers of children are to be better than today's, then we in graduate schools must make a concerted effort to provide future teachers of children with better teachers themselves. If we want to develop competent readers in our population, then we must assume responsibility for preparing college instructors in such a way that they know better than we do how to select, prepare, and teach teachers and future teachers.

REFERENCES

1. Aaron, Ira E. "What Teachers and Prospective Teachers Know about Phonic Generalizations," *Journal of Educational Research,* 53 (May 1960), 323-330.
2. Austin, Mary C., and Coleman Morrison. *The First R: The Harvard Report on Reading in Elementary Schools.* New York: Macmillan Co., 1963.
3. Barton, Allen A., and David E. Wilder. "Research and Practice in the Teaching of Reading: A Progress Report," in Matthew B. Miles (Ed.), *Innovation in Education.* New York: Bureau of Publications, Teachers College, Columbia University, 1964, 361-398.
4. Chall, Jeanne, and Shirley Feldman. "First Grade Reading: An Analysis of the Interactions of Professed Methods, Teacher Implementation and Child Background," *The Reading Teacher,* 19 (May 1966), 569-575.
5. Emans, Robert. "Teacher Evaluations of Reading Skills and Individualized Reading," *Elementary English,* 42 (March 1965), 258-269. .
6. Spache, George D., and Mary E. Baggett. "What Do Teachers Know about Phonics and Syllabication?" *The Reading Teacher,* 19 (Nov. 1965), 96-99.

SPECIAL AREAS

PHILOSOPHY, SOCIOLOGY OF READING, AND TECHNOLOGY

Philosophical Aspects

HENRY P. SMITH
The University of Kansas

MY SPECIAL INTEREST over the past several years has been the *psychology* of reading with occasional ventures into reading's sociological determinants. In this paper, I was asked to discuss the *philosophy* of reading. This assignment has compelled me to consider with some care the possible distinctions between three disciplines—psychology, sociology, and philosophy—each of which contains data and theory of significant interest to teachers of reading.

Let me begin by suggesting how these three areas of knowledge contribute in their special ways to the teaching of reading.

Psychology is concerned with the nature of the individual and how and why he learns. Educational psychology interprets and extends psychological data and principles in an educational setting. In a very real sense a psychology of reading is an educational psychology directed to the tasks of learning to read and reading to learn.

Sociology focuses on the nature of social groups and the impact of a group on its members. Thus a sociology of reading uses the accumulated data and theory of sociology and educational sociology for its applications to the teaching of reading.

Philosophy assumes responsibility for defining the goals of human behavior and suggests methods for directing behavior toward those goals. In identifying the goals of education and in suggesting the educational methodology for reaching them, educational philosophy must be aware of the nature of the individual and the nature of the social order. It must be concerned with both society's need for each individual to make maximum contributions to the social order and the individual's need to receive optimal benefits from his society.

A philosophy of reading as a special segment of educational philosophy must consider the components of the reading act, the purposes of reading, and the educational techniques that promise greatest reader growth. It must have a proper regard for the nature of the individual and the impact of environment on human development. At the same time a philosophy of reading must consider the nature and demands of the current social order and, so far as possible, must attempt to predict changes that are likely to occur in the demands of that social order during the life span of the reader.

As we examine the purposes of reading, we recognize that today's society requires that each child shall be educated to a level far above the level required by the society of fifty or even twenty years ago. And we see that today's society is a rapidly changing society. In a changing society the development of high-level reading, listening, and thinking skills becomes crucial because change can quickly outmode school-taught basic facts and principles and make necessary the constant relearning of specific job skills and even professional knowledge long before a worker reaches the end of his years of greatest productivity. In other words, today's technological changes increasingly outdistance schoolroom education.

A total philosophy of reading must be concerned with many components of the reading act, the various purposes for reading, and with the techniques of effective reading instruction at all age levels. I believe that space limitations here can best be used for a focus in some detail on a special segment of the philosophy of reading—the reading act's dependence upon meaning and society's role in the provision of that meaning.

Although reading requires sensory reaction to graphic symbols, true reading is a perceptual act. Sensation is merely the trigger. Perception's ammunition is the perceiver's experiential background. Printed symbols have no innate power to convey meaning. They can do little more than evoke whatever stored meanings the perceiving individual already possesses. Thus understanding through reading requires a store of appropriate meanings that the reader himself previously has distilled from his experiences. Perception through reading is possible because these stored meanings tend to be associated with and to be evokable by words.

In the perceptual processes of both reading and listening, the meaning that can be evoked in the reader-listener is dependent on the wealth of prior experiences that have become identified with the word and word combinations that are used by the writer or speaker. In one reader-listener a word may evoke no experience, in another, no more than a single experience, whereas in still another, it may evoke the distilled essence of numerous experiences. Thus, when we consider the communicative power of words, the most important factor is the richness and similarity of the experiences underlying the words that are used by the communicators. And as we discuss the importance of meaningfulness, it is well to note that words not only are the tools of communication—words also are the tools of thinking. This recognition, that without appropriate prior experiences words are but barren symbols, compels us to be concerned with society's responsibility to provide each child with an environment rich in the experiences required for effective communication. Only by providing rich experiences for each child can society hope to gain maximum contributions from its members and each individual receive optimal benefits from society. The special stock of meanings that a child must possess if he is to be suc-

cessful in school is the heart of what we refer to as intelligence.

. Experiential background and intellectual ability are not separate and distinct traits. In fact, except for individual differences in the quality of the sense organs and in general physical soundness and health, experiential background may be the *sole determinant* of intellectual ability. And experiential background's impact is extended to the individual's motivation to achieve. The individual's interests, life goals, work habits, and his self-concept are products of his successes and failures during his environmentally delimited experiences. In short, I believe that environment is the casual factor in producing most, and possibly *all,* of the educationally important differences among the children who enter our classrooms.

Recently there has been increased emphasis on the fact that educational tests, particularly intelligence tests, reflect differences in experiential background. Because children in the crowded midcity areas and in culturally impoverished rural areas tend to make low scores, such tests have been called culturally unfair. Unfortunately, however, whenever tests fail to reflect the impact of cultural disadvantage, they fail at the same time to predict school success at any level, elementary through college, in our typical middle class schools. A search for culture-fair tests then, even though directed by high principles of fairness to children, adolescents, and adults of all cultures, may merely obstruct our view of the real problem. It seems likely that it is our educational system, particularly our failure to provide appropriate experience before the child enters school, that is culturally unfair, and our various tests of ability and achievement merely reveal that unfairness!

The typical school of today does a reasonably good job of educating the children of our middle and upper classes. Its hours and its curriculum have been planned for children of educated parents from homes equipped with library, play equipment, and study space and for children who have had special experiences such as summer travel and play experiences with children from middle class background who speak a middle class language Unfortunately, our schools are failing to meet the needs of vast numbers of those children who lack the home and community experiences of the typical middle class child.

To attack ignorance among culturally disadvantaged children and to help them acquire the meanings needed for success in reading and other areas of educational achievement, we must create an educational system that can be tailored to the specific needs of each child that it serves. To remove unfairness, we must recognize that maximal educational opportunity for all greatly requires unequal educational offerings.

Near the turn of the century no more than ten percent of our high school age youth were in school. At that time man's muscles furnished a major portion of the power required to produce his needed food, clothing, and housing. Society at that time did not require universal education beyond the lower grades.

Today man's muscle produces far less than one percent of the power required for meeting his needs. And in the United States more than 90 percent of all youth of ages 14 to 17 are in school. Our society certainly can afford to educate all youth through the high school years and greatly needs the higher-level work and citizenship skills that can result from this education. However, we must be disturbed by the fact that too many of these young persons fail to do well in school and merely serve their time there as they wait to reach the age at which they can legally leave.

If we are to provide each youth with an effective preparation for life, changes must be made and many of these changes must occur long before the high school years. In making these changes we must recognize that much more is needed than simply supplying

culturally disadvantaged children with middle class schools.

In providing equal opportunity nothing is more unequal than equal facilities. The school curriculum, materials, buildings, and teachers must be planned to fit specifically the experiential background and needs of the children who are to be educated. Probably we have done a reasonably good job in the planning of curriculum and in the training of teachers for those children who have lived since infancy in a middle class home and community background. What we must recognize is that when appropriate experiences are not provided by the home and the community, these experiences must be provided by the school. The age at which preschool and school experiences begin, the nature of such experiences, the length of his school day and week, and the months of his school year must be planned to suit the needs of the child. For the culturally disadvantaged child, school-planned experiences starting at age six or even at age five are almost certainly too late; and five hours a day, five days a week, and nine or even ten months a year are too little. And if we must offer him middle class teachers with middle class backgrounds and values—and presently we have little else to offer—somehow his teachers must be taught to know and value his culture, his language, and his needs. Better still, our efforts must be extended to recruit and train a multitude of teachers who grew up in his culture, who will live in his community, who will be identification symbols for him, and who will have a genuine acceptance of him, his parents, and his peers.

To be culturally fair, our schools must be designed to build on the strengths and to remedy as many weaknesses as possible in the experiential background for education that each child's home and community provides for him. The achievement of this objective promises a better educational program for children of all cultures—advantaged as well as disadvantaged.

Traditionally the American educational system has been thought of as a ladder up which a child may climb as far as his energy and his ability allow. However, in offering all children essentially the same ladder we find the rungs too far apart for the culturally disadvantaged. In addition, this ladder has been so greased with middle class values and expectancies that most disadvantaged children have found its climbing impossible or unworthy of their efforts.

In addition to the provision of teachers who know and value the child and his culture, many of the changes that we must make are fairly obvious and some are being implemented. Operation Head Start is an exciting development although so far it is starting too late, stopping too soon, offering too little, and, frequently, evidencing a distressing lack of coordination with the school's program for kindergarten and the primary grades.

Suggestions are being heard for year-round schools for the disadvantaged. An extended school year coupled with more extensive use of school facilities during the school day and week and the provision of skilled teaching and supervisory help for the extended day and week could be important forces in creating a culturally fair educational system.

As I see it, our major task must be to provide appropriate experiences during the child's foundation years. If these foundation years are inadequate, no amount of "shoring up" during later years can produce a structurally sound educational edifice. In addition, effort must be expended to identify and make attractive those educational goals that are attainable by the typical culturally disadvantaged child. Certainly some of these children with proper schooling can and should achieve professional status. And the provision of appropriate early experiences will allow many more of them to do so. Professional status, however, should not be the only socially approved goal even for children from the homes of professional persons. Skilled laborers, trained office workers, technicians, and owners of small business are legitimate and rewarding educational products.

To be completely successful, the provision of experiences that build the background of meaning required by the perceptual processes of reading and listening must begin when the child is born. Ideally, it should begin before that time with better education for his parents. For the intellectual, social, and emotional development of the individual, no other year of life is as important as the first year. The sensory, motor, and emotional experiences of the first year lay the foundation on which the experiences of the second year build. Thus, each year of life, important as it is, probably is less important than was the preceding year.

Meaning is built on prior meaning. Once deficiencies in experiential background arise, they prevent the attainment of full benefit from later experiences. It is for this reason that educators have found that individual differences in achievement increase rather than decrease as children grow older.

Obviously, our examination of the philosophy of reading has had to be limited. We have been concerned here with the importance of meaning and how meaning is acquired. We have recognized that in the perceptual processes of reading and listening the raw materials for all meaning must come from each individual's environmentally delimited experiences. We have noted society's need for good readers and have recognized each individual's great need for high-level reading skills in order to receive optimal benefits from his society.

In keeping with the responsibility of a philosophy of reading, we have suggested goals of reading development and proposed methods for attaining them.

Sociological Influences on Reading

ROY A. KRESS
Temple University

SOCIOLOGICAL ANALYSIS is the realm of the sociologist, not of the reading specialist. Therefore, this paper will focus not on a study of society but on the impact of society on the learner and the reading process. These are the primary concerns of the psychologist and educator involved in children's learning to read.

At the outset of this consideration of sociological influences on reading, it must be understood that they cannot be separated from other factors which bear upon the child and his development. A variety of types of psychological influences plays upon the child from at least the moment of his birth. Physiological factors, resulting from both the child's heredity and environmental conditions, play a large part in the determination of what he is and does. Pedagogical influences shape a large portion of the child's life. In the final analysis, it is not any one factor or a group of factors of any one type which makes the potentially successful child either a reader or a nonreader but the interrelationships among all the factors.

It is the purpose of this paper to indicate some of the ways in which the child's society provides the setting within which various other forces act upon him. Of particular concern here are the effects on his attitude toward himself as a learner, his values and motivations, and his resources for learning.

The child's society

What are the sources of the sociological influences which act upon the child and form the framework within which the other factors operate? One *might* think of them as a series of concentric circles, with the smallest and most intimate society which encircles the child overlapped and surrounded by a series of others, each larger than the last and engulfing all the smaller societies. At the same time, he operates in other social circles which are somewhat "off-center" in that they do not involve all of the people in even his most intimate group. None of these, of course, can act independently on the child but rather within the complex pattern set up by the interactions of all of them.

Suppose, for example, that the child is a member of a close-knit family group which forms his most intimate social setting. The immediate family is part of a larger family, perhaps including numerous grandparents, uncles, great aunts, cousins, and various "near relatives." This group in turn is part of a local community or several local communities, one of many church, business, or political groups, all of which have an impact on its mode of living. As the series of circles grows, the influences become more and more complex and even contradictory at times. Unfortunately, it is not always true that what appears to be good for one of these circles is also good for all the others. Instead, what is perceived by the inner family group as desirable may be viewed by the total family as detrimental to its good. What appears to be expedient for the good of the local community may not actually be in the best interest of the world community.

Further complexities arise as the child finds himself involved in other groups of which even his own immediate family is not really a part. At best they are interested observers or at times fringe members of his play groups, his many school groups, and so on. Here again, there may be some very complex and sometimes conflicting influences acting upon the child. Purposes, values, accepted behaviors— these and many other important things may vary greatly from group to group. Even the language which is most effective for communication within one group may be inappropriate to another.

From his earliest days, then, the child is called upon to function in what can by no stretch of the imagination be called a simple, secure, and constant society. He must adjust more often than even he consciously realizes. The way that he learns to operate in one social setting may be extremely helpful to him in getting along in another or it may actually be a considerable liability. Among other demands which living makes upon him is the necessity to perceive the essential nature of each of the groups of which he is a part so that he can make the most appropriate adjustment possible in each situation. Even the limited degree of success which some children have comes to seem rather remarkable when one considers the tasks which confront them.

Resources for learning

Because they are so obviously influenced by the sociological factors which play upon a child, his resources for learning may be the logical starting point in this discussion. Certainly this area has tended to receive most of the emphasis in the study of the so-called deprived child. A major complaint of the educator has been that the child of this type comes to school ill-prepared for the job of learning. He has been characterized as lacking in background of experience, language facility, and various other essential elements of readiness for academic achievement generally and reading success in particular. Corrective measures have all too often, therefore, been "pouring in" operations. The solution to the child's problems has been considered to be one of giving him broad opportunities to take in the world and the language of the school. Too often, his "language development" has been his acquisition of the ability to mimic the socially acceptable verbalisms of the society into which he is now to be incorporated. Some teachers have felt an unfortunate sense of accomplishment when all the children in their classes can pipe "Good Morning, Miss White" in good standard English. Likewise, they have felt that their children are better prepared for learning because they have visited the zoo, manipulated a variety of concrete objects, colored a variety of geometric forms, or learned to chant the alphabet. All of this kind of "filling in the gaps in the child's background" is actually to little avail if direct attention is not given to determining *what really are* the weak points in his resources for learning.

The basic question to be asked is not where the child has been and what he has seen or what language he has learned. It is, rather, what kind of perceptual-conceptual-language activities has he learned to carry on. The child who has learned to function adequately in his home society but lacks the particular concepts and language of the classroom life is a far cry from the child who is actually perceptually, conceptually, and linguistically deprived. One has already responded in a meaningful fashion to those things which surrounded him. The other has either had limited stimulation of all types or has been unable, for one reason or another, to act in response to the available stimulation. Corrective measures would be quite different in the two cases, even if the ultimate aim of helping the child to succeed in his present school situation were the same for both. Sociological influences acting upon a child could have produced either of these results.

For purposes of getting the spotlight on these sociological factors, assume for the moment that the children under consideration have intact sensory mechanisms and sufficient intellectual potential to allow them to perceive the world around them and organize it into some kind of conceptual structure. Further, assume that there are no physiological or basic psychological factors which would prevent their learning to function in the world of language. What can go wrong? What might interfere with the child's acquiring the kind of perceptual-conceptual-language background which would allow him to become a reader?

Within the framework of these assumptions, it is obvious that the child who has been successful in learning to respond to his own particular environment, lost though he may be in the school setting, is the easier case with which to deal. He has already given evidence of his ability to take in the sensory data which are available to him. He not only has eyes but also sees; he not only has ears but also hears. Furthermore, if he has really learned to function in his own world, as different as it may be from the world of his teacher, he has shown evidence of the ability to abstract from the sensory data which he has gotten—to deal with the elements of his individual experiences in terms of their similarities to or differences from elements of other experiences. He has shown that he can organize these data in a variety of ways so that they become useful to him in his subsequent experiences. In short, he has evolved some kind of conceptual framework which provides a map to guide him through the process of living. Finally, the fact that he can communicate with his family and his peers proves that he has been able to attach meaningful language to his experiences and use it not only to exchange ideas with others but to facilitate his own manipulation of ideas.

If the concepts that he has formed from his experiences and the language in which he communicates about them happen to be foreign to his teacher, as his teacher's may likely also be to him, then the problem becomes one of developing some communality of experience. Perhaps one of the greatest problems posed by sociological differences is that of the teacher who is a foreigner in the classroom rather than that of the child who is a foreigner in the school. Ample proof of this can be gotten by simple observation. Quite frequently, groups of children who would have been judged in the classroom to be lacking in all essential background and language can be observed talking a mile-a-minute to each other on the way home. Often the child who seems totally incompetent in the classroom goes home to quite competently take over household tasks and deal with crisis situations which might

well confound the teacher were she confronted with them. The point is that child and teacher live in different worlds and therefore not only speak different languages but also know different things and have different competencies.

Sad to say, all the burden of learning and changing seems to be placed on the child. Rarely is it considered important for the teacher to learn what the child knows in order to establish communication between them. The net result is to retard the child's adjustment to his new society because the great resources he brings to the learning situation are never discovered, let alone used, and the solid foundation of the known from which he could move on to the acquisition of new learning is never capitalized upon. Instead, he is expected to throw away his life and learnings of six or more years and begin again as an infant in a new society. The final blow to his success sometimes comes in the lack of recognition of the fact that he must continue to live and learn in the society of his more intimate circles, different as they may be from the larger school circle.

Some attention is at last being given to the fact that asking certain pupils to acquire so-called standard English is actually asking them to become bilingual. It does not seem that the point has yet been reached at which recognition will be given to the fact that these pupils may also be carrying a double burden of perceptual and conceptual development. It seems something worse than ridiculously inconsistent to expect those adjudged least prepared for learning to do the most learning.

If the child of this type is ever to learn efficiently in the school situation, he must be able to take advantage of his previous learnings. He must have the opportunity to see that the same perceptual processes which he has been using in his own society are those which he will have to apply to the school learning. He must be able to see the relationships between the thinking processes which he has been using and the solutions to the problems which face him in the school setting. He does not have to be born anew and learn again, as it if were for the first time, how to get meaning from his environment and to use that meaning for successful operation. He does not even have to begin again the long process of language development. However, all of this is true only if his previous learnings are known and can be used to advantage.

Suppose, on the other hand, that the child is one of those who is truly the victim of deprivation in all areas. Granted that he could not have lived to the age of school entrance having seen and heard nothing, gone nowhere, and said never a word—at least this can be taken for granted within the previous assumptions of intact sensory mechanisms and freedom from basic psychological or physiological problems. If severe deprivation, in even the sensory areas, is actually at the root of the child's problems, its solution demands different corrective measures. He has no reservoir of percepts and concepts which can be called upon by the teacher who knows his experiences and his language. He has literally learned only a minimum about taking in the world around him and manipulating the data which he gets. The problem here is one of helping him to perceive—to attend to available stimuli, to select those which are pertinent to his present needs, to examine the sensory data in terms of its significance, to organize it so that it will be useful to him both now and later. This is much closer to the situation of being born again, of beginning at this point to live as a human being.

Such a child may have had only limited opportunity to contact things which seem a part of everyday life— colors, shapes, sound values, textures. Again, there appears to be a serious error made in many of the attempts to help such a child begin to grow. Too often he is surrounded suddenly with such a wealth of stimuli that they serve only to confuse him. He cannot focus sufficiently on any of them to actually learn. Before he has had an opportunity to master one set of stimuli, to find out what they really have to say to him, he is being bombarded by others. The result in this case is usually confusion and sometimes even the building of a protective barrier against the invasion of further stimuli. The process of learning is not one of first building up a tremendous amount of perceptual data, then in another phase of development forming concepts, and finally attaching language to this perceptual-conceptual mass. If the child is to be successful in really learning as he is exposed to a variety of experiences and many kinds of stimulation, he must have an opportunity to carry through to the point of conceptual-language functioning in relation to these new experiences. Rather than attempts to bathe a child in experiences, these "rich experience" programs often turn out to have been attempts to fill a sieve. It is *the conceptual map* which plugs the holes, *not* the sensory data in themselves.

If the child has very limited experience and, consequently, a very poor conceptual background, it is essential that opportunities be provided for him to acquire related experiences at the rate at which he is capable of handling them and that he have direct help in dealing with these experiences. The kind of guidance that he will need includes structuring of his observations within the experience situation—a guide in terms of when and where to look, what to listen to, what kind of tactile stimulation to expect. He cannot be expected to make comparisons and contrasts of related experiences on his own but rather needs careful leading in terms of the kinds of similarities and difference to look for. He cannot be expected to figure out independently what significance his observations, when he finally makes them, might have. Here, too, he will have to rely on the guidance of a good teacher to help him make the discoveries. Furthermore, one successful experience with this kind of activity will not bring mastery. He may need continued reinforcement of the process he has been taken through, repeated experiences in situations which vary only very little from the original, until finally he achieves a degree of self-direction and, therefore, independence.

Obviously, many different sociological factors could have combined to bring about either kind of child just discussed and many other varieties which lie between them. Many of these factors will be mentioned specifically in the discussions of other ways in which the potentially successful reader's actual achievement is influenced.

The child's values and motivation

In this area, as in the case of his resources for learning, the child who is not being successful academically—the child who is not achieving in reading—is often described in purely negative terms. "He is completely unmotivated" and "he has no sense of values" are all too frequently heard. Every living individual is motivated in *some* direction and has *some* set of values. Again, the problem seems to lie in the lack of agreement between the motivations and values of the child and those which would make the job of educating him within the *existing school setting* an easier task. He is motivated in directions other than those in which the school would like to see him moving. His values diverge from those of the teachers and administrators who determine the nature of his program.

The fact that he has incorporated into himself those values and motivations which have been the prevailing ones in his society is often overlooked. Thus in this area, too, the child may be called upon to make major readjustments in his way of living or even to lead a double life. Either may impose on him extremely heavy burdens.

Again, consider some of the possible results which the child's sociological setting may have had upon him. Suppose that in his inner circle, his own immediate culture, there is a great deal of store set on financial status and very little virtue seen in contributions to society as a whole. The child's whole value system and, consequently, his motivation will likely be directed toward his own achievement of outward evidence of what he views as success. Material gain is apt to motivate him rather than inner rewards. Shortcuts to high grades in school will probably be perfectly acceptable to him since the grade in itself rather than the satisfaction of learning is more likely to be the reward that he seeks. In certain socioeconomic brackets of this country, rarely the lower ones, this kind of attitude is apt to be inculcated in the child from an early age and even tied to such seemingly high-minded aims as getting into the right college some years hence. Attaining a high standing in one's class and getting high college entrance scores are the short-term positive values. Very infrequently is there mention of how much the individual learned or what contribution he has made to his school, his community, or his associates. No one would openly suggest that the point is to get ahead even if one must lie, cheat, or trample his peers in the process, but the objective is clearly understood by all concerned.

In other circles, getting ahead is actually looked down upon. The individual who achieves academic, social, or economic status above that of the other members of his group is suspect. He is literally an outcast and viewed as an outsider in the society of his peers. To maintain a secure and comfortable existence requires that one not exceed the general level of the group. To want to learn is to be overly impressed with one's own importance, to think oneself better than the others in the group—an attitude not to be tolerated by the pack. Maintaining status in the inner society requires that one remain a misfit in the larger society.

Still other circles remain almost untouched by any real strivings, neither motivated *to* achieve nor a c t i v e l y *against* achievement or *even* suspicious of it. The members of such groups have simply never had the chance to become aware of the possibilities. They are neither *for* nor *against* academic learning. They do not view with suspicion the active reader, nor do they become concerned about inability to read. Reading and academic pursuits are simply not a part of their way of life.

None of these situations is likely to be productive of the kind of values and motivations which would be positive factors in the child's success in learning to read. In fact each, in its own way, is apt to exert a strong negative influence on his learning. Obviously the child who is simply untouched by reading will have no motivation to succeed with the job of learning to read. He can have no idea what it would mean to him to be able to read. He has not seen members of his society getting enjoyment or any other kind of gain from reading. Neither has he been in a position to find out what they might be able to do if they could read. Perhaps the one fortunate aspect of this situation is that such a child will also not be highly motivated to not learn. If the time comes when he develops values which are related to reading, his motivation to succeed may still be intact.

On the other hand, the child who lives in the society in which achievement in any area is actually disparaged may be motivated to block all possibility of his getting ahead in reading. He probably would not consciously say that this is the direction of his striving, but he may still do everything in his power to insure that he will not become a reader. His concentrated efforts in this direction may lead to his being labeled in the school as lazy, inattentive, argumentative, withdrawn, or a variety of other undesirable things. He may even succeed so completely in shutting himself off from learning that no one ever suspects that he actually has the capacity to learn. Some children can even manage to appear to be trying desperately to learn, and thus earn both pity and a kind of admiration from their teachers, at the same time that they are working very hard at not learning. It is their way of living happily in both worlds.

Perhaps most unfortunate of all is the child who grows up in a society where a high premium is placed on achievement, either true achievement or the outward appearance of it, but who does not find it easy or even only moderately hard to meet the standards set for the group. Certainly the child for whom learning is a relatively easy matter can gain some positive motivation and thereby increase his achievement when he lives in an atmosphere in which learning is valued. However, for the child who cannot, at least without tremendous effort, achieve as he is expected to, this kind of atmosphere can be devastating. He may put forth his best efforts and find that he still falls short of what the school and his inner society want of him. If this continues over a prolonged period, one of two possibilities is apt to become an actuality. The child may suffer such great anxiety and frustration because of his apparent failure that his learning power is decreased with each passing experience. In its extreme form, this kind of anxiety and frustration, no doubt coupled with other negative influences, has led young people to choose suicide as the only possible solution. In less extreme cases, or with a somewhat different combination of personality characteristics and other factors, this kind of anxiety and frustration has led the child to give up completely in his attempts to learn. He has already had ample proof that no matter how he tries he will be found wanting. His giving up may or may not be accompanied by open rebellion against the individuals and the society which have imposed the standards which he cannot maintain. Whatever mode of adjustment he chooses, he does it with the full and firm knowledge that he has failed those who matter most to him.

It is important to note that the final adjustive mechanism which is adopted may be much the same in very different cases. Treatment of the child who has withdrawn from learning to insure that he will not learn, and by learning lose his status, is not the same as treatment of the child who has withdrawn from learning because he is convinced that he can never do well enough. Thus, identical treatments of the symptom of withdrawal from learning might, in one case, help to remove the cause of the withdrawal, and, in another, serve only to aggravate the cause.

The child's concept of himself as a learner

Any good teacher could testify to the fact that even when realistic expectations are set for each child it is virtually impossible to teach him something that he does not want to learn or that he is convinced he is incapable of learning. Therefore, the influences which shape the child's concept of himself as a learner are extremely important to his success. The points made already in relation to motivation and values are definitely pertinent here. However, they can be extended into this specific area and also tied more directly to the learning of the reading process.

How does the child view himself as a potential reader when he first enters school and as he progresses in the acquisition of ability in this area? Does he see himself as growing into something which is a natural and necessary part of life—growing into it naturally and with ever increasing satisfaction? Or does he see himself as someone who probably will not have much need or desire to read and, consequently, may learn only because it is a part of school life? Or does he come to the task already strong in the conviction that the job will be hard and that he probably will not be able to succeed in it? He may even expect that he is going to be able to learn to read in the first few days or weeks of school and that that will take care of that. Many things can happen in his own inner society to cause any one of these attitudes to develop.

The child who has grown up in an atmosphere of healthy curiosity and exploration of ideas—where reading is a normal part of living—stands a good chance of developing a positive concept of himself as a learner and as a potential reader. He has already *learned* from a variety of types of situations, has seen the differences which his learnings can make, and is anxious to continue to extend the realm of his learnings. He is not likely to have developed false notions, however, about the rate at which he can expect to grow, for he will have learned to recognize his own limitations at his particular stage of development and to accept them at least temporarily. He will have learned that he can afford to wait, for a reasonable time, to become prepared for fulfilling a particular role. Meantime, he makes his place by fulfilling some other role which is in keeping with his degree of maturity and still a vital role in his own intimate society. He is ready, willing, and anxious to extend his learnings but not unduly impatient about it.

In contrast to this picture is that of the child who has seen himself as a completely dependent and noncontributing member of his inner circle. He adds nothing but another responsibility to the life of the home. Basically, he has been viewed as incompetent and has come to think of himself in this light. He sees no real place which can be filled through his own efforts and accomplishments. What he might learn or be able to do is actually a matter of little consequence in the main stream of life. Whether or not he becomes a reader will have no particular significance. It is, therefore, in a rather willynilly fashion that he approaches learning to read and other learnings in the school situation. Life will proceed in much the same fashion regardless of what he does. He, in himself, has little importance, and thus his accomplishments cannot truly matter.

Some children come to school with set patterns of expectation of immediate mastery of almost adult abilities and others with fear in their hearts about how different life will be. They may have been filled full of either "When you get to school, you'll learn to read and count, etc." or "They won't let you get away with that when you get to school." In both cases a rather unnatural concept of self as a learner has been built. Neither is apt to lead to real freedom to learn in a developmental sequence.

Basically, the child with a wholesome concept of himself as a learner is the product of a society which has allowed him to recognize his own worth, to develop a feeling of security about his place in his world, to look forward with realistic expectations to what he can accomplish and when he can accomplish it. He wants to increase his independence in all areas, including reading, so that he can broaden his participation in the daily living of his society. Finally, he believes that he can and will achieve because it is a normal part of growing and that this achievement will serve to modify but not threaten his place in each circle of his society.

Conclusion

Certain characteristics of today's society at large make for negative influence in all the areas which have been discussed. One of these is the tremendous amount of mobility in various groups. It is difficult for some children to put down roots and develop a feeling of security about their relationships with others because they are almost constantly on the move. It is not only the child whose family moves in the middle of the night to avoid paying the bills or the one who is constantly shunted from mother to father to grandmother to foster home who suffers from overmobility. Many families are forced to keep on the move in order to carry out the functions of government or some business organization. Economic strivings lead others to change homes frequently in the course of their upward mobility. Others are forced to move from place to place in order just to survive. In any of these situations, the child may find it difficult if not impossible to learn who he is and, consequently, what he might become.

Economic strivings can lead to the parents' virtual withdrawal from the inner society of the home. Some are forced to be out of the home to work so that the family can eat. Others put the home in the hands of a hired mother substitute whose services can be bought cheaply enough to allow a portion of the real mother's earnings to go into the purchase of such "necessities" as a new set of silverware or the extra car or the color television. Regardless of the degree of necessity which motivates the withdrawal from the intimate life of the home, its impact on the child can be much the same.

Various other kinds of pressures can lead to neglect of children and lessening of the opportunity for them to come to the task of reading well prepared to learn. The university professor who chooses to publish rather than perish may find it necessary to shield himself from his family. Perhaps with his promotion may also come the realization that he has a child with a severe reading problem as well as a wife who is not sure that she has a husband. The doctor who always manages to make it to the bedside of the expectant mother may find that he has not been quite so successful in meeting the needs of his own family. The sales manager who never fails to wine and dine the out-of-town client or get to the first tee on time may discover that, in the process, he has sold a lot of goods and also sold down the river his child's chances for academic success.

Sociological influences on reading are far more extensive than is commonly thought. It is not just availability of materials, background of experience, or development of language facility which is affected. It is the core of the child as a human being and as a learner that is at stake. No society which does not recognize the importance of its effects on this learner and take seriously its obligations to him could be considered a satisfactory one in which to live.

Applying Audio-Lingual (Oral) Technology to Beginning Reading

PAUL E. KING
and
EVA KING
Briarcliff College

What is education? A few weeks ago, the *Saturday Review* reported: Education is how kids learn stuff. This definition comes from a seven-year-old, and it is a good definition.

1. It concerns *kids*—not adults, not teachers, not parents.

2. It concerns how kids *learn*—not how we *teach,* not *what* we teach, and certainly not what we *think* we teach them.

3. It concerns the *stuff* which kids learn, the content, the curriculum, the fabric, the material, the program.

4. And finally, it concerns the *how,* the ways and means, the approaches, the techniques—one of them now being education technology which appears to open new avenues of learning and new opportunities within the classroom and beyond the classroom's limitations—so that *kids can learn stuff.*

What can education technology do for children when they first come to school at the age of five or six and when the "stuff" is the vital area of communication; i.e., language in all of its forms—listening and speaking, reading and writing?

It is a well-known fact that a child's success or failure in school and also in adult life is tied to his ability to communicate—to listen, to speak, to read, and to write. The earliest school years—the primary years—are often crucial to later success.

Reading specialists, language specialists, and primary teachers all agree that there is a strong and intimate link between oral language communication and written language communication. By the time he starts school, the five- or six-year-old communicates orally quite adequately, yet he often has great difficulty in linking his oral speech with the written symbols which he is now expected to acquire. There are today some hundred-odd reading methods in use, none of them considered significantly superior to any other; and there are some hundred-odd remedial programs, indicating that no program is as fully successful as hoped for.

Why? Could it be that some of the solutions will have to come through new avenues of learning rather than through yet another method of teaching reading?

This much we already know:

1. *We know* that communication skills develop in sequence.

a. Man has communicated with fellow man through speech for perhaps half a million years; yet, for barely five thousand years has he used graphic symbols.

b. The child parallels the experience of the race: he first listens and speaks, and only years later does he read and write.

c. And once again, this sequence reappears when the six-year-old begins to read: he first listens while being read to; he then mimics and copies the model; he repeats, and finally he relates his first set of symbols, oral speech, to his second set of symbols, written speech.

2. *We also know* that there exists a large gap, a discrepancy, between the six-year-old's already developed skill of listening and speaking and his not-yet-developed skill of writing and reading: there is a sharp contrast between the child's meaningful and often rich oral language and the limited, artificially structured, and often meaningless language of the textbook "readers," whatever they may be, good or bad. They offer, therefore, little motivation to the child.

The divergent speaker is at a particular disadvantage; he must bridge the gap from his regional dialect or his first native language via the detour of so-called "standard" English and continue all the way to the new *third* set of graphic symbols—reading and writing.

3. We also know that reading,

which is "speech written down," is a multisensory, not a monosensory, skill. It is beginning to be recognized that beginning reading cannot be taught and cannot be learned without constant use of ear and mouth. And when we include writing—as we must—we know that a simultaneous and correlated approach is needed for perfecting a truly multisensory skill involving eyes, ears, mouth, and hands.

4. We are also beginning to realize that there exist striking similarities in what it takes to master both of these skills, i.e., oral language and beginning reading.

a. Reading, like oral language, needs extensive, repetitive, audible practice.

b. Reading, like oral language, needs extensive listening practice and audible mimicry of spoken models.

c. Reading, like oral language, must be practiced "out loud" and in short bits or frames.

d. And finally, reading, like oral language, must become "automatic" to fulfill its true function as a means to an end, i.e., as a vehicle of thought communication.

5. We are also beginning to realize that this common requirement of extensive audio-lingual p r a c t i c e—of practicing aloud—needs one-at-a-time performance. This necessity conflicts sharply with the limitations of today's classroom in primary education. "In a class of 30, 29 are idle while one is busy," said Al Hayes years ago in *New Media For Instruction.* How much opportunity does the young child really have for active oral response in the "inhuman" classroom? One minute a day? Or is it two minutes? Research indicates that teachers, not children, use 75 percent of the school day for talking. And, in addition, in trying to adjust to these outdated classroom limitations, curricular programs have, in effect, capitulated to them by sacrificing audio-lingual practice techniques. And, thus, the gap

between oral and written language widens even further.

6. Yet, we also know that for the past twenty years a new education technology has been able to make significant contributions toward reducing classroom limitations on high school and college levels by providing language students with added opportunities for active audio-lingual practice. We, therefore, began to ask ourselves if young children would not make similar gains if they were provided with increased opportunities for language participation and practice—oral and graphic—in a systematic way? Could technology make our "inhuman" classroom conditions just a little bit more human by giving the young child some individual opportunities once again?

What we did not know until recently was whether what worked with teenagers would also work with the young child in early childhood and primary grades. Was it reasonable to assume that the very young child would meet the conditions inherent to programed technology—self-study, individual participation, sustained attention?

The first clues came to us during our just completed USOE Research Project on *Bilingual Readiness In Primary Grades,* and these came from the five- and six-year-olds themselves.

When we needed to extend a curriculum which had proved highly meaningful and motivating in content (it was based on high-quality, early childhood literature) but which was limited through scheduling to 15 minutes a day, we designed a system of electronic "satellites"—a term originated by the children—which incorporated tape recorders, headphones, and cartridge tapes with recorded versions of bilingual stories, songs, and rhythm games. These were made available to the children as reinforcement in both English and Spanish.

We observed that their attention span expanded well beyond age expectations; that they concentrated intensively for extended periods of time; that they thrived on repetition of the programs and of the language patterns within the program; that they showed technical readiness often surpassing that of their teachers; and finally that these five- and six-year-olds started to sing along, respond, and answer their literary story friends on tape even though, with headphones alone, they lacked the facility really to do this. It was soon obvious to us that the children were ready in every way to step beyond the experiences of passive auditory listening into active oral interchange and participation—with the tape.

We, therefore, welcomed the opportunity for expanded experimentation which presented itself last fall when the Virgin Island Department of Education wished to include a pilot project on *audio-lingual (oral) technology and beginning reading* in their language communication project.

The children on St. Thomas are dialectically divergent speakers of English; the children on St. Croix are also dialectically divergent speakers. In addition, well over 50 percent of all first graders are second language learners, Spanish being their native language. A typical first grade class averages 35-40 children.

We are attacking the problem of limited opportunity for oral language expression and beginning reading practice through appropriate technology and supportive programing. Any tool, in any work or profession, is only worthwhile if it can help do the job at hand either better or faster. By providing more one-at-a-time practice, we are increasing the ratio of child participation and are, in effect, giving the child an opportunity for a more human participating relationship within the classroom. In the 18 participating Grade 1 classes, every child is scheduled to get a chance

1) to listen and to speak in undisturbed, uninterrupted, and concentrated privacy, for at least 10 minutes every day;

2) to practice all the skills (audio-lingual and visual-manual) basic to correlating oral language and beginning reading practice: to mimic and repeat, to speak and respond; to sense and discover the tie-in between oral language and its written symbols; to practice in a correlated manner auditory and visual perception and discrimination; and to decipher and to read—in short, to enable every child, individually, for at least 10 minutes every day and for increasingly longer periods later on to experience language in all its forms.

We call our technological corner the ALR (Audio-Lingual) Reading Mini-Lab. There are two sections: a teacher's position and 6 to 10 student positions. The program, which is first presented live and then recorded on a tape cassette, passes to the children's positions electronically, via headphones and microphones, in individual privacy.

Each child sees the teacher and all visual materials presented. While each child hears the teacher (live or taped) and himself, he does not hear his classmates, and they do not hear him. Thus, all 6 or 8 or 10 children speak and read aloud simultaneously, yet individually, without interfering with or waiting for one another.

The children may also be linked to one another for intergroup participation (discussion, choral work, group reading, and so on). There are no controls at the pupils' positions.

As the children work orally at an increased rate, they must also be supervised. A series of buttons, one for each child, permits the teacher or teacher's aid to be in instant contact with the children, individually or as a group.

Also from the teacher's position, the teacher can record any child without interfering in his activity and without his knowledge.

Now this seems like a lot of new avenues, but are they really solutions? Education technology is without value unless programed with content of sufficient significance to make a difference. Jerome Bruner says, "The art of programing a machine is an extension of the art of teaching." This means that only to the extent that there are good teachers in the classroom will there be good programed lessons.

An artfully programed lesson goes well beyond isolated skill items; it is whole and complete in itself, with sequenced and related parts leading up to the next step. Mere practice of unrelated parts is useless; for effective storage of information the human brain requires structured order and meaningful connections in order to function effectively later on during retrieval. In reading, just as in oral language, words and sentences must lead to the ultimate goal of thought communication.

There can be no compromise in this area. Technology amplifies mediocrity. The captured sound, imposed upon a young child, is fraught with danger. It pinpoints; it shows up equally the bad and the good. What may pass as a fleeting oral presentation in the classroom simply does not pass, is not good enough, when captured and framed electronically.

Of course, we are aware that education technology is just as new to the teachers as it is to the children. We can now add to the 3 R's the 3 T's: teachers, tools, and training. The 18 teachers in our pilot project are learners in an innovative enterprise. As they attempt to create a lesson script, they learn once again what a lesson really is; they reevaluate what teaching actually entails, and they gain new insights into how learning takes place. If a teacher goes through the labor pains of creating a programed lesson—a task different from outlining an overall written lesson plan—she then can make the new opportunities of education technology her own.

Some of the efforts of our classroom teachers are already paying off. To quote Jerome Bruner, "A good program has the effect of making one highly conscious of the sequence in which one presents problems and of the aims of the sequence." Out of this teamwork, there is developing among our teachers an awareness that if new avenues are opening up for learning, then teachers must be also prepared to open up new avenues for teaching.

As education technology forces the actual creation of better lessons, these better lessons are brought back by our teachers into the classrooms.

As for the effects on the children, our observations indicate that the nonverbal child who has remained unresponsive in the conventional classroom, speaks and participates in the privacy of the lab; that there is increased and total attention and concentration by all the children; and most exciting of all, there is a realistic, de factor, dialog involvement with a "human" tape and correlated graphic materials. In addition, the child's natural love of repetition and play makes for a self-motivating and self-sustaining avenue of learning.

If the children's apparent concentrated attention and their obvious joy at being able to fully interact as individuals are any indication, then there is good reason to expect that "kids *will* learn stuff."

A Traditional Lexico-Morphemic Orthography and Its Reading Facilitating Qualities

ELIAHU ERELL
Tel-Aviv University, Israel

THE NATURE OF an orthographic system has, of course, a great influence on our treatment and achievements in teaching in general and in reading in particular. An orthographic system, however, is to a large extent a given condition which, contrary to popular belief, cannot be changed easily. Nevertheless, looking into the complex and multiform developments in the history of writing accomplishes more than satisfying an interesting curiosity. It appears that the present phase does not favor the idea of reforming changes in the orthography, and with very good reason: the example of orthography-torn Norway in the present century cannot be very encouraging. [Norway has been torn for decades between two writing systems, both created by cultural authorities and both reformed again and again within short intervals (2).] However, it is certainly justifiable that specialists be equipped with enough knowledge and understanding of the various developments in the writing systems in the history of human culture and the generalizations derived from them.

An argument for a nonphonetic orthography

The case for a phonetic orthography is rather popular. Anybody can see the usefulness of a writing system that yields a perfect duplicate of the spoken sounds. Whether this aim can ever be fully achieved is, however, very doubtful. There is not really any practical way to put on paper, in a readable manner, an exact representation of the tremendous variety and complexity of vocal sounds. Once this ideal is abandoned, the way is open to argue the advantages of different systems which by giving up the phonetic ideal can facilitate reading in other ways. Such an achievement can be gained mainly in the economy of the writing and reading procedures, a feature which is rapidly becoming of cardinal value in the vastly extensive usage of written language in modern life. By short-circuiting the way from written symbols to concepts, leaving out as much as possible of the sound mediator, a much more economic and rapid writing and reading can certainly be achieved. Moreover, there are at least two instances in the history of writing when a writing system could be read equally in two different languages and serve each one of them in an apparently satisfactory manner. One of them, hinted at in the biblical text, was the official Aramaic-Persian administrative script of the Persian empire during the 4th and 3rd centuries B.C. mentioned in the Book of Esther (1). Even though the concept of an interlingual orthography is not very practical, there remains no doubt as to the reading advantages of such a system within the same language. In our own reading we recognize these advantages as the unit or word perception in reading rather than as the letter perception. A very crude illustration of this can be found in the signs and abbreviations, such as, &, etc., e.g., and $. Often their true pronunciations are not generally known. Some of them may have interlingual validity, like $ or &.

The impracticability of an ideographic writing system

All this matter is not intended to propagate an ideographic writing system which uses actual pictures to convey meanings of objects and even ideas. Such systems have been discarded many times in history by different cultures, and even its contemporary remnants are actually escaping from it by passing over to syllable orthography. This is probably the place to make clear some principal distinctions between ideographic writing, syllable writing, and alphabetical, phonetic writing. Syllable writing is not really ideographic, although it is closely derived from it (1). The ancient syllable writing in Egypt, Mesopotamia, China, and Japan made a crucial step forward by using the ideo-pictures as symbols representing sound or a group of sounds. It was a syllable that grouped to express the sounds of actual words (originally only proper and foreign names). The story of these steps can be fairly well conjectured now as illustrated in the Proto-Sinai stone engravements from the 14th century B.C.

These developments had apparently an important role in the later Semitic writing system from which modern Hebrew will here be used as a special example. No nostalgia for ancient ideography is, however, entertained here. The impracticability of such a system in the immensely complex and ever diverging vocabulary of human language in the scientific era need hardly be argued. The notion of putting it into an ideographic system cannot be conceived even by the wildest imagination, although there might have

THE PROTO-SINAI ENGRAVINGS AND THEIR LATER DEVELOPMENTS

Aleph looked like an ox's head, called *eleph*

Bet resembled a house with an open corridor, *bayit*

Gimel was like a camel, *gamal*

Daled was *delet*, door

Vav resembled a hook, a *vav*

Zayin was an olive, *zayit*

Yood looked like a hand, *yad*

Kaf was a palm, *kaf*

Mem looked like water waves, *mayim* (water)

Noon was a fish called *noon*

Ayin an eye, *ayin*

Pay resembled a mouth, *peh*

Resh a head, *rosh*

Shin looked like a tooth, *shen*

and Tav was a sign or mark, *tav.*

Evolution of the Letter "R"

Hieroglyph of "Head"

Sinai "R"

True Alphabetic "R" (North Semitic)

Early Hebrew "R"

Phoenician "R"

Greek "R", called *Rho*

Maccabean "R"

Modern Hebrew "R", called *Resh*

been a primitive phase in the history of writing which contented itself with it. The question to be raised now is whether advantages can be gained from a writing system that will not be ideographic at all, yet will not be entirely avowed to phoneticality by selecting the advantages and trying to avoid the disadvantages of each system.

The theories about the creation of alphabetic writing

The characteristics which will be demonstrated presently are originally common to the Semitic languages, of which only Hebrew and Arabic now enjoy a fully developed literary and writing life. Both have reached the printing era and have experienced phases of revival and expansion. Modern Hebrew has experienced during these very years an extremely vigorous expansion and renovation, guided now by a learned and linguistically-minded professional leadership. The expanding processes show remarkable consistency with the original basic structures of the language. Thus, modern Hebrew furnishes a good example for illustrating a lexico-morphemic orthography which differs very markedly from those generally known in the world today.

These characteristics seem to apply to Arabic in very much the same way as to Hebrew.

The origin of the Hebrew or Phoenician alphabet of 22 letters is still debated. The view held some years ago that the Proto-Sinaic engravings demonstrate the passage from ancient Egyptian picture writing to the Hebrew-Phoenician alphabet is recently being questioned (1), and new theories about the cunneiform origin of that alphabet have been put forward (6). The controversy is, however, not very relevant to our subject. The fact remains that these 22 letters have served for nearly four thousand years and still serve today a tremendous development and inner change in the Hebrew language, and they seem to be adequate for all the needs of a modern language. The 22 letters represent a similar number of *consonants* only; the vowels are not represented principally in the writing system. They combine, in a very regular way, in groups of three to form a great number (estimated about 3,000) of "roots" or word families, each of which is formed on the root in one of a limited number (estimated 250) of very fixed patterns. The following table illustrates, by actual examples, this basic lexicomorphemic structure.

DEMONSTRATION OF THE PRINCIPLES OF HEBREW ORTHOGRAPHY

The 3-root consonants	(the vowels indicated by the inserted small English letters *do not* appear in the Hebrew words) Note: F = P		
Š F T	ŠoFeT (judge)	MiŠPaT (judgment)	ŠaFaT (judged)
D R S	DoReS (tearing)	MiDRaS (torn object)	DaRaS (tore)
Š M R	ŠoMeR (watchman)	MiŠMaR (watch)	ŠaMaR (watched)
Š T R	ŠoTeR (policeman)	MiŠTaR (regime)	ŠaTaR (policed)
"Standard morph. marker"	-O-e-	*Mi--a-	-a-a-

* an auxiliary prefixed consonant

THE HEBREW ALPHABET

Print	Cursive	English Equivalent	Phonetic Value	Print	Cursive	English Equivalent	Phonetic Value
1. א	'	'	'	12. ל	ל	l	l
2. ב	ב	b, v	b, v	13. מ	מ	m	m
3. ג	ג	g	g	14. נ	נ	n	n
4. ד	ד	d	d	15. ס	ס	s	s
5. ה	ה	h	h	16. ע	ע	'	'
6. ו	ו	v	v	17. פ	פ	p, f	p, f
7. ז	ז	z	z	18. צ	צ	ts	ts
8. ח	ח	h.	h.	19. ק	ק	q	k
9. ט	ט	t	t.	20. ר	ר	r	r
10. י	י	y	y	21. ש	ש	sh	sh
11. כ	כ	k	k, ch	22. ת	ת	t, th	t

The absence of vowel-letters

Now, the examples in the above table also show the orthographic method of representing by way of writing only the basic consonants of the root (sometimes also one or two auxiliary consonants belonging to a special group of six consonants). The selection of vowels is left to the reader to be made according to his prior identification of the word, by recognition and context, as illustrated below :

GoDeL (size)	GaDaL (grew)	GiDeL (raised)	— are all written G D L
QoDeM (before)	QaDaM (preceded)	QiDeM (accelerated)	— are all written Q D M

Although this principle governs essentially the whole language, there have always been marginal vocabulary areas, e.g., borrowed words, which were an exception to it. Another exception to this principle involves the two auxiliary methods of representing the vowels—both also borrowed by the Arabic—known as "punctuation" and "full orthography." These latter developments will be dealt with later on.

Lexical function of the root-letters

Attention should be drawn to the unique function of this orthography which uses principally only three-root consonants as a recognition marker. The individual letter does not build the form of the word; the combination of any three consonants forms a lexical category, so to speak. The immediate recognition of this combination puts the word into a limited area of meaning, leaving the decoder to choose next between a very limited number of words within that specific area. The aids for this choice may be auxiliary prefixed or suffixed consonants and to a very large extent the recognition of morphological units helped out by the context; for example,

D V D	H M L Kh — DaViD	HaMeLeKh (David the King)
D V D	M L Kh — DaViD	MaLaKh (David reigned)

These characteristics boil down to what may be described as a lexico-morphemic type of language structure; that is, the morphemic qualities of a word are directly linked with the lexical qualities by obvious rules. In an abstract way it can be said that the meaning of a particular word can be divined on a matrix that has all the roots on one dimension and all the fixed vowel forms on the other. This can be shown on the first table and is realistic enough as an aid for people who have acquired this principle structure of the language.

Rules for the creation of new words

It can be clearly seen that this, so to speak, matrix-like type of a language structure can be a powerful instrument in the creation of new words for objects and concepts. The structurally proper choice of morphemic elements for a new word is in this case very systematically prescribed to a point that makes the new word capable of being almost guessed as to its meaning by the chosen root and vowel form. This method has been widely used in recent decades for creating literally thousands of words to fit the great revolutionary changes in the environment in which old biblical Hebrew is being used nowadays. A word for "procedure," NoHaL, was created in the following way :

MiN H aL (administration)	MiNH aG (custom)
H aN H aLa (management)	HaNH aGa (leadership)
NoHaL (*procedure*)	NoHaG (rule)

We can proceed now to define the qualities of this kind of writing system in terms of the basic classification for phonetic and ideographic writings. Modern Hebrew makes no pretence about representing the pronunciation of words, and this fact is manifested by its original giving up of any vowel representation. The deliberate and consequent discrimination between vowels and consonants in this matter receives an interesting support in a phonetical research of vowel articulation. It has been shown through instrumental measurements (3) that vowel articulation is more fluid in nature than that of consonants and that actually a sound pattern could hardly be perceived in a consequent way if it were to rely on vowels only; it is mainly the consonants that give the word its identification (5). Whether this difference was sensed by the early writers of the Semitic languages and brought them to adopt this system of writing or whether it was just accidental, the outcome might be described as a lexcio-morphemic spelling system, since what is really represented in the spelling is not the sound of a word but its morphological origin. By writing the three-root letters, all that was marked for the reader was this area of meaning, a lexical feature rather than a phonetic one. Thus this system can be justly defined as an intermediary between the purely ideographical sign system and the purely phonetic one by virtue of its using actual phonetic-like letters as signs for an idea, i.e., a definite area of meaning. On the other hand, no phonetic data are supplied for the reader to form the actual phonology of the word.

Economy in writing-reading elements

Here is an illustration of the economy in writing elements in a Hebrew text as compared with an English text:

HŠMŠ ?oLH BMZRKh VŠoQ ?T BM ?RV—24 letters (note: Kh is one letter).

The sun rises in the east and sets in the west—36 letters.

This illustration is hardly needed for understanding how much is gained (in terms of writing elements) by omitting vowels. However, the economy in reading perception is probably even greater due to the ability of the reader to grasp a number of writing elements grouped as a *consonant-root-unit* and denoting the meaning area of the root. Very few extra elements are needed for actual word determination within the mean area of the root.

Standard morphological marker

Little has been said until now about the second marker for decoding meaning—i.e., the extra markers besides the root, which can be defined as "standard morphological markers." This term refers to any marker in the spelling of a word that serves to identify a specific word in the root group and discriminate it from others that have the same root. It is termed morphological because it is specifically such a discriminating element that it gives the word its morphological quality; the three-root consonants are nothing more than phonological raw material to build the word on and virtually cannot be pronounced at all without vowels. The vowels, then, give the words their morphological value (together with a restricted number of prefixed or suffixed consonants). In this way the "standard morphological markers" of any word can be theoretically abstracted from any specific root as a pattern that can be imposed on any given three-consonant root. These patterns are not arbitrary; they comprise, as mentioned previously, a relatively small number of standard morphological units. To those acquainted with Arabic and Hebrew grammar these units are known as "scales"—in Arabic, Wazan and in Hebrew, Mishkal—and play a basic role in the theoretical grammar of these languages.

Difficulties with foreign languages

Foreigners studying Hebrew—who, by the way, comprise the majority of

Hebrew speakers today—might find what they have been trying to present as an advantageous writing system a rather confusing one. The word goes around that a writing system with no vowels is difficult to read. This opinion certainly is shared among native speakers of Hebrew. There hasn't been any proof that this feature of the language hampers the learning of reading or makes this reading more difficult than that in English, for instance. While there is some suspicion that other grammatical characteristics, especially those originating from the fact that the language is being revived from an ancient written dialect, do present some difficulties in acquiring skill in the language, there is some real ground to believe that reading is easier than in other languages (4). In two instances, however, the system is at a disadvantage: one is in the case of adult foreigners who have to learn to read without vowels, and the other is in the case of finding the correct pronunciation of foreign names and words. In extreme cases it has been found that adult learners could never really get over this difficulty of learning to read. The remedy for these difficulties has been provided by auxiliary orthographies used especially in later generations, orthographies which will be described more fully.

Tentative reform

The difficulties in reading Hebrew must have been felt even in ancient times when the exact pronunciation of biblical texts became a subject in school. It was thus that modifications and even reforms were sought. A system of 15 different dot signs representing the vowel system was introduced in the 10th century. This feature lends to certain Hebrew texts the typical "dotted" appearance which is probably familiar to many. Contrary to general belief, however, the system was never really adopted, and it has remained restricted to biblical texts, to poetry, to most children's books, and to such special purposes as the spelling of foreign names. One of the reasons

for its limited use is the mechanical difficulty of having the dot signs inserted into typewriters and printing machines. Since modern research into the psychology of reading was applied in Hebrew schools, the objection to using the vowel punctuation has become founded on more substantial grounds. The late Dr. Yaakov Levy argued in a convincing manner (4) that the vowel punctuation added a frightening and confusing load to the task of reading and that it became entirely superfluous soon after the beginning stages of learning to read. By his counsel certain schools practiced the omission of vowel punctuation altogether, from the very beginning. No evident failure was ever reported on these experiments.

A compromise solution

The views expressed here about the reading advantages of the system were, of course, not always shared by all, although they are gaining ground now. Under the pressure of mass immigration from Europe the Hebrew Academy adopted in the late forties a mild reform that had its beginnings already in biblical orthography. The reformed system is called "full spelling" and can be described as a partial vowel orthography. The spelling uses the four letters A, H, V, I (the first one being a glottal and not a vowel and used much less than the others) as vowel markers in certain cases according to fixed rules. The use of these letters is by no means wide. In no case does it cover even all the occurrences of one single vowel. It hardly upsets the original system of the three root letters. Yet, during a certain period of time it caused a typical discontent among those who were trained in the orthodox spelling. The mild reform is taking over, though.

Transcription to Latin alphabet

The same circumstances brought forward suggestions in favor of dropping the original alphabet altogether and adopting the Latin alphabet for

Hebrew in the same way as it was done in Turkey and elsewhere. For a short time a small newspaper, written in Latin alphabet, was published in Hebrew by a Tel-Aviv journalist*. The issue was never seriously considered. The arguments against such a reform are more than just conservatism. Virtually all Hebrew grammarians agree that whatever gain may come through a full vowel orthography, the loss in decoding feasibility will be very substantial. Writing words as they are pronounced in Latin letters will make morphologically related ones seem quite remote, and vice versa. This realization is, of course, based on the lexico-morphemic qualities described here and appears to be, at least in the mind of the writer, another proof for the reading facilitating qualities of the system.

* A very extraordinary person, Itamar Ben-Avi was the eldest son of the prominent innovator of Hebrew, Eliezer Ben-Yehuda. According to his father's claim, Itamar was the first person in modern times to speak Hebrew as a first natural language.

REFERENCES

1. Diringer, David. *The Alphabet,* (rev. ed.). New York: Philosophical Library, 1953.
2. Haugen, Einar. *Language Conflict and Language Planning.* Cambridge, Mass.: Harvard University Press, 1966.
3. Ladenfoged, P., and D. E. Broadbent. "Information Conveyed by Vowels," *JASA* (1957), *29,* 98.
4. Levi, Yaakov. *Yesodot Psychologyim shel Haqriah be'Ivrit* (Hebrew). Tel Aviv: Hachinuch, 1944.
5. Miller, G. A. *Language and Communication,* Chapter 3. 1951.
6. Tur-Sinai, Naphtali H. *Lashon Vasefer* (Hebrew). Jerusalem: 1954.

Cultural Deprivation: Ideas for Action

THOMAS J. EDWARDS
Science Research Associates

WE WHO ARE COMMITTED to education and to the other behavioral sciences are finding ourselves thrust into history in a way that has never before been true during the development of our various disciplines. No longer are we locked into the somewhat comfortable isolation of our little red school houses or our laboratories or our academic ivory towers. The urgency of shrinking space, or shrinking time, and of social revolution is nudging us with unrelenting persistence. And there is no turning back.

Just a few years ago we suddenly discovered our "wasted Americans"— discovered them or perhaps just dared, finally, to acknowledge their existence. With something like a royal decree, it was ordered that we declare war on poverty and on ignorance. And the *ignorant ones* came under microscopic scrutiny. We asked: "Who are these people? What are they like? Why are they so different and disadvantaged? What are we to call them?"

It was probably inevitable that we should get involved in a semantic battle. We spoke of the "culturally deprived." Anyone who had not been exposed to the experiential and linguistic and value orientation of the normally advantaged segment of our population must indeed be deprived. However, cultural anthropologists argued that no one is truly deprived of a culture. He may simply have come from a culture different from the predominant one.

So the term "culturally deprived" became a dirty word and was supplanted by the term "culturally different." Yes, this terminology was better since it acknowledged the difference among cultures within an essentially heterogeneous society. However, the question was then raised: "Who is different from whom? Who represents the standard and who is the deviant? Is there not a value judgment implied in the term "culturally different"?

Although the terminology became increasingly confusing, the fact still remained: There were significantly large numbers of people within our society who grew up in subcultures that did not prepare them adequately to cope with academic achievement or with the work-a-day world. They were at a decided disadvantage in terms of coping skills. Hence, the term "culturally disadvantaged" came into prominence. However, this proliferation of terms continued with rather wild acceleration: culturally deprived, culturally different, culturally disadvantaged, culturally disabled, culturally debilitated, culturally disenfranchised, and even culturally denuded.

This seemingly ridiculous semantic battle was probably a necessary first step in our attempts to define a rather involved psycho-social and educational problem. However, we were pressed into action because the availability of very tempting federal funds required that program plans be set down in proposals. Deadlines were upon us. And the psychology of crisis catapulted us into action with phenomenal speed.

As programs got underway and live bodies began to appear for help, the stark realities of cultural deprivation became increasingly apparent: Our American society had allowed many millions of its members to remain culturally isolated, locked in their own cultural cocoons, as it were, either by design or neglect. Thus sealed off from contact with the predominant culture, they grew up culturally different. Their self-concept frequently reflected the feelings of inferiority and rejection often characteristic of social outcasts. There was a tendency for them to feel that they had no significant stake in our society. Their experiences had been severely circumscribed and limited. Their linguistic isolation had resulted in their speaking either a markedly divergent dialect of American English or an entirely different language. Their repertoire of concepts tended to be both limited and highly specialized. And their value systems were likely to differ from and even to come into conflict with those of the predominant culture. It soon became apparent, therefore, that any effective attack on the problems of the culturally disadvantaged would have to be interdisciplinary. It would require creative intellectual pragmatism in the application of psychology, cultural anthropology, economics, sociology, linguistics, community development, medicine, and education. The task was a formidable one!

The war on poverty and ignorance within the United States was given further impetus by the fact that the culturally disenfranchised were themselves becoming increasingly aware of their plight and were articulating their discontent. They wanted to burst out of their cultural cocoons and participate with comfort, with dignity, and with effectiveness in the life, culture, and mores of the general society. And this society, in turn, was beginning to recognize the expense of having the disadvantaged on its relief rolls, the wasted manpower resulting from the undereducation of the cultural isolates, and the immorality of denying them optimal self-fulfillment.

Against this backdrop, therefore, it becomes imperative that we generate ideas for action at a rapid rate. And it is the purpose of this paper to sketch broadly a few ideas that might be provocative, if not totally comprehensive. Action must occur in two major dimensions. First of all, intelligently conceived ideas must be programed and implemented, even though they have not stood the acid test of rigorous experimentation. Time is of the essence. We have waited too long and we must get moving. In addition, action programs must be paralleled by more careful experimental investigations of the many variables that may reverse the effects of cultural deprivation. And the interaction that may exist among these variables must also be studied. Further, there must be maximum intercommunication and cross-fertilization between those working on the firing lines in the various programs and those who are doing the more controlled experimental investigations. Feedback from programs will provide significant hypotheses which the experimenters can test. And the findings from experimentation can, in turn, be applied in the action programs.

The phenomenon of spontaneous acculturation

There are numerous examples around us of people who were born in cultural cocoons but who have broken out for no reason that is *apparent*. Unquestionably, some motivational factor has abrogated society's dictum that these people should be doomed to permanent cultural isolation. What could this factor be? Why, for example, might two siblings raised in essentially the same depressed environment differ in their tendency to break out of their cocoon? Is this emancipation based on innate intelligence or might it be some environmental influence that provided for the one a glimpse into a different world and thereby generated for him an elevated level of aspiration with concomitant increased self-confidence?

This phenomenon of spontaneous acculturation is intriguing and is certainly worthy of systematic investigation. Such research should involve the culling of case history and psychological test data from these "cultural breakouts." These data should then be treated with factor analysis in order to determine whether there is a cluster of traits or environmental influences common among those who break out of their various subcultures. If such factors can be isolated and identified, it might follow that we could devise systematically programed cultural emancipation.

Informal investigations by this writer have failed to yield any consistent specific factor common to these "cultural breakouts." Generally, however, there seems frequently to be present some almost fortuitous incident or influence of another person that triggers a change in self-confidence and in goal-setting behavior that is aimed at a raised level of aspiration.

Modified curriculum: content or methodology?

A number of educators look with considerable pessimism at the educational future of the culturally disadvantaged learner. Some feel that significant cultural difference is essentially immutable and that attempts to reverse the effects of this difference would therefore be futile: "Provide them with minimum requirements for some low-level vocation and then turn them loose." This same conclusion is also held by those who are convinced of the innate inferiority of members of the culturally disadvantaged segment of our society. Both points of view often lead to the contention that the curricular goals of educational programs for the disadvantaged should either be lowered or markedly changed.

I would challenge this contention with vigor. First of all, we must assume that good curricula in school systems across the nation embody a systematically sequenced complex of concepts that are regarded by educators as highly desirable for general life adjustment and necessary for employability in most occupations. If this point is tenable, then the already disadvantaged learner must not be deprived of this body of knowledge, lest his deprivation, his failure, his sense of worthlessness, and his economic dependence be perpetuated and even become the legacy of his offspring. This, I am afraid, has already been happening for many generations.

A second assumption held here is that innate intelligence or learning capacity is distributed within the culturally disadvantaged group in the same way that it is distributed within the general American population. It would therefore follow, of course, that the mean IQ for both groups would be 100 and that genius, normalcy, and mental deficiency exist to the same degree among the culturally advantaged and the culturally disadvantaged. To this we might add the assumption that difference in *measured* IQ's reflects the inappropriateness and inaccuracy of our measuring instruments when used with subjects who are culturally different from the dominant population and that the disproportionately high degree of academic underachievement reflects the failure of our schools still to present the curriculum in a way that is palatable and compatible with the unique background, learning style, and cluster of characteristics of the disadvantaged.

If we assume, therefore, that the acquisition of our curriculum content is desirable and that culturally disadvantaged students have normal learning capacity, then we are faced with the exciting challenge of modifying our *approach* rather than our curriculum *content* in presenting the skills and concepts that are traditionally a part of our academic diet. This is indeed *the* crucial task confronting educators of the culturally disadvantaged. And both experimental research and action programs must be directed to the accomplishment of this task.

I have identified elsewhere a number of specific differences or deficiencies that are likely to handicap the disadvantaged learner and militate against his academic achievement (*1*). These fall into two major categories: basic learning deficiencies and psycho-social adjustment needs. The modification of our approach to the education of the culturally disadvantaged should take these kinds of factors into consideration. If, for example, disadvantaged students are likely to have a deficient repertoire of concepts, we should be sensitive, alert, and constantly diagnostic. In this way we can recognize and provide for any deficiencies in the conceptual elements that may be prerequisite to the learning of a new, more advanced, more complex, or more abstract concept. How, for instance, can a student grasp world geography if he does not have the more fundamental concepts of "east," "west," "north," and "south?"

Similarly, if a student's own achievement expectancy and his self-concept are inadequate, it follows logically that he should be given rather constant reassurance of his learning ability and also be provided with success-insured tasks.

In addition, we may need to know a great deal about the unique experiential-conceptual background, the value system, and the linguistic orientation of the disadvantaged student and adjust our pedagogy in a way that will prevent his unique characteristics from hampering his mastery of the curriculum.

Dialectical barriers to learning

Linguistically, we in the United States are not homogeneous. So-called standard American English or "network English" is spoken by only a small minority of Americans. And even the acceptable English of one region of the United States will differ considerably from that of another region. These regional differences in standards of speech generally do not tend to interfere with academic achievement, nor do they usually hamper inter-regional communication.

Because the majority of culturally disadvantaged students have grown up in linguistic cocoons, their isolation from standard American English has resulted in their speaking dialects that differ even from the standard acceptable English of their own regions. In certain cases, as is true, for example, of Americans of Spanish descent or many American Indians, even an entirely different language may be spoken. Dialectical variations from standard English tend to fall into four major categories: vocabulary, pronunciation, syntax, and idiomatic expression. And significant divergence in any of these four categories may seriously penalize a linguistically different student in the school setting.

Ultimately, the educative process involves the communication of a myriad of concepts to learners. These concepts comprise our curriculum content. Communication, in turn, relies very heavily upon language. In the acquisition of concepts, the learner must have proficiency in the *receptive* aspects of communication—that is, listening and reading. On the other hand, when he wants to react, to question, or to demonstrate that learning has taken place, he must rely on *expressive* communication—that is, speaking and writing.

When a learner moves from the familiar dialect of his own linguistic cocoon to the somewhat unfamiliar language of the school, the communicative process often tends to be seriously impaired and, in turn, is quite likely to penalize him in his attempts to acquire the concepts embodied in the curriculum. And even if he is reasonably successful in understanding these concepts, he might be at a loss in communicating the fact that he does understand them if his expressive language skills are deficient as they relate to standard American English. This language barrier is also one of the factors that make it difficult for intelligence tests to measure the learning capacity of culturally different students because language is often one of the fundamental means by which intelligence is assessed.

What, then, must be done in order to arm linguistically different students with the essential communication skills prerequisite to academic achievement?

One answer is *linguistic immersion*. The school must make every effort to provide the student with maximum meaningful contact with the standard American English of his region. He should *hear* a great deal of standard language in order to develop *receptive* communication proficiency. And he should *use* the language for the development of competence in *expressive* communication.

Students who grow up in linguistic isolation learn to master both the *speech sound system* and the *syntax* of their peculiar dialect. When they encounter standard American English, they find themselves suddenly faced with sounds that they have never become accustomed to perceiving or reproducing. And the perception and reproduction of speech sounds are learned acts. The dialectical pronunciations come into conflict with the more conventional standards and interference results.

According to Johnson, ". . . the language of culturally disadvantaged pupils should be considered as a different system that interferes—systematically—with the learning of standard English." And he proceeds to identify characteristic points of conflict between the American Negro dialect and standard American English on which instructional emphasis should be placed. He also suggests specific kinds of instructional activities which can be employed (2).

Conflicts among systems of arranging words into syntactical patterns also present problems for disadvantaged learners, and syntax is probably as much a fixed language habit as are auditory perception and pronunciation. These habits are learned early and are difficult to modify. It is often felt that the various dialects of American English are haphazard and unsystematic. However, careful analysis of nonstandard speech has shown that dialects tend to be both systematic and consistent (3, 4).

In all probability, initial emphasis in language retraining should be at the oral level. First of all, language is learned naturally at the auditory-vocomotor level before written language is ever attempted. In addition, printed symbols are representations of spoken language and should therefore follow the learning of spoken language in the sequence of language development. Any attempts to learn symbols for sounds that have never been mastered at the auditory level would be psychologically and pedagogically un sound.

A culturally different student might question very seriously the school's attempts to change his language habits. And justifiably so. His dialect has served him well. He has communi-cated with it effectively all of his life and has shared it with others as an integral aspect of his unique culture. So, why change? First of all, he should not be encouraged to discard or reject his familiar dialect. Rather, he should strive for linguistic versatility so that he can slide easily and comfortably up and down a language continuum from his own dialect to slang to colloquialisms to more formal standard American English. And he should know in which situations each type of language is appropriate. Standard American English is the lingua franca of the United States and, therefore, provides the relatively uniform and stable system for communication. In addition, marked deviations from linguistic norms tend to stigmatize a person as being uneducated or outlandish. These points should be made clear to culturally disadvantaged students, particularly since their cultural or ethnic difference will in all probability have already been a source of derision or rejection or humiliation once they have ventured outside their own cultural milieu.

A number of practical techniques can be employed to help students add standard American English to their native dialects. Plays, the memorization of interesting poems or even nonsense ditties, songs, and impromptu dialog, all may prove to be helpful. The important consideration is the hearing and reproduction of the pronunciations and the syntactical structures of standard American English. Because there are numerous dialects represented among the various disadvantaged subcultures, it is essential that a teacher listen for frequently recurring deviations from standard English and plan language-learning activities around these deviations.

Language immersion must not be viewed as an isolated curricular area. Rather, it must be woven systematically into a thoroughly integrated program designed to expand students' repertoires of concepts and the cognitive power and reasoning ability with which to manipulate these concepts logically and creatively. This is education.

Self-concept and cultural disadvantage

A person who either peeks out or dares to move out of his cultural cocoon becomes immediately aware of the fact that he is "different." He is a deviant from the acceptable dominant group that enjoys a special place in the societal sun. And his awareness of his difference may be underscored by derisive labels that are hurled at him or by various verbal or graphic caricatures designed to ridicule him. He is often a social outcast.

In his attempts to ease even unobtrusively into the mainstream of general American life, he often encounters a school situation designed for students from quite different backgrounds. Failure ensues, and he learns quickly not to expect much of himself by way of school achievement. As a chronic academic failure, he first becomes a *psychological dropout* at an early age. However, he is required to remain in school until he is old enough to become a physical dropout.

By early adulthood he has already learned to lower his level of aspiration and to adjust his specific goal-setting accordingly. He may give up and get on the relief rolls or possibly settle for an unskilled menial job. On the other hand, he may still have salvaged enough ego strength to compete in the job arena. However, in all probability his background will not have provided him with the myriad of language, conceptual, and technical capabilities necessary to compete effectively for a job. This kind of continuous failure might ultimately drive a culturally disadvantaged person to one of two extremes: he may either give up and withdraw into the comfort of his familiar cultural cocoon and settle for effortless, simple hedonism; or he may lash out in bitterness against a hostile society that refuses him admittance.

What is to be done to salvage culturally disadvantaged Americans who might otherwise be headed toward psychological, social, and economic destitution? Again, we need the combined efforts of both experimental investigators and professionals involved in action programs. Unquestionably, the most advantageous starting point is early childhood. At that stage, a negative self-concept is not likely to have developed with any degree of permanence. Also, experiential conceptual, linguistic, and cognitive versatility can be achieved more easily if hardening of the learning arteries has not yet set in. This need to start at an early age underscores the tremendous importance of the Operation Headstart concept.

Professionals and para-professionals working with the disadvantaged must be helped by either pre- or in-service training to understand the social and psychological dynamics that create the profile of destitution described above. They must become trained observers of the behavioral patterns of the culturally disadvantaged. And they must learn to devise, administer, and interpret both informal and standardized testing instruments in order to make valid assessments of coping skills and deficiencies.

Needless to say, a healthy self-concept cannot develop within a vacuum. Hence, detailed but flexible program guidelines must be formulated to assist in arresting or reversing the deleterious effects of cultural deprivation on human personality adjustment. We must pinpoint the attitudinal traits and the cognitive skills that are prerequisite to success in handling traditional curricula. These, in turn, must be woven into a program that is palatable, stimulating, challenging, success-yielding, and relevant to academic achievement and to general life adjustment. Both within the school and within the larger community, provision must be made to secure older models whom culturally disadvantaged youths can emulate and who can provide these youths with encouragement and specific help. In the school, this model role could be performed either by a teacher or by an older, sympathetic, and more advantaged student.

Within the community, organizations such as Big Brothers of America could perform this function very effectively.

Concluding comment: cultural symbiosis and synthesis

In conclusion, one central principle deserves reiteration here: An all-out, multi-faceted attack must be waged if we are to salvage youngsters who are disadvantaged because of cultural difference and if we are to assist them in realizing optimal self-fulfillment. Such an attack will require careful and continuous assessment of their strengths, their weaknesses, and their progress. Programing must provide for the development of skills and concepts as well as for the expansion of their cognitive power. And all of this must be done in a setting that is conducive to the growth of a healthy self-image.

At long last, we may now be moving toward a new society in which no one will be at a disadvantage because of his identification with a special subculture. Hopefully, we are creating a generation of *cultural straddlers*—individuals who can participate with equal ease and comfort both in their own subcultures and in a common general American culture. Our goal must *not* be the eradication of the richness of our diversification in favor of a bland and colorless homogeniety. Rather, we can indeed enjoy cultural symbiosis and synthesis simultaneously. Our subcultures may remain essentially intact but not as cultural cocoons. As they exist side-by-side, there must be a healthy fluidity of communication and true cross-fertilization. From this kind of cultural reciprocity there can develop a synthesis that will become a superculture in which we can all participate with dignity, with self-acceptance, and with mutual respect.

REFERENCES

1. Edwards, Thomas J. "Learning Problems in Cultural Deprivation," *Reading and Inquiry*, International Reading Association Conference Proceedings, Vol. 10. Newark, Delaware, 1965.
2. Johnson, Kenneth R. "Improving the Language Skills of the Culturally Disadvantaged," *Teaching Culturally Disadvantaged Pupils*. Chicago: Science Research Associates, Inc., 1967.
3. McDavid, Raven I., Jr. "The Dialects of American English," in Francis W. Nelson (Ed.), *The Structure of American English*. New York: The Ronald Press, 1958.
4. Stewart, William A. (Ed.). *Non-Standard Speech and the Teaching of English*. Washington, D.C.: The Center for Applied Linguistics, 1964.

Children Without— Without Motivation

LYDIA B. POOL
Washington County, Georgia,
Board of Education

LET ME TAKE YOU to rural central Georgia. The town is Tennille; population, 1,847. I want you to meet Jimmy, age eight, a member of the third grade class of the Tennille Elementary School. Jimmy first came to the reading center in March of 1967. He informed everyone at the center that he could not read and that, furthermore, he did not want to learn to read. Rapport was not easily established. Verbal approaches failed, but a smile or wink would sometimes result in a positive response. When asked what he liked, his answer was "Nothing." Efforts to find Jimmy's interests continued.

At last Jimmy volunteered to tell about his experiences of the afternoon before. Jimmy talked about Steve, the adult identity in his life. Steve had taken Jimmy to ride on his tractor. Now, Jimmy dictates stories about Steve and about farm life for an experience chart. He enjoys reading his own simple, yet true stories. Jimmy has cut pictures from the *Progressive Farmer* to illustrate stories he has dictated to his classroom teacher.

Vast amounts of materials are not the most essential elements to be considered in motivation. The vital ingredient is a creative, understanding teacher.

In March Jimmy was a child without—without motivation. Jimmy is now learning to read, because reading has become meaningful. He can see himself in what he is reading; he is involved.

There are many *Jimmys* in our schools today. Many of these children without motivation are the much-read-about, much-talked-about, culturally deprived children. How can children who do not like books, who have an aversion to reading, be encouraged and led to read—not because they are forced to do so but because they want to?

Motivation: definition of and factors affecting

A great deal of time could be spent defining the term *motivation*. The definition used here is "the need and desire to know or to do." While there is often a lack of motivational factors operating among the culturally deprived children, the problem is not one of culture alone. There are those whose culture puts little value on "the need to know"; yet there are culturally deprived children who present no motivational problems. Conversely, there are children from environments one would never characterize as culturally poor who also need motivation.

The degree and type of motivation necessary to create a good climate for learning to read depend upon many factors. The individual's interests, physical well-being, emotional stability, and mental alertness are but a few of these. Children who require extensive and imaginative motivational techniques, if they are to be successful readers, are those who are emotionally deprived. These children are truly without. They may be without love; therefore, they feel alone. They are often those who fail; therefore, they feel inadequate. Perhaps they are bored; therefore, they are dull or tired. It could be that they have been pressured to "do better" and have rebelled. They could be ill, sleepy, or hungry, and, therefore, listless. Often they are those who present behavioral problems; therefore, they have been labeled "bad." Perhaps they feel they are different and, as a result, they are ashamed. Could it be that concentration is limited because of energy depletion? In an effort to solve their problems, they may have used up their energy supply. Perhaps these children who are without motivation are troubled and can be characterized by such terms as hyperactive, aggressive, or withdrawn.

Principles of motivation

Whatever the circumstances, the teacher must surmount a problem if our children without—without motivation—are to learn to read. The problem is how to create, on the part of the child, a need and a desire to read. The child must be a success. Reading must be rewarding. The child must become involved. When reading goals become the reader's goals, then reading becomes an integral part of self. These goals must be close at hand. Few, if any, children have learned to read because they want to be able to go to college. The child must read to solve a problem, or he must satisfy a need through reading. A problem may be to find out how to play a game or read a letter. Reading can be the means through which such needs as approval, recognition, and praise are realized. Smith and Dechant in *Psychology in Teaching* said, "A child will learn to read if by doing so he can get the esteem of his parents, his teacher, his peers, or if he can increase his own self-esteem."

Each child—whether culturally deprived, emotionally deprived, or educationally deprived—must be accepted for what he is. When a child's language is not accepted, he will often refuse to use language. He fears ridicule and feels unaccepted in the world in which he finds himself. To be positively motivated, acceptance of the child and his environment is a necessity. If his language is not accepted, he is in effect being told, "Your culture is not acceptable; therefore, you who are a product of this 'poor' culture are not acceptable."

Of all the facets of reading that

come to mind as the writer thinks of motivation, one stands above the rest—appropriateness of the materials used. Not only the reluctant reader but every reader, if learning is to take place, must be presented materials appropriate for his reading level. Nothing yields success like successful experiences; nothing yields failure like continually failing. Nothing can stand in the way of motivation more than being forced to attempt to handle materials that are too difficult. Materials should be appropriate not only in terms of the instructional level but also in terms of interest. Interest and curiosity play vital roles in good motivational techniques.

It is simple to expound on ideas and theories, but let us see what we are doing in our schools about the problems of the culturally, emotionally, and educationally deprived children.

Title III ESEA planning grant

In April of 1966, the Washington County Board of Education in Sandersville, Georgia, was awarded a Title III ESEA Grant by the United States Office of Education. The project, "Developing a Pilot Reading Program," originated with three classroom teachers, Catherine E. Thurston, Kathleen M. Hodges, and the writer.

Twelve school systems from the area joined the Washington County School System in efforts to provide treatment for disabled readers and to improve the developmental reading program. These included the Dublin City System and the county systems of Wilkinson, Johnson, Putnam, Hancock, Emanuel, Jefferson, Baldwin, McDuffie, Warren, Columbia, and Lincoln.

The project now has a full-time director and a full-time bookkeeper-secretary. In addition, a demonstration teacher has been employed three days a week. Part-time personnel include the assistant director, who also teaches afternoon classes; a director of materials, whose responsibilities include some teaching; and a coordinator, Washington County's Director of Curriculum. The principal of the lab-

oratory school also serves in an advisory capacity. Washington County School Superintendent, W. B. Ouzts, Jr., is the representative of the legal applicant. Seventeen persons representing the twelve systems participating with the legal applicant and one person from the Georgia College at Milledgeville compose the advisory board. Byron Callaway, director of the reading clinic at the University of Georgia, is the project consultant. Two nationally known reading consultants, A. Sterl Artley from the University of Missouri and William D. Sheldon from Syracuse University, have visited the center. Others, including Ira E. Aaron of the University of Georgia, have been consulted. Juanita Abernathy, English and reading consultant with the Georgia State Department of Educaton, has provided professional guidance.

Reading center

The planning grant stages a pilot demonstration center operating as a part of the program of the Tennille Elementary School in Tennille, Georgia. Thirty-four children are receiving direct teaching services. No one method or special materials are used. Teaching methods are diagnostic, dynamic, pragmatic, varied, individualistic, creative, flexible, and highly motivative. Each child's program is planned according to his unique needs and interests, beginning with materials having meaning for a child's particular culture and changing as cultural aspirations rise. In general, these thirty-four students first came to the reading center as children without—without motivation. Today many remain deprived; but few, if any, are without motivation. Materials and methods which yield positive results are employed; those yielding negative results are discarded. The philosophy that permeates each teaching session is to respect every child as an individual, to show faith in his ability, and to create a learning environment where success is achieved.

Demonstration teachers work with

groups ranging in size from one to six, for thirty minutes to one hour, on two to five days a week. Participants come to the reading center from their regular classrooms; however, for seven students, work in the reading center means a longer school day. The average IQ of the students, according to standardized tests, is 104. The extent of reading disability ranges from 1.3 to 4.6 years. Achievement test scores and reading expectancy levels were compared to determine disabilities. Reading expectancy levels were determined by a recognized formula.

Other students throughout the thirteen-county area are benefiting from the diagnostic services offered as a part of the pilot program. As children's reading problems are diagnosed, recommendations are made to classroom teachers. Many instruments are used. Among these are

> Wechsler Intelligence Scale for Children
> Stanford-Binet Intelligence Scale
> Peabody Picture Vocabulary Test
> Informal Reading Inventory
> Gray Oral Reading Test
> Durrell Analysis of Reading Difficulty
> Spache Diagnostic Reading Scales
> Gates Reading Survey
> Iowa Work-Study Skills
> Informal Interview
> Parent Interview
> Telebinocular
> Audiometer

Educational laboratory

Throughout the planning grant stage, the pilot center has served as an educational laboratory. Materials have been studied. Research has been conducted. A reading survey of 11,500 children in grades four through seven in the thirteen participating systems has revealed that 25 percent of these students are "severely disabled" readers. A severely disabled reader has been defined as one who is reading more than one and one-half years below his reading expectancy.

A cultural study is also underway. Cultural deprivation is prevalent in this rural central Georgia area. The mid-point of the median family income in the thirteen counties is less than $3,000. The non-white population is 48.4 percent.

In-service education has been an integral part of the project. Approximately 150 visitors, including classroom teachers, have observed in the demonstration center. Project personnel have visited similar programs and attended reading conferences throughout the nation.

Title III ESEA operational grant

As a result of experiences gained and the efforts of the advisory board and the visiting consultants, an operational grant proposal was submitted to the United States Office of Education on January 15, 1967. This grant will make an extension of the present program possible. The pilot reading center will become the parent center with personnel providing guidance for newly created subcenters throughout the participating area. The subcenters will serve as demonstration centers providing direct services for disabled readers.

The title of the operational grant phase, "Progress Thirteen," is an acrostic for Pilot Reading Organization with Guidance through Research, Experimentation, and Scientific Study. *Thirteen* denotes the thirteen participating systems.

A program concerning the prevention of reading disabilities will also be undertaken in the area of early childhood education. Work is to begin with six-year-olds; however, it is anticipated that the program will later involve three-, four-, and five-year-old children.

Project personnel believe the in-service aspects of the project to be a most significant part of the proposed program. In-service education plans include sessions with classroom teachers led by outstanding consultants and demonstrations of the teaching of large groups by means of video tape. Substitute teachers will also free classroom teachers to visit the demonstration centers. Reading supervisors will be available for consultations with classroom teachers. Even though the treatment aspects of the project can be invaluable, prevention of reading disabilities in the classroom is the ultimate goal. It is recognized that the classroom teacher is, and will remain, the backbone of our educational system.

Motivational techniques

In August a reading consultant came to Washington County, Georgia, en route from Florida to California. Upon hearing about the innovative and exemplary project in this rural county, she came to visit the reading center. Her remark was, "I've never been to such a little out-of-the-way place in such a little place and seen such exciting things going on!" Yes, exciting things have gone on, especially for the personnel connected with the project and the thirty-four children who come to the center. You met Jimmy. I would also like to introduce you to the other thirty-three participants of the pilot reading center, but there is time to meet only a few.

Jane is a sixth grade girl who read her first book just for fun in the fall. The only motivation Jane needed was encouragement, praise, and assurance that she would become a better reader. These ingredients were coupled with appropriate materials; Jane is making outstanding progress.

Tom has many emotional problems. Sometimes his problems are so great that Tom and I just talk. Other times, I read to him. Tom needs to succeed. Tom responds to the Language Master and other mechanical aids. Operating the machines is motivating; Tom is in control. This position gives him a sense of power. He learns to spell by typing the words over and over on a primer typewriter.

Phillip has been motivated through art. A book has been written especially for him to illustrate. He found a need to read the book in order to make the illustrations.

Drama and creative play mean motivation for Mike. Mike was a nonreader in December. He learned to read his script on tape in preparation for a pantomime to present in his classroom. Mike, a very sensitive nine-year-old boy, found an identification with the story character, Denny, who found a lost puppy. Being successful before his own peer group has been an extremely valuable motivational aid.

Rod loves cars. He has been motivated with books about cars. Recently he was asked to draw a motor and explain how it worked. This task required much reading and Rod mastered the task.

Joe can be motivated through external rewards. He will work for praise, for good grades, or for positive comments on his papers. He needs and requires much individual attention. His favorite method of receiving this attention is to discuss stories he has read silently or to read orally in a one-to-one relationship.

Johnny's language patterns are not those generally accepted in a middle-class culture. Recently, with the aid of a Language Master, Johnny listened on the instructor's tract to the phrase *"the* baseball game." He in turn recorded on the student's tract *"de* baseball game." As he listened a second time to the instructor's phrase and then to his own, he commented that he needed to record his again. This time he proudly said, *"The* baseball game."

Puppetry has motivated many children. Puppets are used in various ways. A favorite way has been to have the children read scripts for a play as they manipulate their puppet characters. The shy and withdrawn child and the child who daydreams find this especially satisfying.

Conclusion

Yes, we are tackling our education problems as we plan for our children without—the culturally deprived, the emotionally deprived, and the educationally deprived. Next year we look forward to the further refinement and extension of our present program.

We know that if there are to be successful reading experiences, there must be motivation—not only motivation of students but also motivation of teachers. Motivation of students may continue to challenge us. As this goal is accomplished, however, teachers are motivated because there can be no greater motivation than the realization that children who once did not want to read can hardly wait to get out of the hall to run to the reading center. These children are motivated chiefly because they are succeeding; reading has become fun.

There have also been external motivations. We call this reinforcement for learning. What is it? Every child gets a piece of hard candy from the big candy jar every day, not because he did well (we know he will do well; we make sure of that) but because the reading center is a special place and each child is a special person.

Using Continuous Evaluation in the Elementary Program

SOPHIE BLOOM
Gary, Indiana, Public Schools

ABOUT FOUR YEARS AGO, when working in Chicago, I met an extremely bright and sensitive boy named Eddie. In spite of his intelligence, however, at thirteen he lacked the most basic reading skills.

I often think of Eddie and wonder where he is today. I wonder if he has been able to realize his potential or if the system has caught him up again in the cycle of failure producing more failure. When I worked with Eddie, he was a sixth grader who had just come up from the South. He was practically a nonreader who in six months made phenomenal gains. Then he moved. I was able to observe what failure had done to Eddie and how success in learning in just a brief period of time had transformed him from a shy, hesitant, discouraged, and silent boy to a self-confident, outgoing person. While I hope he has maintained his success, I fear that he has reverted. He was on his way to success but had not mastered enough of the necessary basic skills before he moved.

If you have taught for a year, you already must have encountered some students who have had learning difficulties. If you have taught children of disadvantaged backgrounds, you know the problem well.

The magnitude of the problem of failure in our schools is almost unbelievable, and failure is by no means limited to the so-called disadvantaged though the proportion is greater among that group. There are today in the United States about fifty-five million students at all levels, elementary through graduate school. Of this number one third feels great success in school; one third vacillates, does well and poorly, goes up and down; and the last third rarely has *any* feelings of success. About twenty million children each year fail in one or more subjects and have deep feelings of frustration and despair. Failure is destructive. It destroys faith in one's ability to perform. Failure breeds self-distrust and anxiety, and for ten years there is *no escape from this unpleasant,* unrewarding situation. The child is imprisoned in a constantly punishing environment. Attendance at school is required both by law and by society. Under existing conditions there is no way out for these children.

The incidence of failure among disadvantaged students is appalling. The rate of failure among children of disadvantaged backgrounds is indicated by the finding that at the third grade, about two thirds of the children are one year behind in reading, and this gap continues to increase to two, three, four, and sometimes even five years behind at the high school level. Many are forced to drop out.

How can this failure and its debilitating effects on the personality and the development of the individual be reduced and even prevented? From my experience, there are four basic conditions necessary to prevent failure and promote success in school for each child:

1. Instruction must be adapted to the learning needs of each child.
2. Teachers must have a positive

attitude toward each child; that is, the teacher must accept each child as he is and must feel that the child can learn.

3. Each child must have evidence of his success in learning.

4. The parents must have belief in their child's ability to learn and must support the child in his learning.

It is obvious that many factors are needed to meet these four conditions. Materials, instructional methods, administrative support, and evaluation procedures, all play a role in promoting the basic conditions for success in school. In Gary, we used a three-stage cycle to provide the framework for a multiple approach to the problem. In this paper, I will emphasize only the role of continuous evaluation as a key factor in promoting these four basic conditions necessary for success in school. In our program of compensatory education, which included fourteen schools in Gary, Indiana, we found that continuous evaluation actually did play a central role in each.

By continuous evaluation, I mean the use of periodic, systematic evidence to diagnose the needs and progress of the children in the detailed aspects of learning. This use of evaluation parallels the teaching-learning. It does not guarantee change, just as a doctor's accurate diagnosis will not guarantee the recovery of the patient, but it is the first step in determining the direction of the change.

Effective use of continuous evaluation begins with an analysis of the subskills of the s u b j e c t matter, whether it be math, science, social studies, or language arts. Our subject matter in Gary was not just reading but all the language arts which we broke down into the expressive and receptive areas and their sequential subskills.

After the analysis of the subject matter into the subskills, tests and other techniques are required to obtain evidence of the level of instruction for each child. A variety of diagnostic instruments is necessary for the wide range of subskills.

Finally, after obtaining the evidence, we need a graphic way of representing the results so that both teacher and child can see at a glance what has been learned and what is yet to be learned.

The evaluation must be continuous because its purpose is constantly changing. We used it to provide the starting point for the sequence of learning. We used it to check the progress of each child. Finally, we used continuous evaluation to check for mastery.

Not all evaluation is continuous evaluation. Quite in contrast to continuous evaluation is summative evaluation. Summative evaluation is the one to which teachers and schools have been most accustomed. Examples of summative evaluation are standardized achievement tests, such as reading and math. Summative evaluation plays a vital role in education in setting standards and in marking and promotion. In our program in Gary, we have made a great deal of use of summative evaluation, but we have not found this type of evaluation useful in *adapting the instruction*. Nor have we found it useful in promoting positive attitudes on the part of the teachers, students, or parents.

The use of summative evaluation has not helped in implementing the four basic conditions necessary for successful learning. We have found that, at fifth grade, a reading score of 3.2 has not told us much about Jimmy's or Mary's strengths and weaknesses. If Jimmy and Mary are having difficulty, would 3.2 help the teacher develop a positive attitude toward their ability to learn? Of would the child feel adequate as a learner? And you can see how difficult it would be for Jimmy's or Mary's parents to have a positive attitude toward their children's ability to learn if they continue to fail.

We have looked at some of the limitations of summative evaluation. Let us now examine in detail the key role of continuous evaluation in promoting the four conditions basic to success in school.

Think of a child you know who is having great difficulty in learning. This may be a child with whom you are currently working or one you have worked with in the past. As we discuss the use of continuous evaluation in promoting each of the four conditions necessary for success in school, try to see how these ideas and techniques would apply to the child you have in mind. Would continuous evaluation have helped him succeed? Can it still?

Role of continuous evaluation in adapting the instruction to the developmental and learning needs of the children

One of the problems concerning work with the disadvantaged child and other children who are having difficulty in school has been that we have used materials which were developed and which worked well for the more advantaged child. Because the materials have not been based on the learning needs and development of the other type child, both the child and the materials have failed. Continuous evaluation will not change the materials, but it can furnish a basis for adapting the instruction and providing the materials needed. It focuses the instruction and locates the starting point.

The culturally disadvantaged child has disparities in his development. His physical development proceeds at the norm for his age. His emotional and social development are within the normal range for his age, though some of his behavior may be inappropriate for the classroom. His inadequate development in the language area is the major source of his learning problems in school. Bereiter states in his book on teaching the disadvantaged child, "The children have mastered a language that is adequate for meeting their social and material needs, but they do not learn how to use the language for obtaining and transmitting information, for monitoring their own behavior, and for carrying on verbal reasoning" (1). Their special learning needs, then, are in language.

We have tried to obtain diagnostic instruments which would point up these specific language needs of the children. Our program in Gary used oral and written diagnostic instruments for both the receptive and expressive language skills. As you know, there are many diagnostic instruments in the reading area and very few in the other language arts areas. In the reading area, we used teacher-made inventories, Botel Phonics Mastery Test, and tests accompanying basal readers to test word attack skills, comprehension skills, and work study skills. We developed a picture vocabulary inventory for receptive, meaning vocabulary. We are in the process now of adapting an inventory for the written expressive subskills. Each of these inventories broke down the subject matter into small sequential steps to parallel the instruction.

The diagnosis gave us the starting point reported on an easy-to-interpret chart form. This chart determined the level of instruction for each child. We tried to avoid any complex reports which would require much interpretation. Many diagnostic reports I have seen are so complex that it is difficult to use them. For example, a friend of mine recently told me about a seventeen-page report that she had completed on a single child in her reading clinic. It would be impossible for the classroom teacher to use even a condensed version of such a report when she has thirty or more children in her classroom. For the classroom teacher we found color-coded charts gave them the necessary detailed information in easily understood form on the specific needs of the children. We used three colors: blue for mastery, yellow for near mastery, and red for the skill which had not been learned yet. These distinctions are not for the purpose of grading or marking. They are used only to diagnose subskills already learned or not learned yet. These diagnostic tests and recordings of results on charts, then, focused the starting point and pinpointed strengths and weaknesses of individual children as well as groups of children.

Role of continuous evaluation in developing the teacher's positive attitude toward each child and his learning

It is difficult for a frustrated teacher to have a positive attitude toward her students. The main reward in teaching is to have one's students make good progress in learning. Take this away and the teacher's efforts seem meaningless and futile. They lead only to frustration and discouragement. Can a teacher who really feels discouraged about her students' learning convey a positive attitude toward the children and their ability to learn? It would be an understatement to say that it is difficult.

At times every teacher feels discouraged if she cannot reach even one child who is having difficulty. Multiply this by twenty or thirty and you have the picture of the frustration of the teacher in many classes for the disadvantaged.

In face of this existing frustration, how can continuous evaluation help the teacher develop a positive attitude toward each child's ability to learn and toward her own ability to teach?

The breakdown of the subject matter and recording the subskills enable the teacher to focus on small steps that are teachable. Breaking it down makes it possible to communicate each small step to the learner.

A fifth grade teacher who had diagnosed the level of each child in each of the subskills said that, finally, she felt that her feet were on the ground. She knew that she could teach the boys and girls the basic skills which they had previously been taught but had not mastered. At fifth grade, difficulty with such beginning skills as sound-symbol relationship was still preventing the progress of the children. When the teacher was able to break down the process into the first small step, she was able to communicate that precise subskill to the learners, and

they were able to master it within a short time.

Continuous evaluation also informs the teachers of the effectiveness of instruction for the class by observing the number of students who make the same errors. If all students make certain errors, it is an indication that some part of the teaching-learning process needs reexamination. The teacher then looks for solutions which will reduce the probability of error.

At first many teachers resented the use of teaching time for the testing. As they were encouraged by the test results, they made continuous evaluation an integral part of their teaching as it gave them objective evidence for the starting point, feedback on the most appropriate pacing of instruction, and evidence of mastery.

In the evaluation of our program last year, of 126 teachers, over 90 percent felt that the diagnostic tests were very helpful in pinpointing strengths and weaknesses and in helping them understand the subskills in the reading process.

The teachers need clear and visible evidence of success. As the children learned one subskill at a time and the color on the chart changed from red or yellow to blue, the teacher felt that the children could learn and that she could teach. The chart provided visible evidence of success for the teacher.

This need for visible evidence of success also determines the teacher's emphasis. We have observed a tendency for teachers to neglect those areas where they cannot get clear evaluation. If the teachers do not get objective evidence in the areas related to the teaching-learning process, they will seek it in other areas. We found that their teaching energy was devoted to those areas where they could obtain clear rewards. Many teachers depended upon compliments from their colleagues for beautiful bulletin boards or a well-produced program if it was difficult or impossible for them to obtain visible evidence of success in the teaching-learning situation. We found that continuous evaluation helped focus the attention and efforts of the teacher on the more central aspects of learning, and it provided the satisfaction needed to reinforce these efforts.

Finally, the use of continuous evaluation not only shifted the focus of the teacher to the teaching-learning situation but also shifted it from the response from a few children to response from all the children.

We are all aware of the appealing quality of the attractive and responsive child, and we give such children the lion's share of our attention as well as teaching energy. Many times, if the teacher evokes a flattering response from a few students, she often is unaware that many of the other students who have failed to respond may not have learned the topic under discussion. For example, in a recent Head Start follow-up evaluation in kindergarten and first grade, it was discovered that the teachers devoted 85 percent of their time to 50 percent of the children.

We have found continuous evaluation places the focus on each of the children, and, as a result, the emphasis has changed from teacher's attention for a limited number to emphasis on the progress of all the students.

We have seen how continuous evaluation can be instrumental in changing the attitude of the teacher from frustration to hope and satisfaction. Now let us see how it can also help change the self-image of the child.

The role of continuous evaluation in providing each child with evidence of his own success in learning

All children and especially children of disadvantaged backgrounds need reassurance that they can learn. This feeling is especially urgent for those who have experienced failure. The most convincing proof that they are learning is visible evidence of success. Children are not always sure when they are right. Objective evidence reinforces the certainty. As we noted before, teachers need objective evidence of success. If adults need visible evidence of success, children, having less experience and being more sensitive to failure, need it more.

I have described the color-coded charts used with the subskills inventories. We encouraged the teachers to administer tests for mastery as soon as the child was ready for it. This step gave the child a feeling of moving ahead and gave him courage to try new tasks. The color-coded chart also permitted self-evaluation on the part of the child. The children became very excited about learning. The charts motivated many students who had given up before. The children would check the chart to see which skills they had already mastered and which ones they still needed to learn. Each small step seemed possible of attainment.

Since all children are expected to learn, there was no stigma attached to not knowing. The skill with a red color on the chart merely indicated that the child had not learned that skill yet, rather than that he had failed in that skill. The individual differences among the children were reflected not in their achievement of mastery but rather in the amount of time and effort required for mastery. There was every expectation that each child, given a variety of approaches to learn, would master the subskill. All the children have a chance to succeed.

Keeping in mind the child who has learning difficulties, we can ask ourselves whether continuous evaluation helps both teacher and child.

Role of continuous evaluation in promoting a positive parental attitude

Recent research in the United States and in England has provided clear evidence that parental attitude about education accounted for more of the variation in the school achievement than any other single variable. Both the Coleman Report on "Equality of Educational Opportunity" in the United States (2) and the Plowden Report on "Children and Their Primary Schools" in England (3) demonstrate this point unequivocally.

How can continuous evaluation help develop a positive parental attitude?

Many parents of disadvantaged backgrounds feel that school and education *are* important, but due to their own unfortunate school experience or failure on the part of their children, they are not sure that their children *can* learn. Parents frequently react with anger and blame when their child does not learn at school. They often believe that it is willful on the part of the child.

We have found in our own work with parents that using continuous evaluation to break down the learning and combining it with appropriate and varied instructional approaches convinced parents that their children can learn.

Continuous evaluation also formed one of the bases for parent conferences in Gary. Instead of merely reporting that Jimmy is good or bad, learning or not learning, the teacher was able to point out what Jimmy had learned and what he still needed to learn.

Parents have been responsive and encouraged when they have seen the charts and seen the visible evidence of their child's learning. Under the teacher's direction, this information frequently led to specific ways parents could help their children in particular aspects of the learning.

Summary

Continuous evaluation is not a panacea for the learning problems of the disadvantaged. However, it is a most essential part of the multiple approach necessary for the eradication of failure and promotion of success for these children. We found that it was effective when used in the context of our three-stage cycle of diagnosis of need, provision of a variety of instructional materials for specific subskills, and evaluation of mastery.

As we mentioned earlier, children who are culturally disadvantaged have many gaps in the verbal and thinking skills necessary for success in school. Part of our problem in using continuous evaluation for them has been the lack of diagnostic instruments for some of the subskills. In the receptive area, there are many for the reading and a few for the listening.

In the expressive area, except for screening for speech, it has been difficult to find diagnostic instruments for the oral language. One result is that the teaching of oral language has been grossly neglected. This condition is unfortunate since oral language forms the basis for all the language arts. The first diagnostic writing test that we found had been published within the past year.

We are much encouraged in that we do have a paradigm of the process for change, and we do know the parts we need to complete the picture.

We are much encouraged by the change in attitude of the teachers, children, and parents. We feel we have a good start, and we hope to continue to build on it.

REFERENCES

1. Bereiter, Carl, and Siegfried Engelmann. *Teaching Disadvantaged Children in the Preschool.* Prentice-Hall, 1966.
2. Coleman, James. "Survey on Equality of Educational Opportunity," U.S. Office of Education, 1966.
3. Lady Plowden (Chairman). "Report on Children and Their Primary Schools," London, England, 1967.

Marshaling the Forces in a Community

CARRIE B. DAWSON
Gary, Indiana, Public Schools

SOME EDUCATORS BELIEVE that the schools which are located in deprived areas need not accept the slum conditions and their erosive effects on children as unalterable and permanent. They believe that the modern concept of the role of the school includes and commits them to the leadership role of "marshaling the forces" in their communities so that cooperative action programs can be fashioned and conducted in behalf of and in defense of providing good education for children in the depressed area. Such concerned educators realize that environmentally disadvantaged children are deprived of those experiences that are constructs for the development of an adequate foundation for learning to read and that, because of the stultifying conditions under which they live, there is little motivation for learning to read. The schools and communities in which such concerned educators serve are demonstrating that the school can and should assume leadership for reversing the negative effects of environmental deprivation. This movement is basic to any national effort toward *forging ahead in reading*.

The well-documented disparity between the native capacity and the reading achievement of environmentally deprived children and our nation's need for the conservation of all human resources and talent provide the framework for this attempt to take a close look at the techniques now being developed through the commendable leadership of educators as they work to "marshal the forces of the community" in behalf of children.

A question immediately arises: Why have such a discussion among school persons, all of whom have been engaged at their own community levels or through conference, administrative, or advisory capacities with programs specifically designed to aid impoverished children and their parents?

My cautious answer is that precisely because schools have and are making sincere efforts in behalf of rural and inner-city children with dissimilar experiential backgrounds but quite similar learning problems and because we can point to some measure of progress based on considerable evidence contained in voluminous reports of programs underway, there is a very real danger of our being overly optimistic. We may fail to appreciate that each report of dramatic results refers to a particular group's efforts in behalf of a particular group of children under very special environmental conditions, and is not necessarily applicable to an assessment which would permit us to claim more than that we have found fragmentary solutions to the problem of helping children overcome their environmental handicaps. The greater

necessary corollary task of modifying the home and community environments responsible for cultural and educational disadvantage remains a frontier.

Hopefully, we are at least beginning to move in the right direction, but all evaluations must be balanced against the disquieting, if not frightening, prediction that "by 1970 *one out of every two* children in the nation's largest school systems will be disadvantaged" (*1*).

> Furthermore, it should be recognized that some of the handicaps which the disadvantaged suffer cannot be eliminated completely but that their crippling effects may be reduced, the damaging influences minimized, and some compensatory provisions made for overcoming limitations or difficulties. On the other hand, many disabilities can be eliminated by effective planning and by action programs. In fact, some limitations may be turned into advantages when given new perspectives and opportunities for expression (*3*).

As long as there is one small hope that there is a possibility of reversing the negative effects of environmental deprivation, the present discussion must retain a single central focus. It is to demonstrate that when school personnel in a disadvantaged neighborhood establish meaningful relationships with parents and with the community agencies which serve the families, extraordinary breakthroughs occur— documented breakthroughs that have completely changed a community, its adults, and their interrelationships and, in consequence, the achievement, aspiration levels, personalities, and behavior patterns of its students.

Descriptions of individual teachers' efforts or of school-community programs and their successes have been widely reported and sufficiently documented; they would not serve our purposes here. I submit that where changes have occurred within communities, they are the direct result of far more than increased budgets, additional auxilliary equipment, enlarged staffs, specialized personnel, or even excellence of programing. There must become common denominators, some basic principles operative in all successful investigations, and programs which produce positive changes in persons and their perspectives. On this premise, alone, is this paper organized.

As a *first* consideration, the "forces in a community" are briefly indicated mainly to point up the fact that the children live in a restrictive environment that tends to separate them from the mainstream of culture and that the restriction itself creates and compounds the problems with which the school must deal.

A *second* area of discussion tests the hypothesis that there are common threads which are identifiable in all programs making headway in effecting positive community changes. Because educators have access to and are familiar with the full and detailed reports of exemplary programs, the actual descriptions of programs are eliminated. The principles, rather than the practices, are examined.

A *third* and final phase of the discussion examines "motivation and reading" in an attempt to show how carefully and conscientiously educators now use the data available from sound research to establish firm and defensible programs to supplement and provide these educative ingredients which deprived children were previously denied.

Forces in a community

Slum areas remain ineffective communities partially because there are no strong leaders who can and are willing to make sacrificial and sustained efforts toward improving conditions. This fact is understandable when we reflect that potential leaders are discouraged and finally lose initiative because they, too, are victims of the same defeating circumstances which dehumanize their neighbors. As a result, it is necessary that the school take the initiative to coordinate and lend support to the few persons and the established agencies which serve their children and families.

For even the basic requirements of existence, many families must rely on welfare agencies, housing departments, neighborhood or settlement houses, and religious institutions. The school makes deliberate effort, therefore, to plan and work with persons who are responsible for directing the services of such agencies for certainly these agencies are strong "forces in a community."

One of the most comprehensive and disturbing analyses of the needs and characteristics of the environmentally deprived child and the "other forces" which render them incapable of coping with the requirements of school life is included in *The Journal of Negro Education's 1964 Yearbook (4)*. The five articles by Robert Havighurst, Walter G. Daniel, Frank Riessman, Martin Deutsch, and Harold Spears list and intensively define those "forces" which are most destructive of children's innate and insatiable desire to learn. Included are such sociological-psychological forces as a minimum of direct contact with central channels of the main culture, the frequent non-availability of successful adult male models, economic insecurity, few shared or planned family activities, restriction in the variety of stimuli, and many more.

These selected forces are examples of the kind which create deficits which the school can realistically plan to overcome; literature is filled with exciting reports of schools' successes in helping not only deprived children make their first and continuous contacts with the mainstream of culture but helping, also, the adult members grow in the ability and confidence to guide and direct their own children's experiences.

The forces which touch the lives of the disadvantaged are not all negative. Riessman makes this point clear as he writes on "the strengths of the poor" (7). His question is well worth considering:

... if the have-nots have nothing—no culture, no strength, no anger, no organization, no cooperativeness, no inventiveness, no vitality—if they are only depressed, apathetic, fatalistic, and pathological, then where is the force for the social action and self-help to come from?

Riessman rejects the help for the poor if it is to "come only from the outside, to be doled out." Realistically, he acknowledges the need for the poor to align themselves with other groups and forces in the society but stresses their strengths gained through coping with problems—the interdependence, organization, and stability of the female-based family; the maturity of the children, cooperativeness, lessened sibling rivalry, etc. Suggestions are included for further strengthening.

Reports of highly successful, well-coordinated community action programs evidence close planning and programing between the school and all facets of the community; the school reaps an additional benefit by putting to work its knowledge of children without having to assume the responsibility of using its own limited personnel for the persistent and involved follow-up work that must be done.

Common characteristics of successful programs

The programs represent one of the most dramatic and remarkable revolutions in American educational history. Virtually all school systems in every section of the United States have been engaged, simultaneously, in drafting, designing, and implementing programs to accelerate the achievements of disadvantaged children. The intensive efforts, the enthusiasm of participants, the spirit of urgency, and the unusually strong support of the public and the local and federal governments would seem strange if the ideas were not universally accepted. Why is it, we may well ask, that, despite geographic distance, there are great similarities in problems and needs identified, in techniques employed, in goals sought, and in the results so far achieved?

Our seemingly sudden expectation that we can erase or at least mitigate the deficits of disadvantaged children is based in sound philosophy. I submit that all who are now engaged in finding special ways to help these children are, consciously or unconsciously,

working because they have a singular but common perspective. The evidence is explicitly given by Arthur Combs in "The Role of the Teacher in Creating Intelligence" (2). At the risk of devaluing one of the most inspiring messages of our times for educators, I have extracted a few of his statements. It seems to me that these are the guidelines or touchstones on which all new programs for the disadvantaged are founded.

Presented here in Combs' words, the statements serve as the frame of reference reflecting the characteristic beliefs of those who work with new vision for children:

We have had the impertinence to believe that poverty can be eliminated—that human intelligence can be created.
When this idea reaches its full potential, it will change the face of the entire world.
We are beginning to discover that we have been selling people short for a very long time. We have been much too concerned with human limitations and not nearly enough concerned with human possibilities and potentialities.
We are not the victims of the child's intelligence; we are the creator of it. We can, therefore, change a child's capacities to behave or misbehave.
What this new conception means is that there is something we can do for *every* child.
Human adjustment is in very large measure a problem of a person's perception of himself. People with a positive view of themselves are also likely to be more intelligent.
A positive view of self also determines the degree to which a person is able to make use of the learning experiences we subject him to in public school.

Motivation toward reading— the ultimate goal

Never before has it been demonstrated so clearly that the child's physical well-being, concept of self, communicative ability, experiential background; that the parent's concept of self, interest, understanding, and support of the child and the school; that the teacher's attitude, knowledge of the value system operative in the child's community, the teacher's sympathy and concern, all are intrinsically interwoven with the child's intellectual and reading achievement. The school must attend to, remove, or redirect any of these toward positive lines before getting on with the business of promoting learning. Educational planning for the disadvantaged is synonymous, therefore, with "marshaling the forces in a community" in one of the greatest efforts in the school's history to teach all educable children to read.

Variations in approaches, methods, and materials appear because individual and groups of children differ; educators realistically concentrate first and foremost on the removal of those stumbling blocks which interfere the most with the children's becoming excited about (motivated) and acquiring an insatiable thirst for reading: 1) Headstart programs reflect our knowledge, based on research, of the positive effects of enriched early environments on cognitive and motoric abilities required if children are "ready for reading." 2) Medical, dental, general physical examinations, immunizations, and corrections—as well as provisions for breakfast at school or hot lunches—honor the relationship between a healthy body and academic achievement. 3) Parent-education programs are established because parental encouragement and support can take a child a long way toward achievement because positive parent-teacher relationships promote positive child-teacher relationships and because parents can, with the school's assistance, improve their own homemaking and child-rearing skills. 4) Teachers are retrained through NDEA institutes and through local in-service training programs where special attention is given to promoting understanding of the value system of the low-economic groups assuring right attitudes and increasing teachers' knowledge of the best instructional methods for promoting children's interest and power in reading. 5) Field trips, study trips, and cultural excursions give some children their first glimpses at ways of living, working, and enjoying in settings enchantingly different from

their own. 6) Remedial reading programs are incorporated in most programs, especially for those children in upper elementary and secondary school levels who have already been severely retarded or damaged by their environment. 7) Noncertificated aides are used in the classrooms to augment the teachers' efforts and to give children another adult who can listen to them, reassure them, and give them the individual attention needed.

How do we know that even these small random samples of programs designed to interpret and extend the experiences of children will motivate them toward learning to communicate and especially to acquire the desire to and skill in the basic tool—reading? Research is beginning to tell us that we are on sound ground: 1) An English investigator (6), faced with the identical problems now being faced by American educators, found that parental encouragement and support have greater effect on children's progress in school than either the variation in home circumstances or the variation in schools and teachers. 2) A team of investigators (5), in attempting to determine the influence of parental attitudes and child-parent interaction upon remedial reading progress, found that parental attitudes are significantly correlated with reading gains of their respective children. 3) The Institute for Developmental Studies (8), an interdisciplinary unit within the New York College Department of Psychiatry, is "engaged in a long-range investigation of the developmental, psychological, and social determinants of learning and intelligence, with particular emphasis on the role of environmental influences." Established in 1958, sufficient evidence has been gathered to show that the disadvantaged child has not been stimulated to develop the abilities that underlie the *capacity* to learn in a school setting. These and other careful investigations are beginning to validate the new approaches to helping children overcome learning deficits.

Concluding statement

The most significant feature of what is called "education for the environmentally or culturally disadvantaged reader" is the school's deliberate effort to seek the aid of all adults who touch the lives of the children. With urgency, the school is attempting to marshal all the forces of the community in order to expand even more the potential range and breadth of the children's intellectual and cultural lives. Children, seemingly, are becoming excited about and showing promise of achieving levels higher than anticipated. Deepest interest and concern exist for the children's acquisition of power and skill in reading. If we can assure mastery of the skill of reading for disadvantaged children, there is more than reason to hope—there is evidence we are forging ahead in reading.

REFERENCES

1. American Association of School Administrators, *School Programs for the Disadvantaged,* Educational Research Circular No. 1, January 1965, Washington, D.C.
2. Combs, Arthur. "The Role of the Teacher in Creating Intelligence," address delivered at School City of Gary Human Relations Institute, May 1966.
3. Daniel, Walter G. (Ed.). "Educational Planning for Socially Disadvantaged Children and Youth," *The Journal of Negro Education, 33,* No. 3 (Summer 1964). Washington, D.C.: The Howard University Press, 204.
4. *Ibid.* 210-217.
5. Gabriel, Della-Piana; Robert F. Stahmann; and John E. Allen. *The Influence of Parental Attitudes and Child-Parent Interaction Upon Reading Progress,* Cooperative Research Project S-266, University of Utah, Salt Lake City, 1966.
6. Peaker, G. F. *The Regression Analyses of the National Survey,* printed in England for Her Majesty's Stationery Office by McCorquodule, London.
7. Riessman, Frank. "The Strengths of the Poor," *Social Welfare Forum,* 1964.
8. Snyder, Ralph E.; Alfred Freedman; and Martin Deutsch. *Institute for Developmental Studies.* New York: New York Medical College, Department of Psychiatry, Annual Report, 1965.

The New York City Reading Program—A New Attack for Improvement

Helene M. Lloyd
New York City Board of Education

THE NEW YORK CITY SCHOOL SYSTEM is a giant, even among great urban centers. It enrolls more than a million students, ranging from the barely educable to the highly gifted. It includes over 900 schools, ranging from the most modern plants in the educational world to a few that will be demolished as plans on the drawing boards materialize. It employs more than 40,000 professionals, ranging from substitutes in their first day of teaching to veterans nearing retirement.

All of this bigness brings with it great challenges—one of the greatest of which is teaching *each* pupil to read up to his full measure of ability. How successful have we been in the past? As successful as other great cities? Yes, and in some cases more so. As successful as we would like to be? This question we answer with an emphatic *no*! No professional or parent in our city will be or should be satisfied until *all* children are reading up to their full capacity.

It is this determination that lead the Superintendent of Schools, Bernard E. Donovan, to turn the spotlight on New York City's reading program and to announce that the improvement of reading achievement is the number one objective in every school in our city this year. Turning a spotlight on a program pays dividends. Questions were asked; answers had to be ready to stand scrutiny. Let's consider a few of these questions and the answers.

Big city problems

The answers to the question *Why don't some New York City children read better?* are connected, in large part, with the city's bigness:
1. We are a city of great teacher turnover. In 1964-65, the median length of service for elementary school teachers was 6½ years.

One third of the staff has 3 years or less experience. Yet this is the very level of schooling where reading begins and where great ability in teaching is needed.

2. This is a city where "children are on the move." Far too many families in New York City, especially disadvantaged ones, move eight, nine, or ten times in one school year. In the borough of Manhattan, enrolling 175,000 pupils, the average rate of mobility in 1964-65 was 32 percent.

3. This is a city of many socially-disadvantaged children. Because these children are moving into our city in ever increasing numbers, the need becomes more and more urgent.

4. This is a city of many non-English speaking children. Eight percent of New York City's over 1,000,000 pupils are non-English speaking. These children, many of them coming from Puerto Rico and more recently from Cuba and China, come with a multiplicity of backgrounds —rural, urban; educated, uneducated; deprived, advantaged.

Staff needs

What help does the teacher need to teach children in this city to read better? is the second question we asked:

1. Effective guidance from a well-informed supervisor is needed. With this answer in mind, the superintendent asked the principals of several schools enrolling large numbers of disadvantaged children to design a series of refresher workshops for principals in the supervision of a school's reading program. Supplementary materials were prepared; practical assistance to teachers was emphasized. These workshops were held for elementary principals in each of the thirty school districts in our city.

2. A reading bulletin or handbook for teachers that is specific and easy to use was the request of ten superintendents of districts in our city where there are many newly appointed teachers who are having difficulty in the teaching of reading. To meet this request three concise handbooks have been prepared by the office of curriculum this year. These will be in the schools in September—one for the primary grades, one for the intermediate, and one for use at the high school level.

3. A list of reading skills was requested in order that a teacher could understand the skills she is responsible for teaching to specific children. As a result of this need, we developed during the current year and have just sent to the printer a list of sequential reading skills, prekindergarten through grade 12, for use by teachers in our schools. Many readers no doubt appreciate the difficult task this was and understand our feeling of accomplishment.

4. Support from other professionals and paraprofessionals was requested and took the form of 618 teachers of library—at least one to each of our 607 elementary schools; additional teachers of speeech to improve the overall listening and speaking skills of children; additional after-school study centers focusing on the improvement of reading; increased school-aide time to handle the duplication of materials, requests for new readers, preparation of displays of library books, and related work.

Use of personnel

How can we use our staff more effectively to improve reading? is the third question we asked. The answer was found in a shift in emphasis; i.e., the decision not to increase the number of corrective reading positions in our city but to focus on the following:

1. Increasing the number of children enrolled in prekindergarten and kindergarten. Because of space limitation during the regular school year, every effort will be made to increase the number of pupils attending kindergarten in the sum-

mer. During the school year, 9,000 were enrolled in board of education prekindergartens. It is expected that more pupils will be registered this summer. Kindergarten registration will also be pushed this spring.

2. Improving the initial teaching of reading in the primary grades. This decision has already resulted in smaller class size in the early grades of some schools in disadvantaged areas; in those schools where space is not available, two teachers are assigned to one class.

3. Having the classroom teacher responsible for the reading achievement of all pupils in her class except those in need of help from a reading clinic. Children assisted by a clinician would be those retarded two or more years in reading and those emotionally disturbed.

4. Using paraprofessionals and school volunteers in ever increasing numbers. These people would work under the teacher's guidance on a one-to-one basis with children.

New materials

What materials do children need to improve their level of reading achievement for use with our disadvantaged children? was another question raised. The answer was a many-faceted one and included these answers:

1. The materials must be based on experiences to which the child can relate. The Bank Street Readers, the Chandler series, and the Webster series are all moving in this direction.

2. Materials used by *all* children should contain photographs and content promoting integration and the development of a worthy self-image.

3. Materials for use with disadvantage pupils at the initial reading stage should have a strong audiovisual emphasis.

4. Materials should involve the child

in their use so that he gains a feeling of responsibility for his own reading progress. The SRA kits, the Reader's Digest skill texts, Macmillan skill builders, as well as the programed materials in reading skills being developed by the New York City school system for the use of the disadvantaged, use the basic idea of involving the learner in the responsibility for progress.

Publishers are making greater efforts than ever before to develop the types of reading and audiovisual materials needed by urban children. Our unmet needs, however, are still too great. Consequently, we initiated this school year a project known as "A District Adopts a Publisher." Ten of the leading publishers have each been invited to work in one school district in our city; i.e., to visit schools to study the learning materials needed by the children and the teachers and to try out materials in process of development in order to determine whether the items are of value. To date our roster includes the following publishers: Scott, Foresman; McGraw-Hill; Silver Burdett; Holt, Rinehart and Winston; Houghton Mifflin; Harcourt, Brace, and World; Random House; Harper and Row; Doubleday; and Rand McNally. Other publishers who express interest will be invited to work in one of the remaining school districts. The objective is to have publishers, working in every school district in this city, tailoring materials to fit the needs of children and adults at all levels of our school system.

Accountability

How can we emphasize accountability for reading progress? was another in the series of questions raised. It evoked the following answers:

1. In this area the superintendent of schools has been explicit. In his words, "Responsibility for the reading achievement of children rests with the *classroom* teacher, working under the supervision of

the principal and district superintendent. The assistance from a reading clinician, guidance teacher, speech teacher, or other staff member does not detract from the classroom teacher's overall responsibility for the child's reading progress." In addition, the superintendent has asked that the child's reading level be indicated on his report card in order that the parent is aware of progress or lack of progress.

2. The board of education has underscored accountability to parents at the local level by publishing the standardized reading test scores of every school in this city and by providing city-wide conference time in the school's calendar for teachers to meet with parents.

Project Head start has shown us that the effectiveness of the work with children was *directly related* to the extent of parent involvement in this whole area of accountability. We have only scratched the surface in regard to parent participation, but it is a benchmark of progress to note that the scratch is deep and the interest in it is great.

Getting somewhere

We cannot to date point to test scores as evidence that "Our New Attack for Improvement" has had a positive impact on the reading achievement level of New York City's over 1,000,000 children.

The evidence lies in the fact that the administration of a great school system has not been willing to accept today's reading scores but has taken a hard look at what it has been doing and has tailored its entire program to meet need. True, the task ahead is great, but we know where we are going and how we plan to get there. We also know that accountability for progress has been clearly defined with today's classroom teacher spearheading our drive for reading improvement in New York City's schools in 1967.

A Summer Learning Readiness Program in Passaic, New Jersey

DOROTHY D. KOHANSKI
Passaic, New Jersey, Public Schools

LUCY HAD COME TO PASSAIC from a rural southern community; her parents were illiterate and, therefore, were unable to read to her. Maria knew about airplanes. In her short six years of life she had been back and forth to Puerto Rico several times, but she had never been on a train. Bill lived with foster parents; no one knew who his father was and Bill's mother had deserted him. John shared a bed with his mother and four brothers and sisters. Martha spoke only Polish at home. Childhood for all of these children and many, many like them was already a grim experience. They had all had one year's experience with school—in kindergarten—and had met with frustration.

Lucy, Maria, Bill, and the others lived in Passaic, New Jersey. Passaic is a moderate-sized community not far from New York City. It has a large population of Negroes, many of whom are migrants from the South, and a great number of Puerto Ricans and Cubans. There are also a number of small neighborhoods consisting of Hungarians, Poles, Ukranians, Italians, and a smattering of other nationalities who cling to the language and ways of their home countries. These groups are mainly the ones who comprise the "disadvantaged" category, but their disadvantages vary.

Some are disadvantaged because they lack enough money to provide the proper physical environment of food, clothing, and shelter for their families. Some are disadvantaged because their inability to communicate with the English speaking world around them makes it difficult for adults to get jobs and for children to manage in school.

The children of these people are disadvantaged for all the many reasons that have been written about and spoken about in countless books and at countless conventions, as educators across the nation attempt to grapple with the problem that is certainly not exclusive to Passaic.

Recently the United States government has been extending assistance to educators to help them deal with the situation. The Elementary and Secondary Education Act of 1965 suddenly provided one weapon— money—that could help to fight the problem. With money one could buy suitable materials, provide adequate personnel, and do, it seemed, a million wonderful things. In Passaic, as elsewhere, we used our ESEA funds for a massive attack on the reading problem. And in our planning we put aside enough money to plan and carry out a summer program for kindergarten children like Lucy, Bill, and John which we chose to call a "learning readiness program" rather than a "reading readiness" one. Our aim was to prepare these children for a total school experience and not for reading alone.

The children

Our first problem was to decide which children should take part in the experiment. The decision was to take kindergarten children in the culturally depressed areas who had, in a sense, "failed sandbox" and who, according to their readiness tests and the judgment of their teachers, would not be able to manage first grade work. We used the Metropolitan Readiness Test as one basis of choice. All the children who fell into the average (C), below average (D), and poor risk (E) categories received letters to take home inviting them to take part in an exciting summer program.

The response was gratifying: well over 300 parents indicated their interest. By the time the program got under way, however, the number registered had become about 200. The reason for this decrease is that some parents tend to sign anything that comes home from the school. Another reason is that Puerto Rican families tend to commute rather regularly between the main land and the island. And then, family plans often change. In any case, we started our program with 200 eager youngsters from a variety of racial and cultural backgrounds.

The staff

We decided that the youngsters should be divided into small groups of ten to fifteen children and that each group should have a teacher and a teacher aide. The teachers who had volunteered to join in the experiment were from the Passaic School System. We insisted that they be primary or kindergarten teachers. The teacher aides were all college students majoring, for the most part, in primary education. It was to be a learning period not only for the children but also for the teachers and, in many ways, a training ground for future teachers.

In addition, we had several specialists: a gym instructor, whose teacher-aide doubled as visual-aids man; a nurse; a speech therapist; a consulting psychologist; a perception consultant; kitchen and custodial staff; an office secretary; and one director.

The program was based in an elementary school building in the heart of the disadvantaged area. Four buses picked up the children from the other areas of town, and one bus was available every day for field trips which were an essential part of the program.

Teacher preparation

To prepare our staff, we embarked on an in-service training program that began two days before the program started and lasted all through the summer. In the two-day session we met to discuss major goals and techniques, to become acquainted with the many new and varied materials ESEA funds were able to provide, and to begin an understanding of motor-visual-perceptual skills. During the summer the teachers also had an opportunity to participate in a team-teaching approach developed at the Harvard-Lexington program. The former coordinator of the ESEA led this part of the program. By the end of the summer the teachers were not sure whether they or the children had learned the most!

The program begins

July came and with it the busloads of children. To avoid confusion, all children had been sent tags with a symbol and color that matched tags worn by their specific teacher and teacher aide. The children were also issued smaller colored tags by which they identified their buses for the homeward journey. We lost no children during the summer, coming *or* going. Although it took only a day or two for the children to know their teachers, their rooms, and their buses, they were reluctant to part with the tags and wore them day in and day out until the tags fell apart.

The needs of the children and how they were met

In planning a program such as this one, we had to know the needs of the children in order to tailor a curriculum to suit them. We knew from observation and research some of the most serious needs the children had that the school could deal with.

One need of most of the children was nutritional. We know that hungry children can not learn. Therefore, as soon as they arrived in the morning, we provided milk and cookies and a nutritious hot lunch daily. The nurse reported an average gain of 1½ pounds at the end of the six-week period.

A second and very major area was the development of motor-visual-perceptual skills. A characteristic of underprivileged children seems to be a lack of these skills. Florence E. Sutphin of Bridgeport, Conn., listed the following characteristics she found among deprived children: being unable to track a target visually, to negotiate a walking beam or perform on a jump board satisfactorily, to cross-pattern in walking and creeping, to distinguish figure-ground images, and to reproduce a simple rhythm; being kinesthetic learners; and lacking perceptual maturity (2).

To cope with this problem, a major part of our program was devoted to meeting these needs. The gym period involved balance boards, walking beams, and the like, on which children developed a sense of balance and an awareness of their own bodies in space. All the other usual gym activities were done under this new frame of reference. In fact, to distinguish our program from the mere concept of exercise, we dubbed it *kinematics*—the science of motion. Cross patterning was consciously worked on, as were dominance exercises. One of the most interesting features of the kinematics period was the practice of the body alphabet— the actual feeling of the shape of the letters through making the form with one's own body (1). Children also traced letters on one another's back to get a muscle impression of form.

Even the lunchroom proved to be a place to practice balance. Children handling lunch trays for the first time found them something of a problem, but by the end of the summer session to walk with a tray full of food that had to be carefully balanced was a simple matter.

The classroom teachers continued motor-visual-perceptual training in the classrooms. Rhythm instruments, dancing, and singing helped to develop a sense of rhythm. Eye-hand coordination was assisted by the use of workbenches, puzzles, and the like. Perceptual materials of all kinds helped to develop visual discrimination and auditory discrimination. Building blocks were a favorite with the children in discovering size, shape, and relationship in space.

In addition to the need to develop perceptual experiences, there exists in these youngsters a great need for conceptual experiences. In the classroom the children played games and had experiences that developed understandings of time, color, texture, left and right, and so forth. It is well known that deprived children often do not know colors, and so art played an important role in the curriculum.

Of greatest importance was expanding their concept of the world around them. To this end we planned five trips, so arranged that every child went on every trip during the course of the program. The bus trip itself was an experience in group living, for this was not the short trip from school to home that they took every day. This time they went to places that were a half an hour to an hour distant. The trips included a park with a farm, a zoo of wild animals, a zoo of tame animals, a junior museum and a fantasy land park. Intensive preparation took place in the classroom beforehand with film strips, stories, pictures, and records playing a part in the preparation. Then for a day or two following each trip there were follow-up activities in each classroom, including creative dramatics and role playing and a wide variety of art work.

Finally, there was the need for oral communication. The activities involved in developing the skills of communication permeated all the other activities, of course. Nevertheless, there were times when this skill was concentrated upon by pupils and teachers as in teaching English to the non English-speaking children and in the work of the speech therapist. Classroom activities along these lines included listening to stories, learning sequence of events, being able to describe an event such as the trips, play acting with hand puppets, and handling acceptable English speech patterns in all these activities.

Communication with the first grade teachers

It has been the experience of this writer that all too often children have some unusual school experience but the information is not passed on in any useful form to the child's next teacher. To avoid this lack of communication we designed a card which was sent to the schools at the close of the summer program. The card, which was filled in by the staff throughout the summer, included a detailed diagnosis of the child's problem at the beginning of the summer; the results of tests of speech, vision, hearing, and psychology; dominance as developed by that time; observation of motor skills and eye-hand

coordination; scores on pre- and post-readiness tests; the reaction of the child to each trip; his knowledge of the alphabet at the end of the program; and a long array of reading-readiness skills. The card included a record of the child's growth in all these areas during the six-week period. We felt it presented a fairly complete picture.

Results of the program

The schools, as well as the superintendent, the board of education, and the New Jersey Department of Education received a detailed report on the results at the end of the program. All of us who were involved were pleased to report the results because they were rather impressive.

For instance, in comparing the pre-and post-tests, in which alternate forms of the Metropolitan Readiness Test were used, it was found that out of the 132 children tested on both tests, 103 gained. The gains ranged from 2 to 66 percentile points. Six children actually reached the 99th percentile on the second test. There was an average gain of 24 percentile points. Twenty-two children lost ground, with the range of loss from 1 to 25 percentile points. The average loss was 6 percentile points. The median percentile score for the first test was 29 and for the second test, 45.

In order to be reasonably scientific about our testing, we also set up a control group. It was a rough control, consisting of children who had been recommended for the program because of C, D, or E rating on the Metropolitan Readiness Test administered in May of their kindergarten year but who had not attended the program. There were seventy-six public school and fifty-one parochial school children in the control group in September.

The testing showed that there was a much higher percentage of children in the control group that lost ground between the May test and the start of the fall term than in the summer group—nearly twice as great a percentage. And the gains of the summer group outstripped the gains of the control group, except in the case of the parochial school children where the difference was not so great. For instance, 41.3 percent of the public school summer group gained 20 percentile points or more as compared to 7.9 percent of the public school control group. In the parochial group, 53.1 percent of the summer participants gained 20 or more percentile points, compared to 34.5 percent of the parochial control group. In all cases, the summer group did significantly better than the control group on the tests.

Further follow-up

Tests, however, do not tell the full story. Planning was set up to do a follow-up study of the children, both the summer and control groups, through the first grade. A simple questionnaire asked the teachers to indicate their ratings of the children according to what reading group they were in and to indicate their reading level. There were to be three follow-ups during the year.

The first of these was done in October on the summer group only. Fully three quarters of the summer children, including several in the "poor risk" category, were rated in the top or middle of their classes. Even at that early date many were beginning to read in preprimers or even primers.

The second follow-up took place at the beginning of March. At this time both groups were checked. Normal progress for that time of year would show children reading in the primer of their basal series. Of the summer children, 44 percent were in the primers, as compared with 25 percent of the control group. Even more important was that teachers indicated the difference in approach and attitude on the part of the summer group compared to others. They were more secure and eager. Even the slowest children were ahead of a similar group of a year before, according to some of the teachers.

A third follow-up will be conducted in June. The writer fully expects the trend indicated above to continue.

Conclusion

The results appear to justify the concept of a summer learning readiness program, or a transition class, for kindergarten children who do not seem ready for the tasks of first grade. It would also appear from our experiment that intensive training can help to make a child "readier" than he would be if one merely waits for automatic maturation to take place.

It is the feeling of the summer ESEA staff and of its director (the writer) that government money spent in projects such as ours and in other early learning programs such as Head Start is money very well spent. Prevention of learning problems is more effective than are later cures. Of course, it would be naive to say that early learning and readiness programs will eliminate the need for remedial programs later, but we believe that the firm foundation laid in such programs will make for fewer remedial cases later and will very possibly make such cases less severe.

It is the hope of the writer that if and when government funds cease to be available, local school boards will see the beneficial effect of learning readiness programs and will continue them as a regular part of the educational structure.

REFERENCES

1. Kirshner, Abraham. *Visual Motor Game.* Montreal, Canada, Snowden Medical Building.
2. Sutphin, Florence E. "Learning to Learn—First Step in Teaching the Underprivileged," *The Reading Instruction Journal.* New Jersey, January 1967, 5.

Advantaged Education for Disadvantaged Youth

Melvin Howards
Northeastern University

MY CHOICE OF TITLE, Advantaged Education for Disadvantaged Youth, was not intended to preclude concern for advantaged education for the advantaged, for it is my basic contention that substantive change at all levels and in all quarters of American education are desperately needed—changes in curriculum content and structure, teachers, books and materials for instructional purposes, goals and objectives, etc. No matter what you may think of the War on Poverty as a whole, one thing seems clear now, and that is that until the passage of the Economic Opportunity Act in April 1964, very little was happening in the way of innovation in education for the disadvantaged population in our schools. Since that time several types of programs have been developed which are attempting to offer viable alternatives to educating this particular group. One such alternative that I shall describe in some detail is the Northeastern University Laboratory School for high school dropouts which has been in operation since February 1, 1966.

But first, consider the context in which this particular program developed. The War on Poverty is not at all a war on poverty, but it is rather a massive educational movement for the enlightenment of the middle class. For it is, in fact, the middle class which has historically controlled access to almost all of the major institutions of our society, so that unless they were given opportunities to work more directly with the poverty population, no major change could be expected in American life. Just three years ago the Economic Opportunity Act was passed, and most Americans discovered that almost one third of our total population was suffering from the complete syndrome of poverty—inadequate housing, little or no relevant education, hunger, ignorance of basic human and civil rights, medical problems, limited job opportunities, etc. With the advent of the Office of Economic Opportunity (conscience of the middle class) programs and projects were developed which were intended to alleviate and alter (where possible) the basic conditions under which one third of the population was living. Our school for dropouts is one such attempt to meet these young people where they are and to develop jointly a program worth the

time, effort, and money. Many office of economic opportunity and office of education projects and programs, especially CAP and VISTA projects, put the middle- and lower-class populations into very direct contact with each other. New understandings and misunderstandings evolved; but, at least for the first time on a massive scale, continuous contact was set up, new relationships were developed, and success and failure of specific projects took second place to the simple fact that the two groups were in some kind of new relationship. Some communication was beginning. The disadvantaged were no longer invisible or inevitable.

It is worth noting in this connection, that it was, in fact, OEO and not the National Education Association which initiated this massive educational contact and interaction. NEA has apparently become too large and too powerful and institutionalized to generate change within its own membership. But change was inevitable, and the past three years are filled with evidence enough that many attempts to meet the basic educational and vocational—human—needs of one third of our population have been made on a national basis. Our language is now sprinkled with such terms as Head Start, Job Corps, Neighborhood Youth Corps, Title I, Title III, ABE, Title V, Sheuer, et al—an indication that not only OEO but the Office of Education and Department of Labor are involved in this massive educational undertaking to upgrade the basic skills and understandings of millions of Americans who never before had such an opportunity.

All major professions have been touched by this crusade: the AMA and medical students have been participating in various programs, many of them in the summer, to provide medical aid and information in places like Appalachia; law students have been engaged in several projects across the country, as well as lawyers in such projects as bail bond in many major cities; social workers have been nudged rather forcefully by many of these projects, and many seem to be responding differently than they had earlier; colleges and universities have begun to realize their role in assisting in the development and, in some cases, in the implementation of new educational or other programs (scholarship) which have brought some needed support; public schools have their Title I, III, or NDEA projects affecting teachers and students; and so it goes. In three years, OEO has launched a massive review of existing programs and needs among almost every major institution in our society with the schools at the top of that list.

But, alas, change comes slowly to individuals or their institutions. Yet, considering the scope of the undertaking, there is no doubt that significant progress has been made. Now that schools have spent money to buy audiovisual equipment and individualized programed material, perhaps they will mature to the stage where they will be able to use the federal money more effectively to improve teacher education and the basic curriculum at all levels. The next two to three years will tell whether America's educators can respond creatively to the challenge of handling not only disadvantaged youth and adults but the total school population as well. For schools, teachers, and curricula which are inadequate for disadvantaged youth are very likely to be inadequate for other students.

One of the most dramatic and obvious problems is that of the dropout. At least 750,000 youth drop out of the public schools each year and fall into the vortex of low education, poor job opportunities, drugs, antisocial behavior, juvenile delinquency, and, finally, adult crime. Certainly there is not a one-to-one correspondence here, but the correlation between high school dropouts and poor reading and language skills is beyond + .90. And the rest of the syndrome also correlates quite highly, so that it has almost become a cliche to say that most of the youth who do drop out of school have encountered major problems with learning to read and write acceptably —by typical middle-class standards. Nationally, thirty-five percent of the youth who start high school drop out for various reasons. Not until OEO and other federal moneys became available has there been an attempt to build on a large scale special programs for these youths. The most obvious of the new programs to aid the dropout (the *disadvantaged* dropout or the representative of primarily the socioeconomic problems of the lower class and not the drug and delinquency problems of the middle class) has been the Job Corps, rural and urban. Approximately 29,000 youths between the ages of 16 and 21 are currently involved in a Job Corps training program in one of the more than 100 camps around the country. These residential centers provide, at the appropriate levels, education and vocational training in a new environment. Typically the rural or conservation camps enroll between 100 and 200 youths whose reading and language skills levels range from nonreader to about 7th grade, while the urban camps typically enroll youths whose reading and language skills achievement are above the seventh grade level. Generally speaking, the camps I have seen or the camps where I have had VISTA volunteers working full-time for a year or more have done a decent job of rehabilitating these young people. A research study, reported by *The New York Times* in March 1967, indicated that some progress had been made with the majority of these youths in terms of their improving their language abilities as well as in learning some prevocational or vocational skills. Obviously there have been failures, and the Job Corps program does not come across (in the study) as *the* answer to the problem of dropouts, but it does come out as one fairly decent alternative which has a better-than-average chance of succeeding with many of the youths who enroll. The failures I have personally noted in visiting camps have been the quality of the staff teaching in basic education and the materials (Sullivan's, McGraw-Hill programed material) used. Yet success comes in many of the conservation camps because of the special human relationships established by VISTA or other staff people who work with these youths on a personal basis.

Another alternative is the Neighborhood Youth Corps (out-of-school program). This is a Department of Labor program which has some of the same goals and objectives as the Job Corps, with the exception that NYC is nonresidential; the youths live at home or alone.

The program I wish to discuss is connected with the NYC in Boston and Revere, a suburb of Boston. Our students are all in NYC, out of school, and spend about 29 hours a week on a work site where they are learning some prevocational skills, and they spend about eight hours a week in a special school developed for them and with them—the Youth Education Program or the Northeastern University Laboratory School. The school has been operating since February 1, 1966, and has served approximately 400 youths. Currently 150 are enrolled in the program at various reading levels, from nonreader to tenth or eleventh grade.

Before describing in detail how the school works and what its philosophy and psychology of education are, a few general remarks are in order about the population, the curriculum, the teachers, the place of a reading program, and the nature of that reading program for such youths as these.

To my knowledge this Youth Education Program is the only school of its kind for this population and, in the past 14 months or so, we have learned a great deal about the relevance of curriculum, books, and materials; the qualities of teachers who can work successfully with these youths; and learning itself. Perhaps I should sketch briefly the general characteristics of the typical youth representing the population we have been working with: he is male, Negro, average or above-average

in intelligence, and a school dropout in grade nine. Many of our youths have police records; several are currently on probation for such crimes as robbery, assault and battery, and dope addiction. At least 15 of our students are attending a special addicts' clinic, and more than one third of our young girls are pregnant out of wedlock. Babies have been brought to school by their teenage mothers who could not get baby sitters. The vast majority of our students come from broken homes or live alone. In our lower groups are several youths who have been incarcerated (in special classes), the majority of whom seem to be responding to instruction in our school. Approximately fifty of our students are engaged in a program which will lead to a high school diploma, not a GED.

The environment which we have created with their active participation is one in which each student becomes aware that he has a major responsibility for what he does. The curriculum has been developed with their direct participation and assistance. We treat them as adults, and they take as much freedom and responsibility as they can handle at a given time. Not all participate fully, but most do. We have a student council and a newspaper, and both have been somewhat erratic, but they remain and they function most of the time. Progress within the school, academically, is very much their own personal set of choices. If a youth prefers to *goof off* for a couple of weeks, he can and he does. Then he leaves or *digs in*. The vast majority dig in when they discover they can or cannot and that the ultimate choice is theirs, not ours. They sit around tables and smoke and drink coffee or coke during class, and if they insist on wearing hats or handkerchiefs on their heads, that is not forbidden. After several weeks in the program, almost all of them give up these signs and gestures. They are involved almost all of the time they are with us, and many of them hang around to listen to records, or play the piano or guitars, or just sit in the library even when not scheduled to be in school. The environment is such that most of them feel quite comfortable most of the time. They also produce at their own pace; we use no programed material, nor any hardware, just software—well-educated, intelligent, imaginative teachers. The key factor in our success has been our staff.

Our curriculum and the books and materials we use in our small classes (varying from 6 to 12 in size) proceed from student interests and concerns and then are elaborated into massive, integrated learning units (e.g., migration) to be described later. All subjects are related as well as possible to one major conceptual focus; we do not deal with separate and distinct subject areas and we do not have 30 minutes of history, 30 of geography, etc. We have a core period of about two hours which involves reading and language skills, English, and social studies (broadly defined to include sociology, psychology, and anthropology, as well as history, geography, etc.); and we have related science and math for the remainder. We always start where they are, with their language, interests, maturity, knowledge, and ignorance, and build with them outward toward integrated units of study. They do not understand the world in shreds or bits. Our approach is successful to the extent that the youth do not quit in droves. With these youths, if you bore them, you lose them; and they bore easily. We have found them educable and interested when they can participate in all phases of their own learning and when they are treated like the young adults they are. Whatever their experiential reservoir, it becomes relevant in some part of our curriculum building and in our daily instructional activities.

Some of our Northeastern undergraduates and some graduate students have visited the school as have many others from around the country, and the students have asked repeatedly "Why don't we have a curriculum like that?" It is our contention that the type of curriculum we have developed and the educational philosophy on which we have built are relevant for middle-class youths and adults, as well as for these "disadvantaged" youths.

Let me describe in some detail the structure of the school and give you some of our first results on achievement and attendance. We still have much to learn, and I am pleased to say that the staff at the school is most educable. Although most are middle class, they have learned from daily contact with these youths things which do not yet appear in textbooks. We all hope that the methods and the curriculum, which we are dealing with for these disadvantaged youths, will become a model, not only for other such youths but for public schools also.

The Youth Education Program, or Northeastern University Laboratory School, was funded and opened in February, 1966, to enrollees of the Neighborhood Youth Corps of Boston. These youths work an average of 28 to 30 hours a week and attend school 7 hours each week. They are paid the minimum wage for this prevocational training. They are not paid for attending school. A staff of four full-time teachers and the director initiated this unique program. The student body numbered approximately 50 to 65, varying weekly. Turnover was large and attendance, irregular, due to youths quitting the Neighborhood Youth Corps program, or joining Job Corps or the service, or for personal problems. The average attendance was approximately 37 percent in the first four months. A change of location to a university-owned property near the campus, partly renovated by the youths themselves, raised morale and attendance, as did a major shakeup in the city's poverty agency, ABCD (Action for Boston Community Development). By August 1966, the new quarters were occupied, the enrollment rose steadily, and the stability of the population increased. In the past few months the enrollment has risen from 70 to 145, and the average attendance is more than 75 percent. It is anticipated that the enrollment will reach 250 youths within the next six to nine months.

From the outset, the key purpose of the school has been to provide these dropouts between 16 and 22 years with an educational environment totally different from any they had ever experienced. Classes are small; the teachers are hand-picked for skill, experience, and understanding of these youths and the rugged world they inhabit; and a curriculum is provided which is relevant and exciting. Student participation in planning and implementing the curriculum has been basic to the success that has been experienced.

The school is divided into three broad tracks:

Track I—Nonreaders to 4^2 reading levels,

Track II—5^1 to 8^2 reading levels, and

Track III—9th grade and above in reading.

Within each track are several small groups, homogeneously organized in terms of each student's instructional level. Each youth is given an individual informal reading analysis upon entrance; on the basis of that a standardized reading test is administered, the California Reading Test, and then each youth is placed in the appropriate group for optimal instruction. Whichever group and track a youth enters in the program, he may advance at his own pace. Movement is frequent in some cases—several have been outstanding.

Track III is the one designated as high school level, and many of the youths are working toward a high school diploma. Youths in the upper groups of Track II may also earn credits toward a high school diploma.

In the past 14 months of the school's existence more than 400 youths have been involved in the program to some extent. A number of those who started in February, 1966, are still in the program, but most of the original students have moved into other programs or activities. Approximately 25 youths have entered Job Corps; several have gone into the army; approximately 20 have returned to the public school system, and the remainder have either moved into MDTA (Manpower Development and Training Act), OJT (On the Job Training), other training programs, or into regular full-time jobs.

A complete and thorough follow-up of each student is under way in order that we may get some indications as to their long-term progress and achievement. Three of our students have made unusual progress, and, as a result, have been hired as part of the regular full-time staff of the Youth Education Program. They serve as teacher aids and provide, among other services, tutorial assistance to youth in the lower groups. Two of the boys have been enrolled at the Northeastern University (University College since September 1966) and are taking two college courses (English and mathematics). Previously, one of these boys had not completed elementary school; the other had dropped out in ninth grade. Both are progressing well in their courses, and their example has encouraged several youths to inquire as to the possibilities of doing the same thing. A third youth has been accepted at the New England Conservatory of Music for voice training.

The curriculum leading to a high school diploma (consisting of 15½ Carnegie units) is in the process of being certified so that students will be able to earn an accredited high school diploma. Recently, the Office of Economic Opportunity has approved an amendment to our original contract stating that youths not enrolled in the Neighborhood Youth Corps could participate in the Northeastern University Laboratory School. Several communities with Neighborhood Youth Corps programs have wanted to send their youths to the program or have requested our assistance in developing a similar educational component of their own. The school is visited by many educators and other interested people.

We believe, and experience has supported this belief, that many of our students are of average or above-average intelligence and are susceptible to academic motivation if the learning environment—class size, relevance of materials, curriculum, and teachers—encourages each youth to take some of the responsibility for his own learning. Thus, our students take an active role in planning, implementing, and evaluating the learning experiences which are meaningful to them. Adult-level discussions, usually originating in a significant topical issue, spark interests, reveal knowledge in the students, and suggest specific reading and writing assignments in history, literature, or science. The basic context is their life, their concerns, the here and now; from these beginnings we develop with them both the conceptual framework and the skills necessary to deeper and deeper understanding in each subject matter area. Such a structure exploits the experience and maturity of the students to the fullest extent. The ultimate goal is to develop academic independence and sensitive discrimination among life's alternatives.

This type of activity in the classroom setting produces, under the guidance of each teacher, an extended core-type curriculum; that is, English, social studies, reading, and language skills are the basic core context around which the rest of the curriculum tends to organize. For example, a major unit being studied is Migration. This broad concept serves as the unifying force field for the entire curriculum so that in literature the reading of *The Grapes of Wrath* becomes very pertinent to one dimension of American migration. The study of migration in plants, animals, and man from a biological viewpoint is integrated with the work in literature concerning man's movement. In biology, naturally, emphasis is upon adaptation, the way various species protect themselves or fail to and upon the relationship between the species and the total environment as related to their movement. The history of human migration opens many doors of investigation, including such key questions as who moved? why? from where and to where? what happened when the migrant arrived at his home? and was there cultural assimilation or lack of it? Such questions probe a host of social, political, economic, and religious issues which motivated men throughout the ages to move from place to place. Thus, the concept of migration is elucidated in all its dimensions and aspects: history, literature, science, etc. All the information from each field focuses upon the single concept of migration.

The basic skills needed in reading, writing, spelling, and mathematics are all taught within this context. Each unit is planned to cover a 16-week trimester—those youths who cannot complete the work continue until they can, since no one can fail in the old sense of academic failure. It is possible for a youth in Track III to earn one unit of English; one, Social Studies; one, Science; and one, Mathematics, in the Migration unit. Other units provide similar possibilities.

Summary of school population statistics

All meet the Office of Economic Opportunity poverty requirements (less than $3,000 income per year).

Total enrollees (as of March 1, 1967)
145 students
   males   — 93 (64%)
   females — 52 (36%)

Median age for all enrollees—17.6 years
   males   — 17.5
   females — 17.6

Average years in school—
   males   — 8.6
   females — 8.9
   total   — 8.8 (based on 378 students, including those who have left the program)

Negro — 78 (54%)
White — 53 (46%)
   (13, or 9%, are Puerto Rican)

The following, in order of high frequency to low, are some reasons for termination: entrance into full-time employment, advancement to Job Corps (for higher level job training), return to public school (because of greater goal concreteness, at least for some students), pregnancy, marriage, entrance into vocational schools, emotional problems, and ineligibility because of age or change in family income. Three have become part-time college students.

Some preliminary data

The following data represent retest scores on the California Reading Test administered at the end of December and the beginning of January 1967, to 50 percent of the total school population (123 as of February 1). Mean score on the California for the initial test for students in all three tracks was 6.3. Mean gain was nine months for students in all tracks. These gains are more impressive when considered in light of the fact that our students' mean attendance between pre- and post-tests was 17 weeks for a maximum of 7½ hours of instruction each week, a figure which represents approximately one quarter of the time normally devoted to instruction to youth of this age in the public schools. Currently other data are being collected and analyzed relating specifically to students' previous academic performance, personal, social, health, and legal problems. In addition, we hope to be able to measure attitudinal changes toward work and toward academic matters in general.

Average Reading Test Scores
for Sixty Students
Pre- and Post-tests*
Score (grade level)
Pretest   6.34 (standard deviation—2.84)
Post-test   7.2   (standard deviation—2.89)
Average Reading Test Scores
for Track I Students
Pre- and Post-tests*
Score (grade level)
Pretest   2.8   (standard deviation—2.86)
Post-test   3.6   (standard deviation—2.45)
Average Reading Test Scores
for Track II Students
Pre- and Post-tests*
Score (grade level)
Pretest   5.8   (standard deviation—1.78)
Post-test   6.3   (standard deviation—1.74)
Average Reading Test Scores
for Track III Students
Pre- and Post-tests*
Score (grade level)
Pretest   8.5   (standard deviation—1.91)
Post-test   10.8 (standard deviation—1.39)
* Average number of weeks between pre- and post-tests is 17 weeks.

Programed Intervention to Improve Reading in a Disadvantaged Public School System

Edith H. Grotberg
The American University

THE PRINCE EDWARD SCHOOL PROJECT, 1966-1967, was sponsored by demonstration grant No. VA-CAP 66-9201/1 from The Office of Economic Opportunity, under Section 207 of Title 11a of the Economic Opportunity Act of 1964, and by the state of Virginia under Title 1 of the Elementary and Secondary Education Act, 1965. The Reverend L. Francis Griffin and Robert E. Taylor, codirectors of the Prince Edward County Community Action Group, Inc., requested the funds from the Office of Economic Opportunity. Bryant S. Harper, superintendent of the public schools of Prince Edward County, requested Title 1 funds through the state of Virginia.

The Institute of Educational Research, Washington, D. C., was the sole contracted organization with responsibility for carrying out the project. Myron Woolman, director of the Institute of Educational Research, was senior research consultant for the project. The project staff also included: Edith H. Grotberg, project director; Marilyn Outlaw, assistant project director; Paul Barth, field supervisor; and Margaret Barnett, secretary.

The project was essentially to provide a corrective reading program for all the children from grades one through ten in the public schools. All of these children met criteria for the educationally deprived, and all but a few met criteria for socially and economically disadvantaged. Further, most of the children in the public schools had been denied education from 1959 to 1963, as the result of closing the public schools in protest against integration.

Stated in more specific terms, the Prince Edward School Project, 1966-67, was designed to 1) develop and improve reading and language skills for first, second, and third grades; 2) develop and improve reading and language skills for pupils from fourth through tenth grades who were educationally deprived and were reading below grade level; and 3) provide a reading program for dropouts. The project used as its primary materials *The Basal Progressive Choice (1)* and *The Accelerated Progressive Choice Reading Methods (2)*. These materials are programed. The theory and principles underlying the Progressive Choice (PC) Method are concerned with insuring that the learner is given information in doses which are 1) small enough for him to swallow, 2) given at a sufficiently slow pace for him to digest, and 3) agreeable enough to be palatable and to produce real feelings of satisfaction and accomplishment. The method also is designed to provide pupils with evidence of increasing ability to reach clearly defined goals. Finally, and above all, the PC Method is designed to develop increasing independence and responsibility, based on demonstrated mastery of the materials being learned.

The body of information to be learned is broken down into discrete elements which are then organized into a sequence based on the following criteria: 1) the learner is responsible for mastering only one new learning unit at any given time; 2) each successive unit to be learned is as dissimilar as possible from the one preceding it; and 3) the learner must demonstrate that he can integrate the unit he is learning with all previously learned units.

Twenty-eight teachers and nineteen aides who were part of the school project received 15 hours of training in the use of the progressive choice instructional materials by the assistant project director.

Testing

Tests were administered to each student by the teachers in the program and under the supervision of the project staff. Initial testing began March 7 and terminated March 10. The following tests were administered and forms and levels selected for designated grades:

1. Lorge-Thorndike Intelligence Tests
   Level 1—Grades 1- 2 (330 N)
   　　　2—Grades 3- 4 (401 N)
   　　　3—Grades 5- 6 (219 N)
   　　　4—Grades 7-10 (315 N)
2. Stanford Achievement Tests Form W
   Primary Battery I
   　　　Grades 1- 3　Students: 535
   Word Meaning
   Paragraph Meaning
   Vocabulary
   Arithmetic
   Primary Battery II
   　　　Grades 4- 6　Students: 415
   Word Meaning
   Paragraph Meaning
   Arithmetic
   Intermediate Battery I
   　　　Grades 7-10　Students: 315
   Word Meaning
   Paragraph Meaning
   Arithmetic

Interim tests were administered from May 31 through June 3, 1966, at the end of the academic school year. The students had been in the program for two months. Form Y of the SAT was used. Only the SAT and the Lorge-Thorndike Tests were administered on these dates.

On August 15 and 16, 1966, two subtests of the SAT Word Meaning and Paragraph Meaning were administered to the students from grades one through six who attended the summer session. The summer program reached forty percent of the students in the first six grades.

Final tests were administered January 25-27, 1967, to the population which had been in the program since March 1966, except the tenth grade class which left the program in June 1966. These tenth graders became eleventh graders in September and were no longer part of the program. Final testing, then, was conducted with children who had been in grades one through nine in March and who were in grades two through ten in January 1967. The same forms and levels were used in the final testing as in the initial testing. The new first graders, as of September 1966, were tested in

January 1967, but their test results are treated separately.

The progressive choice materials were introduced into the classrooms of the Prince Edward County schools upon the completion of pretesting in each school. The teachers and teacher aides had been trained and, with the help of the assistant project director, through observation visits and group meetings launched the reading program.

Frequency and duration of classroom visits were set up on the basis of informal evaluations. When the teachers and aides seemed secure with the materials and procedures, observation visits were made on a regularly scheduled basis. Conferences with teachers followed the observation visit to discuss the evaluation.

Age-grade placement

The percentages of pupils at the appropriate age-grade placement in March 1966 were obtained from third grade through tenth, since the problem was most acute at these grades. Appropriate age-grade relationship was determined from an eleven-month span consistent with expected age-grade placement for March of a school year.

Only 22.8 percent of all pupils were at the appropriate age-grade placement. In other terms, 77.2 percent of the pupils in Prince Edward County were overage for their grade placement. It may be assumed that the closing of the schools was responsible for this condition since no other school system has reported a similar condition.

The children who were at appropriate age-grade placement had low achievement scores, and the children who were overage for grade placement had even lower achievement scores. There is a strong possibility that the grade placement pattern of Prince Edward schools tended to depress the total achievement of all the students. This situation affected the reading program in terms of testing and materials as well as in interpretation of the test

results. The implications of such a situation for curriculum development and planning are far reaching.

Results and evaluation

The evaluation of the project is based primarily on the degree to which the purpose of the project was achieved. The effectiveness with which the purpose was accomplished may be measured or examined by analyzing the data from a number of perspectives. For purposes of clarity and specificity these perspectives are treated separately.

Reading performance of primary grades

The mean gain in Word Meaning of the Stanford Achievement Tests for the primary grades between March 1966 and January 1967, or six months of school, was .39; for Paragraph Meaning, .48; and for Vocabulary, .84. The combined reading score (WM + PM + V ÷ 3) was .57 which was three tenths of a month below the expected gains according to national norms. These students were in the program for two hours per day.

Reading performance of elementary grades—four through six

The mean gain in Word Meaning of the SAT for the elementary grades between March 1966 and January 1967, or six months of school, was .63 and for Paragraph Meaning, .61. There is no vocabulary subtest for the test at these grades. The combined reading score (WM + PM ÷ 2) was .62, which was two tenths of a month above the expected gains according to national norms. These students were in the program two hours per day.

Reading performance of junior high school— grades seven through nine

The mean gains in Word Meaning of the SAT for the junior high grades between March 1966 and January 1967, or six months of school, was .45 and for Paragraph Meaning, .37. The combined reading score (WM + PM

$\div$ 2) was .41, or almost two months below the expected gains according to national norms. These students were in the program one hour per day.

The mean gains in reading were according to national norms for the primary and elementary grades but not for the junior high grades. If the gains were a result of the intervention of the program, then the program produced desirable results for the primary and elementary grades but not for the junior high grades. The factor of time, however, may be the important factor explaining the difference in gains. Grades one through six were in the program two hours per day while the junior high grades were in the program one hour per day, or half the time. Since the materials used by grades four through six were the same as for the junior high grades, the material differences could not account for the difference in gains. The time factor seems the logical explanation for the difference. In short, students must be in the program more than one hour per day and probably at least two hours per day in order to achieve at a national norm rate.

Transfer effects of reading program to another subject area—arithmetic

The mean gain in the Arithmetic subtest of the SAT for the primary grades between March 1966 and January 1967, or six months of school, was .54. This gain was higher than the mean gain for Word Meaning or Paragraph Meaning but lower than Vocabulary. While it is difficult to isolate what intervention produces what results, the organization and sequence of the programed materials used in the reading program have many of the components of logical symbolic constructs which are also germane to arithmetic.

The mean gain in the Arithmetic subtest for the elementary grades (4-6) for the six months was .41. This gain was lower than for Word Meaning or Paragraph Meaning; however, both the initial and final Arithmetic grade scores were higher than for Word Meaning or Paragraph Meaning. The general effect of the reading program in the elementary grades seemed to be to close the gap between the subtest grade scores.

The mean gain in the Arithmetic subtest for the junior high grades (7-9) for the six months was .20. This was the smallest gain made by any other grouped grades but was a reversal of what occurred at the interim testing after the program had been in effect for ten weeks. At that time the junior high grades showed losses in scores rather than gains. However, by January 1967, the process shifted to gains. Again the initial and final grade scores for the Arithmetic subtest were higher than for Word Meaning and Paragraph Meaning. And again, it may be suggested that the reading program tended to close the gap between the SAT subtest grade scores.

Changes in rate of learning

Changes in the rate of learning were compared in two ways: 1) changes in approximating expected scores for each grade as compared to actual scores at the beginning of the reading program, March 1966, and the end of the program, January 1967; and 2) changes in rate between grades for the March 1966 scores and the January 1967 scores.

For seven of the nine grades, the January 1967 scores are closer to expected scores than the March 1966 scores. Only grades three and seven have January 1967 scores farther below expected scores than the March 1966 scores. For grades five, six, and eight, the differences are sizable in favor of the January 1967 scores. Table 1 provides a picture of the differences.

Table II illustrates the rate of learning for March and January by comparing changes in rate between grades for the two test periods. Thus, the rate of learning between grades one and two is arrived at by subtracting the score of grade one from the score of grade two. (Reading average scores were used.)

TABLE 1

	March 1966		January 1967
Expected Reading Score	Difference between Actual and Expected Reading Score	Expected Reading Score	Difference between Actual and Expected Reading Score
1.6	— .50	*	
2.6	— .88	2.4	— .85
3.6	—1.10	3.4	—1.16
4.6	—1.67	4.4	—1.56
5.6	—2.28	5.4	—1.86
6.6	—2.65	6.4	—2.15
7.6	—2.39	7.4	—2.78
8.6	—4.04	8.4	—2.81
9.6	—4.58	9.4	—4.52
10.6	—4.33	10.4	—4.79

* The first graders of March 1966 were the second graders of January 1967.

TABLE II

Rate of Learning
Average Reading Score

	March 1966		January 1967	
Grades				
1 from 2	.60			
2 from 3	.79	2 from 3	.57	
3 from 4	.41	3 from 4	.67	
4 from 5	.44	4 from 5	.66	
5 from 6	.60	5 from 6	.82	
6 from 7	1.43	6 from 7	.12	
7 from 8	— .78	7 from 8	1.21	
8 from 9	.60	8 from 9	— .69	
9 from 10	1.45	9 from 10	.72	

For January 1967 scores, the first graders had become second graders; the second graders had become third graders; and so on. Thus the first comparison is arrived at by subtracting second grade from third grade, etc. The table provides the actual number difference in rate of learning by months.

The average rate of learning for the ten grades in March was .62 years, and the average rate of learning for the nine grades in January was .60 years or an insignificant difference. Thus, while for seven of the nine grades in January 1967 the grade scores were closer to national norms, the rate of learning remained the same between grades. The majority of the students, then, benefited by the reading program and no dramatic shifts in between-grade rate of learning were made. The very high rate of learning for grade seven in March 1966 was a function of grade placement. Only the more able students were permitted to enter seventh grade. The loss of rate for eighth grade was due to no selective feature for that grade. The same pattern may be seen for the eighth and ninth grades in January 1967. These were the same students who had been seventh and eighth graders in March 1966 and the same explanation applies.

Improvement of intelligence capabilities

The most striking mean gains made as a result of the reading program were made in the Lorge-Thorndike Grade Equivalent, Nonverbal scores. Comparing mean gains in matched scores for March 1966 and January 1967, the following occurred:

Grade	1	.89
"	2	1.28
"	3	1.47
"	4	1.28
"	5	1.94
"	6	.72
"	7	.82
"	8	.98
"	9	.97

The seventh graders made a small mean gain, .82, but they also had very high initial and post-tests when compared to the eighth and ninth graders. Again, the seventh grade was a select group because of grade placement policies which had been operating. The third grade made very high mean gains, 1.47, a fact which was especially interesting since the third grade had not gained proportionately in the achievement subtests. The average overall gain for matched scores was 1.15 years or more than twice the average gain for achievement scores. This increase in intellectual functioning was the major change measured as a result of the reading program.

Changes in attendance

It had been determined that an average thirteen percent absence rate for Prince Edward students did not affect their achievement scores. It was necessary to have a protracted absence before the effects were measurable. However, attendance was recorded during the reading project more to determine the holding power of the materials and the program than to measure effects of absence.

To determine the holding power of the reading program, attendance figures were obtained for two separate months before the reading program and two separate months during the reading program. October 1965 was selected as a month of high attendance. Weather is good in October and the students attended quite regularly. February 1966 was selected as a month of generally poor attendance because of bad weather and illness. April was selected as the second month of the program as a poor month, and October 1966 as a month comparable to October 1965 in terms of tendency to attend in the early fall. Below are the percentages of attendance:

	Oct. 1965	Feb. 1966	Apr. 1966	Oct. 1966
Students				
Boys	87.9	84.8	84.5	90.0
Girls	89.9	84.6	87.9	92.4
Total	88.9	84.7	86.2	91.2

The average attendance increased by more than 2 percent from October 1965 to October 1966. It may be assumed that the reading program contributed to this increase.

Changes in dropout rate and provisions for dropouts

Dropout rates were not changed as a result of the reading program. There had been seventeen dropouts during the 1965-1966 academic year, and, as of February 1, 1967, there were seventeen dropouts during the 1966-1967 academic year.

Dropouts in the community were offered classes in reading after regular school hours. They were to be given two hours of instruction per day, using the Accelerated Progressive Choice reading program. The dropout program was to have begun in June to coincide with the termination of an Adult Literacy Program sponsored by the Prince Edward Community Action Group, Inc.

Facilities were organized; staff was designated; and announcements were made through posters, newspapers and radio. Only a few dropouts attended the first session and so the program was abandoned for the summer. The explanations given for nonparticipation were that dropouts had work and many had already been part of the Adult Literacy Program.

Effects of reading program on teachers

The materials were designed to require the least amount of training necessary for teachers and to provide step-by-step instructions for the teacher by use of the teacher's manual. To some extent, the materials were self-teaching, and where a teacher was needed, careful instructions appeared in the manual.

To determine how teachers felt about themselves as teachers during the reading program compared to their self-evaluation before the reading program, a scale was designed. Only teachers who had taught in Prince Edward County before the reading program were involved in filling out the scale. They felt they were generally better teachers during the reading program and their pupils learned better. The fact that the teachers generally felt closer to their pupils may be attributed to the individualized nature of the materials. Teachers were required to interact individually with students since they progressed at different rates. The teachers felt a loss of freedom because of the requirement to follow the manual, but this feeling did not detract from their recognition of the effectiveness of the program.

Continuing effects of the school closing

The students who had had education during 1959-1963 made considerably higher pre- and post-test scores but made somewhat smaller gains. The project tended to close gaps between subtest scores within and between groups who had different educational experiences.

Concluding statement

The students were still behind national norm scores for grades even though their mean gains showed a national norm rate. Thus, while this kind of intervention does bring about a change in learning, it does not bring sufficient change to compensate for the initial low scores. Further, the students were greatly overage for their grade placement. Indeed, seventy-five percent were overage for their grade. This fact suggests that regrouping of students and revamping of curriculum are necessary to eradicate the education problems of Prince Edward County. In disadvantaged communities where the debilitating effect of the overage problem is not present, the results should be greater.

REFERENCES

1. Woolman, Myron. *Lift-off to Reading.* Chicago, Illinois: Science Research Associates, 1966.
2. _____. *Reading in High Gear.* Chicago, Illinois: Science Research Associates, 1964.

PROGRAMED INSTRUCTION

Let's Be Realistic

LILLIAN PUTNAM
Newark State College

FOR YEARS, EDUCATORS have given lip service to the concepts of providing for individual differences, teaching at the instructional level, and utilizing the effects of motivation and reward. Although sound in theory, these concepts are difficult to implement in actual practice. The purpose of programed materials is to bring about this implementation.

B. F. Skinner, of Harvard, has shown that our behavior is largely shaped or conditioned by the results of our actions. If we are pleasantly or favorably rewarded for some action, we tend to repeat the action; we "learn it well." If the reward or reinforcement comes immediately, it is most effective; if it is delayed, it is less effective, and the effectiveness is reduced as the delay increases. Programed materials are designed to give immediate reinforcement of a correct response by enabling the student to see the correct answer immediately after his response. This satisfaction provides the "spark" to motivate the next trial. If the response is incorrect, the programed materials indicate the error and provide another chance to correct it.

Programed materials are designed so that a child may work independently—without teacher help. This approach enables a child to work at his own instructional level, even if he is an isolate on that level. It enables him to progress at his own rate because the material is presented in "bite-sized" chunks; by meeting one and only one new task at a time, the confusion of multiple stimuli is reduced. He can also get repetition, if his response is incorrect, without being subjected, perhaps, to the increasingly harsh, critical voice of an annoyed teacher. Programed materials are intended to make efficient use of teacher time.

Programed materials are designed to require constant, active participation by the student, the theory being that involvement and participation, as opposed to passive listening, are more likely to result in learning.

Do they really work? What actually happens in classrooms?

The exaggerated claims made by authors and publishers of different materials frequently fall far short in actual practice. There are several different types of programed materials available, and it is not feasible to classify them here. However, my observations of practical classroom use of the different types lead me to conclude that in general they have the following assets:

1. They can and do provide material at the correct instructional level, even for the extreme deviates.
2. They do give immediate reinforcement or correction.
3. The correction occurs without the teacher's becoming annoyed or irritated and without "loss of face."
4. They do enable the child to progress at his own rate.
5. The frames present only one new item at a time and thus reduce confusion. They enable the student to master or cope with each step before he is required to tackle or perform on the next level. One popular magazine reported the reactions of a student who compared his efforts to wade through a traditional college text in chemistry with the ease of using programed materials:

> What a difference! I had been picking at a mountain with a shovel: now I was on a bulldozer, progressing with irresistible force and really moving dirt. After the bulldozer sensation faded, it felt more like tennis. The ball keeps coming back at you, and you hit it again. After an hour or two, you are wrung out but you have had fun (1).

6. By demanding that the student demonstrate mastery of each step before proceeding, they prevent failures from going unnoticed until a crisis is reached.

7. Because the materials are presented in "bite-sized" chunks, they do enable the student to see his chance of success *before* he does the work. This attitude is a prime requisite for remedial readers and is, therefore, one reason why programed materials are so successful in remediation.

8. They seem to be particularly good for people who get "lost in the language maze" of regular books because the style of writing is terse and brief.

9. They seem to be more effective with older children—upper elementary, junior high, senior high, and college students.

10. They do provide for more efficient use of teacher time.

11. The slow learning child seems to be more content than the bright child with programed materials. Porter's study indicated that self-instructional devices were particularly good for the lower intelligence levels (2).

12. They are an easy, effective way for absentees to "catch up" with material already taught.

13. They are an excellent source of "extra practice" for the slow learner. The average teacher simply lacks time to do this work realistically.

14. They are effective in stimulating constant involvement and participation. They convert the student from a passive recipient to an active learner. (I believe this is the most important contribution of programed materials.)

What are the limitations of programed materials?

Despite the assets of programed materials, there are concomitant limitations in actual practice:

1. Programed materials seem to be most effective for the extreme deviates in the class. The average child tends to become bored and lose interest.

2. They are most effective if used for only short daily periods; prolonged usage becomes tedious. They do serve a particular purpose, but they do *not* constitute a whole reading program.

3. They are least effective with young, primary age children who need the "give and take" of human association and discussion.

4. If an error is made, usually another frame repeats the question or directs the child to reread the material. Little or no attempt is made to analyze the *reason* for the error or to teach the concept in a new way.

5. By the very nature of the design, programed materials present learning in a fragmented manner. We still need a teacher to focus and synthesize the ideas into a related gestalt.

6. The student must constantly turn pages and complete many books to "cover" an ordinary program. This busy work can mislead the student into thinking that he has digested much material; in reality it is a minimal amount of content. It cannot be compared to completing a "book" in the ordinary sense.

7. Many students react negatively to the constant demand to stop and *circle* or *write* answers, an overt response. Average and high ability students may find the covert response, or *thinking* the answer, to be just as effective. A study done by Evans, Glaser, and Homme indicated that the group which made covert responses spent less time in learning and showed slightly higher retention scores than the group which responded overtly to each item (3).

Ringler's study with retarded readers showed that pupils who used the covert response mode completed the material in considerably less time than the overt response group, without any loss of reading ability either immediately upon completing the program or after a two-week interval. For the slower ability pupil, the overt response appeared to be the more effective one.

Ringler, therefore, suggests that the high ability pupil should *think* each response and thus complete a skill sequence in less time, while the slower ability pupils should write each response (4).

8. *Gigo*—the term used by programers to explain "garbage in—garbage out," indicates that it is not enough to establish an excellent piping system; the content going *through* the pipes is important, and the programed materials will be no better than the input on each frame.

9. The expense of programed materials as compared with traditional basals is difficult to estimate because the duration value varies with age groups, community types, etc. It is well to remember, however, that the programed materials are totally consumed, while in a basal series the text is reusable and the companion workbook is consumable. One elementary reading program costs $11.73 per child or $351.90 for a class of 30—prohibitive for the entire class. Although the use of programed materials has and will continue to increase, they still constitute only a small fraction of the instructional materials used. An informal survey in New Jersey revealed that only 3 percent of the schools were actually using some from of programed materials.

Need for future research

Although the programed materials have made great strides in enabling teachers to implement several desirable concepts of instruction, there are some fascinating areas to be explored:

1. Because programed materials are designed so that the child works singly, without teacher or peer group, do personality traits of introversion and extroversion affect the effectiveness of the material?

2. The Grimes-Allinsmith study on the relationship of personality traits of compulsiveness and anxiety to phonic methods opened a new vista (5). It seems probable that these same traits would affect the effectiveness of programed materials.

3. Does the immediate reinforcement of programed materials compensate for the lack of intragroup relationships in the learning situation?

4. Finally, there is, as yet, no solid body of research data which prove the superiority of programed materials and there probably never will be. However, future research could certainly establish data on the specific factors or constellation of factors about a student (intelligence, personality traits, etc.) for whom programed materials would be most successful.

Summary statement

If cognizant of these assets and limitations, the reading teacher can utilize programed materials judiciously.

REFERENCES

1. Langewiesche, Wolfgang. "Now You Can Double Your Learning Power," *Reader's Digest,* April 1967, 113.
2. Porter, Douglas. "Some Effects of Yearlong Teaching Machine Instruction," in Eugene Galanter (Ed.), *Automatic Teaching: The State of the Art.* Wiley and Sons, 1959, 85-90.
3. Evans, J. L., Robert Glaser, and L. E. Homme. "A Preliminary Investigation of Variation in the Properties of Verbal Learning Sequences of the Teaching Machine Type," in A. A. Lumsdaine and Robert Glaser (Eds.), *Teaching Machines and Programmed Learning:* A Source Book. Washington, D. C.: National Education Association, 1960, 446-451.

4. Ringler, Lenore. "Verbal Learning Sequences With Retarded Readers," *Educational Horizons*, Winter 1966-67, Vol. 45, No. 2, 68.

5. Grimes, Jesse W., and Wesley Allinsmith. "Compulsivity, Anxiety, and School Achievement," *Merrill-Palmer Quarterly* (1961), 7, 247-269.

Potentialities of Programed Tutoring

D. G. Ellson
Indiana University

PROGRAMED TUTORING is a special form of programed instruction which prescribes and controls the behavior of nonprofessional tutors in order to achieve learning. In programed tutoring, the tutor, rather than a teaching machine, is the vehicle through which the operational programs transmit knowledge to the pupils.

As we have developed the concept of programed tutoring at Indiana University, it is basically a set of teaching operations which can be applied to almost any content but is used primarily as a means to supplement the teaching of beginning reading. Thus, in our operations, the usual storytelling content of reading materials, in and of itself, is not important except as something to teach. Since 1960, we have conducted 20 experiments using this technique to tutor 1260 children in beginning reading. Over this period of time and with this number of children we have had no failures!

These results are even more significant because the majority of children tutored have been from culturally disadvantaged inner-city schools. Furthermore, for the most part these children have been drawn from the lower third of first grade classrooms. They are children judged to be potential reading failures on the basis of their scores on the Metropolitan Readiness tests and their kindergarten teachers' evaluations. Yet all of these children, these nonreaders, have learned to read at least the preprimer and primer basal materials on sight. They can answer comprehension questions, both written and verbal, about what they have read; and they have made a beginning in word analysis.

And, since one of our side concerns has been the relation of dyslexia to reading problems, it may be of particular interest to others concerned with the same problem that up to this time we have not found a single child, among all these 1200, who has been unable to learn to read, when tutored, because of some form or degree of dyslexia.

Before I go further, let us talk about what is meant by standards of success or failure in reading at the end of first grade. In general, a classroom teacher would list as a reading failure a child who can not sightread and comprehend basal reading material at or near a second grade level by the close of the first grade year. A reading success in the first grade classroom, on the other hand, would be one who has read, with a least 80 percent accuracy and comprehension, the preprimers, primer, and first grade readers.

In programed tutoring, however, our definition of a reading failure is a child who, after repeated, prolonged instruction, fails to learn how to read a single word. Or, if he does learn to read a few words, fails to continue the learning process.

Now, if this seems to be too elemental or too unrealistic a definition for reading failure, consider what we demand for a child to be considered a reading success—100 percent perfection in all material presented to be read. By classroom standards then, some of our children who have only completed, under tutoring, the first primer by the end of the first grade may be considered as failures. However, in their reading of the first three preprimers and the primer, these children have performed with 100 percent correctness as compared with the generally acceptable classroom performance standard of 80-90 percent or less. In other words, while our definition of failure is more absolute than the usual one, our definition for reading success is equally more absolute.

With this discussion of definitions of reading success or failure as a background, I will further amend my cate-

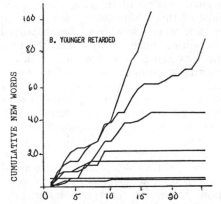

Fig. 1. New words read during tutoring by young retardates; Mean CA 13-4, IQ's 56-29. Individual curves. Exp. VII.

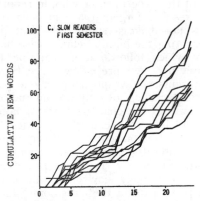

Fig. 2. Cumulative new words learned by "slow readers" during tutoring; individual curves. Exp. VII.

gorical statement about failures. Even by our definition, we have had six failures. This graph shows the evidence. The "failures" shown here are young retardates with a mean CA of 13-4, all with IQ's of 56 or less. We are not, however, using their IQ's as excuses. Rather, we feel they failed to learn to read, or to continue to learn to read, because our operational programs at the time of this study had not been sufficiently developed, rather than because of the children's lack of potential learning capacity. Our other failure in this same experiment is even a bit more embarrassing to our record since he is a "normal" child. We have now learned that much of his failure to progress under tutoring was probably caused by a severe, though temporary, psychological problem in his home environment. When the home situation was solved, the child's learning difficulties disappeared. However, our failure, we feel, was because we did not continue the tutoring of the child, as we would do now.

Having now illustrated what we call our reading failures, let us turn to what happens to the potential reading failures with whom we have done most of our work and see what happens to them through programed tutoring.

These data show individual learning curves for a group of slow readers in an inner-city public school in Indiana. The children in this graph we may call kindergarten failures since they were the lower third of *kindergarten* classes, and, according to their teachers' judgment, none were ready for first grade work. Their mean chronological age was 6-2 and their mean IQ, 91. These children were tutored for 20-minute sessions, twice weekly for 12 weeks. During this time the mean number of different words learned by the group was 74.8 words in 480 minutes, or about four class days if two hours a day were devoted to the teaching of reading. I should add that the reading material we used in this experiment was *The Brown Family* series which, on a Thorndike Readability Scale, works out to third grade level readability. This was the vocabulary which these potential nonreaders learned during the 12-week summer session!

TABLE 1

Psychological Achievement and Test Information

	C.A.	M.A.	I.Q.
Binet (form L-M)	6-11	3-6	46
*WISC	6-11		48
PPVT (Form A)	7-0	3-2	44
Wide Range	C.A.	Reading	Arith.
Achievement Test	7-0	1.2	.9

* Verbal scale discontinued after items on the information subtests were failed.

I am always leery and usually critical of the experimenter who, in reporting results, forgets that one swallow does not make a summary! But, in presenting the highly detailed case history which follows, it is tempting to forget my own prejudices since Sara represents, all wrapped up in one pathetic package, not only a combination of many of the characteristics of nonreaders but some exaggerated ones of her own. She presents a relatively complete clinical picture of an inner-city child. Obviously she is the prototype of the extremely slow child who does not participate in the classroom. Her teacher suggested, even demanded, that the child be put in a special education class or, at the very least, removed from her class as soon as possible. The psychologist who tested Sara said she was a borderline mental defective and agreed that she should be in a special education class. A medical examiner reported that the child seemed to show evidence of considerable brain damage. All in all, she presented a picture of a pathetic, potential non-reader, nonlearner from the school's point of view.

It so happened that we were in the normal process of tutoring Sara while most of this testing was going on and, in fact, were unaware of her reported disabilities until we were notified that she was going to be dropped from the tutoring program to be placed in a special education classroom. At this point we were shown this mass of data displayed here. We, of course, had been keeping our own record of her learning performance in the tutoring program since the beginning of the school year. While we recognized Sara to be a slow learner, our records showed even at the time of her proposed transfer that she had definitely started to make progress. The following graph shows what her reading performance in the tutoring sessions looked like from September 1966 up until April 28, 1967.

When we presented our information and evidence to the school psychologist and the school principal, the psycholo-

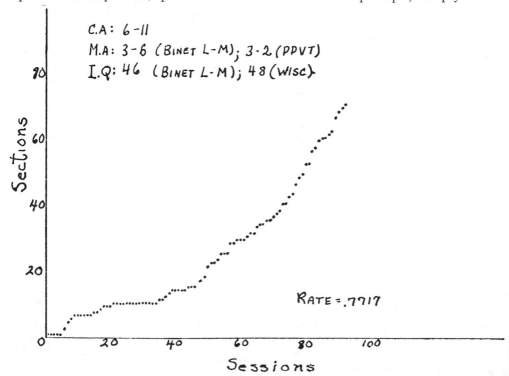

Fig. 3. Section-Session Interaction Learning Curve for Child #20, Sara S. School 36. Exp. XX.

gist literally did not believe us and asked to see for himself. We then invited him to observe Sara in the tutoring situation and were in the room when Sara came in.

First of all, she spoke cordially to us and greeted the tutor with enthusiasm and considerable exchange of conversation, got out the reading materials herself, and told the tutor: "O.K. Let's go!" Then she proceeded to read approximately six pages of reading material without a single error.

The psychologist pulled me aside, saying: "I can't believe it. This can't be the same child. She can't be!"

A few days later, after the psychologist had collected even more data on the child and reexamined his own previously collected data, he returned several more times to observe Sara. His concluding comments to me were, "What I have seen scares me. My recommendation that this child should be placed in a special education classroom seems to have been entirely wrong. She just is not what I thought the evidence showed she was."

Now that we have seen some of the results, let's look at the programs that make programed tutoring work. There are in all, 12 different operational programs: a sightreading program, seven comprehension programs, three word analysis programs, and a free reading program. These operational programs, which are described in a tutor's guide containing the instructions to the tutors, make up the procedures we call programed tutoring. These are our "content." It is through these operational programs that the tutors are able to bring about learning.

The operations of the sightreading program can be applied to almost any content—any material that has words in it that can be taught. What is important is the operation of the sightreading program itself and not the content that is taught—nor, for that matter, the previous educational background of the tutor who carries it out.

For use with the sightreading program, the reader or primer is divided into digestible parts called units and sections in which the number of new words and number of different words per division are carefully controlled. In addition to the reader we use an alphabetical word list of all the different words in the reader, a record keeping system, and the tutor's guide.

The first tutoring session begins with the first small division in the reader, called the first unit. In Step 1 we show this to the child and then ask "Can you read this?" If the unit is read correctly orally, the tutor reinforces by saying "Very good," "Fine," and then proceeds to the next unit, Step 1. If the unit is not read correctly, the tutor proceeds to Step 2.

Step 2 is a teaching step and is repeated for each word missed in Step 1 in alphabetical order as follows: The tutor points to the word in the word list and requires the learner to point to that word in the sentence. The tutor then asks the child to read the word. If he reads it correctly, the tutor reinforces and proceeds to the next word. If the word is not read correctly, the tutor speaks the word, requires the learner to repeat it, and then proceeds to the next word. After the final word, the tutor proceeds to Step 3, another test step essentially the same as Step 1, except that failure to read correctly is followed by Step 4, another teaching step.

Step 4 is repeated for each word missed in Step 3 in alphabetical order. The tutor reads the word aloud and indicates the general area in the word list, requiring the learner to point to the word. The tutor then asks the learner to read the word. If he reads it correctly, the tutor reinforces and proceeds to the next word. If the word is not read correctly, the tutor requires the learner to repeat it orally and proceeds to the next word. After the final word, the tutor proceeds to Step 5 which again is a test step, similar to Steps 1 and 3, except that failure to read correctly is followed by the next unit, Step 1.

We continue to do these five steps where necessary for every unit in the section (about six pages in a pre-primer). When we reach the end of the section, we review each unit that was missed in the first run through. On each following run, we review only the units missed in the run which proceeded it until no unit ' is missed on Step 1. We again start at the beginning of the section and continue this process until the child has read every unit in the section absolutely correctly and consecutively—this is what we mean by our 100 percent criterion of success.

We then go to the next section and repeat the process. However, not every section is purely a sightreading section. As I have mentioned, there are comprehension and word analysis programs as well. These are interspersed between sightreading sections. The sightreading program, however, is the basis for all other programs, and the way we proceed from unit to section in the other programs is exactly the same as is done with the sightreading program—always requiring a performance of 100 percent correctness.

Since space does not permit a detailed description of the other operational programs, those who are interested can find examples in the *Reading Research Quarterly,* Vol. I, No. 1 (Fall 1965). It should be pointed out, however, that since we are still involved in making refinements of details in the various programs, our present ones differ in several instances from those described in the Quarterly. In general, such differences are minor, designed to increase the efficiency of program administration, and do not involve the underlying basic technique of operation. This description is particularly true of our word analysis programs, which, I might add, are now in process of major revision although here, too, the revision involves content and sequencing of content more than basic operational changes.

At this point, rather than continuing a detailed examination of our operational programs, I should like to stress a few significant differences in the philosophy of programed tutoring from the generally accepted practices in the teaching of reading. As indicated earlier, the operational details of programed tutoring are based on laboratory learning principles rather than on teaching doctrine. There is no necessary contradiction here since we feel the learning principles simply emphasize some of the things a *good* teacher does naturally—in so far as it is possible to do so with 30 or more children in the classroom. However, there is one feature of programed tutoring as we practice it which directly contradicts teaching philosophy as generally taught. This is our practice of continuing (as some have expressed it, "stubbornly and stupidly" continuing) the program when the child fails. This practice runs absolutely counter to the "gospel" as given in the training of elementary teachers; namely, if one technique does not work, try another; do it quickly, and then try another.

Our results, particularly as they are mirrored by the success of the poor readers, would seem to indicate that while the "gospel" technique may work with the bright child, for the slow learner the effect is confusing. In the programed tutoring method the child finds himself in a very stable situation as to method and is given whatever time is necessary to learn what is required. Under these conditions, as indicated by our experiences, many of these slow learners, after a long period of seemingly no progress at all, suddenly take off and thereafter learn at a "normal" rate or even a faster than average rate.

Another important characteristic of programed tutoring involves our method of review. While a first look at the operational technique of programed tutoring may seem to give the impression of almost endless repetition, actually the student is required to repeat or review only those words or divisions he has missed—not the entire section in which the errors occur. This method actually diminishes the usual amount of time needed for review and places the emphasis where it is primarily needed—on the actual mistakes.

For anyone who becomes even slightly involved with programed tutoring, the importance of one term in particular becomes immediately clear. That term is "reinforcement." While we do not claim to have reached the Skinnerian goal of 100% reinforcement, we do make a major effort to stress this at every possible jucture of the program. Again, it would seem from our observations and results that the need for such repeated emphasis on reinforcement, and an understanding of what it means, is greater for the disadvantaged child than it is for other children. For many of the inner-city children with whom we have worked, the whole idea of praise for constructive accomplishment is completely foreign. Up to the time they enter school, what little reinforcement they have received in the home environment is of a distinctly negative nature—if they keep quiet, they are not scolded. With many children, a carry-over of this protective behavior results in nonparticipation in the classroom. Some of these children have not even learned the oral vocabulary that indicates praise. One child, for example, who was making very slow progress under tutoring, actually asked her tutor: "What does 'good' mean?" When the tutor was finally able to explain the term, there was an immediate upswing in the child's learning rate and a drastic improvement in her attitude both in the tutoring situation and in the classroom. While, admittedly, this is an unusual case—although unfortunately, not unique—to us it underscores the need to provide as great an amount of reinforcement at every level of the teaching process as is possible and practical, and this is what we attempt to do in programed tutoring.

One other distinctive feature of programed tutoring which will be dealt with in greater detail is our method of record keeping which not only serves as a means of keeping the tutor informed as to the exact place in the program reached by each child but

serves as the research tool by which it is possible to put every step of the learning process under the microscope, so to speak, of the investigator's eye.

Having discussed what programed tutoring is, its philosophy, and the mechanics through which it achieves its results, let us now take a look at a few things for which it may be useful.

On the basis of our experiments involving teaching of beginning reading, programed tutoring is most successful when used in conjunction with classroom teaching. It is a supplement to classroom teaching rather than a replacement for it. Further, programed tutoring seems most effective with the lower third of first grade populations —the potential reading failures as indicated by the Metropolitan Reading Readiness scores and/or teacher evaluations. And, judged by anybody's standards of success or failure, it has been demonstrated to be highly effective in diminishing the number of reading failures, the so-called nonreaders or problem readers in the classrooms *even of inner-city schools.*

As an aid to classroom teaching, for a teacher concerned with having a weekly, daily, or even hourly individual report of the reading performance of her problem readers, programed tutoring can provide a detailed picture of the individual progress, or lack of it, that has never before been readily available.

Furthermore, this kind of information makes it possible for a teacher, if she chooses, to reorganize her classroom reading groups objectively, and it can also be used to help her tailor her instruction toward specific reading problems of individuals within these groups.

Programed tutoring obviously can be highly useful in relieving the classroom workload of the teacher by supplying extra hours of individualized instruction to the children who need it most. Think what this could mean to the teacher with 30 or more children, almost a third of whom need more individual help than she can possibly give. Programed tutoring can provide

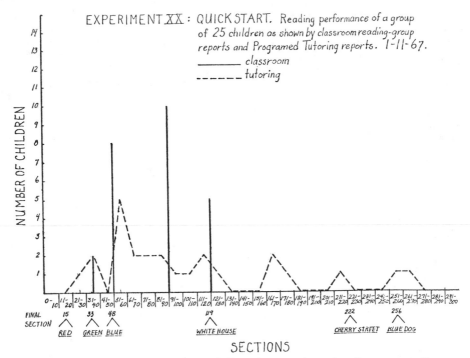

Fig. 4. Reading performance of a group of 25 students as shown by classroom reading-group reports and Programed Tutoring reports, January 11, 1967.

those necessary added hours of individualized instruction to insure a higher probability of success for these children.

As far as the children themselves are concerned, our experience indicates that programed tutoring may be considered unique in that it brings to the child who needs it most all the advantages of individualized instruction programs, and at the same time it provides the systematic presentation of skills and control of comprehension and vocabulary acquisition that are characteristic of the basal approach.

In addition to these preceding specific examples of how programed tutoring can help as a teaching aid, there is one further long-range value that seems highly probable from our evidence to date. Programed tutoring's effectiveness as a technique for teaching beginning reading has been established even for nonreaders among the disadvantaged children in inner-city schools. Since a high percentage of school dropouts comes from such problem readers because of their inability

to make satisfactory progress through the school curriculum, we feel it is reasonable to expect that the use of programed tutoring with beginning readers may well lead to a future reduction among the dropouts caused mainly because of reading difficulties.

Turning from the classroom to the laboratory, let us look at programed tutoring in the role of a research tool.

Each year brings a new flood of recommendations from various sources for changes in educational methodology, theory, or philosophy. One of the chief problems in evaluating these suggestions or testing the validity of their assumptions is that up to now there has been no method of bringing the controls of the laboratory into the organized chaos of the classroom. Because of its fundamental structure, especially its detailed recording system, programed tutoring offers an instrument which can produce experimentally valid evidence in testing hypotheses with a minimum disruption to the classroom itself.

For example, let us assume that there is a genuine value in a pre-first grade summer classroom experience for kindergarten failures—a sort of a remedial head start program. A logical question asks what kind of experience should this be? Some people believe that a pure readiness program is best involving a continuation of the kindergarten program. Others feel that it would be best to introduce actual reading on the grounds that the best readiness for reading is reading itself. Still others feel that a combination of these would be best. In testing these theories, the microscopic view of learning provided by the recording procedures of programed tutoring enables us to gather practical and experimentally significant evidence in support of or disproof. In fact, we have just such a study set up for this summer which we hope will provide definitive answers to these questions.

Actually our decision to do this study on what kind of a pre-first grade summer session would be most helpful to the slow learner stemmed from an earlier experiment which yielded the information shown in this graph.

One of the most interesting things indicated here is the similarity of learning curves by all the subjects, from the fastest learner to the slowest once the slowest had finally caught fire. All the implications of these learning curves are not clear as of now, but one very likely probability seems to exist; namely, that the difference between the so-called nonreaders and the good readers may be that the so-called nonreaders may be instead merely slow starters. The experiment designed for this summer should provide clearcut evidence as to whether this probability is so.

Or, take another research possibility, the area of reading content, and consider these questions: Is preprimer material really necessary? If so, how much is necessary? (We have a study in process where we are testing this hypothesis.) Or, does a visual defect necessarily preclude the possibility of reading success? Or, can a teaching technique such as programed tutoring

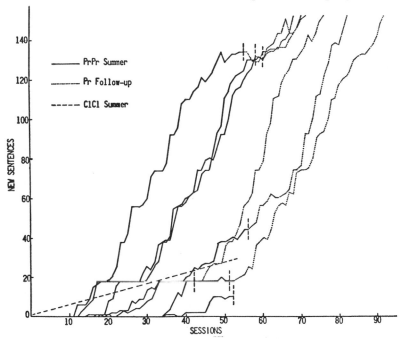

Fig. 5. Individual learning curves for children tutored twice daily, with post-experiment follow-up and estimated maximum performance curve for the group taught twice daily in the classroom.

actually help minimize such problems? (We are currently gathering data on this subject also.)

Even while I have been discussing these research possibilities you may have thought of others. We feel that the possibilities are practically endless. But, in conclusion, whether programed tutoring finds its place in the teaching world as a teaching aid or as a research tool, those of us who have been involved in its development are extremely glad to discuss it with you.

REFERENCE

Ellson, D. G., *et al.* "Programed tutoring: a teaching aid and a research tool," *Reading Research Quarterly, 1,* No. 1 (Fall 1965), 77-127.

Criteria for a Sound Literacy Program

WILLIAM D. SHELDON
Syracuse University

LITERACY PROGRAMS are a relatively recent development in the United States. We were reminded of the inadequate state of literacy of our adolescents and adult males during the recruitment and drafting of men during the Second World War. Thousands of otherwise eligible men could not serve the United States in a profitable or useful manner because they were unable to read or write. Programs which were improvised to serve these men had a ninety-day success and were soon forgotten after 1945.

Less than five years later the need for men in the Korean conflict again served to remind us that hundreds of thousands of young American men were unable to participate fully in the war efforts of the nation because they were illiterate.

From 1952 to the present the movement to bring full literacy to adolescents and adults in the United States has been erratic and ineffective. Now legislation which would provide funds for a comprehensive attack on literacy has been written and for the immediate future, at least, we will see literacy efforts burgeon throughout the United States. Programs will be developed not only for the illiterates but for their teachers and for those who prepare the teachers. Unfortunately the new monies find us unprepared for the gigantic task ahead.

Between 1952 and the present, literacy efforts have not been based on sound procedures. They have lacked an adequate consideration of the basic assumptions which must underlie the criteria for establishing programs. A look at present efforts in literacy testifies to their random nature. We find, in the main, our literacy classes manned on the one hand by untrained volunteers, usually members of church or other welfare groups, who round up available illiterate adolescents and adults and teach them in haphazard fashion, without sound scheduling and often meeting in the basement or parlors of a neighborhood church, or by moonlighting elementary school teachers, lead into teaching the adult illiterate by the director of an adult education program without the structure of a sound program, tested methods, or relevant materials, with classes usually taught a few evenings a week in a local school.

School systems have not in general assumed the responsibility for adult literacy improvement. In some city school systems, no activities take place, even of the most inadequate sort, unless the state or federal government pays the cost.

Because of the lack of support and a central effort, the lack of professional researchers and well-trained teachers, the methods and materials of literacy instruction have been untested, poorly designed, and often unsound. The most popular available materials were originally created for use with slow learning children, remedial elementary or junior high school pupils, or to supply an alphabet and basic vocabulary for peoples who did not have a written language.

The survey made by Barnes and his colleagues has revealed the inadequate nature of methods and materials as well as programs, and certainly the recent book on the disadvantaged published by the NCTE emphasizes the same grave lack of sound programs and the elements needed to develop them (1, 2).

In order to take the first major steps

[1] Robert F. Barnes. "A Review and Appraisal of Adult Literacy Materials and Programs," Report on Research, Project G-029 (unpublished report to U. S. Office of Education, October 1965).

[2] Richard Corbin and M. Crosby. *Language Programs for the Disadvantaged.* National Council of Teachers of English, 1965, Champaign, Illinois.

in developing a sound literacy program we must proceed from valid assumptions to the spelling out of criteria for a program with universal, practical applications.

Major assumptions underlying criteria

1. It is assumed that it is imperative that all Americans become literate. This assumption is based on the necessity of literacy for full citizenship in our democracy where the vote and wish of a well-informed, literate citizenry determines the future course of our government.
2. It is assumed that virtually all individuals can be taught to read and write provided that they are motivated to do so, that the proper learning climate is provided, that well-prepared teachers are available, and that sound materials based on a useful and intelligent methodology can be made available.
3. It is assumed that in order to break the chains of illiteracy in an area such as Appalachia, the Center City, or in abandoned out-of-the-way rural areas a literacy campaign must be launched which embraces adults, adolescents, and children simultaneously.
4. It is assumed that providing literacy programs for all individuals is an important and significant aspect of our school system.
5. It is assumed that because of the urgent need for a literate population the financing of literacy programs is a federal, state, and local obligation and needs a continuing nationwide effort for complete success.

This article will attempt to develop seven major criteria which can be used to appraise the development of a sound literacy program. Financing the adolescent and adult literacy program must be as important a part of the budget of local, state, and national educational agencies as that of providing support to educate children.

The criterion of continuity

Without continuity based on a strong local commitment literacy programs will not develop a professional staff, adequate housing, annual budgetary support, or students who will seek the services which are offered.

It is possible that within the next year or two we will receive temporary funds which will support a rash of literacy programs throughout the nation. If this subsidy is then withdrawn or substantially reduced, the illiterate will be left with disappointments from which he might not recover in terms of his motivation to invest time and energy in becoming literate. Short-term projects will also cause disenchantment of the small but growing group of professional educators who see literacy development as their particular task.

The criterion of the motivated student

Students encouraged to participate in the literacy program must demonstrate a strong desire to learn or be capable of being motivated to learn.

Because many programs will be able to serve only a limited number of illiterates, it is suggested that recruitment of students be active, that inducements be attractive, and that those persons demonstrating the highest motivation to learn be admitted to classes and those who seem to be able to be persuaded be considered next. No student should be involved in an initial or infant program who is aggressively hostile or essentially passive or uncooperative towards upgrading his own literacy status.

The criterion of well-prepared instruction

Our search of the literature and a look at existing programs reveal a drastic lack of well-trained, professional teachers of illiterate adolescents or adults. Also revealed is a lack of programs aimed at training the teachers needed. Heretofore, virtually all instructors in literacy programs have been supplied by volunteer groups composed for the most part of individuals without experience or education as teachers and secondly from the ranks of elementary and secondary teachers who take on the instruction of illiterate adults as an extra or moonlighting activity. The lack of a corps of well-trained, highly motivated literacy teachers has probably been one of the major reasons for the defects in our present and past literacy efforts.

The criterion of research-based methods and materials

The reports available to date on methods and materials and the research base of both suggest that adequate research and a sound rationale for methods and materials are virtually nonexistent. Few, if any, of the currently used materials or methods have been field tested and then revised in accordance with a need to adjust materials for practical usage. The step of making comparative, well-designed studies which would answer questions concerning which material or what method is best suited to specific kinds of students has not been taken on a significant enough scale to give us a methodology or materials supported by research.

The criterion of relevancy

The program must be relevant to the student. Irrelevancy suggests that the program does not provide for either the immediate or long term needs of the student. Programs for adults which use the social spiral in terms of content provided 6-7-8-year-olds or the materials and methods found efficacious for 9-11-year-old remedial readers have virtually no relevance in terms of content, needed procedures, or pace for the mature adult.

An interesting example of the effect of irrelevant procedures versus relevant ones related to a project the writer was involved in several years ago. The aim of the project was the creation of programed materials for illiterate center city adults. During a carefully planned programed sequence using the methods applicable to first grade pupils, little or no excitement or interest and disappointing learning seemed to result. However, when the programers switched to the presentation of advertisements related directly to the buying needs of the illiterate adults, interest picked up immediately.

Another example of relevancy or the lack of it in terms of success relates to the initial development of material for slow-learning adolescents. Units of reading materials were developed related to the specific interests of adolescents, such as, the garage, the shop, automobiles, the service station, building of a home, etc. The units were created simultaneously with a direct involvement with work in the garage, for example. These materials, then printed, were presented for use with adolescent and adult illiterates. The result was failure. The relevancy was gone and the involvement which made the materials successful with one group was not present in the other.

The criterion of evaluation

Programs and individual progress must be properly evaluated before we can really develop a scientific approach to a sound literacy program. Evaluation of programs can be based on the criteria suggested:

1. Financial support
2. Continuity
3. Motivated student
4. Well-prepared instruction
5. Research-based methods and materials
6. Relevancy
7. Evaluation

Individual progress must be measured not only in terms of the progress of the individual in literacy but the application of the new found skills to the illiterate's daily living. We can ask such questions as

1. Is the student able to use his reading skills to identify the signs in his environment?
2. Is the student growing in his ability to handle verbal directions in his work?
3. Can the student read newspaper

reports with increasing accuracy?

4. Has reading become a habit with the student?

5. Can the student use his reading ability to protect his rights as a citizen in terms of knowing political issues, reading pertinent laws, interpreting legal and other contractual papers?

A sound literacy program calls for the establishment of a sound fiscal base which will allow the growth and development of community participation, a permanent effort, skilled teachers, research to identify the most adequate methods and materials, a relevant program which can be periodically evaluated in terms of program soundness and its effect on the individual student.

Reading Instruction in Business and Industry

Frances Beck
University of Chicago

THE HARASSED ADULT in business and industry says he needs help in attacking the mountain of printed matter which confronts him every day. You might argue that this is a narrow, minimal concept of what reading should be for a mature adult and still agree that this narrow concept deserves our serious attention. There have been some attempts to analyze this harassed adult's problem and some attempts to give him additional tools with which to attack it. If we assume that this type of adult reading has been of serious interest and study by experts in reading since the 1930's when Guy T. Buswell (2) studied adults, in and out of industry of that depression era, our next query would naturally focus on the practices followed and the attempts made to enhance the skills of such adult readers.

A lengthy chronological study would be impossible in this paper. It is our purpose to relate to you some of the practices with which we have some knowledge. In preparation each of us spent a good amount of time in studying the published literature of this subject. We searched widely for reports of reading instruction of adults in business and industry. We were, of course, interested in the kinds of persons taught, their motivation, the teaching methods employed, the materials used, and the instruments of evaluation and their validity. We searched in the public domain of print for reports of follow-up studies of the persons who were taught to improve their reading.

Such reports are hard to find. Follow-up studies are harder to find. Research reports are even more elusive. Permit me to report briefly on two different kinds of teaching experiences which I have had. They may serve to point out the reasons for the scarcity of such reports.

Urban adult education setting

The adult reader may choose to enroll in an institutional adult education setting for a course in rapid reading, better reading, rapid reading and comprehension, or some other such entitled course. These courses generally last for one academic quarter, meet once a week for two or more hours, and depend up self-motivation for the necessary private practice on the days without class meetings. For a number of years I taught such a course in an urban setting where adults chose the course "Rapid Reading and Comprehension" from a catalog listing about one hundred and eighty other courses ranging alphabetically from accounting and acting to workshop in creative writing and ranging in interest from cake decorating to camus.

The students in my course, each section of which was supposed to be closed to further registration when it reached twenty-five, represented very well our urban population of literate adults. There was the high school graduate who had been admitted to some college on the condition that, before registration there, he take some reading improvement course. There was the new immigrant whose elementary or secondary education abroad had included some study of the English language but whose English reading was painfully slow. There was a secretary; a minister; a lawyer or an accountant; an office manager; a teacher or a nurse; and about eighteen other equally special individuals who had a great variety of needs, motivations, and experiences for a "rapid" reading course. Their tested reading achievement was generally never good, even for those with considerable education.

On the Van Wagenen Rate of Comprehension test their rate of reading this easy, about fourth-grade material would vary from about 52 to 300 words per minute. On any test of more varied and higher levels of comprehension, as on the old Schrammel Gray, the Dvorak-Van Wagenen Diagnostic Examination, their rate and skills of reading comprehension were below expectancy for their ages and educations. This is a rough oversimplification, but generally one would find that tested comprehension ranged from 40 to 70 percent and rate of reading varied between 50 to 300 wpm. They were slow, inflexible, bewildered readers. They wanted to read better and faster but did not know how; they were convinced, however, that someone outside themselves could lead them to achieve their goal.

There we were with mounds of magazine articles, a textbook, quantities of "graded" reading materials, many duplicated articles, and, by authority of established custom in this particular adult education center, a reading rateometer for every one of them. Let me hasten to tell you that a reading rateometer is a portable pacing device. One of the mounds of magazine articles had been word-counted for use with this machine. Sometimes one or two persons could be said to be ready for such a device. For the most part, as the test scores showed, most of these people needed help on vocabulary building and on all reading skills beyond mere word recognition in order to read to compare, to weigh, to con-sider, to argue, to learn—all normally considered prerequisite skills before undue emphasis on rate or speed which the mere presence of any pacing device is likely to create.

In an attempt to satisfy the catalog description of the course, the rateometers were issued to each student, and part of one class period was devoted to instruction on the use of this pacer, the level of reading for which it was probably appropriate, and its present incongruence for most of their current skills. In most classes the rateometers were taken home by all members and used by some. However, no student report ever indicated that the rateometer was regularly and consistently used throughout the entire period of instruction.

Our class time, nevertheless, was spent in activities not entirely and universally satisfactory. Remember that the initial reading scores showed little, if any, difference between easy and more difficult material on level and rate of comprehension. Remember, also, that our student population in every section was peculiarly diverse so that it was rare that more than two persons could be said to have truly similar reading interests and needs. Nevertheless, being of intrepid and foolish spirit, I lectured on the development of reading skills; they practiced on timed exercises to develop reading skills. We discussed their reading problems as they related to theories of learning. We used a series of short, timed, and graded exercises designed to call attention to reading for certain purposes—for main idea, to learn details, etc. We used a variety of reprints and reproduced or acquired articles of varying length authored by Inez Robb, Farley Mowat, Robert Redfield, and others in an attempt to take advantage of every expressed interest that became apparent in class discussions. Whenever possible, these were read under timed conditions, and some check of comprehension was always made either through objective type tests or short written student summaries.

In short, we were practicing for the post-test scheduled for the final week of the course. Those members of the class who were able to attend each time, who were able to practice about one hour each day, and who read a novel or two during the quarter generally made gains on the post-test. Sometimes those who had to be absent for several weeks because of business trips, surgery, family problems, golf tournaments, or vacations also made gains on the post-test; but because of the difficulty of controls in this hectic urban setting, we never found it possible to test for significance of gains which were at least partly a result of class coaching.

After several quarters of this situation I proposed a change of procedure as one attempt to group persons in accordance with their tested reading competence: to schedule a day of testing for persons who expressed an interest in registering for the course so that the pretesting could be more extensive, more diagnostic, and probably indicative of probable "good" class groupings. The response to this proposal was negative on the grounds that this institution was designed to serve all the people and such a classifying process of prior testing would likely discourage many of those who wanted to learn. Clearly, what this situation needed was a professional person, more courageous and articulate than I, who would ask, expect, and secure better conditions under which learning would have a better chance of taking place.

Industrial setting

Several years later a management consultant requested that I join him in a series of meetings with about twelve men in the management hierarchy of an industrial plant. Although already "in" management, these men were in a sense being groomed for movement within the administrative setup. They were plant managers and industrial relations directors; they were all concerned about the company's future industrial competitiveness. They were mature (35-59), intelligent, and generally would not have been excluded from graduate study even though most of them were not college graduates. They were articulate and alert. They had read those newspaper advertisements which predicted amazing gains in reading rate and comprehension in certain kinds of courses.

In our course, the plan for ten of the twelve weekly meetings was to spend one hour discussing the outside reading which had been previously assigned and to spend one hour in reading skills instruction. The outside reading assignments consisted of several short articles by such management authors as Douglas MacGregor and Walter Chrysler and large portions of three books, *My Years with General Motors* by Alfred P. Sloan, Jr., *Managing for Results* by Peter F. Drucker, and *Classics in Management,* edited by Harwood F. Merrill.

The reading-skills text was *Read Better, Read Faster* by Manya and Eric DeLeeuw. The Van Wagenen Rate of Comprehension and the Cooperative English tests were administered as pre-and post-tests; but of the total number of students, only four of the same men were present at the two testing sessions! Absences were legitimate—family, business travel, etc. Such modest gains as could be determined in the post-tests and in the DeLeeuw exercises could probably be attributed to practice and test sophistication acquired in the course. Therefore, a later test to determine permanence of gain or change in reading seemed unwarranted for such a small tested population. Some attention should certainly be devoted to evaluation of comprehension of the readings for class discussion. Generally, this task would be most difficult because attitude toward the administrative role might well have been named the area for behavior change, and no objective measure of this had been devised.

These two chastening experiences reveal instances of harsh reality and indicate some of the reasons for the paucity of good reports on instruction and the difficulty of controlled research in such circumstances. It is small consolation for me to be able to remove from the context of Emery Bliesmer's "1964 Review of Research in College Adult Reading" (1) such statements as "Cross . . . reported positive results for a number of participants in three reading improvement programs . . . and that Crowell . . . reported 'striking differences' between earlier and later performance of participants in three . . . programs (mostly adults from business and industry); but they reported that regular types of comparisons were invalidated by contamination of tests or test date."

REFERENCES

1. Bliesmer, Emory P. "1964 Review of Research in College Adult Reading," *Yearbook of the National Reading Conference, 14,* 237-256.
2. Buswell, Guy T. *How Adults Read.* Supplementary Educational Monographs, No. 45. Chicago, Illinois: University of Chicago Press, 1937.

Some Problems and Solutions in Teaching Reading for Business and Industry

MIRIAM SCHLEICH
Hofstra University

TEACHING ADVANCED READING SKILLS to professional and business adults is a challenging task which has its problems and its rewards. In my experience the chief problems have been handling the students' ego involvement delicately, allaying their fear of being rated by their superiors on the basis of their reading performance, dispelling unrealistic expectations of rate improvement, finding a time for scheduling a reading course, selecting materials, and evaluating gains. Among the rewards have been the stimulating effect of the give and take that goes on in a reading class for business or industrial executives, the subjective evaluations of some of the students who suddenly discovered that they were capable of far better performance than

they had ever had before, and the unexpected by-products such as the students' awareness that their personal presentation of reports to be read by others had greatly improved in the process of working on the improvement of their reading.

Handling the ego delicately

Reading teachers have long been aware of the close relationship of the students' self-concept to their progress. However, in working with business and professional groups, the problem of ego involvement is sometimes acute. Adults are supposed to know how to read—to have the necessary comprehension skills to meet their needs—and any intimation that speed may not be their only need, or that speed and interpretative skills are inextricably interrelated, may leave the adult student slightly shaken or even antagonistic. Because of the assumption that adult reading improvement should be confined to speed, standardized tests—indeed any kind of legitimate testing of the adults' understanding and grasp of what he reads—tend to be threatening. The professional or business man may see the evaluation of his reading comprehension as a reflection of his intellectual capacity.

Walter B. Pitkin in his introduction to *The Art of Rapid Reading* (Grosset & Dunlap, 1929) recounts his experience with the president of a company for which he had written a report of trade conditions. After reading the report, the business man wrote his comments, revealing that he had completely missed the main points. When asked where he had found the basis for his interpretation, he spent two or three hours rereading and then concluded he must have read too fast. Pitkin comments that the truth was he read poorly.

Since ego involvement is so strong in reading improvement courses for business and industry—indeed for all educated adults—it is very important to establish early in the course a better understanding of the nature of the reading process. Adults need to realize that learning to read is a lifetime process and that a complete mastery of the reading process is like the pot of gold at the end of the rainbow—something to search for but never to attain fully. They need to be helped to accept their present level of skills without embarrassment and without any self-satisfied or complacent smugness. Adults need to be aware of the fact that lack of any formal training in reading since grammar school or junior high almost certainly results in reading skills considerably below their potential capacities, no matter how well they may score on a standardized reading test such as the reading section of the Cooperative English tests.

Allaying the fear of being rated on the basis of reading scores

A second problem I encountered in working with business and industrial groups who were not entirely self-selected was the fear of being rated by their superiors on the basis of the reading course results. In my first class of engineers, which included the president of the firm, one man verbalized his own fears and those of his colleagues before the class began. He indicated that even before the class had started, many of the men were apprehensive because of the composition of the class, and he predicted a difficult time for all, instructor included, unless some way were found to allay the growing fears of the men. This fear of exposure of their weaknesses or of the use of test results in a detrimental way—even to the affecting of the boss's feelings toward them—might make instruction more difficult and could even contaminate test results. Since business firms wanted assurance that they were getting their money's worth for any investment they made, including a training program, it was necessary to turn in a final evaluation of the program and gains made. However, being forewarned, I made an agreement with the training director that all individual results would be given to the individual concerned only and that a composite evaluation, without names, would be given to him. This agreement was made known to all students and was subsequently included in all contracts for business and professional courses thereafter.

Dispelling unrealistic expectations of speed

A third problem that arose in working with adult reading improvement groups was the unrealistic expectations of improvement in speed. This expectation is not surprising in view of the national advertising and publicity given to certain commercial speed-reading programs which make claims that are not only immoderate but impossible. Perhaps, too, students come with unreasonable expectations because of their fond hope that somewhere, someone must have a magic formula for helping them learn in fifteen easy lessons how to get through the mountains of reading materials that daily clutter up their desks at home and in their offices. A guided discussion of the variables in rate and comprehension, together with an explanation of the physiological aspects of the reading process, helped to bring the students' goals to a more realistic level, which was often accompanied with an evident sense of relief. It also helped to point up for them the importance of flexibility in rate, of adjusting one's rate to the material, one's background, and one's purpose.

In this connection I sometimes tell my class an experience I had with my first group of top-level executives of a utility company. We had been discussing flexibility, and during the discussion I had tried to stress the fact that some things should be read very slowly and carefully while others should be skimmed through "practically at the speed of light." I recalled my own reading of *War and Peace*, which I had lived with for almost six months, and I described my writing in the margins and making notes in the back of the book as I read. Rate, it was noted, is in part determined by the reader's personal evaluation of the worth of the material to him.

In the interim between our discussion and the next class, one of my students saw a TV program on speed reading. On the show a reading instructor demonstrated teaching speed reading by means of a tachistoscope device and during the program remarked that he had read *War and Peace* in four hours. At our next meeting, my student recounted this story and asked me pointblank what was the matter with me. During the subsequent discussion on how fast one could see and then process what one saw, I set up an old tachistoscope to prove to the class that theoretically they could read 20 to 30 thousand words a minute, too. "And why don't you read that fast?" they were questioned.

The answer came somewhat as follows, "Well to begin with, we can't actually *see* five words at one fixation, but we can make good guesses from minimal cues when we make effective use of context and configuration clues. Secondly, there is no time lost in interfixation movements and return sweeps at the end of lines, as in normal reading. And last and most important of all, we can't think that fast continuously in significant materials."

Selecting course materials

Still another problem in giving a course for business and industrial executives was the selection of the course materials. The question as to whether to use specific professional materials or materials of a more general nature had to be decided. In the case of the utility company I worked with, a decision was made not to use company materials. The basis of the decision was that for the most part the participants would be engineers, whose general reading tended to be technical in nature and somewhat narrow. The hope was that not only would reading skills, including rate of comprehension, be improved but that interest in a wider range of reading might be stimulated. This decision proved to be a wise one in terms of participant satisfaction and test results.

In the case of a group from the Appellate Division of the Internal Revenue, professional materials were used as part of the total course reading. The decision here was based on the homogeneity of the group—all lawyers and some both lawyers and accountants—and on the fact that their prime need was to increase their case coverage through increased rate of reading skills. This experiment did not appear to be successful mainly because the internal revenue code and case histories at the appellate level tend to be subjectively interpreted and comprehension depends to a large extent on the background of experience of the individual lawyer in terms of previous cases and precedents.

Finding the right time for scheduling classes

A fourth problem that needs consideration in setting up a reading course for executives is the time at which it should be scheduled. Ideally, it should be scheduled in the morning, preferably at the beginning of the day before the participants get involved with their various business problems and get so deep in their work that a reading course comes as an unwelcome interruption. Late hours, after the working day is over, are equally unpropitious.

My first group of executives included the president of the firm, the chief legal counsel, and the industrial relations manager. The president verbalized his difficulty in mentally turning off the day's problems, in unwinding, so that he could concentrate on the work at hand. It was his suggestion that at least one of the two sessions per week be held the first hour of the day. In still another group, both weekly sessions were scheduled early in the morning.

With busy business and professional men and women, four hours a week are difficult to schedule, and any schedule turns out to be a compromise.

Evaluating reading gains

Perhaps most difficult of all the

tasks confronting the instructor of a course in reading improvement for business and industrial personnel is evaluating course results meaningfully, especially if the instructor insists on using the C^2 reading test as one measure of improvement. As those of you who use the C^2 reading test know, it probably measures general reading ability as well or better than most adult reading tests, but it is not an ideal instrument for measuring short-term gains. While there is little difficulty in getting a statistically significant group gain, almost always one or more individual students finish with a score lower than the entering ones.

In some of these cases where entering scores were high to begin with and where the individuals are secure in their positions, the test results can be interpreted satisfactorily in terms of overall appraisal and of the errors inherent in standardized testing. In other cases, the students are disturbed by the results, which seem to prove that they didn't improve as much as they thought they did. I have found using several measures to evaluate helpful in such cases since no one instrument measures all the areas covered in the course anyway. An informal test of the student's ability to read and organize an article from *The Atlantic* at the beginning of the class and at the end makes an impressive measure of gains in reading ability, and a rate test giving a words-per-minute score is also useful.

In general, however, it is probably most useful in evaluating to point out that it is both possible and desirable to include, along with subjective measurements of gains in reading effectiveness, objective measures which sample both individual and group progress in certain specific areas, especially rate and general comprehension. All individual evaluations will be done for the individuals concerned only. The group evaluations will be charted to ascertain how much improvement the group as a whole makes in those areas measured by objective tests.

Developing a Comprehensive Reading Program for the Atterbury Job Corps Center

Erwin F. Stevenson
Westinghouse Management Services

THE ATTERBURY JOB CORPS CENTER is located on the dormant military reservation known as Camp Atterbury. This area is located some 30 miles south of Indianapolis, Indiana, and is serviced by a national highway network. There are over 40,000 acres of land formerly used to train and house troops for World War II and the Korean conflict. The land is gently rolling with the extreme southern portion heavily wooded. The corpsmen are billeted here in "temporary" housing built in 1942.

At the Atterbury Center our typical enrollee has been in school nearly 10 years, but he reads at less than the fifth grade level. Nine of ten have never held a job. The tenth was working for an average of eighty cents an hour. Sixty-three percent never have had a brush with the law. Twenty-seven percent have a record of minor antisocial behavior. Less than ten percent had a conviction of a serious juvenile offense.

They come from 35 states and the District of Columbia. At least 8 of the 10 have never seen a doctor or dentist before coming to Atterbury. Almost half of all new enrollees need emergency dental treatment. Forty-seven percent are not eligible for military service because of their age, their physical weaknesses, or lack of academic achievement. Forty-five percent are from broken homes; sixty-five percent are from families where the head of the household is chronically unemployed. And one of two comes from a family that is living on some form of public welfare.

To give you an even better idea of the type of population we are dealing with in terms of their scholastic achievement, fifty-three percent of all enrollees thus far in 1967 read no higher than the fourth grade level.

The corpsman at Atterbury Center will begin studying to raise his literacy level in our general education department, with his work there related to his choice of vocational training. He is offered vocational courses including electronics, food service, building service, and automotive services. Primary emphasis is placed upon the development of basic skills required for entry-level occupations in his selected field.

A typical corpsman's schedule is as follows:

8:15- 9:45	General Education
10:00-11:30	Physical Education, Driver Education, or Counseling
11:45-12:45	Lunch
1:00- 4:00	Vocational Training
4:15- 5:00	Corpsman Projects

Note that the period of time a corpsman spends in his general education classes is limited to one and one-half hours per day to develop reading, mathematics, and communication skills.

The problem

When Westinghouse Management Services Corporation took over the operation of the Atterbury Job Corps Center in July 1966, it faced problems similar to those of other Job Corps Centers.

In the area of reading, the basic problem was to develop a method of raising the reading level of an educationally, environmentally, and culturally deprived person to a level consistent with his vocational aspirations in as short a time as possible.

In any vocational training program, the matter of literacy quickly becomes paramount. If a person is unable to read material that pertains to his job and his daily life, it is unrealistic to expect him to master anything more than short-term goals.

A nonreader can learn to tune up a specific make and model of car by watching a demonstration and listing the various specifications, but he cannot learn to tune up any car. The skill requires the ability to read a service manual. In the same way, an illiterate, would-be cook can learn to bake a meat loaf by following his instructor's example, but he cannot learn to follow a recipe. Obviously, neither of these men would be an acceptable employee.

The first step taken by Westinghouse in establishing an effective reading program was a comprehensive evaluation of the reading instruction then being given. The following specific weaknesses were noted:

1. There was not in existence a consistent developmental reading program. No specific objectives had been established with which the instructional staff could identify. (In place of this goal, each teacher was operating within his own basic concept of what he considered to be a successful reading program.)

2. The staff, while possessing excellent rapport with the corpsmen, did not have the training needed to teach basic and developmental reading. This fact was accounted for in part by the fact that 90 percent of the staff consisted of secondary teachers trained in a content field which did not require a basic course in reading. Because of their inability to identify reading problems related to individual corpsmen and lacking the understanding necessary for sequential development of the skills needed for success in reading, the obvious result was that corpsmen were poorly motivated to learn; consequently, little learning took place.

3. The corpsmen had no way of evaluating their progress in reading. Consequently, they were becoming apathetic and discouraged; and this attitude in turn led to poor attendance, sleeping in class, and other disciplinary problems.

4. The basic reading materials in the form of linear programs were

inappropriate in format and interest.

Steps toward solution

Related to the goals and overall design of the program, an organizational approach to reading instruction was necessary which would attempt to properly place the corpsman in the program.

Upon arrival at the center, a corpsman is placed in a two-week orientation program. During this period he is administered the Stanford Achievement Test Battery and an oral reading test. Based upon the results of these two tests, the corpsman is assigned to one of three instructional levels, depending on his reading scores, which are as follows:

Level   I—0 to 3.9 grade reading level
Level   II—4 to 6.9 grade reading level
Level III—over 7th grade reading level

Those corpsmen assigned to Level I are placed in class groupings where the teacher/corpsman ratio is approximately 1:10, with additional one-to-one tutoring available for those with complex reading disabilities. Levels II and III classes have a teacher/corpsman ratio of approximately 1:20.

After assignment to a particular class, additional diagnostic testing takes place for completion of an individual progress chart and an individual program planned to meet the particular corpsman's needs.

In order to initiate a successful developmental reading program, it was recommended by the evaluation team that 1) professional teacher training be undertaken immediately and that 2) an evaluation of available materials be started. This resulted in a three-phase in-service teacher training program. Phase I of the program consisted of a thirty-hour basic course in the teaching of reading. Phase II was a thirty-hour workshop designed to give teachers the opportunity to actually work with materials and use techniques used in the teaching of word recognition skills, comprehension skills, and study skills. In addition, they were given the opportunity to participate in the using of materials specifically designed to evaluate and diagnose individual reading problems. Phase III was to be a thirty-hour course in the diagnosis and treatment of learning difficulties.

Working with the Indiana University Reading Clinic, the classroom teachers and supervisors have thus far been given more than sixty hours of instruction in the techniques of teaching reading. An additional thirty-hour course is planned for the very near future.

With our objectives and the characteristics of the population in mind, a careful evaluation of available published materials was begun.

As a result of this evaluation, we adopted a basic adult reading series which was felt would serve as a basis for sequential skill development in the reading program. To supplement this series, there was added a wide variety of commercially prepared materials such as paperbacks, popular magazines, newspapers, comics, and low-level high-interest books.

In addition to the large variety of commercially prepared materials, it was necessary to supplement these with center-developed or rewritten materials, especially in the area of materials related to vocational training.

One of the pitfalls previously encountered revolved around the readability of instructional materials outside the structured reading program. Too often the situation was encountered where corpsmen were correctly placed in reading materials during actual reading instruction, only to find themselves frustrated by the reading of shop manuals, job sheets, or instructional materials in other areas of the general education curriculum.

To eliminate this problem all staff members were trained in the use of the Farr-Jenkins-Peterson revision of the Flesch Readability Formula for use in the grading of all utilized material. The staff benefited from this by having teachers and vocational instructors write a great many vocational correlated materials. As a consequence, now no matter what the content of the material required for a corpsman, the reading level stays consistent.

These supplementary materials serve two basic purposes: 1) to provide enrichment and vocational related reading (vertical growth); and 2) to provide horizontal depth for almost any identifiable skill incurred at all reading levels. Vertical growth provides for the continued development of skills, attitudes, and habits in reading. Horizontal depth provides the opportunity for continued practice of a specific deficient skill until the corpsman's performance reflects proficiency. However, this requirement does not prevent the corpsman's vertical progress in the basic program.

Design of program

In the design of the program considerable attention had to be given to various characteristics of the population. For instance, people were not highly motivated to take part in the academic areas of training in contrast to their desires to participate in vocational training. Therefore, there had to be included in the program problem solving vocational situations which demanded that a student master selected reading skills before he could hope to bring his work to a successful conclusion. The general education teachers were charged with presenting a major portion of the corpsman's shop theory.

It was also known that the population was easily discouraged during the learning process, so initially the program had to provide for correct placement in order to maximize the chances of a corpsman's success. Secondly, each skill level required sufficient depth so that regressions could be held to a minimum. Thirdly, there needed to be a system developed whereby the corpsman could receive immediate reinforcement for any successful accomplishments.

From past experiences it was observed that a higher degree of motivation was maintained when the materials used were not of a textbook nature but rather of single sheets or, at most, small units containing 8 to 10 pages. This requirement was more true for the first two levels of instruction.

Therefore, the program was divided into small skill units corresponding to a set of performance objectives with a progress check administered at the completion of each unit. If the progress check shows that a student has not satisfied a particular objective, the teacher assigns the corpsman work elsewhere in the program that will aid him in satisfying this objective.

This progress check corresponds to a progress chart which is constructed for each corpsman's independent reading level to visually portray for him at all times his reading strengths and weaknesses. As he demonstrates proficiency by overcoming a particular weakness, it is so noted by the teacher. This type of visual reinforcement which identifies progress for the corpsman is a very successful motivator throughout the instructional program.

Because of the short attention span of most of the corpsmen, it was found that it was necessary to have many materials available, as well as a wide variety of techniques for use in their presentation.

Finally, it was necessary that the program be so designed that a corpsman could pursue the lessons with maximum self-help, a situation necessitating definite program lessons in easy bite-size steps. There were many other characteristics considered in the program design; however, the ones mentioned received considerable attention at the time.

Conclusions

Presently, the Stanford Achievement Test measurements indicate that the average corpsman's reading level at the center is rising one and one third academic months per month of training. Considering the fact that the corpsmen only receive thirty hours of general education a month, we are somewhat pleased with these statistics. As our programs become firm and even more comprehensive in scope, it would not be unrealistic to expect these gains to increase.

In summary from this paper, the following conclusions may be drawn:

1. A developmental reading program must have recognizable and measurable goals that are acceptable and understandable by the learner and the instructor.

2. Proper diagnosis and placement techniques are vital to the success of this approach to reading instruction.

3. A developmental reading program should provide the learner with opportunities to constantly check his own progress and fulfill his individual needs.

4. Throughout the program small units of instruction seem to be more acceptable and satisfying to this population group composed largely of the culturally deprived probably because such instruction provides ego gratification on a more consistent basis.

5. The types of instructional materials which can be used with this population are limited only to the extent that they are acceptable to the learner and meet his needs.

6. In this program it was not sufficient to use grade level materials only in the academic or structured reading program. It was necessary to use grade level materials in the vocational training programs as well as the academic areas. This material prevented frustration and loss of effectiveness during the learning process.

7. It was learned that the complexity of a concept and the reading level at which that concept could be explained did not necessarily go together. In other words, highly complex materials, it was found, could be explained at a low reading level if technical terms were limited in number and taught as sight words.

8. In-service training played a crucial role in the development of this program.

9. The experience in this program indicates that a developmental reading program is a continuously developing program which requires constant reevaluation and updating.

RESEARCH

PSYCHOLOGY AND SOCIOLOGY OF READING

The Psychology of Reading

ALBERT J. KINGSTON
The University of Georgia

READING is a complex act performed by humans. Within the traditional meaning of the word, humans seem to be the only fauna which read. Although it is possible, perhaps, to argue that other types of animals read signs while seeking food or searching for mates, most of us likely will stipulate that reading is something that only humans do. Psychology is commonly regarded as the study of behavior. And because reading is one type of behavior, and an extremely important one to modern man, it might be assumed that psychologists have devoted considerable time and effort to studying it systematically. Unfortunately such is not the case. While many psychologists have on occasion studied some aspect of reading which momentarily interested them, few, if any, have devoted their entire professional careers to the study of the reading process. There are perhaps a number of reasons for a lack of interest manifested by psychologists in reading. One reason may be the ascendancy which behaviorism has held in American psychology during the present century, and the reluctance of the behaviorial psychologist to deal with covert behavior. Another reason, undoubtedly, is the obvious difficulties encountered in attempting to explicate. and to study under controlled conditions, many of the more significant aspects of reading behavior. Regardless of the reasons, however, there has not emerged and does not exist at present a systematic, well-formulated psychology of reading.

Yet many aspects of reading as it is taught and discussed today have been influenced by psychology. The familiar concepts of readiness, developmental reading, vocabulary control, drill and repetition, emphasis on meaning and interpretation, and evaluating pupil progress, to mention but a few, have been influenced by psychological findings. Unfortunately, the applications of psychological findings have been piecemeal and sometimes even seem to serve merely as "garnishes," rather than to function as basic or fundamental principles underlying reading pedagogy. At present only one current text uses the word *psychology* in its title. This text entitled *Psychology in Teaching Reading* has three major goals according to the authors. First, it seeks to select data that are most relevant to the teacher's understanding of the reading process; secondly, it seeks to interpret these data in terms of the problems that the teacher will encounter; and finally, it seeks to apply the interpretations to the specific classroom problems that teachers meet (20). Although these objectives are laudatory, it is questionable whether a psychology of reading is sufficiently structured to be of much value to the classroom reading teacher. The text seems to select a number of different aspects of educational psychology which appear to bear upon reading behavior and instruction. As such it falls short of presenting a systematic psychology of reading.

There is, however, no systematic psychology of reading, nor is there an adequate theory of reading, a situation which complicates the task of this author. In attempting to deal effectively with this assignment, the writer deliberately has not attempted to report research bearing upon such familiar reading topics as readiness, perception, sensation, intellectual abilities, etc. Nor has any attempt been made to discuss in detail the research of persons having special interest in reading. Rather, the strategy has been to discuss the work of certain psychologists that may have bearing upon the field of reading and to suggest possible areas where psychology can make significant contributions to reading.

Basically, one major contribution which psychology can make to reading is to provide the impetus needed to develop a more adequate theory of reading. The term *reading* has been applied to such a wide range of behaviors that it has ceased to have a single identifiable meaning. If a science of reading behavior is to be developed it must draw heavily on what has been learned regarding the behavior of humans in a related field such as psychology. Although at present many psychological theories, i.e., personality, learning, psychometrics, growth, and development, have been developed largely in special and limited contexts, there is no reason to suspect that the successful theory building found in social services cannot also be achieved in reading. Much of science has had its great impetus from the discovery of principles that apply to merely a limited range of events. Thus, it might be expected that a psychology of reading may evolve not from a comprehensive treatment, but rather from the discovery of principles or the development of theories which apply to limited segments of reading behaviors. In fact, one difficulty the reading specialist faces is the limited degree to which many current psychological theories appear to be related to any aspect of classroom behavior. However, it is important that the present body of knowledge in the field of reading become so organized that generalizations and laws be applied to a wider range of problems and be testable under a number of conditions.

A major difficulty in achieving this end stems from the very complexity of the human organism. Modern psychologists recognize that the organism functions in a holistic fashion, and that in any given situation behavior is a function of both the attributes of the individual and the situation in which the individual operates at that moment. Both Raygor (*18*) and Weaver (*23*) have suggested that the task is difficult because much reading behavior is cov-

ert, and the researcher must infer what goes on within the organism by studying how an individual reacts to various stimuli. Chomsky (*5*), in an excellent review of Skinner's *Verbal Behavior,* states

> . . . that insights that have been achieved in the laboratories of the reinforcement theorist, though quite genuine, can be applied to complex human behavior only in the most gross and superficial way, and that speculative attempts to discuss linguistic behavior in these terms alone omit from consideration factors of fundamental importance that are, no doubt, amenable to scientific study although their specific character cannot at present be precisely formulated.

It seems likely, however, that because of its adherence to the methods of science, psychology offers the promise of providing the means for explicating the current confusions concerning reading. To date, though, psychology offers the promise rather than the fruits of the scientific method. The writer believes, however, that the major contributions of psychology will result from the theoretical considerations and carefully controlled experimentations of psychologists, which may serve as models for reading research.

Despite the present lack of an adequate psychology of reading, the work of certain scientists seems to bear on the interests of reading specialists or those concerned with reading behavior. Probably one of the most significant areas of congruence is the work of linguists, psycholinguists, information-theorists, and psychologists concerned with language. Carroll (*4*), for example, notes three points at which linguists and psychologists have common interests. These are the possibility of universals in grammar and in language structure, the possibility of significant differences between languages in the kinds of relationship they exhibit between their expression and content systems and the possible implications such differences may have for the cognitive behavior of the speakers of those languages, and the possibility of making a psychological interpretation of grammatical structure. Carroll also suggests that language may be viewed as a communication system. As such, language has two major aspects: one, a physical and biological system in which communication takes place, and, two, a sign system in which messages are formulated. Weaver, who has attempted to apply the rubric of information theory to language and reading, points out the shortcomings of communication theory, but believes that it probably fits as well or better than S-R psychology. He argues that in communication theory neural action (covert though it may be) is considered whereas behaviorism excludes such physiological considerations from its theoretical structures. Today, however, there is a group of neo-behaviorists who attempt to deal with mediating processes.

Most reading specialists would agree that the reading process involves some sort of interaction between writer and reader and that some sort of language system is employed. A genuine problem that must be faced in finding similarities between the interests of language specialists and reading specialists lies in the tendency of linguists to talk mainly about oral language. Auding and reading obviously do involve the two aspects of communication which Carroll stresses, yet there also are certain significant differences between the two modes of behavior. Buswell (2) notes that the major difference in reading and speech is the difference in the sense avenues through which stimuli are received. According to Buswell, the essential difference between knowing how to read and how to understand oral speech is the substitution of visual perception of visual symbols for auditory impressions of the same symbols when spoken. The thoughts expressed are the same, the vocabulary is the same, and the word order is the same. The problem in reading is thought to be one of learning to recognize the visual symbols with accuracy and reasonable speed. Buswell's thesis has more accuracy in describing reading at the earliest

stages of development than it does for the reading behavior of more sophisticated scholars. Many of us, for example, have first discovered words in print long before we have heard them presented orally. Textbooks and published reports in the academic disciplines are filled with specialized vocabulary that has not been previously encountered in oral form by the typical scholar. Carroll, furthermore, even suggests that an individual might learn to read a foreign language fluently without much acquaintance with its spoken form (3). Deaf children also learn to read without previously having heard language in its oral form. It may be that beginning readers rely on some sort of implicit speech to a greater degree than do more proficient or mature readers. At present it only seems safe to say that auding and reading are somehow related, yet the exact nature of the relationship is obscure. The relationships obviously grow out of the mediating processes generally associated with cognition.

Reading, typically, is regarded as a thought process. The relationship of reading to thought was noted by Thorndike (21) fifty years ago. Gray (10), speaking for the Yearbook Committee of the National Society for the Study of Education, stressed the viewpoint that reading and thinking are inseparable as shown by the following quotation:

> The Yearbook Committee believes that any conception of reading that fails to include reflection, critical evaluation, and the classification of meaning is inadequate. It recognizes that reading includes much that psychologists and educators have commonly called thinking.

Unfortunately for reading specialists many psychologists shunned research in thinking and cognition in the years that followed Watson's attacks on Wundt's introspection experiments. Even today many behaviorists avoid research in this area because such covert activities are not thought to be subject to adequate experimentation. Those interested in reading found a greater affinity with psychologists of the Gestalt school who stressed perception and meaning. Unfortunately, the experiments of the classical Gestaltists, although interesting, have yielded little of permanent value concerning the nature of cognition. On the other hand, their experiments in perception have been of more value yet do not answer many important questions concerning reading (19).

Perceptual learning is part of the skill of reading. Particularly significant is the acquisition of the directional scanning habit. Also necessary is letter differentiation and, as with learning the Morse code, there is a second stage of perceptual learning in reading—wherein the letter units now discriminable, are organized into higher-order units so that more is perceived at a glance (9).

During the last decade there has been a resurgence of interest in the psychology of cognition, perhaps because it is becoming more apparent that any psychology of human behavior must deal with this important human attribute. Unfortunately for the reading specialist, there seems to be a number of different positions which are identifiable among those psychologists who work in the area of cognitive investigation. Ausubel, for example, identifies one group as neo-behaviorists as typified by Hebb, Osgood, Hull, Berlyne, and Staats; another group as cognitive theorists including Bruner, Ausubel and Gagné; a group of developmentalists typified by Piaget and Vygotsky; and finally, a group interested primarily in cognitive organization and functioning. A cogent review of these various positions can be found in Ausubel's introduction to a book of readings edited by Anderson and Ausubel (1).

Educators, of course, have been interested in cognition for many years. Evidence of this interest is obvious from even a casual scanning of the current educational literature on curriculum materials in any academic discipline, ranging from reading and language arts to science and mathematics. The keen interest of educators some-times has caused them to accept the theories and experimental findings of cognitive theories prematurely. Currently there seems to be a rather prevalent belief among educators that mediational responses are primarily verbal in nature and that they can be taught by the careful exposure of pupils to various teaching procedures and materials. Unfortunately, the truth is that although some teachers talk blithely about such words as concepts, concept attainment, concept formation, and learning by inquiry or discovery, these terms usually represent merely hypothetical constructs or psychological inferences. Cognition theorists tend to be more reserved concerning the nature of these constructs and their function in mediation and learning. Although the work of cognitive theorists holds promise, the extent to which these terms are misused, overgeneralized, and employed as new labels to describe old behaviors may cause eventual difficulty. Reading, for example, does not necessarily need new terms but rather needs operational statements which more adequately serve to define the behaviors we think we observe.

A number of experimental studies by researchers interested in cognition seem to hold promise for persons interested in reading. Kendler, Kendler, and Leanard (15), for example, studied the mediating responses of children of various chronological ages. They found that children below age six tended to behave predominately on a single S-R basis and that with increasing chronological age an increasing proportion behaved in a mediating manner. The experimenters suggest that since there is a relationship between learning and choice behavior mediators learned more rapidly than did non-mediators. An analysis of the verbalizations of the children after they had completed the presented tasks suggests that there is a relationship between the ability to connect words with actions and the tendency toward mediated choices. This study seems to verify the emphasis placed by reading teachers on the relationship of language and reading and also indicates the need for further research to ascertain the nature of the factors which lead to cognitive differences among children at an early age.

A number of researchers have conceptualized cognitive functioning in terms of principles of control or cognitive styles (24, 25). Such control principles, styles, or strategies as leveling-sharpening, tolerance for unrealistic experience, focusing-scanning, equivalence range, constructed-flexible control, and field dependence-independence have been studied. Holzman and Klein (11) relate leveling and sharpening to modes of organizing stimuli. Leveling implies a low level of articulation in a sequence of stimuli, while sharpening implies a high level of articulation. Tolerance for unrealistic experience has been described by Gardner (6) as acceptance of experiences that do not agree with what one knows to be true. Equivalence range relates to organizing ability as related to the awareness of differences. Focusing-scanning deals with the tendency to narrow awareness, to keep experiences discrete, and a tendency to separate affect from idea and thus to maintain objectivity. Field dependence-independence is employed to describe the ability to abstract an item from the field in which it appears or is embedded (6). In essence, the theory of cognitive principles implies that an individual develops certain characteristic modes of cognitive control as he matures. These styles, then, are employed in coping with various situations which the organism faces. At present most of the research in this area seems to be focused upon the personality, yet the consistency with which these modes of control appear to be manifested in various individuals makes it reasonable to assume that the same controls may function in reading. The work of Kagan (13, 14) bears on this possibility.

Kagan postulates two stable dimensions upon which children and adults are distributed. The first is called reflection-impulsivity and describes the degree to which a child reflects upon alternative classifications of a stimulus or alternative solution hypotheses in situations in which many response possibilities are available simultaneously. In such situations some children have a fast conceptual tempo; they impulsively report the first classification that occurs to them or carry out the first solution that appears appropriate. On the other hand, reflective children or adults characteristically delay before carrying out a solution hypothesis or reporting a classification. They actively consider the alternatives available and compare their validity. The reflective individual behaves as if he cared that his first response is as close to correct as possible. A second dimension, called visual analysis, describes the child's tendency to analyze complex stimuli into their component parts. Some children fractionate a stimulus into small subunits, others label and react to a larger stimulus chunk. According to Kagan, analysis is relatively independent of the reflection-impulsivity dimension and each contributes variance to a variety of cognitive products. Kagan and his associates have conducted a number of interesting and thought provoking experiments to verify these hypotheses. Their findings appear to have important implications for reading specialists.

Reading teachers who have observed how some children will guess at unfamiliar words—even though they have little likelihood of success, while others appear reluctant to guess, even though they probably know the word—should study the work of Kogan and Wallach. Kogan and Wallach have studied the process of decision making in individuals and the types of judgments and the manipulations of alternative solutions which lead toward judgments. Presumably some individuals constantly are more willing to take risks than are others (16).

If reading behavior involves thinking, and apparently it does, cognition and cognitive styles must play some part in the manner in which the reader comprehends and interprets what has been read. Cognitive styles, for example, imply various modes of conception, categorizing of ideas, and organizing significant facts and details. Reading is one mode by which "signs" and cues are inputted to some sort of a categorizing system by the organism. The nature of these categories is not known at present, but apparently the syllogistic or reflective patterns of reasoning long described by philosophers are not satisfactory descriptions of the process. It seems likely that in some types of reading the individual already has many concepts and that reading is a simple task of recognition and association. In another type of reading, the individual has merely a limited number of concepts and is able to organize just a few related associations so that considerable effort is required to either retrieve concepts or search for relationships associated with the inputted cues. In a third case, the reader may have little or no familiarity with the information being processed and must rely mainly upon the information contained in the reading selection for processing. Obviously, the latter type of reading is most difficult and frustrating. Presumably, cognitive styles and previously developed modes of control play a role in the degree of persistence the reader brings to the reading task.

Educators long have recognized maturational influences in the life cycle of the child. Significantly, the previously mentioned research also recognized developmental patterns, perhaps of a type not generally observed by the classroom teacher. It has been said that

> Development is the complex product resulting from the cyclical actions that occur between physiological growth and learning. And because all development, whether it applies to one structure, one skill, a series of behaviors, or an entire personality, follows certain natural laws and consists of universal characteristics, it can best be defined as a rhythmic flow of qualitative changes proceeding in specific directions in a predictable sequence (7).

It is apparent, however, that we have considerable difficulty in identifying many of the important attributes and characteristics of the organism for systematic study. The traditionally employed concepts of intelligence, physical development, psychomotor abilities, personality, and social-emotional adjustment represent extremely broad traits. Maturation and learning are difficult to measure and predict under the best conditions and do not take place in segmented, piecemeal fashion. Rather, development and learning are continuous and constantly interrelated and integrated. In the United States the acquisition of reading behavior generally is regarded as taking place in some developmental fashion that is typically regarded as being akin to and correlated with the process of physical and intellectual development. Much has been made of the concepts of readiness and the apparent relationship between the age of the child and the acquisition of various skills and their integration in subsequent stages. While the research of Piaget (17), Vygotsky (22), Gesell (8), and Ilg and Ames (12) has indicated that development proceeds in certain patterns, two other truths also are apparent. First, there are wide individual differences in developmental rates and, secondly, much significant development takes place prior to the age the child typically enters school. The typical research study, which stresses correlations between reading achievement and other characteristics related to development, has tended to ignore the lack of relationships and variance among traits and/or patterns of development. Such studies have emphasized uniformities and commonalities and ignored differences.

Despite the difficulties of measuring stages of development, it seems safe to assume that the process of maturation, coupled with learning at each stage, is related to reading. As yet, just how the reading process is related is not clear. Typically, one factor is the increasing capacity of the individual to acquire more complex abilities with age. Measurable differences in language, intellectual abilities, and formal social behavior obviously are other facets of the developmental cycles. Many areas of growth and development need some precise study. There seem to be certain "pre-reading" stages, other than those now employed to assess readiness, that should be considered by reading specialists. One example is the development of visual and auditory discrimination abilities related to letters, syllables, words. With skillful readers these abilities appear to be less important by the intermediate and upper elementary grades. At this stage somewhat different response modes and "sign" and language manipulation seem to be more important. In addition to the literal language needed during the primary grades, ability to handle figurative language and more complex structures seems to be necessary for reading success. The reasons why some children have less difficulty in acquiring these abilities is not so simple as many teachers think. It also should be noted that recently there has been a shift in emphasis from the biological concept of maturation to an emphasis on the effects that environment, particularly a stimulating and nurturing one, have on the course of development.

In summary, it has been suggested that, at present, a well formulated psychology of reading has not been developed. Reading specialists have tended to select various psychological positions to support certain of their own practices and beliefs. These are fragmentary and piecemeal. The major help that reading will gain from psychology is the assistance that any science with a more rigorous methodology can offer to any nonscience. The work of current psychologists working in fields which appear to have bearing on the reading process were discussed as examples.

REFERENCES

1. Anderson, Richard C. & David P. Ausubel. *Readings in the Psychology of Cognition.* New York: Holt, Rinehart, & Winston, 1965.
2. Buswell, Guy T. "The Process of Reading." *The Reading Teacher, 13,* 1959, 14-21.
3. Carroll, John B. "Wanted: A Research Basis for Educational Policy on Foreign Language Teaching." *Harvard Education Review, 30,* 1960, 128-140.
4. Carroll, John B. *Language and Thought.* Englewood Cliffs: Prentice-Hall Inc., 1964.
5. Chomsky, Noam. "Review of Skinner's *Verbal Behavior.*" *Language, 35,* 1959, 26-58.
6. Gardner, R. W., *et al.,* "Cognitive Control: A Study of Individual Consistencies in Cognitive Behavior" in G. S. Klein, (Ed.), *Psychological Issues.* New York: International Universities Press, 1959.
7. Garrison, K. C., A. J. Kingston, and H. W. Bernard. *The Psychology of Childhood.* New York: Chas. E. Scribners & Sons, 1967.
8. Gesell, A. and F. L. Ilg. *Child Development.* New York: Harper & Row, 1949.
9. Gibson, Eleanor J. "Perceptual Learning." *Annual Review of Psychology, 14,* 1963, 29-56.
10. Gray, William S. "The Nature and Types of Reading." Guy N. Whipple (Ed.). *The Teaching of Reading: A Second Report. Thirty-sixth Yearbook of the National Society for the Study of Education, Pt. I.* Bloomington: Public School Publishing Co., 1937, 23-28.
11. Holzman, P. S. and G. S. Klein. "Motive and Style in Reality Contact." *Bulletin of the Menninger Clinic, 20,* 1956, 181-191.
12. Ilg, F. L., and L. B. Ames. *School Readiness.* New York: Harper & Row, 1965.
13. Kagan, J. "Developmental Studies in Reflection and Analysis." A. H. Kidd & J. L. Rivoise, (Eds.). *Perceptual Development in Children.* New York: International Universities Press, 1966. 487-522.
14. Kagan, J., H. A. Moss, and I. E. Siegel. "Psychological Significance of Styles in the Basic Cognitive Processes in Children." *Monographs of the Society for Research in Child Development,* No. 28, 1963.
15. Kendler, Tracy S., H. H. Kendler, and Beulah Leanard. "Mediating Responses to Size and Brightness as a Function of Age." *American Journal of Psychology, 75,* 1962, 571-586.
16. Kogan, N. and M. A. Wallach. *Risk Taking: A Study in Cognition and Personality.* New York: Holt, Rinehart & Winston.
17. Piaget, J. *The Origins of Intelligence in Children.* New York: International Universities Press, 1952.
18. Raygor, Alton E. Behavioral Research in Reading: What Does it Offer? J. Allen Figurel (Ed.), *Improvement of*

Reading Through Classroom Practice, Proceedings of Ninth Annual Conference International Reading Association, 1964, 235-238.

19. Spache, George D. "The Perceptual Bases of Reading." Delivered at the World Congress in Reading, Paris, 1966.

20. Smith, Henry P. and Emerald V. Dechant. *Psychology in Teaching Reading.* Englewood Cliffs: Prentice-Hall, Inc., 1961.

21. Thorndike, Edward L. "The Understanding of Sentences: A Study of Errors in Reading," *The Elementary School Journal, 18,* 1917, 98-114.

22. Vygotsky, L. S. *Thought and Language.* Cambridge: Massachusetts Institute of Technology Press, 1962.

23. Weaver, Wendell W. "On The Psychology of Reading." E. Thurston and L. E. Hafner (Eds.), *New Concepts in College-Adult Reading.* Thirteenth Yearbook of the National Reading Conference, 1964, 67-74.

24. Witkin, H. A., *et al. Personality Through Perception.* New York: Harper & Row, 1954.

25. Witkin, H. A., *et al. Psychological Differentiation: Studies of Development.* New York: John Wiley & Sons, 1962.

The Hawthorn Center Longitudinal Reading Study

MURIEL POTTER LANGMAN,
RALPH D. RABINOVITCH,
and others
Hawthorn Center
Northville, Michigan

THIS STUDY was initiated in October 1958. The subjects were 154 children in 6 first grade classes, selected from 3 schools in 2 neighboring small cities, to represent the normal school population. There was excellent rapport with the school systems cooperating because Hawthorn Center is a state-supported psychiatric children's hospital and its personnel are well-known in the area and render many services to the schools.

The teachers whose pupils were to become subjects were oriented in advance to the general purpose of the study; at the time of the administration of the first tests, the subjects were told that they were helping grown-ups to learn more about how to teach children, and many of them remembered this brief orientation over the entire period of the study. Children and adults were unfailingly cooperative. The schools benefited from the study through reports of the annual reading test scores as they were administered each May. A few children in the study whose reading achievement was low attended summer language clinic sessions at Hawthorn for one or two years.

As in any longitudinal study, one problem was attrition of subjects. Each year on follow-up it was found that some children had left the area, while others had moved within about a fifteen-mile radius of Hawthorn. Wherever time permitted, the subjects were followed to the new schools, and by 1961 eighteen schools were included in the examiners' itinerary. By May 1964 only 96 children remained of the original 154 subjects.

In October of the first grade year (1958-59) at the inception of the study, the subjects were given two subtests from a test of memory for orientation of forms and letters (6).

In February 1959 the nonverbal administration of the Otis Alpha test (5) was used to measure ability to categorize.

In April 1959 the Auditory Discrimination and Letter Sounds subtests of the Stroud-Hieronymus-McKee Primary Reading Profiles, Level One (7), were given, along with the Rhymes subtest of the Gates Reading Readiness Test (3).

In May 1959 all three subtests of the Gates Primary Reading Tests, Form 2 (2) were given; the raw scores of the Word Recognition and Sentence Reading tests were summed, and to the sum was added the doubled raw score of the Paragraph Reading Test, in order to give approximately equal weight to each subtest.

The maximum score on the Gates thus became 144, permitting a very wide distribution of the scores. This score became the criterion for the experimental groups. Those subjects whose scores fell at or above the 75th percentile point were thereafter designated 1959 Best Readers; those whose scores fell at or below the 25th percentile were designated the Poor Readers. The movement of the subjects' percentile standings in reading from year to year is the subject of this report. Reading achievement was measured 4 times after the experimental groups were formed; in 1960, by the Gates Advanced Primary Reading Tests, Form 2 (1); in 1961, by the Level of Comprehension and Speed and Accuracy subtests of the Gates Reading Survey, From 1 (4); and in 1962 and 1964, by Form 2 and Form 1 of the Gates Reading Survey, respectively.

In the springs of 1961 and 1962, exhaustive psychological assessments were made of each individual in the experimental groups, and a number of pilot tests and variations on administration were also tried with them. The findings will be reported in a later paper.

Summary over the six-year period (1964 N = 96)

TABLE 1

Best Readers*

	Boys	Girls	Total	% Total
—Best Readers at or above P^{75} on all reading tests	3	5	8	8.3
—Best Readers in 1959 and 1964, but not for all tests between	1	6	7	7.3
—Best Readers above P^{75} through 1962, but in 1964 at or above P^{75} in *comprehension* only	0	2	2	2.1
—Best Readers 1959, variably best through 1962, at or above P^{75} in 1964 in *comprehension* only	1	0	1	1.0
Totals	5	13	18	18.7

*For these children, success in first grade reading predicted success in sixth grade reading.

TABLE 2

Late Emerging Best Readers

	Boys	Girls	Total	% Total
—Children whose reading scores in 1959 fell between P^{26} and P^{74}, whose reading scores ranked at or above P^{75} after one or more years in the study, and who in 1964 were at or above P^{75} in both *comprehension* and *speed*.	2	3	5	5.2
—Children whose reading scores in 1959 fell between P^{26} and P^{74}, and who in 1964 ranked at or above P^{75} in *comprehension* only.	4	2	6	6.3
Totals	6	5	11	11.5

TABLE 3

Lapsed Best Readers

	Boys	Girls	Total	% Total
—Best Readers 1959, variably best through 1962, in 1964 at or above P^{75} in *speed* only.	3	3	6	6.3
—Best Readers 1959 who by 1964 ranked below P^{75} in both *speed* and *comprehension*.	1	2	3	3.1
Totals	4	5	9	9.4

TABLE 4

Late Emerging Partial Success

	Boys	Girls	Total	% Total
—Children with scores between P^{26} and P^{74} in 1959 who by 1964 were at or above P^{75} in *speed* only.	4	1	5	5.2
—Children with scores at or below P^{25} who in 1964 were at or above P^{75} in *speed* only.	2	0	2	2.1
Totals	6	1	7	7.3

TABLE 5

Improved Poor Readers

	Boys	Girls	Total	% Total
—Poor Readers 1959 who after one or more years crossed P^{25} upward, and in 1964 ranked above P^{25} in both *speed* and *comprehension*.	5	4	9	9.4
—Poor Readers 1959 who crossed P^{25} upward after one or more years, and ranked above P^{25} in 1964 in *comprehension* only.	7	0	7	7.3
Totals	12	4	16	16.7

TABLE 6

Readers in the Middle Range

	Boys	Girls	Total	% Total
—Never at any time crossed P^{25} or P^{75}.	3	4	7	7.3
—Crossed P^{25} downward one or two intermediate years.	3	1	4	4.2
—Crossed P^{75} upward one intermediate year.	2	0	2	2.1
Totals	8	5	13	13.6

TABLE 7

Poor Readers*

	Boys	Girls	Total	% Total
—Poor Readers at or below P^{25} for all reading tests.	4	2	6	6.3
—Poor Readers 1959, variably poor through 1962 and at or below P^{25} in 1964.	0	1	1	1.0
—Poor Readers 1959 who in 1964 were at or below P^{25} in *comprehension* only.				
Totals	5	5	10	10.4

*For these children failure in first grade reading predicted failure in sixth grade reading.

TABLE 8

Late Emerging Failure in Reading

	Boys	Girls	Total	% Total
—Children whose reading scores fell between P^{26} and P^{74} in 1959, at or below P^{25} in 1960 or later, and at or below P^{25} in 1964 in both *speed* and *comprehension*.	1	3	4	4.2
—In *comprehension* only.	1	2	3	3.1
Totals	2	5	7	7.3

TABLE 9

Late Emerging Partial Failure

	Boys	Girls	Total	% Total
—Children with scores between P^{26} and P^{74} in 1959 who in 1964 were at or below P^{25} in *speed* only.	3	2	5	5.2

Discussion

From the foregoing analysis it is clear why multiple correlation is an unsatisfactory method of prediction. A summary of our clinical observations of the subjects suggests the following tentative generalizations:

1. No child whose reading score fell in the top quartile of the range at the end of first grade was found in the lowest quartile in sixth grade. Thus to have a score in the top quartile in grade one suggests that reading *failure* is not in one's future.

2. If a child's reading score fell in the lowest quartile at the end of grade one, he was not necessarily going to remain a poor reader. Of 26 first grade Poor Readers for whom we have complete records, 16 children (12 boys and 4 girls) reached and remained in the middle range after one or more years.

3. Consequently, reading success at first grade level is more useful in predicting subsequent reading success over the six-year period than is reading failure at first grade level in predicting reading failure. Of 27 first grade Best Readers for whom there is complete record, 18 children (5 boys and 13 girls) were still or again Best Readers at the end of the sixth grade, while the other 9 scored in the middle range.

4. Only 13 children of the 96 began and ended with scores in the middle range; and of these only 7 remained there consistently. The other 6 moved either into the top or bottom quartile for one or more years. Only 1 boy of the whole population moved from below P^{25} the first year to above P^{75} (in speed) in the sixth. One boy who was in the middle range the first 2 years fell below P^{25} in 1961, then rose again until he was above P^{75} in speed in 1964.

5. The group seems to have been characterized by unexpected variability in reading performance. Of the 29 children (11 boys, 18 girls) who ranked at or above P^{75} on the Gates National Norms at the end of Sixth Grade, only 8 performed consistently at the top level over the whole period (Table 1); 7 others were in the top quartile at the beginning and end of the study, but not during all the intervening years; 3 others not only varied in performance during the intervening years, but were no longer superior in speed of reading by 1964. Eleven (Table 2) entered the top quartile in the second year or later, and in 1964 were found there either in both speed and comprehension or in comprehension only. Nine Best Readers of 1959 were unable to maintain their original superior positions; none of these, however, ever fell below the P^{25} point.

Implications

If any safe and acceptable guidance can be drawn from these results, it is that maturation rates are undoubtedly variable; that they and/or environmental factors appear to work together to make every child uniquely different in reading performance from every other child, just as they operate in all other areas of growth and development. The acceptance of these differences is essential. It must not, however, interfere with our efforts to influence every manipulable element in each child's environment to make his development fulfil not only obvious potentialities but those, too, which may be manifested later than standard expectation (Tables 2, 4, and 5). That 34 children of 96 moved upward a whole quartile in the course of the study indicates the importance of maintaining open minds regarding the potentialities of first grade children.

REFERENCES

1. Gates, A. I. *Gates Advanced Primary Reading Test,* Teachers College (Columbia) Bureau of Publications, New York, 1958.
2. ———. *Gates Primary Reading Tests,* Teachers College (Columbia) Bureau of Publications, New York, 1958.
3. ———. *Gates Reading Readiness Test,* Rhymes Test. Teachers College (Columbia) Bureau of Publications, New York, 1942.
4. ———. *Gates Reading Survey, Speed and Accuracy* and *Level of Comprehension* subtests. Teachers College (Columbia) Bureau of Publications, New York, 1958.
5. Otis, A. S. *Otis Quick Scoring Mental Ability Tests,* Alpha Test, Form A. World Book Company, 1936.
6. Potter, Muriel C. *Perception of Symbol Orientation and Early Reading Success.* Teachers College (Columbia) Bureau of Publications, New York, 1949.
7. *Stroud-Hieronymus-McKee Primary Reading Profiles,* Level One, Tests 2A and 2B. Houghton Mifflin Company, 1957.

Reading and Writing Abilities of High School Students

Dorothy M. Lampard
University of Alberta

WHILE MUCH IS KNOWN about comprehension skills, little is known about the reader's ability to synthesize the ideas from print into written expression. In practice, much of the effectiveness of a student's reading capacity in academic work is based on his ability to formulate ideas gained from reading and express them in continuous prose. From a logical point of view, it would appear that comprehension of reading matter which results in written response is dependent upon an understanding of the meaning of each word, the structure of sentences in which they appear, an appreciation of the significance of the order of the sentences in an author's writing or in the reader's response. Although it is often assumed that standardized tests which assess the amount of content recognized are an indication of the student's functional ability to reorganize and synthesize knowledge, they measure reorganization and synthesis indirectly.

Only recently has research been undertaken to investigate the thoughtful reactions of the reader to what he reads. Moreover, the type of reading material generally used in studies has been of literary content, rather than of a type requiring interpretation and reaction to the expository material that is also typical of school texts. The work that at present is being done on information processing has also not yet been applied to any extent in the schools.

The purpose of this study was to explore, by examining their written responses elicited by question and explanation of events, the extent to which students absorb and integrate what they read. The basic reading and thinking abilities needed for the analysis and synthesis of the material read were also examined. It was considered that such a structured descriptive investigation using experimental methods for evaluation, done on a large sample could provide evidence currently lacking both for teaching procedures and research in the evaluation of reading, writing, and the interpretative processes involved.

Procedures

Seven different tests were administered to a stratified random sample of 447 high school students (229 boys, 218 girls) in grades X, XI, and XII from four high schools in the Edmonton (Canada) area. Each grade was subdivided into three groups of high, average, and low achievers on the basis of their school marks. The sample represented 16.6 percent of the schools tested and 4.2 percent of the total high school population. The material for the study was collected from each grade and achievement level in the following manner:

1. Objective answers were obtained by means of a standardized test (Cooperative Reading Test, Higher Level, Form R) to determine the comprehension and/or signification of words, vocabulary

meaning, and paragraph comprehension.

2. Written answers were obtained by using a different form of the above standardized test Form Z to determine vocabulary signification and/or meaning, and paragraph comprehension. The objective type questions were rewritten as open-ended questions.

3. Written word meanings were obtained by means of a list of words from an individual intelligence test (Stanford-Binet) to estimate the level of ability to understand and define words in writing, and the quality of the understanding of the words.

4. Written responses were obtained to two verbal problems, one requiring convergent (closed) and the other divergent (open) reasoning from the verbal stimuli.

5. Written abstractions of meaning of two expository essays were obtained, one in outline and one in summary form.

6. School records were used to obtain grade, intelligence, and achievement levels of all the students included in the study. An idea of the scoring can be derived from an examination of the 68 variables listed for statistical computations (Table I).

For the sake of clarity in reporting, the tests were grouped under three headings; reading tests (3), reading-writing tests (4), and language ability scores. From the total scores and the subscores on each of the tests, correlation coefficients and analyses of variance were computed. The results were then scrutinized to determine whether patterns of performance and patterns of response were discernible.

Summary of findings

The findings are discussed in relation to four hypotheses. The *first hypothesis* that there would be positive relationships between age, sex, intelligence, general achievement and grade levels (on the tests of general reading

achievement and the ability to write definitions, to write effective outlines and summaries, and solve verbal problems) received major support from the findings.

Age appeared to be the most negligible factor. The results of the girls' scores, showed higher correlation coefficients than that of the boys' between their general reading achievement and their total scores on both the verbal problems, in outlining, and in the measure of fluency. However, the findings indicated that the girls made more errors in thinking, in drawing valid conclusions and logical interpretations, than did the boys.

The relationship between the reading-writing tests and intelligence appeared to be erratic when compared with the conventional objective tests. The tests, designed for this study in an attempt to assess functional reading skills, appear to rely less on capacity than do the objective tests. Thus the ability to abstract and use information derived from reading appears to be relatively independent of both intelligence and maturation.

Though general reading achievement as measured in this study appears to relate to general scholastic achievement, this relationship appears to be complex and variable. The functional reading-writing tests revealed even more inconsistencies with general academic achievement. In contrast the magnitude of the correlation coefficients were remarkably stable for the successive grades.

For the *second hypothesis,* the analysis of variance of the results of each of the tests revealed important evidence. The two Cooperative tests, objective and written, gave the most stable results for each grade of any of the tests, though the means of the total scores on the objective test were higher than those of the written. This growth was not uniform for achievement levels. Between grades the high achievers were well above the average and low achievers but showed no significant development from grade to grade. The low achievers, on the

TABLE I

Constants

1. Name
2. Grade
3. Achievement
4. Sex

Variables

Totals	1. Age	Closed	34. Solution
	2. Intelligence	Problem	35. Use of relevant information
	3. Cooperative Objective		36. Inference Correct
	4. Cooperative Written		37. Inference Incorrect
	5. Binet Vocabulary		38. Interpretation Correct
	6. Closed Problem		39. Interpretation Incorrect
	7. Open Problem		40. Redundancy
	8. Outline		41. Total Information Units
	9. Summary		42. Total Number of Ideas
	10. Fluency	Open	43. Total Number of Ideas
	11. Lack of Verbal Ability	Problem	44. Information Used—
	12. Lack of Thinking Ability		Explained
Cooperative	13. Vocabulary		45. Information Used—
Objective	14. Comprehension		Unexplained
Cooperative	15. Vocabulary		46. Information Correct from
Written	16. Fluency		Experience
	17. Comprehension		47. Inference Correct
	18. Main Idea		48. Inference Incorrect
	19. Understanding Detail		49. Interpretation Correct
	20. Accurate Use of Referents		50. Interpretation Incorrect
	21. Inference		51. Ability to Follow Directions
	22. Interpretation		52. Drawing Conclusions
	23. Author's Purpose	Outline	53. Recognizing Main Ideas
	24. Vocabulary in Context		54. Recognizing Subordinate
Binet	25. Genera		Ideas
Vocabulary	26. Differentia		55. Recognizing Relationships
	27. Genera and Differentia		56. Sequence
	28. Synonym		57. Form
	29. Example		58. Title
	30. Operational	Summary	59. Number of Words
	31. Fluency		60. Title
	32. Form and Sound Errors		61. Recognizing Main Ideas
	33. Accuracy Errors		62. Recognizing Subordinate
			Ideas
			63. Plagiarisms
			64. Wrong Use of Referents
			65. Errors in Using Words
			66. Rearrange Meaning
			67. Group in Unified Patterns
			68. Condense in Logical Order

other hand, developed from grade to grade and equalled the average group from XI to XII. A comparison of the vocabulary scores on the vocabulary section of both versions of the Cooperative test and the written definitions test suggested that students find recognition vocabulary prompted by association of synonyms easier than writing definitions with no aid to recall.

The ability to write an outline differed between achievement levels within each grade, but there was no improvement in this ability from grade to grade. There was, however, more evidence of development in summarizing, with the girls at all levels performing significantly better than the boys. Though there was evidence that grade XII was more competent than the lower grades in verbal problem solving, the overall performance was mediocre and all students experienced difficulty with these tests.

The *third hypothesis* was upheld by the indications of differences in patterns of performance that appeared. A scrutiny of the correlations and the analysis of variance suggested that the patterns might be categorized under the following heading; structured and unstructured tests and the recall of meaning, the ability to abstract information, to solve problems, and general language abilities.

The *fourth hypothesis* stated that measurable qualitative differences on the test scores would indicate patterns of response. The patterns of response were categorized under the headings recall of word meaning, abstracting the meaning of a passage, and variations in problem solving. This systematic qualitative examination of the functional reading skills measured revealed various and serious deficiencies in the abilities of high school students to translate what is read into writing.

Implications and conclusions

It was evident from the study that as the common measures of reading, such as the standardized objective type tests, do not investigate the same abilities as do outline, summary, problem solving, and definition exercises, it might be necessary to design standardized type tests for assessing these language abilities.

The performance of these high school students seems to provide evidence that greater stress should be placed upon teaching all aspects of the particular reading-writing skills defined in this study. Furthermore, it might be concluded that the students become so conditioned by short answer type exercises that their development in the ability to synthesize ideas is inhibited.

Students of high academic achievement do not progress in these reading-writing skills as they pass through the successive grades. This suggests that such skills are not recognized by either teachers or students as essential to academic progress, or, perhaps, that the type and level of achievement demanded in the so-called content areas of the curriculum are not of sufficiently comprehensive dimensions, and therefore conceal the student's basic linguistic inadequacies. The low achievers

on the other hand appear less static, and some improvement seems evident through the grades. The average students fare better than the high achievers but not as well as the low, which suggests that if there is differentiated teaching or a particularized curriculum it tends to benefit the low achievers. It would seem that both the high and average groups need to be challenged in terms of materials and activities demanded of them as well as in the level of expectation.

In terms of writing skills there appears to have been over training in the use of narrative. Perhaps this is a carry-over from the pervasive writing of the elementary school, where little attention is directed to the development of expository writing, or the disciplined objectivity of precis and summary. Much of the students' writing and the comprehension of ideas was complicated by their constant need for self-identification with the author or the main character of the problem. Thus, in certain types of writing, objectivity needs to be fostered. Moreover, students tended to be egocentric in their use of personal experience rather than generalizing it or recognizing its limitations. Training and practice in writing exposition, particularly explanation, appears to be essential for high school students.

Critical thinking has long been an educational objective but from the results of this study, it must be considered to have remained a pious hope rather than having become an actuality. Training in elementary logic, or at least work directed toward the sequencing of thought in the manner basic to problem solving, would seem to be necessary for the majority of the students in this study. Perhaps in this area, too, they were conditioned by the prevailing types of examination and by current attitudes. There was evidence of an inability to withstand ambiguity and to withhold judgment until a reconciliation of the variant facts could be made. The easiest, rather than the most feasible solution was normally preferred.

It was difficult to assess whether confusions in thought occurred because of inaccurate reading, inadequate logic or a failure to communicate due to poor writing ability. There were, however, many elementary writing errors, switches in tense, and failures to appreciate the function of connectors in making the sequences in writing or thinking cohesive. Since precision, accuracy, and facility in reading-writing acitvities are essential for academic development in the high school, more emphasis must be placed upon both teaching and learning in these areas, with some stress on logical form.

The results of this study indicate that training in the written exposition of the author's ideas which demands the integration of the concepts gained from reading appears to need greater emphasis.

Aural Presentation As a Supplement in Programed Instruction for Slow Readers

BURTON L. GROVER
and
KARL D. HESSE
Manitowoc, Wisconsin,
Public Schools

SLOW READERS have difficulty, presumably, in learning by programed instruction when they must read the frames without any aids. If this handicap could be alleviated even partially by aural presentation of the frames, the number of programs of potential value to the slow reader would be increased.

Although this paper attempts to answer the preceding if, the study was conducted in a classroom situation that was not originally organized to solve this particular problem. Another set of circumstances and problems, perhaps more typical of other junior high English classes, set the stage for this query in Manitowoc, Wisconsin. The language arts department, facing the cries and concern of its members about reading instruction on one hand and traditional vs. structural or transformational grammar on the other, established the following two points of policy:

1. A developmental reading program in grade seven for students with corrective deficiencies would be offered as soon as willing English teachers could be trained.
2. All students in English (grades 7-12) in Manitowoc would be confronted with the concepts of usage and grammar as found in *English 2600 (1)* until such time that the teachers and materials are prepared to present concepts of the "new English."

One result of this policy was that four seventh grade sections of low achievers in reading were to be faced with a long programed text in traditional English grammar and usage which was originally designed for tenth grade pupils. Previous experience had indicated that most seventh-grade pupils could achieve reasonable scores on the accompanying tests. But now, with slow readers concentrated in special sections, frustration and failure seemed imminent if the programed grammar was to be thrust upon them in the same manner.

What then should be done if both the policy were to be followed and the self-image of the slow reader were to be developed? That question loomed in a very real sense.

It was these circumstances and problems that led to the question, "If the slow reading students are likely to find little success in working through programed instruction that is all reading, what would be the effect of tape recording the program so it would be a reading-listening program?" With an aural presentation of the frames (aural stimulus) accompanying the sight reading by the pupils (visual stimulus), there was the possibility that the reading handicap in comprehension of the program would be lessened.

Reports of studies relevant to the problem of sensory modality, slow readers, and programed instruction did not appear to be too plentiful, nor helpful in planning an experiment. In a discussion of stimulus-control factors, Lumsdaine (5) reached the same general conclusion that McGeoch and Irion (6) had earlier, namely, that any advantage for either the visual or auditory modality would not be general but would most likely depend upon the interaction with other specific variables. The results of two more recent studies (2, 4) indicated certain advantages for aural presentations or supplements under conditions and with populations different from those in the study reported here. These two studies and the belief that, if effective at all, aural supplementation would be of most help where it could help compensate for a weakness in sight reading, gave some support to the idea that supplementary aural presentations might help the performance of slow readers. Accordingly, the major hypothesis for the experiment was that an aural presentation of the frames to slow readers which accompanied the subject's visual reading of the frames would result in comprehension of the material superior to the subjects who encountered the frames only by reading. This advantage was hypothesized even though the aural presentation eliminated the self-pacing feature of programed instruction.

Procedures

The sixty-four seventh grade pupils in the experiment had all previously been identified as slow readers and scheduled into special English sections. There still remained substantial variation in apparent reading ability among these subjects, so they were subdivided into eight equal blocks according to scores on form 2 of the Iowa Basic Skills reading test. Within each block subjects were then assigned to one of three treatment groups.

All of the subjects in each treatment group worked through the programed text on traditional English grammar and usage, *English 2600* (1) and they were all required to give written (and generally nontrivial) responses to the frames. The instruction was con-

ducted in a room equipped with language laboratory facilities, and each subject in all treatment groups sat in individual booths during the experiment. Completion of the program required 22-minute daily sessions over 45 school days. Responses were written and kept in notebooks to make it possible to check individual progress at any time. In addition there were twelve unit tests administered periodically throughout the program to all subjects on the same dates.

Four subjects in each block were assigned to the aural treatment group. All subjects (n = 32) in this group listened by means of headsets to the frames being read on tape. After each frame, there was a pause to allow a written response. The answer was then heard, followed by the number of the next frame, and then the next frame itself. The rate was approximately 3½ frames a minute.

The aural presentation treatment differed from conventional use of a programed text in at least two important respects. First, there was the difference in the sensory mode of presenting the frames. Secondly, because of technological limitations it was not possible to individualize the rate of presentation, and consequently the possible self-pacing advantage of programed instruction was lost. Because of these two distinctions, the aural presentation treatment was contrasted with two other treatments, one of which retained and one which attempted to eliminate the self-pacing feature.

Two subjects in each of the eight blocks were assigned to the "self-paced treatment" (n = 16). This group worked through the program in the usual manner without wearing headsets or hearing any aural presentations. They took the periodic unit tests along with the other subjects, but they could work the required number of frames within any unit by taking as much or as little time as necessary. The rate was thereby a self-paced one within any one unit and not over the whole program. On only one occasion was there a subject noticed who jumped ahead to the next unit before taking a test on the previous unit. The subjects who finished working the frames of a unit before the aural presentation group were instructed to either read a library book or review previous material in the program. On the average fourteen of the sixteen subjects in the self-paced group completed the unit within ten minutes of the aural presentation group.

The remaining two subjects in each block were assigned to the "forced-pace treatment" ($n = 16$). This group wore headsets as did the aural presentation group. However, as they worked through the program, they heard only the number of the frame, and they were instructed to follow the pace given on the tape. If a subject was found deviating from the prescribed rate, he was advised again to follow the pace given on the tape. This procedure was successful to the extent that an average of fourteen of the sixteen subjects kept an identical pace to the aural presentation group for all units of the program. One subject persisted in keeping a few frames ahead throughout the program, and occasionally other subjects finished either a few frames ahead or behind the pace set for a unit. These deviations were concentrated in the initial units.

The experiment was a relatively long term one in a public school setting, and, in addition to the pacing features, there were some other problems in keeping the treatments as tightly controlled as desirable. Absentees from the experimental group had to catch up by spending extra time working through the frames that they had missed, without the possible benefit of aural presentations. Periodically the instructor, perceiving some general confusion, suspended the programed instruction for all groups in order to reteach the content to the subjects by means of lecture, work sheets, and discussion (this occasional supplementary instruction was conducted simultaneously for subjects from all groups). And, there were the usual changes

from the regular schedule on some days because of school assemblies, administrative conflicts, and blizzards. On the surface none of the noticed problems, aside from those associated with pacing instructions, appeared to bias any of the treatment effects; if these factors did have an effect, it most likely would have been to lessen the distinction between the experimental treatments. However, there was no way to ascertain this from analysis of the data.

The special course for these seventh-grade pupils had been scheduled into four class sections, taught by the same teacher but meeting at different times of the day. The three treatments were administered simultaneously in each section. For various reasons—the fact that all three treatments were administered simultaneously in each section, the belief that the different sections or time of day did not contribute much to the total variation of scores, and the desire to preserve proportional subclass frequencies within treatment-block combinations—the "class-section" factor was ignored in the analysis. Figure 1 illustrates how the frequencies of subjects in the different blocks and treatments were distributed in each class section. Because of the random assignment of subjects and their relative isolation during the experiment, the individual pupil was considered as the experimental unit.

There were two criteria for the experiment. One was the set of twelve unit tests, which accompanied the programed text, that were administered periodically during the experiment. The number of items in each test ranged from 25 to 72, and they were weighted so that the top score for each test was 100 when scored according to the accompanying instructions. The second criterion was a final test containing 72 items, also furnished by the publisher and also scored so that the highest possible score was 100. The tests were administered to all treatment groups simultaneously in each class (except for absentees who made

FIGURE 1

Distribution of Pupils from Different Treatment Groups According to Ability Blocks and Class Sections

A=Pupil assigned to aural presentation group
B=Pupil assigned to self-paced group
C=Pupil assigned to forced-pace group

Ability Blocks

		1	2	3	4	5	6	7	8	Total Pupils
	I	BCC	AAA	AAC	A	ABC	AB	B	A	17
CLASS	II		C		A	AAAB	A	C	ABBCC	13
SECTION	III	AAA	BB	B	C	C	C	AAAABC	A	16
	IV	AB	AC	AABC	AABBC		AABC		A	18
										64

(Because of the desirability of using proportionate cell frequencies in the analysis and the fact that subjects in all treatment groups were present in all class sections, the class section factor was ignored in the analysis.)

up tests at later times) without aural presentation of the questions.

Two criterion measures were used because each appeared to have an advantage over the other. The set of twelve periodic tests was employed because it contained more items than a single final test, because it sampled pupil performance on several occasions, and because it had a fair chance of revealing any interactions between treatment, duration of experiment, and/or the content of separate units. However, the possibility existed that the timing of the unit tests gave an advantage to the aural presentation group over those individuals in the other groups who finished a unit at different times. A final test given after everyone had finished the total program appeared to be less sensitive to such an advantage, if it existed. If analysis of both criterion measures revealed consistent results in the hypothesized direction, the alternate explanation that the test-timing factor gave an advantage to the aural presentation group would be somewhat less plausible.

Results

For the analysis of the unit test scores, the mean score over all twelve tests and over all groups was 62.2; the separate unit test means ranged from 47.2 to 77.0. The mean of the experimental treatment exceeded the means of the other two groups for ten of the twelve tests, as indicated in Figure 2. The scores of the "self-paced controls" exceeded those of the "forced-paced controls" on ten tests.

The major hypothesis of the study was tested by means of a planned comparison between the experimental treatment group and the average of the two control groups. For this comparison, the total of all twelve tests for each individual was used as the criterion score. The mean of all total scores was 746 out of a potential 1200. Experimental subjects' total scores exceeded those of the control subjects by an average of 61.71, and this difference yielded a t score of 2.68, significant in a directional test beyond the .01 level.

The remaining orthogonal comparison among the treatment means was between the two control groups. No directional alternate hypothesis for this comparison was proposed prior to the study, for certain conditions of the forced-paced treatment could conceivably have more than compensated for the loss of the self-pacing feature. Forcing the pace might also have forced some increased attention and induced a Hawthorne Effect because of its closer resemblance to the experimental treatment, if any such effect would persist in any group over a ten week period. As it turned out, the average score in the self-paced group

Figure 2

Average Scores of the Treatment Groups on Unit Tests

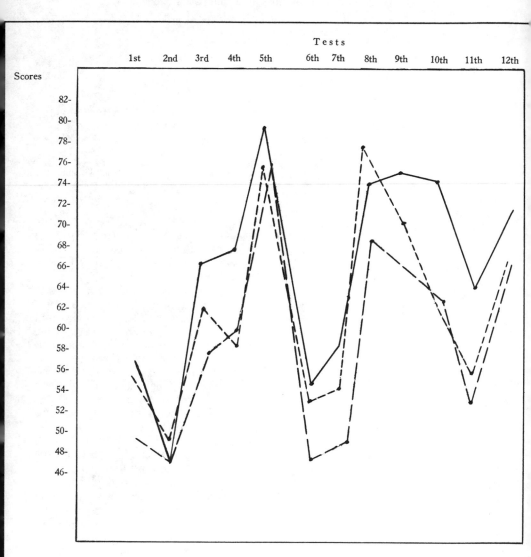

Aural Presentation...56.8   46.6   65.8   67.1   78.8   54.2   57.8   72.9   73.7   72.8   63.1   68.8

Self-Paced...........56.0   48.9   62.1   58.1   75.6   53.0   53.9   76.4   69.6   60.9   54.1   66.0

Forced-Paced........ 50.3   46.7   57.6   58.9   74.8   47.9   48.6   68.5   65.6   61.6   52.0   64.8

over all blocks was 735 compared to 697 in the forced-pace group; this difference was not statistically significant.

The mean square error term used in both comparisons was that taken from an analysis of variance of the total scores which separated out the treatment, block, and treatment-block interaction effects from the overall variation of the total test scores. The comparisons are summarized in Table 1.

A more complete analysis of the data from the unit tests is presented in Table 2. In this analysis, which used a least squares procedure for unequal but proportionate subclass frequencies, the three main effects were treatments, blocks, and separate tests. Unlike the treatment and block effects, the test ef-

fect involved repeated measures on each individual. Blocks of size eight permitted independent estimates of interaction and between-subject error.

This analysis revealed that there were no significant interactions of either blocks or tests with the treatment effects. Within the rather selective nature of the population, slow reading seventh graders, the advantage of the experimental treatment appeared to be consistent for all levels of reading ability. Also, the advantage of the experimental treatments did not appear to depend upon the content or temporal position of any of the separate tests. The varying difficulty of the different tests did, of course, account for a highly significant source of variation. The analysis of data from the final

TABLE 1

Comparisons Among the Treatment Means Over All Unit Tests

TREATMENT	MEAN	N	
Aural Presentation	$X_1 = 777.72$	32	
Self-Paced	$X_2 = 734.63$	16	Error Mean Square =
Forced-Pace	$X_3 = 697.38$	16	8497.45

Ho	H_1	t	P
$2M_1 = M_2 + M_3$	$2M_1 > M_2 + M_3$	+2.68	<.01
$M_2 = M_3$	$M_2 = M_3$	+1.14	n.s.

TABLE 2

Summary of Analysis of Variance on Data from Unit Tests

Source	df	SS	F
Between Subjects	63	82,349	
Treatments (T)	2	6,003	4.24*
Blocks (B)	7	41,009	8.27**
T x B	14	7,010	.71
Subjects within T x B (error between)	40	28,324	
Within Subjects	704	124,560	
Observations (0)	11	57,878	58.22**
T x 0	22	3,072	1.54
B x 0	77	7,985	1.14
T x B x 0	154	15,859	1.14
O x Subjects within T x B (error within)	440	39,763	

test gave some additional support to the results from the unit tests (Table 3). On the final test the differences between the groups were in the same direction, but here the differences were marginally significant at best In seven of the eight blocks of subjects, the total scores of the aural presentation group exceeded the combined totals of the other two groups. The mean for the aural presentation group was 63.8 compared with 60.5 for self-paced group and 57.5 for the forced-paced group. The planned comparison of the aural presentation group with the other two groups yielded a t score of 1.64, significant only between the .05 and .10 levels. The lower significance level of the results from the final test analysis can most easily be attributed to the fact that this analysis was based on only one test whereas the unit test analysis used scores from twelve tests over an extended period of time; however, it is not possible to rule out completely the possibility that a test-timing factor (in addition to the sensory modality factor) gave an advantage to the aural presentation group that was reflected more strongly on unit test performance than on final test performance.

Once statistical significance of the differences among treatment effects had been ascertained, it became of some importance to know the practical significance of these differences; the learning gains resulting from the experimental treatment might or might not justify the extra effort and facilities needed whenever slow readers encountered difficulty programs. An appropriate estimate of the strength of the association between the experimental treatment variable and the criterion variable, signified by W^2 (3), yielded the value .055 for the data in this experiment. In other words, the treatment variable accounted for only about 5.5 percent of the variance in the criterion scores. The aural presentation helped the experimental subjects, but it did not affect their scores nearly as much as prior reading ability and those unanalyzed factors accounted for by the error term.

Discussion

The use of aural presentations of frames to supplement reading of a programed text over a ten-week period resulted in a small but statistically significant advantage for a group of seventh grade slow readers. The advantage of the aural supplement to reading occurred in a rather consistent manner over all unit tests, which involved different content, over all gradations of reading ability within the sample of subjects, and over a relatively long period of time. The advantage also occurred despite certain apparent drawbacks in implementing the aural presentation treatment, namely, the loss of the self-pacing feature and occasional use of the control treatment for absentees in order to make up lost time.

Although the experiment was conducted with quite different conditions, subjects, and materials than in two related studies, one by Budoff and Quinlan (2) and one by Jester and Travers (4), the results corresponded in a general sense with both of them. In the

TABLE 3

Comparisons Among Treatment Means on the Final Test

Treatment	Mean	N
Aural Presentation	$x_1 = 63.78$	32
Self-Paced	$x_2 = 60.5$	16
Forced-Pace	$x_3 = 57.5$	16

H_0	H_1	t	
$2 \quad _1 = {_2 +{_3} \atop _2 = _3}$	$2 \quad _1 > {_2 + _3 \atop _2 \neq _3}$	1.64 .73	.10 > p > .05 n.s.

Jester and Travers study the advantage in using a combined audiovisual presentation of reading passages to college students seemed to be greater when the material was presented at a fast pace by means of a speed compressor. In this study the advantage of the combined presentation showed up in the use of programed learning without any fast delivery of the material, possibly because the material was more difficult relative to the subjects' ability.

The difference between the other two treatments was not statistically significant, but there was a trend favoring the self-paced group. This trend makes it possible to speculate that the small advantage of the experimental treatment would have been greater if it had been possible to retain the self-pacing feature in the aural presentation of the frames. The results of this study do not indicate that the number of programs of potential benefit to slow readers can be greatly increased merely by placing the frames on tape, but there is some support for the idea that with greater technological sophistication, such as use of speed compressors and individualized pacing devices, the aural supplement would additionally increase the number of programs possible for such pupils.

REFERENCES

1. Blumenthal, Joseph C. *English 2600.* (Rev. ed.). New York: Harcourt, Brace and World, Inc., 1960.
2. Budoff, Milton and Donald Quinlan. "Reading Progress as Related to Efficiency of Visual and Aural Learning in the Primary Grades." *Journal of Educational Psychology,* 55: 247-252; October, 1964.
3. Hays, William L. *Statistics for Psychologists.* New York: Holt, Rinehart and Winston, Inc., 1963.
4. Jester, Robert E. and Robert Travers, "Comprehension of Connected Meaningful Discourse as a Function of Rate and Mode of Presentation." *The Journal of Educational Research,* 59: 297-302; March, 1966.
5. Lumsdaine, A. A., "Instruments and Media of Instruction," *Handbook of Research on Teaching,* N. L. Gage (Ed.). Chicago: Rand McNally and Company, 1963.
6. McGeoch, John A. and Arthur L. Irion. *The Psychology of Human Learning.* New York: Longmans, Green and Co., Inc., 1952.

Retention in Educable Mentally Retarded Children of Material Presented by Simultaneous Reading and Listening

DAVID B. ORR
American Institutes for Research

THE AMERICAN INSTITUTES FOR RESEARCH has begun to develop a program of research which has as its long-term goal the investigation and improved understanding of human informational inputs, processing, and storage, and the translation of such improved understanding into both theory and practice. The research described here was part of a project which had two broad aims, 1) to study the effect of using simultaneous, *bimodal* (eye-ear) inputs on the comprehension of connected discourse, both in terms of assimilation and retention of content, and in terms of improvement of reading and listening skills, and 2) to consider the implications of such procedures for the instruction of that portion of the intellectual continuum commonly known as educable mentally retarded (EMR).*

The concept that bimodal presentation (simultaneous reading and listening) might facilitate information transfer and retention had its origin in several previous studies.

In an unpublished paper, Travers (6) reported making a careful review of studies back to 1894 supposedly supporting the idea that the use of several senses simultaneously is more efficient than the use of the senses separately for the transmission of information. Nearly all of these studies concluded that simultaneous use of auditory and visual channels of information transmission is more effective than

* The author wishes to extend his appreciation to Jacques H. Robinson who carried out much of the work herein described, and to the National Institutes for Mental Health for its support under grant No. MH 10819-01.

use of either alone. (These studies form much of the basis for the widespread use of audiovisual aids.) However, most of these studies were found wanting either in design or in tests of significance, and Travers and his students, e.g., Van Mondfrans (7), researched the problem further using more careful controls. Briefly, their results cast doubt on the earlier conclusions of facilitation. Using *simple rote learning of word lists* of varying degrees of meaningfulness, no significant facilitating effect of eye-plus-ear transmission was found. (The influence of degree of meaningfulness was not discussed.) A further study using more rapid rates of transmission appeared to show an interference effect.

Travers maintained that these findings tied in with those of Hernandez-Peon, *et al.* (2), who demonstrated that the sight of a mouse by a cat resulted in a blocking of the nerve impulse produced by an audible click. However, it should be noted that the mouse and the click, far from being identical or complementary in stimulus content, are properly thought of as *competing* stimuli. Thus, the Travers and Hernandez-Peon experiments are based on rather sharply different stimulus conditions, and do not necessarily support each other.

On the other side of the question, Stromer (5) trained one group of subjects extensively in listening alone, and another group in reading silently while listening to the same material presented simultaneously at rates up to 285 words per minute. Both groups were then tested on both narrative and "study" material. Those students given reading-listening training showed a significant increase in rate of reading, a slight improvement in listening comprehension, and no improvement in reading comprehension of study material. For those students given training only in listening there was no significant improvement in reading comprehension, though presumably the group did improve in listening comprehension. However, for both groups, listening to narrative

material while reading it resulted in comprehension that was significantly greater than that for silent reading alone.

In an unpublished paper presented to the Annual Workshop on Reading Research (March 1964) conducted by the Committee on Diagnostic Reading Tests, Heckelman (1) reported as follows on the use of simultaneous oral reading by teacher and student as a remedial reading training procedure:

"Children with severe handicaps in the area of reading were given a maximum of 7¼ hours of instruction by this method during a period of 6 weeks with a resultant average of 2.2 grade levels of growth in functional reading skill." Heckelman termed his system a "Neurological Impress Reading Method," employing visual-linguistic and aural-linguistic networks, and regarded it as a fundamental approach. In any case, it appeared to produce impressive results.

Finally, an exploratory study reported by the present writer (3) has also suggested the importance of simultaneous input of aural and visual information. In this experiment, subjects read silently while a special device presented the same text aurally, without pitch distortion, 375-475 wpm, *well above the average reading rate of the group.* The Nelson-Denny Reading Test was used before and after training. Experimental subjects had no difficulty in keeping up and showed a significant, post-experimental mean increment in reading rate of 90 wpm; this increment was significantly greater than the control group increment (10 wpm at the one percent level. This increment was accomplished with no loss in comprehension score and a significant increment in vocabulary scores as compared to both initial score and control increment.

In summary, the above-cited research seemed to suggest that simultaneous presentation of material via both auditory and visual channels may have a facilitating or an interfering effect on informational transmissions depending on the rate of presentation, the degree of similarity and complexity of the two stimuli, and the continuity and meaningfulness of the material.

The present research was undertaken to examine the possibility that bimodal presentations might enhance the comprehension and retention of content of EMR's, a group that traditionally has extreme difficulty not only in learning to read, but perhaps more importantly *reading to learn*.

Procedures

The experiments were carried out at a public special education school in the Montgomery County, Maryland system. As the present paper is concerned only with the retention phase of these experiments, only procedures relevant to that phase are discussed below.

Subjects

Subjects were selected who had recorded (individual test) IQ's between 54 and 86, ages between 12 years, 11 months and 17 years, 11 months, reading grade level of at least 2.0, and no major auditory or visual defects or known degenerative neurological diseases. Subjects were of both sexes and predominantly white. They were randomly assigned to the various treatment groups used in the experiment.

Materials

Materials consisted of three 600-700 word passages developed and adapted by Spicker (4). These passages were rated at grade levels 3, 5, and 9, respectively. Twenty four-choice multiple-choice tests of appropriate difficulty were developed for each passage.

Treatment groups

Four groups of subjects were constituted:

1. A Machine-Audiovisual (MAV) group, exposed to bimodal presentation of the three passages. Tape recordings slowed by 20 percent (to about 80 wpm) by means of a device which can vary rate without pitch distortion were used for the auditory pres-

entations; 14-point macrotype was used for the same material to be read.

2. A Teacher-Audiovisual (TAV) group, also exposed to bimodal presentations, with the audio portion produced by the teacher reading at his normal speed.

3. A Machine Audio (MAud) group, which received the slowed auditory taped presentation but no reading material.

4. A Control group which did *not* receive the passages, but only the questions.

There were not sufficient subjects available for Teacher Audio or Hawthorne control groups. The rates of presentation used were selected on *a priori* grounds after pilot testing as being "appropriate" in each case. They were not under experimental investigation in this phase of the study.

Experimental method

The three passages were administered, one each day on successive days, in ascending order of difficulty to each of the three treatment groups. They were presented in accordance with the type of treatment prescribed for the group (MAV, TAV, or MAud). After each passage its 20-item test was administered; and the tests only, without the passages, were given to the control group. All tests were given using both the reading and listening modes.

As measures of retention, the "odd" test items were readministered without the passages after about one month, and the "even" items readministered after the second month. As before, these tests were presented on three successive days. Immediately after the collection of the second retention measure, the passages were again presented and all 20 questions again administered to supply a relearn index.

Data collection efforts for this phase of the study had to be limited in time in order to permit carrying out an instructional experiment which took up the time between the initial and final retention testing. Make up sessions were limited to within one calendar week from the group testing. As a consequence, there was a differential N in each of the groups, and, in general, the analyses were simplified by equalizing the N's in each of the cells of the analyses of variance to $N = 8$ by randomly casting out the excess cases.

Results

Tests showed in general that the treatment group means significantly exceeded the control group mean, thus indicating, as expected, that the scores were a function of knowledge gained

from the passages. (It will be remembered that the control group did not receive the passages.) An analysis of variance was done based on the initial score data shown in Table 1. This analysis clearly showed that the two subtests (odds and evens) were not different, at least with respect to initial score data. It may be safely presumed that they were not different for other administrations, and the absence of interaction between split and treatment suggested that the two subtests were appropriate for the comparison of treatments.

TABLE 1

Means and Standard Deviations by Odd and Even Items, Treatment Groups, and Passages for Initial Comprehension Data, Retention Phase

Difficulty (Passage)		Control		MAV		TAV		MAud	
		Even	Odd	Even	Odd	Even	Odd	Even	Odd
3	($\overline{X}$)	3.8	3.6	7.5	7.6	5.2	5.8	5.8	6.0
	(s)	.88	.92	2.07	2.07	1.28	1.39	1.91	2.27
5	($\overline{X}$)	3.3	3.3	6.6	5.7	6.0	5.1	4.0	4.2
	(s)	1.17	.88	1.60	1.98	1.60	2.30	2.07	2.19
9	($\overline{X}$)	2.0	3.0	5.1	5.1	4.6	5.2	3.0	3.1
	(s)	.93	.75	2.10	1.46	2.26	2.66	2.45	2.03

Note: Each entry is based on $N = 8$; data is based on 10-item tests. The Control group did not receive the passages and thus represents a base line estimate.

As expected, the Grade, 3, 5, and 9 passages proved highly, detectably different in difficulty. However, a treatment effect was also detected at the 10 percent level (the level chosen for significance for the entire experiment on several a priori grounds), with MAV > TAV > MAud being the order of the means. Further analyses of the treatment effect were suggested by the treatment by difficulty interaction. Analyses of the simple main effects confirmed the treatment difference at the 10 percent level or better for each of the three difficulty levels. The means were in the order given above for the Grade 5 and Grade 9 passages and MAV > MAud > TAV for the Grade 3. Not all mean differences reached significance, however. The significant ones were as follows: Grade 3,

MAV > TAV, MAud; Grade 5, MAV > MAud; Grade 9, MAV, TAV > MAud.

Having demonstrated that the odd-even subtests were equivalent, the retention data themselves could then be analyzed. The average of the odd-even scores was taken at the initial treatment group, by difficulty (passage). Thus, these analyses were based on 10-item tests or equivalent. The means are shown in Table 2. The purpose of this comparison was to determine whether or not there were significant differences in score after the two intervals of time, and whether or not difficulty and initial treatment differences persisted.

The differences in initial treatment did not hold up over the retention intervals, although the overall differences

TABLE 2

Means and Standard Deviations by Retention Interval,
Difficulty and Treatment Groups (Cell Ns = 8)

Difficulty (Passage)		MAV R_0	R_1	R_2	TAV R_0	R_1	R_2	MAud R_0	R_1	R_2
3	($\overline{X}$)	7.6	6.5	6.4	5.5	6.0	4.8	5.9	5.8	4.0
	(s)	1.76	1.14	2.26	1.20	1.85	1.28	1.90	1.28	1.85
5	($\overline{X}$)	6.2	5.2	5.0	5.6	5.9	4.9	4.1	4.8	4.6
	(s)	1.42	2.19	2.20	1.68	2.95	1.73	1.86	1.28	2.82
9	($\overline{X}$)	5.1	4.4	4.1	4.9	4.0	3.8	3.1	3.6	3.2
	(s)	1.73	1.51	1.36	2.38	2.67	1.49	2.13	1.41	1.58

Note: Data are based on 10-item tests, where R_0 is the average of initial odd and initial even scores.

in the means remained in the same direction. Mean differences by difficulty level were again highly significant. Mean differences at the retention intervals were also significant and in the anticipated direction: initial > one month > 2 months. These analyses suggested that the favorable effects of bimodal presentation were decreased over the retention intervals, but that the bimodal procedure did not adversely affect retention. In other words, the results may be interpreted as a case of the regression of the high groups toward the common mean, across time.

A further measure of retention was obtained by readministering the passages to the three treatment groups, using the original presentation mode, two months after initial exposure.

The data are summarized in Table 3. The analysis of variance showed significantly higher mean scores for the relearning condition than for the initial data. The ANOVA again revealed no differences by treatment group and highly significant differences by difficulty level in the expected direction. However, the nearly significant treatment by test interaction suggested that the initial versus relearning increase be examined by treatment group. In an analysis of simple main effects this difference was found to be significant for TAV and MAud, but not for MAV. A similar analysis showed that while the means remained in the order MAV > TAV > MAud, the significant difference obtained on the initial test did not hold up on the relearning test.

TABLE 3

Means and Standard Deviations for Relearning by
Difficulty and Treatment Group

Difficulty (Passage)		MAV RL_0	RL	TAV RL_0	RL	MAud RL_0	RL
3	($\overline{X}$)	15.1	15.4	11.0	14.4	11.8	13.1
	(s)	3.52	4.00	2.39	2.50	3.81	4.09
5	($\overline{X}$)	12.4	13.2	11.1	13.1	8.2	11.9
	(s)	2.97	5.09	3.36	3.56	3.73	5.17
9	($\overline{X}$)	10.2	12.1	9.9	11.6	6.1	9.4
	(s)	3.45	4.82	4.76	4.53	4.26	4.41

Note: Cell Ns = 8; data based on 20-item tests.

Thus it would appear that the second administration of the passages produced scores at a significantly higher level than the original administration in spite of a two-month interval between administrations. It should be noted, however, that the two-month interval contained 30 instructional periods in which the experimental treatments were used with other materials. The demonstrated increments could thus be attributed to relearning or treatment effects or, probably, both. In any case, these findings emphasize that EMRs *can* profit from suitable learning experiences. The failure of the MAV increase to reach a significant level was again probably due to a regression effect of the highest score level toward the common mean.

A final question which was investigated with these data was whether or not the scores obtained after an interval differed significantly from a chance level. Relevant information can be had by comparing the scores for the treatment groups after one month to those obtained by the control group (which did not receive the passages at all) for the same (odd) items. The relevant means are contained in Tables 1 and 2.

In the analysis of variance, a highly significant difference in the group means was detected. Examination of the means themselves showed that this difference arose because all treatment group means significantly exceed the control group mean, thus suggesting strongly that some of the material was retained by the treatment groups over the interval of one month. Again a significant difference in difficulty was noted.

Although statistical interdependencies precluded a test at the two-month interval, it seems safe to say that EMRs demonstrated a significant capacity for the retention of instructional material over a considerable time span. Means at the two-month interval were in the same direction. This finding may be one of the more important of the study as it indicates the value of continued effort to improve instructional techniques for the EMR.

Summary and discussion

To summarize the retention phase of the study, significant retention was obtained after a one-month interval (and probably after a two-month interval) as compared to a control base line that did not receive the passages. Significant losses with time were also detected, as expected, by comparison with initial scores. The initial differences in the treatment group means in the direction MAV > TAV > MAud did not hold up across the retention interval. A significant improvement over initial score was found on a relearning exercise carried out after a two-month interval, particularly for the TAV and MAud groups. Difficulty levels were significant in all analyses in the expected direction. It was concluded that EMRs are capable of retaining and of significantly profiting by relearning for the instructional materials used; and that the initial treatment group differences tended to regress toward a common mean over time.

It is not possible to come to any definite conclusions on the matter of sensory facilitation on the basis of this small study, though it seems quite clear that the simultaneous sight/sound procedures did not produce an interference effect on retention. Indeed, the persistent tendency for the means to favor the bimodal presentation groups, not only in the phase of the experimentation reported here, but in the instructional phases of this experiment not reported here, suggests strongly the need for further research with a less specialized and more generalizable population to determine the potential value of bimodal presentation for educational communication.

REFERENCES

1. Heckelman, R. G. *A Neurological Impress Method of Reading Instruction* (unpublished). Merced County Schools, California, March 1964.
2. Hernandez-Peon, R., H. Scherrer, and M. Jouvet. "Modifications of electric ac-

tivity in cochlear nucleus during 'attention' in unanesthetized cats." *Science,* 1956, 123, 331-332.

3. Orr, David B. "Recent Research on Reading and the Comprehension of Time-Compressed Speech." *College Reading Association,* Vol. 17, 1966.
4. Spicker, H. "Listening comprehension and retention of intellectually normal and retarded children as a function of speaking rate and passage difficulty," unpublished doctoral dissertation, George Peabody College for Teachers, 1963.
5. Stromer, W. F. "An Investigation into Some of the Relations Between Reading, Listening, and Intelligence," doctoral dissertation, University of Denver, 1952. Abstract: *Speech Monographs,* 21, 1954, 159-160.
6. Travers, Robert M. W. "On the Transmission of Information to Human Receivers" (unpublished). Based on Contract C-997, U. S. Office of Education, Educational Media Branch, 1964.
7. Van Mondfrans, A. "An Investigation of the Interaction Between the Level of Meaningfulness and Redundancy in the Content of the Stimulus Material, and the Mode of Presentation of the Stimulus Material," M. A. thesis, University of Utah, 1964.

Personality and Reading Success: A THEN and NOW Study of Thirty Years Span*

IRENE J. ATHEY
University of Rochester
and
JACK A. HOLMES
University of California

READING is a highly complex skill. The ease and fluency with which the average adult reads printed materials and comprehends their content belies the fact that this virtuoso performance is reached only after years spent in perfecting many different kinds of skills, compounding and recompounding these skills to form the finished product. Holmes (7) and Holmes & Singer (8), Davis (3), and Kling (9) have demonstrated the extent and variety of skills which make up the reading level of different subgroups from junior high school and college populations.

* The research reported in this paper was pursued under Contract No. OE 5-10-450, S-248, U. S. Office of Education, 1967.

Neither the layman nor the reading expert would readily assume that personality characteristics figure prominently in the reading act. When we think of reading, we are apt to concentrate on cognitive abilities and informational background. Yet it is trite to say that the individual develops as a "whole person." Olson (11), for example, has suggested that a child's reading age may be a function of his level of maturation on certain physical indices such as skeletal age, dental age, etc. Haggard (6) and others have shown the relationship between certain personality traits and academic achievement in school. It should occasion no surprise, then, to find such traits to be intimately associated with reading.

Historically speaking, investigation into the relationship between reading and personality received its initial impetus from the psychological clinic. Spurred on by the obvious emotional handicaps of many of their disabled readers, Blanchard (2) and Ladd (10) pioneered some of the earliest studies on the connection between these phenomena. During the almost forty years that have intervened since these early studies, a steady flow of research on this topic has issued from the clinic, the classroom, and the laboratory. In spite of the fact that this field has proved to be notoriously "stony ground," repeatedly yielding negative or inconclusive results, the flow has gained momentum, rather than diminished. For the most part, however, it has consisted of "one-shot" studies, in which specific personality scales are correlated with reading achievement, and the low correlations are taken as evidence of a negligible relationship between reading and personality or emotional adjustment in general. What is demonstrated, of course, is the absence of relationship between reading and the particular adjustment scales used. Such findings do not exclude the possibility, however, that other aspects of personality, for which no scales exist, may be highly and consistently related to reading. "Personality" and "adjustment" are, after all, very broad terms, and one cannot assume *a priori* that those aspects of personality which have most bearing on academic achievement will be the ones of most interest to the clinician. One might, in fact, assume just the opposite. A major phase of the present study was devoted to the attempt to build new scales which would have a more specific and direct relationship to reading ability, and would not be primarily oriented to adjustment *per se*.

In summary, one may say that analytical research into the relationship of personality factors to reading has had four major defects: 1) It has lacked a firm theoretical base with respect to both reading and personality, i.e., generally speaking, the hypotheses tested have not been derived from a theory of reading nor from a theory of personality, much less from an integration of the two types of theory. 2) It has resulted in inconclusive findings because of the unsuitability of the personality scales used. 3) It has generally consisted of "one-shot" studies without proper cross-validation or replication. 4) It has been insensitive to the possibly changing relationship of specific value-saturated personality scales and reading achievement with increasing academic experience and age.

The present study, in seeking to meet these four objections, fell naturally into the following four phases. First, a personality theory was sought which could accommodate a cognitive task such as learning to read. Erikson's (*4, 5*) theory was selected as particularly appropriate for this purpose, and an attempt was made to integrate his major concepts concerning the development of the normal or healthy personality through early childhood and the primary school years with the substrata-factor theory of reading propounded by Holmes (*7, 8*). Second, instead of using conventional personality scales, an attempt was made to build scales which would measure some of Erikson's primary concepts from items which had been

shown to have discriminating power with respect to reading. Third, the scales were cross-validated twice, and the study was replicated on a comparable group at a different point in time. Finally, the two samples were followed longitudinally over a period of three years, making this a then-and-now study of thirty years duration, utilizing a three-year longitudinal sample in the earlier phase, and three comparable cross-sectional groups in the later phase.

The next four sections are devoted to a description of the four phases of the study. A paradigm of the research design is shown in Figure 1.

Theoretical background

Erikson is a neo-Freudian who views man's progress through life as attained only by meeting, with varying degrees of success, a series of challenges posed by his own physical maturing and the cultural expectations of his milieu. Success at any one stage is accomplished at the expense of giving up earlier methods of obtaining gratification which are inappropriate to the higher level, but is rewarded by the addition of new skills to one's repertoire, and by the approval and privileges accorded the new status. Failure involves not only a denial of such perquisites, but it handicaps the individual when he is confronted by new tasks at subsequent levels, giving rise to cumulative emotional and social handicap with its attendant anxieties and implications for learning. A major challenge for the growing child comes around the time of first admission to school. Erikson calls this period the crisis of "industry *vs.* inferiority," the time when the child must obtain mastery of the fundamental tools of learning and acquire habits of work and positive attitudes toward school which will enable him to establish those permanent "patterns of industry" valued by an activity-oriented society. Reading is perhaps the most important of these fundamental tools. On this theory, then, one might expect that success in learning to read would lead

PHASE I

Initial Cross-sectional Sample (9th grade, 1935)

Group	Item pool	Item analysis predicting Reading Ach.	Double cross-validation Selected items	Double cross-validation Total sample	Pooled sample
IN		$N_{g1} = 40$ good readers $N_{p1} = 40$ poor readers	$n_1 = x_1$	$N_{in} = 160$	Significant items from IN & OUT groups combined to form final "then" (1935) inventory. Validation on pooled 9th grade sample: $N_p = 290$
	$n = 328$				
		$N_{g2} = 40$ good readers $N_{p2} = 40$ poor readers	$n_2 = x_2$	$N_{out} = 130$	

PHASE II

Longitudinal Cross-validation

9th grade (1935)   8th grade (1934)   7th grade (1933)

Correlation analysis

Multiple correlation

PHASE III

Current Cross-validation

9th grade (1966)   8th grade (1966)   7th grade (1966)

Correlation analysis

Multiple correlation

Fig. 1. Paradigm of research design.

to a personality syndrome character-ized by industry, self-confidence, and positive attitudes toward school and work. To carry the implications of the theory one step further, one might also infer that good readers would pos-sess the qualities which will ensue from the successful negotiation of Erik-son's earlier stages in the life of the child, namely autonomy, trust, and ini-tiative.

If these personality characteristics can be shown to accompany good read-ing in elementary school children, to what extent can they account for differences in the ability to read? Holmes has hypothesized that, beyond a required minimum level of attain-ment in certain basic skills such as vo-cabulary and information, the reader draws upon many different kinds of abilities and skills to achieve success. He further states that personality characteristics and personal value sys-tems may be found among the constel-lations of factors contributing to the variance in reading performance. In the present study it was hypothesized that characteristics representing Erik-son's concepts of the healthy person-ality would not only discriminate between groups of good and poor read-ers, but would make a significant con-tribution to the variance in reading for the total sample.

In brief, the hypotheses derived from the integrated Erikson-Holmes theory stated: 1) That successful read-ers would exhibit those qualities which characterize the "healthy personality," (viz. positive self concept, mastery of the environment, and freedom from neurotic anxiety), and 2) that each of these qualities would make a signifi-cant contribution to reading success.

Tests

The Stanford Achievement Test, Paragraph Meaning, Form V (1932) was used as the reading criterion.

A double cross-validation following a two-way analyses of the University of California Inventory selected those items which exhibited discriminating power with respect to reading. A third and consolidating item analysis determined the content of the new inventory.

Samples and procedures

In all, five samples were used in the present study. Two samples were drawn from the longitudinal study (1933-1935) at the Institute of Human Development, University of California, Berkeley, and one of these ($N = 160$) was studied longitudinally in Grades 7, 8, and 9 (1933-1935); the other sample ($N = 130$) was used for cross-validation purposes. In addition, three comparable samples were selected from Grades 7, 8, and 9 in 1966 (N's $= 143, 158, 112$).

Construction of reading-
personality scales (THEN)

1. *Item analysis.* The upper and lower 27 percent of Grade 9 (1935) students on the reading distribution were used to make an item analysis of the initial 328 items on the personality protocols of the University of California Inventory ($N = 160$).
2. *Initial cross-validation.* The significant items were cross-validated on a totally new Grade 9 (1935) sample ($N = 130$).
3. *Reciprocal cross-validation.* Procedures 1 and 2 were repeated, using the upper and lower 27 percent of the second sample for the item analysis; and the original sample was now used for the second cross-validation.
4. *Item analysis of pooled samples.* A third consolidating item analysis was performed on the 27 percent of the best and poorest readers in the pooled Grade 9 samples ($N = 290$). An item

was retained if it was a) significant at the 5 percent level on the chi-square test, and b) discriminating in the same direction in this *and* the two former analyses. Of the original 328 items, 70 survived the triple analyses.

5. *Pearson correlation.* All subjects in the two samples were rescored on the 70 discriminating items, and the resulting scores were correlated with reading. These correlations, ranging from .46 to .66, were all significant and also stable for the cross-validating samples. In view of the fact that the correlations of the original UCI scales ranged from -.31 to .19 and, for the most part, tended toward zero, it appears that the selection of items on the basis of the reading criterion considerably improved their power to predict reading achievement.
6. *Factor analysis.* The items were intercorrelated and submitted to a principal components factor analysis to determine whether they would cluster into scales descriptive of the personality characteristics hypothesized from theory. Seven factors were isolated and subsequently purified to form four scales which were interpreted as:
   I. *Social Independence;* II. *Self-Concept;* III. *School Dislikes;* and IV. *Self-Decision.*

Social Independence is so called because the items, when scored in the direction of responses given by good readers, indicate a belief in the ability to lead one's own life, and the desire to make one's own decisions in adult fashion. Self-Concept reflects a highly positive self-image on the part of the good readers extending beyond the academic sphere into the social fields of leadership and popularity. School Dislikes consists of two clusters of items; that of the good readers consists of dislikes with school work and teachers, while that of the poor readers is composed primarily of complaints against behavior of peers. The Self-Decision and Family Orientation factor suggests that the good reader seeks companionship among his peers, while the poor reader looks to his parents and home life for leisure activities. Considered together, the scales present a picture of greater self-confidence, independence, and social maturity on the part of the good readers, as predicted. The total scale was called the Self-Interest Inventory.

Genetic longtitudinal validation
(THEN)

The personality protocols for the original Grade 9 sample were also available at Grades 7 (1933) and 8 (1934). They were rescored for the four new scales, and the resulting scores correlated with reading. In a longitudinal study, however, the researcher is always faced with a loss of subjects. In the present study the missing data phenomenon necessitated a reduction of the sample to an N of 120 if the *same* students were to be compared over the three years.

Table 1 shows the correlations between the new scales and the criterion, reading achievement, for the three grades.

Comparing the correlations for the separate scales with those for the Total "Pure" Factors Scale (I-IV) in Table 1, it is interesting to note that the latter yields the highest r for each year —as would be expected. Further, the

correlation of the Total Scale with reading for Grade 9 yields an r of .465, as opposed to the parallel r's of .322 and .288 obtained in the 7th and 8th Grades, respectively. This drop is explained *not* so much by the fact that the 9th Grade r of .465 is slightly spurious (for it compares favorably with the average r of .480 derived from the reciprocal cross-validation of the IN and OUT Samples), but mainly because the *same* children are indeed somewhat *different* children in the 7th and 8th Grades than they are in the 9th, where the original item analyses were made (see Table 2). The further removed one gets from the original conditions for selecting the items and establishing the original r's, the lower the relationships are likely to be. Table 2 reports the constancy correlations of the criterion with the Self-Interest Inventory scales from year to year. Reading Achievement and Independence appear to be the most stable. The greatest changes from the 7th to the 9th Grades seem to have taken place in the self-concepts of these pupils as measured by this scale. However, the constancy correlations from the 7th to 8th and from 8th to 9th Grades are relatively low, indicating that a general differential development was taking place within this adolescent sample over the three-year period. It should be noted that the developmental correlations are not reliability indices and should not be taken as such.

TABLE 1

Correlations of the New Reading-Personality Scales with Reading Achievement for the *Same* Students on the *Same* Tests at Three Grade Levels

Reading Achievement with	Grades (N = 120)		
	7th (1933)	8th (1934)	9th (1935)
I. Social Independence	.219*	.211*	.219*
II. Self-Concept	.256*	.086	.388*
III. School Dislikes	.136	.077	.077
IV. Self-Decision	.209*	.257*	.345*
Total "Pure" Factors (I-IV)	.322*	.288*	.465*

* Significant at or beyond the .05 level.

TABLE 2

Year-to-Year Self Correlations of the Scales
Showing Development Relationships in the THEN Sample

		Grades		
		7th (1933) r_{7-8}	8th (1934)	9th (1935) r_{8-9}
C.	Reading Achievement	.78*		.85*
I.	Social Independence	.60*		.71*
II.	Self-Concept	.06		.09
III.	School Dislikes	.16		.12
IV.	Self-Decision	.33*		.46*
T.	Total "Pure" Factors (I-IV)	.31*		.42*

* Significant at or better than the .05 level.

The pattern of correlations, in Table 1, suggests that each factor, except III, "School Dislikes," makes a substantial contribution to the overall relationship between reading and the Self-Interest Inventory. Since the inter-scale correlations are relatively low, it appears that the overall inventory is effectively measuring the combined impact of the three major factors. A judgmental analysis by the present writers of the items in Factor Scales I, II, and IV suggests that the junior high school students who hold high values toward their a) Social Independence, i.e., freedom from social dependency, b) Positive Self-Concept, and c) Self-Decision, i.e., need to make their own decisions, will be better readers than those who place a low value on these attributes. It is evident that these three value systems are in one sense factorially different; yet in another sense they are only different facets of a single basic attitude, need, desire, or active role on the part of the student who is seeking to become a confident and competent individual able to make his own decisions now, and looking forward to the time when he can make his own way in the world. To accomplish these objectives it is quite apparent to him that, realistically, he must have an education of *quality*, and consequently he places high value on acquiring such an education. These, then, are the values delineated in this study as bearing a

positive relationship to reading achievement in the 7th, 8th, and 9th Grades in the 1930's. The question remains, "Are these same values (as operationally measured in the Inventory Scales) related to reading success in the same way in the *same* grades today, i.e., in 1966?"

Cross-sectional validation (NOW)

In order to determine whether the personality scales discovered to be related to reading achievement at the junior high school level in the 1930's were constant over time in their relationship to reading achievement, a suitable replication at a later date was needed. Hence, in 1966, samples of 7th, 8th, and 9th graders were drawn from a similar school population. Except for a few Orientals, the student populations of the THEN and NOW schools were composed almost entirely of Caucasians of comparable socioeconomic levels, living in similar geographical locations of the San Francisco East Bay Area.

Table 3 compares the correlations between reading and the personality scales for two samples taken thirty years apart. Inspection of thse correlations in Table 3 will show that 21 of the 30 *r*'s are significantly different from zero ($< = .05$). The most striking aspect of the Table, however, is the remarkably high and consistent corre-

TABLE 3

Comparison of Correlations for Personal-Values Inventory Scales and Reading
for 7th, 8th, and 9th Grades

Reading and		Grades	
	7th	8th	9th
I. Social Independence			
1933, '34, '35[a]	.219*	.211*	.219*
1966[b]	.062	.024	.238*
II. Self-Concept			
1933, '34, '35	.256*	.086	.388*
1966	.169*	.161*	.188*
III. School Dislikes			
1933, '34, '35	.136	.077	.077
1966	.095	.003	.059
IV. Self-Decision			
1933, '34, '35	.209*	.257*	.345*
1966	.308*	.427*	.221*
Total "Pure" Factors (I-IV)			
1933, '34, '35	.322*	.288*	.465*
1966	.245*	.317*	.318*

* Significantly different from zero ($< = .05$).
[a] 1933, 1934, 1935: $N = 120$.
[b] 1966: $N_7 = 143$, $N_8 = 158$, $N_9 = 112$.

lations for the Total (I-IV) Inventory over the three years for both the *then* and *now* groups. Here, possibly for the first time, is evidence that a certain set of personal values is *consistently* related to the achievement of reading success in the junior high school grades—within the limits and conditions of the two populations, sampled over a thirty-year span. This finding, corroborated in a large scale study using a strictly random sample from the 7th, 8th, and 9th Grades at *all* socioeconomic levels, would indeed be a real breakthrough in the field of reading.

The second striking feature of Table 3 is the consistency and strength of the relationships exhibited between Factor IV, Self-Decision, and Reading Achievement in the THEN and NOW samples over the three grades. This scale, more than any of the others, appears to assess willingness to face up to the reality needs for self-fulfillment. The hard fact is that, to strive to fulfill one's self-image as a maturing person, one must strive to be less dependent on one's immediate family for direction, for companionship, and for protection from both the real and fancied dangers

and anxieties of one's external and internal worlds. On the positive side, it assesses the degree to which a young person perceives his parents as developing a basic trust in his ability to make decisions for himself, such as choosing his own friends, deciding on the nature and extent of his own educational goals, and acquiring the ability to deal with anxieties arising from the decision *not* to be a "mother's helper" in order to pursue his own interests and fulfill his own needs.

The third most consistently positive factor is the scale assessing Self-Concept. All but one of these r's are significant beyond the .05 level. Low scores on this scale reveal that a person tends to perceive himself as insignificant and ill-equipped for leadership in either social or academic competition. A high score, on the other hand, does not mean that the person has feelings of superiority or, in fact, considers himself to be the most outstanding individual in his school; it only means that he does not profess deep-seated feelings of inferiority. Although the scoring is dichotomized for each item, in taking the test a student had a 5-point scale on which to record his answers. The poor reader tended to concentrate his responses in the lowest category, while the best and average reader's responses were spread out more or less evenly over the other four categories. Thus the scale tends to assess the poor *vs.* the average, good, and best readers when used in its present context.

Factor I, Social Independence, displays a consistent and educationally important set of correlations for the 7th, 8th, and 9th Grades of the THEN sample and for the 9th of the NOW group. A low score on this scale means the individual wishes to be and professes to be considerate of other people in his actions and, in return, is willing to trust them in their actions toward him. On the other hand, he neither professes nor wishes to be old enough to make his own decisions. In short, he wishes to be, and considers himself to be, rather completely dependent upon others. Thus, a low score would tend to indicate extreme social dependency.

Finally, Factor III, School Dislikes,

is consistently unrelated to Reading Achievement.

Multiple correlation

A step-wise multiple-correlation, using the scales of the Self-Interest Inventory produced the results tabulated in Table 4 for each of the years in the THEN and NOW samples. To facilitate comparison, the multiple R's derived from the best weighting of the subtests are presented with r's obtained by correlating the *sum* of the number of correct *raw* items scored (or simple sum of the raw scale scores for the total) with Reading Achievement. Perusal of Table 4 reveals that the adjusted multiple R's are sometimes higher and sometimes lower than the parallel zero-order r's. The second interesting aspect of the tabled entries, however, is the beta weights given to the three factors in contributing to the various multiple R's.

Theoretically, one would like an *estimate* of just how much of the variance in Reading Achievement at the

TABLE 4

Comparison of Multiple R's, Derived from a Best Weighting of the Subscales of the Inventory for Predicting Reading Achievement, with Zero-order r's derived by Summing Raw Scores of Subscales of the Inventory and Correlating the Total with Reading Achievement

Sample	$\beta.r$		$\beta.r$		$\beta.r$		Comparable correlations	
							Unadjusted	Adjusted
7th Grade								
1933 $\overline{R}_{c \cdot II, I, IV}$ = (.21)	(.26)	+ (.16)	(.22)	+ (	.12)	(.21) =	.377[a]	.302
1933 $r_{c \cdot (I-IV)}$							.322	.322
1966 $R_{c \cdot IV, II, I}$ = (.31)	(.31)	+ (.17)	(.17)	+ (−.02)		(.06) =	.350	.322
1966 $r_{c \cdot (I-IV)}$							.245	.245
8th Grade								
1934 $\overline{R}_{c \cdot IV, I, II}$ = (.23)	(.26)	+ (.19)	(.21)	+ (	.04)	(.09) =	.324	.286
1934 $r_{c \cdot (I-IV)}$							.288	.288
1966 $R_{c \cdot IV, II, I}$ = (.44)	(.43)	+ (.19)	(.16)	+ (−.05)		(.02) =	.464	.447
1966 $r_{c \cdot (I-IV)}$							.317	.317
9th Grade								
1935 $\overline{R}_{c \cdot II, IV, I}$ = (.36)	(.39)	+ (.33)	(.35)	+ (	.04)	(.22) =	.512	.493
1935 $r_{c \cdot (I-IV)}$							.465	.465
1966 $\overline{R}_{c \cdot I, IV, II}$ = (.17)	(.24)	+ (.20)	(.22)	+ (	.18)	(.19) =	.343	.305
1966 $r_{c \cdot (I-IV)}$							.318	.318

[a] I. Social Independence, II. Self-Concept, IV. Self-Decision, (I-IV). Total of "Pure" Factors (including III. School Dislikes).

junior high school level this value-saturated Self-Interest Inventory accounted for under the THEN and NOW conditions. Since both chi-square and Z-tests show that there are no significant differences in the r's in the grade-by-grade THEN and NOW samples *or* between the 7th, 8th, and 9th Grades within each condition for the Total Self-Interest Inventory and Reading Achievement, they may all be averaged by Fisher's z-transformation. When this is done, the averaging procedure yields a mean r of .36, and the best *estimate* is that the value-saturated personality scales assessed in this Inventory could, *on the average,* account for approximately 13 percent of the variance in Reading Achievement in the 7th, 8th, and 9th Grades. In the field of personality and reading research 13 percent is a substantial contribution, especially when it has shown itself to be consistent over the entire range of the junior high school and also in two samples separated by a period of over thirty years.

Socioeconomic status

Socioeconomic status scores were available for the families of the 7th, 8th, and 9th Grade children in the THEN sample. Hence, it was possible to compare the magnitude of the correlations of Reading Achievement not only with the Total (I-IV) Inventory Score, but also with the socioeconomic status of the family. Table 5 presents these data.

Reference to Table 5 shows that at each grade level the Total (I-IV) Inventory Score correlated higher with Reading Achievement than did the socioeconomic status of the family.

Obviously a child's value system— his attitudes toward self-image, freedom from family and social dependency, and the making of decisions— are intimately tied with the attitudes and behavior he observes and reacts to in his family, and these, of course, are dependent on the socioeconomic status of the family. However, the relationship need not be large in all cases, for there are many other individuals and institutions which are also actively engaged in trying to mold the child—the peer culture, the school, the church, and advertising campaigns via mass media, to name only a few. Beyond each child's genetically determined tendencies and the influence stemming from his family's social and economic position, there are these other strong, persuasive elements in the child's life. The degree to which each is successful

TABLE 5

Comparative Correlations between Reading and
(a) Total (I-IV) Inventory and (b) Socioeconomic Status

Variables	THEN sample	r_{ex}
	7th (1933)	
Total (I-IV) Inventory		.322
Socioeconomic Status		— .170*
	8th (1934)	
Total (I-IV) Inventory		.288
Socioeconomic Status		— .277*
	9th (1935)	
Total (I-IV) Inventory		.465
Socioeconomic Status		— .240*

* The correlation is negative simply because the socioeconomic scale weights the occupations in an inverse order:

I & II. Professionals, proprietors, managers with some college education,
III. Small shopkeepers, clerks, salespersons, skilled workers of high educational status,
IV. Skilled manual workers,
V. Unskilled workers with minimal education.

reinforces or diminishes the impact of family pressures on the child. Finally, the evidence from the present study indicates that the composite value-system, no matter how or from what sources it is derived, is somewhat more important in accounting for achievement in reading in junior high school children than the family's socioeconomic status *per se*. It must be held in mind, however, that the present samples are restricted in range as far as socioeconomic status is concerned. Under the condition where the full range of the socioeconomic status was present, undoubtedly the influence of socioeconomic factors would be increased; but under such conditions the range in value-systems might also be greater, in which case the relative picture found here would remain constant.

Future research in this area

The present study has clearly demonstrated that, by isolating and cross-validating only those personality items related to reading, it is possible to construct new personality scales which have a consistent and significant bearing on reading success. Moreover, the characteristics measured by these scales are those which were hypothesized from reading and personality theory, if one assumes that reading is a "developmental task" in western culture. The relative importance of each characteristic at each age level and for different groups is a matter for further research. Especially at kindergarten and grades 1 to 3, when reading assumes tremendous cultural significance, and the relevant personality characteristics are undergoing rapid transformation, the relationships should provide interesting insights into the mutual development and impact of the emotional overlay and language skills. There is no reason to suppose that the factors involved in this study exhaust the total realm of values and personality characteristics which may be related to reading. The hope is that the use of the double cross-validation technique coupled with longitudinal and cross-sectional replications in a THEN and NOW experimental design

have demonstrated a satisfactory way of mining low grade ore. The "payoff" has proven to be substantial, and the present writers submit that it opens possibilities for new and rewarding studies at other levels in this challenging field of inquiry.

REFERENCES

1. Athey, Irene J. and Jack A. Holmes. *Personality and Reading Success at the Junior High School Level.* Final Report Covering Contract No. OE-5-10-450, S-248, 1967.
2. Blanchard, Phyllis. "Reading Disabilities in Relation to Maladjustment," *Mental Hygiene,* 12 (1928), 772-788.
3. Davis, Frank R., Jr. "Speed of Reading and Rate of Recovery in Certain Physiological Subsystems." Unpublished Doctoral Dissertation, University of California, 1963.
4. Erikson, Erik H. *Childhood and Society.* New York: Norton, 1950.
5. Erikson, Erik H. "Growth and Crises of the Healthy Personality," in George S. Klein (Ed.), *Psychological Issues,* Vol. I. New York: International Universities Press, 1959, 50-100.
6. Haggard, Ernest R. "Socialization: Personality and Academic Achievement in Gifted Children," *School Review,* 65 (1957), 388-414.
7. Holmes, Jack A. "The Substrata-Factor Theory of Reading: Some Experimental Evidence," *New Frontiers in Reading;* Proceedings of the Fifth Annual Conference of the International Reading Association, 1960.
8. Holmes, Jack A. and Harry Singer. *The Substrata-Factor Theory of Reading: Substrata Differences Underlying Reading Ability in Known Groups,* Final Report Covering Contracts No. 538, SAE-8176 and 538A, SAE-8660, U.S. Office of Education, 1961.
9. Kling, Martin. "The Generalization of the Substrata-Factor Theory to General Open Systems Theory." Unpublished Doctoral Dissertation, University of California, 1965.
10. Ladd, Margaret R. "The Relation of Social, Economic and Personal Characteristics to Reading," *Teachers College Contributions to Education,* No. 582. New York: Columbia University, 1933.
11. Olson, Willard C. "Reading as a Function of Total Growth of the Child," *Supplementary Education Monographs,* No. 51, 1940.
12. Tryon, Caroline M. "A Study of Social and Emotional Adjustments: The Internal Consistency and Interrelationships of Measures by Different Techniques." Unpublished Doctoral Dissertation, University of California, 1933.

A Continuum of Teaching Strategies for Developing Reading Readiness at the Kindergarten Level

HARRY SINGER, IRVING H. BALOW,
and PATRICIA DAHMS
University of California,
Riverside*

THE DEBATE on when formal reading instruction should be initiated has been with us for many years, and many positions have been taken by the participants. At one extreme are those programs which recommend formal reading instruction in kindergarten (5), (15), or earlier (18, 16)**. At the other extreme, instruction would be delayed until a necessary mental age of six years and six months had been reached (19). Between these extremes a crude continuum can be constructed that represents several other points of view. Close to the extreme of delay is a maturational theory which holds that reading readiness is a function of the individual's biologically-determined time schedule or organismic age (20). According to this theory, readiness is a matter of waiting until the child has attained the necessary organismic age for beginning reading, as evidenced by "seeking" behavior. Near the opposite end of the continuum is the language arts approach of integrating pictures, language, writing, and reading through individual experience charts (27.) This is followed by a program that emphasizes some systematic effort at effecting reading readiness by developing conceptual responses to printed words (25). The next position is represented by the attempt to develop reading readiness by providing for incidental "exposure" to printed stimuli (8, 24). What can, perhaps, be considered the central position on the continuum between formal reading in kindergarten and delay in first grade is the adjustment-to-school philosophy which emphasizes the development of favorable attitudes toward school and utilizes prereading experiences such as oral language and picture interpretation but does not include responses to printed words (8, 24).

This crude continuum represents three segments: 1) initiation of formal reading instruction in kindergarten or earlier without a formal reading readiness period, on the assumption that children are already "ready" for reading; 2) stimulation of reading readiness by several means, on the assumption that readiness is susceptible to improvement through direct instruction; and 3) delay in instruction until the necessary mental or organismic age has been reached, on the assumption that readiness cannot be developed or accelerated through specific instruction.

One result of the debate has been the adoption by teachers of different kindergarten programs as advocated by the various protagonists in the debate. Observation of kindergarten classes suggests that the controversy is now shifting from "when should reading begin" to "what is the most effective method of initiating readiness readiness?" In other words, the debate appears to be less a controversy over "timing" versus "experience" (13), and more a controversy over the most effective curriculum for initiating reading instruction earlier than first grade. Instrumental in shifting the debate has been the hypothesis that "any subject can be taught effectively in some intellectually honest form to any child at any stage of development"

* This study was supported by an intramural research grant from the Research Committee of the Academic Senate of the University of California, Riverside. Appreciation is expressed to the teachers and administrators of Alvord and Riverside Unified School Districts for participating in and cooperating with this study.

** References to the literature are not meant to be exhaustive, but merely representative of positions taken. See Gunderson (1964) and Mason and Prater (1966) for recent summaries of the literature.

(4). Thus, with modified teaching methods *(18)*, materials *(6)*, and learning conditions *(14)*, reading instruction could be initiated at an earlier age than in the past. Hence the concept of reading readiness *(2)* has to be reformulated. Instead of asking when should reading be initiated, the question ought to be: given certain conditions, such as a particular teacher-pupil ratio; a particular medium of instruction, such as traditional orthography; and present-day classroom equipment, what is the relative effectiveness of various strategies for developing readiness?

Problem

The basic assumption of the present study is that reading readiness is an achievement variable and hence susceptible to educational development. The purpose of the study then is to determine which, if any, of six teaching strategies is most effective in developing reading readiness. Since Gates *(9)* has shown that perception of printed words was not highly correlated with perception of numbers of geometric objects, and since perception of printed words at the beginning of first grade is a better predictor of reading achievement than is a general test of intelligence *(1)*, it was hypothesized that a teaching strategy which emphasized development of perception of printed words would be more effective than one which stressed perception of pictures or merely "adjustment" to school. To test this hypothesis, six teaching strategies, at the kindergarten level—which formed somewhat of a continuum from adjustment of children to school to a formal reading program that had been previously used at the first grade level—were selected for the study. The final test of the hypothesis awaits analysis of first grade reading achievement. The present report is only concerned with the effectiveness of the various teaching strategies in the development of reading readiness.

Procedure

All of the kindergarten teachers who participated in the study were volunteers. The rationale for using volunteers rather than taking a random sample of kindergarten teachers and asking them to utilize another method of developing reading readiness was that the teachers who volunteered would presumably be enthusiastic about their own method and consequently the "Hawthorne Effect" would be controlled since all of them would be in the "experimental group"; and further, these methods or teaching strategies represented positions on the continuum described above. No attempt was made to control any other teacher variable, such as age or experience. As it worked out, the most experienced teachers were those at either end of the teaching strategy continuum.

The following teaching strategies were employed in the study:

1. Adjustment. The teacher of this program utilized a "traditional" kindergarten approach. Emphasis was placed upon having children enjoy kindergarten through songs, games, construction activities, and discussion. Some printed words were placed about the room, particularly at holiday time. Although children's books were in the room, these were primarily used for reading stories to children or for children to use voluntarily. No systematic effort was made to teach children to perceive or recognize printed words.

2. Irrelevant Picture-Type Reading Readiness. One teacher who had been teaching for several years had been and preferred to utilize the Scott-Foresman Series: *We Read Picture, We Read More Pictures,* and *Before We Read, (11)*. This approach was categorized as "irrelevant" because the pictures were not related to those used in the basal reader series that the children would get in the first grade.

3. Relevant Picture-Type Reading Readiness. The teacher of this group used the Ginn reading readiness workbook *(22)*. Because the children would go into the Ginn basal reader in

grade one, the materials were labeled "relevant."

4. Development of Conceptual Responses to Printed Words. One beginning kindergarten teacher volunteered to use a set of materials that was designed to develop the initial stage of a conceptual response to printed words. The teaching strategy, described in detail elsewhere (25) consisted of a systematic organization of kinesthetic, visual, auditory and language experiences in temporal contiguity to a particular object and its printed label. The words used in this teaching strategy were taken from the Ginn reading readiness workbook.

5. The Language Arts Approach (27). One beginning kindergarten teacher was an intern who used a language arts approach to reading readiness which essentially consisted of having children draw pictures and learn to write descriptive sentences under their pictures and then read their "stories" to the class.

6. Formal Reading Program. Two experienced teachers were using a set of experimental reading materials modeled after the linguistic approach of Bloomfield-Barnhart's *Let's Read* (3). The words in this experimental material, originally constructed for the initial stages of reading in the first grade, were controlled on phonetic regularity and the content was based on an Indian boy growing up in his own culture (10).

Supervision

The university supervisor for the intern teacher and the beginning teacher using the "conceptual response" materials also visited all the other teachers either to observe or, if asked, to help them improve the method they were using. Thus, an attempt was made to control her supervision of two teachers by having her assist all the teachers. She also kept observational records of her visits. Thus, it was possible to ascertain whether or not each self-selected teaching strategy was, in fact, being employed. In general, she found that the teachers did utilize their teaching strategy rather faithfully.

Tests

The Lee-Clark Reading Readiness Test was administered as a pretest about March 1st and as a post-test about June 1st. All children were tested each time in their own classrooms in groups of five.*

Results

The essential results are shown in Tables 1 and 2. Table 1 shows that reliabilities for the pre- and post-tests were sufficiently high in all groups that confidence could be placed in the consistency of the results. Although there

*Elementary credential candidates Caryl Fisher, Sandra Rosen, Catherine Valentino, Pauline Dilday, and Barbara Smith administered and scored the tests.

TABLE 1

PRETEST AND POST-TEST RESULTS OF SIX STRATEGIES
FOR DEVELOPING READING READINESS

LEE-CLARK READING READINESS RESULTS

Teaching Strategy	N	r_{11}	PRETEST (March 1) Mean	S.D.	r_{11}	POST-TEST (June 1) Mean	S.D.
A. Adjustment	35	.78	45.31	10.0	.77	52.43	7.1
B. Irrelevant Pictures	26	.84	43.9	9.2	.75	51.2	7.4
C. Relevant Pictures	30	.86	48.0	9.0	.82	52.4	6.5
D. Conceptual Response	43	.84	38.0	11.2	.80	48.0	11.3
E. Language Arts	42	.91	41.9	12.1	.78	52.6	7.6
F. Formal Reading	43	.87	47.8	10.5	.91	52.6	11.2

is considerable variation in pretest means, all post-test means are approximately the same, reflecting in part that many children had reached the "top" of the test. Only in the formal reading group was there an increase in the variability of the group; in the other groups the variabilities decreased! Nevertheless, each group had increased significantly in reading readiness.

To test the null hypothesis that there was no significant difference in reading readiness gains that could be attributed to variation in educational treatment, analysis of covariance was used. When variation in initial scores was controlled, the results indicated that the null hypothesis should be accepted.* Even if the differences among the teaching strategies were significant, it would be erroneous to conclude that any strategy should be advocated, and particularly erroneous that any one program should be administered to all kindergarten children. Instead, it should be emphasized that in each kindergarten some children

were ready to read, according to the Lee-Clark norms, at the pretest time; and that many more children were ready to read in each kindergarten at or before the post-test was administered, as shown in Table 2. The implication from this analysis is that provision for such individual differences should be taken into account in each kindergarten. Rather than one program for all children, a differentiated curriculum should be utilized at kindergarten as at every other grade level (21). Hence, one percent of the children who are already reading to some degree when they enter kindergarten (7) should be put into some type of formal reading program when they enter school. Those who are almost ready might have a more informal program, such as the language arts approach. Those who need further perceptual development might profit from

---

*Price Stiffler and Fred Goldstein, programers, assisted in the analysis of the data. The Computer Center staff at the Berkeley and Riverside campuses of the University of California also rendered services.

TABLE 2

READING READINESS STATUS OF PUPILS IN SIX TEACHING STRATEGIES

READING READINESS STATUS*

| | | PRETEST (March 1) | | | POST-TEST (June 1) | | |
| | | DELAY | | | DELAY | | |
Teaching Strategy	N	7 months or more	1-6 months	none	7 months or more	1-6 months	none
A. Adjustment	35	4	5	26	1	0	34
B. Irrelevant Pictures	26	5	3	18	0	2	24
C. Relevant Pictures	30	4	1	25	0	1	29
D. Conceptual Response	43	16	7	20	7	1	35
E. Language Arts	42	9	7	26	0	2	40
F. Formal Reading	43	4	3	36	3	2	38
TOTAL	219	42	26	151	11	8	200
PERCENT		19.1	11.8	69.1	5.0	3.6	91.3

* Based on Lee-Clark Reading Readiness Test norms on reading-grade placements for end-of-year kindergarten pupils: 0-32 = Delay of 7 months or more; 33-39 = Delay of 1-6 months; 40 and up = no delay.

the "conceptual response" program; and those children who did not know how to function in a group or whose language development is quite deficient or whose preschool range of experiences has been constricted could probably benefit from some period of instruction aimed at overcoming their specific deficiencies (26).

Limitations

The findings of this study must, of course, be limited to the particular measure of reading readiness used. An unsuccessful attempt was made to obtain a control group to evaluate the effect of maturation alone on reading readiness. Until such data are collected, the findings of this study must be attributed to the interaction of maturation and instruction. Whether or not the planned follow up of reading achievement at the end of grade one reveals any differential effects that can be attributed to any of the instructional strategies utilized at the kindergarten level remains to be seen.

Summary and conclusions

Six teaching strategies for developing reading readiness, conceived as an achievement variable, were evaluated by means of analysis of covariance. The statistical results showed that the differences among the strategies were not significant.

However, in each strategy, many children were already "ready" for formal reading instruction, according to the test norms, at the pretest time and others became "ready" before the post-test time. It was inferred that instead of being "forced" or "paced," many of these children, in fact, were being "delayed" in reading instruction. Since children are at various stages of readiness for instruction in reading during kindergarten, the conclusion is that provision should be made for such individual differences by adopting the teaching strategy of a differentiated curriculum.

REFERENCES

1. Balow, Irving H. "Sex Differences in First Grade Reading," *Elementary English*, 40 (1963), 303-306; 320.
2. Beckett, Dorothy B. "Philosophical Differences in Reading Concepts," *The Reading Teacher*, 18 (October 1964), 27-32.
3. Bloomfield, Leonard and Clarence L. Barnhart. *Let's Read: A Linguistic Approach*. Detroit: Wayne State University Press, 1961.
4. Bruner, Jerome S. *The Process of Education*. New York: Vintage Books, 1963.
5. Brzeinski, Joseph E. "Beginning Reading in Denver," *The Reading Teacher*, 18 (October 1964), 16-21.
6. Downing, John A. *The Initial Teaching Alphabet*. New York: Macmillan, 1964.
7. Durkin, Dolores. "Children Who Read Before Grade One," *The Reading Teacher*, 14 (January 1961), 163-166.
8. Durkin, Dolores. "Reading Instruction and the Five-Year-Old Child," in J. A. Figurel (Ed.), *Challenge and Experiment in Reading*, Proceedings of the Seventh Annual Conference of the International Reading Association, 7, 1962, 23-27.
9. Gates, Arthur I. "A Study of the Role of Visual Perception, Intelligence and Certain Associative Processes in Reading and Spelling," *Journal of Educational Psychology*, 17 (1926), 433-445.
10. Gearing, Fred. *Big Cat Series*. Riverside, California: University of California, 1964 and 1965. (Multilith)
11. Gray, William S., Marion Monroe, A. Sterl Artley. *We Read Pictures, We Read More Pictures*, and *Before We Read*. Chicago: Scott, Foresman, 1956.
12. Gunderson, Doris. *Research in Reading Readiness*. Bulletin No. 8, 1964. U. S. Department of Health, Education, and Welfare. Washington, D. C.: Superintendent of Documents, Catalog No. 5.230 :30013.
13. Hillerich, Robert L. "An Interpretation of Research in Reading Readiness," *Elementary English*, 43 (April 1966), 359-364; 372.
14. Holmes, Jack A. "When Should and Could Johnny Learn to Read?" in J. A. Figurel (Ed.), *Challenge and Experiment in Reading*, Proceedings of the Seventh Annual Conference of the International Reading Association, 7, 1962, 237-241.
15. Kelley, Marjorie L. "The Effects of Teaching Reading to Kindergarten Children." Unpublished doctoral dissertation, University of California, 1966.
16. McManus, Anastasia. "The Denver Pre-reading Project Conducted by WENH-TV," *The Reading Teacher*, 18 (October 1964), 22-26.

17. Mason, George E. and Norma Jean Prater. "Early Reading and Reading Instruction," *Elementary English,* 43 (May 1966), 483-488.
18. Moore, Omar K. In Helen Rowan. "'Tis Time He Should Begin to Read." *Carnegie Corporation of New York Quarterly,* 9 No. 2 (1961), 1-3.
19. Morphett, M. V. and C. Washburne. "When Children Should Begin to Read." *Elementary School Journal,* 31 (March 1931), 496-503.
20. Olson, W. C. and B. O. Hughes, "Concepts of Growth—Their Significance to Teachers," *Childhood Education,* 21 (1944), 53-63.
21. Pincus, Morris and Frances Morgenstern. "Should Children Be Taught To Read Earlier?" *The Reading Teacher,* 18 (October 1964), 37-42.
22. Russell, Davis H. and Odille Ousley. *Fun With Tom and Betty.* New York: Ginn, 1957.
23. Sheldon, William D. "Teaching the Very Young to Read," *The Reading Teacher,* 16 (December 1962), 163-169.
24. Sheldon, William and Dolores Durkin. "Should the Very Young Be Taught to Read?" ("They Should Have the Opportunity," says Dolores Durkin. "Harm Might Result," warns William D. Sheldon), *NEA Journal,* 52 (1963), 20-24.
25. Singer, Harry. "An Instructional Strategy for Developing Conceptual Responses in Reading Readiness," in J. A. Figurel (Ed.), *Vistas in Reading,* Proceedings of the Eleventh Annual Convention of the International Reading Association, 11, Part 1, 1966, 425-431.
26. Spache, George, *et al.* "A Longitudinal First Grade Reading Readiness Program," *The Reading Teacher,* 19, (May 1966), 580-584.
27. Van Allen, Roach. *Report on the Reading Study Project.* Monograph No. 1. San Diego: Superintendent of Schools, 1961.

An Analysis of Eight Different Reading Instructional Methods Used with First Grade Students

PAUL B. CAMPBELL, HENRY C. HEUSNER, and JUNE J. SLOBODIAN
Livonia, Michigan, Public Schools

SCHOOL DISTRICTS, in approaching the problem of selecting materials on instructional methods for the teaching of reading, are frequently bewildered by the varying claims of publishers and authors of such programs. It is nearly always possible to find in the literature evidence which supports the success of each program with some group of children somewhere. The question for the school district then becomes one of evaluating these claims and reported successes in terms of the particular set of conditions which operate on the local scene.

Systematic study of the output of the various programs, given the local conditions, is a task which is too often neglected. Such a study is not basic research in the traditional sense, although the replication of many local efforts across the country may well provide basic knowledge about the effectiveness of various kinds of programs. It is, nevertheless, a very important and even critical activity in which local school districts should engage.

During the 1965-66 school year, groups of first grade children in the Livonia, Michigan, school system were provided with reading instruction material from eight different publishers, representing eight different approaches and materials, as the first part of a two-year study. The materials were: Lippincott Basic Reading Series (1); Science Research Associates Basic Reading Series (2); Scott, Foresman Basal Reading Sixties Series (3); Ginn Basic Readers (4); Michigan Successive Discrimination Language Reading Program (6); Stern Structural Reading Series (7); McGraw-Hill (Sullivan) Programed Reading Materials (8); and the Initial Teaching Alphabet (i.t.a.) program (9). Preliminary measures were collected on mental ability, reading readiness, socioeconomic status, teacher estimate of reading motivation, interest in reading, dominance, and presence or absence of speech problems.

Materials were assigned by an essentially random procedure among those teachers who were willing to volunteer for new reading materials. The Ginn Basic Readers material served as a control, with an added advantage in that it, too, was a new adoption for the 1965-66 school year. Thus, all of the materials were essentially new to the people who were using them in the classroom, although, in each case, some previous familiarization had taken place before actual teaching began.

The assumption of equivalence among groups was tested by means of an analysis of variance of the pre-measures on mental ability and reading readiness. No significant differences among groups were found on mental ability. A difference appeared, however, on reading readiness. The entire study group was, therefore, divided into subsets for the purpose of analysis.

The Lippincott and McGraw-Hill materials formed a subset with Ginn, while the remaining materials formed another subset overlapping Ginn, but not including Lippincott and McGraw-Hill. In other words, there were no significant differences between the Ginn control group and the Lippincott and McGraw-Hill groups, nor between the Ginn control group and the remaining groups in the study. There were, however, significant differences between Lippincott, McGraw-Hill, and the groups using materials such as the Michigan Successive Discrimination Language Program.

After a year's instruction, during which all teachers were provided with appropriate consultative service and demonstration help when needed, a preliminary analysis of reading achievement was made. The children were tested using the Stanford Achievement Test, Primary Battery I, 1964 edition. Prior to the analysis of the data, the differences in group size were moderated somewhat by random sampling from the population of children who were working with any given material. Test scores were tabulated and the Hartley F_{max} tests were used to assess the validity of the assumption of homogeneity of variance. This assumption was supported for the smaller experimental subset and for the larger experimental subset with one exception, a rather large divergence in the Word Study Skills section of the Stanford Achievement Test. The data were, however, studied by means of the analysis of variance model with the divergence accounted for, where possible, by alternative analyses. Further random samples, categorized on the basis of variables of interest (i.e., male and female, high and and low readiness, etc.) were also drawn; were subjected to the same tests; and were analyzed by appropriate statistical methods, including distribution free statistical tests.

Tentative conclusions

The comparison of the eight commercial materials and reading instruction methods was undertaken to provide a basis for answering the following questions:

1. Which among the eight methods and materials seem to produce the highest level of reading achievement for children in general?

2. Which among the eight methods and materials seem to produce the highest level of writing ability for children in general?

3. Are there reading materials and methods which seem to be uniquely suited for use in instructing children of high or low previous interest in reading?
   Corollary to this question, is it possible to collect accurate information about levels of reading interest?

4. Are there differences among the materials and methods in producing types of reading achievement?

5. Do groups of children categorized by high and low levels of readiness perform better with some materials than with others?

6. Do girls perform better than boys with certain types of materials and methods?

7. Are some materials uniquely suited for teaching children with speech problems?

8. Are some materials and methods better suited for teaching chil-

dren with mixed dominance patterns?

The findings support the following conclusions:

With respect to question one, no significant F ratios were found. The data, therefore, give us reason to believe that Livonia children, in general, have no advantage or disadvantage when they are taught by Lippincott linguistic or McGraw-Hill programed reading as opposed to Ginn reading material.

In the larger experimental subset, however, the groups ranked themselves in the following order:

The i.t.a. group equals or significantly exceeds the Ginn group in all five subtests.

Scott, Foresman Sixties group does likewise, except that the Scott, Foresman group exceeds the Ginn group in only one subtest, Vocabulary, ($t = 2.59$ df 6,120)* while the i.t.a. group exceeds Ginn in three, Spelling ($t = 3.53$ df 6,120), Word Study Skills ($t = 3.86$ df 6,120), and Word Reading ($t = 5.61$ df 6,120).

The group using the Stern material does not differ from the Ginn group in Vocabulary, Spelling, or Word Study Skills. The obtained means were lower than Ginn in Spelling and Word Study Skills, but not significantly so. The Stern material is significantly poorer on Paragraph Meaning ($t = 2.67$ df 6,120) and Word Reading ($t = 2.81$ df 6,120) than the Ginn group.

The Michigan Successive Discrimination program equals the Ginn material on Vocabulary and Word Study Skills. This group does less well than the Ginn group on Paragraph Meaning ($t = 2.67$ df 6,120), Spelling ($t = 3.53$ df 6,120), and Word Reading ($t = 2.81$ df 6,120).

The SRA group equals the Ginn group in Vocabulary; it does not do as well as the Ginn group in Paragraph Meaning ($t = 2.67$ df 6,120), Spelling ($t = 2.64$ df 6,120), and Word Reading ($t = 2.81$ df 6,120). The Word

Study Skills mean is lower than the Ginn mean, but the divergent nature of the variances makes this result uncertain. There is, however, no reason to believe that the SRA material was as successful or more successful than the Ginn material in Word Study Skills.

It would appear from these data that the i.t.a. material is promising enough to be given a further tryout, and that the Ginn and Scott, Foresman Sixties materials succeed quite well in Livonia classrooms. The same statement may be made for the Lippincott and McGraw-Hill materials, although the latter was judged by the staff as quite difficult to employ. The other materials do not offer much general promise in the Livonia school setting. Some cautions are, however, in order. First, previous experience with Stern material seems to indicate that the problem in Paragraph Meaning tends to disappear by the end of the second grade. Second, the i.t.a. material needs to be reevaluated at the end of the second grade likewise, since it is possible that the nature of the test, printed in i.t.a. rather than traditional orthography for the i.t.a. group, favored children who had been trained by the i.t.a. method. There is little doubt, however, that a substantial plurality had a very successful first grade experience with i.t.a. Finally, further testing is essential because these results may be generalized only to the conditions operating this year. A follow up of these children and a replication of the study with the more promising materials is underway.

The second question concerns quality of written expression. On the basis of a significant difference obtained by a nonparametric analysis of variance of judgments of writing samples, it appears that writing ability is best achieved in groups using SRA, i.t.a., Lippincott, and McGraw-Hill materials, in that order. Again, follow-up is required to better assess this finding.

With respect to question three, no method of instruction seems to be

*Reported t values are computed using Dunnett's method for comparing multiple means with a control (10).

uniquely appropriate for high or low interest levels. The data collected do, however, support a conclusion that a measure of interest in reading can significantly predict a subsequent level of achievement after a year's instruction ($F = 18.87$ df 1,123). While this finding answers a question posed as a corollary in this study rather than a direct concern, it does open the possibility for further exploration of methods for improving reading instruction.

Concerning question four, the data support the conclusion that the eight materials of the study do vary considerably in the kind of reading achievement which they most effectively foster ($F = 32.39$ df 4,490). Word Study Skills emerge most consistently strong, and Paragraph Meaning is the most consistently weak aspect of reading achievement. The specific relation between materials and type of achievement is discussed under question one.

The data support conclusions ($H = 254.4$) concerning question five that for Paragraph Meaning, i.t.a, Ginn, and Scott, Foresman materials, in that order, produce better achievement in the low readiness groups, while no significant differences occur in the high readiness groups. The Spelling subtest seems to indicate that in the low group, the i.t.a. material ($t = 3.90$ df 7,62) is associated with the highest success, while the Stern material is associated with the lowest success ($t = 5.46$ df 7,62). Again, no differences appear among the high groups. The previously mentioned caution about the i.t.a. version of the Stanford Achievement Tests applies here. The significant H statistics (263 and 251) for the Word Reading analysis confirm again the differences among materials for all children in the study. No precise probability statement about interaction between levels of readiness and materials is possible here, but the data seem to indicate that Ginn, i.t.a., and Scott, Foresman materials are likely to be more productive in the low groups, and i.t.a., Scott, Foresman, and McGraw-Hill materials seem to fill this specification in the high groups.

Concerning question six, no materials seem to be uniquely suited for boys or girls. In addition, an unpredicted finding appears from these data; it is that there appears to be no difference between boys and girls in reading achievement in the first grade. This is contrary to common assumptions. Furthermore, this finding was duplicated for a different sample of Livonia first graders by a previous study (5). It appears possible that teachers in Livonia in the first grade are at least taking into account some of the differences between boys and girls which effect reading instruction, or else the differences do not exist when instruction begins.

No material appeared to be uniquely better than the others for children when there were speech problems, as question seven asks, nor was any difference in general reading performance found between the speech problem group and the no speech problem group. A slight trend in the direction of lower achievement associated with speech problems is evident, but it cannot be ruled out as a chance occurrence.

Concerning dominance patterns, as posed by question eight, no material emerges as being uniquely best for children with mixed dominance patterns, or conversely, for children with established dominance patterns. Some differences appear among the means between the groups. For example, in Paragraph Meaning, Scott, Foresman, Stern, and i.t.a. materials seem to be most effective for the mixed dominance group, while Ginn, Scott, Foresman, McGraw-Hill, and i.t.a. seem to be best for the established dominance groups. Likewise, in the Word Study Skills, i.t.a., Scott, Foresman, Stern, and Lippincott materials appear to produce the best achievement for the mixed group, while for the established group, Scott, Foresman, i.t.a., McGraw-Hill, and Stern materials seem to do the best job. These occurrences, of course, may be chance orderings, and no firm conclusion should be drawn from them. Again, the lack of differences between the overall achievement of the mixed and established dominance groups, where it could be tested, seems to indicate that these factors are being taken into account fairly well by teaching methods in use in Livonia schools at the present time.

In considering the total pattern which emerges from this study, it appears that the most significant result is the existence of highly significant differences among the materials and methods for all children, as posed by the first question.

It should be further recognized that all such findings as these are probabilistic; in other words, the results may apply to most children, but there will always be exceptions who may profit by an approach which does not show as promising general results as the others which are included in this study. Teachers should continue to try differing approaches when children do not seem to fit with the pattern which works best for the total group.

REFERENCES

1. McCracken, Glen, et al. *Basic Reading Series*. Philadelphia: J. P. Lippincott Company, 1964.
2. Rasmussen, Donald and Lynn Goldberg. *Basic Reading Series*. Chicago: Science Research Associates, Inc., 1965.
3. Robinson, Helen M.; Marion Monroe, and A. Sterl Artley. *Basal Reading Sixties Series*. Chicago: Scott, Foresman and Co., 1963.
4. Russell, David H.; Doris Gates, and Mabel Snedaker. *Ginn Basic Readers*. New York: Ginn and Company, 1964.
5. Slobodian, June J. "An Analysis of Certain Dimensions of Teacher Behavior During Reading Instruction in the First Grade." Doctoral dissertation, Kent State University, 1966.
6. Smith, Donald E. P. and Judith M. Kelingos. *Michigan Successive Discrimination Language Reading Program*. Ann Arbor, Michigan: Ann Arbor Publishers, 1965.
7. Stern, Catherine, et al. *Stern Structural Reading Series*. Syracuse, New York: L. W. Singer Company, Inc., 1963.
8. Sullivan, M. W. and Cynthia Dee Buchanan. *(Sullivan) Programed Reading Materials*. New York: McGraw-Hill Book Company, 1963.
9. Tanyzer, Harold J. and Albert J. Mazurkiewicz. *Initial Teaching Alphabet*. New York: Pitman Publishing Corp., Initial Teaching Alphabet Publication, Inc., 1963.
10. Winer, B. J. *Statistical Principles in Experimental Design*. New York: McGraw-Hill Book Company, 1962, 89.

Some Differences Between Silent and Oral Reading Responses on a Standardized Reading Test

ROBERT E. LEIBERT
University of Missouri
at Kansas City

RESEARCH COMPARING THE ACHIEVEMENT of pupils on standardized reading tests with pupils' performance on informal reading tests has indicated that grade placement is often not equivalent to instructional reading level (*2, 5, 6, 9*).

Purpose

The purpose of this study was to identify some of the differences between the responses on one standardized test (The Gates Advanced Primary Reading Test) and the kinds of responses obtained from an informal reading inventory. Specifically the purpose was to ascertain possible explanations for the answers pupils choose while taking a silent reading test. The following questions were considered in this investigation:

1. Does the measurement of word retention by a recall test result in significantly fewer words correct than when the same words are presented in a recognition test?

2. What types of skills do pupils use to select a word on the word recognition section of the Gates test?

3. Can pupils answer certain items on the paragraph section of the Gates test without having to read the entire item?

4. Can pupils engage in partial or inaccurate reading during the regular administration of the paragraph section of the Gates test, and to what extent are children successful in correctly answering questions on which they read orally in a less accurate fashion than would be acceptable on an informal reading inventory?

Procedure

In the fall term of 1964 sixty-five third grade pupils of the West Babylon, New York, school system were administered the Gates Advanced Primary Reading Test (Form 2) and an informal reading inventory. The pupils were divided into three groups roughly representing pupils whose instructional levels were at, above, or below grade level at the time of testing. Each group was called a Reading Level Section. The reading levels included in each section are listed below:

Reading Level Section I —
    Primer-First Reader Level
Reading Level Section II —2^1-2^2
Reading Level Section III—3^1-3^2

The three groups were found to be statistically equivalent in terms of IQ.

To shed some light on the differences between the two types of tests, the Gates test was administered to some pupils in ways similar to an informal reading inventory. Specifically, the administration of the word recognition portion of the Gates test was changed to study the ways in which the two tests measure the retention of words. The Gates test measures retention through a recognition technique (picture and four word choices) while an informal word recognition test utilizes a recall procedure (words in isolation). Further information about the possible differences between the two tests was sought by having pupils explain certain choices on the word recognition section of the Gates test. The paragraph reading section was administered to investigate the possibility suggested by Dolch (3) and Plessas (7) that pupils can mark the correct answers on a standardized reading test by reading only part of a test item. Second, the accuracy of oral reading was compared with the ability to obtain the correct response on an item.

Word recognition

Retention. The pupils' retention of the words on the Gates Word Recognition section was determined by utilizing three measures of retention, two of which were similar to those on the Gates* and an informal**.

    1. Recall** (words presented in isolation)
    2. Recognition—1 (Selecting a word —pronounce)
    3. Recognition—2* (Picture and selecting one of four words)

Using a table of random numbers, pupils in each reading level section were assigned to one of the three test situations (Recall, Recognition—1, Recognition—2). This provided an equal representation of children from each of the reading level sections in each testing condition.

Recall. To test the recall of words on the Gates test of word recognition, each of the forty-eight correct words was shown in isolation to the twenty-one pupils. The child was asked to pronounce each of the words on the list. Each response, or lack of response, made by the pupils was recorded by the examiner. This testing yielded a number of correct responses and a record of the actual response for each word incorrectly pronounced.

Recognition—1. The twenty-two pupils in this group were instructed to mark the word pronounced by the examiner for each item. This required the child, who was using the regular testing booklet, to find and circle the one word pronounced from among the four printed choices. This task eliminated picture interpretation and excluded the use of meaning in the choice of a response.

Recognition—2. Pupils in the third group received the test under the recommended conditions of administration. That is, these twenty-two pupils were to encircle the word which they decided best fit the pictured idea for each item. When finished, each child in this group was asked to explain how he arrived at certain responses in his test booklet. The remarks by the pupil were then recorded by the examiner on a separate test booklet.

Paragraph reading

The relationship of partial reading and inaccuracy of reading upon test scores was investigated by manipulating the administration of the paragraph reading section of the Gates test. The possibility of reading only part of the material and the extent of inaccurate reading were examined by administering the Gates test in the following ways:

1. Following directions *only* (effect of induced partial reading)

2. Normal administration with oral rereading (check on accuracy of reading).

The pupils were again randomly assigned from each reading level section to one of the two testing conditions by using a table of random numbers. The first method of presentation permitted the pupils to read only the directions for each item. Any preceding written information was concealed to accomplish this end. The pupils were instructed to read and follow the directions as best they could in the absence of other information. As has been previously described, this test consists of a series of items with pictures and a short paragraph. The following is a sample of such an item:

Four pictures which portray:
Boy holding a small fish
Boy holding a large fish
Boy holding a small fish
Boy holding a small fish
(When we went fishing the scout leader said he would give 25¢ to the one who caught the biggest fish.)* Draw a line under the boy who has the biggest fish (4).

For the pupils in the second group, the test was administered in the usual manner. The child was to read each item and follow the directions at the end of the selection as indicated in the sample above. As these pupils finished, they were asked to explain what they did to answer items, 1, 7, 9, 16, 18 and 24. These items include both those which were judged to be answerable without reading the entire item (as in the previous example) as well as some which seemed answerable only when a part of all of the preceding information had been read.

* The section in parentheses was concealed from the children in this testing condition.

The writer then met individually with the pupils in the second group to record the oral reading and explanations by each child. The pupils were directed to read to the examiner just what he read during the silent reading test situation. While the child read the material, the examiner recorded any responses which were at variance with the test material.

To answer the question whether pupils reading only directions would do less well than the pupils reading the entire item, the number of correct responses for each item was computed for both of the testing conditions (partial reading and complete reading). Using the chi-square statistic these frequencies were tested for the hypothesis that the number of correct responses achieved by reading only the directions would be less than the number of correct responses when the entire item was read.

Accuracy. The accuracy of reading for each of the six items for the children who read to the examiner was computed. The number of errors was then categorized according to whether this met, was less than, or was greater than the 95 percent criterion for words in context used in the informal reading inventory. This criterion of accuracy as outlined by Betts (1) was used in scoring the informals administered to these pupils. This information was further separated for both correct and incorrect responses to an item within each reading level section. The resulting breakdown provided a comparison of the effect of accuracy on the ability to correctly complete the test item.

Results

Word recognition

Retention. The analysis of variance indicated that the means of the three measures of retention of words were not equal. Scheffe's test for multiple comparisons clearly indicated that the measurement of word retention was higher when determined by recognition tests than when determined by a recall test. Significant differences between the two tests of recognition suggested the task in Recognition-2 is more difficult than the task required in Recognition-1.

Analysis of responses given during interrogation. The purpose of this interrogation was to explore the pupils' explanations of how they selected an answer. The words chosen for this interrogation included not only words that appeared to the writer as easily pictured, but also those items containing ideas less easily pictured. (picture of a fist—correct word—knuckles)

A total of 201 responses were made by these children, of which 119, or 59 percent, were correct and the remaining 82 were incorrect.

The majority of correct responses were words which were either recognized or worked out through word analysis (96-23). A small number of responses were correct even though the pupil could not identify the picture. The last explanation type in this Table indicates that few responses were correct because of a deliberate attempt to eliminate other responses.

The analyses up to this section have included (as nearly as possible) only known errors. This interrogation provided a way of investigating the pupils' ability to interpret pictures and to determine their approach to selecting answers on the Gates test.

Incorrect responses were categorized in approximately the same manner. In addition, for each explanation type a tabulation was done as to whether the picture was correctly or incorrectly identified. Words which were guessed were further classified as to whether the word chosen was correctly or incorrectly pronounced for the examiner.

The majority of incorrect responses reflected guessing (50-32) because the pupil did not know the meaning of the picture and/or did not recognize the words presented. Often the picture was incorrectly identified (44-6) and the word selected was unknown to the child (44-10). This analysis identified pictures for which pupils were unable to correctly determine the idea represented.

Paragraph reading

Partial reading—accuracy. The question considered here is whether the ability to respond correctly to the items is relative to the degree of accu-

TABLE 1

CLASSIFICATION OF CORRECT RESPONSES FROM INTERROGATION INFORMATION FOR RECOGNITION-2

Word Analysis	Word Recognition	Guess[a]		Process of Elimination
		Picture		
		Right	Wrong	
18	78	2	12	9

[a] Responses which represented a guess were also rated according to whether the picture to that item was correctly or incorrectly identified.

TABLE 2

CLASSIFICATION OF INCORRECT RESPONSES FROM INTERROGATION INFORMATION

Word Analysis (Picture)		Word Recognition		Guess				Process of Elimination	
				Right		Wrong			
Right	Wrong	Right	Wrong	C[a]	In[b]	C	In	Right	Wrong
9	2	18	1	0	6	10	34	2	0

[a] C—Correctly pronounced.
[b] In—Incorrectly pronounced alternative.

racy of reading in which the pupils engage during the task. The majority of responses made by pupils in Reading Level Section I who correctly answered the questions had error scores which exceeded 1 error in 20 running words. In only one case at this level did a pupil correctly respond to an item on which an error score within the instructional level criterion was attained.

In the other two reading level sections the majority of errors of those correctly answering the items fell within the instructional level criterion. A larger majority of pupils in these two reading level sections who answered the items correctly fell within the instructional level criterion. That is, only 32 percent of the responses of pupils answering the items correctly for the Reading Level Section II, and 24 percent of the responses for the Reading Level Section III were made within the frequency range of errors not acceptable on an informal reading inventory.

It is apparent from this analysis that some of the pupils on the Gates test were able to correctly answer items for which their reading was very inaccurate. They were able to adequately follow the directions by reading only part of the material correctly. This occurred mainly for those pupils in the lowest reading level section.

Partial reading—induced. A final analysis was conducted to answer the question as to whether pupils reading directions only could complete certain items on the Gates test with the same frequency of correct responses as those taking the test under the normal conditions.

These items were completed correctly with the frequency of correct responses similar to that of pupils who read the entire item. It is important to note that of items 2 through 24, responses to only item 14, 15, and 24 produced chi-square values of statistical significance. Therefore, these were the only items which could not be answered by partial reading.

Summary and conclusions

Word recognition

The Gates test employs a multiple choice technique which is a recognition test, and the informal reading inventory uses a test of recall to check word recognition. Pupils in this investigation at the same instructional level scored higher in the recognition test than in the recall test. These results were similar to the findings of other investigations in this area of retention. Lastly, from these results lower word recognition scores would be expected on the informal reading inventory than on the Gates test.

Analysis of responses—interrogation. The inability to identify the pictured idea supports a conclusion of Postin and Patrick's (8) investigation, which reported that some pictures did not facilitate the recognition of the intended word. This interpretation assumes the test will be one of word recognition only. Responses of these pupils clearly illustrate that the results of a test, such as the Gates, cannot be fully analyzed unless the manner in which the responses were derived can be determined.

As previously suggested by Dolch and Plessas, answers reflect a variety of skills and guessing. On the informal, where the majority of testing is oral, guessing is held to a minimum and is often detected by the examiner or is verbalized by the child.

Paragraph reading

Partial reading—accuracy. This analysis supports the contention that pupils can read inaccurately and still obtain the correct answer to items on a standardized test such as the Gates. Hence, inaccurate reading alone does not account for correct or incorrect answers on that test, as is also true on an informal reading inventory. Some of the pupils who made the same number of errors when reading completed the item correctly and others did not.

Pupils can read inaccurately to a point where the instructional level criterion is exceeded and still obtain the correct response on the item. This increases the difference between the informal reading inventory and the Gates test. It would seem that for many pupils, especially those at the lowest reading levels, standardized tests scores reflect a maximum level.

The fact that pupils in reading level sections II and III did so well in accuracy suggests that either the items were not as difficult as the level computed or that the practice derived from reading during the testing enabled them to read orally more accurately.

Partial reading—induced. Since it was found that children who read only the directions could answer all but three of these questions, the tentative conclusion that it is possible to partial read on this test and to complete the items correctly is substantiated. This will support the similar conclusion suggested by Dolch.

Thus the Gates test compares the pupil taking the test with norms developed on other pupils who have taken the test, while an informal reading inventory uses a predetermined objective standard to judge reading performance in a graded set of materials.

The general findings of this study indicate that there are sufficient differences between these two tests to conclude that the grade-placement score of the Gates Advanced Primary Reading Tests, Form 2, reflects a more global measure of reading performance than does the instructional level of the informal reading inventory. That is, the range of test difficulty and the variety of skills employed on the Gates test should not be expected to result in a score equivalent to the instructional reading level as determined by a more narrowly conceived performance on an informal reading inventory.

REFERENCES

1. Betts, Emmett A. *Foundations of Reading Instruction.* New York: American Book Company, 1957, 484.
2. Daniel, J. E. "The Effectiveness of Various Procedures in Reading Level Placement," *Elementary English,* 39 (October 1962), 590-600.
3. Dolch, E. W. "Complete vs. Partial Reading," *Elementary English,* 33 (January 1956), 11-12.
4. Gates, Arthur I. Gates Advanced Primary Reading Test, Form 2, Type APR. New York: Bureau of Publications, Teachers College, Columbia University, 3, 1958.
5. Killgallon, Patsy A. "A Study of Relationships Among Certain Pupil Adjustments in Reading Situations," unpublished doctoral dissertation, The Pennsylvania State University, 1942.
6. McCracken, Robert A. "The Oral Reading Performance of a Second Grade Class Using an Informal Reading Test," *Journal of Educational Research,* 55 (November 1961), 113-117.
7. Plessas, Gus P. "Another Look at the Reading Score," *Education,* 83 (February 1963), 344-347.
8. Poston, Freds, and James R. Patric, "An Evaluation of Word and Picture Tests for First and Second Grades," *Journal of Applied Psychology,* 28 (April 1944), 142-152.
9. Sipay, Edward, "A Comparison of Standardized Reading Achievement Test Scores and Functional Reading Levels," unpublished doctoral dissertation, University of Connecticut, 1961.

Determining Reading Levels of Elementary School Children by Cloze Testing

PEGGY E. RANSOM
Ball State University

THROUGH VARIOUS TECHNIQUES of appraisal, elementary teachers attempt to recognize the reader level at which a pupil can learn to read effectively. Standardized tests, informal tests, teacher observations, questionnaires, and records of various kinds are examples of methods teachers rely upon to determine the appropriate grade placement of pupils in reading. In recent years a new tool, cloze testing, has been introduced in appraising the reading techniques of children. This instrument may prove to be a useful tool in helping elementary teachers determine the appropriate instructional reading levels of children in the classroom.

The purpose of this investigation was to compare the relative indicated reading levels of children when two instruments for measuring reading performances had been used. The two instruments used were a cloze test and an informal reading inventory. The study was designed to determine whether or not a significant relationship exists between scores on a cloze test and scores on an informal reading inventory.

One of the elementary teacher's greatest tasks is that of identifying and assigning to students reading materials which are challenging yet not frustrating. Two primary sources presently relied upon by a large number of teachers to determine this instructional reading level are standardized tests and the informal reading inventory. It is generally recognized that standardized tests tend to overestimate a child's reading level, while informal reading inventories, though they are accepted as valid and reliable, are quite time consuming because they must be administered individually. Since evidence indicates that teachers have tended to place children at the frustration level in reading, rather than at the instructional level, it has been deemed advisable to attempt to identify a technique by which teachers can more easily ascertain the instructional reading level of pupils. Children's learning efforts can be increased if they are placed in reading material where they can easily succeed. Cloze testing can be used with a group, it can be administered in a short period of time, and the materials from the test are easily reproduced. It would seem that cloze tests could be the contributory support teachers need for placing children at the reading level where they can read effectively for instruction.

Definitions of terms used

Cloze procedure. Cloze procedure is the random deletion of a portion of the words in a passage, the replacement of deleted words with a blank, and the instruction of the subjects to write in the missing words.

Cloze test. A cloze test contains a series of reading passages including preprimer through ninth reading levels in which every fifth word has been deleted in consecutive order.

Cloze response. The cloze response is the word selected by the reader to fill in the blank found within a cloze test.

Readability. Readability is the relative difficulty of reading materials, as has been determined by applying an accepted formula to samples of reading materials.

Informal reading inventory. An informal reading inventory consists of selections taken from carefully graded material or from a series of basic readers and placed together to form an oral-silent reading evaluation instrument.

Adjustment of reading materials

Teachers can provide for a wide range of reading abilities in a classroom only if they are aware of what differences exist. Instructors need to determine the reading material to be used with each child in accordance with the individual achievement level. In teaching reading, the initial identification of each child's instructional level is only the first step in the process of evaluating continually the specifics of the child's performance (1).

That reading materials be adjusted as far as possible with the reading achievement level of each child is advocated. Consequently, if teachers of reading must adapt materials and methods to the different needs and abilities of individual pupils, there exists the necessity of determining each child's reading achievement levels (2, 3, 4, 5, 6).

Standardized tests are the instruments most frequently used by teachers to estimate reading levels, yet research studies have found that the scores of the standardized tests overestimate the instructional level of children (7, 8, 9, 10, 11).

Informal reading inventories

It would be impractical to list all the writers who advocate the use of an informal reading inventory in a classroom situation. Let it suffice to state that use of an informal reading inventory is suggested in most volumes on the teaching of reading. Emmett A.

Betts, in *Foundations of Reading Instruction,* first explained its value and use as a means for estimating reading levels of children. Various authors have advocated different criteria to use with an informal reading inventory; however, these appear closely related and display no great discrepancies. It has evidently become a matter of choice as to criteria selection when one administers and interprets the informal reading inventory.

For a number of years the validity of the informal reading inventory has been assumed since the materials are equal in readability to that of the instructional material, and the techniques of administration were similar to those used in classroom instruction. McCracken established, statistically, the validity on his standardized reading inventory which includes many features of the informal reading inventory (12).

Informal reading inventories are an important appraisal instrument because they have relationship to a pupil's work and are realistic and more meaningful to the pupils. They do estimate a child's level of reading and can be readily acceptable for use by the teacher.

Cloze tests

The cloze procedure was developed in 1953 by Wilson Taylor, who derived the term "cloze" from the gestalt concept of closure (13). The validity of cloze tests as a readability measure for evaluation of materials designed for adults and for intermediate and primary grade pupils has been explored to a limited extent.

Taylor found that the order or ranking obtained on cloze test scores given to college students were the same as the order or ranking of the same passages by the Dale-Chall and Flesch formulas. He also showed that the cloze scores were a more valid prediction of difficulty than the formulas for selected materials. He used materials in which the ease of the language belied the complexity of the ideas expressed (14). Rankin obtained correlations from .45 to .65 between a cloze test and a reading survey test, but he found a significantly stronger relationship (.78) between the cloze test and an objective test covering the same article (15). Bormuth and Ruddell and Gallant found positive correlations in their studies (16, 17, 18). The reliability of cloze tests has been ascertained by Taylor, Rankin, Ruddell and Bormuth also. Further proof that cloze tests have been accepted as a valid and reliable technique is the recent inclusion of this instrument (for measuring comprehension) in various testing situations.

Procedure of this study

One school in Muncie, Indiana, was used in this study. It was selected by school personnel who identified it as a typical "average" school with children possessing a wide range of achievement levels, and representing varied socioeconomic classes. Six classes (representing grades one through six) were used within the school. These classes were selected by the principal to include teachers with experience and those that were willing to participate in a research study. The six teachers were female.

A total of 178 pupils were used in this investigation. There were 98 boys and 80 girls. On the Lorge-Thorndike Intelligence Test mean intelligence quotient of 101.78 was obtained. The range of scores extended from a high of 135 to a low of 69. The standard deviation of the entire population was 13.37. To establish the silent reading achievement of the subjects, Gates Primary Reading Test, Form 1, Gates Advanced Primary Test, Form 1, and The Gates Reading Survey, Form 1, were administered. The mean reading score of the entire population was 4.3, with scores ranging from 1.5 to 10.2. The standard deviation was 2.04. The Minnesota Scale for Paternal Occupation also revealed the sample population of this investigation to be in the average category.

An informal reading inventory and a cloze test were constructed for use in the study. The material used for content in both instruments was selected from the same basal reading series (19).

Cloze test scoring

In scoring the cloze test a criteria of 50/30/20 was used. The independent reading level was the highest level at which the pupil supplied 50 per cent or more correct responses. If this criterion was not met on the easiest reading passage, an independent level of .5 was assigned. The instructional level was defined as the highest level at which the student had 30 percent or more correct responses. If this criterion was not met, an instructional level of 1.0 was assigned. The frustration level was designated as the first level on the passages considered more difficult than the established instructional level at which the student obtained less than 20 percent correct responses. When the pupil completed the instrument and this percentage was not met on the most difficult passage, a frustration level of 9.8 was assigned.

This assigned criteria of 50/30/20 was arbitrarily set by the investigator after visually examining scores students obtained on a cloze test.

Informal reading inventory scoring

The independent level of reading for the informal reading inventory was determined from the test scores by correct word recognition of 99 percent or better and 90 percent comprehension as reflected by answers to questions on the passages.

The instructional level was determined by correct word recognition of at least 95 percent and at least 75 percent comprehension. The frustration level of reading was assigned to those levels where scores fell below 95 percent correct word recognition or below 75 percent comprehension.

If a child reached an instructional reading level according to the established criteria, then on the following passage his reading scores were such as to place him at the independent reading level, and on a subsequent passage the instructional reading level was attained again, the highest level at which the child met the established criteria was used. If the frustration reading level was established at 1.4, the lowest reading level attainable, then the instructional reading level of 1.0 was assigned, and the independent reading level was designated at .5.

All testing was completed in a six weeks period, by a team of three doctoral students (Clara Kirby, Delbert Patty, and Peggy Ransom).

Testing significance

Readability scores of the cloze test utilizing 50/30/20 were correlated with readability grade level scores of the informal reading inventory to test for significance. Comparison between the two instrument scores was obtained by using the Pearson Product-Moment Correlation measurement and the .01 level of confidence was used as the criterion for significance.

Findings

1. The independent, instructional, and frustration reading levels derived by use of the cloze test correlated with the informal reading inventory at the .01 level of confidence for the total population in grades one through six.

2. With first grade pupils the relationship between cloze test and the in-

TABLE 1

CORRELATION BETWEEN THE CLOZE TEST SCORES AND THE INFORMAL READING INVENTORY FOR THE TOTAL POPULATION GRADES ONE THROUGH SIX (N = 178)

Reading Level 50/30/20 Criteria	Correlation	Standard Error	t	Level of Significance
Independent	.4982	.0565	7.6230	.01
Instructional	.8355	.0226	20.1750	.01
Frustration	.8112	.0256	18.4066	.01

formal reading inventory at the independent, instructional, and frustration reading levels was found to be not statistically significant at the .01 level of confidence, but at the .03 level of confidence the instructional and frustration reading levels were significant.

3. The instructional and frustration reading levels were correlated significantly at the .01 level of confidence from grades two through six, when comparing cloze test and the informal reading inventory.

4. Only at the fourth grade were the pupils' scores on the independent reading level, using the 50/30/20 cloze test criteria, significantly correlated at the .01 level.

5. For the boys, the levels derived from the cloze test, both sets of criteria, and the informal reading inventory scores correlation were significant at the .01 level, at the independent, instructional, and frustration reading levels.

6. Levels derived for the girls' scores for the independent, instructional and frustration reading levels between the cloze test and the informal reading inventory showed correlation at the .01 confidence level.

Conclusions

The correlations between the cloze test scores and the informal reading inventory scores at the instructional and frustration reading levels, grades two through six, were statistically significant. This relationship indicated that a cloze test could aid the teacher in determining the appropriate instructional reading level for children in a classroom for these grades when administered at the beginning of the school year. The cloze test also would indicate the level of material which would be frustrating for children to read in these classes.

Only at the fourth grade were the scores of the pupils predicted at the .01 level of confidence for the independent level of reading. Whether or not independent reading levels can be determined from a cloze test remains doubtful from the results of this investigation.

In the first grade the scores on the two tests were not related at a statistically significant level. A higher relationship might have occurred had the testing been administered nearer the end of the school year.

Cloze testing can be administered, simultaneously, to an entire class, and thereby save time. The average length of time required for administering the cloze test to a group was 40 minutes. This procedure is easily administered and interpreted by qualified teachers who have not had special training in test administration.

Recommendations

It is recommended that cloze tests be utilized in classrooms by teachers and the results subsequently checked against teachers' estimations of the children's level of reading. A documented study of this type, using a significantly large population, should prove valuable.

The cloze test 50/30/20 criteria used in this investigation should be used in further studies, as well as other proportions which may prove to determine more accurately the independent, instructional, and frustration reading levels for pupils.

A comparison of cloze test scores with standardized reading test scores could further establish bases for the future expanded use of the cloze procedure.

It is recommended that cloze testing be administered early in the school year in grades two through six as a tool to aid the teacher in estimating reading levels of pupils and determining appropriate materials for instruction.

An analysis of the types of responses which children supply in a cloze test situation could reflect patterns of speech which children use at various ages.

Since this study represents one of the early exploratory investigations utilizing the cloze test technique to identify discreet reading levels, further basic research in this area is recommended.

REFERENCES

1. Johnson, Marjorie S. "Identifying Individual Needs in the Classroom." *That All May Learn to Read*, 8-12. Roy A. Kress, editor. Annual Reading Conference, No. 1, Syracuse University, 1960.
2. Durrell, Donald D. *Improving Reading Instruction.* New York: Harcourt, Brace and World, Inc., 1956.
3. Bond, Guy L., and Eva Bond Wagner. *Teaching The Child to Read.* Third Edition. New York: The Macmillan Company, 1960.
4. Austin, Mary C., Coleman Morrison, and others. *The First R: The Harvard Report on Reading in Elementary Schools.* New York: The Macmillan Company, 1963.
5. Betts, Emmett A. "Reading Problems at the Intermediate Grade Level." *Education, 40* (March 1951), 737-746.
6. Sartain, Harry W. "Individualized Reading—An Evaluation," in Donald L. Cleland (Ed.), *New Dimensions in Reading,* 55-60. Nineteenth Annual Conference and Course on Reading, University of Pittsburgh, 1963.
7. Killgallon, Patsy A. "A Study of Relationships Among Certain Pupils" Adjustment in Language Situations," unpublished doctoral dissertation, Pennsylvania State University, 1942.
8. Sipay, Edward R. "A Comparison of Standardized Reading Achievement Test Scores and Functional Reading Levels," unpublished doctoral dissertation, University of Connecticut, 1961.
9. McCracken, Robert A. "Standardized Reading Tests and Informal Reading Inventories." *Education, 82* (Feb. 1962), 366-367.
10. Williams, Joan L. "A Comparison of Standardized Reading Test Scores and Informal Reading Inventory Scores," unpublished doctoral dissertation, Southern Illinois University, 1962.
11. Davis, Sister M. Catherine Elizabeth, R.S.M. "The Relative Effectiveness of Certain Evaluative Criteria for Determining Reading Levels," unpublished doctoral dissertation, Temple University, 1964.
12. McCracken, Robert A. "The Development and Validation of the Standard Reading Inventory for the Individual Appraisal of Reading and Performance in Grades One Through Six," unpublished doctoral dissertation, Syracuse University, 1963.
13. Taylor, Wilson L. "Application of 'Cloze' and Entropy Measures to the Study of Contextual Constraint in Samples of Continuous Prose," unpublished doctoral dissertation, University of Illinois, 1954.
14. Taylor, Wilson L. "Cloze Readability Scores as Indices of Individual Differences in Comprehension and Aptitude." *Journal of Applied Psychology, 41* (Feb. 1957), 19-26.
15. Rankin, Earl F. "Uses of the Cloze Procedure in the Reading Clinic," in J. Allen Figurel, (Ed.), *Reading in a Changing Society,* International Reading Association Conference Proceedings, Volume 4, 228-232. New York: Scholastic Magazines, 1959.
16. Bormuth, John R. "Cloze Tests As Measures of Readability and Comprehension Ability," unpublished doctoral dissertation, Indiana University, 1962.
17. Ruddell, Robert B. "An Investigation of the Effect of the Similarity of Oral and Written Patterns of Language Structure on Reading Comprehension," unpublished doctoral dissertation, Indiana University, 1963.
18. Gallant, Ruth M. "An Investigation of the Use of Cloze Tests as a Measure of Readability of Materials for the Primary Grades," unpublished doctoral dissertation, Indiana University, 1964.
19. Betts, Emmett A., Carolyn Welch, *et al. Betts Basic Readers, The Language Arts Series,* Third Edition. New York: American Book Company, 1963.

Implications for Further Research and Practice*

Emery P. Bliesmer
The Pennsylvania State University

ALTHOUGH SOME ATTEMPT to impose commonality among the papers presented here was made when this section was being planned, the topics of the papers vary considerably. At the time this presentation was being prepared, there were available only papers with rather (in some cases, exceedingly) limited information concerning these studies. It is not my purpose to impose further commonality, or to present a broad review of research for each of the areas treated, or even to present a critical analysis of the studies. Rather, I shall present some observations noted and implications seen as I examined and studied the information presented in the papers.

While all of the six readiness programs involved in Singer, Balow, and Dahms' study reportedly resulted in "successful reading readiness develop-

---

* Based on the four preceding research reports.

ment" of the kindergarten pupils, readiness for the sake of readiness obviously was not the goal of the programs. As was seemingly recognized by the investigators, perhaps one of the most significant aspects of the study concerned plans for the follow-up study to determine long range effects of the various programs. This perhaps should be a big part of any readiness program study.

While the importance and necessity of a reading readiness program has been assumed by many in the field of reading for some time, and this assumption has received some support from reported findings in studies, such as those reported some years ago by Baker (1) and by Bradley (2), among others, there have also been in recent years some negative reactions to the idea of reading readiness programs, especially ones entailing a time of some considerable length. Also, some of the newer or more recently developed reading programs for which some success has been reported, such as those published by Houghton Mifflin, Lippincott, Open Court, and Singer, involve or entail relatively little if any, time for formal readiness programs or periods. This suggests or implies the need for further study and analysis of whether formal or other types of readiness programs are necessary for all, for the great majority, or for only a few (if any) beginners. What traits or characteristics of children determine the length of a readiness program which might be needed to best insure later success in reading? To what extent is the intensity and type of readiness program needed a function of the particular beginning reading approach used?

Children were exposed to more formal reading instruction while still in kindergarten in only one of the six programs, although a considerable portion in each of the programs had reportedly gained rather favorable "readiness" status. The reported finding that approximately two-thirds of the children in the various programs had attained "very high" readiness status

by March, and over 90 percent had acquired this status by June, suggests that formal reading instruction programs might well have been implemented in all of the kindergarten programs instead of in only one. What would be or have been the effects of beginning formal reading instruction before the end of the kindergarten year with the "ready" groups in each of the other programs also? What would be the relative advantages or disadvantages of delaying or beginning reading at the kindergarten level in the various programs?

It was noted also that the kindergarten teachers each "had strong commitments to their type of readiness programs." This has often been posited as a factor which influences results. Furthermore, this is also often presented more as a negative criticism concerning studies, or the outcome in studies, than as a favorable one, as if it were wrong for strong commitment to obtain among teachers with respect to programs they are pursuing. There would appear to be a need for more definitive study or research of the influence of strength of commitments to programs being pursued on the relative success of various programs. It would also appear to be worthwhile to investigate possible procedures for promoting or producing strong commitment to particular programs.

Since Taylor's study (6) approximately a dozen years ago, considerable and increasing interest has been shown in various possibilities for use of the cloze procedure. Ransom's efforts would appear to offer another promising area.

Ransom stated that the two main means of drtermining a child's "instructional level" are "standardized tests" and the "informal reading inventory" procedure. She then pointed out that reading achievement test scores have often been considered to be "overestimates." Are reading achievement scores really "overestimates," as Ransom and others have suggested, or do they represent "frustration levels" rather than "instructional levels"?

What about the often advocated and relatively widespread practice of subtracting a year from a recent general reading achievement score and using this score as an estimate of "instructional level"? Over the past twelve to fifteen years, the writer has been directly involved in the relatively detailed diagnostic testing of several thousand elementary and secondary level students and a number of adults with reading problems. The nature of his direct role in the testing has made it possible for him to make informal comparisons of estimates of instructional level ("comfortable level") obtained by use of an informal reading inventory procedure with estimates obtained by subtracting a year from the general reading achievement score obtained at that time also. He has been impressed with how often the two estimates seem to jibe fairly well. The seeming effectiveness of applying this simple subtraction procedure in remedial programs and clinical practicum work, when it is necessary or highly desirable to select appropriate instructional materials before more detailed and further diagnosing and other testing is sometimes possible, has also been relatively impressive.

Part of the concern for finding an appropriate instructional level stems from the assumption or belief that a child can improve more readily if the instructional material used with him is easy rather than if the material is difficult and frustrating. There would appear to be some need for further checking on this assumption. One of the writer's former students has been gathering data for the past year which should have some bearing on this assumption. Pupils in a number of fourth and sixth grade reading classes practiced daily, for a period of six weeks, with reading materials of difficulty levels either a year above, a year below, or at their reading achievement test levels. Reports of preliminary analyses of data gathered, while rather meager and somewhat contradictory, support the need for further checking

in this area and also suggest initial reading level as playing a role.

Ransom has defined instructional level as "materials which are challenging yet not frustrating." There has tended to be some inconsistency with regard to what is meant by "instructional level" in a number of the studies reported in the literature of the past. Ransom's criteria for "instructional" and "independent" levels (50 percent or better and 30 percent or better comprehension, respectively) seem somewhat low in view of criteria used with informal reading inventories. With respect to her informal reading inventory, Ransom's criteria for independent and instructional levels seem rather high with respect to word recognition (99 percent and 95 percent, respectively). There is posed the question of whether we have real justification for these or other criteria. Further and more definitive research with respect to this matter seems called for. The high criteria of 99 percent word recognition and 95 percent comprehension might explain the relatively lower correlation (.50) obtained by Ransom between cloze test scores and informal reading inventory estimates of independent reading level. Relatively higher correlations (.84 and .81) were obtained with respect to instructional and frustrational levels, where the criteria were somewhat lower.

There has also occurred the question of what would happen if the criteria for the cloze tests for various types of levels (independent, instructional, and frustration) were adjusted or varied. Might this result in higher relationships between cloze estimates and IRI estimates?

What might be interpreted as a caution should also be proffered here. A relationship (correlation) between IRI level estimates and cloze level estimates does not necessarily mean that the scores can be interchanged. Relative interchanges of scores would be valid or justified only if the differences between means were also not significant. Data concerning this aspect were not provided in the information available to the writer at the time of preparation of this paper. Perhaps this is an area which might be further explored.

The several different ways of checking word recognition used by Leibert in his study (recall of words presented in isolation, selection of one of four given words to go with a picture, and marking one of four given words pronounced by an examiner) and findings of differences among scores obtained by the three methods highlights the importance of checking word mastery, especially sight vocabulary mastery, in several ways and realizing that different "levels" of mastery are being measured, in a sense. This may also explain, in part, why some pupils at primary levels, especially first and second grade levels, seem to know words at one time but do not know them at another time.

The finding that the three types of word recognition testing produced different scores may also account for differences in scores obtained by elementary school children on different tests. This further suggests that teachers will need to examine and know what kind of testing is involved in word recognition tests before attempting to compare scores obtained on different tests.

Procedures used and findings obtained with respect to word recognition suggest a need for checking and having pupils practice comprehension skills also. On some tests, the examinee is permitted to look back to find answers to comprehension questions; on others he is forced to use his recall skill, without looking back. The latter would appear to pose a more difficult task for readers. There are implications for classroom or teaching practice here also. While tests of comprehension in which the reader is permitted to look back are a type often found in tests, this would appear to be a simpler kind of task than answering without being able to refer back to the context of a selection. However, the former type of task is not always found involved or employed in reading practice activity. While it is perhaps assumed that most readers can readily do this kind of task, the assumption (like many of those we employ in our teaching) is not always a safe one. Observation of remedial program and clinic practicum cases frequently reveals children who cannot find the right answer when permitted to look back in the materials. There have also been revealed children who frequently are able to answer given questions but who cannot identify the specific part or parts of context which provide the basis, either direct or indirect, for the answer.

Leibert's finding that it was possible for third grade pupils to answer all but three items on the Gates Advanced Paragraph Reading Test with only partial reading gives rise to further questions also. Does this necessarily affect scores or norms? Is it not likely that some of the examinees in the original norm or standardizing group might have answered a number of items by doing partial reading also? An attempt to study a number of pupils who actually do tests by doing only partial reading might yield rather interesting results. Work with retarded readers suggests that a considerable number of such readers have developed effective partial reading skills (perhaps as survival techniques). It seems somewhat common to find teachers judging materials as "too easy" for given retarded readers on the basis of finding that these readers are able to answer questions over the material fairly rapidly and successfully. Further checking will often reveal that questions posed can frequently be answered with a minimum amount of reading; when students are asked to read portions of the material aloud, and word recognition errors can thus be more definitely noted and determined, the estimate of "too easy" is frequently negated.

Leibert's study also offers a possible explanation for a seeming and puzzling contradiction in connection with informal reading inventory estimates and reading achievement test scores. As was indicated earlier, Ransom suggested (as have others before her) that standardized reading tests tend to produce overestimates of instructional level. While informal reading inventories are often prepared to be used, and are suggested to be used, with varying degrees of elaborateness, the actual instructional level estimate obtained is based essentially on a tally of word recognition errors. Leibert pointed out that lower word recognition scores would be expected on informal inventories than on the Gates Advanced Primary Reading Test because the former would require recall while the latter required a type of recognition, with the former (recall) being found more difficult by subjects in his study. This would perhaps explain why instructional levels estimated or obtained with informal reading inventories are rather consistently lower than achievement levels obtained with such standardized instruments as the Gates tests. This also may explain why sight word test scores, which are recall test scores, have frequently been found useful and successful for obtaining quick estimates of instructional levels. Leibert also found that pupils could read inaccurately to a point where the instructional level criterion was exceeded but would still be able to obtain correct answers to items, increasing differences between informal reading inventory estimates and Gates test scores. Leibert suggested that standardized test scores may actually reflect a maximum level, rather than an instructional level, especially for poor readers. This would support a suggestion or contention made earlier that achievement test scores represent frustration level rather than the more comfortable instructional level and the explanation for this seeming contradiction between informal reading inventory estimates and reading achievement test scores.

In the Livonia study, reported by Campbell, Huesner, and Slobodian, one of the emphases was on the study of the particular or peculiar set of conditions which operate on a local scene. The appropriateness for the Livonia school system, or the applicability or suitability of findings and aspects to the Livonia system only, was stressed throughout the report; generalizing or making of inferences beyond the local setting was done somewhat hesitantly and limitedly, and findings and conclusions were presented rather conditionally. In view of this and the relatively limited details available, it was rather difficult for the writer to draw further definite conclusions or to make further inferences. However, it appeared that five of the eight programs involved were used with some degree of success in the Livonia schools. These were the i.t.a. material and the programs published by Ginn, Lippincott, McGraw-Hill, and Scott, Foresman. The observation was made that school staff had judged the McGraw-Hill materials as somewhat difficult to employ, even though some degree of success was attained with the materials.

A somewhat similar observation has been made by others who have used and are familiar with the materials. It has been suggested that, if improvements can be made in the program to "get over the hump" at the start or in the initial phase of the program, the materials might enjoy even more success. A further observation presented by Slobodian and her colleagues was that previous experience with one of the materials indicated that one of the seemingly negative aspects in the first year (the "problem in paragraph meaning") tended to disappear by the end of the second grade. This further highlights the importance of extending studies whenever possible through second and third years. The investigators indicated that a second year is being devoted to their study. One wonders if perhaps the same teachers will follow their children into second grade, that is, in the classes involved in the second year. There is also the problem of keeping groups relatively intact in methods studies. This condition has usually been rather difficult to obtain. It is also difficult to carry on a study of methods with sufficiently frequent expert supervision (even when generally adequate supervisory staff is available in a system) and without considerable contamination from other and previous programs. Methods studies in the last two to three years, particularly, have also been even more difficult to carry out because of contamination from projects and programs, and a great influx of new and varied materials, prompted by Title I and other federally subsidized programs.

As was reported, materials utilized in the Livonia study were assigned by "essentially random" procedures, but among "teachers who were willing to volunteer for new reading materials." The "volunteers" aspect could perhaps have affected outcomes somewhat, as could have also the fact that, as was pointed out, some of the materials were ones with which some "previous familiarization had taken place before actual teaching began." This, of course, would be a positive, rather than a negative, factor with respect to conducting a program with maximum effectiveness with a given set of instructional materials. The influence of "volunteer" teachers in a methods study in which various programs or materials are being compared in terms of effectiveness, while often posited as being great, is, however, still in need of further study and clarification.

The "essentially random" procedures used for assignment of materials to the volunteer teachers was a rather unique feature of this study (when compared with most methods studies). This was also one of the several unique features of a methods study conducted and reported earlier by Bliesmer and Yarborough (3). Unlike the latter study, however, the Livonia study stressed comparison of company's or publishers' materials with one another rather than of basic procedures or methods involved in the various programs. The eight programs involved in the study included (as judged on the basis of the writer's familiarity with the eight programs) six synthetic programs (those which begin with the teaching of sounds rather than whole words initially) and only two analytic approaches (those which begin with the teaching of whole words first and smaller sound elements later).

It was suggested that two analytic programs (Ginn and Scott, Foresman) and one synthetic program (i.t.a.) worked most effectively with groups of low readiness status while with groups of high readiness status, two synthetic programs (i.t.a. and McGraw-Hill) and one analytic (Scott, Foresman) worked most effectively. The only program common to both high and low readiness groups in this instance was i.t.a.

It was also pointed out that the best level of written expression was attained in connection with four approaches (i.t.a., Lippincott, McGraw-Hill, and SRA). The four approaches involved may be classified as synthetic and/or linguistic. There would appear to be a need for further study to see how and to what extent there should be integration of writing with reading in beginning programs and just what the nature of such writing activity should be.

The finding of no significant sex differences with regard to reading achievement at the end of the first grade is, as the investigators pointed out, a highly unusual one and is one of the unique findings of the study. If, as the investigators suggest as a possibility, the Livonia first grade teachers really are able to take into account differences between boys and girls sufficiently to avoid the usual significant sex differences in reading achievement, information concerning their procedures and adaptations would perhaps be one of the major contributions made over a period of years to the field of reading instruction.

REFERENCES

1. Baker, Emily V. "Reading Readiness Is Important," *Elementary English,* 32 (January, 1955), 17-23.
2. Bradley, Beatrice V. "An Experimental Study of the Reading Readiness Approach to Reading," *Elementary School Journal,* 56 (February, 1956), 262-267.

3. Bliesmer, E. P., and Betty H. Yarborough. "A Comparison of Ten Different Beginning Reading Programs in First Grade," *Phi Delta Kappan,* 46 (June, 1965), 500-504.
4. Durkin, Dolores. *Children Who Read Early.* New York: Teachers College Press, 1966.
5. McKee, P., J. E. Brzeinski, and M. Lucile Harrison. *The Effectiveness of Teaching Reading in Kindergarten,* (Cooperative Research Project No. 5-0371). Denver, Colorado: Denver Public Schools and Colorado State Department of Education, 1966.
6. Taylor, Wilson L. "Application of 'Cloze' and Entropy Measures to the Use of Contextual Restraint in Samples of Continuous Prose," unpublished doctoral dissertation, University of Illinois, 1954.

New Data on Readability

John R. Bormuth
University of Minnesota

READING AND LANGUAGE SPECIALISTS are avid students of readability research, for this research attempts to discover what makes language easy or difficult to understand. Readability researchers study the correlations between various features of language and the difficulty children have in understanding language. This provides the specialists with the information they need to tailor instructional materials to fit the reading abilities of their students. It also provides them with readability formulas by which they can determine if commercially prepared materials are suitable for their students. Finally, by studying how the many features of language influence comprehension, readability research provides insights into the nature of the comprehension process itself.

The last few years have seen rapid and somewhat startling developments in readability research. For example, the readability formulas available only three years ago could, at best, predict only 25 to 50 percent of the variation we observe in the difficulties of instructional materials. Today, we have not one but two prototype formulas, which are able to predict 85 to 95 percent of the variation. This represents a very high level of precision and an improvement of from 35 to 75 percent over the validities of older readability formulas. The purpose of this paper is to describe some of the results of this research and the efforts currently being made to forge our newly gained knowledge into practical educational tools.

Among the most important events leading up to the present developments was the publication of two books summarizing the readability research done up to that time. One was by Chall (1958) and the other by Klare (1963). From these books it became clear that the future readability research had to concentrate on three problems. First, a more reliable method would have to be developed for measuring the difficulty children have in understanding materials. Second, researchers would have to learn to measure and describe the linguistic features of materials that are really important in affecting comprehension. Third, investigators would have to analyze their data in far more detail than they had up to that time. What follows is an account of what resulted when efforts were made to attack each of these problems.

Measurement of comprehension difficulty

Problem. Until recently, investigators used multiple choice tests to determine the comprehension difficulties of materials. They made a test over each passage they were studying, tested the students after they had read each passage, and then found the mean percentage of questions answered correctly. The test means represented the difficulties of the passages. This method presented two problems. First, because the test was itself a reading task, the investigator was never quite certain whether he was measuring the difficulty of the passage or just the difficulty of the test questions. Second, these tests could tell him nothing about how difficult each word, phrase, or sentence in the passage was.

Construction of cloze tests. Shortly before Chall and Klare published their books, Taylor (1953) reported his first work with the cloze procedure. The cloze readability procedure can be used to make tests from any verbal instructional material. To do so, the investigator selects the passage he wishes to study, deletes every fifth word, and replaces the deleted words with underlined blank spaces of a standard length. The test is given to children who have not previously read the passage, and they are instructed to write in each blank the word they think was deleted. Their responses are scored correct when they exactly match the words deleted, except that misspellings are disregarded.

Advantages. Cloze readability procedure does not confuse the measurement of passage difficulty by injecting an extraneous reading task into the process. It also has the added advantage that investigators could measure the difficulty of every word, phrase, or sentence in a passage.

Research. The cloze readability procedure immediately drew the attention of readability researchers who set about studying cloze tests to see if they were valid and reliable measures of the comprehension difficulties of passages. This research has become far too extensive to review here. Bormuth (1967) and Rankin (1964) have each published detailed analyses of this research. In general, the research showed that cloze readability tests are highly valid and highly reliable measures of the comprehension abilities of students and of the comprehension difficulties of materials.

Description and measurement of language

Early researchers felt a need to make their formulas so simple they could be used even by clerks having little technical knowledge of language. For example, to determine the complexity of a word, the clerk either counted its syllables or looked it up to see if it was on a list of words thought to be easy. To determine the grammatical complexity of a sentence, the clerk had only to count the number of

words, and sometimes prepositions, in the sentence. While it was, at that time, important for formulas to be simple, the old formulas vastly oversimplified the rich array of language features that influenced its comprehension difficulty. The oversimplification also contributed to the fact that the old formulas were inaccurate.

Vocabulary complexity

Present investigators are probing more deeply into the question of what makes a word difficult to understand. It is not enough to say that the words on some list have been shown to be easier to understand, for this leaves us still asking which of a word's many meanings do children understand and why those words are easier for students. Nor is it practical to test all words directly on children, especially when we consider that most words have several meanings. What follows is a discussion of some of the features currently being investigated.

Word length. Children have always thought of long words as hard and short words as easy, and researchers have recently rediscovered this fact and begun investigating word length as a variable. Coleman (1961) found that a word's difficulty has a correlation of -.90 with both the number of letters and the number of syllables in the words. Bormuth (1966) found correlations of -.76 and -.68, respectively, for the same measures.

Morphological complexity. A word is often a complex structure which may be analyzable into a stem and a series of inflectional, derivational, and lexical affixes. It seems that this is an important source of difficulty in understanding words. Coleman (1961) found that word difficulty had a correlation of -.88 with the number of affixes and stems into which a word could be analyzed and a correlation of the same size with the number of inflectional morphemes.

Abstractness. Although there are almost as many meanings of the word abstractness as there are people who use it, nearly everyone agrees that, whatever it is, it has an influence on the difficulty of a word. Coleman (1966) devised a definition which permitted him to count reliably the number of nouns that referred to internal mental states and found that this number had a correlation of -.78 with passage difficulty.

Frequency. It has long been known that the frequency with which a word is used has some influence on the difficulty people have in understanding it. But frequency was thought to be a weak variable since Lorge (1949) had found only a correlation of .51 between it and difficulty. More recently, Bormuth (1966) has shown that frequency and difficulty have a curvilinear relationship and that, when this fact is taken into account, they have a correlation of .66. Klare (1967) has now taken a position that the frequency of a word may directly reflect most of the other characteristics of the word.

Grammatical complexity

The degree of intricacy of the grammatical relationships between the parts of a sentence has always been considered an important source of the difficulty in understanding the sentence. Until recently, the chief means of assessing grammatical complexity consisted of counting the number of words in sentences.

Two major objections can be raised in considering sentence length as the sole factor affecting grammatical complexity. First, it forces us to accept the dubious proposition that all sentences containing the same number of words possess the same degree of complexity. Thus, we are asked to believe that the sentence, *The man saw the boy who found the penny which was lost,* has the same degree of complexity as, *The penny which the boy whom the man saw found was lost.* Second, the number of words in a sentence does not measure a natural unit of language. We cannot simply add or chop off a few words to make the sentence more or less complex.

The grammatical complexity of a sentence actually results from the grammatical structure of the sentence. Consequently, modern researchers are investigating measures of grammatical complexity based on the grammatical structures of sentences. This approach is given firm support by the experiments performed by Martin and Roberts (1966) and Johnson (1966a, 1966b) which demonstrate that people utilize the phrase structure of sentences as they process the sentences.

Syntactic depth. Yngve (1960) developed a measure of syntactic complexity which obtains the number of grammatical facts a reader must temporarily hold in his memory as he reads a sentence. Presumably, the more grammatical facts the reader must remember as he reads a sentence, the more likely he is to forget one of those facts and the more likely he is to fail to comprehend some aspect of the sentence. Bormuth (1964) and Martin (1966) have each shown that people's responses to sentences are closely related to the depth measures of the sentences. Bormuth (1966) found a correlation of -.55 between depth and passage difficulty. Further, he found (1963) that the effects produced by depth were independent of those produced by sentence length.

Modifier distance. A variation on the depth measure was developed by Bormuth (1967) and is being investigated by him and by Coleman and Aquino (1967). This variable measures the number of words occurring between a word or phrase it modifies on the theory that the longer a grammatical fact is held in memory, the more likely it is that it will be forgotten. Preliminary results indicate that there is a correlation of -.80 to -.90 between this feature and passage difficulty.

Transformational complexity. A sentence such as *The little boy ran* may be represented as resulting from a transformation which embedded the kernel sentence *The boy was little,* into the kernel sentence, *The boy ran.* Chomsky (1965) has argued that to interpret a sentence people must transform a sentence back into its kernel sentences.

An interesting aspect of the transformation analysis is the fact that it can be used to measure what early researchers referred to subjectively as being the idea density of materials. Coleman (1966) found that the number of nominalized verb and nominalized adjective transformations had correlations of -.76 and -.57, respectively, with passage difficulty. Many parts of speech represent transformations, also. Bormuth (1966) found that counts of the various parts of speech had correlations as high as .81 with passage difficulty. His present studies are analyzing the effects associated with each of the transformations found in English.

Contextual variables

Modern researchers are looking beyond the word and the sentence to find the features of language that operate over longer segments of text to influence comprehension. Rosenberg (1966) found indications that passages containing words which people tend to associate with each other are easier to recall. Coleman and Aquino (1967) are finding that anaphoric analyses yield variables that predict passage difficulty. Anaphora are repeated references to a concept in a passage. The use of anaphora indicates the extent to which a passage deals in depth with a single topic. Since the work in this area is only beginning, it is still too early to predict its outcomes. But it seems certain that gains in this area will have great value in increasing our ability to predict and control passage difficulty.

Readability formulas

Early investigators had to defer the investigation of many important problems until research in other disciplines had made tools available for studying those problems. As may be seen from the preceding discussion, linguistic research provided readability researchers with new and powerful tools for analyzing language. Similarly, research tools became available for studying the problems involved in designing readability formulas. As a result, we have now learned enough to design much sounder readability formulas.

Readability and reading ability

A problem long plaguing researchers was the question of whether the features that influenced readability for poor readers also influenced the readability of materials for more able readers. If the same features of language influence readability for both and by the same amount, then a single and fairly simple formula can be used to predict readability for all students, regardless of their level of accomplishment in reading. But if different features influence difficulty for students of differing levels of reading achievement or if the same features influence difficulty by different amounts, then we must develop more complex and materially different kinds of formulas. Bormuth (1966) studied this problem and found that, regardless of the person's reading ability, the same features of language that caused difficulty for him caused the same amount of difficulty for others.

Shapes of the relationships

A second question was whether a given amount of increase in a feature of the language increased difficulty regardless of how much was already present. For example, is the difference in difficulty between two and three syllable words as great as the difference in difficulty between 7 and 8 syllable words? If not, the simple correlation techniques used by early researchers yield misleading results. Bormuth (1966) found the differences were not always the same. Figuratively speaking, adding another syllable to a one syllable word increases its difficulty far more than adding another syllable to a seven syllable word. The same is true of many other features. Hence, future readability formulas must include appropriate transformations of measurements taken of these features.

Form of the formulas

The traditional readability formulas

are presented in the form of what is called a multiple variable, linear equation. These equations have a characteristic that makes them unsuitable for use as readability prediction formulas. To use them, the researcher must assume that any correlation observed between two variables, say sentence length and word length, must always exist. This simply is not true of the language features used in most formulas. The result is that the old formulas yield misleading results whenever the correlation is anything other than the correlation the formulas assume. Most future readability formulas will probably be designed to provide a profile of the level of difficulty represented by each of the language features in a passage.

Summary

Readability researchers have made rapid strides in the past few years, increasing the accuracy of readability formulas by as much as 75 percent. The reason lies largely in the fact that researchers in several disciplines have developed research tools which have aided greatly the study of readability. Psychologists have developed the cloze procedure into an accurate and reliable method of measuring language difficulty. Linguists have developed descriptions of various features of language, and these descriptive devices have been further adapted into powerful new techniques for measuring the features of language that influence its comprehension difficulty. Finally, advances in our understanding of the mathematics used in our analyses have led to improved designs for readability formulas. The result of these advances is that, within a year or two, educators will have placed in their hands powerful new tools for determining if instructional materials are suitable for use with their students.

REFERENCES

1. Bormuth, J. R. *Implications of Cloze Procedure for the Evaluation of Instructional Programs.* Los Angeles, University of California Center for the Study of Evaluation of Instructional Programs, Occasional Report No. 3, 1967.

2. Bormuth, J. R. "Development of Readability Analyses." Project in Progress at the University of Minnesota, Sponsored by the U. S. Office of Education, 1967.

3. Bormuth, J. R. "Readability: A New Approach," *Reading Research Quarterly, 1* (1966), 79-132.

4. Chall, Jeanne S. *Readability: An Appraisal of Research and Application,* Ohio State University Educational Research Monograph No. 30, 1958.

5. Chomsky, N. *Aspects of the Theory of Syntax.* Cambridge, Mass.: M.I.T. Press, 1965.

6. Coleman, E. B. "Developing a Technology of Written Instruction: Some Determiners of Complexity of Prose," *Symposium on Verbal Learning Research and the Technology of Written Instruction,* unpublished manuscript, 1966.

7. Coleman, E. B., and M. R. Aquino. Communications Project. Project in Progress at the Southwest Regional Laboratory in Los Angeles, 1967.

8. Johnson, N. F. "The Influence of Associations between Elements of Structured Verbal Responses," *Journal of Verbal Learning and Verbal Behavior, 5* (1966), 361-368.

9. Johnson, N. F. "On the Relationship between Sentence Structure and the Latency in Generating the Sentence," *Journal of Verbal Learning and Verbal Behavior, 5* (1966), 369-374.

10. Klare, G. R. *The Measurement of Readability.* Ames, Iowa: Iowa State University Press, 1963.

11. Klare, G. R. "The Role of Word Frequency in Readability." 1967 (in press).

12. Lorge, I. "Readability Formulas—An Evaluation," *Elementary English, 36* (1949), 85-95.

13. Martin, E. and K. H. Roberts. "Grammatical Factors in Sentence Retention," *Journal of Verbal Learning and Verbal Behavior, 5* (1966), 211-218.

14. Rankin, E. F. "Cloze Procedure—A Survey of Research," *Yearbook of the Southwest Reading Conference, 14* (1965), 133-148.

15. Rosenberg, S. "Recall of Sentences as a Function of Syntactic and Associative Habit," *Journal of Verbal Learning and Verbal Behavior, 5* (1966), 392-396.

16. Taylor, W. L. "Cloze Procedure: A New Tool for Measuring Readability," *Journalism Quarterly, 30* (1953), 415-433.

17. Yngve, V. "A Model and an Hypothesis for Language Structure," *Proceedings of the American Philosophical Society, 104* (1960), 444-466.

Research on Readability and Reading Readiness

E. B. COLEMAN
Southwest Regional Laboratory,
Inglewood, California

WE SHALL DESCRIBE a prototype reading program and two research strategies that are being used to refine it. The general orientation of our research is this: by manipulating characteristics of prose that affect learnability, we are reducing the difficulty of elementary reading materials. We have constructed a progression of pre-preprimers beginning with one so simple that most five-year-olds can learn to read it after a single 20 minute lesson—a series versatile enough to teach simultaneously reading, spelling, phonics, and printing (see Figure 1). In one recent test, over half of the children in a Head Start class were able to take a book

Figure 1

home and read it after a single lesson. Other kindergarten classes have done considerably better.

In short, it is possible to redesign and extend the notion of reading readiness. It is possible to construct a long series of pre-preprimers beginning at such simple level and increasing in difficulty so gradually that a kindergartener can be taught all the concepts of reading readiness—and much, much more—by actually reading entertaining little books. If we teach a child the basic concepts underlying reading and give him books simple enough to read, much of his problem is solved. He begins reading to himself and teaching himself.

Refining the prototype by shaping the instructor

Any student of operant conditioning who has shaped a number of animals to press a bar is aware that his teaching ability increases rapidly. Sometimes it takes a student an hour to shape his first rat, but he usually shapes his second in half the time. As he teaches the animal, the animal is teaching him.

The same teaching process is taking place in most first grade classrooms. Children are teaching the teacher to teach reading. But reading is more complicated than bar pressing, and this teaching ability improves with disappointing slowness.

Part of the problem is complexity; reading is a complex hierarchy of subskills, and few teachers are masters of all of them. Part of the problem is time; it takes so long to teach a child to read that by the time the teacher finishes she has forgotten much of what she learned from the child. Part of the problem is record keeping; paper and pencil are inadequate to record the complexities of reading.

In the laboratory, the complexity problem can be partly solved by specialization. A team of psychologists teaches a child and each of them is responsible for a single subskill of the reading process. One teaches whole word memorization, one teaches the letter-sound relations, one teaches phonic blending, and so on. Each of them is also conducting controlled laboratory experiments in the same restricted area of reading and he tends to become a specialist in that area.

In the laboratory, the problems of time and record keeping can both be solved by videotape. Videotape provides an almost complete record; and furthermore, by cutting two-minute strips from each lesson, we can splice them together and compress a child's reading history into a manageable time span.

Videotape may provide an opportunity to extend analytical techniques to the study of complex skills that have heretofore been investigated by the grosser forms of phenomenology. Videotape may lead to a methodology that combines the strengths of the controlled experiment with those of phenomenology.

A second research strategy for refining the prototype collecting a data base of functional relations

There are characteristics of printed materials that increase or decrease their learnability. Let us call these characteristics stimulus-dimensions. We need to measure the effects of these stimulus-dimensions upon the various responses that make up reading; we need a vast collection of S-R functional relations.

Ever since the publication of *Über das Gedächtnis,* psychologists of verbal learning have been collecting such functional relations. But these relations have yet to be organized into a system that would help an education engineer manipulate characteristics of prose so as to increase its teaching efficiency. What is worse, most of these S-R relations are only generalizable to populations that are of slight interest to an education engineer. The majority of the experiments were performed upon college sophomores memorizing nonsense syllables. To be of use to an education engineer, the experiments must be replicated upon relevant learner populations and relevant language populations upon 5- and 6-year-olds learning reading responses to English words, letters, and phonemes.

To use another terminology, we need to calibrate linguistic units (letters, phonemes, words, phrases, etc.) as to learnability. Learnability would have to be defined in terms of the several subskills making up reading. Then we could select linguistic units for beginning materials so as to maximize learnability.

Selecting materials for an eclectic reading program

As recorded in the professional journals, the history of reading appears to be cyclic. A period of heavy emphasis upon phonics is followed (with apparently little motivation for the change) by a period of emphasis upon whole word, or even whole sentence, learning. The true history of reading, however, (the history of students and classroom teachers) is unrecorded. It is probable that throughout all these cycles the classroom teacher has gone her own way, following an eclectic system, blending together a hodgepodge of analytic phonics, synthetic phonics, look-and-say learning, context, and all the rest. As far as the classroom teacher is concerned, then, there is not too much harm in the academic community's overemphasis of any one teaching method.

The harm of overemphasizing one teaching method lies in the pernicious effect it exerts upon the selection of materials. Materials that are best suited for look-and-say learning are usually poorly suited for teaching phonics and spelling. (The following words—*Tom, ride, Betty, fast, Susan, Bunny, see, Flip, and, Mother, come, airplane, the, can, Pony, Father, apple, get, toys*—selected from one of the more popular basal readers, while excellent ones for look-and-say learning, are very poor for teaching phonics and spelling because of their irregularities). Words selected for a spelling or phonics approach are usually poor ones for look-and-say learning; many of them are too uncommon, and because they are usually generated from a minimum number of letters they are so similar that they are hard to discriminate from one another.

People who prepare reading materials may as well face a basic fact of life: most classroom teachers are going to follow an eclectic approach, probably for the simple reason that their experience proves it to be the most effective one. Therefore, to give them an effective set of materials, the requirements of all approaches must be considered simultaneously when selecting the words (and other linguistic units).

	ɛɛ	I	A	i	e	U
		I	A			
s	see		SAM sat sAd	sit Sis	set	SUN US
M	mee meet		AM MAN mAd MAt	miss	mess met	
s	sees			is		
t			At	it		
n	need		An Nan	in		Nut
th	thee		that	this	then them	
d			And	did	Ed	
w	wee			will with win	wet well	wus
f	feel feet		fAn fAt	fill fish if	fell	fuss fun
l				ill	let	
sh	shee sheet					shut
r			rAn rAt			run
h			hAt			

Table 1, a vowel-by-consonant matrix giving the first 64 words of our program, will serve to illustrate a few of the requirements that must be considered. Note that the words are common ones; selecting according to this characteristic facilitates look-and-say learning. Note that they are regularly spelled and are generated from a relatively small number of letters; selecting according to these characteristics facilitates the teaching of phonics and spelling. Note that they contain most of the common words used in the linguistic series so they permit that approach. They are supplemented, however, by a few function words misspelled in a transitional alphabet so they permit the idiomatic sentence structure of the i.t.a. Note that the number of shapes the child must learn to print has been reduced. Sooner or later the child will have to learn the lower case characters for A, M, N, and L, but there is little need to inflict that learning upon him at the beginning. His time would be better spent learning something more useful.

The most difficult subskills to teach are phonic analysis and phonic blending. The words of Table 1 were selected to facilitate teaching these two subskills. The consonants are arranged in their order of introduction. Note that the first ones are continuants (continuants are sounds that you can continue saying such as s-s-s, m-m-m, etc.). They can be pronounced in isolation and most of them have meaning in English. Note that, with the exception of the final *t,* Table 1 contains no stops (/t, b, p, d, k, g,/). One of the shortcomings of most phonic programs is their early introduction of the stops. The child inevitably learns such sounds as *puh* and *buh.*

The advantage of eliminating stops and beginning with continuants can be made apparent by considering a few examples. The isolated sounds *buh i guh* bear little resemblance to *big,* but the isolated sounds *s-s-s ee-ee* do not differ too much from *see.* Figure 2 illustrates one of the many techniques our program uses for teaching phonics

and spelling, techniques that would not be available if the first words had been *look* or *say* or *here.*

Other factors that would facilitate the teaching of phonic blending were considered in selecting words. Clearly it is easier to teach the child to blend two sounds into a word than to teach him to blend three or more. Perhaps some letter pairs are easier to blend than others. For example, in pronouncing the word *out,* there are great changes in the tongue, lips, and vocal cords as one progresses from the vowel to the consonant. The changes are much less for words such as *in, an, is, as, see,* and *she.* A set of words that involve minimal changes in progressing between vowel and consonant were selected to illustrate phonic blending.

Summary

This paper describes a beginning reading program and two research strategies that are being used to refine it. One strategy uses videotape and pushes the program through a continuous self-correcting cycle of test-refine-test-refine. The second strategy is to collect a data base—a matrix of S-R functions—that will allow the material for first grade communications skills to be engineered. Essentially, these S-R relations will calibrate linguistic units as to various kinds of learnability and thus allow an education engineer to order the low order tasks into a sequence that will facilitate the child's induction of the high order concepts such as phonics and spelling.

With this matrix of S-R relations, education could engineer a "new reading"—a new reading that might be as revolutionary as the new math. Our present program is still a long way from this. Even with its present lack of polish, however, placed on a preschool television program in the form of animated cartoons, it could teach most of the five-year-olds in the United States a rudimentary form of reading before they enter school.

Figure 2.

The Effect of a Thought-Directing Question on Reading Comprehension at Differing Levels of Difficulty

EUGENE B. GRANT
Northern Illinois University
and
MARCIA HALL
Hammond, Indiana, Public Schools

ALTHOUGH THE LITERATURE generally supports the practice of establishing a purpose before reading, comparatively few studies have been done in an attempt to support this practice. Some of the studies which have been conducted provide only partial support. Unquestionably, it is believed by most writers in the field that it is highly important for the reader to establish a purpose for reading before he begins to read. Educators have long insisted that proper motivation and mind-set are influential factors in learning. In expressing this point of view Schubert states, "Too many students are looking for nothing when they read, and end up with it. Seek and thou shalt find seems to be apropos" (6).

Nearly twenty years ago Gray declared, "Very little has been done to determine the patterns of guidance that are most effective in reading for different purposes" (2). Empirical evidence related to the establishment of purpose, and the most effective means of creating an appropriate mind-set among children, need to be compiled.

Observation and inquiry reveal that many college and university freshmen have never learned to establish a purpose for reading other than the shallow purpose of reading to see what is said. Most students of this type are merely compliant and read without seeking understanding. They realize that they are expected to do the reading, and in their way they do so. Their efforts, however, amount only to hoping that they understand, but do not constitute real effort to understand.

Shores (5) reported a study in *Elementary English* in which he found that pupils need help in recognizing the requirements of reading and need practice in adjusting their reading rates and techniques to their purposes. While Shores was primarily concerned with reading for different purposes, as Gray (2) had suggested, he also recommended carrying out empirical and analytical studies of what is involved in ability to read for various purposes.

In an earlier study, Holmes (3) used college students in an effort to determine the comprehension levels of reading when guided by questions, as opposed to careful reading and rereading without questions. The results of her study indicated that guiding questions significantly increased reading ability in both immediate and delayed recall of the answers to the questions used. There was no loss in delayed recall of answers to supplementary questions.

In a 1927 study Distad, studying a group of sixth grade pupils, concluded that, "If the purpose is to measure the immediate recall on the *entire content** of a selection after a single reading, it appears doubtful whether a wide variety of purposes for reading, directing attention to the content, can be justified in view of the relatively large amount of time required for reading" (1). He further concluded, however, that it is valuable to read with a problem or questions in mind. When *definite information** is desired, and when thus used, "directed types of reading are intrinsically worthwhile in that they develop habits of reading effectively for different purposes." Tinker and McCullough (7) define the efficient reader as one who comprehends just what is required by whatever purpose he has in reading, rather than the one who comprehends the most details.

In working with a group of college students, Letson (4) found that when the students were asked to read for complete mastery of a passage, alertness was engendered above normal. He said that such a mental set made the reader capable of reading with greater comprehension and speed.

*Italics provided by present writer.

His study seems to attest to the importance of the mental set or purposeful attitude upon the part of the reader. The problem in part, then, seems to be one of helping children establish a mental set before they begin their reading either in the content areas or in recreational reading.

Purpose of the study

The purpose of this study was to make an appraisal of the value of providing pupils with a broad general thought-directing question prior to reading at different levels of difficulty. In other words, what is the value of a broad thought-directing question to the above average reader, the average reader, and the below average reader? The above average reader was considered to be one who read more than a year above his grade placement; the average reader, one who read on a level within a range of one year below and one year above his grade placement; and the below average reader, one who read more than a year below his grade placement.

Design of the study

This experimental study involved 279 sixth grade pupils from ten classrooms in three different schools in Hammond, Indiana. The children in each classroom had been grouped heterogeneously. Through a random selection of classrooms, the pupils in half of the classrooms in each school became the subjects of the experimental group (Group A) while the children in the remaining classrooms formed the control group (Group B).

Both Group A and Group B pupils were further subdivided into above average readers, average readers, and below average readers on the basis of approximate reading levels. For this purpose the Reading Subtest of the Iowa Test of Basic Skills, Form 2, was used. In the few cases where the grade equivalent scores could not be obtained, the pupils were eliminated from consideration in the study. The

breakdown into the subgroups within groups A and B was accomplished by placing all pupils who read more than one year below grade level into subgroup I; including all pupils who had grade-equivalent scores of 5.1 or lower. Subgroup II pupils had grade-equivalent scores which ranged from 5.2 through 7.1; including pupils who were to read on a level approximating their grade placement. Subgroup III was made up of pupils reading well above the average, and who had earned a grade-equivalent score of 7.2 or above on the test.

As a result of grouping in this manner it was found that the mean grade equivalents for Group A (6.7) and Group B (6.6) were comparable. Since the mean scores showed that there was only one month difference between the average reading abilities of the members of the experimental group and the control group used in the study, it was thought that these pupils represented a good random sampling.

The pupils in both groups were asked to read the article entitled, "The Swiss Government," which was taken from the *Junior Scholastic Magazine*. The content of this article was judged to be appropriate for the average sixth grade pupil. Each of the various subgroups of Group A, the experimental group, was given a broad thought-directing question prior to reading the article. They were informed that they were to answer some questions after the reading. The broad question was, "In what ways is Switzerland's government like our own and in what ways is it different?" After the test, ten follow-up questions of the multiple-choice type were given. The children in Group B were told only that they would be asked to answer the questions after the reading.

The mean score on the multiple-choice test was obtained for each subgroup of Groups A and B. After making a comparison of the subgroup mean scores, the total scores for Groups A and B were compared.

Analysis of the data

In examining the data obtained from this study it was found that the mean of the scores on the test for the experimental group was six points higher than the mean of the scores for the control group. Examination of the mean scores from the three separate schools involved in the study showed a consistent pattern of increased comprehension for the pupils in the experimental group. The t-test was then applied in an attempt to ascertain whether or not the differences in the mean of the two groups was statistically significant. Upon the application of this test it was found that this difference was significant at a level exceeding the five percent level of confidence.

Examination of the data for subgroup I of Group A, the poorest readers, reveals that these pupils not only did not improve in comprehension when presented with the broad thought-directing question, but actually did not comprehend as well. The fact that these pupils were reading on the frustration level may well be of some particular significance in this instance.

A comparison of the data from subgroups II of both Groups A and B reveals that there was a mean difference of eleven points in favor of the experimental subgroup. These groups represent the average readers for whom sixth grade material is very likely on their instructional level. These two subgroups represented the largest of the population groups. When the t-test was applied to the eleven point difference in the mean performance, the results indicated a significant difference at the two percent level of confidence. This seems to attest to the value of the thought-directing question when material is at an average level of difficulty.

Analysis of the results of testing subgroups III, the above average readers, reveals that the difference between the mean performance of the experimental subgroup and the control subgroup was only three points, with the difference favoring the experimen-

tal group. This difference was not significant at the five percent level.

Since the subgroup III pupils were able to read more than a year above the level of difficulty of the material read, it is likely that this material was easy enough to be referred to as independent level material.

Summary and conclusions

An analysis of the results of the test seems to indicate that in general a broad thought-directing question before reading is of value as far as comprehension is concerned. But, as was shown by some of the earlier studies, there are some qualifying conditions. Apparently when pupils read on an easy level, a level some might describe as the independent or free-reading level, the thought-directing question is of very little value since these readers probably formulate their own purpose for reading. Perhaps the material is just so easy that the thought-directing question is superfluous.

For pupils who read material at or near their instructional level, a level at which some help may be needed (the teaching level), the thought-directing question seemed to be significantly valuable. Apparently the thought-directing question gave enough mind-set to enable the pupils to comprehend better. It was quite clear that this group attained better comprehension as a result of the question.

The pupils who read below the level of difficulty of the material to be read were not aided in comprehension by the provision of a thought-directing question. The broad question appeared to affect comprehension adversely. This finding is somewhat in line with earlier studies where a number of questions were used, rather than a single broad question. It should be remembered that these pupils probably were reading on the frustration level, and the question served only to add to their confusion.

In an attempt at a broad interpretation of the findings of this study, it seems that three discreet conclusions may be drawn, namely:

1. A broad thought-directing question may not contribute significantly toward better comprehension when the material is of a low level of difficulty for the particular reader.

2. In general, the broad thought-directing question is of value in comprehending material that is near the instructional level of difficulty for the reader.

3. When the material to be read is on the frustration level, a thought-directing question to give mind-set, is of no value.

REFERENCES

1. Distad, H. W. "A Study of The Reading Performance of Pupils Under Different Conditions on Different Types of Materials," *Journal of Educational Psychology, 18* (April 1927), 247-258.
2. Gray, William S. "Teaching of Reading," *Encyclopedia of Educational Research* (Third edition), 996-998. New York: The Macmillan Company, 1950.
3. Holmes, Eleanor. "Reading Guided By Question versus Careful Reading and Re-Reading Without Questions," *School Reviews, 39* (May 1931), 361-371.
4. Letson, Charles T. "Speed and Comprehension in Reading," *Journal of Educational Research, 52* (October 1958), 49-53.
5. Schubert, Delwyn G. "Helping Students Read to Remember," *The High School Journal, 41* (October 1947), 39-40.
6. Shores, J. Harlan. "Reading of Science for Two Separate Purposes as Perceived by Sixth Grade Students and Able Adult Readers," *Elementary English, 37* (November 1960), 461-468.
7. Tinker, Miles A., and Constance M. McCullough. *Teaching Elementary Reading.* New York: Appleton-Century-Crofts, Inc., 1962.

Effects of Free Reading on the Reading Achievement of Sixth Grade Pupils

HOYLE D. LAWSON
Tennessee Technological University

THE PRIMARY PURPOSE of this three-month study was to determine whether, in a given amount of time, some combination of free reading and basic reading skills instruction could be as effectively used as a program devoted primarily to instruction in the basic skills. A basic premise giving rise to this study—supported by the literature (*4, 5*)—was that children are aided in becoming improved readers by regularly reading books chosen by themselves. A strong case rests on the assumption that one more readily and permanently learns those skills which are realistically utilized and are perceived to be of immediate, personal value. This suggests that the teaching of reading skills should merge with the exercise of these skills in free reading.

All youngsters will not regularly read simply because books are accessible to them. The classroom teacher is ideally situated for providing the time, place, and books, so that children may daily read books of their own choice. Too, the effect on a child of seeing his classmates engaged in reading their personally selected books would likely be a strong incentive to act accordingly.

More specifically, this study was arranged to help determine whether a portion of the daily reading instruction program, in the sixth grade, could advantageously be devoted to the reading of freely selected books.

Procedure

In order to accomplish such an investigation, the experimental population was organized from twelve classrooms of sixth grade children in the Nashville, Tennessee, public school system. They were selected because they attended schools located in neighborhoods judged to be representative of this country's large, intermediate, socioeconomic class; the 1960 federal census provided primary evidence for determining nine socioeconomic similarities among the neighborhoods. Also, the sixth grade supervisor and the five principals deemed these schools to be similar in the effectiveness of their pursuit of the educational goals of the school system. The experimenter found the schools attractive and equipped with accessible, central libraries averaging from eight to ten books per child in each school.

In addition, the teachers were 1)

college graduates, 2) certified to teach at the elementary level, 3) experienced, and 4) subjectively appraised by their principals and supervisor as being better-than-average teachers.

Four methods of reading instruction were employed. Each method was used with students from three classrooms of sixth graders, with no two (different) methods being used in the same school. The four methods of instruction were utilized for twelve weeks. Each of the twelve classes had one assigned library period each week and the pupils were allowed to check out books from the library as needed. In each of the classrooms there was a weekly, thirty-minute, book-sharing period involving the entire class.

Gains in achievement were measured by the 1959 revision of the Metropolitan Achievement Tests, Intermediate Battery; form Am was administered for the pretest on February 4, 1964, form Bm for the post-test on May 4, 1964. By using two subtests, one for word knowledge, and one for reading, two separate criterion measures were obtained. In order to study the relative effectiveness of each of the methods at different levels of intelligence, the individuals under each method were identified by IQ scores.

To appraise the effects at different levels of intelligence, the data for each method were analyzed for three levels of IQ; 118 to 131, 97 to 117, and 72 to 96.

The conventional method

Instruction under the conventional method represented a rather strict adherence to the teacher's guide accompanying the basal reader series used with three or four groups in each room. Each group represented a different level of reading achievement, and used a basal reader which was graded at approximately the mean reading level of the given group. The basal readers for this method, and for the experimental A and experimental B methods, were from a series of developmental readers employing an "eclectic" (*1*) program including im-

provement in comprehension, and instruction in the use of phonetics (analytic), context clues, and structural word analysis. The three or four groups in each classroom under this method had forty-five minutes of systematic instruction each day, but were not allowed free reading time. The children in these three classrooms totaled 95. After 7 were lost due to lack of test results, 88 were included in the study. The findings pertinent to this group were as follows:

1. The gain in word knowledge achievement for this group was significantly less than that for either the experimental A or experimental B group, and was equal to that of the individualized group.

2. The gain in reading achievement for this group was significantly greater than that of either the individualized or experimental B group, and was equal to that of the experimental A group.

The individualized method

This method as described by Veatch (*6*) constituted a severe contrast to the more historically conventional method. Although the daily instruction period was for forty-five minutes also, instruction was primarily based on each individual child's personally selected book. Group instruction occurred for a short period as a teacher became aware that the needs of more than one pupil coincided. Under this method a teacher interviewed one child at a time, for instruction and in order to arrange appropriate reading improvement activities for the child. A greater amount of free reading was likely to have occurred under this method than under the other three methods described in this study. Systematic instruction for this method was minimized as compared to that of the other three methods. The children in these three classrooms totaled 91. After 7 were lost due to lack of test results, 84 were included in the study. The findings pertinent to this group were as follows:

1. The gain in word knowledge

achievement for this group was significantly less than that for either the experimental A or experimental B group, and was equal to that of the conventional group.

2. The gain in reading achievement for this group was significantly less than that for either the conventional or experimental A group, and was equal to that of the experimental B group.

3. This group experienced a loss in achievement for both word knowledge and reading.

The experimental A method

Instruction under this method ran for a period of 45 minutes each day. During the first 30 minutes of the daily period conventional instruction, as described for the conventional method, was provided; the remaining 15-minute portion was devoted daily to free reading. At this time the children read from any books they chose. In this situation there was systematic daily instruction, along with daily free reading. The children totaled 105 in these three rooms. After 18 were lost due to lack of test results, 87 remained. The findings pertinent to this group were as follows:

1. The gain in word knowledge achievement for this group was significantly greater than that for either the conventional or individualized group, but was less than that of the experimental B group.

2. The gain in reading achievement for this group was significantly greater than that for either the individualized or the experimental B group, and was equal to that of the conventional group.

The experimental B method

Instruction under the experimental B method was for a period of 45 minutes each day. During only the first 15 minutes of the daily period conventional instruction, as described for the conventional method, was provided, while the remaining 30-minute block was devoted to free reading. As in the experimental A method, the children at this time read from books personally chosen by them. Here also was systematic daily instruction, and daily free reading, but when compared with the experimental A method, having different proportions of the period devoted to instruction and to free reading. The children totaled 75 in these three rooms. After 5 were lost due to lack of test results, 70 remained. The findings pertinent to this group were as follows:

1. The gain in word knowledge achievement for this group was significantly greater than that for any of the other three groups.

2. The gain in reading achievement for this group was significantly less than that for either the conventional or experimental A group, and was equal to that of the individualized group.

Analysis of the data

Analysis of variance procedures with tests at the .05 level of significance, allowed the following observations to be made:

1. Taken as a group, the 329 children in the study made a significant gain in word knowledge and in reading, as measured by the achievement tests.

2. Considering each of the three levels of intelligence as a group, each higher level maintained significantly greater achievement in word knowledge and in reading, over each lower level.

3. There was no interaction between methods and intelligence levels for word knowledge or reading.

4. The rank order by methods for gain in word knowledge was experimental B, experimental A, conventional, and individualized.

5. The rank order by methods for gain in reading was conventional, experimental A, experimental B, and individualized.

Discussion and conclusions

For the four methods, greater gains in word knowledge seemed to be associated with more time spent in free reading. Greater gains in reading tended to go with more time spent in systematic instruction. The individualized method, having the most free reading but the least amount of systematic instruction for the entire class, actually showed a loss in word knowledge and in reading. The experimental A method, having devoted thirty minutes to conventional instruction and fifteen minutes to free reading each day, exhibited the best overall gain.

The findings seem to indicate that reading ability may be improved by the use of more than a single method of instruction. Methodically pursued free reading, when accompanied by systematic skills instruction, has been shown to improve pupils' achievement scores in word knowledge and in reading. This would tend to justify the inclusion of free reading in the daily program of reading instruction. Also, the data rather well support the necessity for providing each child with systematic reading skills instruction.

All of the teachers in the study, who utilized some type of free reading, were enthusiastic with regard to the apparent results. They reported that not only were many more books read, but the children had shown greater interest in reading.

There is general agreement that consistent and systematic reading instruction decreases with each succeeding grade level (2, 3). To be accepted by many teachers, a method of instruction must be practical and without unnecessary embellishments. It must work without overwork. The results of this and similar studies should help the intermediate teacher make better provisions for reading improvement. Certainly, an elementary teacher should not feel conscience-stricken when allowing children to freely read for pleasure during the school day.

Recommendations

1. Such a study as this might well be considered as a pilot effort, pointing toward similarly patterned projects of a longer term and involving more students.

2. Other, varied combinations of total instruction time and divisions of the time, between methodical skills instruction and daily free reading, might profitably be investigated.

3. Another variation of this study, which alternated each day's reading program between skills instruction and free reading, would seem to be worthwhile.

4. An interesting and valuable adjunct to further investigations of this nature would be a study of the more lasting effects of free reading on sixth graders' subsequent reading habits.

5. There should be a replication of this study at the fourth grade and fifth grade levels.

REFERENCES

1. Bond, Guy L. and Eva Bond Wagner. *Teaching the Child to Read.* New York: The Macmillan Company, 1960.
2. Heilman, Arthur W. *Principles and Practices of Teaching Reading.* Columbus, Ohio: Charles E. Merrill Books, Incorporated, 1961.
3. Hoyt, Jean S. "Fifty Seventh-Graders: A Comparison of their Reading Achievement in Grades One Through Seven," *Journal of Educational Research,* 53 (January 1960), 163-171.
4. McKim, Margaret G. *Guiding Growth in Reading.* New York: The Macmillan Company, 1955.
5. Russell, David H. *Children Learn to Read.* Boston: Ginn and Company, 1961.
6. Veatch, Jeannette. *Individualizing Your Reading Program.* New York: G. P. Putnam's Sons, 1959.

Studies on Reading Disabilities in the Elementary School

Eve Malmquist
National School for Educational Research, Linköping, Sweden

IN RECENT YEARS the leading specialists in reading have emphasized time and again that only very rarely can reading disabilities be ascribed to a single causal factor. Usually it is a question of a whole complex of factors which may be interrelated with each other and with reading disabilities. It is not always possible, however, to determine the relationship between cause and effect.

Factors related to reading disabilities

My own investigations in Sweden some years ago as regards factors related to reading disabilities in the first grade in the elementary school were rather extensive (3). A relatively large number of factors were studied in the same population and at the same test session. In addition to the more conventional methods of investigation (comparisons between different groups of readers with regard to one variable at a time and studies where each factor is considered separately in relation to reading ability) I studied several variables not only in isolation but also in interaction with other variables by the use of analysis of variance technique of higher order (multifactorial design).

I attempted to take into account the child's preschool development (birth, health, speech development, etc.), home background, social and economic status, the educational level of the parents, and other home conditions. Moreover, the respective teachers evaluated a number of personality factors for each pupil. Tests of vision, hearing, reading ability, visual perception, spelling ability, and intelligence were administered. In addition certain teacher and school variables were included in the studies.

Out of more than forty variables investigated the following factors were found to be most intimately related to reading disabilities in the first grade, and further to most clearly differentiate the group of poor readers from the group of good readers.

1. Intelligence, ability to concentrate, persistence, self-confidence, and emotional stability of the child.
2. Spelling ability, according to some spelling tests, and visual perception as measured by five visual perception tests.
3. Social status and educational level of the parents and reading interests in the home.
4. Teaching experience of the teacher as measured by number of years of service in the profession.

By using the case-analysis approach I have found that children with "special reading disabilities" (IQ above ninety according to the Terman-Merrill) deviated negatively, in a very marked manner, from the mean for the total population investigated, with regard to several other variables besides reading ability. Judging from my results, reading disabilities at first grade level are never isolated defects. In all the cases investigated they were found to exist together with deficiencies, disturbances, or unfavorable conditions in several other areas.

Do the poorest readers represent a uniform group with regard to the type of errors in oral reading?

It is often maintained in medical science that qualitative differences exist between the various types of errors in reading made by children who are "wordblind," and those made by children with "reading disabilities of some other type," and by normal readers (2, 1).

In my studies I was unable to find any facts in support of the medical hypothesis that among poor readers there exists a specific group which can be clearly differentiated and which suffers from a special form of disease; and moreover, that the qualitative character of the errors in reading made by this group differs from that of other groups of children with reading disabilities or even of normal readers. All conceivable types of errors in oral reading were found also among good readers, though to a much smaller extent. Our data demonstrated conclusively that the poorest readers were not differentiated from the others as a specific, sharply delimited group. On the contrary, we found a relatively smooth and continuous gradation from the poorest readers of the grade to the best. Thus on the distribution curve for the reading tests used, it was not possible to determine where the best of the poor readers ended and the worst of the medium readers began.

Operational definition of the concept reading disabilities

For purposes of practical education it may prove expedient to draw a line of demarkation through some point on the distribution curve for the reading test administered. The children who fall below this line may be termed children with reading disabilities or children suffering from dyslexia, etc. We should always be fully aware, however, that this delimitation is operationally defined and depends upon the purpose which the delimitation is intended to serve. For example, we might draw the boundary line through a certain point on the distribution curve because, in view of the school's resources, we think we are able to give just this number of children special teaching in reading or because we wish, for scientific purposes, to investigate a group of poor readers limited to a certain size.

Consequently, it is never a question of actual differences in essence, in kind, between the poor readers in the delimited group and the medium readers immediately above the line of intersection, but of differences only in degree.

Can the occurrence of reading disabilities be prevented? A six year study

The research results and practical experiences reached from this study have been the starting point for two further investigations. These concern the development of reading ability at the primary stage and were carried out at the National School for Educational Research in Sweden. Inasmuch as the purposes and the design of these two studies were practically the same and as they were both longitudinal in character, they might be considered as parts of only one investigation, extending over a time period of six years (1958-1964).

Purposes of the investigation

The main aims of this investigation have been the following:

1. To find an answer to the question, of whether it is possible to prevent the occurrence of special reading disabilities in grades 1-3 in the elementary school.
2. To study the prognostic value of school-maturity tests of a conventional type, as very commonly used in the Scandinavian countries, administered prior to the children's entering school before the first grade.
3. To construct and standardize further measuring instruments both for the diagnosis of children's reading and writing readiness before starting school and at the same time giving a satisfactory prediction of the reading and writing ability of children who have completed respectively the first, second, and third grades of the elementary school.

The theory behind the design of the studies follows. The occurrence of special reading disabilities is dependent upon a whole complex of factors which are intimately interrelated, and are frequently difficult to separate, one from the other. In the majority of cases of special reading disabilities there are good prospects of exerting an influence in a positive direction, and at times this may be done to a very considerable extent.

In our special remedial reading classes and in our reading clinics many teachers are performing excellent work, entailing considerable self-sacrifice, in attempting to help children with reading disabilities, and personality maladjustments which often are associated with these difficulties.

Ideally, it would naturally be preferable to forestall and to prevent the occurrence of the reading disabilities in the first instance. One of the conditions for an effective program to prevent reading disabilities would be the ability to diagnose, satisfactorily, even before the child begins school, his qualifications for the learning of reading.

Another necessary condition is, that

it should be made possible for teachers in their methodical planning of instruction, to take into consideration the various aspects of various stages of development of each pupil from his very first day at school. How well the teacher may use findings from diagnostic tests and how effectively he may develop a program based on these findings will naturally be influenced by factors such as the teacher's training and experience, the size and organization of the class, the nature of the educational material.

The following main hypothesis was advanced for our investigations: it is possible to decrease, markedly, the frequency of reading disability cases by a careful diagnosis of the child's reading readiness and general school readiness, and then, on the basis of these diagnostic findings, establish a teaching situation synthesizing ongoing diagnosis—treatment—and teaching for those children who could be expected to experience special reading and writing difficulties.

Pilot study

In order to test this hypothesis experimentally we first administered a pilot study, starting in 1958, with a population of first graders, which was followed up to grade 3 in 1961. Certain organizational and pedagogical arrangements were made.

The four parallel classes of grade 1 at the research school in the school year 1958-1959 were made equivalent as far as possible as regards number of pupils in the class, sex distribution, general intelligence, reading readiness, parents' social and economic status, and teacher-competence. Two classes were assigned to the experimental group at random and two to the control group.

In the population studied even eight grade-one classes for the other compulsory schools of Linköping and eight grade-one classes from rural districts in various parts of the province Östergötland were included.

The results of the school readiness tests could be expected to give only moderate prognostic value. Therefore supplementary testing of the pupils was carried out by using specially constructed reading and writing readiness tests. These tests aim to give an idea of the beginners' level as regards the ability of visual perception, auditive perception, phonetic analysis, sound synthesis, and vocabulary. Further on, the pupils' speech, memory span, motoric manipulation ability, vision and hearing were tested. By interviewing the parents of the beginners according to special rating scales and forms, certain information was obtained about the behavior and development of the children from birth to school start. Data of this kind were mostly not quantifiable but it was nevertheless assumed that they might be of some value for the prediction of the children's reading and writing development.

The children in the experimental group, as well as those in the control group, were given a battery of school readiness tests (may be considered to be a kind of intelligence test) as well as tests of their ability and knowledge in reading, writing, and arithmetic, before entering school, at the age of 7. The results of the studies of the beginners' attainments and proficiency in reading, writing, and arithmetic before the teaching of these subjects was begun at school, have been reported in a special volume (4). From the results of the used diagnostic instruments we anticipated that certain children would get reading disabilities, if no special auxiliary measures were taken.

From the very beginning these children were then given special help by a reading clinic teacher, in cooperation with the teacher in the classroom, if they were part of the experimental group, but not if they belonged to the control group.

The remedial teaching was given by a reading clinic teacher who had to take care of pupils with reading disabilities from all 12 classes at the primary stage within her total service. Out of her weekly service time she devoted 8 hours to children within the experimental group in grade one, 6 hours in grade two, and 5 hours in grade three.

The study was continued until the children had completed the third grade, in 1961.

From the results of the tests given at the end of the first, second, and third grades, we found that the experimental group had reached significantly better results on reading tests, as compared to the control group. The number of cases of reading disabilities, as to the operational definitions used, was much lower in the experimental group than in the control group.

The results from this experiment were evidently very promising. Judging from the experiences of this pilot study we can anticipate that this kind of approach might effectively contribute to the prevention of the occurrence of special reading and writing disabilities.

The main study

In order to test the results reached upon in the pilot study, we started, in 1961, a new study of the same character, and with about the same design, but on a larger scale.

In this study 11 cities with 41 classes and 938 pupils fulfilled the conditions put forward for the comparative study in the first grade. (Control group n = 466, Experimental group n = 472.)

Twelve classes were ruled out from the study during their second and third grade because the local school administrations did not wish to exclude control group pupils from receiving special remedial help as needed.

A total of 218 individual pupils moved to other schools or were absent from school during test sessions. Complete data for grades 1-3 are available for 9 cities with 29 classes and 454 pupils. (Control group n = 230, Experimental group n = 224.)

Each class was divided into two halves and made as equivalent as possible as regards age, number of pupils, sex, intelligence, and socioeconomic status of parents. The two half-classes

had the same teacher. Remedial teaching by a reading clinic teacher was given only to certain pupils belonging to that half of the class, which was randomly assigned to the experimental group, however, and not to pupils belonging to the other half of the class—the control group.

Statistical treatment of data

Raw scores on the different variables included in the investigation were transformed into standard scores (Z-values, according to the formula: $Z_i = (X_i - \overline{X})/S_x$).

Composite indexes have been calculated for various groups of variables by means of addition or subtraction of standard scores.

We have tested the differences between the experimental group (41 half-classes with 472 pupils) and the control group (41 half-classes with 466 pupils) by using analysis of covariance. The effect of possible remaining initial differences between the two matched groups would in this way be statistically eliminated.

We have also used a special method of covariance analysis not depending upon the assumption of common slope for group regression lines, "the matched regression estimates" method as described in Walker-Lev (6).

A series of multiple regression and correlation analyses, with the purpose of investigating the prognostic value of different predictors as regards the level of reading and writing ability in grades 1-3, have been made.

By means of these analyses it has been demonstrated that the number of the predicting instruments could be considerably reduced with an only negligible deterioration as regards prognostic value.

A group of three variables has been crystallized. Each one can be expected to contribute significantly to a good prognosis. First, the battery of reading readiness tests; second, one of the five visual perception tests (visual letter perception); and third, the battery of school maturity tests. Out of 30 criterion variables registered (10 variables at the end of each of grades 1, 2 and 3) we have calculated, with the use of transformation procedures earlier mentioned, composite indexes as regards the following three major groups of variables: reading accuracy, reading comprehension and spelling.

Results

1. *Prognostic values of the predictors used.* The school maturity tests used in this study have notably lower predicting values than the reading readiness tests. This observation applies to each of the three specially studied achievement variables: reading accuracy, reading comprehension and spelling.

Only as far as the prediction of reading comprehension is concerned the school maturity tests seem to be of some value.

Out of the different predictors studied the reading readiness variable has throughout given the highest prognostic values, regardless of which criterion variable was examined.

The simple pair correlations between reading readiness results and different criterion variables are between 0.48 and 0.55 in grade 1, between 0.41 and 0.51 in grade 2, and between 0.39 and 0.51 in grade 3.

Table 1 summarizes the findings as regards the prognostic values of the three predictors: visual letter perception, school maturity and reading readiness.

The squared multiple correlation coefficient (R^2) can be interpreted as a measure of the proportion of the total criterion variance, explained by variances of the three predictors. It is obvious that a substantial part of the criterion variance remains unexplained concerning all criterion variables.

The accuracy of prediction decreases with increasing grade level (1-3) as regards all types of criteria. Between grades 2 and 3, however, this decrease is rather small. The prediction of spelling is more accurate than the prediction of the two reading criteria with the exception as regards grade 1. The prediction of spelling also seems to be the most stable in the long run (there is only a small difference noted between R^2 for grade 1 (.306) and for grade 3 (.277). The table also shows the prognostic values of each predictor when used to predict performance in different criterion variables. Under all circumstances reading readiness is by far the most efficient predictor.

TABLE 1

The prognostic values of the three predictors, visual letter perception, school maturity, and reading readiness, when used to predict performance in different criterion variables.

| | | | | R^2—component due to predictor | | |
Grade	Criterion Type	R	R^2	Reading readiness (1)	School maturity (2)	Visual letter perc. (3)
1	Reading accuracy	.507	.257	.183	.043	.031
1	Reading compreh.	.622	.387	.226	.076	.085
1	Spelling	.553	.306	.251	.023	.032
2	Reading accuracy	.421	.177	.148	.077	.027
2	Reading compreh.	.457	.209	.124	.042	.043
2	Spelling	.529	.280	.223	.013	.044
3	Reading accuracy	.400	.160	.130	.006	.023
3	Reading compreh.	.433	.186	.121	.062	.003
3	Spelling	.527	.277	.237	.002	.038

Note: The squared multiple correlation coefficients (R^2) have been divided into its components using the formula

$$R^2_{y.123} = r_{y1}b_{y1.23} + r_{y2}b_{y2.13} + r_{y3}b_{y3.12}$$

(Symbols and subscripts according to Walker-Lev, Statistical Inference, New York 1953, chapt. 13, pp. 315 ff.)

The prognostic value of all nine criteria is between 58 and 86 percent of the combined prognostic value of the three predictors.

The predictor, school maturity, is evidently of some value as predictor of reading comprehension, but it is of small or no value as predictor of reading accuracy and spelling—especially in grades 2 and 3 (R^2-components between .002 and .013).

The predictor, visual letter perception, is obviously of some value as predictor of spelling and reading accuracy in grades 1-3. As a predictor of reading comprehension it has some value in grades 1 and 2, but practically no value in grade 3 (R^2-component .003).

In a relatively long term prediction (over a three-year period) it seems reasonable to reduce the number of predictors to two for each criterion: namely reading readiness and visual letter perception as predictors of reading accuracy and spelling, and reading readiness and school maturity as predictors of reading comprehension.

2. *Stability of different types of criteria through the grades.* Table 2 shows the coefficients of correlation between all pairs of criterion variables.

Of special interest are the coefficients of correlation between criteria of the same type at different grade levels (these coefficients are found in the 3 x 3 squares along the diagonal of the total matrix).

The criterion, reading accuracy, is obviously the most stable of the three types with a correlation of .774 between grade 1 and grade 3 measures. This coefficient may in fact be interpreted as a long term retest coefficient, since this criterion is measured by means of the same test battery at all three grade levels.

The criteria, reading comprehension and spelling, have been measured through different tests at different grade levels and this may partly explain the lower stability (correlation between grade 1 and grade 3 measures .645 for spelling and .502 for reading comprehension).

The rather low stability of reading comprehension measures may also be due to an increasing complexity in the set of factors that influence reading comprehension performance. The decrease from grade level to grade level in correlation between reading accuracy and reading comprehension (.848 in grade 1, .797 in grade 2, and .523 in grade 3) also seems to indicate that these abilities become more and more differentiated.

Correlations between reading comprehension and spelling at successive grade levels show the same tendency (.661 in grade 1, .576 in grade 2, and .442 in grade 3). Correlations be-

TABLE 2

Coefficients of correlation between different criterion variables.

Type	Type Grade	R.A. 1	R.A. 2	R.A. 3	R.C. 1	R.C. 2	R.C. 3	SP 1	SP 2	SP 3
R.A.	1		.829	.774	.848	.734	.471	.659	.682	.637
R.A.	2	.829		.922	.720	.797	.492	.592	.701	.712
R.A.	3	.774	.922		.654	.768	.523	.554	.667	.716
R.C.	1	.848	.720	.654		.745	.502	.661	.626	.555
R.C.	2	.734	.797	.768	.745		.551	.541	.576	.613
R.C.	3	.471	.492	.523	.502	.551		.462	.449	.442
SP	1	.659	.592	.554	.661	.541	.551		.700	.645
SP	2	.682	.701	.667	.626	.576	.449	.700		.785
SP	3	.637	.712	.716	.555	.613	.442	.645	.785	

Note: 1. Coefficients computed from data for control group (n = 230).
2. R.A. = Reading Accuracy
   R.C. = Reading Comprehension
   S.P. = Spelling
3. The squares of the diagonal parts of the matrix marked above contain coefficients of correlation between criterion variables of the same type.

tween reading accuracy and spelling on the other hand do *not* show any such tendency (.659 in grade 1, .701 in grade 2, and .716 in grade 3).

It therefore seems reasonable to assume that the reading comprehension ability during the primary stage becomes more and more differentiated

Fig. 1

Analyses of differences between the total experimental group and the control group regarding the criterion spelling, grade 3 (y), as a function of reading readiness (x).

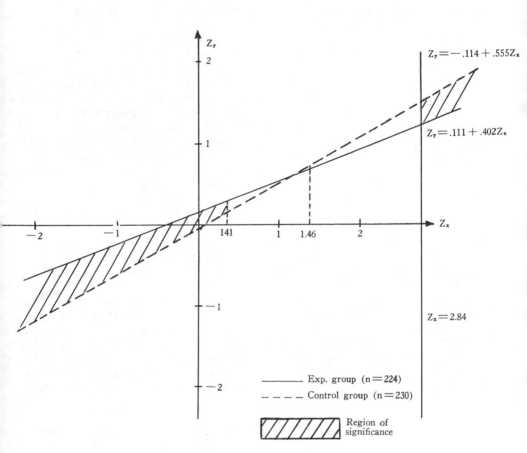

Note: Z_x values limiting the regions of significance and nonsignificance have been computed according to the method of "matched regression estimates" as described in Walker-Lev (6).

Comment: Two different regions of significance have been found. The upper region contains only one case in the control group and is therefore disregarded.

The lower region of significance contains more than 50 percent of the total number of cases (454).

Within this region the experimental group pupils are superior in spelling ability (as measured in this study) in comparison with control group pupils at corresponding reading readiness levels.

It should be noticed that out of the 78 "reading clinic" pupils in the experimental group 72 are found within the lower region of significance.

from the two abilities, reading accuracy and spelling, while these two abilities remain quite closely correlated to one another throughout the period.

3. *Effects of remedial teaching.* Table 3 shows group means and differences as regards the three predictors and the nine criteria studied.

The control group was superior in two out of three predictors, although the differences are nonsignificant.

The experimental group was superior in all nine criterion variables with significant differences in five criteria, reading accuracy, grades 1, 2 and 3, spelling, grade 2 and 3.

The aim of the remedial teaching has been to prevent or eliminate reading and writing difficulties among pupils in the experimental group.

The criteria, reading accuracy and spelling, seem to be most fitted to indicate reading and spelling difficulties at this level. The fact that the analysis of these two types of criteria has yielded significant group mean differences favoring the experimental group in five cases of six strongly supports the hypothesis that the remedial teaching has had the expected effect.

The data also support the hypothesis that there is an additive increase in this effect from grade level to grade level, especially when the criterion is reading accuracy (group mean differences: $+ .191$ in grade 1, $+ .236$ in grade 2, and $+ .255$ in grade 3).

The grade 3 criteria can be regarded as the ultimate criteria of reading and writing performance within this study. Group mean differences in the three criteria have been studied through covariance analysis using all three predictors reading readiness, school maturity, and visual letter perception.

These analyses have yielded highly significant F-values as regards group mean differences in reading accuracy ($F = 9.44$) and spelling ($F = 6.96$) but a nonsignificant F value for reading comprehension ($F = 2.94$).

As the correlation and regression analyses in some cases yielded lower within group regression coefficients for the experimental group than for the control group, we have also used a method of "matched regression estimates" (6) studying reading accuracy and spelling grade 3 with reading readiness as a single predictor.

As regards the criterion variable, reading accuracy, this analysis did not yield any significance region in the predictor, i.e., the superiority of the experimental group in this criterion is about the same at all reading readiness levels.

The corresponding analysis of spelling grade 3 did yield a region of significance (experimental group pupils were better than control group pupils at reading readiness levels *below* $+.4z$) and a region of nonsignificance (no significant difference between groups

TABLE 3

Group means, group mean differences and significance of group mean differences ($n = 454$).

	Variable	Means Exp. group	Contr. group	Diff. E-C	Significance
Predictors:	Reading Readiness	$- 0.026$	$+ 0.026$	$- 0.052$	n.s.
	School maturity	$+ 0.034$	$- 0.034$	$+ 0.068$	n.s.
	Visual letter perc.	$- 0.049$	$+ 0.048$	$- 0.097$	n.s.
Criteria:	Reading accuracy, gr. 1	$+ 0.097$	$- 0.094$	$+ 0.191$	$p < 0.05$
	Reading accuracy, gr. 2	$+ 0.120$	$- 0.116$	$+ 0.236$	$p < 0.05$
	Reading accuracy, gr. 3	$+ 0.129$	$- 0.126$	$+ 0.255$	$p < 0.01$
	Reading compreh., gr. 1	$+ 0.078$	$- 0.076$	$+ 0.154$	n.s.
	Reading compreh., gr. 2	$+ 0.066$	$- 0.064$	$+ 0.130$	n.s.
	Reading compreh., gr. 3	$+ 0.060$	$- 0.059$	$+ 0.119$	n.s.
	Spelling, grade 1	$+ 0.064$	$- 0.062$	$+ 0.126$	n.s.
	Spelling, grade 2	$+ 0.104$	$- 0.100$	$+ 0.204$	$p < 0.05$
	Spelling, grade 3	$+ 0.101$	$- 0.100$	$+ 0.201$	$p < 0.05$

at reading readiness levels *above* + 0.4z).

Thus the total experimental group superiority in spelling ability is mainly due to a superiority of experimental group pupils with low or medium initial reading readiness level. As 72 out of 78 "clinic" pupils belong to this category, it seems reasonable to conclude that this finding supports the hypothesis that the remedial teaching has significantly increased the spelling ability of the "clinic" pupils.

Out of the 78 pupils from the experimental group who received remedial instruction, 42 had initial school maturity test results above — 0.5z.

At the final testing session in grade 3 only 7 out of these 42 pupils reached results as regards reading accuracy below — 1.0z

Using our operational definition of special reading disabilities we find that 83 percent of the cases identified as potential reading disability cases were prevented from occurring.

The study further shows that the optimistic hopes of totally eliminating reading disability cases through remedial procedures such as those used within the experimental group were not fulfilled.

REFERENCES

1. Hallgren, B. (1950) Specific Dyslexia ("Congenital Word-Blindness"). A Clinical and Genetic Study. Diss., Stockholm.
2. Hermann, K. (1955). Om medfødt ordblindhed. Diss., Copenhagen.
3. Malmquist, E. (1958). Factors Related to Reading Disabilities in the First Grade of the Elementary School. Acta Universitatis Stockholmiensis, Diss. Stockholm.
4. ——— (1961). Studies of the Children's Attainments and Proficiency in Reading, Writing, Arithmetic at the Beginning of Their Schooling in the First Grade of the Elementary School. Research Reports from the National School for Educational Research in Linköping, Sweden, No. I. (In Swedish with a Summary in English). Stockholm.
5. ——— (1966). Reading and Writing Disabilities in Children. Analysis and Methodology. Lund.
6. Walker, H. M. and J. Lev., (1953). Statistical Inference. New York.

The Influence of a Head Start Program on Reading Achievement

WALLACE RAMSEY
and
MARGUERITE BOERCKER*
University of Kentucky

AMONG ALL of the programs made possible by a massive infusion of federal funds, the one that has excited much interest and enthusiasm is aimed at giving four- and five-year-olds enriched experiences that will enable them to have a "head start" in school. The states in Appalachia have received a substantial portion of Head Start funds because of the large numbers of disadvantaged children in the region.

The study reported here sought mainly to discover the effects of Head Start on the first grade reading achievement of 152 first grade children in Scott County, Kentucky.

In September, 1965, 152 first graders who had attended an eight-week Head Start program during the preceding summer were intermixed in 15 first grade classrooms with 192 children who had not attended Head Start. Of the latter group twenty-two had attended kindergarten and were not included in the study.

Nature of program

The children had been enrolled in an eight-week Head Start program in classes of fifteen taught by certified primary grade teachers. The latter had received one week of in-service training at the University of Kentucky to qualify them as Head Start teachers. Each was assisted by an aid who was a high school or college student interested in working with children.

The Head Start program to which the children were exposed was experience oriented and designed to increase children's knowledge and understand-

*The study reported here was the doctoral project of Marguerite Boercker at the University of Kentucky.

ing of their life space. A combination of field trips, viewing of films, listening to stories, construction activities, oral language activities, and classroom displays served to increase the children's stock of information and their language facility. Emphasis was given to concept and vocabulary building in an informal atmosphere.

The first grades which the children attended were all in five multigrade consolidated schools and constituted the entire entering first grade enrollment in the two systems. The first grade teachers were graduates of four year teacher education programs in accredited institutions. None had received any training in teaching reading beyond the one course required for certification.

Each classroom was supplied with basal reading textbooks by the State Department of Education under the state adopted textbook system. Charts, supplementary readers, and supplementary phonics materials (when used) were supplied by the local system or were purchased from funds made available from the PTA. Small numbers of trade books appropriate for first grade use were available in each classroom. In both school systems represented in the study the annual per-pupil cost of education was below $400 in 1965-1966.

Classroom equipment could best be described as minimal. A rather formal and traditional approach to reading instruction was followed. In-class ability grouping was used to care for individual differences.

Two hundred forty of the total group of 322 were enrolled in classes in which materials were used that provided for early emphasis on phoneme-grapheme correspondence and synthetic phonics. (*Phonetic Keys to Reading* published by the Economy Co.) The other 82 were in classes using basal materials providing for earliest emphasis on learning to read whole words followed by an analytic approach to phonics. (*Ginn Basic Readers* published by Ginn and Co.) The former group attended school a full day from the beginning of school; the latter group had only half-day sessions until after Thanksgiving vacation.

Gathering data

In order to make sure that the Hawthorne Effect did not have a strong influence on the results of the study, it was decided to do a bare minimum of special testing, to gather information as quietly as possible, and to avoid any publicity concerning the study. Since both Head Start and non-Head Start children were intermixed in about the same proportion in all classrooms, the teacher variable was held constant for both groups.

The only special testing done was the administration of the California Test of Mental Maturity. This was given to all first graders by the researchers in December. This was necessary because the two school systems do not normally give such tests to first grade children.

At the end of the 1965-66 school year the mental maturity test data and other information gathered from cumulative records were analyzed to determine 1) how the Head Start and non-Head Start groups differed, 2) variables correlating with end-of-the-year reading achievement scores, 3) the nature and significance of differences in end-of-the-year reading achievement scores of the two groups, and 4) which approach (the synthetic or analytic) seemed to better exploit the benefits of Head Start. Test results that were available (in addition to the California Mental Maturity) were those from the Metropolitan Readiness Test (administered in October) and the Stanford Achievement Test (administered in May).

Differences in groups

When compared with the non-Head Start group, the Head Start group had a similar proportion of boys to girls (51 percent girls in Head Start versus 52 percent girls not in Head Start), contained a significantly higher proportion of Negroes (30 percent versus 3.5

percent in the non-Head Start group), contained a slightly higher proportion of children of unskilled laborers (37.5 percent vs. 25.5 percent) and a lower proportion of children of parents in the professions (15.7 percent vs. 31.3 percent). The difference between the two groups in occupation of parents was significant at the .02 level. (Occupations of parents were categorized by use of *The Socioeconomic Scale of Occupations* devised by A. M. Edwards.) Figures in the full version of the study clearly revealed that the Head Start distribution clusters towards the unskilled end of the distribution.

In readiness for reading (as measured by the Metropolitan), the Head Start group measured slightly less ready for reading but the difference was only marginally significant at the .15 level. It is noteworthy that over sixty percent of both groups ranked below the fiftieth percentile in readiness. The median score of both groups was in the third decile of the test. The Head Start group had fewer children scoring in the top quartile.

Mental age differences between the two groups were significant at the .02 level—the Head Start group was four months below the other group at the time of testing (December). Fifty-six percent of the Head Start group was below the mental age of 6.6 while only forty-seven percent of the non-Head Start group were below that level—the minimum mental age at which a child is likely to learn to read with ease.

The differences between the mental age and readiness score distributions are interesting. Whereas the mental-ages-in-months pattern is an almost normal curve, the readiness scores pattern is almost random, with peak populations in the 0-10 decile. The correlation between the two scores is only .41. Does this suggest that the readiness test measures results of more formal preschool experiences than any of these children experienced?

In other important variables for which information was available there seemed to be no significant differences in the two groups. These included chronological age, state of the family (whole or broken), number of children in the family, sibling rank of the child, and presence of health limitations.

Achievement results

A comparison of reading achievement scores at the end of the year revealed that there was no significant difference in the mean reading level of the two groups, although a high proportion (over 60 percent) of both groups scored below expected grade level. The Head Start group had a higher proportion of children scoring very low (35.5 percent scoring below 1.5 vs 22.4 percent of non-Head Start group who scored that low).

Five variables were found to correlate positively with reading achievement as follows:

Reading Readiness Score	.52
Mental Age	.49
Race	.35
Approach to Reading	.30
Occupation of Parent	.22

Equating for variables

In order to determine if each of the above variables exerted a real difference on reading achievement, the two groups were equated for each variable and achievement scores compared. When equated for race it was found the Head Start Negro reading mean was a month higher than the non-Head Start Negro mean but the difference was not significant.

Equating the groups for occupation of the wage earner produced an interesting phenomenon. The means of the professional group differed in favor of the non-Head Start group but only at the .12 level. As the skill of the wage earner (in the non-Head Start group) went up the reading scores went up. Head Start scores went up from the unskilled to the skilled category, but dropped again in the professional category. This cannot be explained with the data available.

In the socioeconomic levels for whom Head Start is designed, the two groups exhibited no significant difference in achievement. The same was found to be true when the groups were equated by readiness scores.

When equated for mental age a significant difference in reading achievement was noted in only one mental age group—the 71-80 months group. The difference was in favor of the Head Start group at the .06 level. It appeared that in this study that for the child of approximately 6.6 years of mental age the Head Start experiences were not enough to bring him up to his non-Head Start counterpart in reading achievement at the end of first grade. Yet the brighter Head Start child tended to achieve as well as the brighter non-Head Start child.

Equating for two variables produced interesting results. When groups were equated for occupation and mental age it was found that among the children of skilled workers the Head Start group with mental ages above seventy-seven months achieved significantly higher than the non-Head Start group of the same mental age.

When equated for approach to reading (synthetic vs. analytic) and mental age, the only difference found was in the group using the synthetic approach. In the mental age group below 6.5, the non-Head Start group achieved significantly higher than their Head Start counterparts.

Advantage of approach

One of the objectives of the study was to determine which of the two reading approaches seemed to better exploit the benefits of Head Start. An analysis of the data showed that the non-Head Start group did better than its counterpart in the synthetic groups but the difference was not significant. Among those learning to read by the analytic approach the non-Head Start group achieved significantly better than the Head Start group. It would appear, therefore, that the synthetic approach was better able to exploit the benefits of Head Start.

Summary of findings

In summarizing and drawing implications from the study, several points should be made. The Head Start and non-Head Start children who were intermixed in first grade classrooms differed in several important respects. The Head Start group tended to come from the lower socioeconomic levels and contained a higher proportion of Negroes. The group measured less ready to read and had a lower mental age than the non-Head Start group. At the end of first grade the Head Start group had the larger proportion of poor readers. Although all of the above were true, it is significant to note that *a straight, unequated comparison of the reading scores of the two groups revealed no significant difference in achievement.* This would indicate, to this writer, that the Head Start program achieved signal success in accomplishing one of its goals: preparing children for better academic learning. That it was not more successful is unfortunate but probably explainable.

In all likelihood the factors influencing the usual academic retardation of disadvantaged children are too complicated for an eight week preschool program to make a tremendous difference. In all probability a full-year kindergarten of compensatory quality would better meet the readiness needs of all five-year-olds in Scott County, Kentucky, as well as for most of the children for whom Head Start is intended. Though concrete research evidence is lacking, the same could be said of Head Start programs for four-year-olds.

A look ahead

The intent of legislation to finance Head Start programs is to create an opportunity to enrich the lives of disadvantaged children. By providing programs full of new experiences such children are helped to begin school more nearly ready to read.

An approach to beginning reading that would seem to grow naturally out of the Head Start activities is the language experience approach. Typical basal reader stories in the first grade materials are not suited to the experience-starved, language-underdeveloped six-year-old from Appalachia or the inner city. When taught by teachers who have been using it a number of years, the basal reader approach can be particularly sterile.

A language experience approach would permit children and teachers to create their own stories, using experiences and language patterns that are more typical of the children involved. The experiences of Stauffer (3), Vilscek, Morgan and Cleland (4) in Delaware and Pittsburgh in using the language experience approach with disadvantaged children is evidence supporting this idea.

The level of competence of teachers is an important variable in such a program. Following a basal reader guidebook provides a systematic program in skill development. Working out a skills program to fit language experience stories, as well as the needs of individual children, demands a higher level of knowledge, a greater degree of creativeness, and a deeper degree of self-confidence than many first grade teachers possess. If Head Start is to be followed up in an effective manner, a way must be found to help teachers acquire these traits.

A way must also be found to reduce the pupil load of first grade teachers of Head Start children. A greater sensitivity to individual needs seems required of those working with the disadvantaged first grader. The presence of a large number of poor readers among Head Start children in this study underscores the need.

Many such children come from environments in which they have had very little undivided attention from an adult. Teachers with reasonable pupil loads can find time to listen to them, provide language feedback of a type that will help them alter their speech to fit more mature patterns, and encourage them to engage in the kind of language activity leading to higher levels of linguistic development.

The success of the "Rooms of Twenty" in St. Louis schools (1) provides evidence that reducing the pupil load can result in some rather spectacular results.

About one-third of the children in this study were Negroes. The mean reading achievement of Negro Head Starters was below that of white Head Starters, though not drastically so. This may have been due to the use of the basal approach to reading or to some factors not revealed in this study. The very real difference in phonology and syntax between Negro speech and the speech of white children as revealed in at least one study (2) causes difficulties for the teacher—as several teachers of Title I remedial reading have indicated to the writer. Experimentation with various practices is in order to find what works most effectively in helping these children learn to read.

A study presently underway in Washington will supply information concerning the exact nature of Negro dialect in that area and provide materials for teaching the dialect group. Entitled "The Urban Language Study," the research is under the direction of Dr. J. H. Dillard and is supported by the Center for Applied Linguistics. Accompanying sociological and anthropological studies seek to discover familial, social, group, and other characteristics influencing dialect and holding implications for writing materials for learning to read.

Experimentation with an approach that may seem drastic to many purists is proposed by this writer. Early reading material for disadvantaged dialect groups (and especially Negro) should be written in their dialect—with its phonological and syntactical deviations from standard English represented in the graphic form. In this manner the child who says "Ah needs tin cints by fo' o'clock" or in response to the question "Where is John?" says

"He home" can be helped to read material closely representing his dialect. When he learns to *speak* standard English (perhaps as a second language taught by oral-aural methods in a language laboratory situation), he can be taught to *read* standard English. In the meantime, his development in reading need not wait, or be complicated and retarded by his inability to speak standard English.

In the judgment of the writer Head Start holds a lot of promise for the future. However, experimentation with various patterns of organization and different types and lengths of programs is in order. The approach taken in teaching reading to children, once such instruction is begun, should be one that naturally supplements and follows up what has been begun in the Head Start program. The typical basal program (even when supplemented with synthetic phonics) does not do this. Classes of thirty to thirty-five children are too large to enable teachers to do the kind of teaching that is needed. Some radical approach to teaching reading to children whose normal dialect is nonstandard English is needed. Substantial further experimentation and study will enable us to refine our approaches and techniques so we can help Head Start to fully achieve its promise.

REFERENCES

1. Kottmeyer, William. *Teacher's Guide for Remedial Reading.* St. Louis: Webster Division, McGraw-Hill Book Co., 1959.
2. Labov, William. "Linguistic Research on Non-Standard English of Negro Children" in Anita Dorr (Ed.), *Problems and Practices in New York City Schools.* New York: New York Society for the Experimental Study of Education, 1965.
3. Stauffer, Russell G. "The Effectiveness of Language Arts and Basic Reader Approaches to First Grade Reading Instruction," *The Reading Teacher, 20,* No. 1 (October 1966), 18-24.
4. Vilscek, Elaine, et. al. "Coordinating and Integrating Language Arts Instruction in First Grade," *The Reading Teacher, 20,* 1 (October 1966), 31-37.

A Statewide Summer Reading Program: Second Year

Byron Callaway, Ira E. Aaron, Hazel D. Simpson
University of Georgia
and
Randall C. Hicks
Valdosta State College

During the school year 1963-64 the Georgia State Superintendent of Schools was concerned about the large dropout problem in Georgia. One of the considerations was the reading ability of the dropout and when this disability originated.

This Summer Reading Program was a long range aspect of a program to reduce the dropout rate of Georgia. Actual results can be evaluated only after a period of years, when these children reach the usual dropout age.

The apparent success of the program in 1964 led to continuing the program during the summer of 1965. This report is concerned with the second summer program, 1965. The state program was discontinued after 1965, due to the availability of federal funds to school systems, especially Title I funds. These funds enabled schools to support a more extensive program than was possible from state funds. The two state programs, 1964 and 1965, were judged successful in contributing to improvement of reading instruction. As a result of the experience in this program, the Georgia schools were able to plan more adequately for federal programs.

Teachers

The teachers were selected by the local superintendents, with the approval of the State Director. The State Director was the Reading and English Consultant of the State Department of Education.

Superintendents selected the best teachers available. Criteria used for selection were: 1) A background of study and successful experience in the teaching of reading; 2) an evident understanding of child development and the principles and techniques of the teaching of reading; 3) an interest and desire to participate in the teaching of corrective or remedial reading; and 4) a minimum of a four-year professional certificate (approximately thirty percent had either fifth or sixth year certificates). More than 67 percent of the teachers had in excess of ten years experience.

There were 404 teachers selected and supported by this program. A number of additional teachers were employed by local systems at their expense to expand the program. Data were obtained and analyzed on only those teachers supported by the state program.

Children

Children were selected by teachers and principals using specific criteria and screening devices.

Guidelines used for selecting children were as follows:

1. Enrolled in grades one through three in the 1964-65 school year with priority for first graders, then second graders, and finally third graders.
2. Had average ability or above. (Slow learners were accepted if their reading grade placement was clearly below their intellectual grade placement.)
3. Disabled in reading. (Children finishing the first grade reading at the primer or lower level, children finishing the second grade reading at the low second grade or lower level, and third graders at or below the low third grade level.)
4. Freedom from serious emotional problems.
5. Had parents with a desire for their children to participate, and who agreed to cooperate fully.
6. Recommended by the classroom teacher.
7. Had record of good attendance.

In April, a group intelligence test, a group reading test, and an informal reading inventory were administered

by the regular classroom teacher to aid in screening. The specific standardized tests used varied from one school to another.

A total of 6,118 children participated in the program. Complete data were available on 5,677. Additional children were supported by local systems, but were not included in this study.

The 5,677 children were classified as follows: 2,972 first graders, 1,619 second graders, and 1,085 third graders. There were 3,453 boys and 2,224 girls. Classified as to race, 3,486 were white and 2,191 were Negro.

Program

The Summer Reading Program was scheduled for a total of eight weeks. Two days were used for a briefing session to aid in preparation of teachers for the project. The briefing sessions were conducted by members of the University of Georgia Reading Department and of the Georgia State Department of Education. One day was allotted for preparations for the children at the school. At the end of the program two days were utilized for evaluation sessions held in each of the ten districts. Each district had a supervisor for the program to work with teachers during the project and to conduct the evaluation sessions at the end of the program.

Seven weeks were devoted to actual instruction with the children. Instructional sessions were for three hours in the morning, with adequate breaks and rest periods. None of the classes had more than 16 children and most of them had 15 or less, the recommended maximum for this program. Some teachers worked with a few individual children in the afternoon. In general, however, these afternoon sessions were used for preparations for the following day. Teachers worked a full eight-hour-day in preparation, evaluation, and teaching.

Children were taught with seven different types of materials. Most of the instruction, however, was done with one of ten basal reading series or with one of the series in combination with the SRA Laboratory. Methods of instruction reported as percentage of children were as follows: Basal Readers, 67.8 percent; SRA Laboratory, 1.4 percent; Basal Readers and SRA Laboratory combination, 21.3 percent; Programed Instruction, 4.5 percent; Individualized Reading, 2.2 percent; i.t.a., 0.7 percent; and Language Experience, 2.1 percent.

Birth month

Children are generally admitted to school in Georgia if their birth date is on or before December 31. (Some local systems do require an earlier birth date for admission to the first grade.) A frequency table was made indicating birth month. There were more children born during each of the six months that would place the child in the younger half of the year than were born in any month that would place them in the older half of the year. A total of 55.6 percent of the children were born in the last six months of the year.

Chi-square analysis of birth month by the quarter of the year revealed a significant difference beyond the .001 level with the differences attributable to the higher proportions of Summer Reading Program children born in the latter half of the year as compared to the first two quarters.

This is similar to the findings of the 1964 Summer Reading Program. Of the children participating in each of the two summer programs, more younger children needed help in reading than older children. As indicated above, both standardized tests and teacher opinion based on specific criteria were used to identify these children.

Means of assessing the program

To assess progress made by children participating in the program, equivalent forms of a standardized reading test were administered at the beginning and at the end of the program. The three subtests, Word Recognition,

Sentence Reading, and Paragraph Reading, of the Gates Primary Reading Tests were administered to all children not expected to be reading above beginning third grade at the end of the program. The Gates Advanced Primary, consisting of two subtests, Word Recognition and Paragraph Reading, were administered to all children likely to be reading at or above the third grade level by the end of the program.

The Peabody Picture Vocabulary Test was administered to all participants during the first week of the program. The Peabody Test and the Gates Tests were administered by the Summer Reading Program teacher.

Intelligence test results

Children participating in the program had a median intelligence quotient in the lower part of the average range. The median intelligence quotient for the total group was 93.4; for the first grade 93.8; for the second grade 93.5; and for the third grade 91.8. Scores ranged from the forties to the one hundred fifties with 0.1 percent in each of these extreme groups. These scores did not differ significantly between grades.

Children were classified into subgroups to examine the intelligence quotients. White children, increasingly with grade level, exceeded Negroes about ten IQ points. Boys were somewhat higher than girls, approximately five IQ points for whites and three IQ points for Negroes. The median scores were: white males 99.1, white females 93.7, Negro males 87.5, and Negro females 84.8.

Approximately 39 percent of the children had intelligence quotients below 90, and 18 percent had intelligence quotients below 80, as measured by the Peabody Vocabulary Test. The majority of these children were probably not disabled readers but reading near their expected level. The program was developmental in nature as well as remedial, so these children did continue to show progress. However, it is possible that children with low intelligence quotients affected the growth for the total group significantly.

Reading test results

A total of 4,768 children were administered the three subtests of the Gates Primary at the beginning and at the end of the program. This group consisted of 2,967 first graders, 1,351 second graders, and 450 third graders. They could also be categorized as 2,898 males and 1,870 females, or as 2,838 whites and 1,930 Negroes.

In comparing pretest and post-test scores on Word Recognition, gains were indicated as one month for first graders, two months for second graders, and one month for third graders. For the entire group the median gain was two months. Differences between boys and girls were not significant; however, white children made greater gains than did Negro children.

Comparison of tests of Primary Sentence Reading indicated median gains of two months for first and third graders and one month for second graders. For the total group the median gain was two months. On this test boys were slightly ahead of girls initially, however, girls made greater gains. Whites made greater gains than Negroes.

First graders and second graders made median gains of two months on the Primary Paragraph Reading Test and third graders made one month gain. The median gains for the entire group was two months. Initially, girls were ahead of boys and girls showed more gain than boys. Initially, whites were ahead of Negroes and showed more gain than Negroes.

The above comparisons are based on the differences of pretest and post-test scores with no adjustment to intelligence. These scores indicate that first and second graders made greater gains. However, when the data were treated statistically and gains were adjusted to differences in intelligence the findings were reversed, with third graders making the greater gains. Analysis of covariance was used to test the signifi-

cance. Second graders made more gain than first graders.

In other findings on these test scores, girls' gains exceeded boys', and white children made significantly more gain than Negro children. The month of birth of children was not significantly related to gain.

Gains, as shown by the comparison of the "before" and "after" Gates Primary Reading Tests, are depressed because many children should have been given the advanced primary tests instead of the easier primary tests. Probably few first graders were affected by this. However, indications were that approximately 16 percent of the second graders and 28 percent of the third graders scored so high that comparison of scores did not indicate the true growth made during the program. Thus many children in grades two and three did not have an actual evaluation of true gains.

There were 909 children who took both forms of the Gates Advanced Primary Tests. This group was composed of five first graders, 268 second graders, and 636 third graders. There were 555 males and 354 females, and 648 whites and 261 Negroes. The five first graders will be ignored, as the size of the group is not significant and they were probably not disabled readers.

On the Advanced Primary Word Recognition Test second graders had a median gain of four months, third graders a median gain of three months, and the total group a median gain of four months. There was no significant difference in achievement according to sex. Gains by whites were significantly higher than gains by Negroes.

Comparisons of the pretest and post-test scores on the Advanced Primary Paragraph Reading indicated a gain of three months by second graders, five months by third graders, and five months by the total group.

There was no significant difference indicated by race of the children. Gains significantly favored girls over boys. Third graders made gains that were significantly superior to second graders.

Analysis of covariance with control for initial raw score on the Gates Advanced Primary Reading Tests and the Peabody Picture Vocabulary Test was used to examine score gains statistically with respect to sex, race, grade, and birth month. Gains by third graders were significantly higher than those by second graders. On Word Recognition there was no significant difference between boys and girls, but on Paragraph Reading girls were significantly higher at the .01 level. On Word Recognition white children were significantly higher than Negro children at the .01 level, but these differences were insignificant on Paragraph Reading.

For the Word Recognition subtest of the advanced primary tests, no significant differences were attributable to birth month. Significant differences at the .05 level did occur on Paragraph Reading. The differences were such that children born in June made significantly higher adjusted post-test scores than children born in January, July, August, September, October, or November.

Comparison of different approaches

As previously mentioned, seven different methods of instruction were utilized in various classrooms. Two methods accounted for the teaching of almost 90 percent of the children. The numbers taught by the seven methods were as follows: Basal Readers (10 different series) 3,847; SRA Laboratories 81; Basal Reader and SRA Laboratories combined, 1,210; Programed Reading, 255; Individualized Reading, 123; Language Experience, 120; and i.t.a., 41.

These approaches, though in general they fit the various classifications of method, were not tightly controlled. Teacher enthusiasm and teacher knowledge of the approach used were not equated. Teachers using basal readers were familiar with the material while those using other approaches were not as familiar with their materials, in general. A two-day special briefing session was held for those using i.t.a. materials. Those using other approaches had a one-hour or a two-hour briefing during the briefing session for all teachers of the Summer Reading Program.

Gains within the approach groups were compared for primary tests and advanced primary tests separately, each with scores adjusted to intelligence.

Statistical tests showed method differences for the 4,768 children tested on the three subtests of the primary tests. When the results of the three subtests of the Gates Primary Reading Tests were considered, the order of effectiveness of methods appears to be as follows:

1. Basal Readers
2. Individualized Reading
3. Basal Reader with SRA Reading Laboratories
4. Programed Reading
5. SRA Reading Laboratories
6. Language Experience
7. Initial Teaching Alphabet (i.t.a.)

Scores for the 909 children tested with the two subtests of the Gates Advanced Primary Reading Tests indicated no significant differences. Scores were adjusted to scores on the Peabody Picture Vocabulary Test. There were some differences but none of these were statistically significant.

Results should be considered in light of limitations. Some of these would be: 1) Lack of adequate training for teachers using new methods, 2) Lack of tight controls and adequate supervision, 3) The number of children who should have been administered the advanced primary test instead of the primary test, 4) The duration of the program, (seven weeks of instruction).

Summary

Children ranged in intelligence quotients from below 50 to above 150. The median IQ was slightly above 93. This placed the typical child in the average intelligence bracket but slightly below the midpoint of this average grouping.

On the Gates Primary Reading Tests, administered to 4,768 students, the typical gains were two months for first and second graders and one month for third graders. These gains are underestimates because a number of the second and third grade children were given the primary tests when they should have been administered the advanced primary tests. The primary tests were too easy to assess gains accurately.

The Gates Advanced Primary Reading Tests were given to 909 students who were expected to exceed lower third grade level at the end of the program. The gains made were four months for second graders and three months for third graders on the Word Recognition subtest, and three months for second graders and five months for third graders on the Paragraph Reading subtest.

Statistical tests showed method differences on all three subtests for the children taking the primary tests and no method differences for those children taking the advanced primary tests. For the primary test gains, Basal Readers and Basal Readers plus SRA Reading Laboratories were superior to Language Experience, Programed Materials, and i.t.a.; Individualized Reading gains were superior to those of Programed Materials; and all approaches were superior to i.t.a.

The Effect of a Parent-Training Program upon Reading Achievement of Children

John E. Allen, Gabriel
Della-Piana, and
Robert F. Stahmann
University of Utah

This part of the study describes the hypotheses, the procedures, the design, and the results of the experiment. A description of the parent-training program is presented in the second part of this paper.

Hypotheses. The two basic hypotheses of this study are:

1. Pupils whose parents are involved in a training program will show greater oral and silent reading gains than a control group whose parents are not involved in the program during the experimental period.

2. Mothers' attitudes as measured by the Parental Attitude Research Instrument (PARI), Factors I, II, and III, are significantly correlated with oral and silent reading gains.

Sample. In late spring all children who would be in grades three to six the following year in two elementary schools were tested, and those with reading ability a year or more below grade level were selected. An "Invitational Letter To Parents" was sent to all parents of children so identified. There was approximately a 50 percent return which amounted to a sample of 45. Since we could enroll only 20 students in each school in remedial classes, 40 students were invited to the remedial class on condition that the mother (and if possible father) attend the parent class. Students were then randomly assigned to experimental or control group for the parent treatment. Attrition throughout the period of the experiment reduced the sample to 29. There were 13 experimentals and 16 controls in the final group. Both experimental and control parent groups were taken through a parent-training program. The experimental groups participated first. After post-testing of all pupils in reading (the end of the experiment), control group parents participated in the training program.

Means and standard deviations for the experimental and control groups on the instruments used in the study are included in the Appendix. The California Test of Mental Maturity (CTMM) was used as an intelligence measure. The mean IQ score on the CTMM for the control group are: Language 80.7, Non-language 91.9, Total 84.4. The mean IQ scores on the CTMM for the experimental group are: language 86.6, nonlanguage

99.5, Total 91.5. Although the means of the IQ's for the control and experimental groups are different, a t test analysis applying Welch's correction for degrees of freedom (Winer, B. J. *Statistical Principles in Experimental Design,* New York: McGraw-Hill, 1962, 37) disclosed that the differences are not significant at the .05 level.

The mean grade placement of the control group in September was 3.7. The mean grade level reading achievement scores for the control group in September were: Gilmore Oral Reading Test: accuracy 3.0, comprehension 3.3; California Reading Test: vocabulary 3.9, comprehension 3.5, total reading 3.7. The mean grade placement of the experimental group in September was 4.8. The mean grade level reading achievement scores for the experimental group in September were: Gilmore Oral Reading Test: accuracy 2.6, comprehension 2.7; California Reading Test: vocabulary 2.9, comprehension 2.5, total reading 2.7.

Pupil measures

The students were tested during the week of September 10, 1965, before the remedial reading program or the parent treatment group had begun. During this pretesting each student was administered the California Reading Test, Elementary Level, Form X, on a measure of silent reading achievement. The Gilmore Oral Reading Test, Form A, was also administered at this time to obtain a measure of oral reading achievement. The California Short Form Test of Mental Maturity was administered as a group measure of intelligence.

During the week of January 28, 1966, following the remedial treatment, the students were tested to obtain post-test measures. At this time the California Reading Test, Elementary, Form W, was administered to them as well as the Gilmore Oral Reading Test, Form B.

Design. A simple pretest post-test control group design was utilized. Parents of children in grades 3 to 6 who had reading disability formed the population out of which were selected those who volunteered to participate in a parent training group while their children were enrolled in a remedial class in school. The remedial classes met pupils in groups of two to five students, and the treatment was the same for both experimentals and controls.

The first analysis consisted of getting the correlations between the pre- and post-test scores of the students on the California Reading Test and the Gilmore Oral Reading Test. In this analysis the students in the experimental and control groups were combined into one group for the pretest and one group for the post-test. This correlation analysis was done for two reasons. It enabled us to study the data in correlational manner for each subtest. Secondly, the analysis gave us a basis for predicting post-test scores for each student in the sample, based upon his pretest score on an alternative form of the same test.

A chief focus of this study was the pupil gains in the areas of silent (California) and oral (Gilmore) reading. It was decided for a number of reasons that simple pretest vs. post-test gain scores would be less desirable than a difference score taken as a difference between end-of-treatment predicted score and actual end-of-treatment score. Thus, in each of the subtests for silent and oral reading, regression equations were obtained using as the predictor variables the pretest scores of the subtest. Using this method, a post-test score was predicted for each subject on each of the silent and oral subtests. This score was then subtracted from the actual score giving us a regressed gain score for each subject.

The experimental and control group regressed gain scores for each subtest were then compared by means of the t technique.

At the beginning of the study the PARI was administered to the mothers of the children in the study. This test yielded three factor scores for each of the mothers: Factor I—Approval of maternal control of the child; Factor II—Approval of expressions of hostility; Factor III—Approval of positive attitudes toward childrearing. As part of the data analysis, correlations were obtained between each of the subjects' regressed gain scores on each of the silent and oral subtests and the mothers' scores on each of the three PARI factors.

Analysis of regressed gain scores

Regressed gain scores were computed for each student on each of the test subscores. These regressed gain scores served as the measure of gain as a result of the treatment and were compared for the experimental vs. control students on each subscore by means of the t technique.

The t analysis for the experimental and control on the California Reading Test results are as follows:

	t	Signifi-cance	W²
Reading Vocabulary	— .04	n.s.	.00
Reading Comprehension	— 1.81	p > .10	.10
Total Reading	1.41	n.s.	.05

The difference between the regressed gain scores for the experimental and control groups in the reading vocabulary and total reading scores on the California Reading Test are not significant. The difference between the regressed gain scores for the experimental and control groups on the reading comprehension score is significant at the .10 level. The t (-1.81) also tells the direction of the significance; in this case, that the control group regressed gains are significantly greater than the experimental group on the reading comprehension (silent) subtest.

The t analysis for the experimental and control groups on the Gilmore Oral Reading Test are as follows:

	t	Signifi-cance	W²
Accuracy	2.16	p > .05	.16
Comprehension	2.76	p > .02	.25
Rate	1.95	p > .10	.12

The differences between the regressed gain scores for the experimental and control groups on the Gilmore Oral Reading Test subscores are all significant. The results indicate that the experimental group scores are significantly greater than the control group scores. The level of significance for each of the subtests is different.

The results of the t analysis of the regressed gain scores for the experimental and control groups would enable us to conclude the following:

1. The remedial treatment program apparently had little effect on the gains of the reading vocabulary and total reading subscores of the California Reading Test (silent reading).

2. There was a significant difference (.10 level) between the experimental and control groups on the California Reading subtest, reading comprehension; however, this difference indicated control group gains to be greater than experimental group gains.

3. The treatment program apparently had a significant positive effect on the three subscores of the Gilmore Oral Reading Test. Although the levels of significance are different for each of the three subscores, they are all in the same direction in this analysis indicating that experimental group gains were greater than control group gains.

4. Apparently the treatment program was more effective in increasing oral reading gains than silent reading gains.

The W² columns in the two tables above tell us the percent of variance on the respective reading achievement measures accounted for by the experimental treatments. The formula used

$$\left(\frac{t^2 - 1}{t^2 + N_1 + N_2 - 1} \right)$$

is from Hays, W. L., *Statistics for Psychologists,* Holt, Rinehart and Winston, 1965, 327-328. Both oral reading accuracy and comprehension measures reflect significant treatment differences favoring the experimental group and a substantial amount of variance is accounted for by the treatment. Silent reading measures reflect only one significant treatment difference and that favoring the control group but a rather low degree of association between the treatment and the dependent variables. In summary, we have found the experimental treatment (parent training) to have an impressive effect on oral reading gains; thus, making a follow-up of this finding a promising venture.

Teacher report

There is some evidence that the effectiveness of the training program was in part due to greater parental interest and more regular work on the part of their children. The remedial teacher reported that six children requested material to be sent home regularly for parents to hear them read. All six were experimentals. Nine children did not report regularly on home reading or had to be reminded week after week to bring their reading slips in. All nine were controls. In six out of seven cases where brothers or sisters or cousins of remedial students voluntarily went to the remedial teacher for help, the children were experimentals. The average regressed gain on oral reading comprehension for the six experimentals requesting home material was $+ 1.3$ compared with an average regressed gain of a $- .5$ for the nine controls who did not report regularly on home reading.

Parents made many positive remarks to the remedial teacher after the program was over concerning their appreciation. Of more interest were the negative comments made by some parents. The remedial teacher had post-experimental interviews with most parents. The major negative reactions are illustrated by the following excerpts:

"They used such hard words. I guess I'll have to get used to it."

"What is this negative and positive stuff? I'm positive. When I say 'Do this,' those kids jump. I haven't got time for such foolishness."

"I have no time. I have Scouts on Monday, Church on Tuesday, overtime on Wednesday, and bowling on Friday. Saturday I work half-a-day. Sunday we go to church. I have no time to help the boy."

In spite of attempts to be nontechnical, and shifting of methods when it appeared advisable, early sessions discouraged some parents because of the jargon.

The parent-training program

The parent-training program continued for fourteen formal sessions starting September 15, 1965, and including September 22, 29, October 6, 13, 20, 27, November 3, 10, 17, 24, and December 1, 8, 15. Individual sessions were held with each parent twice during the period September 15 to December 15.

Between December 15 and the beginning of pupil post-testing (January 28) individual appointments in parents' homes and at the University dealt with discussion of their progress and problems in applying contingency management techniques to their children.

Parental pressure for child's schooling enters our training program rather directly. We begin with the assumption that, if a parent does not like the child's behavior, the *parent* needs to behave differently. Thus, one of the first steps in our training program requires the parent to identify child behavior to be accelerated or decelerated. Since we are working with parents of children with reading disability, school behavior is typically on the list. However, we make no attempt to exclude other types of behavior since the general parent-child interaction pattern is of importance for school learning.

The number of cultural activities provided for the child and the child's participation in mealtime conversations enter our training program initially through exercises requiring the parent to record conversations with the child at mealtime, during a child's study activity, in social activities outside the home, and in other settings. These reports often become the focus for devising activities for the parent to try out.

Parental warmth and disapproval enter our training program through the obvious medium of specific parent behavior we attempt to modify in training. It may seem unusual that parents of the higher achievers give more help and warmth as well as withhold more help and show more disapproval. It is, of course, possible that the techniques of giving disapproval and withholding help work best for parents who give much to their children. That is, a child who is given much by a parent may well want to conform to the parent's wishes or care what the parent thinks if there is a threatened loss of approval.

In brief, our training program involved the following:

1. Teach parents a language for talking about the nature and effects of punishment and five alternatives to punishment. The five alternatives include removing the discriminative stimulus, eliciting an incompatible response, allowing time to pass, extinction, and getting a response under the control of a different stimulus or shaping up a new behavior.

2. The parent observes a child's behavior to be changed (accelerated or decelerated), gets a base rate for the behavior, and describes in detail what happened and the circumstances or stimulus conditions under which the behavior occurred.

3. The parent learns to identify *what* is reinforcing for his child. That is, the parent through direct observation and interview makes a list of activities which are reinforcing for the child and puts these in a hierarchy according to response probability.

4. The parent identifies the behaviors to be changed including those deriving from step "2" above plus those deriving from an analysis of the child's reading ability reported to the parent.

5. The parent tries punishment and/or any of the five alternatives to punishment that seem appropriate. Constant contact is maintained with the training staff. Some of the parent attempts at using new techniques are worked out in the home and some in our laboratory.

The program undergoes frequent revisions on the basis of tryouts. Three examples of how the program was revised are presented here in concluding our discussion of the parent training program.

1. In the initial pre-experimental versions of the training program we worked with parents who were paying fees for diagnostic and remedial work on their children. With these highly motivated parents, attendance was no problem. However, when we conducted the training program with a random selection of parents of children with reading disability, we had to change our procedures to maintain attendance. Thus, we had to provide transportation for some parents, and for others we had to modify the highly academic training program to maintain interest and attendance. Much of the program that communicated effectively in written format had to be changed for parents who were poor readers. Technical terminology was supplanted by nontechnical language.

2. We also learned from early versions of our program that it was not very easy for parents to reinforce new behaviors in a child because the parents often chose neutral stimuli which were not reinforcing. Thus, we developed exercises for identifying reinforcers based on the work of Ligon (1959) and Premack (1965). One parent applied these techniques in a creative way. She noticed that her daughter would do almost anything to avoid being late to school (e.g., skip breakfast, run to school, ask for a ride, trade chores). Thus, when the parent made 'getting to go to school on time' contingent on having homework completed, the daughter got her homework completed earlier. In training parents to identify and use reinforcers we have found it more effective to teach them general principles rather than specific techniques. Because behavior is complex, a specific technique may fail to work in a given situation, but a knowledge of principles allows the parent to figure out why and to devise alternative techniques.

3. One problem that came to our attention early in the development of a training program was the practical problem of changing a parent's behavior when a strong previously developed

competing response was interfering. In one case a mother had a tendency to give the child a big lecture when the child erred on a word. Thus, if the child said "place" for "palace," the parent might say "Now Michael I told you that before. You left part of the word out. Now sound it out slowly. . . ." In this particular case the child quit listening to the parent and "tuned in" again after the long lecture. The mother did not respond to our suggestions for her behavior change but expressed a desire to change. Parent and child were brought into our laboratory and placed in a room with a one-way viewing screen. The parent (mother) wore an earphone allowing the trainer to communicate with her. If the parent began a lecture when her child read place/palace, the trainer said (over the earphone) "palace, m-hm," signifying to the parent that she should stop her lecture and say "palace, m-hm." The parent's lectures diminished rapidly in length as a result of such practice.

In each session with parents, whether individually or in a group, there were seven major objectives of the training program.

1. Encourage parent goal setting of specific things to accomplish with respect to themselves and their children.

2. Relate new concepts to their own background of experience with as many common associations as possible.

3. Provide knowledge of their own progress and progress of their children at home and school.

4. Offer personal warmth and support to parents.

5. Establish identification of parents with a new reference group "acquainted with some special terminology, successful in specific skills, in a winning operation, etc."

6. Develop skills in behavioral analysis and management through discussion of their own cases and selected training cases and role playing.

7. Develop awareness of own behavior so they can see how competing habits of their own are being reinforced.

Home visits. We made several visits to the homes of all experimental children. The following is a report of a visit to the home of Norinne.

In the course of discussion Norinne's parents mentioned another family in the experimental group. The child had an operation and was required to wear a cast that kept him home. They wanted to do something for the child, so they gave him some goldfish to watch. This kind of concern for others in the group was quite common and showed itself in offering rides and offering emotional support during the class sessions. A feeling of confidence and identity with the group was established in such encounters. Each person had some uniqueness for which we showed appreciation and recognition. Norinne's mother made some Eskimo Yo Yos and slippers and a coat and showed these to us. Thus, instead of being "a parent of a child with a reading problem," each parent was recognized in his own right and glory.

Another value of the home visit centered around helping them to implement the principles that were discussed in class. Of course, we had quite a bit to go on in these home sessions. Discussion centered around parent descriptions of changeworthy child behavior, descriptions of dinner table conversations, the five-day log of the child's activities, and the child's reading performance on the various tests administered. The specific recommendations for parents were followed up in these home visits. For example, in carrying out the suggested recommendations, Norinne's parents had considerable success but noted that a major problem was the "soft volume" in Norinne's oral reading. This difficulty was noted by the child's teachers as well as the parents. Since it was of concern to both teacher and parent, suggestions were made for increasing the volume of Norinne's vocalizations.

On a follow-up visit parents reported lack of success. At that time the experimenter directed parents to have Norinne prepare some material to read to the experimenter. On a final visit the experimenter listened to Norinne and showed more approval for louder, more fluent reading than for the softer reading. This demonstration followed by a discussion with the parents helped them to increase the amplitude of Norinne's oral reading as well as her fluency.

The mother's ineffectiveness in getting the children to respond to her requests was also discussed in home visits. With parent permission the family agreed to support each other in changing this circumstance. Thus, children responded more immediately to mother when she spoke in a normal tone than when she raised her voice. Also, the mother followed through on her "commands" by not repeating them many times but simply going after the child and "walking them through the required task" after the first request.

Home visits gave the experimenters insight into conditions that were incompatible with homework or conditions that were potentially quite powerful. Parent interaction patterns, TV watching, parental neglect, and other conditions were observed and provided the basis for parent instruction in the general class setting as well as in home visits.

After home visits parents were more responsive in bringing in reports of child behavior. For example, after emphasizing to Norinne's mother the importance of working with Norinne a few minutes a day, and demonstrating what to do, she brought to class brief descriptions of her work as follows:

> Did her spelling today. Had to find out what each word meant. I find it good practice for both of us. Fussed a little cause she had to do the supper dishes, but I only asked her once.
> She seems to be grasping more of the meaning of words today. She enjoys the few minutes we spend together. She comes to me now about things and words she don't understand.

Thus, home visits provided an opportunity for the experimenter to see the situation more clearly, conduct demonstration of techniques and check on the validity of parental "rationalizations" for the difficulty of implementing suggestions. On the last count, for example, one mother with nine children argued she was too busy to supervise her child's reading even for 5 minutes a night. On the evening of the experimenter's visit (by appointment) the entire family was watching TV. It was easy after that to get at least 5 minutes a day from this mother in which she listened to her child read.

School visits. The experimenter visited all experimental and control children in their school remedial reading class. He did not make recommendations to the remedial teacher but simply observed the children. The school visits by the experimenter appeared to have an impact on experimental parents by demonstrating an interest in their children. As reported in the experimental results, experimental children (on urging from parents) requested more reading material to be sent home and did more home work on such material. When experimental parents visited the school, they had specific purposes in mind because of class and private discussions with the experimenter.

Summary and discussion

Objectives. The two major hypotheses tested in this study are:

1. Pupils whose parents are involved in a training program will show greater oral and silent reading regressed gains than a control group whose parents are not involved in the program.

2. Mothers' attitudes as measured by the PARI Factors I, II, III are significantly correlated with oral and silent reading regressed gains.

Sample. A sample of forty remedial reading students in grades three to six in two elementary schools, 20 experimentals and 20 controls—reduced to 13 experimentals and 16 controls due to moving, lack of parental interest, or infrequent attendance during the time of the study.

Pupil measures. In September, all pupils were administered the California Reading Test, Elementary Level, Form X, as a measure of silent reading achievement and the Gilmore Oral Reading Test, Form A. Alternate forms of these tests were administered during the week beginning January 28th.

Parent measures. During the second week of September all mothers were administered the PARI. A post-treatment administration was not carried out as intended because an unexpected contamination occurred when many of the experimentals were found to be involved in another project in which the PARI was administered and discussed.

Design. Parents and children were randomly assigned to experimental and control groups after an initial sample of children and parents was selected as described above. All pupils were in a school remedial reading class receiving instruction in groups of 2 to 5. Mothers of experimentals were in a training program during the course of the study, and controls entered the training program after post-test data on children was obtained.

The parent-training program

Fourteen once-a-week formal sessions from September 15 to December 15 were held with experimental parents. Each parent participated in two individual sessions at their home or the university during that period. From December 15 to January 28 parents met individually with experimenter to discuss the progress of their children. The parent training program is outlined in the body of the report.

Results.

1. There was a significant difference (.10 level) between experimental and control groups on regressed gains on the California Reading subtest, reading comprehension favoring the control group. However, vocabulary and total reading in silent reading measure did not differ significantly between groups.

2. Experimentals had significantly higher regressed gains on Gilmore Oral Reading accuracy (.05), comprehension (.02), and rate (.10).

3. None of the PARI Factor I (approval of maternal control of the child) or Factor II approval of expressions of hostility) were significantly correlated with any of the six reading achievement measures. However, Factor III (approval of positive attitudes toward child-rearing) was significantly correlated with silent reading comprehension (.05) and oral reading rate (.10).

Discussion. The exploratory work in this study has supported previously published data concerning the effect of parent factors on reading achievement. Specifically maternal warmth has been found to be reliably associated with pupil achievement in reading in both a laboratory investigation of actual parent behavior in structured discussions with their own children as well as in the larger treatment study. Putting together the results of our studies and those reviewed, we find the following parent behavior patterns associated with reading performance of children.

1. Parent pressure or aspiration for the extent of the child's schooling.

2. Number and quality of cultural activities provided for the child including books and toys in the home and places visited.

3. Allowing participation by children in mealtime conversations beyond talk about food.

4. Presence of emotionally positive or warm parent interaction with the child.

5. Participation by parents in training programs focused on one or more of the above behavior patterns as well as other behavior patterns characteristic of our own program.

Our studies, though they were small

sample pilot projects, have made several contributions to previous work including use of regressed gain scores, the development of a semi-structured interaction situation on a reading task, the development of hypotheses for further investigation, and the clarification of training problems requiring further development.

One hypothesis generated by this study comes from the result in the laboratory study conflicting with Bing's study showing that mothers of high verbal girls showed significantly more disapproval and withholding of help than mothers of low verbal girls. This discrepancy is of particular interest since the studies were so similar. They both observed behavior in a laboratory interaction situation. Bing's study was on fifth grade girls and boys and ours on sixth grade girls, and her results for girls alone are those reported here. Also, her definition of high and low verbal ability was similar to that used in our study. One plausible and testable exploration of this discrepancy is that withholding help and disapproval is characteristic of mothers of high verbal children when built on a previous history of much warmth and approval in early childhood plus a present history of much warmth along with the disapproval and withholding of help.

Another line of research that follows from the study just completed is the identification of the amount of variance in dependent variable measures accounted for by specific parts of the treatment program. In our study, too, treatment accounted for 16 percent of the variance in oral reading accuracy and 25 percent of the variance in oral reading comprehension. It might well be that a more limited treatment could account for as much variance. Or, if we could find out what part of the treatment accounts for most of the variance, that part might be made even more effective. Or, alternatively, treatment parameters not accounting for dependent variable variance may be studied to determine whether revisions

in the treatment might make it more productive.

Finally, specific problems in implementing the treatment program have been identified. Some of these suggest modifications in the training program. Thus, we found ourselves moving further away from technical jargon as we became involved with parents who had little formal schooling or little interest in our jargon. Also, we found that when we introduced sessions in which they looked at a profile of their own children's performance in reading, we had more attentiveness and more follow-through on treatment suggestions. Thus, we would put specific case data on their children earlier in our next parent program. Many parents were in such conflict with each other or were so busy with two jobs, children, etc. that they could not manage much time on the program. Others who could have arranged more time were, according to their own reports, "too busy," "sick," or "will be there next time." We found ways eventually of getting to many of these parents, but our inexperience caught us unprepared to cope early with the problem. Thus, we would make a major part of our next training program the identification of "foot-draggers" and implementation of ways of getting them out to our sessions. Two of the most difficult problems faced by most parents in implementing contingency management were identifying events that were reinforcing, and trying out new behavior patterns inconsistent with their current

TABLE 1

MEANS AND STANDARD DEVIATIONS FOR THE SEPTEMBER AND JANUARY GRADE PLACEMENT OF THE CONTROL AND EXPERIMENTAL GROUPS

September		
	Mean	Standard Deviation
Control	3.7	0.9
Experimental	4.8	1.1

January		
	Mean	Standard Deviation
Control	4.2	0.9
Experimental	5.3	1.1

TABLE 2

MEANS AND STANDARD DEVIATIONS FOR THE SEPTEMBER AND JANUARY TESTING IN ORAL READING (GILMORE ORAL READING TEST), CONTROL AND EXPERIMENTAL GROUPS

CONTROL GROUP
September Testing

	Mean	Standard Deviation
Accuracy	3.0	1.0
Comprehension	3.3	1.2
Rate	85.9	38.2

January Testing

Accuracy	4.0	1.1
Comprehension	4.5	1.3
Rate	83.5	24.1

EXPERIMENTAL GROUP
September Testing

	Mean	Standard Deviation
Accuracy	2.6	0.6
Comprehension	2.7	0.9
Rate	70.3	24.1

January Testing

Accuracy	4.2	0.7
Comprehension	4.8	1.4
Rate	91.1	18.5

TABLE 3

MEANS AND STANDARD DEVIATIONS FOR THE SEPTEMBER AND JANUARY TESTING IN SILENT READING (CALIFORNIA READING TEST), CONTROL AND EXPERIMENTAL GROUPS

CONTROL GROUP
September Testing

	Mean	Standard Deviation
Vocabulary	3.9	1.3
Comprehension	3.5	1.1
Total Reading	3.7	1.2

January Testing

Vocabulary	4.4	1.5
Comprehension	4.4	1.3
Total Reading	4.5	1.3

EXPERIMENTAL GROUP
September Testing

	Mean	Standard Deviation
Vocabulary	2.9	1.0
Comprehension	2.5	0.5
Total Reading	2.7	0.7

January Testing

Vocabulary	3.4	1.2
Comprehension	3.4	1.0
Total Reading	3.5	1.1

behavior. One of the contributions of our study was the preliminary development of procedures for helping parents to identify reinforcers using the work of Premack and Ligon as our guides. Another contribution was the preliminary development of special procedures for helping a parent to break a habit interfering with her trying out of a new behavior pattern. These two training innovations will be further developed for future training programs.

Other future developments should include emphasis on father participation or, in the case of father absence, some significant other adult follow-up of parent attitude and behavior change as well as pupil gains, and development of measures of more specific behaviors related to the training program.

TABLE 4

MEANS AND STANDARD DEVIATIONS FOR THE CALIFORNIA TEST OF MENTAL MATURITY, CONTROL AND EXPERIMENTAL GROUPS

CONTROL GROUP: N = 16

	Mean	Standard Deviation
Language IQ	80.7	7.8
Nonlanguage IQ	91.9	8.1
Total IQ	84.4	6.8

EXPERIMENTAL GROUP: N = 13

	Mean	Standard Deviation
Language IQ	86.6	6.2
Nonlanguage IQ	99.5	11.5
Total IQ	91.5	8.2

TABLE 5

MEANS AND STANDARD DEVIATIONS FOR THE MOTHERS' PARENTAL ATTITUDE RESEARCH INSTRUMENT FACTOR SCORES, CONTROL AND EXPERIMENTAL GROUPS

CONTROL GROUP

	Mean	Standard Deviation
Factor I	168.7	29.0
Factor II	50.5	7.7
Factor III	64.7	6.5

EXPERIMENTAL GROUP

	Mean	Standard Deviation
Factor I	164.3	23.6
Factor II	58.2	7.0
Factor III	65.4	6.8

The Effect of a Summer Television Reading Program on the Reading Achievement of Children

JACK W. HUMPHREY
Evansville, Indiana,
Reading Center

AT THE END of the critical first grade program, children leave school for the long summer vacation where many of them do little reading. Six- and seven-year-old children usually cannot go to libraries by themselves, and there are comparatively fewer books in most homes for these children than for older pupils in upper grades. Most school systems do not operate summer reading classes for children leaving the first grade, so it would seem that reading skills might not increase over the summer and might even be lower when school starts in the fall.

It seems to be common knowledge among second grade teachers that children lose some of their reading skills during the summer vacation after the first grade. The purpose of this study, which was funded by the U. S. Office of Education, was to determine the amount of reading skill loss that occurs during the summer and to see if a television reading program would help.

Objectives. The objectives of this study involving children during the summer after the first grade were as follows:

1. To determine the reading loss or gain of first grade children during the summers of 1965 and 1966.

   a. To find the loss or gain of boys and girls.

   b. To find the loss or gain of the upper and lower intelligence quarters.

2. To develop and present a summer reading program by television.

3. To test the null hypothesis that there was no difference between the means of reading achievement tests taken by children who did and who did not participate in a summer television program.

Procedure. A steering committee was formed at the beginning of the project. The purpose of the committee was to approve the various phases of the project as well as to give suggestions and comments concerning plans for each phase. It was composed of the superintendent, assistant superintendent in charge of instruction, director of elementary education, director of educational television, accounting supervisor, primary supervisor, and the director of the project.

After the formation of the steering committee in January, 1965, the California Reading Test, Lower Primary, Forms W and X, 1963 norms, and the California Short-Form Test of Mental Maturity, Primary, 1957 S-Form, 1958 norms, were purchased so that all forms would be available for the experimental and control groups. In May, first and second grade teachers met for a presentation of the entire research project which included instruction in how to administer the reading and intelligence tests.

The tests were administered to the control and experimental groups during the same weeks in May and September of 1965 and 1966. Although the teachers had one week to give the tests and to return them to the reading center, most of the tests were given on Tuesday or Wednesday. Written instructions were sent to teachers during the second year of the project as no general meeting seemed necessary. Since no scoring or reading of norms had to be done by teachers, the testing of pupils was a relatively easy task. All teachers received copies of the manual so that they could administer the test properly; the directions in the manuals were clear and easy to follow. All tests were returned to the reading center where secretaries did the scoring.

A book was needed by each child to get him actively involved in the program, to help him become enthusiastic about the program through ownership of a special summer book, and to provide skill lessons to be completed as introduced by the television teacher.

Eight first and second grade teachers, including the television teacher plus the primary supervisor, wrote the lessons in the activity book during the summer of 1965 following an outline developed prior to the workshop. These teachers of different ages had taught and had been taught with a variety of methods, which enabled them to present many different ideas for consideration by the group.

The content of the book was based on the judgment of the workshop participants who knew the problems of first and second grade children and who were aware of the summer loss and resulting fall reading deficiencies. They were concerned about the attitudes of children and suggested fun pages. They knew that many children forget the names and sounds of letters over the summer and that there is confusion between letters such as "b" and "d." Possessives, blends, recreational reading, and other reading skills were included in the final draft.

The title of the activity book, "Ride the Reading Rocket," was selected because of the high interest in space activities of both boys and girls. A special feature was a puppet which was named Rocko by the children at the beginning of the program.

The alphabet was placed on the inside of the front cover as a reference for making correct letters in the book. In the back of the book were pages to record attendance and books read. Addressed postcards were placed in the book for children and parents to mail to the television teacher. They were used to send in a name for the puppet, the name of the books liked best, comments by parents, and other information.

Other pages featured puzzles, coloring, and writing letters and words. Blanks for 40 words of the day were spaced throughout the book. Numerals were spelled and written at the bottom of each page. A note to parents was placed in the front of the book to give them directions on how to help their child during the summer.

The lessons in the activity book were designed so that most of them could not be done by the children without directions from the teacher. Thus, lessons would be done correctly and at the right time.

The vocabulary used in the activity book was generally restricted to words normally introduced in the first grade; other words were used as necessary to develop lessons about special topics. The skills involved in the lessons were those normally used in the first grade by the regular classroom teachers. They were planned to motivate the listener, to give practice in word study and the comprehension skills, to provide a review of the first grade vocabulary, to introduce additional sight words, to develop the ability to follow directions, to furnish opportunities for self-direction, and to stimulate creative expression.

The activity book was illustrated and printed during the winter and spring months. During this time a puppet was designed to be used daily in the program. The purpose of the puppet was to capitalize on the inherent interest that children have in puppets as well as to have someone to assist with the pacing of the program. Pictures of the puppet were also used throughout the activity book.

The television set was designed as the inside of a space ship and included control knobs, chalkboard, flannel board, and space for mounting materials. The costume of the teacher was a space suit which was designed to show up on black and white television, similar to space suits in the U. S. space program.

The teacher was given a week's leave of absence to work at the educational television station. A complete orientation given by the executive producer of the summer program included working in the control room and observing teachers preparing and presenting programs. On her last day at the station the television teacher presented an in-service television program to area teachers. She described the program to teachers, emphasized the importance of the project, and reviewed the role of teachers in gathering data and preparing children for the summer reading class.

On Thursday of the last week of school, a 15 minute television program was presented to all first graders. The children met the puppet and were invited to help select a name for him by sending their suggestions on the post cards in the activity book. Activity books were distributed to children, and their use with the program was described so pupils would not work ahead prior to directions being given with each lesson. The beginning date, time, and channel were emphasized at the end of the presentation.

The next 15 minutes of television time involved only parents, who had been notified earlier in the week to observe the entire 30 minutes. Parents were given information concerning the need for the program as well as how they could help by getting children up on time, by seeing that children had crayons and pencils to work with, and by helping them understand directions when necessary. The importance of recreational reading was emphasized, and parents were encouraged to take children to the library. Parents were also asked to be interested in the activity book which was to be brought home by the child that evening, and they were reminded of the starting date and time.

The theme of the summer television program was a space trip to Jupiter with Miss Sandy as the pilot and a puppet, named Rocko by the children, who was trying to learn to read. All scenes took place on the rocket ship although guests from earth could be zeroed in through special machines and presented to the children.

Each day the children from one of the schools were taken on an imaginary rocket ride. The school was mentioned by name and all of the pupils were invited to climb aboard.

A word of the day was written each day on the chalkboard by the teacher and in the activity book by the children. The word selected related to the lesson presented that day.

A book was usually read to the chil-dren each day. Permission was granted by over 20 publishers for use of their books on the program.

The attendance page was illustrated by the children rather than filled with X's or colored in. A simple picture relating to the day's lesson was drawn by the teacher, and the children made similar pictures for their books. For example, they drew a lamb the day one was shown on the program.

As most of the pages in the activity book were designed so that children could not work them without directions from the teacher, each day's lesson was planned so that there would be entertainment for the children as well as skill lessons.

The majority of the children had television sets in their homes. In the spring of 1965, 97.5 percent of 2,395 first grade children out of 2,455 had television sets in their homes. A higher figure was found in 1966 when 98.7 percent or 2,300 out of 2,330 children surveyed had television sets.

In 1965, 24 of the 60 children without television sets were able to view programs in the homes of neighbors or relatives. In 1966, 17 out of the 30 without television sets were able to view the program in other homes. Thus, only 13 children out of the 30 or one half of one percent were without television sets.

A survey made in May 1966, to determine the favorite television programs of first grade children in the Evansville-Vanderburgh School Corporation, revealed that the majority liked "adult" or family shows presented during prime television time rather than children's programs.

A total of 2,342 postcards and letters were received from children during the program. The following types were received: name the puppet, 532; parent comments, 273; picture requests, 285; library books liked and read, 195; and rhymes and miscellaneous, 1,057.

During the summer 518 children signed up in branches of the public library as "Rocket Readers." This club was limited to children who had just completed the first grade and who participated in the program. They checked out 5,187 books or about 10 books per child. These figures do not include children who got books from bookmobiles or those whose parents or older brothers or sisters checked out books for younger children. A total of 1,036 children visited with the teacher at libraries during the week after the eight weeks program.

All test information for both groups was given to the computer center of a local bank where IBM cards were punched. The cards were run on an IBM 1440 computer, and information concerning means and number of various groups was obtained. The Indiana University Computer Center ran all programs involving further analysis of the data. The CDC3400-3600 Computer System was used to run the analysis of variance and the analysis of covariance. The analysis of variance was computed using the Duncan Multiple Range Biomedical Computer Program O1V. The BMD04V analysis of covariance-multiple covariates program from the Health Sciences Computing Facility, UCLA, version of May 4, 1965, was used for the analysis of covariance. The number of cases exceeded the capacity of the program for covariance, so random numbers were generated by machine to eliminate a small number of cases.

Results. The experimental group contained less boys and girls than did the control group. The average age of children in the experimental group was one month higher than in the control group due to a change in entrance age requirements. The mean IQ of the experimental group was higher than the control group for boys, girls, and the total group. Boys had higher average IQ scores than girls in both groups.

The experimental group had higher scores in all reading categories in the pre-summer tests. Although both groups did better in the vocabulary test than in the comprehension test, girls outscored boys in all areas of reading in the pre-summer tests.

In the post-summer tests, the differences between the two groups was wider than in the pre-summer tests. The control group had losses over the summer in all areas except the comprehension test for girls. The biggest loss was in the vocabulary test where there was a much larger loss than in the comprehension test. The girls not only outscored the boys in all areas of the post-summer control group reading tests but also had less loss over the summer than boys; the boys had a loss of .19 years and the girls, .13 years. The total decline from a pre-summer control group score of 2.02 years to a post-summer score 1.86 years was a loss of .16 years.

The post-summer experimental group had losses in all areas except in the comprehension and total reading scores for girls; these losses were much less than those of the control group. The experimental group had a loss over the summer in vocabulary of .05 years and gained .10 years in comprehension.

All areas of the post-summer experimental group tests were higher than the control group post-summer tests. Boys made higher gains in the experimental group in vocabulary, comprehension, and total reading than girls, but the girls still had higher scores in all areas on the post-summer scores. There were larger differences between the comprehension means of the post-summer tests than between those of the post-summer vocabulary means. There was a gain for the post-summer experimental group over the post-summer control group of .17 years in vocabulary, .21 years in comprehension, and .18 years in the total reading scores. Boys made up 52.1 percent of the control group and 51.9 percent of the experimental group.

In the low quarters of the control and experimental groups, according to IQ, there was a smaller percent of boys in both the control and experimental groups compared to the entire population; there were 50.1 percent boys in the control group and

48.3 percent boys in the experimental group.

The average age of the children in the low quarter was higher than the total group as the control group was four months older and the experimental group three months older than the average for the total population. The boys in the experimental group were an average of two months older than the girls.

The average IQ for the experimental group was higher than the control group as in the total population.

The pre-summer control and experimental groups scored higher in vocabulary than in comprehension as did the total group. The pre-summer experimental group boys scored higher than the control group boys while the control group girls outscored the experimental group girls.

The biggest loss over the summer for the low quarter control group was in the vocabulary test where there was a total loss of .16 years. In contrast, the control group gained .02 years in comprehension. The total loss over the summer for the control boys and girls was .15 years.

The experimental group made its biggest gain over the summer in vocabulary. There were losses in all areas except in the comprehension and total reading scores for girls. In the experimental group, scores were higher in all reading areas as compared to those of the post-summer control groups. Although the largest gains were made in the vocabulary tests, boys made larger gains than girls. Finally there was a gain for the post-summer experimental group over the post-summer control group of .13 years in vocabulary, .12 years in comprehension, and .12 years in total reading.

There was a larger percentage of boys in the upper quarter, according to IQ, than in the total or lower quarter groups as 53.9 percent of the upper quarter control group and 54.4 percent of the experimental group were boys. The children in the upper quarter were younger than the total group. The average IQ in the upper quarter experimental group was slightly higher than the control group. The boys had a higher average IQ than girls in both the experimental and control groups.

In the pre-summer tests the girls scored better than boys in all areas for both the control and experimental groups. Scores were higher on the vocabulary test than on the comprehension test for boys and girls in both groups. The pupils in the control group were superior in the pre-summer tests in vocabulary scores for boys and in the total vocabulary scores. The experimental group scored higher in all areas of comprehension and in total reading for boys and for all pupils combined.

In the post-summer tests the children in the control group had lower scores than in the pre-summer tests in all areas except the comprehension scores for girls. More loss was made in vocabulary scores than in comprehension. The experimental group made gains over the summer in all areas of comprehension and in the total reading scores, although there was a slight loss in each area of the vocabulary scores.

The post-summer experimental group had higher scores in all test areas for both boys and girls than did the post-summer control group. The biggest gains were made on the comprehension tests. Boys made bigger gains in vocabulary, comprehension, and total scores than did the girls. There was a gain by the experimental group over the control group in post-summer scores of .12 years in vocabulary, .19 years in comprehension, and .18 years in the total reading score.

The means for the boys in their pre-summer and post-summer reading and intelligence tests showed that the experimental groups scored higher in all pre-summer and post-summer reading and intelligence tests. The experimental groups scored higher in all pre-summer and post-summer reading tests. The difference between the post-summer groups was larger than the pre-summer difference.

There was a significant difference

shown in the analysis of variance between the control and experimental pre-summer groups of boys in vocabulary, p < .01; comprehension, p < .01; and total reading, p < .05. The groups grew wider apart in the post-summer tests where there was a more significant difference in vocabulary, p < .001; comprehension, p < .001; and total reading, p < .001. There was also a significant difference between the means of the IQ scores for the two groups, p < .001.

The means of the girls in their pre-summer and post-summer reading and intelligence tests showed that the experimental group was superior in all areas. The differences between the reading scores of the groups grew after the summer program.

Analysis of variance for the means of the pre-summer reading tests for the girls showed that none of the differences was significant, but there were higher scores for the experimental group in all areas. In the post-summer tests there was a significant difference in vocabulary, p < .001; comprehension, p < .001; and total reading, p < .001. There was a significant difference between the groups in intelligence, p. < .05.

Analysis of variance revealed a significant difference in intelligence between the groups as well as a significant difference in the pre-summer reading tests for boys. The number of cases of boys and girls in each group was reduced by random sample to allow the BMD04V analysis of covariance program to be used so that the differences in the starting point for both reading achievement and IQ could be corrected.

The analysis of covariance for boys of the post-summer vocabulary test adjusted for the pre-summer vocabulary test and IQ revealed that there was a significant gain, F = 158.033, p < .001, during the summer months. Similar gains were made in comprehension, F = 105.340, p < .001, and total reading, F = 67.649, p < .001. The fact that the F for total reading is smaller than for vocabulary or comprehension

suggests that the summer television program influenced the vocabulary but not the comprehension of some boys, and the comprehension but not the vocabulary scores for other boys. When the scores are combined for vocabulary and comprehension into total reading, the effects seem to be slightly weakened.

The analysis of covariance for girls of the post-summer vocabulary test adjusted for the pre-summer vocabulary test and for IQ revealed that there was a significant gain, F = 22.729, p < .001, for the girls in vocabulary during the summer. There was also a significant gain for the girls in comprehension, F = 11.306, p < .001, and in the total reading score, F = 22.269, p < .001.

The F was larger for both boys and girls in the vocabulary test than in the comprehension test. The television program appeared to have an especially strong effect on boys as all outcomes were higher than those for girls.

The children in the experimental group were asked by their second grade teachers to return their books to school so that the number of days watched could be recorded. The children were divided into three groups according to the number of days watched. Group 1 watched 21 to 40 days; Group 2 did not return their books and may or may not have watched the program, and Group 3 returned their books and watched 0 to 20 days. There were 795 children in Group 1, 818 in Group 2, and 293 in Group 3.

Group 1 had higher pre-summer scores in all reading tests and in IQ than Group 2 or Group 3. Group 3 had higher pre-summer scores in all reading tests and in IQ than Group 2. The vocabulary scores were higher than the comprehension scores for all three pre-summer groups.

The means in all post-summer reading tests for Group 1 were higher than pre-summer scores for the same group. The largest gain, .1875 years, was made in the comprehension test. Group 2 lost in all reading areas over the summer with the biggest loss in vocabulary. Group 3 also lost in all reading areas, but the highest loss was in the comprehension test. Group 2 had less loss than Group 3 during the summer.

Analysis of variance for the means of the pre-summer vocabulary test for experimental Groups 1, 2, and 3 showed that there was a significant difference, $F = 47.0327$, $p < .001$, between the groups. Significant differences were also found in comprehension, $F = 33.7230$, $p < .001$, and in total reading, $F = 50.1129$, $p < .001$.

The analysis of variance for the means of the post-summer vocabulary test for Groups 1, 2, and 3 showed that the difference was wider than in the pre-summer vocabulary test, $F = 102.1042$, $p < .001$. The differences were significant and wider than pre-summer scores for comprehension, $F = 93.0457$, $p < .001$, and in total reading, $F = 106.3714$, $p < .001$.

There was a significant difference between IQ scores for the groups, $F = 34.5893$, $p < .001$. The average IQ for Group 1 was 115.32, 109.07 for Group 2, and 113.03 for Group 3. The total reading means for the pre-summer groups were 2.2024 for Group 1, 1.9093 for Group 2, and 2.1468 for Group 3. The post-summer reading means were 2.2834 for Group 1, 1.8178 for Group 2, and 1.9973 for Group 3.

The data indicate that children who watched over half of the summer television programs had higher intelligence scores; better pre-summer and post-summer reading scores in vocabulary, comprehension, and total reading; and made gains in reading ability in all reading areas during the summer while the average in reading scores for the other groups declined during the summer months.

Conclusions and implications. The following conclusions are based on information reported throughout the study and, specifically, data concerning availability of television sets and television viewing interests, the use of library facilities, and the results of the analysis of the data. All of the conclusions concern children in the Evansville-Vanderburgh School Corporation who just completed the first grade.

1. Most of the children who complete the first grade have television sets in their homes.

2. The favorite television programs of the children are not children's programs but "adult" or family shows which are presented during prime television time.

3. Boys and girls have significant losses in reading ability during the summer vacation months.

4. Girls have less loss during summer vacations than boys.

5. Girls have higher reading scores than boys at the end of the first grade.

6. There is an equal loss in reading ability for the upper and lower quarters based on IQ, but the percent of loss is greater for the lower quarter during the summer months.

7. The summer television program significantly increased library usage during the summer.

8. Boys and girls made significant gains in vocabulary, comprehension, and total reading as a result of the summer television program, as compared to boys and girls who had no formal reading program during the summer.

9. Children who watched over half of the television programs had higher IQ and reading scores at the end of the first grade and made significant gains in all reading tests, as compared to those children who did not watch over half of the programs or who did not return their books to school.

10. The television program had an especially strong effect on boys, as all outcomes for the total group and for the upper and lower quarters were higher for boys than for girls.

The findings of the study show that there is normally a significant loss in reading ability by children during the summer vacation after the first grade. The results suggest that many parents do not utilize library facilities or encourage reading for their children during the summer months.

Even with the availability of activity books and a summer television program, help and encouragement is needed by children from their parents to sustain the interest necessary to benefit from the program. As in most good reading programs, cooperation of the home and school will usually result in better reading achievement for children.

The results of the study show that boys, despite having a higher average intelligence than girls, do not achieve as well as girls in reading during the first year of school. When the content of a program is aimed at the interests of boys—for example, the summer television program with its space theme and boy puppet—boys achieve better than girls. As several authors indicated in the related research, beginning reading materials should be especially concerned with the interests of boys.

Summer television is helpful in maintaining reading achievement during the summer. Good teachers are available; children watch television frequently and enjoy learning, using the medium; and post-first-grade children during the summer are not overburdened with other studies and activities. The cost of a summer television program is much less expensive than normal reading programs. A much larger percentage of the children participated in the television program than has been reported in summer reading programs held in regular classrooms.

Some Difficulties in Transfer of Learning from i.t.a. to t.o.

JOHN DOWNING
Reading Research Unit
London, W.C.1.

THE RESULTS OF five years of basic research on i.t.a. were published in January 1967 by the National Foundation for Educational Research in England and Wales. The research report by Downing (*3*) was reviewed by eleven independent experts from Australia, Britain, Canada, and the United States and all this material is published together in one volume, *The i.t.a. Symposium.*

The most important conclusion from the research is that "the traditional orthography of English is a serious cause of difficulty in the early stages of learning to read and write" (p. 51). The evidence for this conclusion is massive. For example, on the Schonell (*11*) Graded Word Reading test and on the Neale (*10*) Analysis of Reading Ability, administered in the middle of the second school year, the t.o. word recognition and accuracy scores of the t.o. pupils were less than half of the i.t.a. scores of the i.t.a. pupils on the same tests printed in i.t.a.

The report also concludes that "i.t.a. as an example of a transitional writing-system for beginning reading and writing in English generally produces superior results in t.o. reading and in t.o. spelling by the end of the third year of school" (p. 49). But the superiority of the i.t.a. group after transition from i.t.a. to t.o. at the end of the third year, although significant, is small compared with the great difference between i.t.a. attainments and t.o. attainments one and one-half years earlier. What has happened to cut down the dramatic advantage of i.t.a. in the earlier phase?

The i.t.a. Symposium's report examines the children's progress during the transition stage and concludes,

The success of i.t.a. in improving t.o. literacy skills occurs in spite of an important setback in the growth of these basic skills at the stage of transition from i.t.a. to t.o. (p. 49).

While subjective impressions may suggest that the transition from i.t.a. to t.o. is "smooth" and "painless," nevertheless, the objective test results from the basic research in Britain show clearly that the i.t.a. students' t.o. attainments are generally inferior to their i.t.a. attainments—a few weeks earlier in the case of the Neale test, and a few months earlier on the Schonell test.

For example, 152 i.t.a. students who had been transferred from i.t.a books to t.o. materials by their teachers, took the i.t.a. version of Form C of the Neale Test in the middle of the second year and one month later they were tested again on the t.o. version of Form A of the Neale test. The mean score fell from 42.2 on the i.t.a. test to 33.4 on the t.o. test.

Further evidence of this setback in the development of the ability to read the English language was obtained from comparing the i.t.a. and t.o. scores on Schonell's Graded Word Reading test of 135 children who had been transferred from i.t.a. to t.o. materials at least four months prior to the test. The i.t.a. test was administered a little before the middle of the second school year. The t.o. version of the same test was given at the start of the third school year. The mean score fell from 51.6 in i.t.a. to 44.8 in t.o. (Full statistical information is given in *The i.t.a. Symposium* report.

In a second British i.t.a. experiment designed to control the teacher variable more rigorously than was possible in the first one, and thus to check on the results obtained, a similar setback appears to have occurred. All 13 of the i.t.a. classes had lower t.o. scores than i.t.a. scores on the Neale test administered as in the first experiment. These results were published in Downing and Jones (*7*) and are further discussed in a new book by Downing (6) to be published shortly.

The report in *The i.t.a. Symposium* states that the evidence supports the view expressed by some teachers in the i.t.a. classes that "no technique of circumventing t.o. would be as immediately effective as changing to a simple and regular system, through a reform of English spelling" (p. 52). Certainly the setback at the transition stage is still further evidence that t.o. is a serious handicap in learning to read in English-speaking countries.

However, under present circumstances and possibly for many years to come, methods of circumventing the difficulties of t.o. seem likely to be important and therefore the final paragraph of the report in *The i.t.a. Symposium* reads:

> If the Initial Teaching Alphabet or some other transitional system is to be taken up and more widely used, as seems likely from current trends, then urgent consideration should be given to this need for a series of laboratory studies to shape the new system to provide greater effectiveness in transfer to reading and writing in the conventional orthography of English (p. 53).

As a preliminary step towards the proposed laboratory experiments to establish these needed improvements in i.t.a., an analysis of i.t.a. students' errors in t.o. reading has been made in an attempt to answer the question "What are the causes of this setback in skill development in the stage of transition from i.t.a to t.o.?"

What causes the setback?

The three error analyses which have been made are intended only as a preliminary step to answering this question. However, their results may permit us at least to derive some hypotheses for testing in future experiments.

The first two error analyses are based on data from the original British experiment on i.t.a. which commenced in 1961. Full details of the design, methods, and procedures of this experiment are given in Downing's report in *The i.t.a. Symposium* on pages 3-24.

The method of error analysis was to count the number of errors made on each t.o. word by i.t.a. students who had been transferred from i.t.a. to t.o. materials by their teachers. In this way the t.o. words which were most difficult for i.t.a. students could be discovered. Two t.o. tests were used for this purpose; the Neale Analysis of Reading Ability and Schonell's Graded Word Reading test. The complete statistics are provided on pages 63-65 of *The i.t.a. Symposium.*

The design for transfer from i.t.a. to t.o. is based on the similarity of i.t.a. whole-word configurations to t.o. whole-word configurations, especially in respect of the "top coast-line" or upper part of the line of print. A description of the i.t.a. design for transfer to t.o. is given in Downing (2). However, the two error analyses reported in *The i.t.a. Symposium* and discussed further in Downing's (6) later book, at least raise doubts about the theoretical assumptions behind i.t.a.'s design for transfer. The results of these analyses of errors made by i.t.a. pupils in the stage of transition to t.o. suggested that they may have been analyzing and paying attention to details within the whole word at least part of the time. In particular, on the Neale test more of the words which caused difficulty appear to have differed in t.o. from their i.t.a. form in terms of individual letters rather than in terms of overall configuration. For example, in the second test passage of the Neale measure the five most difficult items were:

T.O.	*(i.t.a)*
the center	(ſhe senter)
frightened	(frietend)
to safety	(tω sæfty)
returned	(returnd)
wandered	(wonderd)

The i.t.a. theory of transfer might predict "frightened" as a difficult word at the transition stage because its t.o.

configuration is different from its i.t.a. one, but the other four items have i.t.a. and t.o. configurations which are highly similar. On the other hand, four of the above five especially difficult items have some particular *detail within the t.o. word* which is different from the relevant detail in the i.t.a. word. These and other examples led to the proposal that there is a "need to consider for the study of this problem a smaller unit of transfer than the upper half of the configurations of whole words" (*3,* p. 50).

If one examines the problem of transfer from i.t.a. to t.o. in terms of such smaller units, the possibilities for proactive interference are much greater. Only a relatively few possibilities are obvious from the configurational point of view (e.g. ʃhœ/ *show*), but many of the more difficult words found in the analysis of errors made on the t.o. Neale and Schonell test by "transferred" i.t.a. pupils contained possible sources of proactive interference, e.g., the *s* in island; the *c* in ceiling; the *g* in gnome; and the *ph* in nephew on the Schonell test. In almost every case those t.o. words on the Neale test which produced the greatest number of errors represented *a different sound* in i.t.a., e.g., the *c* in center, the *igh* in frightened, the *a* in safety, the *a* in wandered, the *or* in work, the *t* in action, the *i* in final.

McBride's (*9*) study of transfer from i.t.a. to t.o. provides further evidence that proactive interference from individual letters is an important factor in the transition stage. He found that the six most difficult t.o. words from a list of 100 words from the *Janet & John* i.t.a. basal series were *these, age, huge, whom, fruit, magician,* all of which contain t.o. letters which have different sound values in i.t.a.

The second British i.t.a. experiment which began in 1963 has now produced further results beyond those published in the article by Downing and Jones (*7*). A report of these results from the later stages of the experiment is currently in preparation but the full details as to aims, methods, and procedures may be found in the article already published. One new set of results comes from the administration of the Schonell Graded Word Reading test in t.o. to all experimental (i.t.a.) group pupils and control (t.o.) group pupils at the beginning of the third year in school.

At this stage in the second experiment less than half of the i.t.a. pupils had been changed over to t.o. materials by their teachers but *all* of the Experimental i.t.a. Group were tested in t.o. The method of this third error analysis was different. *All* the childrens' responses were utilized, but errors were only counted if the word read incorrectly on the second test had been read correctly previously, when the same test had been administered approximately nine months earlier. In that previous testing the experimental (i.t.a.) group had been tested on the same test *in i.t.a.* Now, they were given the t.o. version. Thus the errors showed which words read correctly in i.t.a. proved difficult to read in t.o. Parallel data were collected for the control (t.o.) group tested on both occasions in t.o. This provides some control for random guessing. The results are provided in the table.

Naturally the results cannot be regarded as conclusive, but they increase the doubts about the theoretical assumptions underlying the i.t.a. design for transfer to t.o. The words which proved most difficult in transfer from i.t.a. to t.o. generally differed little in their i.t.a. and t.o. upper-half configurations, but they did differ instead in some *detail* within the configuration, this detail being a possible source of proactive interference.

If one breaks down the words in the table into groups of ten, following Schonell's order of grading, the more difficult words in each group can be ascertained. The most difficult word among the easiest first ten words was *playing* (plæiŋ). The t.o. and i.t.a. forms of this word differ in terms of both configuration and detail. The high proportion of failures in transfer on this word could be due to either

SECOND i.t.a. EXPERIMENT ANALYSIS OF ERRORS MADE BY EXPERIMENTAL GROUP (N = 203) AND CONTROL GROUP (N = 211) ON SCHONELL'S GRADED WORD READING TEST

First test administered after one and one-third years in i.t.a. to i.t.a. experimental group subjects and in t.o. to t.o. control group subjects. Retest at start of third year in t.o. to all subjects.

Word (i.t.a./t.o.)	EXPERIMENTAL (i.t.a.) GROUP			CONTROL (t.o.) GROUP		
	Total No. Ss reading word correctly in i.t.a.	Ss who read word correctly in i.t.a. but not in t.o.	Percent failure in transfer	Total No. Ss reading word correctly first test	Ss who read word correctly on first test but not on second test	Percent failure in second test
tree/tree	137	5	3.6	123	7	5.7
littl/little	199	7	3.5	191	5	2.6
milk/milk	135	2	1.5	122	1	0.8
egg/egg	143	4	2.8	122	2	1.6
bcok/book	147	12	8.2	127	4	3.1
scool/school	119	9	7.6	82	2	2.4
sit/sit	142	3	2.1	121	8	6.6
frog/frog	125	10	8.0	100	1	1.0
plæin/playing	134	20	14.9	103	1	1.0
bun/bun	111	2	1.8	103	2	1.9
flouer/flower	100	4	4.0	62	3	4.8
rced/road	119	22	18.5	50	1	2.0
clock/clock	107	8	7.5	87	1	1.1
træn/train	146	17	11.6	110	3	2.7
liet/light	137	48	35.0	39	1	2.6
pictuer/picture	75	3	4.0	5	0	0
thiŋk/think	96	8	8.3	67	1	1.5
summer/summer	82	3	3.7	64	2	3.1
peepl/people	89	11	12.4	42	1	2.4
sumthiŋ/something	120	22	18.3	97	6	6.2
dreem/dream	97	21	21.6	29	1	3.4
dounstærs/ downstairs	52	9	17.3	28	0	0
biscit/biscuit	87	23	26.4	36	0	0
ʃheperd/shepherd	79	13	16.5	35	1	2.9
thirsty/thirsty	41	4	9.8	22	0	0
croud/crowd	85	20	23.5	25	1	4.0
sandwich/sandwich	67	6	9.0	40	1	2.5
beginniŋ/beginning	26	1	3.8	26	5	19.2
pcestæj/postage	52	14	26.9	11	0	0
ieland/island	71	30	42.3	8	0	0
sauser/saucer	55	17	30.9	8	0	0
ænjel/angel	76	35	46.1	8	0	0
seeliŋ/ceiling	70	45	64.3	5	0	0
appeerd/appeared	27	10	37.0	6	0	0
ncem/ghome	82	47	57.3	6	0	0
canæry/canary	18	9	50.0	4	1	25.0
attractiv/attractive	14	7	50.0	5	1	20.0
imajin/imagine	37	9	24.3	12	2	16.7
nevue/nephew	32	15	46.9	4	0	0
gradueally/gradually	21	5	23.8	7	0	0
smcelder/smoulder	35	12	34.3	4	0	0
applaud/applaud	30	17	56.7	2	0	0
dispcesal/disposal	35	16	45.7	2	0	0
nuriʃht/nourished	37	21	56.8	5	0	0
dixeesd/diseased	23	10	43.5	6	0	0
ueniversity/ university	15	3	20.0	6	0	0
orcestra/orchestra	10	5	50.0	2	0	0
noledʒ/knowledge	21	13	61.9	3	0	0
audiens/audience	18	14	77.8	4	0	0
situeæted/situated	14	10	71.4	3	1	33.3

difference, and therefore no conclusion seems possible. The error analysis of the most difficult words in the first group of ten words in the table is also inconclusive. But the second, third, and fourth groups of ten words provide very interesting data.

In the second group of ten words the most difficult in transfer were *light* (liet), *road* (rœd) *something* (sumᚦiᶇ), *people* (peepl), *train* (træn), in that order of difficulty. Only one of these has a markedly different t.o. configuration from that of its i.t.a. version. This was *light*. The other four difficult words have similar t.o. and i.t.a. configurations, but what they do have in common with *light* is some important detail which is a probable source of proactive interference.

The third group of words reveals a similar pattern. The most difficult in transfer were *island* (ieland), *postage* (pœstæj), *biscuit* (biscit), *crowd* (croud), *dream* (dreem). All the t.o. configurations are very similar to the i.t.a. configurations with the possible exception of *postage,* but all contain a detail which is a possible source of proactive interference.

The evidence from the fourth group is perhaps less clear but the trend seems to be in the same direction. Excluding *canary* and *attractive* because of the rather small number of correct responses on the i.t.a. test, the most difficult words in transfer to t.o. were *ceiling* (seeliᶇ), *gnome* (nœm), *nephew* (nevue), *angel* (ænjel). *Gnome* and *nephew* do differ somewhat in their i.t.a. and t.o. configurations, but this is not true of *ceiling* or *angel.* On the other hand, all four words contain a detail which is a possible source of proactive interference.

A study of the easiest words in each group of ten does not add much to this inquiry because generally they have identical or similar i.t.a. and t.o. configurations, but also their details do not contain probable sources of proactive interference (e.g., *bun, milk, sit*).

Conclusions

The object of this study of i.t.a. students' errors in reading t.o. was to seek hypotheses for testing experimentally. Two hypotheses have emerged:
1. i.t.a. students do not transfer to t.o. simply on the basis of the upper-part of whole word configurations. They also perceive details within the t.o. configurations which are different from details within the corresponding i.t.a. configurations.
2. The differences in the details of the i.t.a. and t.o. spellings of words are an important source of proactive interference in transfer from i.t.a. to t.o. Such interference is a significant factor in the setback in skills development at the transition stage.

One more definite conclusion may be added. This further analysis of i.t.a. students' t.o. reading errors confirms the conclusion of the British i.t.a. experiment that there are needed improvements in i.t.a. which through "systematic laboratory studies could be shaped to provide improved proactive facilitation and reduced proactive interference and thus increase the efficiency . . . in the transition phase" (*3*, p. 52.). The difficulties facing those who may seek these improvements in i.t.a. have been outlined in two recent articles by Downing (*4* and *5*,) but strong encouragement to pursue these needed improvements has come from the recent contributions by Artley and by Holmes.

Artley (*1*) states, "Indeed, it would be extremely unfortunate if at this stage in the development of the Initial Teaching Alphabet it were to be assumed that both the code system and the method of its use were fixed and established so that no further work on either would be necessary. Were this to take place, the chances would be great that we would be operating with something less than the best. This, the profession could hardly condone."

Holmes' (*8*) comment is as follows, "In summary, this reviewer heartily agrees with Downing's call for a series of experiments in the 'psychological laboratory' designed to determine how the forms of i.t.a. characters ought to be modified to maximize their transfer value to t.o. and further to find what new materials and teaching techniques should be developed to facilitate transfer from i.t.a. to t.o."

REFERENCES

1. Artley, A. Sterl. "Evaluations—1" in National Foundation for Educational Research. *The i.t.a. Symposium.* Slough, Bucks: National Foundation for Educational Research in England and Wales, 1967.
2. Downing, John. *The Initial Teaching Alphabet Explained and Illustrated.* London: Cassell, and New York: Macmillan, 1964.
3. Downing, John. "Research Report on the British Experiment with i.t.a." in National Foundation for Educational Research. *The i.t.a. Symposium.* Slough, Bucks: National Foundation for Educational Research in England & Wales, 1967.
4. Downing, John. "What's Wrong with i.t.a.?" *Phi Delta Kappan, 48* (February 1967), 262-266.
5. Downing, John. "Can i.t.a. Be Improved?" *Elementary English* (in press).
6. Downing, John. *Evaluating the Initial Teaching Alphabet.* London: Cassell, 1967.
7. Downing, John and Barbara Jones. "Some Problems of Evaluating i.t.a. A Second Experiment," *Educational Research, 8* (1966), 100-114.
8. Holmes, Jack. "Evaluations—6" in National Foundation for Educational Research. *The i.t.a. Symposium.* Slough, Bucks: National Foundation for Educational Research in England and Wales, 1967.
9. McBride, Fergus. "A Preliminary Study of the ability of Children who have been learning to read in i.t.a. to transfer to reading materials in traditional print," in John Downing and Amy Brown (Eds.), *Third International Reading Symposium.* London: Cassell (in press).
10. Neale, Marie. *Neale Analysis of Reading Ability.* London: Macmillan, 1958.
11. Schonell, F. V. and F. E. Schonell. *Graded Word Reading Test.* Edinburgh; Oliver & Boyd, 1949.

An Experimental Study of the Effect of i.t.a. on Reading Achievement of Disabled Readers in Grades Seven and Eight

Wallace D. Miller
Southwest Baptist College

READING IS A COMPLEX PROCESS which includes the recognition of printed or written symbols, understanding of the individual symbol in relation to other symbols, and integration of the symbols into a pattern which will elicit both literal and interpretive responses.

In order to present ideas in a written or printed form, a particular orthography must be adopted. This process is sometimes referred to as encoding. Reading is the converse or decoding process. Therefore, it would seem that the more regular the code the less difficult the decoding process would be.

The purpose of this study was to investigate the effectiveness of the initial teaching alphabet, a simplified alphabet, in facilitating the reading process for students in the seventh and eighth grades who were diagnosed as disabled readers.

Basic hypotheses

1. Disabled readers' speed of comprehension will be significantly increased when instruction is provided through i.t.a.
2. Disabled readers' comprehension skill will be significantly increased when i.t.a. is used as a medium of instruction.
3. Disabled readers' knowledge of individual word meanings will be significantly increased when i.t.a. is used as a medium of instruction.
4. Disabled readers' ability to identify words will be significantly increased when i.t.a. is used as a medium of instruction.

Predictive questions

Data were obtained to answer the following questions:

Major question

Can a medium of instruction to increase reading achievement be identified which is a superior aid to disabled seventh and eighth grade readers?

Sub-questions

(1) Is the influence of various mediums of instruction on speed of comprehension different across the range of speed pretest scores and measured in-

telligence for disabled seventh and eighth grade readers? If not, then:

(2) Is there a constant level of difference in mediums of instruction for disabled seventh and eighth grade readers across the range of speed pre-test scores and measured intelligence?

These two sub-questions were repeated for each of the skills under observation, i.e., speed of comprehension, vocabulary, comprehension, and word recognition.

Need for the study

Modern technological development has greatly increased the need for schools to develop the reading ability of all the students to a level that is commensurate with their capacity for learning. To do this it is necessary to continually evaluate methods and materials which are used for this purpose.

There is considerable agreement among educators that a student must be provided with materials constructed at an appropriate level, and in accordance with what is known of patterns of child development, if he is to acquire efficient reading skills and habits. An appropriate medium for presenting such materials is needed as well.

Even though attempts have been made to provide suitable material for instruction, reading disabilities continue to plague the modern classroom from primary school through the university level (2).

Frequently the reading disability is the result of an individual's inability to recognize words (7).

It has been stated (4) that the one element common in all teaching methods is the traditional printed alphabet and spelling, and it is the belief that its unsystematic nature causes many reading failures.

Several attempts have been made to construct a simplified alphabet to be used as a medium for teaching reading.

Phonotypy, one of the earliest alphabets of this nature, was described as "a system of printing and writing, in which the same sound has always the same symbol, and the same symbol has always the same sound" (6). Using Phonotypy as a base, Sir James Pitman developed the Augmented Roman Alphabet which later became known as the initial teaching alphabet (4).

Several researchers have reported outstanding success in teaching beginning reading using i.t.a. as a medium for instruction (1, 4, 8, 9).

On the other hand, Sebesta (11) found that when he used a simplified alphabet in beginning reading instruction, there were "no statistically significant differences on familiar words, between the groups taught with the new alphabet and those taught with traditional orthography."

Reported studies, where i.t.a. was used with disabled readers, are not only few in number but also present conflicting evidence (1, 5, 12).

The present investigation was designed to obtain empirical evidence of the extent to which mediums of instruction, pretest data, and/or measured intelligence relate to the reading achievement of disabled seventh and eighth grade readers.

Subjects

The population consisted of all seventh and eighth grade students (N = 148 in the Woodland R-IV School District of Lutesville, Missouri, and all eighth grade students (N = 163) of the Jackson R-II School District of Jackson, Missouri, in January 1966.

The sample drawn from the population consisted of 77 subjects (38 girls and 39 boys). The subjects ranged in chronological age from 149 months to 178 months and in IQ from 89-117. Each subject had a reading disability of two or more years as measured by the Wechsler Intelligence Scale for Children and the Gray Oral Reading Test.

Methods

The subjects were divided into four groups as near equal as possible in number and sex.

The subjects were randomly selected with the groups previously established in accordance with the administrative procedures of the schools. A coin was flipped to determine which medium of instruction a group was to receive.

Intra-class grouping was used so that each subject used a text appropriate for his reading level. The subjects in Group I received instruction in "i.t.a. only" during the reading period. The rest of the school day they followed the regular schedule using traditional texts. Group II was divided into two groups, half of them receiving instruction in i.t.a. and the other half in t.o. in the same classroom at the same time. Group III received instruction in t.o. during the reading session as well as at other times during the day. Group IV served as the control group. The subjects in this group received the regular program of the school which did not include any reading instruction. The investigator visited this group as often as he visited the other groups (one period every two weeks).

The subjects received five 50 minute periods of instruction per week for 14 weeks.

The teachers who were using i.t.a. spent five days teaching sound-symbol relationships of the new alphabet before they began instructing through i.t.a.

Each student received instruction at the level indicated by the pretest diagnosis. The teachers used the methods and procedures recommended in the manuals that accompanied the *Sheldon Basic Reading Series.*

The Gray Oral Reading Test and the Gates Reading Survey Test were administered as pretests, at the end of the tenth week of instruction, and as post-tests.

Multiple linear regression analyses were used to determine the level of significance that obtained. The .05 level of significance was adopted for this study.

The data necessary for analysis when multiple linear regression is used include predictor variable scores and criterion variable scores (*3*). In the present study predictor variables were scores representative of mediums of instruction and intelligence. Criterion variables were post-test scores on the Gray Oral Reading Test and the Gates Reading Survey Test.

Four regression models were formulated to test the level of relationship that existed between the predictor variables and the criterion variables. The equation below illustrates an unrestricted linear regression model used in the present study.

Model

$$Y = a_0u + a_1x^{(1)} + a_2x^{(2)} + a_3x^{(3)} + a_4x^{(4)} + a_5x^{(5)} + a_6x^{(6)} + a_7x^{(7)} + a_8x^{(8)} + a_9x^{(9)} + a_{10}x^{(10)} + a_{11}z + e$$

A complete description of the statistical procedure used in this study would be too lengthy for a report of this nature.

Statistical analyses were conducted for each score obtained, i.e., word recognition, speed of comprehension, vocabulary, and comprehension.

In order to determine the statistical significance of the difference between the residual variance of the unrestricted model and the residual variance of the restricted model the F distribution was used (*3, 10*).

Results

After ten weeks of instruction, the restricted model indicated that i.t.a. was a statistically superior medium of instruction to increase speed of comprehension. No other significant relationships obtained at this point in the experiment. However, the correlated T-tests revealed significant gains in all skills under observation except comprehension.

The results at the end of the investigation (14 weeks of instruction) indicated that the only significant difference between mediums of instruction that obtained was on the speed of comprehension scores. The subjects in the control setting made significantly greater gains in speed of comprehension than subjects in any medium of instruction used in this experiment.

While there were no other statistically significant relationships between the mediums of instruction, subjects in all mediums made significant gains in reading achievement.

Discussion of results

The discussion reported in this section is relevant to the findings of this study. There are obviously numerous interpretations which may account for the findings produced by the present study. No attempt has been made to discuss all of the possible circumstances that could account for the findings. The theoretical and empirical explanations offered here were based upon the reported findings of this study in relation to findings reported in previous research which appeared to be relevant to the present study.

Even though the results of this investigation did not provide unequivocal evidence as to the best medium of instruction in reading for disabled seventh and eighth grade readers, there are some aspects of the investigation which deserve attention. Specifically, the variance manifested by this sample suggests that different mediums of instruction produce varied effects upon the functional criterion variables measured in this study. The only medium which produced a significant effect upon the reading achievement of this sample was the control setting. This group made significant gains in speed of comprehension across the range of pretest scores with IQ as a non-interacting covariable.

Results regarding the relationship of pretest scores, mediums of instruction, and/or intelligence seemed quite clear. There were no significant interactions resulting from the use of any of the regression models.

The apparent variance in mediums of instruction used with this sample is especially relevant when evaluated in connection with earlier studies. One such study which was conducted with subjects whose IQ scores were all below 85 reported no statistically significant differences between experimental and control groups (5). Another study found no statistically significant differences with first grade subjects when an artificial alphabet was used for initial instruction (11).

The results of the present study indicated that the subjects in the control group made significantly greater gains in speed of comprehension than did those in any of the instruction groups. A possible explanation of this is that in the schools from which the sample was drawn the students who were not in reading classes were taking courses in science, shop, or home economics. The high interest value in these subjects plus the fact that the students had a choice might have adversely affected the results of the study. It is also possible that the broad experience of these courses supplied information to the subjects which was indirectly related to the test material. One other possible explanation is that the added emphasis on word recognition skills in the reading groups tended to slow the speed of comprehension.

The theory that i.t.a. should reduce the amount of effort needed to recognize unfamiliar words was not verified in this study. While no statistically significant results were obtained, the trend indicated that the subjects instructed through "i.t.a. only" made the least amount of gain in word recognition. A possible explanation of this finding is that the time element was not long enough to allow the groups who were receiving reading instruction to assimilate the new knowledge. A follow-up study will be conducted six months from the close of the experiment to assess the results over a longer period of time.

Conclusions

Nonsignificant results on a substantial number of F ratios indicate that no one medium of instruction is a superior aid to disabled readers in improving all of the skills measured in this study.

Some mediums of instruction yielded greater gains on one skill than they did on another. Care must be used in selecting the medium that promises the best results for the particular skill being taught.

REFERENCES

1. Baker, Marvin. "Remedial Reading with i.t.a. Elementary Level in Albert J. Mazurkiewicz (Ed.), *The Initial Teaching Alphabet and the World of English,* Proceedings of the Second Annual International Conference on the Initial Teaching Alphabet, Hofstra University, August, 1965.
2. Bond, Guy L. and Miles A. Tinker. *Reading Difficulties—Their Diagnosis and Correction.* New York: Appleton-Century-Crofts, 1957.
3. Bottenberg, Robert A. and Joe H. Ward, Jr. *Applied Multiple Linear Regression.* Technical Documentary Report PRL-TDR-63-6. Lackland Air Force Base, Texas, 6570th Personnel Research Laboratory, Aerospace Medical Division, Air Force Systems Command, March, 1963.
4. Downing, John. *The Initial Teaching Alphabet.* London: Cassell, 1965.
5. Downing, John A. and N. J. Georgiades. "Reports on the Uses of the Initial Teaching Alphabet in Remedial Reading Classes in Primary, Secondary and Special Schools." London: Reading Research Unit, University of London Institute of Education. 1964.
6. Ellis, Alexander John. *A Plea for Phonotypy and Phonography.* Bath, England: Isaac Pitman at the Phonographic Institution, 5 Nelson Place, April, 1845.
7. Karlin, Robert. *Teaching Reading in the High School.* Indianapolis: Bobbs-Merrill Company, Inc., 1964.
8. Mazurkiewicz, Albert J. "A Comparison of i.t.a. and t.o. Reading, Writing and Spelling Achievement When Methodology Is Controlled," *The Initial Teaching Alphabet and the World of English,* Proceedings of the Second Annual International Conference on the Initial Teaching Alphabet, Hofstra University, August, 1965.
9. McCracken, Robert A. "A Two-Year Longitudinal Study to Determine the Ability of First-Grade Children to Learn to Read Using the Early-to-Read i.t.a. Program (An Interim Report of the First Year)," in Albert J. Mazurkiewicz (Ed.), *The Initial Teaching Alphabet and the World of English,* Proceedings of the Second Annual International Conference on the Initial Teaching Alphabet, Hofstra University, August, 1965.
10. Miller, Wallace D. "An Experimental Study of the Effect of i.t.a. on Reading Achievement of Disabled Readers in Grades Seven and Eight," unpublished doctor's dissertation, Southern Illinois University, 1966.
11. Sebesta, Sam Leaton. "Artificial Orthography as a Transitional Device in First-Grade Reading Instruction," *Journal of Educational Psychology, 55,* (October, 1964), 256.
12. Tanyzer, Harold J. Personal Letter. Hofstra University, Hempstead, New York, March 9, 1965.

Effects of Practice and Instruction in i.t.a. upon Ability to Transfer from Reading Orally in t.o. to Reading Orally in i.t.a.

THEODORE A. MORK
Western Washington State
College

MANY OF THE proponents of i.t.a. have suggested that transfer from reading in i.t.a. to reading in t.o. takes place readily and without instruction. However, McCracken (1) in studying the abilities of children to transfer in the opposite direction, that is, from t.o. to i.t.a., found that transfer does take place automatically or without instruction if it is accepted that the transfer is at a level one year or more below the child's instructional level as measured by the Standard Reading Inventory or if it is accepted that the child's performance after transfer will be significantly slower and less fluent. This raised the question of how much time might be necessary to effect full, or complete, transfer. Would a small amount of instruction and practice make a sizable difference?

Purpose

This study examined the ability of third and fourth grade children to transfer from reading in traditional orthography to reading in i.t.a. at five intervals of instruction and practice in i.t.a., pretest, 15 minutes, 45 minutes, 105 minutes, and 165 minutes.

Subjects, tests, and procedures

Seventeen third and fourth grade children enrolled in the Campus School of Western Washington State

College were the subjects. Pretests were administered in t.o. and in i.t.a. The children received 165 minutes of instruction and practice in i.t.a. Tests in i.t.a. were administered after 15, 45, 105, and 165 minutes of instruction and practice. The i.t.a. practice materials were the *Early-to-Read Series* produced by Mazurkiewicz and Tanyzer (*2*). The Gray Oral Reading Test (*3*) and the isolated word recognition sub-test of The Standard Reading Inventory (*4*) were used to measure speed of oral reading, errors in oral reading, and isolated word pronouncing ability. Both tests were transliterated into i.t.a.

Results

Speed of i.t.a. reading increased and the number of errors made in i.t.a. reading decreased as the amount of instruction and practice increased. The differences in speed and in the number of errors between initial t.o. reading and i.t.a. reading at each interval decreased, although initial t.o. was still better after 165 minutes. More than 165 minutes of instruction and practice would be necessary for i.t.a performance to equal reading performance in t.o. However the decrease, plotted as a linear relationship, indicated that equal performances would be reached in 6 to 7 hours.

This study indicated that some instruction and practice are necessary in transferring from t.o. to i.t.a. However, the child who is transferring from i.t.a. to t.o. has t.o. "practice" in his natural environment—street signs, TV commercials, newspapers, comics, and books. This would appear to be sufficient practice to effect transfer in reading from i.t.a. to t.o. without special training.

REFERENCES

1. McCracken, Robert A. "A Cross-Sectional Study to Determine the Ability of Children to Transfer in Reading from Traditional Orthography to the New Augmented Roman Alphabet," *The Initial Alphabet and The World of English,* in Albert J. Mazurkiewicz (Ed.). Initial Teaching Alphabet Foundation at Hofstra University, Hempstead, N. Y., 1966.
2. Mazurkiewicz, Albert J. and Harold J. Tanyzer. *The Early-To-Read I.T.A. Program.* New York: i.t.a. Publications, Inc., 1963.
3. Gray, William S. and Helen Robinson. *Gray Oral Reading Tests.* Bobbs-Merrill Company. Inc., 1963.
4. McCracken, Robert A.. *The Standard Reading Inventory.* Pioneer Printing Co., Bellingham, Washington, 1965.

Current Linguistic Research and Its Implications for the Teaching of Reading

RONALD WARDHAUGH
University of Michigan

DURING THE past decade there have been periodic discussions about the relationship of linguistic research to research in reading and to the teaching of reading. Recently, several authors have produced summaries of these discussions and have pointed out what appears to them to be important in the relationship. In one such summary Carroll (6) criticizes reading researchers for their failure to incorporate linguistic findings into the procedures which they have chosen to examine in their research. He points out that even though much reading research has been methodologically sound, it has proved to be of little use because the teaching procedures which were examined in the research were not thoroughly sound. In another summary, Betts (3) points out some of the relationships he perceives between reading and linguistics but at the same time criticizes linguists for being content to dabble in reading and for adopting a rather naive approach to psychological and pedagogical problems. In a most able summary of the whole reading-linguistics controversy, Devine (11) rightly points out that although the controversy has been characterized by opinion rather than by fact, it still gives one good reason to be optimistic that the findings of linguistic research will prove to be of use to reading specialists.

One view of linguistics

Perhaps it would be well at this point to try to characterize just what linguistics and the discoveries of linguistic research appear to be for most of the writers who so far have tried to relate linguistics to reading. According to this characterization, the main findings of linguistics which might have application to the teaching of reading and to reading research might be listed as a) language is speech and writing is a reproduction of speech; b) graphemes and punctuation marks are representations of phonemes and intonation patterns; c) language is patterned, that is grammatical, and although the patterns are relatively few in number, they are almost bewildering in possibilities for variation; d) language is spoken in dialects; and e) linguists prefer description of linguistic data to prescription and introspection. While it is undoubtedly true that many linguists would agree with the above statements, nevertheless, the statements by no means adequately characterize current linguistic thinking and research. Even if they were adequate, current reading procedures lag sadly behind them, and this linguistic lag really deserves a comment or two before any mention is made of current linguistic thinking.

Linguists agree that speech and writing may be considered to be different codes but insist that the speech code is somehow basic to the writing code. Consequently, comments about the sounds of speech and the symbols of writing must be clearly differentiated from each other. In spite of the work of Bloomfield and Barnhart in *Let's Read* (4) and of Fries in *Linguistics and Reading* (13), even these basic facts have not been taken into consideration in the majority of texts on reading. This statement should not be read as a blanket approval of the two books and the positions taken by their authors. Both books overstress the importance of the phoneme-grapheme relationship and both oversimplify the process of reading: learning to read means more than developing high-speed recognition responses to various letter patterns though not, to be sure, as much as some statements, for example those by Gates (14) and Burton (5), make it out to be. However, many of the teaching procedures advocated by Fries, such as, the use of contrast, the stress on vowels, the insistence on whole word patterns, and the separation of reading and writing, seem to be excellent linguistically and pedagogically; and certainly Fries' insistence on a clear use of the terms *phonics, phonetic,* and *phonemics* must be recognized as crucial if there is to be any really worthwhile discussion of those topics by reading specialists. Except for what is basically a sound book by Cordts, *Phonics for the Reading Teacher* (10), books on reading still continue to confuse phoneme and grapheme, phonics, phonetics, and phonemics and to interweave linguistic data and linguistic myth ad nauseam. Heilman's *Phonics in Proper Perspective* (15) is a good example of such confusion: if this is a proper perspective, then reading teachers, like the Habsburgs, have learned nothing and forgotten nothing! And the ones to suffer are the children they would teach. Furthermore, a recent series of articles in *The Reading Teacher* by Clymer (9), Bailey (1), and Emans (12) on phonic generalizations would have benefited from a much closer attention to linguistic data than any of the authors chose to give, for here is a good example of the type of investigation of which Carroll speaks in which adequate methodology is largely wasted on unsound procedures.

Phoneme and grapheme

Reading teachers and particularly reading researchers must make themselves aware of the phoneme-grapheme correspondence; the clear distinctions among phonics, phonetics, and phonemics; and the difference between statements about speech and statements about writing. Happily there is much linguistic research available on these topics. Current work in linguistics does, however, indicate that a word of caution is required at this point on the subject of the phoneme. Linguists in general have always viewed the phoneme as a convenient linguistic fiction, and a hard to define one at that, rather than as an absolute

linguistic fact. Today many linguists manage to do without phonemes because such linguists believe that a distinct phonemic level is not required in describing a language. More important to them than the phonemic is a level of representation which may be called the morphophonemic. For example, instead of picking out the broad phonetic differences among the endings of *cats, dogs,* and *judges,* the [s], [z], and [əz] and calling these differences phonemic differences because of certain contrasts elsewhere in the language, these linguists point out that English plural formation is characterized by a morphophonemic sibilant which is predictably realized in various phonetic shapes according to environment. Likewise, they stress the importance of the morphophonemic connection in English between such pairs of words as *produce* and *production, nation* and *national,* and *long* and *longer.* In each case it seems that a phonemic spelling and an insistence on "traditional" phonemicization conceals rather than reveals the linguistic facts. It might even be said that English spelling in many cases is a good (or at least better than previously acknowledged) representation of the phonological facts of English. What this means for reading specialists is that there is reason to have serious doubts that a child beginning to read is well served by a strict insistence on a one-to-one phonemegrapheme correspondence when current linguistic research suggests, first of all, that the phoneme neither exists nor is a particularly useful fiction and, secondly, that rules for pronouncing are dependent in part on grammatical and lexical information.

There is really nothing new in what has just been said. The lack of novelty is readily apparent if you read an interesting paper by Edward Sapir (24), which first appeared over thirty years ago. Although Sapir claimed in this paper that phonemes have a psychological reality, a close examination of what he says shows that what he was talking about was morphophonemes rather than phonemes. He also seems to have been making a distinction between linguistic facts, that is linguistic reality, and linguistic data, that is, the observable characteristics of language. It will be useful at this point to take up this fact-data distinction in order to gain insight into the nature of current linguistic research.

Current linguistic research

During the period of approximately 1930 to 1960, linguistic research was largely concerned with data, that is, with making observations of linguistic events and with procedures for classifying these observations. Out of this work came considerable development and clarification of such concepts as the phoneme, the morpheme, the sentence pattern, the intonation contour, the linguistic level, the slot and its fillers, and so on. In fact this is just the kind of linguistic research that is referred to in most discussions of linguistics by reading experts. Lefevre's work is based on this type of thinking and his book (*18*) in many ways carries the usefulness of such research to reading about as far as it can be carried. I would suggest that this is neither very far nor far enough and I say this because there are severe shortcomings in such research. Let us look at a few of these.

Do classifications of corpora of English utterances really tell us a great deal about English? Do they account for a speaker's ability to relate some of the sentences to others within a corpus? Do they account for an ability to distinguish between sentences and non-sentences? Do they account for a speaker's feeling that some sentences are confused, or deviant, or ambiguous? Do they allow us in some principled way to predict which sentences might be produced in the future? And so on. The suggestion is that the facts of English may only be accounted for if such questions as these are answered by the grammar. Grammarians concerned merely with the classification of data reject such questions as outside their concern. Books and articles relating linguistics to reading have

favored the data rather than the fact approach. For this reason they find it difficult to demonstrate an insightful and economical relationship between sound and symbol. Similarly, statements that writing is speech put down on paper are not as adequate as they should be. Raw speech is not language, for the data of linguistic performance are not the facts of linguistic competence; and the data of written performance are something else again. Speech performance is characterized by pauses, repetitions, syntactic shifts, and so on, whereas almost all the reading material presented to children is written in full polished sentences, a very different type of performance. The same basic competence apparently underlies performance in both speech and writing but the performances of speech and writing are not easily related to each other. The data are different and they are not easily convertible, and not convertible at all if the underlying reality is ignored.

The point of view just presented is one held by the transformational-generative grammarians. It would be true to say that linguistics has not been the same since 1957, the year of the appearance of Noam Chomsky's *Syntactic Structures* (*7*). In this book and since then (*8*), Chomsky has put forward a theory of language which has revolutionized linguistics but which appears hardly to have touched the reading researcher. Perhaps this is not surprising for the theory is not easy to explain and any simple explanation is very likely to be distorted and misunderstood. The theory stresses the fact that a good explanatory grammar of a language requires a set of explicit syntactic rules which generate sentences of that language together with grammatical descriptions of the generated sentences, and such a set of rules will reveal sentences to have deep structures on which semantic rules operate and surface representations which are mapped out by phonological rules. The phonological and graphemic surface features of sentences are automatic and superficial and contribute nothing to the understanding of sentences. Sentences, the primitive grammatical units in the language, may be understood correctly only if the deep underlying elements are known and if the deep relationships among elements are understood.

Syntax and comprehension

The importance of such a linguistic theory for an understanding of comprehension surely cannot be overestimated. Adequate comprehension of any sentence, spoken or written, requires more than just high-speed recognition, left-to-right linear decoding, or recognition of surface patterns. In order to fully comprehend a sentence a listener, or reader, must be able to relate the correct deep structure to the surface structure of the sentence and to project a consistent semantic reading on the individual words. A reaction to the surface structure alone, that is, a recognition of individual sounds, letters, words, or superficial syntactic patterns, is insufficient for comprehension, since comprehension requires that each sentence be given both syntactic and semantic interpretations in depth.

The following sentences will illustrate a very few of the major syntactic problems that appear to be of interest in an understanding of comprehension.

(1) The man sold the car.
(2) The car was sold.
(3) Who sold the car.
(4) What did the man sell?
(5) What was sold?

The first sentence requires the comprehender to assign a deep reading which will show that *The man* is the deep subject of the sentence; *sold the car,* the predicate; and *the car,* the deep object.

(i) The man sold the car.
(ii) (SOMEONE) sold the car + Passive.

This deep structure accounts for the fact that a correct interpretation of *The car was sold* requires an understanding that an unspecified person did the selling and this unspecified person sold the car, *the car* being the underlying or deep object of the sentence

though the superficial or grammatical subject.

The deep structures of the remaining sentences may be represented as follows.

(iii) Question + SOMEONE sold the car.
(iv) Question + The man sold SOMETHING.
(v) Question + SOMEONE sold SOMETHING) + Passive.

A further group of sentences illustrates the need for the comprehender to understand exactly what is in the deep structure and what is not there.

(6) The dog amazed the boy.
(7) The boy was amazed by the dog.
(8) The boy was amazed.
(9) The dog's strength amazed the boy.
(10) Who was amazed by the boy's strength?

These sentences have deep structures which may be represented as follows.

(vi) The dog amazed the boy.
(vii) The dog amazed the boy + Passive.
(viii) (SOMENOUN) amazed the boy + Passive.
(ix) SOMETHING (The dog was strong) amazed the boy.
(x) Question + SOMETHING (The dog was strong) amazed SOMEONE + Passive.

Accurate comprehension of the above sentences requires an awareness that an unspecified *SOMENOUN* is the deep subject "causing" the amazement in (8), that *SOMETHING* is "causing" the amazement in both (9) and (10), and that this *SOMETHING* is the fact that *The dog was strong,* the only plausible interpretation of *The dog's strength.*

Ambiguity

The linguistic theory alerts us to the fact that a comprehender must be aware of the possibility that a sentence may have more than one interpretation. Compare the following sentences.

(11) The shooting of the hunters disturbed us.

(12) The drinking of the hunters disturbed us.

(13) The drinking of the water disturbed us.

Whereas (11) may have two interpretations and is ambiguous:

    (xia) SOMETHING (The hunters shot (SOMENOUN))
              disturbed us.

    (xib) SOMETHING ((SOMEONE) shot the hunters)
              disturbed us.

(12) and (13) have unique interpretations since (12) will bear only an interpretation analogous to (xia):

    (xii) SOMETHING (The hunters drank (SOMETHING))
              disturbed us.

and (13) will bear only an interpretation analogous to (xib):

    (xiii) SOMETHING ((SOMENOUN) drank the water)
              disturbed us.

Ambiguous sentences therefore can pose serious comprehension problems since a correct interpretation requires the choice of the deep structure intended by the producer of the sentence. Such ambiguous sentences are also interesting linguistically for an adequate theory must surely account for the different possibilities in a way that is both elegant and intuitively satisfactory.

The kind of analysis just illustrated could be carried much further into complement structures, complex sentences, pronominal substitutions, and various kinds of noun and verb classes; but this would lead us too far afield. The analysis does serve the purpose of illustrating the interest that linguists are now taking in accounting for how sentences are understood, particularly in specifying what there must be in sentences and in speakers to make communication possible. A transformational-generative grammar offers an explicit characterization of the grammatical elements in sentences, a characterization which strives for completeness and which is based on a theory of language which clearly distinguishes what is important about the underlying facts of language from what is involved in actual performance.

The theory says nothing about performance, that is, about how a human being actually generates or interprets sentences. It does say though that anyone who wants to understand how a human being does either such task must recognize the facts just presented and that anyone who does not cannot hope to discover anything very revealing about actual sentence production and interpretation.

Semantics and comprehension

Work in transformational-generative grammars has also produced some interesting work in semantics; and since reading is concerned with getting meaning out of a text, the work of Katz and Fodor (*16*) must be mentioned. Katz and Fodor have proposed a semantic theory which relates closely to Chomsky's syntactic theory. How that theory might apply to basic language competency in reading may be characterized somewhat as follows. The comprehension of a sentence requires that that sentence be given a reading of its deep grammatical structure together with a reading of its semantic content. This latter reading requires that the lexical items in a sentence be interpreted in a manner consistent with each other and that inconsistent readings be rejected. The ability to give a consistent reading would imply that sentence production and interpretation require in producers and interpreters a sense of a semantic norm which can be explicitly characterized.

Some illustrations, based on suggestions from Nida (*20*), may serve to clarify these concepts:

(14) The man sat in the chair.

(15) The man died in the chair.

In sentence (14) a correct interpretation of the meaning of *chair* would be one which marked this occurrence of *chair* for such characteristics as "object," "human use," and perhaps "harmless." Sentence (15) might arouse a suspicion that a "harmless" rather than "harmful" distinction cannot be guaranteed because the verb *died* appears in the sentence. Sentence (15) is consequently more likely to pose an interpretation problem than sentence (14). In sentences (16) and (17) the ambiguity of (15) is resolved because "harmful" now replaces "harmless" as a characteristic of *chair:*

(16) He died in the electric chair.
(17) He died in the chair for his crime.

Electric in (16) and *for his crime* in (17) require that *chair* be given a different reading from *chair* in (14) and illuminate some of the difficulties encountered in (15). In sentences (18) and (19) a similar meaning for *chair* to that in (14) seems to be required:

(18) He took the chair.
(19) He accepted the chair.

However, the addition of *at the meeting* to (18) would require a "role" rather than "object" characteristic for *chair* just as would the addition of *at the university* to (19). Furthermore, *chair* in (18) would now require an additional "judicial" characteristic just as *chair* in (19) would require an additional "academic" characteristic.

Understanding figurative language

A general ability to recognize the correct syntactic and semantic interpretations of sentences is also basic to any kind of specific ability to recognize that a particular sentence is incapable of a syntactic or semantic interpretation; that is, it is either ungrammatical or nonsensical. It is also basic to an ability to interpret deviant sentences, particularly the deviant sentences of figurative and poetic language. Sentences (20 to 24) are examples:

(20) My dog passed away yesterday.
(21) Salt is eating away my car's fenders.
(22) All nature sleeps.
(23) He sat in black despair.
(24) The king was a lion in battle.

Normally only human beings pass away; only certain animates eat and sleep; only concrete things are capable of color; and lions are non-humans, whereas kings are human. These sentences deviate from the English norm but not far enough so that they cannot be given interpretations which relate them to that norm. Because such interpretations can be achieved, the sentences can be understood and it is possible to account for the "humanness" of *dog* in (20), the animism of *salt* in (21), and *nature* in (22), the metaphoric blackness of *despair* in (23), and the animal attributes of *king* in (24). Anyone with an interest in poetry can see how that interest and linguistic research come together at this point. Linguists are indeed conducting research which is revelvant to an understanding of poetic and literary style, and some of this research is proving to be most revealing. Again the basic distinctions between competence and performance, and between grammars accounting for facts and grammars accounting for data, provide the insights.

In structures beyond the sentence little has as yet been done by linguists. Transformational-generative grammarians work within the sentence framework at present, and a leading transformationalist, Postal (*23*), has flatly denied the need to become involved in what he calls "discourse contexts." Another group of linguists, the tagmemicists, principally Pike (*22*) and Becker (*2*), have ventured beyond the sentence and concerned themselves with such matters as lexical equivalence chains, parallels, and verb and pronoun sequences. This work holds promise for reading research, particularly as most of it is based on written language rather than spoken language, but as yet it is only a beginning. It is to be hoped too that tagmemicists and transformationalists will come to work together on the problems that are involved in supra-sentence analysis.

The dialect problem

Before summarizing what has been said in order to draw the main threads together, it would be appropriate to mention the dialect work that is being conducted in at least three major northern cities, by Labov and his associates in New York (*17*), by Stewart of the Center for Applied Linguistics and his associates in Washington, D.C. (*25*), and by McDavid (*19*) and his associates (*21*) in Chicago. These investigations are producing descriptions of the English spoken in such cities which will be invaluable for teachers of English and reading. The language of many children in these cities is very different from that of their teachers and their textbooks. The dialect studies tell us what the main phonological and grammatical differences are. The findings suggest that teachers should clearly differentiate the teaching of the language habits of any kind of standard spoken English from the teaching of reading. It is possible to read standard written English in almost any dialect, and a standard printed text can be associated with dialects which show considerable phonological and grammatical variation from what might be considered a standard spoken dialect. There are several reports in the literature of children reading the standard written forms in nonstandard spoken forms which are the dialect equivalents of the standard forms only to be told that the readings are "incorrect" by the teachers. In each instance the child understood what was on the page, understood it in fact so well that he gave the printed words the "correct" phonetic realizations in his own dialect and in each case the teacher revealed her confusion between teaching the child to read and teaching him to speak a different dialect. Likewise, the problem of teaching a child to say *with* not *wif* or to distinguish *den* and *then* is a dialect problem, not a reading problem in most cases, and almost never is it a speech correction problem in the usual sense of that term. Again, a little linguistic knowledge can go a long way in helping teachers to arrive at sensible attitudes and procedures in teaching spoken and written English to such children.

Conclusions

No definition of reading has been offered in this paper but at least two have been rejected: reading as high-speed recognition, on the one hand, and reading as all things to all people, on the other. Reading does involve getting meaning from the printed page. It does require perceptual skills not required in oral communication, particularly, of course, visual skills. A written text is also a special type of linguistic performance; it is not just speech written down. In addition, most of us read and comprehend far faster than we can listen and comprehend, and this fact must be explained somewhere in a theory of reading which incorporates the view of language advanced here. However, no matter what definition of reading is finally agreed to, certain basic linguistic principles must be recognized in such a definition.

The first principle is that a clear understanding of any kind of language use can be based only on discovering answers to the question of what language is and how language works. Transformational-generative theory gives us clues to answer these questions. The second principle is that there is an important distinction between competence and performance. In teaching we are concerned with the former for it is competence which allows one to produce and understand sentences. Performance, on the other hand, is but a record of those particular sentences that were produced along with all the imperfections that occurred in such production. Performance acts, of course, at the same time as a kind of screen through which we must investigate all competence. The final principle is that most, if not all, language behavior is rule governed behavior, and this fact must be taken into account if one is to seek to reinforce or change existing behavior.

Current linguistic research promises much to the reading researcher. It tells him about language; it shows him how graphemics relates to phonological structure; it points out to him what he has to be aware of in talking about comprehension; and it indicates some of the variables that must be taken into account in poetic appreciation. It is not quantitative and computerized, and for that a linguist need make no apology. Instead, the linguist offers the reading researcher and reading teacher insights that do not depend on the computer and on the research design and asks only that reading research be based on sound linguistic understanding, for only in that way can any insights of real interest and real significance be gained.

REFERENCES

1. Bailey, Mildred H. "The Utility of Phonic Generalizations in Grades One through Six," *The Reading Teacher, 20* (Feb. 1967), 413-418.
2. Becker, Alton L. "A Tagmemic Approach to Paragraph Analysis," *College Composition and Communication, 16* (Dec. 1965), 237-242.
3. Betts, Emmett A. "Linguistics and Reading," *Education, 86* (April 1966), 454-458.
4. Bloomfield, Leonard and Clarence L. Barnhart. *Let's Read.* Detroit: Wayne State University Press, 1961.
5. Burton, William H. *Reading in Child Development.* Indianapolis: Bobbs-Merrill Company, 1956.
6. Carroll, John B. "The Analysis of Reading Instruction: Perspectives from Psychology and Linguistics," Theories of Learning and Instruction, N. S. S. E. 63rd Yearbook, Part 1. E. R. Hilgard (Ed.). Chicago: University of Chicago Press, 1964.
7. Chomsky, Noam. Syntactic Structures. The Hague: Mouton & Co., 1957.
8. ———. *Aspects of the Theory of Syntax.* Cambridge, Mass.: M. I. T. Press, 1965.
9. Clymer, Theodore. "The Utility of Phonic Generalizations in the Primary Grades," *The Reading Teacher, 16* (Jan. 1963), 252-258.
10. Cordts, Anna D. *Phonics for the Reading Teacher.* New York: Holt, Rinehart and Winston, Inc., 1965.
11. Devine, Thomas G. "Linguistic Research and the Teaching of Reading," *Journal of Reading,* (March 1966), 273-277.
12. Emans, Robert. "The Usefulness of Phonic Generalizations above the Primary Grades," *The Reading Teacher, 20* (Feb. 1967), 419-425.
13. Fries, Charles C. *Linguistics and Reading.* New York: Holt, Rinehart and Winston, Inc., 1963.
14. Gates, Arthur I. "The Nature of the Reading Process," *Reading in the Elementary School,* N. S. S. E. 48th Year-book, Part 2. N. B. Henry, editor. Chicago: University of Chicago Press, 1949.
15. Heilman, Arthur W. *Phonics in Proper Perspective.* Columbus, Ohio: Charles E. Merrill, Inc., 1964.
16. Katz, Jerrold J. and Jerry A. Fodor. "The Structure of a Semantic Theory," *Language, 39* (April-June 1963), 170-210.
17. Labov, William. *The Social Stratification of English in New York City.* Washington, D. C.: Center for Applied Linguistics, 1966.
18. Lefevre, Carl A. *Linguistics and the Teaching of Reading.* New York: McGraw-Hill Book Company, 1964.
19. McDavid, Raven I., Jr. "Social Dialects: Cause or Symptom of Social Maladjustment," *Social Dialects and Language Learning.* Roger W. Shuy (Ed.). Champaign, Illinois: National Council of Teachers of English, 1965.
20. Nida, Eugene A. *Toward a Science of Translating.* Leiden: E. J. Brill, 1964.
21. Pedersen, Lee A. "Some Structural Differences in the Speech of Chicago Negroes," *Social Dialects and Language Learning.* Roger W. Shuy (Ed.). Champaign, Illinois: National Council of teachers of English, 1965.
22. Pike, Kenneth L. "Discourse Analysis and Tagmeme Matrices," *Oceanic Linguistics, 3* (1964), 5-25.
23. Postal, Paul M. "On So-called 'Pronouns' in English," *Report of the Seventeenth Annual Round Table Meeting on Linguistics and Language Studies.* Francis P. Dinneen (Ed.). Washington, D. C.: Georgetown University Press, 1966.
24. Sapir, Edward. "The Psychological Reality of Phonemes," *Selected Writings of Edward Sapir.* D. G. Mandelbaum (Ed.). Berkely and Los Angeles: University of California Press, 1963.
25. Stewart, William A. "Urban Negro Speech: Sociolinguistic Factors Affecting English Teaching," *Social Dialects and Language Learning.* Roger W. Shuy (Ed.). Champaign, Illinois: National Council of Teachers of English, 1965.

Phoneme-grapheme Correspondences in Monosyllabic Words

RICHARD E. HODGES
University of Chicago

IN THIS STUDY the spellings of all monosyllabic words in the core vocabulary of American English were analyzed in order to determine the degree to which the orthography approximates the alphabetic principle (i.e., a one-to-one correspondence between a phoneme and a single graphemic representation) in this set of words. Most beginning spelling and reading programs, for a number of reasons, typically use vocabularies comprised largely of monosyllabic words. With the proliferation of linguistically oriented spelling and reading programs in which pupils are guided toward gaining an understanding of the alphabetic structure of our writing system, it seems important to describe the orthography of those words which are the basis for the child's introduction to a structural analysis of American English orthography.

Monosyllabic words and the orthography

Monosyllabic words constitute a rich and functional part of our language. Indeed, 340 of the first five hundred most frequently used American English words have monosyllabic structures (5). Why is there a predilection to employ monosyllabic words with high frequency in our language? It seems likely that it is simply easier to remember and to pronounce monosyllabic words than other words having more complex structures. This "principle of least effort" (6), in fact, probably accounts for such highly functional monosyllabic words as *phone, zoo, ad, lab, math,* and *bus* that are clipped forms of polysyllabic words.

Monosyllabic words are therefore characterized by their *functionality* and their *structural simplicity,* and both of these characteristics cause monosyllabic words to be quite useful in beginning spelling and reading programs. Each characteristic, in fact, can be used as the most basic rationale for the selection of words for beginning spellers and readers.

In terms of functionality, it is generally assumed that the child's introduction to written language should begin with the study of words he will most likely be acquainted with and which are useful to him in verbal communication. Numerous studies, the Rinsland study for example (4), have attempted to determine children's uses of words and these studies have, in turn, been important sources for word selection. Because monosyllabic words tend to be among the most frequently used words of the American English core lexicon, it is easy to see why these types of words predominate in beginning spelling and reading programs.

Structural simplicity, on the other hand, refers to the idea that the words a child initially encounters in learning to spell and read should be controlled in terms of their structural complexities. Monosyllabic words, of course, do not necessitate that the child concern himself with such linguistic factors as syllabication and affixation. Monosyllabic words are, in short, the simplest structural forms of the lexicon and therefore are assumed to be the logical starting points for subsequent structural analysis of written language.

Structural simplicity, however, has a second important consequence, particularly in light of recent linguistic insights into the nature of American English orthography. In order to understand this consequence, we should first examine briefly the notion of an *alphabetic orthography,* since this is the principle upon which American English orthography is based.

An alphabetic orthography is based upon the idea that the constituent speech sounds of oral language—the *phonemes* of a language—each have individual graphic representations in writing. The majority of the world's writing systems are of this type chiefly because alphabetic orthographies are more efficient than other types of orthographies. "Word" writing systems (technically, such systems are called *logographic* orthographies), for example, employ graphic symbols to represent the morphemes, or meaning elements, of a language. These writing systems do have the advantage of circumventing various language forces, such as sound change and dialect, that can interfere in the translation of speech into writing and vice versa. But logographic writing systems also require their users to master a prodigious number of graphic symbols if they are to use this type of writing system, for each word of oral language requires its own graphic symbol.

A second type of órthography is called a *syllabary*. In such writing systems, graphic symbols are devised to represent the syllables that, in combination, make up the words of a language. Syllabic writing is an improvement over logographic writing because there are fewer syllables than words in a language and therefore fewer graphic symbols that must be mastered in order to spell and read. Yet, syllabically-based orthographies still require substantial "memory loads."

An ideal alphabetic orthography, on the other hand, employs only as many graphic symbols as there are phonemes (speech sounds) in oral language. A thirty-phoneme language, for example, would use only thirty distinct graphic symbols to represent these phonemes in writing. Theoretically, at least, an individual should be able to spell and read correctly any written representation of a spoken word once he has mastered the ability to differentiate speech sounds and has mastered their graphic representations.

American English orthography is alphabetically *based*. It uses alphabet letters and their combinations to represent the phonemes of American English speech. We are all keenly aware, however, that our writing system does not attain the idealized state of a pure alphabetic orthography; but it is based upon this principle, and for this reason, linguists and others propose that a basic, indeed crucial, aspect of a child's understanding of written language involves his understanding the nature of the American English orthography. Most important, too, it is argued that a knowledge of the alphabetic structure of the orthography can be applied as important components of mastering written American English.

But, because American English orthography does not truly reflect the alphabetic principle, we cannot rely with complete assurance upon the knowledge that a given phoneme is spelled a certain way. In our orthography we are forced to play *odds;* we are obliged to determine which graphemic representation of a phoneme most often represents that phoneme in words, and we must also master those exceptional phoneme-grapheme correspondences which exist in the orthography. The basic reason underlying our orthograpy's disparity with the alphabetic principle lies not only in the fact that we have but twenty-six letters to represent some three dozen or so phonemes but that we use these letters in various combinations, with the consequence that we have far *more* graphic symbols than necessary.

In any case, the notion of structural simplicity, in linguistic terms, also refers to the need to *control* the selection of words for beginning spelling and reading such that the dominant sound-to-letter correspondences are mastered initially by children before they progress toward more complex and less productive orthographic characteristics. Such linguistically based reading programs at the Bloomfield-Barnhardt materials typify this condition.

Differences between spelling and reading processes

The discussion to this point has been directed toward an understanding of the nature of American English orthography. But, particularly in terms of the study reported here, it should also be noted that the processes of spelling and reading differ in an alphabetic orthography. At the risk of oversimplification, spelling is an *encoding* operation. The speller's task is to translate speech sounds into writing, a task that necessitates the development of an ability to select from a set of possible graphic representations of a phoneme that graphic symbol which correctly represents the phoneme in the word to be spelled. Reading processes, on the other hand, involve *decoding* operations. Reading an alphabetic orthography, in short, requires an individual to determine which of several possible phonemes is represented by a given graphic symbol in a word.

In sum, spelling involves sound-to-letter correspondences while reading involves letter-to-sound correspondences. In a pure alphabetic orthography these processes are reciprocal. But in an imperfect alphabetic orthography such as the American English writing system, spelling and reading have their own unique complexities. The distinction, while useful for analytic purposes, also has important educational consequences.

Phoneme-grapheme correspondences in monosyllabic words

The study reported here involves the encoding process of *spelling*. Its purpose is not particularly to identify educational implications for beginning spelling and reading programs but to describe the orthographic structures of monosyllabic words that are or could be used in such programs and to demonstrate a technique that might be useful in examining the orthography for reading purposes.

A recently completed study of phoneme-grapheme correspondences in American English orthography (1) analyzed the spellings of over 17,000 different words to determine the degree to which this core vocabulary of American English approximates the alphabetic principle. The findings of this research have been reported elsewhere in the literature (1, 2, 3); but these findings may be summarized quickly by noting that the researchers found that most phonemes are typically represented at least 80 percent of the time by a particular graphic symbol either anywhere in a syllable or in particular positions in syllables. In other words, recalling that in our imperfect alphabetic orthography we must rely on odds that a graphic symbol will represent a phoneme, American English orthography is alphabetically based; but we must utilize cues in addition to

simple sound-to-letter correspondence to spell correctly American English words, using alphabetic principles.

The Stanford Research Project did not isolate monosyllabic words for critical analysis; rather, all words in the core American English orthography were examined, each word being broken down into syllables, with the result that monosyllabic words were treated as syllables rather than as discrete words. The present study isolated the 3,428 monosyllabic words of the earlier study, and these words were subjected to an examination of their phoneme-grapheme characteristics.

A phonemic classification was devised, a system that employed forty-eight phonemes—twenty-eight consonants and twenty vowels. Conventional phonemic systems, of course, use fewer numbers of phonemes to classify American English phonology. But, it was felt appropriate *for spelling purposes* to include phonemic notations for the occurrence of vowel phonemes before /r/, as well as for the consonant clusters /kw/ and /ks/, which have unique orthographic characteristics.

The possible graphemic representations of phonemes used in American English orthography were then derived from the previous Stanford Research, with some reclassifying of those graphic symbols that include a final letter *e* as in *bake* or *spoke*.

Computer technology was then employed to analyze the phoneme-grapheme correspondences in monosyllabic words in two ways:

1. To examine them in terms of how a given phoneme is spelled *anyplace* in monosyllabic words. This examination was intended to describe the orthography of monosyllabic words as though the orthography were ideally alphabetic. No factors were considered, other than how is a sound spelled when it appears in a monosyllabic word. This classification was termed *simple phoneme-grapheme correspondence.*

2. To examine them in terms of how a given phoneme is spelled in *particular positions* in monosyllabic

words; that is, initial, medial, and final position of monosyllabic words. This examination thus described the orthography of monosyllabic words using additional cues that are needed to ascertain how some phonemes are spelled in our alphabetically *based* orthography. This classification was termed *positional constraints*.

By rank-ordering the spellings of each phoneme at each of these levels of analysis it was therefore possible to assess how nearly each phoneme in monosyllabic words *approximates* the alphabetic principle. In this way, a determination could be made of the odds that a given phoneme would be represented by a particular graphic symbol at least 80 percent of the time in monosyllabic words or in some position in them. The *80 percent criterion* is a useful measure of the degree to which the orthography approximates the alphabetic principle, since it means that any phoneme-grapheme correspondence achieving this criterion could be applied to the spelling of monosyllabic words and the resulting spelling would be correct at least four times out of five.

Findings

In terms of the phonological characteristics of monosyllabic words as compared to polysyllabic words, it was found that

1. All phonemes of the general lexicon are not present in monosyllabic words. The neutral vowel /ə/, occurring in unstressed syllables, for example, does not occur in monosyllabic words since, by definition, all monosyllabic words, when isolated from running speech, have primary stress.

2. More important for spelling purposes, however, is the apparent fact that the number of spellings of certain phonemes in the general lexicon as classified in the Stanford Research are considerably reduced in numbers when monosyllabic words are separately classified. In the general lexicon, consonant phonemes employ 141 graphic symbols, while in monosyllabic words 89 graphic symbols are employed. This is also true of vowel phonemes. In the general lexicon, 234 graphic symbols are employed to represent vowel phonemes, while in monosyllabic words 156 graphic symbols are used. In short, 130 fewer graphic symbols are used in monosyllabic words than in the general lexicon.

Such reductions in the number of graphemes used to represent phonemes in monosyllabic words as compared to the general lexicon would seem to infer that phoneme-grapheme correspondences in monosyllabic words more nearly approximate the alphabetic principle in these words than in all words of the general lexicon. But, is this the case?

3. At the level of simple phoneme-grapheme correspondence, American English phonemes in the general lexicon fail to achieve the 80 percent criterion (73.13 percent) while phonemes in monosyllabic words only exceed this criterion (81.36 percent). Mean percentage tabulations, however, obscure the important information concerning consonant and vowel phonemes, respectively, as well as individual phonemes. Consonant phonemes as a group increase in approximations to the alphabetic principle from 83.99 percent to 88.35 percent at the level of simple phoneme-grapheme correspondence. Vowel phonemes as a group also increase, but from 62.27 percent to 64 percent, well below the 80 percent criterion.

4. In terms of positional constraints, consonant phonemes further approximate the alphabetic principle in each position of monosyllabic words as compared to their occurrences in the total lexicon. Vowel phonemes, on the other hand, also approach this principle although in no position do vowel phonemes exceed the 80 percent criterion. Table I summarizes approximations to the alphabetic principle of the total phonemic system used in this study as well as the separate consonant and vowel classifications. This table

TABLE I

SUMMARY TABLE OF PERCENTAGES OF APPROXIMATION TO ALPHABETIC
PRINCIPLE OF PHONEMES IN MONOSYLLABIC WORDS

Phonological Level:	48 Phoneme Classification		28 Consonant Classification		20 Vowel Classification	
	No. of Phonemes Used	%	No. of Phonemes Used	%	No. of Phonemes Used	%
Simple Phoneme-Grapheme Corres.	48	81.36	28	88.35	20	64.00
Position Factors						
Initial	43	95.17	24	96.00	19	73.77
Medial	39	80.37	19	98.08	20	68.48
Final	33	81.46	23	83.15	10	59.66
Mean %		84.92		91.71		68.05

also points out how position affects the numbers of phonemes that are used in respective positions in monosyllabic words.

Findings such as the foregoing provide us with general information about the orthography. But they do not help us determine the conditions that characterize American English orthography's departure from the alphabetic principle.

5. Twenty-four of the twenty-eight consonant phonemes classified in this study exceed the 80 percent criterion at the level of simple phoneme-grapheme correspondence. The four phonemes that do not are /j/, /k/, /ng/, and /z/. However, *all* consonant phonemes exceed this criterion when positional constraints are considered. That is, even the four errant phonemes which fail to exceed the 80 percent criterion at the level of simple correspondence do so in some position in monosyllabic words. Clearly, then, consonant phonemes as a group are not primarily responsible for American English orthography's departure from the alphabetic principle.

6. On the other hand, only seven of the twenty vowel phonemes classified in this study exceed the 80 percent criterion at the level of simple phoneme-grapheme correspondence, these phonemes being the so-called "short vowel" phonemes and two vowel phonemes occurring before /r/. Even when positional constraints are considered, vowel phonemes as a group do not appreciably increase in approximations to the alphabetic principle, although /oi/, /ou/, and /ɔh/ (the vowel sound in one pronunciation of *law*) exceed the 80 percent criterion in some position in monosyllabic words. In sum, this examination of the orthography of monosyllabic words reveals that the phonemes largely responsible for the orthography's failure to approximate the alphabetic principle in monosyllabic words are the so-called "long vowel" phonemes and certain diphthongs.

Discussion

Such seeming disparities with the alphabetic principle should not require that we "throw the baby out with the bath water." For the fact of the matter is that American English orthography *is* alphabetically based and although *as a system* is more complicated than it might be, contains many sound-to-letter correspondences that, if learned, can ease the burden of mastering our writing system. The consonant and "short vowel" phonemes, for instance, are rich sources for helping children to understand the nature of the orthography and to apply this knowledge in correctly spelling words. In fact, it is precisely these phoneme classifications that are so heavily utilized in linguistically-based beginning spelling and reading programs and are often used to initiate traditional phonics-oriented reading programs.

American English words, however, are obviously comprised of other phonemes having less consistent spellings. What might be done about them? One alternative is to present lists of words, selected for their functionality in writing, in which particular phoneme-grapheme correspondences, although failing to exceed the 80 percent criterion, occur in large numbers of words. This "spelling pattern" approach, for example, could be used to demonstrate one of the several spellings of the "long" vowel /ow/, the so-called "long o" sound spelled oa. Although this spelling of /ow/ occurs only 17 percent of the time in monosyllabic words, 45 of the 51 words in which it occurs are extremely functional words. A number of these words are board, boat, cloak, coach, coal, coast, coat, croak, foam, goat, groan, load, loaf, loan, road, roam, roar, roast, soak, soap, and throat.

In short, one possible solution is to present individual phoneme-grapheme correspondences in terms of the functional words in which they occur. Rare spellings of phonemes would, in this instance, be treated as exceptions and learned by whatever instructional methods appear to be appropriate.

A second alternative suggests itself, however, when we review the degree to which phonemes approximate the alphabetic principle in monosyllabic words as compared to their spellings in the general lexicon, particularly the spellings of those phonemes which depart farthest from the alphabetic principle in monosyllabic words. The vowel phoneme /ey/, for example, (the so-called "long a" sound) in monosyllabic words does not achieve the 80 percent criterion at the level of simple phoneme-grapheme correspondence nor in any position in these words. But, in the general lexicon, this phoneme is spelled a approximately 81 percent of the time in the final position of syllables that are not word final. Examples of this observation are able, crater, lady, radio, acorn, flavor, major, table, baby, gravy, bacon, paper, and cable.

In other words, should we wish to do so, an earlier introduction of the factor of syllabication and affixation into beginning spelling and reading programs would enable children better to understand the alphabetic principle underlying our orthography and to induce useful sound-to-letter correspondences that pertain to the total lexicon. Such an alternative, of course, necessitates that words be selected with precision and with a concern for their functionality. But, the concepts of functionality and structural simplicity which were discussed at the outset of this report are not either-or propositions. What is suggested here is that balanced spelling programs must contend with both criteria; that is, if we wish to provide pupils with spelling content that accurately describes the alphabetic structure of the orthography and has utility for them as well.

The purpose of this study, however, has not been to search for curriculum implications per se but to provide a description of the alphabetic nature of the orthography of American English words and to illustrate a research design and methodology that has potential usefulness for further studies of the orthography in terms of reading. Studies such as this, it is hoped, contribute to a better understanding of the structure of American English orthography; and with such understanding may well emerge more effective and accurate spelling and reading program.

REFERENCES

1. Hanna, Paul R., et al. Phoneme-Grapheme Correspondences as Cues to Spelling Improvement. Washington, D. C., U. S. Dept. of Health, Education and Welfare, Office of Education, 1966.
2. Hodges, Richard E. "The Case for Teaching Sound-to-Letter Correspondences in Spelling," The Elementary School Journal (Mar. 1966).
3. Hodges, Richard E., and E. Hugh Rudorf. "Searching Linguistics for Cues for the Teaching of Spelling," Elementary English, 42 (May 1965), 527-533.
4. Rinsland, Henry D. A Basic Vocabulary of Elementary School Children. New York: Macmillan Co., 1945.

5. Thorndike, Edwarl L., and Irving Lorge. *The Teacher's Word Book of 30,000 Words.* New York: Bureau of Publications, Teachers College, Columbia University, 1944.
6. Zipf, George Kingsley. *Human Behavior and the Principle of Least Effort.* Cambridge, Mass.: Addison-Wesley Press, 1949.

Conditional Responsibilities in the Phonemic Representation of English Words

DONALD A. LETON
Honolulu, Hawaii, Education
Research and Development
Center

IN DISCUSSING the nature and development of reading, Judd (6) explicated the process in this statement, "The printed units must be made to coincide with their oral counterparts." The coincidence of the two systems of language, i.e., the graphic system and the oral system, is effected in the successful teaching of reading; however, the procedures for converting the graphic system to oral language have not been systematically ordered as yet.

Frequency studies of the components of English have been concentrated on the two separate systems, words and sounds. Some studies have been based on counts of entries in dictionaries; but these do not identify the importance of the components in terms of frequency of use. Other counts have been based on running words, either written or spoken. Some of these have been made to determine the frequency of sounds in the language; and others, to determine the frequency of words in various compositions.

Studies of the phonemic structure of American English have been handicapped by the lack of commonly accepted standards. A wide acceptance of the phonemic notation system presented by Trager and Smith (13) has only recently developed among linguists. Most of the basic studies, however, have used earlier systems, for example, Kenyon and Knott (7), Pike (9), or the International Phonetic Alphabet. The information from these studies, therefore, has tended to be noncumulative.

It is a surprising but little known fact that the boundaries of American English have not as yet been identified. Linguistic geographers have made extensive efforts to identify, in phonetic notation, the regional and social variations of American English. Ever since the 1930's, Kurath and his associates (8) have attempted to write an American Linguistic Atlas; however, their investigations of the dialect variations are not as yet complete. The lack of a common standard for phonemic notation and the concern about phonetic variations have probably delayed the systematic study of some of the basic problems in the acquisition of language.

The objective of the International Phonetic Alphabet, which was developed prior to 1900, was to provide a distinctive symbol for every sound in human speech. In spite of minor changes it has maintained a general utility for the phonetic analysis of English. More recently phonemics has evolved as the structural analysis of phonetics. A phoneme is defined as a group of phone types that are phonetically similar and either in complimentary distribution or in free variation. Each member of a phoneme class is an allophone. The numbers of allophones in the phoneme classes vary in different languages.

A grapheme is ordinarily defined as the minimum unit of orthography. Each of the 26 letters of the alphabet and the punctuation marks qualify under this definition as a grapheme.

Bloomfield and Barnhart (1) have recommended phoneme analysis in the teaching of reading; and Stratemeyer and Smith (12) have published a series of primers for elementary school children, which are based on a systematic phonetic translation. Gillingham and Stillman (4) were pioneers in the use of phonetics in remedial reading, and their work has stimulated general methods of instruction in reading.

Gibson and associates (3) have defined grapheme-phoneme correspondence as the critical unit in the reading process. They regard this correspondence as a higher-order unit, with the graphemes and phonemes representing the primary variables. Empirical studies using pseudo words have supported their hypothesis that reading skill is a function of prior knowledge of grapheme-phoneme relationships.

Although there are major correspondences between the English alphabet and English phonemes, there are also a number of inconsistent, arbitrary, and unsystematic relationships between the two systems. The manner in which the regular and irregular associations are learned or the manner in which they should be taught for most efficient learning has not as yet been established.

In developing the Augmented Roman alphabet, Pitnam (10) attempted to establish a more direct relationship between the printed symbols and the phoneme response. The i.t.a. is composed of 43 characters, 14 of which are digraphs. This alphabet is associated with 24 consonant phonemes and 16 vowel and diphthong phonemes.

Venezky (14) used a computer to count the tokens of letters and letter clusters appearing in the 19,607 words in the Thorndike Senior Century Dictionary. In his more recent work with Weir (15) he has been able to identify a high degree of spelling to sound patterning; however, he also acknowledged that the traditional view of orthography, i.e., as 26 letter graphemes, is not adequate for spelling to sound mapping. Their suggestions on the use of "marker letters" and of identifying relational units should hold significant value for further research and teaching methodology.

Hanna and associates (5) have reported on the spelling variations of the phonemes appearing in a list of 17,000 American English words. In a subsequent phase of their work Rudorf (1) developed an algorithm for computer spelling which led to 49 percent accuracy. The works of Venezky

(14) and Rudorf (11) demonstrate the feasibility of systematizing the procedures for converting from one system to another.

Procedure

The phoneme system developed by Trager and Smith (13) was used in this study. The system included 33 segmental phonemes, nine phoneme combinations, one juncture phoneme, and a nonphoneme. There were 24 consonant phonemes: p b t d k g č j f v ө ð s š z ž m n ŋ l r w y h/ nine simple vowels:/i e æ ɨ ə a u ɔ ɔ/, eight vowel-semivowel nuclei /iy ey ay oy aw uw ow ɔh/, one consonant combination /ks/, the transition stop /+/, and the nonphoneme /Ø/. The nonphoneme was used to represent silent graphemes. Stress and pitch phonemes were regarded as suprasegmental and not included at this stage of analysis.

For this study a grapheme is redefined as the minimum unit of orthography to which a segmental phoneme, a diphthong, or the silent phoneme could be tagged. Sixty-five graphemes were identified as the orthographic subunits which generate all of the segmental phonemes. Thirty-eight of these were digraphs, i.e., nine consonant combinations, sixteen vowel-vowel combinations, and thirteen vowel-semi vowel combinations. The other 27 graphemes were the letters of the alphabet and the period. The period was used to include the juncture phoneme. Other punctuation marks can also be included for the same phoneme. For the grapheme <x> the phoneme combination /ks/ is treated as a single phoneme.

It was then postulated that a 65 by 44 matrix is an adequate structure to accommodate all of the pertinent English grapheme-phoneme associations. This matrix is part of the computer output in a reading simulation study. The limits of the matrix for the phoneme analysis of an extensive list of English words has not been tested as yet; however, its use is illustrated in this study.

Results

The associations which occurred in the new words and in the total words of the preprimer and primer program of the Ginn Basic Readers were tabulated and recorded in the matrix. The associations for 6,949 total words in the primer program are presented.

The frequencies in the matrix represent conditional or one-way probabilities. The conditional associations, although these did not occur in the primer data, are illustrated in the following examples. In the word *lead* the grapheme <ea> is associated with the phoneme /e/ and the word is pronounced /l e d/ if it refers to the metal. The same grapheme is associated with the diphthong /iy/ and pronounced /l iy d/ if it refers to the front position or to guide. In this illustration the conditions of the association are not discernible at the word level. Also, since there are noun forms for the two pronunciations, the associations can not be determined through syntactical analysis. The correct grapheme-phoneme association is determined only by the word meaning. At the text level, if the word appeared frequently in a report on mineral resources, the probability that its pronunciation would be /l e d/ could be assigned from prior analyses of other reports on mineral resources. If the word appeared frequently in a report on racing sports or card games, a prediction of /l iy d/ would be fairly reliable.

In one-way probability the relationship between the antecedent conditions and the consequences is not reversible. The conditional association is also illustrated for phoneme-grapheme relationships. For example, the phoneme chain /l e d/ may be presented as the antecedent condition and the required task is to predict the correct orthography, i.e., <led> or <lead>. In this case the prediction can be made through syntactical analysis.

Conditional grapheme-phoneme associations can also be illustrated in words such as <tough> <dough> and <ghost>. In these words the correct phoneme choice for the <gh>

digraph is determined at the word level. The one-way probabilities for phoneme-grapheme associations are again illustrated in the phoneme chains /t u f/ and /d o w/. The orthography for /t u f/ may be <tough> or <tuff>, and the orthography for /d o w/ may be <dough> or <doe>.

Obviously, there are few words that are illustrative of these one-way conditional associations. The grapheme-phoneme associations may be consistent enough, and the conditions or rules which determine the associations may be objectively identified, so that some maximum prediction could be effected.

There are several purposes which the frequency matrix such as that presented for the grapheme-phoneme associations in the Ginn Primer can serve. First, it has an heuristic value. For example, the association between the grapheme < b > and the phoneme /b/ may prevail through the primary grades. It may be considered to be a one-to-one relationship until words such as *debt* and *bomb* are introduced for phoneme analysis. The second purpose which such a matrix can serve is that it can indicate the hierarchy of rules for an efficient algorithm. For example, the associations of the 2,648 occurrences of grapheme < a > in the primer matrix were /ɔ/ /æ/ /e/ /a/ /u/ /ə/ /ey/ /Ø/ and /ɔh/. The frequencies, extracted from the table in their order of magnitude are .313, .291, .128, .096, .088, .039, .022, .018, .005. For the phoneme analysis of similar material the rules underlying these associations should then be applied in descending order for optimum efficiency.

The proportions of phonemes for the < a > grapheme indicated above are row probabilities. The phoneme-grapheme associations are determined on the basis of column frequencies. For example, the phoneme /ə/ appeared 592 times in the 6,949 words in the primer and it was associated with the < e > < a > and < u > graphemes in the following proportions, .806, .174, .020. In this case the phoneme represents the antecedent condition and the graphemes are the consequents. The hierarchy of spelling rules, i.e., rules for orthographic analysis, might be established from the column associations.

Discussion

Although the teaching of grapheme-phoneme relationships has been recommended for the teaching of reading for a number of years, the precise nature of these relationships has not been studied. On the basis of existing definitions of graphemes and phonemes the recommendation could not be carried out. With the traditional definition of a segmental grapheme the letter t in the < th > digraph is not associated with a phoneme; the grapheme < e > in a word such as *bite* is not associated with a phoneme; and the grapheme < x > ordinarily requires two phonemes (except in words such as *xylophone*).

This study of grapheme-phoneme relationships evolved from an effort to develop a computer program for the simulation of reading. The conditional nature of these associations led to a further study of conditional probability (2) as a procedure for phoneme analysis.

A 65 x 44 matrix was used to tabulate the grapheme-phoneme associations appearing in the new words and the total words of the Ginn Basic Reading Series. This procedure should be of practical value to authors of reading texts to obtain objective data on the range and frequency of associations. The row associations represent grapheme-phoneme relationships; the column associations represent phoneme-grapheme relationships. To the extent that rules for orthography, i.e., spelling, and rules for phonemic analysis, i.e., oral reading, coincide the associations are symmetrical and reversible. The joint probability is an indication of the degree of consistency in the graphic and phonemic representations of English. The joint probability matrix appears only to have theoretical meaning; whereas the one-way probability matrices should have practical and research values.

REFERENCES

1. Bloomfield, L., and C. L. Barnhart. *Let's Read: A Linguistic Approach.* Detroit: Wayne State University Press, 1961.
2. Coombs, C. H. *A Theory of Data.* Ann Arbor, Michigan: University of Michigan, 1964.
3. Gibson, E. J. *et al.* "The Role of Grapheme-Phoneme Correspondence in the Perception of Words," *American Journal of Psychology, 75,* No. 4, 1962, 554-570.
4. Gillingham, A., and B. W. Stillman. *Remedial Training for Children with Specific Disability in Reading, Spelling, and Penmanship.* Distributed by authors, 25 Parkview Ave., Bronxville, N. Y., 1940.
5. Hanna, P. R. *et al.* "Needed Research in Spelling," *Linguistic Cues for Program of Spelling Curriculum,* Stanford University, 1964.
6. Judd, C. H. "Reduction of Articulation," *American Journal of Psychology, 39,* 1927, 313-322.
7. Kenyon and Knott. "A Guide to Pronunciation," *Websters New International Dictionary.* Springfield, Massachusetts: Merriam Co., 1951.
8. Kurath, H., *et al.* "Methodology." *Handbook of the Linguistic Geography of New England.* Washington, D. C.: American Council of Learned Societies, 1939, 39-54.
9. Pike, K. L. *Phonemics.* Ann Arbor, Michigan: University of Michigan Press, 1947.
10. Pitnam, J. "Learning to Read," *Journal of Royal Society,* July 1962, 1-32.
11. Rudorf, E. H. "Measurement of Spelling Ability," *Linguistic Cues for Program of Spelling Curriculum.* Newark, Delaware: University of Delaware, 1964.
12. Stratemeyer, C. G., and H. L. Smith. *The Linguistic Science Readers.* Evanston: Harper and Row, 1963.
13. Trager, G. L., and H. L. Smith. *An Outline of English Structure.* Norman, Oklahoma: Battenburg Press, 1951.
14. Venezky, R. L. *A Study of English Spelling to Sound Correlations.* Berkeley: University of California, Nov. 1962.
15. Weir, R. H. *Formulation of Grapheme-Phoneme Correspondence Rules to Aid in the Teaching of Reading.* Cooperative Research Project No. S-039. Stanford University: 1964.

Children's Reading: Syntactic Structure and Comprehension Difficulty

JOANNE R. NURSS
Emory University

CHILDREN'S ACQUISITION and mastery of the reading process are the focus of primary grade education. The problem investigated in this study was one aspect of the relationship between syntactic structure and comprehension difficulty.

Grammatical structure and reading comprehension

Reading comprehension has been shown to be influenced by syntactic structure in a variety of ways, including the relationship of the sentence patterns in the reading passage to those in the children's oral language (8), sentence or independent clause length (4), and the structural depth of the sentences in the reading passage (2). The reader's awareness of grammatical structure (7) and the emphasis on sentence patterns in the reading curriculum (9) have been shown to influence reading comprehension. These studies have been done with intermediate grade, high school, or college students. Little is known about the relationship between syntactic structure and comprehension difficulty in primary grade children.

Readability studies usually find a significant relationship between some measure of sentence structure and reading comprehension. Once a vocabulary measure has been included in a readability formula, a measure of sentence structure adds relatively little to the formula's prediction of reading difficulty. In a study of fourth through eighth grade children's performance on a Cloze procedure test, Bormuth (3) found that mean word depth, computed according to Yngve's procedure, made a significant contribution to the prediction of the comprehension difficulty.

Measures of structural complexity

Yngve (10) has proposed a model for language structure based on his work with computer translation. He defines the depth of a sentence in terms of a tree diagram of its constituent structure. A sentence is analyzed by successive binary divisions. Production of a left-hand branch of a sentence requires temporary storage in memory of the right-hand branch of the node. The structural depth of a sentence is the maximum number of such nodes that must be accumulated in the temporary memory at any point within the sentence. Comprehension involves understanding the grammatical complexity of the passage being read. Structural depth, which reflects the grammatical complexity of a sentence, may be a measure of the difficulty of comprehending that sentence.

An equally promising procedure for measuring structural complexity is based on Allen's sector analysis (1). Allen has suggested that reading comprehension is dependent upon the reader's implicit analysis of the syntactic structure of a sentence. In his analysis of English grammar, Allen first identifies constructions that occupy certain defined positions within the sentence and then analyzes the positions within these constructions on lower levels. This process continues throughout the levels of a sentence until the word level is reached. The structural depth is the maximum number of levels required to go from sentence to word level. Allen has proposed that the sector analysis depth figure may be a measure of the readability of a passage.

The concern of the study being reported (6) was the effect of sentences of varying structural complexity on primary grade children's oral reading, silent reading, and listening comprehension.

Hypotheses

It was expected that sentences of more complex syntactic structure would be more difficult for primary grade children to read than would sentences of less complex syntactic structure, when structural complexity was assessed by

1. structural depth, computed according to Yngve's depth hypothesis;
2. structural depth, computed according to Allen's sector analysis; and
3. structural organization, as defined by traditional grammar.

Materials, procedures, and sample

Thirty-six one-sentence "stories" were written, one half representing varying structural depths and one half representing three types of structural organization. The structural depth stories were written in six different forms and ranked into two high-, two mid-, and two low-depth sentences according to Yngve's analysis. The same six sentences were also ranked into two high-, two mid-, and two low-depth sentences according to Allen's analysis. The ranks given the sentences by the two analyses were not always the same, due to the different conceptions of structural depth in the two analyses. These differences allowed a comparison of the prediction of comprehension difficulty by the two depth analyses. The structural organization stories were written in three different types of organization, as defined by traditional grammar—complex, compound, and simple sentences.

The stories were the same interest and difficulty level, and the sentences were approximately the same length. The vocabulary used in the stories was words from the Dolch Basic Sight Vocabulary of 220 Words and the Dolch 95 Most Common Nouns, supplemented by words from the Ginn cumulative vocabulary for the first grade and the second grade, level one. Twelve of the stories (six structural depth and six structural organization) were read orally. The children read another 12 of the stories silently and had the remaining 12 read to them. The stories in their different forms were rotated over the three tasks. The children's comprehension of each story was tested by a picture comprehension test. Each child was shown three pictures prepared for the story just read so that he could select the one which correctly depicted the events described in the story. The same pictures were used for each story regardless of the syntactic form in which it was read and regardless of the mode of presentation. The children's reading was tape-recorded, and an analysis of their oral reading errors was made as another measure of the comprehension difficulty of the sentences.

The subjects were second graders from a suburban Connecticut school system. They were tested in the spring and the fall of 1966. One sample of 108 children, tested at the end of second grade, was selected on the basis of a vocabulary screening test. These children read orally a list of 20 vocabulary words selected at random from those used in the stories, and only children who could read at least 90 percent of them were used as subjects. When the sentences were administered to this selected group, the between-subjects variation was small and the picture comprehension test was very easy. The reliability coefficients of these scores were severely limited when this screening procedure was used.

A second sample of 36 children, tested at the beginning of second grade, was selected without the vocabulary test. Any vocabulary words that the subjects did not know were supplied by the examiner for both the oral and silent reading tasks. Under these conditions the materials were of more appropriate difficulty for the children and the range of their scores on the picture comprehension test were wider. The split-half reliability coefficients for the total scores, calculated by applying the Spearman-Brown formula to the correlation between each pair of scores, were .81 for the Yngve structural depth sentences, .77 for the Allen structural depth sentences, and .80 for the structural organization sentences.

The reliability coefficients ranged from .43 to .72 for the separate oral and silent reading scores. The correlations of the total picture comprehension scores with the standard scores obtained on the comprehension test of the Gages-MacGinite Reading Test, Primary B, were .57 for the structural depth sentences and .61 for the structural organization sentences. These validity correlation coefficients ranged from .42 to .62 for the separate oral and silent reading scores.

The oral reading tapes for the sample of children screened on the vocabulary test were analyzed for oral reading errors by three experienced reading teachers. The errors tabulated were corrections, substitutions, other errors (additions, omissions, repetitions), total oral errors (the first three categories combined), and hesitations. The percentage of agreement between at least two of the three judges ranged from 54 percent to 85 percent, and the correlations between the subjects' total oral errors and their standard scores on the comprehension Test of the Gates-MacGinite Reading Test, Primary B, were -0.53 for the structural depth sentences and -0.40 for the structural organization sentences.

Results

The hypotheses that sentences of greater structural depth would be more difficult for primary grade children to read were partially supported by the oral reading error data but not by the picture comprehension data. The hypothesis that sentences of more complex structural organization would be more difficult for these children to read was not supported by either comprehension measure.

The scores obtained by the children on the picture comprehension test were analyzed by several three-way analyses of variance, testing the effects of syntactic structure, mode of presentation, and subjects. Because the stories were rotated completely over the subjects, a mixed model analysis of variance was used with subjects as the random effect. No significant differences due to structural complexity were found with the picture comprehension scores under either vocabulary condition. However, there were larger absolute differences between comprehensibility of varying levels of structural complexity with the vocabulary screening test then without.

Significant effects due to mode of presentation were found with the picture comprehension scores under the vocabulary screening conditions. Silent reading comprehension was significantly more difficult than oral reading or listening comprehension. Listening comprehension was also easier than oral or silent reading comprehension when the subjects were not screened on vocabulary. It was not included in the analysis of variance under these conditions, however, because the distribution of scores was quite different from that of the reading comprehension scores.

There also was a significant interaction effect between levels of depth and modes of presentation under the vocabulary screening conditions. For the Yngve depth analysis, oral and silent reading comprehension of sentences of low depth was easier than that of mid or high depth sentences, but listening comprehension of mid depth sentences was easier than that of high or low depth sentences. For the organization analysis, oral reading comprehension of complex sentences was more difficult than that of compound or simple sentences, and silent reading comprehension of complex sentences was more difficult than that of compound sentences. Listening comprehension of complex sentences, however, was easier than that of compound or simple sentences. Syntactic structure affected reading comprehension when the subjects had been screened on the vocabulary test, but the effects varied with the mode of presentation of the stories.

The oral reading tapes for the sample of children who had been screened on vocabulary were analyzed, using the five categories of oral reading errors. They show that the subjects made very few errors per sentence, although there were wide differences among the subjects. These errors were analyzed by several two-way analyses of variance, testing the effects of syntactic structure and subjects.

Significant effects due to syntactic structure were found for hesitations in the Yngve and Allen structural depth sentences, and in the structural organization sentences, for corrections and for total oral errors in the Allen depth sentences, and for substitutions in the structural organization sentences.

Sentences of high Allen depth produced significantly more corrections and hesitations than did those of mid or low depth. Sentences of high Yngve depth also produced significantly more hesitations than did those of low depth. Simple sentences resulted in significantly more substitutions than did compound sentences.

Several additional analyses of oral reading errors were made. The oral reading repetitions were tabulated as a repetition of either a whole structural unit or part of a structural unit. When a child repeated a whole unit, it was assumed that he understood the relationship of that unit to the rest of the sentence. The proportion of whole-unit repetitions decreased with increasing sentence complexity.

When uncorrected substitutions, additions, and omissions occurred, the resulting sentence might or might not be a complete, meaningful sentence—semantically and grammatically. These errors more frequently "made sense" in the sentences of low structural depth and simple structural organization than they did in the more complex sentences.

The hesitations were analyzed as occurring at grammatical or nongrammatical junctures according to the crtieria established by Henderson, Goldman-Eisler, and Skarbek (5). Fewer hesitations occurred at nongrammatical junctures in the sentences of less complex syntactic structure than in those of more complex structure.

Evidence from the analysis of oral reading errors shows that sentences of more complex syntactic structure, according to the Yngve and Allen measures of structural depth and according to the traditional grammar definition of structural organization, are more difficult for primary grade children to read and understand.

Discussion

Vocabulary is a major factor in comprehension difficulty at any level of reading. Its role is especially large in beginning reading where comprehension of materials depends heavily on word knowledge and word attack skills. For this reason, vocabulary was controlled in the initial phases of this study. However, when both the vocabulary range of the materials and vocabulary knowledge of the subjects were controlled, major sources of variability in comprehension difficulty at this level were removed and the range of the picture comprehension scores was restricted. When the subjects were not screened on vocabulary, however, there was more variability in their vocabulary knowledge and the distribution of comprehension scores was wider. The sentences were more difficult for these subjects, in spite of the fact that the vocabulary words which they did not know were supplied during oral and silent reading. However, there were smaller absolute differences between levels of syntactic structure under these conditions than when the subjects were screened on vocabulary.

Additional investigation of the effects of syntactic structure on primary children's comprehension needs to be undertaken using longer passages and other comprehension measures. A significant interaction effect was found in this study between levels of structural complexity and modes of presentation. Within the oral and silent reading modes, complex structures were more difficult to understand but within the listening mode, the simpler structures were more difficult. This interaction finding also needs to be investigated further. This study was initiated, in part, to learn what types of syntactic structure should be used in beginning reading materials. The results indicate that strict control of sentence structure in primary grade materials is probably not necessary. However, these results should not be interpreted to mean that any sentence structures, no matter how complex or long, should be used in these materials. Primary grade reading materials need to continue to give major attention to vocabulary control and development, but the analysis of oral reading errors suggests that sentences must not be unduly long or complex. As more complex syntactic structures are introduced into primary grade reading materials, instruction should be given in ways of handling the increasing complexity of sentences.

REFERENCES

1. Allen, Robert L. "English Grammars and English Grammar." Unpublished manuscript, Columbia University, Institute for Teachers of English, 1964.
2. Bormuth, John R. "Mean Word Depth as a Predictor of Comprehension Difficulty," *California Journal of Educational Research, 15* (November 1964), 226-231.
3. _____. "Relationships Between Selected Language Variables and Comprehension Ability and Difficulty." U. S. Office of Education Cooperative Research Report, 1964, No. 2082.
4. Coleman, Edward B. "Improving Comprehensibility by Shortening Sentences," *Journal of Applied Psychology, 46* (April 1962), 131-134.
5. Henderson, Alan, Frieda Goldman-Eisler, and Andrew Skarbek. "Temporal Patterns of Cognitive Activity and Breath Control in Speech," *Language and Speech, 8* (October 1965), 236-242.
6. Nurss, Joanne R. "Children's Reading: Syntactic Structure and Comprehension Difficulty," unpublished doctoral dissertation, Columbia University, 1966.
7. O'Donnell, Roy C. "A Study of the Correlation Between Awareness of Structural Relationships in English and Ability in Reading Comprehension," *Journal of Experimental Education, 31* (Spring 1963).
8. Ruddell, Robert B. "An Investigation of the Effect of the Similarity of Oral and Written Patterns of Language Structure on Reading Comprehension," unpublished doctoral project, Indiana University, 1963.
9. _____. "Reading Instruction in First Grade with Varying Emphasis on the Regularity of Grapheme-phoneme Correspondence and the Relation of Language Structure to Meaning," *Reading Teacher, 19* (May 1966), 653-600.
10. Yngve, Victor H. "A Model and Hypothesis for Language Structure," *Proceedings of the American Philosophical Society, 104* (October 1960), 444-466.

Improving Comprehension through Study of Syntax and Paragraph Structure in Seventh Grade English Classes

ESTELLA E. REED
Purdue University
Calumet Campus

THE PURPOSE of this investigation was to determine the relative effect of the study of syntax and paragraph structure on reading comprehension of monolingual and bilingual pupils of middle ability in grade seven. This study was done in Washington High School, East Chicago, Indiana, between February 1965 and May 1965, excluding a pilot study which was conducted between September 16 and December 1, 1964. In this investigation, reading comprehension was construed as gaining the general significance of printed passages.

Why study literal comprehension?

The ability to read with comprehension is a prerequisite for success in junior high school. Inability to read at, or near, grade level causes failures, frustration, and limitations in school —and in adult life. Goldenson (6) points out that at least 90 percent of a child's study consists of reading. Penty (10) has shown a direct relationship between poor reading skills and school dropouts. Conant (4) has termed the low-skilled dropout "social dynamite."

Reading is a complex act that involves many skills. Broening (2) and Robinson (11) call attention to the fact that too many skills may be taught at one time. Comprehension has been adjudged a major problem in reading by Brown (3) and Braam and Roehn

(1). Literal comprehension precedes critical comprehension in the hierarchy of skills. Reading to grasp the central idea is one aspect of literal comprehension. Until the literal meaning is achieved, a reader will not advance to the implied level, and ultimately to the creative meaning level.

Why emphasize junior high school?

The seventh grade is a critical stage in a pupil's development in reading because 1) the school organization frequently thrusts the child into a new administrative pattern; 2) formal reading instruction has often been curtailed by the end of grade six; 3) grades seven and eight have been traditionally heavy in content subjects; and 4) skills and attitudes could be nurtured that would make the child a more productive reader in high school and in later life.

In this age of population mobility, there is a growing urgency within the American society to increase educational opportunities for the culturally different pupil. Educators, such as Edwards (5), Passow (9), Niemeyer (8), Traxler (12), and Madeira (7), have called attention to the existing need for modifying both curricula and methods to embrace the culturally different pupil found in the American classroom today. Increased effort in junior high schools might alleviate the dropout rate in high school.

This study supports the contention that a reexamination of method and content in the junior high school curriculum, with respect to reading, is in order.

Two additional general conditions make this study of reading comprehension pertinent to educational needs today: 1) a common complaint among secondary school teachers that pupils cannot read as well as they should; and 2) a prevailing lack of knowledge of methods for teaching reading in the junior and senior high school.

Reading instruction within the English class

This study presents one approach to incorporating reading instruction within the English class of a regular seventh grade curriculum. The relative effect of a planned program of instruction in reading comprehension is compared with a program of incidental reading instruction with intact classes containing both monolingual and bilingual pupils.

A monolingual pupil is one who uses only one language and comes from a home where only English is spoken regularly.

A bilingual pupil is one who uses more than one language (not learned at school) and comes from a home where English is not the only language used regularly.

Reading instruction and syntax

Specific questions for which answers were sought are as follows:

1. Will comprehension of the general significance of a passage be facilitated if reading instruction is based on a) recognition of sentence elements and b) recognition of paragraph structure?

2. Will reading instruction based on recognition of sentence elements and paragraph structure result in greater gain in comprehension for bilingual pupils than for monolingual pupils of middle ability in grade seven?

3. Will reading instruction based on recognition of sentence elements and paragraph structure result in greater gain in comprehension for boys than for girls of middle ability in grade seven?

Statement of the problem

The problem investigated was to compare the reading achievement in comprehension of seventh grade pupils in programs characterized by a contrasting method of reading instruction. In one method there were semiweekly study sheets, designed to emphasize comprehension skills through directed study of syntax and paragraph structure, in addition to the regular textbook lessons and library books for free reading; in the other method the regular textbook lessons and library books were used.

The following hypotheses were tested:

1. There is no significant difference in achievement in reading comprehension between a group characterized by a program of reading instruction based on a) recognition of sentence elements and b) recognition of paragraph structure and a group characterized by incidental reading instruction in a regular English class.

2. There is no significant difference in the reading achievement in comprehension of boys in the two groups.

3. There is no significant difference in the reading achievement in comprehension of girls in the two groups.

4. There is no significant difference in the reading achievement in comprehension of monolingual pupils in the two groups.

5. There is no significant difference in the reading achievement in comprehension of bilingual pupils in the two groups.

6. There is no significant difference in the reading achievement in comprehension between monolingual pupils in the experimental group and bilingual pupils in the experimental group.

7. There is no significant difference in the reading achievement in comprehension between boys in the experimental group and girls in the experimental group.

Procedure

A sample survey of the sixth grade population in April 1964 was taken to ascertain the possible number of subjects, linguality, and sex.

A series of 30 lessons, devised to promote ability in literal comprehension in reading, was written by the experimenter. The materials were tested in a pilot study with one 7A class between September and December, 1964. Modifications were made in the materials.

Eight classes of Track II pupils (Middle ability) were randomly assigned to four regular English teachers by school administrators. Each teacher had one experimental class and one control class as a part of his regular teaching load. The classes were randomly assigned to experimental or control classification by the researcher. A total of 167 pupils were in the eight classes.

Among the 84 subjects in the experimental groups were 47 bilingual pupils and 37 monolingual pupils. The control classes had a total of 83 pupils with 48 being bilingual and 35 monolingual. Linguality was established by two questionnaires to pupils. The predominant language among bilingual pupils was Spanish.

In the experimental group there were 40 boys (21 bilingual) and 44 girls (26 bilingual). In the control group there were 28 boys (17 bilingual) and 55 girls (31 bilingual).

The pretest, Nelson Reading Test, Form A, was administered by the investigator to experimental and control classes in February, 1965. Raw scores from the "Paragraph Comprehension" subtest provided the data. Analysis of data by single classification analysis of variance determined homogeneity of the two groups.

Semi-weekly study materials

The following criteria for writing the study sheets were used in this research:

1. State goals and use models in each lesson.
2. Stress sentence units and main ideas.
3. Use local places, people, and events within the background of the pupils.
4. Use material from geography and science textbooks.
5. Direct attention to punctuation as an aid to meaning.
6. Provide practice for writing as a counterpart of reading.

7. Encourage library usage and reference skills.

8. Repeat goals and items of syntax more than once.

The study sheets were mimeographed and distributed to pupils in the experimental classes.' No grades were assigned to the study sheets by the experimenter, but full corrections and comments were written to the pupils. The study sheets were merely the reading training and no analysis was made of these materials.

A practice booklet, *Gates-Peardon Practice Exercises in Reading, Type A, Book VI,* was used during the last ten lessons.

Pupils in the experimental classes had three days of regular English classwork and two days of reading instruction each week for fifteen weeks.

The control group followed a regular course of study for the seventh grade, Track II.

The post-test, Nelson Reading Test, Form B, was administered by the investigator to experimental and control classes in May, 1965. Using scores from the "Paragraph Comprehension" subtest on Forms A and B, single classification analysis of variance was used to determine the significance of gain scores.

Findings

1. The experimental group was significantly superior to the control group in gain score on the Paragraph Comprehension test at the .01 level.

2. A significant difference at the .05 level existed between the boys of the experimental group and the boys of the control group; the difference favored the experimental boys.

3. A significant difference at the .01 level existed between the girls of the experimental group and the girls of the control group; the difference favored the experimental girls.

4. There was no significant difference between monolingual pupils in the experimental group and monolingual pupils in the control group.

5. A significant difference at the .01

level, favoring the experimental group, existed between bilingual pupils in the experimental group and bilingual pupils in the control group.

6. When the experimental group was considered alone, the bilingual pupils were superior to the monolingual pupils at the .01 level in gain score in comprehension.

7. When the experimental group was considered alone, there was no significant difference between boys and girls in gain score in reading comprehension.

Conclusions

1. The superiority of the experimental program, based on study of syntax and paragraph structure, suggests that this program has much to offer in helping both bilingual and monolingual pupils in grade 7 to gain the literal comprehension of a sentence or paragraph. Since the findings in this study are based upon Tack II, or average ability pupils, the same results might not be achieved with gifted or slow pupils.

2. Since boys in the experimental group excelled boys in the control group in reading achievement, there is evidence (at the .05 level of confidence) that boys benefited from reading instruction based on recognition of syntax and paragraph structure.

3. Girls in the experimental group excelled girls in the control group in paragraph comprehension, at the .01 level of confidence. In comparing Conclusion 2 and 3, the data suggest that girls gained somewhat more in comprehension than boys in the experimental program.

Since no significant difference existed between the sexes in the experimental group singly and since significant differences did exist between the sexes when the experimental and control groups were considered antithetically, the implication is that the treatment reduces differences in comprehension between sexes while increasing the gain scores for both sexes.

Since there was no significant difference between monolingual pupils in the experimental and control groups and since there was a highly significant difference between bilingual pupils in the experimental and control groups, the greatest value of this study may lie in a contribution to the methodology for teaching bilingual pupils.

Summary

In summary, the answers to the original questions in this study are as follows:

Is comprehension facilitated by the treatment? Within the limits of this study, the answer is in the affirmative. A program of reading instruction based on 1) recognition of sentence elements and 2) recognition of paragraph structure did produce greater gains than a program of incidental reading instruction.

Will the treatment result in greater gain in comprehension for boys than for girls? There is no evidence to support the contention that boys will make greater gain in reading comprehension than girls will make.

Will the treatment result in greater gain in comprehension for bilingual pupils than for monolingual pupils? Bilingual pupils did make significantly greater gain than monolingual pupils did, within the limits of this study conducted in East Chicago, Indiana.

REFERENCES

1. Braam, Leonard S., and Marilyn A. Roehm. "Subject-Area Teachers' Familiarity with Reading Skills, *Journal of Developmental Reading, 7,* Spring 1964, 188-196.
2. Broening, Angela M. "Abilities Which Contribute to Effective Reading, *Education, 62,* September 1941, 11-17.
3. Brown, Frank B. *The Non-Graded High School.* Englewood Cliffs, New Jersey: Prentice Hall, Inc., 1963, p. 90.
4. Conant, James B. *The Slums and Suburbs.* New York: McGraw-Hill Book Co., 1961.
5. Edwards, Thomas J. "The Language-Experience Attack on Cultural Deprivation," *The Reading Teacher, 18,* April 1965, 546-551.
6. Goldenson, Robert M. *Helping Your Child to Read Better.* New York: Thomas Y. Crowell Co., 1957.
7. Madeira, Sheldon. "Pennsylvania's Mandated Reading Program," *Journal of Developmental Reading, 5,* Summer 1962, 221-226.
8. Niemeyer, John J. "The Bank Street Readers: Support for Movement Toward an Integrated Society," *The Reading Teacher, 18,* April 1965, 542-545.
9. Passow, Harry A. (Ed.). *Education in Depressed Areas.* New York: Bureau of Publications, Teachers College, Columbia University, 1963.
10. Penty, Ruth C. *Reading Ability and High School Drop-Outs.* New York: Bureau of Publications, Teachers College, Columbia University, 1956.
11. Robinson, H. Alan. "A Cluster of Skills: Especially for Junior High School," *The Reading Teacher, 15,* September 1961, 25-28.
12. Traxler, Arthur E. "What Does Research Suggest About Ways to Improve Reading Instruction?" in "Improving Reading in the Junior High School," *Education Digest, 23,* April 1958, 43-46.

Pupil Understanding of Connectives in Reading

Jean E. Robertson
University of Alberta

STUDENTS in the upper elementary grades are often required to read sentences which have coordinate and subordinate ideas in them, but very little is known about the problems which these sentence structures may present to them in reading. The purpose of this study, therefore, was to investigate children's understanding of connectives, the linguistic form that connects a clause to another clause or some word in it on the printed page. The subjects were children aged eight to twelve studying in grades four to six.

Even though there are a number of ways of associating ideas in English, connectives are widely utilized. Many investigations of clauses children use in their speech and writing have been made but very little research has concentrated on the connectives of the clauses. The concern many felt was voiced by Smith (6:18) when she said, "One wonders whether over-emphasis upon subject and predicate, which appear in both the clause and the sentence as a whole, and too little attention to the meaning signaled by the connective may cause the difficulty."

Children in school are forced to read books written by adults who very often use more mature language structures and thinking processes than those the child can understand. The structural patterns of these printed materials often contain ideas which are linked coordinately or subordinately to other ideas by this linguistic unit called a connective. Any control over the use of these complex sentence patterns does not appear to extend beyond the first few years in school. The result is an imposing array of these reading materials both in the basal developmental reading program and in the functional and recreational reading programs. Although there may be many factors contributing to reading problems, one factor may be the lack of understanding of connectives.

The investigation itself was conducted in three stages. Stage one analyzed stories of basal readers to identify the connectives in them and the type of sentence structures in which they are often found. The second stage was the construction of multiple-choice test items containing selected connectives in sentence structures of basal readers. The administration of the test and the processing of data collected according to selected statistical techniques constituted the third stage of the study. Following a summary of the main hypotheses and definition of the term "connective," each stage of the investigation is summarized briefly, concluding with a statement of some of the main findings, conclusions, and implications.

Summary of main hypotheses and definition of term "connective"

It was hypothesized in the study that there would be no significant increase in pupils' understanding of connectives from grade four, to five, to six and no significant difference in the rate of development of their understanding of different connectives. It was also hypothesized that there would be no significant variation in the pupils' understanding of connectives within each grade and no significant relationship between their understanding of a connective and the three stated types of reading errors. In addition, there was a hypothesis that there would be no significant relationship between the understanding a child would have of connectives and the factors of sex, mental and chronological age, socioeconomic status, and achievement in listening, reading, and written language.

A connective was defined as a linguistic form that linked a clause to another clause or some word in it on the printed page, and the common element appeared to be that these connectives were semantic links basic to the understanding of meaning. The forms of connectives were identified, one-word and phrasal connectives, but the latter were not studied in this investigation. The one-word connectives were divided for the study into groups, classes, and subclasses as shown in Table 1.

A group of one-word connectives was studied as a special case of subordinate clause connectives. They were called "absent" connectives because, although they were "absent" in print, the words or groups of words being connected were present. For example, in the sentence, "The corn the donkey had saved each month had turned to gold" (7:40), the group of words "the donkey had saved each month" is connected to "the corn . . . had turned to gold," but the connective is not present. The purpose of including this construction in the investigation was to investigate whether the absence of connectives hindered the understanding of students in reading. As the connective was absent, it could not be said to have form, so it was entered as a spe-

cial case of the Group 1, Class A, one-word connectives in Table 1.

A review of investigations of children's language with particular reference to their use of clauses, the formal language of print, and possible memory problems revealed close relationships in the development of children's language, reading skills, and thought processes. The selected review of research also identified the factors of chronological and mental age, occupational status of parents, parental education, and language ability of students as significant; and provision was made for their statistical control in this study.

Analysis of sentences in selected basal readers

To substantiate the choice of connectives for this investigation and their use in sentences of particular structures, an analysis of sentences in three basal reader series was considered essential: the *Winston Basic Readers,* the *New Basic Readers* (Canadian Edition), and the *Canadian Parade Readers.* Sentences were taken from the first hundred words on every twen-

TABLE 1

SUMMARY OF THE CONNECTIVE FORMS:
GROUPS AND CLASSES OF THE ONE-WORD CONNECTIVES

Connective Forms and Groups of Connectives	Classes of Connectives	Subclasses of Connectives and Names of Connectives Investigated in Study
Connective is present in graphic form.		
I. Connectives connecting a clause to another clause or some word in it on the printed page.	A. Subordinate Clause Connectives	1. Simple Includer: —although, because, if, so, that, when, where.
		2. Relative Pronoun: —that, which, who.
	B. Coordinate Clause Connectives	—and, but, for, yet.
II. Those connecting one sentence with another.		—however, thus.
Connective is not present in graphic form but the connective "that" could be appropriately inserted.	Subordinate Clause Connective	—"absent", "that"

tieth page of each reader for grades four, five, and six in the three series. In the sample of 2,587 sentences drawn, 957 sentences contained 1,268 connectives. The 77 phrasal connectives (e.g., in spite of) were deleted and the 1,191 one-word and "absent" connectives retained for study. The 957 sentences represented 37 percent of the total sample. Three quarters of them had one connective only and the remaining one quarter had two or more connectives. Forty-two different connectives were identified and 17 connectives were chosen representing the subordinate, coordinate, sentence linkers, and "absent" connectives, as shown in Table 1.

Distribution of connectives in the three reader series did not appear to follow any pattern consistently among grade levels. No sequential program for the introduction of classes of connectives was apparent from one grade level to the next. Nor was there any clearly defined pattern for the progressive introduction of single and multiconnective sentences. A similar distribution was noted within series of basal readers.

The bases for selection of the seventeen connectives included frequency of occurrence in basal readers; the expression of functions such as time, place, concession; and the variety of both meanings and functions expressed by the connective.

Sentences containing the seventeen connectives were analyzed according to a modified structural grammar approach and then each clause was analyzed separately (3, 4). From this analysis, sentence patterns were identified for use as the bases for test items in the Connectives Reading Test.

The construction of the Connectives Reading Test

A multiple-choice reading test was constructed using information from the analysis of sentences containing the seventeen selected connectives. The first draft of the test used in the pilot study consisted of 199 test items set out in four comparable sections. The second and final draft randomly distributed 150 test items equally among three parts of the test, a total of eighty-five single connective items and sixty-five multi-connective items. This test was the Connectives Reading Test. All subjects took all parts of the test.

For the main study a second test was added consisting of twenty test items in which the children supplied only the missing connective(s) to an otherwise complete test item. The name of this test was the Written Connectives Test.

An overall pattern for selection of the test items for each connective took cognizance of direct and indirect discourse, the use of connectives singly and in combination, as well as other features such as passive voice, an imperative format, and an "it" construction.

The construction of any one test item followed a set procedure:

1. The choice of a sentence pattern was determined by the analysis of sentences in the reader series. In many cases one of the sentences from a reader was extracted in its entirety from the reader and only the vocabulary was adjusted.

2. The sentence chosen was then written as far as and including the connective being tested, and the rest of the clause which this connective introduced was written below the sentence as an alternative answer. A student choosing this answer would reveal a good understanding of that connective as it makes a smooth connection of meaning from the clause to the rest of the sentence.

3. The second alternative answer used the connective correctly giving the same smooth transition of meaning to the sentence as the correct answer but incorporating a grammatical error of some type.

4. The third alternative answer also endeavored to use the connective correctly, but the situation expressed in that part of the clause following the connective was incongruent.

5. The fourth and last alternative to the test item was predicated on the use

of an entirely different connective than the one being tested in the item.

6. The four alternative answers were then randomly ordered in each test item.

A vocabulary control in which only words from the first 5,000 words of the Thorndike and Lorge list were used placed the grade level of difficulty of the test items at approximately midpoint in grade five. The Connectives Reading Test was untimed and test instructions were based on those of the Sequential Tests of Educational Progress (STEP) in listening, reading, and writing which were also given in the main study.

A pilot study for the assessment of reliability and validity of scores on the Connectives Reading Test was carried out with 112 students in grades four, five, and six using a test-retest procedure. Kuder-Richardson reliability coefficients (formula 20) were computed, and the biserial coefficients of correlation assessed the validity of each test item. The difficulty index of each test item was ascertained; and for the final draft of the Connectives Reading Test, items which hovered about 0.500 difficulty index and which had the highest possible biserial correlations were retained.

An alternate format for Part One of the test was constructed to see if this format would significantly change the performance of students, but no significant difference between the scores of the students on Part One, regular format of the test, and Part One, alternate format, was found.

The collection and treatment of data

As some research has indicated that children from various population strata may have their own strengths and weaknesses in the language arts, a stratified random sample was drawn proportionate to the population strata of the province of Alberta. A test sample of 402 children aged eight to twelve, grades four to six, was chosen from this population. Fifty-one per-

cent of the subjects were urban dwellers, twelve percent were small town residents, and thirty-seven percent lived in rural areas.

Several types of data were collected. The Connectives Reading Test prepared especially to appraise understanding of connectives in reading was administered to all subjects. Mental ability was assessed by the Cooperative School and College Ability Test (SCAT) Level 5, Form 5A, while the STEP tests, Level 4, Form 4A, in reading, writing, and listening assessed achievement in these three areas. Each subject's father was rated on the Occupational Class Scale (Blishen).

In the analysis of the data, the effects of the variables of sex, chronological age, mental ability, socioeconomic status, and achievement in listening, reading, and written language were controlled statistically. The score on the Connectives Reading Test was used as the criterion variable. The statistical techniques of multiple regression, analysis of variance and covariance, and factor analysis were used to investigate the hypotheses. The statistical procedures summarized in Table 2 were programed for use on the IBM 7040 by the Division of Educational Research Services at the Faculty of Education, University of Alberta.

The children's answers to all tests except the Written Connectives Test were scored by the I.B.M. Optical Mark Reader while test papers for the latter were hand scored. Three markers, the investigator, and two other experienced elementary school teachers assessed the work of 394 students who attempted the Written Connectives Test. The Kendall Coefficient of Concordance: W was computed and found to be 0.936, a high value with $p < .001$ (5: 288-239). Student scores were grouped by grade, sex, and population strata for comparisons.

In a nonstatistical analysis, the percentages of certain language elements and structures in each Connectives Reading Test item by designated difficulty index ranges were computed to isolate possible patterns of language difficulties in the test items.

Significant findings and conclusions of the study

Statistical analyses showed the following:

1. Variables of sex, mental age, and the abilities of listening, reading, and written language exerted significant effects upon the total test scores of students on the Connectives Reading Test.

2. Grade is a highly significant factor, and students developed in their understanding of each of the seventeen connectives from a lower grade to a higher grade. A progression in understanding from grades four to six was also shown in the informal analysis of the Written Connectives Test.

When the sentences in the basal readers were analyzed, it was apparent that the percentage of connectives in them varied negligibly from one grade to another. Writers of basal readers appeared to have concluded that students in grade four have reached a satisfactory level of understanding of connectives, that there is no development of understanding from grade four upwards, and that there is no need to control the introduction or use of connectives in any way. This investigation showed that these factors should be considered by writers of basal readers and by teachers.

3. The development of student understanding of connectives proceeds at a different rate for each of the seventeen connectives. Not only were there different beginning levels of comprehension in grade four but the developmental rates from grades four to six varied also. The analyses of connectives also showed that for students in

TABLE 2

Statistical Procedures Used in the Treatment of the Data

Statistical Procedure	Use of Procedures
Item Analysis	—counter check on the reliability and validity of the test. —identification of student membership of each of five achievement groups in sample. —identification of most difficult test items. —analysis of student achievement on test items.
Correlation Coefficient Computation	—assessment of relationships between total test scores on Connectives Reading Test and scores of test items assessing reading comprehension of each of 17 connectives by grade and sex. —assessment of relationships between Connectives Reading Test and selected variables.
Stepwise Multiple Regression Analysis	—ability of seven covariants to predict total score on Connectives Reading Test (2: 191-203)
One-Way Analysis of Variance	—test of significance of variations in student performance on Connectives Reading Test by grade (9: 48-55).
Three-Factor Experiment with Repeated Measures on One Factor	—determination of effect of three factors of sex, grade, and Connectives Reading Test on test scores, for each of 17 connective subtests and the total test scores of the Connectives Reading Test (1: 347-355).
Three-Way Analysis Variance	—test of significance of variations in student performance on Connectives Reading Test by grade, sex, and place of residence (1).
Analysis of Covariance	—determination as to whether the initial differences on 5 variables identified by Stepwise Multiple Regression Analysis were important to final scores on Connectives Reading Test (1).
Principal-Axis Factor Analysis	—assessment of whether the variance of Connectives Reading Test scores could be accounted for by a number of smaller basic categories than the criterion factor, connective(s) present in each test item (8).

higher achievement groups of the Connectives Reading Test, greater growth in understanding came between grades four and five, while for those in lower achievement groups, it came between grades five and six. As students who are high achievers in the Connectives Reading Test are also high in mental ability, it is evident that there is a close relationship between the understanding of different connectives and mental ability.

4. When the students were divided into five achievement groups according to their test scores on the Connectives Reading Test, most of the group means were significantly different one from the other, both within and across grades. Also, within any one of the five achievement groups the development of understanding of connectives could be traced from grades four to six.

5. There was a consistent relationship between the students' understanding of a connective and their choice of responses on test items for that connective. As students developed in their ability to understand connectives, as shown by an increase in the number of correct answers on test items, a pattern of the three types of errors suggesting increasing semantic awareness of the connectives was noted. At each grade level, ungrammatical answers were chosen in error most frequently, then the wrong connective answers, and finally the situational error answers. This relationship between correct answers and types of errors held not only from grade to grade but also within each of the five achievement groups of a grade.

6. The total student group in grades four to six understood 67 percent of the sentences having connectives. The understanding level rose from 57 percent in grade four, to 66 percent in grade five, and to 75 percent in grade six. Since basal reader stories are materials used at an instructional level, it appears that student comprehension in grades four and five is too low. For independent reading materials such as textbooks in science, social studies, and literature where there may

be very little reading instruction, this comprehension level is very low, even in grade six classrooms.

By connective class, the comprehension problems appear to center on sentence linkers. For six of the seventeen individual connectives, the comprehension levels fell below the 67 percent acquired by the total test group in grades four to six on the Connectives Reading Test. These connectives were however, and, thus, although, which, and yet. When the twenty most difficult test items were ordered, fifteen of them were common to both the total test group and the grade groups.

7. The correlation coefficients between total test scores and test scores for the items of sixteen connectives were all high and positive as were the intercorrelations. The connective *thus* was the exception. There was a high positive correlation between the Connectives Reading Test and the STEP Reading Test.

8. Sixty-three percent of the total variance in the Connectives Reading Test was apparently attributable to one factor, part of which could be a connective. The factor was also common to the three STEP and the two SCAT tests (verbal and nonverbal) suggesting that, basically, the common element in the Connectives Reading Test was one of language.

9. Each analysis of connectives showed the positive effect of the grade factor upon comprehension of connectives. In addition to the development of comprehension by grade reported earlier, there were a number of significant interactions of grade with both sex and population strata. Between grade and sex, for example, the test performance of boys and girls on the Connectives Reading Test in grades four and five revealed that boys lagged significantly behind the girls, suggesting that they may need extended help. The grade by population strata factors revealed that place of residence provides a verbal environment for students at particular grade levels such that development of understanding of connectives is affected.

10. The informal analysis of language features of the most difficult test items in the Connectives Reading Test indicated that multiplicity of both meaning and function of connectives were characteristics of these test items. Test items, in which there were deviations from the oral and written language students use, were also found difficult to read. For example, clauses longer than those students speak or write and featuring adjective clauses or adverb clauses of condition or concession rare in children's language at this age recurred often in the most difficult test items.

Implications of the study

1. Since the reading comprehension level of students in grades four and five as revealed in this study may be termed inadequate, it appears that the developmental reading program should intensify the systematic teaching of comprehension skills. Special provision could then be made for the development of understanding of a) connectives which are characteristic of the formal language of print, or b) connectives which have not yet become a part of the speech of students.

2. As students develop in understanding of connectives from grade to grade at different rates for individual connectives, there is no plateau of comprehension; educators should both expect and aid this development in reading.

3. Different rates of development of understanding among students for individual connectives necessitate flexibility in the conduct of the reading program. Also, as boys in grades four and five appear to develop understanding for connectives more slowly than girls, additional adjustments in the reading program may be necessary.

4. Students who score low on tests of mental ability may need more help with the development of formal language structures which they need as vehicles for logical thought processes. Similarly, students who score high on tests of mental ability should be systematically trained in an earlier grade in the formulation, manipulation, and use of these formal language structures.

5. Development of understanding similar to that in reading can be expected in listening, speaking, and writing, with systematic training in one and a possible aid to their understanding of connectives in another.

This study showed that although children acquire language structures using connectives early in life, they gain mature understanding of them gradually throughout their school years. Children use clauses in speech before they go to school, but they do not develop a sufficient understanding of the meanings of connectives in print for a number of years after that. Therefore, children should be given systematic training through the reading program so they may develop more facility, at an earlier age, in understanding communications from the printed page.

REFERENCES

1. Bottenberg, Robert A., and Joe H. Ward, Jr. *Applied Multiple Linear Regression.* Technical Documentary Report PRL-TDR-6306, March 1963, U. S. Department of Commerce.

2. Efroymson, M. A. "Multiple Regression Analysis," in A. Ralston and H. S. Wilf (Eds.), *Mathematical Methods for Digital Computers.* New York: John Wiley & Sons, Inc., 1960, 191-203.

3. Francis, Nelson. *The Structure of American English.* New York: The Ronald Press Company, 1958.

4. Mellon, John C. *The Grammar of English Sentences, Unit Two: Real Sentences and Their Transforms.* Culver: Indiana, 1964.

5. Siegel, Sidney. *Nonparametric Statistics for the Behavioral Sciences.* Toronto: McGraw-Hill Company, Inc., 1956.

6. Smith, Dora V. "Growth and Sequence of Language," in H. Alan Robinson (Ed.), *Reading and the Language Arts.* Supplementary Educational Monographs, No. 93. Chicago: University of Chicago Press, December 1963.

7. Stauffer, Russell G.; Alvina Treut Burrows; and Dilys M. Jones. *Winston Basic Readers.* New York: Holt, Rinehart and Winston, Inc., 1961.

8. Wilkinson, J. H. "Householder's Method for the Solution of the Algebraic Eigen

Problem," *Computer Journal, 3,* April 1960.
9. Winer, B. J. *Statistical Principles in Experimental Design.* Toronto: McGraw-Hill Book Company, Inc., 1962.

Effectiveness of Four Methods of Increasing Reading Rate, Comprehension, and Flexibility*

ALLEN BERGER
Southern Illinois University

VARIOUS METHODS which claim to increase reading rate, comprehension, and flexibility are now available to the public and to the schools. Most studies that have attempted to evaluate the results or effectiveness of these reading improvement methods have fallen short. Many are in reality only descriptions. Others may lack a needed control group or pilot study or an assessment of retention of gains after a period following the completion of instruction (*1*).

This study was designed to determine 1) the effectiveness of four methods of increasing rate, comprehension, and flexibility; 2) retention of gains after a period following completion of instruction; 3) differences in gains in rate, comprehension, and flexibility; 4) retention of these differences; 5) effect of increase in reading rate on the reading of textbook-like materials; and 6) whether increase in reading rate through a specific method will result in an increased rate of reading both short and long passages. The four methods used in this study are referred to as 1) tachistoscopic, 2) controlled reader, 3) controlled pacing, and 4) paperback scanning.

Objectives

In this study, thirteen hypotheses were tested:

1. No gains in reading rate will result from any of four different methods of instruction.

2. No gains in reading comprehension will result from any of four different methods of instruction.

3. No gains in reading flexibility will result from any of four different methods of instruction.

4. There will be no retention of gains in reading rate resulting from any of four different methods of instruction.

5. There will be no retention of gains in reading comprehension resulting from any of four different methods of instruction.

6. There will be no retention of gains in reading flexibility resulting from any of four different methods of instruction.

7. There will be no differences in gains in reading rate resulting from different methods of instruction.

8. There will be no differences in gains in reading comprehension resulting from different methods of instruction.

9. There will be no differences in gains in reading flexibility resulting from different methods of instruction.

10. There will be no differences in retention of gains in reading rate resulting from different methods of instruction.

11. There will be no differences in retention of gains in reading comprehension resulting from different methods of instruction.

12. There will be no differences in retention of gains in reading flexibility resulting from different methods of instruction.

13. Different methods of instruction will result in no differences in the rates with which short and long passages are read.

In addition, analyses were made of the effect of the variables of verbal and math aptitude and sex.

*The research reported herein was performed pursuant to a contract with the United States Department of Health, Education, and Welfare, Office of Education.

Population sample and procedure

This study, conducted during the first semester of the 1965-1966 school year, is based upon findings and considerations arising from a pilot study conducted the previous semester. Involved in both studies were freshman students enrolled in Improvement of Learning, a one-semester two-credit hour reading-study skills course at Syracuse University. Instruction in this course focuses on improvement of reading rate and comprehension, vocabulary, and study skills.

Twelve sections of the Improvement of Learning course at Syracuse University were involved in the major investigation. Nine sections meet for one 50-minute session three mornings a week; three sections meet for extended sessions two afternoons a week. Total classroom time is 150 minutes a week. Although the course is open to all who wish to enroll, the majority of students are freshmen. Those whose college board verbal scores are below 500 are recommended for enrollment. Only fully matriculated freshmen were considered in the investigation. For the control group, two instructors from the university's English department contributed five sections in response to a request for volunteers from the director of Freshman English. The control group was composed of a total of 76 students. The total number of students in the experimental group was 179; each treatment group was composed of 40 to 45 students. A total of 255 students was included in the study.

The college board scores were comparable among the treatment groups, the range being 483 to 493 for the verbal and 555 to 580 for the math. The initial reading rates were also relatively comparable among the treatment groups, as indicated by the measuring instruments.

The number of sessions required for each major aspect of this investigation is presented:

Major Aspects	Number of Sessions
Orientation to Course	1
Pretesting	3
Training Sessions	17
Post-Testing	2
Post-Post-Testing	2
	25

Lesson plans for these 25 sessions may be found in Appendix B of the final report (2).

Treatment methods were randomly assigned to the experimental sections. Three sections were instructed through the tachistoscope; three, through the controlled reader; three, through the controlled pacing; and three, through the paperback scanning method.

Each method took approximately 30 minutes each session. For the remaining time in all sections under all methods, students read paperbacks with the encouragement to apply their newly acquired skills. The paperbacks used for this transfer reading were not the same titles used for training in the paperback scanning method.

On the first session each week during the time normally allotted for transfer reading, a quiz was given to all sections on specified chapters in a vocabulary text.

With all methods, the intent was to present the programs following as closely as possible the recommendations made by the publishers.

Following is a description of each of the four methods:

Method A—Tachistoscope. Essentially, each lesson involved the use of Classroom Kit VII (RK-7) published by Learning Through Seeing, Inc. (7). The kit contains sets of four types of filmstrips: Seeing Skills, Word Mastery, Phrase Mastery, and Reading Development. Material on the filmstrips is flashed at 1/40 second, and two strips were viewed each session. As an illustration, during the first training session the students viewed the first filmstrip from Seeing Skills and the first filmstrip from Word Mastery. The Seeing Skills strip includes forms and numbers which the students record and then check for accuracy. The Word Mastery strip contains words flashed, recorded, and then checked. The students recorded their words in notebooks. The publisher claims that reading rate and comprehension will be increased through the use of the material.

Method B—Controlled reader. The instruction closely followed the recommendations made by the publisher, Educational Developmental Laboratories (5), which claims that through use of the material reading rate, comprehension and flexibility (referred to as variability) will be increased. Each day's lesson involved building a readiness for the filmstrip to be viewed, discussion of the vocabulary, viewing the strip, and then checking comprehension through multiple choice questions. To correspond to the readability level of the material used in the other methods, Set IJ was used. Each student used an EDL-Study Guide, which corresponded to the filmstrips in Set IJ, so that the program might be followed exactly as recommended. On each training session, the filmstrip was viewed at approximately 30 words faster than the strip on the preceding session. The first filmstrip was viewed at 150 words a minute and, on the seventeenth and final session, the students viewed a filmstrip at 540 words a minute.

During the last six sessions, the speed of the filmstrips combined with the reading rate attained by the students made it necessary to group students. Two groups were formed in each section and the filmstrip was viewed twice by each group—once at a speed 30 words a minute faster than the strip on the preceding session for the faster group. In addition, during the remaining six training sessions, on the recommendation of the publisher, this method incorporated the practice of viewing the last session's filmstrip at the last session's speed before beginning the lesson using the new filmstrip.

Method C—Controlled pacing. The primary difference between this method and Method B was that the reading matter on the filmstrips used in Method B was in this method presented in book form, with the same number of words per line as on the filmstrips. To substitute for the left-to-right visual pacing of the machine, students moved 3 x 5 cards containing slots large enough to reveal half a line, along each line and down the page, to the pacing of a metronome, which was synchronized to the steady click made by the Controlled Reader. As in Method B, there was an introduction of the material about to be read, a discussion of the vocabulary followed by the reading of the passage, and the comprehension check.

During the last sessions, groups were formed as needed. During these last sessions, to remain as close as possible to Method B, the practice was incorporated of reading the last session's reading at the last session's speed before beginning the lesson using the new reading. Each student used an EDL-Study Guide.

Method D—Paperback scanning. In this method, the reader is required to scan each page under time pressure. For the first two minutes of this exercise, the student was allowed 8 seconds a page; for the next two minutes, 7 seconds a page and on down to 2 seconds a page and then immediately up to 10 seconds a page. A metronome was used to click each second, with the instructor indicating the start of a new page, thereby insuring controlled pacing of the material.

Primary objective of this exercise is to accustom the eyes to move vertically. Paperbacks were selected with a particular consideration to a comparable readability level as determined by the Dale-Chall Readability Formula to the material used in the other methods; in addition, consideration was given to type size and line length. To correspond to the other methods, 10-item quizzes based on the paperbacks were prepared. The method, which basically involves a five-minute pretest, the countdown exercise described above, and then a post-test, requires approximately 30 minutes, like the other methods.

Control

Instructors of the control sections gave students standard instruction in Freshman English. To counterbalance the Hawthorne Effect, the control sections were told that they were part of the experiment. A brief statement was read to each treatment group at the first meeting which explained that all sections would cover similar material but through different methods.

In selecting the control group, an attempt was made to have the students in both the experimental and control groups as comparable as possible. To reach this end, answers were needed to two basic questions, one dealing with whether or not the control group should be a part of the Improvement of Learning course. At Syracuse University, there are two main groups of Freshman English students, those scoring above and those scoring below 550 on their college board verbals. After examining the data from the pilot study, it was agreed that the verbal scores of the lower group of English students were comparable to the verbal scores of freshmen in the Improvement of Learning course.

Another question that had to be answered in regard to the comparability of students in the experimental and control groups related to the motivational fact that students were required to take Freshman English but were not required to take Improvement of Learning. However, considerable thought was given to the typical freshman coming to a large campus alone and bewildered and, during orientation week, talking to his faculty adviser who has in his hands the Syracuse University Freshman Test Profile Card; on the IBM card it is recommended that the student take the Improvement of Learning course: the consensus was that when the faculty adviser looked at the card and told the student that he should take the Improvement of Learning course, the typical freshman would feel required to take the course, just as he would feel required to take Freshman English.

It should be noted that a control group was not absolutely essential to the design and scope of this particular study; that is, the effectiveness of the four methods of increasing reading rate, comprehension, and flexibility could have been discerned with only the treatment groups; however, the control group was included to provide additional data and a basis of comparison.

Measuring instruments

The following measuring instruments were selected:

1. The Van Wagenen Rate of Comprehension Test (Forms D, C, and B). Testing Time: 4 minutes. The test is composed of 30-word passages; in each passage there is an incongruous word which the student must cross out. This is almost a sheer rate of reading test since the level of comprehension is such that the reader should attain 100 percent. Reliability is reported between .86 and .96, with a 15-word error of measurement (8).

2. The Robinson-Hall Reading Test of History (Forms Canada and Russia). Testing Time: approximately 20 minutes—10 minutes to read and about 10 minutes to answer questions. The test is approximately 3,000 words in length. The student notes where he is at the end of 10 minutes—or, if finished earlier, notes the time that elapsed—and begins responding to test items, nearly all multiple choice. The reliability is reported as .91 for reading rate (6).

3. The Braam-Sheldon Flexibility of Reading Test (Forms 1, 2, and 3). Testing Time: approximately 40 minutes. The test is composed of five passages selected from different areas (e.g., narrative, literature, science, history, and psychology). The student is required to respond to ten multiple choice items following each passage. Because none of the multiple choice questions and only the first two forms have been published (3), all the material was reproduced in order to have all forms comparable in format. The present investigator obtained an overall rate reliability of .89 between the

first and second forms and .90 between the second and third forms.

From these three measuring instruments, the following data were obtained:

   a. Initial reading rate and comprehension level
   b. Final reading rate and comprehension level
   c. Retention of gains in reading rate and comprehension level
   d. Initial reading flexibility and comprehension level
   e. Final reading flexibility and comprehension level
   f. Retention of gains in reading flexibility and comprehension level.

In addition, Syracuse University Freshman Test Profile Cards provided the following data:

   g. College Entrance Examination Board Scholastic Aptitude Test —verbal and math scores.

General statistical design

The design used for this investigation was the Non-equivalent Control Group Design (4). It was selected because it most closely fit the experimental situation. It was not possible to randomize either students or instructors; the treatment variable, however, for each section was randomly selected.

To compensate for any possible initial differences between groups, the major statistical method used to analyze the data was the analysis of covariance. Attention was given to the variables of verbal and math aptitude and sex. In addition, after significant F values were found, the t-test was applied to all possible combinations of group means. The t-test was also used to determine any significant differences in the level of comprehension scores. The Pearson product-moment coefficient of correlation was used to obtain a correlation matrix and to test reliabilities.

Findings and implications

The major purpose of this study was to test thirteen hypotheses related to reading effectiveness. These hypotheses were built on a hierarchical structure which required the rejection of prior hypotheses in order to test related hypotheses. For example, because there were no gains in reading comprehension, it was not possible to test retention of gains in reading comprehension. Four of the thirteen hypotheses proved to be untestable for this reason.

Following are the hypotheses and results of this study:

1. The first hypothesis, which stated that no gains in reading rate would result from any of our different methods of instruction, was rejected. Significant gains in rate were made as a result of all methods on two measuring instruments.

Implications for designing a program of reading and study skill development may be derived from this finding. Since students seem to like the idea of increasing their reading rate, it may be psychologically advantageous to begin a program with emphasis on this particular skill. Nearly all students can see a marked increase in a relatively short time. The development of an increased reading rate allows an entrance into other areas, such as study skills. For example, to use any of the reading-study skills formulas, such as SQ3R, students must be able to skim. From this point, the instructor may move into a variety of areas, depending upon student need.

2. The second hypothesis, which stated that no gains in reading comprehension would result from any of four different methods of instruction, was accepted. However, it must be noted that the tests in this study were designed to measure comprehension of details, primarily; therefore, it cannot be assumed that increases in rate of reading will have no effect on other kinds of comprehension.

3. The third hypothesis, which stated that no gains in reading flexibility would result from any of four different methods of instruction, was rejected. The gain in flexibility was

anticipated, for the more rapidly the student is able to read, the greater is his potential for flexibility. The reader who can skim some materials at 1,000 words a minute may read other materials at 200 words a minute, whereas the reader whose top rate is 250 words a minute has a limited range.

Support for the view that the more rapidly the student is able to read the greater his potential for flexibility comes from the findings of gains in rate made through the four treatment methods. Although all four methods produced significant gains in rate, the smallest amount of gain was produced by the tachistoscopic method, as indicated by both instruments measuring rate. The finding that the tachistoscopic method produced the smallest amount of gain in rate may account for the fact that the tachistoscopic group made no significant gains in flexibility at the .01 level of confidence, although at a less conservative level gains may be observed.

4. The fourth hypothesis, which stated that there would be no retention of gains in reading rate resulting from any of four different methods of instruction, was rejected. Although gains in rate were retained by all the experimental groups, one must recognize that eight weeks is a relatively short interval. Moreover, during this interval the experimental groups continued in the Improvement of Learning course. Even though reading and study skills other than rate are empha-

sized in this course, it may be assumed that this instruction and practice were supportive of maintenance of gains.

5. The fifth hypothesis, which stated that there would be no retention of gains in reading comprehension resulting from any of four different methods of instruction, was untestable, since no gains in comprehension were made.

6. The sixth hypothesis, which stated that there would be no retention of gains in reading flexibility resulting from any of four different methods of instruction, was rejected. Like the finding of the fourth hypothesis, this finding is encouraging, bearing in mind the limitations of the relatively short interval and the fact that the experimental groups continued in the course.

7. The seventh hypothesis, which stated that there would be no differences in gains in reading rate resulting from different methods of instruction, was rejected.

The following four tables contain data bearing upon this hypothesis. Tables 1 and 3 contain the results of the analysis of covariance with the variable of verbal and math aptitude and sex covaried out, using different measuring instruments. Results of t-tests are reported in Tables 2 and 4.

Because significant F values were found when verbal aptitude, math aptitude, and sex were held constant, the t-test was applied to all possible combinations of pairs of means, with the results reported in Table 2.

TABLE 1

ANALYSIS OF COVARIANCE OF GAINS IN READING RATE ON THE
VAN WAGENEN RATE OF COMPREHENSION TEST

Variable Held Constant	Source of Variation	Sum of Squares	df	Mean Square	F
Verbal Aptitude	Between Groups	64,813.38	4	16,203.35	8.06**
	Within Groups	390,779.84	195	2,004.00	
Math Aptitude	Between Groups	64,994.60	4	16,248.65	8.15**
	Within Groups	390,460.30	195	2,002.36	
Sex	Between Groups	30,871.37	3	10,290.46	5.19**
	Within Groups	335,256.49	169	1,983.77	

**p < .01.

Inspection of Table 2 reveals ten significant differences between pairs of means at the .01 level of confidence when verbal aptitude, math aptitude, and sex were held constant. Nine of the 10 *t*-tests favor the paperback scanning method; of these 9, 7 indicate superiority over other treatment methods and 2 over the control group. The tenth significant *t*-test favors the controlled reader group over the control group.

No significant F value was found when sex was held constant.

Because significant F values were found when verbal aptitude and math aptitude were held constant, the *t*-test was applied to all possible combina-

TABLE 2

CORRELATED *t*-TESTS FOR PAIRS OF MEANS FOLLOWING ANALYSIS OF COVARIANCE ON THE VAN WAGENEN RATE OF COMPREHENSION TEST

Groups	Verbal *t*	Math *t*	Sex *t*
Tachistoscopic Controlled Reader	1.234	.979	.534
Tachistoscopic Controlled Pacing	.407	.485	.174
Tachistoscopic Paperback Scanning**	.960	3.771**	2.954**
Tachistoscopic Control	1.443	1.935	
Controlled Reader Controlled Pacing	.213	.496	.036
Controlled Reader Paperback Scanning**	2.425	2.729**	2.849**
Controlled Reader** Control	2.591	3.528**	
Controlled Pacing Paperback Scanning**	3.148**	3.293**	3.181**
Controlled Pacing Control	1.983	2.398	
Paperback Scanning** Control	5.074	5.604**	

**significantly superior   **$p < .01$ level of confidence

TABLE 3

ANALYSIS OF COVARIANCE OF GAINS IN READING RATE ON THE ROBINSON-HALL READING TEST OF HISTORY

Variable Held Constant	Source of Variation	Sum of Squares	df	Mean Square	F
Verbal Aptitude	Between Groups Within Groups	257,355.86 3,155,804.20	4 202	64,338.97 15,622.79	4.19**
Math Aptitude	Between Groups Within Groups	228,690.23 3,132,622.00	4 202	57,172.56 15,508.02	3.69**
Sex	Between Groups Within Groups	189,756.72 2,907,244.80	3 172	63,252.24 16,902.59	3.74

**$p < .01$.

tions of pairs of means, with the results reported in Table 4.

TABLE 4

CORRELATED t-TESTS FOR PAIRS OF MEANS
FOLLOWING ANALYSIS OF COVARIANCE ON
THE ROBINSON-HALL READING TEST
OF HISTORY

Groups	Verbal t	Math t
Tachistoscopic Controlled Reader	.096	.918
Tachistoscopic Controlled Pacing	1.027	.881
Tachistoscopic Paperback Scanning**	2.985**	2.891**
Tachistoscopic Control	.721	.632
Controlled Reader Controlled Pacing	.912	.766
Controlled Reader Paperback Scanning**	2.835**	2.756**
Controlled Reader Control	.803	.711
Controlled Pacing Paperback Scanning	1.897	2.026
Controlled Pacing Control	1.720	1.491
Paperback Scanning** Control	3.677*	3.496**

**significantly superior	**$p < .01$ level of confidence

Inspection of Table 4 reveals significant differences at the .01 level of confidence in six mean comparisons when verbal aptitude and math aptitude were held constant, all favoring the paperback scanning method. On the basis of the data presented in Tables 1 through 4, the seventh hypothesis was rejected. This finding, however, should not imply ruling out the use of the other methods considered, for certain individuals may learn better through one or a combination of them. In addition, it must be borne in mind that the methods considered are group pacing methods and there may be individuals who would profit more from individual pacing methods.

8. The eighth hypothesis, which states that there would be no differ-

ences in gains in reading comprehension resulting from different methods of instruction, was untestable, since it was contingent on the rejection of a prior hypothesis which was untestable. No significant change in the level of comprehension was found.

9. The ninth hypothesis, which stated that there would be no differences in gains in reading flexibility resulting from different methods of instruction, was accepted. No method produced significantly superior results in reading flexibility at the .01 level of confidence. However, a rank-order was observed, with the paperback scanning method making the greatest gains, followed by the controlled reader, controlled pacing, and tachistoscopic method.

10. The tenth hypothesis, which stated that there would be no differences in retention of gains in reading rate resulting from different methods of instruction, was rejected. It is interesting to observe that, although all changes remained within the measuring instrument's 15-word error of measurement, the control group was the only group showing a loss, while the treatment groups all showed gains.

11. The eleventh hypothesis, which stated that there would be no differences in retention of gains in reading comprehension resulting from different methods of instruction, was untestable, since no gains were made in reading comprehension.

12. The twelfth hypothesis, which stated that there would be no differences in retention of gains in reading flexibility resulting from different methods of instruction, was also untestable, since no differences were found in reading flexibility.

13. The thirteenth hypothesis, which stated that different methods of instruction would result in no differences in the rate with which short and long passages are read, was rejected. A reason for including this hypothesis was to obviate the possibility of a particular method having the effect of teaching for the testing instrument. This hypothesis was also included to

determine if one method might produce significantly superior results in both short and long passages. The paperback scanning method appeared to be significantly superior over all other methods on the two different types of measuring instruments.

Conclusions

The fact that the paperback scanning method produced the most significant results over the other methods has additional educational implications. Of all the methods, the paperback scanning method allows for the greatest amount of reading. The training material is or can be more closely related to material read normally. The cost of the paperback scanning method is far less than the other methods. Virtually no upkeep is required; teachers need not concern themselves with the possibility of burned-out bulbs or short circuits. Costs of replacing 30 copies each of six titles should amount to approximately $100 every two or three years.

In addition, one of the indices of good teaching is that the students should be far more different from one another at the end of instruction than at the beginning of instruction; the paperback scanning method produced a dispersion, as indicated by the standard deviation on a post-test instrument measuring rate, that was approximately three times greater than that produced by the Controlled Reader method.

The work of teachers interested in increasing the reading effectiveness of their students may be coordinated through a reading specialist, who might conduct a program to familiarize reading teachers with the methods considered in this study and with the latest research on increasing rate, comprehension, and flexibility. A peripheral benefit of such a program would be a greater understanding of claims made by commercial reading programs.

In short, then, the findings of this study suggest that the current emphasis on the use of machines to increase reading rate, comprehension, and flexibility should be reevaluated, for there appear to be other, more effective, less complicated, and less expensive approaches to the desired end.

REFERENCES

1. Berger, Allen. "Selected Review of Studies on the Effectiveness of Various Methods of Increasing Reading Efficiency," *Journal of the Reading Specialist, 6,* 2 (December 1966), 74-87.
2. Berger, Allen. "Effectiveness of Four Methods of Increasing Reading Rate, Comprehension and Flexibility," unpublished doctoral dissertation, Syracuse University, 1966, (CRP No. OEC-1-6-068187-0845).
3. Braam, Leonard S. and William D. Sheldon. *Developing Efficient Reading.* New York: Oxford University Press, 1959.
4. Campbell, Donald T. and Julian C. Stanley. "Experimental and Quasi-Experimental Designs for Research on Teaching," in N. L. Gage (Ed.), *Handbook of Research on Teaching.* Chicago: Rand McNally & Company, 1963, 171-246.
5. *Controlled Reader Study Guide.* Huntington, New York: Educational Developmental Laboratories, 1963, 6-7.
6. Robinson, Francis P. and Prudence Hall. *Manual for the Robinson-Hall Reading Tests.* Columbus: College of Education, Ohio State University, 1949, 1-2.
7. *Tachist-O-Films Manual,* Sunland, California: Learning Through Seeing, Inc., 1965, 1-2.
8. Van Wagenen, M. J. and August Dvorak. *Manual of Directions for the Dvorak-Van Wagenen Diagnostic Examination of Silent Reading Abilities.* Minneapolis: University of Minnesota, 1953, 17-18.

The Flexibility of Reading Rate

BEATRICE JACKSON LEVIN
Philadelphia Board of Education

AS FAR BACK as the latter part of the nineteenth century, investigators began to study eye movements in an effort to understand the speed aspect of reading. Interest in this has continued unabated; studies on both the peripheral and the central functions during reading have created contradictory and controversial conclusions. One of the phenomena of the present day is the enormous interest, with attendant misconceptions, concerning rate of reading. The spurt in public attention to this particular aspect of reading has spawned an image of the good reader as a sort of omnivorous chimera, hungrily ingesting books at the rate of thousands of words per minute. The idea of being able to absorb all the intelligence contained on any page of print at the flick of the wrist so fired the public imagination that, too often, form has been confused with substance and a direct result has been the proliferation of speed reading courses and schools throughout the country.

That most people can learn to read faster, just as they can learn other reading skills, has been amply demonstrated. Reading skills do grow and expand with training and practice. The danger here is on the continued and undue emphasis on speed of reading as an end in itself, despite the fact that educators (Artley, 1963; Carlson, 1952; Tinker, 1946) have long recognized that speed is not a unitary process, nor should it be a constant; that unless speed is considered in concert with comprehension, particularly the type of comprehension demanded by the specific reading situation, it becomes little more than an optical exercise. Studies point to the fact that the fast reader is not inevitably the best reader (Shores, 1960; Shores & Husbands, 1950); that the really efficient reader adjusts his rate according to the nature of the reading situation. Most educators agree that it is flexibility of reading rate rather than speed itself that is basic to good reading (Artley, 1963; Ehrenworth & McAuliffe, 1963). Yet there have been relatively few attempts to study this aspect of reading; while many standardized tests of reading include a check on speed, there are few tests, or inclusions in other tests, to check flexibility of rate. This paucity of testing devices must affect the teaching of flexibility; in practical terms, while flexibility is generally included as a goal of good reading instruction, very little is done practically to implement it.

This study attempted to reveal the nature and importance of flexibility of reading rate and, hopefully, to deemphasize the current concentration on speed alone. If flexibility of reading rate is a natural concomitant of efficient reading, as measured by available standardized tests and as concluded by Anderson (1937), Blommers and Lindquist (1944), then it need not be taught as a separate skill. If, as maintained by Carillo and Sheldon (1952), Sister M. Herculane (1961), Letson (1956), and Perry (1959), it does not inevitably accompany "good" reading, then it would appear necessary to teach flexibility, along with other specific skills, as an important part of the reading instructional program. It would also be necessary to have tests of flexibility for diagnostic as well as teaching purposes. Standardized tests of reading would have to be reexamined and reassessed and perhaps be modified, changed, or appended to include a measure of flexibility. If the results of the test constructed proved singularly significant, it might be feasible, with additional research and consequent alteration or modification, to standardize such a test, to adapt it as an informal technique, or to incorporate some of its objectives and features into otherwise acceptable standardized tests.

Statement of the problem

The major purpose of this study was to investigate the flexibility of reading rate among ninth grade students at an academic high school for girls, by estimating the presence and amount of flexibility of rate in two separate groups of readers: "good" readers and "poor" readers, so designated by scores on an accepted standardized test of reading. In order to study the problem, a test of flexibility of reading rate had to be constructed and administered. Results of the two groups and the group as a whole were to be compared and correlated with outside criteria considered relevant. Specifically, the following questions were studied:

1. Is flexibility of reading rate a separate skill, to be taught along

with other reading skills, or is it generally a concomitant of "good" reading? To check this, the following two subordinate areas were evaluated:

a. What is the relationship between scores on a standardized test of reading and flexibility according to difficulty of material, for "good" and for "poor" readers?

b. What is the relationship between scores on a standardized test of reading and flexibility according to purpose, for "good" and for "poor" readers?

2. Is there more flexibility according to difficulty of material than according to purpose, generally? In "good" readers? In "poor" readers?

3. What is the relationship between flexibility of reading rate according to difficulty of material and according to purpose, and mental ability, as measured by a group intelligence test?

4. What is the relationship between flexibility of reading rate according to difficulty of material and according to purpose, and school achievement, as measured by grades in major subjects on the first report period?

Limitations

One hundred subjects were used in the study, all members of the ninth grade class at the Philadelphia High School for Girls, a college preparatory secondary school. At the time of the testing, the subjects ranged in age chronologically from twelve years six months to fourteen years eight months inclusive, with a mean age of thirteen years six months. The group was Negro and white.

Tests administered and materials used were the following:

1. The Cooperative English Test: Reading Comprehension, Form 2A

2. The Flexibility Test, constructed by the investigator

3. The Otis Quick-Scoring Mental Ability Test, Gamma Test, Form EM

4. School records to compute the mean of marks in major subjects for the first report period following the testing.

A two-part test was constructed composed of four subtests: the first two subtests were to test flexibility of rate according to difficulty of material; and the second two subtests were to test flexibility according to purpose. In the first two selections, called A and B, the purpose was to be held constant, but the difficulty level of the selections was divergent (A was at the 5th-6th reading level, and B was at the 11th-12th level). In the second two selections, called C and D, the level of difficulty was the same for both (9th-10th level), but the purpose for which each was to be read was different; for subtest C, the purpose set was to read for main ideas only; and for subtest D, the purpose was to read for complete knowledge of main ideas and supporting facts. An alternate form of the test was constructed at the same time, using similar materials.

Materials were to be moderately interesting and similar to those encountered in normal high school reading. It was decided that social studies material would be most suitable. Each selection was to be of continuous context. The selections were to be of sufficient length to assure a reliable rate but were not to be so long that all subjects could not have the time to finish them. It was decided that selections of approximately 500 words would meet these requirements.

The test was to be timed by marking five-second intervals on the chalkboard. As soon as each subject finished the reading of a selection, she was to copy down on her answer sheet the last time recorded on the board. She was then to turn the page and answer all the questions without recourse to the text. When this was done, she was to close her test booklet and wait for directions to go on. The same procedure was to be repeated for each of the remaining three subtests. Each subject was to be given time to finish the reading and the answering of all the questions on all subtests.

Rate and comprehension were to be measured separately; rate was to be based strictly on minutes and seconds of reading time and recorded in words per minute, and comprehension was to be the percent of questions answered correctly of the total number of questions for that selection. The directions which preceded each selection were precise, with the purpose carefully stressed for each reading.

Procedures

From their scores on the standardized test of reading, the final population of 50 "good" and 50 "poor" readers, to be known as Group I and Group II respectively, was selected. Group I, the so-called "good" readers, ranked between the 95th and 99th percentile. Group II, the so called "poor" readers ranked between the 37th and 53rd percentile.

The flexibility test was administered to Groups I and II on November 17, 1964. The entire test, including the distribution and collection of materials, was completed in one hour and fifteen minutes. For each subject, rate and comprehension were marked and recorded. Indices of flexibility were computed: flexibility according to difficulty of material (the difference in rate between Selections A and B) and flexibility according to purpose (the difference in rate between Selections C and D).

Estimates of reliability and validity of the flexibility test were computed. The internal consistency reliability was computed with the use of the Kuder-Richardson Formula 20. Since the tests were composed of relatively few items, the Spearman-Brown Formula was applied to see how the reliability changed when the length of the test was increased. When lengthened (5 times), subtests A, C, and D seemed relatively reliable with r_{tt}'s of .85, .70,

and .86 respectively, while subtest B, with an r_{tt} of .17 was still quite low. According to Baggaley (1964, p. 84), any measurement represents an interaction of several factors, such as the trait structure of the individual, the nature of the measurement (e.g., the difficulty of the test), the conditions of the testing, and that the range of scores can be affected by any one of these. Subtest B was the most difficult selection of all four subtests and may have been beyond the comprehension level of many subjects, even when they slowed down their rate. The primary purpose of the flexibility test was to measure versatility of reading rate, and while a change in rate should be accompanied by adequate comprehension, the essential interest here was in the ability to vary the rate according to the difficulty of the material and in the consistency of this change in rate.

Since there were no outside criteria considered comparable, the test had to be its own criterion. Analysis of the purpose of the test and of the desired outcomes support the belief that the test was a valid measure of flexibility of rate; the results, showing the differences in rate between subtests A with B and C with D, also support this contention.

An item analysis done on all of the test items composing each subtest yielded results showing an acceptable mean proportion passing each subtest (.76 for subtest A, .68 for B, .52 for C, and .73 for D). Guilford (1956, p. 450), states that reliability tends to be higher when items are equal in difficulty. Items of moderate difficulty, i.e., where p equals .50, yield maximum variance. Since the flexibility test was concerned primarily with versatility of rate, the questions for each subtest were mainly aimed at tapping literal comprehension of material, a type of questioning assumed to be less demanding than that which necessitates a more critical analysis. This type of question should yield a higher proportion passing than questions that probe greater depth of thinking. Any item having less than a .50 proportion passing would be open to question. Only three individual items were slightly under .50.

Item validity, to provide a basis for improving those items which appear weak, was estimated via the proportions of success on the individual test items in the upper and lower 27 percent of the population and the estimation of the validity coefficients (according to Flanagan, 1939). The capacity of a test item to discriminate between good and poor readers is reflected in those items where the proportion passing is higher in the good readers than in the poor readers. An item that fails to have a higher proportion passing in the better readers than in the poorer ones is considered weak. Except for item 7 in subtest C, all the test items did discriminate between good and poor readers. The mean validity coefficients for each subtest (i.e., .47 for subtest A, .35 for subtest C, and .52 for subtest D) appeared satisfactory.

The effectiveness of distractors was also estimated as another check on the accuracy of the test. It was found that only seven distractors failed to attract any subjects. These responses and the questions of which they are part warrant reexamination.

The Otis Quick-Scoring Mental Ability Test: Gamma Test, Form EM, was administered to Groups I and II on November 24, one week following the administration of the Flexibility Test. Results showed that the mean IQ was 129.66 for Group I, 114.98 for Group II, and 122.320 for the group as a whole.

For each student the mean of the numerical marks in major subjects for the first report period, ending on November 23, 1964, was computed. Group I had a mean of 83.20, Group II had a mean of 79.04, and the group as a whole had a mean of 81.12.

The data were organized and then processed by computer. Fisher's t test of significance was applied to test the difference between the mean rates of the two pairs of subtests, A vs B, and C vs D, to see if the mean indices of flexibility according to difficulty of material (the mean difference in rate between subtests A and B) and the mean indices of flexibility according to purpose (the mean difference in rate between subtests C and D) were statistically significant. Since it was hypothesized that reading rate was or should be decelerated by an increase in difficulty of the material, and by a set to read for complete knowledge rather than just for main ideas, a one-tailed t test of significance was calculated for all the indices of flexibility. Scores that were negatively flexible were examined in the light of the comprehension for those scores, and possible reasons for these reversals were hypothesized.

The Pearson product-moment coefficient of correlation was used to examine the relationships for Group I, Group II, and the group as a whole.

Results

Findings relevant to the specific questions posed are as follows:

1. a. The correlation between the index of flexibility A-B and the speed of comprehension section of the Cooperative English Test: Reading Comprehension, Form 2A, yielded a coefficient of .05 for Group I, .05 for Group II, and .08 for the group as a whole.

   b. The correlation between the index of flexibility C-D and the speed of comprehension section of the foregoing test of reading comprehension yielded a coefficient of .05 for Group I, .04 for Group II, and .37 for the group as a whole.

2. The mean index of flexibility A-B (according to difficulty of material) was approximately 35 WPM for Group I, 28 WPM for Group II, and 32 WPM for the group as a whole. The mean index of flexibility C-D (according to purpose) was approximately 42 WPM for Group I, 20

TABLE 9

MEANS AND STANDARD DEVIATIONS OF RATE IN WPM IN ACCORDANCE WITH DIFFICULTY OF MATERIAL AND PURPOSE AND MEAN FLEXIBILITY OF THOSE PARTS

	Group I N = 50	Group II N = 50	Both Groups N = 100
Subtest A			
M	313.120	222.140	267.630
SD	80.335	35.589	77.003
Subtest B			
M	271.480	194.020	232.750
SD	54.089	28.933	58.150
Index of Flexibility A-B			
M	35.340*	28.100*	31.720*
SD	59.967	28.366	47.047
Subtest C			
M	264.800	195.520	230.160
SD	52.988	43.771	59.680
Subtest D			
M	220.880	173.780	197.330
SD	47.191	34.797	47.681
Index of Flexibility C-D			
M	42.180*	19.740*	30.960*
SD	31.883	21.039	29.248

*Significant at the 1 percent level of confidence

WPM for Group II, and 31 WPM for the group as a whole. The *t* ratios (Fisher's) for the difference in mean rates A-B were 3.09 for Group I, 4.28 for Group II, and 3.59 for the group as a whole. The *t* ratios for the difference between the mean rates C-D were 4.33 for Group I, 2.72 for Group II and 3.14 for the group as a whole. These ratios were all found to be significant at the 1 percent level of confidence.

3. The correlation between the mean index of flexibility A-B and IQ yielded coefficients of .10 for Group I, .16 for Group II, and .13 for the group as a whole. The coefficients of correlation for the index of flexibility C-D and IQ were .09 for Group I, .13 for Group II, and .33 for the group as a whole.

4. The correlation between the index of flexibility A-B and the mean of marks in major subjects yielded coefficients of .10 for Group I, .07 for Group II, and .01 for the group as a whole. The coefficients of correlation for the index of flexibility C-D and the mean of marks in major subjects were .12 for Group I, .13 for Group II, and .40 for the group as a whole.

Additional findings relevant to the major facets of this investigation included the following:

1. Comprehension on the Flexibility Test was generally higher on subtest B than on A and on D than on C; while the comprehension of Group I was adequate on all subtests, that of Group II was generally less than adequate.
2. Intercorrelations between rate on subtests A and B, and C and D, yielded coefficients ranting from .51 to .83.
3. Correlations of comprehension between subtests A and B ranged from .27 to .41; between C and D, these correlations ranged from .13 to .46.
4. Correlations between rate and comprehension on the subtests ranged from -.25 to .36.
5. Correlations between the indices of flexbility A-B and the indices of flexibility C-D yielded a range of from .08 to .19.

Conclusions

Within the limitations of the population and of the measures used in this study, the following qualified conclusions can be drawn in terms of the original questions posed:

1. Although a certain amount of flexibility of reading rate is present and is more pronounced in "good" readers than in "poor" readers, it apparently does not inevitably accompany "good" reading. There appears to be little relationship between scores

on a standardized test of reading comprehension and flexibility according to difficulty of material and according to purpose for both "good" and "poor" readers. This supports the theory that flexibility of reading rate is a skill separate from those skills measured in standardized tests of reading; that a high score on such a test is apparently no guarantee of the ability to be flexible.

2. For the group as a whole, there appears to be about the same amount of flexibility according to difficulty of material as there is for flexibility according to purpose. While "good" readers seem to be more flexible in both areas than "poor" readers, purpose appears to affect the rate of "good" readers more than does difficulty of material. In "poor" readers, difficulty of material appears to be more influential on rate than purpose.

3. Flexibility of reading rate for both difficulty of material and for purpose bears little relationship to mental ability, as measured by a group test of intelligence. This suggests that ability to adapt rate of reading to the demands of the reading situation is not related to basic intelligence but is a skill which must be acquired.

4. There appears to be very little relationship between flexibility of rate according to both difficulty of material and purpose and marks in major school content areas. This again suggests that flexibility is not related to school achievement as it is usually measured but is another ability needing training.

Overall findings point to the fact that, within the context of this investigation, flexibility of reading rate does not incontrovertibly accompany mental ability, school achievement, or "good" reading as generally evaluated but is another ability in the total complex of reading techniques needing implementation and development.

Within the same limitations other conclusions can be drawn. While the lower comprehension on subtest B (as compared to A) was probably largely due to the more complex level of the text, had there been more deceleration in rate these comprehension scores might have been higher. Comprehension on the selection read for main ideas was generally lower than that on the selection to be read for more complete knowledge. This may have been due to the fact that the call to read for complete mastery stimulates more alertness. Also, possibly there has been not enough training and practice in reading for main ideas.

Support is given to the contention of other researchers that there is a low, positive relationship between speed and comprehension but that this relationship is not inevitable. Also, apparently adjusting the rate of reading to the difficulty level of the text requires a different adaptation than adjusting the rate to the purpose for which the reading is done.

Educational implications

Since flexibility of reading rate apparently does not inevitably accompany "good" reading, there is a need for instruction in adapting rate of reading to the level of the material and to the purpose for which it is read. Results of this investigation point to the fact that while "good" readers seem to exhibit more flexibility than "poor" readers, there is ample reason to believe that both could profit from such instruction.

Along with the teaching of flexibility, there is a need to have a suitable instrument for testing it. Principles of flexibility should be incorporated into otherwise acceptable tests of reading, or a test such as the flexibility test and its parallel form might be improved, amended, and possibly standardized so that it could be employed diagnostically to measure the effects of teaching of flexibility.

REFERENCES

Anderson, I. H. "An Analysis of the Factors contributing to Individual Differences in Eye Movements During Silent Reading," doctoral dissertation, Iowa State University.

Artley, A. Sterl. "Speed Reading: Its Values and Place in a School Program," School and Community, 14, January 1963.

Baggaley, A. R. Intermediate Correlational Methods. New York: Wiley, 1964, 211.

Blommers, P., and E. F. Lindquist. "Rate of Comprehension of Reading: Its Measurement and Its Relation to Comprehension," Journal of Educational Psychology, 35, November 1944, 449-473.

Carillo, L. W., and W. D. Sheldon. "The Flexibility of Reading Rate," Journal of Educational Psychology, 43, May 1952, 299-305.

Carlson, Thorsten R. "Effect of Certain Test Factors on Measurement of Speed of Reading," Journal of Educational Research, 44, March 1952, 543-549.

Ehrenworth, B. J., and M. M. McAuliffe. "Developmental Reading Program for the High School," Chicago Schools Journal, XLIV, No. 7, April 1963, 315-322.

Flanagan, J. C. "General Consideration in the Selection of Test Items and A Short Method of Estimating Product-Moment Coefficient From Data at the Tails of the Distribution," Journal of Educational Psychology, 30, No. 9, December 1939, 674-681.

Guilford, J. P. Fundamental Statistics in Psychology and Education, 3rd ed. New York: McGraw-Hill, 1965, 565.

Herculane, Sister M. "A Survey of the Flexibility of Reading Rates and Techniques According to Purpose," Journal of Developmental Reading, IV, Spring 1961, 207-210.

Letson, Charles C. "The Construction and Evaluation of a Test to Measure the Flexibility of Reading Rate," unpublished doctoral dissertation, Boston University, 1956.

Perry, William G., Jr. "Students' Uses and Misuses of Reading Skills: A Report to the Faculty," Harvard Educational Review, 29, 1959, 193-200.

Shores, H., and K. L. Husbands. "Are Fast Readers the Best Readers?" Elementary English, XXVII, January 1950, 52-57.

Shores, J. Harlan. "Reading of Science For Two Separate Purposes as Perceived by 6th Grade Students and Able Adult Readers," Elementary English, XXXVII, November 1960, 461-465.

Tinker, Miles. "A Study of Eye Movements in Reading," Psychological Bulletin, 43, March 1946, 93-120.

The Utilization of Accent Generalizations in Identifying Unknown Multisyllabic Words

CAROL K. WINKLEY
Northern Illinois University

THE MAJOR PURPOSE of this study was to assess the extent to which pupils learn and apply certain generalizations concerning the placement of accent when attacking unfamiliar multisyllabic words. To accomplish this purpose the reading of two groups of pupils at the fourth-, sixth-, and eighth-grade levels was compared. Children in the experimental group received systematic instruction in the application of various accent "clues" as a technique of identifying unknown words (the "accent generalization group"). The control group was comprised of pupils who were taught the dictionary skill of reading words which had the accented syllable(s) marked (the "marked accent group").

The chief hypothesis tested by this investigation was that the "accent generalization group" would be significantly superior to the "marked accent group":

1. In ability to attack unfamiliar words of more than one syllable,
2. In level of vocabulary development, and
3. In ability to comprehend printed material.

The significance of the study

This study of one aspect of the word recognition program recommended by some authors of basal reader series was needed since there was no evidence available demonstrating the advisability of teaching the application of accent generalizations as a word attack method. Two recent studies, conducted by Clymer (1) and Groff (6), investigated related aspects of this problem. Both studies raised questions regarding the efficacy of teaching principles of accentuation at either the primary or the intermediate grade levels. Reading teachers, authors of teachers' manuals to accompany basic readers, and reading experts who write textbooks describing and recommending various methods of teaching reading need to know whether children can be taught to make effective use of accent generalizations in identifying unknown words. The absolute lack of any experimental research to substantiate the teaching of this word recognition technique made this study imperative.

Background of the study

A survey of textbooks on reading instruction written by reading authorities confirmed the conclusion reached by Groff (6) that these pedagogues differed in the relative importance they placed on the understanding of accent as a skill in word analysis. Groff divided the authorities into three groups: 1) those who did not mention accent in their discussions of phonic analysis; 2) those who advocated the reading of words in which the accents were marked; and 3) Gray and his followers who favored an extensive study of accent and the teaching of principles of placing accent marks.

In the 1960 edition of *On Their Own in Reading*, (5) Gray presented a detailed plan for teaching numerous "clues to accent." Teaching these accent generalizations was an integral part of the intermediate grade word analysis program of the Scott, Foresman "Curriculum Foundation Series," of which Gray was an author.

Whereas reading specialists have been interested in the stress patterns of isolated words, linguists have been more concerned with the stress patterns in connected speech and have pointed out that these are often different from the accent patterns of the citation forms of words. In addition, the linguists have shown the effects of shifts of accent on intended meaning. Nevertheless, the teaching of the stress patterns of the citation forms or isolated words was investigated in this study.

Procedures of the investigation

Three steps were planned to test the hypothesis of this investigation: 1) the development of the experimental design, 2) the collection of evidence, and 3) the analysis of the data.

1. *The experimental design.* The design was planned as a cross-sectional study involving pupils at the fourth, sixth, and eighth grade levels in two different school systems (one using the Scott, Foresman readers which included accent generalizations; the other using a basal reader in which the pupils learned to read words in which the accented syllables were marked). Both basal readers were to have been used in each respective school system for a period of five years or more. This design made it possible to assess, during the course of one school term, the long-range benefits which pupils gained from instruction in the application of accent generalizations. Thus, a section of the subjects on the basis of "natural variation" (where no change in present practices was involved) made it possible to compare differences in current methods of instruction, thereby eliminating the Hawthorne effect.

Three types of tests were used: 1) the Henmon-Nelson Tests of Mental Ability which served as measures of intelligence; 2) two sections of the Gates Reading Survey—vocabulary and comprehension; and 3) an accent test, constructed by the experimenter, requiring the pupils to perform three tasks in relation to each unknown word—a) to underline the accented syllable, b) to select the right vowel sound for the accented syllable, and c) to choose the correct meaning for the word.

The unknown words for the accent test were secured from two word lists —Dale and Eichholz, Children's Knowledge of Words (3), and a list of words known in grades 11 and 13, compiled by Diederich and Palmer (4). A total of 10,896 multisyllabic words, which could be considered unknown to an average fourth grader, were classified according to the generalization with which they were compiled. Gray's generalizations, as appearing in the Scott, Foresman readers at the intermediate grade level, were used for this purpose and are listed below:

1. *Compound Word Clue.* In compound words, a common pattern of accent is a primary accent on or within the first word and a secondary accent on or within the second word.

2. *Noun-Verb Clue.* In two-syllable words which may be used either as a noun or a verb, the accent is usually on the first syllable when the word is used as a noun and on the second syllables when the word is used as a verb.

3. *"-Ion" Clue.* In words ending with -ion, the primary accent falls on the next-to-the-last syllable.

4. *Varied Suffix Clue.* The primary accent usually occurs on the syllable before the suffixes, -ity, -ic, -ical, -ian, -ial, or -ious, and on the second syllable before the suffix -ate.

5. *Dropped Final "e" Clue.* A single consonant letter following a single vowel letter before an ending or suffix (beginning with a vowel) may be a clue that a final e was dropped and the last syllable of the root word is accented.

6. *Unaccented Syllable Before Ending Clue.* A single consonant letter following a single vowel letter before an ending or suffix (beginning with a vowel) may be a clue to an unaccented final syllable in the root word.

7. *Two Consonants Before Ending Clue.* Two like consonants before an ending or suffix are a clue to an accented final syllble in the root word.

8. *Twin-Consonant Clue.* Two like consonant letters following the first vowel letter are a clue to an accented first syllable.

9. *"Ck" Clue.* The letters ck following a single vowel letter are a clue to an accented first syllable.

10. *Final "e".* Two vowel letters, one of which is final e, in the last syllable of a word, may be a clue to an accented final syllable.

11. *Two Vowels Together Clue.* Two vowel letters together in the last syllable of a word may be a clue to an accented final syllable.

12. *Final "y" Clue.* In a two-syllable word that ends in a consonant followed by y, the first syllable is usually accented.

13. *Common Beginning Clue.* If de-, re-, be-, ex-, in- or a- is the first syllable in a word, it is usually unaccented.

14. *"-Ture," "-Le" Clue.* If the final syllable in a word is -ture, or -le preceded by a consonant, that final syllable is usually unaccented.

15. *Root-Word Clue.* In inflected or derived forms of words, the primary accent usually falls on or with the root word.

16. *Long Word Clue.* In words of three or more syllables, one of the first two syllables is usually accented.

17. *Two-Accent Clue.* In longer words where there is a secondary as well as a primary accent, often the secondary accent falls on the first or second syllable, which is then followed by one unstressed syllable before the primary accent.

The accent test was constructed using a random selection of words from the lists obtained for each generalization. The number of test words exemplifying each accent generalization reflected the percent of words of that type in the total sample at each particular grade level. The "foils," originally used by Dale and Eichholz in their testing, were obtained and used as the multiple-choice items of the test. The administration of the test in pilot studies provided an additional check on the familiarity of the words and made it possblie to improve the content of the test and refine the procedures of administration.

"Face validity," supplemented by evidence obtained in individual interviews with subjects of both groups, and reliability coefficients of .92 and .95 (using the Spearman-Brown "split-half" technique) established the accent test as a dependable instrument. There were seven levels of the test— each containing 50 words. No time limits were set. Each pupil took tests at two consecutive levels, thereby providing a sample of 100 words.

2. *The collection* of *evidence.* The Gates Reading Survey and the accent tests were administered to all subjects in May 1964, while alternate forms had been administered to the fourth graders as pretests in October 1963.

The subjects of the study were 207 pupils from the Aurora Public Schools (West Side) and 202 students from the Batavia Public Schools. The neighboring community of Batavia was selected following a survey of the treatment of accent in eight basal reader series. Inquiries to four companies whose basal reader manuals contained no recommendations for teaching accent generalizations disclosed this nearby school system which met the criteria previously set up as essential for the selection of the control group.

The Aurora pupils, using the Scott, Foresman series of readers, were taught accent generalizations as a part of their word recognition program at the intermediate grade levels; while the Batavia pupils, using the Lyons and Carnahan basal readers, were instructed in pronouncing words which had their accented syllables marked. The investigator had served as a reading consultant in the Aurora schools for a period of six years while Batavia's reading consultant had been there an equal length of time. Both consultants were familiar with the teaching practices in their schools and had urged teachers to follow the manuals in respect to understandings related to accent. Conferences with principals and teachers in both school systems revealed that they concurred with the consultants' beliefs that the manuals had been followed.

All students from 13 classrooms in six different schools in Aurora and 12 classrooms in five different schools in Batavia were tested. Teachers of these classrooms had had at least two years of experience in that school system, had a bachelor's degree and at least one course in the teaching of reading. The pupils in both systems represented a cross section of various socioeconomic levels. The final selection of pupils for the study was made using these additional criteria.

1. They had average mental ability or above (IQ of 100 or more). This was essential since children in the experimental schools, reading at lower levels, were seldom taught the accent generalizations.

2. They had attended their present school system since the beginning of fourth grade.

3. They had been taught by teachers in the intermediate grades who met the standards mentioned earlier for the selection of teachers.

4. Fourth graders, at the beginning of the study, scored above the national norms on the average of the vocabulary and comprehension sections of the Gates Reading Survey.

The groups selected as described were found to be equated at each grade level on three variables—sex, age, and IQ—while the fourth grade groups were also comparable at the beginning of the study in vocabulary, comprehension, and ability to apply accent-generalizations to unknown words, as measured by the accent tests.

3. *Analysis of the data.* All data, including grade-equivalent scores on the vocabulary and comprehension sections of the standardized reading test, raw scores on the accent tests, intelligence quotients, chronological ages, and sex for each subject were coded and punched on IBM cards.

To test the main hypothesis the Harvard Multiple Discriminant Analysis Program (UCSM 336), a revision of three programs described in Cooley and Lohnes, *Multivariate Procedures for the Behavioral Sciences* (2), was used to process the data at the University of Chicago's Computation Center. The output of this program provided means, standard deviations, and all of the information needed for a standard F-Distribution Table. An F-Ratio of the difference between the groups on any variable, which attained the 5 percent level of significance, led to acceptance of the hypothesis. Table 1 pre-

TABLE 1

MULTIPLE DISCRIMINANT ANALYSIS OF VARIANCE

Fourth Grade (Pretest) Overall F-Ratio = 2.2360 df = 4/195 p => .05	Mean in Exper. Group (N = 94)	Mean in Control Group (N = 106)	F-Ratio df = 1/198	p
Accent Test	100.26	99.83	0.01	(Overall
Vocabulary	6.17	6.60	4.23	F-Ratio
Comprehension	6.02	6.03	0.00	not sig.)
Fourth Grade (Post-Test) Overall F-Ratio = 3.2186 df = 6/193 p = < .005	Mean in Exper. Group (N = 94)	Mean in Control Group (N = 106)	F-Ratio df = 1/198	p
Accent Test	142.97	122.92	10.49*	< .005
Vocabulary	6.25	6.20	.07	> .05
Comprehension	6.95	6.52	4.04*	< .05
Sixth Grade Overall F-Ratio = 3.2866 df = 6/108 p = < .005	Mean in Exper. Group (N = 61)	Mean in Control Group (N = 54)	F-Ratio df = 1/113	p
Accent Test	164.49	134.30	13.85*	< .0005
Vocabulary	8.90	8.08	6.50*	< .025
Comprehension	8.90	8.25	5.22*	< .025
Eighth Grade Overall F-Ratio = 4.3002 df = 6/87 p = < .005	Mean in Exper. Group (N = 52)	Mean in Control Group (N = 42)	F-Ratio df = 1/92	p
Accent Test	178.12	170.93	.98	> .05
Vocabulary	11.06	10.52	6.14*	< .025
Comprehension	10.23	10.75	2.49	> .05

*Significant at .05 level or beyond.

sents the data for the analysis of variance, which are basic to the findings and conclusions of this investigation.

Limitations of the study

Various limitations of the study were recognized and considered when the findings were interpreted.

1. Since the sample comprised pupils with intelligence quotients of 100 and above, any generalizations regarding the findings are applicable to a similar population only.

2. Findings based on the results of the accent test may have been affected by the degree of familiarity each child had with the sample words.

3. Appraisals of ability and achievement in various facets of reading were limited to the behavior evoked by the tests which were administered.

4. There was equivocal proof that the quality of instruction, interest in reading, and other motivational factors were comparable in the experimental and control groups.

Chief findings of the study

The following findings, supported by the data presented in Table 1, are related to the hypothesis stated earlier:

1. In ability to attack unfamiliar words of more than one syllable, the fourth and sixth grade "accent-generalization groups" were superior to the "marked-accent groups" at the same grade levels but there was no significant difference between the eighth grade experimental and control groups. Therefore, the first part of the hypothesis was sustained by the data obtained at two grade levels, but not by the data secured for the eighth graders.

2. Sixth and eighth grade students in the "accent generalization group"

were superior in vocabulary development to students in the same grades of the "marked-accent group"; whereas, at the end of fourth grade, neither group demonstrated superiority. Thus, the second part of the hypothesis was partially accepted.

3. In ability to comprehend printed material, superiority was demonstrated again by the subjects of the "accent-generalization groups" at two grade levels. Nonsignificant differences in comprehension at the eighth grade level prevented complete acceptance of the last part of the hypothesis.

Related findings

Findings concerning the relative value of each accent generalization have been reported previously. In an article appearing in the *Academic Therapy Quarterly* (7), the writer reported on the "applicability" of the accent generalizations to the multisyllabic words that children meet in their reading. From a list of words of more than one syllable that children from the fourth to the eighth grade levels must identify, the percentage of words complying with each principle and the percentage of exceptions were computed. Six of Gray's "clues to accent" were found to be applicable to a significant proportion of the words and did not have a high proportion of exceptions (Nos. 3, 4, 8, 13, 15, and 16 listed previously). In addition, the clue "In a word of two syllables the first syllable is usually accented, unless another clue is applicable to the word" was found to help in locating the accented syllable in about 10 percent of the words.

In a second article entitled "Which Accent Generalizations Are Worth Teaching?" (9) the investigator discussed the relative usefulness of each generalization to the children in the study in the identification of unfamiliar multisyllabic words. Following an item analysis of test responses related to each generalization, proportions were computed comparing the total responses that were correct with the total possible responses for all of the

test items exemplifying each generalization. The relative merits of each accent clue were determined by comparing differences between the resulting proportions. Eight of the generalizations had proportions significantly higher than the remaining generalizations (Nos. 7, 9, 10, 11, 12, 13, 14, and 15).

As a result of the findings reported in these two articles, a recommended list of seven accent generalizations was proposed as worth teaching to children. The list included the clues numbered 11, 13, 15, and 16 above. It was suggested that Clues 7 and 8 be combined, thus, "When there are two like consonant letters within a word the syllable before the double consonants is usually accented." Likewise, Clues 3 and 4 could be combined by including "-ion" in the list of suffixes found in Clue 4. The need for teaching Clues 8, 9, 12, 14, and 18 would be eliminated if the principle were taught that "When there is no other clue in a two syllable word, the accent is usually on the first syllable."

Major conclusions

On the basis of the findings enumerated, the following conclusions of this investigation were reached.

Conclusion 1: At the intermediate grade levels, pupils of average ability and above, who received instruction in applying accent generalizations to unfamiliar multisyllabic words, had greater "power" in a) ability to attack unknown words, b) vocabulary development, and c) comprehension than pupils who had learned only the dictionary skill of pronouncing words in which the accented syllables were marked.

Conclusion 2: Knowledge of accent generalizations and the ability to apply them in the identification of unknown words were not acquired by pupils at the sixth grade level and below who had not participated in a word recognition program in which accent principles were taught.

Conclusion 3: Teaching pupils to read words in which the accented syllable was marked did not give children at the intermediate grade levels the degree of independence in attacking unknown words which was provided by instruction in the application of accent generalizations. Pupils must use the dictionary to find the accent marks before they can pronounce the word.

Conclusion 4: The ability to comprehend written material was not adversely affected by attention given to the identification of individual words through the teaching of accent principles.

Conclusion 5: Instruction in the application of accent generalizations at the intermediate grade level ceased to be of great value to students of average ability and above when they reached the eighth grade level.

Implications of the findings

The following implications of this investigation were made considering the limitations, findings, and conclusions presented.

First, accent generalizations should be taught to intermediate grade pupils with average ability and above because pupils capable of using the accent generalizations to attack unfamiliar words enjoy a distinct advantage in reading over pupils who receive no instruction helpful in locating the accented syllable. Thus, teaching the generalizations, even though the advantages may not be maintained at the eighth grade level, is justified.

Second, since learning to apply accent generalizations was found to be a valuable method of word attack for pupils of above average ability, it is likely that pupils with ability below average would benefit from similar instruction at the time that they have acquired the basic word recognition skills usually taught at the primary grade levels.

Third, only the most useful accent generalizations should be taught at the intermediate grade levels. Those principles that have a high proportion of exceptions, that are applicable to a limited number of words, or that are not

helpful to the pupils in the identification of unknown words, should be excluded from the word recognition program or be taught at higher levels.

Fourth, reading authorities, writing textbooks on the teaching of reading, should reexamine their theories and recommendations related to the teaching of accent generalizations. Since the effectiveness of this practice has been demonstrated, practicing teachers and prospective teachers should be familiarized with the technique of applying accent generalizations in their study of various methods of word attack.

Fifth, all authors of basal reader manuals should provide suggestions and exercises which the classroom teachers can use to teach pupils who are reading at the intermediate grade level to apply accent principles when "unlocking" unknown multisyllabic words.

Concluding statement

Since this study is the only investigation known to the experimenter which, based on classroom experimentation, demonstrates the advisability of teaching the accent generalizations as a part of the word recognition program in reading, additional research is needed to verify its findings.

REFERENCES

1. Clymer, Theodore. "The Utility of Phonic Generalizations in the Primary Grades," *The Reading Teacher*, 16, (Jan., 1963), 252-258.
2. Cooley, William W., and Paul R. Lohnes. *Multivariate Procedures for the Behavioral Sciences*. New York: John Wiley & Sons, Inc., 1962.
3. Dale, Edgar, and Gerhard Eichholz. *Children's Knowledge of Words*. Columbus, Ohio: Bureau of Educational Research and Service, 1960.
4. Diederich, Paul B., and Osmond E. Palmer. "Difficulty in Grades 11 and 13 of 4,800 Words from 6,000 Through 20,000 in Frequency." Princeton, New Jersey: Educational Testing Service, 1956.
5. Gray, William S. *On Their Own in Reading*. Chicago: Scott, Foresman, 1960, 121-225.
6. Groff, Patrick. "To Teach or Not to Teach Accents?" *Elementary School Journal*, 62 (Jan. 1962), 218-221.

7. Winkley, Carol K. "The Applicability of Accent Generalizations," *Academic Therapy Quarterly, 2* (Fall 1966), 2-10.

8. Winkley, Carol K. "Utilization of Accent Generalizations in Identifying Unknown Multisyllabic Words," unpublished doctoral dissertation, University of Chicago, 1965.

9. Winkley, Carol K. "Which Accent Generalizations Are Worth Teaching? *The Reading Teacher, 20* (Dec. 1966), 219-224, 253.

Applying Research Findings in Comprehension to Classroom Practice (Elementary)

JOSEPHINE B. WOLFE
University of Scranton

"CHILDREN don't comprehend what they read!" is becoming an increasing complaint among today's competent teachers. Since the perplexity without doubt can be channelled to lack of knowledge and practice, it appears the professionals who educate teachers need to inquire of themselves: 1) do we, as students of reading, understand the process of teaching children to comprehend? 2) are those who educate teachers knowledgeable of the research findings in the area of comprehension? and, 3) do students of reading possess the know-how to apply the significant research findings in comprehension to classroom practice? It is my intent to examine each of these queries.

Comprehension: a definition

To teach children to comprehend one must understand the process of comprehending. Perhaps a definition is necessary. Yet, in arriving at a definition, a definitive explanation, or a conceptualization of the process of comprehending, he who teaches comprehension must recognize the involvement of a great variety of behaviors. Of the many behaviors some are observing and regarding, experiencing a felt problem or task, locating and defining the difficulty, utilizing past knowledge and experience, evolving suggestions for solutions, reasoning about possible outcomes for solutions, verifying solutions in thought, as well as including and taking action after solutions have been made. However, regardless of the behavior or behaviors exhibited, there are three common components present in any behavior that takes place, namely *experience (the material needed for comprehend-ing), thinking (the process of comprehending),* and *language (the product needed to communicate what has been comprehended).* Although these three component parts are unequivocally imperative to any proposed definition, a professional must perform two tasks before making judgments or suggestions: 1) he must review and determine the worthiness of the research that has been completed in comprehension, and 2) he must outline the experiences of educational practitioners who have been successful in utilizing with students "the known" about comprehension.

What research has said since 1960

Two research projects have been completed reviewing the research in READING COMPREHENSION. The first study "Research in Reading Comprehension from 1900-1960" was reported in 1963 by Barbara Binkley Maestle under the direction of James W. Becker, the graduate school, Millersville State College, Millersville, Pennsylvania. The Maestle-Becker Study has been currently updated by the Walsh-Wolfe Study, "Reading Comprehension 1960-1966," a study completed in April 1967 by John J. Walsh under the direction of Josephine B. Wolfe, the graduate school, University of Scranton, Scranton, Pennsylvania. A compilation of studies totaled 119. Of all the studies completed from 1900-1966, 42 were considered valid and 77 were considered invalid when using the criteria listed below:

1. the definition and restriction of the experimental factor
2. the control of the pupil factors
3. the control of important nonexperimental factors
4. the accuracy and validity of measures of differences in achievement
5. the justification of the generalizations.

Of course, the need is great for such studies which are useful to teachers and students of reading. Any attempt to collect, to examine, and to analyze research findings in reading comprehension is valuable for classroom practice, for designing, for developing and/or for examining reading programs within a school as well as teacher education programs which involve the preparation of reading teachers.

Of the 42 studies considered as studies of value to teachers, each was categorized into 5 specific classifications: 5 were related to comprehension and motivation, 12 were related to comprehension and method, 9 were related to comprehension and physical components, 9 were related to comprehension and material, 5 were related to comprehension and format of material, and 2 were related to comprehension and vocabulary. *But,* to possess knowledge is one thing, to place it into practice is another! Therefore, it is imperative that we use "the known."

Using what is known

There are four phases of "the known": 1) the process of comprehending, 2) the kinds of comprehension, 3) the relationship between comprehension and concept development, and 4) the place of word perception in comprehension.

The process

The process of comprehending involves the ability to understand language in its total sense. In fact, a classroom teacher cannot deny that comprehension is a complex process. As everyone who communicates knows, the efficiency of transferring ideas from writer to reader is seldom high for the following reasons:

1. The reader must rely on the printed symbols ONLY. He does not have the advantage of knowing the additional meanings the writer may have intended to employ through the use of personal factors such as the writer's voice, his facial expressions, and his gestures. Therefore, the reader must create his own images and understandings.

2. There is an unavoidable variation in what readers may comprehend because of the differences in background as well as the mental processes among readers and teachers.

3. The reader may experience inaccuracies due to improper word perception, mistaken word meanings, strange differences in sentence structure, inaccurate implications, and lack of practical knowledge in applying his experiences to cultural standards.

Teachers must also know the three *components* of comprehension and be able to apply each to classroom practice.

1. A teacher always must be mindful that *experience* gives meaning to language. Just as the writer lends *his experiences* and *ideas* to his writing symbols, so do readers lend their *experiences* and *ideas* to the printed symbols. Therefore, teachers *must assume* the responsibility of equipping each child with the appropriate experiences for the material he is reading. In other words, the teacher must begin with the experiences of the child and build his experiences to the material he is to read.

2. A teacher must recognize that *thinking* is the *most important component* in teaching children to comprehend. Teaching children to *think* is not easy. It involves too many high level elements such as the *acquisition, organization* and *use* of *experiences.* Following this these experiences must be evaluated and applied to solving the problem "at hand." Thus, teaching children to think becomes no small task!

3. A teacher must never fail to remember that without *language,* the third component part of comprehension, children are unable to communicate what they com-

prehend. Unless children are able to express verbally what they *think*, full understanding and comprehension cannot be expected.

The kinds of comprehension

There are four basic kinds of comprehension with which all teachers should be familiar, teachers who teach children and teachers who teach teachers. In addition to the four kinds of comprehension, teachers should know the specific skills that are included in the program for studying each area of basic comprehension.

The most commonly taught comprehension is *assimilative (factual) comprehension* which involves the use of some ten skills. The next area of comprehension given major consideration by teachers is *critical (inferential) comprehension*. This area of comprehension is usually considered the most difficult of all kinds to teach because it requires greater depth of perception than the others. According to current research studies in comprehension, there are twenty-one specific skills in the area of *critical comprehension*. A third classification of skills, equal in importance to *critical comprehension*, is *organizational comprehension*. This type of comprehension includes such skills as observing the sequence of ideas about what is read, interpreting charts and graphs, and understanding and using the parts of a book. Included in this particular area are twelve specific skills to be learned and used. Finally, we look at the last classification of comprehension skills, those involving the *reading-study* area. Although it is listed as last in this paper, it is by no means less in importance because there are more specific skills to be taught and used in this area of comprehension than in any other area. In fact, there is a total of twenty-five. Thus, it is evident that teaching children to comprehend the printed symbol is no small professional endeavor! However, since there is a direct relation of comprehension to concept development, teaching comprehen-

sion can become a stimulating experience in classrooms at all levels.

The relationship between comprehension and concept development

Concept development is basic to comprehension. The reasons are threefold. 1) If a reader has the appropriate concepts that are basic to understanding the symbols he is to interpret, comprehension will take place with ease. 2) If a reader understands the appropriate concepts of a selection *before* he reads the selection, he will experience a minimum number of word recognition difficulties. Of course, it is an unequivocably known fact that loss in word recognition leads to loss in comprehension. 3) If a reader understands the appropriate concepts of a selection *prior* to his reading the particular selection, he usually will develop broader concepts and/or new concepts as a result of his reading. Therefore, since the building of concepts must be considered a prerequisite to comprehension, teachers must know how concepts can be built.

First, concepts are built basically upon concrete (actual) experiences. When vicarious experiences are used to build a concept, children must be taught that experiences should be related to concrete experiences *if* meaning is expected to be associated with a new printed word. Secondly, a reader must be taught how to organize his experiences.

A child may have been on a boat, in a car, on an airplane, and on a train, yet he may not understand the concept of transportation.

Thirdly, a reader must be taught to recognize the levels of concepts he will experience as he reads, low level concepts and high level concepts as well as the existing variations between each.

A child may understand that milk is white, is something he drinks, is a liquid, is a nutritious liquid, and is a food.

Lastly, regardless of grade levels, book levels, or content areas, teachers must recognize and adhere to the fact that they must begin in terms of a reader's experiences.

It is difficult for a reader to understand the phrase, "Mary's home," if the reader does not have full experience with the word "home."

After this discussion, one might ask, "What about word perception?" Of course, any student of reading would be dilatory not to acknowledge the area of word perception and its importance to comprehending the printed symbol.

Word perception: its importance to comprehension

Although the ability *to think* always will receive priority when comprehending, word forms and other aids are needed by a reader if he is to receive complete conveyance of the writer's ideas. Meaningful aids helpful to a reader include such specifics as anticipating meanings from context, clues from illustrations, language patterns, phonetic "cues," and structural elements, as well as the extension of word meanings by synonyms, homonyms, homographs, and words which have multiple meanings. Each provides the reader with an opportunity for "checking" the accuracy of his experience. Thus, it should be clearly understood that there is no single method or single device for developing comprehension. It is the use the reader makes of each method with emphasis being on "all." Although the process of using these many aids is complicated, permit me to suggest some considerations for helping children in classrooms to comprehend the printed symbol.

Applying "the known" to the classroom

Before delving into the act of teaching children to comprehend, there are prerequisites to which the classroom teacher must be alert.

1. She must be cognizant of *the number* and *the nature* of the experiences the child possesses.
2. She must be aware of the child's ability to organize his experiences.
3. She must be knowledgeable and/or sensitive to the child's ability to think. In other words, the teacher must know whether the child is able *to think* in a concrete (practical) fashion.
4. She must be observant of the child's ability to listen as well as to express himself in oral and written form.

To begin where the learner is and help him to develop his fullest potential in comprehending, the classroom teacher must understand that there is a sequential development in the comprehensive process. Though there are many means of development, let me suggest one sequence.

1. *associative comprehension*—This, perhaps, may represent the lowest level of comprehension, the level of immediate thought which is related to an experience.
2. *concept formation*—This act of comprehending represents the relation of insight to the problem or word which precedes the formulation of a definition to a problem.
3. *problem solving*—This is representative of the process by which a child goes from a task or a problem to a satisfying solution.
4. *critical comprehension*—This phase of comprehending is characterized by the judgments which are made after examination of significant facts and correlated materials.
5. *concentrative comprehension*—This is a depth process by which implications are made after careful examinations of significant facts and correlated materials.
6. *creative comprehension*—This process represents the highest level of comprehension. Here new ideas are produced, reactions to previous ideas and to the ideas of others are utilized. Problem solving is objectively directed toward a goal and more "fixed" with facts. Comprehending becomes more personal, less fixed and provides opportunity for greater insights.

Keeping the above in mind, a simple plan for helping children learn to comprehend in a scientific manner as a group or as individuals might be as follows:

1. Help them to select and/or define a problem.
2. Suggest that they "set up" hunches or guesses about the problem they select.
3. Guide them in selecting procedures for solving their problems.
4. Decide with them how they are going to evaluate and record the results from their "set" procedures.
5. Discuss possibilities for drawing their conclusions and making their generalizations.
6. Describe how their results, conclusions, and generalizations can be used as implications for further study.

Will this plan help children to think? The response from successful practitioners is an enthusiastic, "Aye" accompanied by a preface of "musts."

Too many musts?

Are there too many "musts" to make the teaching of comprehension practical? Do TOO MANY MUSTS appear in this paper? No, I think not if you wish to help your children apply what they learn to their own experiences, to develop other experiences from their learning, and to find the answers to the many problems they are attempting to solve. As teachers we should accept the belief that there are never TOO MANY MUSTS to help our pupils become good comprehenders.

Applying Research Findings in Comprehension to Classroom Practice (Secondary)

HAROLD COVELL
University of British Columbia

COMPREHENSION is something like the weather. We talk about it a great deal, but we do relatively little research on it (14).

Perhaps one reason for the paucity of research on comprehension in reading is that we are not exactly sure what comprehension is (17). Some scholars, in attempting to clarify the concept of comprehension, have resorted to making models, others to drawing diagrams. Research workers have ranged widely in their study of comprehension, from Gray (5), who fifty years ago equated it with getting meaning through reading, to Ruddell (12), who recently discovered that passages with greater frequency of occurrence of syntactical elements are more easily understood than ones with less. We may be well aware of the pitfalls of the circular argument implied in Gray's concept of comprehension. Nevertheless, his seductively simple and illusory definition of comprehension as getting meaning through reading may be the most practical one to orient us to the topic "Applying Research Findings in Comprehension to Classroom Practice."

Selected research in comprehension

While Gray's definition may serve to orient us in a general way to a concept of comprehension its inadequacies soon become apparent when we try to put it into practice. We can not blithely trip along distributing general comprehension goodies to students. We must use methods and materials of instruction and procedures of sound classroom organization, and we must be quite specific. When we face the rigorous reality of teaching comprehension some of the more analytic studies of this process, although incomplete, serve as a basic in research for classroom practice.

Early in his work on the substrata-factor theory of reading, J. A. Holmes (7) listed vocabulary in context, intelligence, and perception of verbal relationships as some of the main factors related to getting meaning in reading. Referring to comprehension as a process, Russell and Fea (13) have organized a succinct summary of research on this topic under the following headings: 1) percepts (sensations and images), 2) concepts (symbolization of meaning), 3) verbals (standardization of symbols), and 4) relationships of verbalized concepts (multiple meanings, denotation—connotation, figurative language, grammar—syntax).

The David (2) factor analysis research on the components of comprehension is one of the earliest of several such studies. He identified the fundamental factors of comprehension in reading as 1) knowing word meanings, 2) seeing relationships, 3) handling explicit statements, 4) identifying the writer's intent, 5) using context to decide on the meaning of unfamiliar words, 6) understanding the literal meaning of words, 7) the writer's organization of his materials, 8) being familiar with literary devices, and 9) recognizing main ideas. This study is a most useful one because it can be applied readily to the classroom situation. Attempts to fragmentize comprehension skills much beyond those related to these nine factors have so far served no practical purpose in the classroom.

A different approach involving introspection and retrospection on the part of her subjects, was used by Piekarz (11) to further our knowledge of the process of comprehension. She identified three areas of comprehension; literal meanings, implied meanings, and critical evaluation. Jenkinson (8) combined the introspective approach with cloze test procedures to analyze the factors that differentiated the high cloze test scorers from the low scorers among her subjects. The high scorers tended to relate more ideas, assume a more active role in interpreting ideas from the author's words, and have a better knowledge of language structure than low scorers.

Perhaps reading comprehension reaches its highest planes as *critical reading* and *creative reading*. Even though many different meanings have been attached by different writers to these terms a few studies have yielded some evidence that 1) critical reading may be distinguished from literal comprehension (16), 2) readers' attitudes affect critical reading ability (6) and creative interpretation of materials (9), and 3) there are specific reading abilities related to critical reading (3) and creative reading (10), and that these require separate, specific practice.

In summary, these selected studies have indicated that comprehension, unlike bologna, does not remain comprehension when we begin to slice it. On close examination we discover that it involves structural elements of language such as breadth and depth of vocabulary and relationships among words in sentences, paragraphs and longer passages. It has been dissected into lexical, literal and interpretive levels of meaning. It is influenced subtly by human factors such as the intent of the author and the biases and stereotyped concepts of the reader. It may be synthesized according to the purpose of the reader into a hierarchy of reading skills such as selecting and relating details, recognizing main ideas, understanding an author's organization, and doing inferential reasoning. Finally, these skills can be applied either separately or in various combinations at any level of maturity of the reader, provided suitable materials of instruction and conditions of learning are employed.

Of these several facets of comprehension we shall observe the applications to classroom practice of research findings in this area only insofar as the relationship of certain aspects of vocabulary development, levels of comprehension, and some of the purposes of the reader are concerned.

Applications to classroom practice

Knowledge of word meanings is the one factor which most research workers seem to agree is basic to reading comprehension. Words are labels symbolizing concepts and concepts depend on accurate percepts. The first practical application of research findings in comprehension, then, is that we must give students direct, vivid experience in building percepts which will endow their concepts with some depth of understanding if we hope that the words they read may be symbols with some richness of meaning. However, it is impossible to develop all of the concepts needed by secondary school students by direct experience alone. Much of their experience must be of the vicarious variety. Therefore, discriminating use of audiovisual aids, experimentation, demonstrations, and dramatizations is vital to concept development. If these kinds of classroom activities are accompanied by discussions students will be helped to understand better and to put into words the many dimensions of the concepts they are considering. And this better understanding of concepts and the verbal symbols used to represent them can only result in better reading comprehension.

We might consider picture reading, an often neglected reading skill in the content subjects, as a specific example to illustrate the use of visual aids in concept, vocabulary, and comprehension development. Students should be given opportunities to think about and discuss the facts and the possible implications of the facts presented by the illustrations in their textbooks. Often the five *W* questions (*Who? What? When? Where?* and Why?) may serve as a conceptual framework for picture reading.

Wide reading is universally recognized as another way of developing vocabulary and, thereby, skill in reading comprehension. This assumption is as common in classroom practice as it is unwarranted in research. Perhaps, one reason for the disappointing results of research about the effects of wide reading on vocabulary development is the tendency for students to do their wide reading in areas of familiar vocabulary. This tendency might be offset if students were encouraged to read widely in familiar contexts containing some unknown words.

Verbalism forms a constant threat to comprehension in reading. Students may be good, glib, accurate word callers with little, or no, or wrong understandings of the concepts for which the words are symbols. This problem can be particularly acute in reading in the content subjects. At the secondary school level this problem can be reduced by inductive teaching of technical vocabulary before students read.

A thread running through all of the research on comprehension is that direct teaching is needed for the student to develop any skill. This generalization is particularly valid in teaching vocabulary in relation to comprehension. The following suggestions by W. S. Gray for direct vocabulary instruction are as pertinent today as they were when he made them sixteen years ago (*4*).

(1) Teachers should constantly direct pupils' attention to words—to appropriateness of the author's choice of words, to accuracy of meaning, to the power of words in appealing to the various senses.
(2) Teachers should offer two choices when a word is required so that pupils may practice selecting the exact word.
(3) Reading material must contain unknown words to afford practice in extending word meaning.
(4) Pupils should be encouraged to build their own lists of technical words.

We have considered in a limited way a number of suggestions for applying to classroom practice some of the findings of research concerning the relationship between word meaning and comprehension. Let us now look at a specific example of developing the various levels of comprehension that have been identified by research.

Students might be asked to read the excerpt below adapted from Rachel Carson's *Under the Sea Wind:*

As Ookpik, the snowy owl, flew silently up the valley he saw among the willows the moving balls that were ptarmigan. The white foe moved nearer, blending into the pale sky, the white prey moved, unfrightened, over the snow. There was a soft *whoosh* of wings—a scattering of feathers—and on the snow a red stain spread, red as a new laid ptarmigan egg before the shell pigments have dried.

Then, an exercise, such as the following addressed to the students, might follow this excerpt:

> To help you to grasp the idea of the three levels of comprehension study the words
> —*on the snow a red stain spread*
>
> The first level of comprehension is the one where you know the *meaning of each word.*
> *on*
> *(the) snow*
> *(a) red*
> *stain*
> *spread*
>
> The second level of comprehension is the one where you understand the *literal meaning of these words as they are used together* in the phrase
> —*on the snow a red stain spread*
> You should be able to imagine a picture of red stain growing outwards from a central point on the snow.
> The third level of comprehension is where you read between the lines, where you go beyond the literal meaning of the words and *interpret the idea implied by the words in the total context within which they are used.*
> What is the idea implied by the words
> *on the snow a red stain spread?*

At the secondary level the skilled reading teacher will help his students to acquire the habit of assessing the nature of the reading task before him and then to adjust his rate and manner of reading according to the difficulty of the material and his purposes for reading it. This habit which has been variously labeled as "previewing" or "surveying" can be learned and maintained only by having many opportunities to practice it.

Four purposes for reading which have been identified with regular frequency by various studies (*15*) are reading for details, for main ideas, for understanding the author's organization, and for making inferences.

Some mental image of a hierarchy of comprehension skills ranging from easy to difficult (*1*) is a useful conceptual structure for framing comprehension questions. A teacher should understand, for example, that, in any given material, questions requiring the location of specific details are usually easiest to answer; that it is usually more difficult to discover the main idea of a sentence, paragraph, or story than to answer a question involving specific details; that understanding a writer's organization involves some synthesis of reading for main ideas and details; and that questions involving inferential reasoning are the most difficult to answer. With this hierarchy in mind the judicious teacher can distribute the kinds of comprehension questions according to an individual's or a group's ability to answer and need for practice.

There is evidence that, while we tend to develop in our students the skill of reading for details, we fail to develop the other three comprehension skills which require the higher mental thought processes. Along with developing meaningful vocabularies, a most practical suggestion for applying research findings in comprehension to classroom practice is providing a balanced comprehension skills development program for each student. This kind of direct comprehension instructional program should enable each student to work with challenging and intrinsically interesting reading materials at his own level of understanding. It should give him opportunities to experience varying degrees of success in answering thought-provoking questions based on those materials.

The hierarchy of the four important and interrelated comprehension skills should be a part of each content subject teacher's professional knowledge as he helps to guide his students' understandings of his subject. He must be aware that the teacher of English can be expected to provide practice in these skills only in a general way insofar as his own subject is concerned. The research facts are that these four skills have different emphases in each subject and that the person most competent to deal with these skills in any subject is the subject matter specialist.

Reading teachers at the secondary level have one distinct advantage over those at the elementary level because they can help their more mature students to understand the concept of the hierarchy of comprehension skills. The secondary school student not only should know how to read well but also he should know something about the reading process itself.

When he undertakes a reading comprehension exercise or test the secondary student should know what skills are being appraised. He should be a partner with his teacher in a process of continuous evaluation of his own progress, continuous diagnosis of his own reading problems and suggestions of possible remedies for those difficulties. All this can be made easier with appropriately designed materials of instruction. While all this can be accomplished under the guidance of a competent teacher, the student himself should understand the nature of the reading comprehension skills he is to learn and the purpose of learning and practising those skills.

Conclusion

An obvious conclusion to the research in comprehension is that good readers are made, not born. At the secondary level it is both possible and practical for students and teachers together to set broad and far reaching as well as specific and immediate goals in reading instruction. Perhaps the most important application of research in comprehension to classroom practice is that secondary students are mature enough to be involved as partners with their teachers in the improvement of reading instruction.

REFERENCES

1. Bell, H. "Comprehension in Silent Reading," British Journal of Educational Psychology, 12 (1942), 47-55.
2. Davis, F. B. "Fundamental Factors of Comprehension in Reading," Psychometrika, 9 (1944), 185-197.
3. Gans, Roma. "Study of Critical Reading Comprehension in the Intermediate Grades," Teachers College Contribution to Education, (1940) No. 811.
4. Gray, William S. "Reading and Understanding," Elementary English, 28, (1951), 148-159. Cited in David H. Russell, and Henry R. Fea, "Research on Teaching Reading," Handbook of Research on Teaching. (N. L. Gage—ed.) Chicago: Rand McNally and Co., 1963.
5. Gray, William S. "The Relation of Silent Reading to Economy in Education," Sixteenth Yearbook Part 1, National Society for the Study of Education. Bloomington, Illinois: Public School Publishing Co., 1917.
6. Groff, P. J. "Children's Attitudes toward Reading and Their Critical Reading Abilities in Four Content-type Materials." Unpublished doctoral dissertation, University of California, Berkeley, 1955.
7. Holmes, J. A. The Substrata-factor Theory of Reading. Berkeley: California Book, 1953. Cited in Russ.
8. Jenkinson, Marion D. "Selected Processes and Difficulties of Reading Comprehension." Unpublished doctoral dissertation, Department of Education, University of Chicago, 1957.
9. Loban, W. Literature and Social Sensitivity. Champaign, Illinois: National Council of Teachers of English, 1954.
10. McCullough, Constance M. "Responses of Elementary School Children to Common Types of Reading Comprehension Questions," Journal of Educational Research, 51 (1957) 583-7.
11. Piekarz, Josephine A. "Getting Meaning from Reading," Elementary School Journal, 56 (1956), 303-9.
12. Ruddell, Robert B. "Reading Comprehension and Structural Redundancy in Written Material," Proceedings of the Annual Convention, International Reading Association 10, (1965).
13. Russell, David H. and Henry R. Fea. "Research on Teaching Reading," The Handbook of Research on Teaching. Chicago: Rand McNally and Co., 1963.
14. Sayles, Daniel G. "Recent Research in Reading: Implications for College and Adult Programs," Journal of Developmental Reading, 4 (Summer 1961), 217-27.
15. Smith, Nila B. "Utilizing Reading Opportunities in the Entire Curriculum," Education, 72 (1952), 73-4.
16. Sochor, Elona E. "Literal and Critical Reading in Social Studies," Journal of Experimental Education, 27 (1958), 49-56.
17. Spache, George. "Reading Rate Improvement—Fad, Phantasy, or Fact?" Proceedings of the Annual Conference, International Reading Association, 9 (1964), 28-30.

Applying Research Findings in Rate of Reading to Classroom Practice (Secondary)

WALTER R. HILL
State University of New York
at Buffalo

EDUCATIONAL RESEARCH, laudable for its earnest efforts to emulate the exactness of the physical sciences, frequently fails to carry its impact to classroom practice. In the area of reading, it is common for three to five decades to elapse between the collection of useful research data and their related application to curriculum, materials, or methods. No doubt many factors contribute to this subcultural lag. No argument is tendered here against professional reticence to change reasonably successful operations until solid evidence of better procedures is available. What is decried is the inconsistent, nearly fickle manner in which the profession furls its sails against the small but orderly winds of empirical evidence, and then races aloft, shakes out its canvas, to run before the tempest created by an opinionated article in one of the national Sunday supplements. Sometimes we come to our senses before we are blown hopelessly off course. It must be admitted, the gale usually does jar us out of our complacency.

Thus has it been in that area of the business known as reading rate and its improvement. Here is a pertinent case in point. As early as 1879, Javal reported that in the process of thorough reading, the eyes moved in a series of small fixations along each line of print. Since Javal's research, hundreds of carefully controlled studies using finite reading instruments have confirmed this fact and its supporting data. This evidence was dutifully reported in research journals, reading theory texts, psychology texts, as well as in general professional sources. Then, in the early 1960's a private reading business, having learned a lesson from the Coca Cola Company, ma-nipulated a set of fortuitous Madison Avenue incidents, and soon the American public (and too many professionals) accepted that it was possible to read at "astronomically" high rates of ten thousand words-per-minute, as one learned how to read an entire page at a fixation. In time, and after further research, certain scholars of reading criticized this generalization and its related practices. A controversy ensued, and the improvement of reading rate, traditionally considered a questionable objective in some quarters, became a dirty professional word.

A little time has passed, egos have calmed, high interest has subsided, and we find ourselves looking at the issue once again. The illustration is pertinent to this introduction, because it enables you to see something of the dilemma of this writer. First, he would like to spare his audience the non-lurid details of statistical summaries, since experience indicates they come to naught in transfer to classroom practice. Evidently the stuff research is made of—the cold hard facts of means, standard deviations, and "significance"—carries little force when matched against the needs of the beating heart. Secondly, he would like to draw some generalizations from his review of the available research, and to avoid being stereotyped as an eyeball mechanic while respectfully suggesting that down where the people live, the world is picking up its pace—and if one wishes to keep with it, he'd better master the survival skills.

We make our start by looking at several observations from three publications not likely to be considered as reading research journals. The first of these sources is a cartoon which appeared in the *Wall Street Journal* several years ago. It depicts a harried traveler aiming his auto along the complex maze of a superhighway. Although moving at a good rate, he is being pressed on all sides by the horns and indignation of those who would go faster. As he looks ahead, he sees three routes, and a decision coming up. The sign over the route to the left says

Montreal, Bangor, Boston and fades into a blur of ten more city names. The sign over the route to the right reads Tallahassee, Washington, D. C., Baltimore, and gradually decreases in size like the Snellen chart. And the one over the route straight ahead states—City Dump and Slow Readers.

The second source is a rather fearful little paperback, entitled *Children Under Pressure*. Here are a few quotations—statements made by high school students.

I don't think there's anything physically wrong with me but I just go through life feeling terribly tired.
There's so much pressure, it seems, that it builds up to a point at which you have to let off steam. So I get nervous twitches, or my hands start shaking, or I start arguing with people.
After studying, I feel tired because I've been reading over and over again the facts I'm likely to be tested on.
When I come home, I feel I have to get to bed early because I stayed up late studying last night. So I start right after school, but the work goes on and on because I'm tired and I seem to have lost my ability.
College seems to have moved down to the high school. In my sophomore year we had a fat notebook full of notes the teacher of biology had taken during a summer institute, plus our regular textbook and a supplementary book that said inside it "This book is for seniors in college who are working in their field of concentration" (6).

These are the students who are most serious and successful academically. The quotes from those who have given up are much less complimentary. The third source is for those who might hold the opinion that these are just idle adolescent complaints. The following comments are from the Gordon's book, *The Blight on the Ivy*, and they reflect something of the emotional state of today's youth. The comparative percentages of males, age 13-24, who attended New Jersey private out-patient psychiatric clinics primarily for reasons of academic pressure read: 1953-55 = 34 percent; 1956-57 = 54 percent; and 1960-61 = 74 percent. Thus, nearly three-fourths of those getting psychiatric care were most concerned with academic pressures. The Gordons

turned up evidence that the increase in the number of adolescents among psychiatric patients has increased from 4 percent in 1953 to 12 percent in 1962. They also cite a considerable increase in psychosomatic illnesses, such as ulcers, in adolescents (7).

Please don't misinterpret me. I don't mean to imply that the answer to societal and personal problems lies in developing flexible reading rate. Rather, I hope that we will keep in mind that the following research generalizations are derived from patterns of empirical statistics—and each statistic represents a live body with dreams and fears.

Rate of reading

Reading rate, as an element of the reading process, has been a part of the literature since the earliest scientific investigations of the process (21). And, if we diligently search the literature, we will find that upper school level teachers identified a need for improved reading rate as early as 1894 (10). Traditionally, we have not viewed a direct emphasis upon the improvement of reading rate to be a basic objective of elementary reading instruction, although a good total program in elementary reading reflects itself in pupil reading efficiency, as in other positive reading attributes. College level programs were the first to accept the improvement of reading rate as a worthwhile objective in itself, and during the period 1945-60, when college reading programs were found at the majority of higher educational institutions in this country, the majority of such programs emphasized rate improvement and study efficiency. High schools tended to follow suit, with some lag in time, and with lesser direct emphasis. A survey of the literature on high school reading programs published by IRA in 1965 indicated that the most frequent pattern of a high school reading program was a class or center primarily directed toward the improvement of reading rate and study efficiency (11). The "dynamic speed reading" boom of the early 1960's and its related controversy appears to be tailing off. Perhaps we are ready to view the improvement of reading rate as one of the several worthwhile objectives of higher level reading development, and to consider any improvement made in this direction to be useful to the reader, even though it does not reach the phenomenal claims of the private enterprisers.

Selected generalizations from reading rate research

It should be recognized that the research on reading rate reflects differences in findings and conclusions. We would be naive to expect perfect consensus from the study of human behavior. The following generalizations represent consistent patterns among the empirical investigations.

1. The meaningfulness of reading rate and the legitimacy of programs directed toward its improvement is quite dependent upon the assumption of adequate comprehension of the material read (14). But this raises an enigma of the entire area of reading instruction—the nature of adequate comprehension. It has been traditional and expedient to use 75 percent accuracy in answering questions constructed for the selection as a criterion of reading adequacy for testing or instructional purposes. This places emphasis on accuracy of comprehension "per-unit-of-material." More importantly, it ignores the instructional goal of the self-directed reader. In the broader life setting, as well as the pressure circumstance of the modern high school, it would seem reasonable to stress adequate comprehension in terms of concepts gained "per-unit-of-time." Reasonable, perhaps, in instructional emphasis, but very difficult in terms of objective measurement (4).

2. We encounter a similar problem of measurement with rate itself. It is traditional and statistically expedient to measure reading rate and its improvement in units of "words-per-minute," whether measured on an "amount-limit" basis (how much time taken to read a selection of certain word length) or on a "time-limit" basis—how many words can be read in a selection when given a certain limit of time in which to read (21). Like the percent accuracy of comprehension measure, the words-per-minute measure is practical in measurement and research. Nevertheless, it would seem instructionally appropriate to develop readers who assimilated concepts-per-hour, or whatever practical period of time is available for such reading.

3. It is widely accepted that the most effective reading rate is that which permits the reader to achieve his reading purposes as adjusted to the nature of the material he reads, his background in the topic, the setting in which he reads, and his pertinent personal characteristics. Thus, long ago, effective reading rate became an intimate consequence of reading flexibility (25).

4. It follows, therefore, that it is fallacious to think of one general appropriate rate of thorough reading for any one individual or group. Rather, it is better to view the individual as having a series of rates of thorough reading. Empirical findings support this (1, 2). However, there is some evidence to suggest that while an individual reader may read different materials at different rates, he will tend to maintain his relative position in comparison with the rates of other readers on those different materials (21). The major exception, of course, would occur when he counters content for which he has little background.

5. Like other aspects of the reading process, reading rate is influenced by, and rate improvement is limited by, personal characteristics of the reader: his intelligence; his general grasp of the language, particularly his meaning and sight vocabulary; his background of concepts; his mastery of the basic skills of reading; his physiological condition; and his effective drive and emotional flexibility (16).

6. Empirical data indicate that the majority of high school students habitually read at rates considerably

below their capacities to perform (15).

7. There is considerable evidence that high school students can increase their reading rates in either short, intensive programs or in longer multi-objective reading programs (18, 20). This increase in reading rates is maintained to a large extent if the individual continues to apply his learned approaches. Further, it does not take a great deal of teaching experience to develop a program which successfully improves reading rate, a finding which has both positive and negative implications for reading professionals.

8. While reading rates can be improved, and most students can learn to read faster, there are limits to the extent of this improvement (3). Spache has presented evidence which places a physiological limit on thorough reading around 800-900 WPM (19). Stroud has indicated that the psychological limit of thorough reading under work conditions is more frequently around 500 WPM (21). In these estimates, the term "thorough reading" is an important consideration. This means that these limits are imposed when the reader covers his material in a progressive series of fixations, line by line, paragraph by paragraph, attempting rather total assimilation of content. If he "skim-reads" the material by skipping certain sentences or even paragraphs, there is no real limit to his rate in terms of words-per-minute (16). The limit in skimming is imposed only by how familiar the individual wishes to be with the author's literal presentation and by how well the reader can generalize understanding from a limited set of cues.

Generalizations emanating from eye-movement studies

Much of what we have learned about reading rate has resulted from eye-movement research. Some of these generalized findings are listed here. It can be seen that they apply to more than the one aspect of the reading program (1, 22, 24).

1. Silent reading is more efficient than oral reading as soon as the reader has mastered a basic sight vocabulary and the fundamental reading process.

2. Words can be recognized as units from partial cues, and are not dependent upon minute analysis as long as the word is a part of the reader's sight vocabulary.

3. Mechanically, total reading time is composed of fixation time and eye-movement time. Of these, the much greater portion, (approximately 9/10 of the total reading time), is spent in fixations. This would include, of course, time spent in regressive fixations, i.e., eye stops.

4. Slower readers make more fixations, more regressions, and spend more time per fixation than faster readers. Were it otherwise, we should be surprised!

5. In the larger setting, good comprehenders reveal more efficient eye-movement performance, better rate, and more flexible adjustment to reading conditions than poor comprehenders. Again, we should be surprised if this were not so, since we recognize that comprehension is the final product of interrelated skills and habits.

6. Eye-movement efficiency and its related aspect of reading rate are adversely effected by certain conditions, as long as the reader accepts the challenge of understanding the material he is reading. These conditions include; a) more difficult material in terms of readability, b) reading purposes of greater complexity, such as critical analysis of material or organizing a structure of ideas as contrasted to general enjoyment of content, c) extremes in intensity of "felt pressure" by the reader; that is, both too little or too much pressure will cause the reader to perform less efficiently.

It is ironic that the eye-movement research process has been employed to justify the use of eye-movement training as a means of improving reading rate, when that very source has provided hard data of the uselessness of such operations. Eye-movement data indicate clearly that with the exception of quite young readers, the eye-movement processes are shaped by the central perceptual and thinking processes of the reader, not vice versa. The futility of attempting to increase reading rate by concentrating upon the reader's "eye-ball" actions is seen in such evidence as; a) time spent in actual movement is fractional, (approximately .003 seconds), b) interfixative movements are reflex action and are uninfluenced by reader volition or training process, and c) eye-span per fixation seldom extends beyond one and a fraction words in the contextual reading situation (22).

It does not follow, necessarily, that mechanical devices such as reading pacers, reading films, or tachistoscopes are useless or dishonest, as some writers would imply. This would depend upon how they are employed, the extent to which they take over the program, the motivation and skill objectives of the instructor, and, since they are relatively expensive, how much their purpose limits the other functions of the reading program (17). Used judiciously, they can provide variety, motivation, and a source of independent practice for secondary students. Many otherwise adequate secondary school readers operate sluggishly and rather rigidly in their attack upon reading content (13). The teacher can employ reading films or pacers as part of a program to gradually condition these students into faster assimilation of content. There is considerable research to support this generalization (23). But we are speaking here of their value in developing faster reading reaction response, not about their value in training specific eye-movement patterns, which is equivocal (8). Surely, the same objective can be reached by well motivated instruction and a variety of reading materials. But, it must be recognized that this takes teacher time, talent, and energy which might better be directed to those aspects of the program for which there are few materials or devices of instruction available.

Nor does it necessarily follow that the use of mechanical devices to condition a faster perception of reading content precludes a total program objective of developing reading flexibility. After all, one of the major detractors from flexibility is that many readers are rigidly slow in their attack on all materials. And, there is no reason why mechanical devices, particularly individual pacers which can be adjusted to purpose and material, cannot be employed to considerable advantage in conditioning the reader to a varied attack.

A note concerning flexibility of reading rate

It was not the specific function of this paper to treat the broad issues of reading flexibility, *per se*. However, it must be obvious that reading flexibility and rate of reading are intimately related. In terms of program objectives, scholars of the area are agreed that our major purpose is to develop a flexible reader, one who adjusts his total reading attack to fit his reading purposes (including consideration of the state of his knowledge about the topic), and to the readability of his material. In this, being capable of reading rather rapidly for some purposes and in some materials enhances his potential for flexibility. Also, we would hope that whatever approach he used, whether it be scanning, skimming, rapid thorough reading, or careful analysis of ideas, he would do each as efficiently as possible!

The concept of reading flexibility is not a recent development (1, 25). However, it has gained considerable emphasis as a major objective of reading instruction during this decade. Partly, this has resulted from the rate vs. comprehension controversy, with the recognition that the concept of flexibility provides both a theoretical and operational catalyst to combine the best elements of both reading rate and reading comprehension.

McDonald and several others have provided good summaries of the research and thinking on the topic of flexibility (5, 16). It may be useful to consider here several implications of flexibility research as they relate to rate of reading.

Even good readers at the high school and college levels are not as diversified in their reading attack as they could be (12, 15). While there has been little controlled study of the most effective nature of flexibility programs, we have evidence that improvement in flexibility can be gained through programs directed to that end (2, 9). As one might expect, a reader's flexibility is influenced by a number of factors, both personal and instructional (16). These are much the same as those which influence reading comprehension and reading rate (10). In a sense, all reasonable reading instruction from the readiness period to the college graduate course which deals with the analysis of specific technical content contributes to the objective of flexible reading behavior. It has been recommended that specific instructional activity to develop conscious reader adjustment of attack, particularly in reading rate, should not be emphasized before the reader is well founded in his fundamental reading skills, somewhere around sixth or seventh grade (5).

Instructional implications

Hopefully, most of the foregoing comment has classroom value for improving flexible rate of reading. A few specific implications for instruction are presented here.

1. As in any good reading program, it is wise to assess the reading skills and developmental characteristics of the pupils. Students with basic reading skill deficiencies should receive more fundamental corrective reading help before undertaking intense instruction in rate. Those with physical and personal anomalies should be referred for corrective aid.

2. Improvement of thorough rate of reading should consist of but one important phase of the development of reading flexibility. Other phases should include instruction and practice in the use of a) a reading-study procedure such as POINT or SQ3R, b) scanning to locate specific information, c) skimming to gain an impression of the total idea structure, d) a rapid noting procedure, and e) critical analysis of content. Of these, the study procedure should be taught first since it can be immediately employed by the pupil and provides a meaningful setting for use of the other phases.

3. In the improvement of thorough reading rate, the practice reading materials are quite important. They should be easier than the student's instructional level (e.g. fewer than 5 percent word hesitations and better than 75 percent comprehension on untimed readings). The materials should be lucid, neatly organized, on topics of interest, but not requiring special background of information. These recommendations are particularly important for materials read under mechanical pacing.

4. The early portion of the rate improvement program should concentrate rather intensively upon jolting the reader out of sluggish reading reaction habits. The four basic elements of this attack are a) instruction in the rationale of flexible reading rate, b) demonstration of procedures, c) controlled guided practice (here the mechanical devices are useful), and d) immediate transfer reading practice (timed but not mechanically controlled).

5. After the initial phase of establishing new patterns, the direction of instruction and materials should move in graduated steps a) from easy to more difficult content, b) from shorter to longer selections, c) from comprehension tasks of general overview to identification of main ideas, to summary organization of the major structure, to specific recall of factual content, and d) from instructor provided purpose to pupil identification of purpose. When the more efficient habits of thorough reading are well established, the instructor would intensify the practice of flexible adjustment of reading rate to a variety of materials and purposes.

6. Motivation is important since the student is being asked to change deeply grooved behavior. To this end,

frequent individual conferences, periodic testing, variety in instructional procedures, reading selections of interesting content, the keeping of progress records, and a personable teacher are quite helpful.

It seems appropriate to end by citing Arthur Heilman's application of Parkinson's Law to the publishing business. It states "When a society develops high productive capacity in paper manufacture and printing facilities, that society will find something to print on the paper" (8). I can think of no better reason why we must teach students to read selectively and rapidly, as well as accurately.

BIBLIOGRAPHY

1. Anderson, I. H. "Studies in the Eye Movements of Good and Poor Readers," *Psychological Monographs*, 48 (1937), 1-35.
2. Braam, Leonard. "Developing and Measuring Flexibility in Reading," *The Reading Teacher*, 16 (January 1963), 247-51.
3. Buswell, G. T. "The Relationship between Rate of Thinking and Rate of Reading," *School Review*, 59 (September, 1951), 339-46.
4. Carlson, T. R. "The Relationship between Speed and Accuracy of Comprehension," *Journal of Educational Research*, 42 (March, 1949), 500-12.
5. Carrillo, L. W. "Developing Flexible Reading Rates," *Journal of Reading*, 8 (April, 1965), 322-25.
6. Doll, Ronald and R. S. Fleming. *Children Under Pressure*. Columbus, Ohio: Charles E. Merrill, 1966, 7-13.
7. Gordon, Richard and Katherine Gordon. *The Blight on the Ivy*. Englewood Cliffs, New Jersey: Prentice-Hall, 1963, 8-11.
8. Heilman, Arthur. "Rapid Reading: Uses and Abuses," *Journal of Developmental Reading*, 5 (Spring, 1962), 157-63.
9. Herculane, Sister M. "A Survey of the Flexibility of Reading Rates and Techniques According to Purpose," *Journal of Developmental Reading*, 4 (Spring, 1961), 207-10.
10. Hill, Walter. "Factors Associated with Comprehension Deficiency of College Readers," *Journal of Developmental Reading*, 3 (Winter, 1960), 84-93.
11. _____. *High School Reading Programs*. Newark: IRA, 1965.
12. _____. "Influencing of Direction upon the Reading Flexibility of Advanced College Readers," *Thirteenth Yearbook of the National Reading Conference*. Milwaukee: 1964, 119-25.
13. Letson, Charles. "The Future of Rapid Reading." *Eleventh Yearbook of the National Reading Conference*. Milwaukee: 1962, 57-67.
14. _____. "The Relative Influence of Material and Purpose on Reading Rates," *Journal of Educational Research*, 52 (November, 1959), 238-40.
15. McDonald, Arthur. "Flexibility in Reading," *Reading as an Intellectual Activity* (J. Allen Figurel, ed.) International Reading Association Proceedings, 8, 1963, 81-87.
16. _____. "Rate and Reading Flexibility," *Journal of Reading*, 8 (January, 1965), 187-91.
17. Noall, Mabel S. "Automatic Teaching of Reading Skills in High School," *Journal of Education*, 143 (February 1961), 1-73.
18. North, Marie. "Measurable Gains Made by High School Students in a Developmental Reading Course," *Journal of Developmental Reading*, 5 (Spring 1962), 208-13.
19. Spache, George. "Is This A Breakthrough in Reading?" *The Reading Teacher*, 15 (January, 1962), 258-63.
20. Summers, Edward. "Evaluation of Reading Gains in a Secondary School Reading Laboratory," *The Reading Teacher*, 17 (January 1964), 255-60.
21. Stroud, James. *Psychology in Education*. New York: Longmans, Green, 1956, 129-64.
22. Taylor, Earl. "The Fundamental Reading Skill," *Journal of Developmental Reading*, 1 (Summer 1958), 21-30.
23. Taylor, Stanford. "Reading Instrument Usage," *The Reading Teacher*, 15 (May 1962), 449-59.
24. Tinker, Miles. *Bases for Effective Reading*. Minneapolis: University of Minnesota Press, 1965, 53-115.
25. Yoakam, Gerald. *Reading and Study*. New York: Macmillan Co., 1928.

Applying Research Findings in Comprehension to Classroom Practice (College)

RICHARD P. WILLIAMS
New Mexico State University

RESEARCH in education began in the nineteen twenties, as one considers the elements of comprehension in reading. Three factors gave rise to the research and contributed to its growth. First, there was a new emphasis on determining a scientific basis for curriculum by determining the extent of individual disciplines. The field of reading was one of the first areas to be analyzed. Secondly, the experience-centered approach in education, proposed by Dewey, Kilpatrick, and Thorndike, emphasized that the school take its cues from the values, needs, and interests of children. Books and associated reading materials were examined to determine whether they actually met the values, needs, and interests of the children. Thirdly, the most important, there was a growing recognition for the need of individualizing instruction due to the enforcement of compulsory school attendance laws. Also, psychologists disclosed that children's abilities develop with age, but that the degrees of attainment of these abilities varied tremendously within a given age.

Therefore, if the democratic idea of education—the greatest good for the greatest number—was to be fulfilled in the reading field, reading material had to be suitable for the majority of the children and yet provide for the deviants within specified chronological age groups. Some forty years of research have followed.

In spite of the generally favorable attitude toward science and research, a considerable time lag is required before an innovation reaches wide acceptance. This is true despite the economic benefits of the innovations studied. For instance, a 40-year time lag was found between the first success of the tunnel oven in the pottery industry and its general use. Over 14 years were required for hybrid seed corn to reach complete adoption in Iowa. About 50 years elapsed after development of a new educational practice before its adoption by all public schools. Put in another way, the average American school lags 25 years behind the best practice. To help close this time lag, classroom practitioners should apply research findings in comprehension to classroom practice.

George Spache has described comprehension as an almost perfect example of a gestalt, a total that is greater than the sum of its parts. It is undoubtedly true that the factors of word meanings, interrelationship of details, and reasoning are significant components of comprehension. These factors are identified in a majority of factor analyses of reading tests. Yet certainly comprehension is more than these three simple elements, for this information leaves unanswered the questions of what thinking processes operate in comprehension and how those processes may be measured or trained.

Thinking and comprehension must be considered as an intellectual process in terms of the individual's personality makeup. Among the factors to be considered are the background of experience of the individual and how readily he can deliver this information into consciousness. The ability to form concepts also vitally affects how well one can comprehend in any learning situation.

Reading comprehension is more than decoding an interpretation of meaning from the printed page. To illustrate that reading comprehension is more than decoding an interpretation of meaning from the printed page, consider Albert Kingston's example of the hypothetical reaction of a group of children who read the following nursery rhyme:

Jack and Jill went up the hill
to fetch a pail of water.
Jack fell down and broke his crown
And Jill came tumbling after.

1. Two lads went up a hill to get some water but both fell down.
2. A boy named Jack and a girl named Jill went up a hill to get a bucket of water from a well, the boy fell down, and hurt his head. Then the girl fell down too.
3. A king and queen went up a hill to get some water. The king fell down and broke his crown. The queen fell too.
4. A man and a woman climbed a mountain. The man whose name was Jack fell and broke a crown the dentist had put in a tooth. The lady whose name was Jill fell down after him as she tried to help him.
5. Two people went up a hill looking for water. The man slipped and

fell down to the bottom. The woman fell down on top of him.

6. A boy and a girl named Jack and Jill ascended a hill seeking water. Jack slipped and fractured his skull. Jill also slipped and rolled down the hill.

In each interpretation there are certain elements of correct average decoding. Each child made associations from his experience background that were meaningful to him. Can we assume which child had the greatest comprehension? Certainly not on the evidence shown here. As classroom practitioners we would seek to elicit more information from each student by questions, discussions, and suggestions.

An early study by Thorndike indicated that comprehension of even simple reading material was a complex process. He analyzed the test responses of several hundred students in grades 3-8 in terms of three dimensions: individual word meaning, the weighting of words or larger elements, and the purpose or mental set of the reader. He concluded that the complex nature of comprehension favored the teaching of silent reading followed by questioning rather than oral reading instruction, since vocalizing was no indication that understanding had occurred.

The nature of reading comprehension has more recently been investigated by means of factor analysis. Davis found nine factors underlying comprehension in his study of the comprehension skills of 421 college students. His experimental materials were tests C1 and C2 of Form Q of the Cooperative Reading Comprehension Tests. He interpreted the nine factors in terms of the following abilities: 1) knowledge of word meanings; 2) ability to select the appropriate meaning for a word or phrase in the light of its particular contextual setting; 3) ability to follow organization of a passage and to identify antecedents and references in it; 4) ability to select the main thought of a passage; 5) ability to answer questions that are specifically answered in a passage; 6) ability to answer questions that are answered in a passage but not in the words in which the question is asked; 7) ability to draw inferences from a passage about its contents; 8) ability to recognize the literary devices used in a passage and to determine its tone and mood; and 9) ability to determine a writer's purpose, intent, and point of view, hence, to draw inferences about the writer.

In contrast to Davis' results, Harris, in his study of the elements underlying comprehension of literature by 112 college students, found one general factor to account for comprehension of both prose and poetry and one general factor underlying seven skills considered by the investigator to be necessary to the comprehension of literary materials. In a somewhat later study, Vernon also found that two factors accounted for the intercorrelation of seven tests of comprehension and vocabulary constructed by him to investigate the reading ability of 183 American and British college students.

A number of studies have been conducted to determine variables that might improve reading comprehension. Arnold investigated the effect of four study techniques—underlining, rereading, outlining, and summarizing—upon the comprehension of history text materials by 242 college students. No method yielded consistently better comprehension scores. Christensen and Stordahl did not find significant differences among groups of comprehension scores when the passages read included headings, underlinings, summaries, or outlines. The subjects for this pair of studies were approximately 800 Air Force trainees. In contrast to the results just summarized, Holmes found that comprehension of history and science material was significantly better when 170 college students were guided by pertinent questions rather than by using a rereading technique. The questioning technique was especially effective for delayed recall.

Factors other than study techniques have been examined in relation to improving reading comprehension.

Bernstein found that comprehension and rate of reading of 100 ninth graders were significantly better on a story designed to be more interesting than on another passage where readability was held constant. In contrast to her finding, Bryant and Barry did not find that varying interest affected either the comprehension or the rate of 57 college freshmen when reading simple (junior high level) narrative style articles.

The effect of programed instruction on reading comprehension has been reported in two studies. Raygor and Wark investigated the effectiveness of two variations of programed instruction as compared with an instructor-centered approach to the teaching of skills in locating the main idea of a passage. Three groups of 24 college freshmen participated in the study. Both programing groups performed significantly better than the third group on a standardized test of reading comprehension. Neither programed approach was more effective than the other. Calvin and Hanley studied the effect of programed instruction in mathematics on the reading comprehension of 408 high school students. When results of the STEP reading achievement of students who had been instructed in mathematics without programed materials were compared with those of the experimental group, the students studying geometry by means of programed materials showed a significant gain in speed of reading comprehension, but none of the experimental group showed a significant gain in total reading score or level of comprehension.

The effect upon reading comprehension when reading material orally or silently was investigated by Collins. He used seven levels of difficulty for both the silent and oral passages. In his study of 60 college freshmen, oral reading yielded significantly higher total comprehension scores. Oral reading was especially effective for "very easy" and "fairly difficult" material.

Another factor was studied by Strom. She correlated the reading

comprehension scores of 327 high school sophomores with their scores on a test of their knowledge of the grammar and syntax utilized in the ten passages read on the comprehension test. She found a significant correlation between comprehension and knowledge of grammar among four classes who attended a university laboratory school where instruction in grammar and syntax was closely integrated with writing and oral expression. No significant correlation was found between comprehension and knowledge of grammar for the other classes drawn from public and private schools.

Investigators have presented evidence which shows that a reader is more likely to accept a statement or argument which harmonizes with, rather than runs counter to, his attitudes and beliefs. Crossen reports that "an unfavorable attitude toward a topic of some personal and immediate concern tends to interfere with the critical reading of material about that topic."

To support the findings of Crossen, Cannell and MacDonald found that the acceptance of the finding of the relationship between smoking and cancer differed significantly on the part of smokers and nonsmokers.

Lefford pointed out that a reader's ability to reason accurately in a non-emotional situation is no indication of his ability to do so in an emotional one. The McKillop study established that answers to questions of fact are far less affected by the reader's attitude than are answers to questions which require value judgments and evaluative conclusions.

Results of the studies reported in this review indicate that reading is not a unitary process, but differing numbers of factors are reported to underlie comprehension. Several inferences should be made from the studies reported concerning classroom practice.

These inferences include

1. Comprehension is a gestalt of reading involving every aspect of the process of reading.

2. Comprehension must be consid-

ered as an intellectual process in terms of the individual's personality makeup to include:

    a. The background of experience of the individual, and

    b. How readily the learner can deliver this past experience to the present experience.

3. Silent reading followed by pertinent questions for the reader to answer is better than oral reading instruction since vocalizing was no indication that understanding had occurred.

4. Factors of comprehension include:

    a. Knowledge of word meanings.

    b. Ability to select the appropriate meaning for a word or phrase in the light of its particular contextual setting.

    c. Ability to follow the organization of a passage and to identify antecedents and references in it.

    d. Ability to select the main thought of a passage.

    e. Ability to answer questions that are specifically answered in a passage.

    f. Ability to answer questions that are answered in a passage but not in the words in which the question is asked.

    g. Ability to draw inferences from a passage about its contents.

    h. Ability to recognize the literary devices used in a passage and to determine its tone and mood.

    i. Ability to determine a writer's purpose, intent, and point of view, hence to draw inferences about the writer.

5. The four study techniques, underlining, rereading, outlining, and summarizing are equally efficient in obtaining comprehension gains.

6. Comprehension gains improve when reading is guided by pertinent questions rather than by using a rereading technique.

7. Varying interest of material read to that of the student caused an improved comprehension score.

8. The programed instruction approach appears to elicit more effective results in comprehension than an instructor-centered approach.

9. At certain levels of difficulty oral reading appears to have advantages over silent reading.

10. A knowledge of grammar and syntax has little value in attaining reading comprehension.

11. The personal emotions of the individual reader will interfere with the comprehension of what is read.

12. The ability to reason accurately in a non-emotional situation is no indication of the ability to do so in an emotional one.

BIBLIOGRAPHY

Arnold, H. F. "The Comparative Effectiveness of Certain Study Techniques in the Field of History," *Journal of Educational Phychology, 33* (September 1942).

Bernstein, Margery. "Relationship Between Interest and Reading Comprehension," *Journal of Educational Research, 49* (December 1955), 283-88.

Bryant, N. Dale and Nel E. Barry. "The Relationship Between Interest and Reading Rate and Between Interest and Reading Comprehension." *Phases of College and Other Adult Reading Programs,* Tenth Yearbook of the National Reading Conference, 1961, 127-30.

Calvin, Allen D. and Charles Hanley. "Exposure to Programed Learning Material and Reading Comprehension," *Psychological Reports, 10* (October 1962), 538.

Cannell, Charles F. and James C. MacDonald. "The Impact of Health News on Attitudes and Behavior," *Journalism Quarterly, 33* 1956, 315-323.

Christensen, Clifford M. and K. E. Stordahl. "The Effect of Organizational Aids on Comprehension and Retention," *Journal of Educational Psychology, 46* (February 1955), 65-74.

Collins, Ray. "The Comprehension of Prose Materials by College Freshmen When Reading Silently and When Reading Aloud," *Journal of Educational Research, 55* (October 1961), 79-82.

Crossen, Helen T. *Effect of Attitudes of Readers Upon Critical Reading Ability,* Chicago: University of Chicago Press, 1947, 94.

Davis, F. B. "Fundamental Factors of Comprehension in Reading," *Psychometrika, 9* (September 1944), 185-97.

Harris, Chester. "Measurement of Comprehension of Literature," *School Review, 51* (June 1948), 332-42.

Holmes, Eleanor. "Reading Guided by Questions versus Careful Reading and Re-Reading without Questions," *School Review, 39* (May 1931), 261-71.

Kingston, Albert J., Jr. "Some Thoughts on Reading Comprehension," *Problems, Programs, and Projects in College-Adult Reading,* Eleventh Yearbook of the National Reading Conference, Milwaukee, Wisconsin, The National Reading Conference, 1962, 20-23.

Lefford, Arthur. "The Influence of Emotional Subject-Matter on Logical Reasoning," *Journal of General Psychology, 34* (May 1946), 127-51.

McKillop, Anne S. *The Relationship Between the Reader's Attitude and Certain Types of Reading Response,* Fort Worth: Texas Christian University Press, 1952, 102.

Raygor, Alton L. and David M. Wark, "An Evaluation of Programed Learning in Teaching Reading Comprehension," *Problems, Programs, and Projects in College-Adult Reading,* Eleventh Yearbook of the National Reading Conference, Milwaukee, Wisconsin, The National Reading Conference, 1962, 68-72.

Rogers, Everett M. *Diffusion of Innovations,* New York: The Free Press of Glencoe, 1962, 367.

Spache, George D. "What is Comprehension?" *Problems, Programs, and Projects in College-Adult Reading,* Eleventh Yearbook of the National Reading Conference, Milwaukee, Wisconsin, The National Reading Conference, 1962, 17-19.

Stordahl, Kalmer E. and Clifford M. Christensen. "The Effect of Study Techniques on Comprehension and Retention," *Journal of Educational Research,* 49 (April 1956), 68-72.

Strom, Ingrid. "Does Knowledge of Grammar Improve Reading?" *English Journal,* 45 (February 1956), 129-33.

Thorndike, Edward L. "Reading as Reasoning: A Study of Mistakes in Paragraph Reading," *Journal of Educational Psychology, 8* (June 1917), 323-332.

Vernon, Philip E. "The Determinants of Comprehension," *Educational and Psychological Measurement, 20* (Winter 1962), 269-86.

Applying Research Findings in Rate of Reading to Classroom Practice (College)

WALTER J. MOORE
University of Illinois

WITH VERY FEW EXCEPTIONS, adults enrolled in reading improvement programs and college students in credit and non-credit courses are reported to have achieved increases in reading speed—as much as one hundred per cent, with some gain, or at least no loss, in comprehension. To the question, "Can adults improve reading rate?" the answer is very definitely, "yes!" The further question "Do these increases in the rate hold up?" can be answered in the affirmative. One reviewer summarized thirty studies in which it appeared that although variability in retention of gain in rate prevailed, the average retention was about seventy percent after one year.

One researcher, Standlee, wondered if it could be shown that improvement detected as a result of intensive course work in reading spilled over—or transferred to other performance areas. He managed to locate some twenty-five studies dealing with academic achievement of college students following reading instruction. Results tended to be positive; that is, college students were reported to have improved their grades and to have continued in college following completion of a reading improvement program. The one researcher, though, who correlated achievement in a reading course with achievement in other courses in the following semester, reported a correlation coefficient of only .08.

Factors influencing the effectiveness of reading improvement programs

Against this background, then, it is interesting to speculate on the factors which influence the effectiveness of reading improvement programs. Obviously, the method of instruction —the mechanical aids, the teaching procedures, the organization—do make a difference and considerable research has been devoted to these aspects of reading programs. There is one factor, however, which cannot be said to have been carefully or exhaustively researched, and this is the motivational factor.

As this writer has stated elsewhere (6),

many of the reported attempts to improve rates have centered on the improvement of word perception skills and to a more limited extent, to the improvement of comprehension. Both word perception and comprehension have been more or less acceptably defined, but less thoughtful attention has been directed at other and more important components of reading. These include the thoughtful reaction involving both critical evaluation and appreciative responses, and assimilation, or the integration with previous experience of the ideas acquired through reading.

It is at this point that most improvement programs have been failures. They may have improved rates, that is, have improved perceptual habits which in turn have made it possible for the reader to proceed more rapidly. Or, such programs may have resulted in improved comprehension as revealed by increased ability—in answering questions aimed at disclosing the reader's ability to literally recount what has been covered.

Such programs have not usually ventured into the realm of motivation. Spache (9), in commenting on the studies of Holmes and Singer, observed that "approximately half of the variability in speed is accounted for by the trainee's vocabulary and word attack skills. Another 44 percent of the variations depend upon *motivational habit or desire for speed.*" [Italics mine].

The motivational factor in reading improvement programs

Without lengthy and profound attempts at a definition of motivation, a useful general description might be "how behavior gets started, is energized, is sustained, is directed, is stopped, and what kind of subjective reaction is present in the organism while all this is going on." (5).

The first major step in getting the learning process under way is to identify intelligently some of the learner's present and prospective problems. Simpson has observed that "the ability on the part of the learner to take this step successfully will be of paramount importance in determining whether he will be intrinsically motivated or whether he will actively help carry on the learning because he sees its probable benefit to him. If the teacher or someone else attempts to take this step for the learner the latter is not likely to

accept responsibility for his learning in a wholehearted fashion. Rather he is likely to learn systematically only as long as the teacher is around and then in a rather passive manner" (7).

Or, as Ausubel has put it, "Doing without being interested in what one is doing results in relatively little permanent learning, since it is reasonable to suppose that only those materials can be meaningfully incorporated on a long-term basis into an individual's structure of knowledge that are relevant to areas of concern in his psychological field. Learners who have little need to know and understand, quite naturally expend little learning effort; manifest an insufficiently meaningful learning set; fail to develop precise meanings, to reconcile new ideas with existing concepts, and to formulate new propositions in their own words; and do not devote enough time to practice and review. Material is therefore never sufficiently consolidated to form an adequate foundation for sequential learning" (1).

Gans has observed "that many of us can recall when some of our teachers considered that they were warming up cooling ardor about school by telling us how important school was. Others may have prescribed more homework to be sure that learning efforts came in for their proportionate share of time. Still others, and unfortunately this is still too prevalent, applied fear as the technique of recharging lagging learners. Low grades, threat of failure, notes to parents, as well as public scolding and ridicule, were (and still are) the processes whereby the inferior teachers attempted to stimulate increased eagerness to learn" (2).

Levels of motivation

Levels of motivation and their uses have been studied by Simpson (7) who envisions a learning-motivation ladder as consisting of six levels:

1) *the lowest level,* here learning is based on fear;
2) *the next to the lowest level* finds people working for extrinsic rewards (credits, marks, etc.) with-

out understanding the purposes of the instructor;

3) *the third level from the bottom* wherein the individual understands the purposes of the instructor directing the work, largely rejects these, but works for extrinsic rewards;

4) *the fourth level*—here the individual sees the purposes of the instructor, accepts them as important, and works to carry them out without having any share in forming them;

5) *the fifth level,* near the top of the ladder, is the individual who with proper guidance, has set up well-thought-out goals and problems and has started to meet them, and,

6) *the sixth or highest level* finds the individual independently setting up his own goals and problems and facing them wisely with a minimum of help from others.

It goes without saying that no competent instructor of a reading improvement program would be satisfied with the so-called lower motivational levels, but it is not always possible to begin operations at the higher levels—or put another way, operations do not usually begin at an appropriate level.

The role of purposes and motivation in reading improvement programs

When a beginning reader is delayed in learning that we *read for meaning,* or for some equally clear purpose, the result can be ineffective reading habits. It can also produce slight to severe retardation in reading achievement. Teacher explanations and children's discussions of why various "reading for meaning" teaching activities are used are important when teaching beginners to read. Young children have limited ability to understand the reason for using these activities. Therefore, the inadequately trained beginning reader may see the reading activities as nothing more than interesting or uninteresting pastimes. This attitude toward reading may *never* change!

What is meant by the term *purpose* as it pertains to reading? There would appear to be two major kinds of purposes for reading: first, the broad, general purposes which are sometimes called the life purposes for which a reader selects and reads particular books or articles. These might be called the *primary purposes;* and second, the different kinds of comprehension skills, or as they are sometimes called, the *secondary purposes.*

Kinds of purposes for reading

Examples of primary purposes according to Smith (8) are to extend one's range of information, to evaluate possible solutions to social or economic problems, to understand one's self, to achieve aesthetic appreciation, and the like. Examples of the secondary purposes include understanding the main idea, noting sequential order, making generalizations, and anticipation of outcomes.

Smith makes the point that reading to understand details and the main idea are considered basic to all other secondary purposes. Reading to understand ideas in sequential order, to follow directions, to make comparisons, to relate cause and effects of ideas and/or phenomena, and to understand or to reach generalizations and conclusions appear to be dependent upon the reader's skill in reading for details and for main ideas. Interrelated with any or all of the foregoing are reading to anticipate ideas or to predict outcomes, to understand characterization and descriptions, to determine the mood or tone of a selection, to distinguish between fact and opinion and fact and fiction, and to understand sensory imagery. It appears that the reader may be called upon to achieve the foregoing purposes by understanding the *literal* meanings, the *implied* meanings, or *both* the literal and implied meanings.

This same writer points out further that both the primary and secondary purposes appear to be interrelated and dependent upon each other. There is no published research which shows the interdependency among the purposes;

yet, subjective opinion points to this assumption. Many extraneous factors which may be important in reading but are not readers' purposes *per se* are noted in the literature, such as writers' purposes, style, content of the selections, writers' point of view, the literary type, and techniques used in reading for different purposes, such as the selection, analysis, organization, evaluation of the content, and relating the content to one's own personal experiences.

Dealing with motivation and purposes in reading improvement programs

It may well be that instructors in reading improvement programs will have to learn how to deal with motivational problems by departing from the literature of reading and delving into the fields of human relations and management. Writers like Giles (*3*) and Gellerman (*4*) who have been working in these respective fields have advanced theories and practical suggestions which may prove to be quite effective in reading improvement situations. In discussing the dynamics of motives, Gellerman observes that

> much of the difficulty we have in understanding motives stems from the way they arrange themselves in any given individual. They seem to acquire a structure and to follow a dynamic all their own. The structure has sometimes been called a hierarchy; that is, one motive will usually be more powerful, and therefore more prominent in influencing the individual's behavior, than the others. Another will be the second most powerful, another the third, and so on. However, this structure is not fixed: A primary motive today may not be primary tomorrow. A reshuffling occurs whenever a motive has been so well satisfied that it sinks into the background and all the others move up a notch to replace it. As long as the 'old' motive gets plenty of gratification it will remain fairly quiescent and much less likely to rouse the individual to action than one of the 'newer' still unsatisfied ones (*4*).

Gellerman sees the kinds of motives which can be diminished when enough rewards are given as *satisfiers*—that is, they press themselves insistently upon the individual when they do not receive enough gratification but lapse into insignificance when they do. Likewise he sees those motives which are not susceptible to being "appeased" as *motivators*. He believes that they can continue to play commanding roles in an individual despite the fact that he enjoys repeated success. Motivators are likely to be "highly subjective, personalized experiences like feelings of growth, achievement, and significance."

Gellerman observes that

> . . . a person learns how to satisfy the needs that one phase of his life thrusts upon him, and having satisfied them, he is no longer very strongly motivated by them. Instead he anticipates newer needs. This is why it is a mistake to continue appealing to individuals by satisfying needs that are already satisfied. Thus a person's motives may not always be the same; at any given time he is likely to have a motivational potential —that is, a capacity for responding to new incentives and rewards—which he has not yet given any hint of possessing. This potential is likely to remain masked until his more basic needs are attended to and will not ordinarily spring forth merely because an incentive has been flourished before him. As a matter of fact, his overt pursuit of a particular goal may give a completely misleading impression of what his true motivation is like. Lastly, time itself will gradually realign the importance of his motives. Motivation is not, therefore, a particularly straightforward process, which is precisely why so many straightforward schemes for motivating individuals achieve such unspectacular results.

Summarizing statement

Certain factors profoundly influence the effectiveness of reading improvement programs and one of the most important but difficult of these factors to deal with is that of motivation. The levels of motivation are inextricably interwoven with the purposes for which individuals read. Not all instructors in reading improvement programs recognize the importance of and interrelations of motivation and purpose. It is reasonable to believe that theories derived from the fields of human relations and management have pertinence for education, and more specifically, for those engaged in work with people in reading improvement programs.

REFERENCES

1. Ausubel, David P. "A Teaching Strategy for Culturally Deprived Pupils: Cognitive and Motivational Consideration," *The School Review, 71* (Winter 1963), 458-459.
2. Gans, Roma. *Common Sense in Reaching Reading.* Indianapolis: Bobbs-Merrill, 1963, 234.
3. Giles, Harry. *Education and Human Motivation.* New York: Philosophical Library, 1957.
4. Gellerman, Saul W. *Motivation and Productivity,* New York: American Management Association, 1963, 175-176, 182.
5. Jones, M. R. *Nebraska Symposium on Motivation.* Lincoln: University of Nebraska, 1955.
6. Moore, Walter J. "Improving Reading Rates," *Improvement of Reading Through Classroom Practice,* Newark, Delaware: International Reading Association, 1964, 135.
7. Simpson, Ray H. *Improving Teaching-Learning Processes.* New York: Longmans, Green, 1953, 41, 43.
8. Smith, Helen K. *Instruction of High School Students in Reading for Different Purposes.* Cooperative Research Project No. 1714. University of Chicago, 1966, 10-14.
9. Spache, George D. "Reading Rate Improvement or Success for the Wrong Reasons," *Journal of Developmental Reading, 6* (Autumn 1963), 6.

AUTHOR INDEX

636